Collins Encyclopedia of Music

Collins Encyclopedia of Music

Sir Jack Westrup and F.Ll.Harrison

revised by Conrad Wilson

CHANCELLOR PRESS

First published in Great Britain in 1959 by
William Collins Sons & Co Ltd
Completely revised and reset 1976

This edition published in 1984 by
Chancellor Press
59 Grosvenor Street
London W1

Reprinted 1985, 1986

ISBN 0 907486 50 9

Printed in Czechoslovakia

50 549/3

INTRODUCTION

Throughout my years as a student and subsequently as a professional musician, I have diligently acquired reference books necessary to my work. I have bought them, borrowed them, and copied from them, and by now my bookshelves are impressively crammed with volumes about every conceivable aspect of music and musicians. However, time has only made it seem more difficult to find a concise, comprehensive volume which is both readable and scholarly at the same time. Many publications, it seems to me, almost delight in using language which resembles a verbatim translation from the Old German, with endless footnotes, and sentences so arcane as to make Henry James ashamed of his simplicity. Conversely, there are hundreds of so-called 'popular' books about music, which seem to be aimed at the 10-year-old child. This book solves a lot of these problems. The research and scholarship are beyond cavil, but the language and approach are concise and even entertaining.

It has been a criterion of mine that any reference book should make fascinating random reading – a difficult test – but this encyclopedia more than meets the requirement. It is actually fun to pick up, open it on any page and peruse the contents. It is simply crammed with information usually obtainable only by cross-checking through quite a few separate books. I suppose a good way to put it is that this volume contains not only facts you *need* to know, but also things you *want* to know, whether they are of the moment's necessity or not.

Music never stands still. It progresses and moves forward all the time, and it is surprising to open reference books of only a few years back and find great gaps. The *Collins Encyclopedia of Music* has taken enormous pains to be current. There are up-to-date listings of performers who have recently come to the fore; the relatively new interest in medieval music is well provided for, and the composers' biographies take full advantage of the latest facts and theories.

The book looks just as up to date – the design is clear and uncluttered, with copious illustrations. Were it only for the beautiful drawings of the instrument families, ancient and modern, this would be an invaluable book. What is more, no other music encyclopedia in this area has such a wealth of musical examples, which can explain problems so much more swiftly than words.

A wonderful addition to any one-volume music encyclopedia is the listing of the plots of major operas. Unless you are an absolutely inveterate opera buff, you will, quite often, be baffled by the story unfolding on the proscenium. I remember once talking to a world-famous baritone who confessed to me that although he had sung in *Trovatore* probably more than a hundred times, he had never been totally sure what it was about. This book would help him! The stories of the operas are admirable concise and are not plagued by the convolutions so often encountered in attempts to relate the twistings and turnings of the operatic dramas.

The biographical listings are as complete as any I have encountered in multi-volume reference works. Open any page at all, and names spring out of the dimming past: names which were once illustrious but tend to be relegated to professional researchers. Annibale Pio Fabri, Franco Faccio, Marie Corneille Falcon; Carlo Farino, Michel Farinel, and Farinelli (did you know that it was his stage name only? – he was actually Carlo Broschi), all vie for attention within a minute's reading time. Are you quite sure of the meanings or significance of faramondo, faburden, *fado*, *falsa musica*, or fa-la? Can you name Fauré's two operas? Are you aware that Liszt's *Faust Symphony* was based on Goethe, but he utilized Lenau's *Faust* when writing the *Mephisto Waltz*? Obviously, my test of random reading has been passed with flying colours.

If you are particularly interested in any given subject, chances are that the *Collins Encyclopedia* will be able to steer you on to more detailed paths. The bibliographical listings are well-chosen and cover material from the past and the present, in most major languages. While I am on the subject of foreign languages, the editors have also kindly seen fit to cross-index titles of compositions, as well as musical terminology. If a friend, steeped in the Stephen Potter tradition, decides to test you by opining that 'the *haute-contre* was not *innig* enough in her singing of the *Durchführung*', a quick glance at this book will even the score and more. Seriously, the cognizance of the possible Babel of the music world is invaluable, and, once again, is too often the province of a specialized separate book.

There is more interest, even fascination, in serious music now than ever before. Although it is certainly true that the mass media of the 20th century have much to answer for, it is an undeniable plus that ubiquitous radios and television sets and world-wide availability of excellent recordings have bred a new generation of music lovers. Young people no longer fear the concert hall ambience as alien territory. They are familiar with current performers and, through recordings, with giants of past decades. Music seems to be everywhere, easily accessible. With this current familiarity, there is a growing interest in the how, where, why, who, and wherefore of the art. A book such as this one is no longer restricted to the needs of the student or the professional. The music amateur (in the true French connotation of the word) is everywhere. Record-buyers, concert-goers, and radio listeners all share a desire to be well informed. The days of casual, passive listening seem to be waning. Information is being sought eagerly, and this volume is a treasure chest, ready to be opened.

ANDRÉ PREVIN
April 1976

PREFACE

Seventeen years may be a short time in the history of music, but they are quite a while in the life of an encyclopedia. When the *Collins Encyclopedia of Music* was first published, in 1959, Sir Michael Tippett had composed only the first of his three operas, and Britten had still to write *A Midsummer Night's Dream*. Pierre Boulez and Hans Werner Henze failed to rate a mention in these pages, and the only Stockhausen was Julius Stockhausen (1826–1906). The most 'modern' Hungarian composer was Bartók, not Ligeti, and it could still be said of Anton von Webern that his music was 'often barely intelligible, even to sympathetic listeners'. Statements such as the above, of course, helped to give the book its own strong character and place in time, and it was with reluctance that the present editor jettisoned some of its inclusions and assessments in order to bring it up to date.

Wherever possible I have sought to preserve its original flavour, while at the same time trying to ensure that it reflects current tastes and attitudes and answers the questions that a listener in the 1970s and 80s is likely to ask. Many minor figures of the early years of the present century have been dropped to make way for what seem to be the major figures of today (some of whom, in their turn, may be dropped by future editors of this book). Room has also been found for some of the key figures of jazz.

Inevitably, many reassessments have had to be made, in the light of our greater understanding today not only of Webern but also of earlier composers, e.g. Berlioz and Bruckner. The greatness of Monteverdi, on the other hand, was fully appreciated by Sir Jack Westrup and F. Ll. Harrison, and their enthusiasm for that composer has been consolidated by the Monteverdi revival that has taken place since the encyclopedia was first published. Indeed the widespread realization that there was great music before Bach has been one of the most remarkable developments since that time. Not only Monteverdi but also much of other, even earlier, music of what we now loosely call the pre-classical period has been brought out of the world of private scholarship into the public domain.

Since the rediscovery and performance of this music has grown into a heavy industry, I have been glad to have the help of Warwick Edwards, lecturer in music at Glasgow University and (as a *gamba* player and director of the Scottish Early Music Consort) a practising exponent of works of the period, in revising all the original entries and providing the many new ones that were needed. Good though the encyclopedia previously was in this field, it has been greatly strengthened by Dr. Edwards's authoritative contributions. He in turn acknowledges the expert assistance of Greta Mary Hair (University of New England, N.S.W.) in subjects related to Gregorian chant. Similarly, in the field of musical instruments, I am grateful to Malcolm Rayment, music critic of the *Glasgow Herald*, and to Neil Ardley, the writer and composer, for bringing these entries up to date and for adding the many extra, often exotic, instruments (especially in the percussion section) used by composers today. Stephen Arnold, who presides over the electronic studio of Glasgow University's music department, has also provided valuable assistance in the field in which he is expert.

'Pronunciation presented several difficulties', declared the encyclopedia's original authors in their preface to the first edition. It did to me, too; and rather than interrupt the flow of articles with pronunciation guides for every difficult entry, we have decided to provide a brief, selective pronunciation glossary as part of the introductory material.

Another difference is that I have abandoned the ruling that titles of operas should be listed in the language employed at their first production. This, in the first edition, resulted in Delius's *A Village Romeo and Juliet* appearing under letter 'R' as *Romeo und Julia auf dem Dorfe*, simply because the work had its première in Berlin, and *The Bartered Bride* appearing academically under its Czech title, *Prodaná Nevěsta*. Foreign titles are admittedly a problem, and it is possible to go to the other extreme and anglicize everything, a ruling which can be just as irritating (such as listing Debussy's *La Mer* as *The Sea*). My own decision has been a pragmatic one. Where possible, I have allowed good popular usage to dictate the language of a title. Thus I have preferred *The Flying Dutchman* to *Der Fliegende Holländer* (only the most tedious of musical snobs would claim to have seen a performance of *Der Fliegende Holländer*) but have been happy to settle for *La Mer*, simply because that is what everyone calls it. On the other hand, I prefer *The Rite of Spring* to *Le Sacre du printemps* because in this case the use of a French title is merely an affectation.

For Russian names in general I have preferred modern transliterations – *Petrushka* rather than *Petrouchka*, Rakhmaninov rather than Rachmaninov or Rachmaninoff, Chaikovsky rather than Tchaikovsky or the Germanic Tschaikowsky. The last of these (though duly cross-referenced) may at first seem eccentric, but does anyone nowadays spell Chekhov as Tchekov? Music does seem to lag behind the other arts in this respect.

Finally, enormous thanks must go to all my helpers, advisers and editors at Collins, especially Chris Gravell, who (along with her predecessor, Jenny Carter) had the fearsome task of collating and correcting every entry. She made numerous constructive suggestions, reminded me of my omissions, tracked down many of the striking pictures with which the book is illustrated, generally smoothed my path (though I did not smooth hers) and patiently put up with my snail-like progress. It was also good to work again with Bill McLeod, who edited my history of Scottish Opera four years ago, and who, as a dedicated music lover and operamane, cast a friendly and critical eye over my efforts, and shared with Chris Gravell and myself the choosing and captioning of the illustrations. Jim Mallory, too, gave me useful advice and encouragement and, to complete my round of thanks, I must pay tribute to Nortons, the American publishers, who provided much practical help about the general balance of the book, and about what it should and should not contain, especially where the American scene is concerned.

CONRAD WILSON
Edinburgh 1976

PREFACE
TO THE FIRST EDITION

The chief difficulty in compiling an encyclopedia of any kind is to decide what to leave out. No doubt this problem does not seriously worry editors who are able to spread themselves over several volumes. But it becomes acute when the material has to be compressed within the covers of a single book. It would have been possible to include more entries in the present volume by reducing the amount of information supplied and by omitting the music examples. But though conciseness in general is a virtue, it can easily reach a point where the elimination of what appears to be unessential leaves little that is of practical value to anyone. As for the music examples, we regard these as indispensable. It is difficult to see how any technical explanation of the elements or the forms of music can be made intelligible without an illustration. To the experienced musician many of our examples may appear superfluous. But it is a basic principle in making an encyclopedia to assume that the reader comes to any article without previous knowledge of the subject.

So far as the biographical entries are concerned, we have made a general distinction between composers who may be presumed to be widely known and others who are less well-known, though without presuming to impose any implied judgment of values on the reader. In the case of composers of the first category we have supplied fairly detailed summaries of their principal works; for those of the second category we have been content to indicate the main fields of composition in which they were active – a method which does not exclude particular mention of works which may be of special interest. The bibliographies, both in the biographical articles and in the technical articles, are admittedly a selection, but we hope they will provide sufficient material to start the reader off on any plan he may have for more detailed study. Though we have naturally given preference to works in English, on the ground that these are likely to be more accessible to the general reader, we have also included a large number of standard works in foreign languages.

The principle on which we have selected musicians for inclusion cannot be stated simply, since each case has had to be decided on its merits. No doubt the specialist on any particular period will be surprised at the omission of persons whom he regards as of considerable importance. Equally, the reader with no specialist knowledge may question the inclusion of musicians of whom he has never heard. But this work is not designed for specialists nor to flatter a reader's ignorance. We believe that every entry in this volume, whether biographical or technical, is likely to be of interest to somebody at some time, and we have tried to provide for this contingency, however remote it may appear.

A large number of foreign words for instruments and for technical terms are included in these pages. The latter may appear unnecessarily numerous. On the other hand, many of them occur in the footnotes to modern editions of classical works published abroad, and recourse to a dictionary does not always tell the reader precisely what they mean. We have also taken into account the fact that many English and American writers today tend to use foreign terms (particularly German terms) in essays on a musical subject. This habit is deplorable; the English language must be a very poor medium for expression if it cannot supply equivalents to German terms (which are, incidentally, often far from precise and not always very good German). But since the practice is now common, it seemed reasonable to offer some assistance towards interpretation.

On the other hand, the number of foreign words indicating tempo or expression has been strictly limited. It would have been quite impossible to include them all, since there is no limit to the directions which a composer may wish to convey in his own language. We have been content to include those which occur most commonly in Italian (traditionally the *lingua franca* of musical expression), French and German. For the rest, particularly those which strain verbosity beyond reasonable limits, the reader must consult a dictionary.

It is hardly necessary to say that we are heavily indebted to the labours of other writers and editors. Among the encyclopedic works which we have found particularly useful are the late Alfred Loewenberg's *Annals of Opera*, *The International Cyclopedia of Music and Musicians* (revised by Nicolas Slonimsky), *Grove's Dictionary of Music and Musicians* (fifth edition, edited by Eric Blom) and *Die Musik in Geschichte und Gegenwart* (edited by Friedrich Blume). The last of these had only reached the letter G when our final revision was completed, but within these limits it proved invaluable on many points of detail. We have to thank many friends and colleagues for answering questions and providing information. It is impossible that a work of this kind should be entirely free from errors; but we hope that any that survive will prove to be the result not of carelessness but of inadvertence.

J. A. W.
F. Ll. H.
Oxford,
June 1959

PRONUNCIATION KEY

Stress is shown by a stress mark placed after the stressed syllable thus:

Haitink hī'tingk

ay	pay	õ	*Fr.* bon	tsh	church
ah	calm	ĩ	*Fr.* vin	hw	what
ee	freeze	ã	*Fr.* dans	j	jam
eh	*Fr.* père	œ̃	*Fr.* un	th	think
ī	bite, try	œ	*Fr.* feu, *Ger.* Flöte	TH	this
ō	rope	ü	*Fr.* tu, *Ger.* Dürer	zh	azure
oo	brook	ə	rotten	CH	loch
y	tune, yes				
oi	boil				
ow	how				

Abba-Cornaglia a'ba-kornal'ya
Abel ah'bəl
Abendmusiken ah'bənt-moozee'kən
Abgesang ap'gəzang
Abschiedssymphonie ap'sheets-zeemfōnee'
Absil apseel
accelerando a-tsheleran'dō
acciaccatura a-tshakatoo'ra
Acis et Galatée asees ay galatay
adagietto adajet'ō
adagio *It.* adaj'yō, *Fr.* adahzh-yō
adagissimo adajee'seemō
Adam *Fr.* adã
Adam de la Hale *or* **Hallé** adã də la al *or* alay
à deux cordes a dœ kord
Adieux, L'Absence et Le Retour, Les layz adyœ, lapsãs ay lə rətoor
a due a doo'e
Africaine, L' lafreeken
agitato ajeetah'tō
agogic ago'jik
Agon agōn'
agréments agraymã
Aguiari, Agujari agooyah'ree
Aguilera de Heredia ageelay'ra day ayray'dee-a
Aichinger eesh'ing-ər
Aida a-ee'da
Ais, Aisis aees', aee'sees
Alain alĩ
Albéniz albay'neeth
Albert, d' dalbehr
Alcina al-tshee'na
Alembert alãbehr
al fine al fee'ne
Alfvén alfvayn'
alla breve ala breh've
allemande almãd
allmählich almay'leeCH
Almenräder al'mənraydər
Also sprach Zarathustra al'zō shpraCH tsaratoos'tra
Amadigi di Gaula amadee'jee dee gow'la
Amor Brujo, El el amōr' broo'hō
amore amō're
Amore dei Tre Re, L' lamō're day tray re'
Amour des Trois Oranges, L' lamoor day trwaz orãzh
Amy *Fr.* amee
Anacréon anakrayō
anche ãsh

An die ferne Geliebte an dee fer'nə gəleeb'tə
André ãdray
Andreae andray'ay
Andriessen andree'sən
Andrieu, D' dãdree-œ
anglaise ã-glez
Anglebert, d' dã-gləbehr
Anglès ã-gles
Animuccia aneemoo'tsha
Annibale Padovano aneebal'e padovah'nō
Anschlag an'shlak
Antheil an'tīl
a piacere a pya-tshay're
appassionato apasyonah'tō
appoggiatura apojatoo'ra
Apprenti Sorcier, L' laprãtee' sors-yay
Après-Midi d'un Faune, L' lapreh meedee dœ̃ fōn
Aquin, D' dakī
Araja, Araia arah'ya
Arbeau arbō
archi ar'kee
arciliuto ar-tsheelyoo'tō
Arezzo, d' dared'zō
Ariadne auf Naxos aree-ad'nə owf nak'sōs
Arie ahr'yə
Arlecchino arlekee'nō
Arlésienne, L' larlayz-yen
arpeggio arpej'yō
arpeggione arpejyō'ne
Arrau arah'oo
Ashkenazy ashkanah'zi
assai asah'ee
Attaignant aten-yã
Attaque du Moulin, L' latak dü moolī
aubade ōbad
Auber, Aubert ōbehr
Aubry ōbree
Audran ōdrã
Auer ow'ər
Auf dem Anstand owf dem an'shtant
Aufstieg und Fall der Stadt Mahogonny owf'shteek oont fal' der shtat' mahagon'ee
Augener ow'gənər
Auric ōreek

Bach baCH
Bach Gesellschaft baCH gəzel'shaft

Bachianas Brasileiras baCHyah'nas brazeelay'ras
badinage badeenazh
badinerie badeenree
Badings bah'dings
baguette baget
balalaika balalī'ka
ballabile balah'beele
Ballard balahr
Balling bal'ing
Ballo in Maschera, Un oon bal'ō een mas'kayra
Banchieri bang-kyeh'ree
Barbier von Bagdad, Der der barbeer' fon bag'dat
Barbiere di Siviglia, Il eel bar-byeh're de seeveel'ya
Bärenreiter bay'rən-rītər
Bargiel bar'geel
Barkarole barkarō'lə
Baron *Ger.* barōn'
Barraqué barakay
Barthélémon bartaylaymō
baryton *Fr.* bareetō, *Ger.* baritōn'
basse chiffrée bas sheefray
basse fondamentale bas fōdamãtal
basson basō
Bassposaune bas'-pozow'nə
Basstrompete bas'-trōmpay'tə
Bataille bata-ee
batterie batree
Bayreuth bīroit'
be bay
Bearbeitung bə-ahr'bītoong
bécarre baykar
Bédos de Celles baydō də sel
Beethoven bayt'hōvən
Begleitung bəglī'toong
Bègue, Le lə beg
Belaiev bayl-yah'yef
Benoit bənwa
Benucci bənoo'tshee
bequadro bekwad'rō
berceuse bersœz
Berenice berenee'tshe
Bériot, de də bayr'yō
Berwald bayr'vald
Bes bes
Besard bəzar
bestimmt bə-shtimt'
bewegt bəvaykt'
bezifferter Bass bə-tsif'ərtər bas'
Bianchi bee-an'kee
Bigot de Morogues beegō də morog
Binchois bī-shwa

Bindungszeichen bin'doongz-tsīCHən
bis bees
bisbigliando beezbeelyan'dō
Bizet beezay
Björling byœr'ling
Blamont blamō
blanche blãsh
Blanchet blãshe
Blangini blanjee'nee
Blasinstrumente blahs'instroomen'tə
Blechinstrumente bleCH'instroomen'tə
Blume bloo'mə
Blüthner blütnər
Bobillier bobeel-yay
bocca chiusa boka kyoo'za
Boccherini bokəree'nee
Boehm bœm
Bohème, La la bō-em
Boieldieu bwal-dyœ
Bois bwa
Boito bō-ee'tō
Bolero bōlay'rō
Boschot boshō
Bote and Bock bō'tə ənd bok'
Botstiber bōt'shteebər
bouche fermée boosh fermay
bouchés booshay
Bouffons boofō
Boulanger boolã-zhay
Boulez boolez
bourdon boordō
Bourgault-Ducoudray boorgō-dükoodray
bourrée booray
branle brã-lə
Bratsche brat'shə
Brautwahl, Die dee browt'vahl
Brustwerk broost'verk
Bukofzer bookof'tsər
Bülow, von fon bü'lō
Bund boont
Busnois bünwa
Buxtehude book'stə-hoo'də

Cabanilles kabaneel'yes
Cabezón kabay-thōn'
caccia kat'sha
Caccini ka-tshee'nee
Cadmus et Hermione kadmüs ay ermyon
caisse kes
Caix d'Hervelois ke derv-lwa

Calzabigi kaltsabee´jee
Cambert kãbehr
Campra kãpra
Cannabich kanabeesh
cantabile kantah´beele
canti carnascialeschi kan´tee karnashales´kee
cantilena kanteelay´na
canzona, canzone *or* canzon kantsõ´na, kantsõ´ne *or* kantsõn´
capriccio kapree´tshõ
Cardillac kardeeyak
Carnaval Romain, Le lǝ karnaval rõmĩ
Caron karõ
Casse-Noisette kas nwazet´
Castil-Blaze kasteel-blahz
Castillon, de dǝ kastee-yõ
Castrucci kastroo´tshee
Caurroy, du dü kõrwa
Cavaillé-Col kava-yay-kol
Cavalleria Rusticana kavaleree´a roosteekah´na
cédez sayday
cembalo tshem´balõ
Cenerentola, La la tsheneren´tola
Cerone tsherõ´ne
Certon sertõ
cervelas serv-la
Ces, Ceses tses, tses´ǝs
Cesti tshes´tee
cetera tshet´era
ceterone tsheterõ´ne
Chabrier shabree-ay
chace shas
Chaliapin shalyah´peen
chalumeau shalümõ
Chambonnières shãbonyehr
Chaminade shameenad
chanson shãsõ
chant *Eng.* tshahnt, *Fr.* shã
chanter shãtay
Charpentier sharpã-tyay
chaunter shãtay
Chausson shõsõ
chevalet, au õ shǝvale
chiavette kyavet´e
chiesa kyeh´za
chitarrone keetarõ´ne
chiuso kyoo´zõ
Chorton kõr´tõn
ciaccona tshakõ´na
cialamello tshalamel´õ
Ciconia tsheekõn´ya
Cid, Le lǝ seed
Cifra tsheef´ra
Cilèa tsheeleh´a
Cimarosa tsheemarõ´za
cimbasso tsheembas´õ
cinelli tsheenel´ee
cinque-pace *Eng.* singk-pays
clairseach, clarsach klahr´saCH
Claudin klõdĩ
Claudio da Correggio klow´dyõ da korej´yõ
clavecin klavsĩ
clavicembalo klavee-tshem´balõ
clavier *Fr.* klav-yay, *Ger., Eng.* klaveer´
Clavierübung klaveer´üboong
Clemens non Papa klaymãs nõn papa
Clément klaymã
Clérambault klayrãbõ
Cliquot kleekõ
clos klõ
colla voce kol´a võ´tshe
come *It.* kõ´me
comes *It.* kõ´mes
com(m)odo kõ´mõdõ
Compère kõpehr
concertant *Fr.*, concertante *It.*, kõsertã, kon-tshertan´te
concertato kon-tshertah´tõ
Concertgebouw konsert´gǝbow
concertino kon-tshertee´nõ
Concert spirituel kõsehr speereetüel

Concertstück kontsert´-shtük
concitato kon-tsheetah´tõ
Conzert kon-tsert´
cor anglais kor ã-gle
cori spezzati ko´ree spedzah´tee
cornet à bouquin korne a bookĩ
Cornett-ton kornet´-tõn
Correa de Arauxo koray´a de arah´ooksõ
Corregidor, Der der kore´geedor
Cortot kortõ
Cosi fan tutte kõzee´ fan too´te
Costeley kost-le
coulé koolay
Couperin kooprĩ
courante koorãt
Courvoisier koorvwaz-yay
Coussemaker koosmakǝr
Cramer krah´mǝr
crécelle kraysel
Crécquillon kraykee-yõ
crescendo kreshen´dõ
Croce krõ´tshe
croche krosh
crotales krõtahl
cruit, crwth kroot, krooth
csárdás tshar´dash
cuivre kwee-vr
cuivré kweevray
Cuzzoni koodzõ´nee
czardas tshar´dash
Czerny tsher´ni

Dame Blanche, La la dam blãsh
Damoiselle Élue, La la damwazel aylü
Damoreau damõrõ
Dämpfer demp´fǝr
Dandrieu dãdree-œ
Danican daneekã
Daquin dakĩ
Dargomijhsky dargamish´kee
Dauprat dõpra
Dauvergne dõvern-yǝ
David *Fr.* dahveed, *Ger.* dah´feet
Davidsbündler dah´feets-bünt´lǝr
Daza dah´tha
De Bériot dǝ bayr-yõ
Debora e Jaele deb´ora e ya-ay´le
Debussy dǝbüsee
déchant dayshã
decrescendo daykreshen´dõ
Dedekind day´dǝkint
dehors, en ã dǝ-or
Deidamia day-eedamee´a
Delannoy dǝlanwa
Delibes dǝleeb
Delvincourt delvĩkoor
Demeur dǝmœr
demiton dǝmee-tõ
Denkmäler der Tonkunst in Bayern/in Österreich denk´maylǝr der tõn´koonst in bĩ´ǝrn/in œs´tǝrĩCH
Denza den´tsa
déploration dayploras-yõ
descort deskor
Deses des´ǝs
Des Prés day pray
Dessau des´ow
dessus dǝsü
Destouches daytoosh
détaché daytashay
Deutsch doitsh
Deutsches Requiem, Ein ĩn doi´tshǝs rek´vee-em
Deux Journées, Les lay dœ zhoornay
Devienne dǝ-vyen
Devin du Village, Le lǝ dǝvĩ dü veelazh
Devrient dǝ-freent´
Dialogues de Carmélites, Les lay dee-alog dǝ karmayleet
Diaments de la Couronne, Les lay dee-amã dǝ la kooron
diapason *Eng.* dee-apay´son, *Fr.* dee-apazõ

Dichterliebe deeCH´tǝrlee´bǝ
Die *Ger.* dee
dièse dee-ez
Dies Irae dee´ays ee´rĩ
diesis *Eng.* dĩ-ee´sǝs, *It.* dee-ays´ees
Dieupart dyœpar
diferencia deeferen´thee-a
Dirigent deereegent´
divertissement deeverteesmã
Dobrowen dõbrõven´
Doctor und Apotheker dok´tõr oont apõtay´kǝr
Dohnányi doCH´nanyi
dolce dol´tshe
Doles dõlǝs
Domaine Musical domen müzeekal
Don Juan don hwan´
Don Quichotte dõ kee-shot
Doppelschlag dop´ǝl-shlak
doublé dooblay
double croche doob-lǝ krosh
doucement doosmã
Dreigroschenoper, Die dee drĩgrõ´shǝn-õ´pǝr
drohend drõ´ǝnt
Dumont dümõ
Duni, Duny *It.* doo´nee, *Fr.* dünee
Duport düpor
Du Pré, Dupré, Duprez dü-pray
Du Puy dü-pwee
Dur *Ger.* door
Durand dürã
Durchführung doorCH´füroong
Durchkomponiert doorCH´kompõneert´
Dušek doosh´ek
Dushkin doosh´kin
Dussek doosh´ek
Dutilleux dütee-yœ
Dvořák dvõr´zhak
Dzerjinsky jerzhin´ski

Eberlin ay´bǝr-leen
Eccard ek´art
échappée ay-shapay
échiquier aysheek-yay
Écho et Narcisse aykõ ay narsees
École d'Arcueil aykol darkœ-ee
écossaise aykosehz
Egge eg´ǝ
Eichheim ĩCH´-hĩm
eilen ĩ´lǝn
Einleitung ĩn´lĩtoong
Eis, Eisis ay´ǝs, ay´ǝsǝs
Eisteddfod eesteTH´võd
embouchure ãbooshür
Empfindsamer Stil empfĩnd´zahmǝr shteel´
enchaînez ãshenay
Encina, del del enthee´na
enclume ãklüm
Enesco enes´koo
Enfance du Christ, L' lãfãs dü kreest
Enfant et les sortilèges, L' lãfã ay lay sorteelezh
ensemble ãsãbl
entr'acte ãtrakt
entrée ãtray
Enzina, del del enthee´na
Épine, L' laypeen
equale ekwah´le
Érard ayrar
Erbe deutscher Musik, Das das er´bǝ doi´tshǝr moozeek´
Erlebach er´lǝbaCH
Erlkönig erl-kœ´neeCH
Eroica erõ´eeka
Erwartung ervar´toong
Erzlaute erts´lowtǝ
España espan´ya
essercizi eser-tshee´tsee
Estampes estãp
estampie estãpee
Este, Est eest
Étoile du Nord, L' laytwal dü nor
étouffez aytoofay
Étranger, L' laytrãzhay

etwas et´vas
Eulenburg oy´lǝnboork
Euridice, L' *It.* le-ooreedee´tshe
Euryanthe oiree-an´tǝ
Expert *Fr.* ekspehr

Faccio fah´tshõ
Falcon falkõ
Falla fal´ya
Fanciulla del West, La la fantshool´a del west
fantasia *It.* fantazee´a
Fantasiestück fantazee´shtük
Faschingsschwank aus Wien fash´ingz-shvank ows veen´
Fauré fõray
Faust *Ger.* fowst, *Fr.* fõst
Fauxbourdon fõboordõ
Favart favahr
Feen, Die dee fay´ǝn
feierlich fĩ´ǝrleeCH
Ferroud feroo
Fétis faytees
Feuermann foi´ǝrman
Feuersnot foi´ǝrz-nõt
Février fayvree-ay
Fidelio feedayl´yõ
Fille du Regiment, La la fee dü rayzheemã
fine *It.* fee´ne
Finke fing´kǝ
Finot fee´nõ
Finta Giardiniera, La la feen´ta jardeenyeh´ra
Finta Semplice, La la feen´ta sem´pleetshe
Firkušny firkoosh´ni
fisarmonica feezarmõ´neeka
Fischer-Dieskau fishǝr-dees´kow
Flageolett-töne flazhõlet´tönǝ
flatté flatay
Flatterzunge flat´ǝr-tsoong-ǝ
flebile fleh´beele
Fledermaus, Die dee flay´dǝr-mows
Fliegende Holländer, Der der flee´gǝndǝ hol´endǝr
Flöte flœ´tǝ
Flothuis flõt´hüs
flûte flüt
flûte-eunuque flüt-œnük
folia *Sp.*, follia *It.* fõlee´a
Forellenquintet forel´ǝn-kvintet´
Förster fœr´stǝr
forza for´tsa
forzando fortsan´dõ
Fournier foornyay
Françaix frãse
Frauen-Liebe und Leben frow´ǝn-leebǝ oont lay´bǝn
Frauenlob frow´ǝn-lõp
Frau ohne Schatten, Die dee frow´ õnǝ shat´ǝn
Freischutz, Der der frĩ-shoots
Friedenstag free´dǝnz-tak
Friedheim freet´hĩm
Friedländer freet´lendǝr
friska, friss frish´ka, frish
Froschquartett frosh´kvartet´
Frühlingssonate frülingz-zonah´tǝ
Frühlingssymphonie frülingz-zeemfõnee´
Fuenllana foo-en-lyah´na
Fuge foo´gǝ
Furtwängler foort´veng-lǝr
Fux fooks

Gade gah´dǝ
Gagliano galyah´nõ
gagliarda *It.*, gaillarde *Fr.* galyar´da, ga-yard
galant galã
Galanterien galantǝree´ǝn
Galli-Curci gal´ee koor´tshee
Ganz gants
Ganze Note gan´tsǝ nõ´tǝ
Ganzton gants´-tõn
Garcia garthee´a
Garlande, de dǝ garlãd

Gaspard de la Nuit gaspar də la nwee
Gastoué gastoo-ay
Gaubert gōbehr
Gaultier gōtyay
Gaveau, Gaveaux gavō
Gazza Ladra, La la gad′za lad′ra
Gazzaniga gadzanee′ga
Gebrauchsmusik gəbrowCHs′-moozeek′
Gédalge zhaydalzh
geheimnisvoll gəhīm′nisfol
gehend gay′ənt
Geige gī′gə
Geisslerlieder gīs′lər-leedər
gemächlich gəmeCH′leeCH
Geminiani jemeenyah′nee
gemütlich gəmütleeCH
Generalpause generahl′pow′zə
Genoveva gaynofay′fa
Gerhard zhayrar
Gérold gayrolt′
Gesamtausgabe gəzamt′-owsgah-bə
Gesamtkunstwerk gəzamt′koonstverk
gesangvoll gəzang′fol
Geschöpfe des Prometheus, Die dee gəshœp′fə des prōmay′tayüs
geschwind gəshvint′
Gesellschaft der Musikfreunde gəzel′shaft der moozeek′froində
Gesellschaft für Musikforschung gəzel′shaft für moozeek′forshoong
Geses ge′səs
Gesius gayz′yoos
gestopft gəshtopft′
Gesualdo jezoo-al′dō
Gevaert gay′vahrt
Gewandhauskonzerte gəvant′hows-kontser′tə
Gianni Schicchi jan′ee skee′kee
Gieseking gee′zəking
giga jee′ga
Gigault zheegō
Gigli jeel′yee
gigue zheeg
Ginastera geenastay′ra
giocoso jōkō′zō
gioioso joi-ō′zō
Giovanni da Cascia jōvan′ee da kah′sha
Giulio Cesare in Egitto jool′yō tshay′zare een ejee′tō
giustiniana joosteenyah′na
giusto joos′tō
Glasharmonika glahs′-harmō′neeka
Glière glyehr
Glocke glok′ə
Glogauer Liederbuch glog′owər lee′dərbooCH
Gluck glook
Glückliche Hand, Die dee glük′leeCHə hant′
Godard godahr
Gombert gombehr
Gombosi gōmbō′shi
Götterdämmerung gœ′tər-dem′əroong
Goudimel goodeemel
Gounod goonō
gradevole gradeh′vole
Grande Messe des Morts grād mes day mor
Grand Prix de Rome grā pree də rom
Graner Messe grah′nər mes′ə
Grassineau graseenō
Graun grown
Graupner growp′nər
grave grah′ve
grazioso gratsyō′zō
Grenon grənō
Grétry graytree
Grigny green-yee
Grocheo grok′ay-ō
Grosse Fuge grōs′ə foo′gə

Grosse Orgelmesse grōs′ə or′gəlmesə
Grovlez grovlay
Grumiaux grümyō
Guadagni gwadan′yee
Guadagnini gwadanyee′nee
Guarneri gwarneh′ree
Guédron gaydrō
Guerre des Bouffons, La la gehr day boofō
Guerrero geray′rō
Guglielmi goolyel′mee
Gui goo′ee
Guido d'Arezzo gwee′dō dared′zō
Guillaume Tell gee-yōm tel
Guilmant geelmā
Giraud geerō
Gurrelieder goo′rə-leedər
Guttoveggio gootō-vej′yō
Gwendoline *Fr.* gwīdōleen
Gyrowetz gee′rōvets

habanera abanay′ra
Habeneck ab′ənek
Haitink hī′tingk
Halbe hal′bə
Halbton halp′-tōn
halévy alayvee
Hälfte, Die dee helf′tə
Hallén halayn′
Handschin hant′sheen
Hanuš han′oosh
Harfe har′fə
Harfenquartett har′fən-kvartet′
Harmonie der Welt, Die dee harmonee′ der velt′
Harmoniemesse harmonee′mesə
Háry János hah′ree yah′nōsh
Hasse has′ə
Haugtussa hōg′toosa
Hauk howk
Haupt howpt
Hauptmann howpt′man
Hausmusik hows′moozeek′
hautbois ōbwa
haut-dessus ōdəsü
haute-contre ōt-kōtr
Haydn hī′dən
Haym hīm
Hebenstreit hay′bən-shtrīt
Heger hay′gər
Heimkehr aus der Fremde, Die dee hīm′kayr ows der frem′də
Heise hī′zə
Henry VIII *Fr.* ãree weet
Henze hen′tsə
Heredia ayray′deea
Héritier, L' layreet-yay
Hérodiade ayrōdyad
Hérold ayrold
Hervé ervay
Hervelois, d' derv-lwa
hervorgehoben herfōr′gəhōbən
Hesdin aydī
Heugel *Fr.* œzhel
Heure Espagnole, L' lœr espanyol
Heydn hī′dən
Hidalgo eedal′gō
Hindemith hin′dəmit
Hochzeit des Camacho, Die dee hōCH′tsīt des kamah′tshō
Holmès olmez
Holzbauer holts′-bowər
Homme armé, L' lom armay
Honegger oneger
hongroise, à la a la ō-grwaz
Hotteterre ot-tehr
Hubay hoo′ba-ee
Huë ü-ay
Hufnagelschrift hoof′-nah-gəl-shrift
Hugo von Reutlingen hoo′gō fon roit′ling-ən
Huguenots, Les lay üg-nō
Hunnenschlacht hoon′ən-shlaCHt
hupf auf hoopf′ owf′
Huré üray
Hurlebusch hoor′ləboosh

Iberia eebay′reea
Ibert eebehr
idée fixe eeday feeks
Idomeneo, Re di Creta eedōmay′nay-ō, re dee kreh′ta
Illuminations, Les layz eeloomeenasyō
Images eemazh
Incoronazione di Poppaea, L' leen′koronatsyō′ne dee popay′a
incudine eenkoo′deene
Indes Galantes, Les layz īd galāt
Indy, d' dīdee
Ingegneri eenjenyeh′ree
Inghelbrecht īgelbresht
Isouard eezoo-ahr
Italiana in Algeri, L' leetalyah′na een aljeh′ree

Jacopo da Bologna yak′ōpō da bolon′ya
Jacques de Liége zhak də lee-ezh
Jacquet zhake
Jadassohn ya′dasōn
Jagd yahkt
Jahn yahn
Jahreszeiten, Die dee yar′əs-tsītən
Janáček yan′a-tshek
Janequin zhan-kī
Jarnach yar′nak
Järnefelt yer′nəfelt
Jean de Garlande zhã də garlãd
Jemnitz yem′nits
Jensen yen′zən
Jenufa yenoo′fa
Jeppesen yep′əsən
jeu zhœ
Jeune zhœn
Joachim *Ger.* yō-aCH′im, *Eng.* yō′akim
Jolie Fille de Perth, La la zhōlee fee də pert
Jommelli yomel′ee
Jongen yong′ən
jongleur zhō-glœr
Jonny spielt auf yon′ee shpeelt owf′
Josquin des Prés zhoskī day pray
jota hō′ta
Jour d'Éte à la Montagne zhoor daytay a la mōtan-yə
Jullien zhülyī

Kade kah′də
Kadosa kod′oshō
Kaiserlied kī′zər-leet
Kaiserquartett kī′zər-kvartet′
Kajanus kayah′noos
Kalliwoda kal′ivōda
Kammermusik kam′ər-moozeek′
Kammersymphonie kam′ər-zeemfonee′
Kammerton kam′ər-tōn
Karajan kar′ayan
Kastagnetten kastanyet′ən
Katchen kat′CHyən
Kaun kown
Keilberth kīl′bert
Kempe kem′pə
Kerle ker′lə
Khachaturian ka′tshatoo′ryan
Khovanschina kövansh′tsheena
Kiene kee′nə
Kiesewetter kee′zəvetər
Kilpinen kilpee′nən
Kinderscenen kin′dər-tsay′nən
Kindertotenlieder kin′dər-tōtən-leedər
Kirchenkantate keer′CHən-kantah′-tə
Kitezh keet′ezh
Kjellstrom shel′strœm
Kjerulf sher′oolf
Klavier klaveer′
Klavierauszug klaveer′ows-tsook
Kleine Nachtmusik, Eine īnə klīnə naCHt′-moozeek′

Kleine Orgelmesse klīnə or′gəl-mesə
Kleinmichel klīn′-mishəl
Klenau klay′now
Klindworth klint′vort
Klose klō′zə
Knaben Wunderhorn, Des des knah′bən voon′dər-horn
Köchel kœCH′əl
Kodaly kō′da-ee
Koechlin kœCHlī
Köhler kœ′lər
Königin von Saba, Die dee kœ′neegeen fon zah′ba
Konzert kon-tsert′
Konzertstück kon-tsert′-shtük
kräftig kref′teeCH
Krebskanon krebs′kanōn′
Krejči krezh′tshee
Křenek krzhen′ek
Kretzschmar kretsh′mar
Kreutzer kroit′sər
Kreuz kroits
Křička krzheetsh′ka
Kuhlau koo′low
Kuhnau koo′now
Kuhreigen koo′rīgən
Kunst der Fuge, Die dee koonst′ der foo′gə
Kurth koort
Kutchka kootsh′ka
Kyrie kee′ree-ay

Lablache lablash
Lage lah′gə
laissez vibrer lesay veebray
Lakmé lakmay
Lalande lalãd
La Laurencie la lōrãsee
Lamoureux lamoorœ
Lampe lam′pə
Lampugnani lampoonyah′nee
Ländler lent′lər
Landre lãdrə
Lange lang′ə
Langlais lã-gle
langsam lang′zam
Lantins, de də lãtī
larigot lareegō
lasciare vibrare lash-yah′re veebrah′re
lassú losh′oo
Laudon low′don
Laute low′tə
Lautenclavicymbel low′tən-klavi-tsümbəl
Lavallée lavalay
Lebewohl, Das das lay′bəvōl
lebhaft layb′haft
Leclair ləkler
Leeuw löv
Lefébure-Wély ləfaybür-vaylee
Lefebvre ləfeh-vrə
légèrement layzhermã
leggero, leggiero lejeh′rō
legno, col kol layn′yō
Léhar lay-ar
Lehrstück layr′shtük
Leibowitz lī′bōvits
Leider lī′dər
Leier lī′ər
leise lī′zə
Leitmotiv līt′mōteef
Leitton līt′tōn
Le Jeune lə zhœn
Lekeu ləkœ
Lélio layl-yō
Le Maistre lə meh-trə
lent lã
Lenz lents
Leonore layōnō′rə
L'Épine laypeen
Leroux ləroo
Le Roy lə rwa
Leschetizky lesheteet′ski
Les Six lay sees
Lesueur ləsü-œr
Lesur ləsür

L'Héritier layreet-yay
Libuše lee'booshe
Licenza lee-tshen'tsa
Liebe der Danae, Die dee lee'bə der dah'na-ay
Liebesflöte lee'bəs-flötə
Liebeslieder lee'bəs-leedər
Liebesoboe lee'bəs-ōbō'ə
Liebestod lee'bəs-tōt
Liebestraum lee'bəs-trowm
Liebesverbot, Das das lee'bəs-fərbōt'
lieblich leeb'leecH
Lied leet
Lied von der Erde leet' fon der er'də
Liederbuch lee'dər-booCH
Lieder eines fahrenden Gesellen lee'dər īnəs fah'rəndən gəzel'ən
Liederkreis lee'dər-krīs
Liederspiel lee'dər-shpeel
Liedertafel lee'dər-tah'fəl
Linda di Chamounix leen'da dee shamoonee'
Liniensystem leen'yən-züstaym'
Liszt list
Liuzzi lyood'zee
Lobgesang lōp'gəzang
Loeillet lœyay
Loewe lœ'və
Loewenberg lœ'vənberk
Logier lōjeer'
Logroscino logroshee'nō
Lohengrin lō'əngrin
Loriod lor'yō
Lourié loor-yay
Lucia di Lammermoor lootshee'a dee lamərmoor'
Lucio Silla lootshee'ō seel'a
Lucrezia Borgia lookrets'ya bor'ja
Ludwig lood'veecH
Luftpause looft'-powzə
Lully lülee
lustig loost'eecH
Lustigen Weiber von Windsor, Die dee loost'igən vī'bər fon vin'tsor
Luth lüt
Luther *Ger.* lü'tər, *Eng.* loo'thər
Luython loi'ton
Luzzaschi loodzas'kee
Lyraflügel lü'ra-flügəl

Machaut mashō
Macque, de də mak
Maelzel mel'tsəl
maestoso mīstō'zō
maestro al cembalo mī'strō al tshem'balō
maestro de capilla mī'strō day kapeel'ya
maestro di capella mī'strō dee kapel'a
Maggini majee'nee
maggiore majō're
Magnard manyar
Mahillon ma-eeyō
main *Fr.* mī
maître de chapelle meh-tr də shapel
maîtrise metreez
majeur mazhœr
Majorano mayorah'nō
malagueña malagayn'ya
Maldeghem, van van mal'dəgəm
Malherbe malerb
Malibran maleebrã
malinconia maleenkōnee'a
Ma Mère l'Oye ma mehr lwa
Manchicourt, de də mãsheekoor
Mancinelli man-tsheenel'ee
Mandyczewski mandi-tshev'ski
Manieren maneer'ən
Manon manō
Manon Lescaut manō leskō
Maometto II mah-ōmet'ō sekon'dō
Marais ma-re
Marazzoli maratsō'lee

Marcello martshel'ō
Marchand marshã
Marchesi markay'zee
Marchetto market'ō
marcia mar'tsha
Marseillaise, La la marsay-ez
Marteau sans Maître, Le lə martō sã meh'tr
martelé martəlay
Martenot martənō
Martin *Fr.* martī
Martinon marteenō
Martinu morteenoo'
Martin y Soler marteen' ee soler'
Martucci martoot'shee
Martyre de Saint Sébastien, Le lə marteer də sī saybastyī
Marziale marts-yah'le
Mascagni maskan'yee
Maskarade maskarah'də
Massenet masnay
mässig mes'eecH
Masson masō
Mathis der Maler matees' der mah'lər
Matin, Le lə matī
Matteis mateh'ees
Mattheson *Ger.* mat'əzōn
Mauduit mōdwee
Mayr mīr
Mazzocchi matsok'ee
medesimo tempo medeh'zeemō tem'pō
Mefistofele mefeestof'ayle
Megli mehl'yee
Mehrstimmigkeit mayr-shtim'eecH-kīt
Méhul may-ül
mélodie maylōdee
menuet mənü-eh
Menuhin men'ooən
messa di voce mes'a dee vō'tshe
Messager mesazhay
Messiaen mes-yã
mesure məzür
Meyerbeer mī'ərbayr
mezzo med'zō
Michael meesh'-a-el
Micheli meekeh'lee
Midi, Le lə meedee
Mignon meenyō
Migot meegō
Milhaud mee-yō
Millöcker mil'əkər
minacciando meenatshan'dō
minaccevole meenatshe'vole
Minnesinger min'əzing-ər
Mireille meeray
mirliton meerleetō
Moiseiwitsch mō-eezay'əvitsh
Moments Musicaux mōmã müzeekō
Mompou mompō'oo
Mondonville mōdōveel
Moniuszko monyoosh'kō
Monsigny mōseen-yee
Montalant mōtalã
Monte, de də mon'te
Montéclair mōtayklehr
Montemezzi montemed'zee
Monteux mōtœ
Monteverdi montever'dee
montre mōtr
Moór mōr
Morales mōrah'ləs
morceau morsō
Moreau morō
Morhange morīzh
Morin morī
Morlacchi morlak'ee
Moscaglia moskal'ya
Moscheles mosh'eləs
Mosè in Egitto mōze' een ejeet'ō
motif mōteef
Mouton mootō
mouvement moovmã
Mozart mō'tsart
Muette de Portici, La la mü-et

də port'eesee
Muffat *Ger.* moo'fat
Munch münsh
Mundharmonica moont'harmō'neeka
Muris, de də moo'rees
musette müzet
Musikalischer Spass moozeekah'lishər shpas'
musique concrète moozeek kōkret
musique de chambre moozeek də shombr

nachgehend naCH'gay-ənt
Nachschlag naCH'shlak
Nachtmusik naCHt'moozeek'
Nachstück naCH'shtük
Nagelclavier nah'gəl-klaveer'
Nagelgeige nah'gəl-gīgə
Namensfeier nah'mənz-fīər
Narvaez, de də narvah'əth
Naumann now'man
neben nay'bən
Neefe nay'fə
Neue Liebeslieder noi'ə lee'bəs-leedər
Neues vom Tage noi'əs fom tah'gə
Neukomm noi'kom
Neusiedler noi'zeedlər
Niccolò neekolō'
niente nyen'te
Nivers neever
Noces, Les lay nos
Noches en los Jardines de España nō'tshes en los hardeen'əs day espan'ya
Nocturnes noktürn
noire nwahr
Nonnengeige non'ən-gīgə
Non più andrai non pyoo' andrī'
notes égales notsaygal
note sensible not səseebl
notes inégales notseenaygal
Nottebohm not'əbōm
Nozze di Figaro, Le le not'se dee fee'garō
Nuits d'été nwee daytay
Nuove Musiche noo-ō've moo'zeeke
Nystroem nü'strœm

Oberwerk ō'bər-verk
ochetto oket'ō
Ochsenmenuette, Die dee ok'sən-menoo-et'ə
Ockeghem ok'əgem
Octandre oktãdr
oeuvre œvrə
offrandes ofrãd
ohne ō'nə
Oiseau de feu, L' lwazō də fœ
Oiseaux exotiques wazō egzoteek
Okeghem ok'əgem
Oktave oktah'və
Oktavgeige oktahv'gīgə
Ombra mai fu ōm'bra mī foo'
O namenlose Freude ō nah'mənlōzə froi'də
ondeggiando ondejan'dō
Ondes Martenot ōd martənō
ondule ōdül
ongarese, all al ōgaray'ze
Orff-Schulwerk orf'-shool-verk
Orgelbüchlein or'gəl-büCHlīn
Orgelwalze or'gəl-valtsə
orgue org
Orphée orfay
Ortiz orteeth'
O soave fanciulla o swah've fantshool'a
Othmayr ōtmīr
Ours, L' loors
ouvert oover
ouverture oovertür

Pacini patshee'nee
Pacius pah'tsioos
padiglione cinese padeelyō'ne tsheenay'ze

Padilla padeel'ya
Paer pah'er
Pagliacci 'palyat'shee
Paisiello pa-eezyel'ō
Paladilhe paladeel
Papillons papeeyō
Paradies paradees'
pardessus de viole pardəsü də vyol
Paride e Elena pah'reede ay elay'na
parte par'te
partita partee'ta
pasodoble pas'ōdō'ble
passacaglia pasakal'ya
passamezzo pasamed'zō
passecaille paskī
passepied pas-pyay
Pasticcio pasteetsh'yō
pastorale *It.* pastōrah'le
Pauken pow'kən
Paukenmesse pow'kən-mesə
Paukenschlag pow'kən-shlak
Paukenwirbel pow'kən-virbəl
Paumann pow'man
Paumgartner powm'gartnər
Paur powr
pausa pow'za
pause *Fr.* pōz
pavillon chinois paveeyō sheenwa
pedale paydah'le
pédalier paydal-yay
pedaliera pedalyay'ra
Pedalpauken pedahl'-powkən
Peeters pay'ters
Peitsche pīt'shə
Pénélope paynaylop
perdendosi perden'dōzee
Péri, La la payree
Persée persay
pes pays
pesante pezan'te
Pescetti peshet'ee
Petit Chaperon Rouge, Le lə pətee shapərō roozh
Petit Riens, Les lay pətee ree-ī
Peuerl poi'ərl
Pfeife pfī'fə
Phaéton fa-aytō
Philémon et Baucis feelaymō ay bōsees
Phinot feenō
piacere pya-tshay're
piacevole pya-tshev'ole
piangendo pyanjen'dō
Picchi pek'ee
Piccini pee-tshee'nee
Pierné pyernay
Pierrot Lunaire pyerō lünehr
Pijper pīpər
pincé pīsay
Pincherle pīsherl
Pistocchi peesto'kee
piston *Fr.* peestō
più pyoo
piuttosto pyootos'tō
Pizzetti peetset'ee
pizzicato peetseekah'tō
plainte plīt
plein jeu plī zhœ
pleno play'nō
pochette poshet
pochettino poketee'nō
poème symphonique pō-em sīfoneek
Poglietti polyet'ee
point d'orgue pwī dorg
pointe pwīt
Ponce pon'the
Ponchielli ponkyel'ee
Ponte, da da pon'te
ponticello pontee-tshel'ō
Poot pōt
port de voix por də vwa
portée portay
Posaune pozow'nə
positif pozeeteef
Positive pozeetee'və
Pothier potyay

Pougin poozhĭ
Poulenc poolĭk
Pouplinière poopleenyehr
poussez poosay
Pré aux clercs, Le lə pray ō klehr
près de la table pre də la tabl
prestant prestä
principale *It.* preen-tsheepah'le
Prinzipal printsipal'
Prise de Troie, La la preez də trwa
Prix de Rome pree də rom
Prodana Nevesta pro'dana nev'yasta
Prokofiev prokof'yev
Prophète, Le lə profet
Proporz prōports'
Provenzale proven-tsah'le
Prunières prün-yer
Puccini poo-tshee'nee
Pugnani poonyah'nee
Pujol poo'hol
Pulcinella pool-tsheenel'a
Pult poolt
punta poonta

quadruple croche kwodrüplə krosh
Quagliati kwalyah'tee
Quantz kvants
Quartettsatz kvartet'-zats
Quartfagott kvart'-fagōt'
Quartgeige kvart'-gīgə
Quartposaune kvart'-pozow'nə
Quatorze Juillet, Le lə katorz zhwee-ye
Quattro Rusteghi, I ee kwat'ro roo'stehgee
Querflöte kvayr'-flœ'tə
Querstand kvayr'-shtant
Quinet keenay
Quintaton kvin'ta-tōn
quinte kĭt
Quintenquartett kvin'tən-kvartet'
quinto kveen'tō
quinton kĭtō
Quintposaune kvint'-pozow'nə
Quintsaite kvint'-zītə
quintuor kwĭtüor

Rabaud rabō
Rainier rayn-yay
Raison rezō
Rákóczi rah'kōtsi
Rameau ramō
Ramis de Pareja rah'mees day pareh'-ha
Ranz des Vaches räts day vash
rappresentativo raprezentatee'vō
Rappresentazione raprezentatsyō'ne
Rasiermesserquartett razeer'-mesər-kvartet'
Rathaus rat'-hows
Ratsche rat'shə
Rauzzini ra-oo-tsee'nee
récit raysee
recitativo re-tsheetatee'vō
recueilli rakœ-yee
Reger raygor
régisseur rayzheesœr
Regnart rek'nart
Reicha *Ger.* rī'sha, *Fr.* resha
Reinecke rīn'ekə
Reizenstein rī'tsən-shtīn
réjouissance rayzhweesäs
relâche rəlash
Reményi rem'ay-nyee
Rencontre Imprévue, La la räkōtr īprayvü
Re Pastore, Il eel re pastō're
répétiteur raypayteetœr
répétition raypaytees-yō
reprise rəpreez
Respighi respee'gee
Reszke, de də resh'kə
Reubke roip'kə
Reyer rī'ər

Rezitativ retseetateef'
Reznicek rez'nee-tshek
Rhau row
Rhené-Baton rənay-batō
Riccardo I reekar'dō pree'mō
Ricci ree'tshee
Riccio ree'tshō
ricercar ree-tsherkar'
Richafort reeshafor
Rienzi, der Letzte der Tribunen ree-en'tsee, der lets'tə der treeboon'ən
Ries rees
Riesco ree-es'kō
Rieti ree-eh'tee
rigaudon reegōdō
Riisager rees'ahgər
Rippe reep'e
ripresa reepreh'za
risvegliato reezvayl-yah'tō
Rivier reev-yay
Robert le Diable rober lə dee-abl
Roger-Ducasse rozhay-dükas
Rohrwerk rōr'verk
Roi de Lahore, Le lə rwa də la-ōr
Roi d'Ys, Le lə rwa dees
Roi l'a Dit, Le lə rwa la dee
Roi Malgré Lui, Le lə rwa malgray lwee
Roland rōlä
Roland-Manuel rōlä-manüel
Rolland rōlä
Rolle rol'ə
Roman roo'man
Rondeau rōdō
Rondes de Printemps rōd də prītä
Rondine, La la ron'deene
Ronger rōzhay
Rore, de də rō're
Rosamunde rōzamoon'də
rossignol roseenyol
Rouget de Lisle roozhay də leel
Roulade roolad
rovescio, al al rovesh'yō
Roxolane, La la roksōlan
Roy, Le lə rwa
Rózsa rō'zha
Ruckpositif rük'-pozeeteef'
Rue, de la də la rü
ruggiero roojeh'rō
Rust roost
Ruthe roo'tə
Ruy Blas *Sp.* roo'ee blahs, *Fr.* rwee bla

Sacchini sakee'nee
Sackpfeife zak'pfīfə
Sacre du Printemps, Le lə sakrə dü prītä
Saint-Foix, de də sī-fwa
Saint-Saëns sī-säs
Saite zītə
Salome *Ger.* zal'ōme
Salón México, El el salōn' me'heekō
Sances san'tshes
Sandrin sädrī
sarabande sarabäd
Sarasate sarasah'te
saudades sa-oodah'des
Sauguet sōge
sautillé sōtee-yay
Sauveur sōvœr
Scacchi skak'ee
scena sheh'na
Schalmei shal'mī
Scharwenka sharveng'-ka
Schauspieldirektor show'shpeel-deerektōr'
Schellengeläute shel'ən-gəloi'tə
Scherchen sher'CHən
scherzando shertsan'dō
Scherzi, Gli lyee sher'tsee
scherzo sher'tsō
Schicksalslied shik'zahlz-leet

Schikaneder sheekanay'dər
Schildt shilt
Schipa shee'pa
Schlag shlak
Schlägel shlay'gəl •
Schlaginstrumente shlak'-instroomen'tə
Schlagobers shlahg'ōbərs
Schlagzither shlahg'tsitər
Schleife shlī'fə
Schlüssel shlüsəl
Schoeck shœk
Schoenberg shœn'berk
Schöne Melusine, Die dee shœ'nə meloozee'nə
Schöne Müllerin, Die dee shœ'nə mü'lərən
Schöpfung, Die dee shœp'foong
Schöpfungsmesse, Die dee shœp'foongz-mesə
Schottische shot'ishə
Schott und Söhne shot oont zœ'nə
Schröder-Devrient shrœ'dər-dəfreent'
Schulwerk, Das das shool'verk
Schuppanzigh shoop'an-tseeCH
schwach shvaCH
Schwanengesang shvan'ən-gəzang'
Schweigsame, Frau frow shvīg'zahmə
Schwung shvoong
sciolto shol'tō
Scipione sheepyō'ne
scorrevole skoreh'vole
Scriabin skree-ah'been
Sechzehntel zeCH'tsayntəl
segno, dal dal sayn'yō
segue seg'we
Seguidilla segeedeel'ya
sehr zayr
Seiber shī'bər
semiramide semeerah'meede
semiseria semee-say'reea
semplice sem'plee-tshe
Senaillé sena-yay
sensibile *It.* sensee'beele
senza sen'tsa
Seraglio, Il eel seral'yō
serpent droit serpä drwa
serré seray
Serse ser'se
Shaporin shapō'reen
Shebalin shebah'leen
Si see
Siciliano see-tsheelyah'nō
Sieben Worte, Die dee zee'bən vor'tə
Si j'étais Roi see zhayte rwa
simile see'meele
Simone Boccanegra seemō'ne bokaneg'ra
sinfonia concertante seenfōnee'a kon-tshertan'te
Sinfonie zinfōnee'
sinfonietta seenfōnyet'a
Singakademie zing'-akademee'
Singspiel zing'-shpeel
Sinigaglia seeneegal'ya
sino see'nō
Siroe, Re di Persia seerō-eh', re dee pers'ya
sistema seestem'a
Sitzprobe zits'prōbə
Six, Les lay sees
sixte ajoutée seekst azhootay
Skazka o Tsare Saltane skazh'ka ō tsar'ye saltan'ye
Skryabin skree-ah'been
slancio zlan'tshō
Smetana smet'ana
soave swah've
soggetto sojet'ō
Soirées Musicales swaray müzeekal
Soir et la Tempête, Le lə swar ay la täpet
solenne solen'e
Soler soler'

Solesmes solem
solfeggio solfej'ō
Solti shol'ti
Sommernachtstraum zom'ər-naCHts-trowm
Sonate Pathétique sonat patayteek
Sonnenquartetten zon'ən-kvartet'ən
sons bouchés sō booshay
sons étouffés sōz aytoofay
sons harmoniques sō armoneek
Sordun zordoon'
Sosarme, Re di Media sōzar'me, re dee med'ya
sotto voce so'tō vō'tshe
soupir soopeer
sourdine soordeen
Souterliedekens soo'tərlee'dəkənz
spassapensieri spasapensyay'ree
Spataro spatah'ro
spezzato spedzah'tō
Spieltenor shpeel'tenōr'
Spitta shpeet'a
Spitze shpit'sə
Spohr shpōr
Sprechgesang shpreCH'-gezang
Sprechstimme shpreCH'-shtimə
Squarcialupi skwar-tshaloo'pee
Staatsoper shtahts'-ōpər
Städtische Oper shtet'ishə ōpər
Stadtpfeifer shtat'-pfīfər
Stahlspiel shtahl'-shpeel
Ständchen shtent'CHyən
stark *Ger.* shtark
Steg shtek
Steibelt shtī'bəlt
stile *It.* stee'le
Stimme shtim'ə
Stölzel shtœl'tsəl
Strandrecht shtrant'reCHt
strascinando strasheenan'dō
Straube shtrow'bə
Streich shtrīCH
Streit zwischen Phöbus und Pan, Der der shtrīt tsvish'ən fœ'boos oont pan'
Striggio stree'jō
stringendo streenjen'dō
Strungk shtroongk
Stück shtük
Sturm und Drang shtoorm' oont drang'
style galant steel galä
Suggia soo'ja
suivez sweevay
sulla scena sool'a sheh'na
sulla tastiera sool'a tastyeh'ra
sul ponticello sool pontee-tshel'ō
Suppé süpay
sur la touche sür la toosh
Süssmayr züs'mīr
Swieten, van fan sveet'ən
symphonie *Fr.* sīfōnee, *Ger.* zeemfōnee'
System züstaym'
Szell sel
Szigeti sig'eti
Szymanowski sheemanov'ski

table *Fr.* tabl
tabourin taboorĭ
Tabourot taboorō
Tafelmusik ta'fəl-moozeek'
taille ta-ee
Taillefer ta-yəfehr
Taktstrich takt'shtriCH
talon, au ō talō
Tamagno taman'yō
tambour tāboor
tambourin tāboorĭ
tampon tāpō
tañer tanyer
Taneyev tan-yay'ev
Tannhäuser tan'hoizər
Tanz tants
Tapissier tapees-yay
Taste tas'tə
Tauber tow'bər

Tausig tow´zeecH
Tcherepnin tsherep´neen
tema teh´ma
temps tä
Terradellas teradel´yas
Terz terts
Tessier tes-yay
Teutsch toitsh
Thais ta-ees
Thalberg tahl´berk
Thamos tah´mōs
Theresienmesse teray´ziən-mesə
theses thee´sis, thes´is
Thibaud teebō
Thoinan twanä
Thomas *Fr.* tōma
Thomé tōmay
Thuille tweel´ə
tierce de Picardie tyers də peekardee
Tiersot tyersō
Tietjens teet´yənz
Till Eulenspiegel til´ oi´lən-shpeegəl
timbales tībal
timbre tībr
tirade teerad
tirasse teeraś
tiré teeray
Titelouze teetlooz
Tod und das Mädchen, Der der tōt oont das mayd´cHyən
Tod und Verklärung tōt oont fərklay´roong
Toëschi tō-es´kee
Togni ton´yee
Tomášek tō´mashek
tombeau tōbō
ton *Fr.* tō, *Ger.* tōn
tonadilla tōnadeel´ya
Tonart tōn´art
Tondichtung tōn´-deecHtoong
Tonkunst tōn´-koonst
Tonreihe tōn´-rī-ə
Tortelier tortəl-yay
Toteninsel, Die dee tō´tən-inzəl
Totenmesse tō´tən-mesə

Tote Stadt, Die dee tō´tə shtat´
touche toosh
Tournemire toorn-meer
Trabaci trabah´tshee
Traetta tra-et´a
Träumerei troi´mərī
träumerisch troi´mərish
tremblement trâblə-mä
Triebschener Idyll treep´shənər idül
Trinklied tringk´leet
Triole tree-ō´lə
triolet tree-ole
triple croche treeplə krosh
Triumphlied tree-oomf´leet
Trompete trompay´tə
trompette trōpet
trouvères troover
Trovatore, Il eel trovatō´re
Troyens, Les lay trwa-yī
Tschudi tshoo´dee
Tunder toon´dər
Turandot *It.* toorandōt´, *Eng.* tshoo´rəndot
turba toor´ba
Turchi toor´kee
tutte le corde toot´e le kor´de
tutti toot´ee
tympanon tīpanō
Tyrwhitt-Wilson tir´it-wil´sən

Ubung ü´boong
Uhr, Die dee oor´
Umkehrung oom´kayroong
Umlauf oom´lowf
umore oomō´re
Un di felice oon´ dee faylee´tshe
unruhig oonroo´eecH
unter oon´tər

Vaccai vaka´ee
Vaet vaht
Valen valayn´
Vallin valī
Varèse varez
Vecchi vek´ee
veloce velō´tshe
Ventil venteel´

Verdelot verdlō
Verklärte Nacht fərklayr´tə nacHt´
Verschiebung fərshee´boong
Verschworenen, Die dee fərshvō´rənən
Vesti la giubba vest´ee la joob´a
Viaggio a Reims, Il eel vee-aj´yō a rīs
Vicentino vee-tshentee´nō
Vida Breve, La la vee´da breh´ve
vide veed
Vier Grobiane, Die dee feer grōbyah´nə
Vierhebigkeit feerhay´beecH-kīt
Viertel feer´təl
Vieuxtemps vyœ-tä
vihuela vee-oo-eh´la
villancico veelyanthee´kō
Vinci veen´tshee
Viñes veen´yəs
Vin Herbé, Le lə vī erbay
Violine vee-ōlee´nə
violon vee-ōlō
Virdung feer´doong
Visions fugitives veezyō fü-zheeteev
vite veet
vivace veevah´tshe
voce vō´tshe
Vogelweide, von der fon der fō´gəl-vīdə
Voi, che sapete voi´ kay sapay´te
Voix Humaine vwa ümen
volante volät
Volkslied folks´leet
Volles Werk fol´əs verk´
Von Heute auf Morgen fon hoi´tə owf mor´gən
Vorschlag fōr´shlak
Vorspiel fōr´shpeel

Waelrant val´rant
Wagner vag´nər
Waldmärchen valt´-mercHən
Waldteufel valt´-toifəl
Walküre, Die dee valkü´rə

Wally, La la val´ee
Walter, Walther val´tər
Walzer val´tsər
Wanhal van´hal
Weber vay´bər
Wechsel vek´səl
Weihe des Hauses, Die dee vī´ə des how´zəs
Wellesz vel´es
Werle ver´lə
Wert vert
Werther ver´tər
Weyse vī´zə
Widor vee´dor
Wiegenlied vee´gən-leet
Willaert vil´ahrt
Windgassen vint´gasən
Winter *Ger.* vin´tər
Winterreise, Die dee vin´tər-rīzə
Wolf, Wolff volf
Wozzeck vot´sek
Wurstfagott voorst´fagōt

Yradier eeradyehr´
Ysaÿe eeza´ee

Zachow tsak´ow
Zaïde za-ee´də
Zampa zăpa
Zampogna dzampōn´ya
Zandonai zandōna´ee
zapateado thapatayah´dō
zart tsart
zarzuela thar-thoo-eh´la
ziemlich tseem´leecH
zingarese, alla ala tseeng-gareh´-ze
zoppa, alla ala tsop´a
Zugposaune tsoog´-pozow´nə
Zukunftsmusik tsoo´koonfts-moozeek´
Zumsteeg tsoom´shtayk
zurückhaltend tsoorük´-haltənt
Zweiunddreisigstel tzvī-oont-drī´sigstəl
Zwischenspiel tsvish´ən-shpeel
Zwölftonsystem tsvœlf´-tōn-züstaym´

ACKNOWLEDGEMENTS

The editor and publishers wish to thank the following for their help with the illustrations to this book:

Ashmolean Museum, Oxford: 47; reproduced by permission of the British Library Board: 50, 70, 180, 238, 241, 247, 265, 389, 407, 529, 563; the Trustees of the British Museum: 150, 259, 262, 304; Camera Press: 155; courtesy of Contemporary Films: 27; David Redfern: 41, 156, 191, 290; English National Opera: 90 (photograph by Angus McBean), 281 (photograph by Dominic); Keystone Press Agency: 81, 521, 554; Mansell Collection: 42, 69, 79, 157, 174, 184, 235, 237, 240, 262, 330, 373, 433, 459; Mary Evans Picture Library: 578; reproduced by courtesy of the Trustees, the National Gallery, London: 451; Peters Editions: 99 (photograph by James Klosty); Popperfoto: 72, 83, 112, 277, 351, 388, 490; Radio Times Hulton Picture Library: 32, 145, 230, 232, 269, 272, 307, 337; Raymond Mander and Joe Mitchenson Theatre Collection: 56, 62, 106, 117, 172, 218, 226, 349, 403, 473, 474, 506, 507, 557, 564; Royal College of Music, London: 64B; G. Schirmer Ltd.: 56, 107, 287; Schott & Co. Ltd.: 550 (photograph by Mischa Scorer); Scottish Opera: 189, 562 (photographs by Bryan and Shear Ltd.); Victoria and Albert Museum: 234.

The specially commissioned drawings of musical instruments are by Anthony Valbonesi.

ABBREVIATIONS AND CROSS REFERENCES

Names of languages are given in abbreviation in brackets following the head-word – Cz. for Czech, Dan. for Danish, Du. for Dutch, Eng. for English, Fr. for French, Ger. for German, Gr. for Greek, It. for Italian, Lat. for Latin, Russ. for Russian, Sp. for Spanish.

Cross references are indicated by (1) *see* plus word(s) in small capitals; (2) Word(s) in small capitals in the course of an entry.

A (Eng., Ger.; It., *la*), (1) the sixth note (or submediant) of the scale of C major. In the early middle ages the letter A came to be attached to

in preference to other notes, because this had been the lowest note of the two-octave scale system of the Greeks. The practice of using the letters A to G for successive octaves dates from the 10th century. In Germany it is common to use *A* for A major and *a* for A minor, and similarly with other letters. This practice has also begun to be followed (to a limited extent) in Britain.

is the note (normally given by the oboe) to which an orchestra tunes. By international agreement its pitch is 440 cycles a second.

See KEY, NOTATION, PITCH, SCALE.

(2) as an abbreviation *A.* = alto, associate.

Aaron, Pietro (c. 1490–1545), Italian theorist, who was active as a teacher in Rome. One of the most progressive writers of his time, he refused to accept many of the conventions of medieval practice which still survived in the 16th century. Aaron recommended, among other things, that accidentals should always be written in the music and not left to the performers. His best known work was *Thoscanello de la musica* (1523; facsimile edition 1969), which went into several editions.

Abaco, Evaristo Felice Dall' (1675–1742), Italian violinist and composer. From 1714 he was director of the court music at Munich. He wrote trio sonatas, violin sonatas and orchestral concertos. His son, Giuseppe Clemens Ferdinand Dall' Abaco (1709–1805), was a cellist, and from 1738 director of court music at Bonn.

Abba-Cornaglia, Pietro (1851–94), Italian composer and historian. His compositions include several operas (including *Isabella Spinola* and *Maria di Warden*), a Requiem and chamber music.

Abbado, Claudio (born 1933), Italian conductor. He studied in Milan and Vienna, and in 1958 won the Koussevitsky prize for conducting at Tanglewood. Later he won the Dmitri Mitropoulos conducting prize in New York, which helped to establish his international reputation. His first British appearance was with the Hallé Orchestra in 1965. In the 1970s he consolidated his European success by achieving the dual distinction of the musical directorship of La Scala, Milan, and the conductorship of the Vienna Philharmonic. Though he is one of the most gifted Verdi and Rossini conductors of the day, his repertory ranges much wider than that – from his own arrangement of Bach's *Musical Offering* to the latest opera by Luigi Nono.

Abbatini, Antonio Maria (c. 1597–1680), Italian composer, active as a church musician in Rome. He published Masses, psalms, motets and antiphons, and was joint composer with Marco Marazzoli of one of the earliest known comic operas, *Dal male il bene* (Rome, 1653).

Abbé, Joseph Barnabé Saint-Sevin l' (1721–1803), French virtuoso violinist, a member of the orchestra of the Comédie-Française at the age of twelve. He wrote music for violin and *Les Principes du violon* (1761).

abbellimenti (It.), ornaments.

Abbey, John (1785–1859), English organ-builder who lived in Paris from 1826 and built many organs for French cathedrals and churches.

ABEGG Variations, work for piano, op 1, by Schumann, written in 1830 and dedicated by him to 'Countess' Abegg (really Meta von Abegg, a friend of the composer). In tribute to her, he derived the theme of the variations from her name, using the notes A–B flat–E–G–G (the German *B* being the same as the English B flat).

Abel, Carl Friedrich (1723–87), German composer, son of a violinist in the court music at Cöthen. He worked at the Dresden court from 1748 until 1758. He became a distinguished performer on the bass viol and appeared in this capacity in London, where, in association with Johann Christian Bach, he gave several series of subscription concerts. His works include symphonies and chamber music. His portrait was painted by Gainsborough.

Abell, John (1653–1724), Scottish counter-tenor singer in the service of Charles II and James II. He travelled on the Continent during the reign of William III, returning to England in 1700. His publications include three collections of songs. His reputation as a singer was high (*see* Evelyn, *Diary*, January 27, 1682).

Abendmusiken (Ger.), evening musical performances, in particular those given every autumn in the Marienkirche at Lübeck. They are first mentioned in 1673, when Buxtehude was organist. They consisted of organ solos and a cycle of five church cantatas for voices and instruments, performed on the last Sunday after Trinity, the Sunday next before Advent, and the second, third and fourth Sundays in Advent (*see* Albert Schweitzer, *J. S. Bach*, volume i, pages 76–9). In 1705 Bach (aged twenty) obtained leave of absence from Arnstadt (about 230 miles from Lübeck) in order to hear the *Abendmusiken* under Buxtehude. He was so impressed by what he heard that he overstayed his leave.

Abert, Hermann (1871–1927), German historian and musicologist who held professorships at Halle, Leipzig and Berlin. He wrote studies of Greek and medieval music, a biography of Schumann, and an authoritative study of the life and work of Mozart (based on Jahn).

Abgesang (Ger.), 'aftersong'. The concluding portion of a stanza of a MINNESINGER or MEISTERSINGER song. *See* BAR (3)

Abraham, Gerald Ernest (born 1904), English musicologist, whose special field is Russian music. From 1947 until 1962 he was professor of music at Liverpool University, and from then until 1967 assistant controller of music with the B.B.C. His books include *Masters of Russian Music* (with M. D. Calvocoressi, 1936), *A Hundred Years of Music* (1938), *Chopin's Musical Style* (1939), and *Eight Soviet Composers* (1943). He has edited several volumes of the *New Oxford History of Music*.

Abschiedssymphonie, *see* FAREWELL SYMPHONY

Absil, Jean (born 1893), Belgian composer. He studied at Brussels Conservatoire and in 1931 became professor there. His compositions, unconventional in rhythm and harmony, include five symphonies, concertos for violin, viola, cello, piano, choral and chamber music.

absolute music, a term commonly used as the opposite of PROGRAMME MUSIC, to indicate music that has no admitted association with anything outside itself. The great majority of instrumental music comes into this category of 'purity'. The distinction is, however, unsound, since music, being a product of the human mind, can never be wholly divorced from human experience.

absolute pitch, or **perfect pitch,** the gift of recognizing the pitch of any note that is heard, or of singing any note at the correct pitch without help from an instrument. Though it derives largely from a constant association with music performed at the standard pitch, it is also found in precocious children, and may decline with advancing years. It is particularly useful to singers and conductors but may prove embarrassing when music is transposed. There is no justification for regarding it as a sign of outstanding musical ability.

Academic Festival Overture, Brahms's *Akademische Fest-Ouvertüre* for orchestra, op 80 (1880), written in recognition of the conferment of an honorary Ph.D. on the composer by the University of Breslau in 1879. A number of German students' songs are introduced into the score, including 'Gaudeamus igitur', with which the piece ends. The work was first performed in Breslau in 1881.

a cappella (It.), 'in the church style'. Traditionally, the term is applied to choral music which is either (1) entirely without accompaniment or (2) without any independent accompaniment. Today, however, it is used only in the first sense.

accelerando (It.), 'quickening (the time)'. Often abbreviated *accel.*

accent, (1) the rhythm of music, as of verse, is made clear by accent. Where the structure is symmetrical, as in most 18th century music, the accent will recur at regular intervals, e.g. in 4/4 time on the first beat of the bar and, with lesser force, on the third; in 3/4 time on the first beat of the bar. But even in 18th century music this is by no means universal:

HANDEL, *Messiah*

This is equivalent to:

i.e. an accent on the word 'hath' would distort the rhythm. A further example:

MOZART, *Sonata in F major*, K 332

Here the departure from the normal rhythm in the third and fourth bars is made clearer by the alternation of *f* and *p*. Modern composers tend to express such changes of rhythm by altering the lengths of the bars.

Although bar-lines represent a fundamental rhythm (similar to the scansion of a line of verse), there is no reason why accent should coincide with the 'strong' beats, any more than the words in poetry exactly represent the scansion by feet. This distinction is clearly marked in 16th century music. Here, in spite of the absence of bar-lines, there is a fundamental rhythm which governs the treatment of consonance and dissonance, while at the same time the rhythm of any individual phrase pursues an independent course. The opening of Palestrina's *Stabat Mater* is barred in modern editions as follows:

This represents the fundamental rhythm of the piece. But the rhythm of the phrase is more clearly seen if we remove the bar-lines and write:

In this example all the voices have the same rhythm; but where the vocal lines are independent of each other we find contrasted rhythms, with the accent occurring in different places in the different voices:

BYRD, *Gradualia*, Book I, i, 2

In such cases intelligent singers will require no signs to show where the accent lies.

Accent signs are properly used to indicate special emphasis, in whatever part of a bar it may be required. Those in current use are: (1) > (2) — (3) ∧ or ∨ . Composers are not always consistent in using them; but > normally indicates a strong accent, — stress or pressure, ∧ or ∨ heavy pressure. > and — are written over or under the note, whichever is more convenient; ∧ is written over, ∨ under. These signs indicate relative intensity and may occur in a passage marked *pianissimo*. They are also found, rather unnecessarily, in combination, e.g. △, and in association with the sign for *staccato*, e.g. —. The following abbreviations also indicate strong emphasis: *sf* or *sfz* (*sforzando*, 'forcing'), *sfp* or *fp* (*sforzando piano* or *forte piano*. an accent followed immediately by *piano*), *rf* or *rfz* (*rinforzando* 'reinforcing'). The sign *pf*, used by Brahms, has nothing to do with emphasis; it is an abbreviation of *poco forte*, 'moderately loud'.

(2) (Fr.), an ornament used in French music of the 17th and 18th centuries, equivalent to the German NACHSCHLAG.

acciaccatura (It.), a 'crushing' (implying violent pressure); (1) a keyboard ornament current in the 17th and 18th centuries.

A dissonant ornamental note, of the shortest

possible duration, is struck at the same time as the chord which it decorates. The ornamental note is often printed as part of the chord, in which case it is for the interpreter to guess the composer's intention:

BACH, *Partita no 3*

Here the G sharp, in the chord marked *, must be released as soon as it is struck, leaving the A minor chord to sound without further interference. In music in slower tempo it was customary to play the chord arpeggio. The conventional sign for the acciaccatura was an oblique stroke to represent the dissonant note, e.g.

as written:

as played:

BACH, *English Suite no 1*

French composers also used the following sign (which now indicates a simple arpeggio):
as written:

as played:

(2) the name is now applied to the short APPOGGIATURA, an ornamental note of minimum duration, sounded either immediately before, or simultaneously with, the main note, and notated by using an auxiliary note in smaller type, with a stroke through its stem.

accidental, a comprehensive term for a SHARP, DOUBLE SHARP, FLAT, DOUBLE FLAT or NATURAL prefixed to a note in the course of a composition. An accidental placed against a note applies also to all subsequent repetitions of that note (if any) in the same bar, unless cancelled by another accidental. In FIGURED BASS, accidentals are placed before or after the figures; an accidental by itself, without any figure, applies to the third from the bass.

accompaniment, a subordinate part or parts, most frequently instrumental, added to a principal part or parts. Such accompaniment may be merely a duplication, as often happens with the organ accompaniment of vocal church music, in which case it can be dispensed with at will. More often it is independent, though it may incorporate some details of the principal part or parts. In the 17th and early 18th centuries keyboard accompaniment was normally from FIGURED BASS and hence involved an element of improvisation. With the decline of figured bass, such accompaniment was less likely to be purely subordinate. In many 19th and 20th century songs the accompaniment is at least as important as the vocal line; such works are rather duets for voice and piano than songs with piano accompaniment. The popular view that an accompanist is a person inferior in skill and importance to the person accompanied has no justification. In the 18th century sonatas for violin (or flute) with harpsichord (or piano) were commonly said to be for keyboard instrument with accompaniment, e.g. J. C. Bach's op 10: *Six Sonatas for the Harpsichord or Piano Forte; with an Accompagnament for a Violin.*

See ADDITIONAL ACCOMPANIMENTS, OBBLIGATO

F. T. ARNOLD: *The Art of Accompaniment from a Thorough-Bass* (1931)

accordion, piano-accordion (Fr., *accordéon*; Ger., *Ziehharmonika*; It., *fisarmonica*), a portable reed organ, invented by Friedrich Buschmann of Berlin in 1822, who gave it the name Handäoline. The sounds are produced by metal reeds freely vibrating within frames, the air being supplied by bellows which the player operates by pulling and pushing the instrument – hence the nickname 'squeeze-box'. There are two basic types of accordion. In the first both hands are used to press studs, which produce either single notes or chords, while in the other the right hand plays on a keyboard. Only the second type, which is in more general use, is correctly described as a piano accordion. Although largely confined to popular music, the instrument has been used by such composers as Chaikovsky, Shostakovich, Gerhard and Roy Harris, who has written a concerto for it.

Achtel (Ger.), quaver.

Acis and Galatea, a masque, or pastoral opera, for soloists, chorus and orchestra by Handel, first performed at Cannons, near London, between 1718 and 1720. The libretto by John Gay (with additions by Dryden, Hughes and Pope), is based on Ovid. It tells how Acis loves the nymph Galatea but is crushed to death by the monster Polyphemus beneath a rock; Acis's blood is transformed into a river. The most famous aria in the work is 'Oh ruddier than the cherry', sung by the bass, Polyphemus.

Handel's Italian cantata, *Aci, Galatea e Polifemo* (Naples, 1708) is an entirely different composition, though when Handel revised it for performance in London in 1732 he incorporated parts of the English work.

Acis et Galatée (Fr., *Acis and Galatea*), opera with a prologue and three acts by Lully, to a libretto by Jean Galbert de Campistron, first performed by the Duke of Vendôme for the Dauphin at Anet in 1686. Another opera on the subject was written by Haydn (1790).

acoustic bass, an organ stop in which the pipes of a sixteen foot pedal stop sound with a rank a fifth above, producing a RESULTANT TONE an octave below the sixteen foot pipes.

acoustics, the science of sound. Sound, in music, consists in the impact on the ear of air vibrations set in motion by (1) the vibration of some elastic material, (2) the vibration of an air column in a pipe, or (3) vibrations electrically produced or transmitted. The elastic material may be (*a*) a gut string or wire, set in motion by a bow (violin), or plucked with the fingers (harp) or a plectrum (mandoline) or a quill (harpsichord), or hit with a metal tongue (clavichord) or a hammer (piano); (*b*) a reed or reeds set in motion by air pressure (oboe, clarinet); (*c*) a membrane set in motion by air pressure, such as the vocal chords (human voice) or the lips (brass instruments), or struck with a beater (drums); (*d*) a solid body, set in motion by striking (bells, triangle, xylophone).

The *intensity* of a note is determined by the amplitude of the vibration. The greater the amplitude of the vibration, the louder the sound. Hence force is needed to produce a loud note.

The *pitch* of a note is determined by the frequency of the vibration. A low note vibrates slowly, a high one quickly. The frequency of the vibration may depend (1) on the length, thickness, tension and density of the vibrating material, (2) on the length and density of the air column and the nature of the tube enclosing it, or (3) may be directly produced by electrical processes. Thus, other things being equal, a short string will produce a higher note than a long one, a taut string a higher note than one less taut. A short air column will produce a higher note than a long one: the piccolo is shorter than the flute and so higher in pitch.

On the other hand, the clarinet, though approximately the same length as the flute and oboe, is much lower in pitch than either. This is because it has a cylindrical tube stopped at one end (the mouthpiece), whereas the flute, though cylindrical, is open at both ends and the tube of the oboe, though stopped at one end, is conical or expanding. String and wind instruments are differently affected by temperature. A rise in temperature causes strings to expand, so that their tension is relaxed and they drop in pitch; but the expansion of air decreases its density, so that the pitch of wind instruments rises, the expansion of their material not being sufficient to counteract this.

The *resonance* of a note depends on the presence of some auxiliary material or an air column that will vibrate either in sympathy or by direct contact with the original vibrations. Thus the violin owes its resonance to its belly, the oboe to the air column contained in its tube. There is, however, an important difference. In the violin the belly has to vibrate as the strings dictate. In the oboe (as in other wind instruments) the vibrating air column, being of a definite length, controls the vibrations of the reed; so that in this case the resonator determines the pitch.

The *quality* of a note depends on the complex character of the vibrations. A stretched string does not merely vibrate as a whole. It also vibrates simultaneously in sections, which are in an exact mathematical relationship to the length of the string. These sections are the halves, thirds, quarters, fifths and so on. The halves produce a note an octave higher than the note sounded by the whole string, the thirds a note a twelfth higher, the quarters a note two octaves higher, and so on. The 'overtones' sounded by the respective sections fall into a series known as the HARMONIC SERIES. If the principal note or 'fundamental' is ♩ the series will run as follows:

(The notes marked x are not in tune with our ordinary scale).

The numbers of the series indicate exactly the mathematical relationship between the frequencies of the notes. Thus the ratio between:

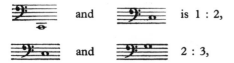

and so on. The sound of the overtones is very much fainter than that of the note produced by the whole string, but without them the note heard by the listener would lose its lustre. The air-column of a wind instrument or an organ pipe also vibrates in sections. If it is stopped at one end, as in some organ pipes, only alternate sections vibrate, so that a stopped pipe produces only nos 1, 3, 5, 7 etc. of the harmonic series. Much the same thing happens with the clarinet, with its cylindrical tube stopped at one end. The characteristic tone-quality of instruments is thus due to the extent to which the 'upper partials' (the overtones of the harmonic series) are present or absent and to their relative intensity. This makes it possible, in electronic instruments like the Hammond organ, to imitate closely the sound of orchestral instruments by presenting an artificial selection of the appropriate upper partials and giving to each the necessary intensity. In some instruments the overtones do not fall into the harmonic series and are therefore 'inharmonic'. The result may be a confused but recognizable sound, as in a bell, or one of indeterminate pitch, as in most percussion instruments.

By touching a string lightly at a point half-way from the end the player can prevent the string vibrating as a whole, while leaving the two halves free to vibrate. A similar result can be achieved by touching the string at other sectional points. The notes so produced are known, for obvious reasons, as HARMONICS. In the same way a wind-player, by increased lip-tension (known technically as 'over-blowing'), can split the air column in his instrument into one of its component parts, so that instead of sound no 1 of the harmonic series it produces one of the upper partials as its principal

note. This is done to a limited degree on woodwind instruments and extensively on brass instruments. The horn, for example, has a choice of upper partials from the second to the sixteenth harmonic. This explains why horn-players sometimes seem uncertain about their notes. The higher harmonics lie very close together, so that the selection of the right one by lip-tension calls for considerable skill. The extent to which members of the harmonic series are available on brass instruments depends on the relation between the diameter of the tube and its length. Neither the horn nor the trumpet, being narrow-bored instruments, can sound no 1 of the series.

When two notes are sounded simultaneously the difference between their frequencies produces a faintly sounding note known as a DIFFERENCE TONE, and this in turn combines with them to produce further difference tones. With a chord of three notes there will be even more difference tones, which may conflict with the notes of the chord. The difference tones set up by the major triad merely confirm the harmony, but the difference tones set up by the minor triad include notes completely alien to the chord:

This explains why the minor triad sounds less smooth and restful than the major triad. An additional reason is to be found in the clashes between the upper partials of notes heard in combination:

There are obvious clashes between the upper partials of the notes of the major triad; but in the minor triad the third of the chord (emphasized by its second and fourth harmonics) itself clashes strongly with the prominent fifth harmonic of the bass note, i.e. in this example E flat, the third of the chord, clashes with E natural, the fifth harmonic of C. Such clashes are apparent in a resonant building. It was a sure instinct that led 16th century composers of church music to avoid ending a piece with a minor chord. They preferred in such cases either to leave the final chord without any third at all or to substitute a major third, the so-called *tierce de Picardie*.

A further result of the combination of two notes is a very much fainter sound produced by the sum of their frequencies and therefore known as a SUMMATION TONE. Difference tones and summation tones are together known as COMBINATION or RESULTANT TONES. The principle of difference tones is applied in a number of electrical instruments, which by combining two high frequencies produce an audible difference tone which can then be amplified. For a clumsy application of the same principle to organ building, see ACOUSTIC BASS, ORGAN.

The science of acoustics is practical. It is responsible for improvements in the manufacture of instruments, in wireless transmission and gramophone recording, and in the building of concert halls – though the acoustical success of a hall still seems to be as much a matter of luck as of science. The 'acoustics' of a concert hall or theatre are good if the building provides an adequate but not an excessive amount of resonance. Resonance is affected both by the shape of the building and by its material and interior decoration.

H. BAGENAL and A. WOOD: *Planning for Good Acoustics* (1931)

L. L. BERANAK: *Music, Acoustics and Architecture* (1962)

P. C. BUCK: *Acoustics for Musicians* (1918)

J. JEANS: *Science and Music* (1937)

LL. S. LLOYD: *Music and Sound* (1937)

H. LOWERY: *The Background of Music* (1952)

E. G. RICHARDSON: *The Acoustics of Orchestral Instruments and of the Organ* (1929)

A. WOOD: *The Physics of Music* (1943)

action, the mechanism of a keyboard instrument, especially the pressure required to sound a note.

act tune, a term used in Britain in the 17th and early 18th centuries to indicate a piece of instrumental music (generally in dance rhythm) performed between the acts of a play. There are a large number of examples in Purcell's music for the theatre. The modern term is the French word *entr'acte*.

acute, an ornament in 17th century English music.
See SPRINGER

acute mixture, an organ stop giving overtones tuned slightly sharp.

adagietto (It.), slightly faster than *adagio*.

adagio (It.), 'at ease', i.e. slow. Hence used often to describe the slow movement of a symphony, sonata or concerto.

Adagio for Strings, short orchestral piece by Samuel Barber, originally the slow movement of a string quartet. In its inflated (and admittedly very beautiful) version, it was first performed in 1938.

adagissimo (It.), very slow.

Adam, Adolphe Charles (1803–56), French composer, teacher and critic, most successful as a composer of *opéra comique*. He was the son of a pianist and composer, Jean Louis Adam, and a pupil of Boieldieu. His attempt to found a new opera house in 1847 was ruined by the Revolution of 1848. He was professor of composition at the Paris Conservatoire from 1849. His most famous operas are *Le Postillon de Longjumeau* (1836), with its high-flying tenor part, and *Si j'étais roi* (*If I were King*, 1852), though today it is for his ballet, *Giselle*, that he is most widely known.

Adamberger, Johann Valentin (1743–1804), German tenor singer and teacher. He sang first in Italy under the name Adamonti, then in Vienna from 1780. Mozart wrote the part of Belmonte in *Die Entführung aus dem Serail* (1782) for him.

Adam de la Hale or **Hallé** (c. 1230–88), *trouvère* and composer, who wrote both solo songs and polyphonic motets and rondeaux. He was nicknamed 'le bossu d'Arras' (the hunchback of Arras), but himself denied the deformity. In the last years of his life he was in the service of Count Robert II of Artois and followed him to Naples. His dramatic pastoral *Li Gieus de Robin et Marion* (The Play of Robin and Marion), in which popular songs were incorporated, remained in favour long after his death. His works were published by E. de Coussemaker (1872) but more recently his *Lyric Works* have been edited by N. E. Wilkins (1967). An English translation of *The Play of Robin and Marion* is included in R. Axton and J. Stevens, *Medieval French Plays* (1971).

added sixth (Fr., *sixte ajoutée*), a term invented by Rameau to describe the addition of a sixth from the bass to the subdominant chord in a plagal cadence, i.e. in the key of C major:

He thus distinguished the chord by its function from the same combination of notes followed by the dominant chord:

where he regarded it as the first inversion of the supertonic seventh:

Later theorists have failed to observe this distinction, so that the term 'added sixth' no longer has any significance and might with as much, or as little, justification be applied to similar combinations of notes on other degrees of the scale.

See CHORD, FIGURED BASS, HARMONY

additional accompaniments, parts for extra instruments added to the scores of 17th and 18th century works, which through the employment of a figured bass and modest orchestral resources are thought by a later age to lack fullness. Handel has been the chief victim of this practice, though Bach has also suffered considerably on the Continent. Mozart wrote additional accompaniments for performances of *Messiah* where no organ was available, and further additions were made to these by other hands. Ebenezer Prout's edition (1902) was an ineffective compromise between additional accompaniments and a return to the original text. Sir Henry Wood ignored compromise and rescored the whole work. He also applied the same principles to other works by Handel. A common defence of rescoring is that choirs today are much larger than in Handel's time. This is clearly no defence at all, since there is no reason why any of Handel's works should be sung by a large choir. Bach's *St. Matthew Passion* is regularly sung without any additional accompaniments whatever, and there is no reason why Handel's oratorios should not be treated in the same way – fortunately there are now more scholarly editions of *Messiah* (e.g. by Watkins Shaw) which have begun to win favour, though inflated performances of *Messiah* are still put on.

à deux cordes (Fr.; It., *a due cordes*), on two strings.

Adieux, L'Absence et Le Retour, Les, *see* LEBEWOHL

Adler, Guido (1855–1941), Czech-Austrian historian and musicologist who in 1898 succeeded Hanslick as professor at Vienna University. There he founded the institute of musical history, directing it until 1927. His pupils include a large number of distinguished scholars. In 1894 he founded the *Denkmäler der Tonkunst in Osterreich* (monuments of music in Austria) and acted as general editor of the series for 44 years, as well as editing sixteen volumes himself. He wrote books on Wagner and Mahler and on methods of historical study in music. His *Handbuch der Musikgeschichte* (1924, second edition in two volumes, 1930), with contributions by 47 writers, is indispensable to the student of musical history.

M. CARNER: *Of Men and Music* (1944)

Adler, Larry (born 1914), U.S. mouth-organist – the only such exponent of world rank. His qualities as a performer inspired Milhaud, Vaughan Williams, Malcolm Arnold and others to write works for him.

ad libitum (Lat.), 'at pleasure'. Generally abbreviated *ad lib.* According to the context the performer has complete freedom (1) to interpret a passage as he wishes, without regard for strict time (It., *a piacere*), or (2) to make use of an alternative note or notes provided by the composer, or (3) to improvise. Also applied to a part (generally instrumental) which may be omitted at will or exchanged for another; in this sense it is the opposite of OBBLIGATO.

Adlung, Jacob (1699–1762), German organist (at Erfurt from 1727) and teacher. Of his theoretical works the most important is *Musica mechanica organoedi* (two volumes, 1768), a treatise on the manufacture and care of keyboard instruments: facsimile edition by C. Mahrenholz (1931). Facsimile edition of his *Anleitung zur musikalischen Gelahrtheit* (1758) by H. J. Moser (1953).

Admeto, Re di Tessaglia (It., *Admetus, King of Thessaly*), opera in three acts by Handel, to a libretto by Nicola Francesco Haym or Paolo Antonio Rolli (altered version of an earlier Italian text by A. Aureli). First performed in 1727 in London, the work is notable for the beauty of its arias.

a due (It.), 'in two parts'. The term is generally written *a 2*: (1) in wind parts it indicates that a single melodic line is to be played by two instruments in unison;

(2) in string parts it indicates that a passage in two parts is to be played *divisi* (the term normally used today). So also *a 3* and *a 4*.

Aeolian harp, a zither-like instrument with strings of different thickness all tuned to the same note. It is not played but placed outside, often on a windowsill, to catch the wind. The wind makes the strings vibrate with various harmonics depending on its speed, producing a series of chords. The Aeolian harp was known in ancient times and is named after Aeolus, the mythological god of the winds; its present form was developed at the end of the 16th century.

Aeolian mode, (1) in ancient Greek music one of the names given to:

(2) from the 16th century onwards applied to:

The tonic (or final) and dominant are marked respectively T and D.

See GLAREANUS, GREEK MUSIC, MODE

aeolina, aeoline, a soft organ stop, so named because the tone produced resembles the sound of an Aeolian harp.

aeoliphone, *see* WIND MACHINE

aerophone, an instrument in which the movement of air causes sound production. In free aerophones, a reed is made to vibrate by the passage of air across it and produce the sound. Examples include the harmonium, mouth organ and reed section of an organ. In wind instruments, a column of air is made to vibrate and produce the sound. There are three kinds of wind instruments: brass instruments, such as the horn and trumpet, in which vibration of the lips inside the mouthpiece sets a column of air vibrating; reed pipes such as the clarinet and oboe in which the vibration of a reed (single or double) in a mouthpiece causes an air column to vibrate; and flutes and whistles, such as the recorder and flue section of an organ, in which air is blown across the edge of an aperture to set the air column within the pipe vibrating.

aerophor, device enabling wind instrumentalists to play continuously without pausing for breath. Air from a bellows, operated by the player's foot, is pumped through a tube into the corner of his mouth and then into his instrument while he breathes through his nose.

aetherophone, etherophone, *see* ELECTRONIC INSTRUMENTS

Affektenlehre (Ger.), a system of musical aesthetics, formulated in Germany in the 18th century and widely accepted, according to which compositions were judged by the extent to which they portrayed and aroused specific emotions.

affetto (It.), 'affection'.

affettuoso (It.), 'affectionate', i.e. with tender emotion.

affrettando (It.), 'hurrying', i.e. increasing the speed.

Africaine, L' (Fr., *The African Girl*), opera in five acts by Meyerbeer, to a libretto by Augustin Eugène Scribe, first performed in 1865 in Paris. Meyerbeer's last opera (which took him about twenty years to write) concerns Vasco da Gama – shipwrecked on the African coast in this story – and the captive African girl with whom he falls in love. In the end she sacrifices her life for him. Though very popular in the 19th century, the work is known today mainly for the aria which Vasco da Gama sings in Act 4 as an apostrophe to the island of Madagascar. The original words were French, but Italian tenors have established it firmly by the title, 'O paradiso'.

agitato (It.), 'agitated', i.e. restless and wild.

Agnus Dei, (Lat.), 'Lamb of God'. The concluding portion of a musical setting of the Roman Mass, a three-fold petition ending with the words 'dona nobis pacem' (grant us thy peace). In a Requiem Mass the petition ends with the words 'dona eis requiem sempiternam' (grant them rest eternal) and is followed by *Lux aeterna* (Light eternal).

agogic, term introduced by H. Reimann in his *Musikalische Dynamik und Agogik* (1884) to describe the deviations from strict tempo and rhythm that are necessary if the performance of a musical phrase is to have any subtlety. The German term *Agogik* is used in reference to all such subtleties of performance brought about by the intelligent employment of *rubato*, etc.

Agon, ballet score by Stravinsky, written for George Balanchine and first performed in 1957 by the New York City Ballet. The music marks a turning-point in the composer's career, from the neo-classical works which had preceded it to the serialism which was to follow.

Agostini, Paolo (1583–1629), Italian organist in Rome. He was a prolific composer of church music, some of it for several choirs.

agréments (Fr.), ornaments.

Agricola, Alexander (c. 1446–c. 1506), Flemish composer, a pupil of Ockeghem. His real name was Ackermann. He served in succession Charles VIII of France, Lorenzo de' Medici, the Duke of Mantua, and Philip I of Castile. He composed church music, chansons and instrumental part-music. His complete works have been edited in five volumes by E. R. Lerner (1961–70).

Agricola, Johann Friedrich (1720–74), German organist and composer. He studied under J. S. Bach at Leipzig and Quantz at Berlin, and became court composer to Frederick the Great. His compositions, mostly unpublished, include operas and choral and instrumental works. He married the celebrated soprano Benedetta Molteni.

Agricola, Martin (real name Sore) (1486–1556), Flemish author of books on music. His most notable work was *Musica instrumentalis deudsch*, of which six editions were published (1529 and 1545 editions reprinted by R. Eitner, 1896). He also composed hymns, motets and instrumental music.

   H. FUNCK: *Martin Agricola ein frühprotestantische Schulmusiker* (1933)

Agrippina, opera in three acts by Handel, to a libretto by Vincenzo Grimani, first performed in 1709 in Venice. This opera was the main theatrical outcome of Handel's three-year stay in Italy, and with its amorous plot, still seems one of his most human.

Aguiari or **Agujari, Lucrezia** (1743–83), a remarkable Italian soprano, nicknamed – because of her illegitimacy – 'La Bastardella'. In a letter of 24 March, 1770, Mozart paid tribute to her powers, praising her 'lovely voice, flexible throat and incredibly high range' – which spanned three octaves above middle C. She was popular in London (where her fee for singing two songs was £100) as well as in Italy. She married the opera composer Giuseppe Colla.

Aguilera de Heredia, Sebastian (born 1560–70), Spanish composer. He published a volume of settings of the Magnificat for four to eight voices (1618; three settings reprinted in *Das Chorwerk*, cvi), and composed Versets and *Tientos* for organ. Examples of his organ pieces have been published in Pendrell's *Antologia de Organistas Espanoles*, i (1908) and in Bonnet's *Historical Organ Recitals*, vi (1940).

Ahle, Johann Rudolph (1625–73), German organist at St. Blasius Church, Mühlhausen and composer. He wrote a great number of works (many of a simple character) for voices and instruments. A selection is published in *Denkmäler deutscher Tonkunst*, v. One of his tunes, used for the hymn 'Liebster Jesu, wir sind hier' (Beloved Jesu, we are here), became very popular (*English Hymnal*, no 336, *Songs of Praise*, no 457).

Aichinger, Gregor (1564–1628), German composer

Aida: the great Zenatello as Radames

of church music. Strongly influenced by the Venetian school of Gabrieli, his selected works are printed in *Denkmäler der Tonkunst in Bayern*, x (1).

Aida, opera in four acts by Verdi, to a libretto by Antonio Ghislanzoni and the composer. Reputedly written for the celebration of the opening of the Suez Canal, Verdi's Egyptian opera was in fact commissioned by the Khedive of Egypt to open the new Cairo Opera House the same year (1869). Unfortunately the Franco-Prussian war delayed the first performance – the sets and costumes could not be transported from Europe – and the première did not take place until 1871.

Aida is a story of warfare between Egypt and Ethiopia, and of the love of Aida, daughter of the Ethiopian king and a slave at the Egyptian court, for Radames, the Egyptian commander-in-chief. For both of them there is a conflict between love and patriotism. Yielding to love, Radames is convicted of treachery through the jealous fury of Amneris, daughter of the Egyptian king. He is sentenced to be buried alive, and Aida, though she has escaped, prefers to share his punishment.

For many years *Aida* seemed likely to be Verdi's last opera. He wrote it, one of the grandest of his works, at what seemed to be the height of his powers. But sixteen years later, at the age of 74, he shook the opera world with *Otello* and, six years after that, capped his achievement with *Falstaff*.

air (Eng., Fr.), (1) a tune;

(2) a song, either for one voice or for several voices. The term was common in this sense in the 17th century, when the normal English spelling was 'ayre';

(3) a song or *aria* (It.), in an opera or oratorio;

(4) an instrumental piece whose melodic style is similar to that of solo song.

P. WARLOCK: *The English Ayre* (1926)

Air on the G String, the name originally given to an arrangement by August Wilhemj of the second movement of Bach's Suite no 3 in D major for orchestra. In this version the first violin part becomes a solo with accompaniment and is transposed down so as to be suitable for playing on the lowest string of the instrument. The nickname caught on, and today the piece, even in its authentic version, is still familiarly (if erroneously) known by this title.

Ais (Ger.), A sharp (A ♯).

Aisis (Ger.), A double sharp (A ×).

Akademische Fest-Ouvertüre, *see* ACADEMIC FESTIVAL OVERTURE

Akhron, Joseph (1886–1943), Lithuanian born violinist, composer and teacher (whose surname is also sometimes spelt Achron). A pupil of Auer and Lyadov, he taught at Kharkov University before settling in the United States in 1925. His compositions include three violin concertos, the *Golem Suite* for chamber orchestra, and a sinfonietta for string quartet.

Akimenko, Feodor Stepanovich (1876–1945), Ukrainian composer, a pupil of Balakirev and Rimsky-Korsakov. He later became Stravinsky's first composition teacher. He lived for many years in France. His works include a symphony, a violin concerto, an opera, chamber music, piano music and songs.

à la hongroise, *see* ALL' ONGARESE

Alain, Jean, *see* ALEYN

Alain, Jehan Ariste (1911–40), French composer, pupil of Dupré, Dukas and Roger-Ducasse at the Paris Conservatoire. For some years he was a church organist in Paris, but was killed in action during World War II. His compositions, original in idiom and distinguished in execution, include choral works, three volumes of organ music, three volumes of piano music, chamber music and songs.

B. GAVOTY: *Jehan Alain, musicien français (1911–40)* (1945)

alalá (Sp.), a type of Galician folk melody, sung in free rhythm and often ornamented with grace notes. It appears to have melodic affinities with plainsong.

Alanus, Johannes, *see* ALEYN

Alayrac, D', *see* DALAYRAC

Albanesi, Licia (born 1913), Italian born soprano, who became a member of the Metropolitan Opera House, New York, in 1940, and took U.S. citizenship in 1945. She was one of Toscanini's favourite singers, and took part in several of his recordings.

Albéniz, Isaac (1860–1909), Catalan pianist and composer. He began his career as a child prodigy, then studied at Madrid, Brussels and Leipzig – also at Budapest with Liszt. He wrote a number of operas, including one to an English libretto, *The Magic Opal* (London, 1893), but is now remembered mainly by his later piano works (notably the twelve-movement suite *Iberia* composed in 1909), which borrow effectively the rhythms and idioms of Spanish popular

music. Altogether he composed some 250 piano pieces, but did not succeed in bringing such industry to what would have been his most ambitious work – an operatic trilogy based on Arthurian legends, left unfinished.

Albert, Eugène Francis Charles d' (1864–1932), Scottish born pianist and composer, of Franco-English descent. He studied at the National Training School for Music (later the Royal College of Music) in London, and appeared as a concert pianist at the age of sixteen. Having won the Mendelssohn Scholarship he went abroad and studied with Liszt. He settled in Germany and became director of the Berlin Hochschule in 1907 in succession to Joachim. During World War I he repudiated his British birth, declared himself to be German, and established the spelling of his first name as Eugen. His numerous compositions include 21 operas, of which the most successful were *Tiefland* (Prague, 1903), *Die toten Augen* (Dresden, 1916), and the comic operas *Die Abreise* (Frankfurt, 1898) and *Flauto Solo* (Prague, 1905). The use of jazz idioms won for *Die schwarze Orchidee* (Leipzig, 1928) a temporary success. He also composed two piano concertos, a violin concerto, a symphony, chamber music and piano solos. He transcribed several of Bach's organ works and edited piano works by Beethoven and Liszt. He died in Riga.

Albert, Heinrich (1604–51), German poet and composer, a cousin and pupil of Heinrich Schütz. He published eight collections of *Arien* – sacred and secular songs with German words for one or more voices with accompaniment (reprinted in *Denkmäler deutscher Tonkunst*, xii and xiii). An adaptation of the melody of his 'Gott des Himmels' was used by Bach in the *Christmas Oratorio* and is in current use (*Hymns Ancient and Modern*, nos 368 (i) and 551). For the original form of the melody see *English Hymnal*, no 132, and *Songs of Praise*, no 32 (i).

Albert Herring, comic opera in three acts by Benjamin Britten, to a libretto by Eric Crozier, after Guy de Maupassant's short story *Madame Husson's May King*. First performed in 1947 at Glyndebourne, Britten's first comedy describes the emancipation of Albert, the young East Anglian shopkeeper who has been browbeaten by his mother. Being more virtuous than any of the local girls, he is elected King of the May. During the ceremony, however, he inadvertently becomes the worse for drink, and plucks up enough courage to shake himself free from his mother and other local puritans. Though Britten's opera has a happy ending, Maupassant's story did not; there the hero died of delirium tremens.

Alberti, Domenico (1710–40), Italian singer, harpsichordist and composer. In his keyboard sonatas he was addicted to the use of a conventional figuration for the left hand, which, though purely harmonic in effect, suggests the bustle of contrapuntal elaboration:

ALBERTI, *Sonata no 6*, op 1

The formula, known as the 'Alberti bass', (though it was not invented by him or peculiar to him) became part of the stock-in-trade of late 18th century and early 19th century composers, not excluding Mozart (as in the slow movement of his C major piano sonata – the familiar 'sonata facile').

Albertini, Giovacchino (1751–1812), Italian opera composer and director of music at the Polish court. His *Don Juan*, to a Polish text, was performed in Warsaw in 1783, four years before Mozart's *Don Giovanni*.

Alberto de Ripa, Alberto Mantovano, *see* RIPPE

Albicastro, Henrico, late 17th century Swiss violinist, who wrote a number of sonatas and orchestral concertos. His real name was Weyssenburg.

Albinoni, Tommaso (1671–1750), Italian composer and violinist. Born in Venice, he became one of the first composers to write concertos for solo violin. He wrote prolifically – his output included about fifty operas – and was much admired by Bach, who wrote keyboard fugues on themes by him (*Bach Gesellschaft*, xxxvi, pages 173, 178).

Alboni, Marietta (1826–94), celebrated Italian contralto, one of the greatest in operatic history. She studied Rossini's operas with the composer and was one of the singers at his funeral in Paris in 1868. She sang frequently at Covent Garden, and on one occasion sang the baritone role of Carlos in Verdi's *Ernani* there, after it had been turned down by two male singers.

alborada (Sp.; Fr., *aubade*), 'morning song'. A form of instrumental music popular in Galicia, where it is played on the bagpipes (*gaita*) with side-drum (*tamboril*) accompaniment. A modern sophisticated example is the *Alborada del gracioso* (*The Clown's Aubade*), no 4 of Ravel's *Miroirs* for piano (1905).

Albrechtsberger, Johann Georg (1736–1809), Austrian organist, composer and teacher. He was appointed court organist in Vienna in 1772 and was *Kapellmeister* of St. Stephen's Cathedral. He had a great reputation as a teacher. Beethoven had counterpoint lessons from him during the two years 1794–5 but was not, in Albrechtsberger's opinion, a promising pupil. He composed many religious and instrumental works, and wrote a text book entitled *Grundliche Anweisung zur Composition*.

Albumblatt (Ger.), 'album leaf'. A title frequently used by 19th century composers and their successors for a short piece of an intimate character. Wagner's was at one time one of the most popular of its kind.

Alceste, (1) opera in three acts by Gluck. His original setting of Ranieri Calzabigi's Italian libretto was performed at Vienna in 1767 and a revised version, with French adaptation by François du Roullet, was given at Paris in 1776. The plot is borrowed from the Greek legend of the wife who offers to die in place of her husband, Admetus, and is subsequently restored to life. The dedication of the Italian version of *Alceste*, published in 1769, contains a historically important statement of Gluck's artistic principles, probably written by Calzabigi (see A. Einstein, *Gluck*, pages 98–100);

(2) opera by Lully with a prologue and five acts, to a libretto by Philippe Quinault, first performed in 1674 in Paris.

Alcestis, *see* ALKESTIS

Alchemist, The (Ger., *Der Alchymist*), opera in three acts by Spohr, to a libretto by 'Fr. Georg Schmidt' (pseudonym for Karl Pfeiffer), founded on a story by Washington Irving. It was first performed in 1830 at Cassel.

Alcina, opera in three acts by Handel, to a libretto by Antonio Marchi (from Ariosto's *Orlando Furioso*). First performed in 1735 in London, the opera concerns a sorceress, Alcina, who uses her supernatural powers to win the love of Ruggiero, but finds that things do not work as she planned. *Alcina* has been successfully revived in recent years as a vehicle for Joan Sutherland.

Alcock, John (1715–1806), English organist and composer. He was organist of Lichfield Cathedral (1750–60) and wrote instrumental music, glees and church music. His son John (c.1740–91) was also an organist and composer.

Aldrich, Richard (1863–1937), U.S. music critic. A graduate of Harvard, he served as critic on several papers, becoming eventually music editor of the *New York Times* (1902–23). Among his publications were a volume of essays, and two books on Wagner.

aleatoric, present-day widely used but bastard word meaning ALEATORY.

aleatory music, music containing chance or random elements – a trend in many compositions written since 1945. Aleatory elements may sometimes be fairly closely controlled by the composer (as in certain works by Lutoslawski) or the music may be so indeterminate that no notes are written down at all (as in certain works by Stockhausen). In the latter case the performers have to make do with written directions, though often such music can only be adequately performed when the composer is present in person to direct it. The chance elements are sometimes decided by dice throwing, interpretation of abstract designs, or by mathematical laws of chance. John Cage, for example, used the *I-Ching*, an ancient Chinese method of divination by random numbers, for his *Music of Changes* (1951), the first widely-known 20th century example of aleatory music.

Alembert, Jean le Rond d' (1717–83), French philosopher and mathematician, a contributor to the *Encyclopédie* and author of several works on music. He was one of the advocates of that operatic reform which we now associate principally with Gluck.

Alessandri, Felice (1742–98), Italian composer and conductor. A prolific composer of operas (of which he wrote some 35) and instrumental music, he travelled widely and from 1789–92 was second conductor at the Berlin Opera. His most successful comic opera was *Il vecchio geloso* (Milan, 1781).

Alessandro, opera in three acts by Handel, to a libretto by Paolo Antonio Rolli, first performed in 1726 in London. It was in this work that Faustina Bordoni made her important début.

Alessandro della Viola, Alessandro Romano, *see* MERLO

Alessandro Stradella, opera in three acts by Flotow, to a libretto by 'W. Friedrich' (Friedrich Wilhelm Riese), first performed in 1844 at Hamburg. The work is based on dramatic incidents in the life of the 17th century composer, Stradella.

Alexander Balus, oratorio by Handel, to a libretto by Thomas Morell, first performed in 1748 in London.

The 'Battle on ice' sequence in Eisenstein's film *Alexander Nevsky*, powerfully depicted in Prokofiev's film score and in the cantata he subsequently created out of his film music

Alexander Nevsky, cantata by Prokofiev for soprano, chorus and orchestra, first performed in 1939, and using material from Prokofiev's famous film score. The hero of the title was the Russian patriot who defeated the Teutonic knights in the 13th century, and the climax of the work occurs in the famous sequence of the 'Battle on Ice'.

Alexander's Feast, ode for soloists, chorus and orchestra by Handel, to words by John Dryden (originally written for St. Cecilia's Day, 1697). The first performance was in London in 1736.

Alexandrov, Anatol Nikolayevich (1888–1946), Russian composer. He studied at the Moscow Conservatory where he later taught composition. His works, which are on the whole conservative in style, include two operas (*Two Worlds* and *The Forty-First*), incidental music for Maeterlinck's *Ariadne and Bluebeard*, two orchestral suites, film music, piano music, and songs.

Aleyn, John (Jean Alain, Johannes Alanus) (died c. 1373), English composer and theorist. A member of the Chapel Royal from the middle of the 14th century until his death. A Gloria by him is in *The Old Hall Manuscript*. His only other known composition is a motet 'Sub Arthuro plebs vallata' (printed in *Denkmäler der Tonkunst in Osterreich*, lxxvi, Jg. xl), which contains in one voice references to several English musicians; a second voice lists musical theorists including himself.

    B. TROWELL: 'A Fourteenth-Century Ceremonial Motet and its Composer,' *Acta Musicologica*, xxix (1957)

Alfano, Franco (1876–1954), Italian opera composer, educated at Naples and Leipzig. He became director of the Liceo Musicale, Bologna, in 1919, and of the Liceo Musicale, Turin, in 1923. His most successful operas are *Risurrezione* (Turin, 1904) and *La leggenda de Sakuntala* (Bologna, 1921), for the latter of which he wrote the libretto. Today he is best remembered for his completion of the third act of Puccini's *Turandot* (Milan, 1926) from sketches left by the composer.

al fine (It.), 'to the end'. Most commonly in the phrases *da capo al fine* (from the beginning to the end) and *dal segno al fine* (from the sign to the end).

    See DA CAPO and DAL SEGNO

Alfonso el Sabio, Alfonso X, nicknamed 'the Wise' (1221–84), king of Castile and Leon (1252–84). A patron of music and poetry, he compiled a collection of more than 400 *Cantigas de Santa Maria* (hymns to the virgin). The music of these shows the influence of Provençal troubadours but has also specifically Spanish characteristics, in which Moorish influence has been suggested, though without any precise evidence. The miniatures in the manuscripts suggest the use of a wide variety of instruments, though the melodies appear without accompaniment, as in troubadour manuscripts. A transcription and critical study of the collection, together with a facsimile of one of the principal manuscripts, is in H. Anglès, *La Música de las cantigas de Santa Maria del Rey Alfonso el Sabio* (four volumes, 1943–64).

    J. B. TREND: *Alfonso the Sage* (1926)

Alfonso und Estrella (Ger., *Alfonso and Estrella*), opera in three acts by Schubert, to a libretto by Franz von Schober, first performed in 1854 at Weimar, 26 years after the composer's death.

Alfvén, Hugo (1872–1960), Swedish composer. He studied at the Stockholm Conservatory and in Brussels, and was director of music at Uppsala University (1910–39). His works include five symphonies, choral works, chamber music, piano pieces and songs. Outside Sweden he is best known for his colourful *Midsommarvaka* for orchestra, the first of a series of three Swedish rhapsodies written by him.

Algarotti, Francesco (1712–64), Italian scholar. His experience of opera led him to write an essay, *Saggio sopra l'opera in musica* (1755), advocating the abandonment of the outworn conventions of early 18th century opera along lines similar to those of Gluck.

Alkan, Charles Henri Valentin (1813–88), French composer and pianist (of Alsatian-Jewish ancestry) whose real name was Morhange. His brilliance as a pianist was such that he was admitted to the Paris Conservatoire at the age of six. As an adult, however, he resisted the life of a great public virtuoso – though he was a friend of Liszt, Chopin and George Sand – and preferred for the most part to be one of Paris's leading piano teachers and a composer of piano pieces of daunting technical complexity and adventurousness. Many of his 'Lisztian' and 'Brahmsian' ideas predated those of Liszt and Brahms.

Though at one time neglected (except by Busoni and Egon Petri) the music of Alkan has again begun to attract pianists with the technical apparatus to cope with it. One of these, Raymond Lewenthal, has described the *Grand Sonate*, op 33, as the longest and most difficult piano sonata since Beethoven's *Hammerklavier* and the strangest one before the Ives sonatas. Alkan also composed a set of *Twelve Studies in Minor Keys*, op 39 (1857), the last of which is a stunning set of 25 variations entitled *Aesop's Feast* (*Le Festin d'Esope*). The fourth, fifth, sixth and seventh of these studies form a four-movement symphony for solo piano. Apart from his piano works, Alkan's output includes pieces for *pédalier*, or pedal-piano; characteristically these pieces include footwork as difficult as their finger-work – some of them are four-part fugues for pedals alone. Alkan died in Paris as curiously as he lived: he was crushed by a bookcase which fell on him while he was trying to remove from its top shelf a volume of the Talmud, of which he had been a devoted scholar.

Alkestis, (1) opera in two acts by Rutland Broughton, to a libretto from Euripides' tragedy in Gilbert Murray's English version, first produced in 1922 at Glastonbury;

(2) opera in one act by Wellesz, to a libretto by Hugo von Hofmannsthal (based on Euripides's tragedy), first performed in 1924 at Mannheim.

alla breve (It.), this expression, which defies literal translation, means that the BREVE is to be taken as the standard of mensuration instead of the SEMIBREVE, i.e. that the music is to be performed twice as fast as its notation would suggest. In the following example from Handel's *Messiah* the minims are to be treated as though they were crotchets, i.e. there will be two beats in each bar, not four:

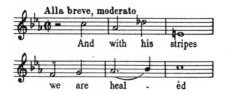

This is the equivalent of:

The term originated in the 16th century, when the corresponding term *alla semibreve* was also used to indicate that the notes had their normal value. Diminution of note values was represented by alterations in the time-signature. A vertical stroke indicated that the notes had only half their written value. Thus the sign C indicated 'imperfect' (or, as we should say, duple) time, in which one breve equalled two semibreves; but the same sign with a vertical stroke through it, ₵ , meant that the two semibreves to a breve became in effect two minims to a semibreve. The other proportional signs became obsolete; so did the term *alla semibreve*. But the sign ₵ survived as the equivalent of what we should call 2/2, just as C survived as the equivalent of 4/4. (*See* NOTATION). In the 18th century, ₵ is the normal time-signature for a piece marked *alla breve*. But even then the term did not necessarily imply two beats in a bar. The following extract from the aria 'Es ist vollbracht' in Bach's *St. John Passion* shows it was used simply as an indication of relative speed:

Here *alla breve* means that the crotchet of the 3/4 section is equivalent to the slow quaver of the *Molto adagio* – in other words, the quaver of the 3/4 section is to be taken twice as fast as the quaver of the *Molto adagio*.

allargando (It.), 'getting broader', and, in consequence, slower.

alla tedesca (It.), short for *alla danza tedesca*, i.e. in the style of the German dance or ALLEMANDE of either type. Beethoven uses *alla tedesca* in the first movement of his piano sonata in G major, op 79, and *alla danza tedesca* in the fourth movement of the string quartet in B flat major, op 130. Both movements represent the later type of allemande – the *deutscher Tanz* in triple time, current in the late 18th and early 19th centuries.

alla turca (It.), 'in the Turkish style'.

See JANISSARY MUSIC

alla zingarese (It.), in the style of gypsy music (from *zingaro*, a gypsy).

alla zoppa (It.), literally 'in a limping manner', i.e. syncopated. Applied particularly to the rhythm

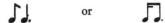

(known also as the 'Scotch snap' or the 'Lombardy rhythm'), familiar in songs like 'Comin' thro the rye' or in pieces like the following:

LISZT, *Hungarian Rhapsody no 14*

allegretto (It.), diminutive of ALLEGRO, indicating a moderately quick movement, somewhat slower than *allegro*.

Allegri, Gregorio (1582–1652), Italian priest who was at first attached to the cathedral of Fermo and in 1629 became one of the papal singers. He composed a quantity of church music. A nine-part *Miserere*, sung annually in Holy Week in the Sistine Chapel, was greatly prized, although its effect was due more to the method of performance than to the music. See Charles Burney, *The Present State of Music in France and Italy* (1771), pp. 275–81, and Emily Anderson, *The Letters of Mozart and his Family* (1928), p. 187.

allegro (It.), 'lively'. Used to indicate a brisk movement, often in association with other adjectives or qualifying expressions, e.g. *allegro moderato*, *allegro con brio*.

Allegro, il Penseroso ed il Moderato, L' (It., The lively man, the thoughtful man, and the moderate man), cantata for soloists, chorus and orchestra by Handel, first performed in 1740 in London. The words were compiled from Milton by Charles Jennens, with the addition of *Il Moderato*.

allemande (Fr.), short for *danse allemande*, 'German dance':

(1) a moderately slow dance of German origin in duple time, adopted in the 16th century by the French, and from them by the English (Eng., almain, alman, almand; It., *allemanda, tedesca*). Described by Thomas Morley (1597) as heavier than the GALLIARD and 'fitlie representing the nature of the people, whose name it carieth'. Here is a characteristic Elizabethan example from the *Fitzwilliam Virginal Book* (no 61):

BYRD, *Monsieur's Alman*

In the 17th and early 18th centuries it was normally the first of the four contrasted dances which formed the basis of the SUITE. Composers did not always adhere to the slow tempo. Corelli has allemandes marked *allegro* and *presto*, as well as *largo* and *adagio*. But by the 18th century it had settled down into a stylized instrumental form, described by Mattheson as representing 'a contented mind that delights in order and calm,' e.g.:

BACH, *English Suite no 1*

The initial semiquaver is typical.

(2) a brisk dance in triple time, current in the late 18th and early 19th centuries and still popular among the peasantry of Swabia and Switzerland (Ger., *deutscher Tanz*; It., *danza tedesca*), e.g.

The allemande is the prototype of the WALTZ. The third of Beethoven's *Bagatellen* (op 119) is marked *à l'allemande* = ALLA TEDESCA. The *presto assai* from Haydn's *Trio No 5 in Eb* shows the line of development admirably:

HAYDN, *Trio no 5 in E flat*

E. MOHR: *Die Allemande* (two volumes, 1932)

Allen, Hugh Percy (1869–1946), English musical scholar, who in 1918 succeeded Parry as director of the Royal College of Music, London, and Parratt as professor of music at Oxford. He was specially active in spreading enthusiasm for the works of Bach.

allentando (It.), 'slowing down'.

Allison, Richard (fl. 1600), English composer. He published *The Psalmes of David in Meter* (1599), a harmonization for voice (or voices) and instruments of the melodies to which the metrical psalms were sung (*see* PSALTER), and *An Howres Recreation in Musicke* (1606; modern edition in *The English Madrigal School*, xxxiii), a collection of madrigals for four and five voices. He also wrote several pieces for mixed consort of lute, pandora, cittern, bass viol, flute and treble viol, some of which are printed in Morley's *First Booke of Consort Lessons*, edited by S. Beck (1959).

allmählich (Ger.), 'gradual, gradually'.

all' ongarese (It., Fr., *à la hongroise*), in the style of Hungarian (gypsy) music.

all' ottava (It.), 'at the octave' (above or below).
See OTTAVA

all' unisono (It.), 'in unison', i.e. two or more instruments are to play the same notes.

almain, alman, almand, *see* ALLEMANDE

Almeida, Francisco Antonio d' (flourished 1740), Portuguese composer. His comic opera *La Spinalba* (Lisbon, 1739) is the first Italian opera by a Portuguese to be preserved intact. The third act of an earlier work, *La pacienza de Socrate* (Lisbon, 1733) has also survived. He also composed church music.

Almenräder, Karl (1786–1843), German bassoonist. He made considerable improvements in the structure of the instrument, which are described in his *Abhandlung über die Verbesserung des Fagotts*. *See* Adam Carse, *Musical Wind Instruments* (1939), pages 196–200.

Almira, opera in three acts by Handel, to a libretto by Friedrich Christian Feustking (based on an Italian libretto by Giulio Pancieri). First performed in 1705 at Hamburg, this was Handel's first opera, containing forty-one German and fifteen Italian airs.

Alphorn (Ger.), 'alpine horn'. A primitive instrument still used by herdsmen in Switzerland and other mountainous countries. It is made of wood, bound with bark, is either straight or slightly curved, with an upturned bell, and may be as much as ten feet long. It produces the notes of the HARMONIC SERIES, with certain modifications due to the material of which it is made and its irregular diameter. The practice of yodelling is though to be an imitation of the sounds of the alphorn.

Alpine Symphony, (Ger., *Eine Alpensinfonie*), symphony by Richard Strauss, vividly depicting events in the course of a mountain climb. This, the last of the composer's big descriptive works, was first performed in Berlin in 1915.

Also sprach Zarathustra (Ger., *Thus spoke Zarathustra*), symphonic poem by Richard Strauss, op 30, inspired by Nietzsche's work of the same title. It was first performed in 1896 in Frankfurt.

alt, (1) in the phrase *in alt*, an English adaptation of the Latin *in alto* (in the height), applied to notes from

The notes in the octave above are said to be *in altissimo*;
(2) (Ger.), ALTO.

Altenburg, Johann Ernst (1734–1801), German trumpeter and organist, author of *Versuch einer Anleitung zur heroisch-musikalischen Trompeter-und Pauker-Kunst* (1795; reprinted in facsimile, 1911).

alteration, (1) a conventional augmentation of the value of the breve, semibreve or minim in mensural notation before 1600. (*See* RHYTHMIC MODES, MENSURAL NOTATION);
(2) chromatic alteration is the raising or lowering of a note of the scale by means of an ACCIDENTAL.

Althorn (Ger.), a brass instrument of the SAXHORN family.

Altnikol, Johann Christoph (1719–59), German harpsichordist, organist and composer, a pupil and son-in-law of J. S. Bach, whose last composition – the chorale prelude 'Vor deinen Thron' – was written out by Altnikol from dictation when the composer was on his death-bed.

alto (It.), literally 'high', (1) the highest adult male voice, now employed mainly in church choirs and male-voice choirs. The range of the voice is roughly two octaves, from

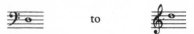

though the lower notes lack resonance. The upper part of the compass is made possible by the cultivation of the FALSETTO voice. In 17th century England the alto (known also as counter-tenor) was popular as a solo voice;
(2) a low female voice (properly called contralto), covering a slightly higher range than the male alto, which it has supplanted in music for mixed voices;
(3) (Fr.), viola;
(4) prefixed to the name of an instrument it indicates one size larger than the treble (or soprano) member of the family, e.g. alto saxophone;
(5) the alto clef is the C clef (indicating middle C) on the third line of the stave:

It was at one time in general use for any vocal or instrumental part of the appropriate range and was also employed in keyboard music. It is now used only for the viola, for which it is the normal clef.

alto basso, see TAMBOURIN DU BEARN

Alto Rhapsody, work by Brahms, op 53, for solo contralto, male-voice chorus and orchestra. Based on Goethe's philosophical poem, 'Harzreise im Winter', it was first performed in 1870 in Jena.

Alwyn, William (born 1905), English composer, pupil of McEwan. His works, in traditional style, include four symphonies, a symphonic poem (*The Island*, after Shakespeare's *Tempest*), an impressive piano sonata and much film music.

Amadigi di Gaula (It., *Amadis of Gaul*), opera in three acts by Handel, to a libretto probably by John James Heidegger (signature on dedication), first performed in 1715 in London.

Amadis, opera with a prologue and five acts by Lully, to a libretto by Philippe Quinault, first performed in 1684 in Paris.

See also AMADIGI DE GAULA

Amahl and the Night Visitors, the first opera designed for television production. Written by Menotti, with a text by the composer, it was first performed by the U.S. National Broadcasting Company in 1951. Its sentimental story, using the legend of the Magi (involving a crippled child whom they encounter on their way to Bethlehem), has ensured its world-wide popularity ever since.

Amati, a famous family of violin-makers at Cremona in Italy in the 16th and 17th centuries. The earliest known is **Andrea Amati** (b. 1500–5; d. 1575–9), who established a design and standard of craftsmanship to which his descendants adhered. **Nicolo Amati** (1596–1684), the most celebrated member of the family, was the master of Antonio Stradivari.

Ambros, August Wilhelm (1816–76), a brilliant and versatile Czech musician, who managed to combine his work as historian, composer and pianist with regular employment in the Austrian Civil Service. His *Geschichte der Musik* (four volumes, 1862–81), of which the last volume was compiled from his notes, is a standard work, though the first and fourth volumes have since been extensively revised. It ends with the 16th century. A fifth volume of examples was compiled after his death, and two volumes by Wilhelm Langhans were added to bring the history down to the 19th century. His compositions include an opera, *Bratislav and Jitka*, and an overture to Shakespeare's *Othello*.

Ambrose (340–97), bishop of Milan. He appears to have introduced into the Western Church the Syrian practice of antiphonal singing, as well as encouraging the singing of hymns. None of the melodies of the so-called Ambrosian chant (or plainsong) can be attributed to him with certainty.

America, symphony by Bloch, described by him as an 'epic rhapsody' and summing up his impressions of the first eleven years of his life in the United States. The carpet-bag score quotes Indian music, Negro music, songs of the American Civil War and much else. At the end, the audience are invited to rise to their feet and sing an anthem in praise of America.

American organ, a free-reed keyboard instrument, originally known as the Melodeon, introduced by Mason and Hamlin of Boston (Massachusetts) about 1860. The principal difference between the HAR-MONIUM and the American organ is that in the former the air is forced through the reeds, while in the latter it is drawn through by suction. The American organ is nearer in tone-quality to the organ, but is less expressive than the harmonium. It is also made with two manuals and pedals, in which case the air supply has to be provided by a separate hand-blower or by electricity.

Amico Fritz, L' (It., *Friend Fritz*), opera in three acts by Mascagni to a libretto by 'P. Suardon' (pseudonym of Nicolo Daspuro), based on Erckmann-Chatrian's novel. First performed in 1891 in Rome, this work differs from the blood-and-thunder of *Cavalleria Rusticana* (written the previous year) by being a light pastoral comedy about a confirmed bachelor (Fritz) and the girl he eventually falls in love with. Inevitably overshadowed by its popular predecessor, *L'Amico Fritz* is still performed in Italy, though very rarely elsewhere.

Amner, John (1579–1641), English organist, choirmaster of Ely Cathedral from 1610. He composed a number of services and anthems, and published *Sacred Hymns of 3, 4, 5, and 6 parts, for Voyces and Vyols* (1615).

A. J. GREENING: 'Amner Reconsidered', *Musical Times*, cx (1969)

Amor Brujo, El, see LOVE, THE MAGICIAN

amore (It.), 'love'. *Con amore*, lovingly.

Amore dei Tre Re, L' (It., *The Love of the Three Kings*), opera in three acts by Montemezzi, to a libretto by Sen Benelli (from his play of the same title). The first performance, at La Scala, Milan, in 1913, was conducted by Toscanini (who also conducted its New York Metropolitan première the following year).

amoroso (It.), lovingly.

Amour des Trois Oranges, see LOVE FOR THREE ORANGES.

Amphion Anglicus, a volume of songs by John Blow (1649–1708), published in 1700 with a dedication to Princess Anne. A facsimile was published in 1965.

Amy, Gilbert (born 1936), French composer and conductor, pupil of Milhaud, Messiaen and Boulez, and director since 1967 of the concerts of the Domaine Musical, which Boulez founded with Jean-Louis Barrault and Madeleine Renaud in 1954 for the promotion of new music. Though a Boulez disciple, Amy has shown himself to have a strong musical voice of his own. His works, many of them orchestral, include *Antiphonies* (1963), which sets two orchestras in competition, with a third orchestra to arbitrate between them; *Trajectories* (1966), in which each section of the orchestra follows its own 'curve', with a solo violin acting as a link between them; and *D'un espace déployé*, (1973), in which a small solo group is split off from the main body of the orchestra, with a solo soprano to fill the space between them, the results being, in essence, a rich, various, and enormously complicated concerto grosso. He has also written *Alpha-Beth* for wind sextet, *Mouvements* for chamber orchestra and *Epigrammes* for piano.

Anacréon, *opéra-ballet* in two acts by Cherubini, to a libretto by R. Mendouze, first performed in 1803 in Paris. Today it is known mainly for its overture, which makes pioneering use of what later became known as the 'Rossini crescendo'.

anche (Fr.), reed, reed instrument, reed pipe (in an organ).

ancient cymbals, also known as **antique cymbals,** small cymbals, usually found in pairs, producing definite notes. They were much used by dancing girls in ancient Egypt, Greece and Rome. In marked contrast to ordinary cymbals, they are capable of producing only soft, delicate sounds. Berlioz, in *Romeo and Juliet* and *The Trojans*, was perhaps the first to introduce ancient cymbals into the orchestra. They have been used many times since, notably by French composers, including Debussy and Ravel.

andamento (It.), (1) 'movement'.

(2) an 18th century term for a fugue subject of substantial length, which will often fall naturally into two contrasted sections, e.g.:

BACH, *48 Preludes and Fugues*, Book I, no 20

(3) an episode in a fugue;

(4) a movement in a suite.

andante (It.), 'going, moving'. Generally used today of a moderate tempo, inclining to slowness ('at a walking pace') rather than actually slow. Hence used as the title of a piece or movement in this tempo. *Più andante* means properly 'moving more', i.e. slightly faster. (*See* the slow movement of Brahms's G major sonata for violin and piano, op 78).

andantino (It.), diminutive of ANDANTE. An ambiguous term, since it is impossible to know whether it implies a movement slightly faster than *andante* or slightly slower. Most composers and performers, however, interpret it as 'slightly faster'.

Anderson, Marian (born 1902), U.S. contralto – the first Negro singer to appear at the New York Metropolitan (as Ulrica in Verdi's *Masked Ball* in 1955).

Marian Anderson, one of the great contraltos of her day

Toscanini regarded her as 'the voice that comes once in a hundred years'. Mostly, the voice was heard in the concert hall rather than the opera house: her interpretation of Sibelius's songs, as well as of Negro music, made her world famous.

An die ferne Geliebte (Ger.), 'to the distant beloved'. Song-cycle by Beethoven, op 98 (1816), to words by A. Jeitteles. These six songs form what is usually considered to be the first genuine German song cycle, pre-dating Schubert's famous examples by several years.

André, a German publishing firm. The family included **Johann** (1741–99), who composed a large number of operas, among them *Belmonte und Constanze, oder die Entführung aus dem Serail* (1781), a setting of the libretto which, with modifications and additions, was reset by Mozart a year later.

His third son, **Johann Anton** (1775–1842) was like his father, a composer. He also wrote books on harmony, counterpoint and composition. He purchased all Mozart's surviving manuscripts from the composer's widow.

Andreae, Volkmar (1879–1962), Swiss composer and conductor, principal of the Zurich Conservatoire from 1914 until 1939. His works include two symphonies, two operas – *Ratcliff* (Duisburg, 1914) and *Abenteuer des Casanova* (Dresden, 1924), chamber music, choral music and songs.

Andriessen, Hendrik (born 1892), Dutch composer and organist. His works, many of them religious, include Masses and a Te Deum. He also wrote three symphonies, chamber music and songs.

His son, **Juriaan Andriessen** (born 1925), is a composer, pianist and conductor. He has written a sinfonia concertante for brass and orchestra, incidental music and chamber music.

Andriessen, Willem (1887–1964), Dutch composer and pianist, who became director of the Amsterdam Conservatory in 1937. He wrote a piano concerto, a scherzo for orchestra, and choral music.

Andrieu, D', *see* DANDRIEU

Anerio, Felice (c. 1560–1614), Italian composer to the Papal Chapel from 1594 to 1602. His works include madrigals and church music. His brother, **Giovanni Francesco Anerio** (c. 1567–1630) was also a composer. He wrote large quantities of sacred music and madrigals.

Anet, Jean-Baptiste (c. 1661–1755), French violinist, who studied with Corelli in Rome and who was described by Philippe-Louis Daquin (son of the composer) as the greatest violinist that had ever existed. He was one of the first violinists to appear at the *Concert spirituel*, founded by Philidor in Paris in 1725. His compositions, apart from the evidence of virtuosity, are unimportant.

Anfossi, Pasquale (1727–97), Italian opera composer, a pupil of Piccinni, whose influence shows itself in an inclination to sentimentality. Anfossi in turn influenced the young Mozart, particularly through his *La finta giardiniera* (Rome, 1774), the libretto of which was reset by Mozart in the following year.

Angeles, Victoria de los (born 1923), Spanish soprano. She studied at Barcelona Conservatorio, and made her first appearance (as a student) in Monteverdi's *Orfeo*. Her official début was in 1945, as the

Countess in *Figaro* at the Teatro Liceo, Barcelona.
Five years later she sang Mimi in *La Bohème* at Covent
Garden, and in 1951 made her New York Metropolitan
début. In Rossini's *Barber of Seville* she made a
speciality of singing the role of Rosina in the original
key at a time when it was usually transposed upwards
for more birdlike sopranos. In the concert hall, her
career has been as distinguished as in the opera house.
In particular she has drawn the attention of listeners
all over the world to the riches of the Spanish song
repertory.

angelica (Fr., *angélique*), a type of lute in use during
the late 17th and early 18th centuries.

Angel of Fire, The (also known as **The Fiery Angel**),
opera in five acts by Prokofiev, with a libretto based on
a story by Valery Bryusov. Though Prokofiev composed it in 1925, it did not achieve its first performance
until thirty years later – in a concert version in Paris.
The first stage production followed in 1955 in Venice.
Prokofiev considered this to be his best opera (as do
several other authorities) though its subject matter –
diabolical possession and sorcery, culminating in an
exorcism rite in a convent – has always aroused controversy.

anglaise (Fr.), short for *danse anglaise*, English dance:
a dance in quick duple time, one of the dances of
foreign origin (cf. POLONAISE) introduced in the 17th
century and so incorporated in the SUITE as one of the
Galanterien or optional dances added to the normal
allemande, *courante*, *sarabande* and *gigue*, e.g.:

BACH, *French Suite no 3*

The name '*anglaise*' was also applied to other dances
of English origin.

Anglebert, Jean Henry d' (c. 1628–91), French harpsichordist, organist and composer, a pupil of Chambonnières. He was in the service of the duc d'Orléans
in 1661, and of Louis XIV in 1664. His *Pièces de
clavessin* (1689; facsimile edition, 1965), including
both original compositions and transcriptions of
works by Lully, is a valuable record of contemporary
ornamentation: a modern edition is in *Publications
de la Société française de Musicologie*, viii.

Anglès, Higini (1888–1969), Catalan musicologist. He
was professor of musical history, Barcelona Conservatory from 1927 until 1933, and subsequently at
Barcelona University. In 1947 he became director of
the Pontifical Institute of Sacred Music, Rome.
Among the works he has edited are *El Còdex Musical
de Las Huelgas* (three volumes, 1931), *Monumentos de
la Musica Española* (two volumes, 1941 and 1944),

La Música de las Cantigas del Rey Alfonso el Sabio
(1948), and a complete edition of the works of Morales
(1953).

Anglican chant, a harmonized setting, designed to be
used for successive verses of the canticles and psalms
in the English Prayer Book. A *single chant* consists
normally of seven bars, unequally divided into three
and four, the caesura in the middle corresponding
to the colon in the text, e.g.:

Adapted from Richard Farrant

This is repeated for each verse of the canticle or psalm.
A *double chant* serves for a pair of verses, a *triple* or
quadruple chant for groups of three or four respectively. If a double chant is used for a psalm (or section
of a psalm) that has an odd number of verses, the
second half of the chant will be repeated for the odd
verse. This may be done at the end of psalm (or section)
or at any convenient place suggested by the words.
Similar modifications may be necessary in the case of
triple and quadruple chants, though examples of
these forms are not common.

The difficulty of accommodating verses of different
lengths to the same tune is solved by treating the first
and fourth bars of the single chant, and the first,
fourth, eighth and eleventh of the double chant, as
reciting notes of indefinite length, e.g.:

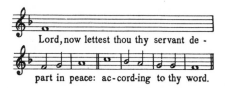

Lord, now lettest thou thy servant depart in peace: ac-cord-ing to thy word.

This may easily result in a hurried gabbling of the
syllables sung to the reciting notes and a rigid, metrical
interpretation of the rest of the chant. Modern practice
strives to avoid this by aiming at a flexible rhythm
dictated by the natural rhythm of the words and,
if necessary, ignores the caesura, making the whole
chant continuous. To secure a uniform interpretation
from a choir a system of 'pointing' is used, indicating
how the syllables of each verse are to be allotted to the
chant. The publication of psalters with pointing dates
from the first half of the nineteenth century, when the
cathedral service was beginning to be copied in parish
churches. The system of pointing differs from one
psalter to another, in accordance with the editors'
views on interpretation. Among the devices used in
printing the words have been bar-lines, figures to
indicate grouping, and miniature minims and crotchets placed above the syllables.

The Anglican chant is an imitation of the Gregorian
tones used for the musical recitation of the psalms
in the Roman Catholic church, e.g.:

8th tone, 1st ending

It was the practice to use the complete tone only for the first verse of the psalm: in the others the initial 'intonation' was omitted. Harmonizations of the Gregorian tones were current in the 16th century, and the practice was adopted by English composers and applied to the English psalter after the Reformation. The following harmonization of the eighth tone, with the melody in the tenor, exhibits the shortened form without 'intonation'.

MORLEY, *A Plaine and Easie Introduction*, page 148

When English composers began writing original chants at the Restoration they took this shortened form as their model and established a type which has remained constant to the present.

anima (It.), 'spirit'. *Con anima*, with spirit.

animando (It.), becoming animated.

animato (It.), 'animated'.

Animuccia, Giovanni (c. 1500–71), Italian composer, *maestro di cappella* at St. Peter's, Rome, from 1555 to 1571. He was a friend of St. Philip Neri, for whose Oratory he composed *laudi spirituali* (*see* LAUDA, ORATORIO). He also composed church music and madrigals. A facsimile reprint of his first book of Masses (1567) was published in 1972.

Annibale Padovano (1527–75), Italian organist and composer. He was organist at St. Mark's, Venice, from 1552 to 1566, and afterwards was in the service of the Archduke Karl at Graz. He composed church music, madrigals and instrumental music. His collection of four-part *ricercari* (1556) has been edited by N. Pierront and J. P. Hennebains (1934).

Anschlag (Ger.), (1) literally, 'touch', i.e. either the way in which a player depresses the keys of a keyboard instrument or the way in which they respond;

(2) an ornament, sometimes known as the double APPOGGIATURA, consisting of two successive grace notes, one lower than the principal note, the other a second above it. Since about 1750 it has been represented by two small notes, the first of which is played on the beat. The first note is normally either (*a*) a repetition of the preceding note or (*b*) a second below the principal note, e.g.:

as written:

as played:

C. P. E. BACH, *Versuch uber die wahre Art das Clavier zu spielen* (1753)

The example illustrates two points in 18th century practice: (i) in type (*a*) the grace notes were played a little slower than in type (*b*); (ii) in both types the grace notes were played more softly than the principal note.

Ansermet, Ernest (1883–1969), Swiss conductor. He was teacher of mathematics in Lausanne from 1906 until 1910 and began his career as a conductor by directing the Casino concerts at Montreux in 1911. From 1915 he was conductor with Diaghilev's Russian ballet, and in this capacity he conducted the first performances of many works by Stravinsky. In 1918 he founded the Orchestre de la Suisse Romande in Geneva, and established it as Switzerland's leading symphony orchestra. Though famed as a conductor of 20th century music, he wrote a controversial book in 1961 criticising many aspects of modern music. In later life his friendship with Stravinsky became strained.

answer, in the exposition of a FUGUE the answer is the second entry of the subject, which is presented while the first entry continues in counterpoint to it. In a four-part fugue the second and fourth entries of the subject will normally be transposed and so answer respectively the first and third entries, e.g.:

BACH, *48 Preludes and Fugues*, Book II, no 9

If the transposition of the subject is exact, as in the previous example, the answer is called a 'real' answer.

If the transposition is modified in some way, whether at the beginning or the end or both, the answer is called 'tonal', e.g.:

BACH, *48 Preludes and Fugues*, Book I, no 7

Antarctic Symphony (*Sinfonia Antartica*), Vaughan Williams's seventh symphony (1953), based on the music he wrote for the film *Scott of the Antarctic*.

Antheil, George (1900–59), U.S. composer and pianist, pupil of Bloch. He spent part of his life in France, winning notoriety by the performance in Paris of his *Ballet mécanique* (1925). The score includes various mechanical devices for producing sound, among them aeroplane propellers and motor-horns. His first opera, *Transatlantic* (Frankfurt, 1930), made use of jazz rhythms. His other operas include *Helen Retires* (New York, 1934), and *Volpone* (after Jonson). Two works for solo piano, the *Sonata Sauvage* and *Airplane Sonata*, created a scandal when first performed, but his later music proved more conservative. From 1939 he wrote a quantity of music for Hollywood films, and in 1945 produced an extremely entertaining autobiography, *Bad Boy of Music*. Apart from music, his interests included glandular criminology (on which he wrote two books) and military prophecy (which also yielded a book); in addition he wrote a regular 'advice to the lovesick' column.

anthem (an English corruption of ANTIPHON), a setting of non-liturgical English words used in the Anglican church services of morning and evening prayer, where its proper place is after the third collect, in accordance with a rubric which first appeared in the Prayer Book of 1662. It derives from the Latin MOTET of the Roman church, but ever since its first appearance at the English Reformation it has developed on independent lines. The introduction of passages for solo voice with accompaniment in the late 16th century led to the creation of a type known as the 'verse' anthem, in which any section sung by one or more solo voices was technically a 'verse'. Contrasted with

this was the 'full' anthem, in which the voices supplied all the necessary harmony and there was no independent accompaniment. Restoration composers developed an elaborate type of anthem, in which solo recitative and instrumental interludes· played a part, the whole forming a cantata for voices and instruments. In modern practice the anthem is not confined to settings of English words nor to pieces specifically written for the purpose. Latin motets and excerpts from oratorios and similar works are often used.

E. H. FELLOWES: *English Cathedral Music* (4th edition, 1948)

anthologies, *see* HISTORY OF MUSIC

anticipation, the sounding of a note (or notes) before the chord to which it or they belong e.g.:

BEETHOVEN, *Sonata in C sharp minor*, op 27, no 2

where the first D flat in the treble is an anticipation of the chord of D flat in the second bar.

antiphon, a plainsong setting of sacred words, sung before and after a psalm or canticle in the Latin church service with a view to emphasizing its significance. It was originally a refrain occurring after every verse of the psalm and was so called from the method of performing the psalm, which was antiphonal, i.e. by two bodies of singers in alternation. In course of time the refrain was omitted from the body of the psalm and sung only at the beginning and end. A further restriction was the curtailment of the antiphon before the psalm to the first two or three words, leaving the complete melody to be sung when the psalm was over. This is the current practice. The INTROIT and COMMUNION were originally antiphons with psalms attached, but the psalms disappeared from the Mass except for one verse in the case of the introit. The name 'antiphon' was also applied to certain processional melodies and to four hymns in honour of the Virgin. Polyphonic settings of such pieces were also known as antiphons, or, in a typically English corruption of the word, as 'anthem'. Hence the use of the word 'ANTHEM' in the Anglican church service to indicate a musical setting independent of the liturgy.

antiphonal, the book containing the music sung by the choir in the Office of the Roman church i.e. in all services other than the Mass. The choir music for the Mass is contained in the GRADUAL. Today, the word antiphonal is widely applied to musical effects brought about by groups of performers being positioned in different places in the auditorium or on the platform – one group 'responding' to the other group(s). Many 18th and 19th century symphonies employ antiphonal effects between their first and second violin parts – though the sound of these is weakened by the modern practice of massing all the violins to the left of the conductor, instead of on both sides of him (some conductors, e.g. Boult and Kempe, still insist on the authentic seating arrangement).

anvil (Fr., *enclume*; Ger., *Amboss*; It., *ancudine*), an instrument composed of steel bars struck with a hard wooden or metal beater. It is intended to represent the sound of the blacksmith's anvil and has been used for this purpose by several 19th century composers, including Verdi in Act 2 of *Il Trovatore*. The sound is normally of indefinite pitch, but Wagner in *Das Rheingold* wrote for anvils of different sizes tuned to specific notes.

Apel, Willi (born 1893), German born musicologist. He studied mathematics at Bonn, Munich and Berlin, and settled in the United States in 1936, teaching at Harvard and Boston, and holding the professorship at Indiana University from 1950 until 1963. His books include *The Notation of Polyphonic Music, 800–1600* (fifth edition, 1961) *Harvard Dictionary of Music* (with A. T. Davison, revised edition, 1969), and *Masters of the Keyboard* (1947).

apertum, *see* OUVERT

a piacere (It.), 'at pleasure', the same as AD LIBITUM.

Apollonicon, a particularly elaborate type of BARREL ORGAN, provided with keyboards for six performers and fitted with stops designed to imitate the sound of orchestral instruments. It was made by Flight and Robson, organ-builders, and first exhibited in London in 1817.

Apostles, The, oratorio by Elgar, op 49, dealing with the calling of the apostles, the crucifixion and resurrection of Christ, and the ascension. First performed at the Birmingham Festival in 1903. It was intended to be the first part of a trilogy. The second part is *The Kingdom* (1906); the third part was never completed.

Appalachia, 'variations on an old slave song with final chorus' – orchestral piece by Delius, originally written in 1896 and revised in 1902. The first performance took place at Elberfeld, Germany, in 1904. The title refers to the old Indian name for North America.

Appalachian Spring, ballet by Copland, inspired by Hart Crane's poem about a marriage in a rural part of the United States. The Martha Graham company presented it in New York in 1945. Copland's sensitive use of an old U.S. song, 'Simple Gifts', has helped to ensure the success of the music in the concert hall as well as in the theatre.

appassionato (It.), 'impassioned'. *Sonata appassionata*, the title given (though not by the composer) to Beethoven's piano sonata in F minor, op 57.

Appia, Adolphe (1862–1928), Swiss operatic designer and disciple of Wagner. His pioneering reforms – involving a reduction of stage 'clutter' and emphasis on subtle lighting – paved the way for Wieland Wagner and the more abstract presentation of Wagnerian (and other) opera today. His designs for *The Ring* (1899) were especially influential. A rich Parisienne, the Countess de Béarn, had a theatre built for him in the grounds of her home. His philosophy as a designer is set down in his writings: *La Mise-en-Scène du Drame Wagnérien*, published in Paris in 1895, and *Die Musik und die Inszenierung* published in Munich four years later.

appoggiatura (It.; Ger., *Vorschlag*), literally a 'leaning'. There are three principal forms (1) the *long appoggiatura*, now known simply as appoggiatura.

A note of varying length, alien to the harmony against which it sounded but subsequently resolving on the harmony note, e.g.:

CHAIKOVSKY, *Symphony no 6 in B minor*

where the appoggiaturas are marked*. Here the appoggiatura is anticipated by a harmony note in the previous chord, e.g. the D in the treble on the first beat of the bar is prepared by the D in the previous bar. In such cases an appoggiatura is very similar to a SUSPENSION, the only difference being that in a suspension the two D's would have been tied together:

But very frequently an appoggiatura is not anticipated by any harmony note in the previous chord, e.g.:

MOZART, *Symphony no 40 in G minor*

In such cases the effect of the appoggiatura is more striking, because it is unprepared. The systematic use of appoggiaturas over a long period has enriched the harmonic vocabulary, since the chords they create become familiar and so can be used by themselves without resolution of the 'alien' note (*see* CHORD).

The length of an appoggiatura is now precisely indicated by the notation, but in the 17th and 18th centuries it was a convention to allow the harmony note to occupy the whole of the time to be shared between it and the appoggiatura, and to indicate the appoggiatura by a stroke or a curve or a note of smaller size. The reason for this was that the appoggiatura was regarded as an ornament and hence subordinate to the main melodic line. The following examples all mean that the C must be less than a minim, to allow room for a preceding B on the beat:

What remains to be determined in such cases is the length of the appoggiatura. In the latter part of the 18th century precise rules were formulated for doing this, and the practice arose of showing exactly the value of the small note, e.g.:

MOZART, *Violin Sonata in E flat major*, K 380

is to be played:

Earlier practice, however, was less rigid, and the interpretation of the texts is made more difficult by the fact that the same signs were also used for the short appoggiatura. The following examples from Quantz's *Versuch einer Answeisung die Flöte traversiere zu spielen* (1752) will give some idea of conventional interpretation about the middle of the 18th century:

as written:

as played:

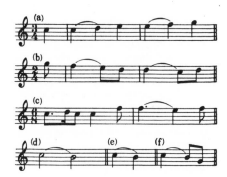

A problem for modern performers is that many 18th century composers (e.g. Mozart in his operas) fre-

quently left appoggiaturas unwritten, because they were able to rely on the taste and musical knowledge of their performers to insert them where appropriate. The practice of observing these appoggiaturas later fell into neglect, but was revived in the 1960s by Charles Mackerras and other conductors in Britain (e.g. in Mackerras's famous Sadler's Wells performances of *The Marriage of Figaro* in London, and Alexander Gibson's of *Cosi fan tutte* in Scotland), greatly enhancing the music and jettisoning the so-called blunt endings which so often misshape a Mozart line, as in Susanna's Act 4 aria in *Figaro*:

(2) the *short appoggiatura*, now known inaccurately as the ACCIACCATURA. A very short note of indeterminate length, originally played on the beat (like the long appoggiatura) and indicated by the same signs. Among the cases in mid-18th century music where the appoggiatura is short are: (i) when it precedes short notes, (ii) when it decorates repetitions of the same note, (iii) when it resolves on to a note dissonant with the bass, so that it is itself consonant with the bass:

C. P. E. BACH, *Versuch uber die wahre Art das Clavier zu spielen* (1753)

The following passage illustrates both the short appoggiatura (*b*) and the long appoggiatura (*c*), as well as the SLIDE (*a*):

as written:

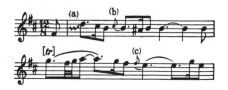

as played:

BACH, *St. Matthew Passion*

(The long appoggiatura has not been translated in accordance with Quantz's rules, which do not necessarily apply to Bach). In the latter part of the 18th century the practice arose of distinguishing the short appoggiatura by an oblique stroke across the note:

but it was some time before this became universal. In the 19th century there was a growing tendency to play the short appoggiatura before the beat, and this is now the normal method of execution, though it is naturally incorrect to apply it to older music. The result of this development is that the short appoggiatura has become similar in execution to the passing appoggiatura;

(3) the *passing appoggiatura*, current in the 18th century (though condemned by C. P. E. Bach), occurred normally when the principal notes of a melody formed a sequence of thirds. It was indicated by a curved sign identical with that used for the ordinary appoggiatura, or by a small quaver or semiquaver. Unlike the short appoggiatura, it was played before the beat. In this example (*a*) is the passing appoggiatura, (*b*) the ordinary long appoggiatura:

as written:

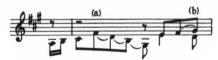

as played:

BACH, Organ Prelude on 'Allein Gott in der Hoh sei Ehr'

Quantz recommends a similar interpretation where the ornamental note precedes a long appoggiatura written in ordinary notation:

as written:

as played:

where the notes marked* are long appoggiaturas.

Appoggiaturas may occur simultaneously in more than one part, e.g.:

BEETHOVEN, *Sonata in E major*, op 109

In the second bar A, F sharp and D sharp are all appoggiaturas.

The name *double appoggiatura* is sometimes given to the ornament whose German name is ANSCHLAG.

E. DANNREUTHER: *Musical Ornamentation.*

A. DOLMETSCH: *The Interpretation of the Music of the XVIIth and XVIIIth Centuries.*

Apprenti Sorcier, L' (Fr., *The Sorcerer's Apprentice*), symphonic scherzo by Dukas (after a ballad by Goethe), first performed in 1897 in Paris.

Après-Midi d'un Faune, L', *see* PRÉLUDE À L'APRÈS-MIDI D'UN FAUNE

a punta d'arco (It.), with the point of the bow.

Aquin, D', *see* DAQUIN

Arabella, opera in three acts by Richard Strauss, to a libretto by Hugo von Hofmannsthal, first performed in 1933 in Dresden. This was the last of the six operas on which Strauss and Hofmannsthal worked together, and was not performed until four years after Hofmannsthal's death. Like *Der Rosenkavalier* it is a Viennese comedy of love and complications. Arabella is the daughter of an impoverished count who wants her to make a profitable marriage.

arabesque (Fr., Eng.; Ger., *Arabeske*), in architecture an ornament in the Arabic style. Hence in music: (1) decorative treatment of thematic material; (2) a lyrical piece in a fanciful style. In the latter sense first used by Schumann (op 18) and subsequently by other composers, including Debussy.

Araja, or **Araia, Francesco** (1709–70), Italian opera composer, resident in Russia from 1735 until 1759. His *La forza dell' amore e dell' odio* was the first Italian *opera seria* to be given in St. Petersburg (1736). His *La clemenza di Tito* (St. Petersburg, 1751 – forty years before Mozart set it in Italian) was the first opera with a Russian libretto.

Arbeau, Thoinot (1519–95), French priest, whose name is an anagram of Jehan Tabourot (J represented by I). He wrote a treatise on dancing, entitled *Orchésographie et traité en forme de dialogue par lequel toutes personnes peuvent facilement apprendre et pratiquer l'honnête exercise des danses* (1589). This includes descriptions of the dances, directions for playing the appropriate instruments, and a number of dance-tunes, some of which were arranged by Peter Warlock in his suite *Capriol*. The treatise has been edited by L. Fonta (1888), and translated into English by M. S. Evans with corrections and additional notes on the dance steps by J. Sutton (1967).

Arbos, Enrique Fernandez (1863–1939), Spanish violinist and conductor, a pupil of Vieuxtemps and Joachim. From 1894 until 1916 he was professor of the violin at the Royal College of Music, London. For many years he was conductor of the Madrid Symphony Orchestra. He orchestrated music by Albeniz, including *Iberia*. His compositions include a comic opera, *El centro de la tierra* (Madrid, 1895).

Arcadelt, Jacob (c. 1504–after 1567), composer, probably of Flemish origin. He was one of the papal singers in Rome from 1540 to 1549. From 1555 he was in the service of the Duc de Guise in Paris. A famous composer of Italian madrigals, he wrote also French *chansons*, motets and masses. The so-called 'Ave Maria', transcribed by Liszt, is a 19th-century adaptation, with altered harmony, of the *chanson* 'Nous voyons que les hommes' (published in 1554). His complete works have been edited in ten volumes by A. Seay (1965–70).

Archduke Trio, nickname for the piano trio in B flat major by Beethoven, op 97 (1811), dedicated to the Archduke Rudolph.

archet (Fr.), bow.

archi (It.), literally 'bows', the word is used to denote any group of stringed instruments played with bows.

archlute (Fr., *archiluth*; Ger., *Erzlaute*; It., *arciliuto*), a large bass lute, with two necks, one for the stopped strings running over the fingerboard, the other for the independent bass strings (*see* LUTE). It was much used in the 17th century for playing the bass part in concerted compositions.

arch viol, a 17th century keyboard instrument designed, to quote Samuel Pepys, 'to resemble several vyalls played on with one bow'. It was not successful.

arciliuto (It.), ARCHLUTE.

arco (It.; Fr., *archèt*; Ger., *Bogen*), bow (of a string instrument); *coll'arco*, with the bow (generally abbreviated to *arco*), as opposed to *pizzicato*, plucked with the finger; *strumenti d'arco* (or the plural *archi* alone), string instruments; *arcata*, a stroke of the bow; *arcato*, bowed.

Arditi, Luigi (1822–1903), Italian composer and conductor, particularly of opera. His waltz-song 'Il bacio' (the kiss) achieved an extraordinary popularity. His reminiscences, compiled by Baroness von Zedlitz, were published in 1896.

Arensky, Anton Stepanovich (1861–1906), Russian composer. He studied at St. Petersburg Conservatory under Rimsky-Korsakov, and became teacher of harmony and counterpoint at Moscow Conservatory (1883), and director of the Imperial Chapel, St. Petersburg (1895–1901). His compositions include three operas (one of them based on Ostrovsky's *Voyevoda*), a ballet (*Egyptian Night*), incidental music for Shakespeare's *Tempest*, two symphonies, a violin concerto, cantatas, church music, chamber music, piano solos and songs. In Britain his best-known works are the piano trio in D minor (op 32) and the variations on Chaikovsky's 'Legend' from the second string quartet in A minor (op 35). Though he made some use of folk tunes, his work in general is nearer to the mainstream of Western European music than to the ideals of the Russian nationalists.

Arezzo, Guido d', *see* GUIDO D'AREZZO

Argyll Rooms, the name of three successive buildings in London used for the performance of music in the early part of the 19th century. The first stood in Argyll Street (adjoining Oxford Circus tube station) and was the first home of the Philharmonic Society (now the ROYAL PHILHARMONIC SOCIETY), which was formed in 1813. The second, designed by John Nash, was in Regent Street and from 1818 till 1830, when it was destroyed by fire, was the principal concert hall in London. The third, built on the same site, failed to achieve the same success.

aria (It.; Eng., Fr., air; Ger., *Arie*), (1) a song for one or more voices, now used exclusively of solo song. It came into current use in the early 17th century, when it was used in opera and the chamber CANTATA to describe a symmetrical piece of vocal music, as opposed to the declamatory recitative. The attraction of such pieces for listeners, who were apt to find recitative tedious, was such that by the early 18th century the aria completely dominated opera. There were a large number of accepted types, designed to exploit the capabilities of singers and to afford contrast within a single work. Structure had also become stereotyped. The use of a form in which a contrasted middle section is followed by a repetition of the first section – an obvious symmetrical device – had become general. This form was known as the *da capo* aria, since after the middle section the singer began again 'from the beginning' (*da capo*). An early English example of this form on a small scale is Belinda's song 'Pursue thy conquest, love' in Purcell's *Dido and Aeneas* (1689). From opera the *da capo* aria was transferred naturally to oratorio. In both it was the practice of singers to vary the *da capo* by adding improvised ornaments. The modern habit of shortening a *da capo* by playing only the instrumental introduction, in order to save time, is indefensible, since it destroys the symmetry of the piece.

Since the structure of the *da capo* was primarily musical it did not always harmonize with the words. There were cases where the repetition of the first section weakened the effect made by the words of the middle section. Hence protests were made in the later 18th century against the domination of the *da capo* aria in opera as something unnatural. These protests took practical shape in the work of Gluck; but the principle of using lyrical pieces to intensify the emotion of dramatic situations was not challenged, until Wagner in his later operas demonstrated the possibility of a new continuity, in which set vocal pieces are abandoned and the function of establishing symmetry is assigned to the orchestra.

(2) an instrumental piece of a song-like character, e.g. the theme of Bach's *Goldberg Variations*.

Ariadne auf Naxos (Ger., *Ariadne on Naxos*), opera in one act with a prologue by Richard Strauss, to a libretto by Hugo von Hofmannsthal. The first version of the work, without the prologue, was designed to follow a performance of Molière's *Le Bourgeois Gentilhomme* and was written as a musical thanksgiving to the theatrical producer, Max Reinhardt, who had been helpful to the composer and librettist. In this form the work was first produced in 1912 at Stuttgart. But the hybrid nature of the evening satisfied neither the opera-lovers nor the theatre-lovers in the audience, so a second version was written in which the Molière was replaced by an operatic prologue. This was first performed four years later in Vienna, and is the version most frequently staged today. In it we are introduced to an idealist composer (a 'breeches' role, sung by a soprano or mezzo-soprano) who learns to his horror that his *opera seria* on the subject of Ariadne is to be performed simultaneously with an entertainment featuring a *commedie dell' arte* troupe.

This philistine demand has come from the owner of the house in which the performance is due to take place, because he wants the music to be finished in time for a firework display. When the prologue is over, the Composer does not reappear: what follows is the opera itself (in this case an opera-within-an-opera) in which the main plot is the familiar story of Ariadne, abandoned on Naxos by Theseus and delivered by Bacchus. But this, as predicted in the prologue, suffers comic interruptions from the *commedia dell'arte* players, led by the flirtatious Zerbinetta (soprano).

Though the juxtaposition of comic and serious elements has irritated some opera-lovers, *Ariadne auf Naxos* remains one of Strauss's most popular works, and the role of the Composer has been a favourite among singers ever since Lotte Lehmann first performed it.

Ariane et Barbe-Bleue (Fr., *Ariadne and Bluebeard*), opera in three acts by Paul Dukas – an almost literal setting of the play by Maeterlinck. First performed in 1907 in Paris, this was Dukas' only opera. Though rarely staged, it is nevertheless considered by many authorities to be one of the great operas of the 20th century. The story tells how Ariadne, the sixth of Bluebeard's wives, opens the forbidden door and releases her five predecessors. Instead of revenging themselves on Bluebeard, they show sympathy for him when he is attacked and wounded by the peasants. Ariadne, however, abandons him. The U.S. première of the work, in New York in 1911, was conducted by Toscanini.

Arianna, L', opera with a prologue and eight scenes, by Monteverdi to a libretto by Ottavio Rinuccini. It was first performed at Mantua on May 28, 1608. The only surviving fragment is the 'Lamento d'Arianna' which was separately published in 1623, and was also adapted by Monteverdi as a madrigal in his Sixth Book of Madrigals (1614) (*see* LAMENT).

Arie (Ger.), air, ARIA.

arietta (It.), diminutive of ARIA, (1) a term in use since the early 17th century to indicate a short song, simpler in character and structure than the aria;

(2) an instrumental piece of a similar kind, e.g. the theme of the variations which form the second movement of Beethoven's Sonata in C minor, op 111.

ariette (Fr.), (1) a short aria;

(2) in early 18th-century opera, a brilliant aria in Italian style, and even with Italian words;

(3) in late 18th century *opéra comique*, a song introduced into a scene in dialogue.

arioso (It.), 'like an aria', (1) a piece of recitative which has characteristics demanding a more song-like interpretation than the declamatory style proper to recitative. These characteristics are likely to include an expressive melodic line and rhythmical definition. The change from strict recitative to *arioso* is common in Bach. He also uses the word to describe a piece wholly in this style. A typical example of the latter is no 31 of the *St. John Passion* – 'Betrachte, meine Seel'

(Consider, O my soul) – for bass solo accompanied by lute, two viole d'amore and continuo. An *arioso* style has also been widely exploited by many present-day composers of opera or other vocal music, e.g. Hans Werner Henze in *Elegy for Young Lovers*;

(2) a short vocal solo in a lyrical style, e.g. no 37 of Mendelssohn's *Elijah* – 'Ja, es sollen wohl Berge weichen' (For the mountains shall depart);

(3) in instrumental music a piece similar in style to vocal *arioso*. In the third·movement of Beethoven's sonata in A flat major, op 110, the plaintive melody in A flat minor is marked *arioso dolente* to distinguish it from the preceding *recitativo*.

Ariosti, Attilio (1666–c. 1740), Italian opera composer. After some years in Berlin he travelled to England and was, with Handel and G. B. Bononcini, one of the musical directors of the Royal Academy of Music – a company for the production of Italian opera which was formed in 1720 and came to an abrupt end in 1728. Among the operas written for London by Ariosti were *Cajo Marzio Coriolano* (1723) and *Teuzzone* (1727). The old story that he collaborated with Handel and Bononcini in writing *Il Muzio Scevola* (1721) is without foundation.

Arlecchino (It., *Harlequin*), opera in one act by Busoni, to a libretto by the composer, first performed (with the same composer's *Turandot*) in 1917 in Zürich. In spite of the Italian title, this 'theatrical capriccio' is written in German. The story concerns Harlequin's successful defiance of conservative attitudes.

Arlésienne, L' (Fr., *The Girl from Arles*), a play of Provençal life by Alphonse Daudet (1840–97) with incidental music for small orchestra by Bizet, first performed in 1872 in Paris. Though the play is very rarely staged, Bizet's delightful pieces have long enjoyed a life of their own in the form of two orchestral suites – the first prepared by Bizet himself, the second an arrangement made by Guiraud after the composer's death. The music is notable for the pioneering use of the saxophone in the scoring.

Armida (It.; Fr., *Armide*), operas of this title have been written by several composers, with Tasso's poem of the Crusades, *La Gerusalemme liberata* (Jerusalem delivered) as their inspiration. Among the composers have been Lully whose work (with a libretto by Quinault) was first produced in 1686 in Paris; Gluck (again with Quinault as librettist) Paris, 1777; Haydn (libretto in Italian by Durandi), Eszterház, 1784; Rossini (libretto by Schmidt), Naples, 1817; and Dvořák (with a libretto by 'Jaroslav Vrchlický', i.e. Emil Bohuš Frida, based on a Czech translation of Tasso), Prague, 1904. Handel's *Rinaldo* was also inspired by the characters in Tasso's poem.

armonica, *see* HARMONICA (1)

Armstrong, Louis (1900–71), U.S. Negro jazz trumpeter, one of the greatest and most ebullient figures in jazz history. Born in New Orleans, he developed his abilities as a trumpeter in the brass band of the Waifs' Home to which he was sent as a child. In the 1920s he reached peak form in Chicago, appearing with Fletcher Henderson, and organizing his own Hot Five and Hot Seven with which he made his finest recordings. In later life he remained an immensely popular figure, but success and too many world tours weakened his creative talent and ultimately he was more a superb

Louis Armstrong, pictured at the height of his fame, when he had become the most lovable and humorous jazz trumpeter in the world. Musically, however, his most creative period was in the 1920s – the time of his Hot Five and Hot Seven – and many Armstrong devotees consider that his later public success brought with it an artistic decline from jazz into vaudeville

entertainer than the important jazz figure he was in his youth. Among his great performances, available on disc, are *Willie the Weeper*, *West End Blues*, *Weather Bird* and *Tight Like This* – Armstrong's memorable farewell to Chicago (and to his own heyday as a musician) just before he left for New York. Among his autobiographical writings, *Satchmo: My Life in New Orleans* gives a vivid impression of his early years.

arm viol, *see* VIOLA DA BRACCIO

Arne, Thomas Augustine (1710–78), English composer. He was educated at Eton and intended for the law, but studied music privately and adopted it as a profession. His first opera was a setting of Addison's *Rosamond* (London, 1733), previously set by Thomas Clayton. His most ambitious work was the opera *Artaxerxes*, to a text adapted by the composer from Metastasio (London, 1762). His comic opera *Thomas and Sally* (London, 1760) – the first English opera with clarinets – has been successfully revived in the present century. In addition to a very large number of works for the stage he also wrote two oratorios and instrumental music. His masque *Alfred* (1740) includes the patriotic song 'Rule Britannia'. His settings of 'Under the greenwood tree', 'Blow, blow, thou winter wind' and 'When daisies pied' were written for a revival of *As you like it* in 1740, and 'Where the bee sucks' for a revival of *The Tempest* in 1746. He was attached as composer to Vauxhall Gardens in London, to Drury Lane, and to Covent Garden, and received an Oxford doctorate in 1759. See illustration on p. 42.

His illegitimate son **Michael Arne** (1740–86), was a singer and composer of dramatic music. His most successful work was the music for Garrick's *Cymon* (1767). He also dabbled in chemistry, attempting to discover the philosopher's stone.

Thomas Arne's sister, **Susanna Maria Arne** (1714–66), was a singer and actress. She married Theophilus Cibber, son of Colley Cibber, but the marriage was not a success. Her interpretation of 'He was not despis'd', which she sang at the first performance of *Messiah* in Dublin in 1742, made a great impression. Handel wrote the part of Micah in *Samson* for her.

H. LANGLEY: *Doctor Arne* (1938)

Arnell, Richard Anthony Sayer (born 1917), English composer, pupil of John Ireland. He lived in the United States from 1939 until 1947, during which period he was music consultant to the B.B.C.'s North American services. His numerous compositions include a ballet, *Punch and the Child*, commissioned in 1947 by the Ballet Society of New York. He has also written two other ballets (*Harlequin in April* and *The Great Detective* – the latter after Conan Doyle), five symphonies, a violin concerto, a symphonic poem (*Lord Byron*), chamber music and piano pieces.

Arnold, Madeleine Sophie (1740–1802), French singer and actress. She was the first Iphigenia in Gluck's *Iphigenie en Aulide* (1774) and the first Eurydice in the Paris version of his *Orfeo*, produced in the same year. She owed her success more to her ability as an actress than to her voice, which was not outstanding. Her portrait was painted by Greuze.

Arnold, Malcolm Henry (born 1921), English composer, pupil of Gordon Jacob. He was formerly a trumpeter in the London Philharmonic and B.B.C. Symphony Orchestra. His compositions, mainly in a straightforwardly melodious and often humorous style, include six symphonies, concertos for horn and clarinet, symphony for strings, overture – *Beckus the Dandipratt*, chamber and film music, and a concerto for piano duet.

Arnold, Samuel (1740–1802), English organist, composer and editor. He was organist of the Chapel Royal (1783), and Westminster Abbey (1793). He wrote several oratorios and a great quantity of music for the stage. He also published a subscription edition of Handel's works (incomplete and in many respects inaccurate) and a collection of *Cathedral Music* in four volumes.

Aron, *see* AARON

arpa (It.), harp.

arpeggio (It., *arpeggiare*, 'to play the harp'), (1) the notes of a chord played not simultaneously but in rapid succession – 'broken' or 'spread out' – as on the harp. The former English name was 'battery'. Among the signs in use in the 17th and 18th centuries were the following:

as written:

as played:

(*See also* ACCIACCATURA). A vaguer indication was to mark a chord *arpeggio* and leave the interpretation to the player, who was free to play ascending and descending arpeggios as he wished and to interpolate acciaccaturas. The modern practice is to play all arpeggios ascending and to use one of the following signs (of which the second is the least common):

Dr. Arne playing 'Rule Britannia': a contemporary cartoon which comments on the patriotic popularity of tune and composer

The question whether the arpeggio begins before or on the beat is one that now depends on the context. In piano music the following distinction should be observed between chords in which the right and left hands play arpeggios simultaneously and those in which there is a single arpeggio divided between the two hands:

as written:

as played:

(2) the term is also applied to the successive notes of a chord, ascending and descending, written out in full and performed in strict time. The practice of such passages forms part of the technical training of every singer and instrumentalist.

arpeggione (It.), instrument, invented by Staufer of Vienna in 1823, which would be forgotten today had not Schubert written for it a sonata with piano the following year. It had six strings, tuned as for a guitar, but it was played with a bow. Schubert's sonata is nowadays usually performed on a cello.

arpicordo (It.), an early name for the HARPSICHORD.

arpo (It.), harp.

arrangement, (1) the adaptation of a piece of music so as to make it suitable for performance by forces other than those for which it was originally composed. The purpose of such an arrangement may be (*a*) to facilitate study or domestic performance, as with the vocal score of an opera or oratorio; (*b*) to enlarge the repertory of a particular medium, as with organ arrangements of orchestral works; (*c*) to enable a work written for a large number of performers to be given with more limited resources. In the last of these three cases arrangement is unlikely to involve more than transference from one instrument to another and the omission of unessential details. In the other two cases it involves a modification of the original text. An orchestral score not only has to be compressed if it is to be playable on the piano; many of its details will also have to be translated into pianistic terms. Conversely, much that is effective on the piano will need considerable adaptation if it is to be equally effective in the orchestra. Arrangers often go far beyond such necessary modification, elaborating details in the original text until they acquire a new significance and adding extraneous material of their own. The criterion of an arrangement is not only technical skill but good taste.

The practice of arrangement is ancient and many composers have arranged their own works. As early as the first half of the 14th century we find examples of organ arrangements of motets in a manuscript from

Robertsbridge Abbey, Sussex (*see* H. E. Wooldridge, *Early English Harmony*). Organ arrangements of vocal works occur also in the 15th century, e.g. in the *Buxheim Organ Book* (1470). In the 16th century, arrangements of vocal works for lute solo or for solo voice with lute accompaniment are very common. In the 18th century, Bach was particularly active in arranging his own works and those of other composers, e.g. Vivaldi's violin concertos, which he arranged for the keyboard. Beethoven arranged his own violin concerto in D major (op 61) as a piano concerto. Brahms adopted the unusual course of issuing two of his works in two different forms: the piano quintet in F minor (op 34) appeared also as a sonata for two pianos (op 34a), and the 'ST. ANTHONY' VARIATIONS were published both for orchestra (op 56a) and for two pianos (op 56b). Schoenberg's orchestral arrangement of Brahms's G minor piano quartet is sometimes known as 'Brahms's fifth symphony'. Ravel's orchestration of Mussorgsky's *Pictures at an Exhibition* makes a fascinating comparison with the piano original.

(2) a harmonized setting, whether for voices or instruments, of an existing melody. Folk song provides obvious material for such treatment, which may range from the provision of a simple piano accompaniment to the most ingenious polyphony. Here, too, good taste is essential, since a setting that is out of keeping with the character of the melody will deform it instead of enhancing its beauty.

Arrau, Claudio (born 1903), Chilean pianist. Known as a child prodigy, he later studied in Berlin under Krause, a pupil of Liszt, and gave his first recital in Germany in 1914. He taught at Stern's Conservatorium, Berlin from 1925 until 1940. Subsequently he opened a school of piano-playing in Santiago, Chile. Today he travels on a diplomatic passport and has a street in Santiago named after him. He is one of the 20th century's greatest interpreters of the music of Beethoven, Schumann, Chopin, Brahms and Liszt.

Arriaga, Juan Crisóstomo Antonio (1806–1826), Spanish composer (full surname Arriaga y Balzola) who, but for his early death, would almost certainly have become one of the major figures of his period. His opera, *Los Esclavos Felices*, was performed at Bilbao when he was thirteen. In 1821 he was sent to the Paris Conservatoire to study. His three string quartets provide tantalizing evidence of an eloquent maturity of expression and a fine sense of musical proportion. He also wrote a symphony and an eight-part *Et Vitam Venturi*, described by Cherubini as a masterpiece.

Arrieta y Corera, Emilio (1823–94), Spanish opera composer. He was professor of composition at Madrid Conservatorio from 1857 and director from 1868. His light opera *Marina* (1855) was later enlarged into a three-act opera with recitatives (1871) – the first opera to be sung in Spanish at the Madrid Court Theatre.

Ars antiqua (Lat.), 'the old art'; music of the late 12th and 13th centuries, in contrast with ARS NOVA, the music of the 14th century. The two terms were originally used by early 14th century writers to distinguish the music of the late 13th century from that of their own time.

Ars nova (Lat.), 'The new art'. The name of an early 14th century treatise ascribed to Philippe de Vitry.

The term was used by theorists of the period to describe the music of their own time in contrast to that of the late 13th century (ARS ANTIQUA). It is now generally applied to the whole of 14th century music.

arsis (Gr.), (1) literally 'a raising' (of the hand or foot), hence an up-beat, in contrast to *thesis*, a down-beat. The Romans, however, used *arsis* of a strong accent, and this interpretation was followed not only by medieval theorists but by many modern writers. Hence the use of the word today may easily create confusion, though there is a growing tendency to accept the meaning of the original Greek;

(2) the expression *per arsin et thesin* was formerly applied to imitation by contrary motion, since one part goes up where the other goes down, and vice versa, e.g.:

BACH, *The Art of Fugue*, Contrapunctus V

Artaria, a Vienna music-publishing firm, of Italian origin. Their publications, which began in 1778, included many works by Haydn, Mozart and Beethoven.

Artaxerxes, opera in three acts by Arne, first performed in 1762 in London. The libretto is an English adaptation, by the composer, of Metastasio's *Artaserse*.

Art of Fugue, The (Ger., *Die Kunst der Fuge*), a work by J. S. Bach, written in 1749 and published after his death in 1750. The first edition had no sale; of the second, published with a preface by F. W. Marpurg in 1752, only about thirty copies were sold in four years. In 1756 C. P. E. Bach sold the copper plates for their value as metal.

The work demonstrates by example almost every possible kind of contrapuntal treatment of the following theme:

It consists of thirteen fugues (for which Bach uses the term *contrapunctus*), two of which are also inverted, and four canons. The published text includes also an unfinished fugue on three subjects (none of which is the subject of *The Art of Fugue*) and the chorale prelude

'Vor deinen Thron', which Bach dictated shortly before his death to his son-in-law J. C. Altnikol. The chorale prelude clearly has no connection with *The Art of Fugue*, and there is no evidence that the unfinished fugue was intended to form part of the work, the engraving of which was largely completed before Bach died. It has been shown, however, that the subject of *The Art of Fugue* can be combined contrapuntally with the three subjects of the unfinished fugue and a conjectural completion on these lines is published in Tovey's edition.

The original text is in score, without any indication of the instruments for which it is intended, except that Bach himself provided an arrangement for two harpsichords (with a fourth part added) of Contrapunctus XIII and its inversion. The whole work, however, with the exception of Contrapunctus XII and Contrapunctus XIII and the concluding bars of Contrapunctus VI, can be performed on the keyboard by a single player. Modern transcriptions include one for orchestra by Wolfgang Graeser and another for string quartet by Roy Harris.

D. F. TOVEY: *A Companion to the Art of Fugue* (1931)

Artusi, Giovanni Maria (c. 1540–1613), Italian theorist and composer. He was a canon of San Salvatore, Bologna, in 1562. His most celebrated work was *Delle imperfettioni della musica moderna* (1600–3), in which he attacked the music of his more advanced contemporaries, particularly Monteverdi.

As (Ger.), A flat (A♭).

Asafiev, Boris (1884–1949), Russian composer and musicologist. He studied at St. Petersburg conservatory, and, after the Revolution, took an active part in propagating the official Soviet attitude towards composition. His own works are chiefly for the stage, and include operas and ballets. Under the name 'Igor Glebov' he was active as a music critic and published several books, mainly on Russian music.

Ases (Ger.), A double flat (A♭♭).

Ashkenazy, Vladimir (born 1937), Russian pianist, joint winner with John Ogdon of the International Chaikovsky Competition in Moscow in 1962. The following year he settled in the West (first in Britain, then in Iceland – his wife is Icelandic) and soon established himself as one of the leading pianists of his generation, with a special flair for the music of Mozart, Beethoven and Chopin.

Ashton, Hugh, *see* ASTON

Aspelmayr, Franz (1728–86), the second German to have a work included in the repertory of the Vienna *Nationalsingspiel*, funded in 1779. This was his opera *Die Kinder der Natur* (1778). He was also one of the first Viennese composers to practise the new instrumental style associated particularly with the Mannheim school.

aspiration (Fr.; Eng., *springer*; Ger., *Nachschlag*), an ornament current in the 17th and 18th centuries, indicated by various signs:

as written:

as played:

assai (It.), 'very', e.g. *allegro assai*, very fast.

Aston or **Ashton, Hugh** (c. 1485–after 1549), English composer. He was master of the choristers at St. Mary Newarke Hospital and College, Leicester, from about 1525 to 1548. His compositions include a Hornpipe for virginals (printed in *Schott's Anthology of Early English Keyboard Music*, ed. F. Dawes), which anticipates by a good many years the methods of Elizabethan and Jacobean composers, and some church music (printed in *Tudor Church Music*, x).

Astorga, Emanuele Gioacchino Cesare Ricón Baron d' (1680–1757), Sicilian nobleman (of Spanish descent) and composer. His works include a single opera, *Dafni* (Genoa, 1709), a *Stabat Mater* (1707) which appears to have been first performed at Oxford in 1752, and a number of chamber cantatas. An opera dealing with his life by J. J. Albert (1832–1915), was produced at Stuttgart in 1866.

Atalanta, opera in three acts by Handel (librettist unknown), first performed in London in 1736. The work was adapted from Belisario Valeriani's *La Caccia in Etiola*, and ends with a firework display.

a tempo (It.; Fr., *au mouvement*), 'in time'. Used to restore the normal tempo of a piece after it has been interrupted by a *rallentando, allargando, a piacere*, etc., or by a section marked to be played at a faster or slower speed than that indicated at the beginning of the piece.

Athaliah, oratorio by Handel, to a libretto by Samuel Humphreys, first performed in 1733 at Oxford.

Athalie, incidental music by Mendelssohn, op 74, written for Racine's tragedy of the same name. The first performance was in Berlin in 1845.

atonality, a term often used loosely of any music whose harmony appears unfamiliar, but properly applied to music which rejects traditional tonality, i.e. which abandons the use of a tonic or key-centre to which all the notes and chords of a piece are related.

What is often described as the 'breakdown' in tonality began during the second half of the 19th century, particularly in the works of Wagner (where the amount of modulation was sufficient at times to disguise the true tonal centre of the music) and Debussy. From Wagner's *Tristan* it was just a short step to Schoenberg's *Transfigured Night*. Yet *Transfigured Night* is not to modern ears an exceptionally atonal work, however strange it may have sounded to some of its early listeners. Schoenberg, though he was the crucial composer in the evolution of atonality, disliked being called an atonalist. He preferred to talk of *pantonality* (meaning the synthesis of all keys rather than the absence of any) though the term never caught on. Schoenberg's suspension of tonality ultimately led to his conscious systemization of atonality in the form of twelve-note music.

R. LEIBOWITZ: *Schoenberg, et son école* (1947)

G. PERLE: *Serial Composition and Atonality* (1962)

R. RETI: *Tonality, Atonality, Pantonality* (1958)

attacca (It.), 'attack', i.e. start the next movement or section without any break. So also *attacca subito*, begin suddenly.

attacco (It.), a short figure used as a subject for imitation in a fugue or other polyphonic composition, e.g.:

BACH, *48 Preludes and Fugues*, Book II, no 3

Attaingnant, Pierre (died c. 1551), French music publisher, the first in Paris to print from movable types. His publications include a large quantity of chansons, motets, Masses, lute music and organ music, mainly by French composers, especially Sermisy, Certon and Janequin. A historical study and bibliographical catalogue of his publications (including details of modern reprints) is in D. Heartz, *Pierre Attaingnant: Royal Printer of Music* (1969).

Attaque du Moulin, L' (Fr., *The Attack on the Mill*), opera in four acts by Bruneau, to a libretto by Louis Gallet (based on a story in Zola's *Soirées de Médan*), first performed in 1893 in Paris.

Atterberg, Kurt (born 1887), Swedish composer, conductor and critic. Originally trained as an engineer, he studied music at the Stockholm Royal Academy of Music and in Germany, with the aid of a state grant. In 1919 he became music critic of the *Stockholms Tidningen*. His works include niné symphonies, concertos for violin, cello, horn and piano, five operas, choral cantatas and miscellaneous orchestral and chamber works. His sixth symphony in C major, op 31, won the first prize of £2000 offered by the Columbia Gramophone Company in 1928 to commemorate the anniversary of Schubert's death.

Attey, John (died c. 1640), last of the English lutenist songwriters. His only published work, *The First Booke of Ayres* (1622; facsimile edition, 1967), includes the well-known 'Sweet was the song the virgin sang'. The songs in the collection are designed to be sung by four voices with lute, or as solos with accompaniment for lute and bass viol. A modern edition is in *The English School of Lutenist Songwriters*, second series.

At the Boar's Head, opera in one act by Holst, to a libretto by the composer, first performed in 1925 in Manchester. The text of the opera is drawn from Shakespeare's *Henry IV*, and much of the musical material from English folk song.

Attwood, Thomas (1765–1838), English composer and organist of St. Paul's Cathedral, London, from 1796. His numerous compositions include anthems for the coronations of George IV and William IV and a large number of works for the stage. He was a favourite pupil of Mozart, with whom he studied in Vienna (1785–7), and a close friend of Mendelssohn, who dedicated to him his three Preludes and Fugues for organ, op 37.

Atys, opera with a prologue and five acts by Lully, to a libretto by Philippe Quinault, first performed in 1676 at St. Germain.

aubade (Fr.; Sp., *alborada*), morning music, as opposed to serenade, which is properly evening music. Often used as the title of short instrumental pieces.

Auber, Daniel François Esprit (1782–1871), French composer. His early years were spent as a clerk in London, where his songs had some success in society. He returned to Paris in 1804 and began to write operas, but without success until the performance of *La Bergère châtelaine* (1820). From 1823 onwards he collaborated with the librettist Augustin Eugène Scribe. He produced in all 45 operas, of which the most successful were *Le Maçon* (1825), *La Muette de Portici*, known in Britain as *Masaniello* (1828), *Fra Diavolo* (1830), *Le Cheval de bronze* (1835), *Le Domino noir* (1837), *Les Diamants de la couronne* (1841), *Haydée* (1847) and *Le Premier jour de bonheur* (1868). *La Muette de Portici* was the first of the French romantic 'grand operas' of the 19th century and is remarkable in that the heroine is dumb. It was much admired by Wagner for its dramatic intensity. Its representation of the spirit of revolt against tyranny was so striking that a performance at Brussels in 1830 precipitated the revolution which established Belgian independence. Apart from this work Auber was at his best in *opéra comique*. His *Fra Diavolo*, dealing with the adventures of English tourists among Italian bandits, is still admired. In 1842, Auber became director of the Paris Conservatoire, and in 1857 of the Imperial Chapel.

CH. MALHERBE: *Auber* (Paris, 1911)

Aubert, Jacques (1689–1753), French violinist and and composer, a member of the king's band of 24 violins and the Opéra orchestra. He wrote violin concertos and a considerable amount of instrumental music for the Concert Spirituel, as well as ballets for the Opéra and music for the *Théâtre de la foire*.

Aubert, Louis François Marie (1877–1968), French composer, pupil of Fauré at the Paris Conservatoire. His most important work is the fairy-tale opera *La Forêt bleue* (Geneva, 1913), which was not performed in Paris until 1924. It combines impressionist harmony with considerable melodic charm. His other works include an orchestral *Habañera* (1919).

Aubry, Pierre (1874–1910), French musicologist, whose special field was medieval music. In his book *Trouvères et troubadours* (Paris, 1909) he advocated the interpretation of troubadour melodies in accordance with the rhythm of the words. According to his interpretation, which was also advanced by J. B. Beck and is now widely accepted, the music is to be transcribed in one of the RHYTHMIC MODES. Aubry also published *Les plus anciens monuments de la musique française* (1903), *Estampies et danses royales* (1906), *Le Roman de Fauvel* (1907), *Cents Motets du XIIIe siècle* (3 vols., 1908) and *Le Chansonnier de l'Arsenal* (1909), of which the last remained unfinished at his death.

au chevalet (Fr.; Ger., *am Steg*; It., *sul ponticello*), on the bridge (of a string instrument), i.e. play near the bridge, thus producing a glassy, brittle tone.

Audran, Edmond (1840–1901), French composer, whose reputation rests on a large number of comic operas, of which *La Mascotte* (Paris, 1880) and *La Poupée* (Paris, 1896) were the most popular. He also wrote church music and was for some years organist of a church in Marseilles.

Auer, Leopold (1845–1930), Hungarian born violinist and teacher, a pupil of Joachim. He was a professor of the violin at the Imperial Conservatory, St. Petersburg, from 1868 until 1917. In 1918 he settled in New York, where he continued to teach. His pupils included Mischa Elman, Jascha Heifetz, Efrem Zimbalist and Isolde Menges.

Auf dem Anstand (Ger.), 'at the hunting station', nickname for Haydn's symphony no 31 in D major (1765), also known as *Mit dem Hornsignal*, 'with the horn call'. It includes prominent, and sometimes elaborate, parts for four horns, and opens with a hunting fanfare.

Aufstieg und Fall der Stadt Mahagonny, see RISE AND FALL OF THE CITY OF MAHAGONNY

Augener, a London music-publishing and printing firm, founded in 1853 by George Augener (died 1915).

augmentation, the presentation of a theme in notes double the value of those originally assigned to it. In the following example the fugue subject and its augmentation are combined:

BACH, *48 Preludes and Fugues*, Book II, no 2

(*see* CANON); the opposite is DIMINUTION.

augmented interval, the following intervals can be augmented by sharpening the upper, or flattening the lower, note: major second, major third, fourth, fifth, major sixth, major seventh, octave, e.g.:

fourth: augmented fourth:

major sixth: augmented sixth:

The augmented fourth occurs between the fourth and seventh notes of every major scale, e.g.:

The other augmented intervals necessitate notes foreign to the key.

augmented sixth, see AUGMENTED INTERVAL. The so-called chord of the augmented sixth has three forms hallowed by tradition, known respectively (for no good reason) as Italian, French and German:

Since on keyboard instruments it is impossible to distinguish between the sound of F sharp and G flat the last of the three may also be treated as a DOMINANT SEVENTH chord (in this case in the key of D flat):

Such ambiguity appealed particularly to 19th century composers, who exploited it for the purpose of modulation.

The 'Italian' sixth originated in the 17th century as the result of the combination of two alternative progressions:

A more pathetic effect was produced by combining the sharpened sixth with the flattened bass:

The frequent use of a chromatically descending bass in movements built on a *basso ostinato* (ground bass) encouraged the adoption of this progression.

augmented triad, a chord composed, in its simplest form, of two major thirds, e.g.:

The notes of the chord can also be rearranged as follows:

See CHORD, INVERSION

Augustine (real name Aurelius Augustinus) (354–430), one of the fathers of the Latin church, who also wrote about music. In his early years he taught at Carthage, Rome, and Milan, where he was baptised in 387. He returned to Carthage in 388 and was ordained priest in 391, becoming bishop of Hippo in 396. His *Confessiones* and *De civitate Dei* date from the latter part of his life, after his appointment as bishop. The treatise *De musica* was written between about 387 and 389. It deals principally with metre. An English translation has been published by R. Catesby Taliafero (1939).

A girl playing an aulos – a detail from a red-figure stamnos from Gela

aulos, a generic term used by the ancient Greeks for a wind instrument (Lat., *tibia*). The term was used more particularly for a double-reed instrument, the most important wind instrument of the ancient Greeks. It had a cylindrical bore, and the numerous pictures show that it was usually played in pairs by a single performer. The double reed was not held between the lips, as in the modern oboe, but inside the mouth. Inflation of the cheeks, which acted as bellows was often controlled by a leather band, called *phorbeia*, which passed round the player's head. It is thought that the second *aulos* was used to provide a drone bass, as on the bagpipe. The *aulos* was used in the Greek drama, in musical competitions, at marriage ceremonies and for entertainment. Girls playing the *aulos* were popular at banquets. The tone of the instrument was shrill and penetrating, like that of the medieval shawm.

K. SCHLESINGER: *The Greek Aulos* (1939)

au mouvement, *see* A TEMPO

aural training, the purpose of aural training is to teach pupils to recognize the sounds and rhythms they hear and to write them down on paper. The ability to do this is indispensable for the study of harmony and counterpoint, and no one can properly be called a musician who cannot do it. There are a number of books on the subject, but what the student needs most is constant practice with a good teacher.

B. C. ALLCHIN: *Aural Training*

Auric, Georges (born 1899), French composer. He studied at the Paris Conservatoire and at the Schola Cantorum. He was influenced by Erik Satie and became one of the group of young composers known as *Les Six*, the others being Darius Milhaud, Louis Durey, Arthur Honegger, Francis Poulenc and Germaine Tailleferre (see SIX). His compositions pay tribute both to popular music and to Stravinsky and Ravel. Notable for their wit and charm, they include songs, piano music, chamber music, ballets (including *Les Matelots* and *Les Noces de Gamache* – the latter from *Don Quixote*), and music for films (including René Clair's *A Nous la liberté* and Bernard Shaw's *Caesar and Cleopatra*).

Aus Italien (Ger., *From Italy*), symphony by Richard Strauss, op 16, inspired by a visit to Italy. Composed in 1886, the music quotes Denza's 'Funiculi, funicula' in the belief that it was an Italian folk song.

Austin, Frederic (1872–1952), English baritone and composer. From 1908 he sang in opera under Richter and Beecham and became a member of the Beecham Opera Company in 1915. From 1924 he was artistic director of the BRITISH NATIONAL OPERA COMPANY. His version of *The Beggars' Opera* (London, 1920), in which he sang as Peachum, was extraordinarily successful.

au talon (Ger., *am Frosch*), with the nut (or heel) of the bow (i.e. the end nearer the hand).

authentic mode, *see* MODE

autoharp, a kind of zither in which chords are obtained by pressing keys that stop or damp the strings. It was invented in the late 19th century.

Ave Maria (Lat.), 'Hail, Mary', (1) a prayer to the Virgin in use in the Roman Catholic Church, beginning with the salutations of the angel Gabriel and Elizabeth. It has often been set to music;

(2) among the popular pieces known by this title are (a) 'Arcadelt's *Ave Maria*', a transcription by Liszt, with altered harmony, of Arcadelt's *chanson* 'Nous voyons que les hommes' (1554); (b) a setting by Schubert, op 52, no 6 (1825) of a translation by P. A. Storck of one of Ellen's songs in Scott's *Lady of The Lake*; (c) a *cantabile* melody superimposed by Gounod on the first prelude, in C major, from Bach's *Well-Tempered Clavier*.

Avison, Charles (1709–70), English organist and composer. He published a number of instrumental concertos but is principally known by his treatise *An Essay on Musical Expression* (second edition, 1753), which, though opinionated, is valuable for the evidence it affords of contemporary taste and practice. He was a pupil of Geminiani, whom he praises warmly in his *Essay*. For his 'Grand March' *see* Robert Browning, *Parleyings with certain people of importance in this day* (1887).

ayre, *see* AIR (2)

B (Eng., Fr.; It., *si*; Ger., *H*), (1) the seventh note (or leading note) of the scale of C major. In the 10th century a distinction was established between ♭ (*B molle* or *rotundum*, 'soft' or 'rounded' B), representing B flat, and ♮ (*B durum* or *quadratum*, 'hard' or 'square' B), representing B natural (*see* HEXACHORD). From these two signs the ♭ and ♮ respectively were derived. The modern French and Italian names for the flat (*bémol* and *bemolle*) and for the natural (*bécarre* and *bequadro*) have a similar origin. The adjectives *molle* and *durum* are also perpetuated in the modern German terms for major and minor *dur* and *moll*. In the 16th century the Germans came to write ♭ as ♮; hence in German nomenclature *B* is B flat and *H* is B natural; e.g. 'Klarinette in B' means 'Clarinet in B flat'.

(2) as an abbreviation *B.* = Bass, Bachelor (*B. Mus.* or *Mus. B.* = Bachelor of Music).

Babbitt, Milton (born 1916), U.S. composer, born in New York. At Princeton he was a pupil of Roger Sessions, and himself taught there (music and mathematics) between 1938 and 1945. Webern was the main influence on his early music. More recently, he has turned to electronic music. His works, sometimes seeming as cool as their titles, include *Composition for twelve instruments* (1948), *Composition for four instruments* (1948), *Composition for viola and piano* (1950) and *Composition for synthesizer* (1961). His *Vision and Prayer* has words by Dylan Thomas and an electronic tape accompaniment. He has also written three string quartets (the most recent in 1969), a string trio and a wind octet.

Babell, William (c. 1690–1723), English composer and performer on the harpsichord and violin. He made a reputation by issuing showy transcriptions for the harpsichord of popular operatic arias, for which Burney had the greatest contempt (*General History of Music*, volume four, pages 648–9). He also published sonatas of his own compositions for violin or oboe.

Babin, Victor (1908–72), Russian born pianist and composer, pupil of Schnabel. He appeared as a solo pianist and in works for two pianos with his wife, Vitya Vronsky. His compositions are mainly instrumental. From 1961 he was director of the Cleveland Conservatory in the United States.

Baborák (Czech.), a Bohemian national dance, consisting of alternating sections in 3/4 and 2/4 time.

Baccusi, Ippolito (c. 1545–1609), Italian composer. He was *maestro di cappella* at Mantua Cathedral in about 1580, and at Verona in 1592. His works consist of Masses, motets and madrigals. He contributed to a number of 16th-century collections, including the *Psalmodia vespertina* dedicated to Palestrina (1592) and *Il trionfo di Dori* (1592), the collection of Italian madrigals which suggested the publication of the English collection *The Triumphes of Oriana*.

Bach, family of Thuringian musicians, important from the 16th to the 18th centuries, of which Hans Bach, 'der Spielmann', was the first professional musician. Of his large family, his sons Christoph and Heinrich are notable, Christoph as J. S. Bach's grandfather and Heinrich as the father of **Johann Christoph** and **Johann Michael**, famous in their own right. Johann Christoph (1642–1703), an organist at Eisenach from 1665 till death, wrote the motet *Ich lasse dich nicht* ('I wrestle and pray') among other vocal and instrumental works. Johann Michael (1648–94), organist at Arnstadt, was a composer of motets and organ music. He was the father of J. S. Bach's first wife, Maria Barbara (1684–1720).

Johann Sebastian Bach (1685–1750) thus inherited a family talent. His father, Johann Ambrosius, was first cousin of Johann Michael and Johann Christoph Bach. Born at Eisenach, he became a pupil of his brother (also called Johann Christoph) in Ohrdruf after their father's death in 1695. At the age of fifteen he became a choirboy at the Michaelis-Kirche, Lüneburg, where he is thought to have had organ lessons from Böhm. In 1703 he became a violinist in the Weimar court orchestra, but left in the same year to become organist of the Bonifacius-Kirche, Arnstadt – from where, in 1705, he made his famous journey to Lübeck to hear Buxtehude play. In 1707 he moved to Muhlhausen, becoming organist of the Blasius-Kirche and marrying his cousin, Maria Barbara. The following year he returned to Weimar as court organist, an appointment he held until 1717, when he became director of music to the court of Prince Leopold of Anhalt-Cöthen. His acceptance of this post provoked his Weimar employer to arrest him, but the matter was cleared up. During his Weimar period, Bach wrote the bulk of his organ music; during his Cöthen period, he concentrated on secular instrumental works, because that was where the prince's interests lay – he had his own small orchestra for which Bach wrote suites and concertos (among them six composed for the Margrave of Brandenburg). In 1720 his wife died, and the following year he married Anna Magdalena Wilcken. Prince Leopold, too, married during this period (to an unmusical princess) and this seems to have caused Bach again to go job-hunting. In 1723 he succeeded Kühnau as cantor of St. Thomas's, Leipzig, where he remained for the rest of his career, composing church music and making occasional visits to other parts of Germany. In 1747, with his eldest son, Wilhelm Friedemann, he visited the court of Frederick the Great at Potsdam, where his second son, Carl Philipp Emanuel, was harpsichordist In 1749 his eyesight began to fail, and in 1750, after an unsuccessful operation, he spent the last months of his life totally blind. His wife died the following year. Of his twenty children, ten died in infancy or at birth.

Bach's work, vast in bulk, contains every kind of music current at the time, except opera – though there is a strong link between such works as the Matthew and John Passions and Wagner's music dramas of a century later.

The chief influences in Bach's music are the Lutheran chorale, the church and organ music of his predecessors and the contemporary French and Italian styles in instrumental music. In his lifetime he had a great reputation as an organist, but his music was considered by many to be over-elaborate and old-fashioned. He combined extraordinary contrapuntal skill with a mastery of picturesque and passionate expression. His genius required no special stimulus; it overflowed the channel of his daily employment. His music was written for a practical purpose – for the court orchestra at Cöthen, for the Sunday service at Leipzig, for the instruction of his sons, for the gratification of patrons, and for his own use. Among his didactic works *The Well-Tempered Keyboard* (*Das wohltemperierte Clavier*) and *The Art of Fugue* (*Die Kunst der Fuge*) are particularly important. The former supports the argument for EQUAL TEMPERAMENT with two sets of preludes and fugues in all the major and minor keys; the latter demonstrates with a wealth of ingenuity the possibilities latent in a single fugue subject (*see* ART OF FUGUE). Both achieve beauty. Bach was a universal musician, whose music has a universal appeal. It is steeped in the flavour of its period, yet belongs to all time (*see* BACH GESELLSCHAFT).

Bach's principal compositions are:

(1) Church music: Magnificat; *St. John Passion* (1723); *St. Matthew Passion* (1729); *Christmas Oratorio* (1734); *Mass in B minor*; 198 cantatas; six motets.
(2) Secular choral music: 23 cantatas;
(3) Orchestra: six Brandenburg concertos (1721); four overtures (or suites); two violin concertos; concerto for two violins; concertos for one or more harpsichords; concerto for harpsichord, flute and violin;
(4) Chamber music: six sonatas for solo violin; six suites for solo cello; flute sonatas; violin sonatas; *viola da gamba* sonatas; *Musikalisches Opfer* (1747);
(5) Harpsichord or clavichord: seven toccatas; chromatic fantasia and fugue; fifteen two-part inventions; fifteen three-part inventions (symphonies); six French suites; six English suites; *Das wohltemperierte Clavier* (1722 and 1744); six partitas (1731); Italian concerto (1735); Goldberg variations (1742); *Die Kunst der Fuge* (probably intended for the keyboard);
(6) Organ: six sonatas; 143 chorale preludes; fantasias, preludes, fugues, toccatas.

Wilhelm Friedemann Bach (1710–84), was the eldest and one of the most distinguished of Johann Sebastian's sons. He received his early musical training from his father, who wrote for him the *Clavier-Büchlein vor Wilhelm Friedemann Bach* (which includes the two-part and three-part inventions). Later he studied at Leipzig University, and in 1733 was appointed organist of the Sophien-Kirche, Dresden. From 1746 until 1764 he was organist of the Liebfrauen-

Johann Sebastian Bach

Kirche, Halle. After resigning from that post he made a living by teaching and giving recitals – he was an outstanding organist. But he could not make ends meet as a freelance, and died in poverty in Berlin. In spite of his restless temperament, his compositions are considerable in number and include works for harpsichord and organ, trio sonatas, symphonies and cantatas.

Johann Sebastian's second son, **Carl Philipp Emanuel Bach** (1714–88) was educated at St Thomas's School, Leipzig, and at the universities of Leipzig and Frankfurt-on-Oder, where he studied law. He was taught music by his father, and in 1740 became harpsichordist to Frederick the Great in Berlin and Potsdam. But since his duties were confined to keyboard work, he grew bored and moved to Hamburg in 1767 as director of music at the five principal churches. His music is characteristic of the middle of the 18th century in its reaction against the habits of polyphonic writing to be found in his father's work. He himself expressed contempt for mere counterpoint. The essence of his work is taste and refinement, and in particular an understanding of the expressive possibilities of keyboard instruments. He had remarkable skill in improvisation. He wrote a large number of vocal and instrumental works, including two oratorios – *Die Israeliten in der Wüste* (The Israelites in the Wilderness, 1775) and *Die Auferstehung und Himmelfahrt Jesu* (The Resurrection and Ascension, 1787), fifty keyboard concertos, and several collections of keyboard sonatas (*see* A. Wot-

Bach's 'Fugue in A flat' from the *Well-Tempered Keyboard*, Book II: his own beautifully written manuscript

quenne, *Catalogue thèmatique de l'oeuvre de C. Ph. Em. Bach*, 1905). His sonatas show the growth of thematic treatment of contrasted keys, from which classical SONATA FORM developed. The influence of opera is to be detected in his sentimental andantes and in the occasional use of instrumental recitative. His treatise *Versuch über die wahre Art das Klavier zu spielen* (Essay on the proper method of playing keyboard instruments, two parts, 1753 and 1762) is a valuable guide to the contemporary style of keyboard-playing and in particular to the interpretation of ornaments (modern edition by W. Niemann (1925); translation by W. J. Mitchell (1949)). For a first-hand account of C. P. E. Bach see C. Burney, *The Present State of Music in Germany* (1773), volume 2, pages 244–72.

Johann Christoph Friedrich (1732–95), was the eldest surviving son of Johann Sebastian's second marriage. He was educated at St. Thomas's School and Leipzig University, where he studied law. He was taught music by his father, and in 1750 was appointed chamber musician to Count Wilhelm of Schaumburg-Lippe at Bückeburg, where he remained the rest of his life, becoming *Konzertmeister* in 1758. His compositions include oratorios, *Die Kindheit Jesu* and *Die Auferweckung Lazarus*, on words by Johann Gottfried Herder. He also wrote cantatas,

motets, symphonies, keyboard concertos, keyboard sonatas, chamber music and songs.

Johann Christian (later John Christian) **Bach** (1735–82) was the youngest son of Johann Sebastian by his second wife. Johann Christian studied under his father, and then, after his father's death, under his brother C. P. E. Bach in Berlin. In 1756 he went to Italy, and became a pupil of Padre Martini in Bologna. He was appointed organist of Milan Cathedral in 1760, and composed his first opera, *Artaserse*, for Turin the following year. In 1762 he moved to London, where he remained for the rest of his life, thus earning himself the nickname of the 'English' or 'London' Bach. His first opera for London, *Orione*, was produced in 1763, and in that year he became music-master to Queen Charlotte, wife of George III. In 1764, with C. F. Abel, he founded a series of subscription concerts which continued until 1781. He showed much kindness to Mozart, who visited London as a boy of eight in 1764. Mozart, for his part, was much impressed by the London Bach, who was one of the early influences on his style – Mozart's piano concertos, in particular, have their roots in Bach's works. His compositions include eleven operas (produced at Turin, Naples, London, Mannheim and Paris), an oratorio, about forty piano concertos, more than ninety symphonies and other orchestral works, chamber music, piano solos and songs. He pioneered the use of the piano (then relatively new) as a solo instrument in Britain. His portrait was painted by Gainsborough.

N. CARRELL: *Bach's Brandenburg Concertos* (1963)

H. T. DAVID & A. MENDEL: *The Bach Reader* (1945)

J. N. FORKEL: *Johann Sebastian Bach: His Life, Art and Work* (translated C. S. Terry, 1920)

K. GEIRINGER: *The Bach Family* (1954); *Johann Sebastian Bach* (1967)

H. GRACE: *The Organ Works of Bach* (1922)

E. & S. GREW: *Bach* (1946)

C. H. H. PARRY: *Johann Sebastian Bach* (second edition, 1934)

A. ROBERTSON: *The Church Cantatas of J. S. Bach* (1972)

A. SCHWEITZER: *J. S. Bach* (translated by E. Newman, two volumes, 1911)

C. S. TERRY: *Bach: a Biography* (second edition, 1933); *Bach's Orchestra* (1932); *The Origin of the Family of Bach Musicians* (1929); *John Christian Bach* (includes a thematic catalogue, 1929)

J. A. WESTRUP: *Bach Cantatas* (1966)

W. G. WHITTAKER: *Fugitive Notes upon some Cantatas and the Motets of J. S. Bach* (1925)

P. WILLIAMS: *Bach Organ Music* (1972)

Bach Gesellschaft (Ger.), 'Bach Society', an organization formed in 1850 to publish a complete edition of the works of J. S. Bach. The last of the 46 volumes was issued in 1900. Its formation was an indirect result of Mendelssohn's pioneer work in reviving the *St. Matthew Passion* in 1829. The *Neue Bach Gesellschaft* (New Bach Society), founded in 1900, has issued performing editions of a large number of Bach's works and from 1904 an annual *Bach-Jahrbuch*, containing important critical articles on various aspects of Bach's works. A new complete edition was initiated by the Johann-Sebastian-Bach-Institut, Göttingen, in 1954.

Bachianas Brasileiras, name given by the Brazilian composer, Villa-Lobos, to a series of works combining Bachian procedures with elements of Brazilian traditional music. One of them is scored for soprano and eight cellos; another is the delightful *Little Train.*

Bach trumpet, a modern instrument designed to make practicable for modern day performers the high and florid trumpet parts to be found in the works of Bach and other composers of his time.

See TRUMPET

Backer-Gröndahl, Agathe Ursula (1847–1907), Norwegian pianist and composer. Among those with whom she studied the piano were Kjerulf, Kullak and von Bülow, who had a great admiration for her gifts. Her compositions consist of songs and piano pieces.

backfall, a term current in 17th century England for the short APPOGGIATURA, where the ornamental note is one degree of the scale above the principal note. It was written:

                        or

and played:

The *double backfall* was equivalent to the SLIDE taken from above, i.e. with two ornamental notes above the principal note:

as written:

as played:

Backhaus, Wilhelm (1884–1969), German pianist, who studied at the Leipzig Conservatory until 1899, and then with d'Albert in Frankfurt. It was as an exponent of the German classics – especially the sonatas of Beethoven – that he achieved world fame.

Bacon, Ernst (born 1898), U.S. pianist, conductor and composer. He studied in Chicago and Vienna and has held academic appointments at the Eastman School of Music, Rochester, New York, and the University of Syracuse, N.Y. His compositions include two symphonies, the musical play *A Tree on the Plains*, a piano quintet and choral works.

badinage (Fr.), = BADINERIE.

badinerie (Fr.), 'frolic', a term used by 18th century composers for a quick, frivolous movement in duple time, e.g. in Bach's suite in B minor for flute and strings. In the SUITE it is one of the optional dances or *Galanterien.*

Badings, Henk (born 1907), Dutch composer and teacher, born in the East Indies. He was originally a mining engineer but studied composition with Willem Pijper while attending the Technical University at Delft. One of the best established of modern Dutch composers, he has written an opera *The Night Watch* (after Rembrandt), ballets, ten symphonies, concertos for violin, two violins, and cello, two string quartets, chamber music, piano pieces and vocal music. In recent years he has experimented with electronic music. He has held various academic appointments in Holland.

bagatelle (Fr.), 'trifle'. A short piece, usually (but not necessarily) written for piano, and usually of a light, humorous or whimsical character. Beethoven composed three sets of *Bagatellen* for piano (op 33, op 119 and op 126 – 26 pieces in all).

bagpipe (Fr., *cornemuse*, Ger., *Sackpfeife*, It., *cornamusa*), a reed instrument, with one or more pipes, to which air is supplied from a skin reservoir or bag inflated by the player. It is probably of Asiatic origin, and was introduced to Europe by the Romans in the 1st century A.D. In course of time it became popular in every European country. Various forms exist: (1) the bag may be inflated by the player's breath through a pipe or by a bellows held under the arm; (2) the pipes may have single reeds (like the clarinet) or double (like the oboe) – in some types both are found in the same instrument; (3) since the 14th century it has been normal for the bagpipe to have not only a pipe with finger holes (sometimes two), called in English the 'chanter' (or 'chaunter'), on which the melody

Scottish bagpipe

is played, but also one or more 'drone' pipes, each tuned to a single note, which provide a simple and monotonous accompaniment.

In the past the bagpipe has been used as a military instrument and for popular music-making. These two functions survive in Scotland. It was also used in association with other instruments in the 16th century, and at the courts of Louis XIV and Louis XV an aristocratic type, known as the *musette*, became popular as a result of the fashionable craze for pastoral entertainments (the name *musette* was also given to a type of rustic oboe). But it never became a member of the standard orchestra, and once the French fashion had become obsolete it disappeared from polite society, though musicians might call upon it for special purposes, as Verdi did for the peasants' serenade in the second act of *Otello*. On the other hand two of its characteristics have been widely imitated in instrumental and vocal music: (1) the drone bass, which it shares with the hurdy-gurdy, (2) a melodic ornament of short duration, known as the 'cut' or 'snap'. The piece marked 'The bagpipe and drone' in Byrd's *The Battell* (*My Ladye Nevells Booke*, no 4) is not particularly characteristic, but Elizabethan viriginal music generally is rich in examples of the drone bass, and in the 17th and 18th century the popularity of the *musette* led to the composition of a large number of pieces bearing the same name, e.g.

BACH, *English Suite no 3*

HANDEL, *Alcina*

The first of these examples illustrates the drone bass, the second the 'snap'. Another dance of the same period, the LOURE, takes its name from an earlier type of bagpipe current in France. The 'Pastoral Symphony' in Handel's *Messiah*, called 'Pifa' in the score, is an imitation of rustic Italian bagpipe music, *piva* or *piffero* being one of the Italian names for the instrument. Many composers have written 'Pastorales' in the same idiom.

    C. SACHS: *The History of Musical Instruments* (1940)

baguette (Fr.), drumstick.

Baird, Tadeusz (born 1928), Polish composer of Scottish ancestry. He studied at Lódz Conservatory. His works, many of them orchestral, include two symphonies, *Four Essays for Orchestra*, a piano concerto, *Expressions* for violin and orchestra, *Cassation for Orchestra* and *Variations without a Theme*.

Baker, Janet (born 1933), English mezzo-soprano, formerly contralto, who won the Kathleen Ferrier Memorial Prize in 1956 and has become one of Britain's most sensitive operatic and concert-hall singers. Though she excells in tragic roles (e.g. Dido in Purcell's *Dido and Aeneas* and Berlioz's *Trojans*), she has shown that her range extends through character parts (Octavian in *Rosenkavalier*, the composer in *Ariadne*) to comedy (Dorabella in *Così fan tutte*). In the concert hall, she is associated particularly with the music of Mahler, Schumann (*Frauenliebe und Leben*), and songs and cantatas of the 17th and 18th centuries. In 1976 she was created Dame of the British Empire.

Bakfark, Balint (Valentin) (1507–76), Hungarian lutenist and composer. He was in the service of King Sigismundus Augustus of Poland between 1549 and 1566. From his early years he travelled extensively in Europe, visiting France and Italy. His published works for the lute include both original compositions and transcriptions; his fantasias have been edited by O. Gombosi (1935).

Balakirev, Mily Alexeyevich (1837–1910), leader of the group of Russian nationalist composers known as the *Kutchka* ('The Five' or 'The Mighty Handful') the others being Borodin, Cui, Mussorgsky and Rimsky-Korsakov. As a boy he owed much to Alexander Oulibishev (author of a three-volume study of Mozart), who gave him the run of his library. He arrived in St. Petersburg in 1855 and began to make his name as a pianist, but preferred to devote himself to teaching. To the other members of the *Kutchka* he gave not only instruction but encouragement – though his difficult temperament sometimes estranged him from his pupils and friends. He was the first director of the Free School of Music in St. Petersburg, but the venture was not financially successful and in 1872 – after a nervous breakdown – he became a railway clerk. For some years he lived a secluded life but later became a school inspector and from 1883–95, when he retired on a pension, was director of the Court Chapel. His teaching followed the lines of his own education in being founded on the study of the classics. His compositions, which show the influence both of Russian folk-music and of the Romantic composers of Western Europe, particularly Liszt, include two symphonies, two symphonic poems (*Russia* and *Tamara*), an overture to *King Lear*, a piano sonata, an Oriental fantasy, *Islamey*, for piano solo, and songs.

    M. D. CALVOCORESSI and G. ABRAHAM: *Masters of Russian Music* (1936)

    G. ABRAHAM: *Studies in Russian Music* (1935); *On Russian Music* (1939)

    E. GARDEN: *Balakirev: a Critical Study of his life and music* (1967)

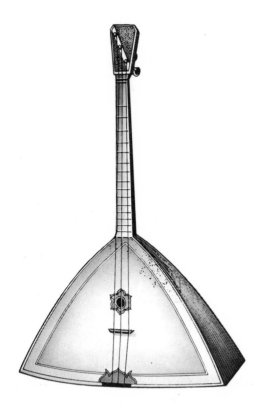

Balalaika

balalaika (Russ.), a triangular guitar, of Tartar origin, very popular among the Russian peasantry. It normally has three strings and is made in several sizes.

Balfe, Michael William (1808–70), Irish composer, baritone and violinist. Born in Dublin, he was the son of a dancing master, and by the age of seven he was playing the violin at his father's dancing classes. After his father's death, he moved to London to study with C. E. Horn. He began his career as a violinist in the orchestra at Drury Lane. At the age of seventeen he was taken to Italy by an Italian count for singing lessons, and in 1827 appeared as Figaro in Rossini's *Barber of Seville* in Paris. His first opera, *I rivali di se stessi*, was produced at Palermo in 1829. The majority of his 29 operas, including *The Siege of Rochelle* and *The Maid of Artois* (in which Malibran sang – the work was based on Prévost's *Manon Lescaut*), were written for London. The only one now remembered is *The Bohemian Girl* (1843).

W. A. BARRET: *Balfe – His Life and Work* (1882)

Balfour Gardiner, *see* GARDINER

Ball, George Thomas Thalben (born 1896), Australian born organist. He studied at the Royal College of Music, London, and was appointed organist of the Temple Church there in 1923. Subsequent appointments included the Royal Albert Hall, London (1933) and the City of Birmingham (1948). In addition to his regular duties in England he soon established himself as a world famous recitalist.

ballabile (It.), a dancing manner.

ballad, (1) a narrative song, either traditional or (as in the 19th century) specially written in imitation of traditional forms. From the 16th to the 19th centuries the words of ballads, which often dealt with contemporary events, were printed on sheets and sold at fairs, markets and other public gatherings;

(2) a sentimental, drawing-room song of the late 19th and early 20th centuries;

(3) an instrumental piece = BALLADE (2).

S. NORTHCOTE: *The Ballad in Music* (1942)

ballade (Fr.), (1) a type of medieval French verse in which the refrain comes at the end of the stanza. *Ballades* were set to music for solo voice by the TROUVÈRES, and in two or more parts, for voices and instruments, by Guillaume de Machaut (14th century) and other polyphonic composers of the later middle ages;

(2) in the 19th and 20th centuries an instrumental piece, sometimes of considerable length, of a lyrical and romantic character. Chopin pioneered this type of *ballade* and wrote four splendid examples – in G minor (op 23), F major (op 38), A flat major (op 47) and F minor (op 52) – said to have been inspired by the poetry of Mickiewicz. In some cases the influence of the traditional poetic ballad is strongly marked, e.g. in Brahms's op 10, no 1 for piano, which is preceded by the text of the Scottish ballad *Edward*.

ballad opera, a type of opera popular in Britain in the mid 18th century, in which dialogue was interspersed with songs set to popular tunes. The term 'ballad opera' is misleading, since the popular tunes were often taken from the works of well-known composers. The best-known of these works is John Gay's *The Beggar's Opera* (1728), the music for which was arranged by Johann Pepusch. This has been successfully revived in the 20th century in editions by Frederic Austin, Edward J. Dent and Benjamin Britten. In England it was succeeded in the latter part of the 18th century by a similar form of entertainment in which the music, however, was original, not borrowed.

F. KIDSON: *The Beggar's Opera* (1922)

W. E. SCHULTZ: *Gay's 'Beggar's Opera'* (1923)

Ballard, a French publishing firm, active from the middle of the 16th to the end of the 18th centuries. Their publications included the scores of Lully's operas.

ballata (It.), a 14th century Italian verse-form, with a refrain which occurs at the beginning and end of the stanza. A large number of such poems were set by 14th century Italian composers, notably Francesco Landini.

ballet, a dramatic entertainment presented by dancers in costume with musical accompaniment. Such entertainments existed in the ancient world and the middle ages and were an important part of the ceremonial festivities associated with French and Italian courts at the Renaissance. A landmark in the history of French ballet was the production of *Circe*, described as *Balet comique de la Royne* (The queen's dramatic ballet), for the marriage of the Duc de Joyeuse and Margaret of Lorraine at Versailles in 1581. The title does not mean that it was a comic ballet but indicates that it combined dancing (*ballet*) with a dramatic plot (*comédie*) to form an organic whole. As such it was an innovation, consisting not only of dancing and instrumental music, but also of spoken declamation and singing, and hence a forerunner of opera. The *ballet de cour*, as it was called, on account of its association with the French court, was extremely popular in the 17th century, and led in England to the cultivation of the Jacobean masque. In France spoken declamation was abandoned at the beginning of the 17th century in favour of sung recitative. A large number of ballets were composed by Lully (1632–87), himself a dancer as well as a musician, who also joined with Molière to write *comédies-ballets*, a combination of spoken drama and ballet. When Lully turned to writing opera in 1673, it was only natural that he should incorporate ballet in the new form.

The association of ballet with opera continued in the 18th century, but ballet also maintained its existence as an independent art, in which vocal music was superfluous. It was saved from developing into a conventional medium for virtuosity by Jean Georges Noverre (1727–1810), who published his *Lettres sur la danse et les ballets* in 1760. It was for Noverre that Mozart wrote his ballet *Les petits riens* in Paris in 1778. In the meantime other countries had adopted the French ballet, including Russia, where an Imperial School of Ballet was founded in the 18th century. Chaikovsky's *Swan Lake* (1876), *The Sleeping Beauty* (1889) and *Nutcracker* (1892), are evidence of the popularity of ballet in Russia in the 19th century. It was from Russia that a new reform came at the beginning of the 20th century in the work of Sergei Diaghilev (1872–1929), who not only adapted existing music, such as Schumann's *Carnaval*, but also encouraged young composers to write ballets for him. Works like Stravinsky's *Firebird* (1910), *Petrushka* (1911) and *The Rite of Spring* (1913), and Ravel's *Daphnis et Chloé* (1912) owe their origin to Diaghilev. The British revival of ballet similarly led a number of well-equipped composers to take an interest in the form, e.g. Vaughan Williams with *Job* (1931), Arthur Bliss with *Checkmate* (1937) and *Miracle in the Gorbals* (1944), and Britten with *The Prince of the Pagodas* (1957). Moreover, with the rise of choreographers of the calibre of Sir Frederick Ashton and Kenneth Macmillan, important ballets have been created out of such works as Elgar's *Enigma Variations* and Mahler's *Song of the Earth*. In the United States the great creative force has been George Balanchine, who, with the New York City Ballet, gave Stravinsky the incentive to compose *Agon* (1957), and whose name has become synonymous with many of that composer's ballet scores. Among ballets by native-born U.S. composers, some of the best established examples are by Copland, whose works include *Billy the Kid* (1938), *Rodeo* (1942) and *Appalachian Spring* (1944); and by Bernstein, who wrote *Fancy Free* in 1944. Russia's great ballet tradition was continued by Prokofiev, whose masterpieces were *Romeo and Juliet* (1935) and *Cinderella* (1945).

The hey-day of ballet as a part of opera was in the latter part of the 19th century, when it was considered an essential part of the Paris *grand opéra*. Italian composers who wrote operas for Paris therefore had to incorporate ballets in them, whether it seemed dramatically appropriate or not (e.g. Rossini's *William Tell* and Verdi's *Don Carlos*).

Modern taste, however, and the extraordinary development of ballet as an independent art combined to favour the separation of opera and ballet into distinct categories, though the influence of ballet technique is often to be observed in the production of operas and some modern composers have re-admitted vocal music to the ballet, e.g. Stravinsky in *The Wedding* (1923) and Lord Berners in *A Wedding Bouquet* (1937).

C. W. BEAUMONT: *Complete Book of Ballets* (1937 and 1942).

J. G. NOVERRE: *Letters on Dancing and Ballets*, tr. C. W. Beaumont (1930)

H. PRUNIÈRES: *Le Ballet de cour en France* (1914)

H. SEARLE: *Ballet Music: an Introduction* (1958)

S. SITWELL and C. W. BEAUMONT: *The Romantic Ballet* (1938)

ballett (It., *balletto*), a composition for several voices, mainly homophonic in character, generally with a refrain to the words *fa la*. It originated in Italy at the end of the 16th century and is associated particularly with the name of Giovanni Gastoldi. It was imitated in other countries, including England. Thomas Morley, who mentions the ballett in his *Plaine and Easie Introduction to Practicall Musicke* (1597), published a set in 1595, of which the best known is 'Now is the month of maying'. Italian and German editions of Morley's balletts appeared in 1595 and 1609. The refrain *fa la*, which is purely Italian in origin, became domesticated in other countries and in England survived as a symbol of light-hearted gaiety. From the prevalence of this refrain the ballett was often known by the title 'fa la'. The name 'ballett' indicates that the music, which was generally in a lively, square-cut rhythm, was suitable for dancing, as Morley points out. Three of Gastoldi's balletts were adapted in Germany to Lutheran hymns. One of them, 'A lieta vita', was fitted to David Spaiser's 'O Gott, mein Herre' in 1609, and later in the 17th century to 'In dir ist Freud', the words of which may be by Johann Lindemann. Bach included a prelude on 'In dir ist Freude' in his *Orgelbüchlein* (Little Organ Book).

balletto (It.), (1) *see* BALLETT;

(2) a dance movement in a suite. The term was current in this sense in the 17th and 18th centuries;

(3) ballet.

Balling, Michael (1866–1925), German conductor, associated with the Bayreuth Festival (1906–14), and Richter's successor with the Hallé Orchestra in Manchester (1912–14). He edited the complete works of Wagner, published by Breitkopf & Härtel.

ballo (It.), dance. *Tempo di ballo*, in dance time.

Ballo in Maschera, Un, *see* MASKED BALL

Baltzar, Thomas (c. 1630–63), German violinist. This brilliant musician was in the service of Queen Christina of Sweden in 1653 and came to England shortly afterwards, where his virtuosity created a sensation (*see* Evelyn, *Diary*, March 4, 1656). He was appointed a member of Charles II's private music in 1661. He was buried in Westminster Abbey.

bamboo pipe, a simple wooden pipe resembling a recorder. There are six front fingerholes and a rear thumbhole.

Banchieri, Adriano (1568–1634), Italian composer, theorist and poet. He was organist of the monastery of S. Michele in Bosco, near Bologna, and founder of the

Accademia de' floridi in Bologna. His compositions include madrigal dramas (similar to Orazio Vecchi's *L'Amfiparnaso*), concerted instrumental music, organ works (see L. Torchi, *L'arte musicale in Italia*, iii) and church music. He was one of the first writers to give instruction in playing from FIGURED BASS in his treatise *L'organo suonario* (second edition, 1611).

band, a term once applied to any large-scale group of instrumentalists but now reserved for ensembles other than the concert orchestra.

See BRASS BAND, JAZZ BAND, MILITARY BAND, OR-CHESTRA

bandurria (Span.), a Spanish instrument of the guitar family, similar to the English CITHER, with six double strings generally played with a plectrum.

bandora, a bass instrument very similar to the CITTERN.

Banister, John (died 1679), English violinist. He was sent abroad by Charles II in 1661 to study French instrumental music and appointed director of a select band of twelve string-players on his return in 1662. Banister lost this position in 1667 (*see* Pepys, *Diary*, Feb. 20, 1667) but remained in the king's service until his death. In 1672 he began a series of public concerts (among the first of their kind) in Whitefriars. His compositions include music for the stage.

banjo, a U.S. Negro instrument of the guitar family. Its body, unlike that of the guitar, consists of a shallow metal drum, covered with parchment on the top side and open at the bottom. Its strings, which vary in number from five to nine, are played either with the fingers or with a plectrum. It is supposed to have been brought to America by slaves from West Africa and to have owed its origin to the activities of Arab traders in Africa. As a result of its introduction into jazz bands a tenor model has been made with four strings, tuned like the viola.

banjolin, a kind of BANJO with a short neck and four strings.

Banks, Don (born 1923), Australian composer. He studied at Melbourne and later with Seiber and Dallapiccola in Europe. In 1950 he settled in London. His works include a horn concerto, a divertimento for flute and string trio, a violin sonata and three studies for cello and piano.

Bantock, Granville (1868–1946), English composer. Born in London, he was educated for the Civil Service but entered the Royal Academy of Music in 1889. He was principal of the Birmingham and Midland Institute School of Music (1900–34) and professor at Birmingham University (1908–34). He was knighted in 1930. As a conductor he worked untiringly to further the interests of young British composers. As a composer he was very prolific and attracted by the local colour of a number of different countries, from Scotland to China. His works, which are in the romantic tradition, include *Fifine at the Fair, Dante and Beatrice* and other symphonic poems, a *Hebridean Symphony*, choral works based on *Omar Khayyám* and *The Pilgrim's Progress*, an opera (*The Seal Woman*) and a setting of Swinburne's *Atalanta in Calydon* for unaccompanied choir.

bar, (1) properly a vertical line drawn across one or more staves of music, now generally known in Britain as 'bar-line' (Fr., *barre*; Ger., *Taktstrich*; It., *barra*). The original purpose of the bar-line was to guide the eye when music was presented simultaneously on several staves or in TABLATURE. Hence it was used in 16th century keyboard music but was not necessary for the separate parts of concerted music for voices or instruments. When concerted music began to appear in score at the end of the 16th century the bar-line was naturally employed there also, and it was found convenient to draw the lines at regular intervals. The increasing rhythmical symmetry of the 17th century, which became stereotyped in the 18th and 19th centuries, led to a false association between the bar-line and ACCENT. As a result, when 20th century composers came to abandon the regular rhythmical periods current in the 18th and 19th centuries, they were supposed to be in revolt against the 'tyranny of the bar-line'. In fact, in one sense, they submitted to the 'tyranny' more wholeheartedly then their predecessors, since they found it necessary to change the length of the bars whenever the rhythm changed. It is more logical, and more practical, to regard the bar-line as a convenient sign of subdivision, which may or may not coincide with the rhythmical accent of the moment. This does not exclude the use of bars of different lengths where the change is appropriate. The essential in all musical notation is that the composer's intentions should be perfectly clear to the performer.

(2) the space between two bar-lines, known in the United States as 'measure' (Fr., *mesure*; Ger., *Takt*; It., *battuta*). (In the United States a bar-line is known simply as 'bar').

(3) Ger., the name commonly given to a song-form borrowed by the German MINNESINGER from the French TROUVÈRES, and used by them and their successors, the MEISTERSINGER. It consists of two *Stollen* (literally, 'props'), each set to the same music, and an *Abgesang* ('after-song'), the whole forming a complete stanza or *Gesätz* (cf. Wagner, *The Mastersingers*, i, 3 and iii, 2). The form may be represented by the formula *a a b*. It is quite common, however, for the *Abgesang* to end with part or the whole of the melody of the *Stollen*:

ich je___ bat: Ich byn ___ kom-en ___ an die stat Da Got men-is — -li-chen trat. ___

WALTHER VON DER VOGELWEIDE (c. 1200)

Here we have the germs of the principle of recapitulation, which in one form or another has played an important part in musical structure, particularly in instrumental music.

Samuel Barber

Barber, Samuel (born 1910), U.S. composer and former singer. Born at West Chester, Pennsylvania, he studied piano and composition at the Curtis Institute, Philadelphia. Among his many awards were the *Prix de Rome* (1935) and the Pulitzer Prize (1935 and 1936). His works, which show a respect for romantic tradition as well as an original mind, include two major U.S. operas – *Vanessa* (1958) and *Antony and Cleopatra*, commissioned for the opening of the new Metropolitan Opera House in New York in 1966. He has also written several ballets for Martha Graham, though the bulk of his output has been for the concert hall. His orchestral works include a symphony in one movement (1936) and two other symphonies, the overture to *School for Scandal* (1932), a violin concerto (1940), two *Essays* for orchestra, *Capricorn Concerto* (1944), cello concerto (1945) and piano concerto (1962), though perhaps the most internationally popular of all his pieces is the *Adagio for Strings* (1936), adapted from the slow movement of a string quartet. His early *Dover Beach* (1931), a setting for voice and

string quartet of Matthew Arnold's poem, was written for himself to sing. He has also written choral music, chamber music and a large-scale piano sonata (1948).

Barber of Baghdad, The (Ger., *Der Barbier von Bagdad*), comic opera in two acts by Cornelius, to a libretto by the composer, first performed in 1858 at Weimar, where Cornelius was a protégé of Liszt. Liszt was responsible for the première, but this genial *Arabian Nights* entertainment caused such a storm in a teacup that he resigned as court conductor.

Barber of Seville, The (It., *Il Barbiere di Siviglia*), comic opera in two acts by Rossini, originally entitled *Almaviva ossia L'inutile precauzione* (Almaviva, or the Fruitless Precaution). The libretto, by Cesare Sterbini, is founded on Beaumarchais's play, *Le Barbier de Séville*. The first performance was in Rome in 1816, with Giorgi-Righetti, a coloratura mezzo-soprano, in the role of Rosina. Today the part is often sung by a soprano, though this alters its musical colouring.

The story tells how Count Almaviva is in love with Rosina, the ward of Dr. Bartolo, and succeeds with the help of Figaro (the barber of Seville) in defeating the doctor's attempts to separate them.

The opera had a violent reception at its first performance, for the supporters of Paisiello's rival version of the story made sure that their presence was felt in the theatre. Nevertheless the work later came to be recognized for what it is: the high watermark of Rossini's comic genius. Mozart's *Marriage of Figaro* (1786) is founded on Beaumarchais's *Le Mariage de Figaro*, which is a sequel to *Le Barbier de Séville*. An earlier adaptation of *Le Barbier de Séville* by Giuseppe Petrosellini, with music by Paisiello, was first performed at St. Petersburg in 1782.

barbershop quartet, a quartet of amateur male singers who specialize in close-harmony arrangements of popular songs. Barbershop quartet singing developed from the informal music-making (instrumental as well as vocal) to be found in barber shops in Britain and Europe during the 16th and 17th centuries. In the 18th century, barbershop music declined there but the tradition was maintained in the United States, developing into the highly organized vocal style of the barbershop quartet. Contests are held in barbershop quartet singing in the United States every year.

The Barber of Seville: lithograph from a piano score of 1850

Barbiere di Siviglia, Il, see BARBER OF SEVILLE

Barbier von Bagdad, see BARBER OF BAGHDAD

Barbieri, Francisco Asenjo (1823–94), Spanish composer and musicologist. He began his career as a clarinettist and a café pianist. He wrote a number of comic operas, of a characteristically Spanish type, of which the one act *Pan y Toros* (Madrid, 1864), dealing with the painter Goya, proved the most successful. He also edited *Cancionero musical de los siglos XV y XVI*, an important collection of Spanish part-songs of the 15th and 16th centuries.

Barbingant, 15th century composer of a Mass and some *chansons*, whose identity was for long confused with that of Jacques BARBIREAU.

C. W. FOX: 'Barbireau and Barbingant: a Review', *Journal of the American Musicological Society*, xiii (1960)

Barbireau, Jacques (c. 1408–91), Flemish composer. He was master of the choristers at Antwerp Cathedral from 1448, and composed church music and *chansons*. A complete edition in two volumes has been published by B. Meier (1954–7); it includes some compositions by Barbingant, who has been identified, without much justification, with Barbireau.

C. W. FOX: 'Barbireau and Barbingant: a Review', *Journal of the American Musicological Society*, xiii (1960)

Barbirolli, Sir John (1899–1970), English conductor of Italian origin – his real name was Giovanni Battista Barbirolli. After studying at Trinity College of Music and the Royal Academy of Music in London, he began his career as a cellist. He first appeared as a conductor in 1925, and joined the British National Opera Company in 1926. He was conductor of the Scottish Orchestra from 1933 until 1937, and then succeeded Toscanini as conductor of the New York Philharmonic. In 1943 he returned to Britain to take on the task of rebuilding the Hallé Orchestra in Manchester, and was associated with that orchestra for the rest of his life, imposing his stamp on it very strongly. For five years, from 1962 until 1967, he was also conductor of the Houston Symphony Orchestra in Texas. His repertory was based mainly on romantic and late-romantic music, and he was particularly associated with works by Elgar, Mahler, Brahms, Delius, Sibelius, and Vaughan Williams. But his range was wider than that: he could conduct Haydn superbly. It was sad that, in later life, he rarely conducted opera. His performances of *Tristan and Isolde* and *Aida* with the Covent Garden company in the 1950s were memorable, and he was fortunately coaxed into recording *Madama Butterfly*. He was knighted in 1949.

barcarola (It.), *barcarolle*.

barcarolle (Fr.; Ger., *Barkarole*; It., *barcarola*), from It., *barca*, 'boat'. A *barcarolle* is properly a boating-song sung by the gondoliers at Venice, but the name has come to be applied to any piece of vocal or instrumental music in the same rhythm (6/8 or 12/8). Familiar examples are Chopin's for piano (op 60) and Offenbach's in *The Tales of Hoffmann* (1881). Fauré wrote thirteen *barcarolles* for piano. A large number of compositions are in fact *barcarolles*, though not so described, e.g. Schubert's song *Auf dem Wasser zu singen* and some of Mendelssohn's *Lieder ohne Worte* (op 19, no 6, op 30, no 6, op 62, no 5).

bard, originally a Celtic minstrel, whose duties included the composition of extempore songs in honour of a patron. In medieval Wales bards also had considerable political influence. An early 17th century manuscript of instrumental music, entitled *Musica neu Beroriaeth* (Music of the Britons) and written in TABLATURE (facsimile edition, Cardiff, 1936; see T. Dart's article in *Galpin Society Journal*, xxi, 1968), purports to record the practice of a much earlier age, but its authority as a record of medieval bardic music is obviously uncertain. The practice of bardic gatherings was revived in the 19th century at the Welsh *Eisteddfodau* (plur. of *Eisteddfod*, 'session'), which are now very largely musical competition festivals.

P. CROSSLEY-HOLLAND: 'Secular Homophonic Music in Wales in the Middle Ages', *Music & Letters*, xxiii (1942)

Bardi, Giovanni (1534–1612), Count of Vernio. A Florentine nobleman, himself a composer, whose house was a meeting place of poets, musicians and scholars interested in the problem of creating a music-drama on the lines of Greek tragedy. The first operas originated from these gatherings.

Barenboim, Daniel (born 1942), Argentine born pianist and conductor, who made his first appearance at Buenos Aires at the age of seven. His career in Europe began in 1954, and he soon established himself as an important exponent of the music of Mozart and Beethoven. He recorded all Mozart's piano concertos with the English Chamber Orchestra, conducting the performances from the keyboard. As a conductor, his interpretations of the 19th century and early 20th century repertory, especially of works by Beethoven, Berlioz, Brahms, Bruckner and Elgar, have at times an almost Furtwänglerian grandeur and reveal a talent of exceptional promise.

Bärenreiter, a firm of music-publishers founded at Augsburg in 1924 by Karl Vötterle.

Bargiel, Woldemar (1828–97), German teacher and composer, a step-brother of Clara Schumann. He held appointments in Cologne, Rotterdam and Berlin. His compositions, strongly influenced by Schumann, include a symphony, three orchestral overtures, chamber music, piano music and choral works.

baritone, (1) a high bass voice – midway between bass and tenor – with a range of roughly two octaves:

(2) a brass instrument of the SAXHORN family (Fr., *bugle ténor*; Ger., *Tenorhorn*; It., *flicorno tenore*). It is built in B flat at the same pitch as the EUPHONIUM, but has a smaller bore and only three valves. It is used only in wind bands and is written for as a transposing instrument. The written compass is

sounding:

(3) the baritone clef is the F clef on the third line:

now obsolete;

    (4) baritone oboe, *see* HECKELPHONE;

    (5) baritone saxophone, *see* SAXOPHONE

Barkarole (Ger.), *barcarolle*.

bar-line, *see* BAR (1)

Bärmann, Heinrich Joseph (1784–1847), German clarinettist, for whom Weber and Mendelssohn wrote pieces.

Barnard, John (fl. early 17th century), a minor canon of St. Paul's Cathedral. He published in separate part-books the first printed collection of English cathedral music, under the title *The First Book of Selected Church Musick* (1641). A second collection survives in manuscript in the Royal College of Music library. A manuscript score of the contents of the first collection, made from the printed part-books and other sources, is in the British Library (Add. 30,087).

Barnby, Joseph (1838–96), English composer, conductor and organist, who did valuable pioneer work in introducing Bach's Passions to English audiences.

Barnett, John (1802–90), English opera composer, the son of German and Hungarian parents (the father's name was originally Beer) and a second cousin of Meyerbeer. His most important work was *The Mountain Sylph* (London, 1834), the first of a series of English romantic operas by Balfe, Benedict, Wallace and other composers.

Barnett, John Francis (1837–1916), English pianist and composer, nephew of John Barnett. He studied at the Royal Academy of Music in London and Leipzig Conservatorium. His works include a symphony, chamber music, piano music, and a number of cantatas, among them a setting of Coleridge's *The Ancient Mariner* (1867). He completed Schubert's symphony no 7 in E major (sometimes said to be in E minor on account of its opening Adagio) from the composer's sketches.

Baron, Ernst Gottlieb (1696–1760), German lutenist, who held a number of court appointments and published several theoretical works, including the important *Historisch-theoretische und practische Untersuchung des Instruments der Lauten* (1727).

Baroni, Leonora (born 1611), famous Mantuan singer and gamba player, said to have been the mistress of Cardinal Mazarin, who brought her to Paris in 1644 to further his efforts to establish Italian opera at the French court. Baroni's praises were sung by a number of poets, including Milton (*Ad Leonoram Romae canentem*), who met her in Rome in 1638. Her mother, Adriana, and her sister, Catarina, were also well-known as singers.

baroque (Port., *barroco*, 'rough pearl'), originally 'grotesque', but now used as a technical term to describe the lavish architectural style of the 17th and early 18th centuries. It has been borrowed by musicians as a general description of the music of the same period. A distinction is common between early baroque music (Gabrieli, Monteverdi, Frescobaldi, Carissimi, etc.) and late baroque music (Alessandro Scarlatti, Bach, Handel etc.). The pre-baroque period (late 15th and

Béla Bartók: The somewhat austere exterior of his later years belies the warmth of understanding and sympathy that enabled Bartok to write the best keyboard teaching pieces since Bach

16th centuries) is generally called RENAISSANCE, the post-baroque (late 18th century), ROCOCO. 'Baroque' applied to music has no pejorative overtones.

Barraqué, Jean (1928–73), French composer, a pupil of Jean Langlais and Messiaen. He worked in the experimental laboratories of the Radiodiffusion Française in Paris. His most famous work is his piano sonata, a densely-packed score of enormous vigour. The rest of his output includes *Sequence* for soprano and chamber ensemble, *Le Temps restitué* for voices and orchestra, *Au delà du hasard* for voices and instrumental groups, and *Chant après chant* for percussion.

barrel organ, a mechanical organ, in which air is admitted to the pipes by means of pins on a rotating barrel. It was very common in England in the late 18th and early 19th centuries and was used in village churches, where the provision of interchangeable barrels made it possible to play a limited number of the best-known hymn-tunes. A complete chromatic compass was unusual, so that the choice of keys was restricted. The term was applied incorrectly to the 19th century street piano, also operated by a barrel-and-pin mechanism, and is currently used in this sense.

Bartered Bride, The (Czech, *Prodaná Nevěsta*), comic opera in three acts by Smetana, to a libretto by Karel Sabini, first performed in 1866 in Prague (though the work did not reach its definitive version until four years later, when the spoken dialogue included in the original was replaced with sung recitatives). Today this Bohemian rustic comedy remains the most internationally popular of all Czech operas. The story tells of Jeník's love for Mařenka, whose parents want her to marry instead the stupid, stammering Vašek – because he is the son of the wealthy Micha. Jeník agrees with the marriage-broker Kecal to give up Mařenka in return for a sum of money, on condition that Mařenka shall marry only Micha's son. As Jeník himself turns out to be a son of Micha by an earlier marriage he gets the best of the bargain.

Barthélémon, François Hippolyte (1741–1808), French violinist and composer, active in England (where he was leader of the orchestra at the opera and Marylebone Gardens), Ireland and France. He was associated with Haydn when the latter visited London in 1791–2 and 1704–5. His works include music for the stage, violin sonatas and concertos and a hymn-tune, 'Awake, my soul'.

Bartók, Béla (1881–1945), Hungarian composer and pianist. Born at Nagyszentmiklós in the district of Torontál (now part of Romania), he was the son of the director of a school of agriculture, who died while Bartók was a child. He received his first piano lessons from his mother, a schoolteacher and musician, and made his first public appearance as a pianist at the age of ten, by which time he was already composing. After studying with Laszlo Erkel, he was offered a scholarship to the Vienna Conservatory, but on the advice of Dohnányi he turned it down and went instead to the Royal Hungarian Musical Academy in Budapest. There he was taught composition by Koessler and devoted much time to the piano. With Zoltan Kodály he devoted himself to the study and collection of genuine Hungarian folk music, as opposed to the international gypsy music generally known as 'Hungarian'. He also studied Romanian and Slovak folk music. These studies helped to emancipate his creative talent from earlier influences (which included Liszt and Strauss). The great bulk of his work is the product of a highly original mind, which sometimes finds expression in an almost aggressive objectivity. His music was 'modern' not in obedience to any fashionable creed or artificial system but in its new attempts to solve the problems of composition. He was a sincere artist wrestling with the raw material of composition (significantly, he even wrote a piano piece entitled *Wrestling*). The result may sometimes be forbidding, but it is always impressive. His writing has an authority and intensity which, combined, have helped to establish him as one of the major figures of 20th century music. In 1940 the increasing Nazi domination of Europe drove him to the United States, where he held university appointments at Columbia and Harvard, and wrote his *Concerto for Orchestra* (1943) for the Boston Symphony Orchestra, and the third of his three piano concertos (1945, unfinished). He died, in poverty, of leukaemia in West Side Hospital, New York.

Bartók's toughest, most dissonant music was written in his middle years. His first piano concerto (1926) is a gritty, clattering work, as awkward to play as it sounds. The second (1931), though no less energetic, shows greater awareness of tonal beauty and contains, in its slow movement, some fascinating passages of 'night music' – the outcome of Bartók's interest in insects and birds. This work paved the way for the *Music for Strings, Percussion and Celesta* (1937) and second violin concerto (1938), in which his style grew more lyrical and he developed a bitter-sweet quality that was to become just as characteristic of him as his punchier style. The various facets of his musical personality are heard at their purest in his string quartets. His output of these was smaller than Beethoven's, and smaller still than Haydn's. Yet the six masterpieces he wrote in this form occupy a place in the progress of 20th century music just as important as Beethoven's in the 19th century and Haydn's in the 18th. Like Haydn's and Beethoven's, they span most of his career as a composer, and are receptacles for his most experimental thoughts; indeed there is a direct link between Beethoven's late quartets and Bartók's works. But because Bartók was a fine pianist, his piano music equally repays study. An impression of his work as a teacher is to be found in the collection of graded piano pieces called *Mikrokosmos*, the six volumes of which contain, in concentrated form, the essentials of his style.

Bartók's principal works are:
(1) Orchestra: rhapsody for piano and orchestra; two suites; three piano concertos; two rhapsodies for violin and orchestra; *Music for Strings, Percussion and Celesta*; *Divertimento* for strings; concerto for orchestra; two violin concertos; viola concerto (unfinished);
(2) Stage: *Duke Bluebeard's Castle* (opera); *The Wooden Prince* (ballet); *The Miraculous Mandarin* (pantomime);
(3) Chamber music: six string quartets; two violin sonatas; rhapsody for cello and piano; sonata for two pianos and percussion;
(4) Piano: sonatina; sonata; *Allegro barbaro*; *Mikrokosmos*; bagatelles, sketches, études, etc.;
(5) Choral: *Cantata profana*.
   Also numerous arrangements of folksongs for voices and instruments.
   B. BARTÓK: *Hungarian Folk Music*, tr. M. D. Calvocoressi (1931)
   J. DEMÉNY: *Béla Bartók, Letters* (1971)
   E. HARASZTI: *Béla Bartók* (1938)
   L. LESZNAI: *Bartók* (1961, English translation 1973)
   H. STEVENS: *The Life and Music of Béla Bartók* (1953, second edition 1964)

baryton (Ger.; It., *viola di bordone*), a bowed string instrument in use in Germany during the 18th century. It originated in the late 17th century and became obsolete in the 19th. Its foundation was a bass viol with six bowed strings, but to these were added a large number of additional strings which vibrated in sympathy (as on the VIOLA D'AMORE). As the neck of the instrument was open the sympathetic strings could also be plucked from behind by the player's left thumb. It was a favourite instrument of Prince Nicolas Esterházy, for whom Haydn composed 125 trios for baryton, viola and cello.

bass (Fr., *basse*; Ger., *Bass*; It., *basso*), in general, 'low' as opposed to 'high'. The term is used particularly of the lowest part of a composition, whether for one or more instruments or for voices – the foundation on which the harmony is built. It is also used in the following special senses:

(1) the lowest adult male voice, with a range of roughly two octaves, from

to

(2) prefixed to the name of an instrument it indicates either the largest member of the family or (in cases where a contrabass instrument exists) one size smaller than the largest, e.g. bass viol, bass clarinet;

(3) short for double bass, also (in military bands) for bass tuba;

(4) the bass clef is the F clef on the fourth line:

See FIGURED BASS

bassadanza (It.), *see* BASSE DANSE

Bassani, Giovanni Battista (c. 1657–1716), Italian organist at Ferrara Cathedral and composer of oratorios, operas, church music and instrumental works.

bass-bar, a strip of wood glued inside the belly of members of the viol and violin families immediately under the left foot of the bridge.

See VIOLIN

bass-baritone, a term sometimes used to indicate a bass voice with a good command of the higher register.

bass clarinet (Fr., *clarinette basse*; Ger., *Bassklarinette*; It., *clarinetto basso, clarone*) a single-reed instrument, built an octave lower than the clarinet, with a metal bell turned upwards for convenience. It was formerly made in B flat and A but is now made only in B flat. The compass is from

sounding

See TRANSPOSING INSTRUMENTS

A. CARSE: *Musical Wind Instruments* (1939)

bass drum (Fr., *grosse caisse*; Ger., *grosse Trommel*; It., *gran cassa*), a percussion instrument of indeterminate pitch. It consists of a large wooden shell, cylindrical in shape, covered on one or both sides with vellum. It is normally beaten with a stick having a large felt-covered knob, but it can also be played with timpani sticks if a roll is required (*see* TIMPANI).

basse chiffrée (Fr.); figured bass.

basse danse (Fr.), literally 'low dance', so called because the feet were kept close to the ground, in contrast to leaping dances such as the GALLIARD. The

basse danse was a court dance current in France in the 15th and early 16th centuries. The earlier music consisted of a melody (or 'tenor') in long notes of equal duration, around which one or more instruments improvised in a style featuring rapid figuration and frequent syncopations. For a modern edition of two 15th century choreographies which include *basse danse* tenors see J. L. Jackman, *Fifteenth Century Basse Dances* (1964). A few examples of the similar Italian *bassadanza* survive with written out parts embellishing the tenors (see M. Bukofzer, 'A Polyphonic Basse Dance of the Renaissance' in his *Studies in Medieval and Renaissance Music*, 1950, and the Introduction to O. Gombosi's edition of the *Capirola Lute-Book*, 1955). In the early 16th century the musical style of the *basse danse* changed. The examples in Attaingnant's collection of *Dixhuit basses dances garnies de recoupes et tordions* (1530; modern edition in D. Heartz, *Preludes, Chansons and Dances for Lute*, 1964) are for solo lute in triple time. Attaingnant's *Second livre de danceries* (1547) includes the following example, entitled *Par fin despit*, for four-part instrumental ensemble:

ANON. (*Les Maitres musiciens de la Renaissance française* volume xxiii, page 6)

It was this type of *basse danse* that Thoinot Arbeau described in 1588 as 'a manner of dancing full of honour and modesty', but by this time it had ceased to be fashionable, having been replaced by the stately PAVANE.

D. HEARTZ: 'The Basse Dance: Its Evolution circa 1450 to 1550', *Annales Musicologiques*, vi (1958–63)

basse fondamentale, *see* FUNDAMENTAL BASS

basset horn (Fr., *cor de basset*; Ger., *Bassethorn*; It., *corno di bassetto*), an alto clarinet, invented in the late 18th century. It is generally built in the key of F, and the notes are written a fifth higher than they sound. The compass is from

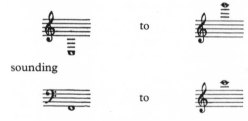

It was used by Mozart (e.g. Requiem, *Die Zauberflöte*) and has been revived by Richard Strauss (*Elektra*).

The name is probably due to the fact that the shape was originally curved.

See TRANSPOSING INSTRUMENTS.

A. CARSE: *Musical Wind Instruments* (1939)

bass flute (Fr., *flûte alto*; Ger., *Altflöte*; It., *flautone*), an instrument built a fourth lower than the normal FLUTE, sometimes known more correctly as the alto flute. The compass is from

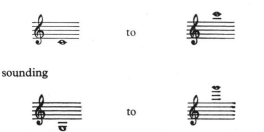

See TRANSPOSING INSTRUMENTS.

A. CARSE: *Musical Wind Instruments* (1939)

bass horn (Fr. *serpent droit*; Ger., *Basshorn*), an obsolete instrument, dating from the late 18th century. It consisted of a SERPENT of wood or brass made in the shape of a bassoon. It was also known as the RUSSIAN BASSOON.

Bassklarinette (Ger.), bass clarinet.

basso (It.), bass. *Basso continuo* (literally 'continuous bass'), figured bass, i.e. the bass line of a composition marked with figures to indicate the harmonies to be played on a keyboard instrument – see FIGURED BASS. *Basso ostinato* (literally 'obstinate bass'), ground bass, i.e. a figure repeated in the bass throughout a composition, or part of a composition, while the upper parts change. The lament at the end of Purcell's *Dido and Aeneas* ('When I am laid in earth') is a good example.

See GROUND BASS

basso continuo, see BASSO

basson (Fr.), bassoon. *Basson russe*, Russian bassoon.

bassoon (Fr., *basson*; Ger., *Fagott*; It., *fagotto*), a double-reed instrument dating from the 16th century, with a compass from

It is made of a wooden tube doubled back on itself, hence the name *fagotto*, a bundle of sticks. The double bassoon (Fr., *contrebasson*; Ger., *Kontrafagott*; It., *contrafagotto*) is built an octave lower and is made either of wood or of metal. There is a solo for the double bassoon in Ravel's *Ma Mère l'Oye*.

A. CARSE: *Musical Wind Instruments* (1939)

L. G. LANGWILL: *The Bassoon and Contrabassoon* (1965)

basso ostinato, see BASSO

Bassposaune (Ger.), bass trombone.

bass trombone, see TROMBONE

Basstrompete (Ger.), bass trumpet.

bass trumpet, see TRUMPET.

bass tuba, see TUBA.

bass viol, see VIOL

Bastien and Bastienne (Ger., *Bastien und Bastienne*), *Singspiel* in one act by Mozart, to a libretto by F. W. Weiskern from C. S. Favart's *Les Amours de Bastien et Bastienne* (a parody of Rousseau's *Le Devin du Village*). This short tale of rustic love was written when Mozart was twelve, and first performed in the garden theatre of Anton Mesmer (inventor of animal magnetism) in 1768 in Vienna.

Bataille, Gabriel (c. 1575–1630), lutenist at the French court. A selection from his *Airs de différents autheurs mis en tablature de luth* (1608–18) has been published by Peter Warlock.

Bate, Stanley (1913–59), English composer and pianist. He studied at the Royal College of Music, London, and subsequently with Nadia Boulanger and Hindemith. From 1942 until 1949 he was in the United States, where he appeared as soloist in his own works. His substantial output includes four symphonies, three piano concertos, three violin concertos, harpsichord concerto, cello concerto, piano works and several ballets.

Bateson, Thomas (c. 1570–1630), English organist. He was successively organist at Chester and Dublin Cathedrals, and apparently the first B.Mus. of Trinity College, Dublin. He composed two sets of madrigals (1604 and 1618; modern edition in *The English Madrigal School*, xxi and xxii).

Bathe, William (1564–1614), English writer. Author of *A Briefe Introduction to the True Art of Musicke* (1584), the first book on the theory of music printed in England, and of *A Briefe Introduction to the Skill of Song* (1600). He was at first in the service of Queen Elizabeth, but subsequently became a Jesuit priest.

baton (Fr.), the stick with which a conductor gives directions to the performers. Today it is slim and light and able to be used with great finesse. But at one time a roll of music was used, and in the 17th century a heavy stick which was beaten loudly on the floor (Lully, wielding such a stick, struck his foot in error and caused an abscess from which he subsequently died).

Batten, Adrian (1591–1637), organist of St. Paul's Cathedral and a composer of church music. He is thought to have compiled an organ score containing a large number of 16th century church compositions, known as the Batten Organ Book (now in St. Michael's College, Tenbury, ms 791).

J. BUNKER CLARK and M. BEVAN: 'New Biographical Facts about Adrian Batten', *Journal of the American Musicological Society*, xxiii (1970)

batterie (Fr.), BATTERY. Also, the percussion section of the orchestra.

battery, a 17th and 18th century term for ARPEGGIO.

battle music, descriptive pieces dealing with war were popular from the 16th to the 19th century. They include Janequin's part-song *La Guerre* (1529, reprinted in H. Expert, *Les Maîtres musiciens de la Renaissance française*, vii), Andrea Gabrieli's *Aria di battaglia* for wind instruments (1590, reprinted in *Istituzioni e monumenti dell' arte musicale italiana*, i), William Byrd's *Battell* for virginals (in *My Ladye Nevells Booke*), Johann Kaspar Kerll's *Battaglia* for harpsichord (17th century, printed in *D.T.B.*, ii (2),), Kotzwara's *The Battle of Prague* for piano (1788) and Beethoven's *Wellington's Sieg oder die Schlacht bei*

Vittoria (Wellington's Victory or the Battle of Vittoria) for orchestra (1813).

Battle of the Huns, *see* HUNNENSCHLACHT

battuta (It.), (1) 'beat'. *A battuta*, in strict time. *Senza battuta*, without any regular beat, i.e. in free time (e.g. in recitative);

(2) particularly the first beat in the bar, hence 'bar'. *Ritmo di tre battute*, three-bar rhythm, i.e. with the main accent falling at the beginning of every three bars.

Bauer, Harold (1873–1951), pianist, of mixed German and English parentage. He was a pupil of Paderewski, and for a time was associated with Thibaud and Casals in the performance of piano trios. He founded the Beethoven Association of New York (1919), a society for the performance of chamber music, and was an early devotée of the music of Debussy.

Bax, Arnold Edward Trevor (1883–1953), English composer. Born in London, he studied at the Royal Academy of Music under Frederick Corder. Knighted in 1937, he became Master of the King's Music in 1942. His style was romantic and powerfully influenced by his affection for Ireland and Irish folklore. His compositions include seven symphonies which, though unfashionably rhapsodic, nevertheless have many supporters. His other principal orchestral works are the symphonic poems *The Garden of Fand*, *Tintagel* and *November Woods*, the *Overture to a Picaresque Comedy*, the violin concerto and cello concerto. He also composed a nonet, octet, string quintet, oboe quintet, three string quartets, piano quintet, trio for flute, viola and harp, three violin sonatas, four piano sonatas and other instrumental works, and a large number of songs and folksong arrangements. He wrote an autobiography of his early years under the title *Farewell, My Youth* (1943).

Bayreuth, the town in Germany where Wagner built his festival theatre, provided by public subscription, for the performance of his own operas. With its hooded orchestra pit, and its 1800-seat auditorium resembling a classical amphitheatre, the Bayreuth Festspielhaus has acoustics ideal for Wagner's music. Indeed it could be said that unless you have heard Wagner at Bayreuth, you have never really heard Wagner – the acoustical quality of the auditorium remains unique and unrivalled. The first production was the tetralogy *Der Ring des Nibelungen*, performed in 1876. After Wagner's death in 1883 the theatre was controlled in turn by his widow Cosima, his son Siegfried and his daughter-in-law Winifred. In 1951 a new era began at Bayreuth under the auspices of his grandsons, Wieland and Wolfgang. Wieland's death in 1966 – after the creation by him of a whole new style of Wagner production – left Wolfgang in artistic command of the theatre.

B.B.C. Symphony Orchestra, founded in 1930 by the British Broadcasting Corporation. In addition to studio broadcasts, which provide its principal activity, it also appears at public concerts, including the Promenade Concerts. Its first conductor was Sir Adrian Boult (1930–49), whose successors have been Sir Malcolm Sargent, Rudolf Schwarz, Antal Dorati, Colin Davis, Pierre Boulez and Rudolf Kempe.

be (Ger.), flat. So called because the sign for the flat was originally shaped like a small rounded B.

See HEXACHORD

Beach, Amy Marcy (1867–1944), generally known as Mrs. H. H. Beach (her maiden name was Cheney). U.S. pianist and composer, who showed great precocity as a child. Her works include a Mass in E major and other choral music, a piano concerto and a *Gaelic Symphony* (1896) – the first symphonic work by a U.S. woman.

Bear, The, nickname for Haydn's symphony no 82 in C major (1786) – one of his *Paris* series and thus also known as *L'Ours*. The name derives from the sound of the last movement, thought to resemble a bear dancing to a bagpipe tune.

Bearbeitung (Ger.), arrangement.

Bayreuth: The theatre soon after its completion. The set is the Temple of the Grail from the last act of *Parsifal*

beat, (1) the unit of measurement in music, indicated in choral and orchestral works by the motion of the conductor's stick (Fr., *temps*; Ger., *Zählzeit, Schlag*; It., *battuta*). The number of beats in a bar depends on the time-signature and on the speed of the movement. A movement in 4/4 time may have eight beats if very slow, four if the speed is moderate, two if it is very fast. In exceptional cases there may be only one beat in the bar. This occurs most frequently in very quick movements in 3/4 or 3/8 time. (*See also* DOWN-BEAT.)

(2) an early English name for more than one kind of ornament. The following are the signs and explanations given respectively by (a) Christopher Simpson (1659), (b) Purcell (1696), (c) Geminiani (1749):

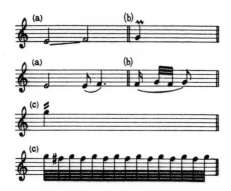

Beatles, The, group of four young British pop singers and poet-composers, John Lennon, Paul McCartney, George Harrison and Ringo Starr, who made a sensational series of discs during the 1960s and performed all over the world before separating. Their discs – one of them a genuine song cycle, *Sergeant Pepper* – have attracted considerable attention from professors as well as pop enthusiasts. And though the Beatles as a group are no longer extant, the sets of songs assembled under such titles as *Revolver, Rubber Soul, Help!, The Magical Mystery Tour* and *Let It Be* contain enough feeling, sharpness and inventiveness for them to be considered as pop classics.

W. MELLERS: *The Twilight of the Gods*

Béatrice et Bénédict (Fr., *Beatrice and Benedick*), opera in two acts by Berlioz, to a libretto by the composer, based on Shakespeare's *Much Ado about Nothing*. This was Berlioz's last opera, written, he said, as a relaxation after *The Trojans*. It was first performed in 1862 at Baden-Baden, but did not reach Britain until 1936 (an amateur performance in Glasgow) nor the United States until 1960 (at Carnegie Hall).

Bebung (Ger.), a form of VIBRATO used on the CLAVICHORD. The finger repeatedly presses the key without releasing it, and the metal tangent, by alternately increasing and decreasing the tension of the string, produces minute variations of pitch, similar to those produced on the violin by the player's finger. The *Bebung* was indicated by a special sign over or under the notes to be so treated:

bécarre (Fr.), natural, so named because the sign for the natural was originally a square-shaped B, i.e. a *bé carré*.

See HEXACHORD

Bechstein, a firm of piano-makers founded in Berlin by Friedrich Wilhelm Carl Bechstein (1826–1900) in 1856. The Bechstein Hall in Wigmore Street, London, opened by the sons of F. W. C. Bechstein in 1901, became the Wigmore Hall in 1917.

Beck, Conrad (born 1901), Swiss composer. He studied at Zürich, Paris and Berlin, and befriended Roussel and Honegger. His works include seven symphonies, concertos, *Der Tod des Oedipus* (chorus and orchestra), *Angelus Silesius* (oratorio), *La Grande Ourse* (ballet), and four string quartets.

Beck, Franz (1723–1809), German composer, a pupil of Johann Stamitz. He moved to France, where he became known as François Beck, and settled at Bordeaux in 1761. He wrote a large number of symphonies, which are important for the early history of the form.

Becken (Ger.), cymbals.

Bédos de Celles, Dom François (1709–79), Benedictine monk, author of *L'Art du facteur d'orgues* (1766–78), an important work on 18th century organ-building, which also contains valuable information about the interpretation and tempo of music of the period (*see* A. Dolmetsch, *The Interpretation of the Music of the 17th and 18th Centuries*); modern edition by C. Mahrenholz (1936).

Bedyngham, John (early 15th century), English composer of church music. Some of his compositions are preserved in the so-called Trent Codices and are printed in *Denkmäler der Tonkunst in Österreich*, xiv-xv (Jg. vii), xxii (Jg. xi, 1), lxi (Jg. xxxi).

Beecham, Thomas (1879–1961), English conductor, born in St. Helens. He was educated at Rossall School and Oxford, and first appeared as a conductor in London in 1905. He was knighted in 1914, and two years later succeeded to his father's baronetcy. He was founder and conductor of the London Philharmonic (1932) and Royal Philharmonic (1946). From 1910 he was active in promoting the cause of opera in Britain and introduced a large number of unfamiliar works to British audiences, including Strauss's *Elektra, Salome* and *Der Rosenkavalier*. These activities at various times involved him in financial difficulties. Apart from his special predilection for the works of Mozart, Handel and Delius (for whom he did a great deal of pioneer work) his sympathies in general lay with the romantic composers – he was a gifted interpreter of Berlioz, Bizet and other French composers.

Bee's Wedding, The, a name given (though not by the composer) to Mendelssohn's *Song without Words*, no 34 in C major. In Germany it is known as the *Spinnerlied*, an equally inauthentic title.

Beethoven, Ludwig van (1770–1827), German composer of Flemish descent. He was born in Bonn, where his grandfather and father were musicians in the service of the Elector of Cologne. His father, a drunkard, bullied him into long hours of keyboard practice, in the hope of making him a *Wunderkind* like Mozart. At the age of eleven, he left school; by thirteen he was harpsichord player in the court orchestra (under Neefe), by fourteen he was second court organist, and

Two views of Beethoven: the genius as public hero and as his friends saw him – a genius who was somewhat diminutive, somewhat cantankerous and more than somewhat individualistic (a sketch by Lyser, c. 1823)

by eighteen a viola player in the opera orchestra. In 1790 Beethoven and other court musicians were entertained to dinner by Haydn, *en route* between Vienna and London. As a result, Beethoven was permitted in 1792 to go to Vienna to study with Haydn and remained there the rest of his life. A previous visit to Vienna, to study with Mozart, had been cut short by his mother's fatal illness in 1787. His studies with Haydn, too, were curtailed – pupil and master did did not get on with each other – and he took lessons from Albrechtsberger, Salieri and Schenk instead. In 1795 he made his first public appearance in Vienna as composer and pianist, playing his B flat major piano concerto, op 19. Though he was friendly with many aristocrats – including Count Waldstein and the Archduke Rudolph – and though he was willing to accept the support of individuals, he rebelled against the 18th century system of patronage, whereby a musician was tied to the service of an employer. As a freelance musician in Vienna, he was more successful than Mozart – in spite of the personality problems from which he obviously suffered. His increasing deafness, which he recognised to be incurable, resulted in 1802 in the pathetic 'Heiligenstadt Testament', in which he contemplated suicide, ironically at the time of composing one of his sunniest symphonies, no 2 in D. During the next few years he reconciled himself to the fact that he could never now become a great public performer, and instead devoted himself largely to composition. His battle with his affliction is waged in his *Eroica* symphony (1804), the biggest and most powerful symphony written up to that time. His failure to find a wife (though he was regularly in love, often with one or another of his rich pupils) increased his sense of isolation, and his temper was not improved by the cares of acting as guardian to his feckless nephew Karl. In manner he was excessively brusque, and in his business relations with publishers inclined to be unscrupulous. By 1819 he was completely deaf, and it was during this last period of his life that he produced some of his greatest, most thoughtful works, including the last five string quartets, the last five piano sonatas, the ninth symphony and the *Missa Solemnis* – music in which he rose above the agonies of his private life, and reached into the future of his art. Naturally such works were misunderstood in their time, though their influence on future generations was enormous. The ninth symphony was one of Wagner's main sources of inspiration, the string quartets influenced Bartók, and Sir Michael Tippett has declared his debt to the piano sonatas and other works. In 1826, after his nephew had attempted suicide, Beethoven's health began seriously to deteriorate. By the following year he was bed-ridden, and though a cheque for £100 from the London Philharmonic Society inspired him to sketch a tenth symphony, he failed to make headway and died of what has been diagnosed as dropsy. For a full study of Beethoven's medical history, including a detailed examination of his deafness, readers are recommended to Martin Cooper's *Beethoven: The Last Decade*, with a 28-page medical appendix, written by Dr. Edward Larkin.

As a composer, Beethoven worked with difficulty, tirelessly revising his original sketches until he was satisfied. His sympathy with the liberal ideas of the times found expression in works like *Egmont*, *Fidelio* and the ninth symphony, and in an outlook on life that would have been unthinkable on the part of a composer in the years before the French Revolution. In this respect, Beethoven was the first great 'subjective' composer: his C minor piano concerto, written in 1800, marked the dawn of a new century and an attitude to music very different from the objectivity of the classical period. *Fidelio*, his only opera, cost him more effort than any of his other works. He was not a natural opera composer (and on the whole we can be thankful that he resisted an invitation to produce one opera every year for Vienna), yet here he created one of the greatest of all masterpieces. *Fidelio* upholds all Beethoven's most cherished beliefs. Its subject – the courage of a faithful wife who saves her husband from execution at the hands of a Spanish oppressor – is made all the more moving because it is allowed to grow out of the homely background of a German *Singspiel*. Along with *The Magic Flute* (said to be the only opera Beethoven really admired), it forms the foundation-stone of the German operatic repertory, but the universality of its theme transcends musical nationalism and the work is regarded everywhere as a symbol of love and liberty.

Many of Beethoven's works, especially those of his middle period (e.g. the *Appassionata* sonata), reflect his tempestuousness, and often his dissatisfaction with things as they were; but with all his rebellion against convention, there is also in his work a deep sincerity and a native simplicity. The tyranny of his ideas made him impatient of technical restrictions, and he could be merciless to voices and instruments, as in the *Grosse Fuge* for string quartet, the finale of the ninth symphony and the *Missa Solemnis*. On the other hand some of his slow movements have a sense of calm and what the Germans call an *Innigkeit* that disclose a different side of the composer. Perhaps the supreme examples of this kind of music are the slow movements of the ninth symphony and the A minor string quartet, op 132, the latter being Beethoven's great and very touching hymn of thanksgiving, written on recovery from illness.

Beethoven was one of the most original of all composers. His most popular works are:

(1) Orchestra: nine symphonies (the last with chorus); violin concerto; five piano concertos; concerto for piano, violin and cello; overtures – *Coriolan*, *Leonore* nos. 1, 2 and 3, *Namensfeier* (Name-Day), *Die Weihe des Hauses* (The Consecration of the House) and overtures to works mentioned in (3); fantasia for piano, orchestra and chorus; two romances for violin and orchestra;

(2) Choral works: two Masses (C major and D major); oratorio – *Christus am Ölberge* (The Mount of Olives); also the ninth symphony;

(3) Stage works: opera – *Fidelio*; incidental music to *Egmont*, *König Stephan* (King Stephen), *Die Ruinen von Athen* (The Ruins of Athens); ballet – *Die Geschöpfe des Prometheus* (The creatures of Prometheus);

(4) Chamber music: septet; quintet for piano and wind; string quintet; sixteen string quartets and *Grosse Fuge*; four string trios; serenade for flute, violin and viola; six piano trios; trio for clarinet, cello and piano; ten violin sonatas; five cello sonatas; horn sonata;

(5) Piano: 32 sonatas; 21 sets of variations; *Bagatellen*;

(6) Songs: *An die ferne Geliebte* (To the distant beloved – song-cycle); *Ah, perfido* (Ah, faithless one – *scena* for soprano and orchestra); other songs for voice and piano.

D. Arnold and N. Fortune (editors): *The Beethoven Companion* (1971)

P. Bekker: *Beethoven* (1925)

E. Blom: *Beethoven's Pianoforte Sonatas Discussed* (1938)

E. Closson: *The Fleming in Beethoven* (1936)

M. Cooper: *Beethoven: The Last Decade, 1817–1827* (1970)

R. Fiske: *Beethoven Concertos and Overtures* (1970)

G. Grove: *Beethoven and his Nine Symphonies* (1896)

A. C. Kalischer: *Beethoven's Letters* (two volumes, 1909)

J. Kerman: *The Beethoven Quartets* (1967)

B. Lam: *Beethoven String Quartets* (two volumes, 1975)

G. R. Marek: *Beethoven: Biography of a Genius* (1969)

J. de Marliave: *Beethoven's Quartets* (1928)

D. Matthews: *Beethoven Piano Sonatas* (1967)

P. Mies: *Beethoven's Sketches* (1929)

H. C. Robbins Landon: *Beethoven* (1970)

A. F. Schindler: *Beethoven as I knew him* (1860, translated by C. S. Jolly, edited by D. W. MacArdle, 1966)

M. M. Scott: *Beethoven* (1934)

R. Simpson: *Beethoven Symphonies* (1970)

J. W. N. Sullivan: *Beethoven – His Spiritual Development* (1927)

A. W. Thayer: *The Life of Ludwig van Beethoven* (edited by H. E. Krehbiel, 1921; revised and edited by E. Forbes, 1967)

Beggar's Opera, The, a ballad opera by John Gay, first produced in London in 1728. It consists of a play, interspersed with nearly seventy songs set to tunes popular at the time, some of them by well-known composers such as Purcell and Handel. In addition to satirizing the vices of the town it also makes fun of the conventions of Italian opera of the day, e.g. the habit of introducing extravagant similes into arias. The songs were arranged for the original production by Johann Christoph Pepusch, who also composed an overture, in which he utilized the melody of one of the songs. The work has frequently been revived. In the 20th century new editions of the music have been made by Frederic Austin, Edward J. Dent and Benjamin Britten.

See Ballad Opera, Threepenny Opera

F. Kidson: *The Beggar's Opera: its Predecessors and Successors* (1922).

W. E. Schultz: *Gay's Beggar's Opera: its Content, History and Influence* (1923).

Begleitung (Ger.), accompaniment.

Bègue, *see* Le Bègue

Beinum, Eduard van (1901–59), Dutch conductor who succeeded Mengelberg as conductor of the Concertgebouw Orchestra, Amsterdam, in 1945. He was also associated with the London Philharmonic and

Los Angeles Philharmonic. He had a special flare for the music of Bruckner and of French composers ranging from Berlioz to Roussel.

Bekker, Paul (1882–1937), German writer on music, active as a music critic from 1906. His most important works, published in English translations, are *Beethoven* (1925) and *Richard Wagner* (1931).

Belaiev, Mitrophane Petrovich (1836–1904), Russian publisher, the son of a timber merchant. He founded a publishing firm in Leipzig in 1885, and issued a very large number of works by Russian composers.

bel canto (It.), literally, beautiful song, beautiful singing. The term is usually applied to singing finely sustained in the Italian manner, with emphasis on beauty of tone and phrasing, on agility and the ability to take high notes without strain. Composers whose works depended on such singing included Bellini, Donizetti and Rossini.

bell, most public bells are made of bell metal, a bronze consisting of four parts of copper to one part of tin, and cast to produce a characteristic mixture of harmonics on being struck. The largest bell is the famous Tsar Kolokol (Emperor Bell) in Moscow, cast in 1733 and weighing 193 tons. Unfortunately, it has cracked, and no other bell approaches even half its weight. Bells are chimed by moving a clapper or wielding a mallet to strike the side of the bell, or rung by swinging the bell to cause a free-swinging clapper to strike it. Many churches and public buildings have sets of bells that are rung or chimed to mark the hours or special occasions. A CARILLON of bells can produce a tune. Changes of bells are often rung by many churches, the ringers attempting to progress through some or all of the permutations of ringing order possible. For five bells, there are a total of 120 changes ($5 \times 4 \times 3 \times 2 \times 1$), for six bells 720 ($6 \times 5 \times 4 \times 3 \times 2 \times 1$) and so on. Tunes and changes may also be rung by a group of people using handbells.

In orchestras, tubular bells made of long tubes of brass are struck with a mallet to simulate the sound of bells. A set is tuned chromatically and suspended in the same arrangement as a keyboard.

See also CHIMES, COW BELL

Bell Anthem, the name given to 'Rejoice in the Lord alway', an anthem for voices and strings by Purcell (*Purcell Society*, xiv), which begins with repeated descending scales in the bass, suggesting the tolling of bells.

Belle Hélène, La (Fr., *Beautiful Helen*), operetta in three acts by Offenbach, to a libretto by Henri Meilhac and Ludovic Halévy, first performed in 1864 in Paris. The work is one of the most spirited of Offenbach's satirical comedies.

Bellérophon, opera with a prologue and five acts by Lully, libretto by Thomas Corneille, first performed in 1679 in Paris.

bell harp, a kind of zither invented in England early in the 18th century. It was gripped with the fingers and swung through the air while plucking the strings with plectrums attached to the thumbs. The word 'bell' probably referred to the swinging motion.

Bellini, Vincenzo (1801–1835), Italian composer, born at Catania, Sicily. The son of an organist, Bellini with financial assistance from a Sicilian nobleman was

Vincenzo Bellini

sent to Naples Conservatorio to study with Zingarelli. In Naples he came into contact with Donizetti and Mercadante. His first opera, *Adelson e Salvina* (1825), immediately attracted attention and resulted in the commission of *Bianca e Fernando* (1826), from Barbaia, the impresario of La Scala, Milan, and San Carlos, Naples. This was performed before King Francis I, and led to the commission of *Il Pirata* (1827) for performance at La Scala. In *Pirata*, and in such subsequent works as *La Straniera* (1829), *Zaira* (1829), *I Capuletti ed i Montecchi* (1830, based on the story of Romeo and Juliet), *La Sonnambula* (1831) and *Norma* (1831), Bellini's lyrical gifts quickly reached maturity. His last opera, *I Puritani* (1835, inspired by Scott's *Old Mortality*), was composed for Paris, where he died of dysentery.

bell lyra, bell lyre, a portable glockenspiel played in military bands. It contains metal bars attached to a lyre-shaped frame with a handle. The player holds the handle in one hand and a mallet in the other.

bell tree, a set of small bells mounted one above the other on a long rod. It is usually played by running a stick along the set to produce an arpeggio of light bell sounds.

belly (Fr. *table*), the upper part of the soundbox of a string instrument, often known as the table, in imitation of the French term.

Belshazzar, oratorio by Handel, to a libretto by Charles Jennens, first performed in 1745 in London.

Belshazzar's Feast, oratorio by Walton, with words selected by Sacheverell Sitwell (mainly from the

Bible). First performed in 1931 at the Leeds Festival, Walton's abrasive score gave the English choral tradition a much-needed injection of vitality. An orchestral suite on the same subject was composed by Sibelius drawn from his incidental music to a play by Procope (1906).

bémol (Fr.; It., *bemolle*), flat. The word is a modification of the Latin *B mollis* (soft B). The sign for the flat was originally a rounded B.

   See HEXACHORD

bemolle, *see* BÉMOL

Benda, Jiři Antonin (1722–95), Czech composer, pianist and oboist, most famous member of the large family of musicians. He was *Kapellmeister* to the Duke of Gotha (1750–78) and became known in Germany as Georg Benda. He wrote church music, orchestral works, chamber music, operettas and three melodramas (i.e. spoken plays with instrumental accompaniment), two of which, *Ariadne auf Naxos* (1775) and *Medea* (1775), were extraordinarily successful. The latter was much admired by Mozart (Emily Anderson, *The Letters of Mozart and his Family*, page 937).

Benedicite (Lat.), the canticle known as the 'Song of the Three Children', appointed as an alternative to the Te Deum in the Morning Service of the Anglican Church. (Generally pronounced in Britain 'ben-ni-dice'-it-i'.)

Benedict, Julius (1804–85), English composer and conductor. Born in Germany, he settled in London in 1836 and later took British citizenship. A pupil of Hummel and Weber, he wrote a large number of instrumental works, oratorios and operas but is remembered today only by *The Lily of Killarney* (London, 1862). Benedict also wrote a life of Weber (1881), which is valuable for its personal reminiscences. He was knighted in 1871.

Benedictus (Lat.), (1) the second part of the *Sanctus* of the Roman Mass. It begins *Benedictus qui venit in nomine Domini*, 'Blessed is he that cometh in the name of the Lord';

   (2) the canticle *Benedictus Dominus Israel*, 'Blessed be the Lord God of Israel', appointed as an alternative to the Jubilate in the Morning Service of the Anglican Church.

Benet, John (15th century), English composer. His works (a Mass, motets and Mass movements) appear principally in Continental manuscripts.

Benevoli, Orazio (1605–72), Italian composer. He was court musician to the Archduke Leopold Wilhelm in Vienna from 1643 to 1645, and *maestro di cappella* at the Vatican from 1645 to 1672. He composed a quantity of large-scale church music, some of it for several choirs. His Mass in 53 vocal and instrumental parts, written for the dedication of Salzburg Cathedral in 1628, is printed in *Denkmäler der Tonkunst in Österreich*, xx (Jg. x, 1). A complete edition of his works was begun by L. Feininger in 1966.

Benjamin, Arthur (1893–1960), Australian composer and pianist. He studied at the Royal College of Music, London, and taught there from 1926. His works, which show a lively sense of humour as well as an accomplished technique, include the operas *The Devil Take Her* (1931), *Prima Donna*, *A Tale of Two Cities* and *Tartuffe*, concertino for piano and orchestra, violin concerto, *Overture to an Italian Comedy*, a symphony, chamber music, and songs. Benjamin also wrote a good deal of film music. His *Jamaican Rumba* has become widely popular.

Bennet, John (c. 1575–after 1614), English composer. He published a set of four-part madrigals in 1599 (reprinted in *The English Madrigal School*, xxiii). His 'All creatures now are merry minded', contributed to *The Triumphes of Oriana* (1601) is one of the best-known of all English madrigals. He also contributed to Ravenscroft's *Brief Discourse* (1614) and wrote five hymn-tunes for William Barley's Psalter.

Bennett, Richard Rodney (born 1936), English composer and pianist. He studied at the Royal Academy of Music, London, with Lennox Berkeley and Howard Ferguson, and in Paris with Boulez. He has written prolifically, employing serialism with both polish and vigour. His most important pieces have been his operas, especially his atmospheric spook story, *The Mines of Sulphur* (1965), which has been successful in London and elsewhere in Europe. His subsequent operas, the comedy *A Penny for a Song* and the Conrad-inspired *Victory*, have further established his considerable theatrical talent. In the concert hall he has had a considerable success with his piano concerto, his first symphony and his *Aubade* for orchestra. He has also written four string quartets, *Calendar* for chamber ensemble, piano pieces and a large quantity of fluent film music.

Bennett, Robert Russell (born 1894), U.S. composer, pupil of Carl Busch and Nadia Boulanger. In addition to film music his works include the opera *Maria Malibran* (1935), an *Abraham Lincoln Symphony* and a *Symphony in D for the Dodgers* (the title referring to the Brooklyn baseball team), chamber music and choral works.

Bennett, William Sterndale (1816–75), English composer and pianist. He visited Germany at Mendelssohn's suggestion (1836) and was warmly received by Schumann. He returned to Britain to teach at the Royal Academy of Music in 1837, founded the Bach Society (1849) and gave the first performance in England of Bach's *St. Matthew Passion* (1854). His works, which are strongly influenced by Mendelssohn, include a symphony in C minor, four piano concertos, overtures – *The Naiads* and *The Woodnymphs*, *The Woman of Samaria* (oratorio), piano music, choral music and songs.

   J. R. STERNDALE BENNETT: *The Life of William Sterndale Bennett* (1907)

Benoît, Pierre Léopold Léonard (1834–1901), Belgian composer, known in Flemish as Peter Benoît. He was a pupil of Fétis at the Brussels Conservatoire. Benoît promoted a national movement which led to the foundation in 1867 of the L'Ecole Flamande de Musique, Antwerp, of which he became director. His numerous works include three operas, three oratorios and several choral cantatas.

   C. VAN DEN BORREN: *Peter Benoît* (1942)

Bentzon, Jørgen (1897–1948), Danish composer, a pupil of Carl Nielsen. He also studied at Leipzig Conservatorium with Karg-Elert. His works include two symphonies (the first on Dickens), orchestral variations, five string quartets, and other chamber compositions.

Bentzon, Niels Viggo (born 1919), Danish composer

and pianist, cousin of Jørgen Bentzon. He studied at Copenhagen Conservatory, became a champion of Schoenberg, and in 1950 wrote a book on twelve-note technique. A prolific composer, he has written fourteen symphonies, of which the fourth (entitled *Metamorphoses*) proved a milestone in his career. Many of his works – including seven concertos and eleven sonatas – are for piano. The rest of his output includes an opera (*Faust III*), two violin concertos, nine string quartets and other chamber music, and a cantata entitled *Bonjour Max Ernst*.

Benvenuto Cellini, opera in two acts by Berlioz, to a libretto by Léon de Wailly and Auguste Barbier, first performed in 1838 in Paris. The Italian sculptor and writer was one of Berlioz's earliest heroes, and a natural choice for the subject of his first opera. Its initial failure at the Paris Opéra was a daunting blow – more than twenty years were to pass before he wrote another opera. Liszt, however, presented *Cellini* at Weimar in 1852, though for many years the music was known only by way of the concert overture, *Roman Carnival* (1844), which uses material from the opera. Today *Cellini* is in the repertory of Covent Garden, and has come to be recognized as the masterpiece it is.

bequadro (It.), natural.

berceuse (Fr.; Ger., *Wiegenlied*), 'cradle song'. A piece suggesting by its rhythm the gentle rocking of a cradle, e.g. Chopin's op 57 for piano.

Berenice, opera in three acts by Handel, to a libretto by Antonio Salvi, first performed in 1737 in London. In spite of its famous minuet (heard in the overture) and consort of recorders, this opera about the wife of an ancient Egyptian king was not a success.

Berg, Alban (1885–1935), Austrian composer. Born in Vienna of a cultured family, Berg showed early talent as a composer, greatly impressing Schoenberg who taught him from 1904 to 1910. Schoenberg exerted a profound influence on Berg, most evident in his development of atonality and serialism, and in his writings in defence of Schoenberg's music. His first opera, *Wozzeck* (1917–21), a free-atonal work, established his reputation. Shortly afterwards he adopted the TWELVE-NOTE SYSTEM, using it distinctively in, e.g., his violin concerto (1935) and unfinished opera *Lulu* (1929–35, after Wedekind). Berg's violin concerto, one of the most important 20th century concertos, was dedicated 'to the memory of an angel' – the angel being the 19-year-old Manon Gropius, daughter of Mahler's widow. The first of its two movements depicts the girl's gentle character; the second, marked *Catastrophe* and *Resolution*, consists of a violent allegro followed by an adagio based on a Bach chorale. The concerto was Berg's last work. He died before hearing it. He was a slow, careful, sensitive composer, whose few works reveal great intelligence and technical mastery combined with a greater warmth of imagination than his master – he was the most romantic of Schoenberg's disciples. He was also a gifted and devoted teacher. His principal works are:

(1) Operas: *Wozzeck* (1921), *Lulu* (1929–35);
(2) Orchestra: three orchestral pieces, chamber concerto for piano, violin and thirteen instruments, violin concerto;
(3) Chamber music: string quartet, *Lyric Suite* for string quartet;

(4) Piano: sonata.

He also wrote a number of songs, with piano and orchestra.

W. REICH: *Alban Berg* (1963)
M. CARNER: *Alban Berg* (1975)
A. BERG: *Letters to his Wife* (edited, translated and annotated by Bernard Grun, 1971)

bergamasca (It., Fr. *bergamasque*), a popular dance, so called from Bergamo in north Italy, current in the 16th and early 17th centuries. In the second half of the 16th century it was normally constructed on a recurring pattern of tonic-subdominant-dominant-tonic harmonies. The melody varied until the early 17th century, when the dance became associated with the following tune:

Frescobaldi wrote an organ canzona on this theme in his *Fiori musicali* (1635, modern edition by J. Bonnet, p. 88). Other composers used the harmonic scheme of the *bergamasca* as the basis for variations, as with the chaconne or passacaglia. Shakespeare refers to the dance in *A Midsummer Night's Dream*, v, 1.

(2) a 19th century dance in quick 6/8 time, similar to the tarantella.

(3) in Debussy's *Suite bergamasque* for piano the adjective seems to have no special significance. It is obviously suggested by Verlaine's 'Clair de lune', which begins:

Votre âme est un paysage choisi,
Que vont charmant masques et bergamasques
Jouant du luth et dansant . . .

bergerette (Fr., *berger* = shepherd), (1) 16th-century dance in brisk triple time;
(2) an 18th century French song dealing with shepherds and shepherdesses.

bergomask, *see* BERGAMASCA

Berio, Luciano (born 1925), Italian composer and conductor, a pupil of Ghedini and Dallapiccola. Though siding with the avant-garde, and employing all the most advanced techniques, Berio has at the same time managed to achieve exceptional world-wide popularity with a succession of colourful and dramatic works in which an underlying Italian lyricism is almost always distinguishable. He made his name in the early 1960s with *Circles* for woman's voice, harp and percussion, to a text by E. E. Cummings, in which he used spatial effects. His series of *Sequenze* are virtuoso but at the same time poetic monologues for a variety of solo instruments – piano, flute, oboe, viola, trombone, voice, etc. The trombone piece, written for Vinko Globokar, is a portrait of Grock the clown. His other works include *Recital*, a psycho-study of a recitalist's career, written for his former wife, Cathy Berberian; *Tempi Concertati* for flute and chamber ensemble; a large-scale *Sinfonia* written for the New York Philharmonic and the Swingle Singers, one movement of which is a musical collage created out of the scherzo of Mahler's second symphony (which proceeds underneath all the other activity and occasionally rises to the surface); a concerto for two pianos; *Nones* for orchestra; a series of pieces entitled *Allelujah*, for different ensembles; *Bewegung*, which has gradually expanded out of a short piece written for the Scottish

Berlioz (standing on the left) plays homage to Liszt. Next to Berlioz stands Czerny. The violinist is Heinrich Ernst, and the drawing was made by Kriehuber (seated on the left) in 1846

National Orchestra in 1971; and electronic works including *Mutations* and *Perspectives*. His music for the stage includes an opera, *Allez, Hop!*, and a work-in-progress, *Amores*, commissioned by the Holland Festival and so far unperformed, partly because it will need a special theatre built for it.

Bériot, Charles Auguste de (1802–70), Belgian violinist, teacher and composer. He married first the singer Maria Malibran, 1836, having lived with her from 1830, and then Marie Huber, daughter of a Viennese magistrate. Bériot taught the violin at Brussels Conservatoire (1843–52). He was a brilliant performer, with considerable influence on his successors. His compositions included concertos, studies and instruction books. Henri Vieuxtemps was his pupil.

Berkeley, Lennox Randal Francis (born 1903), English composer, pupil of Nadia Boulanger in Paris from 1927 until 1933. His works, which were originally influenced by Stravinsky and show a French regard for clarity, precision and a deep sympathy for the human voice, include the oratorio *Jonah*, the operas *Nelson*, *A Dinner Engagement* and *Ruth*, the ballet *The Judgement of Paris*, a *Stabat Mater*, three symphonies, concertos for piano, two pianos and flute, a witty orchestral divertimento, two violin sonatas, three string quartets, and some piano works of great civility.

Berkshire Festival, annual festival of music founded in 1937 at Tanglewood, Mass., by Koussevitsky, with the Boston Symphony as resident orchestra. From 1940 courses have also been held in composition, conducting and performance.

Berlin, Irving, originally Israel Baline (born 1888), Russian-born composer, who settled in the United States in 1893. Composer of some of America's finest pop songs, he scored one of his first international successes with 'Alexander's Ragtime Band' in 1911. His most famous song is probably 'White Christmas' (1942), and the most imposing large-scale receptacle for his talents was the musical, *Call Me Madam* (1950).

Berlin Philharmonic Orchestra, founded 1882, with Franz Wullner as its first conductor. His successors have been Joseph Joachim, Karl Klindworth, Hans von Bulow, Arthur Nikisch, Wilhelm Furtwängler and, since 1955, Herbert von Karajan.

Berlioz, (Louis) Hector (1803–69), French composer. Born at La Côte St. André, among the mountains near Grenoble, he was the son of a doctor. As a boy he learnt the flute and guitar, but his musical training at that time was haphazard: his father wanted him to join the family profession, and accordingly sent him in 1821 to the École de Médecine in Paris. He was an unwilling student, however, and could not bear the gorier side of his studies. In spite of parental opposition he became a private pupil of the composer Lesueur and in 1826 entered the Paris Conservatoire, where he immediately flung himself into composition. His progressive views soon made him an enemy of Cherubini (whom he ripped to pieces in his *Memoirs*) and of the Conservatoire's more conventional minds. He failed several times to win the *Prix de Rome*, but triumphed in 1830 with his cantata, *Sardanapale*. By that time he had fallen in love with the Irish actress, Harriet Smithson, whom he had seen in Shakespeare in Paris and who was the inspiration of his *Fantastic Symphony* (1830). Before he succeeded in meeting her, however, he got engaged to someone else – the pianist Marie Moke, who was in two minds about marrying a person of Berlioz's temperament, and instead married Camille Pleyel while Berlioz was absent in Rome (he vowed to return and kill her, and set out from Rome carrying pistols and poison, but changed his mind *en route*). In 1833 he succeeded in marrying Harriet Smithson, whose career was now in decline, but it was not a happy marriage. By 1842 they had separated, and in 1854 (immediately after Harriet's death) he married the singer Marie Recio. Meanwhile, to keep himself solvent, he had worked as a music critic – a profession he despised, though he was one of its most outstanding practitioners – and in 1838 had been given 20,000 francs by Paganini to enable him to devote more time to composition. Though he held no official appointment until 1859, when he became librarian of the Conservatoire, and though conservative musicians of the day consistently frowned on him, he was subsidised by the French Government for the composition of his Requiem and his *Symphonie Funèbre et Triomphale* – the latter commissioned for outdoor performance in celebration of the tenth anniversary of the 1830 revolution.

With this money he was able to travel extensively, conducting performances of his music and causing a sensation wherever he went – his success in Germany particularly delighted him. In 1855 his *Te Deum* was performed at the Paris Exhibition and in the same year he visited Liszt at Weimar, where his opera,

Benvenuto Cellini, had been presented in 1852 and where the Princess Sayn-Wittgenstein then suggested that he compose an opera on the subject of the Trojans, using Virgil's *Aeneid* as inspiration. By 1858 he had completed this greatest of all his masterpieces (and the one which he himself cherished above all others) but when he offered it to the Paris Opéra he was promptly cold-shouldered. In the end the second part of the work was staged at the Théâtre Lyrique in 1863 in a brutally truncated version which even omitted the Royal Hunt and Storm. It was the only production the work received in his lifetime. The failure of *The Trojans* so dispirited Berlioz that he practically ceased composing. A touching passage in his *Memoirs* tells how a promising musical idea came to him one night, but he did not have the mental energy to write it down; by morning it had gone. His last years were dogged by loneliness, and an increasingly serious nervous affliction. In 1862 his second wife had died, and in 1867 he received news that his much-loved 33-year-old son, Louis, who was in the French Navy, had died in Havana. This finally broke his spirit, and his health steadily deteriorated until his death two years later.

Though France has always maintained a love-hate relationship with its greatest composer – even as recently as 1969 *The Trojans* had failed to achieve a complete performance in that country – Berlioz's greatness has not gone unrecognised elsewhere. Old-fashioned objections to him have gradually faded away, partly because conductors and orchestras are at long last learning how to perform his music properly. Berlioz himself once spoke of how he heard a performance of his *King Lear* overture in Prague, where the players got it more or less right; but 'more or less right', he added, was all wrong. And indeed, unless conductor and players can master the phrasing of the

A Berlioz memento: an autographed version of the theme of the March of the Pilgrims from *Harold in Italy*

music, the swerving rhythms, the delicacy of orchestration and the passionate melancholy that tends to lie at the heart of even Berlioz's most exuberant works, then the current will fail to flow.

At one time it was fashionable to speak of the brassy brilliance of Berlioz, but it is now realised what an abundance of really quiet music he wrote. Even some of his supposedly grandest works make their most memorable effects by stealth. Thus in the Requiem the most overwhelming moment may come with the sound of the four brass bands from all corners of the platform in the Dies Irae, but it is not characteristic of the work as a whole. Much more so is the passage for widely spaced flutes and trombones or, in the Sanctus, the soft swish of six pairs of cymbals, a precisely calculated and, in its context, deeply moving effect. Yet not until he wrote *L'Enfance du Christ* did the Parisian public recognise the restraint and purity of Berlioz's music, and the shock was so great that they thought he had mended his ways and changed his style – to which Berlioz sadly replied that it was only his subject he had changed. Similarly in the case of the *Fantastic Symphony* it took many people a long time to recognise the classical masterpiece that lies behind the work's romantic programme.

Though rightly renowned for his qualities as an orchestrator – he wrote the most famous of all treatises on orchestration (*Traité de l'Instrumentation*) – Berlioz was not a proficient performer on any instrument. The writing of concertos failed to attract him, and the nearest he got to it was in *Harold in Italy* where the role of the solo viola was so unostentatious that Paganini (who commissioned it) declined to perform it. The loss was his, because *Harold* remains one of the most poetic and picturesque of all works for solo instrument and orchestra. Poetry, too, stamps almost all Berlioz's vocal music. His *Nuits d'Été* (1841–56), settings of Gautier, was the first important song cycle ever written for voice and orchestra, as opposed to voice and piano; it thus paved the way for Mahler's song cycles. Its subject, romantic love seen from various aspects, is explored with exquisite delicacy and atmosphere, whether in the wistful little 'Villanelle' which opens the cycle or in the darker reaches of 'Sur les lagunes'. Operatically, Berlioz was consistently daunted by Paris's lack of sympathy with him. Though not all composers have been the best judges of their own work, Berlioz was surely right to regard *The Trojans* as his masterpiece. In duration as long as Wagner's longest operas, it is in many ways the obverse of those works: a classical drama treated with a classical intensity that links it powerfully with Mozart's *Idomeneo* and with the best of Berlioz's beloved Gluck. It is perhaps the most passionate *opera seria* ever written.

Berlioz's principal compositions are:

(1) Operas: *Benvenuto Cellini* (1838); *Les Troyens* (The Trojans, 1865–9); *Béatrice et Bénédict* (1862);

(2) Orchestra: *Symphonie Fantastique*; *Harold en Italie* (for viola and orchestra); overtures – *Le Roi Lear* (King Lear), *Le Corsaire*, *Le Carnaval Romain*, *Les Francs Juges*, *Waverley*, *Rob Roy*;

(3) Choral works: *Sara la baigneuse* (Sara the Bather), *Lélio ou le retour à la vie* (sequel to the *Fantastic Symphony*) for actor, soloists, chorus, pianists and orchestra, *Roméo et Juliette* (a dramatic symphony),

Symphonie funèbre et triomphale, *La Damnation de Faust*, *Grande Messe des Morts* (Requiem Mass), *L'Enfance du Christ* (The Childhood of Christ), *Te Deum*, *L'Impériale*;

(4) Song cycle *Les Nuits d'Eté*, two scenas, *Herminie* and *Cléopatra*, for voice and orchestra; songs and works for small vocal ensemble.

J. BARZUN: *Berlioz and the Romantic Century*, two volumes (1950, revised third edition 1969); *Berlioz and his Century* (1956)
H. BERLIOZ: *Memoirs* (1865; translated, edited and introduced by David Cairns, 1969; earlier translation by Ernest Newman); *Evenings in the Orchestra* (1852; translated by C. R. Fortescue with an introduction and notes by David Cairns, 1963)
A. E. F. DICKINSON: *The Music of Berlioz* (1972)
H. MACDONALD: *Berlioz Orchestral Music* (1969)
E. NEWMAN: *Berlioz, Romantic and Classic* (writings selected and edited with an introduction by Peter Heyworth, 1972)
HUMPHREY SEARLE (editor): *Hector Berlioz: A selection from his letters* (1966)
W. J. TURNER: *Berlioz – the Man and his Work* (1934)
T. S. WOTTON: *Hector Berlioz* (1935)

Bermudo, Juan (fl. 16th century), Spanish author of an instruction book on music and musical instruments, *Libro llamado declaración de instrumentos* (1555; facsimile edition, 1958), which also contains biographical information about Cristobal Morales. Some of the book appeared previously as an instruction manual for the use of a convent of nuns, *El arte Tripharia* (1550).

R. STEVENSON: *Juan Bermudo* (1960)

Bernardi, Steffano (died before 1638), Italian composer. He was *maestro di cappella* at Verona Cathedral in 1615, and *Kapellmeister* at Salzburg Cathedral from 1628 to 1634. He composed church music, madrigals and instrumental music, and also published a successful primer of counterpoint (1615). Some of his church music is printed in *Denkmäler der Tonkunst in Osterreich*, lxix, (Jg. xxxvi, 1).

Berners, Lord, originally Gerald Hugh Tyrwhitt-Wilson (1883–1950), English composer, painter and author who was ten years in the diplomatic service (1909–19) and succeeded to the barony in 1918. As a composer he was largely self-taught, though he had some encouragement from Stravinsky. His music is often ironical and parodies the conventions of romanticism, but it is evident that he was himself a romantic at heart. His Gallic leanings were revealed in the French titles he frequently chose for his works. He was most successful as a composer of ballets, which include *The Triumph of Neptune* (1926), *Luna Park* (1930), *A Wedding Bouquet* (1937) and *Cupid and Psyche* (1939). He also wrote a one-act opera, *Le Carosse du Saint-Sacrement* (Paris, 1924), a *Fantaisie Espagnole*, Fugue in C minor for orchestra, piano music, and songs. His piano pieces often bear Satie-like titles such as *Fragments psychologiques*, *Valses Bourgeoises* and *Petites Marches funèbres*.

Bernhard, Christoph (1627–92), German tenor singer and composer. He entered the service of the elector of Saxony in 1649, and studied singing in Italy, where he met Carissimi. He was vice-*Kapellmeister* at Dresden in 1655, cantor at Hamburg in 1664, and

Kapellmeister at Dresden in 1674. A Mass by him is printed in *Das Chorwerk*, xvi, and some of his Protestant church music is in *Denkmäler deutscher Tonkunst*, vi.

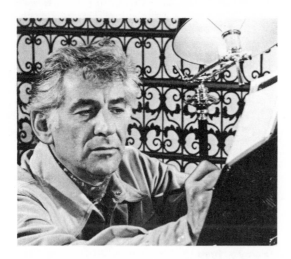

Leonard Bernstein, composer, conductor and pianist: 'a very American *Wunderkind*'

Bernstein, Leonard (born 1918), American conductor, composer and pianist, born at Lawrence, Massachusetts. He studied at Harvard University and the Curtis Institute of Music, New York. His teachers included Walter Piston (composition) and Serge Koussevitsky and Fritz Reiner (conducting). In 1942 he became Koussevitsky's assistant at the Berkshire Music Center, and thereafter quickly showed his qualities as a conductor. In this capacity he rose in 1957 to be co-conductor (with Dmitri Mitropoulos) of the New York Philharmonic, and in 1959 to be the musical director of that orchestra; he is now its 'laureate' conductor, specializing in such composers as Mahler, Ravel, Sibelius and early Stravinsky. He is also a notable, if less frequent, opera conductor, and his career as a composer has likewise been divided between concert hall and theatre. His most successful pieces have been his musicals, *On the Town* (1944), *Wonderful Town* (1952) and above all *West Side Story* (1957); his adaptation of Voltaire's *Candide* (1956) was overshadowed by the latter, though it is a work of considerable sophistication, with a racy overture sometimes performed in the concert hall. More controversial have been his concert pieces, which include three symphonies: no 1, the *Jeremiah* (1942); no 2, *The Age of Anxiety* (1949); and no 3, *Kaddish* (1963). In these, Bernstein has sometimes seemed excessively ambitious. The rest of his output includes the ballets *Fancy Free* and *Facsimile*, *Chichester Psalms* for chorus and orchestra, a modern Mass (first performed, in a dramatized version, at the Kennedy Center, Washington) and the opera, *Trouble in Tahiti*. He wrote the film score for *On the Waterfront*, is a popular television lecturer, and is author of several books.

Bertolotti, Gasparo di, *see* SALA

Berton, Henri Montan (1767–1844), French composer and violinist. He taught at the Paris Conservatoire from 1795 and was conductor at the Opéra-Comique from 1807. In spite of financial difficulties, due partly to conditions under the Terror, he produced a large number of compositions. Of his almost fifty operas, *Aline, Reine de Golconde* (Paris, 1803) was the most successful, and was translated and performed in other European countries.

Bertoni, Ferdinando Giuseppe (1725–1813), Italian composer of operas, oratorios, and instrumental works, a pupil of Martini. He became organist at St. Mark's, Venice, in 1752, and *maestro di cappella* in 1785. His *Orfeo* (Venice, 1776) was a setting of the libretto by Calzabigi which had previously been set by Gluck in 1762.

Berwald, Franz Adolf (1796–1868), Swedish composer and violinist. He studied the violin with Du Puy, but as a composer was self-taught. He was a member of the king's orchestra, Stockholm, from 1812 until 1828. In that year he went to Berlin, where he wrote two operas, and in 1841 to Vienna, where three of his symphonic poems were performed. From 1849 he taught composition in Stockholm. Though little appreciated during his lifetime, Berwald's music is now more frequently performed and rightly so, because it speaks with a quite distinctive voice. His works include four symphonies (two entitled respectively *Symphonie serieuse* and *Symphonie singulière*), several symphonic poems, concertos, chamber music, and several operas, one of which, *A Rustic Betrothal in Sweden*, was given with Jenny Lind. His other operas included *Estrella di Soria*, *Leonida*, *The Traitor* and *The Queen of Golconda*.

Bes (Ger.), B double flat.

Besard, Jean Baptiste (born c. 1567), French doctor of law, who was also an accomplished lutenist and composer. In addition to writing works on other subjects, he published an anthology of lute music (including his own compositions) entitled *Thesaurus harmonicus* (1603) and a sequel *Novus partus sive concertationes musicae* (1617). These are valuable sources for our knowledge of early 17th century lute music. A number of *airs de cour* from *Thesaurus harmonicus* are printed in O. Chilesotti, *Biblioteca di rarità musicali*, volume vii.

Besseler, Heinrich (1900–69), German musicologist. He held academic posts at Freiburg, Heidelberg and Jena, and specialized in the study of medieval music.

Besson, Gustave Auguste (1820–75), French manufacturer of brass instruments, in which he introduced several improvements. He also constructed in 1890 a contrabass clarinet, described as a *clarinette-pedale*, with a compass an octave below that of the bass clarinet. This instrument was used by d'Indy in his opera *Fervaal* (1897).

bestimmt (Ger.), decisively.

Betz, Franz (1835–1900), German operatic baritone. He sang Hans Sachs at the first performance of Wagner's *Die Meistersinger* (Munich, 1868) and Wotan at the first performance of *Der Ring des Nibelungen* (Bayreuth, 1876).

Bevin, Elway (1554–c. 1639), English organist. He was organist of Bristol Cathedral, probably from 1587 to 1638, when he was dismissed (*see* J. E. West, *Cathedral Organists*, second edition, 1921, page 7). He was described in Laud's visitation of 1634 as 'a verie olde man, who, having done good service in the church is not now able to discharge the place, but that hee is holpen by some other of the qhier' (*Historical Manuscripts Commission*, iv, page 141). He wrote *A brief and short instruction of the art of musicke* (1631). His Service in the Dorian mode is still sung in cathedrals.

bewegt (Ger.), 'moved', i.e. with animation (It., *mosso*). *Bewegter*, faster (It., *piu mosso*). *Massig bewegt*, at a moderate speed.

beziffterer Bass (Ger.), figured bass.

Bianchi, Francesco (1752–1810), Italian opera composer and conductor. He was harpsichordist at the Théâtre Italien, Paris (1775–8), second *maestro di cappella* at Milan Cathedral (1783), second organist at St. Mark's, Venice (1785–93) and subsequently conducted at the King's Theatre, London, and in Dublin. Of his numerous operas the most popular was *La Villanella rapita* (Venice, 1783). Sir Henry Bishop was his pupil. He committed suicide in Hammersmith, London.

Biber, Heinrich Ignaz Franz von (1644–1704), German violinist and composer. He was in the service of the archbishop of Salzburg in 1673, becoming vice-*Kapellmeister* in 1680 and *Kapellmeister* in 1684. His works, which are often of considerable technical difficulty, consist of chamber compositions for various groups of instruments, including sonatas for violin and figured bass. Fifteen of the violin sonatas are associated with incidents in the life of Christ and his mother. There is also a Passacaglia for unaccompanied violin. Biber made considerable use of *scordatura*, i.e. modifications of the accepted tuning of the violin. Modern editions of his works are in *Denkmäler der Tonkunst in Osterreich*, xi (Jg. v, 2), and xxv (Jg. xii, 2), violin sonatas), xlix (Jg. xxv, 1), Mass), llix, (Jg. xxv, 2, lute music), (Jg. xxx, 1, Requiem), xcii, xcvi and xcvii (instrumental music).

bicinium (Lat.; *bis*, twice, and *canere*, to sing), a term used in Germany in the 16th century for a composition for two voices. It could equally well, however, be played on instruments, and extended in the early 17th century to include purely instrumental music in two parts.

Biggs, Edward George Power (1906–77), English organist, who became a U.S. citizen in 1938. He was known for his performances of Bach's works.

Bigot de Moroguès, Maria, *née* **Kiene** (1786–1820), Alsatian pianist who married M. Bigot, librarian to Count Rasumovsky in Vienna, where she met Haydn and Beethoven (1804–9). Beethoven seems to have been very much attached to her (*see* A. C. Kalischer, *Beethoven's Letters*, translated by J. S. Shedlock, volume 1, pages 136–8). In 1809 she and her husband moved to Paris, where Mendelssohn (aged seven) had lessons from her in 1816.

Billington, Elizabeth, *née* **Weichsel** (1765–1818), English operatic soprano, a pupil of J. C. Bach. Her father, Carl Weichsel (a native of Saxony), was principal oboe at the King's Theatre, London. Her debut, in 1783 in Dublin, was as Polly in *The Beggar's Opera*. She appeared at Covent Garden from 1786, and starred in Bianchi's *Ines de Castro* in Naples in 1794. The publications in 1792 of *Memoirs of Mrs. Billington*, reputed to be letters written to her mother, created a considerable scandal. She was at one time intimate with the Prince of Wales (later George IV). Her manners are said to have been 'distinguished by the utmost grossness, and in many instances by the most positive indelicacy', but she was a remarkable singer and had a great reputation on the Continent, as well as in England. Her portrait was painted by Reynolds.

Billy Budd, opera in four acts by Britten, to a libretto by E. M. Forster and Eric Crozier, after a story by Herman Melville. First performed in 1951 in London, the action takes place largely on board an 18th century man-o'-war, and tells of the execution of the gentle sailor, Billy, for the accidental killing of his tormentor, Claggart. The work is written for an all-male cast. A revized version, in two acts, was produced in 1961. A slightly earlier operatic setting of Melville's story was made by the Italian composer, Ghedini. His opera, in one act, has a libretto by Salvatore Quasimodo and was first performed in 1949 in Venice.

binary form, as the name implies, a piece of music in binary form is one that can be divided into two sections. This division is characteristic of a good deal of early dance music, where the structure is further emphasized by the repetition of each section. Dance forms were frequently employed by 17th century composers, both in keyboard music and in works for instrumental ensemble, and it was natural that they should transfer the form to pieces which had no association with the dance. In 17th century music, the first section may end (a) in the tonic key (b) on a half close (c) in a related key, i.e. the dominant or (in a piece in a minor key) the relative major. The second section naturally ends in the tonic key. The following is a miniature example, with the first section ending on a half close:

CORELLI, op 4, no 5

Of the possible endings of the first section mentioned above, the first, in the tonic key, was not wholly satisfactory, because it suggested a premature ending to the piece. The second type of ending, on a half close, was apt to sound indefinite. Hence the standard way of ending the first section came to be the third, i.e. the music modulated in the course of the section and the section ended with the establishment of a related key. As a result of this procedure, the first part of the second section had to be devoted to a modulation back to the tonic; and as modulation offered considerable opportunities for development, the second section came to be noticeably longer than the first, and the music frequently passed through several keys before reaching the tonic. This was the standard procedure in movements in binary form in the early 18th century.

Since recapitulation was a feature of the *da capo* aria, composers introduced it also into pieces in binary form, i.e. the whole (or a substantial part) of the first section would be repeated at the end of the second section but modified so that what was previously in the related key would now be in the tonic key. An example of this procedure is the prelude in D major from Book 2 of Bach's *Well-Tempered Clavier*. A further development, which occurred in the middle of the 18th century, was to make the contrast between the two key centres of the first section more vivid by a contrast of thematic material. This procedure was the basis of SONATA FORM as practised by composers in the second half of the 18th century, though even then there are examples (e.g. in Haydn's works) of movements in which there is very little thematic contrast or even none at all. Since the second section of a movement in sonata form was by now considerably longer than the first, the practice of repeating it soon died out. The practice of repeating the first section, however, survived till the end of the 19th century.

Binchois (de Binche), Gilles (c. 1400–60), Flemish composer, who was at first a soldier, then a priest. He was in the service of the Earl of Suffolk in Paris in 1424, and was chaplain to Philip, Duke of Burgundy, in 1430. He also held several canonries. Binchois excelled as a writer of songs, at which his fame rivalled that of Dufay. He also wrote sacred music. He was quick to adopt the 'English style' of Dunstable, Leonel Power and Bedyngham, and no doubt had close contacts with English musicians during his employment by the Earl of Suffolk. His songs have been edited by W. Rehm (1957), and sacred music by him is printed in C. van den Borren, *Polyphonia Sacra* (1932) and J. Marix, *Les Musiciens de la Cour de Bourgogne* (1937).

Bindungszeichen (Ger.), *see* SLUR (1)

bird organ, a miniature forerunner of the barrel organ originally made to teach songbirds to sing tunes. It was invented in the 17th century and is also known as the *serinette* (from the French word *serin*, meaning canary). Later bird organs were constructed to imitate bird song and built into cages of mechanical birds.

Birmingham Symphony Orchestra, City of, founded in 1920, this English orchestra was known originally simply as the City of Birmingham Orchestra. Its earliest conductor was Appleby Matthews (1902–4). His successors have included Sir Adrian Boult, Leslie Heward, George Weldon, Rudolf Schwartz, Andrzej Panufnik, Hugo Rignold and Louis Frémaux.

Birtwistle, Harrison (born 1934), English composer, born in Lancashire. Like Alexander Goehr, Peter Maxwell Davies and John Ogdon, he studied at the Royal Manchester College of Music and was a member of the so-called Manchester School. His works, which offer some uncompromisingly tough sonorities, include

an opera, *Punch and Judy*, which was hailed after its première as the only truly modern opera to have been composed in Britain up to that time. His abrasive chamber piece, *Tragoedia*, shares material with that opera. His other works include *Refrains and Choruses* for wind quintet, *Monody for Corpus Christi* for soprano, flute, violin and horn, and *The Triumph of Time*.

bis (Fr.), 'twice' (Lat., *bis*). An indication that the passage over which the word is written (generally with a bracket for the sake of clearness) is to be played twice. It is still to be found as a convenient abbreviation in manuscript music, but in printed music is obsolete.

bisbigliando (It.), 'whispering'. Term used by Strauss in his *Symphonia Domestica* to indicate the method of playing a quiet tremolando on the harp, and by Britten in *Peter Grimes* for a background figure on the celesta.

biscroma (It.), demisemiquaver.

Bishop, Henry Rowley (1786–1855), English composer and conductor. He held a number of appointments at London theatres, as well as professorships at Edinburgh and Oxford. He was knighted in 1842, the first British musician to be thus honoured. Bishop wrote and adapted a very large number of works for the stage and was responsible for vandalized versions of *Don Giovanni*, *The Barber of Seville* and *Fidelio*, into which he introduced music of his own. Though he composed some sixty operas, he is now known only by the songs 'Lo, here the gentle lark' (with flute obbligato) and 'Home, sweet home' (from the opera *Clari, or the Maid of Milan*, London, 1823).

bitonality, the use of two keys simultaneously, whether indicated by different key signatures or not. The following example illustrates the practice in its simplest form:

VAUGHAN WILLIAMS, *Flos Campi*

It will be noticed that the viola's A flat and G flat fit comfortably into the oboe's key as G sharp and F sharp. This use of notes which can have two different asso-

ciations is common in bitonality. However clear the
distinction may be between the two keys, the ear
instinctively seizes on any points that they may have
in common. Famous examples of bitonality are to be
found in Stravinsky's *Petrushka* and *The Rite of Spring*,
and in pieces by Milhaud. *See* also POLYTONALITY.

biwa, the Japanese LUTE.

Bizet, Georges, originally Alexandre César Léopold
Bizet (1838–1875), French composer. His musical
gifts became evident very early and his parents (also
musicians, his father being a singing teacher) sent him
to the Paris Conservatoire to study at the age of ten.
His teachers there included Marmontel, Gounod and
Halévy (whose daughter he later married). In 1857 he
won the *Prix de Rome*, by which time he had already
written (at the age of seventeen) his sparkling Symphony in C – a piece which did not come to light until
the present century but is now part of the standard
orchestral repertory – and his operetta, *Le Docteur
Miracle*, had won a prize in a competition sponsored by
Offenbach. During his three years in Rome he decided
that his future lay in opera, but when he returned to
Paris he had difficulty making his way. *The Pearl
Fishers*, staged at the Théâtre Lyrique in 1863, was
attacked by the critics. *Ivan the Terrible* (1865),
reputed to have been destroyed by the composer,
turned up during World War II and was performed in
Germany. In 1869, the conductor Pasdeloup recognized his qualities and invited him to write an orchestral
work, the *Roma* suite, and later conducted his *Patrie*
overture. In 1872, Bizet was commissioned to write
incidental music for Daudet's Provencal play, *L'Arlésienne*. The play was a failure, but the music lives on in
the form of two suites which contain the essence of
Bizet's musical personality. That essence also appears
in his last work, *Carmen*, on which he was already
engaged at the time of *L'Arlésienne*. This was unveiled
at the Opéra-Comique in 1875, where it had a run of
37 performances, in spite of opposition; on the day of
the 31st performance Bizet died. Though one of the
greatest of all French composers, Bizet was also a
tantalizing one. Public recognition failed to keep pace
with his musical gifts, which resulted in a lack of
self-confidence on his part. This resulted, in turn, in
his failure at times to make the most of his gifts. A
comparison with Berlioz, who was also badly treated,
would be apt, though Berlioz was a tougher musical
personality than Bizet. In the circumstances, we can
be thankful that he managed to complete a work as
vivid and dramatically true as *Carmen*, and as alive and
exquisitely coloured as *L'Arlésienne*. The rest of his
output included the operas *Don Procopio*, *The Fair
Maid of Perth*, *Djamileh*, *Jeux d'enfants* (the Children's
Games) suite for two pianos, a Nocturne and Chromatic Variations for solo piano, and a number of characteristic songs.

> *Lettres de Georges Bizet* (1907)
> G. BIZET: *Lettres à un ami* (1909)
> M. COOPER: *Georges Bizet* (1930)
> M. CURTISS: *Bizet and his World* (1959)
> W. DEAN: *Bizet* (1948)
> D. C. PARKER: *Georges Bizet – his Life and Works*
> (1926)

Björling, Jussi (1911–60), Swedish tenor, one of a
family of singers. He studied at the Royal Opera
School, Stockholm, and made his début there in
1930, as Ottavio in *Don Giovanni*. Later he sang at the
Metropolitan Opera, New York, La Scala, Milan,
Covent Garden, and other opera houses. He excelled
in Italian opera.

Blacher, Boris (born 1903), German composer born
in China. He studied in Berlin, and in 1954 became
director of the Hochschule für Musik, Berlin. His
music, freely contrapuntal in style and involving an
ingenious system of variable rhythmic metres, has
had a considerable influence on other composers.
His works include a 'scenic oratorio' on *Romeo and
Juliet*; an oratorio *The Grand Inquisitor* (after Dos-
toevsky's *Crime and Punishment*), two piano concertos,
a very successful set of orchestral variations on a
theme of Paganini, string quartets, piano music and
songs.

black pudding, another name for the serpent.

bladder and string, a folk instrument consisting of a
pole to which is attached an inflated bladder. A taut
string fastened to each end of the pole passes over the
bladder, and is bowed to give a sound. A bladder and
string is depicted in Hogarth's print *The Beggar's
Opera Burlesqued*.

Blamont, François Colin de (1690–1760), French
composer, pupil of Michel de Lalande. He was *Surin-
tendant* of the royal music (1719); *Maître de la musique
de la chambre* (1726). His works include ballets,
pastorales, cantatas and motets. His *divertissement*,
Le Retour des Dieux sur la Terre, was written for the
marriage of Louis XV in 1725.

blanche (Fr.), minim.

Blanchet, Elisabeth-Antoinette, *see* COUPERIN

Blangini, Giuseppe Marco Maria Felice (1781–
1841), Italian singer, teacher, and composer. He was
director of music to King Jerome of Westphalia
(Napoleon's brother) at Cassel (1809–14). Of his
numerous operas, the most important is *Nephtali
ou Les Ammonites* (Paris, 1806).

Blasinstrumente (Ger.), wind instruments.

Blavet, Michel (1700–68), French flautist and composer. His *Le Jaloux corrigé* (Berny, 1752) is mainly
compiled from arias in Italian comic operas which
were being performed at Paris at that time. It is one
of the earliest French *opéras-comiques*.

Blaze, *see* CASTIL-BLAZE

Blech, Harry (born 1910), English conductor and
violinist. From 1936 until 1950 he was leader of the
Blech Quartet, and since 1949 directed the London
Mozart Players.

Blech, Leo (1871–1958), German conductor and
composer, a pupil of Humperdinck. He held posts in
Prague, Berlin and Vienna. Blech's compositions
include symphonic poems, choral works, songs and
several operas, of which the one-act *Versiegellt*
(Hamburg, 1908) was the most popular.

Blechinstrumente (Ger.), brass instruments.

Bliss, Arthur (1891–1975), English composer, educated at Rugby and Cambridge, and at the Royal College
of Music, London, where he was a pupil of Stanford,
Vaughan Williams and Holst. He served in the army
during World War I, and during the succeeding years
composed a series of works – including *Rout* for
soprano and ten instruments (1919) and *Conversations*
(1919) – which suggested that a daringly experimental

talent had been born in Britain. His *Colour Symphony* (1922), based on the heraldic symbolism of primary colours, was also striking, but Bliss's later works revealed a change of direction. The independence and vigour of expression were still there, but were now related rather to the English romantic tradition. His knighthood in 1950 and his appointment as Master of the Queen's Music in 1953 seemed to consolidate his conservatism. Nevertheless, Bliss was a major British composer of his generation, and his output included impressive works in many forms. Among the most important of these are his *Music for Strings*, his dramatic piano concerto (New York, 1939), the orchestral *Variations on a theme by John Blow*, the clarinet and oboe quintets and the choral *Pastoral* (*Lie strewn the white flocks*). His stage works – the opera, *The Olympians* (with its libretto by J. B. Priestley, 1949), and the ballets *Checkmate*, *Miracle in the Gorbals* and *Adam Zero* – are currently in eclipse but may prove worthy of revival.

Blitheman, William (died 1591), English composer, noted as an organist and teacher of John Bull. He was a Gentleman of the Chapel Royal. Examples of his work are in the MULLINER book and the *Fitzwilliam Virginal Book*.

Blitzstein, Marc (1905–64), U.S. composer and pianist, a pupil of Nadia Boulanger and Arnold Schoenberg. His works, often politically motivated, include a choral opera (*The Condemned*) and several other operas, including *The Cradle will rock* (1937) and *No for an Answer* (1940). His symphonic poem, *Freedom Morning*, was dedicated to Negro troops of World War II; *The Airborne*, a choral work, was written for the U.S. Air Force. He also wrote a piano concerto, a string quartet and a piano sonata. In 1954 he produced a version of Kurt Weill's *Threepenny Opera*.

Bloch, Ernest (1880–1959), Swiss born composer, originally a pupil of Jaques-Dalcroze. He studied at Brussels Conservatoire and the Hoch Conservatorium, Frankfurt, and taught at Geneva Conservatoire before settling in the United States. After teaching at the David Mannes School, New York, he became director of the Cleveland Institute of Music in 1920 and at the San Francisco Conservatory (1925–30). He then returned to Switzerland for a spell, but – having already become a U.S. citizen – he moved back to the United States at the start of World War II. His music has been called typically Jewish in its intensity and conscious pathos, as well as in its love of orchestral colour. His best-known work is his Jewish rhapsody, *Shelomo* (Solomon) for cello and orchestra. He also wrote an opera on *Macbeth* (Paris, 1910), *Avodath Hakdesh* (Sacred Service) for baritone, chorus and orchestra, an *Israel Symphony* for voices and orchestra, a violin concerto, *Concerto Symphonique* for piano and orchestra, an *American Symphony*, concerto grosso for piano and strings, four string quartets, *Baal Shem* and other works for violin and piano, a piano quintet, piano sonata and songs.

M. TEBALDI-CHIESA: *Ernest Bloch* (1933)

block chords, a harmonic procedure whereby the notes of the chords move simultaneously in 'blocks', instead of in different contrapuntal directions. Debussy made use of the device in his piano pieces, and it was subsequently taken up by many modern jazz pianists (e.g. George Shearing).

Blockflöte (Ger.), recorder or beaked flute (Fr., *flûte-à-bec*).

Blockx, Jan (1851–1912), Belgian composer. He studied at the Flemish School of Music, Antwerp, and Leipzig Conservatorium, and in 1902 became director of the Royal Flemish Conservatoire. Like Peter Benoît, his predecessor as director, he was an enthusiastic supporter of Flemish nationalism. His compositions include a symphony, a symphonic triptych, cantatas and operas, one of them based on *Till Eulenspiegel*. His *Bruid der Zee* (*La Fiancée de la mer*, 1901) was successfully revived in Brussels in 1958.

Blodek, Vilem (1834–74), Czech flautist and composer. His numerous works include the one-act comic opera *V studni* (In the Well, Prague, 1867), in which there is an *intermezzo sinfonico* – a device which Mascagni used later in his *Cavalleria Rusticana* (1890).

Blom, Eric Walter (1888–1959), English critic. He was music critic of the *Birmingham Post* (1931–46) and of *The Observer* (1949–53), and editor, *Music and Letters* (1937–50, 1954–9). His books include *Mozart* (1930), *The Music Lover's Miscellany* (1935), *Beethoven's Sonatas Discussed* (1938), *A Musical Postbag* (1941), *Everyman's Dictionary of Music* (1946). He edited the fifth edition of Grove's *Dictionary of Music and Musicians*.

Blomdahl, Karl-Birger (1916–68), Swedish composer. His most famous work is his space-opera, *Aniara*, of which the Royal Opera, Stockholm, created a striking production. He also wrote three symphonies (no 3 entitled *Facets*), concertos for violin and viola, chamber music, and piano pieces. He was awarded a state grant in 1941. For a short time before his death, Blomdahl was director of the Swedish radio.

Blow, John (1649–1708), English composer and organist. He was brought up as a chorister in the Chapel Royal, where he was later master of the children (1674), organist (1676), and composer (1699), all three appointments being held till his death. He was also organist at Westminster Abbey from 1668 to 1679, and from 1695, and was master of the choristers at St. Paul's Cathedral from 1687 to 1693. He had several pupils, including Henry Purcell.

His music, which, though in general less vivid than Purcell's, has a similar independence of convention, includes numerous court odes, anthems, songs, harpsichord solos and a masque (which is virtually a miniature opera), *Venus and Adonis* (modern edition by Anthony Lewis, 1949). He published a collected edition of his songs under the title *Amphion Anglicus* (1700; facsimile edition, 1965) – an obvious imitation of Purcell's *Orpheus Britannicus*. A modern edition of his organ music by H. Watkins Shaw was published in 1958. His coronation anthems are printed in *Musica Britannica*, vii.

blues, the, the 'classical' Negro basis of American jazz. Evolving partly from spirituals (or black soul music as it is now called), but differing from these in that its emphasis was on solo voice rather than on choral utterances, the blues quickly established its own musical form: strictly, twelve bars long (instead of the usual eight or sixteen featured in much pop music), with each verse of the song consisting of three lines of four bars each (the second line usually repeating the first line), and with an unvarying chord-sequence acting as a ground bass. The occurrence of 'blue notes' – the minor third and seventh of the scale – is another characteristic feature, as is the use of the 'break' at the end of lines. Far from limiting its practitioners, the discipline of the blues has been one of the great incentives to jazz musicians, from the days of such primitive but superb blues singers as Bessie Smith and Ma Rainey right through to the more intellectual jazz spawned by the Charlie Parker revolution. A basic misconception about the blues is that it is sad. It often is, especially in the songs of Bessie Smith (though these are never self-pitying). But it is also often exuberant and joyous.

Blume, Friedrich (1893–1975), German musicologist. Among his several academic appointments was the professorship at Kiel University (1934–58). He edited the complete works of Praetorius and the collection of old choral music entitled *Das Chorwerk*. His most important book is his history of Protestant church music (1931) in Bücken's series, *Handbuch der Musikwissenschaft*. He edited the encyclopedia *Die Musik in Geschichte und Gegenwart*.

Blüthner, a firm of piano manufacturers, founded at Leipzig in 1853 by Julius Ferdinand Blüthner (1824–1910).

B minor Mass, a setting of the Latin text of the Mass for soloists, chorus and orchestra by Bach. The popular title is misleading, since only five of the twenty-four numbers are in B minor. The *Kyrie* and *Gloria* were written in 1733 to support Bach's application for the title of *Hofcomponist* (court composer) to Frederick Augustus II, Elector of Saxony, who also succeeded his father as King of Poland under the title Augustus III (*see* H. T. David and A. Mendel, *A Bach Reader*, pages 128–9). Augustus was a Roman Catholic, but the two movements set by Bach were equally suitable for the Lutheran liturgy. Bach subsequently completed the work by adding settings of the *Credo*, *Sanctus* and *Agnus Dei*. He adapted the following numbers from earlier works:

no 6: *Gratias agimus* from Cantata no 29, *Wir danken dir*.

no 8: *Qui tollis* from Cantata no 46, *Schauet doch und sehet*.

no 13: *Patrem omnipotentem* from Cantata no 171, *Gott, wie dein Name*.

no 16: *Crucifixus* from Cantata no 12, *Weinen, Klagen*.

no 19 (second part): *Et exspecto resurrectionem* from Cantata no 120, *Gott, man lobt dich in der Stille*.

no 21: *Osanna* from the secular cantata *Preise dein Glucke*.

no 23: *Agnus Dei* from Cantata no 11, *Lobet Gott in seinen Reichen*.

no 24: *Dona nobis pacem* from no 6, *Gratias agimus*.

In addition to the B minor Mass, Bach wrote four other Masses, each consisting of settings of the *Kyrie* and *Gloria* only.

C. S. TERRY: *Bach – the Mass in B minor* (1924)

D. F. TOVEY: *Essays in Musical Analysis*, volume 5 (1937), pages 20–49

Boatswain's Mate, The, comic opera in one act by Ethel Smyth, to a libretto by the composer (founded on a story by W. W. Jacobs); first performed in 1916 in London.

Bobillier, Antoinette Christine Marie, *see* BRENET

bocca chiusa (It.), singing with closed lips (Fr., *bouche fermée*).

Boccherini, Luigi (1743–1805), Italian composer and cellist, born in Lucca. His father was a double-bass player who sent him to study in Rome. Later he toured widely as a cellist, and in 1768 won a great reputation in Paris, where he published his first chamber music. In 1769 he settled in Madrid, where the Infante Don Luis became his patron. From 1786 until 1797 he was chamber composer to Friedrich Wilhelm II of Prussia, but subsequently suffered neglect and died in poverty in Madrid. He was a prolific composer of string quintets (125 in all, one of them including the famous Boccherini minuet), and almost equally prolific in other forms. He wrote 102 string quartets, sixty string trios, 27 violin sonatas and much other chamber music. Of his four cello concertos, the one in B flat major is a staple of the cello repertory. He also composed oratorios, cantatas and other church music, and an opera, *Clementina*.

Bodansky, Arthur (1877–1939), Austrian conductor who studied at the Vienna Conservatorium and became assistant to Mahler at the Imperial Opera. After holding a number of European posts, he moved on to become a conductor at the New York Metropolitan in 1915 and was conductor of the New York Society of the Friends of Music from 1918 until 1931.

Boehm, *see also* BÖHM

Boehm, Theobald (1794–1881), German flautist. He was attached to the Munich court and invented an improved mechanism for the flute, since known as the Boehm system and applied to other instruments, including the clarinet. In the Boehm system, an elaborate mechanism allows the holes to be pierced in the correct positions and at the same time to be easily controlled by the fingers (for details see Adam Carse, *Musical Wind Instruments*, pages 94–9). The effect of this is to facilitate accurate intonation and also the playing of passages in keys that were formerly difficult.

Boethius, Anicius Manlius Severinus (c. 480–524), Roman philosopher and statesman. He was consul in 510, and *Magister officiorum* at the court of Theodoric at Ravenna in 522. He was executed by Theodoric. His best-known work is *De consolatione philosophiae*. His treatise *De institutione musica*, based on Greek sources, was a standard text book throughout the Middle Ages; it is included in the Teubner edition of his works, edited by G. Friedlein (1867).

bogen (Ger.; It., *arco*), 'bow' – in string parts used, like *arco*, to contradict a preceding *pizzicato*.

Bohème, La (Bohemian Life), opera in four acts by Puccini, to a libretto by Giuseppe Giacosa and Luigi Illica (founded on Henri Murger's *Scènes de la vie de Bohème*). The first performance, conducted by Toscanini at Turin in 1896, was not the instant success one might have expected. The work took time to establish itself, though it is now one of the three most popular of Puccini's operas. The story deals with the life of the Latin Quarter in Paris and is particularly concerned with the respective love affairs of Rodolfo and Mimi, and Marcello and Musetta, which are not uniformly happy. Rodolfo and Mimi separate. When they are finally reunited it is too late; Mimi dies of consumption. Leoncavallo's *La Bohème* (Venice, 1897) deals with the same subject, but has been over-shadowed by Puccini's opera.

Böhm, *see also* BOEHM

Böhm, Georg (1661–1733), German organist and composer, who worked at Hamburg and Luneburg (from 1698). His compositions include church music and a large number of works for organ and harpsichord, including chorale preludes and suites.

Böhm, Karl (born 1894), Austrian conductor. He studied at the Graz Conservatorium and in Vienna, and became conductor of the Graz Opera in 1918. Later appointments were at Munich (1921), Darmstadt (1927), Hamburg (1931), Dresden (1934) and the Vienna State Opera (1954). Today he is the *éminence grise* of the Salzburg Festival, and has long been regarded as one of the world's leading conductors of Mozart and Strauss – whose *Schweigsame Frau* (1935) and *Daphne* (1938) had their first performances directed by him.

Boieldieu, François Adrien (1775–1834), French opera composer. He studied with the organist of Rouen Cathedral and his first opera, *La Fille coupable*, was produced at Rouen in 1793. He taught piano and composition at the Paris Conservatoire, and was conductor of the Imperial Opera, St. Petersburg, from 1803 until 1811. Of his numerous operas, the most successful were *Le Calife de Bagdad* (Paris, 1800) and *La Dame blanche* (Paris 1825), the latter founded on Scott's *Guy Mannering* and *The Monastery*. He also wrote a certain amount of instrumental music.

bois (Fr.), wood. *Instruments de bois* (or *bois* alone), woodwind instruments.

Boito, Arrigo (1842–1918), Italian composer, poet

Arrigo Boito, composer and poet turned librettist who inspired Verdi to write his two greatest works after the composer had considered himself retired

and librettist. He studied at the Milan Conservatory, and in France and Germany (with a travelling scholarship). His first opera, *Mefistofele*, was performed at Milan in 1868, without success in spite of the enthusiasm of a minority. After revision it became more popular. His (unfinished) second opera, *Nerone* (Nero), was not performed until 1924. Championed by Toscanini at La Scala, Milan, it failed to hold its place in the repertory, though its sincerity and intelligence won it some dedicated admirers. Boito is likely to be remembered chiefly for his brilliant librettos, closely modelled on Shakespeare, for Verdi's *Otello* and *Falstaff*.

bolero, a Spanish dance in moderate triple time, the characteristic rhythm being marked on the castanets, e.g.

The dance has been made particularly popular in the concert by Ravel's orchestral piece with this title (1928). He uses an unremitting bolero rhythm as the basis of a long, slow orchestral crescendo.

bombard, a double-reed instrument, now obsolete, the bass of the SHAWM family.

bombarde, an organ reed stop of great power made at eight foot, sixteen foot and 32 foot pitches.

bombardon, a term used in military bands for the bass TUBA.

bones, pairs of small sticks held in each hand and clicked together rhythmically. Bones are primitive castanets and have been known since medieval times. They were made originally of ox rib, hence their name.

bongo (pl. **bongoes**), a small Cuban drum usually played in pairs and with the fingers.

Bonno, Giuseppe (1710–88), Austrian composer, who studied in Naples and became composer to the Imperial court at Vienna (1739) and *Kapellmeister* there (1774). His numerous compositions include twenty works for the stage, and three oratorios. Mozart spoke of him with affection (see Emily Anderson, *Letters of Mozart and his Family*, page 1076).

Bononcini, Giovanni Maria (1642–78), Italian composer and theorist. He was court musician to the Duke of Modena, and *maestro di cappella*, Modena Cathedral. His works include chamber sonatas, solo cantatas and a treatise on counterpoint, *Musico prattico* (1673; facsimile reprint, 1969).

His son, **Giovanni Bononcini** (1670–c. 1747), was a composer and cellist. After holding various posts in Italy, Austria and Germany he moved to London in 1720 and was supported by the Duke of Marlborough. Though he wrote operas for the newly founded Royal Academy of Music (a company for performing Italian opera), of which Handel was one of the directors, a rivalry grew up between him and Handel, which was encouraged by his aristocratic supporters for political reasons. The rivalry is commemorated in John Byrom's epigram:

Some say, compar'd to Bononcini,
That Mynheer Handel's but a ninny;
Others aver that he to Handel
Is scarcely fit to hold a candle.
Strange, all this difference should be
'Twixt Tweedledum and Tweedledee.

(The verb 'to tweedle' meant to play an instrument in a trifling manner). Bononcini left England in 1732 and subsequently lived in Paris, Vienna and Venice. He wrote a large number of operas (several for London), oratorios, cantatas, etc. His one-act opera *Polifemo* (1702) is the first extant opera produced at Berlin (modern edition by G. Kärnbach, 1938).

The younger son, **Antonio Maria Bononcini** (1674–1726), was also a composer. In 1721 he became *maestro di cappella* to the Duke of Modena. His works include twenty operas and three oratorios. His most successful opera, *Il trionfo di Camilla* (Naples, 1696), was one of the first Italian operas to be given in London, where it was performed (at first in English) in 1706.

Bonporti, Francesco Antonio (1672–1749), Italian composer of chamber music, including trio sonatas and solo sonatas. He trained for the priesthood in Rome from 1691, and studied music with Corelli and Pitoni. Four of his *Invenzioni* for violin and figured bass (1712) were copied by Bach and mistakenly published by the *Bach Gesellschaft*.

boogie-woogie, sometimes abbreviated to 'boogie', a JAZZ style, a special type of piano BLUES which became popular in the late 1930s and early 1940s. It is characterized by a continuous, sharply rhythmic *ostinato* bass played by the left hand, while the right hand provides melody, adhering to a twelve bar period, although with great rhythmic variety and improvisation within that framework.

Boosey, a London firm of music-publishers and manufacturers of musical instruments, founded in 1816 by Thomas Boosey and since 1930 amalgamated with Hawkes and Son as Boosey and Hawkes, Ltd.

bop (**bebop, rebop**), JAZZ style which was developed in New York at the end of World War II. It is distinguished by solos using dissonant chords, complex rhythms, and a continuous, mainly improvised melodic line. Through the charismatic playing of Dizzy Gillespie, Miles Davis and Charlie 'Bird' Parker, bop revolutionized jazz.

Bordoni, Faustina (1700–1781) Italian soprano, a pupil of Gasparini. She first appeared in opera in Venice in 1716 (where she was nicknamed 'The New Siren'), and subsequently in Naples, Florence and Vienna. She was taken to London by Handel in 1726 and sang there for two seasons. She married the composer Johann Adolf Hasse in 1730. Her notorious rivalry with Francesca Cuzzoni in London was satirized in *The Beggar's Opera* (1728).

bore (It.), **boree,** *see* BOURRÉE

bore, the diameter of the tube of a wind instrument.

Boris Godunov, opera with a prologue and four acts by Mussorgsky, to a libretto by the composer (after Pushkin's *Boris Godunov* and Karamzin's *History of the Russian Empire*). Though rejected by the St. Petersburg Opera in 1870, and thereafter subject to much revision by the composer and others, *Boris Godunov* is well established today as the greatest of all Russian operas. The story dates from about 1600. Boris Godunov has murdered Dmitri, heir to the throne, and has become Tsar. A young monk, Gregory, pretends to be Dmitri, and wins support from the people. Boris, overcome by remorse and terror, entrusts the succession to his son Feodor and dies.

Of the several versions of the opera, including a long-established one by Rimsky-Korsakov and a more recent one by Shostakovich, the best can be described as the one that comes closest to Mussorgsky's own intentions. In other words, conductors and producers should take Mussorgsky as their starting point, rather than, say, the Rimsky disarrangement, which over-colours the orchestration, 'corrects' the harmony, and throws the emphasis on Boris rather than on the Russian people, who, in their tremendous choruses, reveal themselves as the real heroes (and villains) of the piece. Properly the opera should end with the scene in the Kromy Forest, and with the Idiot bewailing the fate of Russia, rather than with the more 'operatic' (if moving) death of Boris, as preferred by Rimsky.

Alexander Borodin divided his creative ability between chemistry and music, but was one of the influential group who put Russian national music firmly on the European map

Borodin, Alexander Porfirevich (1833–87), Russian composer and scientist. Born in St. Petersburg, he was the illegitimate son of a prince, who registered him as the son of one of his serfs. In 1862 he became assistant professor of organic chemistry, Academy of Medicine, St. Petersburg, and two years later he rose to professor. He had begun composing as a boy and was much stimulated by meeting Balakirev in 1862. Between 1862 and 1867 he wrote his first symphony, which was performed under Balakirev in

1869. His other works, which were not numerous, include two more symphonies (the third unfinished but performable as a torso in Glazunov's arrangement), *In the steppes of Central Asia* for orchestra, two string quartets, two operas – *Bogatyri*, a parody (Moscow, 1867) and *Prince Igor* (completed after his death by Rimsky-Korsakov and Glazunov), and songs. He also published a number of scientific papers. He was one of the most strongly national of all the 19th century Russian composers, drawing his inspiration from Russian folksong and also owing something to Oriental influences.

> G. ABRAHAM: *Borodin: the Composer and the Man* (1922); *Studies in Russian Music* (1935)
>
> M. D. CALVOCORESSI & G. ABRAHAM: *Masters of Russian Music* (1936)

Borren, Charles Jean Eugene van den (1874–1966), Belgian musicologist. His numerous books include *L'Oeuvre dramatique de César Franck* (1907), *Les Origines de la musique de clavier en Angleterre* (1912, published in English as *The sources of keyboard music in England*), *Les Origines de musique de clavier dans les Pays-Bas* (1914), *Orlande de Lassus* (1920), *Guillaume Dufay* (1925), *Etudes sur le quinzième siècle musical* (1941). His editions of old music include *Polyphonia Sacra: a continental miscellany of the fifteenth century* (1932) and several of the works of Philippe de Monte.

borry, *see* BOURRÉE

Boschot, Adolphe (1871–1955), French music critic, who specialized in the study of Berlioz. His books include a life of Berlioz, entitled *Histoire d'un romantique* (three volumes, 1906–13), *Chez les musiciens* (*du xviii siècle à nos jours*) (three volumes, 1922–6), *Mozart* (1935) and *Musiciens poètes* (1937).

Bösendorfer, a firm of piano manufacturers, founded in Vienna in 1828 by Ignaz Bösendorfer (1796–1859).

Bossi, Marco Enrico (1861–1925), Italian organist and composer. In addition to organ works, he wrote operas, choral music, orchestral music and chamber music.

His son, **Renzo Bossi** (1883–1965), was also a composer. His compositions include operas (one of them, *Rosa Rossa*, after Oscar Wilde, and another based on Shakespeare's *Taming of the Shrew*), orchestral works and chamber music.

Boston Symphony Orchestra, founded at Boston, Massachusetts, by H. L. Higginson in 1881. Its first conductor was Sir George Henschel (1881–4), whose successors have included Wilhelm Gericke, Artur Nikisch, Emil Paur, Karl Muck, Max Fiedler, Henri Rabaud, Pierre Monteux, Serge Koussevitzky, Charles Münch and Erich Leinsdorf.

Bote and Bock, a Berlin firm of music publishers, founded in 1838 by Edouard Bote and Gustav Bock.

Botstiber, Hugo (1875–1942), Austrian musicologist. He held various important administrative posts in Vienna, and completed C. F. Pohl's biography of Haydn by adding a third volume (1927). He also wrote a history of the overture (1913).

Bottesini, Giovanni (1821–89), Italian double-bass virtuoso, conductor and composer. His execution and beauty of tone were much admired. His compositions include several operas, of which *Ero e Leandro* (Turin, 1879) was the most successful, and an oratorio, *The Garden of Olivet* (Norwich Festival, 1887).

Bottrigari, Ercole (1531–1612), Italian author. He wrote the dialogue *Il desiderio, overo de' concerti di varii strumenti musicali*, which gives a valuable picture of musical life and practice in an Italian court of the late 16th century. The first edition (1594) was published under a pseudonym. A facsimile of the second edition (1599) was edited by K. Meyer in 1924, and an English translation by C. MacClintock was published in 1962.

bouche fermée (Fr.), singing with closed lips (It., *bocca chiusa*).

bouchés, *see* SONS BOUCHES

bouffe, *see* OPÉRA-BOUFFE

Bouffons, *see* GUERRE DES BOUFFONS

Boughton, Rutland (1878–1960), English opera composer. He studied at the Royal College of Music, London under Stanford and Walford Davies and taught at the Midland Institute School of Music, Birmingham (1904–11). He settled at Glastonbury, Somerset, with a view to writing a series of operas on the Arthurian legends and establishing a permanent home for their performance. The scheme was never completed, but his two-act opera *The Immortal Hour* was performed there in 1914, followed in subsequent years by other productions. *The Immortal Hour*, produced in Birmingham (1921) and London (1922), was for a time extremely popular, largely on account of its tunefulness and romantic colouring. In London it ran for more than 200 performances. The later operas, which include *Alkestis* (1922), *The Queen of Cornwall* (1924) and *The Lily Maid* (1934), were less successful.

Boulanger, Juliette Nadia (born 1887), French composer and teacher, famous for having taught many distinguished musicians. She studied at the Paris Conservatoire, where she was later appointed professor. During World War II she lived in the United States. She has been active in reviving old music, including the works of Monteverdi.

Her sister, **Lili Juliette Marie Olga Boulanger** (1893–1918) was also a composer. She studied at the Paris Conservatoire, and was the first woman to win the *Grand Prix de Rome* (1913). Her compositions include symphonic poems; a cantata, *Faust and Helen*; chamber music and songs.

Boulez, Pierre (born 1925), French composer, conductor and pianist, one of the most important figures of modern music. Born at Montbrison, he began his career as a mathematician, but abandoned this in favour of studying music under Messiaen at the Paris Conservatoire. He also took a course in serial technique under René Leibowitz. In 1953, with Jean-Louis Barrault and Madeleine Renaud, he founded the Domaine Musical in Paris, an organisation specializing in the promotion and performance of new music. Previously, he had been director of music at Barrault's Paris theatre.

Though he no longer works for the Domaine, he has continued to promote 20th century music in his concerts with the New York Philharmonic, and, in London, the B.B.C. Symphony Orchestra. A typical Boulez programme might include an 18th or 19th century work in which he is interested (e.g. a piece of Handel or Schubert), a 20th century 'classic' by Schoenberg, Berg, Webern, Bartók or Stravinsky, and a modern work by himself or someone else.

Pierre Boulez; conductor and composer, a creative force in French musical life since 1950

In recent years it has seemed that Boulez's active career as a conductor has prevented him from devoting enough time to composition. More cynical observers have claimed that his conducting is a compensation for a loss of compositional steam. Be that as it may, he has already composed enough to make him one of the most challenging and widely-discussed composers of the day. His early *Marteau sans Maître* (The Hammer without a Master) for voice and chamber ensemble, which seemed so daunting when first performed, has already become a modern classic; and the same can be said for the large-scale *Pli selon pli* (Fold upon fold), a setting of Mallarmé for soprano and orchestra, composed in stages between 1958 and 1962. His other works include *Le Soleil des eaux* for voices, chorus and orchestra, after René Char; three piano sonatas (1946, 1948 and 1957); *Structures* I and II for two pianos (1952 and 1961); and *Livre* for string quartet.

Boult, Adrian Cedric (born 1889), English conductor. He studied at Christ Church, Oxford, and Leipzig Conservatorium, and joined the staff of Covent Garden in 1914. He conducted the first performance of Holst's *The Planets* in 1918. Four years later Boult became conductor of the City of Birmingham Orchestra. From 1930 until 1942 he was musical director of the B.B.C. in London, and from 1930 until 1949 was conductor of the B.B.C. Symphony Orchestra. Boult conducted many orchestras in Europe and the United States. He excels in performances of the classics and of the music of Elgar, Vaughan Williams and Walton. He published a short *Handbook on the Technique of Conducting*, and a volume of autobiography, *My own Trumpet*.

bourdon, Fr., literally 'burden': (1) a drone bass, such

as that produced on the lowest strings of the HURDY-GURDY;

(2) a soft organ stop, employing stopped pipes generally of sixteen feet tone.

Bourgault-Ducoudray, Louis Albert (1840–1910), French composer. He studied at the Paris Conservatoire and won the *Grand Prix de Rome* in 1862. He was one of the first to draw attention to the possibilities for composers of modal and non-European scales. His numerous compositions include five operas, choral works and orchestral pieces. He also published collections of Greek, Breton, Welsh and Scottish folksongs.

bourrée (Fr.; Eng., borry, boree; It., *bore*), (1) a French dance in brisk duple time, starting on the third quarter of the bar:

BACH, *Suites for Cello Solo no 3*

It appears to have originated about the beginning of the 17th century. In the 18th century suite it was one of the *Galanterien*, or optional dances inserted between the SARABANDE and the GIGUE. Two bourrées were often written to form a contrasted pair, as was also done with the MINUET and the GAVOTTE.

(2) a dance in triple time, still current in Auvergne:

PURCELL (*Purcell Society*, volume vi, page 55)

bouzouki, a fretted string instrument of Greece. It is played by plucking the strings with much use of tremolo to prolong the notes. The *bouzouki* enjoyed a great revival in the 1960s when several Greek composers, notably Mikis Theodorakis, exploited the sound of the instrument and made it known internationally.

bow (Fr., *archet*; Ger., *Bogen*; It., *arco*), instruments of the viol and violin families are played with a bow, which consists of horse-hair strung on a wooden stick. The name 'bow' is due to the fact that the original shape of the stick was convex. The tension of the hair can be varied by means of an adjustable nut attached to one end of the stick. The shape of the bow has varied from time to time. In Bach's day, for example, a slightly convex bow was in use in Germany, so that the playing of chords in works like the unaccompanied sonatas and partitas for solo violin was much easier than it is today. The modern bow was established by François Tourte (1747–1835) at the end of the 18th century. It is a little longer than the earlier 18th-century bows; the stick tapers towards the point (i.e. the end furthest from the hand) and is slightly curved towards the hair. The bows used for the viola, cello and double-bass are similar to those used for the violin, but progressively heavier. Cello bows are also shorter, and double-bass bows shorter still.

bowed harp, a primitive violin first depicted in a Norwegian carving of the 12th century. The strings, two to four in number, passed over a bridge, and were stopped by passing the hand through a hole in the top of the rectangular body. The instrument was held vertically on the knee and bowed so that the strings sounded simultaneously to give a drone beneath a melody. Very similar is the six-stringed CRWTH or crowd of ancient Wales and Brittany, which survived until the last century.

bowing, in general, the technique of playing a string instrument with a bow.

In particular, the method of playing notes or passages, indicated by conventional signs, a 'goalposts' sign indicating a down-bow, i.e. the arm moving from left to right, and a 'V' sign indicating an up-bow, i.e. the arm moving from right to left. A strong down-bow ensures a good attack; the increased pressure possible with an up-bow, after the bow has already touched the string, helps to produce a steady crescendo. If two or more notes are to be played without changing the direction of the bow, a slur is placed over them, e.g.:

ELGAR, *Symphony no 2*

This passage begins with an up-bow. The D, B flat and C in the second bar are played with a single down-bow, the D and C following are played with a single up-bow, the E flat and D at the end of the bar are played with a down-bow and up-bow respectively, and the passage ends with a down-bow on the C in the third bar.

There is normally no perceptible break between two consecutive notes, one of which is played with an up-bow and the other with a down-bow. If a note is to be detached from its neighbour a horizontal stroke is placed above it, e.g.:

ELGAR, *Enigma Variations*

It is also possible to detach notes slightly without changing the direction of the bow. This is indicated by combining the slur and the horizontal stroke, e.g.:

CHAIKOVSKY, *Symphony no 5*

Notes can also be played staccato without changing the direction of the bow; in this case the slur is combined with dots, e.g.:

CHAIKOVSKY, *Symphony no 6*

Unfortunately composers are not always consistent in their use of these signs, nor are their indications of bowing always practicable. It is one of the duties of the leader of an orchestra, or of a particular section of the strings, to ensure that the bowing marks are adequate and to correct or amplify them where necessary. Some conductors carefully mark the bowing in their scores and then have the marks transferred to the parts. Preparation of this kind contributes a good deal to an effective performance.

The following terms indicate particular methods of using the bow: (a) *col legno*, lit. 'with the wood', i.e. bouncing the stick on the strings instead of playing with the hair of the bow (e.g. Holst, *The Planets*, no 1, *Mars*); (b) *a punta d'arco*, with the point of the bow; (c) *am Frosch* (Ger.) *au talon* (Fr.), with the nut or heel of the bow (i.e. the end nearest the hand); (d) *sul tasto* or *sulla tastiera* (It.), *sur la touche* (Fr.), *am Griffbrett* (Ger.), on the fingerboard, i.e. play near, or actually above the fingerboard, thus producing a rather colourless tone; (e) *sul ponticello* (It.), *au chevalet* (Fr.), *am Steg* (Ger.), on the bridge, i.e. play near the bridge, thus producing a glassy, brittle tone; (f) *martellato* (It.), *martelé* (Fr.), literally 'hammered', heavy, detached up-and-down strokes, played with the point of the bow, without taking the bow from the string; (g) *flautando* or *flautato*, playing like a flute, i.e. producing a light, rather colourless tone, which is done by playing gently near the end of the fingerboard; (h) *spiccato*, literally 'clearly articulated', a light staccato played with the middle of the bow and a loose wrist; (i) *saltando* (It.), *sautillé* (Fr.), allowing the bow to bounce lightly on the string.

Boyce, William (1711–79), English composer and organist. He was a chorister of St. Paul's Cathedral and a pupil of Maurice Greene. He held various organ posts in London, became Composer to the Chapel Royal in 1736, conductor of the Three Choirs Festival in 1737, Master of the King's Musick in 1755 and organist of the Chapel Royal in 1758. He suffered from deafness which increased as time went on. His compositions include church music, cantatas and odes, twenty symphonies, chamber music, and works for the stage. His music for the play *Harlequin's Invasion* (1759) includes the song 'Heart of oak', commemorating the British victories of that year, the *annus mirabilis*. He completed a collection of church music begun by Maurice Greene and published it in three volumes under the title *Cathedral Music*.

Boyd Neel Orchestra, *see* NEEL

Brabançonne, La, the Belgian national anthem written in 1830, when Belgium was struggling free from Holland.

brace, a vertical line, generally accompanied by a bracket, used to join two or more staves together:

Brade, William (c. 1560–1630), English viol-player
and composer, who held several court appointments in
Denmark and Germany. He published on the Continent several volumes of concerted instrumental
music, mostly dance movements, including *Newe
ausserlesene Paduanen, Galliarden, Cantzonen, All-
mand und Coranten* (1609; reprinted in C. R. B.
Engelke, *Musik und Musiker am Gottorfer Hofe*,
1930).

Braham, John (1777–1856), English tenor of Jewish
birth (originally Abraham). He first appeared at Covent
Garden as a boy soprano in 1787, and as a tenor at
Drury Lane in 1796. He was the original Sir Huon in
Weber's *Oberon* (London, 1826). In his later years he
lost much money through theatrical speculations. His
music for *The Americans* (1811) includes the song 'The
Death of Nelson'. According to Leigh Hunt, his voice
in Handel's arias 'became a veritable trumpet of
grandeur and exaltation.'

Brahms, Johannes (1833–97), German composer.
Born in Hamburg, he was the son of a double-bass
player in the orchestra of the Hamburg Stadttheater.
He received his first music lessons from his father, and
(unlike Beethoven's) his home life seems to have been
happy, if humble. Though intended to be an orchestral
player, he soon showed such aptitude for the piano that
his parents hoped to make a prodigy of him. This
ambition was thwarted by Brahms's teacher, Cossel.
After leaving school, Brahms eked out his living for a
while by playing in sailors' taverns and dancing saloons.
In 1853 his career advanced when he toured North
Germany with the Hungarian gypsy violinist, Eduard
Reményi, and composed his first substantial work, the
C major piano sonata, op 1. That year also marked the
start of his friendship with the great violinist, Joseph
Joachim, who arranged for him to meet Liszt and
Schumann – the latter prophesied his genius in the
Neue Zeitschrift für Musik. Schumann's attempted
suicide in 1854, and subsequent madness, deeply
disturbed Brahms, which can be heard in his D minor
piano concerto (1858) and other works he was sketch-
ing around that time; his mental turmoil was increased
by his (largely suppressed) love for Clara Schumann,
who took great professional interest in him, though
neither of them was prepared to let their relationship
blossom into marriage after Schumann's death (Brahms
remained a bachelor all his life). In 1857 he became
director of music to the Prince of Lippe-Detmold, a
part-time post, which gave him time to write his two
orchestral serenades, the first version of his G minor
piano quartet, op 25, and to complete his D minor
piano concerto. But Hamburg remained his home
base until in 1863 he was invited to become conductor
of the Singakademie in Vienna. Having recently
failed to win the conductorship of the Hamburg
Philharmonic, he accepted the Vienna appointment
and spent the rest of his life in the Austrian capital,
leaving it only for his concert tours and holidays. The
death of his mother in 1865 inspired part of his
German Requiem, on which he had been working since

Johannes Brahms: not the stock avuncular likeness but a
study of a more intense figure from a period when he was
already forty and still had his major symphonic works to
write

1857 and which he completed in 1868, using texts from
Luther's German translation of the Bible. In 1872 he
was appointed artistic director of the Gesellschaft der
Musikfreunde in Vienna, in succession to Rubinstein.
The orchestral version of his *Variations on the St.
Anthony Chorale* (formerly known as the *Variations on
a theme of Haydn*), a work which also exists in a version
for two pianos, was given its première the following
year by the Vienna Philharmonic. In 1875, Brahms
resigned from Gesellschaft der Musikfreunde, and
worked on his first symphony during a holiday near
Heidelberg. Brahms took his responsibilities as a post-
Beethoven symphonist with the utmost seriousness.
Though he began his first symphony in his early
twenties, he did not complete it until he was 43. After
its première at Karlsruhe, it was soon being hailed as
'Beethoven's Tenth'; and when someone spotted the
similarity between the main theme of the finale and the
corresponding theme in Beethoven's ninth symphony,
Brahms said 'any donkey can see that'. Certainly the
Beethoven comparison did not deter him from completing his second symphony the following year (1877),
his violin concerto in 1879, his second piano concerto in
1881, and the third and fourth symphonies in 1883 and
1885. His later years, though uneventful in themselves, enhanced his reputation as one of the greatest
composers of the day. His music at that time gained a

touching autumnal beauty, and a new intimacy of expression, in such works as the clarinet quintet and clarinet trio (1891), written for the Meiningen clarinettist, Richard Mühlfeld. In 1896 he attended the funeral of Clara Schumann at Bonn, a journey that damaged his already weak health. Cirrhosis of the liver was diagnosed, and he died the following year.

Brahms's music reflects both the austerity of his North German home and the sensuous charm of Vienna. Both these facets of his work are illustrated in one of his largest compositions, the *German Requiem*. He was also influenced by his early experience of Hungarian gypsy music, not only in his so-called Hungarian Dances but also in passages of such works as the clarinet quintet. Another influence was German folksong, detectable in many of his works and the subject of his delightful and substantial collection of *Volkslieder* for voice and piano. Of all the romantic composers, Brahms was the most successful in reconciling the conflicting claims of lyricism and classical form. His unwillingness to join the musical 'progressives' of the period, and the tactless stand he made during his earlier years against the 'New German' school headed by Liszt, resulted in his being disparaged by some musicians (e.g., Hugo Wolf) and admired by others (e.g., Hanslick), who used him as their principal weapon against unhealthy Wagnerism. In the long run, however, his reputation did not suffer too much from all this – neither did Wagner's – and modern listeners are able to accept both composers as major figures of 19th century music.

Brahms's principal compositions are:

(1) Orchestra: two serenades; four symphonies; two piano concertos; violin concerto; concerto for violin and cello; *Variations on the St. Anthony Chorale*; *Academic Festival Overture*; *Tragic Overture*;

(2) Choral works: *Ein deutsches Requiem*; *Rinaldo*; Rhapsody (alto solo, male chorus and orchestra); *Schicksalslied* (Song of destiny): *Triumphlied* (Song of triumph); *Gesang der Parzen* (Song of the Fates);

(3) Chamber music: two string sextets; two string quintets; three string quartets; clarinet quintet; piano quintet; three piano quartets; three piano trios; trio for clarinet, cello and piano; trio for violin, horn and piano; three violin sonatas; two cello sonatas; two clarinet sonatas;

(4) Piano solos: three sonatas; variations (a) on a theme of Schumann (b) on an original theme (c) on a Hungarian theme (d) on a theme by Paganini (two sets); variations and fugue on a theme of Handel; three rhapsodies; intermezzi, capriccios, ballades, etc.;

(5) Piano duet: variations (a) on a theme of Schumann (b) on a theme of Haydn (for two pianos); sonata for two pianos (= the piano quintet); *Liebeslieder* waltzes and *Neue Liebeslieder* waltzes (with optional voice parts); Hungarian dances.

(6) Organ: eleven chorale preludes.

(7) Songs: nearly two hundred solo songs; duets; folksong arrangements.

Brahms was keenly interested in the revival of old music and edited Couperin's keyboard works for Chrysander's *Denkmäler der Tonkunst*.

J. A. FULLER MAITLAND: *Brahms* (1911)

H. GAL: *Brahms* (1968)

K. GEIRINGER: *Brahms; his Life and Work* (1936)

J. HARRISON: *Brahms and his Four Symphonies* (1939)

B. JAMES: *Brahms: a Critical Study* (1972)

P. LATHAM: *Brahms* (1948, revised 1966)

D. E. MASON: *The Chamber Music of Brahms* (1933)

F. MAY: *The Life of Johannes Brahms* (two volumes, second edition, 1948)

W. MURDOCH: *Brahms – with an analytical study of the complete pianoforte works* (1933)

W. NIEMANN: *Brahms* (1929)

E. SAMS: *Brahms Songs* (1972)

R. SPECHT: *Johannes Brahms* (1930)

Brain, Dennis (1921–57), English horn player. He studied at the Royal Academy of Music, London, and became the most famous horn player of his day. He played in the Royal Philharmonic and Philharmonia Orchestras. Among the works specially written for him were Britten's *Serenade* for tenor, horn and string, and Hindemith's concerto.

Branco, Luis Freita (1890–1955), Portuguese composer and teacher. He studied in Lisbon, Berlin (with Humperdinck) and Paris. Branco's compositions include five symphonies, five symphonic poems, a violin concerto, and oratorio, chamber music, piano and organ music, and songs. He wrote several books.

Brandenburg Concertos, six orchestral concertos written by Bach in 1721 for Christian Ludwig, Margrave of Brandenburg. For the original title and dedication see H. T. David and A. Mendel, *The Bach Reader* (1945), pages 82–3. The scoring is as follows:

no 1 in F major: two horns, three oboes, bassoon, *violino piccolo*, strings and continuo.

no 2 in F major: trumpet, recorder, oboe, violin, strings and continuo.

no 3 in G major: three violins, three violas, three cellos, double bass and continuo.

no 4 in G major: violin, two recorders, strings and continuo.

no 5 in D major: flute, violin, harpsichord, strings (without second violin) and continuo.

no 6 in B flat major: two violas, two bass viols, cello, double bass and continuo.

Brandenburgers in Bohemia, The (Czech., *Braniboři v Cechách*) opera in three acts by Smetana, to a libretto by Karel Sabina; first performed in 1866 in Prague.

branle (Fr.; It., *brando*; Eng., brawl, brangill), originally, in the 15th century, a step in the BASSE DANSE (from *branler*, to sway), hence a dance with a swaying movement, current in France in the 16th and 17th centuries and popular also in other countries, including England (as in Shakespeare, *Love's Labour's Lost*, iii, 1). It could be sung as well as danced and existed in a variety of forms, e.g. *branle de Bourgogne*, *branle de Champagne*, *branle simple*, *branle double*, *branle gai*. Some *branles* were in duple time, e.g. the *branle simple*:

CLAUDE GERVAISE (*Les Maitres musiciens de la Renaissance francaise*, xxiii, page 43)

Others were in triple time, e.g. the *branle gai*:

IBID., page 76

brass band, a band consisting of brass instruments and drums, as opposed to the MILITARY BAND, which includes woodwind instruments. The standard organization in England is: 1 E flat cornet, 8 B flat cornets, 1 B flat flügelhorn (a treble saxhorn), 3 E flat saxhorns, 2 B flat baritones, 2 euphoniums, 2 tenor trombones, 1 bass trombone, 2 E flat bombardons (bass tubas), 2 B flat bombardons. With the exception of the bass trombone, which is written for at the actual pitch in the bass clef, all the instruments are treated as transposing instruments and their parts are written in the treble clef (even the bombardons). The written note:

will sound:
E flat cornet

B flat cornet

B flat flügelhorn

E flat saxhorn

B flat baritone

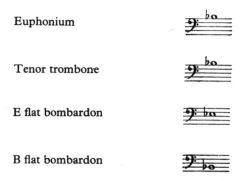

Euphonium

Tenor trombone

E flat bombardon

B flat bombardon

The popularity of the brass band in England dates from the early part of the 19th century and is a direct consequence of the invention of valves for brass instruments, which enabled them to play a complete chromatic scale. Brass bands are amateur organizations, generally coached by experts and often receiving material support from the factories and collieries from which the large majority of the players are drawn. There are at present some 5000 brass bands in Great Britain, apart from the Salvation Army, which has more than 1000. Standards of performance, which are extremely high, are maintained by the competition festivals, which date from the early 19th century. For these a number of distinguished composers have been commissioned in recent years to write test pieces. The normal repertory of the brass band depends largely on arrangements, and a good deal of the music specially written for it is not of a high standard. The general effect of the movement is to encourage musical activity among a large section of the population and to develop individual skill in performance, but not to promote good taste to a love for music in general.

    J. F. RUSSELL & J. H. ELLIOT: *The Brass Band Movement* (1936)

brass instruments (Fr., *instruments de cuivre*; Ger., *Blechinstrumente*; It., *strumenti d'ottone*), instruments made of metal, in which the sound is produced by vibration of the lips, transmitted to a tube by a cup-shaped or funnel-shaped mouthpiece. Usually known in the orchestra simply as 'brass'. In all instruments of this type successive notes of the HARMONIC SERIES are produced by increased tension of the lips. The intervening notes are produced by lengthening the sounding tube, either with a movable slide (trombone) or with valves which open extra lengths of tubing (all other brass instruments). *See* BARITONE, CORNET, EUPHONIUM, FLÜGELHORN, HORN, SAXHORN, TROMBONE, TRUMPET, TUBA, and illustrations, pages 86–8.

    A. CARSE: *Musical Wind Instruments* (1939)

Bratsche (Ger.), viola. The name is an adaptation of the Italian *viola da braccio*.

Brautwahl, Die (Ger., *The Choice of a Bride*), opera in three acts and an epilogue by Busoni, to a libretto by the composer (based on a story by E. T. A. Hoffmann); first performed in 1912 in Hamburg.

bravura (It.), literally, bravery, swagger; in music, the term implies display. A *bravura* passage in a composition is one which requires some feat of virtuosity on the part of the performer.

brawl, *see* BRANLE

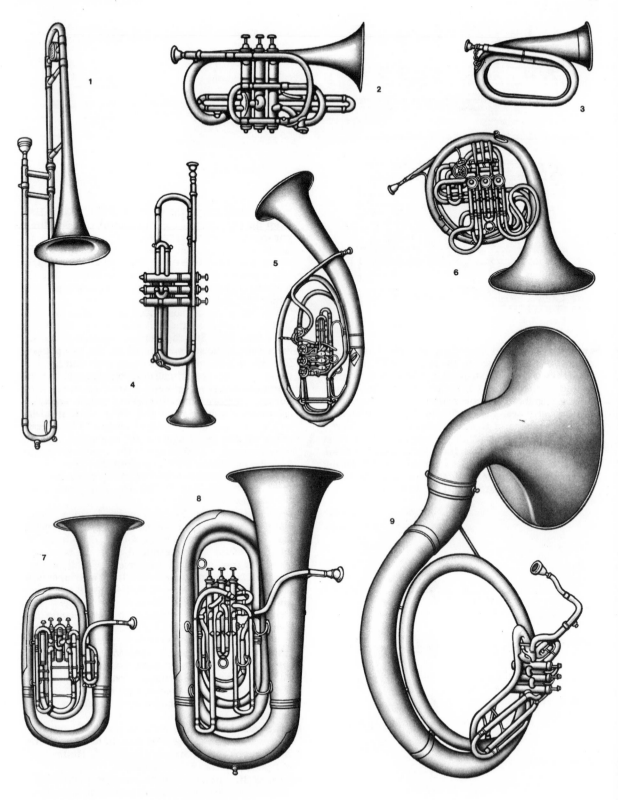

Brass instruments: (1) trombone (2) cornet (3) bugle (4) trumpet (5) Wagner tuba (6) French horn (7) B flat euphonium (8) double B flat tuba (9) sousaphone

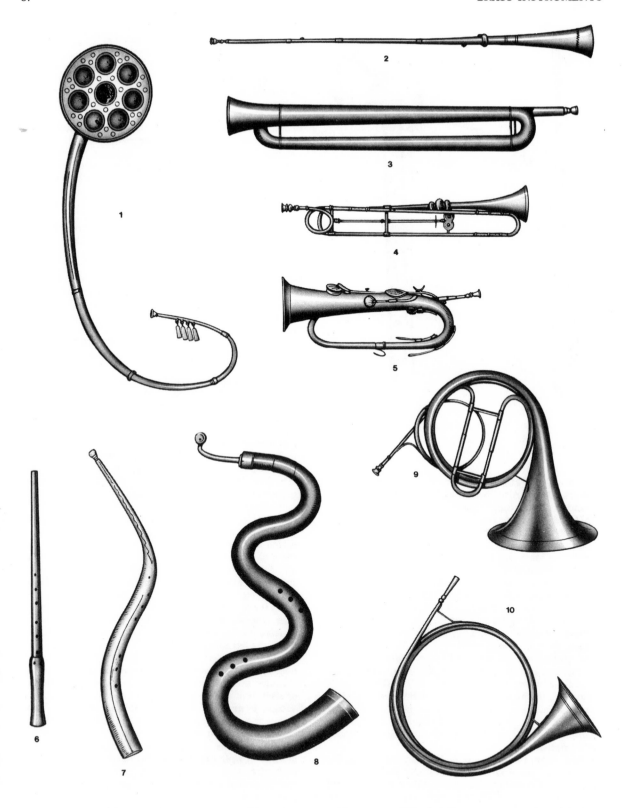

Old brass instruments: (1) lur (2) *buisine* (3) *Alphorn* (4) slide trumpet (5) key bugle (6) straight cornett (7) tenor cornett (8) serpent (9) hand horn (10) natural horn. (Nos 6, 7 and 8 are not, strictly speaking, brass instruments, but are related, being blown with cup-shaped mouthpieces)

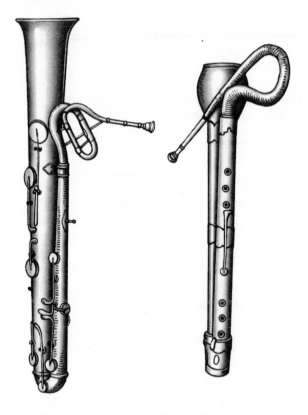

Old brass (cont'd.): (left) ophicleide; (right) bass horn

Breitkopf und Härtel, a Leipzig firm of music publishers. Bernhardt Christoph Breitkopf (1695–1777) founded a printing business in 1719, which was enlarged to include music-printing by his son Johann Gottlob Immanuel Breitkopf (1719–94). J. C. I. Breitkopf's son Christoph Gottlob Breitkopf (1750–1800) assigned the business to Gottfried Christoph Härtel (1763–1827). The firm's outstanding achievement is the publication of complete editions (some still incomplete) of the works of the great composers, from Palestrina to Wagner. They also published the original edition of Vaughan Williams's *Sea Symphony*.

Brenet, Michel, pseudonym of Antoinette Christine Marie Bobillier, (1858–1918), French musicologist. She published a large number of historical works, including biographies of Grétry, Palestrina, Haydn and Handel, a history of the symphony before Beethoven, a sketch of the history of the lute in France, *Les Musiciens de la Sainte Chapelle du Palais* (1910), *Musique et musiciens de la vieille France* (1911) and *La Musique militaire* (1917). Her life of Haydn has been translated into English.

Bretón, Tomás (1850–1923), Spanish composer. He studied at the Madrid Conservatory, and in Rome, Paris and Vienna, and became director of the Madrid Conservatory in 1903. An enthusiast for Spanish national music, he wrote a large number of operettas (*zarzuelas*), of which the most successful was *La Verbena de la Paloma* (Madrid, 1894). His other

compositions include nine operas, an oratorio – *El Apocalipsis,* a violin concerto and chamber music.

Bréval, Jean Baptiste (1756–1825), French cellist and composer. He was first cellist at the Paris Opéra, and taught at the Conservatoire until 1802. His compositions include orchestral music, chamber music, a comic opera, and an instruction book for the cello, which was also translated into English.

breve (Lat., *brevis,* 'short'), originally a short note. Introduced in the early 13th century when a distinction between the lengths of notes became necessary, it became increasingly longer with the introduction of notes of still shorter value – such as the semibreve (Lat., *minima,* 'smallest') – until it was the longest not surviving from the old notation. There is now little need for a note equal to eight crochets, but it still occurs in compositions where, in imitation of 16th century practice, the minim is used as the unit of measurement. It is written ⊨ or ▯
See ALLA BREVE, NOTATION

Bréville, Pierre Onfroy De (1861–1949), French composer, a pupil of César Franck. His compositions, which are chiefly notable for a sensitive lyricism, include a large number of songs, chamber music, choral works, and a three-act opera, *Éros vainqueur* (Brussels, 1910). He was also active as a teacher (at the Schola Cantorum and the Paris Conservatoire) and as a critic.

Brian, William Havergal (1877–1972), English composer, born in Dresden. Mainly self-taught as a composer, he became an organist and music teacher in Staffordshire. His compositions, some of which demand very large forces and suffer from the extravagance characteristic of the early 20th century, include *A Gothic Symphony* (the second of his 32 symphonies), an opera (*The Tigers*), comedy overture (*Dr. Merryheart*), *By the waters of Babylon* (chorus and orchestra), piano music and songs.
R. NETTEL: *Ordeal by Music* (1945)

bridge (Fr., *chevalet*; Ger., *Steg*; It., *ponticello*), a piece of wood standing on the belly of string instruments and supporting the strings. In instruments of the viol and violin families it is not fixed to the belly but retains its position through the tension of the strings. It has two feet: the right foot (on the side of the highest string) stands almost over the soundpost; the left foot, on the other hand, is free to vibrate. The transmission of the vibrations to the belly is assisted by the bass-bar glued inside the belly underneath the left foot of the bridge (*see* VIOLIN).

Also, a passage in a composition forming a connecting link between two important statements of thematic material and often consisting of a modulation or a series of modulations from one key to another.

Bridge, Frank (1879–1941), English composer, viola player and conductor. He studied at the Royal College of Music, London, and was for several years a member of the English String Quartet. His compositions include symphonic poems, *A Prayer* for chorus and orchestra, four string quartets, string sextet, piano quintet, phantasy quartet for piano and strings, two piano trios, violin sonata, cello sonata, works for piano and organ, and songs. His earlier works are in the romantic tradition; his later works (including the third and fourth string quartets) turn aside from traditional tonality and are less accessible to the ordinary music lover. He was Benjamin Britten's composition teacher.

Bridgetower, George Augustus Polgreen (1780–1860), Polish born violinist, the son of an African father and a European mother. He first appeared in Paris in 1789, and subsequently played at several concerts in London. He visited the Continent in 1803 and gave the first performance of Beethoven's 'Kreutzer' sonata (with the composer) in Vienna in 1803 (see A. W. Thayer, *Beethoven*, ii, page 299). From that time, he lived partly in England and partly on the Continent.

Brigg Fair, 'English rhapsody' on a Lincolnshire folk song by Delius (1907).

brindisi (It.), drinking song, in opera usually a toast to someone's health.

Brinsmead, a firm of piano manufacturers, founded by John Brinsmead (1814–1908) in London in 1836.

brio (It.), vigour; *con brio*, vigorously.

brisé (Fr.), 'broken' – used of an arpeggio in keyboard and harp music, and of détaché bowing in string music.

British National Opera Company, company formed in 1922 to perform operas throughout Britain. It came to an end in 1929. Among the operas by English composers produced were Holst's *The Perfect Fool* and *At the Boar's Head*, Boughton's *Alkestis* and Vaughan Williams's *Hugh the Drover*.

Britten, (Edward) Benjamin (1913–77), English composer. Born at Lowestoft, in a house facing the North Sea, he revealed musical aptitude in early childhood and started composing at the age of five. His father, a dentist, enjoyed music but was not a musician. His mother, secretary of the Lowestoft Choral Society, gave him his first piano lessons. Later, while attending Gresham's School, Holt, he travelled to Eastbourne during his holidays to have composition lessons from Frank Bridge – a humanitarian figure whose influence on him was profound. He also studied under Harold Samuel and, at the Royal College of Music in London, under Arthur Benjamin and John Ireland. His earliest published work was his sinfonietta for chamber orchestra (1932), written with great aplomb and still worth performing today. From 1935 until 1937 he worked with the G.P.O. film unit, and wrote the score for *Night Mail* – one of the most famous documentaries of the period. A pacifist from boyhood, he spent the early years of World War II in the United States, during which time he was awarded the Coolidge Medal, but returned to Britain in 1942. By then he already had a number of brilliant works to his credit, some of them written in collaboration with W. H. Auden (e.g. the song cycles *Our Hunting Fathers* and *On This Island*) but it was not until *Peter Grimes* was produced in London in 1945 that he fully established himself. For British music, at the end of the war, it seemed as if a new era had dawned. In *The Rape of Lucretia* (1946), *Albert Herring* (1947), *Billy Budd* (1951), *Gloriana* (1953), *The Turn of the Screw* (1954) and *A Midsummer Night's Dream* (1960), Britten consolidated his position as the leading British opera composer of the day, and his flair for setting words to music was also revealed in many concert works, ranging from song cycles (e.g. *Winter Words* based on poems by Hardy, *The Poet's Echo* based on Pushkin,

and the *Songs and Proverbs of William Blake*) to the *War Requiem*, combining bitter war poems by Wilfred Owen with the Latin words of the Roman Catholic Requiem, first performed at the opening of the new Coventry Cathedral in 1962. Britten's subsequent output has included his three church parables – *Curlew River* (1964), *The Burning Fiery Furnace* (1966) and *The Prodigal Son* (1968) – each inspired by plainsong and designed to be staged in a church rather than an opera house. *Owen Wingrave* (1970), based like *The Turn of the Screw* on a supernatural story by Henry James, was written in the first place for television but later adapted for performance at Covent Garden. Then, after considering operas on *King Lear* and *Anna Karenina*, he produced *Death in Venice*, based on Thomas Mann's novella (1973). Before this achieved its first performance, an operation for heart trouble left Britten in precarious health and cut short his career as conductor and pianist – in both of which spheres he had excelled. Fortunately, he subsequently resumed composing, adding a setting of T. S. Eliot to his series of vocal canticles, producing a third string quartet (after a gap of thirty years), and revising a scintillating operetta, *Paul Bunyan*, originally written in 1941 to words by Auden. Though he no longer took an active part in the Aldeburgh Festival (which he founded in 1948) he was still very much its presiding genius, just as the little coastal town and the North Sea are still major sources of his inspiration.

Britten wrote most of his works for specific performers. Much of his vocal music was designed for the voice and musical personality of the tenor, Peter Pears – to such an extent that Pears could be said to have been a dominating influence on his style. An important series of works, including the cello symphony and cello suites, were similarly inspired by the Russian cellist, Mstislav Rostropovich, and one of the ideas behind the *War Requiem* was that the three soloists should comprise a Russian (Galina Vishnevskaya), a Briton (Peter Pears) and a German (Dietrich Fischer-Dieskau). Britten was such a brilliant and productive composer, and such a famous one, that the staying power of his music has become a topic of wide discussion. The easy success of the *War Requiem* resulted in its being compared, maliciously, with Mendelssohn, and in Stravinsky's caustic gibe about Kleenex music; in a good performance, however, the simplicity of its message, its humanity and pathos continue to be affecting. Attempts to detect an element of dryness in some of his later works (e.g. *Death in Venice*) may seem to have proved successful, but such findings should be treated with caution: the same, after all, was said of Debussy's later music, though today's opinion of it is very different. Since some of Britten's earlier works – especially the powerful *Sinfonia da Requiem*, the violin concerto and the first two string quartets – have come increasingly into focus in recent years, and seem much more important than they once did, it may be that his later music, too, will prosper as time goes by. Certainly his operas remain the backbone of the modern British repertory, and have been widely performed in other countries. *Peter Grimes*, with its complex hero (or antihero), its big Verdian choruses and vivid seascapes, has established itself as a 20th century classic; *Albert Her-*

ring is one of the few successful comedies of our time; and *The Turn of the Screw* (written, like *Herring* and many of Britten's other stage works, for chamber forces) is both a masterly psycho-study and perhaps the most tightly and fascinatingly constructed opera since Berg's *Wozzeck*.

Britten's compositions include:

(1) Operas: *Paul Bunyan* (1941); *Peter Grimes* (1945); *The Rape of Lucretia* (1946); *Albert Herring* (1947); *Billy Budd* (1951); *Gloriana* (1953); *The Turn of the Screw* (1954); *A Midsummer Night's Dream* (1960); *Owen Wingrave* (1970); *Death in Venice* (1973). Also *Let's Make an Opera*, *Noye's Fludde*, *Curlew River*, *The Burning Fiery Furnace*, *The Prodigal Son*, and an arrangement of *The Beggar's Opera*;

(2) Choral works: *A boy was born*; *Ballad of Heroes*; *Hymn to St. Cecilia*; *A Ceremony of Carols*; *Rejoice in the Lamb*; *Saint Nicolas*; *Spring Symphony*; *Cantata Academica*; *Cantata Misericordium*; *War Requiem*; *Voices for Today*;

(3) Orchestra: *Sinfonietta*; *Simple Symphony*; *Variations of a theme of Frank Bridge* (strings); piano concerto; violin concerto; *Sinfonia da Requiem*; *Young Person's Guide to the Orchestra* (Variations and fugue on a theme of Purcell); cello symphony; overture, *The Building of the House*;

(4) Chamber music: three string quartets; *Phantasy Quartet*; two suites for solo cello;

(5) Song cycles and songs: *Our Hunting Fathers*; *On This Island*; *Les Illuminations*; *Serenade for tenor, horn and strings*; *Nocturne*; *seven Sonnets of Michel-angelo*; *The Holy Sonnets of John Donne*; *A Charm of Lullabies*; *Winter Words*; *six Holderlin Fragments*; *Songs and Proverbs of William Blake*; *The Poet's Echo*; canticles, folk-song arrangements and other songs.

R. BLYTHE (editor): *Aldeburgh Anthology* (1972)

A. GISHFORD (editor): *Tribute to Benjamin Britten on his Fiftieth Birthday* (1963)

I. HOLST: *Britten* (1966)

P. HOWARD: *The Operas of Benjamin Britten* (1969)

D. MITCHELL and H. KELLER (editors): *Benjamin Britten* (1953)

E. W. WHITE: *Benjamin Britten, his life and operas* (1970)

Benjamin Britten (above) and the court scene from the première (Sadler's Wells, 1945) of his major first opera *Peter Grimes*, with Peter Pears as Grimes, Joan Cross as Ellen

Broadwood, a firm of piano manufacturers, founded by Burkat Shudi (1702–73) in London for the manufacture of harpsichords about 1728. John Broadwood (1732–1812), who was employed by Shudi, became his partner in 1770, having married his daughter in the previous year. The firm first began making pianos in 1773. Grand pianos were made from 1781 onwards, and several patents for improvements were taken out in the latter part of the 18th century.

broken chord, a chord in which the notes are not sounded simultaneously but performed one after the other. The term is often used today in preference of the Italian *arpeggio*.

broken consort, *see* CONSORT

broken octaves, a passage of octaves performed not simultaneously but alternating between the two registers – much used in piano music.

Brossard, Sebastien de (c. 1654–1730), French composer and writer on music. He was *maître de chapelle* at Strasbourg Cathedral in 1689, and at Meaux Cathedral in 1698. His compositions include songs, church music and chamber music. He was the author of an important *Dictionnaire de musique* (1703), which went into six editions; an English translation appeared in 1740.

Browne, John, 15th century English composer. Nothing is known for certain about his life; he may be the John Browne (born 1452) who was elected King's Scholar at Eton on July 8, 1467. His surviving compositions comprise seven complete antiphons, two incomplete antiphons and an incomplete Magnificat (all in the Eton choir-book), and three carols (printed in *Musica Britannica*, xxxvi).

Bruch, Max (1838–1920), German composer of Jewish birth. He studied at Bonn and Cologne, where he taught from 1858–61. He was *Kapellmeister* to the Prince of Schwarzburg-Sondershausen (1867–70), director of the Liverpool Philharmonic Society in England (1880), director of the Orchesterverein, Breslau (1883–90), and teacher of composition at Berlin Hochschule, (1892–1910). His compositions include three symphonies, three violin concertos (of which the first, in G minor, op 26, is still one of the most popular works in the repertory), operas, an operetta, choral works (including the cantata *Odysseus*) and chamber music. His setting of the Hebrew melody *Kol Nidrei* for cello and orchestra, op 47, is well known.

Bruckner, Anton (1824–1896), Austrian composer. Born at Ansfelden, he was the son of a village schoolmaster and during his childhood received scanty musical education. When his father died in 1837, however, he went as a choirboy to the monastery of St. Florian, where he studied the organ and was appointed organist in 1845. Ambitious to compose, he moved in 1855 to Vienna to study counterpoint with Simon Sechter (from whom Schubert had wanted to learn counterpoint during the last year of his life) and from 1856 until 1868 was organist at Linz Cathedral. During that period he visited Munich, where he saw Wagner's *Tristan* – an experience which profoundly influenced him as a composer. From 1868 he worked in Vienna, teaching organ and theory at the Conservatory. By that time he had composed the first of his nine numbered symphonies, as well as an unnumbered one (usually known as no 0). His work as an organist and his admiration for Wagner helped him to forge a style of symphonic composition that was peculiarly his own – though his detractors (of whom at one time there were many) complained that his symphonies were like organ improvisations writ large, or that they were like Wagner without the drama. In a way, the latter accusation was true. Bruckner's music can sound like Wagner purged of its conflict and eroticism (it is said that when Bruckner attended a Wagner performance, he was uninterested in the plot and even averted his eyes from the stage). At heart his symphonies, as well as his choral and organ music, are religious works, proclaiming his simple faith as a Roman Catholic. They are symphonies about God – which is one reason why some people still find them harder to tackle than Mahler's, which are about the world. Their size, and the originality of their form, resulted in their being misunderstood during the composer's lifetime. Bruckner permitted well-intentioned friends to make cuts in them, and to alter the orchestration, with the result that their magnificent cathedral-like structure was weakened: paradoxically, a cut version of a Bruckner symphony can sound longer than an uncut one, simply because its natural proportions, and the logic of its thought, have been disturbed. Today, tainted versions of Bruckner's symphonies are still performed – sometimes by very famous conductors – but true Brucknerians always prefer the composer's own original ideas. The International Bruckner Gesellschaft, founded in 1929, promoted a new edition of Bruckner's works in their original form. These are the versions used by the Dutch conductor, Bernard Haitink, in his performances of the symphonies. Holland, even more perhaps than the composer's native Austria, has become the country most closely associated with Bruckner's music – perhaps there is a natural affinity between the wide lowland behind the dykes and the spaciousness of Bruckner's symphonic form – but Bruckner appreciation has developed everywhere in recent years, and no longer is an entire audience likely to walk out during a performance of his music, as happened at the première of one of his symphonies in Vienna.

Bruckner's principal works are:

(1) Symphonies:

no 0 in D minor (1863–4); no 1 in C minor (1865–6); no 2 in C minor (1871–2); no 3 in D minor (1873); no 4 in E flat major (Romantic) (1874); no 5 in B flat major (1875–6); no 6 in A major (1879–81); no 7 in E major (1881–83); no 8 in C minor (1884–5); no 9 in D minor (unfinished) (1887–1894).

(The dates quoted above are for the original versions of the symphonies; for details of the numerous revisions, one of the Bruckner authorities listed below should be consulted)

(2) Choral music: Mass in D minor (1864); Mass in E minor (1866); Mass in F minor (Grosse Messe) (1867–8); Te Deum in C major (1881); Psalm CL (1892); numerous smaller sacred works.

(3) Chamber music: string quartet in C minor (1862); string quintet in F major (1878–9).

Also organ music, male-voice choruses and songs.

M. AUER: *Anton Bruckner – sein Leben und Werk* (1934)

R. SIMPSON: *The Essence of Bruckner* (1967)

H. F. REDLICH: *Bruckner and Mahler* (1955, revised 1963)

H. H. Schonzeler: *Bruckner* (1970)

D. Watson: *Bruckner* (1974)

Brüll, Ignaz (1846–1907), Austrian pianist and composer, who toured Europe as a soloist and also taught in Vienna. His compositions include a symphony, two piano concertos, a violin concerto, and several operas.

Brumel, Antoine (c. 1450–c. 1520), Flemish composer. He was master of the choristers at Chartres Cathedral in 1483, and at Notre Dame, Paris, from 1498 to 1501. From 1505 he was attached to the court of Alfonso, Duke of Ferrara. He composed numerous Masses, printed in the early 16th century, and polyphonic chansons. His works have been edited in six volumes by B. Hudson (1969–72).

Bruneau, Alfred, originally Louis Charles Bonaventure (1857–1934), French composer and critic. He studied cello at the Paris Conservatoire, where he won the first prize and was also a pupil of Massenet for composition. He won his reputation chiefly as a composer of operas, some of which were considered bold, even crude, when they first appeared. Three of them – *Messidor* (Paris, 1897), *L'Ouragan* (Paris, 1901) and *L'Enfant Roi* (Paris, 1905) – had libretti by Emile Zola. *Le Rêve* (Paris, 1891), *L'Attaque du moulin* (Paris, 1893), *Naïs Miscoulin* (Monte Carlo, 1907) and *Les Quatre Journées* (Paris, 1916) were founded on works by Zola. Of Bruneau's works other than operas the most important is the *Requiem Mass*.

brunette (Fr.), a pastoral song of an amorous character, current in the late 17th and 18th centuries. Three volumes of *brunettes* were issued (1703–11) by the publisher Christophe Ballard, with the alternative title *petits airs tendres*.

Brustwerk (Ger.), one of the manuals in old German organs, with stops of a quieter tone than those on the Great organ (*Hauptwerk*). Also known as *Brustpositiv*. There is no exact English equivalent.

buffo (It.; fem. *buffa*), 'comic'; *opera buffa*, comic opera. The word is now often used as an English adjective, e.g. 'buffo party', 'buffo singers'. As a noun, it means a comic actor or singer.

bugle, a brass instrument with a conical tube and a cup-shaped mouthpiece, used for giving military signals. The regulation bugle of the British Army is in B flat, and as it has no pistons or keys can sound only the notes of the HARMONIC SERIES, i.e.:

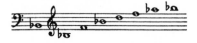

Of these the first and the last two are not used for bugle calls, so that the working compass is from

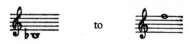

Bugles are also built in G and occasionally in F. In the early 19th century an attempt was made to give the bugle a complete chromatic compass by adding keys (see KEY BUGLE and illustration on page 85).

bugle à clefs (Fr.), key bugle.

Bühne (Ger.), stage or theatre. Wagner called *Parsifal* a *Bühnenweihfestspiel*, i.e. a sacred festival drama.

Bull, John (1563–1628), English organist and composer. He was a chorister of the Chapel Royal, and in 1582 was organist at Hereford Cathedral. In 1586 he became a gentleman of the Chapel Royal. He was the first professor of music at Gresham College, London, from 1596 to 1607. He left England in 1613, and became one of the organists in the archduke's chapel at Brussels; in 1617 he was organist at Antwerp Cathedral. His compositions include church music and a large number of keyboard pieces, some of which were published in PARTHENIA (1611), a collection of works by Byrd, Bull and Gibbons. Many of his keyboard works require considerable virtuosity and also show individuality in the treatment of harmonic progressions. They have been edited by T. Dart in *Musica Britannica*, xiv and xix.

Bull, Ole Børneman (1810–80), Norwegian violinist, largely self-taught. His determination to become a great virtuoso was the result of hearing Paganini play in Paris. He appeared as a soloist in Paris, 1832, and subsequently toured in Europe and the United States. In public recitals he displayed his virtuosity almost exclusively in his own compositions, very few of which were published. His special interest was Norwegian folk music, in which sphere he was an influence on Grieg.

S. C. Bull: *Ole Bull – a Memoir* (1886)

Bülow, Hans Guido von (1830–94) German pianist, conductor and composer, originally a student of law at Leipzig University. He became a devoted adherent of Wagner after hearing *Lohengrin* at Weimar in 1850. He studied piano with Liszt in 1851, and toured Germany and Austria as a solo pianist in 1853. Bülow taught piano in Berlin (1855–64), conducted the Munich Opera, (1864) and directed the Munich Conservatorium (1867). His first wife was Cosima, daughter of Liszt, whom he married in 1857 and divorced in 1870, after she had left him for Wagner. He was *Kapellmeister*, of the Hanover Court Theatre (1878), director of the court music to the Duke of Meiningen (1880–5) and conducted also in England, the U.S. and Russia. Usually considered to have been the world's first virtuoso conductor, he gave first performances of *Tristan und Isolde* (Munich, 1865) and *Die Meistersinger von Nürnberg* (Munich, 1868). As a pianist he had a remarkable repertory and an extraordinary memory. His greatest achievement as a conductor was with the Meiningen Orchestra, which he trained to a high degree of excellence. In addition to his own compositions, he made arrangements of some of Wagner's works and edited a large number of piano works by classical composers.

Bund (Ger.), fret (on a viol, lute, etc.). *Bundfrei*, 'unfretted', a term applied to a CLAVICHORD in which each note has a separate string.

Buononcini, *see* BONONCINI

Burgundian school, the name given to a number of composers of the first half of the 15th century, of whom Guillaume Dufay and Gilles Binchois were the most important. The court of the dukes of Burgundy at Dijon played an important part in the cultural life of the time, and their territories embraced the Netherlands and eastern France. Examples of the work of these composers are printed in J. Stainer, *Dufay and* his *Contemporaries*, C. van den Borren, *Polyphonia Sacra*, and J. Marix, *Les Musiciens de la Cour de Bourgogne*.

Burkhard, Willy (1900–55), Swiss composer, pianist and conductor. He studied at Berne, Leipzig, Munich and Paris, and was teacher of piano and theory at the Berne Musikschule (later Conservatorium) until 1937. His compositions, which incline to an austere simplicity (somewhat reminiscent of Hindemith) and show also a respect for traditional forms, include two symphonies, 'Ulenspiegel Variations' for orchestra, concerto for string orchestra, two string quartets and other chamber music, and several works for chorus and orchestra, among them *Musikalische Ubung* (1934), the oratorio *Das Gesicht Jesajas* (1935) and the 93rd psalm (1937).

burla, burlesca (It.; Fr. *burlesque*; Ger. *Burleske*), literally, 'jest'. A short piece of a lively and frolicsome character, e.g. Schumann's *Albumblätter*, op 124, no 12, and the fifth movement of Bach's *Partita no 3 in A minor*. The term is also applied to an extended composition in a playful style, e.g. Richard Strauss's *Burleske* for piano and orchestra, op 16.

Burney, Charles (1726–1814), English historian and composer. He studied with his half-brother, James Burney, and Arne. He was organist at St. Dionis-Backchurch, London, (1749) and at King's Lynn, (1751–60). From 1770 until 1772 he toured Italy, France and Germany to collect material for his *A General History of Music* (four volumes 1776–89), the first work of its kind in English, though John Hawkins' *A General History of the Science and Practice of Music* was published in five volumes four months after Burney's first volume in 1776. Burney also wrote an abridged account of his tours – *The Present State of Music in France and Italy* (1771) and *The Present State of Music in Germany, the Netherlands and the United Provinces* (two volumes, 1773). His other works include *An Account of the Musical Performances in Westminster Abbey and the Pantheon in Commemoration of Handel* (1785), *Memoirs of the Life and Writings of the Abate Metastasio* (1796) and musical articles contributed to Rees's *Cyclopaedia* (1802–c. 1820).

    C. BURNEY: *A General History of Music*, F. Mercer, two volumes (1935)
    F. BURNEY: *Memoirs of Dr. Burney*, three volumes (1832)
    C. GLOVER: *Dr. Burney's Continental Travels* (1927)
    P. A. SCHOLES: *The Great Dr. Burney*, two volumes (1948).

Busch, Fritz (1890–1951), German conductor. He studied in Cologne, and was director of music at Aachen (1912), conductor of Stuttgart Opera (1918), and director of Dresden State Opera (1922–33). As an anti-Nazi, he settled in Denmark but was principally known in his maturity as a conductor at Glyndebourne in England, where he worked from 1934 until 1939 and again after World War II.

    His brother, **Adolf Georg Wilhelm Busch** (1891–1952), German violinist and composer, was leader of the Busch Quartet. He studied at Cologne and Bonn, was leader of the orchestra of the Konzertverein, Vienna (1912), and taught at the Berlin Hochschule (1918–22). In 1935 he took Swiss nationality as he was also anti-Nazi. His numerous compositions include a choral symphony, concertos and variations for orchestra, violin concerto, piano concerto, many chamber works, and songs, but it was as a violinist that he was best known.

Bush, Alan Dudley (born 1900), English composer, teacher and writer. He studied at the Royal Academy of Music in London, where he was born, and with John Ireland. After further education at Berlin University, he became teacher of composition at the R.A.M. (1925), conductor of the London Labour Choral Union and Chairman of the Workers' Musical Association (1936). His compositions, many of which reflect his Communist sympathies, include the operas *The Press-gang*, *Wat Tyler*, *The Spell* and *Men of Blackmoor*. He has also written two symphonies, a piano concerto (with a male-voice declaiming a left-wing text), violin concerto, incidental music, chamber music, a choral work (*The Winter Journey*), and songs. His works, in a generally approachable style, have been performed in Eastern Europe.

Busnois, Antoine (died 1492), Flemish composer, a pupil of Ockeghem. For some time he was attached to the court of Charles the Bold of Burgundy and his successor Marie. His compositions include church music and part-songs; for examples see *Denkmäler der Tonkunst in Osterreich*, xiv–xv (Jg. vii, p. 105), and *Oxford History of Music*, ii (1932), page 56.

Busoni, Ferruccio Benvenuto (1866–1924), Italian composer and pianist who spent much of his life in Germany. He appeared as a child prodigy in Vienna at the age of nine and studied composition with Wilhelm Mayer at Graz. He was a member of the Accademia Filarmonica of Bologna for composition and piano-playing in 1882 (the youngest to be admitted since Mozart), and thereafter taught piano at Helsinki Conservatory (1889), at the Moscow Conservatory (1890) and at the New England Conservatory, Boston (1891–4). From 1894 until 1913 he lived in Berlin, apart from giving concert tours. He conducted orchestral concerts in Berlin (1902–9) introducing a number of new works and works performed for the first time in Germany. He was director of the Liceo Musicale, Bologna from 1913 until 1914 and then lived in Zurich from 1915 until 1920, in which year he returned to Berlin, where he was based until his death. As a pianist, he was remarkable not only for his virtuosity but also for his intellectual approach to the problems of interpretation. He had a great admiration for the music of Liszt, but his large repertory contained the works of many other composers, including Alkan, Bach, Beethoven, Chopin, Mozart, Schumann and Weber.

    His compositions, which also provide evidence of his intellectual stature, include the operas *Die Brautwahl* (Hamburg, 1912), *Turandot* (Zurich, 1917), *Arlecchino* (Zurich, 1917) and his masterpiece, *Doktor Faust* (completed by Philipp Jarnach, Dresden, 1925), orchestral suites, piano concerto with male-voice chorus, six piano sonatinas, *Fantasia contrappuntistica* for two pianos (inspired by Bach's *Art of Fugue*), chamber music, songs and a large number of arrangements and transcriptions. He wrote the librettos of his operas and also published an essay on aesthetics – *Entwurf einer neuen Aesthetik der Tonkunst* (1907) – and a collection of articles entitled *Von der Einheit der*

Musik (1922). Throughout his career, his Italian birth and German predilections exerted an element of conflict on his musical personality. At Bologna he hoped to prove himself an 'Italian' composer and place his stamp on Italian musical life, but soon retreated to Germany. He was recognized around the world as a great musical teacher, and his master classes were famous. As a composer, he still has a number of dedicated admirers, though the wider public have so far failed to find his musical personality strong enough to maintain a hold on their affections.

F. BUSONI: *Letters to his Wife* (1938)
E. J. DENT: *Ferruccio Busoni* (1933)
H. H. STUCKENSCHMIDT: *Busoni*
B. VAN DIEREN: *Down among the Dead Men* (1935)

Büsser, Paul Henri (1872–1973), French composer and conductor. He studied at the Paris Conservatoire, and won the Grand Prix de Rome in 1893. For some time he was director at the Paris Opéra, and director of the Opéra-Comique. His compositions include several operas, among them *Daphnis et Chloé* and two works after Merimée, as well as church music, orchestral pieces and songs.

Bussotti, Sylvano (born 1931), Italian composer, who studied music in Florence and painting in Paris. A member of the Italian avant-garde, he has written *Torso* for voice and orchestra, *Pour clavier* for piano and *Five Piano Pieces for David Tudor*.

Butterworth, George Sainton Kaye (1885–1916), English composer. Born in London, he studied at Eton, Oxford and the Royal College of Music. His compositions include two song-cycles on poems from Housman's *A Shropshire Lad*, an orchestral rhapsody with the same title, and an idyll for small orchestra, *The Banks of Green Willow*, which reflects his interest in English folksong. He was killed in action on the Somme during World War I.

Buus, Jachet or **Jacques de** (died 1565), Flemish composer. He was organist at St. Mark's Venice, from 1541 to 1550, and organist to Ferdinand I, Vienna, from 1553 to 1564. He published a number of important instrumental works (including *ricercari*), both for organ and for instrumental ensembles (*see* O. Kinkeldey, *Orgel und Klavier in der Musik des 16. Jahrhunderts*, page 141).

G. SUTHERLAND: 'The Ricercari of Jacques Buus', *Musical Quarterly*, xxxi (1945)

Buxtehude, Dietrich (1637–1707), Danish composer and organist. He was organist at Helsingborg in 1657, at Helsingör in 1660, and at the Marienkirche, Lübeck, in 1668. At Lübeck he became famous as a player and also as director of the ABENDMUSIKEN, from 1673. The nineteen-year-old J. S. Bach walked two hundred miles to hear Buxtehude play, and was greatly influenced by him in composing for the organ. Buxtehude's compositions include church cantatas, organ music and sonatas for instrumental ensembles. There are several editions of the organ music, and selections of the church cantatas and instrumental sonatas are in *Denkmäler deutscher Tonkunst*, volumes xiv and xi, respectively. Seven volumes of a projected complete edition of Buxtehude's works appeared between 1925

and 1937, and the project was resumed in 1958. A thematic catalogue of his music by G. Karstädt was published in 1974.

Byrd, William (1543–1623), English composer and organist. He was organist at Lincoln Cathedral from 1563 to 1572 and also a gentleman of the Chapel Royal in 1570, and subsequently joint organist there with Tallis. In 1575 he and Tallis obtained a monopoly of printing and selling music, which remained his after Tallis's death in 1585. In spite of his appointment at the Chapel Royal, he was a Roman Catholic and was more than once cited as a recusant. He managed to remain in Queen Elizabeth I's personal favour, however. His compositions include three Masses, Latin church music (notably the two volumes of *Gradualia*, published in 1605 and 1607), English church music, consort songs and part-songs, music for viols, and pieces for the virginals. Some of his keyboard pieces were printed in PARTHENIA (1611), together with works by Bull and Gibbons.

Byrd was one of the great masters of 16th century polyphony. He excelled in the composition of church music, and particularly music for the Roman Catholic church, where supreme technical mastery is combined with an intimate understanding of the texts and their associations. His songs grew out of an indigenous English tradition which may be traced back to Fayrfax, and show little influence from the madrigal and other Italianate styles which were popular in England after 1588.

Byrd's complete works were edited by E. H. Fellowes in twenty volumes (1937–50); most volumes have subsequently been revised by various editors, and volumes xviii to xx, containing the keyboard music, have been superseded by Alan Brown's edition in *Musica Britannica* xxvii–xxviii.

E. H. FELLOWES: *William Byrd* (second edition, 1948)

Byzantine music, the music of the Christian church in the Eastern Roman Empire, so called from Byzantium, which was made the capital by Constantine in the 4th century with the name Constantinople (now Istanbul). The music of the Byzantine liturgy survives in a notation of ancient origin, which uses NEUMES, though of a different kind from those found in Western manuscripts. These neumes survived in use for many centuries; the earliest examples date from the 10th century. A number of correspondences between Byzantine and Gregorian music show that the influence of the Eastern Church on the Western was strong in the early centuries of our era. A further contribution to the West was the organ, though this was used at Byzantium only for secular purposes. The *Monumenta Musicae Byzantinae* (in progress) include a number of facsimiles of manuscripts and several volumes of transcriptions.

E. WELLESZ: *Eastern Elements in Western Chant* (1947); *A History of Byzantine Music and Hymnography* (1949); *The Music of the Byzantine Church* (1959)
E. WELLESZ and M. VELIMIROVIĆ (eds.): *Studies in Eastern Chant* (three volumes, 1966–73)

C (Eng., Ger.; Fr., *ut, do*; It., *do*), (1) the key-note or tonic of the scale of C major;

(2) as an abbreviation = *cantus* (It., canto), contralto, *con* (with), *col* or *colla* (with the). *c.B.* = *col Basso*, an indication that the cellos are to play with the double-bases. *C.B.* = *contrabasso* (double-bass). *C.F.* = *cantus firmus* (It., canto fermo), i.e. a given theme (generally in long notes) to which counterpoints are added (*see* CANTUS FIRMUS, COUNTERPOINT);

(3) the C clef, an ornamental form of the letter C, indicates middle C or

It may be placed on any line of the stave, and is still so used in some modern library editions of old music, but only the following three positions are used in recent scores:

These are (1) soprano clef, still used for the soprano voice in late 19th century German scores; (2) alto clef, formerly used for the alto voice and alto trombone and in regular use today for the viola; (3) tenor clef, formerly used for the tenor voice and in regular use today for the tenor trombone and the upper register of the bassoon, cello and double bass. A knowledge of the alto and tenor clefs is indispensable for reading chamber music or orchestral scores. The easiest way to acquire that knowledge is by learning to play an instrument that uses them. A tenor-trombone player today must be able to read alto, tenor or bass clefs with equal facility;

(4) the sign

is a time signature and means that there are four crotchets (quarter-notes) in the bar (4/4). Its original form was a half circle, indicating 'imperfect time' (breve = 2 semibreves), as opposed to the complete circle indicating 'perfect time' (breve = 3 semibreves). If a vertical stroke is drawn through the C, thus:

it generally indicates that the minim is to be taken as the unit of measurement (2/2) instead of the crotchet.
See ALLA BREVE, MENSURAL NOTATION, TIME-SIGNATURE

cabaletta (It.), formerly a simple operatic aria, with an incisive and continuously repeated rhythm, often found in Rossini. In later 19th century Italian opera, however, the term came to be used for a showy concluding section of an aria in which the principal emphasis is on an incisive and reiterated rhythm.

The derivation of the word is disputed. It seems unlikely that it has any connection with *caballo*, a horse, nor is it easy to see why it should be regarded as a corruption of *cavatinetta*, diminutive of *cavatina*.

Cabanilles, Juan (1644–1712), Spanish composer of organ music, who was organist of Valencia Cathedral from 1665 till his death. His complete organ works have been edited in three volumes by H. Anglès (1927–36).

Cabezón, Antonio de (1510–66), Spanish organist and composer, blind from birth. He was organist to Charles V and Philip II. His compositions are mainly for keyboard, and consist of liturgical pieces and variations on secular songs. Most of them were published posthumously by his son Hernando in 1578 under the title *Obras de musica para tecla arpa y vihuela* (Musical works for keyboard, harp and lute; modern edition in F. Pedrell, *Hispaniae Schola Musica Sacra*, iii, iv, vii and viii), but some appeared earlier in Henestrosa's *Libro de cifra nueva para tecla, harpa, y vihuela* (1557; modern edition by H. Anglès in *La música en la corte de Carlos V* in *Monumentos de la Música Española*, ii, 1944). A collected edition of his works was begun by C. Jacobs in 1967. For further information on Cabezón *see* the commemorative issue of *Annuario Musical*, xxi (1966).

caccia (It.), literally 'chase' or 'hunt': (1) a 14th century Italian poem dealing with hunting, fishing or scenes of popular life, set to picturesque and lively music for two voices in canon, generally with a third part (instrumental) providing an independent accompaniment. These pieces seem to have been imitated originally from earlier examples current in France under the name *chace* at the beginning of the century.

W. T. MARROCCO: *Fourteenth Century Italian Caccie* (second edition, 1961)

(2) *corno da caccia, oboe da caccia, see* HORN, OBOE

Caccini, Giulio (c. 1550–1618), Italian singer and composer. For many years he was in the service of the Grand Duke of Tuscany at Florence. He was a member of the circle of scholars, musicians and poets who met at the house of Count Bardi in Florence and wished to recreate the music and drama of ancient Greece. One result of this movement was the composition of solo songs with figured bass accompaniment, designed to reproduce as completely as possible the accents and emotions of the poetry. Caccini published a number of settings of this type in 1602 under the title *Le Nuove Musiche* (facsimile edition, 1934; modern edition by H. W. Hitchcock, 1970). In the preface he declared that it had been his object to write a type of music in which one could, so to speak, talk in music (*in armonia favellare*), allowing mere song to take second place to the words. He also contributed part of the music of Peri's opera *L'Euridice* (Florence, 1600), in which the same principles were practised, and in the same year published a complete setting of the same libretto (modern edition in R. Eitner, *Publikationen älterer praktischer und theoretischer Musikwerke*, x), which was performed in 1602.

His daughter, **Francesca Caccini** (born 1588), was also a singer and composer. Her compositions include sacred and secular cantatas for one and two voices, two ballets and the opera *La liberazione di Ruggiero dall' isola d'Alcina* (Florence, 1625; modern edition by Doris Silbert, *Smith College Music Archives*, vii).

cachucha, a Spanish solo dance in 3/4 time, with a rhythm somewhat like a bolero.

cacophany, sounds of the utmost dissonance. The word is usually used in a derogatory sense. Thus Strauss's early operas and symphonic poems and Stravinsky's *Rite of Spring* were originally attacked for being cacophanous. Yesterday's cacophany – if the product of a great musical mind – has a way of turning into today's classic.

cadence, literally 'a falling' (Lat., *cado*, 'I fall'). The name seems to originate from the fact that in unharmonized melody (e.g. plainsong or folksong) it is common for a tune to end by falling to the tonic or keynote (cf. *Twelfth Night*, i, 1: 'That strain again! it had a dying fall'). Hence it is applied to a concluding phrase, whether at the end of a section or at the end of a complete melody, and, by a natural transference, to the harmonization of such phrases. A number of conventional formulae for such harmonization have acquired currency at different periods. In consequence 'cadence' has come to mean a harmonic progression which suggests a conclusion, if only temporary, irrespective of whether the melody rises or falls or remains stationary. In this matter opinions vary from one period to another: what would have seemed inconclusive, if not unintelligible, at one time may very well appear the opposite a hundred years later. To provide a complete index of cadences would be difficult, since there is hardly any limit to the possible variations; in particular, composers have not been slow to enhance the effect of a final close by interpolating something unexpected at the last moment.

Conventional names have been given to certain simple types of cadential formulae current in the classical and romantic periods, e.g. (in the key of C major or C minor):

(1) perfect cadence (or full close) – dominant to tonic:

(2) imperfect cadence (or half close) – tonic to dominant:

(this will normally occur in the middle of a composition, not at the end – hence the name);

(3) plagal cadence – subdominant to tonic:

(4) interrupted cadence – dominant to some chord other than the tonic, e.g.:

(this is strictly not a cadence at all, since it is not conclusive; the name alludes to the fact that the ear is expecting the tonic chord, but the expected cadence is interrupted by the substitution of another chord). The names given above are those most commonly in use in Britain, but there is no absolute uniformity of nomenclature; for instance, nos 1 and 3 are often referred to as 'perfect (authentic)' and 'perfect (plagal)', the use of the word 'plagal' by itself being in fact an abbreviation.

The following are actual examples of the cadences described above:

(1) perfect:

SCHUBERT, *Quartet in D minor*

(2) imperfect:

BACH, *Partita in B flat major*

(3) plagal:

HANDEL, *Messiah*

(4) interrupted:

BRAHMS, *Ein deutsches Requiem*

Among the many possible modifications of these basic formulae one of the commonest is the substitution of a minor chord for a major, or vice versa, in the plagal cadence, e.g.

(1) subdominant minor in a major key:

BRAHMS, *Symphony no 3*

(2) tonic major in a minor key (the so-called *tierce de Picardie*):

BEETHOVEN, *Quartet in C sharp minor*, op 131

The substitution of the tonic major in a perfect cadence in a minor key is also very common:

BACH, *48 Preludes and Fugues*, Book I, no 24

The approach to these simple cadences can be varied by the use of chords extraneous to the key; e.g. in the perfect cadence:

BEETHOVEN, *Sonata in F minor*, op 57

SCHUBERT, *Quartet in D minor*

The 20th century revival of interest in modal folk song (*see* MODES) led to the frequent use of a perfect cadence in which the seventh degree of the scale is not sharpened, e.g.:

and of other cadences using the same melodic idiom, e.g.:

A simple example is the following:

VAUGHAN WILLIAMS, *The Wasps*

This practice contrasts with the medieval and Renaissance practice of sharpening the seventh degree of the modal scales, where necessary, in polyphonic music (*see* MUSICA FICTA). The use of cadences in the course of a composition played an important part in defining the structure of 16th century motets and madrigals. The sharpening of the seventh in cadences was normal in the Dorian (D to D), Mixolydian (G to G) and Aeolian (A to A) modes. It was unnecessary in the Lydian (F to F) and Ionian (C to C) modes, where the seventh was already sharp, and was avoided in the Phrygian (E to E) mode, where the following typical harmonization of the cadence was adopted (with sharpened third in the final chord, in accordance with normal 16th century practice):

This cadence, which came to be known as the 'Phrygian cadence', survived the break-up of the modal system and was often used as a cadence on the dominant in minor keys, i.e. the second chord in the above example would be treated as the dominant of A minor.

The sharpening of the seventh in modal scales did not exclude the use of the flat seventh proper to the mode, either in close juxtaposition to the sharp seventh or simultaneously. This practice is particularly common in British music of the 16th and 17th centuries:

BYRD, *Gradualia*, Book I, ii, 3

PURCELL, 'My heart is inditing'

A. CASELLA: *The Evolution of Music, through the History of the Perfect Cadence* (1924)

cadenza (It.), literally 'cadence' though in musical usage the term came to have a related but different meaning. It was first used to describe the improvisation introduced by operatic singers in the 18th century before the final cadence at the end of an aria. The practice was borrowed by soloists in instrumental concertos. In both cases an instrumental *ritornello* normally followed the final cadence for the soloist. The convention was to pause on a $^6_4$ chord on the dominant, i.e. in the key of C major:

then embark on the improvisation and conclude with the cadence which had been deferred. In the classical concerto the cadenza occurs most frequently in the first movement; though there can be additional cadenzas later in the work. The player was expected not only to display his virtuosity but also to make allusions to the thematic material of the movement. Although these cadenzas were normally improvised, Mozart left written cadenzas for several of his piano concertos. These are often included as an appendix in printed scores of Mozart's concertos. Beethoven wrote cadenzas (and sometimes alternative cadenzas) for all his piano concertos. The one in the first movement of the *Emperor* concerto is an integral part of the work. The ones he wrote for the other concertos are optional, but remain superior to attempts by later composers and pianists to write cadenzas for these works. Post-Beethoven composers, taking the *Emperor* concerto as their example, have tended to write built-in cadenzas for their concertos. In Mendelssohn's violin concerto, Schumann's piano concerto and Elgar's violin concerto – to take only three examples – the cadenza is an integral part of the composition; in Elgar's work it is actually accompanied by the orchestra. Brahms's violin concerto is an exceptional example of the survival of the old practice of leaving the cadenza to the player – though in fact most players settle for the same cadenza in this work. The cadenza in modern works has become in fact an anachronism, since the conditions to which it originally owed its existence no longer exist. The practice of improvising cadenzas to classical concertos has now completely disappeared. Players either write their own beforehand, or use published examples by others. In such cases the disparity of style between the cadenza and the work it is supposed to adorn is often very marked. Benjamin Britten's cadenza for Haydn's C major cello concerto is a good example of this. It is a fascinating piece of music, but it tells us more about Britten than about Haydn.

Cadman, Charles Wakefield (1881–1946), U.S. composer, organist and critic. In his compositions he has made use of American Indian themes. His works include orchestral pieces – one of them a *Pennsylvania Symphony* in which an iron plate has to be banged – music for piano and organ, songs and the operas *Shanewis* (New York, 1918) and *A Witch of Salem* (Chicago, 1926).

Cadmus et Hermione (Fr., *Cadmus and Hermione*), opera with a prologue and five acts by Lully, to a libretto by Philippe Quinault, first performed in 1673 in Paris.

Caffarelli (1710–83), the professional name of Gaetano Majorano, a celebrated Italian *castrato* singer. He was a pupil of Caffaro (from whom he took his name) and Porpora, who considered him the greatest singer in Europe. He had an enormous reputation in Italy, and appeared also in London (in two of Handel's operas) and Paris. He was noted for the beauty of his voice and for his skill in singing embellishments, particularly chromatic scales. Dr. Bartolo mentions him in the lesson scene in Rossini's *Barber of Seville*.

John Cage, the *enfant terrible* of modern music

Cage, John (born 1912), U.S. composer and pianist, born in Los Angeles. A pupil of Adolph Weiss, Henry Cowell, Arnold Schoenberg and Edgard Varèse, he established himself as the pioneer of the prepared piano (his own invention), in which various objects are placed on or between the strings of a conventional instrument, thus changing its tone and sound. He

has held teaching appointments at Cornish School, Seattle, the Chicago School of Design, and the New School for Social Research, New York. In 1944 he became musical director of the Merce Cunningham Dance Company.

A tireless experimenter and musical nonconformist, Cage has explored ALEATORY MUSIC, ELECTRONIC MUSIC and silent music, all of which reduce, or do away with in some cases, the role of the composer. His works include *Winter Music* for one to twenty performers, *Radio Music* for one to eight radios, and *Imaginary Landscape* (1951) for twelve radios with twenty-four performers (each radio needing two people to control it). He has also written a piano concerto, *Music of Changes* for prepared piano, and a large-scale work for amplified harpsichord entitled HPSCHD. His *4′ 33″* is the most famous silent piece ever written. His *0′ 0″* has been designed 'to be performed in any way to anyone'. Cage has also written several books, including *Silence* (1961) and *Notations* (1969).

caisse (Fr.), drum; *grosse caisse*, bass drum.

Caix d'Hervelois, Louis de (c. 1670–c. 1760), French player on the *viola da gamba*, in the service of the Duke of Orleans. He wrote pieces for the *viola da gamba* and for the flute.

calando (It.), giving way, both in volume and speed, a combination of *diminuendo* and *ritardando*.

Caldara, Antonio (1670–1736), Italian cellist and composer, a pupil of Legrenzi. He became vice-*Kapellmeister* to Fux at the Imperial Court, Vienna, in 1716. He wrote about one hundred operas (including *Ifigenia in Aulide*, *Don Chischiotte* and *Sancio Panza*) and oratorios, church music (including a 'Crucifixus' in sixteen parts), and chamber music.

Caletti-Bruni, *see* CAVALLI

Caliph of Baghdad, The (Fr., *Le Calife de Bagdad*), opera in one act by Boieldieu, to a libretto by Claude Godard d'Aucour de Saint-Just, first performed in 1800 in Paris.

Callas, Maria (1923–77), soprano, born in the United States of Greek parents (her original name was Kalogeropoulou). She studied in Athens, where she made her operatic début in 1938 as Santuzza in *Cavalleria Rusticana*. Her first Italian appearance was at Verona in 1947 as La Gioconda in Ponchielli's opera. In that year she married Signor Meneghini, and during the years of her marriage to him called herself Maria Meneghini Callas. During the 1950s and early 1960s she sang regularly at La Scala, Milan, and established her international reputation as the finest dramatic soprano of the day. She excelled in works of the *bel canto* period – e.g., Bellini's *Norma*, *La Sonnambula* and *Il Pirata*, Donizetti's *Anna Bolena* and Cherubini's *Medea* – and did much to revive public interest in them. Though her vocal technique was not unflawed, her qualities as an operatic actress more than compensated for this, as in her memorable portrayal of Violetta in *La Traviata*. At the height of her powers she sang in London, New York, Chicago and Dallas. In the later 1960s, realising that her voice was fading, she withdrew from the operatic stage, and though comebacks were promised (e.g. 'Callas will sing at Dallas'), none took place. A brief concert appearance in London in the 1970s confirmed that she had been wise to retire gracefully, and to concentrate on teaching and giving master classes. Her numerous recordings give an incomplete impression of her qualities: she was a great stage presence, a singer of high dramatic intelligence whom one needed to see as well as hear.

Callcott, John Wall (1766–1821), English composer and organist, famous as a writer of glees.

calliope, an organ powered by steam instead of air. It can be played manually or operated mechanically and, because it produces a very loud sound, has been used in fairgrounds. It first appeared in the United States in 1856.

Calvé, Emma (1858–1942), French soprano, who sang in opera in France, Belgium, Italy, England and the United States until 1910, when she retired from the stage and appeared only on the concert platform. Her interpretation of the title role of *Carmen* was famous.

    E. CALVÉ: *My Life* (1922)

Calvocoressi, Michael D. (1877–1944), English critic, of Greek parentage. His speciality was Russian music. His published works include *Masters of Russian Music* (with G. Abraham, 1936), *A Survey of Russian Music* (1944), *Mussorgsky* (completed by G. Abraham, 1946) and another larger study of Mussorgsky (1956).

calypso, song from Trinidad, originating in the island's plantations in the 18th century. The words were often topical and satirical, the rhythms syncopated, the music employing primitive instruments (e.g. the bottle and spoon), and these elements are preserved in the more sophisticated calypsos being composed today.

Calzabigi, Raniero da (1714–95), Italian critic and author who spent part of his career in Paris and Vienna and wrote the librettos of Gluck's *Orfeo*, *Alceste* and *Paride ed Elena*. He was the force behind a number of Gluck's operatic reforms.

Cambert, Robert (c. 1628–77), French composer and organist, a pupil of Chambonnières. He became associated with the poet Pierre Perrin; they produced jointly *La Pastorale d'Issy* (1659) and *Pomone* (1671), pioneer works in the history of French opera. Cambert also set *Les Peines et les Plaisirs d'Amour* (1672) to a libretto by Gabriel Gilbert. After Perrin had fallen out of favour with Louis XIV in 1672 Cambert went to London, where his activities are uncertain.

cambiata (It.), short for *nota cambiata*, changed note. The term, used mainly of 16th century counterpoint, implies the use of a dissonant note where one would normally expect a consonant note. It is currently used in two senses:

    (1) of an accented passing dissonance, e.g.:

PALESTRINA, *Suscipe verbum*

In Palestrina's practice it occurs, as here, on the even beats (second or fourth) of the bar and in a descending passage. Other composers show greater freedom in its use, e.g.:

BYRD, *Gradualia*, Book II, 20

(2) of a sequence of notes, also known as 'changing note group', which occurs most frequently in the following forms:

    (a)   (b)

The second note is dissonant with one or more of the other parts, but instead of moving by step to the third note (in accordance with the normal treatment of passing dissonance) it leaps, e.g.:

PALESTRINA, *Missa Assumpta est Maria*

(The sequence of notes may occur without any dissonance, but it is not then strictly a *cambiata*).

    The following example illustrates both types of *cambiata*:

TALLIS, *Domine, quis habitabit?*

camera (It.), 'room'. Used in the 17th and early 18th centuries to distinguish music suitable for performance in secular surroundings from that suitable for performance in church, e.g. *sonata da camera*. The English term 'chamber music' is a literal translation of *musica da camera*.

See SONATA

Cameron, Basil (1884–1975), English conductor. He studied at the Hochschule für Musik, Berlin, and in 1940 became assistant conductor of the Henry Wood Promenade Concerts in London.

campana (It.), bell. Diminutive, *campanella*.

campanelli (It.), Glockenspiel.

campanology, the study of BELLS or the art of bell ringing.

Campion (Campian), Thomas (1567–1620), English poet and song writer, a doctor by profession. He was educated at Cambridge. He published four books of lute songs, a fifth in association with Philip Rosseter, and a treatise on counterpoint. He also wrote the music for several court masques. The lute-songs are reprinted in facsimile (*English Lute Songs*, iv, v and xxxvi) and in modern editions (*The English School of Lutenist Songwriters*, second series), and the treatise on counterpoint is in the edition of his works by Percival Vivian (1909).

M. M. KASTENDIECK: *England's Musical Poet, Thomas Campion* (1938)

E. LOWBURY, T. SALTER and A. YOUNG: *Thomas Campion* (1970)

Campra, André (1660–1744), French composer. He was *maître de chapelle* at Toulon (1679), Arles (1681), Toulouse (1683), and Notre Dame, Paris (1694). He composed some distinguished church music but is best known for his *divertissements* and operas, of which *L'Europe galante* (1697), *Les Fêtes vénitiennes* (1710) and *Tancrède* (1702) have been published in vocal score in *Chefs-d'oeuvre de l'opéra français*.

M. BARTHÉLEMY: *André Campra: sa vie et son œuvre* (1957)

canarie (Fr.), a French dance, current in the 17th century, which takes its name from the Canary Islands. It is very similar to the gigue, being in 3/8 or 6/8 time, with a persistent dotted rhythm. Examples occur in keyboard works by French and German composers, and in operas, e.g.:

PURCELL, *Dioclesian*

cancan, a French (especially Parisian) dance of the late 19th century, which grew out of the quadrille and reached its high water-mark in Offenbach's *Orpheus in the Underworld*. Written in quick 2/4 time, cancans were famed for their lasciviousness.

cancrizans, 'crab-like' (Lat., *cancer*, 'crab').

See CANON (5), RETROGRADE MOTION

Cannabich, Christian (1731–98), German violinist, composer and conductor, a pupil of Johann Stamitz. He worked at Mannheim and Munich. His conducting was much praised by his contemporaries, including Mozart, who described him as 'the best conductor I have ever seen' (letter of July 9, 1778), and composed a piano sonata for Cannabich's daughter.

canon (Gk., rule), a polyphonic composition in which one part is imitated by one or more other parts, entering subsequently in such a way that the successive statements of the melody overlap, e.g.:

BIZET, *L'Arlésienne*

If the imitation is exact in every detail the canon is 'strict'; if it is modified by the introduction or omission of accidentals it is 'free'. It is common for such compositions to end with a short coda, in which imitation is abandoned, in order to make a satisfactory conclusion. If, on the other hand, each part, on coming to the end of the melody, goes back to the beginning again and repeats, the result is a 'perpetual' or 'infinite' canon, popularly known as a 'round' (e.g. 'Three blind mice'). Canons are often accompanied by one or more independent parts, e.g.:

BACH, *Musikalisches Opfer*

Here the independent part is a pre-existing melody, given to Bach for improvisation by Frederick the Great. Canons have also been written on a ground bass:

PURCELL, *Dioclesian*, Act 3

The problems to be solved in canonic writing have fascinated composers of all ages, some of whom (particularly in the 15th century) have invested the art with mystery by providing only the melody and adding enigmatic instructions for which a solution must be found before the canon can be scored. The part which imitates may begin at the same pitch as the original melody or at an interval above or below it; hence the terms 'canon at the unison', 'canon at the fifth', etc. (for examples see particularly Bach's *Goldberg Variations*).

Among the possible varieties of canon are

(1) canon by inversion, or contrary motion (*canon per arsin et thesin*). The part which imitates is the same as the original melody but upside down, e.g.:

CLEMENTI, *Sonata in G major*, op 40, no 1

(2) canon by augmentation. The part which imitates is in longer notes than the original, e.g.:

PURCELL, *Sonatas of 3 Parts no 6*

(this example illustrates also double augmentation);

(3) canon by diminution. The part which imitates is in shorter notes than the original;

(4) a combination of (1) and (2) or (1) and (3), e.g. the following canon by augmentation and inversion:

BACH, *Musikalisches Opfer*

(5) crab canon (*canon cancrizans*) or retrograde canon. The part which imitates is written backwards, beginning with the end;

(6) crab canon by inversion. The part which imitates is written backwards and upside down.

Two or more canons may be combined. A simple canon between two parts is called a 'canon two in one', because both parts are singing the same melody. If two two-part canons are combined, making four parts in all, the result will be a 'canon four in two':

PURCELL, *Te Deum in B flat*

cantabile (It.), 'singable'. Applied to an instrumental piece it indicates that the player should make the music sing.

cantata (It., *cantare*, 'to sing'), properly a piece which is sung, as opposed to 'sonata', a piece which is played. In the early 17th century the word was used of extended pieces of secular music, for one or two voices with accompaniment, in which contrasting sections of declamatory recitative and aria were normal. The style of such pieces was similar to that of opera, but they were intended purely for concert performance. In the course of the 17th century the cantata was imitated by French, German and English composers. It was also extended to include settings of religious texts and became increasingly elaborate. In Germany the Lutheran chorale was introduced into the cantata as the basis for extended treatment. This type of cantata, written for soloists, chorus and orchestra and owing much to the example of opera, was the model adopted by J. S. Bach, of whose church cantatas some two hundred survive. The older practice of writing dialogues survives in many of the duets in Bach's cantatas. Bach also wrote a few secular cantatas on the same plan. Since the late eighteenth century the term 'cantata' has generally been used for secular or sacred choral works, with or without soloists, accompanied by orchestra, which are similar in conception to the oratorio but less extended. In the present century, cantatas have continued to be written. Among the most important are Bartók's *Cantata Profana* (1930), Webern's two cantatas (op 29 and 31), and Stravinsky's *Cantata* (1952), *Canticum Sacrum* (1955) and *Threni* (1958). Britten has written a *Cantata Academica* and *Cantata Misericordium*.

A. SCHWEITZER: *J. S. Bach*, two volumes (1911)

W. G. WHITTAKER: *Fugitive Notes on Certain Cantatas and the Motets of J. S. Bach* (1924)

Cantelli, Guido (1920–56), Italian conductor, protégé of Toscanini. He established himself after World War II as one of the most exciting conductors of his generation, and made impressive appearances in Britain (especially the Edinburgh Festival), La Scala, Milan and in New York. His exceptionally promising career was cut short when he was killed in an air-crash in Paris.

Canteloube, Joseph (1879–1957), French composer, active in the collection of folk songs. He studied at the Schola Cantorum in Paris. His compositions include instrumental works, songs and the operas *Le Mas*

(Paris, 1929) and *Vercingétorix* (Paris, 1933). Today he is best known for his delightful collection of *Songs from the Auvergne*.

canti carnascialeschi (It.), 'carnival songs': part-songs of a popular character written in the early part of the 16th century to be performed at court festivals during the annual carnival. Examples are printed in P. M. Masson, *Chants de Carnaval florentin*, and *Das Chorwerk* (ed. F. Blume), xliii.

F. GHISI: *I canti carnascialeschi* (1937)

Cantiga, *see* ALFONSO EL SABIO

cantilena (It.), a sustained, flowing melodic line.

canto fermo, *see* CANTUS FIRMUS

cantor (Lat.), 'singer'. Hence the chief singer in a choir, or in cathedrals and collegiate churches and similar establishments the director of the music (in English 'chanter' or 'precentor'). Though the office of precentor still exists in English cathedrals, and carries with it certain responsibilities, the actual work of training the choir is normally undertaken by the organist. The genitive *cantoris* is used in England to indicate that half of the choir which sits on the same side as the precentor; the other half, sitting on the dean's side, is called *decani*. This division of the choir is used regularly in the antiphonal chanting of the psalms, and frequently in anthems and services.

cantus firmus (Lat.; It., *canto fermo*), 'fixed song'. A pre-existing melody used, often in long notes, as the foundation of a polyphonic composition for voices (with or without instruments), for an instrumental ensemble, or for a keyboard instrument. Plainsong melodies were extensively used in the Middle Ages and later for this purpose. Among the other materials drawn upon by composers were secular songs, Lutheran chorales, scales, and solmization syllables representing the vowels in a verbal text. The practice of using a *cantus firmus* survives today mainly in organ pieces based on hymn-tunes. Mozart used a chorale melody as a *cantus firmus* in his opera *Die Zauberflöte* (1791). A *cantus firmus* in semibreves, to which other parts have to be added, is used in the traditional method of teaching 'strict' counterpoint.

See COUNTERPOINT, TENOR

canzona, canzone or **canzon** (It.; Fr., *chanson*) 'song'. Used either of a vocal piece or of an instrumental piece modelled on a vocal form. In particular:

(1) in the 16th century a polyphonic setting of a secular poem, simpler and more popular in style than the madrigal;

(2) the name used in Italy at the same period for the polyphonic French *chanson* (*canzon francese*);

(3) from the 17th century a solo song with keyboard accompaniment;

(4) in opera a song of a simple type, in contrast to the normally elaborate aria, e.g. 'Voi che sapete' in Mozart's *Marriage of Figaro*;

(5) a 16th century transcription for lute or keyboard of a French *chanson*;

(6) an instrumental piece in the same style written for keyboard or an instrumental ensemble (late 16th and early 17th centuries), sometimes described as *canzon per sonar* (for playing) or *da sonar*. From the contrasted sections introduced into such pieces developed the separate movements of the sonata;

(7) an instrumental piece (or movement in a sonata) of a polyphonic character (17th and early 18th centuries);

(8) an instrumental piece or movement in the style of a song, e.g. the slow movement of Chaikovsky's fourth symphony, op 36, marked 'Andantino in modo di canzone'.

canzonetta (It.; Eng., canzonet), diminutive of CANZONA:

(1) a short piece of secular vocal music, light in character, for two or more voices, with or without instrumental accompaniment. 16th century examples were normally constructed in the form AABBCC, and include Morley's *Canzonets or little short aers to five and six voices* (1597). 17th century examples include the *canzonetta a due voci concertata* and the *canzonetta a quattro concertata* in Monteverdi's seventh book of madrigals (1619). An 18th century example is Mozart's *canzonetta* 'Più non si trovano' (Metastasio), for two sopranos and bass, with three basset horns, K 549;

(2) a solo song of a similar character, e.g. Haydn's *Six Original Canzonettas* (1794), followed by a second set of six in 1795;

(3) an instrumental piece, e.g. Buxtehude's keyboard *canzonette* (17th century), which are in the same style as CANZONA (6).

Caplet, André (1878–1925), French composer and conductor, a close friend of Debussy, whose *Children's Corner* he arranged for orchestra. His compositions include orchestral works (among them a symphonic poem on Poe's *Mask of the Red Death*), chamber music, songs and church music. He was conductor of the Boston Opera from 1910 until 1914.

capotasto (It.), 'head (*capo*) of the finger-board (*tasto*)' of a string instrument. Also a mechanical device, consisting of a cross bar of wood, metal or ivory (Fr., *barre*), for shortening all the strings simultaneously and hence raising their pitch. It has the practical advantage of simplifying the performance of pieces in extreme keys. It can be conveniently applied only to instruments with FRETS, to which it can be attached. In cello-playing the thumb is used as a temporary *capotasto* to facilitate playing in the high register.

cappella, *see* A CAPPELLA, MAESTRO DI CAPPELLA

capriccio (It.; Fr., *caprice*), in general a piece in which the composer follows the dictates of fancy. In particular:

(1) in the late 16th and 17th centuries an instrumental piece, fugal in character, similar to the *ricercar*, *fantasia* and *canzona*, though sometimes more fanciful in the choice of themes, e.g. Frescobaldi's *Capriccio sopra il cucu* (capriccio on the cuckoo);

(2) a piece which does not fall into one of the conventional forms of its period, e.g. Bach's *Capriccio sopra la lontananza del suo fratello dilettissimo* (capriccio on the departure of his beloved brother), which consists of several movements with descriptive titles;

(3) a technical study, e.g. Paganini's 24 *capricci* for violin solo, op 1;

(4) an original piece of a lively character, e.g. the sixth movement of Bach's keyboard Partita no 2 (which might equally well be called an 'invention'), or nos 1, 3, and 7 of Brahms's *Fantasien*, op 116, for piano;

(5) a potpourri or rhapsody, e.g. Chaikovsky's *Capriccio italien*, op 45, for orchestra, which is based on popular tunes.

Capriccio, opera in one (full-length) act – today usually divided into two – by Richard Strauss, to a libretto by Clemens Krauss and the composer, first performed in 1942 in Munich. This golden autumnal score was Strauss's last opera. Its story, set in the 18th century, takes as its starting point the old question of whether words or music are the more important in opera. A poet and composer are rival suitors to a young widowed countess. At the end the outcome seems unresolved: Strauss's ravishing music naturally suggests that the composer will win her, though the sophisticated libretto (not unlike one of Anouilh's *Pièces Roses*) reveals the poet as no dullard either.

Cardew, Cornelius (born 1936), English composer, pianist and guitarist, pupil of Howard Ferguson at the Royal Academy of Music, London. In 1958 he went to Cologne to study electronic music and became a disciple of Stockhausen. His music, which shuns conventions other than his own, includes *Octet 1961* and other pieces in which final decisions are left to the performers. He was founder of the Scratch Orchestra, whose performances caused outrage among conservative-minded listeners.

Cardillac, opera in three acts by Hindemith, to a libretto by Ferdinand Lion (based on E. T. A. Hoffmann's *Das Fräulein von Scuderi*). First performed in 1926 in Dresden, the work was revised and given a new libretto (written by the composer himself) in 1952 for a production at Zürich. The story tells of a master goldsmith who steals back from his customers the jewellery he has sold to them. An excellent 'mystery' opera, with an attractive neo-classical score, *Cardillac* deserves to be much better known than it is. Apart from a sensational production by the Deutsche Oper am Rhein during the 1960s, the work has been largely neglected by the world's opera companies.

Cardus, Neville (1889–1974), English critic. He joined the Manchester Guardian in 1917 as Samuel Langford's assistant, and worked for that paper for the rest of his life, ultimately becoming senior London music critic. His books include a study of Mahler's first five symphonies, *Ten Composers* and two fascinating volumes of autobiography.

Carestini, Giovanni (c. 1705–c. 1760), Italian *castrato*, with a remarkable contralto voice. He was in London from 1733 until 1735 and sang in several of Handel's operas. He also sang in Rome, Prague, Berlin and St. Petersburg. His compass is said to have been from

Carey, Henry (c. 1690–1743), English composer and dramatist. His numerous works include operettas, songs and cantatas. His opera *The Dragon of Wantley*, the music of which was by J. F. Lampe (London, 1737), was a very successful satire on Italian opera. He wrote the words and tune of 'Sally in our alley' (part of the tune is used in the scene in the condemned hold in *The Beggar's Opera*). The melody to which the song is now sung is traditional; it became associated with Carey's words in the late 18th century.

carillon, (1) a set of bells hung in a bell tower and struck by hammers connected to a keyboard and pedalboard, or to an automatic mechanism powered by clockwork or electricity, so producing a tune.

(2) an organ stop with a bell-like sound.

Carissimi, Giacomo (1605–74), Italian composer, active for the greater part of his life in the direction of church music in Rome. He played an important part in the cultivation of the solo cantata, and was one of the first to write extended oratorios which break away from the early 17th century practice of opera on sacred subjects. His oratorios, though often dramatic in treatment, were intended for the church, not the stage, and therefore include a narrator, who sings in recitative. The oratorios *Jephteï Judicium Salomonis, Jonas* and *Baltazar* (all with Latin texts) have been published in a modern edition by F. Chrysander. A complete edition of all the oratorios is in course of publication by the Istituto Italiano per la Storia della Musica.

Carl Rosa Opera Company, founded in 1873 by Carl Rosa (originally Karl Rose), a German violinist from Hamburg, for the performance of opera in English. It was active until 1958 as a touring company, visiting many British cities which would otherwise have been cut off from live opera. It gave the first British performances of *Manon* (1885) and *La Bohème* (1897). In 1958 it was superseded as a touring company by Sadler's Wells.

Carlton, Nicholas, early 17th century English composer, who wrote one of the earliest known examples of a keyboard duet under the title 'A Verse for two to play on one Virginal or Organ' (printed in *Two Elizabethan Keyboard Duets*, edited by F. Dawes, 1949).

H. M. MILLER: 'The Earliest Keyboard Duets', *Musical Quarterly*, xxix (1943)

Carlton, Richard (c. 1558–c. 1638), English composer, who was master of the choristers at Norwich Cathedral. He published a set of five-part madrigals (1601; modern edition in *The English Madrigal School*, xxvii), remarkable for their free use of dissonance, and contributed to *The Triumphes of Oriana* (1601).

Carmen, opera in four acts by Bizet, to a libretto by Henri Meilhac and Ludovic Halévy (after the story by Prosper Mérimée). First performed in Paris in 1875, it originally included spoken dialogue, which was replaced by recitative written by Ernest Guiraud when it was first given in Vienna in 1875 (after Bizet's death). But the recitatives weakened the flavour of the piece, and many companies today prefer to revert to Bizet's original ideas. The story is set in Seville and in the neighbouring mountains. Carmen, a gypsy girl employed in a cigarette factory, exercises a fatal fascination on Don José, a sergeant of the guard, who allows her to escape after she has been arrested for disorderly behaviour. José joins Carmen and her smuggler friends in the mountains but soon longs to return home. Carmen, wearying of him, transfers her affections to Escamillo, a bull-fighter. At the bull-ring in Seville, where Escamillo has been successful, José makes a last appeal to Carmen. When she refuses he stabs her.

Carmen, Bizet's last opera, brought a new vitality to French *opéra-comique*. The theory that it was initially a flop, thus causing Bizet to die of a broken heart, was

Carmen. Galei-Marié as Carmen and Duchaise as Frasquita in the first performance at the Opéra-Comique in Paris in 1875

not wholly correct. True, he did die (of a throat infection) soon after the première, but by that time it had already (in spite of criticism) notched up 23 performances at the Opéra-Comique, and was later to go from strength to strength. Today it stands as one of the greatest and most popular of all French operas.

Carmina Burana, scenic oratorio or cantata by Carl Orff, first performed in 1937 at Frankfurt. In Britain it is usually presented in a concert version, but in Germany it is often staged. The work is based on 13th century Latin poems (with ancient French and ancient German interpolations) on the subject of love, drink and kindred pleasures. Orff later wrote two other works, *Catulli Carmina* (1952) and *Trionfi dell' Afrodite* (1953), which form a trilogy with *Carmina Burana*.

Carnaval, a set of twenty piano pieces by Schumann, op 9 (1835), bearing the subtitle *Scènes mignonnes sur quatre notes* (dainty scenes on four notes). The four notes are derived from Asch, the home town of Ernestine von Fricken, with whom Schumann was in love at the time. The letters A S C H can represent either A, E flat (Ger., Es), C, B (Ger., H) or A flat (Ger., As), C, B. By a curious coincidence, of which Schumann was aware, these are also the only letters in his own name which can represent notes. The music depicts a ball attended by the composer (in his conflicting disguises as Florestan and Eusebius), Chopin, Paganini, Clara Wieck (later to become Clara Schu-

mann) and various *commedia dell'arte* figures.

Carnaval Romain, Le (*The Roman Carnival*), concert overture by Berlioz, op 9 (1844), based on material from the opera *Benvenuto Cellini*, op 23 (1834–8). The *cor anglais* solo is derived originally from the early scena *Cléopâtre* (1829).

Carnival, concert overture by Dvořák, op 92 (1891), dedicated to the Czech University, Prague, second of a set of three which he originally intended to call *Nature, Life and Love*. The others are *In Nature's Realm*, op 91 (1891) and *Othello*, op 93 (1892).

Carnival Jest from Vienna (Ger., *Faschingsschwank aus Wien*), a set of five piano pieces by Schumann, op 26 (1839). The title may have been originally designed for the set of pieces published as *Carnival*, op 9, possibly because it includes the letters ASCH on which the latter work is based (*see* CARNIVAL).

Carnival of the Animals (Fr., *Le Carnaval des Animaux*), satirical suite by Saint-Saëns for two pianos, string quintet, flute, clarinet and xylophone, described as a *fantaisie zoologique*. The animals depicted include the Swan (the cellist's friend), Tortoises (an Offenbach cancan played slowly by double-basses), Fossils (hackneyed tunes including one from Saint-Saëns's own *Danse Macabre*) and Pianists (doing their exercises). In many performances, Saint-Saëns's chamber scoring is inflated to symphony-orchestra proportions. Though composed in 1886 it was not published until 1922 (after his death).

carol (Fr., *noël*; Ger., *Weihnachtslied*), the word is now used in the same sense as *noël* and *Weihnachtslied* to mean a song for Christmas. In medieval English it meant any song with a burden (or refrain), whether related to the church festivals or not; in this sense the Agincourt Song is a carol (see John Stevens's edition of *Medieval Carols* in *Musica Britannica*, iv). The music of Christmas carols is drawn from many sources; principally (1) traditional folksong (2) secular music in general, including opera (3) tunes specially composed. The practice of setting or arranging carols for two or more voices is as old as the 15th century. Some of the carol melodies in popular use today, e.g. that associated with 'Good King Wenceslas', were borrowed in the late 19th century from a 16th century hymn-book, *Piae Cantiones* (1582; modern edition by G. R. Woodward, 1910). Among modern English collections are *The English Carol Book* (1913 and 1919), *The Cowley Carol Book* (1902 and 1919) and *The Oxford Book of Carols* (1928). The latter includes notes on the words and tunes. Traditional carols are printed in C. Sharp's *English Folk Carols* (1911).

> H. BACHELIN: *Les Noëls français* (1927)
> J. A. FULLER-MAITLAND: *English Carols of the 15th Century* (1891)
> R. L. GREENE: *The Early English Carols* (1935)
> E. B. REED: *Christmas Carols printed in the 16th Century* (1932)

Caron, Philippe, composer of the latter half of the 15th century, probably a pupil of Dufay and of Flemish nationality. He composed *chansons* and Masses, including one on 'L'homme armé' (modern edition in *Monumenta polyphoniae liturgicae*, Ser. 1, Tom. 1, Fasc. 3). A complete edition of his works in two volumes was begun by J. Thomson in 1971.

Carpani, Giussepe Antonio (1752–1825), Italian

Elliot Carter

Carter, Elliot (born 1908), U.S. composer, born in New York. A pupil of Walter Piston and of Nadia Boulanger in Paris, he has held teaching appointments at the Peabody Conservatory of Music, Columbia University, Yale University and the Juilliard School of Music. As a composer he has emerged in recent years as one of the major figures of U.S. musical life, admired as much abroad as at home. Though he writes in traditional forms – concerto, symphony, string quartet, sonata – he has used these as receptacles for ideas of remarkable freshness and power. Among the most important of his works are the *Variations for Orchestra* (1955), the double concerto for harpsichord and piano (1956), the piano concerto (1965), the *Concerto for Orchestra* (1970), and the three string quartets. In these the writing is often exceptionally complex, but in a good performance is invariably meaningful, intense and finely judged. His chamber music, indeed, is of a quality surpassed by no other composer in the world today. It includes, apart from the string quartets, a sonata for flute, oboe, cello and harpsichord, a woodwind quintet, a piano sonata, and a sonata for cello and piano. He has also written two ballets, *Pocahontas* (1939) and *The Minotaur* (1947).

Caruso as Canio in *Pagliacci*. His recording of 'Vesti la giubba' was the most important single influence in popularizing the gramophone and contains the famous sob so frequently imitated by less gifted performers.

born author of several opera libretti. A friend of Haydn in Vienna, he wrote a study of Haydn's music entitled *Le Haydine* (1812). Henri Beyle published a French adaptation of this, entitled *Lettres écrites de Vienne en Autriche sur le célèbre compositeur Joseph Haydn* (1814), as his own work under the pseudonym C. A. L. Bombet, and in spite of the author's protests issued it again under the pseudonym Stendhal, with the title *Vies de Haydn, Mozart et Metastase* (1817).

Carpenter, John Alden (1876–1951), U.S. business-man who was also active as a composer. In spite of his dual activity, there is nothing amateurish about his music. He wrote a jazz pantomime, *Krazy Kat* (1922), and a 'ballet of modern American life', *Skyscrapers* (1926). His other ballet, *The Birthday of the Infanta* (1919), is based on a story by Oscar Wilde.

Carse, Adam (1878–1958), English composer and writer on music. His numerous compositions include two symphonies, but he is best known for his arrangements of old music (particularly early classical symphonies), text-books on the theory of music, and a number of books on the history of the orchestra and orchestral instruments, particularly *Musical Wind Instruments* (1939), *The Orchestra in the 18th Century* (1940), and *The Orchestra from Beethoven to Berlioz* (1948).

Caruso, Enrico (1873–1921), Italian tenor, the most famous in history. His first public appearance was in Naples (his hometown) in 1894. In 1902 he reached Covent Garden and in 1903 the New York Metropolitan, where he subsequently made more than 600 appearances and sang the role of Dick Johnson in the

première of Puccini's *Girl of the Golden West*. His
beauty of tone and perfection of phrasing can be heard
on his many recordings – he has been called 'the first
true gramophone tenor', and was certainly the first to
make a fortune from his discs (his royalties are said to
have amounted to nearly £500,000). Among the many
books about him is one by his widow, Dorothy Caruso.

> D. CARUSO: *Enrico Caruso: his Life and Death* (1945)
> P. U. R. KEY AND B. ZIRATO: *Enrico Caruso* (1923)
> T. R. YBARRA: *Caruso* (1953)

Carver, Robert (born c. 1487), Scottish composer, a
canon of Scone Abbey. He composed a number of
Masses and motets, including a Mass on the secular
song 'L'homme armé' (used by many other 15th and
16th century composers) and a motet in nineteen
parts, 'O bone Jesu' (modern editions in *Musica
Britannica*, xv).

> K. ELLIOTT: 'The Carver Choir-book', *Music and
> Letters*, xli (1960)

Casals, Pau (also known as **Pablo**) (1876–1974),
Catalan cellist, conductor and composer, the son of an
organist. He studied at the Madrid Conservatorio and
joined the Paris Opéra Orchestra in 1895, and first
appeared as a concert soloist in Paris in 1898. In the
same year he appeared in London, and in 1901 made his
U.S. début. In 1905 he joined the piano trio founded by
Alfred Cortot. He formed his own orchestra in
Barcelona in 1919 and conducted it until 1936. In 1940
he left Spain in protest against Franco's government.
Subsequently he lived at Prades in the French Pyrenees,
where in 1950 he founded a Casals Festival, and in 1956
he settled in Puerto Rico.

His remarkable gifts of execution and interpretation
(particularly of Bach's unaccompanied suites) did more
than anything else in the present century to raise the
prestige of the cello as a solo instrument. He married
(1) the Portuguese cellist Guilhermina Suggia, 1906,
(2) the U.S. singer Susan Metcalfe, 1914, (3) Marta
Montanez (Puerto Rico), 1957. In addition to his cello-
playing and conducting he was also a remarkable
accompanist. His compositions include works for cello
and choral works, *La Visión de Fray Martin* and *The
Manger*. His pupils included Cassadó and Eisenberg.

> L. LITTLEHALES: *Pablo Casals* (1948)
> H. L. KIRK: *Pablo Casals* (1975)

Casella, Alfredo (1883–1947), Italian composer, conductor, pianist and critic. He studied at the Paris
Conservatoire, where he was a pupil of Fauré. From
1915 until 1923 he taught at the Conservatorio di
Santa Cecilia, Rome. He took an active part in further-
ing the cause of modern Italian music (in 1924 he
founded with d'Annunzio and Malipiero an association
for this purpose) and in organizing the *Biennale*
festivals at Venice. His music, eclectic in style,
includes three operas – *La donna serpente* (after Gozzi,
1932), *La favola d'Orfeo* (1932) and *Il deserto tentato*
(1937, glorifying the Abyssinian war). He also wrote
ballets (one of them, *La giara*, after Pirandello), three
symphonies, concertos and other orchestral works, a
cello sonata and other instrumental music, piano
pieces and songs. He was the author of books on
Stravinsky (1928), the piano (1937) and himself (1930).

Casimiri, Raffaele (1880–1943), Italian choral conductor, composer and musicologist. After holding
various posts as teacher and chorusmaster he became

director of music at St. John Lateran, Rome, in 1911.
He edited a considerable amount of old music, notably
a new edition of the works of Palestrina, wrote studies
of Palestrina and Lassus, and founded two periodicals,
Psalterium (1907) and *Note d'archivio* (1924).

cassa (It.), drum.

Cassadó, Gaspar (1897–1966), Catalan cellist and
composer, a pupil of Casals. His compositions include
three string quartets, a piano trio and a *Rapsodia
catalonia* for orchestra.

cassation (It., *cassazione*), a term used in the 18th
century for an instrumental suite suitable for performance in the open air and therefore similar to the
serenade or divertimento. Mozart wrote works in the
form. The origin of the word is disputed.

Casse-Noisette, *see* NUTCRACKER

castanets (Fr., *castagnettes*; Ger., *Kastagnetten*; It.,
castagnette), a percussion instrument, characteristic of
Spain, consisting properly of two shell-shaped pieces
of hard wood, joined by a cord, which passes over the
thumb, and struck together by the fingers. In the
orchestra a modified form is normally used, in which
the clappers are attached to a stick. The word 'castanet'
comes from the Spanish *castañeta*, a diminutive of
castaña, 'chestnut'.

Castelnuovo-Tedesco, Mario (1895–1968), Italian
composer, a pupil of Pizzetti. His opera *La Mandragola*
(Venice, 1926) won a prize offered by the Italian
Government in 1925. In 1939 he was compelled, as a
Jew, to leave Italy, and settled in the United States,
where he became naturalized. His compositions include
two piano concertos, two violin concertos, several
overtures to Shakespeare's plays, sonatas for violin,
cello, clarinet and bassoon and other chamber music,
piano music and songs. Among the latter are a number
of songs from Shakespeare's plays and settings of 27
of the sonnets, all with the original text. His most
consistently popular work, however, has been his
delightfully melodious guitar concerto.

Castil-Blaze, François Henri Joseph (1784–1857),
French writer on music and composer. He studied at
the Paris Conservatoire and adapted (not always
scrupulously) a large number of Italian and German
operas for the French stage. His critical works include
De l'Opéra en France (two volumes, 1820), *Dictionnaire de la musique moderne* (1821), *Théâtres lyriques de
Paris* (three volumes, 1847–56), and *Molière musicien*
(two volumes, 1852).

Castor et Pollux, opera in five acts by Rameau, to a
libretto by Pierre Joseph Justin Bernard, first performed in 1737 in Paris.

castrato (It.), an adult male singer – now defunct –
with a soprano or contralto voice, produced by castra-
tion before the age of puberty. This had the effect of
preventing the voice from 'breaking', as it would
normally do at that time. In consequence the castrato
combined a boy's range with the power and capacity of
a man. Castrati were known in church music in the
16th century, but their principal field of activity was in
Italian *opera seria* in the 17th and 18th centuries, when
many of them were famous for their virtuosity and the
beauty of their voices. They were often exceptionally
vain, and were adulated by the public. The fact that
these singers were used regularly for male parts is one
of the difficulties that have to be faced in reviving operas

of that period. Among important roles written for castrati were the title-role in Monteverdi's *Orpheus*, Nero in the same composer's *Coronation of Poppaea*, Caesar in Handel's *Julius Caesar*, the title-role in Gluck's *Orpheus*, and Idamante in Mozart's *Idomeneo*. Castrato roles are today usually transposed down an octave and sung by a tenor, though this often damages the texture of the music (as in the love duet at the end of the *Coronation of Poppaea*, where Monteverdi clearly wanted the two high voices to intertwine). The casting of a female soprano or mezzo-soprano in such a role is usually preferable, even if it causes some slight loss of dramatic credibility.

A. HERIOT: *Castrati in Opera* (1956)

Castro, Jean de, 16th century composer, probably Walloon. He wrote church music, madrigals and *chansons* (including settings of Ronsard).

Castro, Juan José (1895–1968), Argentinian composer, a pupil of d'Indy in Paris. His compositions include a *Sinfonia Argentina*, a *Sinfonia Biblica*, ballet music and operas. He was also active as conductor at the Colón Theatre and at Montevideo. His opera *Proserpina y el extranjero* (Milan, 1952) won the Verdi prize offered by La Scala, Milan.

Castrucci, Pietro (1679–1752), Italian violinist, a pupil of Corelli. He moved to England in 1715 and led the orchestra in Handel's opera performances for several years. His compositions include twelve *concerti grossi* and thirty violin sonatas. He died in poverty. His brother Prospero (died 1760), also a violinist, was the original of Hogarth's picture 'The Enraged Musician'.

catalán, Spanish dance from Catalonia.

Catalani, Alfredo (1854–93), Italian composer who studied at the Paris Conservatoire and later taught in Milan. His most famous work was his last opera, *La Wally* (1892), which so impressed Toscanini that he called his daughter Wally in tribute to it.

Catalani, Angelica (1780–1849), celebrated Italian soprano, who made her first appearance in opera at Venice, 1797. She travelled widely, and in England sang Susanna in the first performance there of Mozart's *Marriage of Figaro*. Her singing is said to have been remarkable for its execution and beauty of tone but extravagant in the liberties she took with the music. Lord Mount-Edgcumbe (*Musical Reminiscences*, 1825) described her taste as 'vicious'.

catch, a round for three or more voices. The earliest to be printed appeared in Thomas Ravenscroft's *Pammelia : Musicke's Miscellanie, or mixed varietie of Pleasant Roundelayes and delightful Catches* (1609; facsimile edition, 1961). Catches were also published during the Commonwealth and became still more popular after the Restoration, when they were remarkable not only for the ingenuity shown in their composition but also for the coarseness of their words. Purcell wrote more than fifty (*Purcell Society*, xxii). By the 18th century it had become the custom to introduce puns and other humorous devices into the catch. The most plausible derivation of the word is from the Italian CACCIA.

Catel, Charles-Simon (1773–1830), French composer. During the Revolution he was active as a composer of military music and works in celebration of the new régime. He taught harmony at the Paris Conservatoire. Of his ten operas, *Les Bayadères* (Paris,

1810) was the most successful. His *Traité d'harmonie* (1802) was for long a standard text-book.

Caurroy, François Eustache du (1549–1609), French composer. He began his career as a singer in the royal chapel, eventually becoming master of the music. He had a great reputation in his day as a composer. He was one of the group of French composers who experimented in writing music in longs and shorts in imitation of classical scansion. His works include polyphonic vocal music, sacred and secular, and instrumental fantasias. Twenty pieces from his *Mélanges de musique* (1610), consisting of *chansons*, *noëls* and *vers mesurés à l'antique* are printed in *Les Maîtres musiciens de la Renaissance française*, xvii (1903).

Caustun, Thomas (died 1569), one of the earliest composers to write for the services of the Anglican Church. Anthems and services by him are in John Day's *Certain notes set forth in foure and three parts* (1560) and settings of the metrical psalms in the same publisher's *The whole psalmes in foure parts* (1563).

Cavaillé-Col, Aristide (1811–99), member of a French firm of organ-builders, influential in improving the technique of organ-building in France in the 19th century.

Cavalieri, Emilio De' (c. 1550–1602), amateur Italian composer, one of the Florentine *camerata* who were interested in recreating in music the spirit of Greek drama, and one of the first to write the new declamatory solo song with figured bass accompaniment. Of his extant works the most important is *La rappresentazione di anima e di corpo* (1600), a morality play set to music in recitative, interspersed with choruses in the style of popular hymns and instrumental movements; a modern edition by G. F. Malipiero was published in 1919, and a facsimile edition appeared in 1967. The work was first performed in the Oratory of St. Philip Neri (1595) in Rome.

E. J. DENT: 'La Rappresentazione di Anima e di Corpo', in *Papers read at the International Congress of Musicology*, 1944)

Cavalleria Rusticana (rustic chivalry), opera in one act by Mascagni, to a libretto by Guido Menasci and Giovanni Targioni-Tozzetti (founded on a play by Giovanni Verga). First performed in Rome in 1890, the work was the winner of a contest for one-act operas organised in Italy the previous year; and though Mascagni wrote many other operas after it, it was to prove his only enduring international success. As the composer declared later: 'It was a pity I wrote *Cavalleria* first; I was crowned before I became king'. With its fierce story of love and revenge in a Sicilian village, the work was to become the foundation-stone of the Italian *verismo* style. The hero, Turiddu, is ostensibly in love with Santuzza, but has not forgotten his former sweetheart, Lola, now married to Alfio. Santuzza informs Alfio of Turiddu's duplicity. Alfio challenges Turiddu to a duel and kills him (off-stage). The famous intermezzo, performed with the curtain up, occurs halfway through the opera. *Cavalleria Rusticana* is traditionally staged as part of a double-bill with that other short *verismo* masterpiece, Leoncavallo's *I Pagliacci* (1892).

Cavalli, Pietro Francesco (1602–76), Italian composer. His real name was Caletti-Bruni, but he took the name Cavalli for his patron Federico Cavalli, mayor of

Crema. He became a singer at St. Mark's, Venice (under Monteverdi), in 1617, was second organist there in 1640, principal organist in 1665, and *maestro di cappella* in 1668. The opening of the first public opera house in Venice in 1637 gave him the opportunity of writing for the stage. He wrote more than forty operas, of which the first, *Le nozze di Teti e di Peleo*, appeared in 1639. His *Ercole amante* was specially written for performance in Paris in 1662, an indication of the international fame he achieved as an opera composer. The style of his operas, as of Monteverdi's later works, illustrates the growing importance of song (as opposed to recitative) in Italian opera at this time. He also composed some church music which was published in two major collections, the *Musiche Sacre* of 1656 and the *Vesperi* of 1675. Performing editions of several works have been prepared by Raymond Leppard, including the opera *L'Ormindo* (1967), the eight-part *Messa Concertata* (1966), and the motets *Laetatus sum* and *Salve Regina* (1969).

R. J. LEPPARD: 'Cavalli's Operas', *Proceedings of the Royal Musical Association*, xciii (1966–7)
H. PRUNIERES: *Cavalli et l'opéra vénitien au xviie siècle* (1931); *L'Opéra italien en France avant Lulli* (1913)
S. T. WORSTHORNE: *Venetian Opera in the Seventeenth Century* (1954)

cavata (It.), literally a carving or engraving. In music the term was used in the 18th century for the epigrammatic ariosos sometimes found at the end of a long recitative. Good examples of the cavata can be found in Bach's cantatas.

cavatina (It.), diminutive of *cavata* (literally 'extraction') – a term used in the 18th century for an *arioso* section occurring in recitative:

(1) originally a song in an opera or oratorio which is less elaborate in structure and treatment than a *da capo* aria e.g. Barbarina's 'L'ho perduto' at the start of Act 4 of Mozart's *Marriage of Figaro*. But since the Countess's 'Porgi amor' in Act 2 of the same opera is also described as a cavatina, we should beware of supposing that a cavatina is 'less important' than aria;

(2) an instrumental piece or movement of a similar character, e.g. the fifth movement of Beethoven's string quartet in B flat, op 130.

Cavazzoni, Marco Antonio (before 1490–after 1559), Italian composer, known as Marcantonio Cavazzoni da Bologna, *detto* d'Urbino. He was for a short time organist of Chioggia Cathedral (1536–7), and later a singer at St. Mark's, Venice. He published *Recerchari, Motetti, Canzoni* (1523; facsimile edition, 1974) for the organ, dedicated to his patron, Francesco Cornaro; a modern edition is in K. Jeppesen, *Die italienische Orgelmusik am Anfang des Cinquecento* (1943).

His son, **Girolamo Cavazzoni** (c. 1509–after 1577), was also a composer. He published *Intavolatura cioè Recercari Canzoni Himni Magnificati* (1543; modern edition in two volumes by O. Mischiati, 1959–61) for the organ.

Cavendish, Michael (c. 1565–1628). English composer of lute songs and madrigals, published in a single volume in 1598 (facsimile edition, 1971). His madrigal 'Come gentle swains' was the first work by an English composer to include the refrain 'Long live fair Oriana' (borrowed from the English version of Giovanni Croce's 'Ove tra l'herb' i fiori' which was printed in the second book of *Musica Transalpina* in 1597). It was rewritten for inclusion in Morley's anthology *The Triumphes of Oriana* (1601). A modern edition of the lute songs is in *The English School of Lutenist Songwriters*, second series; the madrigals are in *The English Madrigal School*, xxxvi.

Cazzati, Maurizio (c. 1620–77), Italian composer, who held various posts as *maestro di cappella* at Mantua, Bozolo, Bergamo and Bologna. In addition to a large amount of secular and sacred vocal music he also wrote a number of sonatas for various instrumental combinations which are important for the early history of the form. G. B. Vitali was his pupil.

cédez (Fr.), 'give way,' i.e. go a little slower.

celesta, a keyboard instrument invented in 1886 by Auguste Mustel in Paris. The hammers strike steel bars, underneath which are a series of wooden resonators. Its ethereal tone is heard to the best advantage in the higher register. Its written compass is from

but the actual sound is an octave higher. First used in the orchestra by Chaikovsky in the 'Danse de la Fée-Dragée' (Dance of the Sugar-Plum Fairy) in the ballet *Casse-Noisette* (Nutcracker), op 71 (1892).

céleste pedal, a device invented by Sebastien Érard (1752–1831) for reducing the tone on a piano by damping the strings with a strip of pedal. This method is now obsolete. The modern practice is either to check the impact of the hammers or to move the keyboard slightly to the right (*see* CORDA).

cembalo (It.), (1) dulcimer;

(2) abbreviation of *clavicembalo* (*see* HARPSICHORD).

Cenerentola, La (*Cinderella*), opera in two acts by Rossini, to a libretto by Jacopo Ferretti, first performed in 1817 in Rome. Rossini's is the greatest and most human of the several stage works based on the Perrault fairy-tale. The title-role, like Rosina in *The Barber of Seville*, was written for the clarinet-like tones of a coloratura mezzo (or contralto). Other operas on the same subject include Massenet's *Cendrillon* (1899) and Wolf-Ferrari's *Cenerentola* (1900). Prokofiev's ballet dates from 1945.

cents, the units by which musical intervals are measured. If a cent is a hundredth part of a semitone in a well-tempered scale, it follows that an octave contains 1200 cents. The method of scientifically measuring intervals in this way was developed by A. J. Ellis in the 19th century.

Céphale et Procris (Fr., *Cephalus and Procris*), opera in three acts by Grétry, to a libretto by Jean François Marmontel, first performed in 1773 at Versailles.

Cerone, Domenico Pietro (1566–1625), Italian singer and writer on music. He was a singer at Oristano Cathedral (Sardinia), and in the service of Philip II and Philip III of Spain (1592–1603). From 1604 he was a priest and singer at the church of the Annunciation, Naples. His principal theoretical work, written in Spanish, was *El Melopeo y Maestro* (The Musician and Master), published at Naples in 1613 (facsimile edition, 1969) – a voluminous treatise of 1160 pages, which offers not only instruction but also a good deal of information about contemporary music and musicians.

Certon, Pierre (died 1572), French composer, a pupil of Josquin des Prés. He was a singer at the Sainte-Chapelle in 1532, and *magister puerorum* (master of the boys) there in 1542. He wrote Masses, motets, psalm settings (preserved in arrangements by G. Morlaye for voice and lute, published in 1554) and *chansons*. A modern edition of the three Masses is in H. Expert, *Monuments de la musique française au temps de la Renaissance*, ii (1925). Morlaye's versions of the psalm settings have been reprinted in an edition by F. Lesure and R. de Morcourt (1957). Ten four-part *chansons* have been edited by A. Seay in *Das Chorwerk*, lxxxii.

cervelas, *see* RACKET

Ces (Ger.), C flat (C♭).

Ceses (Ger.), C double flat (C♭♭).

Cesti, Pietro Antonio (1623–69), Italian opera-composer, who became a Franciscan monk. He was *maestro di cappella* at Volterra from 1645 to 1649, a singer in the Papal chapel from 1659 to 1662, and vice-*Kapellmeister* to the Imperial court at Vienna from 1666 to 1669. His operas are an important contribution to the development of the *aria* in music-drama. The most elaborate, *Il pomo d'oro*, was written to celebrate the marriage of the Emperor Leopold I to the Infanta Margherita of Spain at Vienna, 1667; a modern edition is in *Denkmäler der Tonkunst in Österreich*, vi, Jugend iii (2) and ix, Jugend iv (2). A modern edition (incomplete) of *La Dori* (Florence, 1661) is in *Publikationen älterer praktischer und theoretischer Musikwerke*, Jugend xi, and his *Orontea* (Venice, 1649) has been edited by W. Holmes (1973). He also wrote solo cantatas and chamber duets, selections from which have been edited by D. Burrows (1963 and 1969, respectively).

cetera (It.), CITTERN.

ceterone (It.), a large cither.

Chabrier, Alexis Emmanuel (1841–94), French composer who took music lessons while studying law. For eighteen years he worked for the Ministry of the Interior in Paris, before devoting himself entirely to composition. He was an enthusiastic admirer of Wagner – it is said that when he first heard the opening notes of *Tristan* he burst into tears – and some of his works (e.g. the opera *Gwendoline*, 1866) show Wagner's influence. But it was in his comic operas – *L'Etoile* (1877), *Une Education Manquée* (1879) and *Le Roi Malgré Lui* (1887) – that he was most delightfully himself. In these his Gallic wit (*L'Etoile* incorporates a superb parody of Berlioz's *Nuits d'Eté*), charm of melody and deftness of orchestration had a chance to flower. They are well worth performing today, though few opera companies seem inclined to do so. As a result, most people know Chabrier only through his vivacious orchestral rhapsody *Espana* (1883) and his *Marche Joyeuse*. His songs (especially his animal ones) and piano pieces are also of high quality.

chace, *see* CACCIA

chaconne (Fr.; It., *ciaccona*), a stately dance in triple time, which appears to have been imported into Spain from Mexico in the late 16th century. Like the PASSACAGLIA, from which it is often indistinguishable, it was habitually written in the form of a series of variations on (*a*) a ground bass (*basso ostinato*) or (*b*) a stereotyped harmonic progression. It was particularly popular in the 17th century, when it occurs frequently in operas and keyboard music. Examples are also found which are chaconnes without being so described, e.g. the 'Triumphing Dance' in Purcell's *Dido and Aeneas*. The most famous example of type (*b*) is the chaconne in Bach's Partita in D minor for solo violin.

chacony, a 17th century English version of CHACONNE.

Chadwick, George Whitefield (1854–1931), U.S. composer, who studied at Boston and in Germany. He taught at the New England Conservatory, Boston, from 1880, and became director in 1897. His works, in the romantic tradition but with their own U.S. quality, include a number of operas (*The Quiet Lodging*, *Tabasco*, *Judith*, *The Padrone* and *Love's Sacrifice*), choral pieces (*The Viking's Last Voyage*, *The Song of the Viking*, *Lovely Rosabel* and *The Lily Nymph*), three symphonies, symphonic poems ranging from *Cleopatra* to *Tam o' Shanter* in their inspiration, five string quartets and other chamber music, songs and keyboard music.

Chaikovsky, Piotr Ilyich (1840–93), Russian composer. Born at Votkinsk, a mining town on the borders of the Vyatka Province, he was the son of a chief inspector of mines who encouraged him from early childhood to learn the piano. When he was eight, the family moved to St. Petersburg, where Chaikovsky was sent to a boarding school. His sensitive personality, however, was ill-suited to institutional life and at ten he was transferred to a school of jurisprudence. When he was fourteen his mother (whom he adored) died of cholera, and in the same year he began to compose. At nineteen he became a clerk in the Ministry of Justice, but continued his private study of music and took lessons from Zaremba and Anton Rubinstein at the newly-opened St. Petersburg Conservatory. Progress was rapid. By 1866 he was professor of harmony at the new Moscow Conservatory, directed by Anton Rubinstein's brother Nicolai, and in the same year he wrote his first symphony, known as the *Winter Dreams* – though the stress of composing it resulted in a nervous breakdown. In 1868 he came into contact with Rimsky-Korsakov, Balakirev and other members of the Russian nationalist school, but tended to regard them (with the exception of Rimsky) as talented, rather presumptuous amateurs. They, for their part, were inclined to think him a somewhat dull eclectic, even though he was already writing music as profoundly Russian as any of them. In the same year he completed the first of his operas, *The Voyevoda*, and the following years yielded a number of outstanding masterpieces, including *Romeo and Juliet* (1870), the second symphony (1872), the first piano concerto (1874), the third symphony (1875) and *Francesca da Rimini* (1876). While working on the greatest of his operas, *Eugene Onegin*, in 1877, he married an infatuated admirer, Antonina Ivanovna Milyukova – mainly, it seems, because he considered Onegin's aloofness towards the infatuated Tatyana (in Pushkin's 'novel in verse' on which he was basing his opera) to be utterly heartless. But Chaikovsky's by now definite homosexuality meant that the marriage was doomed from the start, and in despair he attempted suicide by walking into the Volga. Compensation, however, came around the same time from a sympathetic admirer and patroness, Nadezhda von Meck, with whom he corresponded but never talked. She provided him with a regular income, which enabled him to escape from teaching (which was proving increasingly frustrating) and devote himself to composition; from this period date the fourth symphony (1877), violin concerto (1878), second piano concerto (1879–80), *Italian Caprice* (1880), *1812 Overture* (1880), *Manfred* symphony (1885), fifth symphony (1888), and *The Sleeping Beauty* ballet music (1888–89). In 1890, Mme. von Meck abruptly terminated his allowance – which upset him, because he valued their strange friendship – but he was now well enough established to be able to fend financially for himself.

Piotr Ilyich Chaikovsky: his haunted and introspective nature found the path between the make believe of fairy tale and real life both painful and treacherous

In 1891 he toured the United States, conducting concerts in New York, Baltimore and Philadelphia. In 1892 he visited Hamburg to hear Mahler conduct *Eugene Onegin* (very impressively, he thought). The *Nutcracker* ballet had its première at St. Petersburg in December of that year, and early in 1893 he set to work on his sixth symphony, the *Pathetic*. Nine days after conducting its première in St. Petersburg (in October 1893) he drank a glass of unboiled water at

lunch. As a result of this (perhaps deliberate) rash act he developed cholera and died a few days later. He was buried in the Alexander Nevsky monastery, near Glinka, Borodin and Mussorgsky, and a performance of the *Pathetic* symphony was (inevitably) given in his memory.

Chaikovsky described what he considered to be one of his weaknesses as a composer when he observed: 'I cannot complain of lack of inventive power, but I have always suffered from want of skill in the management of form.' Though pedants have always been prepared to agree with him in this assessment of himself, the supposed structural weakness of many of his works has hardly affected their popularity. In fact, with their warm, open-hearted melodies, their dramatic sweep, and their brilliant and picturesque orchestration, Chaikovsky's works dictate their own form. If they do not obey pedantic rules, so much the worse for pedantry. His well of melodies was bottomless, and we should try to remember, in listening to his orchestral pieces and ballet music, that these represent only two sides of his output. He himself considered his opera, *Eugene Onegin*, to be the finest of all his works. But *The Queen of Spades* (1890) is scarcely less fine, and some of his other operas, too, are worth exploring, as are his songs and chamber music.

Finally, a word about the spelling of his name. Though the traditional transliteration is Tchaikovsky, the introductory 'T' (as Gerald Abraham and other authorities have pointed out) is unnecessary. The standard spelling of 'Tchekhov' today is Chekhov, and it is only conservatism which makes people want to hang on to the familiar Tchaikovsky rather than use a more modern and accurate Chaikovsky.

Chaikovsky's principal compositions are:

(1) Stage works: eleven operas, including *Vakula the Smith* (1876; revived as *The Little Shoes*, 1887; published as *Les Caprices d'Oxane*), *Eugene Onegin* (1879), *Joan of Arc* (1881), *Mazeppa* (1884), *The Enchantress* (1887), *The Queen of Spades* (1890), *Iolanthe* (1892); three ballets – *Swan Lake* (1876), *Sleeping Beauty* (1889), *Nutcracker* (1891–2); incidental music for *Snow-maiden* (1873) and *Hamlet* (1891);

(2) Orchestra: six symphonies (no 4, 1877; no 5, 1888; no 6, 1893); *Manfred* symphony (1885); overture-fantasia *Romeo and Juliet* (1869; final revision, 1880); fantasias: *The Tempest* (1873) and *Francesca da Rimini* (1876); overtures: *The Storm* (1864) and *The Year 1812* (1880); three suites (1879, 1883, 1884); symphonic poem *Faet* (1868); symphonic ballad *The Voyevoda* (1891); *Capriccio Italien* (1880); serenade in C for string orchestra;

(3) Orchestra and solo instrument: three piano concertos (B flat minor, 1875; G 1880, revised 1893; E flat, in one movement, 1893); concert-fantasia for piano and orchestra (1884); violin concerto (1878); *Variations on a Rococo Theme* for cello and orchestra (1876);

(4) Chamber music: three string quartets (D, 1871; F, 1874; E flat minor, 1876); piano trio in A minor (1882); string sextet *Souvenir de Florence* (begun 1887; revised 1892); *Souvenir d'un lieu cher* for violin and piano;

(5) Piano: sonata in C sharp minor (1865); *The*

Seasons (1876); sonata in G (1878); *Children's Album* (1878); *Dumka* (1886);

(6) Songs: nine sets of six songs (1869, 1872, 1874, 1875, 1878, 1884, 1887, 1893); seven songs (1880); sixteen songs for children (1881–3); twelve songs (1886); six French songs (1888); six duets (1880); Also church music, cantatas, and other choral works; translations of Gevaert's *Traité d'Instrumentation* (1865) and J. C. Lobe's *Musical Catechism* (1869); *Guide to the Practical Study of Harmony* (1871); *Short Manual of Harmony, adapted to the study of religious music in Russia* (1874); *Autobiographical Descriptions of a Journey abroad in 1888.*

G. ABRAHAM: *On Russian Music* (1939); (editor): *Tchaikovsky: a Symposium* (1945)

E. BLOM: *Tchaikovsky: Orchestral Works* (1927)

C. D. BOWEN and B. VON MECK: *Beloved Friend* (1937)

E. EVANS: *Tchaikovsky* (1935)

E. GARDEN: *Tchaikovsky* (1973)

W. LAKOND: *The Diaries of Tchaikovsky* (1945)

R. NEWMARCH: *Tchaikovsky, his Life and Works* (1900)

J. WARRACK: *Tchaikovsky* (1973)

J. WARRACK: *Tchaikovsky Symphonies and Concertos* (1969)

H. WEINSTOCK: *Tchaikovsky* (1943)

chair organ, a term used in England in the 17th and 18th centuries for a small organ (Fr., *positif*) used in conjunction with a larger instrument, known as the 'great organ'. The two instruments were originally separate, but in course of time became incorporated, the great organ being played from one manual, the chair (or choir) organ from another. It has been supposed that 'chair' is a corruption of 'choir', but it is just as likely that 'choir', used in this sense, is a corruption of 'chair'. In that case 'chair' (often written 'chayre') is probably the same as the Fr. *chaire* (Lat., *cathedra*), though it is not clear why a word meaning a seat, throne or pulpit should be applied to an organ. The explanation that the chair organ was so called because it was placed at the back of the organist's seat (Ger., *Rückpositif*) is not convincing (*see* CHOIR ORGAN).

Chaliapin, Fedor Ivanovich (1873–1938), Russian bass, the son of a peasant. He began to sing in opera at the age of seventeen, but first won a reputation in Moscow in 1896. Though he sang in Italian opera he was best known for his interpretation of the principal bass parts in Russian opera, particularly Mussorgsky's *Boris Godunov*. He possessed not only a remarkable voice but also an unrivalled sense of the stage.

F. CHALIAPIN: *Pages from my Life* (1927); *Man and Mask* (1932)

chalumeau (Fr.), (1) generic term for a rustic reed-pipe (Lat., *calamellus*, diminutive of '*calamus*', a reed; Eng., shawm), in use up to the 18th century (*see* A. Carse, *Musical Wind Instruments*, pages 148–152);

(2) in the first half of the 18th century also used to mean 'clarinet';

(3) now applied to the lower register of the clarinet (*see* CLARINET, SHAWM).

chamber music (Fr., *musique de chambre*; Ger., *Kammermusik*; It., *musica da camera*), properly music suitable for a room (It., *camera*) in a house, as opposed to music for a church or theatre. At one time it included

vocal as well as instrumental music, e.g. Martin Peerson's *Mottects or Grave Chamber Musique* (1630) but the term is now generally applied – though not exclusively so – to instrumental works written for a limited number of performers, in which there is only one player to each part. Such music is necessarily intimate in character even though performed (as it is today) in a public concert hall. Characteristic forms are the fantasia or ricercar for viols (16th and early 17th centuries), the trio sonata for two violins and bass with organ or harpsichord (17th and early 18th centuries), and the string quartet for two violins, viola and cello (late 18th century to the present day).

In addition to the string quartet compositions have also been written (*a*) for fewer or more than four string instruments (string duo, string trio, string quintet, etc.), (*b*) for strings with one or more wind instruments (e.g. clarinet quintet = a work for clarinet and string quartet), (*c*) for piano with string or wind instruments (e.g. piano trio = a work for piano, violin and cello). There is no foundation for the view that chamber music is the 'purest' form of instrumental music, but the limitation of the means employed does present a serious challenge to the composer's invention and necessarily involves a type of composition in which emphasis is laid on clarity of texture.

See DUO, TRIO, QUARTET, QUINTET, SEXTET, SEPTET, OCTET, NONET

W. W. COBBETT: *Cyclopedic Survey of Chamber Music* (two volumes, 1929–30); supplement edited by C. Mason (1963)

H. ULRICH: *Chamber Music* (1948)

chamber opera, an opera written for reduced forces – a small cast, a small orchestra – suitable for performance in a theatre more intimate than a grand opera house. Though a number of chamber operas were written in reaction against the large-scale Wagnerian pieces, an important reason for the rise of chamber operas in the present century has been a simple one of economics. That is not to say, however, that chamber operas are inferior to full-scale operas any more than string quartets are inferior to symphonies. In *Albert Herring, A Midsummer Night's Dream* and above all in *The Turn of the Screw*, Benjamin Britten responded to the discipline of the genre and used it to telling effect. Moreover, since the oldest known opera (Peri's *Dafne*) is a chamber opera, it could be argued that this is the purest of all operatic forms.

chamber orchestra, *see* CHAMBER MUSIC

Chambonnières, Jacques Champion de (c. 1602–c. 1672), harpsichordist to the French court under Louis XIII and Louis XIV. His works for harpsichord, published in 1670 though written many years earlier, rank high among the keyboard music of the 17th century and had a great influence on younger composers. His pupils included d'Anglebert and Louis Couperin. A modern edition of his works by P. Brunold and A. Tessier was published in 1926.

Chaminade, Cécile (1857–1944), French pianist and composer, a pupil of Godard. Her compositions included orchestral music, chamber music and *Les Amazones* (a *symphonie lyrique* for chorus and orchestra), but her reputation rests on her songs and piano pieces.

Chandos Anthems, a series of anthems by Handel, composed between 1716 and 1720 for the Earl of

Carnarvon, later Duke of Chandos, for performance in his private chapel at Canons, near Edgware.

change ringing, *see* BELL

changing note, *see* CAMBIATA (2)

Chanler, Theodore (1902–61), U.S. composer, pupil of Bloch at the Cleveland Institute of Music and of Nadia Boulanger in Paris. His works include a chamber opera, *The Pot of Fat* (1955), a violin sonata and other chamber music, song cycles (*Epitaphs* and *The Children*) and other songs. The latter have been hailed by Virgil Thomson as among the finest in English of our time.

chanson (Fr.), song, whether for a single voice or for a vocal ensemble. Also applied, like AIR, to instrumental pieces of a vocal character. The normal word in modern French for a solo song with piano accompaniment is *mélodie*.

chant, (1) in general, music which is sung in accordance with prescribed ritual or tradition;

(2) in particular, the unaccompanied vocal music used for the services of the Christian church, e.g. Ambrosian chant, Gregorian chant (also known as 'plainchant' or 'plainsong');

(3) in the Anglican church used only of the music to which the psalms and canticles are sung;

(4) (Fr.), song, singing, voice.

See ANGLICAN CHANT, PLAINSONG, GREGORIAN CHANT

chanter or **chaunter,** (1) part of a BAGPIPE: the pipe with finger holes on which the melody is played, as opposed to the 'drone' pipes, which merely sustain single notes;

(2) obsolete term for 'precentor' in a cathedral.

Chappell, a London firm of music-publishers and piano-manufacturers, founded in 1812 by Samuel Chappell (died December 1834), in association with J. B. Cramer and F. T. Latour.

character piece (Ger., *Charakterstück*), an instrumental piece, very often for piano, portraying a specific mood, attitude, or literary conception. Many types of piece – Beethoven's bagatelles, Schubert's *Moments Musicaux*, Mendelssohn's *Songs Without Words*, Debussy's *Préludes* – could be said to fit this generalised title, though perhaps the pieces that fit it best are the *Fantasiestücke, Nachtstücke, Bunte Blätter, Kinderszenen*, etc. by Schumann.

Charpentier, Gustave (1860–1956), French composer who studied at Lille Conservatoire and Paris Conservatoire under Massenet. Though he wrote instrumental music and songs his reputation rests on the opera *Louise* (Paris, 1900), which adds romantic music to a realistic subject – the life and loves of working-class people in Paris. By the end of 1931 it had had eight hundred performances in Paris alone. In 1902, Charpentier founded the Conservatoire Populaire de Mimi Pinson, with the aim of giving working-class girls like Louise an opportunity to learn music and drama. His second opera, *Julien, ou la Vie du Poète,* was presented in Paris in 1913, but failed to achieve the same success. After the production of *Julien,* Charpentier virtually abandoned composition.

M. DELMAS: *Gustave Charpentier et le lyrisme français* (1931)

Charpentier, Marc-Antoine (1634–1704), French composer. He was a pupil of Carissimi in Rome, becoming director of music to the Jesuits of the *Maison professe* in Paris, and in 1698 director of music to the

Sainte-Chapelle. His compositions include two operas – *Les Amours d'Acis et de Galatée* (1678) and *Médée* (1693) – and other stage music, several oratorios (a form not otherwise cultivated in France at this time) and a large quantity of church music. A complete edition of his works by G. Lambert was begun in 1948.

Chasse, La (Fr., *The Hunt*), title given to two of Haydn's instrumental works containing themes based on a hunting-call idiom: (1) String quartet in B flat major, op 1, no 1 (c. 1755); (2) Symphony no 73 in D major (1781).

chaunter, *see* CHANTER

Chausson, Ernest (1855–99), French composer, a pupil of Massenet and Franck. His compositions, sensitive and romantic in style, include the opera *Le Roi Arthus* (Brussels, 1903), a symphony, *Poème* for violin and orchestra (his best-known work), the *Poème de l'amour et de la mer* for voice and orchestra, a concerto for piano, violin and string quartet, and songs. He died after a bicycle accident.

Chávez, Carlos (born 1899), Mexican composer and conductor who became director of the National Conservatorio, Mexico City, and conductor of the Orquesta Sinfónica de México from 1928 until 1952. Much of his work consists of a presentation in modern terms of the characteristic elements of Indian folk music. His compositions include symphonies, a piano concerto, a violin concerto, string quartets and other chamber music, ballets, choral works, piano music and songs.

chef d'attaque (Fr.), leader of an orchestra.

chef d'orchestre (Fr.), conductor.

chekker (O. Fr., *éschaquier*), a keyboard instrument with strings in use in the 14th and 15th centuries, described towards the end of the 14th century as *istrument semblant d'orguens, qui sona ab cordes* (an instrument like the organ in appearance, which sounds with strings). Its exact nature is unknown, nor has any convincing explanation been given of the name.

Cherepnin, Nicolai (1873–1945), composer, pianist and conductor; studied under Rimsky-Korsakov at the St. Petersburg Conservatoire. He was conductor for the Diaghilev Ballets (1909–14), returned to St. Petersburg (1914–18), and settled in Paris in 1921. He composed operas, ballets, two symphonies, symphonic poems and other orchestral works, a piano concerto, two Masses, piano pieces and songs, and completed Mussorgsky's *Sorochintsi Fair.*

His son, **Alexander Cherepnin** (1899–1977), composer and pianist, studied at the St. Petersburg Conservatoire under his father, visited Tiflis and lived in Paris (from 1921), where he studied at the Conservatoire. He toured extensively as a pianist, lived in China and Japan (1935–37), where he published collections of modern oriental music, and later settled in New York.

Cherubini, Maria Luigi Carlo Zenobio Salvatore (1760–1842), Italian composer, born in Florence, and pupil of Sarti at Venice. He visited London (1784–6) and was appointed composer to the king. In 1788 he settled in Paris, where he remained for the rest of his life, and where (from 1822) he was director of the Conservatoire. Of his numerous operas seven belong to his early years in Italy, two were written for London, one was written for Brescia in 1786, one for Turin in the winter of 1787–8, one for Vienna in 1806, and twelve for Paris. In the Paris operas he showed, e.g. in *Médée* (1797), that the old traditions of *opéra comique* with spoken dialogue were not inconsistent with a tragic subject. His *Les Deux Journées* (1800) known in English as *The Water-Carrier*, is a classic example of the so-called 'rescue' opera, inspired by the hazards and heroism of the French Revolution. He was much admired by Beethoven (*see* A. C. Kalischer, *Beethoven's Letters*, translated by J. S. Shedlock, volume ii, page 234) who shows the influence of Cherubini in his own work, e.g. in *Egmont* and *Fidelio* (also a 'rescue' opera). He was less admired by Berlioz, who considered Cherubini an obstacle to his progress at the Paris Conservatoire. After 1813 Cherubini devoted himself mostly to church music, including several Masses with orchestral accompaniment and two Requiems, one of them for male voices. Among his other works are six string quartets and six piano sonatas. He also published a *Cours de contrepoint et de la fugue* (1835).

E. BELLASIS: *Cherubini* (second edition, 1912)
B. DEANE: *Cherubini* (1965)

Chester, a firm of music-publishers, founded at Brighton in 1860 and transferred to London in 1915.

chest voice, the lower 'register' of the voice, as distinct from the higher register ('head voice').

Cheval de Bronze, Le (*The Bronze Horse*), opera in three acts by Auber, to a libretto by Augustin Eugène Scribe (*opéra-féerique*), first performed in 1835 in Paris.

chevalet (Fr.; Ger., *Steg*; It., *ponticello*), bridge of a string instrument. *Au chevalet*, on the bridge, i.e. play near the bridge, thus producing a glassy, brittle tone.

chiavette (It.), plural of *chiavetta*, diminutive of *chiave* (key, clef). First used by Paolucci (1726–76) to indicate the use of clefs other than those normal for the voices in 16th and early 17th century music, e.g. the use of the tenor clef:

for a bass part instead of

or the use of the G clef on the second line:

for a soprano part in place of the normal

The use of such clefs avoided the necessity for leger-lines, but since notes on leger-lines might well lie outside the effective compass of the voice they were used also to indicate transposition down a fourth or fifth, e.g. a soprano part written in the G clef with this compass:

might indicate that it was to be sung at this pitch (which is not necessarily the same as the standard pitch today):

with a similar transposition indicated by the *chiavette* of the other parts. Though the word *chiavette* does not appear before the 18th century, the principle of transposition when 'high clefs' are used is precisely stated by Praetorius in his *Syntagma Musicum*, vol. iii (1619).

Chicago Symphony Orchestra, one of the United States' leading orchestras. It was founded in 1891 by Theodore Thomas, who was its conductor until his death in 1905. His successors have been Frederick Stock, Désiré Defauw, Artur Rodzinski, Rafael Kubelik, Fritz Reiner, Jean Martinon and Sir Georg Solti. The orchestra has its own concert hall (1904).

chiesa (It.), 'church'. Used in the 17th and early 18th centuries to distinguish music suitable for performance in church from that suitable for performance in secular surroundings, e.g. *sonata da chiesa*.

See SONATA

Child, William (c. 1606–97), English organist and composer. He was a lay-clerk at St. George's Chapel, Windsor, and was organist there from 1630 to 1643 and from 1660. He was also organist at the Chapel Royal from 1660. His compositions consist mainly of church music, which shows an adherence to traditional styles but also accepts the new manner of Restoration music. He published in 1639 *The first set of Psalms of iii voyces, fitt for private chappells, or other private meetings with a continuall Base, either for the Organ or Theorbo, newly composed after the Italian way.*

F. HUDSON and W. ROY LARGE: 'William Child (1606/7–1697) – a new Investigation of Sources', *Music Review*, xxxi (1970)

Child of Our Time, A, oratorio by Tippett for soloists, chorus and orchestra. First performed in 1944 in London, the work has its source in the shooting of a German diplomat by a Jewish refugee shortly before World War II, and the persecution of Jews in Germany which followed that event. The work, in three parts, has a text by the composer. It incorporates Negro spirituals at key points in the score, after the fashion of Bach chorales.

Children's Corner, the title of a suite of piano pieces by Debussy (1908), dedicated to his infant daughter. The separate pieces are: *Gradus ad Parnassum* (a satire on technical exercises), *Jimbo's lullaby* (for a toy elephant, who ought presumably to have been called Jumbo), *Serenade of the doll* (a mistake for 'Serenade to the doll'), *The snow is dancing, The little shepherd* and *Golliwog's cake walk* (including a malicious quotation from *Tristan*). The suite was orchestrated by André Caplet in 1911.

chimes, a small set of bells. Stone chimes have been known since ancient times; their orchestral equivalent consists of the tubular bells. Wind chimes or aeolian bells are hung in the open to strike against each other and sound as the wind blows.

Chinese block, a hollowed block of wood, struck with a drum-stick to give a hard resonant tap. It is also known as the wood block.

Chisholm, Erik (1904–65), Scottish composer and conductor, who studied at Edinburgh University. As conductor of the Glasgow Grand Opera Society from 1930 he directed the (belated) British premières of such works as Mozart's *Idomeneo* and *La Clemenza di Tito,* and Berlioz's *Trojans* and *Beatrice and Benedick.* In 1946 he became professor of music at Cape Town University, where he continued his policy of arousing interest in opera and modern music. His compositions include a trilogy of operas entitled *Murder in Three Keys,* two symphonies, two piano concertos, a violin concerto and piano music.

chitarrone (It.), a large LUTE.

chiuso, *see* CLOS

choir, (1) the place in a cathedral where the singers are stationed;

> (2) a body of singers;
>
> (3) In the United States a particular section of the orchestra, e.g. 'brass choir';
>
> (4) short for CHOIR ORGAN.

choirbook, a large medieval manuscript volume designed so that the separate parts of a choral composition could be read by a number of singers standing in front of a lectern. The music was not written in score: the parts were written separately on two facing pages, using as much or as little space as might be necessary. The system originated on a smaller scale in the 13th century. It was found to be economical to write out a motet in this way, since the upper parts took up far more space than the slow-moving tenor. The large choirbook was in general use in the 15th century and continued to be used in the 16th century, when printed examples are also found, but its use inevitably declined in favour of the more practical system of separate PART-BOOKS. A modification of the choirbook system, however, persisted in domestic music for voices and instruments, which was often printed with the parts facing various ways, so that a small group of performers could sit round a table and read them (*see* illustration for DOWLAND, JOHN).

choir organ (Fr., *positif*; Ger., *Unterwerk*; It., *organo di coro*), in modern use a section of the organ played from the lowest of three or more manuals. It consists generally of quieter stops, some of which will be suitable for solo work, and is frequently enclosed in a box with movable shutters (like the SWELL ORGAN) which enables the player to make a *crescendo* or *diminuendo.* If the organ has no SOLO ORGAN the choir organ may include a powerful reed stop (trumpet or tuba), or alternatively the trumpet stop on the GREAT ORGAN may also be available on the choir organ. This makes it possible to provide a trumpet solo with a heavy accompaniment on the great organ.

> *See* CHAIR ORGAN, MANUAL, ORGAN

choke cymbal, *see* HI-HAT CYMBAL

Chopin, Frédéric François (originally **Fryderyk Franciszek**) (1810–49), Polish born composer, the son of a French father, living in Poland, and a Polish mother. Born at Zelazowa Wola, near Warsaw, he received his first piano lessons (at the age of six) from Adalbert Zywny, composed his first polonaise (in G minor) at the age of seven, and played in public at the age of eight. His father, a teacher of French, held various appointments in Warsaw and insisted that Chopin have a general as well as musical education. At ten, the singer Catalini was moved by Chopin's playing to give him a watch, and at fifteen the boy played before Czar Alexander I, who gave him a diamond ring. At sixteen he entered the Warsaw Conservatory, where he studied composition under Joseph Elsner. Polish folk music, the *bel canto* lines of Italian opera, and the style of Hummel were now exerting their influence on him, and in 1829 he composed his F minor piano concerto (usually known as his second concerto, though in fact written before the E minor, published as no 1). In that year he gave two concerts in Vienna, visited Dresden and Prague, and on his return revealed his love for the singer Konstancja Gladkowska. The following year, however, he left Russian occupied Poland, after playing both his concertos in Warsaw, and in 1831 settled in Paris, where he began to give lessons and appear at concerts. He also made the acquaintance of Liszt, Mendelssohn, Berlioz and Bellini, and began his association with the novelist, George Sand, in 1837. His secret engagement to Marya Wodzińska had just ended. He lived with George Sand in Majorca during the winter of 1838–39, but the poor weather and primitive living conditions affected his health; thereafter he suffered from steadily worsening tuberculosis. From 1840 until 1847, however, he continued to live with George Sand, in Paris and in her country house at Nohant. Six years older than he was, she looked after him devotedly and helped his genius to flower. Many of his finest works, including the 24 preludes, the B flat minor and B minor sonatas, and the F minor fantasy, were written during the period of their liaison. When their relationship broke up (after a quarrel provoked by George Sand's two children) Chopin's inspiration deteriorated along with his health, but he continued to teach and give private recitals. In 1848, though very ill, he toured England and Scotland. His pupil, Jane Stirling, took him for a rest to the country-house of her brother-in-law, Lord Torphichen, and gave him a (by then) much-needed gift of 15,000 francs. In London he played before Queen Victoria, but the social life of Britain exhausted him. He died in Paris the following year.

Chopin's compositions are almost entirely for the piano. Though he owed something to the example of Field and Hummel, and had obviously profited from his study of Bach, he owed almost nothing to the major composers of his own period. He succeeded in creating an individual art of keyboard-writing, which makes a virtue of the evanescent tone of the instrument and uses melodic decoration as an enrichment of the harmonic texture. He was a master of the art of suggestion, and explored a harmonic territory going far beyond the conventional boundaries of his time. Other influences include the folk music of Poland, noticeable particularly in the mazurkas, and the melodic style, often demanding considerable virtuosity, of Italian opera. Chopin took care, however, to point out that his mazurkas were 'not for dancing'. In fact they are his most personal works, a kind of private journal in which, throughout his career, he worked out

Frédéric Chopin – 'the poet of the piano'

his harmonic and rhythmic experiments, explored the most delicate and varied pianistic colours, and jotted down all his changes of mood. The first mazurka was written before he left his homeland in 1830; the last, a poignant little reflection in F minor, was the last piece he ever wrote. Chopin made the mazurka, as a pianistic form, something peculiarly his own; and he did the same with the ballade (of which he wrote four, inspired in a general way by Mickiewicz's poetry) and the keyboard scherzo, to which he brought a sharp, sardonic quality very different from Beethoven's scherzi. His 24 preludes, one in each key, were Chopin's creative tribute to Bach. But though he recognised that his genius lay mainly in the world of short, perfectly proportioned piano pieces, to which he brought a wealth of poetic intensity, Chopin proved in his sonatas that he could sustain a large design without losing grip of his material. Pedants could argue that they are not 'strict' sonatas (though each conforms to a traditional pattern of several movements) but one would not wish them otherwise, for they are constructed with a satisfying logic of their own. The same can be said for his (often underrated) concertos, whose orchestration, far from being the embarrassment some commentators have claimed it to be, is always apt and sensitive, and sometimes (as in the use of the bassoon) positively original. His playing was incomparable, remarkable both for its delicacy and its intensity and giving a magical significance to passages which his contemporaries found incomprehensible on paper.

Chopin's principal compositions are:

(1) Piano and orchestra: two concertos; *Andante spianato* and *Polonaise*; fantasia on Polish airs; *Rondo à la Krakowiak*; variations on 'Là ci darem'.

(2) Piano solo: four *Ballades*; three *Ecossaises*; 27

Etudes; three impromptus; 51 Mazurkas; nineteen Nocturnes; twelve *Polonaises*; 25 preludes; four scherzos; three sonatas; seventeen waltzes; *Barcarolle*; *Berceuse*; *Fantaisie* in F minor; *Fantaisie-Impromptu*.

(3) Chamber music: piano trio; cello sonata; Introduction and *Polonaise* for cello and piano.

(4) Songs: seventeen Polish songs.

   G. ABRAHAM: *Chopin's Musical Style* (1939)
   A. HEDLEY: *Chopin* (1947)
   W. MURDOCH: *Chopin: his Life* (1934)
   A. WALKER (editor): *Chopin* (1966)

Chor (Ger.), choir, chorus.

choral, (1) adjective used in music involving a chorus, e.g. choral cantata;

   (2) (Ger.), (*a*) plainsong (Gregorian chant); (*b*) hymn-tune of the Lutheran church (*see* CHORALE).

chorale (English phonetic spelling of Ger. *Choral*), a hymn-tune of the Lutheran church. The earliest publications date from 1524. The materials used in Lutheran hymnody in the 16th century included (1) adaptations of Latin hymns already in use in the Catholic Church, (2) adaptations of pre-Reformation popular hymns in German, (3) adaptations of secular songs, (4) original hymns. Examples of these four categories are (1) 'Nun komm, der Heiden Heiland' (Lat., 'Veni, redemptor gentium'), (2) 'Christ ist erstanden', (3) 'Herzlich thut mich verlangen' (from Hassler's 'Mein G'müt ist mir verwirret'), (4) *Ein' feste Burg*. In the 16th century the melodies showed considerable rhythmical freedom, but by the 18th century their shape had acquired a four-square symmetry, familiar to us in Bach's harmonizations. Bach made no attempt to preserve the original flavour of the tunes, so that in his hands they become virtually 18th century compositions. The Bach revival in the 19th century led to the incorporation of a certain number of Lutheran chorales in English hymn-books, sometimes in a modified form. The process of adaptation and transformation may be illustrated by one of the best-known of the chorales – 'Herzlich thut mich verlangen' (the so-called 'Passion Chorale'). The original melody, as it appears in Hassler's *Lustgarten Neuer Teutscher Gesäng* (1601), set to secular words, is:

The following is one of nine harmonizations of the tune made by Bach:

BACH, *St. Matthew Passion*

From the 17th century onwards the chorale was used as the basis of two main types of extended music: (1) the church cantata, (2) preludes, partitas or varia-

tions for organ. Both served a liturgical purpose, since the congregation would be familiar with the tunes employed, and would relate them to the words associated with them. The majority of Bach's church cantatas use chorales, either in a four-part harmonization, or as the *cantus firmus* of a choral movement, or in association with solo voices. For organ works based on chorales *see* CHORALE PRELUDE.

> F. BLUME: *Geschichte der Evangelischen Kirchenmusik* (1965); *Hymns Ancient and Modern – Historical Edition* (1909)
> C. S. TERRY: *Bach's Chorals*, three volumes (1915–21); *Bach's Four-part Chorals* (1928)

chorale cantata, a type of church cantata which makes use of the text, and probably also the melody, of a Lutheran hymn or chorale. The greatest cantatas of this kind were composed by Bach, who brought considerable variety of approach to his treatment of these chorales – simple in some cases, but grand and complex in a work like *Ein' feste Burg*.

chorale fantasia or **fantasy,** an organ piece in which a chorale melody is freely treated.

chorale prelude (the spelling 'choral prelude' is misleading because it suggests that 'choral' is an English adjective instead of a German noun), a generic term for a piece of organ music based on a hymn-tune. It originated in Germany in the 17th century, when it was the custom in the Lutheran church to play on the organ an introduction to the hymn (or chorale) to be sung by the congregation. Various types of treatment were employed. The melody might be used as a *cantus firmus*, round which counterpoints were written, or it might appear in ornamented form as a solo with accompaniment, or it might be subjected to fugal treatment or used as a theme for variations. Contrapuntal devices such as canon were also used. All these types of treatment are to be found in Bach's chorale preludes. Among later composers of chorale preludes Reger and Karg-Elert were specially prolific. Chorales have also been used in works which do not strictly fall into the category of chorale preludes, e.g. in Mendelssohn's sixth organ sonata, which makes use of the chorale 'Vater unser im Himmelreich'.

> H. GRACE: *The Organ Works of Bach* (1922)
> A. SCHWEITZER: *J. S. Bach*, translated by E. Newman, two volumes (1911)
> S. DE B. TAYLOR: *The Chorale Preludes of J. S. Bach* (1942)

Choral Fantasia, (1) a work by Beethoven for piano solo, chorus and orchestra, op 80 (1808), consisting of a theme and variations, with improvisatory introduction for the piano. The words of the choral section are a poem in praise of music by Christoph Kuffner. The work is prophetic of the Choral Symphony;

(2) a setting by Gustav Holst, op 51 (1930) of words by Robert Bridges for chorus, organ, brass, strings and percussion.

Choral Symphony, (1) the popular name for Beethoven's ninth symphony in D minor, op 125 (1823), the last movement of which consists of a setting of Schiller's ode *An die Freude* (To joy) for soloists, chorus and orchestra. The original title was *Sinfonie mit Schlusschor* (Symphony with final chorus);

(2) a setting of poems by Keats for soprano solo, chorus and orchestra by Gustav Holst, op 41 (1924).

It is entitled *First Choral Symphony* but had no successor;

(3) symphonies written for chorus and orchestra, though not specifically entitled 'choral', include Mahler's eighth symphony (1907), and Vaughan Williams's *A Sea Symphony* (1910);

(4) symphonies with choral finales include Liszt's *Faust Symphony* (1857) and Mahler's second symphony. Mendelssohn's Hymn of Praise, op 52 (1840), is a 'symphony-cantata', consisting of three symphonic movements followed by a choral cantata.

chord, a term normally used of three or more different notes sounded simultaneously. A chord may be represented by only two different notes, but in that case a third note is implied. The classification of chords and their relation to each other forms part of the study of harmony. A *diatonic chord* is one that uses only notes proper to the key. A distinction between consonant and dissonant chords is arbitrary, since different standards of consonance and dissonance have prevailed at different times.

A chord of three notes in which the lowest note is accompanied by the third and fifth above it is known as a *triad*, e.g.:

Major triad:

Minor triad:

augmented triad:

diminished triad:

Of the diatonic triads in the key of C major, three are major, three are minor and one is diminished:

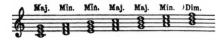

All other triads are chromatic in this key. The range of diatonic triads in a minor key is wider since the minor scale includes both flat and sharp sixths, and both flat and sharp sevenths, i.e. in the key of C minor, A natural as well as A flat, and B natural as well as B flat (*see* MINOR). There are therefore thirteen diatonic triad, in a minor key – five major, four minors one augmented, and three diminished:

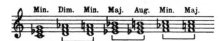

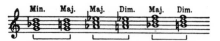

The chords in the above examples are generally said to be in *root position*. Major and minor triads in root position are known as *common chords*. The disposition of the notes above the bass does not affect the nature of the chord. The following are possible versions of the triad of C major in root position:

Where the harmony is in more than three parts it will obviously be necessary to double one or more notes of a triad, either at the unison or at the octave. The following illustrates some possible arrangements of the triad of C major in root position in four, five, six and seven parts:

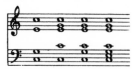

In three-part harmony, and in four-part harmony if the movement of the parts makes it desirable, the fifth of a major or minor triad is often omitted and the bass note doubled:

In 16th and 17th century music for several voices or instruments it is not uncommon to find the third omitted in the final chord, in which case the major third is supplied by the accompanying keyboard instrument or by the natural resonance of the building (*see* ACOUSTICS, TIERCE DE PICARDIE).

If the notes of a chord in root position are rearranged so that one of the upper notes becomes the lowest, the result is generally known as an *inversion*. There are only two possible inversions of a triad, e.g.:

root position:

first inversion:

second inversion:

On a keyboard instrument it is not possible to tell, without the context, whether an augmented triad is in root position or inverted, e.g.:

root position of augmented triad on C:

first inversion of augmented triad on A flat:

Second inversion of augmented triad on E:

On the piano or organ these three chords are identical. This makes possible a variety of harmonic progressions, e.g.:

In FIGURED BASS the first inversion of a triad is called a $\frac{6}{3}$ chord (or more simply, *chord of the sixth*), since its two upper notes are respectively a sixth and a third above the lowest note. Similarly the second inversion of a triad is called a $\frac{6}{4}$ chord. If the sixth in a minor $\frac{6}{3}$ chord is sharpened, e.g. if

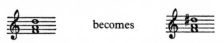

becomes

the result is called an *augmented sixth* chord (*see* AUGMENTED SIXTH). A major $\frac{6}{3}$ chord on the fourth degree of the scale is known as a *Neapolitan sixth* chord (*see* NEAPOLITAN SIXTH).

If an additional third is added above a triad in root position, thus producing a chord of four notes, the result is called a *chord of the seventh*, because the highest note is a seventh above the lowest. The seventh chords in the key of C major are:

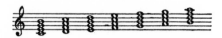

These may be classified as follows:

(1) major triad with major third superimposed:

(2) major triad with minor third superimposed:

(3) minor triad with minor third superimposed:

(also the seventh on D).

(4) diminished triad with major third superimposed:

All these are *diatonic sevenths*, because they do not involve any note foreign to the key. (2) is called the *dominant seventh* chord, because its lowest note is the dominant of the key (*see* DOMINANT). The introduction of chromatic notes makes possible further combinations, e.g.:

diminished triad with minor third superimposed:

This is known as the *diminished seventh* chord.

In three-part harmony it will be necessary to omit one of the notes of a seventh chord. Since the seventh cannot be omitted, it follows that either the fifth or, less frequently, the third will be omitted. Thus the dominant seventh chord in the key of C major may be represented by one of the following:

The same thing may happen in four-part harmony if the movement of the parts make it desirable, in which case the bass note will most probably be doubled, e.g.:

The theory of inversions is applied also to four-note chords. There are three possible inversions of these, e.g.:

root position:

first inversion:

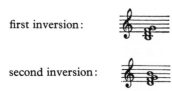

second inversion:

third inversion:

On a keyboard instrument the inversions of a diminished seventh chord are indistinguishable from transpositions of the same chord in root position, e.g.:

This makes it possible to use any diminished seventh chord as a means of modulating to (and consequently from) any major or minor key, e.g.:

The superimposition of a third on a seventh chord will produce a *chord of the ninth*. A ninth chord with a third added becomes a *chord of the eleventh*. An eleventh chord with a third added becomes a *chord of the thirteenth*, e.g.:

These can be inverted. A third added to a thirteenth chord does not produce a new chord, since the note added is merely the bass note doubled two octaves higher, e.g.:

Inversion and the superimposition of thirds makes it possible to build up the chords described above, but it does not explain their origin or their function. The chord did not arise from the conscious rearrangement of the notes of the triad. It arose naturally in the middle ages from the use of a passing note in three-part writing, e.g. in cadences of this kind:

The combination of a sixth and a third proved so attractive that we find British composers of the late 13th and early 14 centuries writing successions of such chords e.g.:

M. BUKOFZER, *Geschichte des englischen Diskants*, E 18

The conception of the $\frac{6}{3}$ chord as composed of a sixth and third combined explains why in the 16th century the diminished triad:

was avoided, because of the diminished fifth between the upper and lower parts, whereas:

(described by later theorists as its first inversion) was freely used.

The $\frac{6}{4}$ chord also occurred as a result of the free use of passing notes, e.g. in the following examples dating respectively from the 13th and 15th century:

G. REESE, *Music in the Middle Ages*, page 334

J. STAINER, *Dufay and his Contemporaries*, page 64

In 16th century practice this chord was normally used only as the result of a suspension requiring resolution (*see* SUSPENSION), e.g.:

PALESTRINA, *Missa Assumpta est Maria*

or as a decoration of a perfect cadence, e.g.:

PALESTRINA, *Ascendens Christus*

Chords other than triads also arose from the practice of using suspensions or passing notes. The following example shows the seventh treated as a dissonance to be resolved or one merely occurring in passing:

It is evident that in four-part harmony one note will have to be omitted from the chord of the ninth, two notes from the chord of the eleventh, and three notes from the chord of the thirteenth. The resulting four-part chords, though conventionally known as chords of the ninth, eleventh and thirteenth, are not in fact mere selections from the notes of those chords but, like the chord of the seventh, are the product of suspensions or passing notes, e.g.:

The same is true of the inversions of four-note chords:

Familiarity with the sound of chords produced and of chords in five or more parts and their inversions in this way led to their use as normal elements in a harmonic progression. The use of chromatic notes as suspended dissonances, appoggiaturas or passing notes led to a further extension of the harmonic vocabulary. Chords once regarded as dissonant came to be accepted as concords on two which more strongly dissonant chords could resolve, e.g.:

WAGNER, *Tristan und Isolde*

Every chord has a function, but that function may differ according to the context in which it occurs. For example, the $\frac{6}{3}$ chord on the subdominant (or fourth degree of the scale) i.e. in the key of C major:

has two distinct functions, resulting from its dual origin (*a*) as a $\frac{6}{3}$ chord sounded simultaneously with a suspended fifth:

(*b*) as a $\frac{5}{3}$ chord against which a passing sixth is heard:

The resulting functions of the chord are:

Another illustration is provided by two further forms of the augmented sixth chord, in which a fourth note has been added to the three mentioned above:

The first of these could be regarded as the second inversion of a seventh chord on the supertonic (or second degree of the scale) in the key of A minor, with the top note sharpened:

or as the second inversion of a dominant seventh chord in the key of E major, with the lowest note flattened:

or as the second inversion of a seventh chord on the leading note (or seventh degree of the scale) in the key of C major, with the top note sharpened:

The other augmented sixth could be regarded as the first inversion of a seventh chord on the subdominant in the key of A minor, with the top note sharpened:

or as a diminished seventh with the lowest note flattened:

or as the first inversion of a seventh chord on the supertonic in the key of C major, with the top note sharpened:

But whatever form of vertical analysis we adopt, these progressions derive in fact from the following simple cadences:

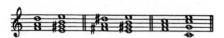

modified by the use of one or more passing notes or anticipations, e.g.:

Awareness of chords must go hand in hand with awareness of part-writing, since it is often the individual movement of the parts that determines the chords. The following examples, both from the 17th century, will make this clear:

MONTEVERDI, *Madrigals*, Book V

PURCELL, *Dioclesian*

See HARMONY, INVERSION

chordophone, any instrument in which a string vibrates to produce a sound. There are basically four groups of chordophones. In zithers, the string is stretched between two ends of a board and plucked or struck to produce a sound; this class of chordophones includes the piano and harpsichord as well as zithers of all kinds. In lutes, the strings are strung from a neck over a bridge to the body and may be plucked (as in the guitar) or bowed (as in the violin). The remaining two groups are lyres and harps.

chord symbol, a simple notation for harmonic progressions often used in popular music. Each symbol consists of a letter that may be followed by a number. The letter indicates the root note of a basic triad and the number the interval between an added note and the root note. For example, C indicates a C major triad (C-E-G) and Cm or C– a minor triad (C-E♭-G). C6 indicates that the sixth (A) is added; C7 the minor seventh (B♭); C maj, C maj 7 or C △ the major seventh (B); C9 the ninth (D); C11 the eleventh (F); and C13 the thirteenth (A). The added notes may be sharpened, indicated by ♯ or +, or flattened, indicated by ♭ or –. C maj 13 ♯ 11 would therefore indicate the chord C-E-G-B-D-F♯-A. The abbreviation 'sus' means a suspension; C sus is C-F-G. The chords may be played in any inversion.

Chorton (Ger.), 'choir pitch', i.e. the pitch to which church organs in Germany were formerly tuned. This pitch was neither constant nor universal. By the beginning of the 17th century it was generally high in the Protestant churches of North Germany, about a minor third higher than our standard pitch today, though naturally there were local variants. In Prague, on the other hand, it was a tone lower at the same period, i.e. about a semitone higher than our standard pitch; this is the pitch advocated by Praetorius in his *Syntagma Musicum*, volume ii (1619) and is the actual pitch of the contemporary organ at Frederiksborg in Denmark, which still survives. Elsewhere, for example in a number of Catholic chapels, a pitch was in use which was a semitone lower than the Prague pitch and a minor third lower than the North German *Chorton*, i.e. approximately the same as our standard pitch today. The following table shows approximately the sounds that would be produced in our standard pitch by playing the note

on the different organs mentioned above:
Protestant churches in North Germany:

Prague and Frederiksborg:

Catholic chapels:

The following table shows the notes that would have to be played to sound approximately the note

in our standard pitch:
Protestant churches in North Germany:

Prague and Frederiksborg:

Catholic chapels:

The inconvenience of different pitches for organs, of which those quoted above are merely instances, became much greater when orchestral instruments were used in church music, as happened frequently in the 17th and early 18th centuries. The highest of the *Chorton* pitches mentioned above (which Praetorius insists on calling *Kammerton*, or 'chamber pitch', in defiance of contemporary German usage) was unsuitable for strings and wood-wind instruments; and even the second, in which the A is roughly equivalent to our B flat, came to be regarded as too high. According to Quantz, in his *Versuch einer Anweisung die Flöte traversiere zu spielen* (1752), the introduction of a lower pitch for orchestral instruments in Germany was due to the influence of French wood-wind manufacturers. Some of the new organs built in the early 18th century were built to the lower pitch, known as *Kammerton*, but the pitch of older organs could not easily be changed. Where older organs were used for the performance of works for voices, organ and orchestra two alternatives were possible: (1) if the high pitch of the organ (*Chorton*) were accepted, the woodwind parts had to be transposed into a higher key, while the strings had to tune up to the organ; (2) if the low orchestral pitch (*Kammerton*) were accepted, the organ part had to be transposed down. Both these expedients are found in Bach's cantatas, the former in works written for the ducal chapel at Weimar between 1708 and 1717, the latter in works written for the Leipzig churches between 1723 and 1750.

See KAMMERTON, PITCH

A. MENDEL: 'Pitch in the 16th and early 17th Centuries', *Musical Quarterly*, xxxiv (1948); 'On the

Pitches in Use in Bach's Time', *Musical Quarterly*, xli (1955)

C. S. TERRY: *Bach's Orchestra* (1932)

chorus (Fr., *choeur*; Ger., *Chor*; It., *coro*), (1) a body of singers (male or female or both) in which there are several performers to each part, as opposed to the soloists in an opera, oratorio, cantata or other concerted work. A *semi-chorus* is a smaller body of singers used in association with, or in contrast to, a large chorus;

(2) music written for a body of singers of this kind;

(3) in a solo song a refrain intended for a number of singers;

(4) medieval Latin name for the CRWTH.

Chou, Wen-chung (born 1923), Chinese composer who went to the United States in 1946 and became a U.S. citizen in 1958. He was a pupil of Edgard Varèse for five years, and held various academic appointments in America. His works, in which his Chinese origins are prominent, include *Metaphors* for wind and symphony orchestra, *The Dark and the Light* for piano, percussion and strings, *Cursive* for flute and piano, *Yu Ko* for nine players, a chamber concerto (entitled *Pien*) for piano, wind and percussion, *To a Wayfarer* for clarinet and strings, and *Seven Poems of T'ang Dynasty* for high voice and instrumental ensemble.

Christmas Concerto, a *concerto grosso* by Corelli, op 6, no 8 (1712), entitled *Concerto fatto per la notte di natale* (Concerto made for Christmas Eve). The last movement is a PASTORALE.

Christmas Oratorio (Ger., *Weihnachtsoratorium*), (1) a series of six church cantatas by Bach (1734), designed to be performed on the three days of Christmas, New Year's Day, the Sunday after New Year's Day, and Epiphany;

(2) the name sometimes given to Schütz's *Historia der freuden- und gnaden-reichen Geburt Gottes und Mariens Sohn Jesu Christi* (1664), printed in the complete edition, supplement I.

Christ on the Mount of Olives (Ger., *Christus am Ölberge*), oratorio by Beethoven, op 85 (1802), to a text by F. X. Huber.

Christophe Colomb (Fr., *Christopher Columbus*), opera in two parts (27 scenes) by Milhaud, to an original French text by Paul Claudel. The first performance (in a German version by Rudolf Stephan Hoffman) took place in 1930 in Berlin. Another opera on the subject was written by Werner Egk.

chromatic (Gr., *chrōmatikos*), literally, 'coloured', hence 'embellished'. In particular:

(1) in ancient Greek music used to describe a modification of the diatonic tetrachord (or descending scale of four notes), by which the second note from the top was flattened a semitone:

diatonic tetrachord:

chromatic tetrachord:

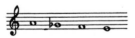

(2) by a natural transference applied in Western European music to notes foreign to the mode or key, produced by the use of accidentals, whereas 'diatonic' refers to notes forming part of the ordinary scale of the mode or key. The sharpened sixth and seventh used in a minor key, e.g. in C minor:

were originally chromatic notes, but they became so firmly established as regular alternatives to the sixth and seventh of the diatonic scale:

that they ceased to be regarded as chromatic.

(3) chromatic chord: a chord which includes one or more notes foreign to the key. A chord which is chromatic in one key may be diatonic in another, e.g. the chord of D flat major is chromatic in the key of C major, where it needs accidentals, but not in the key of A flat major, where it needs none:

This means that a chord which is merely an embellishment of one key may be an integral part of another, so that after using such a chord it is equally possible to remain in the first key or to modulate to the second, e.g.:

See CHORD, HARMONY

(4) chromatic harmony: harmony which makes substantial use of chromatic chords. The use of chromatic notes for melodic purposes does not necessarily produce chromatic harmony, since they may be merely a decoration of diatonic harmony, e.g.

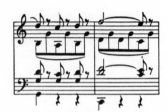

MOZART, *Symphony in C major*, K 551

Contrast the following from the same movement, where the use of a similar melodic progression in four different parts produces chromatic harmony:

MOZART, *Symphony in C major*, K 551

For the origin and development of chromatic harmony, *see* HARMONY.

(5) chromatic instrument: an instrument whose normal compass includes all the notes of the chromatic scale (*see infra*). A chromatic compass is now normal on all instruments. Before the invention of valves for the HORN and TRUMPET in the early 19th century these instruments were incapable of playing a chromatic scale. The HARP in normal use in the modern orchestra is chromatic in the sense that all the semitones are available, but they cannot be played in rapid succession; this is possible only on the so-called chromatic harp. The word 'chromatic' is also applied to TIMPANI fitted with a mechanical device which makes possible an immediate change of tuning.

(6) chromatic scale: a scale proceeding entirely by semitones. It is convenient to write this with sharps if it ascends:

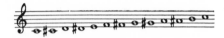

and with flats if it descends:

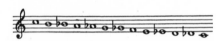

but the application of this principle will depend on the key of the piece. In a flat key, for example, it is obviously simpler in an ascending scale to use the notes which are already flattened by the key-signature and subsequently

to sharpen them with naturals, since the naturals would be required in any case: e.g. in the key of E flat it is simpler to write

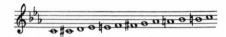

than

In all such cases the object should be to achieve the maximum of intelligibility with the minimum of trouble.

(7) in 16th century Italy *cromatico* was also used to refer to the use of black notes, i.e. notes of smaller value (*croma* is still the word for 'quaver' in Italian). Thus *madrigale cromatico* meant a madrigal employing the smaller note values and hence sung at a brisk speed (*see* A. Einstein, *The Italian Madrigal*, volume 1, pages 398–401).

Chromatic Fantasia and Fugue, a keyboard work in D minor by Bach, composed around 1720–3. The original title is *Fantasia cromatica e fuga*. The adjective refers to the considerable use made of chromatic harmony in the fantasia.

chromatic harp, *see* HARP

chrotta, *see* CRWTH

Chrysander, Karl Franz Friedrich (1826–1901). German historian and musicologist; editor of a complete edition of Handel's works. He studied at Rostock University, and devoted his life to the study of Handel. His biography of Handel (three volumes, 1858–67) remained incomplete at his death. He also published the text of four oratorios by Carissimi and a number of works from which Handel borrowed material.

church modes, *see* MODE

Chybinski, Adolf (1880–1952), Polish historian who studied at Cracow University and Munich and became professor at Lwow in 1921. He took an active part in the publication of old Polish music, including the *Monumenta Musices Sacrae in Polonia*, and wrote extensively on the history of Polish music and on Polish folksong.

ciaccona (It.), chaconne.

cialamello (It.), shawm.

Cibber, Susanna Maria, *see* ARNE

cibell (cebell), a dance form in gavotte rhythm, current in England in the late 17th and early 18th centuries. The name originates from transcriptions of a passage in Lully's opera *Atys* (1676), where the scene is the temple of Cybele. The majority of pieces described as 'cibell', however, have no connection with this passage beyond the fact that they imitate the rhythm, which is common in French music of this period.

Ciconia, Johannes (c. 1335–1411), Walloon composer and theorist, who was born and spent much of his life at Liège, but also lived in Italy. From 1402 till his death he was at Padua. His name is apparently a Latinized form of *Ciwange*, a dialect form of *Cigogne* (stork). His works include Mass movements, motets, and songs in Italian and French. A study of his life and works, together with a complete edition has been published by S. Clercx (two volumes, 1960).

Cid, Le (*The Cid*), opera in four acts by Massenet, to a libretto by Adolphe Philippe d'Ennery, Louis Gallot and Edouard Blau (based on Corneille's tragedy), first performed in 1885 in Paris. Farinelli, Pacini and Cornelius also wrote operas on the subject.

Cifra, Antonio (1584–1629), prolific Italian composer mainly of church music, who held various appointments in Rome and at Loreto.

Cilèa, Francesco (1866–1950), Italian composer. He studied at the Naples Conservatorio, and held academic posts in Florence, Palermo and Naples. He composed several operas, of which *Adriana Lecouvreur* (Milan, 1902) was the most successful.

Cimarosa, Domenico (1749–1801), Italian opera composer, the son of a bricklayer. He studied at the Conservatorio Santa Maria di Loreto. His first opera, *Le stravaganze del conte*, was performed at Naples in 1772. He rapidly became one of the foremost opera composers of the time. He worked mainly in Rome and Naples, but was also for a time in the service of Catherine II of Russia, and subsequently of the Emperor Leopold II in Vienna. His most famous work was the comic opera *The Secret Marriage* (It., *Il matrimonio segreto*, Vienna, 1792) which is still performed. Its idiom is Mozartian but lacks Mozart's genius. The Emperor Leopold II, however, liked it well enough to ask for an immediate repeat of the whole work after the première (though he was thoughtful to fortify the cast with supper first). In addition to some sixty operas he also wrote Masses, oratorios, cantatas, songs and piano sonatas.

   M. Tibaldi Chiesa: *Cimarosa e il suo tempo* (1939)
   R. Vitale: *Domenico Cimarosa: la vita e le opere* (1929)

cimbalom, a form of DULCIMER used in Hungary. It consists of a series of metal strings which are strung on pegs fixed into a wooden box. The strings are struck with sticks held in the player's hands. It has been used by Stravinsky in *Renard* and *Ragtime*, and by Kodály in the *Háry János* suite.

cimbasso (It.), bass tuba.

cinelli (It.), cymbals. The more usual term is *piatti*.

cinque-pace (from Fr., *cinq pas*, 'five steps'), a term used for the GALLIARD by Elizabethan writers, who adapted it from the French original but apparently pronounced it as an English word, as it is often written 'sink-a-pace' (there are several other spellings). Cf. Shakespeare, *Much Ado about Nothing*, ii, 1, and *Twelfth Night*, i, 3.

circle of fifths (Ger., *Quintenzirkel*), the clockwise arrangement of the twelve keys in an order of ascending fifths. Thus, beginning with C, the order of major keys would be C, G, D, A, E, B (or C flat), F sharp (or G flat), C sharp (or D flat), A flat, E flat, B flat, and F. After twelve such steps, the original key is reached again. Composers have sometimes used a circle of fifths as a source of inspiration, as in the *Kleines harmonisches Labyrinth* usually ascribed to Bach, or in the movement entitled *Circle of Fifths* which ends Duke Ellington's *Such Sweet Thunder* suite.

circular breathing, a technique of sustaining a note on a wind instrument by breathing in while playing the note.

cistre (Fr.), CITTERN.

cittern, cither, cithern (Fr., *cistre*; Ger., *Zither*; It., *cetera*), a plucked string instrument similar to the LUTE, but with a flat back and wire strings, popular in the 16th and 17th century. It was played either with a plectrum or with the fingers. The music was written in TABLATURE. In the 18th century it was known in England as the English guitar. The modern German ZITHER is a different instrument.

Clair de lune (Fr., *Moonlight*), popular piano piece by Debussy, actually the third movement of his *Suite Bergamasque*.

clairseach, the Irish HARP. An ancient brass-stringed instrument, reputed to be that of King Brian Boru, is preserved at Trinity College, Dublin. A portable gut-strung harp was developed in Ireland in the 19th century. It has finger levers instead of pedals.

clarinet (Fr., *clarinette*; Ger., *Klarinette*; It., clarinetto), a single-reed instrument, dating from the late 17th century. As the tube is cylindrical, the lowest octave is reproduced a twelfth (not an octave) higher by 'overblowing', i.e. the series:

becomes:

The notes between these two series are produced by opening a thumb-hole and by using keys, which also extend the compass downwards a minor third. The complete compass is:

Clarinets were originally made in several sizes, in order to facilitate playing in different keys, and to save the player the trouble of learning a different fingering for each instrument were treated as TRANSPOSING INSTRUMENTS. By Beethoven's time (late 18th and early 19th century) only three sizes were in normal use – in C (sounding as written), in B flat (sounding a tone lower) and in A (sounding a minor third lower). The clarinet in C is now obsolete in the orchestra, though it has been occasionally revived for performances of old music: the B flat and A clarinets are in regular use, though some players prefer to use only the B flat clarinet, with an extra key to obtain the extra semitone at the bottom. The sounding compass of the B flat clarinet is:

and of the A clarinet:

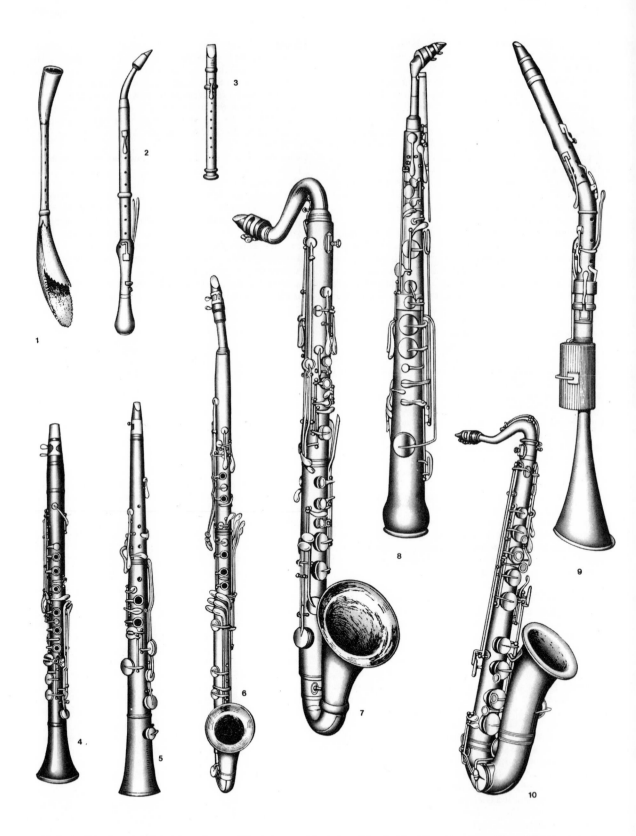

Clarinets: (1) pibgorn (2) *clarinette d'amour* (3) *chalumeau* (4) clarinet (5) *tarogato* (6) modern basset horn (7) bass clarinet (8) *Heckelclarina* (9) old basset horn (10) saxophone

to   8ve higher

A smaller clarinet in E flat (sounding a minor third higher than written) is used in military bands and occasionally in the orchestra: a similar instrument in D has also been made for orchestral use. Larger members of the family are the BASSET HORN, the BASS CLARINET and the CONTRABASS or PEDAL CLARINET. The first of these was in use principally in the late 18th and early 19th century; the last, a 19th century invention, has remained virtually an experiment. Mozart was one of the first composers to realize the expressive possibilities of the clarinet (e.g. in his clarinet concerto and quintet for clarinet and strings). Brahms's chamber music includes two sonatas for clarinet and piano, a trio for clarinet, cello and piano, and a quintet for clarinet and strings.

A. CARSE: *Musical Wind Instruments* (1939)
F. G. RENDALL: *The Clarinet* (1954)

clarinet quintet, a work, generally in several movements, for clarinet and string quartet. Among the best known examples are those by Mozart (K 581), Brahms (op 115) and Bliss.

clarinette (Fr.), clarinet.

clarinette d'amour (Fr.), an alto clarinet in A flat or G with a bulb-shaped bell (like the *oboe d'amore*), current in the late 18th century.

clarinetto (It.), clarinet. The word is a diminutive of *clarino* (trumpet) and was used originally because the tone of the 18th century clarinet suggested at a distance the sound of the trumpet.

clarino (It.), (1) TRUMPET. Applied particularly, in the 17th and early 18th century, to the high register of the trumpet, for which players were specially trained;

(2) clarinet, on account of the similarity of tone in the early 18th century. The diminutive *clarinetto* is the normal term.

Clarke, Jeremiah (c. 1673–1707), English composer and organist, pupil of Blow at the Chapel Royal. He was organist at Winchester College from 1692, at St. Paul's Cathedral from 1695, and at the Chapel Royal from 1704. His compositions include anthems, odes, music for the stage, and harpsichord pieces. Among the keyboard pieces is 'The Prince of Denmark's March', which was falsely attributed to Purcell and is widely known under the title 'Trumpet Voluntary'.

clarone (It.), bass clarinet.

clarsach, Scottish CLAIRSEACH.

classical music, the term 'classical' is used by historians to distinguish music which accepts certain basic conventions of form and structure, and uses them as a natural frame work for the expression of ideas, from music which is more concerned with the expression of individual emotions than with the achievement of formal unity, i.e. ROMANTIC MUSIC. In practice the term is generally restricted to 18th and early 19th century music, i.e. roughly speaking, from Bach to early Beethoven. In so far as the works of the great masters of this period are constantly performed and may be said to have stood the test of time, they are 'classical' also in the sense in which one speaks of the 'classics' of literature. The historical distinction, however, is not strictly valid, since many works of the romantic period (roughly, from 1830 to 1910) show considerable preoccupation with formal design, while equally romantic elements are apparent in a good deal of 18th century music, and in 17th century music as well. It would probably be truer to say that the romantic composers were often self-conscious, whereas the 'classical' composers of the 18th century were not. Beethoven, in whose work the struggle between formal unity and intensely individual expression is often strongly marked, may be said to stand at the junction of the two periods. In the present century, the term 'classical music' is often applied to serious, as opposed to popular music. It is also applied to works which are 'classics' because they are well established. Thus Bartók's Concerto for Orchestra and Berg's *Wozzeck* have come to be known as '20th century classics'.

Classical Symphony, title given by Prokofiev to his first symphony, first performed in 1918 at St Petersburg. Though no more than a witty pastiche, the work has held its place in the repertory on account of its pace, piquancy and melodiousness.

Claudio da Correggio, see MERULO, CLAUDIO

clausula (Lat.), literally, (1) 'close', (2) 'clause' or 'section.' Hence (1) CADENCE, in music in two or more parts (cf. Eng., full close, half close).

(2) in the *organa* or polyphonic compositions of the late 12th and early 13th centuries (associated particularly with Notre Dame, Paris) a clearly defined section, complete in itself (also known as *punctum*). Applied by some modern writers particularly to the new metrical sections written by Perotin and his contemporaries (c. 1200) to replace similar sections in the older *organa* of Leonin, and hence known as 'substitute *clausulae*' (Ger., *Ersatzklauseln*). The 'tenors' of such sections were taken from melismatic portions of the plainsong on which the whole composition was based, i.e. portions where there were several notes to one syllable. These notes were arranged in regular rhythm and so formed a metrical framework to which the added counterpoints conformed. These metrical sections formed a contrast to others where the notes of the plainsong were sustained so as to provide a foundation for rhythmically independent counterpoint (see H. Besseler, *Musik der Mittelalters und der Renaissance*, page 99, G. Reese, *Music in the Middle Ages*, pages 296 following). Perotin's 'substitute *clausulae*' were the immediate forerunners of the 13th century MOTET.

See PUNCTUM, ORGANUM

clausum (Lat.), see CLOS

clavecin (Fr.), harpsichord.

claves, short wooden cylindrical sticks clicked together to emphasize the beat. One is held in each hand. Claves originated in Cuba.

clavicembalo (It.), harpsichord; often found in the abbreviated form *cembalo*.

clavichord (Fr., *clavicorde*; Ger., *Clavichord, Klavichord*; It., *clavicordio*), a keyboard instrument, first mentioned by this name at the beginning of the 15th century. It appears to have been a development of the monochord, a scientific instrument consisting of a stretched string of variable length, which was known to the Greeks and has been used for acoustical demonstrations from the middle ages to the present day (hence the old names for the clavichord: Fr., *manicorde, manicordion*; It., *manicordio*). In the clavichord, which is oblong in shape, there is a series of stretched strings running roughly parallel with the front of the instrument. The depression of a key presses a small blade of brass (known as a 'tangent') against the string. This divides the string into two lengths, one of which is free to vibrate while the other is damped by a piece of cloth. Since the tone is produced by pressure, it can to some extent be controlled by the player, who by repeated pressure on the key can produce minute variations of pitch, similar to the violinist's *vibrato* (*see* BEBUNG).

In pre-18th century clavichords a single string may do duty for more than one note. If two notes are not likely to be required to sound simultaneously, two tangents can be arranged to operate on the same string – an economical device which reduces the number of strings necessary. A clavichord of this type was called *fretted* (Ger., *gebunden*). The clavichord with a separate string for each note (Ger., *bundfrei*) was introduced in the early 18th century. Clavichords with pedals (like an organ) were also made in the 18th century. The clavichord was praised by C. P. E. Bach (1714–88) in his *Versuch über die wahre Art das Clavier zu spielen* (1753), and his performance on it elicited the admiration of Burney (*The Present State of Music in Germany*, 1773, volume ii, page 269). With the increasing use of the piano the clavichord came to be neglected. It has been successfully revived in the 20th century for the performance of old keyboard music, and new compositions have been written for it, e.g. Herbert Howells's *Lambert's Clavichord*. Its small tone makes it ineffective in the concert hall, but it is admirable for intimate music-making and for broadcasting.

P. JAMES: *Early Keyboard Instruments* (1930)

clavicymbal, Eng. for It. *clavicembalo*, harpsichord.

clavier, (1) (Fr.), keyboard;

(2) (Ger., also *Klavier*), (a) keyboard (cf. CLAVIER-ÜBUNG); (b) keyboard instrument with strings, i.e. clavichord, harpsichord or piano. There is nothing in the title of Bach's *The Well-tempered Clavier* to show whether the pieces are for clavichord or harpsichord;

(3) (Eng.), (a) often used by modern writers, particularly in the United States, as the equivalent of the German word; (b) a keyboard designed for finger practice, e.g. the Virgil practice clavier, patented in the United States by A. K. Virgil in 1892. This instrument produces no sound, but the pressure of the keys can be regulated, and a series of clicks, made as the keys rise and fall, enables the ear to detect whether a strict legato is being achieved.

Clavierübung (Ger.), literally, 'keyboard practice'. The title of a collection of keyboard music by Bach, one of the few works to be published in his lifetime. It was issued in four parts:

Part I (1731): six partitas (previously issued separately).

Part II (1735): Italian concerto and overture in the French style (partita in B minor).

Part III (1739): organ prelude in E flat major, twenty-one chorale preludes on hymns illustrating the catechism, four *duetti* for harpsichord, organ fugue in E flat major (known in England as 'St. Anne's').

Part IV (1742): Goldberg variations.

See GOLDBERG VARIATIONS, ITALIAN CONCERTO

clef (borrowed from Fr. *clef*, 'key': Ger., *Schlüssel*; It., *chiave*). a sign used to determine the pitch of a particular line on a stave, from which the pitch of the remaining lines and of the spaces can be deduced. The three clefs now in use:

are ornamental forms of the letters g, c and f (*see* NOTATION) and represent respectively the notes *g'* (an octave above the fourth string of the violin), *c'* (the so-called 'middle C', a fifth below *g'*) and *f* (a fifth below *c'*). Medieval scribes found that letters were more convenient than the coloured lines which were originally used to indicate *c'* and *f*, as their position on the stave could easily be changed. All three clefs were used in a variety of positions until the latter half of the 18th century. Since that time the position of the G (treble) and F (bass) clefs has been invariable, except in some modern reprints of old music which retain the original positions of the clefs. The G clef is placed on the second line of the stave:

the F clef on the fourth line:

The C clef is placed either on the third line (alto clef) or on the fourth line (tenor clef):

The alto clef, formerly used for the alto voice and the alto trombone, is now used only for the viola. The tenor clef, formerly used for the tenor voice, is now used only for the tenor trombone and for the upper register of the bassoon, cello and double bass.

The C clef on the first line (soprano clef):

was in use in Germany as late as the end of the 19th century for the soprano voice, but is now obsolete, except in some modern reprints of old music.

In modern vocal scores, and in solo vocal music, the G clef is also used for the tenor voice, with the understanding (expressed or implied) that the music will sound an octave lower than the written pitch. Modifications of the G clef intended to express this transposition more precisely are:

The first of these is the most satisfactory, since the figure 8 indicates the octave transposition. It is used increasingly in modern editions of old music. For transposition in instrumental notation *see* TRANSPOSING INSTRUMENTS.

Though the old practice of changing the position of a clef in the course of a composition has been abandoned, there are many occasions when a change of clef is necessary to avoid the excessive use of LEGER LINES. Thus, in keyboard music, where the right hand normally has the treble clef and the left hand the bass, it may be necessary to use the bass clef for the right hand or the treble clef for the left. In music for the viola the treble clef is used instead of the alto when the range of the music makes it desirable. Similarly, the tenor clef is used when necessary for the bassoon, cello and (more rarely) the double bass, and in music for the horn the bass clef may temporarily replace the treble.

Clemens non Papa, Jacobus (Jacques Clément) (c. 1510–57), one of the most distinguished Flemish composers of his time. Little is known of his life, beyond the fact that he worked in Ypres and Dixmuiden. His compositions, which are remarkable for their expressive quality, include polyphonic Masses, motets, *chansons* and Flemish psalms. He is supposed to have added the words 'non Papa' to his name to distinguish himself from the poet Jacobus Papa, who lived in Ypres at the same time. The fact that Clemens non Papa can be translated literally as 'Clement, not the Pope' may be taken as an example of the delight in double meaning which was common in the 16th century. The view, formerly expressed, that there was any need to distinguish a Flemish composer from Pope Clement VII is too absurd to be accepted seriously. A complete edition of his works by K. P. Bernet Kempers was begun in 1951.

> E. LOWINSKY: *Secret Chromatic Art in the Netherlands Motet* (1946)

Clément, Jacques, *see* CLEMENS NON PAPA

Clementi, Muzio (1752–1832), Italian composer and pianist, born in Rome, the son of a silversmith. At the age of fourteen, having already showed considerable talent as a composer, he was brought to England by Peter Beckford and continued his studies there. His first three piano sonatas, op 2, were published in 1773. He also won outstanding success as a performer. After serving as harpsichordist at the Italian Opera in London (1777–80), he toured on the Continent (1781–2). He lived in England from 1782 to 1802, and in 1800 founded a firm of music publishers and piano manufacturers (known after his death as Collard & Collard). His next Continental travels (1802–10) included a visit to St. Petersburg with his pupil John Field. He knew personally Haydn, Mozart and Beethoven (all of whom he survived), as well as many other musicians of the time. Mozart's opinion of his playing was unfavourable:

> He is an excellent cembalo-player, but that is all. He has great facility with his right hand. His star passages are

thirds. Apart from this, he has not a farthing's worth of taste or feeling; he is a mere *mechanicus*. (January 16, 1782, *Letters of Mozart and his Family*, translated by E. Anderson, page 1181; cf. pages 1267–8).

This, however, was before he had developed his later style of playing, characterized by its mastery of cantabile and legato.

His influence on other pianists and composers for the piano was considerable. He did more than anyone to develop a style of writing which exploited the characteristics of the piano, as opposed to the harpsichord. His numerous compositions include symphonies, some sixty piano sonatas, and *Gradus ad Parnassum*, a series of piano studies which achieved a remarkable union of technical instruction and artistic expression. His sonatas were sometimes descriptive: one of them, for example, bore the subtitle *Didone abbandonata*. He died in Evesham.

> K. DALE: 'Hours with Muzio Clementi' (*Music and Letters*, July 1943)
> J. S. SHEDLOCK: *The Pianoforte Sonata* (1895)

Clemenza di Tito, La (It., *The Clemency of Titus*), opera in two acts by Mozart, to a libretto adapted from Metastasio by Caterino Mazzolà, first performed in 1791 at Prague. Written in haste for the coronation of Leopold II as King of Bohemia, *La Clemenza di Tito* was Mozart's last opera (though its première took place three weeks before that of *The Magic Flute*). For the occasion, the composer reverted to the form of *opera seria*, which he had abandoned after *Idomeneo*, but which provided him with a tactfully chosen libretto: at a time when royal heads were rolling elsewhere in Europe, it was diplomatic to write an opera about a Roman emperor who forgave those who conspired against him. However, the fortunes of *La Clemenza di Tito* have varied over the years. On the one hand, it was the first Mozart opera ever performed in Britain (in London in 1806). On the other, it was long considered to be cold and uninspired, the work of a dying man written in a form that straitjacketed his dramatic genius. Received opinion in the present century used to declare that *La Clemenza* was not worth performing but a series of successful productions, in Germany, London and elsewhere during the 1960s and 1970s, have proved otherwise. The work may lack the sustained richness of *Idomeneo*, but it is nevertheless a masterly score, with many passages – e.g. Sesto's two arias, one of them with clarinet obbligato – written in Mozart's most mature and expressive vein.

Clérambault, Louis Nicolas (1676–1749), French organist and composer, a pupil of André Raison. He became organist of St. Sulpice, Paris. His compositions include cantatas and works for harpsichord and organ.

Cleveland Orchestra, The, one of the leading symphony orchestras in the United States. It was founded in 1918 by the Musical Arts Association of Cleveland. Before and during World War II its conductors were Sokoloff, Rodzinski and Leinsdorf, but it was not until after the war that it reached the peak of perfection during the long reign of George Szell (1946–70). Since Szell's death, the orchestra's main conductors have been Pierre Boulez and Lorin Maazel.

Cliquot, François Henri (1728–91), French organ-builder, who succeeded his father, uncle and grandfather in this profession. He built organs for a number of churches in Paris, including Sainte-Chapelle, St. Sulpice and Notre Dame, as well as in the provinces. Much of his work survives today.

clochette (Fr.), *see* GLOCKENSPIEL

'Clock' Symphony, the nickname given to Haydn's Symphony no 101 in D major. In the slow movement the accompanying instruments suggest the ticking of a clock.

clos (Fr.; Lat., *clausum*; It., *chiuso*), 'closed', a medieval term used in dance music, and in vocal pieces similar in structure, to indicate a final cadence at the end of a repeated section, in contrast to an intermediate cadence (Fr., *ouvert*; Lat., *apertum*, It., *verto*) used when the section is performed the first time, e.g.:

LANDINI, *Works*, edited by L. Ellinwood, no 103

Ouvert and *clos* thus correspond to what is now called 'first time' (or 'first ending') and 'second time'.

close, cadence. *Half close,* imperfect cadence. *Full close,* perfect cadence.

See CADENCE

close harmony, harmony in which the notes of the chords are kept close together – often as close as an octave.

coach horn, a straight HORN three to four feet long comprising a conical wide-bore tube of copper and a funnel-shaped bell. It is played with a cup mouthpiece.

Coates, Albert (1882–1953), English (Russian born) conductor and composer, the son of an English father and a Russian mother. He studied science at Liverpool University, and music at Leipzig Conservatorium, where he was in the conducting class held by Artur Nikisch. He held appointments at Dresden and St. Petersburg before settling in Britain in 1919. His compositions include the operas *Samuel Pepys* (Munich, 1929) and *Pickwick* (London, 1936).

Coates, Edith Mary (born 1908), English mezzo-soprano, a member of the opera company at Sadler's Wells from 1931, and of Covent Garden from 1946. She created the role of Auntie in Britten's *Peter Grimes,* and was a famous Countess in *The Queen of Spades.*

Coates, Eric (1886–1957), English composer and viola player. He studied at the Royal Academy of Music, London, and became principal viola of the Queen's Hall Orchestra in 1920. From 1918 he worked solely as a composer. His works, many of which are for orchestra, are light in substance but impeccable in workmanship.

Cobbett, Walter Willson (1847–1937), English busi-

nessman and amateur violinist, who rendered considerable service to the cause of chamber music by (1) offering prizes for new works by English composers, (2) founding the Chamber Music Association, which is connected with the British Federation of Music Festivals, and (3) editing a *Cyclopedia of Chamber Music* (two volumes, first published in 1929).

Cobbold, William (1560–1639), English composer, who was organist of Norwich Cathedral until 1608. He harmonized five of the tunes in Thomas East's *The Whole Booke of Psalmes,* 1592 (modern edition by Musical Antiquarian Society, 1844), wrote a number of consort songs (*see Musica Britannica,* xxii), and contributed a madrigal to *The Triumphes of Oriana,* 1601 (reprinted in *The English Madrigal School,* xxxii).

Cockaigne, concert overture by Elgar, op 40, subtitled *In London Town.* First performed in 1901, the work is an evocation of Edwardian London.

Coclicus, Adrianus (Adrian Coclico) Petit (c. 1500–c. 63), Flemish composer and singer, a pupil of Josquin des Prés. He migrated to Wittenberg in 1545 and became a Protestant. He was a member of the Chapel Royal, Copenhagen, in 1556. His *Compendium musices* (1552) is a valuable exposition of current musical practice (facsimile edition by M. Bukofzer, 1954; English translation by A. Seay, 1973), and his collection of psalms entitled *Consolationes Piae* (1552; modern edition by M. Ruhnke in *Erbe deutscher Musik,* xlii) contains the first known use of the term MUSICA RESERVATA on its title-page to indicate a particular type of music, suitable for connoisseurs and private occasions.

M. VAN CREVEL: *Adrianus Petit Coclico* (1940)

E. LOWINSKY: *Secret Chromatic Art in the Netherlands Motet* (1946)

coda (It.), literally 'tail' (from Lat., *cauda*) a passage, long or short, at the end of a piece or movement, which extends the ideas which have already received logical or symmetrical expression and brings the work to a satisfying conclusion, e.g.:

(1) in a CANON a short concluding passage in which strict imitation is abandoned in order to construct a convincing cadence;

(2) in a FUGUE a similar passage, often based on a PEDAL POINT, which sums up and clinches the arguments already presented by the polyphonic treatment of the subject, and so corresponds roughly to the peroration of a speech or the conclusion of an essay;

(3) in a movement in SONATA FORM a passage added to the end of the recapitulation. In 18th century music the coda was generally short, but in Beethoven was often expanded to a considerable length, e.g. in the first movement of the *Eroica* symphony.

codetta (It.), diminutive of CODA. Applied particularly to (1) a short passage forming a tail-piece to a particular section of a composition;

(2) an extension of a fugue subject which serves to delay the next entry, e.g.:

BACH, *48 Preludes and Fugues*, Book I, no 16

col, coll', colla, colle, an Italian term meaning 'with the' as in *colla voce* (with the voice), indicating that an accompaniment be played to the lead of a voice. Where two lines in a score are identical, the first may be written out but the second simply given the word *col* followed by the name of the first instrument. This is done as an instruction to the copyist by hard-pressed composers to save time.

Colasse, Pascal (1649–1709), French composer of operas, as well as church music. He is said to have helped to write the inner parts (i.e. those between treble and bass) of Lully's music.

Colbran, Isabella Angela (1785–1845), Spanish dramatic soprano, with a European reputation, which began to decline after 1815 as a result of uncertain intonation. She was *prima donna* at Milan, Venice, Rome and Naples, and also sang in Vienna, London and Paris. In 1822 she married Rossini, who wrote *Elisabetta, Regina d'Inghilterra* for her. She also sang the leading soprano roles in the première of *Semiramide, Otello, Armida, La Donna del Lago* and other Rossini works.

Coleman, *see* COLMAN

Coleridge-Taylor, Samuel (1875–1912), English composer. His father was a native of Sierra Leone, his mother was English. He studied at the Royal College of Music, London, and made his reputation with his choral setting of Longfellow's *Hiawatha's Wedding Feast* (1898), still his most popular work, followed by *The Death of Minnehaha* (1899) and *Hiawatha's Departure* (1900). His other compositions include the oratorio *The Atonement* (1903), the cantata *A Tale of Old Japan* (1911), orchestral music, chamber music, and incidental music for stage.

colla parte (It.), 'with the part', i.e. the accompaniment is to follow any modifications of tempo made by the soloist. cf. COLLA VOCE.

colla punta dell'arco (It.), with the point (i.e. the end furthest from the hand) of the bow.

coll' arco (It.), 'with the bow', a term used in string music to contradict the previous designation *pizzicato* (plucked with the finger). It is generally abbreviated to *arco*.

Collard, a London firm of piano manufacturers originally founded by CLEMENTI. F. W. Collard was one of five partners of the firm in 1802. By 1823 the firm was known as Clementi, Collard and Collard, and after Clementi's death in 1832 as Collard and Collard.

colla voce (It.), 'with the voice'. The same as *colla parte*, but used exclusively in the accompaniment of a vocal solo.

collegium musicum (Lat.), a society for the practice of music, generally associated with a university. The term was in use in Germany in the 17th and 18th centuries and has been revived in the present century. The purpose of a *collegium musicum* is primarily to study music (particularly old music) by playing it, rather than to give public performances. Its activities form a normal part of musical education in any German university today.

col legno (It.), 'with the wood'. A direction to string players to bounce the stick of the bow on the string instead of playing with the hair (e.g. Holst, *The Planets*, no 1, *Mars*).

Colles, Henry Cope (1879–1943), English critic and historian. He studied at Oxford and the Royal College of Music, London, and became principal music critic of *The Times* in 1911. He edited the third (1927) and fourth (1940) editions of Grove's *Dictionary of Music and Musicians*. His books include *Brahms* (1908), *The Growth of Music* (three volumes, 1912–16), *Voice and Verse* (1928), *Walford Davies* (1942) and *Essays and Lectures* (1945).

Collingwood, Lawrance Arthur (born 1887), English conductor and composer. For some years he was assistant to Albert Coates at the St. Petersburg Opera. From 1931 until 1947 he was principal conductor at Sadler's Wells Opera. His compositions include the opera *Macbeth* (London, 1934), a setting of Shakespeare's text.

coll' ottava (It.), doubled at the octave (above and below).

See OTTAVA

Colman (Coleman), Charles (died 1664), court musician to Charles I and Chalres II, and one of the composers of the instrumental music in the first English opera, *The Siege of Rhodes* (1656). Seven songs by him are printed in *Musica Britannica*, xxxiii.

He had two musical sons, **Charles Colman** (died c. 1694) who was court musician to Charles II and James II, and **Edward Colman** (died 1669). Edward was court musician to Charles II, and sang in *The Siege of Rhodes*. His wife was also a singer and is mentioned in Pepys's *Diary* (October 31, 1665). Two songs by him are printed in *Musica Britannica*, xxxiii.

Colonne, Edouard (originally Judas) (1838–1910), French violinist and conductor, founder of the Concerts Colonne (at first known as Concert National), 1873, at which a large number of works by French composers (particularly Berlioz) were given. He also conducted at the Opéra (1891–3), and in other European countries.

color, *see* ISORHYTHM

coloratura (It.; Ger., *Koloratur*), elaborate ornamentation of the melodic line in music for solo instruments or (more frequently) voices. Arias including such ornamentation occur constantly in 18th and 19th century opera, particularly in Italy. A coloratura singer is one who specializes in the virtuosity which such arias demand. The word does not apply solely to a high soprano, as some people seem to think. There can just as easily be a coloratura contralto or a coloratura bass.

colour, a word used, by analogy with painting, to describe the individual tone-quality of instruments and voices, or their association together, e.g. orchestral colour.

Colour Symphony, A, symphony by Bliss (1922), the movements of which are headed Purple, Red, Blue and Green.

combination pedals, (1) properly a device invented in France for bringing into action several rows of organ pipes by admitting air to the soundboard on which they are placed;

(2) also used in the same sense as COMPOSITION PEDALS, which control the movement of stops.

combination tone, a faint note resulting from sounding two notes simultaneously (known also as *resultant tone*). Combination tones are of two kinds: (1) *difference tones*, resulting from the difference between the frequencies of the notes sounded, (2) *summation tones* (fainter than difference tones), resulting from the sum of their frequencies. In the following examples the two notes which are sounded together are represented by semibreves and the combination tones by black notes:

Difference tones:

Summation tones:

The two notes originally sounded together also combine with the combination tone to produce further combination tones.

If three or more notes are sounded together the number of combination tones will be proportionately increased.

See ACOUSTICS

come (It.), as; *come prima*, as at first; *come sopra*, as above; *come stà*, as it stands, i.e. without any modification of the text.

comes (It.), 'companion'. The name given by older theorists to the second part to enter in a CANON or FUGUE, because it serves as a companion to the first part, known as *dux* (leader), which it imitates.

commodo, an obsolete form of COMODO.

common chord, a major or minor triad in root position, e.g.:

See CHORD

common time, four crotchets in a bar, indicated by the time-signature $\frac{4}{4}$ or C.

See C, TIME.

communion (Lat., *communio*), an antiphon sung after communion at Mass. Originally an antiphon to the verses of a psalm.

comodo (It.), 'convenient', i.e. at a convenient speed, neither too fast nor too slow. Often combined with *allegro*.

compass, the complete range of pitch of a voice or an instrument.

Compenius, a firm of organ builders active in the late 16th and early 17th century. A Compenius organ built in 1612 still survives at Frederiksborg in Denmark (gramophone records by Finn Vider, H.M.V.).

Compère, Loyset (c. 1450–1518), Flemish composer, possibly a pupil of Ockeghem. He became canon and chancellor of St. Quentin Cathedral. His numerous compositions include Masses, motets and *chansons*. A complete edition in six volumes was begun by L. Finscher in 1958.

L. FINSCHER: *Loyset Compère* (1964)

competition festivals, meetings for competitive performance (with or without prizes) of choral music, songs, chamber music and solo instrumental music. Such festivals were first organised in Britain by J. S. Curwen at Stratford, East London, 1882 and by Mary Wakefield in Westmorland, 1885. The Welsh Eisteddfod, in its modern form, dates from the early 19th century, as do the brass band festivals. Similar festivals are also held in the United States and the Commonwealth.

composition pedals, a set of metal pedals, or buttons operated by the feet, used in the organ to bring into action one or more stops without having to draw them individually by hand. Each pedal, in addition to bringing on the stops which it controls, automatically puts out of action any others which happen to be drawn at the time. In modern organs composition pedals generally operate on pedal stops and couplers, but can also be adjusted to bring on manual stops appropriate to the pedal combinations. The electrical action now in use makes it possible for the player to select his own combinations by means of switches, instead of being compelled to use the builder's selection.

composition pistons, these are similar in action to composition pedals, but are placed below the manuals and are controlled by fingers or thumbs. They generally operate on manual stops and couplers, but can also be adjusted to bring on pedal stops appropriate to the manual combinations.

compound time, time in which each beat in the bar is divisible into three, e.g.:

as opposed to SIMPLE TIME, in which each beat is divisible into two, e.g.:

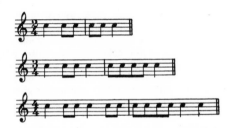

Comte Ory, Le (Count Ory), opera in two acts by Rossini, to a libretto by Augustin Eugène Scribe and Charles Gaspard Delestre-Poirson. First performed in 1828 in Paris, this was the first of Rossini's two French operas, and the second-last opera he wrote. The story tells how Count Ory disguises himself first as a hermit, then as a Mother Superior, in order to woo the Countess Adèle, whose husband has left her in a carefully guarded castle while he is away at the Crusades.

Comus, masque by John Milton, with music by Henry Lawes. It was first performed at Ludlow Castle on September 29th, 1634. An adaptation by John Dalton, with new music by Arne (modern edition in *Musica Britannica*, iii), was performed in London on March 4th, 1738.

con (It.), 'with'; *con affeto*, with tender emotion; *con amore*, lovingly; *con anima*, with spirit; *con brio*, vigorously; *con fuoco*, with fire.

concert, the public performance of music other than opera or church music; in particular a performance by a group of singers or players, as opposed to a RECITAL by a soloist. Until the late 17th century, such performances were to be heard only at the courts of kings and princes or in the private houses of wealthy patrons. A pioneer of public concerts, which anyone could attend on payment of a charge for admission, was John Banister, who started a series at Whitefriars, London, in 1672. Banister's experiment was imitated by others and led in course of time to more ambitious undertakings, e.g. the series of orchestral concerts organized by Salomon in London in the late 18th century, for which Haydn wrote his 'London' symphonies. Similar concerts were organized in France under the title *Concert spirituel*, founded in 1725 by Anne Philidor. The growth of public concerts made it necessary to provide buildings in which they could be given. The oldest hall in Europe specially built for this purpose appears to have been the Holywell Music Room in Oxford, opened in 1748 and still in regular use.

The French *concert* can mean 'concerto' as well as 'concert'.

See PROMENADE CONCERTS, ROYAL PHILHARMONIC SOCIETY

M. BRENET: *Les Concerts en France sous l'ancien régime* (1900)
J. H. MEE: *The Oldest Music Room in Europe* (1911)
G. PINTHUS: *Die Entwicklung des Konzertwesens in Deutschland bis zum Beginn des 19. Jahrhunderts* (1932)

concertant (Fr.), **concertante** (It.), (1) as an adjective, used to describe a work, whether for orchestra or for two or more performers, in which one or more solo instruments are prominent, e.g. Mozart's *Symphonie concertante* for violin, viola and orchestra (K 364), Weber's *Grand Duo concertant* for piano and clarinet (op 48), Walton's *Sinfonia concertante* for piano and orchestra;

(2) the Italian *concertante*, used as a noun, = *sinfonia concertante*.

concertato (It.), CONCERTANTE. *Coro concertato*, a group of solo singers used to form a contrast to the full choir (17th century). *Stile concertato*, the 'modern' style of the early 17th century, in which solo instruments or voices were exploited, with figured-bass accompaniment.

concert band (U.S.), a band of wind and percussion instruments.

Concertgebouw (Dutch), literally 'concert building'. The Concertgebouw is Amsterdam's main concert hall, acoustically one of the finest in Europe, with a resonance ideal for the Bruckner symphonies which the Dutch are so adept at performing. The Amsterdam society of the same name was founded in 1883 for giving public orchestral concerts. The Concertgebouw Orchestra was directed from 1895 to 1945 by William Mengelberg, and until 1959 by Eduard van Beinum. The present conductor is Bernard Haitink.

concertina, a form of ACCORDION, patented by Sir Charles Wheatstone in 1829. It is hexagonal in shape. Small pistons or studs, placed at each end of the instrument and operated by the fingers, take the place of a keyboard.

concertino (It.), diminutive of CONCERTO:

(1) the group of soloists in a *concerto grosso* (17th and 18th centuries);

(2) a work of one or more solo instruments with orchestra, less formal in structure and often shorter than an ordinary concerto (Ger., *Konzertstück*), e.g. Weber's concertino for clarinet and orchestra, op 26;

(3) the title given by Stravinsky to a work for string quartet, in which the first violin has a prominent solo part (1920).

concert instruments, instruments are said to be in concert or in C if their notation is at the same pitch as the music sounds. Other instruments are called TRANSPOSING INSTRUMENTS. Concert instruments include all keyboard and string instruments, the flute and oboe among woodwind, and the trombone among brass instruments.

concert-master (Ger., *Konzertmeister*), the title given in the United States to the first violin (Eng., leader) of an orchestra.

concerto (It.; Fr., *concert*; Ger., *Konzert*)

(1) originally a work for one or more voices with instrumental accompaniment, either for figured bass or with the addition of other instruments, e.g. Banchieri's *Concerti ecclesiastici a otto voci* (1595), Viadana's *Concerti ecclesiastici a una, a due, a tre & a quattro voci, con il Basso continuo per sonar nell'organo* (1602). Monteverdi's seventh book of madrigals (1619) is entitled *Concerto*, indicating that it contains vocal pieces with instrumental accompaniment, not madrigals in the conventional sense. This use of the word *concerto* survived till the early 18th century. It was the name given by Bach to several of his church cantatas.

(2) a work for several instruments, supported by figured bass and offering opportunities for contrast

(17th and early 18th centuries), e.g. Bach's third Brandenburg concerto. In particular:

(3) *concerto grosso*, an orchestral work in several movements, in which it was customary to have passages for a group of solo instruments (*concertino*) as a contrast to the *tutti* for the main body (*concerto grosso*). The favourite group of solo instruments consisted of two violins and cello (accompanied, like the *tutti*, by figured bass), but many other combinations are found, e.g. in Bach's second Brandenburg concerto, where the solo instruments are trumpet, recorder, oboe and violin.

(4) the solo concerto (i.e. for one instrument with orchestra) dates from the early 18th century, when the violin was the most favoured solo instrument. Keyboard instruments, being used to play the figured bass accompaniment, were not at first thought of as suitable for playing solos in a concerto. Bach's concertos for one or more harpsichords were a novelty at the time, and most of these were transcriptions of violin concertos by himself or other composers. Handel's organ concertos were written for his own use, to provide interludes in his oratorio performances. By the late 18th century the solo concerto had become the normal type, and many keyboard concertos were written, e.g. by C. P. E. Bach, Haydn and Mozart. Works of the same character for more than one solo instrument were also written, e.g. Mozart's concertos for flute and harp (K 299) and for two pianos (K 365). By Mozart's time the figured bass for a keyboard instrument had ceased to be an indispensable part of an orchestral composition, but it was still customary for a harpsichord or piano to play with the or hestra, even in concertos for a keyboard instrument.

The use of a solo instrument had obvious similarities to the use of a solo voice in the operatic aria. Hence contrasts between *ritornelli* for full orchestra and sections where the soloist took command were normal, and opportunities for improvised display were offered at the cadence before the final *ritornello* (*see* CADENZA). Mozart, however, achieved a much closer integration of the soloist and the orchestra, and there are many places in his piano concertos where the soloist provides the accompaniment to solos by wind instruments in the orchestra. In this respect his example has been followed by many subsequent composers, but not always with the same success. The increased power of the modern piano and the growth of the orchestra resulted in the composition of concertos in which there seemed at times to be a pitched battle between the soloist and the orchestra. In Thea Musgrave's clarinet concerto the soloist moves around the platform, forming splinter groups with other players 'against' the conductor. This element of mobility she developed further in her horn concerto, where there are calls and responses between the soloist and the orchestral horns – the latter placed in different parts of the hall.

(5) the word *concerto* has also been used by modern composers in a sense similar to (2) above, i.e. a composition for an instrumental ensemble, though without the implication of a figured bass, e.g. Bartók's concerto for orchestra, which highlights different instruments and sections of the orchestra, and is one of many works of its kind in the modern repertory.

(6) Bach's *Concerto nach Italienischen Gusto* (Concerto in the Italian style), popularly known as the *Italian Concerto*, is a work for harpsichord solo, which imitates the style of the solo concerto with orchestra by reproducing the contrast between soloist and *tutti*.

   C. M. GIRDLESTONE: *Mozart et ses concertos pour piano*, two volumes (1939); also in English (1948)
   A. HUTCHINGS: *Companion to Mozart's Piano Concertos* (1950)
   A. SCHERING: *Geschichte der Instrumental-konzerts* (second edition, 1927)
   A. VEINUS: *The Concerto* (1944)

concerto grosso (It.), (1) in the 17th and early 18th centuries, a composition for orchestra in several movements generally with passages for a group of solo instruments to form a contrast with the *tutti* (*see* CONCERTO (3)).

(2) the main body of instruments in a work of this kind, as opposed to the *concertino* of solo instruments.

concert overture, a form originating in the 19th century and consisting of an orchestral piece similar to the overture to an opera or play but intended purely for the concert room. Beethoven's overtures to *Egmont* and *Coriolan* and his *Leonore* no 3 overture (originally intended for the opera *Fidelio*), all of which reflect vividly the spirit of the dramas which they introduce, had a considerable influence on the composers of concert overtures, which often have a title and are associated, more or less definitely, with a programme. Typical examples are Mendelssohn's *The Hebrides* (*Fingal's Cave*), Brahms's *Tragic Overture*, Chaikovsky's *Romeo and Juliet* and Elgar's *Cockaigne*.

concert pitch, a conventional term for standard international pitch, according to which the note:

is fixed at 440 cycles a second. Brass bands in Britain use a higher pitch (*see* PITCH).

Concert Spirituel (Fr.), literally 'sacred concert'. An organization founded in Paris in 1725 by Anne Philidor to give concerts on religious festivals when the Opéra was closed. Before long the introduction of secular works made the original title a misnomer. Mozart composed his *Paris* symphony (no 31) for the Concert Spirituel. The concerts came to an end in 1791.

Concertstück, *see* KONZERTSTÜCK

concitato (It.), agitated.

concord, a combination of sounds agreeable to the ear – the opposite of discord. As, however, there have been widely different opinions as to what is agreeable to the ear, not only at different periods but also at one and the same period, any precise definition or list of concords is arbitrary and has no absolute validity.
   See CONSONANCE, DISCORD

Concord Sonata, work by Charles Ives, which does not owe its title to its harmoniousness. It is inscribed 'Concord, Massachusetts, 1840–60' and is written in an experimental style, incorporating note-clusters produced by laying a strip of wood along the keyboard. Its four movements are entitled *Emerson*, *Hawthorne*, *The Alcotts* and *Thoreau*.

concrete music, *see* MUSIQUE CONCRÈTE

conducting, the direction of a performance given by a group of singers or players or both. It involves not only precise indications of speed, dynamics and phrasing, but also careful preparation to ensure that the balance is correct and that the intentions of the composer are adequately represented. These requirements are not always observed, but a good performance is impossible without them. Unlike the singer or instrumentalist, the conductor has to persuade others to accept his view of the music and so help him to shape it into a unified and convincing whole. The method by which this is achieved varies according to the individual. Some conductors make detailed annotations in the orchestral parts or vocal scores, indicating details of bowing to the string-players or of breathing to the singers. Others rely on verbal instruction at rehearsals and on the impress of a strong personality.

The use of a baton, though at least as old as the 15th century, did not become the almost universal method of directing a performance until the second half of the 19th century. Other methods before that time included the hand, a roll of paper, or a violin bow. When a stick was employed it was sometimes used to beat time audibly, e.g. at the Paris Opéra in the 17th and 18th centuries. Elsewhere in the 18th century it was normal for opera to be directed from the harpsichord, which was in any case necessary for playing the recitative, and for symphonies to be directed by the principal first violin (still known in Britain as 'leader' of the orchestra). When the baton was introduced to London by Spohr in 1820 and to Leipzig by Mendelssohn in 1835, it was regarded as a novelty. The increasing complication of orchestral writing and the growth of the forces employed made a clear and visible direction indispensable, and the use of the baton soon became general. Even today, however, there are a few conductors – e.g. Boulez – who prefer to dispense with it and use their hands.

The original purpose of conducting was simply to keep the performers together, and hence it was very necessary when large forces were employed for church or court festivals. By the latter part of the 18th century, however, the growing subtlety of orchestral expression called for something more than the mere indication of time. By the middle of the 19th century the conductor had become an interpreter. Berlioz, Wagner, von Bülow and Richter showed that a conductor needed to be a consummate musician, with an intimate understanding of every detail of the score and the power to communicate his understanding to others. Hence the rise in the 20th century of the 'star' conductor, who is worshipped as intensely as the operatic singer in the 18th and 19th centuries.

The only satisfactory training for conducting is continual practice, which naturally depends to some extent on opportunity. Among the other indispensable requirements are practical familiarity with orchestral instruments and a knowledge of their capabilities and limitations, ability to read a full score and to hear it mentally, and an intimate knowledge of the style of widely different composers and periods. Methods vary from one conductor to another. The normal practice, however, is to use the right hand for beating time with the baton and the left to indicate entries, dynamics and expression in general. The eyes play an important part in securing the attention of the performers (though Herbert von Karajan conducts with his eyes shut), and for this reason a good conductor uses the score only for reference. To dispense with the score altogether makes a good impression on the audience and may help the conductor to concentrate wholly on the details of performance, but it can cause anxiety to the players, who have reason to fear the consequences of a lapse of memory. Moreover, if a soloist forgets his part during a concerto, the scoreless conductor may find that he is unable to meet this crisis quickly enough.

    A. CARSE: *The Orchestra in the XVIIIth Century* (1940); *The Orchestra from Beethoven to Berlioz* (1940)

    A. T. DAVIDSON: *Choral Conducting* (1941)

    H. SCHERCHEN: *Handbook of Conducting* (1933)

    H. SCHONBERG: *The Great Conductors* (1968)

    G. SCHUNEMANN: *Geschichte des Dirigierens* (1913)

    B. SHORE: *The Orchestra Speaks* (1938)

conductus (Lat.), in the 12th and 13th centuries, a metrical Latin song, sacred or secular, for one or more voices. The polyphonic examples are rarely for more than three voices and are generally characterized by simple part-writing, in which all the voices move together. Unlike other polyphonic forms of this period *conductus* is not usually founded on a pre-existing liturgical melody. The precise meaning of the word, an early example of which is in the 12th century musical drama on the subject of Daniel (from Beauvais), is disputed, though its derivation from the verb *conducere* is obvious.

Conforto (Conforti), Giovanni Luca (born c. 1560), Italian singer in the Papal choir. He was the author of *Breve et facile maniera d'essercitarsi ad ogni scolare . . . a far passaggi* (facsimile edition by J. Wolf, 1922), a valuable source of information about the late 16th century practice of improvised ornamentation in vocal music.

conga, (1) a tall narrow drum, usually single handed and played with the fingers, often in pairs, to emphasize the beat in rhythmic music;

    (2) a dance in which people form a long winding line.

conjunct, opposite of disjunct. Both terms refer to the succession of notes of different pitch. A melody is said to move by conjunct motion if its notes proceed to adjacent degrees of the scale (e.g., the opening of 'Three Blind Mice'), and by disjunct motion if its notes form intervals larger than a second (e.g., the opening of Brahms's fourth symphony).

Consecration of the House, The (Ger., *Die Weihe des Hauses*), overture in C major by Beethoven, op 124, written for the opening of the Josephstadt Theatre, Vienna, in 1822.

consecutive intervals, if any interval between two parts, whether vocal or instrumental, is followed immediately by the same interval between the same two parts, the two intervals are described as 'consecutive' or 'parallel', e.g.:

consecutive thirds:

consecutive fourths:

consecutive fifths:

Consecutive fifths and octaves, though frequent in medieval music, came to be avoided in the 15th century, presumably because they were felt to prejudice the independence of the parts. In the 16th century they were common in popular part-songs, such as the Italian *villanella*, but were avoided in cultured polyphony, whether secular or sacred. This practice established a tradition which was maintained, with occasional exceptions, until the late 19th century and is still incorporated in the teaching of elementary harmony, which is based on 18th and 19th century styles.

In 16th century polyphony it is common to find consecutive fifths which (1) occur by contrary motion, i.e. a fifth followed by a twelfth or *vice versa* (generally in music in five or more parts), or (2) are separated by the interposition of a harmony note, or (3) are avoided by a suspension which does not create a dissonance, e.g.:

LASSUS, *Salve regina* (*Works*, volume 13, page 125)

PALESTRINA, *Missa Assumpta est Maria*

PALESTRINA, *Stabat Mater*

Consecutive octaves are also found treated in the same way, e.g.:

TALLIS, *Lamentations* II

BYRD, *Alleluia, ascendit Deus* (*Gradualia* Book II)

PALESTRINA, *Surge, illuminar*

In the case of contrary motion, however, it is more usual to find a unison proceeding to an octave than an octave proceeding to a fifteenth.

conservatory (Fr., *conservatoire*; Ger., *Konservatorium*; It. and Sp., *conservatorio*), school specialising in musical training. In Italy a *conservatorio* was originally an orphanage, where children were 'conserved' and given an education with emphasis on music. The *ospedali* of Venice were institutions of this type (Vivaldi taught at the *Conservatorio dell' Ospedale della pietà*).

console, that part of the organ from which the player controls the instrument, i.e. the keyboards, pedals, stops, music desk, etc. In modern organs with electrical action it is often placed apart from the rest of the instrument and is sometimes mounted on wheels to enable it to be moved.

consonance, consonance and dissonance provide a valuable contrast in music, one suggesting repose, the other stress. There is, however, no absolute agreement as to which intervals or chords are consonant and which are dissonant. The ear is the final judge, and musicians' ears have reacted in different ways at different periods. Traditionally the major and minor thirds, the perfect fourth, the perfect fifth, the major and minor sixths and the octave are classed as consonant, and all other intervals (e.g. the second, the diminished fifth) as dissonant. Various scientific theories have been advanced to justify this distinction, but they are not convincing. In actual fact only the unison and the octave are mathematically consonant;

all other intervals are dissonant in a greater or less degree.

con sordino, an Italian term meaning 'with mute'. It is countermanded by the instruction *senza sordino*. The terms are often abbreviated to *con sord* and *senza sord*.

consort, in the 16th and 17th centuries, a chamber ensemble, especially of instruments alone, e.g. a consort of viols. An ensemble of instruments from different families is now often incorrectly called a 'broken consort', as distinct from a 'whole consort' of like instruments. There is no evidence that these terms were so used in the 16th and 17th centuries, although the expression 'broken music', used by Shakespeare and Francis Bacon, may have had some connection with the mixed consort of lute, pandora, cittern, bass viol, flute and treble viol, used by Morley in his *Consort Lessons* (1599).

Consul, The, opera in three acts by Menotti, to a libretto by the composer, first performed in New York. Magda Sorel is the wife of a member of the resistance movement in an unspecified European state, who has had to flee to escape the secret police. The story, which ends in her suicide, is concerned with her continually frustrated attempts to procure a visa so that she can cross the frontier to freedom. The consul himself is never seen.

Contes d'Hoffmann, Les, *see* TALES OF HOFFMANN

continuo (It.), abbreviation for *basso continuo* (literally 'continuous bass'), i.e. the bass line of a composition marked with figures to indicate the harmonies to be played on a keyboard instrument (*see* FIGURED BASS). Popular usage today often restricts the term to the keyboard accompaniment of recitative, e.g. in Bach's *St. Matthew Passion*. This is quite incorrect. In 17th century and 18th century music the *continuo* is played throughout the work, unless there is any indication to the contrary.

contrabass, (1) as a prefix indicates an instrument built an octave lower than the normal bass of the family, e.g. contrabass trombone;
   (2) as a noun = DOUBLE BASS, the largest member of the violin family.

contrabass clarinet, also known as 'pedal clarinet'. A 19th century invention designed to extend the lower range of the clarinet family. In its present form it dates from 1890. It is built in B flat, an octave below the bass clarinet, and has the following compass:
   written:

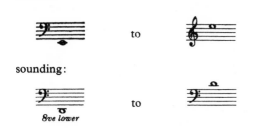

sounding:

8ve lower

There is a part for it in D'Indy's opera *Fervaal* (1897), but owing to its unwieldy size and the heavy demands it makes on the player it has never become a normal member of the orchestra.

   A. CARSE: *Musical Wind Instruments* (1939)

contrabasso (It.), double bass.

contrabass trombone, contrabass tuba etc., *see* TROMBONE, TUBA etc.

contradanza (It.), contredanse.

contrafactum, in medieval music a vocal composition in which the original words are replaced by others of a different character. A common practice was to replace sacred words by secular; the reverse practice also occurred.

contrafagotto (It.), double BASSOON.

contralto, (1) the lowest female voice, with a compass of roughly two octaves from

   (2) in the 16th and 17th centuries a male alto or countertenor.

contrapunctus (Lat.), (1) counterpoint;
   (2) a piece of contrapuntal style, e.g. the fugues in Bach's *Art of Fugue*.

contrapuntal, the adjective deriving from COUNTER-POINT.

contrary motion, *see* MOTION

contratenor, in 14th and early 15th century music the name for a part with roughly the same range as the tenor, which it often crosses. In the course of the 15th century a distinction developed between *contratenor altus* (high contratenor) and *contratenor bassus* (low contratenor), with a prevailing range respectively above and below the tenor. These terms were subsequently reduced to *altus* (alto) and *bassus* (bass).

contrebasse (Fr.), double bass.

contrebasson (Fr.), double BASSOON.

contredanse (Fr.; Ger., *Kontretanz*; It., *contradanza*), a corruption of the English country dance. A lively dance popular in France and Germany in the 18th century. Mozart and Beethoven wrote several (*see* EROICA SYMPHONY).

Converse, Frederick Shepherd (1871–1940), U.S. composer, who studied at Harvard University and Munich, and later held teaching posts at Harvard and Boston, where he became Dean of the New England Conservatory in 1938. His numerous compositions include six symphonies, several symphonic poems, chamber music, and several operas including *The Pipe of Desire, The Sacrifice*, and *Sinbad the Sailor*.

Conzert (Ger.), *see* KONZERT

Cooke, Arnold (born 1906), English composer who studied at Cambridge and with Hindemith in Berlin, and later became teacher at the Royal Manchester College of Music and Trinity College of Music, London. His *Concert Overture no 1* won a prize in the *Daily Telegraph* competition in 1934. He has also written an opera, *Mary Barton* (after Mrs Gaskell's novel), an oboe concerto, clarinet concerto, piano concerto, two string quartets, a piano sonata, sonata for two pianos and several chamber works.

Cooke, Deryck (1919–76), English musicologist who has written a successful 'performing version' of Mahler's unfinished tenth symphony. He is the author of *The Language of Music* and is an authority on Wagner and Bruckner as well as on Mahler.

coperto (It.), 'covered'. *Timpani coperti*, timpani covered with a cloth in order to mute the sound.

Copland, Aaron (born 1900), U.S. composer, conductor, pianist, lecturer and author. Born in Brooklyn, New York, he studied piano with Paul Wittgenstein and Clarence Adler, and composition with Rubin Goldmark and (in Paris) Nadia Boulanger. He has held academic appointments at the New School for Social Research, New York (1927–37), the Berkshire Music Center (from 1940) and at Harvard. He has worked tirelessly as a champion of U.S. music in particular and of modern music in general. Leonard Bernstein has said of him that 'he is the best we have.' Though some of his works (e.g. his piano sonata) are written in what might be called an international abstract idiom, much of his music is immediately indentifiable as 'American'. This includes his folk opera *The Tender Land* (1954) and the ballets *Billy the Kid* (1938), *Rodeo* (1942) and *Appalachian Spring* (1944). In these, regional U.S. idioms are employed with great colour, vitality and warmth of feeling. He has also paid tribute to Latin-America, in *El Salon Mexico* (1936) and to jazz, in *Music for the Theatre* (1925). His other orchestral works include a *Dance Symphony* (1925), piano concerto (1926), *Statements* (1935), *Outdoor Overture* (1938), *Quiet City* (1940), *Connotations* (1963) and *Music for a Great City* (1965), all of which contain to a greater or lesser degree his own special vein of poetry. He has also written chamber music (including a piano quartet, 1950, and string nonet, 1962) and songs and imaginative folk-song arrangements, in which field (e.g. 'I bought me a cat') he has been the U.S. equivalent of Britten. He is the author of *What to Listen for in Music* (1939, revised 1957), *Our New Music* (1941, revised 1968), *Music and Imagination* (1952), *The Pleasures of Music* (1959) and *Copland on Music* (1963).

cor (Fr.), French horn, generally known simply as HORN.

cor anglais, *see* OBOE

coranto (It.), *see* COURANTE

corda (It.), string. *Una corda* (in piano music), 'one string', i.e. use the left-hand pedal, which on grand pianos normally shifts the whole keyboard slightly to the right, so that the hammers can strike only one or two of the two or three strings assigned to each note. The effect is to reduce the volume of sound; on upright pianos the left-hand pedal produces a similar result by bringing the hammers nearer to the keys, so that they strike with less force. There is also another system, now obsolete, which damps the strings with a strip of felt. *Tre corde* (three strings) or *tutte le corde* (all the strings) is an indication that the left-hand pedal is to be released. *See* MUTE

corde (Fr.), string. *Instruments à cordes* (or *cordes* alone), string instruments. *Quatuor à cordes*, string quartet.

cor de basset (Fr.), basset horn.

cor de chasse (Fr.), literally 'hunting horn', 18th century name for the French HORN.

Corelli, Arcangelo (1653–1713), Italian violinist and composer. He studied at Bologna and travelled as a young man in Germany. He returned to Rome about the age of thirty and there enjoyed the patronage of Cardinal Pietro Ottoboni. He had a European reputation as violinist and composer. In his trio sonatas

(*sonate da chiesa* and *sonate da camera*), solo violin sonatas and *concerti grossi* he not only showed a talent for vivacious and intimate expression but also helped to establish a characteristic style of writing for the violin both as a solo instrument and in the orchestra. His works were edited in five volumes by J. Joachim and F. Chrysander (1888–81).

Coriolanus (Ger., *Coriolan*), a play by Heinrich Joseph von Collin, for which Beethoven wrote an overture (op 62) in 1807.

cori spezzati (It.), 'divided choirs'. A term used of the antiphonal choruses which are a characteristic feature of the style of church music practised by Venetian composers of the 16th and 17th centuries.

See WILLAERT

Corkine, William, English composer of two sets of lute-songs and instrumental pieces (1610 and 1612; facsimile editions, 1970). A modern edition of the songs only is in *The English School of Lutenist Songwriters*, second series. Some of the instrumental pieces are reprinted in *Musica Britannica*, ix.

cornamusa (It.), bagpipe.

cornamuto torto (It.), Krummhorn.

Cornelius, Peter (1824–74), German composer and writer on music, originally intended to be an actor. He studied in Berlin and became a close friend of Liszt and later of Wagner, whom he followed to Munich in 1865. In his literary works he championed the 'new music' of which these two composers were the chief representatives. His compositions include a number of songs and part-songs, which are still sung, and three operas – *The Barber of Baghdad* (Weimar, 1858), *The Cid* (Weimar, 1865) and *Gunlöd* (completed by Carl Hoffbauer, Weimar, 1891). The production of *The Barber of Baghdad* under Liszt in 1858 aroused such strong opposition that Liszt resigned his position at the Weimar court.

cornemuse (Fr.), bagpipe.

cornet, (1) a brass instrument with three valves (Fr., *cornet à pistons*, *piston*; Ger., *Kornett*; It., *cornetta*), dating from the early 19th century. Its written compass is from

It is normally built in B flat (*see* TRANSPOSING INSTRUMENTS), in which case its sounding compass is from

By using a larger CROOK or by turning a switch on the instrument its pitch can be lowered a semitone and it becomes a cornet in A, with a sounding compass from

A cornet in E flat is used in brass bands, with a sounding compass from

to

The cornet is a standard instrument in the brass band and military band, where its flexibility makes it particularly suitable for light and rapid passages. In the orchestra it has often been used in addition to the trumpet, e.g. in Franck's symphony and Elgar's *Cockaigne* overture, but outside France is not a normal member of the symphony orchestra. In the hands of a good player it is capable of producing a very expressive tone in *cantabile* passages. There is an early example of a cornet solo in Donizetti's opera *Don Pasquale* (Paris, 1843).

A. CARSE: *Musical Wind Instruments* (1939)

(2) an organ stop with several ranks (i.e. with several pipes of different pitches for each note, cf. MIXTURE), very popular in the 18th century for florid solos.

(3) = CORNETT.

cornet à bouquin (Fr.), the obsolete cornett.

cornet à pistons (Fr.), the modern cornet.

cornett (Fr., *cornet à bouquin*; Ger., *Zink*; It., *cornetto*), a wind instrument, now obsolete, used in the middle ages, in the Renaissance period and as late as the early 18th century. The spelling 'cornett' is used to distinguish it from the modern CORNET, an entirely different instrument. The normal type was slightly curved and made of wood, or less frequently of ivory, with holes which were stopped by the fingers. The mouthpiece was cup-shaped. It was made in several sizes, the commonest of which had the compass

to

with a possible extension upwards, and served as a treble to the trombone family, with which it was frequently associated. Contemporary accounts and the music written for it indicate that it had a wide range of expression – gentle in *piano*, brilliant in *forte*. Two types of straight cornett also existed – the *cornetto diritto* (*gerader Zink*), which had a detachable mouthpiece, and the *cornetto muto* (*stiller Zink*), where the mouth-piece was an integral part of the instrument.

A. CARSE: *Musical Wind Instruments* (1939)

cornetta (It.), the modern CORNET; *cornetta a chiavi*, key bugle; *cornetto*, the CORNETT.

Cornett-ton (Ger.), a pitch used by the German *Stadtpfeifer* in the early 18th century. It appears to have been the same as CHORTON.

Cornish, William, *see* CORNYSHE

corno (It.), HORN. In the 18th century frequently known as *corno da caccia*, 'hunting horn', or French horn.

corno da tirarsi (It.), literally 'slide horn', a term found in a few of Bach's cantatas. The same instrument is implied in a considerable number of other cantatas,

where a horn (described simply as *corno*) is required to play a chorale melody in unison with the sopranos – an impossibility on the natural horn of Bach's time. There is no evidence that a horn fitted with a slide existed in Bach's time. Two explanations of the term have been suggested: (a) that it indicates a slide trumpet (*tromba da tirarsi*) played with a horn mouthpiece (*see* C. S. Terry, *Bach's Orchestra*, pages 34–6), (b) that it was simply an equivalent of *tromba da tirarsi* (*see* C. Sachs, *The History of Musical Instruments*, page 385). The latter explanation, however, makes it difficult to understand why in Cantata no 46 Bach should have prescribed *tromba o corno da tirarsi* (slide trumpet or slide horn).

corno di bassetto (It.), basset horn. Used by Bernard Shaw as a pseudonym when he was writing musical criticism for the *Star* in 1888–9.

Cornyshe or **Cornish, William** (c. 1468–1523), English playwright and composer. He was a gentleman of the Chapel Royal in 1496, and master of the children in 1509. He attended Henry VIII at the Field of the Cloth of Gold in 1520. His compositions consist mainly of secular part-songs (mostly printed in *Musica Britannica*, xviii and xxxvi) and antiphons (mostly printed in *Musica Britannica*, x–xii).

coro (It.), choir, chorus; also used of a body of instrumental players, e.g. Handel's *Concerti a due cori* (concertos for two instrumental ensembles).

See also CORI SPEZZATI

corona (It., Lat., crown), the pause sign placed above a note, so called because it resembles a crown.

Coronation Anthems, four anthems by Handel composed for the coronation of George II in 1727 and performed in Westminster Abbey. The most famous is the first, *Zadok the Priest*. The others are *The King shall rejoice*; *My heart is inditing*; and *Let thy hand be strengthened*. An earlier anthem on *My heart is inditing* was composed by Purcell in 1685 for the coronation of James II.

Coronation Concerto (Ger., *Krönungskonzert*), the name given to Mozart's piano concerto in D major, K 537, composed in 1788, on the ground that he is said to have performed it at Frankfurt in 1790, on the occasion of the coronation of Leopold II.

Coronation Mass (Ger., *Krönungsmesse*), Mozart's Mass in C major, K 317 (1779), said to have been composed in commemoration of the crowning of a miraculous image of the Virgin at Maria Plain, near Salzburg, about 1744.

Correa de Arauxo, Francisco (c. 1576–1663), Spanish organist of San Salvador, Seville, from 1598 to 1633. His *Facultad orgánica* (1626) contains 69 compositions for organ; a modern edition is in *Monumentos de la Música Española*, vi and xii.

Corregidor, Der (*The Corregidor*), opera in four acts by Hugo Wolf, to a libretto by Rosa Mayreder (founded on Pedro Antonio de Alarcón's story *The Three-cornered Hat* – later used by Falla in his ballet). It was first performed in 1896 at Mannheim, and was Wolf's only completed opera.

corrente (It.), *see* COURANTE

Corrette, Michel (1709–95), French organist and composer. He held various organist's posts, the last as organist to the Duc d'Angoulême (1780). In addition to a large number of instrumental works, church music and works for the stage he also published a series of tutors for instruments and one for singing, and issued an anthology of violin solos under the title *L'Art de se perfectionner dans le violon* (1782).

Cortot, Alfred Denis (1877–1962), Swiss born pianist and conductor, the son of a French father and a Swiss mother. He studied at the Paris Conservatoire. After serving as *répétiteur* at Bayreuth, he founded in Paris the Société des Festivals Lyriques (1902) and conducted performances of Wagner's *Tristan und Isolde* and *Die Götterdämmerung* (the latter for the first time in France). He also founded the Société des Concerts Cortot (1903) and the École Normale de Musique, Paris (1918). From 1905 for many years he played piano trios with Thibaud (violin) and Casals (cello). His Chopin performances were famous, though notable more for their character and intelligence than for their accuracy. He edited many piano works, and was a distinguished lecturer on piano technique and interpretation.

Cosi fan tutte, comic opera in two acts by Mozart. Its full title is *Cosi fan tutte, ossia La scuola degli amanti* (literally translated as 'Thus do all women, or the School for Lovers'). This, the third of the three operas Mozart wrote in collaboration with the librettist, Lorenzo da Ponte, was first performed in 1790 in Vienna. The story tells of an elderly philosopher, Don Alfonso, who makes a wager with two officers, Ferrando and Guglielmo, that the ladies they love, Dorabella and Fiordiligi respectively, will not remain true to them in their absence. To test the truth of this it is announced that the officers must leave for military service. With the connivance of Alfonso and the maid, Despina, they return disguised as Albanians and woo the ladies. When they are rejected they pretend to take poison; Despina, disguised as a doctor, restores them by magnetism (a topical reference to Dr. Mesmer). The ladies' hearts are softened. First Dorabella gives in and agrees to marry Guglielmo, then Fiordiligi agrees to marry Ferrando. Alfonso, however, announces that the officers are returning. Guglielmo and Ferrando escape and re-enter in their own persons. The bogus marriage contracts signed by the ladies prove that Alfonso has won his wager. Though considered indecent by 19th century performers (who often bowdlerised it) and audiences (Beethoven, among many others, was appalled by it), *Cosi fan tutte* is recognised today as one of the greatest of all human comedies, a sublime statement about human nature and experience, fidelity and infidelity. Musically, it is the most perfectly fashioned and balanced of all Mozart's works, the characters carefully studied and contrasted, the orchestral writing (especially the woodwind parts) intensifying the drama and wit of the events on stage.

Costa, Michael Andrew Agnus (originally Michele Andreas Agnus) (1808–84), Italian born conductor and composer who studied at the Real Collegio di Musica, Naples. By the time he was 21 he had already composed several operas and other large-scale works. He first came to Britain in 1829 and rapidly established himself as a conductor. His appointments included: King's (later Her Majesty's) Theatre (1832–46); Royal Italian Opera, Covent Garden, (1847); Philharmonic Society (1846–54); Handel Festivals, Crystal Palace (1859–80). He was knighted in 1869. His efficiency and discipline appear to have been in striking contrast with the slovenly character of much English conducting at the time: he aroused the enthusiasm not only of the public but also of many distinguished musicians.

Costeley, Guillaume (c. 1531–1606), French composer and organist at the French court. He wrote some keyboard music, but his reputation rests on his polyphonic *chansons*, of which he wrote more than a hundred; 62 of these are reprinted in H. Expert, *Les Maîtres musiciens de la Renaissance française*, iii, xviii and xix.

Cosyn, Benjamin, English organist at Dulwich College (1622–4) and Charterhouse (1626–43). His manuscript collection of virginal music (in the Royal Music Library at the British Library) contains music mostly by Bull, Gibbons and himself. It is an important source for English keyboard music of this period. 25 pieces from it were edited by J. A. Fuller-Maitland and W. Barclay Squire in 1923.

Cotton, John (Johannes Cotto), early 12th century theorist, whose treatise *De musica cum tonario* contains a section on organum. He is though to have been an Englishman who was born about 1065 and became a monk at Bec in Normandy. This is not universally admitted, however, and he may alternatively have been a monk at Afflighem, near Brussels (Johannes Affligemensis); for the arguments *see* J. Smits van Waesberghe's modern edition of the treatise (1950), L. Ellinwood in *Notes*, viii (1951), Van Waesberghe in *Musica Disciplina*, vi (1952), and E. F. Flindell in *Musica Disciplina*, xx (1966) and xxiii (1969).

coulé, (Fr.), *see* SLIDE (1)

counterpoint, (1) the combination of two or more independent parts in a harmonious texture. Independence is of two kinds, melodic and rhythmic. The second of these is more forceful than the first; on the other hand rhythmic independence without melodic characterization is not sufficient to produce counterpoint. The combination of two or more melodic lines results in a series of related chords. The relationship between the notes of each individual chord and the relationship between the chords themselves constitutes HARMONY. Counterpoint is therefore inseparable from harmony; but since it is possible to write a series of chords without melodic or rhythmic interest in every individual part, harmony can exist without counterpoint. On the other hand the conventions of harmony are historically the product of counterpoint (*see* CHORD), i.e. certain conventions of contrapuntal writing resulted in harmonic relationships which became so familiar that they were stereotyped and came to exist in their own right. Harmony is therefore the crystallization of counterpoint. The following examples illustrate the difference between treatment which is primarily harmonic, and treatment which is primarily contrapuntal. In the first a melody is accompanied by two parts which have virtually no melodic or rhythmic interest. In the second each of the three parts has an independent life of its own:

staccato

BACH, *St. Matthew Passion*, no. 58

BACH, *St. Matthew Passion*, no 33

In the earliest known music in parts (late 9th century) there is no rhythmic, and hardly any melodic, independence. Every note in one part is accompanied by a single note in the other, and the melodic lines are either wholly, or substantially parallel (*see* ORGANUM). From these beginnings there developed, in the early middle ages, first melodic, and then rhythmic, independence. By the 13th century we find a fully mature art of counterpoint (*see* MOTET), side by side with the preservation of what may well be a popular tradition consisting of simple successions of similar chords without either melodic or rhythmic independence in the parts, as in the following late 13th century English example:

Quo - ni - am tu so - lus san - ctus,

tu   so - lus Do - mi nus

A. HUGHES, *Worcester Medieval Harmony* (1928), page 40

The later history of contrapuntal writing is basically

merely a further development of the principles already established. In the 14th century we find a new rhythmic freedom (following the abandonment of the RHYTHMIC MODES), in the 15th the growing use of IMITATION (already familiar in the CANON), which became an integral part of 16th century writing and formed the basis of the 17th century fugue. By the 18th century the conception of tonality (or key relationships) as a vital element in the structure of a piece of music had its influence on contrapuntal writing, without weakening its basic principles. This is true also of 19th century music. The present century has seen a marked tendency to free counterpoint from its dependence on traditional harmony, and to allow it to develop on its own lines, and in doing so to create new harmonic relationships and to establish new harmonic conventions.

Some forms of composition, for example canon and fugue, are by their very nature essentially contrapuntal. Others, such as the 16th century motet and madrigal, may be wholly contrapuntal in conception; but it is very common to find a contrast between sections which exhibit counterpoint, in the strict sense of the word, and others in which there is virtually no melodic or rhythmic independence in the parts. Sections of the first type are polyphonic (*see* POLYPHONY), of the second type homophonic (*see* HOMOPHONY). Counterpoint, in fact, is not a musical form: it is a manner of organizing musical material which may form the basis of a complete piece or may be used intermittently, as the composer desires. In the later 18th century tradition dictated that a considerable amount of church music should be contrapuntal in texture; but contrapuntal methods, even complete fugues, were constantly employed by the best composers in instrumental music as well. To think contrapuntally, to be aware of the potential energy and independence of individual parts is a necessary discipline for any serious composer, whatever style or idiom he may favour.

The teaching of counterpoint was systematised as early as the 16th century. Zacconi, in his *Prattica di musica* (two volumes, 1592 and 1619) gives a series of examples of two-part counterpoint in which a given melody (or CANTUS FIRMUS) in semibreves is treated in various ways: (1) *nota contra nota* (note against note), with the added part in semibreves also; (2) with the added part in minims; (3) with the added part in crotchets; (4) *contrappunto sincopato*, with the added part in semibreves but a minim's distance after the *cantus firmus*, i.e. syncopated:

and other varieties which need not be mentioned here. This system of progressive study was the basis of the five 'species' or types of counterpoint established by Fux in his *Gradus ad Parnassum* (1725). Fux's method, which consisted of adapting 16th century practice to the harmonic conventions of the 18th century, became widely accepted as the foundation of what is called 'strict' counterpoint. The rediscovery of Bach in the 19th century led to a different method of instruction, based largely on his practice, which came to be known as 'free' counterpoint. The terms 'strict' and 'free' are, however, illogical, since art cannot exist without limitations: it is simply a question of deciding what those limitations are to be. The discipline of observing certain conventions is valuable to any student of composition. 20th century teaching, however, has been inclined to relate such discipline to the works of the great masters. Instead of being forced to obey arbitrary rules and to work mechanically at the solution of problems in one or other of the five 'species', the student is encouraged to observe at first hand the methods of the great masters of contrapuntal writing. In this way the study of counterpoint is also the study of history and of style.

If counterpoint is so written that the parts can be interchanged, for example the treble becoming the bass, and the bass the treble, it is called invertible (*see* INVERSION). Invertible counterpoint between two parts is called DOUBLE COUNTERPOINT. Where three parts can be so interchanged, each making a suitable bass for the remaining two, the result is TRIPLE COUNTERPOINT. Similarly with four or more interchangeable parts (quadruple, quintuple counterpoint, etc.). A simple calculation will show that the possible permutations increase rapidly according to the number of parts: in double counterpoint there are two possible arrangements of the parts, the original and the inversion; in triple counterpoint there are six, in quadruple 24, and so on.

(2) a contrapuntal part added to an existing part, i.e. part B is said to be a counterpoint to part A.

K. JEPPESEN: *Counterpoint: the Polyphonic Vocal Style of the Sixteenth Cevtury* (1939)

C. H. KITSON: *The Art of Counterpoint* (second edition, 1924)

R. O. MORRIS: *Contrapuntal Technique in the Sixteenth Century* (1922)

W. PISTON: *Counterpoint* (1947)

E. RUBBRA: *Counterpoint* (1960)

F. SALZER and C. SCHACHTER: *Counterpoint in Composition* (1969)

A. SCHOENBERG: *Preliminary Exercises in Counterpoint*, edited by L. Stein (1963)

countersubject, a melody which is designed as a counterpoint to the subject (or principal theme) of a FUGUE. Its first appearance is normally in association with the ANSWER (or second statement of the subject), so that it is in fact a continuation of the subject as well as a contrast to it, e.g.

Subject

BACH, *48 Preludes and Fugues*, Book II, no 16

This association continues regularly until the EXPOSITION is complete. Later appearances of the countersubject in association with the subject are not determined by any hard and fast principle but depend on the inclination of the composer. The countersubject may also supply thematic material for the episodes or intermediate passages which occur between the recurrent appearances of the subject. Since it is convenient to be able to use a countersubject both above and below the subject, it is generally designed so that it makes DOUBLE COUNTERPOINT with the subject.

A countersubject is not essential in a fugue: several of Bach's are without one. Equally there may be more than one countersubject, in which case the additional ones must necessarily enter later than the first: for an example of a fugue with two countersubjects, *see* FUGUE. Cases occur where a countersubject enters simultaneously with the subject at the beginning of the fugue; but here the countersubject has the characteristics of a subject, so that a fugue of this kind may be described as a fugue with two subjects.

counter-tenor, the highest male voice (also known as alto), produced by using the head register. English composers of the late 17th century – e.g. Purcell – frequently wrote solos for this voice which demand not only a mastery of expression but also a brilliant, ringing tone. A revival of interest in counter-tenor singing was created in the present century by Alfred Deller, and new music has been written for such a voice, e.g. the role of Oberon in Britten's opera, *A Midsummer Night's Dream*.

country dance, the name given to a traditional English dance of popular origin. The term first appears in the glossary to Spenser's *Shephearde's Calendar* (1579). The first printed collection was *The English Dancing Master*, published by John Playford in 1651 (modern edition by L. Bridgewater and H. Mellor, 1933), which was followed by several further editions up to 1728. In the 20th century, Cecil Sharp enlarged the repertory by collecting surviving examples of folk dances, which he published in *The Country Dance Book* (six parts, 1909–22). He also revived the practice of folk dancing and founded the English Folk Dance Society (1911), now amalgamated with the Folk Song Society as the English Folk Dance and Song Society. A form of English country dance also became popular on the Continent: *see* CONTREDANSE.

coupler, a device used to augment the resources of the organ. Couplers, which are controlled by stops or tabs, are of three kinds:

(1) octave and sub-octave couplers, which automatically double in the octave above or below any note which is played;

(2) manual couplers, which enable the player to combine the resources of two manuals, e.g. the Swell to Great coupler automatically transfers to the Great manual all the stops on the Swell. These couplers also exist as octave and sub-octave couplers, e.g. if the Swell to Great sub-octave coupler is drawn, any note played on the Great manual will automatically bring into action the note an octave lower on the Swell;

(3) pedal couplers (Fr., *tirasse*, pl. *tirasses*). These operate in a similar way to the manual couplers, e.g. the Choir to Pedal coupler makes available on the pedals any stops drawn on the Choir manual. Pedal couplers working the reverse way, i.e. transferring pedal stops to the manuals, are also found, but they are not part of the normal equipment of an organ.

Couperin, French family of musicians whose talent stretched over five generations, from the 17th to 19th

François Couperin, 'le Grand': the five generations of the Couperin family were as important to French music as the Bachs to German music

century. All worked in Paris, and at least nine of them were organists of the Church of St. Gervais. The most famous was the second generation's François, known as 'Couperin le Grand'.

The first generation consisted of three brothers, Louis, François and Charles.

Louis Couperin (c. 1626–61) was a viol player and organist. A pupil of Chambonnières, he became organist of St. Gervais in 1653; he was also a string player in the royal service. His works survive only in manuscript (modern edition by P. Brunold, 1936; *see also* T. Dart's revised edition of the keyboard pieces, 1959). One of the most accomplished keyboard composers of his time, he was also one of the first French composers to write solo and trio sonatas for strings. His brother, **Charles Couperin** (1638–78 or 9), succeeded him as organist of St. Gervais in 1661. The third brother, François (1630–c. 1700), was an organist and violinist and is not to be confused with François 'le Grand'.

François ('le Grand') Couperin (1668–1733) was, like his father Charles, organist of St. Gervais (1685–1733), and in 1693 became organist to the king at Versailles, succeeding Thomelin. He taught several children of the royal family. He excelled as a composer of keyboard music, works for instrumental ensemble, secular songs and church music. His harpsichord music, arranged in *ordres* (or suites) is a model of refinement, skill and charm; many of the pieces bear fanciful titles (Couperin called them portraits) which suggest a romantic imagination, disciplined however by a scrupulous regard for formal symmetry.

An argument between the organists of Paris and the corporation of minstrels (*Confrérie de Saint-Julien des Ménestriers*) provoked the composition of the satirical and descriptive suite *Les Fastes de la grande et ancienne Mxnxstrxndxsx*(i.e. *Ménestrandise*): *see* FASTES. Couperin also exercised his talent for description and irony in his chamber music, e.g. in *Le Parnasse ou l'Apothéose de Corelli* (1724) and its companion the *Apothéose de Lully* (1725), in which he imitates the style of Corelli and Lully respectively. His church music is noble, dignified and profoundly impressive. He also published *L'Art de toucher le clavecin* (1716 facsimile of the 1717 edition, 1969) – an instruction book dedicated to the young Louis XV, which is valuable not only for the light it throws on contemporary practice in harpsichord playing but also for its grace and humour. A complete edition of Couperin's works is published by the Lyre-Bird Press, Paris, under the direction of M. Cauchie (twelve volumes).

François 'le Grand' had two musical daughters, Marie-Madeleine (1690–1742), organist of the Benedictine nunnery at Maubuisson, and Marguerite-Antoinette (1705–c. 1778), harpsichordist to Louis XV and teacher of his daughters.

The remaining members of the family of musical note were direct descendants of the first François, cousins of François 'le Grand'. They included Marguerite-Louise (1676 or 1679–1728), singer and harpsichordist; and Nicolas (1680–1748), who succeeded his cousin as organist of St. Gervais in 1733.

Armand-Louis Couperin (1725–89) was the son of Nicolas, whom he succeeded as organist of St. Gervais in 1748. He also became organist to the king at

Versailles (1770) and first organist (1782). Armand had a great reputation as a performer. He composed keyboard music primarily. His wife, Elisabeth-Antoinette (1729–1815), was an organist and pianist, who continued active to the end of her life. They had three children. Pierre-Louis (1755–89) succeeded his father as organist of St. Gervais in 1789, but died within the year. Antoinette-Victoire (c. 1760–1812) was an organist, singer and harpist.

Their best-known child, however, was **Gervais-François Couperin** (1759–1826), who succeeded his brother Pierre as organist of St. Gervais in 1789. His duties were interrupted by the Revolution, but he managed to save the organ from being destroyed and resumed his post in 1795. His compositions include variations on the Revolutionary song, 'Ah, ça ira' (1790). His daughter, Céleste-Thérèse (1793–1860), was an organist, singer and pianist.

C. BOUVET: *Les Couperins* (1919); *Nouveaux documents sur les Couperins* (1933)

W. MELLERS: *François Couperin and the French Classical Tradition* (1950)

A. PIRRO: *Les Clavecinistes* (1925)

F. RAUGEL: *Les organistes* (1923)

J. TIERSOT: *Les Couperins* (1926)

courante (Fr.; It., *coranto, corrente*), short for *danse courante*, a running dance. A lively dance in triple time, which originated in the 16th century and was immensely popular in the 17th and early 18th century, becoming one of the regular members of the SUITE, the others being the ALLEMANDE, SARABANDE and GIGUE. In the 17th century a distinction appears between the Italian *coranto* (or *corrente*) and the French *courante*:

(1) the *coranto* (or *corrente*) is written in $\frac{3}{4}$ (or $\frac{3}{8}$) time, often with quaver (or semiquaver) figuration, e.g.:

CORELLI, *Sonate de Camera*, op 4, no 1

The rhythm of the *coranto* also had a strong influence on secular song of this period;

(2) the French *courante* was more subtle. The time alternated between $\frac{3}{2}$ and $\frac{6}{4}$ (i.e. between three accents in a bar and two), and in keyboard music the broken-chord texture of lute music was frequently imitated, as in other movements of the suite, e.g.:

COUPERIN, *Premier livre de clavecin*, 2ᵉ ordre

Both types, the Italian and the French, occur in Bach's suites and partitas.

Courvoisier, Walter (1875–1931), Swiss composer. He began his career as a surgeon, but turned to music in 1902. His compositions include the operas *Lancelot und Elaine* (Munich, 1917) and *Die Krähen* (Munich, 1921), choral works, orchestral and chamber works, piano music and songs.

Coussemaker, Charles Edmond Henri de (1805–76), French musicologist. Throughout his life he pursued a legal career, but was also active in the study of medieval music. His historical works and transcriptions of medieval music have long since been superseded. On the other hand his collection of *Scriptores*, in spite of its numerous inaccuracies, is still indispensable.

Cousser, Johann Sigmund, *see* KUSSER

cow bell, (1) a clapper bell, made by bending and soldering sheet metal, hung around the necks of animals to locate them on wide pastures;

(2) a square metal bell struck with a stick to emphasize the beat in rhythmic music.

Cowell, Henry Dixon (1897–1965), U.S. composer and pianist, born in California. He studied at the University of California and the Institute of Applied Music, New York, visited Berlin with a Guggenheim Fellowship (1931) and studied comparative musicology there. Between 1923 and 1933 he toured Europe as a pianist. Later he taught at various U.S. institutions, and became director of the department of composition at the Peabody Institute, Baltimore, in 1951. Cowell was one of the 20th century's great experimenters. As a teenager he developed a technique employing note-clusters (or tone-clusters), played by striking the keyboard with the fist, forearm and elbow. He was also a pioneer of sounds produced by plucking or stroking the strings inside a piano. With Lev Theremin he invented the 'rhythmicon', an electrical instrument designed to produce different, conflicting rhythms simultaneously. The variety of Cowell's sources and composing methods has been described (by Virgil Thomson) as 'probably the broadest of our time'. He composed prolifically. His works include nineteen symphonies, a piano concerto (1929) and other piano works employing note-clusters and other devices, a series of pieces for various instrumental groupings collectively entitled *Hymn and Fuguing Tune*, pieces with bizarre or synthesized titles (*Continuations, Synchrony, Tocanta* etc), two ballets (*The Building of Banba* and *Atlantis*) and an opera (*O'Higgins of Chile*). He also composed five string quartets and other chamber music, and was author of several books, including *New Musical Resources* (1930), *American Composers on American Music* (1933) and, in collaboration with Sidney Cowell, *Charles Ives and his Music* (1955).

Cowen, Frederic Hymen (1852–1935), English composer and conductor, born in Jamaica. He studied at the Leipzig Conservatorium and the Stern Conservatorium, Berlin. He conducted the Hallé Orchestra (1896–9), the Liverpool Philharmonic Society (1896–1913), the London Philharmonic Society (1900–7), and the Scottish Orchestra. His compositions include four operas, seven oratorios, several cantatas, six symphonies, four overtures, piano concerto, orchestral suites, and nearly three hundred songs.

Cox and Box, opera in one act by Sullivan to a libretto by Francis Cowley Burnand (from John Maddison Morton's farce *Box and Cox*), first performed in London in 1867. Cox and Box are alternate tenants (day and night) in the same house.

crab canon, *see* CANON, RETROGRADE MOTION

Craft, Robert (born 1923), U.S. conductor and writer, closely associated with Stravinsky during the composer's latter years. His conversation-books with the composer, all published, provide valuable insight into Stravinsky's musical personality and ideas. Craft has also written an equally valuable journal of his travels with the composer, chronicling Stravinsky's habits and meetings with other people.

Cracovienne (Fr.), *see* KRAKOWIAK

Cramer, Johann Baptist (1771–1858), German pianist and composer, living mostly in London, a pupil of Clementi, and son of Wilhelm Cramer. He had a considerable reputation as a performer and as a teacher. Of his numerous compositions only his studies survive in use. He founded the publishing firm of J. B. Cramer & Co. (1824).

Cramer, Wilhelm (1745–99), German violinist. After several years as a member of the Mannheim court orchestra he settled in London in 1772 where he rapidly acquired a reputation as a soloist and as an orchestral leader.

crash cymbal, a suspended cymbal struck with a stick to produce a brilliant crash.

Creation, The (Ger., *Die Schöpfung*), oratorio by Haydn, first performed in 1798 in Vienna. The German text by Baron van Swieten is a translation of an English libretto selected from the Book of Genesis and Milton's *Paradise Lost*.

'Creation' Mass (Ger., *Schöpfungsmesse*), mass in B flat major by Haydn (1801), no 11 in the complete edition of the Haydn Society Inc. (no 4 in Novello's edition in vocal score). The work owes its nickname to the fact that two bars of the *Agnus Dei*, at the words 'tollis peccata', bear a resemblance to bars 7–8 of the duet for Adam and Eve, 'Graceful consort' (*Holde Gattin*) in *The Creation* (no 32).

crécelle (Fr.), rattle.

Crecquillon, Thomas (c. 1490–1557), Flemish composer, at one time in the service of Charles V. He was a prolific composer of *chansons* and church music. A facsimile of Susato's *Tiers livre de chansons à quatre parties* (1544), devoted to Crecquillon's compositions, was published in 1970. His four-part motets have been edited, with a critical study, in four volumes by H. Lowen Marshall (1970–1). A complete edition of his works by N. Bridgman and B. Hudson is announced for future publication by the American Institute of Musicology.

credo (Lat.), the initial word of the Creed in the Roman Mass – in full, 'Credo in unum Deum' (I believe in one God). These opening words were sung by the priest; hence in polyphonic settings of the 15th and 16th centuries the choir regularly begins with the words 'patrem omnipotentem' (the Father almighty). This tradition was later abandoned, though the plainsong intonation of the opening words still survives in Bach's Mass in B minor, where it is used as a *cantus firmus* for the choir. The length of the Creed influenced its treatment by composers. Examples are found in the 15th century of 'telescoped' settings, in which different parts sing different words simultaneously, and also of incomplete settings, in which some of the words were omitted. With English composers of the early 16th century the practice of omitting some of the words was quite common. The normal solution of the problem in the 16th century was to treat certain sections, for example 'Deum de Deo, lumen de lumine' (God of God, light of light), in a simpler, homophonic style, and so save the time that would otherwise be employed in contrapuntal elaboration.

crescendo (It.), 'increasing', i.e. getting louder. Often abbreviated *cresc.* The opposite of *crescendo* is *decrescendo* or *diminuendo*.

crescendo pedal, a pedal on the organ which when applied successively adds more and more stops. The name is inappropriate, since a true *crescendo* (a gradual increase of power) cannot be achieved by an artificial increase of resources which necessarily proceeds by stages, however rapidly these may succeed each other.

Creston, Paul (born 1906), U.S. composer, of Italian origin, whose baptismal name was Joseph Guttoveggio. Originally a bank clerk, he became a church organist and subsequently devoted himself to composition, teaching and criticism. His many compositions include five symphonies, concertos and other works for a variety of unusual instruments (including marimba, trombone, accordion and harp), a *Chthonic Ode* for percussion, piano and strings, a fantasy on Finnish folk songs for symphonic band, choral works, piano pieces and songs. He had also written two textbooks, *Principles of Rhythm* and *Creative Harmony*.

Cries of London, some of the traditional melodies to which itinerant traders in London proclaimed their wares were arranged as rounds or catches by early 17th century composers. More elaborate settings of a series of such melodies, in the form of fantasias for voices and instruments, were made by Weelkes, Gibbons, Dering (who also wrote a similar composition on country cries) and others, and are printed in *Musica Britannica*, xxii.

J. F. BRIDGE: *The Old Cryes of London* (1921)

Cristofori, Bartolomeo (1655–1731), Italian harpsichord and piano manufacturer, for many years in the service of the Medici at Florence. In 1709 he invented the characteristic mechanism of the PIANO – the striking of a string by a mechanically controlled hammer which is immediately forced to rebound or 'escape' by means of a 'hopper' attached to a spring, while a 'damper', withdrawn from the string at the moment of percussion, returns to it and terminates the vibration.

criticism, musical, the reasoned discussion, in a periodical or book, of public performances or compositions, new or old. Published criticism, in the modern sense of the word, first appeared in Germany in the early 18th century with Mattheson's periodical *Critica Musica* (1722–5), which was followed by similar publications by other authors (including Scheibe and Marpurg). In England Charles Avison, in his *Essay on Musical Expression* (1753) suggested that 'it might not be altogether foreign to the Design of some periodical Memoir of Literature, to have an Article sometimes, giving an Account and Character of the best musical Compositions' (page 99), but the suggestion bore no immediate fruit. Musical criticism in daily newspapers was a product of the 19th century, no doubt in consequence of the increased interest in music taken by the middle classes. In Britain *The Times* seems to have been the first newspaper to employ a music critic. In Vienna Eduard Hanslick, active as a critic from 1848 onwards, came to exercise a strong influence on opinion, particularly through his support of Brahms and opposition to Wagner. At the same time the lead given by Mattheson and others in the 18th century had been followed up by the foundation of musical periodicals in several countries, e.g. in France the *Journal de musique française et italienne* (1764), in Germany the *Allgemeine musikalische Zeitung* (1798) and the *Neue Zeitschrift für Musik*, founded by Schumann (1834), in Britain the *Quarterly Musical Magazine and Review* (1818) and the *Harmonicon* (1823). In the course of the century the number of such periodicals, some devoted to music in general, others to specific aspects of it, increased enormously. Inevitably many of these publications enjoyed only a relatively short life; a few, however, have survived to the present day, among them the *Musical Times* in Britain.

The function of the critic is to assess value, to maintain standards, to sift, define and educate, and to say, simply, what it was like to be listening to music at a certain time. The assessment of performance, however valuable for the performers and however instructive for the public, is clearly less important than the assessment of compositions, since creative art endures and performances do not. In both, the essential requisites are the widest possible knowledge, a cultivated taste and complete sincerity. Attempts have been made to reduce criticism to an exact science. In so far as every critic is an individual human being, with his own private reactions to what he hears, this is clearly an impossibility. Even though there is often general agreement about the value of particular compositions or particular composers, there have been, and still are, many cases of individual critics taking a markedly different line from their colleagues; and there is also plenty of examples of judgements almost universally accepted in one age and rejected in the next. The annals of musical criticism are full of exaggerated expressions of enthusiasm for works which now seem to us of very little account. No criticism is universally and permanently valid. On the other hand any criticism which is informed and sincere is valuable, provided we can understand the author's premises. The best critics not only tell us a good deal about themselves; they also stimulate us to form our own judgements. Today there are not so many 'thundering' critics, as in the 19th century, and it has been said that modern critics suffer from a 'Hanslick complex' – the fear that what they write may be derided by future generations. Yet Hanslick, in spite of his prejudices, is still worth reading, and the same can be said for Bernard Shaw who, though he scoffed at Brahms, provides a wonderfully vivid and witty picture of musical life in London at the end of the 19th and beginning of the 20th century.

From the early part of the 19th century onwards musical criticism has been a profession in itself. It has, however, often been combined with other musical occupations. Several composers have been active in this capacity, among them Weber, Schumann, Berlioz, Liszt, Wagner, Wolf and Debussy. At the same time composers rarely make the best critics, probably because their affinities with certain kinds of music, however unconscious, are particularly strong. The writings of Wolf and Debussy, for example, are more valuable as an expression of their authors' personalities than as a serious contribution to our knowledge of the period.

Criticism is also part of the function of the historian. This has often been denied, on the ground that history is an objective science, concerned with what has happened and not with its value. On the other hand, since all history is of necessity selective, there must be some criterion for selection; and it is difficult to see how selection can operate without an assessment of values.

M. D. CALVOCORESSI: *The Principles and Methods of Musical Criticism* (second edition, 1931)

E. NEWMAN: *A Musical Critic's Holiday* (1925)

O. THOMPSON: *Practical Music Criticism* (1934)

Croce, Giovanni (c. 1557–1609), Italian composer, a pupil of Zarlino. He was a singer in the choir of St. Mark's, Venice, in 1565. Subsequently he was ordained a priest, and became second *maestro di cappella* at St. Mark's in about 1595; he was first *maestro di cappella* in 1603. In addition to a number of Masses, motets and other church compositions he also published several books of madrigals. His madrigal 'Ove tra l'herb' e i fiori' (modern edition in J. Kerman, *The Elizabethan Madrigal*, 1962, page 286), originally published in the anthology *Il trionfo di Dori* (1592), was included in Yonge's *Musica Transalpina*, book ii (1597), with the English words 'Hard by a crystal fountain'. The concluding lines of the Italian poem:

Poi concordi seguir Ninfe e Pastori, Viva la bella Dori.

are represented in the English version by:

Then sang the shepherds and nymphs of Diana:
Long live fair Oriana.

This refrain was adopted by Michael Cavendish for his madrigal 'Come gentle swains' (1598) and occurs in the madrigals which comprise the English anthology

The Triumphes of Oriana (1601). Morley, the editor of that collection, included in it his own setting of 'Hard by a crystal fountain', which is in fact a musical elaboration on Croce's 'Ove tra l'herb' e i fiori'.

See TRIUMPHES OF ORIANA

croche (Fr.), quaver (the word for crotchet is *noire*). *Double croche*, semiquaver.

Croche, Monsieur, an imaginary person invented by Debussy as a mouthpiece for his own critical opinions: see *Monsieur Croche the Dilettante Hater* (1927).

Croft, William (1678–1727), English composer and organist. He was organist of St. Anne's, Soho, from 1700 until 1712, of the Chapel Royal (1704) and Westminster Abbey (1708). He published his doctoral exercise for Oxford (1713), consisting of two odes, under the title *Musicus apparatus academicus*, and a selection of his anthems in two volumes under the title *Musica Sacra* (1724). His keyboard compositions appeared in *A choice collection of ayres for the harpsichord* (1700) and *The Harpsichord Master*, ii & iii (1700–2). As a young man he wrote music for four dramatic productions. His setting of the Burial Service, in a simple, syllabic style, is still used at state funerals. His church music includes the famous hymn-tune, 'St. Anne' ('Oh God our Help in Ages Past').

croma (It.), quaver. Hence the adjective *cromatico*, which not only means 'chromatic' but also in the 16th century was applied to compositions which made liberal use of black notes.

See CHROMATIC (7)

cromorne (Fr.), Krummhorn.

crook, a piece of tubing inserted into a brass instrument between the mouthpiece and the body of the instrument. The pitch of the instrument varies according to the size of the crook. Thus a horn with an A crook will sound a major third higher than the same instrument with an F crook. In the 18th and early 19th centuries, before the introduction of valves or pistons on horns and trumpets the use of crooks was necessary in order to enable these instruments to be played in a variety of keys. A horn in F, for example, was for all practical purposes restricted to the HARMONIC SERIES in that key, i.e.:

None of the notes, except A, would have been any use in the key of E. By exchanging his F crook for an E crook the player could produce the same series a semitone lower:

The same principle applied to the trumpet. On the trombone crooks were not required, since the slide made available a complete chromatic compass.

Horn-players today normally confine themselves to a single crook (in F), since notes which are not in the harmonic series can be produced by valves. Occasionally, however, they use smaller crooks (in A or B flat) for 18th century works where the high range of the parts makes their performance hazardous or uncomfortable. To facilitate this change horns are now regularly built in F and B flat (i.e. with two crooks incorporated in a single instrument), with a device enabling the player to switch from one to the other. Trumpets are made in B flat and A with a switch to change from one to the other. For the high trumpet parts to be found in the works of Bach and Handel and their contemporaries a smaller instrument (in D) is used.

See TRANSPOSING INSTRUMENTS

crooning, a soft, sentimental style of singing, amplified by microphone and supported by a dance band, popular during the 1930s and 1940s.

Cross, Joan (born 1900), English soprano who sang for many years at Sadler's Wells and Covent Garden and was a founder member of the English Opera Group. One of the leading British opera singers of the 20th century, she created the roles of Ellen Orford in Britten's *Peter Grimes*, the female Chorus in *The Rape of Lucretia*, Lady Billows in *Albert Herring* and Queen Elizabeth in *Gloriana*. In 1948 she founded with Anne Wood the National School of Opera in London.

Crosse, Gordon (born 1937), English composer, a pupil of Wellesz and Petrassi. He made his name with two works for children, *Meet my Folks* and *Ahmet the Woodseller*, both of which involve child singers and instrumentalists. He has also written *Changes*, inspired by bell-ringing, *Symphonies* for chamber orchestra, and two operas, *Purgatory* and *The Grace of Todd*.

cross relation, the U.S. equivalent of FALSE RELATION.

cross rhythms, conflicting rhythmic patterns performed simultaneously, as in the slow movement of Sibelius's third symphony or some of Brahms's piano pieces.

crot, *see* CRWTH

crotales, (1) a set of small bells tuned to the chromatic scale and played with sticks;

(2) *cymbales antiques*; *see* CYMBALS (3).

Crotch, William (1775–1847), English composer and organist. He was an infant prodigy and gave organ recitals in London at the age of four. Later he held various academic appointments, and was professor at Oxford from 1797 until his death. His compositions include the oratorios *Palestine* (1812) and *The Captivity of Judah* (1834), an ode on the accession of George IV, anthems and keyboard works.

crotchet (U.S., quarter-note; Fr., *noire*; Ger., *Viertel*; It., *semi-minima*), fourth part of a semibreve, represented by the sign ♩ – the crotchet rest is written either 𝄽 or 𝄾. The word is French in origin, *crochet* = hook. The name was given to it since in the 14th century the minim was represented by a lozenge-shaped black note with a stem, and the crotchet was distinguished from it by the addition of a hook at the top of the stem. With the introduction of white notation in the 15th century the minim became a white note (𝅗𝅥), and the crotchet adopted the earlier form of the minim (♩). The hooked note (♪) became the quaver – hence the French word for a quaver is *croche*.

crowd, *see* CRWTH

Crüger, Johannes (1598–1662), German composer and theorist. He studied theology at Wittenberg, and was cantor at St. Nicolaus, Berlin, from 1622 till his death. In addition to a number of theoretical works he published several collections of Lutheran hymns with music. Many of his settings have remained in use to the present day. Among those which are familiar in England are 'Nun danket alle Gott' (Now thank we all our God) and 'Jesu, meine Freude' (Jesu, joy and treasure).

cruit, see CRWTH

Crumb, George (born 1926), U.S. composer of *Ancient Voices of Children* and a series of piano pieces entitled *Makrokosmos* in tribute to Bartók.

Crwth: a reconstruction from the 7th century remains found in the Sutton Hoo ship burial

crwth, the Welsh name of a bowed lyre, known in Irish as *crot* or *cruit*, in English as *crowd* and in Latin as *chorus*, which had a considerable vogue in the middle ages and survived in Wales as late as the 19th century. In its later form it had four strings passing over a finger-board (as on the violin) and two additional unstopped strings at the side. It has been argued that the Latin word *chrotta*, which has often been regarded as the same thing as the *crwth*, indicates in fact a form of harp (*see* C. Sachs, *The History of Musical Instruments*, p. 262).

csárdás, a Hungarian dance, consisting of two alternating sections – the first slow and melancholy (*lassú*), the second fast and vivacious (*friss*). Liszt's familiar *Hungarian Rhapsody* no 2 provides a characteristic example.

cuckoo, a short pipe with a single fingerhole giving two notes a major third apart in imitation of the cuckoo's call.

Cui, César Antonovich (1835–1918), Russian born composer, the son of a French (army) father and Lithuanian mother. By profession an engineer in the army (becoming eventually Lieutenant-General and an authority on fortifications), he enjoyed the friendship of Balakirev and found time to compose a large number of works, including several operas. Though he was a member of the nationalist group known as 'The Five' and was severely critical of other composers, his own works were neither strongly nationalist in feeling nor particularly distinguished. He was primarily a lyrical composer, who was at his best in song and piano pieces. His operas were *The Mandarin's Son, The Captive in the Caucasus* and *A Feast in Time of Plague* (after Pushkin), *William Ratcliff* (after Heine), *Angelo* (after Hugo), *Le Flibustier, The Saracen* (after Dumas senior), *Mam'zelle Fifi* (after Maupassant) and *The Captain's Daughter*. In addition he completed Dargomizhsky's *The Stone Guest* and made

one of the several completions of Mussorgsky's *Sorochintsy Fair*.

cuivre (Fr.), brass. *Instruments de cuivre* (or *cuivres* alone), brass instruments.

cuivré (Fr.; Ger., *schmetternd*), 'brassy'. An indication to horn-players to play with a harsh, blaring tone.

Cunning Little Vixen, The (Czech, *Příhody Lišky Bystroušky*), opera by Janáček, to a libretto by R. Těsnohlídek, first performed in 1924 in Brno. Janáček's animal opera was inspired by a Czech strip-cartoon and by the sights and sounds of a nature reserve, where the composer lived for a time. Since the story mingles animals and humans, and since the animals are played by singers (the vixen is the heroine of the piece), performers have to take care that the work does not slide into the world of Walt Disney; but Felsenstein, in a famous production at the Komische Oper, East Berlin, treated it with sensitivity and revealed it as a masterpiece.

Cupid and Death, a masque by James Shirley, with music by Matthew Locke and Christopher Gibbons (modern edition in *Musica Britannica*, ii). It was first performed in 1653 in London.

Curlew River, the first of Britten's three parables for church performance, first performed at Orford Church, Suffolk, in 1964. The work was inspired by a Japanese Noh play, which William Plomer's libretto skilfully transfers to the English Fens. The touching story concerns a mother's pursuit of her lost child – the role of the mother being played by a tenor (at the first performance, Peter Pears). Britten's other parables are *The Burning Fiery Furnace* and *The Prodigal Son*.

curtall, the English name given in the 16th and 17th centuries to a small bassoon. A larger form, corresponding roughly to the modern bassoon, was called *double curtall*. The name seems to derive from the Low German *kortholt* (short wood), the shortness resulting from the folding back of the tube.

Curwen, John (1816–80), a Nonconformist English minister who founded the Tonic Sol-Fa Association and the publishing firm of J. Curwen and Sons.

His son, **John Spencer Curwen** (1847–1916), continued his work as principal of the Tonic Sol-Fa College and director of the publishing firm. He was a pioneer of the competition festival movement, which he started in Stratford, East London, in 1882.

Curzon, Clifford (born 1907), English pianist, a pupil of Artur Schnabel, Wanda Landowska and Nadia Boulanger. He is specially notable for his performances of Mozart, Beethoven, Schubert and Brahms.

custos (Lat.), see DIRECT

Cuzzoni, Francesca (1700–70), Italian operatic soprano. She was engaged by Handel to sing in London and first appeared there in his *Ottone* (1723). She won great popularity, though her rivalry with Faustina Bordoni led to violent demonstrations in the theatre.

cyclic, an adjective which implies some unity between the various sections or movements of an extended work, more particularly the unity which arises from thematic connection of some kind. In the 15th century composers began to write Masses with thematic resemblances between the openings of the sections (*Kyrie, Gloria,* etc.), or with the same *canto fermo* (plainsong or secular) in all the sections, or with both together. Such Masses are now commonly described by historians as 'cyclic' (*see* MASS). Thematic association also occurs in 16th and 17th century dance suites. In symphonic music it was introduced by Beethoven (in his fifth symphony) and developed further by romantic composers, such as Mendelssohn, Schumann, Berlioz, Dvořák, Chaikovsky, Franck and Elgar. Works of this kind are often said to be in 'cyclic' form.

cymbals, (1) an early English name for chime-bells, which were used in monasteries and schools in the middle ages and often appear in miniatures and figure in sculpture (Fr., *cymbales*; Ger., *Zimbeln*; It., *cymbala*);

> J. SMITS VAN WAESBERGHE: *Cymbala* (*Bells in the Middle Ages*) (1951)

(2) percussion instruments of great antiquity, still used in the modern orchestra and in military bands (Fr., *cymbales*; Ger., *Becken*; It., *piatti, cinelli*). They consist of two metal plates, held in the hands and clashed together. An alternative (but unsatisfactory) method is used when there is only one performer to play both the bass drum and the cymbals: one of the cymbals is fixed horizontally on the top of the drum and the other is clashed against it. There are also two ways of using a single cymbal: (a) hitting it with a stick, hard or soft, in the manner of a gong, (b) performing a roll on it with timpani or side-drum sticks. The two cymbals can also be clashed rapidly together so as to produce a persistent vibration. The range of dynamics, from very soft to very loud, is considerable. It can be further modified by using smaller or larger cymbals, according to the nature of the composition;

(3) small cymbals were used like castanets by dancers in the ancient world. Berlioz introduced a pair of these (*cymbales antiques*), tuned to two different notes, in the 'Queen Mab' scherzo of his *Roméo et Juliette* symphony (1839).

czakan (Ger. *Stockflöte*), a device for enabling gentlemen *amateurs* to practise music while walking. It consisted of a walking stick which contained a flute-like instrument and was popular in central Europe in the first half of the 19th century.

Czar and Carpenter (Ger., *Zar und Zimmermann*), opera in three acts by Lortzing, to a libretto by the composer, based on a French play. First performed in 1837 at Leipzig, it tells how Peter the Great disguises himself as a carpenter. Complications ensue when a diplomat negotiating a treaty mistakes another carpenter for the Czar.

czardas, *see* CSÁRDÁS

Czar's Bride, The, *see* TSAR'S BRIDE

Czerny, Karl (1791–1857), Austrian born composer and pianist, the son of a Czech piano teacher who settled in Vienna in 1786. He was taught by his father and Beethoven (see *Beethoven: Impressions of Contemporaries*, pages 25–31). Instead of making a name for himself as a virtuoso he preferred to devote himself to teaching and earned a great reputation. Liszt was among his pupils. He was an astonishingly prolific composer in every form (including church music) and arranged an enormous number of works by other composers for two, four or eight hands, but is now known only by his technical studies, which are still in use. He left in manuscript an autobiography, *Erinnerungen aus meinem Leben.*

d, in TONIC SOL-FA d = *doh*, the first note (or tonic) of the major scale.

D, the second note (or supertonic) of the scale of C major. As an abbreviation D. = discantus, doctor, dominant. D. Mus. or Mus.D. = Doctor of Music. *D.C.* = *da capo* (go back again to the beginning). *D.S.* = *dal segno* (go back to the sign). *m.d.* = *mano destra*, *main droite* (right hand). D. is also the symbol applied to Otto Deutsch's numerical catalogue of Schubert's works.

da capo (It.), literally, 'from the head', i.e. go back again to the beginning of the piece. Often abbreviated D.C. A *da capo* aria is a song which repeats the first section after an intermediate section (generally of a contrasted character) – a form very common in 17th and 18th century opera and oratorio and also imitated in instrumental music. Traditionally the first section would be decorated by the singer on its return.

Dahl, Viking (born 1895), Swedish composer and critic. He studied in Stockholm, Paris, Munich and Berlin. His works include the opera *Sjömansvisa*, ballets, orchestral and chamber music, piano music and songs.

Dalayrac, Nicolas (1753–1809), French opera composer (originally d'Alayrac). He wrote nearly sixty *opéras comiques*, beginning in 1781 and continuing through the Revolution, of which he was a supporter. Among the most successful were *Tout pour l'amour* (based on *Romeo and Juliet*), *Les Deux petits Savoyards* (1798), *Adolphe et Clara* (1799), *Maison à vendre* (1800), *Gulistan* (1805) and *Deux Mots* (1806). In 1781 he also wrote a set of string quartets (*quatuors concertants*).

D'Albert, *see* ALBERT

Dale, Benjamin James (1885–1943), English composer. He studied at the Royal Academy of Music, of which he became warden in 1936, and made his reputation with a piano sonata in D minor (1902). Among his compositions, which are romantic in style and marked by fine craftsmanship, the best known are the suite for viola and piano (1907) and the cantata *Before the paling of the stars* (1912).

Dalibor, opera in three acts by Smetana, to a German libretto by Joseph Wenzig, translated into Czech by Erwin Spindler. First performed in Prague in 1868, *Dalibor* is one of Czechoslovakia's great national operas. The story tells how the hero, Dalibor, has been imprisoned as a revolutionary, and how his beloved Milada tries to rescue him and is killed in the process. In essence, then, *Dalibor* is a Czech *Fidelio*, and though for many years it was thought to be more localised in its interest than Beethoven's universal masterpiece, it has recently come to be recognised as a work of remarkable power and beauty. The third of Smetana's eight operas, *Dalibor* was written two years after *The Bartered Bride*.

Dall'Abaco, *see* ABACO

Dallam, Ralph (died 1673), English organ builder. He built organs after the Restoration, including St. George's, Windsor.

Dallam, Robert (1602–65), English organ builder, probably a son of Thomas Dallam. He built several organs before the Civil War, including York Minster, St. Paul's Cathedral and Durham Cathedral.

Dallam, Thomas, English organ builder of the early 17th century. He built organs for King's College, Cambridge (1606) and Worcester Cathedral (1613). He also built a mechanical organ, operated either by keys or by a clock, which Queen Elizabeth sent as a present (with Dallam as escort) to the Sultan of Turkey. For Dallam's diary of his journey to Constantinople see *Early Voyages and Travels in the Levant*, edited by J. T. Bent (Hakluyt Society, 1893).

Dallapiccola, Luigi (1904–75), Italian composer. Born at Pisino, in Istria, he was interned at Graz during World War I, after his family had been moved there for political reasons. His decision to become a composer was brought about by a performance there of *The Flying Dutchman*. When his family returned to Italy (in 1921), he studied at the Florence Conservatory, where he later became professor. In 1935 he attended the International Society for Contemporary Music Festival at Prague, heard Schoenberg's Variations, op 31, Berg's *Lulu* suite and Webern's concerto, op 24, and was profoundly impressed by them. He was the first Italian composer to adopt Schoenberg's methods, successfully applying serial techniques to his fundamental Italian lyricism. This lyricism found a natural outlet in his operas, the first of which was the one-act *Volo di Notte* (Night Flight), based on Saint-Exupéry's book (1937–39).

His *Canti di prigionia* (Songs of Captivity), completed in 1941, were an early expression of his antifascist feelings – their texts are drawn from the prayers of Mary, Queen of Scots, and the writings of Boethius and Savonarola. His *Sex Carmina Alcaei* (Six Songs of Alcaeus) were dedicated to Webern, whom Dallapiccola had met in 1942; they had their first performance in 1944 in Rome. It was not until after the fall of the fascist regime that Dallapiccola began to receive the recognition he deserved. His one-act opera *Il Prigionero* (*The Prisoner*), begun during World War II, was based on *La Torture par l'espérance* by Villiers de l'Isle Adam and *La Légende d'Ulenspiegel* by Charles Coster. First performed in 1950 at Florence, it expresses, more powerfully than any of his other works, Dallapiccola's compassion for political prisoners. In 1951 and 1952 he taught at Tanglewood, and in 1956 was appointed professor at Queen's College, New York. In 1968 he completed *Ulisse*, the largest of his operas, which treats the great legend not in the style of a 19th century spectacle but as a psychological study more reminiscent of *Pelléas et Mélisande*. He had already revealed his interest in the subject in 1941, when he completed his modern performing edition of Monteverdi's *Il ritorno di Ulisse in patria*. Though much of Dallapiccola's music – including the four Machado settings (1948), the *Three Poems* (1949) and the *Five Songs* (1956) – was written for the voice, he also wrote a number of orchestral and instrumental works. His *Piccolo musica notturna* (*Little Night Music*) dates from 1944, and his cello *Dialoghi* from 1960. He was a fine pianist, and his works for that instrument include a canonic sonatina (into which are compressed the essentials of his style) and the *Quaderno Musicale di Annalibera* (*Annalibera's Musical Notebook*), a collection of pieces written during 1952 and 1953 for his eight-year-old daughter.

    G. M. GATTI: 'Luigi Dallapiccola', *Monthly Musical Record* (Feb. 1937)

Dallery, a family of French organ-builders active in the 18th century.

dal segno (It.), 'from the sign', i.e. go back to a point in the music marked by the sign ·$·. It is often abbreviated *D.S.*

Daman, *see* DAMON

Dame Blanche, La (Fr., *The White Lady*), opera in three acts by Boieldieu, to a libretto by Augustin Eugène Scribe. First performed in 1825 in Paris, the book is an adaptation of Sir Walter Scott's *Guy Mannering* and *The Monastery*.

Damnation of Faust, The (Fr., *La Damnation de Faust*). A *légende dramatique* (dramatic legend) for soloists, chorus and orchestra by Berlioz, op 24, also described by the composer as an *opéra de concert* (concert opera). The text is an adaptation of Gérard de Nerval's French translation of Goethe's *Faust*, with additions by the composer and Almire Gandonnière. It was first performed in 1846 in Paris. A stage adaptation was made by Raoul Gunsbourg in 1893 and performed at Monte Carlo. Today the work is performed both in the theatre and in the concert hall, and though its critics regard it as an awkward hybrid, it can nevertheless make a powerful impact in either medium. The music includes such familiar pieces as the *Hungarian March*, the *Dance of the Sylphs* and the *Minuet of the Will o' the Wisps*.

Damoiselle Elue, La (Fr., *The Blessed Damozel*), cantata by Debussy for soloists, chorus and orchestra (1887–8), based on a French translation of Rossetti's poem.

Damon or **Daman, William** (c. 1540–91), Walloon composer who went to England about 1564. He was first in the service of Lord Buckhurst, and then of Queen Elizabeth (see *The Musical Antiquary*, 1912, pages 118–9). His harmonizations of metrical psalm-tunes were published in two editions (1579 and 1591). He also wrote church music (reprint of a 'Miserere' in G. E. P. Arkwright, *The Old English Edition*, xxi).

Damoreau, Laure Cynthie (1801–63), French operatic soprano, known as La Cinti. She first appeared at the Paris Opéra in 1826, singing principal roles in Rossini's *Count Ory* and *William Tell*, Auber's *Masaniello* and Meyerbeer's *Robert le Diable*. She taught singing at the Paris Conservatoire from 1834 until 1856 and published a *Méthode de chant*.

damper, a piece of felt, glued to a strip of wood, which covers a piano string and prevents it from vibrating. It is automatically removed from the string when the key is struck and covers it again as soon as the key is released. The right-hand pedal removes the dampers from all the strings and so increases the sonority of the instrument by permitting sympathetic vibration.

    See ACOUSTICS, PIANOFORTE

Dämpfer (Ger.), mute (It., *sordino*). *Mit Dämpfer*, with mute (*con sordino*). *Dämpfer weg*, without mute (*senza sordino*).

Damrosch, Leopold (1832–85), German conductor and violinist. He studied medicine at Berlin University, graduating in 1854, then became a professional violinist, playing in the Weimar orchestra under Liszt (1857). After working in Breslau, he moved to New York, where he founded the Oratorio Society in 1874 and the Symphony Society in 1878, both of which he conducted. He directed a season of German opera at the Metropolitan Opera House (1884–5), and conducted the U.S. première of *Die Walküre*. He was an intimate friend of Wagner and Liszt, who dedicated to him the *Le Triomphe funèbre du Tasse*. He wrote a large number of vocal and instrumental works, including a violin concerto.

    His sons, **Frank Heino Damrosch** (1859–1937) and **Walter Johannes Damrosch** (1862–1950), were also prominent in New York musical life. The first was active as a conductor of choral societies and was chorus master of the Metropolitan Opera from 1885 until 1891. The other was assistant conductor of the Metropolitan Opera (1884), conductor of the Oratorio Society (1885–98) and New York Symphony Society (1885–94), founder of the Damrosch Opera Company (1894–9), conductor of the New York Philharmonic (1902–3) and Symphony Orchestra (reorganised) (1903–26). He was a pioneer of broadcast concerts in the United States. He directed the U.S. premières of Wagner's *Meistersinger*, *Tristan*, *Rheingold*, *Siegfried* and *Götterdämmerung*, and composed five operas himself – *The Scarlet Letter* (1896), *The Dove of Peace* (1912), *Cyrano de Bergerac* (1913), *The Man without a Country* (1937) and *The Opera Cloak* (1942). His memoirs, *My Musical Life*, were published in 1923.

dance band, a band that plays for strict tempo dancing. It usually consists of a brass section of trumpets and trombones, a reed section of saxophones doubling clarinets, and a rhythm section of piano, bass and drums.

Dandrieu, Jean François (1682–1738), French organist and composer. He wrote music for harpsichord and organ (including arrangements of *noëls*) and chamber music. A modern edition of organ music is in A. Guilmant, *Archives des maîtres de l'orgue*, vii; harpsichord music in H. Expert, *Les Maîtres du clavecin des XVII et XVIII siècles*.

D'Anglebert, *see* ANGLEBERT

Danican, François André, *see* PHILIDOR

Daniel or **Danyel, John** (1564–after 1625), English composer, the brother of the poet, Samuel Daniel. He graduated B.Mus. at Oxford in 1603. He was musician to Queen Anne, consort of James I (1612), and to Charles I (1625). He published *Songs for the Lute, Viol and Voice* (1606), including the elaborate and pathetic setting, with chromatic harmonies, of 'Can doleful notes'; a modern edition is in *The English School of Lutenist Songwriters*, second series.

Danse Macabre, an orchestral piece (op 40) by Saint-Saëns (1874), based on verses by Henri Cazalis, and quoting the 'DIES IRAE'. It represents Death playing the violin for a dance of skeletons – a legendary conception which goes back to the middle ages. Liszt's *Totentanz* for piano and orchestra deals with the same subject.

Dante Sonata, abbreviated name for Liszt's piano work, *Après une lecture du Dante* (Fr., *After a reading of Dante*), which forms part of the Italian volume of his *Années de Pèlerinage* (*Years of Pilgrimage*). Laid out in a single movement, it was considered by the composer to be a mixture of sonata and fantasia. It was written between 1837 and 1839, and revised in 1849.

Dante Symphony (Ger., *Eine Symphonie zu Dante's Divina Commedia*), orchestral work by Liszt, with female chorus in the final section. There are two movements, *Inferno* and *Purgatorio*, leading to *Magnificat*. The work was dedicated to Wagner, and first performed in 1857 at Dresden.

Danyel, see DANIEL

danza tedesca (It.), 'German dance'; see TEDESCA, ALLEMANDE, DEUTSCHER TANZ.

Daphne, opera in one act by Richard Strauss, to a libretto by Joseph Gregor, first performed in 1938 at Dresden. Described as a 'bucolic tragedy', the opera is an adaptation of the classical legend of the daughter of the Thessalian river-god Peneus who escapes the pursuing Apollo by being turned into a laurel tree.

Daphnis et Chloé (Fr., Daphnis and Chloe), ballet by Ravel, first performed in Paris, with choreography by Michel Fokine and decor by Léon Bakst. The work, which calls for chorus as well as orchestra, was inspired by a Greek legend of pastoral love and abduction. Two suites from the ballet were subsequently arranged by the composer for concert performance.

Da Ponte, see PONTE

Daquin, Louis Claude (1694–1792), French organist and composer, a pupil of Louis Marchand. He began his career as a child prodigy, and became organist at the French Chapel Royal in 1739. He wrote *Premier livre de pièces de clavecin* (1735; modern editions in *Le Trésor des pianistes*, edited by Farrenc, ix), which includes the well known 'Le coucou' (The cuckoo) and *Nouveau livre de Noëls pour l'orgue et le clavecin* (modern edition in *Archives des maîtres de l'orgue*, edited by Guilmant).

Dardanus, opera in five acts by Rameau, to a libretto by Charles Antoine Leclerc de La Bruère, first performed in 1739 in Paris. Along with *Les Indes Galantes* and *Castor et Pollux*, dating from the same period, this work established Rameau with the French public as one of the major operatic composers of the day.

D'Arezzo, see GUIDO D'AREZZO

Dargomizhsky, Alexander Sergeivich (1813–69), Russian composer. Initially a civil servant, he was largely self-taught as a musician but received encouragement from Glinka. His first opera, *Esmeralda* (Moscow, 1847), produced eight years after its composition, was not a success. *The Russalka* (St. Petersburg, 1856) made a much stronger impression. His most individual work is *The Stone Guest* (St. Petersburg,

1872), which was completed by Cui and orchestrated by Rimsky-Korsakov; the text, which is the story of Don Juan, is set to a sort of continuous recitative. Though essentially an amateur he had a considerable influence on the nationalist school of Russian composers, as well as on Chaikovsky. In addition to his operas he also wrote a number of songs, some satirical, and three characteristic orchestral fantasias.

G. ABRAHAM: *Studies in Russian Music* (1935); *On Russian Music* (1939)

Dart, Thurston (1921–71), English harpsichordist, organist, conductor and scholar. In 1962 he became professor of music at Cambridge (where he had been lecturer since 1947), and from 1964 until his death was the first full-time professor of music at London University. He travelled widely as a solo harpsichordist, and was an outstanding continuo player. His book, *The Interpretation of Music*, was published in 1954. His edition of Bach's Brandenburg Concertos (recorded by the Academy of St. Martin-in-the-Fields, with Dart as harpsichordist in some of the works) is exceptionally interesting, if controversial.

Das, for German titles beginning thus, see the second word of the title.

Daughter of the Regiment, The, (Fr., *Fille du Régiment*), opera in two acts by Donizetti, to a libretto by Jules Henri Vernoy de Saint-Georges and Jean François Albert Bayard, first performed in 1840 in Paris. The story concerns a regimental 'mascot' who turns out to be a Countess's niece. Donizetti's first French opera has attracted coloratura sopranos ever since Anna Thillon created the title-role. Jenny Lind appeared in it in London in 1847; other singers who have starred in it have included Albani, Hempel, Pons, Tetrazzini and, in our own day, Joan Sutherland.

Dauprat, Louis François (1781–1868), French hornist and composer. He worked at the Paris Opéra (1808–31) and taught at the Paris Conservatoire (1816–42). In addition to five horn concertos and other works for the instrument he wrote a *Méthode de cor alto et de cor basse*, which was for many years a standard work.

Dauvergne, Antoine (1713–97), French violinist and composer. He became master of the king's chamber music and manager of the Paris Opéra, as well as one of the directors of the Concert Spirituel. After having written a considerable amount of instrumental music he turned his attention to opera in 1752. His one-act *Les Troqueurs* (Paris, 1753) was said to be the first French comic opera in the style of the Italian intermezzo, with recitative instead of dialogue.

Davenant, William (1606–68), English poet and dramatist. He was author of the libretto of the first English opera, *The Siege of Rhodes* (London, 1656).

David, Félicien César (1810–76), French composer. He studied at Aix and the Paris Conservatoire. Of his numerous compositions, which include two symphonies, 24 string quintets and several operas, the one which made his reputation was *Le Désert* for chorus and orchestra (1844) with its remarkable gift for oriental colouring – the result of several years residence in the Near East.

R. BRANCOUR: *Félicien David* (1911)

David, Ferdinand (1810–73), German composer and violinist, a pupil of Spohr and a friend of Mendelssohn. In 1836 he became leader of the Leipzig Gewandhaus orchestra under Mendelssohn. He advised Mendelssohn during the composition of the latter's violin concerto and gave the first performance at Leipzig in 1845. His pupils included Joachim and Wilhelmj. In addition to a large number of compositions, including five violin concertos, he wrote a *Violinschule* and a *Hohe Schule des Violinspiels* (both standard works) and edited numerous works for the violin by older composers.

David, Johann Nepomuk (born 1895), Austrian composer, organist and writer. He became teacher at the Leipzig Conservatorium in 1934 and later worked in Salzburg and Stuttgart. His compositions include eight symphonies and other orchestral pieces, two violin concertos, a *Requiem Chorale* for soloists, chorus and orchestra, chamber music and organ pieces.

Davidov, Karl (1838–89), Russian composer and cellist, who became principal cello of the Leipzig Gewandhaus Orchestra in 1859. He was director of the St. Petersburg Conservatoire from 1876 until 1886. His compositions include four cello concertos.

Davidovsky, Mario (born 1934), Argentine composer, who studied in Buenos Aires and with Copland in the United States. He has held various academic appointments and is noted for his ELECTRONIC MUSIC, which includes a series of studies and what the composer describes as *Synchronisms* (or *Sincronismi*). He has also written works for chamber ensemble.

Davidsbündler (Ger., Members of the League of David), an imaginary association invented by Schumann, which was supposed to fight against Philistines in music. The names of some of the members, however, represented real people, including Schumann himself and Mendelssohn. A 'Marche des Davidsbündler contre les Philistins' occurs in Schumann's *Carnaval*, op 9, and in 1837 he wrote a set of eighteen characteristic dances entitled *Davidsbündlertänze*, op 6, and signed with the initials 'F' or 'E', i.e. Florestan and Eusebius (names adopted by the composer to represent two different sides of his personality).

Davies, Fanny (1861–1934), English (Guernsey born) pianist, a pupil of Clara Schumann. Her first public appearance in England was in 1885. She excelled in the music of Schumann and Brahms, the latter of whom she knew well; but her tastes were catholic, and she included a great deal of early keyboard music in her programmes.

Davies, Henry Walford (1869–1941), English organist and composer. He was a chorister at St. George's Chapel, Windsor, and assistant there to Walter Parratt, from 1885 until 1890. He held various academic and organist's appointments (including St. George's Chapel, 1927–32) and was Master of the King's Music from 1934 until 1941. He was knighted in 1922. Among his numerous compositions are several works for chorus and orchestra written for various festivals; the most successful of these was *Everyman* (Leeds, 1904). He was active in providing music for the forces in World War I and became Director of Music to the Royal Air Force in 1917. His *Solemn Melody*, for organ and strings, was written for the celebration of Milton's tercentenary at Bow Church, 1908.

H. C. COLLES: *Walford Davies* (1942)

Peter Maxwell Davies, British composer and conductor of the Fires of London, the progressive music group he founded for the performance of his own music and that of like-minded modern composers

Davies, Peter Maxwell (born 1934), English composer. After studying at the Royal Manchester College of Music – where, with Birtwistle, Goehr and others he was to become one of the so-called 'Manchester School' – he spent two years in Italy as a pupil of Petrassi and a period studying under Roger Sessions in the United States. From 1959 until 1962 he was director of music at Cirencester Grammar School, where he wrote his *O Magnum Mysterium* (a milestone of modern British choral music) for the school choir and orchestra.

Davies has always liked composing music for specific performers, and it was for that reason that he formed his own ensemble, the Pierrot Players – later renamed the Fires of London – with himself as director. His music has been greatly influenced by medieval and Renaissance techniques, which he employs in a modern context, often with a keen sense of parody. His opera, *Taverner*, is based on the life of the 16th century English composer and heretic, John Taverner. His other works include two fantasies on Taverner's *In Nomine*, *Prolation* and *Worldes Blis* for orchestra, *St. Michael Sonata* for seventeen wind instruments, and settings of Leopardi for soprano, alto and chamber ensemble. His *St. Thomas Wake* is a foxtrot for orchestra (foxtrots, like medieval music, have exerted their influence on his style).

The works he has written for the Fires of London often contain strong elements of music theatre, e.g. *Eight Songs for a Mad King* for voice and chamber ensemble, *Vesalii Icones, Revelation and Fall, Ante-*

christ and the *Missa super l'homme armé.* Recently he has found a new source of inspiration in the geography and history of the Orkney islands, resulting in such works as *From Stone to Thorn* for soprano and chamber ensemble (a setting of a text by the Orkney poet, George Mackay Brown, in which the ritual of the Stations of the Cross is paralleled with the older ritual of agriculture) and *Stone Litany* (with its atmospheric seascapes) for orchestra.

Davis, Colin (born 1927), English conductor. He began his studies at the Royal College of Music, London, as a clarinettist, and developed his conducting abilities with the Chelsea Opera Group. From 1961 until 1965 he was musical director of Sadler's Wells Opera, and in 1966 he made his New York Metropolitan début with *Peter Grimes.* In 1967 he became chief conductor of the B.B.C. Symphony Orchestra, and in 1971 musical director of the Royal Opera House, Covent Garden. He is specially associated with the music of Mozart, Berlioz and Tippett.

Davis, Miles (born 1926), U.S. Negro jazz trumpeter and flügelhorn player, who began as a disciple of Charlie Parker and soon developed into one of the major and most individual figures of modern jazz. He has worked with his own small groups and in the richer musical context of the Gil Evans Orchestra, contributing creatively to Evans's *Porgy and Bess* suite. Much of his playing is cool, melancholy and muted (though by no means exclusively so), and he is heard at his best in such recordings as *Sketches of Spain,* in which his Negro musical culture is thoroughly integrated with that of Spain. The delicacy of Davis's playing, in comparison with the healthy vigour of Louis Armstrong's, led to one critic comparing him to 'a man walking on eggshells'.

Davison, Archibald Thomson (1883–1961), U.S. conductor and musicologist. He studied at Harvard, where he was a member of staff from 1909 and professor of music from 1940 until 1954. His published works include *Choral Conducting* (1940), *The Technique of Choral Composition* (1945) and *Historical Anthology of Music* (with W. Apel, two volumes, 1946 and 1950).

Davy, Richard, English composer of the late 15th and early 16th centuries. He was organist of Magdalen College, Oxford, from 1490 to 1492, and subsequently became a priest. He was a vicar-choral at Exeter Cathedral from 1497 to 1506. His compositions, mainly for the church, include an incomplete setting of the Passion, six complete and one incomplete antiphons, and one incomplete Magnificat (all in the Eton choirbook; *see Musica Britannica,* x–xii), and carols and part-songs (printed in *Musica Britannica,* xxxvi).

Daza, Esteban, 16th century Spanish lutenist. His *Libro de Musica en cifras para Vihuela, intitulado el Parnasso* (1576) contains a number of fantasies for *vihuela,* as well as arrangements of motets, madrigals and *villancicos* for voice and *vihuela;* excerpts are published in G. Morphy, *Les Luthistes espagnols du XVIᵉ siècle* (1902).

Death and the Maiden (Ger., *Tod und das Mädchen*), song by Schubert (1817) to words by Matthias Claudins; also the nickname of Schubert's D minor string quartet, whose slow movement uses the song as the subject of a set of variations.

Death and Transfiguration (Ger., *Tod und Ver-* *klärung*), symphonic poem by Richard Strauss, op 24, composed in 1889 and first performed the following year at Eisenach. The poem by Alexander Ritter which is placed at the head of the score was written after the work was composed.

Death in Venice, opera in two acts by Benjamin Britten, to a libretto by Myfanwy Piper, based on the story by Thomas Mann. It was first performed at the 1973 Aldeburgh Festival, with Peter Pears in the role of the novelist Gustav von Aschenbach.

De Bériot, *see* BERIOT

Debora e Jaele (It., *Deborah and Jael*), opera in three acts by Pizzetti, to a libretto by the composer, first performed in 1922 in Milan, with Toscanini as conductor. Though hardly known outside Italy, this work

Miles Davis, a leading exponent of modern jazz, at the 1973 Montreux Jazz Festival

is usually considered to be the finest of Pizzetti's music dramas.

Debussy, Claude Achille (1862–1918), French composer. Born at St. Germain-en-Laye, near Paris, from the age of eight he received piano lessons from Mme Mauté de Fleurville, a pupil of Chopin and Verlaine's mother-in-law. In 1873 he entered the Paris Conservatoire, studying under Lavignac, Marmontel and Durand. Though his failure to win a piano prize at the age of seventeen caused his parents to despair of his ever becoming a virtuoso, he won first prize in score-reading the following year – a success which enabled him to enter a composition class. Thereafter, for two years, he became domestic musician to Nadezhda von Meck, Chaikovsky's former patroness. In 1884 he won the *Prix de Rome* with *L'Enfant prodigue*. This 'lyric scene' and *La Damoiselle élue* (1888, the text translated from Rossetti's *The Blessed Damozel*) show the influence of Massenet, though a more individual style was detectable in *Printemps* (1886) and his musical personality developed even more strongly in his string quartet (the only one he wrote, 1893) and the orchestral *Prélude à l'après-midi d'un faune* (1894), written to illustrate a poem by Mallarmé. In 1899 he married a dressmaker, Rosalie (Lili) Texier (whom he left five years later) and in 1901 became music critic for the *Revue Blanche*. By this time he had composed his three orchestral *Nocturnes* (1899). The kaleidoscopic harmonies and shifting tone-colours of these and other pieces are the counterpart of the elusive style of the impressionist painters and the symbolist poets. Debussy's impressionism became the ruling principle of his work, developed in a large scale in the opera *Pelléas et Mélisande*, a setting of Maeterlinck's play (Paris, 1902), for which he had already written some incidental music and which represented his reaction to Wagnerism – the work is the obverse of *Tristan*. It was also to be found in such orchestral works as *La Mer* (1905), a set of three seascapes, and in the *Images* (1906–12), consisting of *Gigues*, *Ibéria* and *Rondes de Printemps*. The same style is found in his songs and his music for piano, in which he discovered sonorities to which earlier composers had paid little or no attention. For all its power of suggestion, his music is not vague but shows every sign of precise and methodical workmanship. Thus, though there was once a fashion to perform his works smudgily, many of today's performers (e.g. the conductor Boulez and the pianist Michel Béroff) have demonstrated how successfully the music responds to being played with absolute clarity. The laconic style of Debussy's later chamber music, written during World War I, was at one time thought to bear the marks of the ill-health which dogged his final years – he died of cancer in 1918. But in fact such works as the cello sonata, the sonata for flute, viola and harp, and the violin sonata, far from showing a decline in inspiration, suggest that he had entered an important new phase in his career, and it is sad that he did not live to write the three other sonatas he was planning at that time.

Debussy's critical writing, though sometimes prejudiced, is frank and witty – for instance he compared Grieg's music with 'a pink sweet stuffed with snow'. His principal compositions are:

(1) Orchestra: *Printemps* (1886); *Prélude à l'Après-midi*

Claude Debussy, photographed by Pierre Louÿs in 1909. A musician photographed by a writer in a way that consciously sets out to reflect the visual qualities of contemporary Art Nouveau and admirably shows how Debussy and his friends felt themselves to be at the centre of the aesthetics of their time

d'un faune (1894); *Nocturnes* (1899); *La Mer* (1905); *Images* (1912).

(2) Chamber music: String quartet (1893); cello sonata (1915); sonata for flute, viola and harp (1915); violin sonata (1916–17).

(3) Piano: *Suite bergamasque* (1905); *Pour le piano* (1901); *Estampes* (1903); *Images* (1905 and 1907); *Children's Corner* (1908); *Preludes* (book i, 1910; book ii, 1913); *Études* (1915); *En blanc et noir* for two pianos (1915).

(4) Choral works: *L'Enfant prodigue* (1884); *La Damoiselle élue* (1888); *Le Martyre de Saint Sébastien* (1911).

(5) Opera: *Pelléas et Mélisande* (1902).

(6) Songs: more than fifty.

A. CORTOT: *The Piano Music of Debussy* (1922)

C. DEBUSSY: *Monsieur Croche the Dilettante Hater* (1927)

E. LOCKSPEISER: *Debussy* (1936)

O. Thompson: *Debussy, Man and Artist* (1937)
L. Vallas: *Claude Debussy: his Life and Works* (1933); *The Theories of Claude Debussy* (1929)

Decani (Lat.), literally 'of the dean', i.e. that half of the choir in an English cathedral which sits on the dean's side, as opposed to *Cantoris*, the precentor's side. Alternations between the two halves of the choir are common in English cathedral music of all periods. The abbreviations *Dec.* and *Can.* are in common use for *Decani* and *Cantoris*.

déchant (Fr.), descant.

decrescendo (It.), 'decreasing', i.e. getting softer, the opposite of *crescendo*. The word is often abbreviated *decresc.*

Dedekind, Constantin Christian (1628–1715), German poet and prolific composer of sacred and secular songs. He was attached to the Dresden court from 1654 to 1675, first as a singer, then as *Konzertmeister*. Four of his sacred concertos for voice and continuo were edited by A. Rodemann in 1929.

Deering, *see* Dering

De Falla, *see* Falla

Defesch, William (1687–1761), Flemish composer. Dismissed from his post as *maître de chapelle* at Notre Dame, Antwerp, he came to London, c. 1732, where an oratorio by him was performed. His works include concertos and chamber music, among which are several cello sonatas.

degrees in music, these are peculiar to universities in the English-speaking world. At Oxford and Cambridge they date from the 15th century; they are now awarded by most British universities. The following degrees are found: Bachelor of Music (B.Mus., Mus.B. or Mus.Bac.), Master of Music (M.Mus. or Mus.M.), Doctor of Music (D.Mus., Mus.D., or Mus.Doc.). At Oxford and Cambridge the B.Mus. is a post-graduate degree: at the former the examination consists only of composition, but is open only to those who have gained first- or second-class honours in the B.A. in music; at the latter it embraces also research and performance. At most other universities the B.Mus. corresponds to the B.A. in arts subjects or the B.Sc. in science. The D.Mus. is an advanced degree, involving normally composition (sometimes with an examination in the history of music as well); at some universities it is awarded also for research or performance. The M.Mus., which exists only at certain universities, is a degree intermediate between the B.Mus. and the D.Mus.; it is also awarded by the Royal College of Music. The Archbishop of Canterbury has the right to confer the degree of Doctor of Music without examination; such a degree is generally known as a Lambeth degree and is represented by the abbreviation D.Mus. Cantuar. The degrees of B.Litt., M.Litt., Ph.D. (at Oxford D. Phil.) or D.Litt. may be awarded for research in music.

In the United States the degree of D.Mus. was until recently awarded only as an honorary degree. At several universities, however, it is now possible to obtain this degree, or A.Mus.D. (Doctor of Musical Arts), by examination. The qualifications for these degrees and for the degrees of B.Mus. and M.Mus. vary considerably from one university to another. The Ph.D. is awarded, as in England, for research.

In Germany there are no degrees specifically for music, though the Ph.D., which is the normal university degree, can be awarded to students who have passed certain examinations and submitted a thesis. In France and Switzerland the Dr. ès Lettres may be awarded for musical research, as for other subjects studied at an advanced level.

Dehn, Siegfried Wilhelm (1799–1858), German musicologist and teacher. From 1842 he was in charge of the music section of the Royal Library at Berlin. He edited a large number of works of the 16th and 17th centuries, as well as several of Bach's works, at a time when these were little known. His theoretical works include *Theoretisch-praktische Harmonielehre* (1840) and *Lehre vom Kontrapunkt* (1859). Among his many pupils were Glinka, Cornelius and Anton Rubinstein.

dehors, en (Fr.), literally 'outside'. Instruction to a performer to emphasize a melody or some other aspect of a piece, so that it stands out from its surroundings.

Deidamia, opera in three acts by Handel, to a libretto by Paolo Antonio Rolli, first performed in London. This was Handel's last opera, whose intention seems to have been to deflate ironically the tradition of *opera seria* which had served Handel throughout his career as an opera composer. Though not a success in its time – it was withdrawn after three performances – it has been successfully revived in recent years.

Deiters, Hermann (1883–1907), German writer on music, by profession a schoolmaster and inspector of schools. He edited the third and fourth editions of Jahn's life of Mozart, and translated and revised Thayer's life of Beethoven.

Delibes, Clément Philibert Léo (1836–91), French composer, pupil of Adam at the Paris Conservatoire. He held various opera and organ posts from 1853 to 1872 and in 1881 was appointed professor of composition at the Paris Conservatoire. His best known works are the operas *Le Roi l'a dit* (Paris, 1873) and *Lakmé* (Paris, 1883) and the ballets *Coppélia* (1870) and *Sylvia* (1876), containing a wealth of charming light music and colouring which so appealed to Chaikovsky that he deemed Delibes a better composer than Brahms.

H. de Curzon: *Léo Delibes* (1927)

Delius, Frederick (1862–1934), English composer, born in Bradford of German parentage, the son of a wool-merchant. He migrated to Florida as an orange-planter in 1884, but abandoned this for music after a year, making a living as teacher and organist. In 1886 he went to Leipzig to study at the Conservatorium where he met Grieg and Sinding. Two years later he moved to Paris to live with his uncle, and settled permanently in France. In Paris he met Strindberg, Gauguin, Florent Schmitt and Ravel, and married the artist Jelka Rosen. An orchestral work, *Sur les cimes* (1892), was performed at Monte Carlo in 1893, followed by *Over the hills and far away* (1895) at Elberfeld in 1897. A concert of his works was given in London in 1899, but it was some time before his music became generally known in Britain. Many of his compositions had their first performance in Germany – among them the operas *Koanga* (Elberfeld, 1904), *A Village Romeo and Juliet* (Berlin, 1907) and *Fennimore and Gerda* (Frankfurt, 1919), the orchestral works *Paris* (Elberfeld, 1901), *Appalachia* (Elberfeld, 1904) and *Brigg Fair* (Basel, 1907), and the setting of Whitman's *Sea-Drift* (Essen, 1906). The growth of Delius's popularity in Britain was due very largely to Sir Thomas Beecham's enthusiasm and unusually intimate understanding of his music: a Delius festival, organized by Beecham, was given in London in 1929. In his later years Delius became blind and paralysed, but with the assistance of his amanuensis, Eric Fenby, he managed to dictate a number of compositions before his death at his home at Grez-sur-Loing near Fontainebleau.

Frederick Delius, blind and paralysed, towards the end of his life: a portrait by Ernest Procter

Though he was influenced by Grieg in his earlier days, his work falls into no ready-made category. It is marked particularly by a luscious use of shifting chromatic harmonies and by a style which prefers rhapsody to calculated construction; the basis of his melodic style, however, is diatonic, and often shows an affinity with folk song. Like many other romantic composers of his generation he demands an extravagantly large orchestra, which he used often with a deeply poetic feeling for nature, as in *A Mass of Life* and in the orchestral interludes in *A Village Romeo and Juliet*, though some of his climaxes were coarse and overloaded. His music is, perhaps, most characteristic when it is intimate, but it is also frequently marked by a robust vigour. The *Mass of Life* (to a text from Nietzsche's *Also Sprach Zarathustra*, first performed complete in 1909) and the subsequent Requiem (also drawn from Nietzsche, 1914–16) both reflected Delius's religious scepticism, and were at one time among the most controversial of his compositions. Today the importance of these pieces is better appreciated, though since the death of Beecham (in 1961) Delius's complete works have lacked a really persuasive champion.

His principal compositions are:

(1) Orchestra: *Over the hills and far away* (1895); piano concerto (1897, revised 1906); *Paris* (1899); *Appalachia* (1896; revised, with chorus, 1902); *Brigg Fair* (1907); *North Country Sketches* (1914); concerto for violin and cello (1916); violin concerto (1916); *Eventyr* (1917); cello concerto (1921).

(2) Choral works: *Sea-Drift* (1903); *A Mass of Life* (1905); *Songs of Sunset* (1907); *Song of the High Hills* (1912); *Requiem* (1916); *Songs of Farewell* (1930).

(3) Operas: *Irmelin* (1892); *Koanga* (1897); *A Village Romeo and Juliet* (1901); *Fennimore and Gerda* (1910).

(4) Chamber music: three violin sonatas; cello sonata; two string quartets.

C. DELIUS: *Frederick Delius* (1935)
E. FENBY: *Delius as I knew him* (1936, revised 1966)
P. HESELTINE: *Frederick Delius* (1923)

De Koven, *see* KOVEN

Delannoy, Marcel François Georges (1898–1962). French composer, mainly self-taught, who began his career as a student of painting and architecture. His works include several ballets and operas, including *Le Poirier de misère* (Paris, 1927) and *Puck* (Strasbourg, 1949), and a ballet-cantata (*Le fou de la dame*).

Deller, Alfred George (born 1912), English counter tenor. He became a lay clerk at Canterbury Cathedral in 1940, and joined the choir of St. Paul's Cathedral, London in 1947. In addition to his valuable services as a cathedral singer he has done much for the revival of late 17th century English music by his brilliant and expressive performance of the solo music of Purcell and his contemporaries. He has also specialized in the performance of lute-songs of the early 17th century and has sung in several works by Handel (including operas). His frequent broadcasts and a number of gramophone recordings familiarized a wide public with the potentialities of the counter tenor voice and have encouraged others to follow his example. Britten wrote the role of Oberon in *A Midsummer Night's Dream* for him. The Deller Consort was formed in 1948.

Dello Joio, Norman (born 1913), U.S. composer, pianist, and organist, pupil of Wagenaar and Hindemith. He won a number of awards for composition in the United States, and taught at various colleges. His lyrical gifts attracted him frequently to write for the stage. His operas include *The Ruby* (1953), *The Lamentation of Saul* (1954) and two works about Joan of Arc, *The Triumph of St. Joan* (1950) and *The Trial at Rouen* (1955). He also wrote ballets, incidental music, *New York Profiles* for orchestra (1949), a clarinet concerto, chamber music, choral music, *Proud Music of the Storm* for organ, brass and chorus (1967), piano pieces and songs.

Delvincourt, Claude (1888–1954), French composer, pupil of Widor at the Paris Conservatoire, where he won the *Grand Prix de Rome* in 1913. Severely wounded in World War I, he lost an eye and did not resume composition until 1922. In 1941 he became director of the Paris Conservatoire, and played an active part in the resistance movement in World War II. His compositions, which show a capacity for humour and for vivid colouring, include the oriental ballet *L'Off-*

rande à Siva, the comic opera *La Femme à barbe*, chamber music and songs. He died in a car accident.

Demeur, Anne Arsène (1824–92), French operatic soprano. She created the roles Béatrice in Berlioz's *Béatrice et Bénédict* (1862) and Dido in *The Trojans* (1863).

demisemiquaver (Fr., *triple croche*; Ger., *Zweiunddreissigstel*; It., *biscroma*), half a semiquaver, or the thirty-second part of a semibreve – U.S. 'thirty-second note'. A single demisemiquaver is written

a group of four

demiton (Fr.), semitone.

De Monte, *see* MONTE

Denkmäler der Tonkunst in Bayern (Ger., *Monuments of Music in Bavaria*), a series supplementary to DENKMÄLER DEUTSCHER TONKUNST. The first volume appeared in 1900.

Denkmäler der Tonkunst in Osterreich (Ger., *Monuments of Music in Austria*), a series of publications of old music, analogous to the *Denkmäler deutscher Tonkunst*, including works by foreign composers written in Austria or found in Austrian libraries. It includes six volumes of 15th-century music from the so-called TRENT CODICES, operas by Monteverdi, Cesti and Gluck and two volumes of early 18th-century Viennese instrumental music. The first volume was published in 1894. The series was interrupted by the *Anschluss* but resumed after World War II.

Denkmäler deutscher Tonkunst (Ger., *Monuments of German Music*), a series of publications of old music by German composers, as well as works by foreign composers resident in Germany. The first volume was published in 1892; the third did not appear till 1900, after the inauguration of the similar *Denkmäler der Tonkunst in Osterreich*. The supplementary series *Denkmäler der Tonkunst in Bayern* started in 1900. With the accession to power of the Nazi government in 1933 the two series came to an end and were replaced in 1935 by *Das Erbe deutscher Musik* (*The Heritage of German Music*), subdivided into two series: (1) *Reichsdenkmale* (national monuments), (2) *Landschaftsdenkmale* (regional monuments); the latter ceased publication in 1942.

Denner, Johann Christoph (1655–1707), a maker of woodwind instruments at Nuremberg, who, according to Doppelmayr's *Historische Nachricht von den Nürnbergischen Mathematicis und Künstlern* (1730), 'invented' the clarinet about 1700, possibly by improving a less artistic instrument already in existence.

Dent, Edward Joseph (1876–1957), English musical historian, teacher and opera translator, educated at Eton and Cambridge, where he was professor of music from 1926 until 1941. In addition he was president of the International Society for Contemporary Music (1922–38) and of the International Society for Musical Research (1932–49).

His lifelong research work was devoted principally to the study of opera. In his capacity as president of two international societies he also did much to foster relations between musicians of different countries and to arouse a lively interest in the music of our time. To the public he is best known by his idiomatic and often witty translations of opera (many of them still in regular use) which successfully killed the belief that opera in English is absurd. He was responsible for the revival of many neglected works at Cambridge, including Mozart's *Magic Flute* (1911) and Purcell's *The Fairy Queen* (1920). His books include *Alessandro Scarlatti, his Life and Works* (1905), *Mozart's Operas* (1913; second edition, 1947), *Foundations of English Opera* (1928), *Ferruccio Busoni* (1933), and *Handel* (1934). A bibliography of his writings by L. Haward was published in the *Music Review* in November, 1946.

Denza, Luigi (1846–1922), Italian composer of a single opera, *Wallenstein* (Naples, 1876), and more than five hundred songs, but remembered only for his Neapolitan song 'Funiculi funicula' (1880), which Richard Strauss borrowed in his orchestral fantasia *Aus Italien* (1887).

déploration (Fr.), a lament. In the 15th and 16th centuries the word was used for a piece written on the death of a musician – often it would be a tribute from a pupil to his (deceased) teacher.

Der, for German titles beginning thus *see* the second word of the title.

De Reszke, *see* RESZKE

Dering or **Deering, Richard** (c. 1580–1630), English composer, who studied in Italy, possibly because he was an illegitimate child. He was organist at the English Convent of the Blessed Virgin, Brussels, in 1617. In 1625 he was back in England as organist to Queen Henrietta Maria. Two books each of motets and *canzonette* by him were published in Antwerp. A further volume of two-part and three-part motets with *basso continuo* was published in London in 1662. He also wrote several Italian madrigals, and music for viols. His *Cantica Sacra* (1618) have been reprinted in an edition by P. Platt (1974), who has also edited his secular vocal music in *Musica Britannica*, xxv, except for his *City and Country Cries* (*see* CRIES OF LONDON) which are in *Musica Britannica*, xxii. Examples of his consort music are in *Musica Britannica*, ix.

Des (Ger.), D flat (D♭).

De Sabata, *see* SABATA

descant (Fr., *déchant*), a translation of the medieval Latin *discantus*, literally 'a different song':

(1) a melodic line, or counterpoint, added to an existing melodic line (*cantus prius factus*), whether extempore or on paper;

(2) in the 13th and 14th centuries '*discantus*' (usually translated 'discant' in modern writings as nearer to the Latin, and also to distinguish it from other senses) referred particularly to the note-against-note style of one discanting voice against a tenor, predominantly in contrary motion. *Discantus* was thus distinct from melismatic polyphonic styles such as ORGANUM (12th and 13th centuries) and the so-called 'cantilena style' of the 14th and 15th centuries. In England the style persisted into the 15th century long after it had been abandoned on the Continent (see 'The Theory of Discant' in S. W. Kenney, *Walter Frye and the Contenance Angloise*, 1964, page 91);

(3) the term 'English Descant' was introduced by Manfred Bukofzer in his *Geschichte des englischen*

Diskants und des Fauxbourdons (1936) to describe a particular type of three-part writing used by English composers from the late 13th to the early 15th centuries. The two upper parts preserve mainly parallel movement with the melody in the lowest part, or tenor – at intervals respectively of a sixth and a third. The usefulness of the term, however, has been subsequently diminished by the awareness that most compositions of the period in parallel style are not in fact built on a *cantus prius factus*. Instead, 14th century English settings of plainsong tenors tend to be in *discantus* style as described above (2), with the plainsong most often in the middle voice;

(4) in the 16th and 17th centuries the upper part of a polyphonic composition (Ger., *Diskant*); hence an instrument which plays the upper part, e.g. descant recorder;

(5) in modern English practice a contrasted melody to be sung simultaneously with one which is already familiar, such as a hymn or folksong. It is designed particularly for occasions when the voices of trained singers can be combined with those of an audience or congregation, but is suitable also for school choirs which can divide into two groups.

See COUNTERPOINT, FABURDEN, FAUXBOURDON, SIGHT, RECORDER

Descort, *see* LAI

Déserteur, Le (Fr., *The Deserter*), opera in three acts by Monsigny, to a libretto by Jean Michel Sedaine, first performed in 1769 in Paris. This was Monsigny's last and most important opera, which looked forward to the 19th century in its grandeur and intensity.

Deses (Ger.), D double flat (D♭♭).

Désir, Le, *see* TRAUERWALZER

desk, a pair of string players in an orchestra, so called because they share a single music stand.

Des Prés, *see* JOSQUIN DES PRÉS

Dessau, Paul (born 1894), German composer and conductor. He studied in Berlin and Hamburg, lived in France and the United States during the Nazi era, and returned to Europe in 1948, when he settled in East Germany. There he was closely associated with Bertolt Brecht, who wrote the libretto of his opera, *The Trial of Lucullus* (Ger., *Das Verhor des Lukullus*). His other works include children's operas, incidental music (to plays by Brecht), orchestral and chamber music, songs and film music.

dessus (Fr.), treble. *Dessus de viole,* treble viol.

Destinn, Emmy (1878–1930), Czech operatic soprano, a pupil of Marie Loewe-Destinn, whose surname she borrowed for professional purposes (her real name was Kittl). She first appeared in Berlin in 1898, at Bayreuth in 1901 (as Senta in the first Bayreuth *Flying Dutchman*), in London in 1904 and in New York in 1908. She sang Minnie at the first performance of Puccini's *La Fanciulla del West* (New York, 1910). After World War I she changed her name to Destinnova. In addition to her outstanding gifts as a singer and actress she was also a dramatist, poet and novelist.

Destouches, André Cardinal (1662–1749), French opera composer who became a pupil of Campra, having previously been a sailor and a soldier. His first work, *Issé* (Fontainebleau, 1697), a *pastorale héroïque,* was very successful. He later wrote several operas and ballets, solo cantatas with orchestra, and church music. He was much favoured by Louis XIV and held several posts under him, including the directorship of the opera. Modern editions of *Issé, Omphale* (opera) and *Les Éléments* (ballet) in the collection *Chefs d'oeuvre classiques de l'opéra français*.

détaché, a style of playing a string instrument so that a noticeable bow change is made on every note. The notes are not necessarily so detached as to produce a staccato effect.

Dettingen Te Deum, a setting by Handel for soloists, chorus and orchestra, written to commemorate the victory at Dettingen on 26 June 1743, and first performed in November that year. Much of the music is borrowed or adapted from a *Te Deum* by Francesco Antonio Urio (modern edition by F. Chrysander); for the contrary opinion that Urio's work is actually by Handel see P. Robinson, *Handel and his Orbit* (1908).

Dett, Robert Nathaniel (1882–1943), U.S. Negro composer and pianist, who studied at the Eastman School of Music, Rochester (New York) and in Paris with Nadia Boulanger. He was teacher at Hampton Institute, Virginia, from 1913 and director of the choir. His compositions include several choral works, among them the oratorio *The Ordering of Moses* (1937). He was active in the study of Negro music and in promoting the interests of Negro musicians.

Deutsch, *see* DEUTSCHER TANZ

Deutsch, Otto Erich (1883–1967), Austrian bibliographer, who made a special study of Schubert. He was librarian of the Hoboken collection of facsimiles of musical manuscripts, Vienna, from 1926 until 1935, but settled in Britain after the *Anschluss* (though he returned to Austria in 1954). He was author of *Schubert – a Documentary Biography,* translated by Eric Blom (1946), a revised version of *Franz Schubert: Die Dokumente seines Lebens und Schaffens* (1913–14); also *Schubert – Thematic Catalogue of all his Works* (1951), which resulted in the old and often misleading opus numbers being replaced by 'Deutsch' (or 'D') numbers. Among his other publications are the complete Handel and Mozart documents, a study of Mozart editions (with C. B. Oldham) and the letters of Leopold Mozart (with Bernhard Paumgartner).

Deutscher Tanz (Ger.; It., *danza tedesca*), 'German dance'. In the late 18th and early 19th centuries this was a brisk dance in waltz time, often known simply as *Deutsch* or *Teutsch*. Examples occur in the works of Mozart, Beethoven and Schubert, e.g.

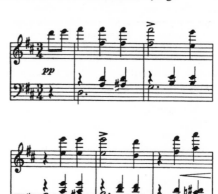

SCHUBERT, *12 Deutsche Tänze no 3*

See also ALLEMANDE, LÄNDLER, WALTZ

Deutsches Requiem, Ein, German title for Brahms's GERMAN REQUIEM.

Deutschland über Alles, German national anthem written just before the upheavals of 1848 and sung to the tune Haydn wrote for the Austrian national hymn.

Deux Journées, Les (Fr., *The Two Days*), opera in three acts by Cherubini, known in English as *The Water Carrier*. The libretto, by Jean Nicolas Bouilly, concerns a water carrier, Michele, who enables Armand to escape from Paris in a barrel after he has fallen into disfavour with Mazarin. Though Armand is subsequently caught, he is given a pardon. First performed in 1800 in Paris, this was Cherubini's most important opera, much admired by Beethoven (whose *Fidelio* was influenced by it).

development, the exploiting of the possibilities of thematic material by means of contrapuntal elaboration, modulation, rhythmical variation, etc. In a movement in SONATA FORM the development section follows the exposition (in which the principal themes are stated): it may be short or long, may discuss all the themes of the exposition or select from them, may present them whole or break them up into sections; it may also (less frequently) merely continue the general character of the movement without precise reference to any of the themes of the exposition, and may introduce new themes which have not been heard before. There are also compositions, e.g. Sibelius's *Tapiola*, in which practically the whole piece is devoted to the development of one simple theme. Works of this kind are known as 'monothematic'. Early examples of this process are the first movements of many of Haydn's symphonies. Beethoven sometimes, as in the first movement of his *Eroica* symphony, widened the scale of sonata form by introducing further extensive development of his material into the coda of a movement. In symphonies of the later 19th century, e.g. Chaikovsky's, the main theme of the first movement may recur in later movements and receive further development. In symphonic poems development is often influenced by a programme, i.e. it not only presents the themes in new ways and new combinations but illustrates episodes in a story at the same time.

The first movement of Mozart's symphony in G minor, K550, will serve as an example of development The opening theme of the movement is:

The development, represented here in outline, is concerned entirely with this theme:

[Recapitulation]

Devienne, François (1759–1803), French flautist, bassoonist and composer. He played a prominent part in the music of the Revolution, was a member of the band of the Garde Nationale and became teacher of the flute at the Institut National de Musique (known as the Conservatoire from 1795). He composed several operas, music for the *fêtes nationales*, concertos for flute, bassoon and horn, *sinfonies concertantes* for various wind instruments and orchestra, and an enormous amount of chamber music. He also wrote a *Méthode de flute théorique et pratique* (1795).

Devil and Kate, The (Czech, *Čert a Káča*), opera in three acts by Dvořák, to a libretto by Adolf Wenig, first produced in 1899 in Prague. Kate is a garrulous country wench who, failing to win a dancing partner at a fair, offers to dance with the devil. The latter (called Marbuel in this story) at first reckons her to be a suitable victim to take to the Underworld, but is later more than happy to return her to earth.

Devil's Trill, The (It., *Trillo del Diavolo*), the title of a violin sonata in G minor by Tartini (published posthumously in J. B. Cartier's *L'Art du violon*, 1798), supposedly inspired by a dream. The composer, in his dream, sold his soul to the devil, who proceeded to give a remarkable performance on the violin. When Tartini woke he attempted to write down what he heard, but the result (he claimed) was far inferior. The title alludes to a passage in the last movement, where the famous trill occurs.

Devin du Village, Le (Fr., *The Village Soothsayer*), opera in one act by Rousseau, to a libretto by the composer, first performed in 1752 at Fontainebleau. It was the Swiss philosopher–composer's most important and most successful work for the stage. A parody by Charles Simon Favart, *Les Amours de Bastien et Bastienne*, was translated into German by Friedrich Wilhelm Weiskern. Weiskern's version was set by Mozart in 1768 under the title *Bastien und Bastienne*.

Devrient, Eduard (1801–77), German operatic baritone, and subsequently theatre director. He was librettist of Marschner's opera *Hans Heiling* (Berlin, 1833), in which he sang the title role. His memoirs of Mendelssohn, *Meine Erinnerungen an Felix Mendelssohn Bartholdy* (1869), include an account of the revival of Bach's *St. Matthew Passion* in 1829, in which he sang the part of Jesus (see H. T. David and A. Mendel, *The Bach Reader*, pages 377–86).

Devrient, Wilhelmine, *see* SCHRÖDER–DEVRIENT

Diabelli, Anton (1781–1858), Austrian composer and founder of a firm of music publishers. He was a chorister at Salzburg, where he was a pupil of Michael Haydn. Subsequently educated in Munich and intended for the priesthood, he abandoned the idea and settled in Vienna in 1803. In 1818 he became partner in Peter Cappi's publishing firm; after Cappi's withdrawal the firm became Diabelli and Co., 1824. His first independent publication was the *Vaterländischer Künstlerverein*, variations by 51 composers on a waltz-theme of his own composition, published in two books: book 1 consists of 33 variations by Beethoven, the *Diabelli Variations*, op 120 (previously published, 1823), book 2 contains single variations by fifty composers, including Czerny, Hummel, Liszt (aged twelve at the time of publication), Moscheles, W. A. Mozart, jun., Schubert and Tomášek, with a coda by Czerny (*see* O. E. Deutsch, *Schubert – a Documentary Biography*, pages 348–51). For the theme see WALTZ. Later owners of the Diabelli firm were C. A. Spina (1857–72) and A. Cranz of Hamburg (1876).

Diabelli Variations, *see* DIABELLI

diabolus in musica (Lat.), literally, 'the devil in music'. This ominous term originated in medieval times as a warning against the use of the tritone (the interval of the augmented fourth, e.g. C–F sharp), which was regarded as a 'dangerous' progression.

Dialogues de Carmélites, Les (Fr., *The Carmelites*), opera in three acts by Poulenc, to a libretto by Georges Bernanos inspired by Gertrude von le Fort's novel *Die letzte am Schafott* (1931). First performed in 1957 at La Scala, Milan, the work deals with the martyrdom of Carmelite nuns during the French Revolution.

Diamants de la Couronne, Les (Fr., *The Crown Diamonds*), opera in three acts by Auber, to a libretto by Augustine Eugène Scribe and Jules Henri Vernoy de Saint-Georges, first performed in 1841 in Paris. This was one of Auber's most successful works.

Diamond, David Leo (born 1915), U.S. composer who studied at the Cleveland Institute, Eastman School of Music (Rochester), the Dalcroze Institute (New York), and with Nadia Boulanger in Paris. His compositions include eight symphonies, concertos for piano, violin and cello, *Rounds* for string orchestra, *Hommage à Satie* for chamber orchestra, *A Night Litany* for chorus (to a text by Ezra Pound), six string quartets and other chamber music, piano pieces and songs.

diapason, (1) in Greek and medieval theory, the interval of the OCTAVE;

(2) (Fr.), tuning-fork. *Diapason normal*, concert pitch (*see* PITCH);

(3) the generic term for a family of flue-pipes on the organ, which provide the substantial foundation of organ tone. *Open diapason* (Fr., *principal*, *montre*; Ger., *Prinzipal*): (1) on the manuals normally of eight foot pitch, with metal pipes; (2) on the pedals normally of sixteen foot pitch, with wood or metal pipes. The corresponding stop of four foot pitch is generally called Principal or Octave (Fr., *prestant*; Ger., *Oktave*, *Prinzipal 4 Fuss*, *Kleinprinzipal*). *Double diapason*: a manual stop of sixteen foot pitch, similar to the Bourdon. *Stopped Diapason*: a manual stop of eight foot pitch and a mellow flute-like tone; the pipes are the same length as those of a four foot stop, but being closed at one end sound an octave lower (*see* ACOUSTICS, ORGAN).

diaphony, (1) the original Greek word means 'dissonance', and was used in this sense by some medieval writers;

(2) used generally by early medieval theorists to describe the simple form of polyphony known as ORGANUM. By the 13th century, when polyphony had become more elaborate, the Latin word *discantus* was generally preferred (*see* DESCANT).

diatonic, in the strict sense used of notes proper to a key, e.g. in the key of D major the following notes are diatonic and constitute a diatonic scale:

Any other notes involve accidentals (sharps or flats) and are CHROMATIC (which is thus the opposite of diatonic). In minor keys the sharpened sixth and seventh are in such common use, though not strictly proper to the key, that they are also regarded as diatonic, e.g. in the key of D minor the notes:

are added to the proper diatonic scale:

Diatonic chord, a chord composed of notes proper to the key. *Diatonic harmony*, strictly harmony which employs only diatonic chords; more generally, harmony which is predominantly based on diatonic chords and their association. *Diatonic tetrachord*, in ancient Greek music a descending scale of four notes, the successive intervals being a tone, a tone, and a semitone, e.g.:

See CHROMATIC (1), ENHARMONIC (1)

Dichterliebe (Ger., *Poet's Love*), cycle of sixteen songs by Schumann, op 48 (1840), to words by Heinrich Heine.

dictionaries of music, *see* HISTORY OF MUSIC

Dido and Aeneas, opera in three acts by Purcell to a libretto by Nahum Tate, first performed in 1689 in London 'at Mr. Josias Priest's Boarding School at Chelsey'. Inspired by Virgil, the story tells how Aeneas, fleeing from Troy, takes refuge at Carthage, where he falls in love with the queen, Dido. He is impelled, however, by his destiny to leave Carthage for Italy. Dido, deserted by her lover, dies – though not before singing her great lament, 'When I am laid in earth'. *Dido and Aeneas* is usually described as Purcell's 'only opera' – his other (and today less viable) works for the stage being masques.

Die, for German titles beginning thus, *see* the second word of the title.

Diepenbrock, Alphons (1862–1921), Dutch composer,

Dido and Aeneas: the 1962 English Opera Group revival of England's first significant opera, with Janet Baker as Dido

self-taught, who had a considerable influence on his contemporaries. His compositions include a Stabat Mater, a Mass and other church music, incidental music for plays (e.g. Sophocles' *Electra*) and songs.

Dieren, Bernard van (1884–1936), composer, the son of a Dutch father and a French mother. He began his career as a scientist, and did not study composition seriously until he was twenty. After settling in London in 1909, as correspondent of the *Nieuwe Rotterdamsche Courant*, he took British nationality. His compositions, admired by a limited circle, include a *Chinese Symphony* for soli, chorus and orchestra (1914), a comic opera – *The Tailor* (1917), six string quartets and other chamber music, and numerous songs. His style, alternating between elaborate polyphony and impressionism, was intellectual and impersonal. His volume of essays, *Down among the Dead Men* (1935), a substantial part of which is devoted to memories of Busoni, is provocative, verbose and sometimes violent.

Dies Irae (Lat., day of wrath), an early 13th century SEQUENCE, the words of which are attributed to Thomas of Celano. It forms part of the *Missa pro defunctis*, or Requiem Mass. The plainsong melody begins as follows:

16th century composers who wrote Requiem Masses generally preferred not to set the 'Dies Irae' but to leave it to be sung to the plainsong melody. In common with the rest of the Requiem Mass it was set to new music, often of a dramatic character, by later composers, e.g. Mozart, Berlioz, Verdi.

The plainsong melody has been used in orchestral and choral works by several modern composers, e.g. Berlioz, *Symphonie fantastique* (1830); Liszt, *Totentanz* (1849); Rakhmaninov, *Rhapsody on a Theme of Paganini* (1936).

dièse (Fr.), sharp (♯).

diesis (Gr.), (1) in Pythagorean theory the difference between a fourth and two 'major' tones (*see* TONE), i.e. a semitone slightly smaller than that of the scale based on the harmonic series. Also known as *limma*;

(2) in Aristotelian theory the quarter-tone of the ENHARMONIC tetrachord;

(3) in modern acoustics the *great diesis* is the interval between four minor thirds, i.e.

$$\left(\frac{6}{5}\right)^4 = \frac{1296}{625}:$$

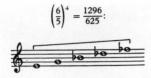

and an octave, i.e.

$$\frac{2}{1}:$$

by this reckoning F flat is sharper than E, and the interval is

$$\frac{1296}{625} \div 2 = \frac{648}{625}$$

The *enharmonic diesis* is the interval between an octave, i.e.

$$\frac{2}{1}$$

and three major thirds, i.e.

$$\left(\frac{5}{4}\right)^3 = \frac{125}{64}$$

By this reckoning B sharp is flatter than C, and the interval is

$$2 \div \frac{125}{64} = \frac{128}{125}$$

See HARMONIC SERIES, TEMPERAMENT

(4) (It.), sharp (♯).

Dietrich, Albert Hermann (1829–1908), German composer, a pupil and friend of Schumann. He collaborated with Schumann and Brahms in writing a violin sonata for Joachim in 1853: the four movements are (1) allegro, A minor (Dietrich); (2) intermezzo, F major (Schumann); (3) scherzo, C minor (Brahms); (4) finale, A minor and major (Schumann). His compositions include two operas – *Robin Hood* (Frankfurt, 1879) and *Das Sonntagskind* (Bremen, 1886), a symphony, concertos for horn, violin and cello, choral works, piano pieces and songs.

Dietrich, Sixt (c. 1492–1548), German composer. He was a chorister at Constance, returning there as a teacher in the choir-school in 1517. He was a prominent adherent of the Reformation, and composed a considerable quantity of church music, including a collection of antiphons (1541; modern edition by W. E. Buszin, 1964), and a collection of Latin hymns (1545; modern edition by H. Zenck, 1960). Five pieces by him were printed by Glareanus in his *Dodecachordon* (1547; modern edition by C. A. Miller,

two volumes, 1965), and four of his songs were published in Georg Rhau's *Newe deudsche geistliche Gesenge* (1544; facsimile edition, 1969).

Dieupart, Charles (died c. 1740), French composer, violinist and harpsichordist. He settled in London and took an active part in the introduction of Italian opera to England at the beginning of the 18th century. He also gave concerts (*see The Spectator*, nos 258 and 278) and was in demand as a teacher. He wrote for harpsichord *Six suittes de clavessin*, which were clearly known to Bach, who made a copy of no 6 in F minor (*see* ENGLISH SUITES).

diferencia (Sp.), in the 16th century a VARIATION or DIVISION. Many sets of *diferencias* were written for lute and keyboard instruments by Spanish composers in the latter half of the century.

difference tone, a faint note resulting from the difference between the frequencies of two notes sounded simultaneously.

See ACOUSTICS, COMBINATION TONE

diminished interval, a perfect or minor interval reduced by flattening the upper note or sharpening the lower, e.g.:

perfect fifth:

diminished fifth:

minor seventh:

diminished seventh:

On keyboard instruments diminished intervals are indistinguishable from the augmented or major interval immediately below, e.g.:

diminished fifth:

sounds the same as augmented fourth:

diminished seventh:

sounds the same as major sixth:

The harmonic function of the intervals, however, remains distinct.

diminished seventh chord, a chord composed of three minor thirds, or a diminished triad with a diminished seventh superimposed, e.g.

By means of enharmonic changes, e.g. writing G sharp for A flat, a chord of this kind can be used a transition to any major or minor triad, e.g.:

diminished triad, a minor triad with the fifth flattened, e.g.:
minor triad:

diminished triad:

The triad on the seventh note of the major scale, e.g. in the key of C major:

is the only diminished triad proper to the key; all others require accidentals. In minor keys the same triad occurs if the seventh note is sharpened, and the triad on the second note of the scale is also diminished, e.g. in the key of C minor:

diminuendo (It.), 'diminishing the tone', i.e. getting softer. It is often abbreviated *dim.* or *dimin.*

diminution, (1) the presentation of a theme in notes of smaller time-value, as in the example below from Handel's *Messiah,* where the theme in the lower line moves at double the speed of the same theme in the top line.

HANDEL, *Messiah*

See AUGMENTATION, CANON.

(2) in 16th and 17th century music the ornamentation of a simple melodic line, in vocal or instrumental music, by breaking it up into notes of smaller value. Such ornamentation was often improvised and was applied to the separate parts of a polyphonic composition as well as to solo pieces. We may take as an example the opening of a five-part *chanson* by Lassus (1560):

Complete Works, volume xiv, page 29

followed by three different adaptations of the text:

AMMERBACH, *Orgel oder Instrument Tablatur* (1571)

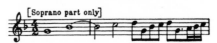

BASSANO, *Motetti, Madrigali et Canzoni francese . . . diminuiti* (1591)

A. GABRIELI, *Canzoni alla Francese*, Book V (1605)

See DIVISION

di molto (It.), 'extremely'. *Allegro di molto,* extremely fast.

D'Indy, *see* INDY

di nuovo (It.), 'again'. *Poi a poi di nuovo vivente,* gradually getting lively again.

Dioclesian, opera with dialogue, adapted from Beaumont and Fletcher by Thomas Betterton, with music by Purcell. It was first performed in 1690 in London. The full title is *The Prophetess, or the History of Dioclesian.* Diocles (later Dioclesian), a Roman soldier, fulfils a prophecy by killing the murderer of the late emperor, and becomes emperor himself. Victorious over the Persians, he hands over the empire to his nephew Maximinian. Maximinian, who is jealous of Dioclesian's popularity, attempts to kill him but is prevented by the prophetess, Delphia. The opera ends with an elaborate masque, designed as an entertainment for Dioclesian.

diplomas in music, certificates of proficiency awarded by colleges of music or accredited bodies after examination in performance, theoretical subjects, composition or teaching. They may also be conferred *honoris causa* on persons who have rendered services to a particular institution or to music in general. Most of them are open to external as well as internal students. There is no absolute consistency in the nomenclature of diplomas: thus the A.R.C.M. (Associate of the Royal College of Music) and L.R.A.M. (Licentiate of the Royal Academy of Music) represent approximately the same standard. Reputable diplomas are those recognized by the Incorporated Society of Musicians. A diploma represents the achievement of a certain standard in a specific branch of music; it is no guarantee of ability in any other branch or of a wide knowledge of music in general.

direct, a sign rather like an ornamental W, formerly used in manuscripts and printed music, (1) at the end of a line or page, to indicate in advance the pitch of the next note, (2) in the middle of a line, to draw the per-

former's attention to a change of clef (Lat., *custos*). Thus, if the following example were the end of a line, the sign would indicate that the first note of the next line would be D:

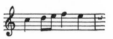

Accidentals can be added, exactly as if the sign were an actual note. The practice is now obsolete except in examination papers and incomplete musical quotations in books, where it indicates what the next note would be if it were printed, though without, of course, specifying its duration.

Dirigent (Ger.), conductor.

Diruta, Girolamo (born c. 1560), Italian organist and teacher, a pupil of Zarlino, Porta and Merulo. He was organist at Chioggia Cathedral in 1597, and at Gubbio Cathedral in 1609. One of the foremost players of his time, he is known today by his elaborate treatise on organ-playing, written in the form of a dialogue, *Il Transilvano* (two volumes, 1593 and 1609).

    E. DANNREUTHER: *Musical Ornamentation*

    C. KREBS: 'Girolamo Diruta's Transilvano', *Vierteljahrschrift für Musikwissenschaft,* viii (1892)

Dis (Ger.), D sharp (D♯).

discant, *see* DESCANT

discantus (Lat.), descant. *Discantus supra librum,* 'descant on the book', i.e. the improvisation of a counterpoint to an existing melody – a practice common from the Middle Ages to the end of the 16th century.

    See SIGHT

discord, a combination of notes which includes at least one dissonant interval. In popular use applied to music in which the relationship between a series of dissonances is not intelligible to the listener, e.g. in the familiar phrase 'modern music is all discord'.

    See CONSONANCE, DISSONANCE

Disis (Ger.), D double sharp (D ×).

disjunct, opposite of conjunct. Both terms refer to the succession of notes of different pitch. A melody is said to move by conjunct motion if its notes proceed to adjacent degrees of the scale (e.g. the opening of 'Three Blind Mice'), and by disjunct motion if its notes form intervals larger than a second (e.g. the opening of Brahms's fourth symphony).

Diskant (Ger.), soprano, treble. *Diskantmesse,* a modern term for a 15th century Mass in which the plainsong, generally freely embroidered, appears not in the tenor but in the upper part. *Diskantschlüssel,* the soprano clef, i.e. the C clef on the first line of the stave:

Dissoluto Punito, Il (It., *The Rake Punished*), subtitle of DON GIOVANNI.

dissonance, etymologically a jarring sound, or 'discord'. The term is incapable of precise definition, since a jarring sound must be judged by the ear, and not all ears agree. The ways in which dissonance can occur in music, however, remain constant: (1) by introducing a passing note which is dissonant with the rest of the chord, (2) by tying over, or suspending, from one chord a note which is dissonant with the succeeding chord, (3) as an essential note of the chord. If for the sake of argument we regard the major seventh as dissonant, the following examples will illustrate the three types of dissonance:

(1)

(2)

(3)

Historically type 3 is the result of types 1 and 2, i.e. dissonances which are familiar as passing notes or suspensions come in time to be accepted without preparation. A series of unprepared dissonances may create difficulties for the listener, if their relationship is unfamiliar or obscure.

See CONSONANCE

'Dissonance' Quartet, nickname for Mozart's string quartet in C major, K465 (1785), whose slow introduction makes remarkable use of dissonance.

Distler, Hugo (1908–42), German composer and organist, who studied at Leipzig, became organist at Lübeck in 1921, and professor of composition at the Stuttgart Conservatory in 1937. He committed suicide in Berlin during World War II. His works, mainly religious, include more than fifty motets, a Passion, an oratorio entitled *Nativity*, a harpsichord concerto and music for organ.

Distratto, Il (It., *The Absent-minded Man*), nickname for Haydn's Symphony no 60 in C major (1774–5), used as incidental music for a comedy of that title produced in Vienna.

Ditson, U.S. firm of music-publishers in Boston, Massachusetts, originally Parker & Ditson (1832), then Oliver Ditson & Co. (1857), after the name of its founder, Oliver Ditson (1811–88).

Dittersdorf, Karl Ditters von (1739–99), Austrian violinist and composer, originally Karl Ditters but ennobled in 1773. After gaining experience in the private orchestra of Prince von Hildburghausen and the Imperial Opera he became *Kapellmeister* to the Bishop of Grosswardein (1765–9) and to the Prince Bishop of Breslau (1769–95). He was one of the most prolific composers of his time. His numerous compositions include about forty operas – among them the still fairly popular *Doctor und Apotheker* (Vienna, 1786), and a version of *The Marriage of Figaro* which may have predated Mozart's. He also wrote oratorios, Masses, more than one hundred concertos, chamber music and piano sonatas. His symphonies include twelve on subjects from Ovid's *Metamorphoses*. His autobiography, *Lebensbeschreibung* (1801; English edition, 1896), though marked by an excess of vanity, is

an entertaining picture of 18th century life and music. Michael Kelly recalled hearing a string quartet played by Haydn, Dittersdorf, Wanhal and Mozart (*Reminiscences of Michael Kelly*, volume 1, page 241).

divertimento (It.), a term originating in the late 18th century for a suite of movements for a chamber ensemble or orchestra, designed primarily for entertainment. Some of the greatest divertimentos were written by Mozart. Of these, some are sublime entertainment music, but others – such as the masterpiece in E flat major for string trio, K563 – seem more serious in intention. The title has continued to be used into the present century, by composers including Bartók and Lennox Berkeley.

divertissement (Fr.), (1) an entertainment in the form of a ballet, with or without songs, interpolated in an opera or play for the sake of variety;
(2) a fantasia on well-known tunes, e.g. Schubert's *Divertissement à la hongroise*, op 54, for piano duet;
(3) divertimento.

Divine Poem, The, symphonic poem by Skryabin, also known as his Symphony no 3. First performed in 1905 in Paris, the music describes the soul's struggle to achieve divinity.

division, (1) a term current in England in the 17th and 18th centuries for the ornamental elaboration of a simple melodic line, whether for voice or instrument: cf. Shakespeare, *Henry IV Part I*, 3., i. 207:

> Thy Tongue
> Makes Welsh as sweet as ditties highly penn'd,
> Sung by a fair queen in a summer's bower,
> With ravishing division, to her lute.

(2) in particular, a variation on a GROUND BASS, written or improvised. The favourite medium for divisions of this kind in 17th century England was a solo bass viol, accompanied by harpsichord or organ, with a second bass viol playing the bass line; but the practice was not restricted to this combination. The standard work is Christopher Simpson's *The Division Violinist* (1659); the second edition (1667) is entitled *The Division Viol*. John Playford published *The Division Violin* (second edition, 1685), 'containing a collection of divisions upon several grounds for the treble violin, being the first musick of the kind make publick'.

See DIMINUTION

division viol, a bass viol slightly smaller than the normal size, suitable for playing divisions. 'A Viol for Division, should be something a lesser size than a Consort Bass; so that the Hand may better command it' (Christopher Simpson, *The Division Viol*, pages 1–2).

See DIVISION, VIOL

Dixie, song by Daniel Emmett written in 1859 for Negro minstrel shows. Surprisingly, it was later associated with the Confederate Army during the American Civil War. 'Dixieland' is a name for the 'classical' jazz produced in the early years of the 20th century in New Orleans, and usually performed by small groups.

Dixieland, a style of jazz derived from the music that originated in New Orleans at the turn of the century. It is simple and cheerful in character.

Dixon, Dean (born 1915), U.S. Negro conductor, who

studied in New York at the Juilliard School of Music. He has worked mainly outside the United States, with the Goteborg Symphony Orchestra (1953–60), the Frankfurt Radio Symphony Orchestra (1961–74), the Sydney Symphony Orchestra (1964–7) and the Dutch Radio Society.

Dobrowen, Issay Alexandrovich (1894–1953), Russian conductor and composer, who studied in Moscow and with Godowsky in Vienna. Among his various appointments was the conductorship of the San Francisco Symphony Orchestra (1930–5). His compositions include a piano concerto, a violin concerto, piano music and songs.

Doctor und Apotheker (Ger., *Doctor and Apothecary*), opera in two acts by Dittersdorf, to a libretto by Gottlieb Stephanie, first performed in 1786 in Vienna. The comedy remains the most popular of Dittersdorf's numerous works for the stage.

Dodecachordon (Gr.), a book published in 1547 by Heinrich Loriti, writing under the name Glareanus. It is so called because it upholds the theory that there were not eight church modes but twelve (the name means twelve string), with examples from polyphonic compositions of the late 15th and early 16th centuries and commentaries on them. The four additional modes accepted by Glareanus were the Aeolian and Hypoaeolian (with final on A) and the Ionian and Hypoionian (with final on C). An English translation by C. A. Miller, with transcriptions of the examples, was published in 1965.

See also MODE

dodecaphonic, term referring to the twelve-note method of composition.

'Dog Waltz', nickname for Chopin's waltz in D flat major, op 64, no 1, also known (no more accurately) as the 'Minute Waltz'. Its title is explained by the theory that the music represents George Sand's dog chasing its tail.

doh, anglicized form of the Italian *do* (C). In TONIC SOL-FA the first note (or tonic) of the major scale.

Dohnányi, Ernö (formerly Ernst von) (1877–1960), Hungarian composer and pianist. He studied at the Royal Academy of Music, Budapest, under Koessler. His first symphony was performed in Budapest in 1897; in the same year he made his début as a solo pianist in Berlin. He frequently toured Europe and the United States and taught the piano at the Berlin Hochschule (1905–15) and in Budapest (1916–19). In 1931 he became general director with the Hungarian Radio, and in 1949 settled in the United States, where he became composer-in-residence at Florida University. His principal compositions are in the German (and especially Brahmsian) tradition rather than in the Hungarian national idiom favoured by Bartók and Kodály. Today he is remembered more for his *Variations on a Nursery Theme* for piano and orchestra rather than his other works, which include three operas (among which *The Tenor* is still occasionally performed; the others are *Aunt Simona* and *The Tower of Voyvod*), three symphonies, an orchestral suite in F sharp minor, a violin concerto, *Ruralia Hungarica* for orchestra, a piano quintet, three string quartets, instrumental music and piano pieces. All these, however, are notable for their polish. As a pianist he was exceptionally able, and in this capacity

visited the Edinburgh Festival towards the end of his life.

Doktor Faust, opera by Busoni, completed after his death by Philipp Jarnach, and first performed in 1925 in Dresden. The libretto, by the composer, is based on the original Faust legend, not on Goethe's drama. Faust, practising magic arts at Wittenberg, summons six spirits, the last of whom, Mephistopheles, persuades him to sign a pact. He pays a visit to the court of Parma, where he displays his magic arts and elopes with the Duchess. By the end of the year agreed on with Mephistopheles he is back in Wittenberg, where he intervenes in a quarrel between Catholics and Protestants. In the street he meets a beggar-woman, who proves to be the Duchess; she gives him their dead child and vanishes. By magic Faust manages to transfer his personality to the dead child. At midnight he dies. From the child's body rises a youth with a green twig in his hand.

Though widely admired and discussed, Busoni's masterpiece is very rarely performed. The most famous production in recent times was Berlin's, with Dietrich Fischer-Dieskau, in 1955. Two excerpts – the *Sarabande* and *Cortège* – are played sometimes in the concert-hall.

dolce (It.), sweet, gentle. *Dolcissimo*, very sweet.

dolcian (also *dulcian, dulzian*), one of the names by which the bassoon was known in the 16th and 17th century, presumably on account of its gentle tone.

dolente (It.), sorrowful.

Doles, Johann Friedrich (1715–97), German composer and organist, a pupil of Bach at Leipzig. From 1756 until 1789 he was cantor of St. Thomas's. In 1744 he wrote a cantata, *Das Lob der Musik*, to celebrate the first year of the Leipzig Gewandhaus concerts. On the occasion of Mozart's visit to Leipzig in 1789 he performed for his benefit Bach's motet *Singet dem Herrn* (*see* H. T. David and A. Mendel, *The Bach Reader*, pages 359–60). In 1790 he dedicated to Mozart and J. G. Naumann his cantata *Ich komme vor dein Angesicht*. He also wrote Masses, Passions, motets and other church music.

Dolly, suite of six children's pieces for piano duet by Fauré, op 56 (1893), dedicated to the daughter of Madame Bardac, who subsequently became Debussy's second wife. The work was later orchestrated by Rabaud as a ballet.

Dolmetsch, Arnold (1858–1940), Swiss born musicologist, instrument-maker and violinist, the son of a Swiss father and a French mother. He studied at Brussels with Vieuxtemps. Having begun to collect and repair old instruments, he started making harpsichords and clavichords. He was employed by the firm of Chickering in Boston (1902–9) and by Gaveau in Paris (1911–14). In 1914 he settled in Britain at Haslemere, where he inaugurated in 1925 an annual festival of old music, played on the appropriate instruments, in which members of his family took part. In addition to keyboard instruments he also made viols, lutes and recorders. The present popularity of the recorder is due entirely to his work. He published a valuable account of *The Interpretation of the Music of the XVIIth and XVIIIth Centuries* (1915) supplemented by a volume of examples.

His younger son **Carl Dolmetsch** (born 1911),

French born (anglicized) recorder-player. As a boy he played at the Haslemere Festivals, and has since become the foremost exponent of his instrument. He succeeded his father as director of the Haslemere Festival, and became managing director of the workshops for making old instruments.

R. DONINGTON: *The Work and Ideas of Arnold Dolmetsch* (1932)

doloroso (It.), sorrowful.

Domaine Musical, society founded by Pierre Boulez, Jean-Louis Barrault and Madeleine Renaud in Paris in 1954 to promote concerts of new music. In 1967 Boulez was succeeded as director by Gilbert Amy.

Domestic Symphony, orchestral work by Richard Strauss (to which he gave the title *Symphonia Domestica*) first performed in 1904 in New York. Like *Ein Heldenleben* (1898) it is an autobiographical symphonic poem in several movements, but concentrating in this case on the composer's private life rather than his public one.

dominant, (1) the fifth degree of the major or minor scale. In the key of C, the dominant is therefore G. *Dominant chord* or *dominant triad*, the triad on the dominant, i.e. in the key of C major the notes G, B, D.

Dominant seventh chord, the dominant triad (G, B, D) with the addition of a seventh (F) from the bass:

The convention of harmonizing the melodic cadence:

with the dominant and tonic triads dates from the latter half of the 15th century. This is the so-called perfect cadence or full close. Its air of finality is due to (1) the melodic cadence, sinking by step to the tonic, (2) the upward semitone progression of the leading note (B to C), (3) the juxtaposition of two major triads. This close relationship between the dominant and tonic triads plays an important part in establishing a new key (*see* MODULATION). The substitution of the dominant seventh chord for the dominant triad in a perfect cadence:

originated in the introduction of the seventh as a passing or ornamental note:

(2) the name given to the reciting note (properly *repercussio, tenor* or *tuba*) of each of the Gregorian psalm-tones, and hence to the degree of the scale in each mode on which this note falls. In the authentic modes the dominant is the fifth degree of the scale, except in the third mode (E to E), where it is the sixth degree, in order to avoid the note B. In the plagal modes it is a third below the dominant of the corresponding authentic mode, except in the eighth mode (D to D), where it is a tone below (C instead of B).

See MODE, TONE

dompe, *see* DUMP

domra or **dombra,** a kind of balalaika. In Russia, it usually has a round body with three metal strings tuned a fourth apart and played with a plectrum. Two-string instruments are also played.

Donato, Baldassare (c. 1530–1603), Italian organist, composer and singer, whose entire working life was spent at St. Mark's, Venice. He was a member of the choir there in 1550, and held the post of *maestro di cappella piccola* from 1562 to 1565. In 1580 he became director of the seminar, and in 1590 he succeeded Zarlino as *maestro di cappella*. He published a volume of motets and several books of madrigals. Two of his madrigals were printed, with English words, in Yonge's *Musica Transalpina* (1588). Modern editions of his madrigals are in L. Torchi, *L'Arte musicale in Italia*, i, and A. Einstein, *The Italian Madrigal* (1949), volume iii.

Donatoni, Franco (born 1927), Italian composer who has made use of most of the progressive musical forms, from the Bartokian qualities of his early pieces through serialism to the aleatory techniques of his most recent works. His output has included *Per Orchestra, Strophes* and *Sezioni* for orchestra, a concerto for kettledrums with strings and brass, chamber music, and *Black and White* for two pianos (in which the performers are told which fingers to use, but are given no actual notes or durations).

Don Carlos, opera in five acts by Verdi, to a libretto by François Joseph Méry and Camille du Locle (after Schiller's play), first performed in 1867 in Paris. Verdi composed the work, in French, for the Paris Opéra. In 1884 he revised it for La Scala, Milan, omitting the (important) opening Fontainebleau scene – though this was restored three years later. In both these versions the work was sung in Italian – which is still the language favoured for it today, even though Verdi deliberately wrote it 'in the French style', and, in doing so, gave the world one of the greatest and grandest French operas ever written.

Don Carlos is the heir to the Spanish throne, betrothed to Elizabeth de Valois. He visits France incognito to see her, and falls in love. But his father, Philip II of Spain decides to marry her himself. One of her ladies-in-waiting, Princess Eboli, is herself in love with Don Carlos. She discovers his love for Elizabeth and determines to have vengeance. Don

Don Carlos: the first London performance, in 1867, at the Royal Italian Opera, Covent Garden, with Pauline Lucca, Fricci, Naudin, and Grazziani. The first New York performance was in 1877.

Carlos espouses the cause of the Flemings and asks to be appointed governor of Flanders. The king refuses, and Don Carlos, who becomes threatening, is disarmed and imprisoned. Through the intrigue of Eboli, the king discovers that Elizabeth was once in love with Don Carlos. He threatens her but repents of his violence. Rodrigo, Don Carlos' closest friend and associated with him in supporting the cause of Flanders, is killed. The crowd demands the release of Don Carlos and is prevented from violence only by the arrival of the Grand Inquisitor. Don Carlos, about to escape to Flanders, takes leave of Elizabeth at the monastery where Charles V is buried. The king and the Grand Inquisitor arrive to arrest him, but a monk dressed like Charles V and presumed to be an apparition saves him.

Don Giovanni, comic opera (*dramma giocoso*) in two acts by Mozart. The full title is *Il dissoluto punito, ossia Don Giovanni* (The Rake Punished, or Don Juan). The second of three masterpieces Mozart composed in collaboration with the librettist Lorenzo da Ponte, *Don Giovanni* was inspired by the Don Juan legend and in particular by Bertati's play *Don Giovanni, ossia Il Convitato di Pietra* (1775). Its first performance was in Prague in 1787, with Luigi Bassi in the title-role. When the work reached Vienna the following year, Mozart composed two new arias for it: Don

Ottavio's 'Dalla sua pace' and Donna Elvira's 'Mi tradi'.

The scene of the action is laid in Seville. Don Giovanni, in pursuit of Donna Anna, is surprised by her father, the Commendatore, whom he kills. Donna Anna and her lover, Don Ottavio, vow vengeance. Don Giovanni, having further escaped from the recriminations of a former mistress, Donna Elvira, joins a peasant's wedding party, invites them to his house and attempts to seduce the bride, Zerlina. Donna Anna, having met Don Giovanni again and recognised him, denounces him, in company with Donna Elvira and Don Ottavio, but he makes his escape. Don Giovanni persuades his servant, Leporello, to change clothes with him. In this disguise he gives Masetto, Zerlina's betrothed, a beating. Leporello, being left to escort Elvira, is discovered by Don Ottavio, Masetto, Donna Anna and Zerlina. Donna Elvira, imagining him to be Don Giovanni, pleads with him, declaring that he is her husband; but he reveals himself, and she joins in denouncing him. He escapes and meets Don Giovanni in the cemetery, where there is a statue of the Commendatore. Don Giovanni invites the statue to have supper with him and the answer is 'Yes'. Meanwhile Don Ottavio offers Donna Anna marriage, but she begs him to wait. At Don Giovanni's supper Donna Elvira makes a last appeal to him but is answered with ridicule. The statue enters according to the pact and after a climactic aria Don Giovanni is dragged down to hell. The remaining characters enter and make an appropriate commentary on the situation.

Mozart conducted the première of *Don Giovanni* (composing the overture, it is said, only hours before the performance) and won great acclaim for it in Prague, where he was much admired.

Don Juan, (1) *See* DON GIOVANNI;

(2) symphonic poem by Richard Strauss, op 20, after a poem by Nicolaus Lenau. The work, one of Strauss's earliest successes, was first performed in 1889 at Weimar.

Don Pasquale, comic opera in three acts by Donizetti, to a libretto by the composer and an unknown collaborator, after Angelo Anelli's *Ser Marc' Antonio*. First performed in 1843 in Paris, Donizetti's greatest comedy tells what befalls Don Pasquale, an elderly bachelor, when Dr. Malatesta offers him his sister's hand in marriage. In fact Dr. Malatesta's sister is nothing of the kind, but a young lady beloved of Ernesto, Pasquale's nephew. When the marriage contract has been signed, Norina behaves intolerably and embarks on reckless extravagance. In despair Pasquale asks Ernesto to marry Norina in his place, which is precisely what Dr. Malatesta had intended. The plot had been successful, and Ernesto wins his bride. The highlight of the work is the patter duet between Pasquale and Malatesta 'Cheti, cheti'.

Don Quichotte (Fr., *Don Quixote*), opera in five acts by Massenet, to a libretto by Henry Cain. Based on Cervantes' *Don Quixote* and on Jean Le Lorrain's comedy *Le Chevalier de la longue figure*, the work was first performed in 1910 in Monte Carlo.

Don Quixote, (1) *see* DON QUICHOTTE;

(2) symphonic poem by Richard Strauss, op 35, based on Cervantes' novel. Described as *Fantastische Variationen über ein Thema ritterlichen Charakters* (Fantastic variations on a theme of knightly character), it includes an important part for solo cello (representing Don Quixote) and another part, somewhat less important, for solo viola (representing Sancho Panza).

The work, first performed in 1898 in Cologne, is one of Strauss's most descriptive symphonic poems – in its course we hear the bleating of sheep and the tilting of windmills. The large orchestra includes a part for wind machine.

Doni, Giovanni Battista (1594–1647), Italian writer on music. He studied the humanities at Bologna and Rome, and in 1621 and 1622 visited Paris. He entered the service of Cardinal Barberini in Rome in 1623, with whom he again visited Paris and Madrid. In 1640 he returned to Florence, and became professor of rhetoric at the university. He made a special study of Greek music and published *Compendio del trattato de' generi e de modi della musica* (1635), *Annotationi sopra il compendio* (1640) and *De praestantia musicae veteris* (1647). A number of miscellaneous works were published posthumously in two volumes in 1763. Extracts from his writings dealing with the early history of opera are printed in A. Solerti, *Le origini del melodramma* (1903).

Donizetti, Gaetano (1797–1848), Italian composer, born in Bergamo, where he studied with Salari, Gonzales and J. S. Mayr (he also studied in Bologna under Pilotti and Padre Mattei). His first opera, *Enrico, conte di Borgogna*, was performed at Venice in 1818. A prolific composer, he wrote some 75 operas with a rapidity remarkable even for the 19th century. In consequence his work, though often charming, is generally superficial, depending to a large extent on the virtuosity of soloists. His best-known works are the serious operas *Anna Bolena* (Milan, 1830), *Il Furioso all'isola di San Domingo* (Rome, 1833), *Lucrezia Borgia* (Milan, 1833), *Torquato Tasso* (Rome, 1833), *Maria Stuarda* (Naples, 1834), *Marino Faliero* (Paris, 1835), *Lucia di Lammermoor* (Naples, 1835), *Roberto Devereux* (Naples, 1837), *La Favorite* (Paris, 1840) and *Linda di Chamounix* (Vienna, 1842), and the comic operas *L'elisir d'amore* (Milan, 1832), *La Fille du Régiment* (Paris, 1840) and *Don Pasquale* (Paris, 1843).

Though it is for his comedies – and for *Lucia di Lammermoor*, with its dramatic sextet and famous Mad Scene – that Donizetti is most widely loved

Don Giovanni: an engraving from the first edition of the score; and a contemporary print of Teresa Saporiti, the first Donna Anna

today, a number of his serious works (especially the Schiller-inspired *Maria Stuarda*) have regained lost ground, now that a new generation of virtuoso singers has risen to perform them, and conductors, producers and audiences to find new interest in them. Among his other operas are *Zoraide di Granata* (1822), *Alfredo il Grande* (1823), *Emilia di Liverpool* (1824), *Elisabetta al Castello di Kenilworth* (1829), *Parisina* (1833), *Belisario* (1836), *Il Campanello* (1836), *Pia de' Tolomei* (1837) and *Maria di Rohan* (1843).

Gaetano Donizetti: he is remembered mainly for his comic operas but the bulk of what he wrote – and what he valued most – was serious grand opera

Donizetti composed for all the leading Italian opera houses, and for important theatres outside Italy as well. In 1839, trouble with the Neapolitan censors over his opera, *Poliuto*, resulted in his moving to Paris, where the work was produced the following year under the title of *Les Martyrs* – the story was based on Corneille's tragedy, *Polyeucte*. Thereafter Donizetti wrote several works for France, culminating in *Don Pasquale* and *Don Sebastiano* (the former one of the most perennial operatic comedies, the latter once described as a 'funeral procession in five acts').

After the death of his wife in 1837, Donizetti suffered from increasing melancholia. During the last four years of his life he composed no more operas. He died, insane and paralysed, in his native Bergamo, where a monument by Vincenzo Vela was erected to him in 1855. The theory that Donizetti was of Scottish ancestry (the grandson of one Don Izett) has been exploded – see *Donizetti* by William Ashbrook, page 5.

    W. ASHBROOK: *Donizetti* (1965)

    H. WEINSTOCK: *Donizetti* (1964)

Donna Diana, opera in three acts by Rezniček, to a libretto by the composer, after Moreto's comedy, *El Lindo Don Diego* (1654). Donna Diana is the daughter of the mayor of Barcelona. First performed in 1894 in Prague, the work is today known mainly for its racy overture.

Doppelschlag (Ger.), the ornament known in English as TURN.

doppio movimento (It.), twice as fast.

doppio pedale (It.), 'double pedal', a term used in organ music to indicate that the two feet play simultaneously. An outstanding example is Bach's chorale prelude 'An Wasserflüssen Babylon'.

Dorati, Antal (born 1906), Hungarian born conductor, a pupil of Bartók and Kodály at the Budapest Academy of Music. In 1948, after becoming a U.S. citizen, he took charge of the Minneapolis Symphony Orchestra. From 1963 until 1967 he was chief conductor of the BBC Symphony Orchestra in London. Since then he has worked with the Stockholm Philharmonic, the National Symphony Orchestra of Washington, and the Royal Philharmonic Orchestra, of which he became conductor in 1975 in succession to Rudolf Kempe. Though he is an outstanding interpreter of Hungarian music, Dorati's range as a conductor is wide, one of his recent achievements being the recording of all Haydn's symphonies with the Philharmonia Hungarica.

Dorian mode, (1) in ancient Greek music:

(2) from the middle ages onwards applied to:

The tonic (or final) and dominant are marked respectively T and D. *See* GREEK MUSIC, MODE

Dorian Toccata and Fugue, the name given to an organ toccata and fugue in D minor by Bach, presumably because (although plainly in D minor) it was originally written without a key signature, thus giving the appearance that it was in the DORIAN MODE.

Dorn, Heinrich Ludwig Egmont (1804–92), German composer, conductor, teacher and critic, who studied in Königsberg and Berlin, and held various posts as teacher and conductor. He conducted the Royal Opera, Berlin (in succession to Nicolai) from 1849 until 1869. Schumann studied counterpoint with him at Leipzig (1830–2). Among his numerous operas was *Die Nibelungen* (Berlin, 1854), written independently of Wagner, of whom he was a severe critic. He published his memoirs and collected essays under the title *Aus meinem Leben* (1870–9).

dot, (1) written above or below a note, e.g.

(*a*) it normally indicates STACCATO, i.e. the following passage:

is played approximately:

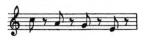

(*b*) in 18th century violin music a series of dots with a slur, e.g.:

indicates that the notes are to be detached but without changing the bow. The normal notation today is:

(*c*) in 18th century clavichord music a series of dots with a slur, placed over or under a single note:

indicates the BEBUNG, i.e. the gently repeated movement of the finger on the key which produces an effect similar to the vibrato of a guitar.

(*d*) in 18th century French music it often has a rhythmical significance: *See* 2 (iv) below.

(2) written after a note, a dot indicates a prolongation of the normal length by one-half. Hence:

In older music the dot was used to indicate such a prolongation not only within a bar but also beyond a barline, e.g.:

This practice was still used by Brahms but is now obsolete.

The double dot, first suggested by Leopold Mozart in 1756 (*see* his *Treatise on the Fundamental Principles of Violin Playing*, translated by Editha Knocker, page 42), indicates a prolongation of the normal length by three-quarters, e.g.:

The dot and double dot are also used after rests, though less frequently after semibreve and minim rests than after those for the crotchet, quaver and semiquaver, e.g.:

In music of the 17th and early 18th centuries the use of the dot was neither precise nor consistent. A number of theorists of the period deal with the ambiguity and give advice on interpretation. The following points should be noted:

(i) in passages of the following kind:

a dot is assumed after the rest, and the first note loses half its written value, i.e. the interpretation is:

A good example of this convention is the chorus 'Surely he hath borne our griefs' in Handel's *Messiah*.

(ii) in movements where triplets occur consistently, the rhythm

is generally, though not invariably, to be interpreted as

e.g.:

BACH, *Brandenburg Concerto no 5*

is to be played:

(iii) in general, however, the value of a dotted note is to be prolonged, and the value of the subsequent note or notes reduced accordingly. This applies particularly to dotted quavers and dotted semiquavers, but it may also apply to dotted crotchets. Much depends on the character and tempo of the piece. It was with the object of providing a precise notation for this convention that Leopold Mozart invented the double dot.

(iv) in French music, and music in the French style, it became the fashion to play successions of quavers or semi-quavers (sometimes also crotchets) unevenly, i.e. alternately long and short. In certain cases this would mean that

would be played

but the lengthening was not always so considerable, and cannot in fact be exactly represented in notation. Notes which were to be altered in this way were called *notes inégales*, and the rhythm was termed *pointé*. Where alteration of rhythm was not required, the notes often had dots over them, or were marked *notes égales*.

(3) in the notation of late medieval and Renaissance music (roughly from 1300 to 1600) the dot was used (a) as in modern notation, to prolong by half the value of an 'imperfect' note (e.g. a semibreve equal to two minims); (b) to clarify, where necessary, the notation of triple time by performing the function of a modern barline, i.e. by separating off one group of three equal notes (or its equivalent) from another.

See MENSURAL NOTATION

R. T. DART: *The Interpretation of Music* (1951)
R. DONINGTON: *The Interpretation of Early Music*

double, (1) (Eng.), an octave lower, e.g. double bassoon, built an octave lower than the bassoon; double diapason, an organ stop sounding an octave lower than the DIAPASON.

(2) (Eng.), prefixed to an instrument it may also signify one that combines two instruments in one, double horn, an instrument which combines the essential features of a horn in F and a horn in B flat alto (see HORN).

(3) (Eng.), an 18th century term for a variation (of an air or dance movement), consisting primarily of melodic ornamentation of new figuration, e.g.:

SARABANDE

BACH, *English Suite no 6*

A set of such variations would be labelled Double I, Double II, Double III, etc.

doublé (Fr.), turn.

double bar, a sign used to indicate the end of a composition or the end of a section:

It is not necessarily equivalent to a barline, as it may occur in any part of a bar. It is often accompanied by dots indicating that the preceding or succeeding section or both are to be repeated:

double bass (Fr., *contrebasse*; Ger., *Kontrabass*; It., *contrabasso*), the largest bowed string instrument and the foundation of the string ensemble. In shape it differs from the other members of the violin family, being modelled on the old double-bass viol (or *violone*) – the sloping shoulders are a characteristic feature. Music for it is written an octave higher than the real sounds, in order to avoid the constant use of leger lines. The modern instrument has four, sometimes five, strings. If there are four strings they are generally tuned:

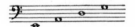

(sounding an octave lower), though some players prefer:

if there are five strings they are tuned:

or even:

In orchestral music before about 1800 the parts for cellos and double bases are very largely identical (apart from the difference in pitch), except that the cellos often play without the double basses. In more recent music the association of the two instruments has continued down to the present day, but there has been an increasing tendency to exploit the independence of the cellos. Extended passages for double basses alone, without any other instruments, are relatively uncommon: a good example occurs in the last act of Verdi's *Otello*, where Othello enters to murder Desdemona:

In chamber music the double bass has rarely been used, apart from works for large ensembles, such as Schubert's 'Trout' quintet for violin, viola, cello, double bass and piano, Dvořák's quintet in G major for two violins, viola, cello and double bass, and van Dieren's quartet no 4 for two violins, viola and double bass.

double bassoon (Fr., *contrebasson*; Ger., *Kontrafagott*; It., *contrafagotto*), a double-reed instrument, of wood or metal, built an octave lower than the BASSOON.

double cadence (Fr.), turn.

double chant, an Anglican CHANT consisting of four sections, to which two verses of a psalm or canticle are to be sung.

double concerto, a concerto for two solo instruments and orchestra, e.g. Brahms's concerto for violin, cello and orchestra, op 102.

double counterpoint, the name given to invertible counterpoint in two parts. It consists in adding to an existing melody a second melody which will fit equally well above or below the first. In theory the added melody can move up or down any interval to its new position, but in practice the commonest intervals are those of the octave, tenth and twelfth. It is not uncommon for the first melody to move at the same time an octave, or even two octaves, in the opposite direction, either to prevent a crossing of parts, or to make room for additional parts in between. Double counterpoint occurs frequently in fugues, since the COUNTER-SUBJECT may be required to enter above the subject in one place and below it in another.

(a) double counterpoint at the octave:

BACH, *Two-Part Inventions no 9*

(b) double counterpoint at the tenth:

BACH, *Art of Fugue*

(*c*) double counterpoint at the twelfth:

BACH, *Ibid.*

double croche (Fr.), semi-quaver.

double diapason, *see* DIAPASON (3)

double dot, indication that the time-value of a note is to be lengthened by three-quarters, e.g.

See also DOT

double flat, the sign $\flat\flat$, indicating that the pitch of the note to which it is prefixed is to be lowered two semitones, e.g. on a keyboard instrument

will sound the same as

double fugue, (1) properly, a FUGUE in which a new theme is introduced in the course of the piece and after being itself treated fugally is finally combined with the original subject, to which it forms in fact a counter-subject;

(2) the name sometimes given to a fugue in which the

subject and counter-subject appear simultaneously at the beginning and are regularly associated throughout the piece.

double reed, two pieces of cane, the lower and thicker ends being bound round a metal tube, while the upper ends, which are very thin, practically meet, leaving however a small aperture through which the player's breath is forced. This method of tone production is used in the oboe, cor anglais, heckelphone, bassoon, double bassoon and sarrusophone.

double sharp, the sign ×, indicating that the pitch of the note to which it is prefixed is to be raised two semitones, e.g. on a keyboard instrument

will sound the same as

See SHARP

double stop, a chord of two notes played on a bowed string instrument (such as the violin) by using two adjacent strings. The name is applied not only to chords where both the notes are stopped with the finger, but also to those in which one or both can be played on an open string.

double tonguing, a means of achieving a rapid articulation of successive notes (particularly repeated notes) on the flute and brass instruments. It consists in articulating alternately the consonants T and K. It is not possible on reed instruments, such as the oboe, clarinet and bassoon, where the mouthpiece is held inside the mouth.

See TRIPLE TONGUING

double touch, a system employed by some modern organ-builders, by which a heavier pressure on the keys can be used to bring into action new registration, without the necessity for changing stops. In this way it is possible for a solo and accompaniment to be played on the same manual in two contrasted tone-colours. The system is common on cinema organs.

doucement, (Fr.), sweetly, gently.

Dowland, John (1563–1626), English composer and lutenist. From 1580 to 1584 he was in the service of the English Ambassador at Paris, where he became a Roman Catholic. He graduated B.Mus. at Oxford in 1588. Unsuccessful in obtaining a place at the English court in 1594, on account of his religion, he travelled widely on the Continent. His *First Booke of Songes or Ayres* was published in 1597, followed in due course by three further collections. From 1598 to 1606 he was lutenist to Christian IV of Denmark. He was in the service of Lord Walden in 1611, and of James I and Charles I from 1612 to 1626. He had a great reputation both as a performer and as a composer. His four books of ayres are the most important English contribution to the literature of the solo song with lute accompaniment (modern editions in *The English School of Lutenist Songwriters*, first series); some of them were printed in alternative versions for four voices with lute (reprinted in *Musica Britannica*, vi).

He also published a collection of instrumental ensemble music, under the title *Lachrimae, or Seaven Teares figured in seaven passionate Pavans* (1605; facsimile edition, 1974; modern edition by P. Warlock, 1927). A number of ensemble pieces and lute solos were published in foreign collections, but much of his lute music survived only in manuscript until the publication of his *Collected Lute Music*, edited by D. Poulton, in 1974. See illustration on p. 180.

His son, **Robert Dowland** (c. 1585–1641), was, like his father, a lutenist and composer, and succeeded his father as lutenist to Charles I in 1626. He edited *Varietie of Lute-Lessons* (1610; facsimile edition, 1958; modern edition by E. Hunt, 1957) and *A Musical Banquet* (1610; facsimile edition, 1969; modern edition by P. Stroud, 1968). The latter is a collection of songs in several languages.

D. POULTON: *John Dowland* (1972)

down-beat, the downward movement of a conductor's stick or hand, marking the first beat of the bar.

down-bow, the drawing of the bow across the strings of a string instrument. The opposite – the pushing of the bow in the other direction – is called the up-bow.

Draghi, Antonio (1635–1700), Italian composer. He was in the service of the Imperial Court of Vienna from 1658 onwards (*Kapellmeister* from 1682). One of the most prolific composers of his time, he wrote an enormous number of operas and oratorios, and also some opera librettos. His selected church music is printed in *Denkmäler der Tonkunst in Osterreich*, xlvi, Jg. xxiii (1).

Draghi, Giovanni Battista (c. 1640–c. 1710), Italian musician, resident in London in the Restoration period (*see* Pepys, *Diary*, February 12, 1667). He was successively master of Charles II's Italian musicians, organist to Catherine of Braganza, and organist to James II's Roman Catholic chapel. His compositions include a setting of Dryden's ode for St. Cecilia's day, *From Harmony, from heavenly Harmony*.

Dragonetti, Domenico (1763–1846), Italian double-bass virtuoso and composer. As a young man he was appointed to St. Mark's, Venice. In 1794 he moved to London and played in opera and concerts there until his death. Throughout this period he played with the cellist Robert Lindley. He had a great reputation, and was acquainted with both Haydn and Beethoven.

Drdla, František (also known as Franz) (1868–1944), Czech violinist and composer. He wrote two operas, but is best known by his violin solos, some of which, e.g. *Souvenir*, have become widely popular.

Dream of Gerontius, The, oratorio by Elgar, op 38, to a text taken from the poem by Cardinal Newman, first performed in 1900 at the Birmingham Festival.

Dreigroschenoper, Die (Ger., *The Threepenny Opera*), opera with a prologue and eight scenes by Kurt Weill. The work is a modern version (jazz-tinged) of John Gay's *The Beggar's Opera*, founded on a German translation by Elisabeth Hauptmann, with lyrics by Bertolt Brecht – who also used ballads by François Villon and Rudyard Kipling. The first performance, in Berlin in 1928, starred Lotte Lenya. Among the songs in the opera (several of them frequently performed out of context, in watered-down arrangements) is 'Mack the Knife'.

Dreiklang (Ger.), triad.

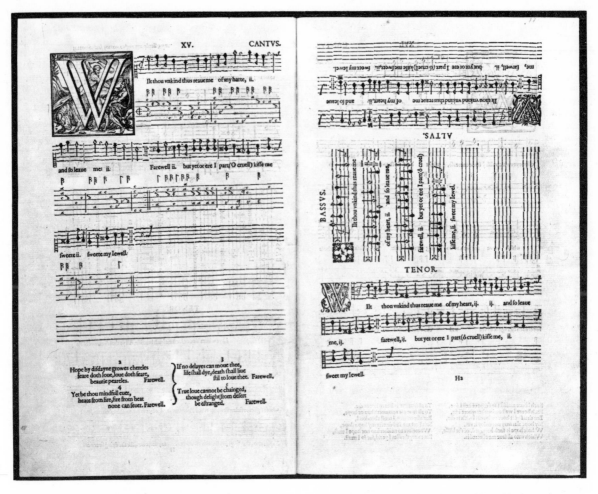

A song from John Dowland's *First Books of Ayres* (1597): the book is designed to be placed on a table, with the performers seated around it

dringend (Ger.), pressing onwards, urgent.

drohend (Ger.), threatening.

drone, the lower pipes of the bagpipe, each of which produces a single persistent note.

drone bass, a bass part which imitates the drone of a bagpipe by remaining on the same note, e.g. the opening of the finale of Haydn's symphony no 104 in D major:

Druckman, Jacob (born 1928), U.S. composer, associated (like Gunther Schuller) with the so-called 'third stream' movement in which post-serial techniques are combined with elements of modern jazz.

drum, for the various kinds of drum used in the orchestra *see* BASS DRUM, SIDE DRUM, TABOR, TENOR DRUM, TIMPANI.

drum kit, a set of drums and cymbals arranged so that they may all be played by one person. The drummer sits behind a snare drum around which are arranged a tenor drum, a bass drum operated by a foot pedal and a hi-hat cymbal operated by the other foot. Crash cymbals are fixed to the drums or supported on stands, and all are played by sticks, mallets or wire brushes. Other drums and such accessories as temple blocks may be included. A good performance on a drum kit is a marvel of coordination.

Drum Mass (Ger., *Paukenmesse*), nickname for Haydn's Mass in C major (1790) in which kettle drums are prominently featured.

Drum Roll Symphony (Ger., *Symphonie mit dem Paukenwirbel*), nickname for Haydn's Symphony no 103 in E flat major (1795) which opens with a kettledrum roll (*Paukenwirbel*) – repeated near the end of the first movement.

Düben, a family of musicians of German origin who settled in Sweden in the 17th century. The most important are Andreas (Anders) and Gustaf.

Andreas Düben (c. 1590–1662) was organist of St. Thomas's, Leipzig. He studied with Sweelinck in Amsterdam from 1614 to 1620. He was court organist at Stockholm in 1621, and *Kapellmeister* there in 1640. His compositions include an eight-part motet, 'Pugna triumphalis', for the burial of Gustavus Adolphus.

His son, **Gustaf Düben** (1624–90), became a member of the court chapel at Stockholm in 1648, and succeeded his father as *Kapellmeister* in 1663. In addition to his own compositions, he made a collection of contemporary music which is preserved in the library at Uppsala.

Ducasse, *see* ROGER-DUCASSE

Du Caurroy, *see* CAURROY

Dudelsack (Ger.), bagpipe.

duet, composition for two singers or players, with or without accompaniment. Early examples of vocal duets are (*a*) without accompaniment: Morley's Canzonets for two voices (1595), (*b*) with accompaniment: several pieces in Monteverdi's seventh and eighth books of madrigals (1619 and 1638). The term 'duo' is more generally used for instrumental music, with the exception of the PIANO DUET.

Dufay, Guillaume (c. 1400–74), Flemish composer. He was a chorister at Cambrai Cathedral in 1409, and in the service of the Malatesta family of Rimini from at least 1420 till 1426. It was probably at about this time that he took his degree, perhaps at the University of Bologna, and became a priest. From 1428 to 1433 and from 1435 to 1437 he was a singer in the Papal Chapel. During the intervening period, and from 1437 to 1439, he was employed at the court of Savoy. In 1436 he was provided with a canonicate and prebend at Cambrai Cathedral but did not reside there until 1439. In 1450 and from 1452 he was again at the court of Savoy, but returned to Cambrai in 1458 to spend the rest of his life there. Dufay was the most important composer of his time, a master both of church music and of secular song. During his creative life span of over fifty years he absorbed an impressive range of styles and made them his own. The earliest works may be regarded as standing at the end of the middle ages, while his mature compositions signify the flowering of the Renaissance. His complete works have been edited by Heinrich Besseler in six volumes (1951–66).

C. VAN DEN BORREN: *Guillaume Dufay* (1926)

C. WRIGHT: 'Dufay at Cambrai: Discoveries and Revisions', *Journal of the American Musicological Society*, xxviii (1975)

Dukas, Paul (1865–1935), French composer and critic. He studied at the Paris Conservatoire, and was subsequently in charge of the orchestra class there for a short time. He also taught composition at the École Normale de Musique, and contributed criticism to several newspapers. A severe self-critic, he published comparatively little. He was strongly influenced by impressionism, but without sacrificing the characteristic clarity of his style. His best-known works are the orchestral scherzo *The Sorcerer's Apprentice* (1897),

the opera *Ariadne and Bluebeard* (Fr., *Ariane et Barbe-Bleue*) (Paris, 1907) and the ballet *La Péri* (1912). He also wrote a remarkable piano sonata in E flat minor. *Ariane et Barbe-Bleue*, a setting of a libretto by Maeterlinck, is one of the outstanding operas of the 20th century, though it has not so far achieved wide popularity.

dulcian, *see* DOLCIAN

dulcimer (Fr., *tympanon*; Ger., *Hackbrett*; It., *cembalo, salterio tedesco*), an instrument of Eastern origin which came to Europe in the middle ages. Like the psaltery, it consists of strings stretched over a wooden frame, but these, instead of being plucked, are struck with hammers held in the hands. The pianoforte is an adaptation of this principle, the hammers being controlled by a keyboard, with a separate hammer for each note. An enlarged type of dulcimer, called the Pantaléon, was invented by Pantaléon Hebenstreit (1667–1750) and had a considerable vogue in the 18th century. The dulcimer is still current in Hungary under the name CIMBALOM.

dulcitone, a keyboard instrument, in which tuning-forks are struck by hammers.

Dulichius, Philipp (1562–1631), German teacher and composer of church music. A modern edition of his *Centuria octonum et septenum vocum harmonias sacras . . . continens* (1607–12) is in *Denkmäler deutscher Tonkunst*, xxxi and xli.

Dumbarton Oaks Concerto, concerto in E flat major for fifteen instruments by Stravinsky (1938). The title refers to the residence of R. W. Bliss near Washington D.C., where the work was first performed. The music is in the style of a modern *concerto grosso*.

dumka, (1) a Slavonic term for a folk ballad, generally of a sentimental or melancholy character (plural *dumky*);

(2) used by Dvořák of an instrumental movement alternating between elegiac melancholy and exuberance (*see* DUMKY TRIO).

dumb keyboard, silent keyboard (often portable) used by some pianists for finger practice. Sometimes also called 'dummy keyboard.'

Dumky Trio, piano trio by Dvořák, op 96 (1891), consisting of six movements, each in the form of a dumka.

Dumont, Henry (1610–84), Walloon composer. He was organist of St. Paul, Paris, from 1639 to 1684, and director of the Chapel Royal, Paris, from 1665. He was a priest, and became canon of Maastricht Cathedral. He published five Masses, a large number of motets, chansons and instrumental music.

H. QUITTARD: *Un Musicien en France au XVIIe siècle: Henry Du Mont* (1906)

dump, 16th and 17th century musical term, probably denoting an elegy or lament. The original meaning of 'dump' is a fit of melancholy or depression, and this is still current in the colloquial phrase 'to be down in the dumps'. The poem by Richard Edwards quoted by Shakespeare in *Romeo and Juliet* is a good example of this primary sense:

Where gripyng griefs the hart would wound
& dolful domps the minde oppresse,
There Musick with her silver sound,
Is wont with spede to give redresse.

Shakespeare's reference elsewhere in the same play (iv, 5) to a 'merry dump' is obviously intended as a paradox. The word is also widespread as a literary term; the poem for Weelkes's madrigal in memory of Morley – 'Death hath deprived me of my dearest friend' (*The English Madrigal School*, xiii, no 26) – was originally entitled 'A Dump upon the death of the most noble Henry Earl of Pembroke'. Musical examples of dumps often carry the name of a person in their titles and may likewise be memorial pieces. All are instrumental, and most are constructed over a simple GROUND BASS. The earliest known example, 'My Lady Carey's Dompe' (*c*. 1543?) for harpsichord, is printed in *Historical Anthology of Music*, edited by A. T. Davison and W. Apel, no 103.

> J. M. WARD: 'The "Dolfull Domps"', *Journal of the American Musicological Society*, iv (1951)

Dunhill, Thomas Frederick (1877–1946), English composer and teacher, pupil of Stanford. His works include a symphony, chamber music, songs and operas, of which *Tantivy Towers* (London, 1931), to a libretto by A. P. Herbert, was very successful. He also wrote the following books: *Chamber Music* (1913), *Sullivan's Comic Operas* (1928) and *Sir Edward Elgar* (1938).

Duni, Egidio Romoaldo (1709–75), Italian born opera composer, a pupil of Durante. He settled in Paris in 1757, and became a leading composer of *opéra-comique*. His first opera, *Nerone* (Rome, 1735), was a successful essay in *opera seria*. Of his numerous *opéras-comiques* the best known is probably *Les Moissonneurs* (Paris, 1768).

Dunstable, John (died 1453), English mathematician and musician. He was one of the most important composers of the early 15th century, with a considerable reputation on the Continent. He was in the service of the Duke of Bedford (regent of France, 1422–35). His compositions, found mainly in Continental manuscripts, appear to be almost entirely for the Church: the beautiful setting of 'O rosa bella' (*Historical Anthology of Music*, edited by A. T. Davison and W. Apel, no 61) is attributed to him in only one manuscript (other sources give Bedyngham as the composer). A complete edition of his musical works by M. Bukofzer is in *Musica Britannica*, viii (revised edition by M. Bent, I. Bent and B. Trowell). He also wrote treatises on astronomy.

> M. BUKOFZER: 'John Dunstable and the Music of his Time', *Proceedings of the Musical Association*, lxv (1938–9)
> F. LL. HARRISON: *Music in Medieval Britain* (1958)

Duny, *see* DUNI

duo, duet.

Duparc, Henri (full name Marie Eugène Foucques-Duparc), (1848–1933), French composer, a pupil of César Franck. For reasons of health (he suffered from a chronic nervous disorder) he abandoned composition after 1885. His reputation rests on some fifteen songs, which date from his twenties; but these are among the finest products of 19th century lyricism. They include 'Invitation au voyage' and 'Phydilé'. Among his other works, few in number, is a symphonic poem, *Lénore* (1875), inspired by Bürger's poem.

duplet, a group of two notes occupying the time normally taken by three, e.g.:

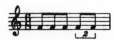

duple time, TIME in which the number of beats in the bar is a multiple of two, e.g. 2/4, 4/4, 2/2. (Time in which there are four beats in the bar is also known as 'common' or 'quadruple' time). If the beats are divisible by two, the time is 'simple'; if they are divisible by three, it is 'compound', e.g.

simple duple time:

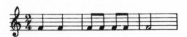

compound duple time:

duplum (Lat.), the part immediately above the tenor in 12th century organum. A third part above these two was called *triplum*. In the 13th century motet the *duplum* came to be known as *motetus*.

Duport, Jean Louis (1749–1819), French cellist brother of Jean Pierre Duport. He held various European appointments and for a time taught at the Paris Conservatoire. On the outbreak of the Revolution he moved to the Prussian court in Berlin. He is the founder of the modern technique of cello playing: his teaching was embodied in his *Essai sur le doigter du violoncelle et la conduite de l'archet*. It was with him (or his brother) that Beethoven played his two cello sonatas, op 5.

His brother, **Jean Pierre Duport** (1741–1818), was also a cellist. He worked in Paris and later in Berlin, where he was principal cellist in the orchestra of Frederick the Great. Mozart composed piano variations on a minuet by J. P. ('Monsieur') Duport, K 573.

Du Pré, Jacqueline (born 1945), English cellist, pupil of William Pleeth and winner (at the age of ten) of the Suggia Gift. She made her début at the Wigmore Hall, London, when she was sixteen. She quickly established herself as an outstanding interpreter of the Elgar and other cello concertos, and of many works in the duo and trio repertory, but ill-health in recent years has hampered her career.

Dupré, Marcel (1886–1971), French organist and composer, member of a family of musicians. He made his mark as a player when still a boy, and won several prizes at the Paris Conservatoire, including the *Prix de Rome* in 1914. He was assistant to Widor at St. Sulpice (1906); and Widor's successor at St. Sulpice (1934). From 1954 until 1956 he was director of the Paris Conservatoire. He toured widely as a recitalist and showed remarkable skill in improvisation. In addition to organ works he composed chamber music, choral works and songs.

Duprez, Gilbert (1806–96), French tenor, one of the leading opera singers of his time. He studied at the Paris Conservatoire and sang Edgardo in the first performance of *Lucia di Lammermoor* (Naples, 1835). He also created the title-role in Berlioz's *Benvenuto*

Cellini (Paris, 1838). His numerous compositions, which had little success, include eight operas, an oratorio and other choral works.

dur (Ger.), 'major', as opposed to 'minor' (*moll*). The word derives from the Latin B *durum* (hard B), the name given to the square-shaped B used in medieval times to indicate B natural.

See B, MOLL

Durand, a French firm of music publishers, founded in Paris in 1869.

Durante, Francesco (1684–1755), Italian composer, one of the most important figures of the 'Neapolitan' school. He was a famous teacher, and was *maestro di cappella* at the Conservatorio de Santa Maria di Loreto (1742–55) and the Conservatorio di Sant' Onofrio (1745–55). His works consist principally of church music, but he also wrote six harpsichord sonatas – the only compositions to be printed in his lifetime. Among his pupils were Paisello, Pergolesi and Piccinni.

Durchführung (Ger.), literally 'through-leading'. German term for the development section of a sonata movement. Confusingly, however, the same term is used for the exposition of a fugue.

Durchkomponiert (Ger.), 'composed throughout' or 'through-composed'. A term applied to songs in which there is fresh music for each verse, as opposed to strophic songs, where the same music is repeated for each verse.

Durey, Louis Edmond (born 1888), French composer, for a few years a member of the group known as 'Les Six' (*see* SIX). His output includes an opera on Mérimée's *L'Occasion* but his best work is to be found in more intimate music, such as chamber pieces and songs, which show both individuality and refinement.

Duruflé, Maurice (born 1902), French composer and organist, pupil of Dukas. In 1930 he was appointed organist of St. Etienne du Mont. He is widely known as a brilliant recitalist. His compositions include some very effective organ pieces and chamber music.

Dušek, František Xaver (also known as Franz) (1731–99), Bohemian pianist and composer, a pupil of Wagenseil in Vienna. He had a considerable reputation as a teacher. He and his wife were close friends of Mozart, who worked on *Don Giovanni* at their home in Prague.

Dušek, Jan Ladislav, *see* DUSSEK

Dušek, Josepha (1754–1824), Bohemian soprano, wife of František Xaver Dušek. Mozart composed for her the concert aria 'Bella mia fiamma', K 528 (1787). She also gave the first performance of Beethoven's *scena* 'Ah perfido' (1796).

Dushkin, Samuel (born 1896), Polish-Russian violinist, who became a U.S. citizen. A pupil of Auer and Kreisler, he gave recitals with Stravinsky, and gave the first performance of the latter's violin concerto in 1931 and *Duo concertant* in 1932.

Dussek, Jan Ladislav (originally Dušek) (1760–1812), Czech pianist and composer, the son of an organist and teacher. He showed great skill as a pianist and organist while still a child. After studying theology at Prague he held organist's posts at Malines and Berg-op-Zoom. In Hamburg he was the pupil of C. P. E. Bach. He won great success as a pianist in Amsterdam and the Hague, and composed a number of works for the piano. As a

soloist he visited Berlin, St. Petersburg, Paris (where he played for Marie Antoinette in 1786), Milan and London, where he stayed for nearly twelve years. He joined his father-in-law's music-publishing firm, Corri & Co., but financial difficulties compelled him to leave for Hamburg in 1800. He continued to travel as a soloist and was befriended by various patrons, the last of whom was Talleyrand. The beauty of his touch was much praised by his contemporaries. In addition to piano concertos and sonatas he wrote a considerable amount of chamber music including about twenty piano trios. His piano sonatas, some of which have programme titles, foreshadow the characteristics of romantic piano music, particularly in their use of pathetic chromaticism.

Dutilleux, Henri (born 1916), French composer. He studied at the Paris Conservatoire and in 1938 won the *Prix de Rome*. In 1944 he began working for the French radio, and more recently was appointed as a professor of composition at the Paris Conservatoire. His music, dissonant but not 'advanced' in style, and notable for its technical brilliance, includes two symphonies, *Métaboles* for orchestra, an important piano sonata, and a cello concerto which Rostropovich has done much to popularise.

Duval, François (c. 1673–1728), French violinist and composer, a member of the orchestra of Louis XIV. He was the first French composer to publish sonatas for violin and continuo: he wrote five books, of which the first appeared in 1704.

dux (Lat.), 'leader'. The name given by older theorists to the first part to enter in a CANON or FUGUE. The second part to enter, which imitates it, was known as *comes* (companion).

Dvořák, Antonin (1841–1904), Czech composer. Born at Nelahozeves, near Prague, he was the son of a village innkeeper and butcher. As a child he heard only popular and simple church music (his father played the zither), but at the village school he learnt enough of the rudiments of violin, viola and organ playing to impress his father, who (in spite of extreme poverty) encouraged him to attend the Prague organ school instead of entering the family business. After studying for three years, he became a viola player in the orchestra of the Prague National Theatre in 1862. During his eleven years with the orchestra he was active as a composer. His patriotic *Hymnus* (op 30) for chorus and orchestra, performed in 1873, was so successful that he left the National Theatre to devote himself to composition and teaching. In 1875 he received a government grant, on the recommendation of Brahms and Hanslick. Brahms thereafter continued to encourage him and helped him to get his works published by Simrock. In 1884 Dvořák made the first of several visits to England, and conducted his *Stabat Mater* in London. He subsequently composed for various English musical societies his D minor symphony (1885), the cantata *The Spectre's Bride* (1885) and the oratorio *St. Ludmilla* (1886). In 1891 he was made an honorary doctor of music by Cambridge University, and in the same year was appointed professor at Prague Conservatory (where, ten years later, he became director). From 1892 until 1895 he was director of the National Conservatory of Music in New York, and spent some time at the Czech colony of Spillville, Iowa. His experiences in the United States, and his responsiveness to the music of the U.S. Negroes and Indians, were reflected in the last of his nine symphonies (*From the New World*, 1893) and in the so-called *American* string quartet in F major (1893). His profound love for his homeland, and for his country estate at Vysoka, soon made him return to Czechoslovakia, however. In 1901 he was appointed director of the Prague Conservatory (a post he held until his death) and his sixtieth birthday was celebrated as a national event.

Antonin Dvořák, aged 38, when his music was becoming known in Vienna through the help of Brahms

Dvořák was a spontaneous composer: all his music has a natural freshness which sometimes conceals the skill with which it is constructed and the scrupulous care he took over the shaping of a theme – very often an apparently God-given melody was the result of arduous trial and error, as Dr. John Clapham has revealed in his book on the composer. The principal influences in his life were the music of Smetana, Brahms and Wagner, and Czech folk song. None of these influences dominated him; but his appreciation of folk song made it easier for him to welcome the Negro and Indian idioms with which he became acquainted in the United States. So true to himself did he remain, however, that it is hard to separate the U.S. elements of his music from the Czech ones. Like Schubert, Dvořák could be discursive and even in some of his most famous and well-loved works – such as the G

major and New World symphonies, and the cello concerto – he had an exasperating habit of saying the same thing twice. This was not a fault, however, of his great D minor symphony (no 7), the tautest and most powerful of all his works, and one of the outstanding symphonic masterpieces of the later 19th century. The lyrical side of his personality found a handsome outlet in his operas, though of these only *Rusalka* – the story of the watersprite – has proved popular outside Czechoslovakia. In recent years the re-numbering of Dvořák's symphonies, in order to incorporate four early works into the official canon, has caused some confusion. The correct chronological numbering of the nine works now runs as follows:

No 1 in C minor (*The Bells of Zlonice*) (formerly unnumbered)
No 2 in B flat (formerly unnumbered)
No 3 in E flat (formerly unnumbered)
No 4 in D minor (formerly unnumbered)
No 5 in F major (formerly no 3)
No 6 in D major (formerly no 1)
No 7 in D minor (formerly no 2)
No 8 in G major (formerly no 4)
No 9 in E minor (*From the New World*, formerly no 5)

Dvořák's principal compositions are:

(1) Operas: *Křál a Uhlíř* (*King and Collier*, 1874); *Tvrdé Palice* (*The Pigheaded Peasants*, 1874); *Vanda* (1875); *Selma Sedlák* (*The Peasant a Rogue*, 1877); *Dimitrij* (1882); *Jakobin* (1888, rev. 1897); *Čert a Káča* (*The Devil and Kate*, 1899); *Rusalka* (1900); *Armida* (1904);

(2) Choral works: *Hymnus* (1872); *Stabat Mater* (1877); *The Spectre's Bride* (1884); *St. Ludmilla* (1886); Mass in D (1887); Requiem Mass (1890); *Te Deum* (1892);

(3) Orchestra: nine symphonies, *Symphonic Variations* (1877); six overtures, including *Carnival* (1891); five symphonic poems; three Slavonic rhapsodies; two cello concertos (1865 & 1895); piano concerto (1876); violin concerto (1880);

(4) Chamber music: four piano trios (the last is the *Dumky* trio); string trio; two piano quartets; thirteen string quartets; piano quintet; two string quintets; string sextet.

Also many songs and duets, piano solos and piano duets.

J. CLAPHAM: *Antonin Dvořák, Musician and Craftsman* (1966)
V. FISCHL (editor): *Antonin Dvořák* (1942)
R. NEWMARCH: *The Music of Czechoslovakia* (1942)
A. ROBERTSON: *Dvořák* (1945)

dynamics, (1) degrees of loudness or softness in a musical performance; (2) the signs by which these are indicated in the score. Those in ordinary use, with their abbreviations, are: *pianissimo* (*pp*), very soft; *piano* (*p*), soft; *mezzo piano* (*mp*), moderately soft; *mezzo forte* (*mf*), moderately loud; *forte* (*f*), loud; *fortissimo* (*ff*), very loud; *poco forte* (*pf*), moderately loud; *forte piano* (*fp*), loud and immediately soft; *sforzato* and *sforzando* (*sf*, *sfz*), heavily accented; *crescendo* (*cres.*, or ◁), getting louder; *decrescendo* and *diminuendo* (*decresc.* and *dim.*, or ▷), getting softer. For signs used for accentuation, *see* ACCENT.

Indications of dynamics began to appear in the early

17th century, and were used to a large extent to indicate contrasts, particularly a soft repetition in the form of an echo. A persistent increase or decrease in volume was marked by indicating the several stages, e.g. *forte*, *piano*, *pianissimo*. The terms *crescendo* and *diminuendo* began to come into use about the middle of the 18th century – largely, no doubt, as the result of orchestral practice. Burney, in his *Present State of Music in Germany* (1773), i, page 94, gives a vivid account of the effect of *crescendo* and *diminuendo* as practised by the Mannheim orchestra. From that time the use of dynamic signs increased, as composers realized more and more the desirability of exactly indicating their intentions if they were not themselves to be in charge of the performance.

R. E. M. HARDING: *Origins of Musical Time and Expression* (1938)

Dyson, George (1883–1964), English composer and teacher. He held various academic appointments and was director of the Royal College of Music in London from 1937 until 1952. He was knighted in 1941. His compositions include a symphony and several choral works, among them *In Honour of the City*, *The Canterbury Pilgrims*, *St. Paul's Voyage to Melita*, *Nebuchadnezzar* and *Quo Vadis*. His critical writings include *The New Music* (1924) and *The Progress of Music* (1932).

Dzerjinsky, Ivan (born 1909), Russian composer, best known for his opera *Quiet Flows the Don*, based on Sholokhov's novel, composed in 1923–4 and first performed at Leningrad, 1935. Another opera by him, *Virgin Soil Upturned*, was also inspired by Sholokhov. He studied at Leningrad Conservatory, but without acquiring a thorough technical equipment. His music is improvisatory in style and derives what character it has from its imitation of folk song.

G. ABRAHAM: *Eight Soviet Composers* (1943)

E, the third note (or mediant) of the scale of C major.

Eagles, *see* ECCLES

East, Michael (c. 1580–1648), English composer and organist of Lichfield Cathedral. His compositions include madrigals, music for viols and church music. Modern editions of the madrigals are in *The English Madrigal School*, xxix-xxxi.

East (Est, Este), Thomas (died c. 1608), music-publisher, who issued some of the most important works by late 16th and early 17th century English composers. Among the many collections which he published were Byrd's *Psalmes, Sonets and Songs* (1588), *Musica Transalpina* (1588 and 1597; facsimile edition, 1972), *The Triumphes of Oriana* (1601), Byrd's *Gradualia*, part i (1605), and madrigals by Morley, Wilbye, Weelkes and Bateson.

Eastman School of Music, part of the University of Rochester, New York State. It was founded and endowed in 1918 by George Eastman (1854–1932), head of the Eastman Kodak Company. Later, Howard Hanson became its director.

Eberl, Anton (1765–1807), Austrian pianist and composer. He travelled widely as a soloist, and from 1796 until 1800 was *Kapellmeister* at St. Petersburg. His compositions, much admired in his day, include five operas, symphonies, concertos, chamber music and piano sonatas. Eberl was a close friend of Mozart, and his piano sonata in C minor, op 1, and other piano works were originally published under Mozart's name. His symphony in E flat was performed at the same concert as Beethoven's *Eroica* symphony, April 7, 1805, and was much more successful.

F. EWENS: *Anton Eberl* (1927)

Eberlin, Johann Ernst (1702–62), German composer and organist. In 1729 he became organist at the court and cathedral, Salzburg, and in 1749 was appointed *Kapellmeister*. His compositions include a large number of oratorios, Masses and other church music, and keyboard works. Mozart wrote of some of his fugues in 1782:

> They are unfortunately far too trivial to deserve a place beside Handel and Bach. With due respect for his four-part compositions I may say that his keyboard fugues are nothing but long-drawn-out voluntaries.

E. ANDERSON, *The Letters of Mozart and his Family*, page 1194

Ebony Concerto, work written by Stravinsky for the jazz clarinettist, Woody Herman, and his band, first performed at Carnegie Hall, New York, in 1946.

Eccard, Johann (1553–1611). German composer, a pupil of Lassus. He was in the service of Jakob Fugger at Augsburg in 1578. About 1580 he was appointed vice-*Kapellmeister* at Königsberg, becoming *Kappelmeister* there in 1604. He was *Kapellmeister* to the court of Brandenburg, Berlin, in 1608. Most of his compositions are for the Lutheran church and include settings of chorales, but he also published a certain number of secular part-songs. His *Newe Lieder mit fünff und vier Stimmen* (1589) have been edited by R. Eitner (1897), his *Geistliche Lieder auff den Choral* (two parts, 1597) by E. von Baussnern (1928), and his *Preussische Festlieder* (two parts, 1642 and 1644) by G. W. Teschner (1858).

Eccles or **Eagles,** family of English musicians. **Solomon Eccles** (1618–1683), taught the virginals and viol during the Commonwealth, became a Quaker, and published the tract called *A Musick-Lector* (1667; see P. Scholes, *The Puritans and Music*, pages 52–4). He later migrated to the West Indies and America.

His son, possibly his eldest, was also called **Solomon Eccles,** and was a violinist and composer. He was in the service of Charles II, James II and William III. Some violin pieces of his were printed in the second edition of *The Division Violin* (1695).

The younger Solomon had two sons. **Henry Eccles** (c. 1670–c. 1742) was a violinist. He was appointed musician to William III in 1689. About 1715 he migrated to France where he published a volume of violin sonatas (1720), which borrow freely from an earlier set by Giuseppe Valentini.

The other son, **John Eccles** (1668–1735) was also a violinist and composer. He was appointed musician to William III in 1696, and Master of the King's Music in 1700. He won second prize in a competition opened in 1700 for a setting of Congreve's pastoral *The Judgment of Paris*. He wrote music for a large number of plays, including parts i and ii of *Don Quixote* (in association with Purcell, 1694).

échappée (Fr.), abbreviation of *note échappée*, i.e. 'escaped note'. The term is used in the theory of harmony to describe a progression between two adjacent notes which first takes a step in the 'wrong' direction and then reverts to the note originally aimed at by the interval of a third.

échiquier (Fr.), *see* CHEKKER

echo attachment, a device that adds artificial echo to the sound of an electric instrument. In one kind, a drive unit is connected to a long coil of wire. The signal from the instrument operates the drive unit, which vibrates the coil. The vibrations pass along the coil and actuate a pickup at the other end. The signal from the pickup is superimposed over the original sound, but is delayed by the time it takes to travel along the coil and so sounds like an echo of the original sound. Another kind of echo attachment uses a tape recorder to return a recording of the original sound after a certain delay. This method can also give multiple echoes for special effect.

Echo attachments produce some distortion – which

may be desirable – but for the highest quality echo, an ECHO CHAMBER must be used.

echo chamber, a device for adding echo or reverberation in recording and broadcasting. It consists of a sealed chamber containing a loudspeaker and microphone. The sound is fed to the echo chamber, where it is reproduced by the loudspeaker and picked up with reverberation from the walls of the chamber by the microphones inside. An acoustic delay line, which consists of a long pipe with a loudspeaker at one end and microphones spaced along it, works on the same principle. Each microphone gives a different delay time depending on its distance from the loudspeaker.

Écho et Narcisse (Fr., *Écho and Narcissus*), opera in three acts by Gluck, to a libretto by Louis Theodore de Tschudy, first performed in Paris in 1779.

echo organ, a set of pipes placed further away than the main body of the organ and designed to suggest an echo. In modern organs they may be placed a considerable distance away, e.g. in the triforium, and be controlled from a separate manual, with several stops.

École d'Arcueil, a group of French musicians, disciples of Satie, who called themselves the 'Arcueil School' after the suburb of Paris in which Satie lived. The members of the group, founded in 1923, included Roger Desormière, Maxime Jacob and Henri Sauguet.

écossaise (Fr.), short for *danse écossaise*, 'Scottish dance'. A quick dance in 2/4 time, popular in Britain and on the Continent in the late 18th and early 19th centuries. Examples occur in the works of Beethoven and Schubert, e.g.:

SCHUBERT, *Eleven Ecossaises no 5*

There seems to be no evidence that it has any Scottish connection. It is not to be confused with the SCHOTTISCHE.

Edinburgh Festival, a summer festival of music and drama held in Scotland, one of the largest in the world. First held in 1947, it was responsible for the reunion between Bruno Walter and the Vienna Philharmonic after World War II. The Glyndebourne Opera Company initially made an important contribution to its success. Later, opera companies were imported from all over Europe, and from 1967 Scotland's own recently-founded national company – Scottish Opera – began to appear there. Orchestras and soloists of world class perform at the Edinburgh Festival each year, and a number of important works (by Tippett among others) have been commissioned. The festival's first director was Rudolf Bing; his successors have included Lord Harewood, Peter Diamand and John Drummond.

Egdon Heath, symphonic poem by Holst, inspired by Thomas Hardy's description of a Dorset landscape in *The Return of the Native*. It was first performed (in New York) in 1928.

Egge, Klaus (born 1906), Norwegian composer, a pupil of Valen. From 1932 to 1945 he taught singing in Oslo, and from 1935 to 1938 was editor of the magazine *Tonekunst*. His compositions, which are strongly influenced by folk music, include five symphonies, two piano concertos, the oratorio *Sveinung Vreim*, chamber music, piano works and songs.

Egk, Werner (born 1901), German composer. He was conductor of the Berlin State Opera from 1936 until 1941, and director of the Hochschule fur Musik, Berlin, from 1950 until 1953. His operas include *Die Zaubergeige* (1934), incorporating Bavarian songs and dances, *Peer Gynt* (1938), based on Ibsen's play, *Irische Legende* (1954), inspired by W. B. Yeats, and *Der Revisor* (1957), based on Gogol's *Government Inspector*. His concert music includes an oratorio, *Columbus*, a violin concerto, and a French Suite (after Rameau) for orchestra.

Egmont, a tragedy by Goethe, dealing with the revolt of the Netherlands against the Spanish domination, for which Beethoven in 1810 wrote an overture and incidental music (op 84) incorporating *entr'actes* and songs.

Ehrling, Sixten (born 1918), Swedish conductor. He was chief conductor of the Swedish National Opera from 1953 until 1960, and became musical director of the Detroit Symphony Orchestra in 1963.

Eichheim, Henry (1870–1942), U.S. violinist and composer, who devoted himself particularly to the study of Oriental music. He was a member of the Boston Symphony Orchestra from 1890 until 1912. His compositions, which are influenced heavily by Eastern music, include three ballets (*Chinese Legend, Burmese Pwe* and *The Moon, My Shadow and I*) and a number of orchestral works employing oriental instruments.

Eighteen Twelve (*The Year 1812*), concert overture by Chaikovsky, written in 1882 for the commemoration of the 70th anniversary of Napoleon's retreat from Moscow – which the music depicts in graphic terms, with the 'Marseillaise' ultimately put to flight by the Tsarist Russian national anthem. The first performance was given at the consecration of the Cathedral of the Redeemer in the Kremlin. The score incorporates optional parts for cannon and military band, though in many performances nowadays (especially if they take place at the Royal Albert Hall in London) the optional parts are treated as obligatory.

eighth-note, U.S. term for 'quaver' (calculated on the basis that a semibreve is a whole-note).

eilen (Ger.), 'to hurry'. *Nicht eilen*, do not hurry.

Einem, Gottfried von (born 1918), Swiss born Austrian composer, son of Austrian military attaché in Switzerland. In 1938 he joined the staff of the Berlin State Opera. He was to become Hindemith's pupil, but Hindemith was suspended by the Nazis. Later Einem and his mother were arrested by the Gestapo. After his release he studied with Boris Blacher in Berlin. In 1948 he moved to Salzburg. His compositions include the operas *Dantons Tod* (*Danton's Death*) (Salzburg, 1953), *The Old Lady's Visit* (after Durenmatt), a ballet *Prinzessin Turandot* (after Gozzi), a *Philadelphia* symphony and other orchestral works.

einfach (Ger.), simply.

Einleitung (Ger.), introduction.

Einstein, Alfred (1880–1952), German born historian and critic. He was music critic of the *Munchener Post* (1917), *Berliner Tageblatt* (1927–33) and editor of the *Zeitschrift für Musikwissenschaft* (1918–33). He was editor of Riemann's *Musik-Lexikon*, ninth to eleventh editions (1919, 1922, 1929). In 1933 he went into exile, and after living in London and Florence settled in the United States in 1939, where he was professor at Smith College, Northampton, Mass. until 1950. His numerous publications include the third edition of Köchel's catalogue of Mozart's works (1937), books on Gluck, Mozart and Schubert, *Music in the Romantic Era* (1947) and *The Italian Madrigal* (three volumes, 1949). His *Geschichte der Musik* (1917) first appeared in English in 1936 as a *Short History of Music* (new edition with music supplement, 1948).

Eis (Ger.), E sharp (E♯).

Eisis (Ger.), E double sharp (E ×).

Eisler, Hanns (1898–1962), German composer, of Austrian parentage. In 1919 he became a pupil of Schoenberg in Vienna, and from 1925 until 1933 he taught in Berlin. After persecution by the Nazis, he emigrated to the United States. There he wrote film and theatre music of notable quality, but gained notoriety for his leftist views – he was a close friend of the Marxist dramatist, Bertolt Brecht. In 1947 he was brought before the Committee for Un-American Activities and given a prison sentence; but a committee (including Chaplin, Copland, Albert Einstein and Thomas Mann) was formed for his rehabilitation, and in the end he was deported. In 1950 he settled in East Berlin.

His works include two operas (*Goliath* and *Johannes Faustus*), a *German Symphony* for solo voices, chorus and orchestra, a *Lenin Requiem*, an instrumental quintet entitled *14 Ways of Describing Rain* and other chamber music, and many songs, often in collaboration with Brecht. His book, *Composing for the Films*, was published in 1942.

Eisteddfod (Welsh), literally 'assembly' or 'session'. The name is applied particularly to a gathering of Welsh bards. Such gatherings were held in very early times. In its modern form the Eisteddfod is a competition festival, not necessarily confined to music. The National Eisteddfod, the most important of these gatherings, is a revival dating from the early 19th

century. An artificial link with the past is maintained by the use of ceremonial and bardic costume.

Eitner, Robert (1832–1905), German lexicographer and musicologist. He founded the Gesellschaft für Musikforschung (Society for Musical Research) in 1868, and edited its journal, *Monatshefte für Musikgeschichte* (1869–1904) as well as a series of musical and theoretical works of the past entitled *Publikationen alterer praktischer und theoretischer Musikwerke*. His *Bibliographie der Musiksammelwerke des 16. und 17. Jahrhunderts* (1877), though incomplete, is still indispensable. His *Quellen-Lexikon* (ten volumes, 1900–4) – a biographical and bibliographical dictionary of musicians up to the middle of the 19th century – was a valiant attempt to lay the foundations for a scientific study of musical history.

Ek, Gunnar (born 1900), Swedish composer whose works include three symphonies and a *Swedish Fantasy* for orchestra.

electronde, an electronic instrument similar to the THEREMIN, but incorporating mechanism designed to interrupt the *glissando* from one note to another and to control amplification. Tone is produced by utilizing the difference between two frequencies. Invented by Martin Taubmann (1929).

electrone, an electronic organ, first produced in 1939 by the John Compton Organ Co. It is provided with stops and couplers like an ordinary organ, but the sound is produced by amplifying electrically generated vibrations.

electronic instruments, there are three principal ways in which electricity is used to produce (as distinct from merely reproducing) musical sounds:

(1) by amplifying existing vibrations, e.g. in the Everett Orgatron (1934), which amplifies the vibration of harmonium reeds, and the Neo-Bechstein piano (1931), which amplifies the vibration of strings and also makes possible sustained tone and a crescendo. The same principle has also been applied to string instruments;

(2) by generating frequencies corresponding to the vibrations of notes and converting them into sound, e.g. in the Hammond organ (1934), where a system of intensifying or suppressing the individual members of a limited HARMONIC SERIES makes possible the artificial representation of the tone of a large number of different instruments;

(3) by utilizing the difference between two frequencies, e.g. in the Theremin (1924), where the difference is controlled by the movement of the hand through the air.

F. W. GALPIN: 'The Music of Electricity', in *Proceedings of the Musical Association*, lxiv (1937–8)

E. G. RICHARDSON: 'The Production and Analysis of Tone by Electrical Means', ibid. lxvi (1939–40)

electronic music, a general term embracing any type of music where composers work with sounds electronically produced and/or treated, usually in special studios. Such music began to be produced in the 1950s, and includes to date more than ten thousand works whose stylistic characteristics vary from the commercial jingle to the most rigorous *avant garde* art music. Using technical criteria, three main types may be distinguished:

(1) pre-recorded tape music, (a) of purely electronic

production and treatment; (b) of MUSIQUE CON-CRETE, i.e. taped compositions of 'naturally' produced sounds electronically treated;

(2) live electronic music either (a) combining the use of performers and tapes, or (b) using simultaneous modulation of 'live' (instrumental) and/or electronic sounds;

(3) computer music including (a) digitally synthesized compositions; (b) compositions created as in (1), but in a studio where a computer is used to control various electronic components and to sequence the work; (c) instrumental compositions, the scores of which were prepared with the aid of a computer.

At present there are thought to be more than five hundred electronic music studios around the world (some two hundred in the United States alone) and more than two thousand composers who have created works involving some aspect of electronic music. Among the most important studios, and composers associated with them, are:

(1) in Europe: the Paris radio studio, founded by Pierre Schaeffer, pioneering musique concrète, and the Centre Beauberg (also in Paris), a lavish project under the direction of Pierre Boulez and Luciano Berio, which opened in 1976; the West German Radio studio in Cologne, originally pioneering the field of 'pure' electronic music, founded in 1951 by Herbert Emert, with Stockhausen as its artistic director and Goevaerts, Hambraeus, Koenig and Pousseur as associated composers; the Milan Radio studio in Italy, founded in the late 1950s by Luciano Berio and Bruno Maderna; the Warsaw radio studio in Poland, where Penderecki, among others, has worked; the EMS studio in London, the most advanced in the U.K., where Peter Zinovieff, Harrison Birtwistle and Tristram Cary have worked; a studio at Liège university, founded by Henri Pousseur;

(2) in the United States: the Princeton Electronic Music Centre at Columbia University in New York, a complex of several studios (one housing the RCA Mk II synthesizer), with Milton Babbitt, Otto Luening and Vladimir Ussachevsky as co-directors, and Mario Davidovsky, Alcides Lonza, Edgar Varèse and Charles Wuorinen as associated composers; the California Institute of the Arts' studio, where Morton Subotnik has worked; Princeton University, a pioneering digital synthesis centre, with James K. Randall as director, and Hubert Howe, Barry Vercoe and Godfrey Winham as associated composers; other important studios are at the Bell Telephone Laboratories in New Jersey, and at the University of Illinois;

(3) in Japan, an active studio in Tokyo, with Mayuzumi, Moroi, Okuyama, Ichiyanagi, and Takemitsu as associated composers.

In 1951, when Pierre Schaeffer established the first purpose-designed studio in Paris, compositions had to be built piece by piece through editing and splicing tapes. Since then there have been many developments, such as multi-track tape recorders, voltage control, and SYNTHESIZERS. The composer now has much greater control and flexibility, and increasing possibilities of access to sophisticated equipment. Electronic music has come to be seen as a valuable extra resource for established composers, and the only possible area for young composers to hear their composition fully realized. Probably the next significant step forward is the development (mainly U.S.) of digital synthesis, using specially designed programs and computers. This process can create very accurate simulations of conventional instruments, which is impossible with analogue synthesis. At the moment digital synthesis can be expensive and time-consuming, and has some drawbacks. Recent research may overcome these problems.

M. V. MATHEWS and others: *The Technology of Computer Music* (1969)

Elegy for Young Lovers: a scene from Scottish Opera's imaginative production for the 1970 Edinburgh Festival (produced by Henze himself) showing John Shirley-Quirk as Mittenhofer and Ralph Koltai's controversial but effective tubular steel Hammerhorn

Elegy for Young Lovers, opera in three acts by Henze, to a libretto by W. H. Auden and Chester Kallman, first performed (in German translation) at Schwetzingen in 1961. The story concerns an egotistical poet who destroys or damages (or, at the very least, exploits) those around him for the sake of his art. The first singer to portray this evil genius was Dietrich Fischer-Dieskau. *See* illustration on p. 189.

Elektra, opera in one act by Richard Strauss, to a libretto by Hugo von Hofmannsthal (after Sophocles), first performed in Dresden in 1909.

Elektra, daughter of Agamemnon, wishes to avenge his death. Her own mother, Clytemnestra, was his murderer. She awaits the coming of her brother Orestes, though Clytemnestra has been told that he is dead. When he returns he kills Clytemnestra and Aegisthus, formerly her lover and now her husband. Elektra rejoices that her father's murder is avenged and in her frenzy dances herself to death.

Elektra was Strauss's fourth opera, and the first in which he collaborated with the Austrian dramatist, Hofmannsthal.

eleventh, the interval of an octave and a fourth, e.g.:

For the so-called 'chord of the eleventh', *see* CHORD

Elgar, Edward William (1857–1934), English composer, son of a music-dealer and organist in Worcester. He had no formal musical training but learned the organ, violin and bassoon. He intended to become a professional solo violinist and had some lessons in London from Adolphe Pollitzer, but abandoned the idea. Among his early posts were the conductorship of the Worcester Glee Club (1879), Worcester County Lunatic Asylum Band (1879) and Worcester Amateur Instrumental Society (1882). In 1885 he became organist of St. George's Roman Catholic Church, Worcester. He married Caroline Alice Roberts, and went to live in London, but finding it impossible to make a career there, he settled in Malvern in 1891. His first important performance was the concert overture *Froissart* at the Three Choirs Festival, Worcester (1890). This was followed by various choral works: *The Black Knight* (Worcester, 1893), *Scenes from the Bavarian Highlands* (Worcester, 1896), *The Light of Life* (Worcester, 1896), *The Banner of St. George* (London, 1897) *Caractacus* (Leeds, 1898). His reputation as a composer of the first rank was established by the *Enigma Variations* for orchestra (1899) and the oratorio *The Dream of Gerontius* (Birmingham, 1900) – one of the several works inspired by his Catholicism. The performance of the latter, however, was inadequate: it was not until it had been given at Dusseldorf in 1902 that it took its place as an acknowledged masterpiece. The next twenty years (until the death of his wife in 1920) were notable for the composition of two more oratorios, several large-scale orchestral works and some chamber music. After 1920 he wrote little of importance. A third symphony, commissioned by the B.B.C., and an opera, *The Spanish Lady*, survive only in sketches. He was the professor of music at Birmingham University (1905–8) and Master of the King's

Music (1924). He was knighted in 1904 and became a baronet in 1931.

He began his career as a romantic, and remained one to the end, though the exuberance of his maturity mellowed into the wistful nostalgia of old age. He delighted in colour and showed a mastery of the orchestra unsurpassed by anyone of his time. His generous display of emotion repelled some who felt that English music should be reserved, but to many more the discovery of his rich humanity was like a new

Sir Edward Elgar: one of the first important composers to record his own music, so producing authoritative documents for posterity

awakening. He created for himself a style and an idiom so personal as to win the epithet 'Elgarian'. His studies of others – in the *Enigma Variations* and in the symphonic poem *Falstaff* – were in reality projections of himself. His second symphony, often regarded as a picture of the Edwardian age, is in fact a revelation of its author. He was not afraid to be popular, and many who never heard his serious works were familiar with his marches. His oratorios are a confession of the faith in which he was brought up. Of these *The Dream of Gerontius* is traditionally regarded as the finest, because it is a consistent whole. But its successors have come in for reappraisal in recent years and *The Kingdom* is regarded by at least one authority, Sir Adrian Boult, as structurally superior to *Gerontius*. Elgar's principal compositions are:

(1) Oratorios: *The Light of Life* (1896); *The Dream of Gerontius* (1900); *The Apostles* (1903); *The Kingdom* (1906).

(2) Other choral works: *The Black Knight* (1893); *Scenes from the Bavarian Highlands* (1896); *King Olaf* (1896); *The Banner of St. George* (1897); *Caractacus* (1898); *Coronation Ode* (1902); *The Music Makers* (1912); *The Spirit of England* (1916).

(3) Orchestra: *Froissart* (1890); Serenade for strings (1893); *Enigma Variations* (1899); *Cockaigne* (1901); *In the South* (1904); Introduction and Allegro for strings (1905); *The Wand of Youth* (1907–8); two symphonies (1908, 1911); violin concerto (1910); cello concerto (1919); *Falstaff* (1913); *Nursery Suite* (1933).

(4) Brass band: *Severn Suite* (1930; also arranged for orchestra and for organ solo).

(5) Chamber music: Piano quintet (1919); string quartet (1919); violin sonata (1919).

(6) Organ: two sonatas (1896, 1933; second arranged from the *Severn Suite*).

(7) Songs: *Sea Pictures*, with orchestra (1899); songs with piano; part-songs.

R. J. BUCKLEY: *Sir Edward Elgar* (1905)

T. F. DUNHILL: *Sir Edward Elgar* (1938)

M. KENNEDY: *Portrait of Elgar* (1968)

B. MAINE: *Elgar: his Life and Works* (two volumes, 1933)

D. MCVEAGH: *Edward Elgar: his Life and Music* (1955)

E. NEWMAN: *Elgar* (1922)

R. POWELL: *Edward Elgar: Memoirs of a Variation* (1937)

W. H. REED: *Elgar as I knew him* (1936); *Elgar* (1939)

P. M. YOUNG: *Elgar O. M.* (1955)

Elijah, oratorio by Mendelssohn, op 70, first performed in Birmingham in 1846. The first German performance was at Hamburg the following year.

Elisir d'amore, L' (It., *The Elixir of Love*), opera in two acts by Donizetti, to a libretto by Romani, first performed at Milan in 1832. Along with *Don Pasquale*, this comic opera represents the highwater mark of Donizetti's inspiration. The story, based on Scribe's *Le Philtre*, tells how a bashful young man buys an 'elixir' from a quack doctor. It is only cheap wine, but he wins the heroine's love all the same.

Elizalde, Federico (born 1907), Spanish composer and conductor, who was born in the Philippines and studied under Bloch and other composers. His works include an opera, *Paul Gauguin*, a sinfonia concertante for piano and orchestra, and a violin concerto.

Elkin, a London firm of music publishers, founded in 1903 by William Wolfe Alexander Elkin.

Ellinwood, Leonard (born 1905), U.S. musicologist. He studied at the Eastman School of Music, Rochester and taught successively at Mount Hermon School (1927), University of Rochester (1934) and Michigan State College (1936–40). He joined the staff of the Library of Congress in 1940 and was ordained deacon in 1948. His special field is medieval music. He edited *Musica Hermanni Contracti* with English translation (1936) and the complete works of Francesco Landini (1939).

Ellington, 'Duke' (1899–1974), U.S. jazz composer, pianist and band leader, the greatest musical 'colourist'

in jazz history. His real name was Edward Kennedy Ellington, the nickname of 'Duke' referring to the aristocracy of his style and personality. His career straddled several eras of jazz history, and (uncommon among jazz musicians) his style developed from period to period, though that is not to say that his early

Duke Ellington, the greatest of all jazz colourists, who used the piano not so much as a solo instrument but as part of the orchestral palette from which he drew and mixed the colours he needed as a composer

performances (many of them marvellously preserved on disc) were inferior to his later ones. Each phase of Ellington's career, indeed, produced great jazz, from the grittiness of his output during the 1920s to his experiments with Shakespeare (the *Such Sweet Thunder* suite) during the 1950s and the subsequent jazz impressions of 'classical' works such as Chaikovsky's *Nutcracker* suite. Among Ellington's masterpieces are the *Black and Tan Fantasy, Mood Indigo, Creole love call, Creole Rhapsody*, and *Concerto for Cootie*. Constant Lambert's *Music Ho!*, a wrong-headed book in many ways, is brilliantly right-headed on the subject of Ellington's *Hot and Bothered*, which it compares favourably with Ravel and Stravinsky, adding that the combination of themes at the end is 'one of the most ingenious pieces of writing in modern music'. Ellington always worked with brilliant bandsmen, whose qualities contributed to the unique colouring of the performances. For example, there was the rich saxophone playing of Johnny Hodges or the trumpet playing of Cat Anderson, who produced almost incredibly high notes. His portrait of Hamlet in *Madness in Great Ones* has to be heard to be believed – though it is said of Anderson that he produces notes which only a dog can hear.

Elman, Mischa (1891–1967), Russian violinist. He studied at Odessa, and with Auer at the St. Petersburg

Conservatory. He toured throughout the world and in 1923 became a U.S. citizen.

Elmendorff, Karl (1891–1962), German conductor. He studied at the Cologne Hochschule für Musik and was active as an opera conductor in many German cities. From 1927 until 1942 he appeared regularly at Bayreuth.

Elsner, Joseph Xaver (1769–1854), Polish composer, German by birth but Polish by residence. He studied medicine at Breslau and Vienna, but also studied violin and harmony. Deciding on music as a career he joined the theatre orchestra at Brno in 1791. He was appointed conductor of the Lwow Theatre in 1792 and of the Warsaw National Theatre in 1799. He was the first director of the Warsaw Conservatory (1821–30) – the result of a society for the encouragement of music which he founded in 1815. His numerous compositions include operas, church music, symphonies, concertos, chamber music and ballets. His pupils included Chopin, who studied at the conservatory from 1826 until 1829.

embellishments, *see* ORNAMENTS

embouchure, (1) the mouthpiece of a wind instrument;

(2) the correct shaping of the lips necessary to produce accurate intonation and good tone. It is acquired only by persistent practice.

Emmanuel, Marie François Maurice (1862–1938), French composer and musicologist. He studied at the Paris Conservatoire and in Brussels, and taught history of music at the Paris Conservatoire from 1909 until 1936. His compositions include two symphonies and two operas – *Prométhée enchaîné* (1918) and *Salamine* (1929), both after Aeschylus. His historical studies include *Histoire de la langue musicale* (two volumes, 1911), a work of outstanding importance.

'Emperor' Concerto, nickname given in Britain and the United States to Beethoven's fifth piano concerto in E flat, op 73, composed in 1808.

'Emperor' Quartet (Ger., *Kaiserquartett*), nickname given to Haydn's quartet in C, op 76, no 3, the slow movement of which consists of variations on the EMPEROR'S HYMN. The work was composed around 1799.

Emperor's Hymn (Ger., *Kaiserlied*), patriotic hymn by Haydn, to words by Leopold Haschka, composed in 1797. Haydn used it as a theme for variations in the slow movement of his C major string quartet, op 76, no 3 (1799). Later it was sung to the words 'Sei gesegnet ohne Ende', by Ottokar Kernstock. It was adopted as the national anthem of Austria ('Gott erhalte Franz den Kaiser'). In Germany Haydn's music was used for 'Deutschland, Deutschland über alles', words by Hoffmann von Fallersleben (1841); the words now sung in Western Germany begin 'Einigkeit und Recht und Freiheit'. In Britain it is used as a hymn tune, e.g. for 'Praise the Lord, ye heavens adore him' and 'Glorious things of thee are spoken'.

Empfindung (Ger.), 'feeling'. *Mit Empfindung*, with feeling. *Empfindungsvoll*, full of feeling.

empfindsamer Stil (Ger.), sensitive style. The term refers to the 18th century style of C. P. E. Bach, Quantz and other composers who tried to make their music expressive of 'true and natural' feeling, thereby paving the way for 19th century romanticism.

enchainez (Fr.), 'link up', i.e. go straight to the next movement or section.

Encina, *see* ENZINA

enclume (Fr.), anvil.

encore (Fr.), again. The cry of English-speaking audiences (though, oddly, not French ones) who want to hear more music than they paid for. If the performer complies – either by repeating a piece already performed or by adding an extra one – the result is called an 'encore'. Dietrich Fischer-Dieskau has been known to sing as many as seven at the end of a recital. There are times, however, when an encore would damage the proportions or character of a programme, and on such occasions the audience's demands should be ruthlessly resisted.

Enesco (Enescu), George (1881–1955), Romanian composer, conductor and violinist. He studied at the Vienna Conservatorium, which he entered at the age of seven, and at the Paris Conservatoire, where he won the *premier prix* for violin-playing, 1899. He was active as a composer, and toured widely as a violinist and a conductor. Yehudi Menuhin was his pupil. His compositions include the opera *Œdipe* (Paris, 1936), three symphonies, two Romanian rhapsodies and chamber music. In 1912 he founded a prize for works by young Romanian composers.

Enfance du Christ, L' (Fr., *The Childhood of Christ*), a sacred trilogy for soloists, chorus and orchestra by Berlioz, op 25.

The three parts are: (1) *Le Songe d'Hérode* (Herod's Dream); (2) *La Fuite en Egypte* (The Flight into Egypt); (3) *L'Arrivée à Sais* (The Arrival at Sais). It was first performed in Paris in 1854.

Enfant et les sortilèges, L' (Fr., *The Child and the Magic Spells*), opera (*fantaisie lyrique*) in two parts by Ravel, to a libretto by Colette, first performed at Monte Carlo in 1925.

Engel, Carl (1818–82), German writer on musical instruments. He first came to England as a piano teacher in his twenties, but soon turned his attention to historical research and the collection of musical instruments. His most important works are *The Music of the Most Ancient Nations* (1864), *An Introduction to the Study of National Music* (1866) and *Descriptive Catalogue of the Musical Instruments in the South Kensington Museum* (1874), where many of the instruments in his own collection are now preserved.

Engel, Carl (1883–1944), U.S. musicologist, of German origin. He was chief of the Music Division, Library of Congress, Washington from 1922 until 1934 and editor of *The Musical Quarterly* from 1929 until 1944. He was active in promoting musical research in the United States and was president of the American Musicological Society (1937–8). He wrote two books, *Alla Breve* (1921) and *Discords Mingled* (1931).

Engführung, *see* STRETTO (1)

English Descant, *see* DESCANT (3)

English fingering, a system of fingering piano music (now obsolete) by which the figures 1, 2, 3, 4 represented the four fingers, while the thumb was indicated by a cross. In the so-called Continental fingering, which is now universal, the thumb is represented by the figure 1, and the four fingers by 2, 3, 4, 5.

English flute, an 18th century name for the RECORDER

or beaked FLUTE, as a distinction from the *flauto traverso* (the ordinary orchestral flute), which was known as the German flute.

English Folk Dance and Song Society, an amalgamation, in 1932, of the Folk Song Society (founded 1898) and the English Folk Dance Society (founded 1911), based at Cecil Sharp House in London. Its activities include the arranging of lectures, meetings and festivals, and the publication of the *Journal of the English Folk Dance and Song Society*.

English horn, *see* OBOE

English Madrigal School, The, an edition by E. H. Fellowes of all the English madrigals published in the reigns of Elizabeth I and James I. 36 volumes were published between 1913 and 1924, many of which have been subsequently revised by Thurston Dart.

English Opera Group, an organization founded in 1947 with the object of producing operas with a small instrumental ensemble instead of the usual large and costly orchestra. Benjamin Britten, who founded it in association with Eric Crozier and John Piper, had already written *The Rape of Lucretia* (1946) as an experiment in the use of such resources. Among the works specially written for the group are Britten's *Albert Herring*, *Let's Make an Opera*, *The Turn of the Screw* and *Death in Venice*, Berkeley's *A Dinner Engagement* and *Ruth*, and Harrison Birtwistle's *Punch and Judy*. The Group also performed revivals of older works, including Blow's *Venus and Adonis* and Purcell's *Dido and Aeneas*. It had no permanent theatre but had close links with Covent Garden and with the Aldeburgh Festival.

English School of Lutenist Song-Writers, The, an edition by E. H. Fellowes of songs for solo voice (or duet) with lute accompanist published by English composers between 1597 and 1622. The first series includes the original TABLATURE for the lute, which is omitted in the second series. The alternative versions for four voices found in some of the original songbooks are not included. The original edition was published between 1920 and 1932. A programme of revisions and additions to the series was begun in 1959.

English Suites, the name given to a set of six keyboard suites by J. S. Bach. They are on a larger scale than the FRENCH SUITES, and have preludes for first movements – which the French Suites do not. Forkel, Bach's earliest biographer, suggests that they are so called 'because the composer wrote them for an Englishman of rank' (*Johann Sebastian Bach*, translated by C. Sanford Terry, page 128), but there is no evidence to support this. There are clear traces of the influence of a set of six keyboard suites by Charles Dieupart, a French composer who was active in London in the early years of the 18th century (*see* E. Dannreuther, *Musical Ornamentation*, volume i, pages 137–9), but this hardly explains why Bach's suites should be nicknamed 'English'. The words 'fait pour les Anglois' (made for the English), written over the first suite in an early manuscript copy, may provide a clue (*see* C. H. H. Parry, *Johann Sebastian Bach*, page 463).

engraving, *see* PRINTING OF MUSIC

enharmonic, (1) in Greek music the enharmonic *genus* was the oldest of three ways of sub-dividing a tetrachord, the other two being the diatonic and the chromatic. In its original form it seems to have consisted simply of a major third with a semitone below:

but in quite early times the semitone was divided into two quarter-tones, so that there were four notes in all, instead of three:

(The quarter-tone above E has been represented here by the sign ‡, i.e. half a sharp.) The existence of these small intervals, which were in use until Hellenistic times, is evidence of the close association between Greek music and Oriental music;

(2) in modern acoustics the enharmonic *diesis* is the interval between an octave, i.e. $\frac{2}{1}$:

and three major thirds, i.e. $(\frac{5}{4})^3 = \frac{125}{64}$:

B sharp is therefore flatter than C, and the interval is $2 \div \frac{125}{64} = \frac{128}{125}$

On keyboard instruments, however, B sharp and C are identical, and this has encouraged composers to use harmonic changes which exploit this identity, e.g.:

BACH, *St. Matthew Passion no 60*

where D sharp becomes E flat. Substitution of this kind is known as an *enharmonic change*. An *enharmonic modulation* is one which makes use of such a change to facilitate the progress from one key to another, e.g. instead of writing:

we may treat the B flat as A sharp and turn the progression in another direction:

Enigma Variations, 'variations on an original theme for orchestra' by Elgar, op 36, first performed in London in 1899. The description on the title-page is as quoted above. The word 'Enigma' appears only on the first page of the music, underneath the single word 'variations'. The page after the title-page bears the words: 'Dedicated to my friends pictured within'. Each variation is in fact a description of the character or habits of an individual. They are mostly represented by initials or nicknames, which stand for the following:

(1) C. A. E. – Caroline Alice Elgar (the composer's wife).

(2) H. D. S.-P. – H. D. Steuart-Powell (amateur pianist).

(3) R. B. T. – R. B. Townshend (author).

(4) W. M. B. – W. M. Baker (country squire).

(5) R. P. A. – R. P. Arnold (son of Matthew Arnold).

(6) Ysobel – Isabel Fitton (amateur viola-player).

(7) Troyte – A. Troyte Griffith (architect).

(8) W. N. – Winifred Norbury.

(9) Nimrod – A. J. Jaeger (on the staff of Novello's).

(10) Dorabella – Dora Penny (later Mrs Richard Powell).

(11) G. R. S. – G. R. Sinclair (organist, Hereford Cathedral).

(12) B. G. N. – B. G. Nevison (amateur cellist).

(13) (***) – Lady Mary Lygon (later Trefusis).

(14) E. D. U. – 'Edu', the name by which Elgar was called by his wife.

Variations 10, 13 and 14 are respectively subtitled 'Intermezzo', 'Romanza' and 'Finale'.

The subtitle 'Enigma' appears, according to the composer, to refer not merely to the initials prefixed to the variations, but also to the fact that both theme and variations are closely associated with another theme which is never heard. The identity of this other theme is not known, though some musical detectives believe it to be 'Auld lang syne'.

Enoch, a London firm of music publishers, founded in 1869 by Emile Enoch. It was bought up by Edwin Ashdown Ltd. in 1927, and incorporated with this firm in 1936.

ensemble, (Fr.), (1) a group of singers and players, e.g. an instrumental ensemble, a vocal ensemble;

(2) in opera, a movement for several singers, with or without chorus;

(3) the artistic co-operation of the individual members of a group. A 'good ensemble' means that they are well-matched and the parts well-balanced, and that they have been successful in achieving a unified performance.

Entführung aus dem Serail, Die (Ger., *The Abduction from the Harem*), comic *Singspiel* (opera with dialogue) in three acts by Mozart, libretto by Christoph Friedrich Bretzner (previously set by Johann André, 1781), adapted by Gottlieb Stephanie. It was first performed in Vienna in 1782, and is the first important opera to have been written in the German language. The story concerns Constanze and her maid Blonde, who are imprisoned in the palace of Pasha Selim. The Pasha wants to marry Constanze, but her beloved Belmonte gets into the palace with his servant Pedrillo to try to rescue her. In doing so, he is frustrated by Osmin, the guardian of the palace. The Pasha (who has only a speaking part) recognises Belmonte as the son of an old enemy, but magnanimously sets him free along with Constanze, Blonde, and Pedrillo (who loves Blonde).

The opera is fully discussed in Mozart's letters (*see* E. Anderson, *The Letters of Mozart and his Family*, pages 1123 and following).

entr'acte (Fr.), music played between the acts of a play or opera. Among the most famous *entr'actes* ever written are Schubert's for *Rosamunde*.

entrée (Fr.), a term used mainly in 17th and 18th century French music:

(1) an introductory piece in a ballet or opera, for the entry of the characters on the stage;

(2) an independent piece of instrumental music, similar in character to (1);

(3) a section of a ballet or opera, the equivalent of 'scene' or even 'act'.

entry, in a fugue, the 'entrance' of the theme, not only at the beginning but also on its later appearances; also a 17th century term for a prelude.

Enzina (Encina), Juan Del (1468–1529), Spanish poet, dramatist and composer. Although a priest, he is known only by secular compositions. He studied at the University of Salamanca, and for some time was in the service of the first Duke of Alba. He was archdeacon of Málaga in 1509, and prior of León in 1519. Compositions by him are in *El cancionero musical de Palacio*, edited by H. Anglès, three volumes (1947–53) and *Cancionero de Upsala*, edited by J. Bal y Gay (1944).

Epine, L', *see* L'EPINE

episode, (1) in a FUGUE, a passage forming a contrast to the entries of the subject and serving as a link between one entry and the next, often modulating to a related key. The thematic material may be derived from the subject or counter-subject, or may be entirely independent. The first episode will normally occur after the EXPOSITION, in which the entries of the subject in the various parts (or 'voices') are heard in succession. It is quite possible, however, to have a fugue without any episodes, e.g. the fugue in C major in book I of Bach's 48 *Preludes and Fugues*.

(2) in a rondo, a section separating the entries of the

principal theme or section and contrasted with it.
See RONDO

equale (old It.), 'equal'. As a noun, a piece for EQUAL VOICES or for instruments of the same kind, especially trombones, Beethoven wrote three *equali* for four trombones for All Souls' at Linz in 1812.

equal temperament, the tuning of keyboard instruments in such a way that all the semitones are equal. This has the effect of putting all the intervals except the octave slightly out of tune. The advantage of the system, which is universally accepted, is that intervals have the same value in all keys. Any other system of tuning favours some keys at the expense of others and makes modulation difficult outside a restricted range.

Equal temperament, or a near approximation to it, was advocated by theorists as early as the 16th century, and some keyboard compositions of the 17th century seem to demand it, if they are to be tolerable to the ear. But it was not until the 18th century that the development of modulation and the general use of a wider range of keys made it a practical necessity for all keyboard music (and hence for music played or sung with a keyboard instrument). Bach's collection of preludes and fugues in all the major and minor keys entitled *The Well-Tempered Clavier* (part I, 1722) was clearly designed as a practical demonstration of the advantages of equal temperament. J. K. F. Fischer had given a similar demonstration in his *Ariadne musica neo-organoedum* (*c.* 1700). It was a long time, however, before equal temperament was universally adopted. In Britain it was not introduced until *c.* 1845.

See TEMPERAMENT

equal voices, (1) voices of the same range, e.g. three sopranos or three basses.

(2) voices of the same kind, i.e. male voices as opposed to female voices, and *vice versa*.

Erard, Sébastien (1752–1831), founder of a firm of instrument makers. Born in Strasbourg of German origin, he went to Paris in 1768, and worked with a harpsichord manufacturer. He was patronised by the Duchesse de Villeroi, who provided him with a workshop; here he made the first piano conctructed in France (1777). With his brother Jean-Baptiste he established his own business in Paris, and opened a branch in London in 1786. Among the improvements which he introduced into the manufacture of pianos were the double ESCAPEMENT and the CÉLESTE PEDAL. He also perfected the double-action harp, which is still the type in normal use.

R. E. M. HARDING: *The pianoforte: its history traced to the Great Exhibition of 1851* (1933)

Erbach, Christian (*c.* 1570–1635), German organist and composer. From 1602 he held the post of city organist and head of the *Stadtpfeifer* at Augsburg. His principal compositions are motets. He also wrote secular part-songs and keyboard music. A modern edition of the keyboard compositions is in *Denkmäler der Tonkunst in Bayern*, iv (2), and a new five-volume edition of them by C. G. Rayner began to appear in 1971.

Erbe deutscher Musik, Das (Ger., *The Heritage of German Music*), a series of publications of old German music, inaugurated by the National Socialist government in 1935 and designed to replace the earlier DENKMÄLER DEUTSCHER TONKUNST.

Erkel, Ferencz (1810–93), Hungarian opera composer. He became conductor of the National Theatre, Budapest, in 1836, and later director. His operas, in a strongly marked national vein, were enthusiastically received by his compatriots. The most successful was *Hunyady László* (Budapest, 1844), which occupies much the same position in Hungary as Smetana's *The Bartered Bride* does in Czechoslovakia. He also composed the music of the Hungarian national anthem, 'Ysten áldd meg a Magyart' (1845).

Erlebach, Philipp (1657–1714), German composer, *Kapellmeister* to the court of Rudolstadt. His works include vocal cantatas, instrumental suites and sacred and secular songs.

Erlkönig (Ger., *Alder King*), song by Schubert, a setting of Goethe's ballad of the same name. It was one of the first important manifestations of Schubert's genius as a song composer – he was only eighteen when he wrote it in 1815. Goethe, however, appeared not to have been impressed by Schubert's achievement. When the composer sent him a manuscript copy of the song, he did not bother to acknowledge it.

Ernani, opera in four acts by Verdi, to a libretto by Francesco Maria Piave, based on Victor Hugo's drama *Hernani*. This was Verdi's fifth opera and, after its première in Venice in 1844, it was the first of his works to bring him fame outside Italy. The story, set in Aragon, concerns the outlaw Ernani's love for Donna Elvira, who is betrothed to an elderly Spanish grandee. The work is a stirring example of early Verdi, though Hugo considered it a travesty of his play.

Eroica, (It.), the popular abbreviation of the title of Beethoven's third symphony in E flat major, op 55 (1804) – *Sinfonia eroica, composta per festeggiare il sovvenire d'un grand' uomo* (heroic symphony, composed to celebrate the memory of a great man). The title on the original manuscript was *Sinfonia grande Napoleon Bonaparte*, but Beethoven angrily changed it when he heard that Napoleon had taken the title of emperor (*see Beethoven – Impressions of Contemporaries* pages 51–2). The thematic material on which the last movement is built comes from no 7 of Beethoven's twelve *Contretänze* (probably written *c.* 1800):

Beethoven also used this theme and bass (1) in the finale of his ballet *Die Geschöpfe des Prometheus* (The creatures of Prometheus), op 43 (1801);

(2) as the basis of fifteen variations and fugue in E flat major for piano solo, op 35 (1802), sometimes known as the *Eroica variations*, although they were written before the symphony. It is interesting to compare the opening theme of the first movement of Clementi's piano sonata in G minor, op 7, no 3 (1782):

which in the development section becomes:

Erwartung (Ger., *Expectation*) monodrama in one act by Schoenberg, to a libretto by Marie Pappenheim, composed in 1909 but not produced until 1924 (in Prague). It was Schoenberg's first opera, and its story – containing only one character – concerns a woman who is searching for her lover in a dark wood. She stumbles upon his dead body, and sings over it of the other woman who stole him from her. Really a drama of the mind, this work for soprano and large orchestra does not lend itself readily to stage performance; it is therefore heard more often in the concert hall.

Erzlaute (Ger.), archlute.

Es (Ger.), E flat

escapement, mechanism in the piano which enables the hammer to 'escape' after the string has been struck, so leaving the string free to vibrate. The *double escapement*, invented by Sébastien Erard, makes it possible to strike the string a second time without waiting for the key to rise to its normal position of rest.
  See PIANOFORTE

Eschig, a Paris firm of music publishers, founded in 1907 by Maximilian Eschig (1872–1927), who was born in Czechoslovakia.

Eses (Ger.), E double flat (E $\flat\flat$).

España (Sp., *Spain*), rhapsody for orchestra by Chabrier, based on Spanish tunes collected by the composer during a visit to Spain. One of the most striking works of its kind, it was composed in 1883 and first performed in Paris. Waldteufel later created a waltz out of the same material.

espressivo (It.), expressively. The usual abbreviation is *espresso*.

Essercizi (It.), literally, 'exercises', the title under which thirty of Domenico Scarlatti's harpsichord sonatas were published in 1738.

Estampes (Fr., *Engravings*), a set of three piano pieces by Debussy, composed in 1903. They are:
  (1) *Pagodes* (pagodas);
  (2) *Soirée dans Grenade* (evening in Granada);

(3) *Jardins sous la pluie* (gardens in the rain).

estampie, (Fr.; Provençal, *estampida*), a dance form current in the 13th and 14th centuries. It consists of several sections, or *puncta*, each of which has a first ending (OUVERT) and a second ending (CLOS).
  P. AUBRY: *Estampies et danses royales* (1906)

Este, Est, *see* EAST

Esther, oratorio by Handel. It was originally called *Haman and Mordecai*, and performed as a masque, with a libretto attributed to Alexander Pope (after Racine). This performance took place at Canons, near Edgware, about 1720. Later the work was revised and enlarged (with additional words by Samuel Humphreys) and performed as an oratorio in London in 1732. The original advertisement for this performance announced: 'There will be no acting on the Stage, but the house will be fitted up in a decent manner for the audience.'

estinto, (It.), literally 'extinct', i.e. so soft that the music can hardly be heard.

ethnomusicology, the study of the different kinds of music to be found in any particular area, in relation to their cultural or racial context. The term is often applied to the study of music outside the European tradition, e.g. Chinese, Japanese, or Indian music, and early music within that tradition. The term could equally describe a study of the music of Paris, say, which included every form, pop, folk, classical, to be found within that area. Ethnomusicology is a relatively young discipline, and there are many developments in methodology, areas of application, and concepts to come before a comprehensive study of the world's music can be attempted.

Etoile du Nord, L' (Fr., *The Star of the North*), opera in three acts by Meyerbeer, to a libretto by Augustin Eugène Scribe, first performed in Paris in 1854. The work describes the relationship between Tsar Peter and the village girl, Katherine, who becomes his Tsarina. Some of the music was later incorporated by Constant Lambert in his ballet *Les Patineurs*.

Eton Choirbook, a manuscript of polyphonic music compiled about 1500 for the use of the chapel choir of Eton College, which has been preserved, though in an incomplete form, in the library of the College. It originally contained 92 compositions for four to nine voices (comprising 67 antiphons, 24 Magnificats, and a *St. Matthew Passion*) and a setting of the Apostle's Creed by Robert Wylkynson in the form of a thirteen-part round. Among the 25 composers were Browne, Walter Lambe, Davy, Wylkynson, Cornysh, Fayrfax, Turges, Horwud, Baneaster, Dunstable, Hacumplaynt, Hampton, Hygons, Nesbett, and Sturton. Nearly half the leaves were lost, apparently during the 16th century, and there remain 43 complete compositions and 21 in various states of incompleteness. Davy's Passion is among the incomplete pieces. In execution and decoration it is the finest English manuscript of polyphonic music which has survived. A modern edition by F. Ll. Harrison is in *Musica Britannica*, x–xii.

étouffez (Fr.), imperative of *étouffer*, 'to damp'. An indication to the player of a harp, cymbal, etc. that the sound must be immediately damped (the opposite of *laissez vibrer*). So also *sons étouffés*, 'damped notes'.

Etranger, L' (Fr., *The Stranger*), opera in two acts by d'Indy, to a libretto by the composer, first performed in Brussels in 1903.

étude, *see* STUDY

Etudes Symphoniques (Fr., *Symphonic Studies*), title given by Schumann to a set of variations for piano, op 13. It was composed in 1834, first published in 1837, and revised in 1852. The full title is: *Etudes en forme de Variations (XII Etudes symphoniques).* Five additional variations, not included by Schumann in the original publication, are printed in the supplementary volume to his complete works (1893) and in other modern editions. The theme is by an amateur, Baron von Fricken. The dedication is to William Sterndale Bennett, in whose honour Schumann used in the finale a theme borrowed from Marschner's opera *Der Templer und die Jüdin* (where the words are in praise of England).

etwas (Ger.), somewhat, rather.

Eugene Onegin (Rus., *Evgeny Onegin*), opera in three acts by Chaikovsky, op 24. The libretto, by the composer and Konstantin Shilovsky, is based on Pushkin's 'novel in verse' of the same title. A student performance was given in Moscow in 1879, though the professional première did not take place until two years later (at the Bolshoi). *Onegin* was Chaikovsky's fifth opera, and the most masterly of his ten works in the form.

The story concerns Tatyana, a sensitive young girl, who falls in love with Onegin, a cold and selfish man of the world. She declares her passion in a letter, but he will not accept her love. At a ball on her birthday he amuses himself by flirting with her sister Olga and is challenged to a duel by Lensky, who is his friend and in love with Olga. Lensky is killed and Onegin leaves the country. Some years later he returns, to find Tatyana married to the elderly Prince Gremin. He falls in love with her and begs her to go away with him. She admits that she loves him but will not desert her husband. He is left alone despairing.

Eulenburg, firm of music publishers, founded in Leipzig by Ernst Eulenburg (1847–1926) in 1874. In 1892 they took over the series of miniature scores of chamber music published by Albert Payne (also a Leipzig publisher), and by adding orchestral works, oratorios, operas, etc., greatly extended its usefulness. The firm is now owned by Schott.

eunuch flute, *see* MIRLITON

euphonium, a brass instrument of the saxhorn type, generally with four valves and a compass from

 to

It is a normal instrument in the military band and the brass band, but in the orchestra is used only occasionally, generally for the performance of parts marked 'tenor tuba', e.g. in Strauss's *Don Quixote* and Holst's *The Planets.*

See TUBA

eurhythmics, a system of rhythmic education through bodily movement, invented by JAQUES-DALCROZE, who founded an institute for this purpose in Germany in 1910.

Euridice, L' (It., *Eurydice*), (1) opera by Caccini, with libretto by Ottavio Rinuccini. It was published in

1600, before Peri's opera, although it did not receive its first performance until December 5th, 1602, in Florence. A modern edition is in R. Eitner's *Publikationen älterer praktischer und theoretischer Musikwerke,* x. An English translation of the dedication to Giovanni Bardi is in O. Strunk, *Source Readings in Music History* (1952), pages 370–2;

(2) opera by Peri, with the same libretto as used by Caccini. It was first performed in Florence on October 6th, 1600, and published in the same year (facsimile editions, 1934 and 1973). A modern edition by C. Perinello appeared in 1919. An English translation of the foreword is in Strunk, *op. cit.,* pages 373–6.

Euryanthe, opera in three acts by Weber, to a libretto by Helmine von Chézy, first performed in Vienna in 1823. Euryanthe, the heroine of the story, is loved by her husband Adolar and also by Lysiart. The treacherous Eglantine betrays to Lysiart a secret of Euryanthe's. Lysiart uses his knowledge of this secret to claim that Euryanthe has been faithless to Adolar. Euryanthe is taken away to the desert by Adolar to be killed, but he spares her life. The king, meeting Euryanthe, discovers Eglantine's treachery. Adolar, confronting the wedding procession of Lysiart and Eglantine, denounces them both. Eglantine, hearing that Euryanthe is reported dead, declares her passion for Adolar and is stabbed by Lysiart. Lysiart is led away to justice, and Adolar is united to Euryanthe. Though saddled with an intractable plot, *Euryanthe* contains some of Weber's most magnificent music. Various attempts have been made to create a theatrically viable version of the score, but the work remains the delight and despair of all who have recognised its musical potential.

Evans, Sir Geraint (born 1922), Welsh baritone who studied in Hamburg with Theo Hermann and Geneva with Fernando Carpi. He made his Covent Garden début in 1948 as the Nightwatchman in *The Mastersingers,* and has sung with that company ever since. Among his most famous roles are Falstaff in Verdi's opera of that title, Figaro in *The Marriage of Figaro,* Leporello in *Don Giovanni* and Wozzeck in Berg's opera of the same name. He has appeared frequently at the Salzburg Festival and the Vienna Opera, and also sings regularly in the United States.

Evans, Gil (born 1912), Canadian jazz arranger and band leader, famous for his work with the trumpeter Miles Davis. His arrangements (often employing instruments such as French horns and tubas, not usually associated with jazz) have a richness surpassed only perhaps by Duke Ellington, whose natural successor Evans is often reckoned to be. His qualities are heard at their best in his recording, with Miles Davis, of a suite of numbers from Gershwin's *Porgy and Bess.*

Ewer, London firm of music-publishers, founded in the early 19th century by John Ewer. In 1867 the business was acquired by NOVELLO, who published under the name of Novello, Ewer & Co., from 1867 until 1888.

Expert, Henri (1863–1952), French musicologist. He studied and later taught at the Ecole Niedermeyer, Paris, and was librarian of the Paris Conservatoire from 1920 until 1933. His principal achievement was the publication of two series of old French music: *Les Maîtres musiciens de la Renaissance française,* 23 volumes (1894–1908); and *Monuments de la musique au temps de la Renaissance*, ten volumes (1924–9). His other publications include *Le Psautier huguenot du XVI*ᵉ *siècle* and *Les Maîtres du clavecin des XVII et XVIII*ᵉ *siècles*.

exposition, the initial statement of the musical material on which a movement is based:

(1) in a FUGUE it consists in introducing the subject to each part (or 'voice') in turn, i.e. if the fugue is in three parts, the exposition is complete when all three parts have announced the subject for the first time;

(2) in a movement in sonata form it is more extended and traditionally consists of the presentation of the principal thematic material partly in the tonic key and partly in a subsidiary key or keys. Thereafter the material undergoes DEVELOPMENT, and then in a recapitulation it is generally restated in the tonic key.

It is a convention in classical works in SONATA FORM that the exposition should be repeated. The practice continued far into the 19th century, and can be found in many of Brahms's and Dvořák's works in this form. In such cases there is very often a 'first ending' which leads back to the beginning, and a 'second ending' which leads into the development. The omission of such repeats in modern performance is to be condemned on the ground that it violates the composer's expressed intentions, and often seriously damages the structure and argument of the music.

expression marks, indications provided by the composer as an aid to the accurate interpretation of his text. They are concerned primarily with (1) DYNAMICS – e.g. *forte* (loud), (2) TEMPO – e.g. *lento* (slow), (3) mood – e.g. *appassionato* (passionate). The vogue of Italian music in the 17th century meant that Italian terms came to be used by composers in other countries – for instance, Britain. The practice was not universal: many French composers preferred to use their own language. But the obvious convenience of having an international language led to the general adoption of Italian for this purpose; and even those composers who have preferred their own language for marks of tempo and mood have been content to use the Italian dynamic signs, either in full or in their commonly accepted abbreviations. The use of German, French and English for marks of tempo and mood makes things easier for composers and interpreters to whom these languages are native; but it complicates the task of performers who lack this natural advantage. On the other hand composers who use Italian sometimes produce curious results, either through misspelling unfamiliar words or through failing to understand exactly what they mean.

R. E. M. HARDING: *Origins of Musical Time and Expression* (1938)

extension organ, sometimes called the unit organ, an organ in which the pipes are constructed to give more than one note each. The number of pipes is reduced, resulting in a saving of space.

f, in TONIC SOL-FA f = *fah*, the fourth note (or subdominant) of the major scale.

F, the fourth note (or subdominant) of the scale of C major. As an abbreviation F. = Fellow; *f* = *forte* (loud), *ff* = *fortissimo* (very loud); *fp* = *forte piano* (loud and immediately soft again), *fz* = *forzando* (literally 'forcing', i.e. accenting), *mf* = *mezzo forte* (moderately loud), *pf* = *poco forte* (moderately loud), *sf* or *sfz* = *sforzando* (the same as *forzando*).

The F clef originated as an ornamental form of the letter F and indicates the note a fifth below middle C:

fa (Fr., It.), the note F; also the fourth note of the Guidonian hexachord (*see* SOLMIZATION).

Fabri, Annibale Pio (1697–1760), Italian tenor, a pupil of Pistocchi. He was several times president of the Academia Filarmonica, Bologna. He came to Britain in 1729, and sang in several of Handel's operas with great success. Mrs. Pendarves (later Mrs. Delany) wrote of him:

> Fabri has a tenor voice, sweet, clear and firm, but not strong enough, I doubt, for the stage. He sings like a gentleman, without making faces, and his manner is particularly agreeable. He is the greatest master of music that ever sang upon the stage.

He was subsequently appointed to the Chapel Royal at Lisbon, where he died.

faburden, English term for a 15th century technique of improvising two parts on a plainsong. Using the SIGHT method the 'faburdener' sang a third below the plainsong melody, except for certain isolated notes at the fifth below including the first note and final notes at cadences. The treble part doubled the plainsong throughout at the fourth above. Some 16th century English CANTUS FIRMUS compositions are built on faburden parts in preference to the original chant. For example, the *cantus firmus* of John Redford's *O lux on the faburden* (*Musica Britannica*, i, no 28) is a melody alternating a third and a fifth below the Sarum hymn 'O lux beata Trinitas'. The origin of the term and its relationship with Continental FAUXBOURDON is disputed.

F. LL. HARRISON: 'Faburden in Practice', *Musica Disciplina*, xvi (1962)

B. TROWELL: 'Faburden and Fauxbourdon', *Musica Disciplina*, xiii (1959)

Façade, a series of poems by Edith Sitwell, recited to the accompaniment of music for flute, clarinet, saxophone, trumpet, cello and percussion by Walton. First performed in London in 1923, the music was revised in 1926 and some of the pieces (which were originally designed to match the rhythm of the verse) were issued as a suite for full orchestra. A second suite was published in 1938.

Faccio, Franco (1840–1891), Italian composer and conductor. He was a close friend of Boito, who wrote the libretto of his opera *Amleto* (Genoa, 1865), and he was partly responsible for the collaboration of Boito and Verdi in *Otello*. He became conductor at La Scala, Milan, and directed there the first performance in Europe of Verdi's *Aida* (1872) and the first performance of *Otello* (1887).

fado (Port.), type of café song or street song which has flourished in Portugal. Also known as *fadhino*, it originated in Lisbon and usually incorporates dancing as well as singing, with guitar accompaniment.

Fagott (Ger.), **fagotto** (It.), bassoon.

fah, anglicized form of the Italian *fa* (F). In TONIC SOL-FA it is the fourth note (or subdominant) of the major scale.

Fairfax, *see* FAYRFAX

Fair Maid of Perth, The (Fr., *La Jolie Fille de Perth*), opera in four acts by Bizet, to a libretto by Jules Henri Vernoy de Saint-Georges and Jules Adenis (based – remotely – on Scott's novel). The first performance was in Paris in 1867.

Fair Maid of the Mill, The, *see* SCHÖNE MÜLLERIN

Fair Melusina, The, *see* SCHÖNE MELUSINE

Fairy Queen, The, operatic masque with dialogue, adapted from Shakespeare's *A Midsummer Night's Dream*, with music by Purcell. It was first performed in London in 1692, but the score was lost in 1700. At the time a reward of twenty guineas was offered for its recovery, but it was not until 1901 that the music came to light in the library of the Royal Academy of Music. A modern edition by J. S. Shedlock, revised by Anthony Lewis, was published in 1958 (*Purcell Society*, xii).

fa-la, name given to a popular type of part-song current in the late 16th and early 17th centuries, known also in Italy as *balletto* and in England as BALLETT. The name is derived from the use of a refrain composed of the syllables 'fa la la'.

Falcon, Marie Cornélie (1812–97), French operatic soprano. She first appeared at the Paris Opéra as Alice in *Robert le Diable*, 1832. Six years later she lost her voice and had to abandon the stage. During her short career she sang leading parts in the first performances of several operas – including Halévy's *La Juive* and Meyerbeer's *Les Huguenots* – and had a great reputation as a singer and actress. Her name became so closely associated with dramatic soprano roles that the term '*falcon*' survives to this day to describe her type of voice.

Falla, Manuel de (1876–1946), Spanish composer and pianist (whose surname should be referred to as Falla, not de Falla). A pupil of Pedrell and Tragó, he made his reputation with the opera *La vida breve*, which was awarded a prize in 1905 but was not performed until 1913 at Nice. From 1907 until 1914 he lived in Paris and then in Spain until the Civil War, when he moved to South America. He died in Argentina.

Falla was the outstanding Spanish composer of his time, skilful in the adoption of Andalusian idioms without becoming their slave. His acquaintance with Debussy in Paris inclined him towards impressionism, but in his later works he turned rather towards a neo-classical idiom, which avoids equally impressionism and the more obvious nationalism of his youth. Severely self-critical, he published comparatively little. His orchestration is vivid and precise. His principal works are:

(1) Operas: *La vida breve* (*Life is Short*, 1905); *El retablo de Maese Pedro* (*Master Peter's Puppet Show*, 1923); *La Atlántida* (completed after his death by E. Halffter);

(2) Ballets: *El amor brujo* (*Love, the Magician*, 1915); *El sombrero de tres picos* (*The Three-cornered Hat*, 1919);

(3) Orchestra: *Noches en los jardines de Espagna* (*Nights in the Gardens of Spain*, 1916) for piano and orchestra; harpsichord concerto (1926);

(4) Piano: *Fantasia bética* (1919).

J. B. TREND: *Manuel de Falla and Spanish Music* (1930)

falsa musica, *see* MUSICA FALSA

false relation, the name given in classical harmony (i.e. late 18th and early 19th century) to (1) a progression in which a note in one part in the first chord is followed by a chromatic alteration of the same note in another part in the second chord, e.g.:

In the above example, the note B flat in the bass of the first chord becomes B natural in the soprano of the second.

(2) the simultaneous sounding in a single chord of a note and its chromatic alteration, e.g.:

'False relations' of both kinds are frequent in late 16th and early 17th century music, particularly in England, e.g.:

BYRD, *Songs of Sundrie Natures no 27*

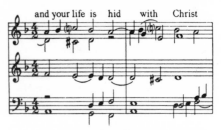

GIBBONS, *Tudor Church Music, iv, page 217*

In harmonic practice, false relations have always offended the pedantic mind. Nevertheless, they can be put to effective use. In the United States the standard (and perhaps more appropriate) term for false relation is 'cross relation'.

falsetto (It.), an adult male voice, used not in the normal range but in a higher register, in such a way that only the edges, as opposed to the whole mass, of the vocal cords vibrate. If this type of singing is seriously cultivated, the voice becomes a male alto (or counter-tenor). Falsetto singing is used occasionally by tenors for notes which lie above their normal range, and sometimes also for comic effect. A good falsetto singer can command a compass up to:

falso bordone, *see* FAUXBOURDON

Falstaff, (1) comic opera in three acts by Verdi, to a libretto by Arrigo Boito (after Shakespeare's *The Merry Wives of Windsor* and *Henry IV* (part 1)). It was first performed in Milan in 1893, with Victor Maurel in the title role. The action of the opera is substantially the same as the play, except that Anne Page, in love with Fenton, becomes Anne (Nannetta) Ford, and some minor characters, such as Shallow and Slender, are eliminated. This was Verdi's last opera, written in his eightieth year, and his only comedy since *Un Giorno di Regno*, 44 years earlier.

(2) symphonic study for orchestra by Elgar, op 68 (after Shakespeare's *Henry IV* and *Henry V*), first performed in Leeds in 1913.

Fanciulla del West, La, *see* GIRL OF THE GOLDEN WEST

fancy, the name given in England in the late 16th and early 17th centuries to the FANTASIA for strings or keyboard instruments.

E. H. MEYER: *English Chamber Music* (1946)

fandango (Sp.), a lively dance in triple time, accompanied by guitar and castanets. In symphonic music, an example of the use of a fandango can be found in Rimsky-Korsakov's *Capriccio Espagnol*.

fanfare, a flourish for trumpets, or for other instruments emulating the character of trumpets. Fanfares are often used as ceremonial preludes, and are sometimes incorporated in extended compositions, e.g. in Act 2 of Beethoven's *Fidelio*. The term, in its French form, also refers to a brass band.

fantasia (It.; Fr., *fantaisie*; Ger., *Phantasie, Fantasie*), in general a piece in which the composer exercises his imagination without following any conventional form. In particular:

(1) in the 16th and 17th centuries, the name was frequently used for a composition, either for strings or for a keyboard instrument (the English term was 'fancy'), in which the composer, instead of adopting a dance form or writing variations, lets his imagination play freely in developing his theme contrapuntally. Morley says in his *Plaine and Easie Introduction to Practicall Musicke* (1597): 'In this may more art be showne then in any other musicke, because the composer is tide to nothing but that he may adde, deminish, and alter at his pleasure' (page 181);

(2) a work for keyboard or lute of an improvisatory character, e.g. Bach's *Chromatic Fantasia*;

(3) an extended work, freer in form than the normal sonata, e.g. Beethoven's *Sonata quasi una Fantasia* in C sharp minor, op 27, no 2;

(4) a short piece similar to an intermezzo, capriccio, etc.

(5) a work based on an existing theme or themes, e.g. Liszt's *Fantaisie sur les motifs favoris de l'opéra 'La Sonnambula'*, or Vaughan Williams's *Fantasia on a theme by Thomas Tallis*;

(6) the development section of a movement in sonata form is sometimes known as 'free fantasia'.

Fantasiestück (Ger.), = FANTASIA (4).

Fantastic Symphony, *see* SYMPHONIE FANTASTIQUE

Faramondo, opera in three acts by Handel, to a libretto by Apostolo Zeno (with alterations), first performed in London in 1738.

farandole (Fr.), a dance of ancient origin still current in Provence. The dancers – men and women – advance in a long chain, preceded by a player (or players) on the *galoubet* and *tambourin* (pipe and tabor). There is a well-known example in Bizet's music to Daudet's play *L'Arlésienne*, beginning:

The original title is *Danse dei chivau-frus* (Dance of the cardboard horses). Though very famous, this example of a farandole is not wholly typical – it is in 2/4 time, whereas most farandoles are in 6/8.

farce (Eng., Fr.; from Lat. *farcire*, to stuff), (1) originally the practice of interpolating TROPES into plainsong or polyphonic settings of the liturgy, so that one can speak of, e.g., a 'farced *Kyrie*';

(2) in 18th century opera, a comic scene introduced into a serious work; about 1800, Italian comic operas in one act were called *farsa*.

Farewell Sonata, *see* LEBEWOHL

Farewell Symphony (Ger., *Abschiedssymphonie*), symphony no 45 in F sharp minor by Haydn (1772). The finale emphasises the desire of Prince Esterházy's musicians to obtain leave of absence in order to visit their families. The instruments stopped playing in turn, and the players put out their candles and left the room. At the end only two violins were left. When the work is played today, the niceties of the original performance are still frequently observed.

Farina, Carlo, Mantuan violinist and composer, who flourished in the early 17th century. He was for a time in the service of the Dresden court, and later had an appointment at Danzig. He was one of the first composers to exploit virtuosity in solo violin music. His 'Capriccio stravagante' (1627) includes not only double stops but also *pizzicato, col legno* and harmonics. The following is an extract:

Farinel, Michel (born 1649), French violinist and composer. He was one of the earliest of the many composers who wrote chaconnes or variations on the theme known as FOLIES D'ESPAGNE, which for that reason was known in England as 'Farinel's Ground'.

Farinelli (real name **Carlo Broschi** – 'Farinelli' was his stage name) (1705–82), famous Italian castrato singer, born in Naples. A pupil of Porpora, he rapidly acquired a reputation in Southern Italy and made his first appearance in Rome, with enormous success, in his master's opera *Eumene* (1721). Subsequently he had some instruction from Bernacchi and appeared in a number of European cities, including London. Visiting Spain in 1737 he was engaged to sing to Philip V and remained there under Philip and his successor, Ferdinand VI, until the accession of Charles III in 1759, when he returned to Italy and settled in Bologna. He told Burney that for ten years he sang the same four songs every night to Philip V (*see* C. Burney, *The Present State of Music in France and Italy*, published in 1771, pages 205–17), thus curing Philip's melancholia and at the same time earning himself 50,000 francs a year.

Farmer, John, late 16th and early 17th century English composer, who published a set of canons on a plainsong (1591) and a set of madrigals (1599; modern edition in *The English Madrigal School*, viii), of which

'Fair Phyllis I saw sitting all alone' is well-known. He also contributed to Thomas East's *Whole Booke of Psalmes* (1592).

Farnaby, Giles (c. 1566–1640), English composer. He published an original set of canzonets for four voices (1598; modern edition in *The English Madrigal School*, xx). His keyboard pieces, which show an equally individual imagination, especially in the smaller forms of which he was a master, have been edited by R. Marlow in *Musica Britannica*, xxiv.

His son Richard (born c. 1594), composed keyboard pieces, only four of which have survived. They are printed with those of his father in *Musica Britannica*, xxiv.

Farrant, Richard (died 1581), English composer, principally of church music. He was master of the choristers at St. George's, Windsor, and a gentleman of the Chapel Royal. His anthems 'Call to remembrance' and 'Hide not thou thy face' are still sung.

Fasch, Johann Friedrich (1688–1758), German organist and composer. He studied at St. Thomas's School, Leipzig, and became *Kapellmeister* to the court at Zerbst in 1722. His numerous compositions include church cantatas, Masses, overtures (suites), concertos and chamber music.

His son, **Karl Friedrich Christian Fasch** (1736–1800), was a harpsichordist and composer. His first important appointment was as accompanist to Frederick the Great at Potsdam in 1756 (in conjunction with C. P. E. Bach), but the outbreak of the Seven Years' War (1756–63) soon brought his duties to an end. He was *Kapellmeister* of the Royal Opera (1774–6) but for the most part maintained himself by teaching.

Faschingsschwank aus Wien (Ger., *Carnival Jest from Vienna*), a set of five piano pieces by Schumann, op 26 (1839). The title *Faschingsschwank* seems to have been originally designed for the set of pieces published as CARNIVAL, op 9, possibly because it includes the letters A S C H on which the latter work is based.

fasola, a form of SOLMIZATION, used in Britain and colonial America during the 17th and early 18th centuries, before the development of tonic sol-fa. The system employed only four syllables, *fa, sol, la, mi*, with repetitions of three of these syllables to fill out the rest of the scale.

Fastes de la Grande et Ancienne Ménestrandise, Les (Fr., *Annals of the Great and Ancient Order of Minstrelsy*), satirical suite for harpsichord published by François Couperin (le grand) in the second volume of his *Pièces de clavecin* (1717). In the original the vowels in the last word are replaced by crosses: *mxnxstrxndxsx*. The suite refers to a dispute between the organists of Paris and the corporation of minstrels (*Confrérie de Saint-Julien des Ménestriers*), which was settled in 1707. The titles of the pieces are:

1er Acte: *Les notables et jurés mxnxstrxndxurs* (The notable and sworn members of the corporation of minstrels) – *Marche*.

2e Acte: *Les viéleux et les gueux* (The hurdy-gurdy players and the beggars).

3e Acte: *Les jongleurs, sauteurs et saltimbanques, avec les ours et les singes* (The jugglers, tumblers and mountebanks, with the bears and monkeys).

4e Acte: *Les invalides, ou gens estropiés au service de la grande mxnxstrxndxsx* (The invalids, or people

crippled in the service of the great minstrelsy).

5e Acte: *Désorde et déroute de toute la troupe, causés par les yvrognes, les singes et les ours* (Disorder and rout of the whole company, caused by the drunkards, monkeys and bears).

Fauré, Gabriel Urbain (1845–1924), French composer, organist and teacher, the son of a schoolmaster. Born in Pamiers, he studied at the Ecole Niedermeyer, where he was a pupil of Saint-Saëns. After holding various organist's posts he became *maître de chapelle* at the Madeleine in Paris in 1877, and organist in 1896. In the same year he was appointed teacher of composition at the Paris Conservatoire; from 1905 until 1920 he was its director. The last twenty years of his life were marred by deafness, which became so acute in the end that he was unable to hear his own music.

As a composer he was one of the most original minds of his time. He began as a romantic, but the idioms of Schumann and Mendelssohn were clarified and refined in his hands till they took on an aspect that was typically French. His harmony, though never revolutionary, is constantly surprising, because of his gift for associating familiar materials in a new way. In this respect he showed an extraordinarily sensitive ear. In his later years, he continued the refining process. His zest for experiment remained and one still has the impression that every note was exactly weighed and calculated.

His operas, in spite of Wagnerian overtones, have their own distinctive personality – a pity they are so neglected today. He excelled in writing songs, many of which exhibit a magical economy of means. He was less at home with the orchestra, and a good deal of his orchestral music was scored by others. As a teacher he had a great influence on younger men. Among his pupils were Florent Schmitt, Louis Aubert, Nadia Boulanger, Georges Enesco, Roger-Ducasse, Gabriel Grovlez, Charles Koechlin and Maurice Ravel. His principal compositions are:

(1) Operas: *Prométhée* (1900); *Pénélope* (1913);

(2) Incidental music: *Shylock* (1889); *Pelléas et Mélisande* (1898);

(3) Orchestra: *Pavane* (1887); *Dolly*, suite (1893–6); *Masques et bergamasques*, suite (1920); *Ballade*, piano and orchestra (1881); *Fantaisie*, piano and orchestra (1919);

(4) Chamber music: two piano quartets (1879, 1886); two piano quintets (1906, 1921); piano trio (1923); string quartet (1924); two violin sonatas (1876, 1917); two cello sonatas (1918, 1922).

(5) Piano: five impromptus; thirteen nocturnes; thirteen barcarolles; nine preludes;

(6) Church music: Requiem Mass (1887);

(7) Songs: three song-cycles – *La Bonne Chanson* (1891–2), *La Chanson d'Eve* (1907–10), *Le Jardin clos* (1915–18); *Mirages* (four songs, 1919); *L'Horizon chimérique* (four songs, 1922); numerous single songs.

P. FAURÉ-FREMIET: *Gabriel Fauré* (1929)

V. JANKÉLÉVITCH: *Gabriel Fauré et ses melodies* (1938)

C. KOECHLIN: *Fauré* (1927)

N. SUCKLING: *Fauré* (1946)

M. COOPER: *French Music from the death of Berlioz to the death of Fauré* (1951)

Faust, opera in five acts by Gounod, to a libretto by Jules Barbier and Michel Carré (after Goethe). It was first performed in Paris in 1859. Originally an *opéra-comique* with dialogue, the recitatives were added in 1860. Faust, an elderly scholar, wins from Mephistopheles the gift of youth, in exchange for his own soul. He falls in love with Marguerite, but having ruined her deserts her. Her brother Valentine, returning from the wars, fights a duel with Faust and is killed. Marguerite, having killed her baby, is condemned to death. She refuses to escape with Faust. As she dies, the voices of an angelic choir are heard, while Mephistopheles claims from Faust the promised payment of his soul.

Though one of the most popular operas ever written, Gounod's *Faust*, with its sentiment and sanctimony, can hardly be said to achieve the grandeur of the original. Other works inspired by Goethe's drama include Berlioz's *The Damnation of Faust*, Schumann's *Scenes from Faust*, Liszt's *Faust Symphony*, Mahler's eighth symphony, Wagner's *Faust Overture*, and Pousseur's opera, *Votre Faust*. Spohr's opera, *Faust*, pre-dated Part 2 of Goethe's play, and was based on the Faust legend, as was Busoni's *Doktor Faust*. Hervé's operetta *Le Petit Faust* was a parody both of Goethe's drama and of Gounod's opera.

Faust Overture, A (Ger., *Eine Faust-Ouvertüre*), orchestral piece by Wagner, based on Goethe (1840). It was not intended as the overture to an opera.

Faust Symphony, A (Ger., *Eine Faust-Symphonie*), orchestral work by Liszt with chorus in the final movement (based on Goethe). It was first performed at Weimar in 1857. The score is dedicated to Berlioz. The three movements are portraits of Faust, Gretchen, and Mephistopheles, in that order. Liszt also composed two orchestral 'Episodes' from Lenau's *Faust*, the second of which is more familiarly known as the *Mephisto Waltz* no 1.

Fauvel, *see* ROMAN DE FAUVEL

fauxbourdon (Fr.; It., *falso bordone*), literally 'false bass' (*faux bourdon*). A term used in the following senses:

(1) in the 15th century to indicate a simple form of three-part harmony in which a plainsong melody in the treble is accompanied by two lower parts, one moving mainly in parallel sixths, the other, to be supplied by the singer, a fourth below the melody, e.g.:

DUFAY (in H. BESSELER, *Bourdon und Fauxbourdon*, page 264)

The name presumably refers to the fact that the bass is not the foundation of the harmony, since the plainsong is assigned to the treble. The aural impression of this kind of harmony is similar to that of English improvised FABURDEN where the plainsong is in the middle part, but it is far from certain whether Continental *fauxbourdon* originated from the English practice or *vice versa*, or whether the two techniques evolved independently;

(2) through the use of this kind of harmony for psalm tones the Italian name *falso bordone* came to be applied to a simple four-part harmonization of plainsong, without any polyphonic elaboration:

PALESTRINA, *Complete Works*, volume xxxi, page 169

(3) in modern English hymnody the name *fauxbourdon* is often given to a counterpoint (or descant) for treble voices superimposed on the melody sung by the congregation.

H. BESSELER: *Bourdon und Fauxbourdon* (1950)

A. BESSER SCOTT: 'The Beginnings of Faux-bourdon: a New Interpretation', *Journal of the American Musicological Society*, xxiv (1971)

S. CLERCX: 'Aux Origines du Faux-Bourdon', *Revue de Musicologie*, xl (1957)

B. TROWELL: 'Faburden and Fauxbourdon', *Musica Disciplina*, xiii (1959)

Favart, Charles Simon (1710–1792), French librettist. He was a pioneer of the French *opéra-comique*, who wrote the librettos for a large number of pieces of this kind. Among the composers for whom he worked were Gluck and Grétry. He was director of the Opéra-Comique in Paris from 1758 until 1769.

Favorite, La (Fr., *The Favourite*), opera in four acts by Donizetti (originally in three acts and called *L'Ange de Niside*), to a libretto by Alphonse Royer, Gustave Vaëz and Augustin Eugène Scribe, first performed in Paris in 1840. The story tells how a novice in a 14th century Spanish monastery falls in love with the mistress of the king of Castile. Since *La Favorite* is a French opera, it should not be called *La Favorita* unless it is being performed in Italian translation.

Fayrfax, Robert (1464–1521), English composer. He was organist of St. Albans Abbey, and a gentleman of the Chapel Royal. He was awarded the D.Mus. degree at Cambridge in 1502, and at Oxford (by incorporation) in 1511. He had a great reputation in his lifetime. His music includes Masses, a Magnificat, and motets, which show considerable dignity and feeling for sonority. He also wrote secular songs. His complete works have been edited in three volumes by E. B. Warren (1959–66).

Fedra (It., *Phaedra*), opera in three acts by Pizzetti, to a libretto by Gabriele d'Annunzio (published as a play in 1909), first performed at La Scala, Milan, in 1915.

Feen, Die (Ger., *The Fairies*), opera in three acts by Wagner, to a libretto by the composer after Gozzi's comedy *La Donna Serpente*. First performed at Munich in 1888 – 54 years after it was written – this was Wagner's earliest completed opera. The story concerns a prince who falls in love with a fairy, and himself becomes king of Fairyland. Today the piece has no more than curiosity value.

feierlich (Ger.), solemn, exalted.

Feldman, Morton (born 1926), U.S. composer, pupil of Stefan Wolpe and Wallingford Riegger. A disciple of John Cage, he was one of the first U.S. composers to introduce elements of chance into his music, as in his *Projections* and *Projections 2* for flute, trumpet, violin and cello (1951). His other works include *Durations I-V*, *Extensions I-V*, *Vertical Thoughts I-V*, a ballet (*Ixion*) and *The Swallows of Salangan* for chorus and an orchestra of 76 instruments.

Feldmusik (Ger.), literally field music. An old German term for music performed in the open air by wind instruments. A *Feldpartie* or *Feldpartita* was thus a suite of pieces for open-air performance. Haydn wrote several works of this nature.

Fellerer, Karl Gustav (born 1902), German musicologist who has written extensively on Catholic church music. He has held academic appointments in Münster, Freiburg and Cologne. In addition to works in his special field he has also written studies of Puccini and Grieg.

Fellowes, Edmund Horace (1870–1951), English musicologist, educated at Winchester and Oxford. His publications of English music of the past include *The English Madrigal School* (36 volumes), *The English School of Lutenist Songwriters* (1st series, fifteen volumes; 2nd series, sixteen volumes), the complete vocal and instrumental works of Byrd, and a number of compositions published in *Tudor Church Music*. His books include *English Madrigal Verse* (1920), *The English Madrigal Composers* (1921), *William Byrd* (1936), *English Cathedral Music* (1941), *Orlando Gibbons* (revised edition, 1951).

feminine cadence, feminine ending, a cadence, or ending, in which the final chord is reached on a weak beat of the bar instead of the more usual strong beat.

Fenby, Eric (born 1906), English composer and writer, who from 1928 until 1934 acted as amanuensis to the blind and paralysed Delius at Grez-sur-Loing, helping him to complete his last works, including *A Song of Summer* for orchestra, *Songs of Farewell* for chorus and orchestra, and the third violin sonata. He also arranged some of Delius's music (e.g. the *Aquarelles* for strings) and wrote *Delius as I Knew Him* (1936, revised 1966), describing his experiences in the Delius household and his work as amanuensis. His own compositions include a parody overture, *Rossini on Ilkla Moor*.

Fennimore and Gerda, opera in two episodes by Delius, to a libretto (originally in German) by the composer (after Jens Peter Jacobsen's novel *Niels Lyhne*, published in English as *Siren Voices*). The first performance took place at Frankfurt in 1919, though the work had been completed nine years earlier. The story concerns a poet (Niels) and a painter (Erik) who both love the same girl (Fennimore). The poet marries her, but later loses her to the artist; when the artist dies, the poet finds happiness, not with his ex-wife but with a childhood sweetheart (Gerda).

Feo, Francesco (1691–1761), Italian composer of the so-called Neapolitan school. In addition to many operas he wrote a considerable amount of church music. For a time he was director of one of the Naples *Conservatori*.

Ferguson, Howard (born 1908), Northern Irish composer and teacher, who studied at the Royal College of Music in London under R. O. Morris and later settled in that city. His works include a ballet, *Chaunteclear*, a partita and four *Diversions on Ulster Airs* for orchestra, a concerto for piano and strings, an octet and other chamber music, piano pieces and songs.

fermata (It.), pause, represented by the sign ⌒.

Fernandez, Oscar Lorenz (1897–1948), Brazilian composer and teacher. His works in nationalistic tradition, include an opera (*Malazarte*), a symphonic suite on popular themes, a *Trio brasileiro* and numerous piano pieces.

Ferrabosco, Alfonso (1543–88), Italian composer, who came to England at an early age and entered the service of Queen Elizabeth. There is some evidence that he was employed by Elizabeth as a secret service agent. He left England in 1578 and received an appointment from the Duke of Savoy, leaving his two children in England. He published two volumes of Italian madrigals (1587), several of which appeared with English versions in the two volumes of *Musica Transalpina* (1588, 1597); a modern edition of them is in *Old English Edition*, volumes xi and xii. He also wrote motets and a few pieces for viols which remain mostly in manuscript, although in their time they were an important influence on William Byrd.

His son (probably illegitimate), also called **Alfonso Ferrabosco** (c. 1575–1628), was an English composer and viol-player. He was in the service of James I and Charles I, and was music-master to Henry, Prince of Wales, and his brother Charles (later Charles I). His compositions include a book of lute songs (modern edition in *The English School* of *Lutenist Songwriters*) and music for viols (examples in *Musica Britannica*, ix). He also wrote music for several of Ben Jonson's masques.

> G. E. P. ARKWRIGHT: 'Notes on the Ferrabosco Family', *Musical Antiquary*, iii (July, 1912) and iv (October, 1912)
>
> G. LIVI: 'The Ferrabosco Family', *Musical Antiquary*, iv (April, 1913)

Ferrari, Benedetto (1597–1681), Italian poet and composer. His librettos include *L'Andromeda*, set by Francesco Manelli (Venice, 1637) – the first opera to be given in a public theatre. The music of the operas for which he wrote the music is lost. Among his surviving works are an oratorio *Sansone* (see A. Schering, *Geschichte des Oratoriums*, page 104) and three books of solo cantatas.

Ferrier, Kathleen (1912–53), English contralto, the

most famous of her generation. Born in Lancashire, she studied originally as a pianist and did not have lessons in singing until 1940. She rapidly acquired a reputation as one of the finest singers of her time, and confirmed it by her tours on the Continent and in Canada and the United States after World War II. She appeared as Lucretia in Britten's *The Rape of Lucretia* (which, amongst other Britten works, was written for her) and as Orpheus in Gluck's *Orfeo* (Glyndebourne, 1947; Covent Garden, 1953) but her principal activity was in the concert hall, where she was a renowned exponent of Brahms and Mahler. Bruno Walter accompanied her in recitals. She was awarded the C.B.E. in 1953, shortly before she died of cancer.

Ferroud, Pierre Octave (1900–36), French composer and critic, pupil of Florent Schmitt. His works include an opera (*Chirurgie*, after Chekhov), ballets (*Jeunesse* and *Le Porcher*), a symphony and other orchestral pieces, chamber music and songs. He was killed in a car accident.

Fervaal, opera with a prologue and three acts by d'Indy, to a libretto by the composer, first performed in Brussels in 1897.

Fes (Ger.), F flat.

Fesch, De, *see* DEFESCH

Festa, Costanzo (after 1490–1545), Italian composer, a member of the Papal choir in 1517. He composed Masses, motets and hymns (modern editions in *Monumenta Polyphonica Italica*, ii and iii) and madrigals. His madrigal 'Quando ritrovo la mia pastorella' is well known to English choral societies as 'Down in a flowery vale'. His Masses and Magnificats have been edited by Alexander Main in the first two volumes of a projected complete edition of his works to be continued by A. Seay (1962 onwards).

Fêtes, the second of Debussy's three *Nocturnes* for orchestra. The pieces were first performed as a set in 1901.

Fétis, François Joseph (1784–1871), Belgian teacher, musicologist and composer. He studied at the Paris Conservatoire, where he taught counterpoint and fugue (1821) and became librarian (1827). In 1833 he was appointed director of the Brussels Conservatoire. He founded and edited the *Revue Musicale* (1827–33) and organised historical concerts in Paris. In addition to a large number of theoretical works he published a *Biographie universelle des musiciens*, eight volumes (1835–44) and a *Histoire générale de la musique*, five volumes (1869–76).

Feuermann, Emanuel (1902–42), Austrian cellist, a pupil of Klengel. He made his reputation as a soloist at an early age. He taught the cello at the Cologne Conservatorium (1919–23) and the Berlin Hochschule für Musik (1929–33).

Feuersnot (Ger., *No Fire in the City*), opera in one act by Richard Strauss, to a libretto by Ernst von Wolzogen, first performed in Dresden in 1901. The work is based on a Flemish legend, *The Quenched Fires of Oudenarde*.

Fevin, Antoine de (died 1512), French composer of the school of Josquin des Prés. A number of his Masses and motets survive. A modern edition of the Mass *Mente tota* is in H. Expert, *Les Maîtres musiciens de la Renaissance française*, ix. The Mass *Ave Maria* has been edited with a biography, by J. Delporte (1934).

Février, Henri (1875–1957), French composer, pupil of Fauré and Massenet. His nine operas and operettas include *Monna Vanna* (after Maeterlinck) and *Carmosine* (after Musset).

Ffrangcon-Davies, David Thomas (1855–1918), Welsh baritone. He was the original Cedric in Sullivan's opera *Ivanhoe* (London, 1891). He sang frequently at concerts and in oratorio in England, the United States and Europe. His *Singing of the Future* was first published, with a preface by Elgar, in 1906; it was reissued in an abridged form with a short biography by his daughter and correspondence with Elgar, under the title *David Ffrangcon-Davies – his Life and Book*, 1938.

fiato (It.), 'breath'. *Strumenti a fiato*, wind instruments.

Fibich, Zdeněk (1850–1900), Czech composer. He studied at the Leipzig Conservatorium, where he was a pupil of Moscheles and Jadassohn. He was assistant conductor at the National Theatre, Prague, from 1875 until 1878, and was subsequently choirmaster at the Russian Church, Prague, for three years. Apart from these posts, he devoted himself wholly to composition. His works, romantic in style, include seven operas (among them *The Tempest*, after Shakespeare, and *Hedy*, after Byron's *Don Juan*), a melodrama trilogy – *Hippodamia*, three symphonies, several symphonic poems and overtures, chamber music, songs and numerous piano pieces. *Hippodamia* consists of three separate melodramas (i.e. spoken drama with continuous orchestral accompaniment).

fiddle, a colloquial term for the violin or any similar string instrument, particularly when used in folk music. A three-string fiddle is still played in Greece and the Balkans, where it is known as the lira. It is held on the knee and bowed vertically.

Fidelio, opera in two (originally three) acts by Beethoven. Full title: *Fidelio, oder Die Eheliche Liebe* (*Fidelio, or Wedded Love*). The libretto originally by Josef Sonnleithner (after Jean Nicolas Bouilly's *Léonore, ou l'Amour conjugal*), was reduced to two acts by Stefan von Breuning (1806), and further revised by Georg Friedrich Treitschke (1814). The première of the original version was given in Vienna in 1805, the second version in 1806 and the final version in 1814.

Florestan is a political prisoner in the hands of Pizarro. His wife, Leonora, disguised as a young man with the name Fidelio, enters the service of the prison gaoler, Rocco, in order to find her husband. Pizarro, learning that the governor, Fernando, is to visit the prison, orders Florestan to be killed. Leonora helps Rocco to dig the grave. When Pizarro arrives, she defies him and reveals herself as Florestan's wife. At that moment a trumpet announces the arrival of Fernando. Florestan and his wife are free.

For the four overtures which Beethoven wrote for this, his only opera, *see* LEONORE.

See illustration on p. 206.

Fiedler, Arthur (born 1894), U.S. conductor, born in Boston, where from 1930 he has been in charge of the 'Boston Pops' Orchestra. His regular summer series of concerts soon established him as one of music's great popularisers, and his many recordings have made him a household name all over the world.

Field, John (1782–1837), Irish pianist and composer, the son of a violinist and grandson of an organist and

Fidelio: title-page of the original edition of the score,
Vienna, 1805

pianist. He was apprenticed at the age of eleven to
Clementi, whom he accompanied to France, Germany
and Russia, his duties being to demonstrate the
excellence of the pianos which Clementi sold. Field
lived in Russia as a teacher (Glinka had lessons from
him) and soloist until 1832, when he returned to Britain
and subsequently toured on the Continent. After a
long illness in Naples he returned to Russia to die. His
reputation as a performer was high. His compositions
include seven piano concertos, four sonatas, and a
number of other works for the piano, of which his
twenty nocturnes (whose name and form he invented)
are the most characteristic. The influence of his
nocturnes on Chopin's is unmistakable: the common
factor is a *cantabile* melody – sometimes simple, sometimes ornamented – with an unobtrusive accompaniment for the left hand.

    P. PIGGOTT: *The Life and Music of John Field,*
      Creator of the Nocturne (1973)
Fiery Angel, The (Russ., *Ognenny Angel*), opera in

five acts by Prokofiev, to a libretto by the composer
after a story by Valery Bryusov. Though written 1919–
27, the work was not heard until 1954, when it received
a concert performance in Paris; the first stage performance, at the Fenice Theatre in Venice, took place
the following year. Also known as *The Angel of Fire*,
the work is one of the most important of Prokofiev's
operas. The story deals with diabolical possession,
religious hysteria, and exorcism in the 16th century.
The heroine, Renata, is in love with an angel – fire,
but in the end she is sent to the stake for having
dealings with evil spirits. Prokofiev worked material
from this opera into his third symphony (1928).

fifara (It.), a 17th century name for the transverse
flute (also spelled *fiffaro*), as opposed to *flauto*, the
beaked flute or recorder.

fife, a small flute, still used, as for centuries past, in the
'drum and fife' band. In its modern form it is built a
tone lower than the orchestral piccolo and has one or
more keys.

fiffaro, *see* FIFARA

fifteenth, (1) the interval of two octaves, e.g.:

(2) an organ stop pitched two octaves higher than
the normal (or 8 ft.) pitch, in other words a 2 ft. stop.

fifth, the interval reached by ascending four steps in
the diatonic scale, e.g.:

In the HARMONIC SERIES it is the interval between the
second and third notes of the series, and therefore has
the ratio $\frac{3}{2}$. A series of twelve fifths, beginning on:

8ve lower

will reach B sharp:

On keyboard instruments this note is the same as C,
but if the fifths are accurately tuned there will be a
small difference, since twelve fifths: $(\frac{3}{2})^{12} = \frac{531441}{4096}$
are larger than 7 octaves: $(\frac{2}{1})^7 = 128$. In other words
B sharp by this reckoning is sharper than C, the
difference being $\frac{531441}{4096} \div 128$, i.e. $\frac{531441}{524288}$
The following terms are in use:

    Augmented fifth: a fifth of which the upper note is
      sharpened or the lower note flattened, e.g.:

Diminished fifth: a fifth of which the upper note is flattened or the lower note sharpened, e.g.:

Perfect fifth: the interval defined above, e.g.:

See also CONSECUTIVE INTERVALS

'Fifths' Quartet, *see* QUINTENQUARTETT

figuration, the consistent use of a particular melodic or harmonic figure, e.g.:

HANDEL, *Suite no 5 in E major*

figure, a short musical phrase – too short to be a genuine 'theme' – but achieving, through repetition, a distinctive character in the course of a composition.

figured bass (Fr., *basse chiffrée*; Ger., *bezifferter Bass*; It., *basso continuo*), formerly known also as 'thorough bass' (a literal translation of *basso continuo*). A bass part (intended primarily for a keyboard instrument) with figures to indicate the harmonies to be played above it; for example, the following figured bass:

implies these harmonies:

The system originated at the beginning of the 17th century and was universally employed until about the middle of the 18th century, after which it was little used outside church music. It was designed to facilitate (*a*) the accompaniment of one or more solo voices or instruments, e.g. in the solo cantata, or the trio sonata for two violins and bass, (*b*) the enrichment of a texture provided by a chorus or an instrumental ensemble or both (*see* CONTINUO).

Practice was not always consistent, but the following principles were generally observed:

(1) a note without figures implies the fifth and the third above;

(2) the figure 3 by itself implies 5 as well;

(3) the figure 4 by itself implies 5 as well, e.g.:

(4) the figure 6 by itself implies 3 as well;

(5) the figure 7 by itself implies 3 as well;

(6) accidentals are indicated either by the normal signs placed next to the figures, or by the addition of strokes to the figures, e.g.:

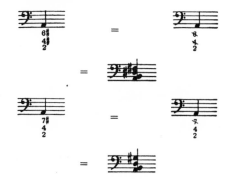

An accidental without any figure refers to the third of the chord, e.g.:

(7) a horizontal stroke indicates that the harmony used above the preceding note is to be continued above a changing bass, e.g.:

The stroke, however, is often omitted where it is obvious that notes in the bass are passing notes.

Provided that he uses the correct harmony, the performer is free to dispose the notes of the chord as he likes, i.e. close together or widely spaced. It is essential, however, that any melodic line or lines that he is accompanying should not be obscured. The same is true of melodic figuration or imitations of the solo part, which can be very effective provided that they do not monopolize the listener's attention. Since the practice of playing from figured bass is now no longer widely cultivated, modern editions of old music generally include a fully written out part of the harpsichord, piano or organ. No written part, however, can be a completely adequate substitute for 'realization' at the keyboard of the composer's shorthand; and many written parts of this kind do positive harm by neglecting to observe the conventions of the period or by introducing an extravagant amount of original material.

F. T. ARNOLD: *The Art of Accompaniment from a Thorough-Bass* (1931).

R. DONINGTON: *The Interpretation of Early Music* (new version, 1974), pages 288ff.

figured chorale, a setting of a chorale melody for organ, in which a particular figuration is employed throughout, e.g.

[Chorale : 'Ach wie nichtig, ach wie flüchtig']

BACH, Orgelbuchlein

Fille du Régiment, La, *see* DAUGHTER OF THE REGIMENT

film music, the use of music to accompany films dates from the early part of the 20th century. Silent films needed music, normally that of a piano, to accentuate the action, and to drown the noise of the projector; often 'special effects', such as gunfire, birdsong,

thunder, etc., were provided by a percussionist. By about 1920 the practice began of employing other instruments, even complete orchestras in larger cities. With the building of large cinemas, organs were also installed, either to bear the whole burden of accompaniment or to alternate with the orchestra. Piano or organ accompaniment was often improvised. For instrumental ensembles (as well as for pianists and organists) there was available a whole library of short extracts, suitable for every conceivable emotion or situation (e.g. 'Help, help', 'Love's Response', or 'Broken Vows'). The accompaniment to a silent film was a sort of potpourri, in the compilation of which considerable ingenuity was often shown. The practice, however, was inartistic, and dissatisfaction with it led, after World War I, to the occasional composition of original music for a complete film, or to the adaptation of existing music – as in the case of the film version of Strauss's *Der Rosenkavalier*, for which the composer made a special arrangement of his own score (1925). Other composers of this period who wrote for films include Satie and Honegger.

The opportunity for a more complete association of film and music came with the development of the sound film in 1926–27, but it was only gradually realized that music could be used as an integral part of the film and only gradually that reputable composers were commissioned to provide it. Among British composers who have written film music of this kind are Arnold Bax, Arthur Bliss, William Walton and Vaughan Williams. In the United States, important film scores have been composed by Aaron Copland, Virgil Thomson and Leonard Bernstein. Russia's musical contribution to the cinema has included three masterly scores by Prokofiev – *Alexander Nevsky*, *Lieutenant Kijé* and *Ivan the Terrible*. Several of these works have proved capable of standing on their own feet in concert-hall versions – e.g. Vaughan Williams's *Sinfonia Antartica* (drawn from *Scott of the Antarctic*), Walton's *Spitfire Prelude and Fugue* (from *The First of the Few*) and Bernstein's *On the Waterfront* suite (from the film of the same title). Schoenberg's *Music for a Film Scene* (1930) was not written for an actual film, but it is a fascinating exercise in the genre.

Some films have used already existing works to creative effect – e.g. the music of Vivaldi in Cocteau's *Les Enfants Terribles*, of Strauss and Ligeti in *2001, A Space Odyssey*, and of Bach in Bergman's *The Silence*. Recent film scores have made increasing use of electronic music, often very effectively, as in Kagel's witty *Ludwig van* (1970).

In the great majority of commercial U.S. and British films, however, the music tends to be imitative of such late romantics as Rakhmaninov, Strauss, and Delius. It describes a scene or mood, tends to repeat certain phrases, and is often a constant background to the film, only noticed at climactic moments.

H. EISLER: *Composing for the Film* (1947)

L. LEVY: *Music for the Movies* (1948)

R. MANVELL and J. HUNTLEY: *The Technique of Film Music* (1957)

Filtz, Anton (c. 1730–60), cellist and composer, probably of Bohemian origin, who joined the Mannheim orchestra in 1754 and established himself as one of the symphonists at the Mannheim court. He wrote about forty works in the form, as well as choral and chamber music.

final, in the church modes the note on which a melody comes to an end, i.e. the tonic. In the authentic modes the final is the first degree of the scale, in the plagal modes it is the fourth degree, e.g.:

Mode I (*protus authenticus*):

Mode II (*protus plagalis*):

finale (It., but now used in English), (1) the last movement of a work in several movements, e.g. a symphony, concerto, string quartet, etc. In the 18th century finales were generally brisk and cheerful. Beethoven challenged this convention in a number of works (e.g. his last piano sonata, op 111) and subsequent composers have shown a similar freedom of treatment. Chaikovsky's sixth symphony has a finale which is marked *Adagio lamentoso* and ends *pppp*;

(2) the concluding section of an act of an opera, often of considerable length and subdivided into smaller sections, with contrasts of tempo and key. An outstanding example is the finale of Act 2 of Mozart's *Marriage of Figaro*. An operatic finale generally involves several singers, and often the chorus as well.

Finck, Heinrich (1445–1527), German composer. He was educated in Poland, where he was also in the service of the court for several years. Subsequently he was *Kapellmeister* at Stuttgart and Salzburg. His compositions include Masses, motets and secular part-songs. Modern editions of selected works are in R. Eitner, *Publikationen älterer . . . Musikwerke*, viii, and in *Erbe deutscher Musik*, 1 Reihe, lvii. He was described by his great-nephew as learned and inventive, but hard in style.

His great nephew, **Hermann Finck** (1527–58), was a composer and theorist. He studied at Wittenberg University and was appointed organist there in 1557. He is best known for his treatise *Practica Musica* (1556; facsimile reprint, 1970) which includes a substantial section on canon. Three of his compositions are in Eitner's volume mentioned above.

fine (It.), 'end'. In the *da capo* aria and similar compositions, where the recapitulation of the opening section is not written in full but indicated by a sign to go back to the beginning, the direction *fine* indicates the point at which the piece comes to an end.

Fine, Irving (1915–62), U.S. composer, pupil of Walter Piston and Nadia Boulanger. He held university appointments at Harvard and Brandeis, and from 1946 was on the Berkshire Music Center faculty at Tanglewood. His works include a symphony (1962), an orchestral 'diversion' entitled *Blue Towers*, three choruses from *Alice in Wonderland*, chamber music and songs.

Fingal's Cave, *see* HEBRIDES

Finger, Gottfried (Godfrey) (c. 1660–after 1723),

Moravian composer. He travelled to England in about 1685 and became an instrumentalist in the Catholic chapel of James II. He published instrumental chamber music in London and wrote music for several plays. Having been awarded the fourth prize in a competition for setting Congreve's *Judgment of Paris*, he left England in disgust, saying that 'he thought he was to compose musick for men, and not for boys' (*Roger North on Music*, edited by J. Wilson, 1959, page 354). He was in the service of Queen Sophia Charlotte of Prussia in 1702, and subsequently of the Elector Palatine.

A. W. MARSHALL: 'The Chamber Music of Godfrey Finger', in *The Consort*, xxvi (1970)

finger-board (Fr., *touche*; Ger., *Griffbrett*; It., *tasto*), the part of a string instrument on which the fingers of the left hand press down the strings at any chosen point and so shorten their vibrating length and raise the pitch.

finger cymbals, a pair of tiny cymbals strapped to the thumb and finger; they give a high bell note of definite pitch.

fingering, any notation that indicates which fingers should be used in playing a piece of music. In piano playing, 1 usually indicates the thumb, 2 the index finger and so on up to 5 for the little finger. Old instruction books may still contain an obsolete fingering in which + stands for the thumb and 1 to 4 for the index to little fingers.

Finke, Fidelio (1891–1968), Sudeten composer, a pupil of Novák. He studied at the Prague Conservatory, and taught there, from 1915 until 1920. In that year he became teacher of composition at the German Academy of Music, Prague, and was director from 1927 until 1945. As a composer he began as a romantic and developed into a disciple of Schoenberg. His compositions include an opera, *Die Jakobsfahrt*, orchestral works, chamber music, choral works and piano pieces.

Finlandia, orchestral tone-poem by Sibelius, op 26. It was first performed in 1899 as the finale of a series of pieces illustrating patriotic 'Tableaux from the Past' (other numbers from the same series were published as *Scènes historiques*). In 1900 it was revised and performed separately as a concert piece under the title *Suomi* (Finland). Though patriotic in character, the melodies of this piece are Sibelius's own, not folk tunes.

Finot, *see* PHINOT

Finta Giardiniera, La (It., *The Girl in Gardener's Disguise*), opera in three acts by Mozart, to a libretto by Raniero de' Calzabigi, altered by Marco Coltellini. It was first performed in Munich in 1775. This early Mozart comedy contains some striking foretastes of *The Marriage of Figaro*.

Finta Semplice, La (It., *The Pretended Simpleton*), Mozart's first opera, K51, performed at Salzburg in 1769, when the composer was thirteen years old – though it had been written a year earlier, in the expectation of a Vienna première. The work is a comic opera in three acts, with a stock Goldoni plot and a text by Coltellini.

Finzi, Gerald (1901–56), English composer, a pupil of Bairstow and R. O. Morris. He taught composition at the Royal Academy of Music, London, from 1930 until 1933. His works, mainly in the smaller forms, include settings for voice and piano of poems by

Thomas Hardy and a cello concerto. His lyrical, pastoral style is heard at its best in *Dies Natalis*, for voice and strings (1940).

fioritura (It.), literally 'flowering' (plural *fioriture*), i.e. an embellishment or ornamentation, whether improvised or written down.

fipple flute, *see* FLAGEOLET, RECORDER

Firebird, The (Russ., *Zhar Ptitsa*), ballet with music by Stravinsky, first performed in Paris in 1910, with choreography by Fokine. The story is based on a Russian fairy tale. This was Stravinsky's first important ballet, musically rooted in the style of Rimsky-Korsakov, but containing ample evidence of Stravinsky's own developing personality. A concert suite, based on the ballet, was made by the composer in 1911, and revised in 1919 and 1947. The French title, *L'Oiseau de Feu*, is relevant only to French audiences; its use in English-speaking countries is a pretention.

'Fire' Symphony, nickname for Haydn's symphony no 59 in A major, composed c. 1766–8. The work may have been used as overture to a play, *The Conflagration*, produced at Esterház during Haydn's period as staff composer there. The name is believed to derive from that event.

Fireworks Music, familiar title for Handel's *Music for the Royal Fireworks*, originally written for wind band and performed in the Green Park, London, in 1749, as an accompaniment to a fireworks display celebrating the Peace of Aix-la-Chapelle. String parts were subsequently added by the composer for concert performances. The movements are: Overture, Bourrée, 'La Paix', 'La Réjouissance', Menuet I, Menuet II.

Firkušny, Rudolf (born 1912), Czech pianist and composer, pupil of Janáček, in the performance of whose piano music he excels. Later he studied under Schnabel and Suk, and composed a piano concerto and solo piano pieces.

first-movement form, *see* SONATA FORM

Fis (Ger.), F sharp.

Fischer, Carl (1849–1923), founder of the New York publishing firm which bears his name.

Fischer, Edwin (1886–1960), Swiss pianist and composer. He studied at the Basle Conservatoire and in Berlin, where he subsequently taught. As a performer he toured widely and was greatly admired for his intelligent interpretations of the classics, especially Mozart and Bach (whose concertos he often conducted from the keyboard, at a time when this practice was out of fashion).

Fischer, Johann Kaspar Ferdinand (c. 1665–1746), German composer, *Kapellmeister* to the Markgraf of Baden. Of his compositions the keyboard works are particularly interesting (modern edition by E. von Werra). They include harpsichord suites in the French style and *Ariadne musica neo-organoedum* (1715) – a collection of twenty preludes and fugues, each in a different key, and a forerunner of Bach's *Well-tempered Clavier*. His *Journal du printemps*, for orchestra with *ad lib.* trumpets, has also been edited by E. von Werra.

Fischer-Dieskau, Dietrich (born 1925), German baritone. He studied at the Berlin Hochschule für Musik, and first appeared in Brahms's *Requiem* at Freiburg in 1947.

He is the most famous German baritone of his generation, and is equally at home in opera house and concert hall. In the former, his repertory ranges from Mozart to Berg's *Wozzeck* and Mittenhofer, the selfish poet in Henze's *Elegy for Young Lovers*. His *Lieder* repertory includes the (more or less) complete songs of Beethoven, Schubert, Mendelssohn, Brahms, Wolf and Strauss – a record total – and he is also a noted exponent of Bach and Mahler's orchestral songs.

fisarmonica (It.), accordion.

Fisher, F. E., 18th century English composer, possibly of German origin (precise name and dates unknown). He worked in London between 1748 and 1773, composing trio sonatas and other instrumental pieces, and performing them himself as violinist and cellist. Some authorities believe he was Friedrich Ernst Fischer, an itinerant German composer of the period.

Fisis (Ger.), F double sharp (F ×).

Fitelberg, Grzegorz (1879–1953), Polish composer and conductor. He took charge of the Warsaw Philharmonic concerts in 1908, and was associated with the Polish nationalist movement. He wrote two symphonies, a *Polish Rhapsody* for orchestra, and other works.

His son, **Jerzy Fitelberg** (1903–51), was also a composer. After studying at the Warsaw Conservatory and playing percussion in his father's orchestra, he became a pupil of Schreker in Berlin. In 1933 he settled in Paris, and in 1940 moved to New York, where he died. He wrote a sinfonietta, two piano concertos, two violin concertos, a cello concerto, two suites and other orchestral works, five string quartets and other chamber music.

Fitzwilliam Virginal Book, the most extensive manuscript collection of keyboard music (almost entirely English) of the late 16th and early 17th centuries, containing 297 pieces. It was copied by FRANCIS TREGIAN, probably during the period of his imprisonment in the Fleet (c. 1609–19). Among the composers represented are Bull, Byrd, Farnaby, Morley, Philips and Tomkins. A modern edition in two volumes by J. A. Fuller-Maitland and W. Barclay Squire was published in 1899, and reprinted in 1949.

Five, The, name sometimes given to the group of Russian nationalist composers of the 19th century, known in their own country as the *moguchaya kutchka* (mighty handful). The term was coined by Strassov, and applied to Balakirev, Borodin, Cui, Mussorgsky and Rimsky-Korsakov, all of whose works were thought to differ from those of more 'westernised' composers, such as Chaikovsky and Anton Rubinstein.

five-three chord, the basic, or common, triad. In figured bass it is denoted by the figures $^5_3$, referring to the third and fifth above the root.

flageolet, a small beaked flute (or recorder), with six holes – four in the front and two at the back, the latter covered by the player's thumbs. It dates from the late 16th century and was much in vogue in the 17th century. There are frequent references in Pepys's diary (*see* C. Welch, *Six Lectures on the Recorder*, pages 47–77).

Flageolett-Töne (Ger.), harmonics on string instruments.

Flagstad, Kirsten (1895–1962), Norwegian soprano, daughter of a conductor. She studied in Oslo and Stockholm, and first appeared in opera at the age of eighteen. She sang as Sieglinde in *Die Walküre* at Bayreuth in 1934, and as Isolde in New York in 1935. Her first Covent Garden appearance was in 1936. The purity and strength of her voice made her one of the outstanding singers of her day. Though she excelled in opera, particularly in Wagner, she was also a gifted interpreter of solo works and made excellent records of Grieg's *Haugtussa* cycle. Her autobiography was published in 1953.

flam, a drum stroke used to mark an accent. It consists of two notes played very closely together.

flamenco, or **cante flamenco** (Sp.), a species of Spanish song, from Andalusia, performed with guitar accompaniment. There are various sub-species named after different areas of Andalusia, e.g. MALAGUENA, Sevillana, etc. The mood of the music is often (though not necessarily) sad, and many of the songs begin with a prolonged exclamation of 'Ay!'. Solo guitarists often play in 'flamenco style', as opposed to 'classical style'. Though the popular expression, 'flamenco dancer', is in a sense a contradiction in terms, flamencos are in fact often danced to as well as sung.

Flanagan, William (1923–61), U.S. composer, pupil of Honegger, Copland and David Diamond, among others. His works, noted for their lyricism, include a one-act opera, *Bartleby* (completed 1957), after the Melville short story; *Song for a Winter Child* (1950), to words by Edward Albee; *The Weeping Pleiades* (1953), a song cycle based on poems by A. E. Housman; *The Lady of Tearful Regret* (1958), in which Albee's words are set for coloratura soprano and chamber ensemble. His orchestral works include *A Concert Ode* (1951), *Notations* (1960) and *Narrative for Orchestra* (1964). He wrote incidental music for Albee's plays, *The Sandbox*, *The Ballad of the Sad Café*, and *The Death of Bessie Smith*.

flat (Fr., *bémol*; Ger., *Be*; It., *bemolle*), (1) the sign ♭, indicating that the pitch of the note to which it is prefixed is to be lowered by one semitone. It holds good for the whole of a bar, unless contradicted. If it forms part of the KEY SIGNATURE it holds good, unless contradicted, until there is a new key signature which omits it. The origin of the sign is the 'soft' or rounded B (*B molle* or *B rotundum*) used in the Middle Ages to indicate the fourth degree of the hexachord beginning on F:

as opposed to the 'hard' or square B (*B durum* or *B quadratum*) used to indicate the third degree of the hexachord beginning on G:

The use of the natural sign (♮) to contradict either a ♯ or a ♭ was not normal until the 18th century. Before that time the ♭ was used to contradict a ♯, as well as to lower the pitch of an uninflected note (i.e. one without ♯ or ♭). Two flats side by side (♭♭) are a double flat and lower the pitch of the note to which they are prefixed by two semi-tones. In French and Italian, flattened notes are referred to by the name of the note followed by the word for a flat, as in English: in German, the suffix '-s' or '-es' is added to the name of the note, e.g. E♭ = Fr. *se bémol*; Ger. *Es*; It., *si bemolle*. There is one exception to this rule: Ger. B (without any suffix) = B♭ (B ♮ is represented by H; B♭♭ is *Bes*);

(2) applied to an interval = minor, e.g. flat seventh = minor seventh, flat third = minor third. This use of the word, though not completely obsolete, is old-fashioned;

(3) a 'flat key' is now one which has one or more flats in the key signature, e.g. F (one flat), B♭ (two flats), E♭ (three flats), etc. It formerly meant a minor key, just as 'flat third' meant minor third. Cf. the following passage: 'They plaid us some flat Tunes . . . with a general applause, it being a thing formerly thought impossible upon an Instrument design'd for a sharp Key' (*Gentleman's Journal*, January 1692);

(4) an instrument or a voice is flat if the notes produced are lower than the normal pitch. A single note can also be flat, as a result of faulty tuning or careless performance.

flatté, *see* SLIDE (1)

Flatterzunge (Ger.), literally 'flutter tongue'. A method of tone production sometimes used on wind instruments. It consists in rolling the tongue as though saying *drrr*. The result, if applied to a single note, is a rapid tremolo. It appears to have been introduced originally by Richard Strauss in *Don Quixote* (1898), where it is prescribed for the flutes and combined with a rapid chromatic scale.

flautando (It.), 'playing like a flute'. A direction to string-players, used in two senses: (1) playing harmonics; (2) playing gently near the end of the fingerboard.

flautato (It.) = FLAUTANDO.

flauto (It.), flute. *Flauto piccolo*, piccolo. In the time of Bach and Handel (and earlier) *flauto* = *flauto dolce*, *flauto d'éco*, beaked flute or recorder; the transverse flute is indicated by *flauto traverso* or *traversa* alone. In Bach's Brandenburg concertos, nos 2 and 4 require *flauto*, i.e. recorder, no 5 requires *flauto traverso*, i.e. flute. *Flauto d'amore*, a transverse flute built a minor third lower than the normal size, now obsolete.

flautone (It.), bass flute.

Flavio, Re de' Longobardi (It., *Flavio, King of the Lombards*), opera in three acts by Handel, to a libretto by Nicola Francesco Haym (partly founded on Corneille's *Le Cid* and altered from Stefano Ghigi's earlier Italian libretto). It was first performed in London in 1723.

flebile (It.), mournful.

Fledermaus, Die (Ger., *The Bat*), operetta in three acts by Johann Strauss, to a libretto by Carl Haffner and Richard Genée (based on Meilhac and Halevy's French vaudeville *Le Réveillon*, which had been taken from *Das Gefängnis*, a German comedy by Roderich

Benedix). It was first performed in Vienna in 1874, and established itself as the 'waltz king's' most successful work for the stage.

Baron von Eisenstein, who has been committed to prison for five days, is persuaded by Falke to postpone it in order to go to a ball at Prince Orlofsky's. After his supposed departure for prison Rosalinda (his wife), is visited by Alfred (the singing teacher). When Frank (the prison governor) comes to take Eisenstein to jail, Alfred (in order not to compromise Rosalinda) pretends that he is Eisenstein and goes to jail. Falke (wishing to have revenge for the ridicule made of him by Eisenstein when he was at a former ball dressed as a bat) has also invited Frank, Adele (Rosalinda's maid) and Rosalinda herself to the ball. The next day they all find themselves at the prison for various reasons: Eisenstein wishes to begin his prison sentence, Rosalinda wants to begin an action for divorce, and Frank is very drunk. Finally Falke appears with all the guests of the ball and declares the whole to be an act of vengeance for the joke played on him by Eisenstein. Thus all the confusion is resolved and Eisenstein is left to serve his term in jail.

Flesch, Carl (1873–1944), Hungarian violinist, son of a doctor. He studied in Vienna and Paris and first appeared as a soloist in Vienna in 1895. He taught violin at the Bucharest Conservatory (1897–1902); Amsterdam Conservatory (1903–8); Curtis Institute, Philadelphia (1924–8); and Berlin Hochschule (1929–34). He toured widely as a soloist, and also gave a series of historical concerts in Berlin. His book on *The Art of Violin-playing* (1923–8) is a standard work.

flexatone, a simple instrument consisting of a steel blade and a small clapper mounted on a flexible strip. On shaking, the clapper strikes the blade to produce a bell sound, and the pitch is varied by pressing the blade.

flicorno, Italian equivalent of the SAXHORN.

Fliegende Holländer, Der, *see* FLYING DUTCHMAN

fliessend (Ger.), flowing.

Flight of the Bumble-Bee, The, orchestral interlude in Rimsky-Korsakov's opera, *The Legend of the Czar Saltan* (1900), often performed out of context, and in arrangements for all kinds of instruments (Harry James, for instance, transformed it into a virtuoso solo for jazz trumpet). The story of the opera concerns a prince who turns into a bee and stings his irksome relatives.

Flonzaley Quartet, a string quartet founded by a U.S. banker of Swiss origin, Edward de Coppet (1855–1916), in 1902 and maintained by him and his son André; so called from the name of de Coppet's summer residence in Switzerland. The members of the quartet devoted themselves entirely to the study and practice of chamber music; they accepted no individual engagements and took no pupils. The quartet disbanded in 1928.

Floridante, Il (It., *Prince Floridantes*), opera in three acts by Handel, to a libretto by Paolo Antonio Rolli, first performed in London in 1721.

Florimo, Francesco (1800–88), Italian historian and composer. He studied at the Real Collegio di Musica, Naples, where he became librarian in 1826. He was Bellini's closest friend, and later in his long career he became a friend of Wagner. He wrote studies of both composers, and also a funeral symphony on the death of Bellini. More important than his compositions are his historical works, which include *Cenno storico sulla scuola musicale di Napoli*, two volumes (1869–71), issued in a revised and enlarged edition as *La scuola musicale di Napoli e i suoi Conservatorii*, four volumes (1880–4).

Flos Campi (Lat., flower of the field), suite in six movements by Vaughan Williams for viola, chamber orchestra and (wordless) chorus, inspired by the Song of Solomon, and first performed in London in 1925.

Flöte (Ger.), flute. *Kleine Flöte*, piccolo.

Flothuis, Marius (born 1914), Dutch composer and critic. His works include concertos for flute, horn, piano and violin, a sinfonietta concertante for clarinet, saxophone and chamber orchestra, a string quartet, cello sonata and songs.

Flotow, Friedrich von (1812–83), German opera composer, son of a nobleman. He studied in Paris, where he had his first public success with *Le Naufrage de la Méduse*, written in collaboration with Grisar and Pilati, 1839 (subsequently rewritten by Flotow as *Die Matrosen*, Hamburg, 1845). His *Alessandro Stradella* (Hamburg, 1844) established his position in Germany. His most popular work was *Martha* (Vienna, 1847). He was director of the court theatre at Schwerin from 1856 until 1863.

flourish, a FANFARE; the term can also be used to describe a decorative musical figure, either written into a piece of music or improvised by the performer.

Floyd, Carlisle (born 1926), U.S. composer and teacher, noted mainly for his operas, all to his own libretti. Of these the most famous is *Susannah* (1955); others are *Wuthering Heights* (1958), *The Passion of Jonathan Wade* (1962), *Markheim* (1966) and *Of Mice and Men* (1970).

flue pipes, in an ORGAN all pipes other than reed pipes, so called because the air passes through a narrow aperture, or flue. The principle is similar to that of the tin whistle.

See ORGAN.

Flügel (Ger.), 'wing'. Hence a harpsichord or a grand piano, both of which are wing-shaped.

flügelhorn (Ger.), (1) a soprano saxhorn in B flat, similar in shape to the bugle, but provided with three pistons. It has the same compass as the B flat cornet, but a fuller tone. In Britain it is used only in brass bands, where it is a recognised member of the ensemble. Tippett, however, incorporated a flugelhorn part in his third symphony. The instrument is also sometimes used in jazz (e.g. by Miles Davis) as an alternative to the trumpet.

(2) in general the German equivalent of the SAXHORN family.

flute (Fr., *flûte*; Ger., *Flöte*; It., *flauto*),

(1) the beaked flute or English flute (Fr., *flûte à bec*, *flûte douce*; Ger., *Blockflöte*; It., *flauto dolce*, *flauto d'éco*), now known exclusively as the RECORDER;

(2) the transverse or German flute (Fr., *flûte traversière*, *flûte allemande*; Ger., *Querflöte*; It., *flauto traverso*), now known simply as the flute. A 'woodwind' instrument, generally made either of wood or silver. One end of the tube is stopped, and sound is produced by blowing across an aperture cut in the side at that end. The compass is normally from

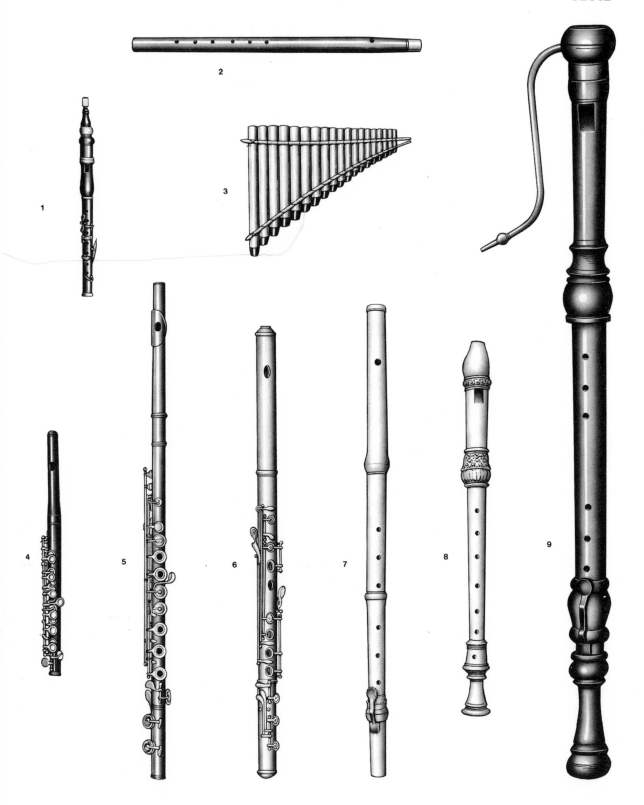

Flutes: (1) keyed flageolet (2) fife (3) panpipes (4) piccolo (5) metal flute (6) wooden flute (7) 18th century flute (8) alto recorder (9) bass recorder

though instruments are also made with an extra semitone at the bottom, i.e. going down to B natural. The modern flute owes much to the work of Theobald Boehm (1794–1881), who made it possible to pierce the finger-holes in acoustically correct positions and at the same time to provide a convenient means of controlling them with the fingers. In addition to the normal-sized flute there are also (a) the *piccolo* (Fr., *petite flûte*; Ger., *kleine Flöte*; It., *flauto piccolo, ottavino*), built an octave higher, and (b) the *bass flute*, also known as the *alto flute* (Fr., *flûte alto*, Ger., *Altflöte*; It., *flautone*), built a fourth lower. The *flûte d'amour* (Ger., *Liebesflöte*; It., *flauto d'amore*), built a minor third lower, is obsolete. Flutes built a minor third or a semitone above the normal pitch were at one time used in military bands and treated as transposing instruments (*see* TIERCE FLUTE). Though an instrument of great antiquity the flute did not come into general use in chamber and orchestral music until the early 18th century (note that at this period *flauto* by itself means 'recorder': the transverse flute is indicated by *flauto traverso* or *traversa*).

See also MIRLITON

A. CARSE: *Musical Wind Instruments* (1939)

flûte (Fr.), flute. *Flûte à bec, flûte douce*, recorder. *Flûte allemande, flûte traversière*, transverse flute (the ordinary orchestral flute). *Flûte alto*, bass flute. *Flûte d'amour*, a flute built a minor third below the normal size, now obsolete.

flûte-eunuque, *see* MIRLITON

flutter tongue, *see* FLATTERZUNGE

Flying Dutchman, The (Ger., *Der Fliegende Holländer*), opera in three acts by Wagner, to a libretto by the composer (after Heinrich Heine's *Memoiren des Herrn von Schnabelewopski*). It was first performed in Dresden in 1843. The Dutchman, for an act of defiance, has been condemned by Satan to sail the seas for ever, unless he can be redeemed by a woman's love. Allowed to come on shore every seven years, he is entertained by the Norwegian sea-captain, Daland. Senta, Daland's daughter, who already knows the legend, agrees to marry the Dutchman. The latter, overhearing a scene between Senta and her former lover Erik, believes that she has betrayed him and puts to sea. Senta hurls herself into the sea and by her sacrifice, brings him at last redemption.

Originally Wagner intended *The Flying Dutchman* to be a one-act opera of heroic dimensions. Later he settled for a three-act version, though the possibilities of his original conception have been explored by some companies (e.g. the Welsh National) in recent years.

Foerster, Josef Bohuslav (1859–1951), Czech composer, teacher and critic who worked in Hamburg and Vienna (where he was a friend of Mahler) before returning to Prague and becoming director of the Prague Conservatory in 1922. A prolific composer, he wrote several operas – including *Deborah*, *Eva*, *Jessica* (after Shakespeare's *Merchant of Venice*), *The Invincibles*, *The Heart*, and *The Fool*. Among his other works are a Stabat Mater, symphonies, symphonic poems, violin concertos, suites and other orchestral

pieces, string quartets and other chamber music, instrumental pieces, incidental music, songs and *Ten Recitations* with piano accompaniment.

Földes, Andor (born 1913), Hungarian pianist, pupil of Dohnányi. In 1939 he settled in the United States. He has also composed piano pieces, and written a book on piano technique.

folía (Sp.; It., *follia*), a Portuguese dance – 'the folly' – which was the origin of the stylized instrumental form known as FOLIES D'ESPAGNE. As the name implies it was originally of a wild and abandoned character.

folies d'Espagne (Fr.), a musical form in dance rhythm, current in the 17th century and derived from the Portuguese dance known as FOLÍA. As often happens when dance forms become stylized the wild character of the original dance gave place to a stately tempo more in accordance with 17th century conventions. The basic formula was as follows:

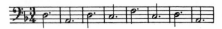

The following examples show two different treatments of this formula, the first, a simple German working:

J. WOLF, *Handbuch der Notationskunde*, ii, page 140

the second a more sophisticated version by an Italian composer:

CORELLI, op 5, no 12

In Britain the piece acquired the name 'Farinel's Ground' from a version by the French composer Michel Farinel. These varied treatments of a basic formula derive from popular practice in improvised dance music. They may be compared with similar treatment of the PASSAMEZZO and the ROMANESCA.

folk song (Fr., *chanson populaire*; Ger., *Volkslied*; It., *canto popolare*), a term implying a song of no known authorship which has been preserved in a community by oral tradition. Some songs which have been preserved in this way are by known composers, many more exist also in printed song books, and there are many more still which presuppose an original author. Oral tradition is valuable in that it often appears to preserve forgotten idioms, without being affected by the changing fashions of succeeding centuries. On the other hand it may easily corrupt both words and tune – and often does. The fact that quite a number of folk songs are modal may be evidence of extreme antiquity; but it may equally be evidence of the fact that medieval peasants imitated the melodic idioms of plainsong which they heard in church (*see* MODES). The irregular rhythms of melodies which have been collected from singers do not necessarily point to an ancient tradition of rhythmical freedom; it is equally possible (and in many cases practically certain) that they are the result of traditional carelessness in singing a tune which is in regular rhythm – carelessness which is quite understandable with songs which have no accompaniment. The antiquity of any folk song is a matter that can hardly be proved; it is certainly not possible to assign confidently a date earlier than its first appearance in a manuscript or in print. Survival suggests that it was once popular, even though it may now be remembered only by a mere handful of people or be saved from extinction only by the collector's notebook. Certainly the great majority of Western folk songs still current shows the influence of written music, probably through a process known as 'seepage'.

Folk songs have often been introduced into serious music or been used as themes for variations. It was not, however, until the 19th century that the use of them became identified with nationalist sentiment and that composers not only used them but imitated their idioms – in Russia, Bohemia, Norway and elsewhere. The new interest in folk songs led to systematic attempts to collect them in most European countries. In Britain the Folk Song Society was founded in 1898, and extensive collecting was undertaken by Cecil Sharp in the first twenty years of the present century – not only in Britain, but also in the Appalachian Mountains in America, where many old British songs and ballads had survived in a simple, isolated community of immigrants. There was considerable activity in collecting folk songs in Ireland and in the Hebrides. Since those early days, the study of folk song has extended to explore that of communities all over the world, and has developed into a separate discipline, ETHNOMUSICOLOGY.

Among composers who have been specially interested not merely in using and imitating folk songs, but also in collecting them, may be mentioned Bartók in Hungary and Vaughan Williams in England. For extended bibliographies, *see* Grove's *Dictionary of Music and Musicians*, and *Oxford History of Music*.

follia, *see* FOLIA

foot, in organ pipes, a measure of pitch. A two-foot pipe sounds middle C, and four-foot, eight-foot, sixteen-foot and 32-foot pipes respectively sound a C an octave lower than the pipe before.

Foote, Arthur William (1853–1937), U.S. composer and organist who wrote cantatas on Longfellow's *The Farewell of Hiawatha* and *The Wreck of the Hesperus*. He also composed orchestral works, chamber music, organ and piano pieces, and songs.

Force of Destiny, The (It., *La Forza del Destino*), opera in four acts by Verdi, to a text by Piave, after the drama *Don Alvaro, ó La Fuerza del Sino* (1835) by Angel de Saavedra Ramírez de Banquedano, Duke of Rivas. Written for the St. Petersburg Court Theatre in 1862, this is one of the grandest of Verdi's middle-period operas, a story of love, war and revenge, which spreads itself from country to country, from monastery to battlefield, and from tragedy to comedy – its richness is almost Shakespearian. The plot tells how the hero, Don Alvaro, accidentally kills the father of his beloved, Leonora. Destiny pursues him in the form of the heroine's brother, Don Carlo, who swears vengeance. In Act 3 the two men, failing to recognise each other, meet and become friends on a battlefield (the scene incorporates one of Verdi's greatest tenor-baritone duets); but Don Carlo, discovering the truth, later resumes his pursuit, which leads to the death of both his sister and himself.

Ford, Thomas (died 1648), English composer and lutenist. He was in the service of Henry, Prince of Wales, and subsequently of Charles I. His only published work was *Musicke of Sundrie Kindes* (1607; modern edition of the songs in *The English School of Lutenist Songwriters*, first series) which includes one of the best-known of all English lute-songs, 'Since first I saw your face'.

Forellenquintett, *see* TROUT QUINTET

Forkel, Johann Nikolaus (1749–1818), German historian, the son of a shoemaker. He studied law and music at Göttingen University and was director of music there, from 1778 until his death. His numerous publications include *Musikalisch-kritische Bibliothek*, three volumes (1778–9), *Allgemeine Geschichte der Musik*, two volumes (1788, 1801), *Allgemeine Literatur der Musik* (1792) and – his best known work – the first biography of Bach, *Uber Johann Sebastian Bachs Leben, Kunst und Kunstwerke* (1802). This, though based on incomplete knowledge, is valuable as a pioneer work and stimulating for the enthusiasm shown by the author at a time when Bach's music had been forgotten.

forlana (It.; Fr., *forlane*), (1) a lively dance in $\frac{6}{8}$ or $\frac{6}{4}$ time, originating in Friuli in north-eastern Italy. The following examples represent its use by composers of the 18th and 20th centuries respectively:

CAMPRA, *Les Festes Venitiennes* (1710)

RAVEL, *Le Tombeau de Couperin* (1917)

There is also an excellent example in Bach's Suite no 1 in C major for orchestra;

(2) in the late 16th century the name *ballo furlano* is found applied to a dance in $\frac{4}{4}$ time and moderate tempo.

form, in music, as in the other arts, this means intelligible shape. The basic elements in musical form are (1) repetition, (2) variation, (3) contrast (whether of material, of speed, or of dynamics). Repetition is essential (though some 20th century composers would dispute this), because the stuff of music is transient and cannot be captured by the ear as a picture can by the eye. Variation is necessary, because unvaried repetition would be intolerable. Contrast is necessary, because even varied repetition of the same material would become monotonous. These three principles operate in the field of (*a*) melody, (*b*) harmony, (*c*) rhythm, (*d*) tone-colour, and can therefore be used simultaneously, e.g. a rhythm can remain persistent while the melody is changed, harmony can change while the melody remains the same, melody and harmony can be repeated with a change of tone-colour. A particular form of melodic repetition which is effective in music but has no equivalent in poetry is overlapping repetition or imitation, which is known as CANON if it is exact and also plays an important part in FUGUE. A particular function of harmony is to establish contrasts of KEY.

Among the influences which have helped to shape musical forms are (1) the dance, (2) words, (3) improvisation. Some dances consist of nothing but simple or slightly varied repetition. But a very large number fall into contrasted sections and exhibit a simple symmetry. These characteristics naturally appear in the music written for them, and in turn influence music not specifically written for dancing but organized on the same principle. Very characteristic of dances is the practice of varying a repetition by turning an inconclusive ending into a final one; in medieval France the inconclusive ending was called *ouvert* (open), the final one *clos* (closed): for a 14th century example, *see* CLOS.

In course of time these melodic conventions were matched by harmonic ones: e.g. a cadence which ended on the tonic chord would be final, one which ended on the dominant would be intermediate (*see* CADENCE). From this contrast developed naturally the division of a piece into two sections, using the same melodic material – the first section ending on a chord

other than the tonic (usually the dominant, or in a minor key the relative major), the second bringing the piece to an end in the proper key (*see* BINARY FORM). Return of the tonic key suggested recapitulation of material from the first section, with the ending altered from the dominant (or relative major) to the tonic. Immediate recapitulation might be too abrupt or too simple: hence the practice of exploring other keys in the second section before returning to the tonic key. The general procedure is then: (*a*) first section beginning in tonic and modulating to dominant, (*b*) second section modulating through related keys to a recapitulation of the material of the first section, but in the tonic key throughout. This procedure is the basis of SONATA FORM, so called because it was used extensively by composers of sonatas (and symphonies, concertos, quartets, etc.) in the late eighteenth century.

The influence of words leads to contrasts in mood in vocal music, and this in turn leads to similar contrasts of mood in instrumental music. If these contrasts are pursued for any length of time they become independent sections. These provide one of the origins of the separate 'movements' of sonatas, symphonies, etc., in the 18th and 19th centuries; the other is to be found in the contrasted dance of the SUITE. Such movements are often distinguished not only by contrast of tempo and material but also by contrast of key. The influence of improvisation also results in contrasts, since no performer will wish to persist in the same mood: it also results in a love of decoration, in giving elaborate clothing to a simple idea.

The desire for intelligibility and the infinite variety possible in music has led composers of all periods to use a limited number of basic forms as skeletons for their ideas, just as poets have used the sonnet or the ballad. Among the forms which became standardized in this way were the RONDO, where there is recurrent repetition, and the DA CAPO aria (or song form) which was not only the foundation of 18th century opera and oratorio but proved fruitful in instrumental music as well. The experience of centuries has shown that there is no limit to the possibilities of simple structures of this kind. They are not conventions to which the composer has to submit; on the contrary, they are the servants of his invention.

In addition to the forms mentioned above, *see* CANTO FERMO, CHACONNE, CHORALE, FANTASIA, FUGUE, MADRIGAL, MOTET, OVERTURE, PRELUDE, RICERCAR, SYMPHONIC POEM, TOCCATA. For works in several movements or parts which exhibit the principles of form on a large scale, *see* CANTATA, CONCERTO, MASS, OPERA, ORATORIO, SONATA, SYMPHONY.

formes fixes, collective name for the ballade, virelai and rondeau, which were the three main forms of late medieval French poetry and music. Guillaume de Machaut was the principal exponent of *formes fixes* in the fourteenth century, and his successors included Eustache Deschamps and Charles d'Orléans. The *formes fixes* show an intimate relationship between poetry and music and indeed poet and musician.

Förster, Emanuel Aloys (1748–1823), Silesian composer, author of an *Anleitung zum Generalbass* (1802). His compositions consist mainly of chamber music and keyboard works. Beethoven acknowledged the value of his example in writing string quartets. __

Forster, Georg (c. 1514–68), German doctor who edited a collection of songs entitled *Ein Ausszug guter alter und newer teutscher Liedlein* (five sets, 1539–56), a volume of psalms. A modern edition of the second set of secular songs is in *Publikationen älterer praktischer und theoretischer Musikwerke*, xxix, Jugend xxxiii.

Förster, Josef Bohuslav (1859–1951), Czech composer, studied in Prague, taught in Hamburg, Vienna and Prague; director, Prague Conservatory 1922–31.

forte (It.), loud (generally abbreviated *f*). *Forte piano*, loud and immediately soft again (*fp*); *fortissimo*, very loud (*ff*); *mezzo forte*, moderately loud (*mf*); *più forte*, louder (*più f*); *poco forte*, moderately loud (*pf*).

fortissimo (It.), very loud.

Fortner, Wolfgang (born 1907), German composer. He studied in Leipzig and became teacher of composition at Heidelberg in 1931 – subsequent academic appointment have been at Detmold and Freiburg-im-Breisgau. His compositions – initially influenced by Reger and Hindemith, but later using serial techniques – include a symphony, concertos for harpsichord, piano, two pianos, violin and cello, three string quartets and other chamber music, a number of important choral works and music for the stage. Two of his operas, *Der Wald* (*The Wood*) and *Die Bluthochzeit* (*Blood Wedding*), were inspired by Lorca, and his ballet, *Die Weisse Rose* (*The White Rose*) by Oscar Wilde.

Fortspinnung (Ger.), 'continuation'. Term for the process of continuation or development of musical material in symphonies and other works, as opposed to symmetrical repetition of that material.

Forty-Eight, The, the name by which Bach's *The Well-Tempered Clavier* is commonly known. It consists of two parts, each containing 24 preludes and fugues for a keyboard instrument.

See WELL-TEMPERED CLAVIER

forza (It.), 'force'. *Con forza*, emphatically, vigorously.

forzando (It.), 'forcing', i.e. strongly accenting (generally abbreviated *fz*).

Foss, Hubert James (1899–1953), English critic. He was music editor of Oxford University Press from 1924 until 1941. He wrote *Music in my Time* (1933) and *Ralph Vaughan Williams* (1950), and edited *The Heritage of Music* (three volumes, 1927–51).

Foss, Lukas (born 1922), composer of German parentage – originally Fuchs. He studied at the Paris Conservatoire and the Curtis Institute, Philadelphia. He was a pupil of Hindemith. His compositions, which have been widely performed in America, include the opera *The Jumping Frog of Calaveras County*, based on Mark Twain's short story (1950), two symphonies and two piano concertos. His orchestral *Recordare* was written after Gandhi's assassination. His oratorio, *A Parable of Death*, has words by Rilke.

Foster, Stephen Collins (1826–64), U.S. self-taught composer of popular songs which became so widely known that they could almost be classed as folk songs. Many of them are as familiar in Britain as in the United States, e.g. 'The Old Folks at Home' ('Swanee Ribber'), 'My Old Kentucky Home', and 'Camptown Races'. Equally durable have been some of his drawing room songs, of which 'Jeanie with the Light Brown Hair' and 'Beautiful Dreamer' are classic examples.

Fountains of Rome, The (It., *Fontane di Roma*), orchestral work by Respighi in four sections depicting four famous fountains. It was first performed in 1917, pre-dating by seven years its companion-piece, *The Pines of Rome*.

Fournier, Pierre (born 1906), French cellist, one of the most distinguished of the century. He studied in Paris, made his début there in 1925, and became professor of cello at the Paris Conservatoire. His performances of Bach, Beethoven, Brahms, Debussy and Elgar have been internationally acclaimed.

Four Saints in Three Acts, opera by Virgil Thomson, to a libretto by Gertrude Stein, first performed in Hartford, Connecticut in 1934. In spite of its title, the work contains four acts and more than four saints; and though the action takes place in Spain, and concerns St. Theresa and St. Ignatius (among others), the first performance was given by an all-Negro cast wearing cellophane costumes.

Four Seasons, The (It., *Le Quattro Stagioni*), a set of four violin concertos by Vivaldi (1725). They are full of charming pictorial effects – bird songs, storms, ice, and so on. During the 1950s, these concertos (which usually, though not necessarily, are performed as a group) helped to develop public interest in Vivaldi and did much to speed the baroque revival.

Four Temperaments, The, (1) title of Carl Nielsen's second symphony (1902), in which each 'temperament' is allotted a separate movement;

(2) title of a work for piano and strings by Hindemith (1940), consisting of a theme and variations in which each 'temperament' is allotted a variation. Neither work is concerned with temperament in the musical sense (i.e. the tempering of musical intervals) but with temperament in the sense of mood – choleric, phlegmatic, melancholic and sanguine.

fourth, the interval reached by ascending three steps in the diatonic scale, e.g.:

In the HARMONIC SERIES it is the interval between the third and fourth notes of the series, and therefore has the ratio $\frac{4}{3}$.

The following terms are in use:

Augmented fourth: a fourth of which the upper note is sharpened or the lower note flattened, e.g.:

Diminished fourth: a fourth of which the upper note is flattened or the lower note sharpened, e.g.:

Perfect fourth: the interval defined above, e.g.:

fourth chord, term for a chord consisting of super-imposed fourths, or of fourths in combination with other intervals. Skryabin's so-called 'mystic' chord (C–F sharp–B flat–E–A–D) was a chord of this kind, and was intended to replace normal major and minor chords. Other composers, including Bartók and Hindemith, have also made special use of fourth chords as elements in their harmonic idiom.

Fox Strangways, Arthur Henry (1859–1948), English critic. He studied at Oxford and Berlin, and wrote *The Music of Hindustan* (1914) after a visit to India. He held appointments on two London newspapers, *The Times* and *The Observer*, and was founder and editor of *Music and Letters* (1920). He wrote a biography of Cecil Sharp (1934) and made English translations of many German songs.

foxtrot, a dance of U.S. origin in duple time, which first became popular in 1912. Several variants appeared, and the word came to lose its limited application to a specific dance. From these variants two main types emerge – one fast, the other slow.

Fra Diavolo, ou L'Hôtellerie de Terracine (Fr., *Brother Devil, or The Inn at Terracina*), comic opera in three acts by Auber, to a libretto by Augustin Eugène Scribe, first performed in Paris in 1830.

Lord and Lady Allcash, having been robbed on the road from Rome to Naples, reach an inn at Terracina. The innkeeper's daughter Zerlina is in love with Lorenzo, a sergeant, who sets off to find the robbers, while she takes care of the reward offered for the recovery of the jewels. The Marquis di San Marco, who has been pressing his attentions on Lady Allcash, is discovered hiding in a closet after dark and is suspected of improper intentions both by Lord Allcash and by Lorenzo. Lorenzo discovers that at a given signal (the ringing of the chapel bell) the robber chief, Fra Diavolo, intends to kill Lord Allcash and abscond with his money and his wife. He orders the signal to be given. Fra Diavolo, who is none other than the Marquis, falls into the trap and is arrested, while Lorenzo marries Zerlina.

Fra Gherardo, opera in three acts by Pizzetti, to a libretto by the composer. First performed in Milan in 1928. The work is based on the 13th century *Chronicles of Salimbene de Parma,* and its première was conducted by Toscanini.

Françaix, Jean (born 1912), French composer, a pupil of Nadia Boulanger. His compositions, in a neo-classical style, include a symphony, a comic opera – *Le Diable boiteux,* an oratorio – *L'Apocalypse de St. Jean,* several ballets, *concertino* for piano and orchestra (1934), a piano concerto (1936) and chamber music. Though many of his works are succinctly written, he has produced one large-scale opera in four acts, *La Main de Gloire* (1950).

Francesca da Rimini, symphonic fantasy by Chaikovsky, op 32, inspired by Dante and first performed in Moscow in 1877. Chaikovsky originally intended to write an opera on the tragedy of Francesca; Rakhmaninov later did so (1906), using Pushkin's play as the basis of his libretto, with additions by Chaikovsky's brother, Modest. Other operas on the subject were written by Generali (1829), Goetz (1877, completed by Ernest Frank), Nápravník (1902) and Zandonai (1914).

Franchetti, Alberto (1860–1942), Italian composer of noble birth, whose spectacular operas earned him the nickname of the Meyerbeer of modern Italy. He studied in Dresden and Munich, where he was a pupil of Rheinberger. He was director of the Florence Conservatorio from 1926 until 1928. Among his operas are *Asrael* (Reggio d'Emilia, 1888), *Cristoforo Colombo* (Genoa, 1892) and *Germania* (Milan, 1902). *Giove a Pompei* (Rome, 1921) was written in collaboration with Giordano.

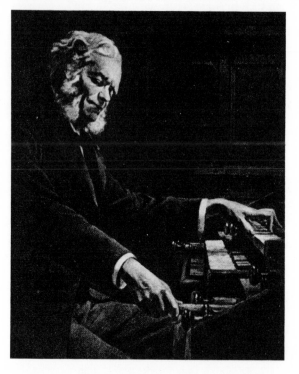

César Franck at the organ: 'Ah, we knew it well, we who were his pupils, the way up to that thrice-blessed organ-loft!'

Franck, César Auguste (1822–1890), Belgian composer and organist. After studying at the Liège and Paris Conservatoires he lived in Paris from 1844, becoming choirmaster at St. Clotilde (1853), organist (1859) and teacher of the organ at the Paris Conservatoire (1872). His music is romantic in style and expansive in manner, with a plentiful use of characteristic chromatic harmony, and much emphasis on cyclic form, in which thematic material employed in one movement of a work is brought back in later movements. His orchestral and chamber music, though admirably written for the medium, sometimes betrays the influence of the organ in its use of contrasts of colour and in a fondness for repetition and short-breathed phrases. At the age of 63 he was awarded the Légion d'Honneur, but for his organ playing, not his work as a composer. His principal compositions are:

(1) Oratorios: *Ruth* (1846), *La Tour de Babel* (1865), *Rédemption* (1872), *Les Béatitudes* (1880), *Rébecca* (1881).

(2) Church music: Mass for three voices; motets; offertories; *Psalm* 150.

(3) Operas: *Hulda* (Monte Carlo, 1894); *Ghiselle* (Monte Carlo, 1896).

(4) Orchestra: Symphony in D minor; *Variations symphoniques* for piano and orchestra; symphonic poems: *Les Eolides*, *Le Chasseur maudit*, *Les Djinns* (piano and orchestra), *Psyché* (chorus and orchestra).

(5) Chamber music: string quartet; piano quintet; four piano trios; violin sonata.

(6) Piano: *Prélude, choral et fugue*; *Prélude, aria et final*.

(7) Organ: Three chorales; miscellaneous pieces.

Also songs, miscellaneous piano solos, and pieces for harmonium.

    C. VAN DEN BORREN: *L'Oeuvre dramatique de César Franck* (1907)

    V. D'INDY: *César Franck* (1906)

    L. VALLAS: *César Franck* (1952)

Franck, Johann Wolfgang (born 1644), German composer. He was *Kapellmeister* at Ansbach from 1673 to 1678, and active as an opera composer in Hamburg from 1679 to 1686. From 1690 to 1695 he was in London where he gave concerts in conjunction with Robert King. A modern edition of his opera *Die drey Töchter Cecrops* (Ansbach, 1679) is in *Das Erbe deutscher Musik*, *Landschaftsdenkmale, Bayern*, ii; a modern edition of his *Geistliche Lieder* (sacred songs, 1681) is in *Denkmäler deutscher Tonkunst*, xlv. He published a collection of secular songs in London under the title *Remedium Melancholiae* (1690).

    W. B. SQUIRE: 'J. W. Franck in England' in *Musical Antiquary*, July 1912

Franck, Melchior (c. 1573–1639), German composer of church music, songs and instrumental works. He was *Kapellmeister* at Coburg in 1603. A modern edition of selected instrumental works is in *Denkmäler deutscher Tonkunst*, xvi.

Franco de Colonia (Franco of Cologne), 13th century theorist, whose treatise *Ars cantus mensurabilis* (modern edition by G. Reaney and A. Gilles, 1974; English translation in O. Strunk, *Source Readings in Music History*, pages 139–59) systematized the notation of mensural music and did away with many ambiguities, particularly in the interpretation of LIGATURES. For a detailed account of his system *see* W. Apel, *The Notation of Polyphonic Music, 900–1600* (fifth edition, 1961), chapter 5.

Frankel, Benjamin (1906–1973), English composer and teacher, the son of a synagogue beadle. After studying at the Guildhall School of Music, he was active for several years in the field of popular music as violinist, pianist, conductor and arranger of scores. His serious compositions, most of which date from the post-war years, include a violin concerto, eight symphonies, five string quartets, unaccompanied sonatas for violin and viola, and a considerable amount of film music.

Franz, Robert (1815–92), German composer. Because of parental opposition, his musical education was desultory, apart from two years with Friedrich Schneider in Dessau. In 1841 he was appointed organist at the Ulrichskirche in his hometown of Halle, and in 1859 he became university director of music. Deafness and nervous troubles compelled him to retire in 1868. He composed more than 250 songs, the quality of his work in this medium being quickly recognised by Schumann and Liszt. His enthusiasm for the works of Bach and Handel led him to write additional accompaniments to Bach's *St. Matthew Passion*, *Magnificat*, and ten cantatas, Handel's *Messiah* and *L'Allegro*, and other works.

Fraser, Marjorie Kennedy, *see* KENNEDY FRASER

Frau ohne Schatten, Die (Ger., *The Woman without a Shadow*), opera in three acts by Richard Strauss, to a libretto by Hugo von Hofmannsthal (based on his story with the same title). It was first performed in Vienna in 1919. This long and complicated allegory on the subject of unselfishness has been hailed by some authorities as Strauss's masterpiece. The story concerns a fairy princess who has to find her shadow (symbol of fertility) to prevent her husband, an Eastern emperor, being turned to stone. In the end she earns her shadow through the unselfishness of her actions. For a full analysis of the piece, *see* William Mann's *Richard Strauss* (1964).

Frauenliebe und Leben (Ger., *Woman's Love and Life*), cycle of eight songs by Schumann, op 42 (1840), depicting the emotional experiences of a woman's life, from falling in love to the death of her husband. Words by Adalbert von Chamisso.

Frauenlob (Ger., praise of ladies), the name given to Heinrich von Meissen (c. 1260–1318), one of the last of the *Minnesinger*. Examples of his melodies are in *Denkmäler der Tonkunst in Osterreich*, xli, Jg. xx (2), and in B. G. Seagrave and W. Thomas, *The Songs of the Minnesingers* (1966).

Frederick the Great (1712–86), King of Prussia, otherwise known as Frederick (or Friedrich) II. He studied music under Gottlob Hayn, organist of Berlin Cathedral, and in 1728 received flute lessons from Quantz. He established a private band at his Rheinsberg castle (1734) and on his accession (1740) created a court band at Berlin and Potsdam. C. P. E. Bach and Quantz were among his employees. While C. P. E. Bach was in his service, J. S. Bach visited him (1747) and subsequently dedicated *The Musical Offering* to the musical king. Frederick himself was a prolific composer. His enthusiasm for the flute inspired him to compose as many as 100 works featuring that instrument.

Freischütz, Der (Ger., *The Marksman*), *Singspiel* (opera with dialogue) in three acts by Weber. The libretto by Friedrich Kind is based on a story in Johann August Apel and Friedrich Laun's *Gespensterbuch* (1811). The first performance was in Berlin in 1821.

Agathe, daughter of the head forester, is to be the prize in a shooting contest. Max, uncertain of his skill and anxious to win her hand, is persuaded by Caspar to visit the Wolf's Glen, where seven magic bullets are cast under the direction of the evil spirit Samiel. When the contest is held Samiel directs the seventh bullet towards Agathe, but her bridal wreath saves her: his victim is Caspar, whose soul is forfeit to the devil.

Der Freischütz, with its scenes (macabre or otherwise) from provincial life, is a milestone of German opera, opening up a new world of romanticism and using the orchestra with a new vividness which was soon to win the admiration of Berlioz. Its influence was far-reaching – Wagner's *Flying Dutchman* was one of the works it later helped to inspire.

French horn, *see* HORN

French overture, *see* OVERTURE

French sixth, *see* AUGMENTED SIXTH

French Suites, the name given to a set of six keyboard suites by J. S. Bach, probably written (about 1722) for his second wife, Anna Magdalena Bach. Forkel, Bach's earliest biographer, says that they were so called 'because they are written in the French style' (*Johann Sebastian Bach*, translated by C. Sanford Terry, page 128). They are on a smaller scale than the ENGLISH SUITES.

Frere, Walter Howard (1863–1938), English liturgiologist, educated at Cambridge and ordained in 1887. His publications include two volumes of facsimiles – *Graduale Sarisburiense* (1894) and *Antiphonale Sarisburiense* (1901–24), a catalogue of liturgical manuscripts in the British Isles – *Bibliotheca Musicoliturgica* (two volumes, 1901–32), an edition of the text (not the music) of *The Winchester Troper* (1894), and the introduction to the historical edition of *Hymns Ancient and Modern* (1909).

Frescobaldi, Girolamo (1583–1643). Italian organist and composer, a pupil of Luzzaschi. He visited Flanders in 1607 and 1608, and was organist at St. Peter's, Rome, from 1608 to 1628 (apart from a few months absence at the court of Mantua in 1615). In 1628 he was appointed organist to the Grand Duke of Tuscany, Florence, but he returned to St. Peter's, Rome, in 1634, remaining there until his death. He was one of the outstanding organists of his time, and his pupils included Froberger. His keyboard compositions have been edited in five volumes by P. Pidoux. They include *ricercari, canzoni francesi,* toccatas, capriccios, and a collection entitled *Fiori musicali*. He also published *canzoni* for instrumental ensemble, arias for one or more voices, and a set of madrigals.

> A. MACHABEY: *Girolamo Frescobaldi Ferrarensis* (1952)
>
> H. F. REDLICH: 'Girolamo Frescobaldi', *Music Review*, xiv (1953)
>
> L. RONGA: *Girolamo Frescobaldi* (1930)

fret (Fr., *touche*; Ger., *Bund*; It., *tasto*), a thin piece of material fitted to the finger-board of a string instrument to facilitate the stopping of the string. Each fret marks the position of a specific note in the scale, and the effect of stopping on a fret is to produce a quality similar to that of an open note. Frets are used on the viol, lute, guitar and similar instruments, but not on members of the violin family. They were formerly made of pieces of gut tied tightly round the finger-board, but are now generally made of wood or metal fixed permanently in position.

Fricker, Peter Racine (born 1920), English composer. He studied at the Royal College of Music in London and privately with Mátyás Seiber, making his mark in 1947 with a wind quintet which won the Alfred Clements prize. As a teacher of composition at the R. C. M. from 1951 and as director of music at Morley College he had a considerable influence on younger musicians. In 1965 he was appointed professor at the University of California. His compositions, which are highly concentrated and individual in idiom, include three symphonies, a violin concerto and a *Rapsodia*

Concertante for violin and orchestra, a viola concerto, chamber music, piano music and songs. His first symphony won the Koussevitsky award.

Fricsay, Ferenc (1914–63), Hungarian conductor. He was a pupil of Kodály and Bartók, and was a gifted exponent of their music. He worked principally in Germany, especially West Berlin and Munich, but died too soon to fulfil his obvious potential.

Friedenstag, (Ger., *Peace Day*), opera in one act by Richard Strauss, to a libretto by Joseph Gregor, first performed in Munich in 1938. Based on Calderón's drama, *La redención de Breda* (1625), the work deals with a besieged city during the Thirty Years War, and culminates in a hymn to peace. *Friedenstag* was the last opera completed by Strauss before the outbreak of World War II. Though it has failed to hold a major place in the Strauss canon, it was initially very successful, in spite of Hitlerian disapproval.

Friedheim, Arthur (1859–1932), Russian pianist, a pupil of Liszt, in the interpretation of whose works he excelled. He lived at various times in Germany, the United States and England.

Friedländer, Max (1852–1934), German baritone and writer on music. He studied under Garcia in London, and taught in Berlin and at Harvard. His books include *Das deutsche Lied im 18 Jahrhundert* (three volumes, 1902) and *Brahms's Lieder* (1922; English edition, 1928).

Friedman, Ignacy (1882–1948), Polish pianist and a pupil of Leschetizky. He edited the piano works of Chopin (Breitkopf & Härtel), Schumann and Liszt (Universal Edition). His compositions, totalling nearly 100, are mainly for the piano.

Friml, Rudolf (1879–1972), Czech composer and pianist. He settled in the United States in 1906, and wrote a series of popular operettas, including *The Firefly, Rose Marie* and *The Vagabond King*.

friska, friss (Hung.), *see* CSÁRDAS

Froberger, Johann Jakob (1616–67), German organist and composer, a pupil of Frescobaldi. He was court organist at Vienna in 1637 (for nine months only), from 1641 to 1645, and from 1653 to 1657. During the intervening periods he travelled extensively; for example, between 1649 and 1653 he visited Rome, Brussels, Paris and London. His later years were spent in the house of Duchess Sibylla of Württemberg at Héricourt. His keyboard works, consisting of toccatas, fantasias, *canzoni,* capriccios, *ricercari* and suites, were published after his death. Many of them are reprinted in *Denkmäler der Tonkunst in Osterreich*, viii (Jg. iv, 1), xiii (Jg. vi, 2) and xxi (Jg. x, 2).

> G. B. SHARP: 'J. J. Froberger', *Musical Times*, cviii (December, 1967)

frog (U.S.), the NUT of a violin and violin bow.

Frog Galliard, the name given to a popular Elizabethan tune, possibly by Dowland who set it as a lute solo and adapted it to the words 'Now, oh now I needs must part'.

'Frog' Quartet (Ger., *Froschquartett*), the nickname given to Haydn's string quartet in D major, op 50, no 6, because of the supposedly 'croaking' theme in the finale.

From Bohemia's Fields and Groves, *see* MÁ VLAST

From my Life (Cz., *Z mého zivota*), title of Smetana's string quartet no 1 in E minor (1876), indicating that the work has autobiographical associations. In particular the sustained high E for the first violin in the last movement alludes to the composer's deafness. The German title, *Aus meinem Leben*, need not be used in English-speaking countries.

From the House of the Dead, opera in three acts by Janáček, to a text by the composer, based on Dostoyevsky's *Memoirs from the House of the Dead*. Janáček's last opera, completed by Bretislav Bakala and O. Zitek, was first performed at Brno in 1930, two years after his death. Though the work has no real plot, it gives an extraordinarily powerful and human picture of life in a Siberian prison camp. At the head of the score, the composer inscribed the words, 'In every human being there is a divine spark' – a statement which perfectly sums up the opera itself.

From the New World, the title of Dvořák's symphony no 9 in E minor, op 95, composed in the United States in 1893 and published in 1894. There is no basis for the popular belief that some of its melodies are those of U.S. Negro music, though there are allusions to idioms of such music.

Frosch, am, (Ger.) played 'at the nut' of the bow.

Froschquartett, *see* 'FROG' QUARTET

frottola, It., literally 'little mixture'. A type of strophic song of a popular character current in aristocratic circles in late 15th and early 16th century Italy – a forerunner of the MADRIGAL. It was marked by clearly defined rhythms and simple harmony in three (or more frequently four) parts, intended either for a vocal ensemble or for a solo voice with instrumental accompaniment. Many *frottole* were also issued for solo voice with lute accompaniment (for example, by F. Bossinensis, 1509 and 1511; modern edition by B. Disertori, 1964). The subject-matter was generally amorous. Eleven books of *frottole* were published by Petrucci (1504–14). A modern edition of books i and iv is in *Publikationen älterer Musik*, viii; books i, ii and iii have also been edited, by G. Cesari (1954).

    A. EINSTEIN: *The Italian Madrigal*, three volumes (1949)

Frühlingssonate, *see* SPRING SONATA

Frühlingssymphonie, *see* SPRING SYMPHONY

Fuenllana, Miguel, blind Spanish lutenist and composer of the early 16th century. His collection *Orphenica Lyra* (1554) includes original compositions (lute songs and instrumental pieces) and transcriptions of madrigals and motets by contemporary composers: examples are in G. Morphy, *Les luthistes espagnols du xvie siècle* (1902).

fuga, (1) (Lat.), in 15th and 16th centuries = CANON. (2) (It.), fugue.

fugato (It.), literally 'fugued'. The name given to a section of a composition which is treated fugally, though the composition as a whole is not a fugue. The slow movement of Beethoven's seventh symphony incorporates a *fugato*.

Fuge (Ger.), fugue.

fughetta (It.), a short fugue.

fugue (Fr., *fugue*; It., *fuga*; Ger., *Fuge*), a contrapuntal composition in two or more parts or 'voices', built on a SUBJECT – a theme (short or long) which is introduced at the beginning in imitation and recurs frequently in

the course of the composition. The second entry of the subject (generally a fifth higher or a fourth lower, but sometimes a fourth higher or a fifth lower) is called the ANSWER: it is often slightly modified to preserve the tonality of the piece or to facilitate the third entry of the subject, which will be identical with the first, though in a higher or lower octave. The third entry is often deferred for one or more bars, the intervening space being occupied by a CODETTA. When the answer enters, the subject continues with a counterpoint to it, which if it is used in the rest of the fugue is called the COUNTERSUBJECT. A countersubject is generally so designed that it can be treated in DOUBLE COUNTERPOINT with the subject. The initial entries of the subject are generally as many as the number of parts (or 'voices') in the fugue; sometimes, however, there is an additional entry, known rather illogically as a 'redundant' entry. When all the parts have made their entries (including a redundant entry, if any), the EXPOSITION of the fugue is complete. The following examples of expositions will serve to illustrate the description given above:

BACH, *48 Preludes and Fugues*, Book II, no 17

BACH, *48 Preludes and Fugues*, Book I, no 21

The rest of the fugue consists of further entries of the subject, several of which will be in related keys for the sake of modulation, normally interspersed with contrapuntal EPISODES based on material derived from the subject or countersubject or both, or entirely independent of either. Among the devices which may be used in the presentation of the subject in the course of a fugue are AUGMENTATION (lengthening the note values), DIMINUTION (shortening the note values), INVERSION (presenting it upside down) and STRETTO (two or more entries in close imitation). None of these devices is essential for a fugue, nor are countersubjects (Bach wrote several fugues without them). Bach's 48 *Preludes and Fugues* show an inexhaustible variety of treatment; the first fugue of Book I even dispenses with episodes.

Sometimes one or more countersubjects appear at the beginning of the fugue simultaneously with the subject, in which case the subject and countersubject (or countersubjects) form a unity and the fugue may be said to have a subject in two (or more) parts. Such a fugue is often described as a double (or triple, or quadruple) fugue. The term 'double fugue', however, is more properly applied to one in which a second, independent subject appears in the course of the fugue and is subsequently combined with the first subject. A triple fugue is one in which three subjects appear independently and are then combined, a quadruple fugue one in which four subjects are similarly treated.

A fugue may be written for voices (unaccompanied, or doubled by instruments, or with independent instrumental accompaniment), for an instrumental ensemble, or for a keyboard instrument. It may occur as an independent piece, or in association with a prelude, or as a movement in a suite, sonata or symphony or as part of an oratorio, cantata or opera (e.g. the finale of Verdi's *Falstaff*). It may also be written so as to form the accompaniment to a CANTUS FIRMUS, e.g. a plainsong melody, a hymn-tune, or a theme used for a set of variations.

The origin of the fugue is to be found in the imitative entries introduced in polyphonic vocal music in the late 15th century and imitated in the instrumental *ricercar*, and subsequently in the *canzona* and capriccio. As an independent form the fugue may be said to date from the 17th century.

A. GÉDALGE: *Traité de la fugue* (1901)
C. H. KITSON: *The Elements of Fugal Construction* (1929); *Studies in Fugue* (1909)
G. OLDROYD: *The Technique and Spirit of Fugue* (1948)
E. PROUT: *Fugal Analysis* (1892)

full anthem, an ANTHEM in which the voices (whether the full choir or an ensemble of solo voices) supply all the necessary harmony, without the need for any independent accompaniment, in contrast to the VERSE ANTHEM, where important sections are assigned to one or more solo voices with independent accompaniment.

full close, another name for the perfect CADENCE.

Fuller-Maitland, John Alexander (1856–1936), English critic and editor, educated at Cambridge. He was music critic of *The Times* from 1889 until 1911. He edited the second edition of Grove's *Dictionary of Music and Musicians* (1904–10). He also edited *English County Songs* (with Lucy Broadwood, 1893), *English Carols of the Fifteenth Century* (with W. S. Rockstro), and *The Fitzwilliam Virginal Book* (with W. B. Squire, two volumes, 1899), as well as two volumes and part of a third in the Purcell Society's edition.

full score, an orchestral SCORE, in which the parts for the various instruments appear on separate staves arranged in a (usually) conventional order on the page.

fundamental, the first, or lowest, note of the HARMONIC SERIES. On wind instruments it can be produced satisfactorily on the trombone, euphonium and tuba.

fundamental bass (Fr., *basse fondamentale*), a term employed by Rameau to indicate the 'root' of any chord, or the 'roots' of a series of chords. Any two chords composed of the same notes, in whatever vertical order these notes may be arranged are considered to have the same fundamental bass, e.g. in the following series of chords:

the fundamental bass would be:

This interpretation is the foundation of the theory of INVERSIONS, which is generally accepted in modern textbooks on HARMONY. Its fallacy lies in the fact that harmony results from the combination of melodic lines, not from a preconceived association of chords.

Funeral Ode, see TRAUER-ODE

fuoco (It.), 'fire'. *Con fuoco*, with fire.

furiant, a Czech dance, in quick triple time with syncopation. There are several examples in the works of Smetana and Dvořák, e.g.:

DVOŘÁK, *Symphony in D*, op 60

furlana, see FORLANA

Furtwängler, Wilhelm (1886–1954), German conductor and composer, son of the archaeologist Adolf Furtwängler. Born in Berlin, he studied in Munich with Rheinberger and Schillings, and acquired experience of conducting in various centres, including Zurich and Strasbourg. After holding posts in Lubeck, Mannheim and elsewhere, he succeeded Nikisch as conductor of the Leipzig Gewandhaus concerts (1922–8) and from 1922 until 1945 was conductor of the Berlin Philharmonic. He conducted frequently at the Bayreuth and Salzburg festivals, and as guest conductor with numerous orchestras. In the opera house he was noted specially for his Wagner interpretations, and in the concert hall for his conducting of Beethoven, Brahms and Bruckner. His grasp of the structure of the music he conducted has never been surpassed, though the flexibility of his tempi often aroused controversy, as did his position of importance during the Nazi era. His qualities as a musician, however, enabled him to rebuild his career after World War II, and his death at the age of 68 left the musical world the poorer. Posthumously he remains one of the most influential conductors of the century, his recordings (which he himself never rated highly) being pored over and his interpretations emulated by a new generation of musicians.

His compositions include two symphonies, a piano concerto, a *Te Deum* and chamber music. He also published books on Brahms and Bruckner and a volume of essays entitled *Gespräche über Musik* (1948).

future, music of the, see ZUKUNFTSMUSIK

futurism (It., *futurismo*), a movement started by the Italian writer F. T. Marinetti in 1911. The first concert of futurist music was given by him and the composer Luigi Rossolo in Milan in 1914. The programme consisted of 'four networks of noises' with the following titles:

(1) Awakening of Capital.
(2) Meeting of cars and aeroplanes.
(3) Dining on the terrace of the Casino.
(4) Skirmish in the oasis.

The instruments employed were bumblers, exploders, thunderers, whistlers etc., specially invented to perform the works. The concert ended in a violent battle between the performers and the audience. Futurist music was defined by Marinetti, who appears to have been a passionate admirer of Mussolini, as 'a synthetic expression of great economic, erotic, heroic, aviational, mechanical dynamism'.

Fux, Johann Joseph (1660–1741), Austrian composer and theorist. He was court composer at Vienna in 1698, second *Kapellmeister* at St. Stephen's in 1705, *Kapellmeister* there from 1712 to 1715, vice-*Kapellmeister* at the court in 1713, and *Kapellmeister* there in 1715. His compositions include a considerable amount of church music, ten oratorios, eighteen operas and instrumental music. A modern edition of the opera *Costanza e fortezza*, written to celebrate the coronation of the Emperor Charles VI as King of Bohemia (Prague, 1723), is in *Denkmäler der Tonkunst in Österreich*, xxxiv–xxxv, Jugend xvii. Other volumes in the same series contain his selected Masses and motets (i, Jugend i, 1, and iii, Jugend ii, 1), his selected *sonate da chiesa* and overtures (xix, Jugend ix, 2), his *Concentus musico-instrumentalis* consisting of seven partitas for orchestra (xlvii, Jugend xxiii, 2), his keyboard works (lxxxv), and his solo motets (ci–cii). A complete edition of his works by the Fux society of Graz was begun in 1959. His treatise on counterpoint, *Gradus ad Parnassum* (1725; facsimile edition, 1966; modern English edition, 1943) was long a standard work.

E. WELLESZ: *Fux* (1965)

G (Eng., Ger.; Fr., It., *sol*), the fifth note (or dominant) of the scale of C major. As an abbreviation *m.g.* = *main gauche* (left hand), G.P. = *Generalpause* (a rest for the complete orchestra).

The G clef, now invariably placed on the second line of the stave, is the treble clef, marking the G above middle C:

Gabrieli, Andrea (c. 1515–86), Italian composer and organist, a pupil of Willaert. He succeeded Merulo as second organist of St. Mark's, Venice. His compositions include madrigals, motets, Masses and a number of instrumental works (see *Istituzioni e monumenti dell'arte musicale italiana*, i). Ten madrigals edited by D. Arnold were published in 1970. Selections from his keyboard works have been edited by P. Pidoux in five volumes (1952–9).

Giovanni Gabrieli (?1557–1612), nephew and pupil of Andrea, became a composer and organist. He was appointed first organist of St. Mark's, Venice in 1585. Among his pupils was Heinrich Schütz. His numerous compositions include some elaborate motets with instrumental accompaniment, ensemble works for up to 22 instruments (which show a lively appreciation of colour), and organ works. A complete edition of his music was begun by D. Arnold in 1956. His instrumental publications of 1597 and 1615 have been reprinted respectively in *Istituzioni e monumenti dell'arte musicale italiana*, ii, and in an edition by M. Sanvoisin (1971). His keyboard works have been edited by G. S. Bedbrook (1957).

E. KENTON: *Life and Works of Giovanni Gabrieli* (1967)

Gabrielli, Caterina (1730–96), Italian soprano, a pupil of Porpora. She sang at Venice (1754) and in Vienna (1755–61), where she appeared in operas by Gluck and Traetta. Later she visited St. Petersburg and London. She was a brilliant coloratura who was less well qualified for passages demanding a sustained tone.

Gabrilovich, Ossip Salomonovich (1878–1936), Russian born pianist and composer. He studied with Anton Rubinstein, Liadov and Glazunov in St. Petersburg, and with Leschetizky in Vienna. He was conductor of the Munich Konzertverein (1910–14), Detroit Symphony Orchestra, (1918) and the Philadelphia Orchestra (with Stokowski, 1928). His wife was the singer, Clara Clemens, daughter of Mark Twain.

Gaburo, Kenneth (born 1926), U.S. composer, whose works have made increasing use of electronic music.

He has written two tape operas (concrete and electronic) as well as more conventional ones – *The Snow Queen* (1952) and *The Widow* (1959). A series of works entitled *Antiphony* employ a mixture of instrumental and electronic forces. His chamber music includes a series of *Ideas and Transformations* for string duo, a string quartet in one movement (1956) and *Line Studies* for flute, clarinet, trombone and viola (1957). He founded the New Music Choral Ensemble in 1964, and has won Pierre Boulez's enthusiasm for his activities in the vocal sphere.

Gade, Niels Wilhelm (1817–90), Danish composer who studied in Copenhagen and became a violinist in the Royal Orchestra. He won a prize for composition with his overture *Ossian* (1840) and went to Leipzig, where he received much encouragement from Mendelssohn. From 1844 until 1848 he was conductor (partly with Mendelssohn) of the Leipzig Gewandhaus concerts. On the outbreak of war between Germany and Denmark in 1848, he returned to Copenhagen, where he established himself as organist and conductor. A gentle rather than a forceful composer, he was one of the many who drew their inspiration mainly from the example of Mendelssohn and Schumann, though there are also traces of national colour in his work. His compositions include eight symphonies, six overtures, violin concerto, several cantatas, chamber music, piano solos and songs.

Gafori, Franchino (1451–1522), Italian theorist and composer, known also by the Latinized form of his name, Franchinus Gafurius. He was *maestro di cappella* at Milan Cathedral in 1484. His most important works are *Theorica musicae* and *Practica musicae*, of which facsimiles were published in 1967. An English translation by Clement A. Miller of *Practica musicae* was published in 1968. Gafori's compositions include Masses, Magnificats and motets. The Masses have been edited in two volumes by L. Finscher (1955–60).

Gagliano, a firm of violin-makers active in Naples in the late 17th and 18th centuries.

Gagliano, Marco da (c. 1575–1642), Italian composer. He was *maestro di cappella* at San Lorenzo, Florence, in 1608, and subsequently to the Grand Duke of Tuscany. He published six books of madrigals, as well as motets and a Mass, but is best known today as one of the first opera-composers. His *Dafne* (a setting of Rinuccini's libretto) was first performed at Mantua, 1608 (reprinted in part in *Publikationen älterer praktischer und theoreticher Musikwerke*, x).

gagliarda, gaillarde, *see* GALLIARD

Gál, Hans (born 1890), Austrian composer and teacher, a pupil of Mandyczewski. Gál won a State prize for composition in 1915 and went on to become the director of the Musikhochschule, Mainz, in 1929. From 1938, after the *Anschluss*, he lived in Edinburgh, where he became a lecturer at the University in 1945 until 1956. His compositions include the operas *Der Arzt der Sobeide* (Breslau, 1919), *Die heilige Ente* (Düsseldorf, 1923), *Das Lied der Nacht* (Breslau, 1926) and *Die beiden Klaas*, two symphonies, choral and orchestral works, violin concerto and chamber music.

galant, *see* STYLE GALANT

Galanterien (Ger.), a name given in the 18th century to dances in a suite which were added optionally to the regular allemande, courante, sarabande and gigue. Their place was normally after the sarabande and before the gigue. Thus, Bach's six *English Suites* comprise:

(1) Prelude, allemande, courante I & II (with two doubles), sarabande, bourrée I & II, gigue.

(2) Prelude, allemande, courante, sarabande (with variant), bourrée I & II, gigue.

(3) Prelude, allemande, courante, sarabande (with variant), gavotte I & II, gigue.

(4) Prelude, allemande, courante, sarabande, menuet I & II, gigue.

(5) Prelude, allemande, courante, sarabande, passepied I & II, gigue.

(6) Prelude, allemande, courante, sarabande (with double), gavotte I and II, gigue.

Galilei, Vincenzo (c. 1520–1591), Italian lutenist and composer, father of the astronomer, Galileo Galilei. He was prominent among the Florentines who, at Count Bardi's house, discussed the question of the revival of Greek drama and contributed to the creation of the declamatory song for solo voice which played an important part in the first operas. He published madrigals and lute music (see *Istituzioni e monumenti dell'arte musicale italiana*, iv), a collection of instrumental duos (1584; modern edition by L. Rood, 1947), and two dialogues – *Fronimo* (1568), dealing with lute tablature, and *Dialogo della musica antica et della moderna* (1581; facsimile edition, 1934). The latter is an attack on the theories of his former teacher, Gioseffo Zarlino, who published a reply in his *Sopplimenti musicali* (1588). This prompted a further attack from Galilei, *Discorso intorno all'opere di messer Gioseffo Zarlino* (1589). An English translation of part of the *Dialogo* is in O. Strunk, *Source Readings in Music History* (1950), pages 302–22.

gallant style, *see* STYLE GALANT

galliard (Fr., *gaillarde*, It., *gagliarda*), a lively dance, generally in triple time, which takes its name from the French *gaillard*, 'merry', and is first found in the early 16th century, for example:

CLAUDE GERVAISE (*Les Maitres musiciens de la Renaissance française*, xxiii, page 43)

From the second half of the 16th century it was regularly used to provide a contrast to the slow PAVANE, which it followed, and with which it was often thematically connected:

BYRD, *My Lady Nevell's Booke*, nos 20–1

Galliard, John Ernest (Johann Ernst) (c. 1680–1749), oboist and composer, of German origin. He came to England in the early 18th century as musician to Prince George of Denmark. In addition to numerous compositions he translated into English Pier Francesco Tosi's *Opinioni de' cantori antichi e moderni, o sieno osservazioni sopra il canto figurato* (1723) under the title *Observations on the Florid Song* (1742).

Galli-Curci, Amelita (1882–1963), Italian coloratura soprano. She studied at the Milan Conservatorio but was self taught as a singer. She first appeared in *Rigoletto* in Rome in 1909, and subsequently in South America and Spain. Her first appearance in the United States was at Chicago in 1916. She never performed in opera in Britain.

Gallus, *see* HANDL

galop, a quick dance in 2/4 time, popular in the 19th century, especially in Germany (where it originated) and France (where Offenbach parodied it).

galoubet (Fr.), a three-hole whistle-flute, held in the player's left hand; with the right hand he beats the tabor (TAMBOURIN), a small drum suspended from the left arm. Many composers have imitated the effect of this popular music-making.

Galpin, Francis William (1858–1945), English musicologist and collector of musical instruments. Educated at Trinity College, Cambridge, he was ordained in 1883 and spent some fifty years of his life as a parish priest. His interest in musical instruments, of which he had practical knowledge, ranged from the Sumerians' to the latest developments of electronic sound-production. His books include *Old English Instruments of Music* (1910; third edition, 1932), *A Textbook of European Musical Instruments* (1937) and *The Music of the Sumerians, Babylonians and Assyrians* (1937). In 1946, in his memory, the Galpin

Society was founded for the investigation of the history of musical instruments.

Galuppi, Baldassare (1706–85), Italian composer, pupil of Lotti in Venice. He was frequently known as 'Il Buranello', from his birthplace, Burano, an island near Venice. Between 1728 and 1740 he produced a large number of operas for Venice and Turin. He also produced several operas in London between 1741 and 1743. He became second *maestro di capella* at St. Mark's, Venice, in 1748, and first *maestro di capella* in 1762. In the same year he became director of the Conservatorio degli Incurabili. From 1766 until 1768 he was in St. Petersburg, where he produced several operas; he then returned to the directorship of the Conservatorio in Venice. His comic operas are a notable contribution to the history of the form. He also wrote several oratorios, symphonies, concertos, and keyboard sonatas. The 'Toccata' to which Browning devoted a poem is an imaginary work.

gamba, abbreviation for VIOLA DA GAMBA.

Gambler, The, opera in four acts by Prokofiev, to a text by the composer, after Dostoyevsky's story. It was first produced at Brussels in 1929, after the projected Leningrad première was cancelled because of the Revolution.

gamelan orchestra, the orchestra of Indonesia. Gamelan orchestras are principally composed of xylophones and marimbas, gongs and drums. Each community possesses its own gamelan orchestra, which may number up to about thirty players performing on three times as many instruments. The music is based on simple five-note scales, but is highly sophisticated in texture and rhythmically very complex.

gamme (Fr.), scale.

gamut, (1) in medieval theory the note

a combination of *gamma* (the letter G in Greek) and *ut*, the first note of the HEXACHORD. The Greek capital letter   (G) was assigned to this note, because it was below the lowest note of the two-octave scale system of the Greeks, to which medieval theorists had assigned the letter A;

(2) the scale beginning on the note *gamma ut*, and hence more generally the range or compass of a voice or instrument;

(3) the key of G, e.g. Purcell's 'Ground in Gamut' is in the key of G major, his 'Overture, Air and Jig in Gamut ♭', in the key of G minor (*see* FLAT).

Ganassi, Silvestro di, 16th century Italian theorist, resident in Venice. He was author and publisher of a tutor for the recorder, *La Fontegara* (1535; facsimile edition 1934), and a tutor for the viols, *Regola Rubertina* (1542–3; facsimile edition by M. Schneider, 1924).

Ganz, Rudolph (1877–1972), Swiss pianist, conductor, and composer, who became a naturalized U.S. citizen. He studied in Zürich, Lausanne, and Strasbourg, and subsequently with Busoni in Berlin. He taught piano at the Chicago Musical College from 1901 until 1905, and became its president in 1934. He was conductor of the St. Louis Symphony Orchestra from 1921 until 1927.

Ganz, Wilhelm (1833–1914), German pianist, con-

ductor and singing teacher, resident in Britain from 1850. He accompanied Jenny Lind and many other famous singers. As a composer he introduced Berlioz's *Symphonie fantastique* and Liszt's *Dante Symphony* to Britain. He published *Memories of a Musician* (1913).

Ganze Note (Ger.), semibreve.

Ganzton (Ger.), whole TONE.

garbato (It.), graceful.

Garcia, Manuel del Popolo Vincente (1775–1832), Spanish tenor, composer, and conductor. After his first appearance in Paris in 1808, he became well-known as an opera singer, touring widely in Italy, the United States, and Mexico. He also established a school of singing in London. The part of Almaviva in Rossini's *The Barber of Seville* was written for him. In 1826 he gave the United States première of Mozart's *Don Giovanni* in the presence of the librettist Da Ponte. His numerous operas had considerable success. His pupils included his children, Maria (MALIBRAN), Pauline (VIARDOT), and Manuel II.

His son, **Manuel Patricio Rodriguez Garcia** (1805–1906), invented the laryngoscope, and published *Mémoire sur la voix humaine* (1840) and *Traité complet de l'art du chant* (1847), both works of outstanding importance. As a teacher, his pupils included Jenny Lind, Mathilde Marchesi, Julius Stockhausen and Charles Santley.

M. STERLING MACKINLAY: *Garcia the Centenarian and his Times* (1908)

Gardano, Venetian music publishing firm, founded by Antonio Gardano. Their numerous publications of secular and sacred music appeared during the years 1538–1619.

Mary Garden in the title role which she created in the first performance of *Pelléas et Mélisande* in Paris in 1902

Garden, Mary (1877–1967), Scottish operatic soprano. She went to the United States as a child and studied singing in Chicago. In 1895 she moved to Paris, where she made her début in Charpentier's *Louise* in 1900, and was chosen by Debussy to sing Mélisande in *Pelléas et Mélisande* in 1902. Other roles she created included Massenet's Sapho and Saint-Saëns's Hélène. She made her first New York appearance in 1907 as Thaïs, and was director of the Chicago Opera from 1919 until 1920. Her entertaining biography, *The Mary Garden Story*, was published in 1951.

Garden of Fand, The, symphonic poem by Bax, first performed (in Chicago) in 1920. The work was inspired by an Irish legend, about a magic island which emerges from the sea before the approach of ships.

Gardiner, Henry Balfour (1877–1950), English composer. He was educated at Oxford, and also studied music with Ivan Knorr in Frankfurt. Though remembered chiefly for his *Shepherd Fennel's Dance* for orchestra (1911), he did great service for British music by promoting at his own expense orchestral concerts for the performance of works by contemporary composers.

Gardiner, William (1770–1853), English writer on music. A stocking-manufacturer by profession, he acquired an extensive knowledge of the works of Continental composers, particularly Beethoven, and adapted music by them to sacred words under the title *Sacred Melodies* (six volumes). In admiration for Haydn, he sent him six pairs of stockings into which were woven themes from Haydn's works.

Gardner, John (born 1917), English composer whose reputation was established with the performance of his first symphony at the 1951 Cheltenham Festival. He has written two operas, *The Moon and Sixpence* (inspired by Somerset Maugham's novel about Gauguin) and *The Visitors*; a ballet (*Reflection*); a piano concerto, orchestral variations on a waltz of Carl Nielsen, choral music, chamber music and songs.

Garlande, Jean de (**Johannes de Garlandia**), 13th century French theorist. He was the author of *De mensurabili musica* (modern edition by E. Reimer, Wiesbaden, 1972), the oldest extant treatise on MENSURAL NOTATION. Other musical writings have been conjecturally assigned to a younger writer of the same name, but without documentary authority. He is not to be identified with the grammarian Johannes de Garlandia who was born in Oxford about 1195 and was active in Paris and Toulouse.

R. A. RASCH: *Johannes de Garlandia* (1969) (in Dutch, with summary in English)

Gaspard de la Nuit (Fr., *Gaspard of the Night*), a set of three piano pieces by Ravel, written in 1908 and inspired by the prose-poems of the same title by Aloysius Bertrand, subtitled 'Fantasies in the style of Rembrandt and Callot'. Gaspard, or Caspar, is another name for Satan. The poems, morbid in nature, influenced Baudelaire in his *Spleen de Paris*. Ravel's pieces are (1) *Ondine*, a portrait of the water-nymph who lured young men to their death; (2) *Le Gibet* (the gallows); and (3) *Scarbo* (a diabolic clown).

Gasparini, Francesco (1668–1727), Italian composer, a pupil of Corelli and Pasquini, and teacher of Marcello. He wrote several oratorios and operas (one of which, *Ambleto*, was based on Shakespeare's *Hamlet*) and also published *L'Armonico pratico al cimbalo* (1708), a treatise on accompaniment from figured bass.

Gasparo da Salò, *see* SALÒ

Gassmann, Florion Leopold (1729–74), Sudeten composer. He left home at the age of twelve and studied for two years in Bologna with Martini. After a long period in private service in Venice, he became composer of ballets to the Vienna court and in 1772 court *Kapellmeister*. In 1771 he founded the *Tonkünstler-Sozietät* (now the *Haydn-Sozietät*) – a charity for the widows and orphans of musicians. His compositions include 54 symphonies, chamber music, church music and some 25 operas, of which *L'Amore Artigiano* (1769) and *La Contessina* (1770) are the most famous.

Gast, Peter (1854–1918), German composer, whose real name was Johann Heinrich Köselitz. He studied at the Leipzig Conservatorium and in Basel, where he became the friend and secretary of Nietzsche, whose letters he subsequently helped to edit. His best-known work is the opera *Die heimliche Ehe* (Danzig, 1891), founded on the libretto of Cimarosa's *Il matrimonio segreto*; it was revived under the title *Der Löwe von Venedig* (Chemnitz, 1933). His other compositions include chamber music, songs and a symphony.

Gastoldi, Giovanni Giacomo (c 1550–1622), Italian composer of church music, madrigals and balletts. He was *maestro di cappella* at Mantua from 1582 to 1609. His most popular work was his *Balletti a cinque voci con li suoi versi per cantare, sonare, e ballare* (1591, which was many times reprinted; modern edition by M. Sanvoisin, 1968). These gay, cheerful part songs, with 'fa la' refrain, had a considerable influence on other composers, notably in England. Morley's *First Booke of Balletts to Five Voyces* (1595) is a very close imitation of the style.

Gastoué, Amédée (1873–1943), French writer on music, a pupil of Lavignac and Guilmant. His special subject was Gregorian chant, which he taught for many years at the Schola Cantorum, Paris. He wrote many books on the subject.

Gatti, Guido Maria (1892–1973), Italian writer on music. He founded in 1920 the magazine *Il Pianoforte*, later known as *Rassegna Musicale*. He also organized the first Maggio Musicale in Florence in 1934. His books include studies of Schumann, Bizet, Pizzetti, French music and modern Italian music.

Gatty, Nicholas Comyn (1874–1946), English composer and critic, pupil of Stanford. He was for a time on the staff of Covent Garden Opera House, and was music critic of the *Pall Mall Gazette* from 1907 until 1914. His numerous compositions include several operas, among them *Greysteel*, *Duke or Devil*, *The Tempest* and *Prince Ferelon*.

Gaubert, Philippe (1879–1941), French flautist, conductor and composer. He studied at the Paris Conservatoire, where he taught the flute from 1919. He was conductor of the Société des Concerts du Conservatoire from 1919 until 1938. His compositions include operas, ballets, an oratorio, orchestral works, chamber music and songs.

Gaultier, Denis (died 1672), French lutenist and composer. His works include a manuscript collection entitled *La Rhétorique des dieux* (facsimile and modern edition in *Publications de la Société française de musicologie*, vi-vii), which consists of dance tunes for lute arranged in groups or suites. This method of arrangement occurs also in the works of the French harpsichord composers. Further evidence of the influence of Gaultier on harpsichord music is the imitation of his technique of broken chords (particularly suitable for the lute and almost equally effective on the harpsichord) and the use of fanciful names for the separate pieces.

Jacques Gaultier was a 17th century French lutenist and composer and a relative of Denis. He came to England in 1618 to escape the consequences of having killed a French nobleman, and entered the service of the Marquess (later the Duke) of Buckingham and subsequently of Charles I. Herrick, in his poem 'To M. Henry Lawes', refers to him as 'the rare Gotire.'

Gaveau, a firm of instrument makers in Paris, founded in 1847 by Joseph Gaveau (died 1903). In addition to making pianos the firm played a prominent part in the revival of the harpsichord. Étienne Gaveau, son of Joseph, built the Salle Gaveau in Paris in 1907. Another son, Gabriel, established an independent business in 1911.

Gaveaux, Pierre (1761–1825), French composer. After appearing as a tenor at the Paris Opéra-Comique in 1789, he devoted himself to composition. His numerous operas include *Léonore, ou l'Amour conjugal* (Paris, 1798), a setting of the libretto by J. N. Bouilly which, translated into Italian, was used by Paer for *Leonora ossia l'amore coniugale* (Dresden, 1804), and in German by Beethoven for *Fidelio oder die eheliche Liebe* (Vienna, 1805).

gavotte, a French dance, the popularity of which dates from its introduction by Lully into ballets and operas in the late 17th century. It retained its popularity in the 18th century: there are several examples in Bach's instrumental suites. It is in fairly quick 4/4 time and generally (though not invariably) starts on the third beat of the bar, e.g.:

BACH, *English Suites no 6*

Where two gavottes occur together in a suite, the second is often in the form of a MUSETTE.

Gazza Ladra, La (It., *The Thieving Magpie*), opera in two acts by Rossini, to a libretto by Giovanni Gherardini (after *La Pie voleuse* by Jean Marie Théodore Baudouin d'Aubigny and Louis Charles Caigniez).

It was first performed in Milan in 1817. The story concerns a maidservant who is condemned to death for thefts which in fact have been carried out by a magpie. A *deus ex machina* (in the form of the magpie itself) saves her in the nick of time. Though now known principally by its overture – one of Rossini's most scintillating – the opera has had a number of successful revivals in recent years.

Gazzaniga, Guiseppe (1743–1818), Italian composer, a pupil of Porpora and Piccinni. Of his numerous operas the one-act *Don Giovanni Tenorio ossia il convitato di pietra* (Venice, 1787) was very successful; the libretto, by Giovanni Bertati, was plainly familiar to Da Ponte, librettist of Mozart's *Don Giovanni,* which was performed at Prague later in the same year.

Gebrauchsmusik (Ger.), literally 'music for use' or 'utility music'. The term arose in Germany in the 1920s to describe music which was intended primarily for social or educational purposes rather than as a form of self-expression – particularly music suitable for domestic or amateur use. By its nature such music is free from elaboration or technical difficulties and is often so designed that instrumental music, for example, can be performed by any convenient ensemble that is available. Hindemith (who coined the term, later disowning it) and Weill were among the composers who devoted themselves to 'utility music'.

Gédalge, André (1856–1926), French composer and teacher at the Paris Conservatoire. His pupils included Ravel, Milhaud, Honegger and Schmitt. His most important educational publication is the *Traité de la fugue* (1901), which is a standard work in France. He also composed a considerable amount of instrumental music and works for the stage.

gedampft, (Ger.), muted.

gehalten (Ger.), sustained. *Gut gehalten,* well sustained.

geheimnisvoll (Ger.), mysterious.

gehend (Ger.), 'going'. i.e. moving at a moderate speed – the same as *andante*.

Geige (Ger.), fiddle, violin. *See* GIGUE (1)

Geiringer, Karl (born 1899), Austrian writer on music who moved to the United States and became professor at Boston University in 1941. His books include studies of Haydn, Brahms and the Bach family.

Geisslerlieder (Ger.), 'flagellants' songs'. Songs sung in procession by flagellants in 14th century Germany, a parallel to the *laudi spirituali* in Italy. They have been edited by P. Runge in *Die Lieder und Melodien der Geissler des Jahres 1349* (1900).

Geistertrio, (Ger.), 'Ghost Trio', a nickname given to Beethoven's piano trio in D major, op 70, no 1, on account of the mysterious character of the slow movement.

geistlich (Ger.), religious, sacred. *Geistlicher Lieder,* sacred songs.

gemächlich (Ger.), comfortable – the equivalent of *comodo*.

gemessen (Ger.), literally 'measured', hence held back, sustained in tempo.

Geminiani, Francesco (c. 1679–1762), Italian violinist and composer, a pupil of Corelli. He had a great success as a soloist, particularly in England, where he arrived in 1714. He lived in Dublin from 1733 to 1740 and from 1759 to 1762; the rest of his life was spent partly in London and partly in Paris. In addition to his numerous compositions (sonatas, trios, concertos and harpsichord solos) he published *Guida armonica o dizionario armonico* (1742), *Rules for Playing in a True Taste on the Violin, German flute, Violoncello and Harpsichord* (?1745), *A Treatise of Good Taste in the Art of Musick* (1749; facsimile edition, 1969), *The Art of Playing on the Violin* (1751; facsimile edition by

D. Boyden, 1952), *The Art of Accompaniment* (1756–7), *The Art of Playing the Guitar* (1760). *The Art of Playing on the Violin* is important as a record of the established practice of violin-playing at the time and as one of the first published tutors for the instrument (see D. Boyden, 'Geminiani and the First Violin Tutor' in *Acta Musicologica*, xxxi, 1959). *The Art of Accompaniment* is discussed in F. T. Arnold, *The Art of Accompaniment from a Thorough-Bass* (1931), pages 438–9, 463–8.

R. DONINGTON: *The Interpretation of Early Music* (new version, London, 1974)

gemütlich (Ger.), comfortable, easy-going.

Generalbass (Ger.), thorough-bass.

Generalpause (Ger.), general pause, a rest of one or more bars for the complete orchestra, generally indicated in older scores and parts by the abbreviation G.P. placed above the rest.

Genoveva, opera in four acts by Schumann, to a libretto by Robert Reinick based on Tieck's tragedy *Leben und Tod de heiligen Genoveva*, and Hebbel's tragedy, *Genoveva*. Schumann's only opera was first performed in Leipzig in 1850, and the Florence Festival in 1951. The story, a triangular drama, tells how Prince Siegfried goes off to war, leaving his wife, Genoveva, in the care of his treacherous friend, Golo, who tries to seduce her. Failing in this aim, Golo tries to bring about Genoveva's destruction, but is himself destroyed.

Gerber, Ernst Ludwig (1746–1819), German lexicographer, author of *Historisch-biographisches Lexicon der Tonkünstler* (two volumes, 1790–2) and *Neues historisch-biographisches Lexicon der Tonkünstler* (four volumes, 1812–4), a supplement to the preceding. The two dictionaries were for long standard works. Gerber's substantial library was bought by the Gesellschaft der Musikfreunde in Vienna.

Gerbert (von Hornau), Martin (1720–1793), German historian. He entered the Monastery of St. Blaise in the Black Forest in 1737 and became a priest and prince-abbot. He wrote a history of church music under the title *De cantu et musica sacra* (two volumes, 1774). In addition to theological works, liturgical works and an account of his travels in Germany, Italy and France, he also wrote in 1784 a collection of medieval treatises on music, to which Coussemaker's series later formed a supplement. Two facsimile editions of these *Scriptores ecclesiastici* have been published – 1905 and 1931.

Gerhard, Roberto (1896–1970), Catalan composer, son of a Swiss father and a French mother. A pupil of Pedrell and Schoenberg, he was a teacher and music librarian in Barcelona from 1929–38. After the Spanish Civil War he travelled to Britain and settled in Cambridge (1939). There he spent the rest of his life, establishing himself, along with Britten and Tippett, as one of the most vital forces in British music. Always a musical progressive, he was one of the most constructive and picturesque exponents of twelve-note technique, and later of electronic music, which he used in successful conjunction with the symphony orchestra. His works include an opera, *The Duenna* (1948), after Sheridan; ballets (one of them on *Don Quixote*); four symphonies (the third of which opens electronically with a vivid evocation of a transatlantic flight; a violin concerto and concerto for orchestra; a concerto for eight instruments, including accordion; a setting of Edward Lear's *The Akond of Swat* for singer and two percussionists; and, towards the end of his life, a cycle of chamber works (*Leo, Libra*, and so on) containing the essence of his style.

Gerhardt, Elena (1883–1961), German concert soprano. She learned much from the conductor Arthur Nikisch, who frequently accompanied her. Her reputation was founded on her performance of songs by Schubert, Schumann, Brahms and Wolf.

Gerle, Hans (died 1570), German lute maker and lutenist. He published *Musica Teusch, auf die Instrument der grossen unnd kleinen Geygen, auch Lautten* (1532), an instruction book for viols and lute, which appeared in a revised and enlarged edition in 1546, *Tabulatur auff die Laudten* (1533), and *Eyn newes sehr künstlichs Lautenbuch* (1552). The pieces in the first edition of *Musica Teusch* consist almost entirely of transcriptions of German songs and dances; in the revised edition French *chansons* are substituted for the German songs. *Tabulatur auff die Laudten* includes both German and foreign pieces; *Eyn newes sehr künstlichs Lautenbuch* includes a substantial number of Italian pieces.

German, Edward (1862–1936), English composer, whose name was originally Edward German Jones. After working as an orchestral player (violin), he became conductor at the Globe Theatre, for which he wrote his incidental music to *Richard III*. His music for later productions at other theatres – *Henry VIII* (1892) and *Nell Gwyn* (1900) – won great popularity. In 1901 he completed *The Emerald Isle*, a light opera which had been left unfinished by Sullivan. He had considerable success with the operettas *Merrie England* (1902), *A Princess of Kensington* (1903) and *Tom Jones* (1907). His instrumental compositions include two symphonies, the symphonic poem *Hamlet*, the *Welsh Rhapsody* and *Theme and Six Diversions*. He was knighted in 1928.

Germani, Fernando (born 1906), Italian organist – principally at St. Peter's, Rome (a post he held from 1948 until 1959) but also as a recitalist all over the world. He has also held teaching appointments both in Italy and the United States, (where he became professor at the Curtis Institute of Philadelphia in 1936). He enjoys the reputation of being one of the outstanding performers of the present day.

German Requiem, A (Ger., *Ein deutsches Requiem*), memorial cantata in seven movements for soloists, chorus and orchestra by Brahms, op 45. The words are compiled from Luther's translation of the Bible. The work is therefore not a Requiem Mass. Though written in memory of the composer's mother, it offers consolation to mourners rather than prayers for the dead. Composed between 1866 and 1868, it was first performed in Leipzig (though portions of it had been heard earlier in Vienna and Bremen) and soon established itself as a concert work of universal appeal.

German sixth, *see* AUGMENTED SIXTH

Gérold, Théodore (1866–1956), French historian and musicologist, lecturer at Basel University (1914–18) and Strasbourg (1919–36). His numerous books include studies of early music, 17th century French song, Bach and Schubert.

George Gershwin – the United States' greatest melodist, whose music matched the wit and charm of the words of his songs, written by his brother Ira

Gershwin, George (1898–1937), U.S. composer and pianist. Beginning as employee of a music-publishing firm, he began to write songs, and from 1919 onwards a series of musical comedies. He also wrote a series of concert works – *Rhapsody in Blue* for piano and jazz orchestra (1924), piano concerto in F major (1925), *An American in Paris* (1928) and *Second Rhapsody* (1932), and *Cuban Overture* (1934). His opera *Porgy and Bess* (Boston, 1935), a kind of U.S. *Carmen* written for a Negro cast, has been successful all over the world. Within a limited field he had a delightful melodic talent, beautifully matched to the polished lyrics supplied by his brother Ira. The most famous of the shows for which he wrote songs are *Lady, Be Good!* (1924), *Oh, Kay!* (1926), *Funny Face* (1927), *Girl Crazy* (1927), *Strike up the Band* (1930), and *Of Thee I sing* (1931). With Cole Porter, Jerome Kern, Irving Berlin, and Richard Rodgers, Gershwin represents the highwater mark of U.S. popular song.

Gervaise, Claude, 16th century French violinist and composer. His published works consist of dance tunes for instrumental ensemble and *chansons*. Modern editions of the third, fifth and sixth *livres de danceries* have been published by B. Thomas (1972–3). A further selection of dance tunes is in H. Expert, *Les Maîtres musiciens de la Renaissance française*, xxiii.

Ges (Ger.), G flat (G♭).

Gesamtausgabe (Ger.), complete edition.

Gesamtkunstwerk (Ger.), literally, 'complete art work', or what we would nowadays call total theatre. Wagner chose this portmanteau title for his music dramas, in which he gave as much thought to the words, decor and overall presentation as to the music.

gesangvoll (Ger.), songful – the same as *cantabile*.

Geschöpfe des Prometheus, Die, *see* PROMETHEUS

geschwind (Ger.), quick.

Gesellschaft der Musikfreunde (Ger., Society of the Friends of Music), a society in Vienna formed in 1812 by Joseph von Sonnleithner. It was responsible for founding the Vienna Conservatorium, 1817, the Singverein (a choral society), 1859, and a regular series of concerts known as the Gesellschaftskonzerte, 1859. The Society has a valuable museum and library, which includes a number of autograph compositions.

Gesellschaft für Musikforschung (Ger., Society for Musical Research), (1) an organization founded by F. Commer and R. Eitner in 1868. It was responsible for the series known as *Publikationen älterer praktischer und theoretischer Musikwerke*, which came to an end in 1905;

(2) a society founded by F. Blume after World War II. Its official publication is *Die Musikforschung*, which first appeared in 1948.

Geses (Ger.), G double flat (G♭♭).

Gesius, Bartholomaus (c. 1560–1613), German composer of church music. Having first studied theology, he became cantor at Frankfurt on the Oder in 1592. His publications include volumes of Masses, Magnificats, motets, Lutheran hymns, and a Passion according to St. John (1588).

gestopft (Ger.), stopped. A term used in music for the HORN to indicate that the hand is inserted into the bell. This method was formerly employed to obtain notes not in the natural harmonic series, but is now used only to produce a muffled tone-quality.

Gesualdo, Carlo (c. 1560–1613), Italian composer, the second son of Fabrizio Gesualdo, Prince of Venosa. He became heir to the title through the early death of his elder brother, and succeeded his father as Prince in 1591. As a young man he developed an interest in music and poetry and became an expert performer on the archlute. He was an intimate friend of Tasso, who addressed three poems to him; he also set several of Tasso's poems to music. In 1586 he married his cousin Maria d'Avalos, whom he murdered in 1590 on account of her infidelity. In 1594 he married Eleonora d'Este. He published six books of five-part madrigals, two books of motets and a volume of *responsoria*. A book of six-part madrigals appeared posthumously in 1626, but only one part-book has survived. In his madrigals he went even further than his contemporaries in his desire to give complete expression to the mood of the text, and made considerable use of chromatic harmony and abrupt modulation. His works have been edited in ten volumes by W. Weismann and G. Watkins (1957–67).

A. EINSTEIN: *The Italian Madrigal*, three volumes (1949)

C. GRAY and P. HESELTINE: *Carlo Gesualdo, Musician and Murderer* (1926)

G. WATKINS: *Gesualdo* (1973)

getragen (Ger.), slow and sustained – the equivalent of *sostenuto*.

Gevaert, François Auguste (1828–1908), Belgian historian, musicologist and composer. He studied at the Ghent Conservatoire and was director of the Brussels Conservatoire from 1871 until his death. After serving as an organist while still in his teens he won a composition prize and the *Prix de Rome*, 1847, and travelled in France, Spain and Italy, 1849–52. Several operas were performed with success in Paris, 1853–64. He was director of music, Paris Opera, 1867–70; director, Brussels Conservatoire, 1871 till his death. By thorough reorganization he succeeded in raising the reputation of the Conservatoire to a high level. He wrote a large number of historical and educational works, notably *Traité général d'instrumentation* (1863), revised under the title *Nouveau traité général d'instrumentation* (1885), *Cours méthodique d'orchestration* (two volumes, 1890), *Histoire et théorie de la musique d'antiquité* (two volumes, 1875–81), *Traité d'harmonie théorique et practique* (two volumes, 1905–7). Among his editions of old music are *Gloire d'Italie* (1868), a collection of vocal solos from the 17th and 18th centuries, and *Recueil de chansons du XVe siècle* (1875, in collaboration with Gaston Paris).

Gewandhauskonzerte (Ger.), a series of orchestral concerts at Leipzig, first given privately in 1743. From 1781 until 1884 they were held in the Gewandhaus (Cloth Hall), from which they took their name. A new concert hall was opened in 1885. Among the conductors of the concerts have been Mendelssohn, Nikisch, Furtwängler, Walter and Abendroth.

Ghedini, Giorgio Federico (1892–1965), Italian composer. He studied at Turin and Bologna and was successively teacher at the conservatories of Turin, Parma and Milan. His compositions include the operas *Maria d'Alessandria* (Bergamo, 1947), *Re Hassan* (Venice, 1939), *La pulce d'oro* (Genoa, 1940) *Le Baccanti* (Milan, 1948) and *Billy Budd* (one act, Venice, 1949). A later opera *L'ipocrita felice* (1956), was based on Max Beerbohm's *The Happy Hypocrite*. He also wrote orchestral and chamber music, choral works, piano pieces, songs and film scores. His numerous transcriptions include works by Bach and early Italian composers.

Gherardello da Firenze (Ghirardellus da Florentia) (died c. 1363), Italian composer. His surviving works, comprising a *Gloria* and *Agnus Dei*, and several madrigals, *ballate* and *cacce*, have been edited by N. Pirrotta in *The Music of Fourteenth Century Italy*, i (1954). The secular works are also edited by W. T. Marrocco in *Polyphonic Music of the Fourteenth Century*, vii (1971).

Ghiselin-Verbonnet, Johannes (c. 1458–after 1508), Flemish composer, who seems to have been known both as Ghiselin and Verbonnet. He was at the ducal court of Ferrara in 1491, at the French court in 1501, and back at Ferrara in 1503. Later he returned to Flanders. His works consist of Masses, motets, and songs to French, Dutch, Italian and Latin texts. They have been edited in four volumes by C. Gottwald (1961–8).

    C. GOTTWALD: *Johannes Ghiselin – Johannes Verbonnet* (German text) (1962)

Ghisi, Federico (born 1901) Italian musicologist and composer. He studied at the Turin Conservatorio, and became a lecturer at Florence University in 1937. His published works include *I canti carnascialeschi nelle fonte musicali del XV e XVI secoli* (1937) and *Feste musicali della Firenze Medicea* (1939). His compositions include chamber music and a *Sinfonia italiana*.

Ghost trio, *see* GEISTERTRIO

Giannini, Vittorio (1903–1966), U.S. composer. He studied in Milan and New York. His compositions include concertos for piano and organ, a symphony *In Memoriam Theodore Roosevelt*, Requiem, *Stabat Mater*, chamber music and the operas *Lucedia* (Munich, 1934), *The Scarlet Letter* (Hamburg, 1938) and *The Taming of the Shrew* (Cincinnati, 1953). His *Frescobaldiana*, for orchestra, is based on Frescobaldi's organ works.

Gianni Schicchi, comic opera in one act by Puccini, to a libretto by Giovacchino Forzano, first performed (together with *Il Tabarro* and *Suor Angelica*) in New York in 1918. The three operas together are known by the collective title *Trittico* (triptych), though their stories have nothing in common. Gianni Schicchi, an unscrupulous lawyer, is asked by the relatives of Buoso Donati, a wealthy Florentine, newly deceased, to prevent the execution of his will, in which he left a fortune to the Church. He impersonates the dead man and dictates a new will before witnesses, in which he leaves the relatives virtually nothing and takes the bulk of the property for himself. The relatives are helpless since they have themselves connived in the felony.

    The work is Puccini's comic masterpiece, brilliantly and succinctly written, but finding room for touches of typical Puccini lyricism – as in the aria 'O mio babbino caro' ('Oh my beloved daddy'), sung by Schicchi's daughter.

'Giant' Fugue, a nickname for Bach's chorale prelude for organ on 'Wir glauben all' an einen Gott, Schöpfer' (We all believe in one God, Creator) from the *Clavierübung*, part 3 – so called because of the recurrence on the pedals of an imposing figure which properly symbolizes unshakeable faith.

Giardini, Felice de (1716–96), Italian violinist. He toured as a soloist in Germany (1748) and Britain (1751). He played frequently in London as leader of the orchestra at the Italian Opera (which he also managed for several seasons). Having failed to establish a company for the performance of comic opera at the Haymarket Theatre (1790) he emigrated to Russia with his singers. He died in Moscow. His compositions include operas and a considerable amount of string music. He collaborated with Charles Avison on the oratorio *Ruth*.

Gibbons, 16th–17th century English family of musicians and composers, two of whom were organists of Westminster Abbey.

    Orlando Gibbons (1583–1625), the composer and organist, is the most famous member of the family. He was a chorister at King's College, Cambridge, where he matriculated in 1598. He was organist at the Chapel Royal from 1605 to 1619, and at Westminster Abbey from 1623 to 1625. He died when attending Charles I on the occasion of the arrival of Henrietta Maria. The works published in his lifetime were *The First Set of Madrigals and Mottets of 5 Parts* (1612) and *Fantasies of Three Parts* for viols (c. 1620). He also contributed two anthems to William Leighton's *The Teares or Lamentacions of a Sorrowfull Soule* (1614) and six keyboard pieces to *Parthenia* (c. 1612). A large number of anthems, chamber pieces for strings, and keyboard pieces survive in manuscript.

    There is in his music a certain reserve, which does

not however exclude emotion. His secular songs, the words of which are serious or satirical, have an austerity which is not common among the madrigalists of his time. His church music includes both 'full' and 'verse' ANTHEMS. Several of the verse anthems have an accompaniment for strings. His instrumental music, of fine quality, forms a substantial and important part of his output.

Orlando Gibbons, from the painting in the Music School at Oxford

A modern edition of his church music is in *Tudor Church Music*, iv; the verse anthems have been edited by D. Wulstan (1964). The *Madrigals and Mottets* are reprinted in *The English Madrigal School*, v. His keyboard music has been edited by G. Hendrie in *Musica Britannica*, xx. Examples of his chamber music are in F. J. Giesbert, *Altenglische Violinmusik zu drei Stimmen* (1953–4) and *Musica Britannica*, ix.

Orlando's elder brother, **Ellis Gibbons** (1573–1603), was a composer also. Two madrigals by him are in *The Triumphes of Oriana* (1601).

Orlando's second son, **Christopher Gibbons** (1615–76), was also an organist and composer. He was organist of Winchester Cathedral in 1638, and of the Chapel Royal and Westminster Abbey in 1660. His compositions include anthems, fantasias for strings, and keyboard music. He also collaborated with Matthew Locke in the music for Shirley's masque *Cupid and Death* (modern edition in *Musica Britannica*, ii). His keyboard compositions have been edited by C. G. Rayner (1967).

E. H. FELLOWES: *Orlando Gibbons* (second edition, 1951)

C. G. and S. F. RAYNER: 'Christopher Gibbons: "that famous musician"', in *Musica Disciplina*, xxiv (1970)

Gibbs, Cecil Armstrong (1889–1960), English composer. He was best known for a number of sensitive and imaginative songs, though he also wrote large-scale choral works, e.g. *Deborah and Barak* (1937) and the choral symphony *Odysseus* (1938).

Gibson, Alexander (born 1926), Scottish conductor, educated in Glasgow and London, and musical director since 1959 of the Scottish National Orchestra. In 1962 he founded Scottish Opera, Scotland's first professional opera company, which (with Gibson as principal conductor) now occupies the Glasgow Theatre Royal – the first full-time British opera house outside the London area. He has been responsible for introducing to Britain a variety of music by Schoenberg, Stockhausen, Henze, Berio, Lutoslawski and Ligeti.

Gieseking, Walter Wilhelm (1895–1956), German pianist and composer. He was born in France and studied in Hanover. He made his début in 1915 and excelled in the works of Debussy and Ravel. His compositions consist mainly of chamber music and songs.

giga, *see* GIGUE

Gigault, Nicolas (c. 1625–1707), French composer and organist at several Paris churches. He published *Livre de musique dédié à la très-sainte Vierge* (1683 – a collection of *noëls* arranged for instruments) and *Livre de musique pour l'orgue* (1685; modern edition in A. Guilmant, *Archives des maîtres de l'orgue*, iv).

Gigli, Beniamino (1880–1957), tenor, one of the outstanding singers of the 20th century. The son of a shoemaker, he studied in Rome, and made his début in La Gioconda at Rovigo in 1914. He sang in most of the principal opera houses of the world – notably La Scala, Milan, and the Metropolitan Opera, New York, where he was acclaimed as Caruso's successor. He also made many concert appearances, especially in his later years – when his voice remained in remarkably good repair.

gigue (Fr.), medieval name for a bowed string instrument. Hence possibly the German word *Geige*, fiddle.

gigue, a lively dance (It., *giga*). The word appears to be adapted from the English 'jig'. Examples of the dance are found in English sources, c. 1600, e.g.:

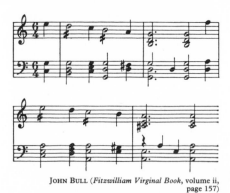

JOHN BULL (*Fitzwilliam Virginal Book*, volume ii, page 157)

but on the Continent not until the middle of the 17th century. As standardized in the late 17th and early 18th centuries, the dance was in 6/8 rhythm, though the music might be noted in a variety of ways, e.g. (1) with notes of larger or smaller value, 6/4 or 6/12, (2) with each 6/8 bar divided into two, 3/8, (3) with two 6/8 bars joined together, 12/8, (4) in 2/4 or 4/4 time with the beats subdivided into triplets or their equivalent.

The gigue was the last of the four regular dances found in the SUITE – allemande, courante, sarabande and gigue. When optional dances (or GALANTERIEN) were added they were generally placed between the sarabande and the gigue. Like the other dances in the suite, the gigue was in binary form, each of the two sections being repeated. There were two main types: (1) generally straightforward in character and simple in texture, e.g.:

HANDEL, *Suite no 7*

(2) more elaborate, with fugal imitation; it was a convention in this type to invert the subject at the beginning of the second section, e.g.:

1st section begins:

2nd section begins:

BACH, *Partitas no 3*

The gigue in Bach's Partita no 1 in B flat (published in the *Clavierübung*, part 1, 1726) had a curious sequel. It was adapted by Gluck for an aria in the opera *Telemacco* (1765), which was subsequently transferred to *Iphigénie en Tauride* (1779):

BACH, *Partitas no 1*

Fièrement, un peu animé

GLUCK, *Iphigenie en Tauride*

W. DANCKERT: *Geschichte der Gigue* (1924)
J. PULVER: *A Dictionary of Old English Music* (1923)

'Gigue' Fugue, nickname given to a fugue in G major for two manuals and pedal in 12/8 time, generally regarded as an early work by Bach. The subject is:

Gigues (Fr.), first of Debussy's IMAGES for orchestra.

Gilbert, Henry Franklin Belknap (1868–1928), U.S. composer, a pupil of MacDowell. His interest in Negro folk music finds expression in his works, of which the best known is the ballet *The Dance in Place Congo* (New York, 1918).

Gillis, Don (born 1912), U.S. composer, conductor, brass player and teacher. His works, written in a popular idiom, include a Symphony no $5\frac{1}{2}$, subtitled 'Symphony for Fun'.

Gilman, Lawrence (1878–1939), U.S. critic. He wrote for many magazines, and for the *New York*

Herald-Tribune from 1923 until 1939. His books include *Edward MacDowell* (1905; second edition, 1909), *Aspects of Modern Opera* (1908). *Music and the Cultivated Man* (1929), *Wagner's Operas* (1937) and *Toscanini and Great Music* (1938).

Ginastera, Alberto (born 1916), Argentine composer, who studied with Athos Palma at the National Conservatory of Buenos Aires. His works, written often in a nationalistic idiom, include two operas (*Don Rodrigo* and *Bomarzo*), two ballets (*Panambi*, based on an American Indian legend, and *Estancia*), an *Argentine Concerto* for piano and orchestra, a violin concerto, psalms for chorus and orchestra, chamber and instrumental music and songs. He is the leading Argentine composer of the day.

giocoso (It.), merry.

gioioso (It.), joyful.

Giordani, Giuseppe (1753–98), Italian composer. His works include numerous operas, oratorios, church music, and instrumental compositions. The well-known aria 'Caro mio ben' is attributed to him.

Giordani, Tommaso (c. 1730–1896), Italian composer. He was active chiefly in London and Dublin, where he composed (or contributed to) some fifty works for the stage, including songs for Sheridan's *The Critic*. He also wrote instrumental pieces.

Giordani, Tommaso (c. 1730–1806), Italian composer. He studied at the Naples Conservatorio, and made his name with *Mala vita* (Rome, 1892), an example of the 'veristic' type of opera then popular in Italy. Of his other nine operas the best known are *Andrea Chénier* (Milan, 1896), *Fedora* (Milan, 1898), and *Madame Sans-Gêne* (New York, 1915).

Giovanelli, Ruggiero (c. 1560–1625), Italian composer. He succeeded Palestrina as *maestro di cappella* of St. Peter's, Rome. In addition to his church music he wrote a considerable number of madrigals, four of which were published with English translations in Morley's *Madrigalls to five voyces: selected out of the best approved Italian Authors* (1598).

Giovanni da Cascia (da Firenze), early 14th century Italian composer, also known by the Latin name Johannes de Florentia. A prominent member of the group of composers who were active in the composition of secular vocal music at the time. His surviving works, mainly madrigals, have been edited by N. Pirrotta in *The Music of Fourteenth Century Italy*, i (1954) and by W. T. Marrocco in *Polyphonic Music of the Fourteenth Century*, vi (1967).

giraffe piano, an early 19th century piano, somewhat like a grand, but with an upright body. The part enclosing the bass strings resembles the neck of a giraffe.

Girl of the Golden West, The (It., *La Fanciulla del West*), opera in three acts by Puccini, to a libretto by Guelfo Civinini and Carlo Zangarini. It was first performed in New York in 1910. Based on David Belasco's play of the same title, the story is laid in California, in the days of the gold rush. The heroine, Minnie, falls in love with an outlaw, Johnson, and hides him in her cabin. When he is found by the sheriff, she plays cards for his life and wins by cheating. Johnson is captured and is only saved from hanging by Minnie's appeal to the miners, who let them go free.

In this opera Puccini pays tribute to Debussy by making use of the whole-tone scale. The first performance

had Toscanini as conductor, and Emmy Destinn and Enrico Caruso in the leading roles.

Gis (Ger.), G sharp (G♯).

Gisis (Ger.), G double sharp (G ×).

gittern, medieval English name for a four-stringed instrument of the GUITAR family, played with a plectrum. A 14th century example is preserved at Warwick Castle. In Tudor and Stuart times the name seems to have been used rather loosely to refer to more than one kind of instrument, including the Spanish guitar, which became popular in England in the 16th century. The title of John Playford's *A Booke of new lessons for the Cithren and Gittern* (1652) makes it clear, however, that the gittern was not necessarily identical with the CITTERN.

Giulini, Carlo Maria (born 1914), Italian conductor, the most important to achieve international distinction since Victor de Sabata. He studied at the Accademia di Santa Cecilia in Rome, and became a first violinist with the Augusteo Orchestra. From 1946 until 1951 he was musical director of Radio Italiana. After receiving encouragement from Toscanini, he was appointed assistant to de Sabata at La Scala, Milan, and later became principal conductor at that opera house. His

Giraffe piano: this elaborate example, now in the Victoria and Albert Museum, London, was made in Amsterdam by Van der Hoef early in the 19th century. Note the six pedals giving an array of special effects (bassoon, drum, celeste, bells, soft pedal, sustaining pedal)

first British appearance was when he conducted *Falstaff* at the 1955 Edinburgh Festival. His subsequent performances of *Don Carlos* and *La Traviata* at Covent Garden consolidated his British reputation. In the United States he has worked with the Chicago Symphony Orchestra as Sir Georg Solti's partner, and more recently has been associated with the Vienna Symphony Orchestra. A man of immense modesty, he never tackles a work until he believes he is ready for it. For this reason, his repertory has built up slowly, though it now includes most of the great symphonic classics, in interpretations of remarkable expressiveness and absolute integrity.

Giulio Cesare in Egitto, *see* JULIUS CAESAR

giustiniana (It.), a popular three-part song current in Italy in the 16th century. According to Morley (*A Plaine and Easie Introduction to Practicall Musicke*, page 180) they 'are all written in the *Berganasca* language', i.e. in dialect. He adds: 'A wanton and rude kinde of musicke it is.' *See* VILLANELLA

giusto (It.), proper, reasonable, exact. *A tempo giusto* or *tempo giusto*, (1) in the proper time, at a reasonable speed, (2) in strict time.

Glareanus, Henricus (1488–1563), Swiss theorist, who took his name from the canton of Glarus, in which he was born. His real name was Heinrich Loriti. He taught mathematics at Basle and philosophy in Paris, returning to Switzerland in 1522. He is chiefly known for his treatise DODECACHORDON published in 1547.

Glasharmonika, *see* HARMONICA

Glazunov, Alexander Konstantinovich (1865–1936), Russian composer, son of a publisher. He studied privately with Rimsky-Korsakov and became a teacher at the St. Petersburg Conservatory (1900) and later its director (1906). In 1928 he settled in Paris, although the Soviet government had conferred on him the title of 'People's Artist of the Republic'. He remained in France until he died. His first symphony was performed in 1882 when he was only sixteen. From that time he continued to compose industriously, and his works rapidly became known outside Russia. Although he was associated with the Russian nationalist composers, the FIVE, most of his work belongs to the main stream of European music. Quick to absorb the influence of others, he never developed a really individual voice. Brilliance, charm and technical skill are the characteristics of his work rather than originality. His compositions are:

(1) Orchestra: eight symphonies; two piano concertos; violin concerto; cello concerto; concerto for saxophone, flute and strings; six suites (including *Chopiniana* and *The Seasons*); six overtures; symphonic poem, *Stenka Razin*; serenades, fantasias, etc.;

(2) Chamber music: seven string quartets; string quintet; quartet for brass;

(3) Choral works: *Memorial Cantata* (Leeds, 1901); *Hymn to Pushkin* (female voices), also works for the piano and organ, songs and incidental music.

He also helped Rimsky-Korsakov to complete Borodin's unfinished opera *Prince Igor* and reconstructed the entire overture from memory.

> M. D. CALVOCORESSI and G. ABRAHAM: *Masters of Russian Music* (1936)

Mikhail Ivanovich Glinka, 'the father of Russian music'

Glebov, Igor, *see* ASAFIEV

glee (from Old English *glíw* or *gléo*, 'entertainment, music'), a simple part-song, generally for male voices. The term first occurs in printed music in Playford's *Select Musicall Ayres and Dialogues* (1652). A popular form of music in England in the 18th and early 19th centuries.

glee club, (1) a society for singing glees, founded in London in 1787 and dissolved in 1857;

(2) the name was also adopted subsequently by other societies with the same objects. In U.S. universities today it generally means a male-voice choral society: those of Harvard and Yale are particularly famous.

Glière, Reinhold Moritzovich (1875–1956), Russian composer of Belgian origin. After studying at the Moscow Conservatory, he became director at the Kiev Conservatory (1914) and in 1920 a teacher at the Moscow Conservatory. In 1939 he became chairman of the Organizing Committee of Soviet composers. His compositions include the opera *Shah Senem* (Baku, 1934), which incorporates Azerbaijan melodies, the ballet *The Red Poppy*, on the Russian revolution (Moscow, 1927), three symphonies, violin concerto, harp concerto, *March of the Red Army*, *Victory Overture*, four string quartets and other chamber works, and numerous songs and piano pieces. In his later works he made use of folk melodies from the eastern provinces of the Soviet Union.

Glinka, Mikhail Ivanovich (1804–57), Russian composer son of a wealthy landowner. He was educated in St. Petersburg, where he studied music privately. He worked in the Ministry of Communications from 1824 until 1828, when he resigned in order to devote himself to music. After visiting several Italian cities and studying in Milan, Vienna and Berlin, he returned to St. Petersburg where he produced his two operas, then visited Paris (1844) where he made friends with Berlioz, Spain (1844), Warsaw (1848), France again (1852–4), and died on his last visit to Berlin (1856–7).

His first opera, *A Life for the Tsar* (St. Petersburg, 1836), now known as *Ivan Sussanin* (its original title), is not strikingly Russian in character, though it makes some use of local colour; its strength is its simplicity – a reaction to the conventions of Italian opera, which were dominant in Russia at the time. It was the second opera, *Russlan and Ludmilla* (St. Petersburg, 1842) which first created a characteristically Russian style, including the oriental elements which came to figure so prominently in later Russian music. Glinka also showed in his orchestral fantasia *Karaminskaya* how folk song could be used as the basis of instrumental composition. His *Jota Aragonesa* was inspired by his visit to Spain. He also wrote chamber music, piano music (for a time he was a pupil of John Field) and songs.

G. ABRAHAM: *On Russian Music* (1939)

M. D. CALVOCORESSI and G. ABRAHAM: *Masters of Russian Music* (1936)

glissando (It.), literally 'sliding' (from Fr., 'glisser'):

(1) on the piano the finger-nail is drawn rapidly over the keys (in either direction), without any articulation of individual notes. On the white keys the procedure is simple and effective; on the black keys it is uncomfortable and less effective, on account of the gaps between the notes. It is also possible for one hand to play a glissando in two (or even three) parts on the white keys. Of the available two-part intervals sixths are the most effective;

(2) on the HARP the finger slides rapidly across the strings. The variety of tuning possible makes available quite a number of different scales;

(3) on instruments of the violin family the finger slides rapidly up or down the string. The term is also used, however, to indicate a chromatic scale played with one finger by rapidly sliding from one note to the next, e.g.:

STRAUSS, *Till Eulenspiegel*

(4) on the trombone the glissando is played with the slide;

(5) on other wind instruments an imitation of a glissando can be produced by increased lip pressure which raises the pitch of each individual note until the next one is reached;

Glissando is often abbreviated *gliss.* or indicated by an oblique stroke (straight or wavy) between the highest and lowest notes, e.g.:

on the harp it is necessary for the exact notes to be specified, either by writing a specimen octave, e.g.:

RIMSKY-KORSAKOV, *Pan Voyevoda*

or by indicating the tuning with letters.

Globokar, Vinko (born 1934), Yugoslav trombonist and composer. He studied at the conservatories of Ljubljana and Paris, his teachers including René Leibowitz and Luciano Berio. The latter composed for him a *Sequenza* for solo trombone, portraying Grock the Clown. Globokar's own works include *Plan, Voie, Accord, Traumdeutung, Fluide* and *Etude pour Folkora I and II*, using various combinations of vocal and instrumental forces.

Glocke (Ger., plural *Glocken*), bell.

Glockenspiel (Ger.; Fr., *carillon, jeu de clochettes, jeu de timbres*; It., *campanelli*), percussion instrument consisting of a series of steel plates of different sizes, arranged like the keyboard of the piano so as to provide a complete chromatic compass (there are various sizes). The steel plates are struck by wooden hammers held in the player's hands. The instrument was at one time fitted with a keyboard (like the CELESTA) and in this form is required in Handel's *Saul* (1738) and Mozart's *Die Zauberflöte* (1791). The German name has by now become virtually an international term.

Glogauer Liederbuch (Ger.), a 15th century German collection of songs and dances, arranged for vocal or instrumental ensemble. The German songs and the instrumental pieces in the collection have been published in *Das Erbe deutscher Musik, Reichsdenkmäler*, iv. A selection of the Latin pieces is in volume viii of the same series.

Gloria (Lat.), (1) the initial word of 'Gloria in excelsis Deo' (Glory to God in the highest), the second part of the Ordinary of the Mass. These opening words were sung by the priest; hence in polyphonic settings of the 15th and 16th centuries the choir regularly begins with the words 'et in terra pax' (and on earth peace). This tradition was later abandoned, as it was in the *Credo*;

(2) the *Gloria Patri* (or doxology) sung at the end of a psalm or canticle.

Gloriana, opera in three acts by Britten, to a libretto by William Plomer, first performed in London in 1953. The story concerns the relationship between Elizabeth I and the Earl of Essex. *Gloriana* was commissioned by Covent Garden for the coronation of Queen Elizabeth II, and was produced at a gala performance in her presence, with Joan Cross and Peter Pears in the principal parts. The music at first aroused considerable antagonism (as did the libretto, which was considered insulting to Elizabeth Tudor) and the opera was allowed to languish for several years after its première. In the 1960s, however, it rightly began to establish itself as one of the most masterly of Britten's scores. The first U.S. performance was at Cincinnati in 1955.

Gloucester, *see* THREE CHOIRS FESTIVAL

Christoph Willibald Gluck, born in Bavaria, reformed 18th century opera first in Vienna and finally in Paris as a result of discovering Handel on a visit to London in 1745

Gluck, Christoph Willibald (von) (1714–87, German composer. After studying in Prague he entered the service of Prince Melzi in Vienna, and went with him to Italy. He completed his studies under Sammartini, and from 1741 until 1744 he produced a number of operas in the accepted Italian style. With Prince Lobkowitz he went to London and produced there (in 1746) two unsuccessful operas and gave concerts on the glass harmonica. He worked with the Mingotti travelling opera company, and in 1750 married and settled in Vienna, becoming *Kapellmeister* to the Prince of Sachsen-Hildburghausen (1752) and at the Court opera (1754) for which he produced a series of Italian pastorals and French light operas. In *Orfeo* (1762) he created a new style of Italian opera which incorporated the choruses and ballets of French opera and abandoned conventional virtuosity for dramatic truth and a moving simplicity of expression. His adoption of this style was largely due to his librettist, Raniero de' Calzabigi, who in turn derived some of his ideas from the writings of Algarotti.

The principles of their 'reform', which sought to 'restrict music to its true office of serving poetry by

means of expression', were set out in the prefaces to *Alceste* (1767), and *Paride ed Elena* (1770), and were pursued in the operas which Gluck wrote for Paris – *Iphigénie en Aulide* (1774), *Armide* (1777) and *Iphigénie en Tauride* (1779). In Paris he also produced French versions of *Orfeo* and *Alceste*. The influence of French traditions is strongly marked in the Paris operas, and it was natural that in the controversy which still raged on the rival merits of Italian and French opera he should have been regarded as the champion of the latter. However, his last opera for Paris, *Echo et Narcisse*, was a failure, and he returned thereafter to Vienna, where he died.

Though Gluck had no immediate imitators, his work had a considerable influence on the operas of Mozart, Gossec, Cherubini, Beethoven, Spontini and Berlioz. Berlioz also wrote essays on *Orfeo* and *Alceste*, and Wagner in his Dresden period (1847) produced a revised version of *Iphigénie en Aulide*.

Gluck was one of the major figures of operatic history. In addition to more than a hundred operas, many of which are now lost, he composed ballets, eleven symphonies, seven instrumental trios, a setting of *De profundis* for choir and orchestra, seven odes by Klopstock for solo voice and keyboard, and a flute concerto.

Gluck's Italian operas include:
Artaserse (1741), *Demetrio* (1742), *Demofoonte* (1742), *Il Tigrane* (1743), *La Sofonisba* (1744), *Ipermestra* (1744), *La caduta de' giganti* (1746), *Artamene* (1746), *La Nozze d'Ercole e d'Ebe* (1747), *Semiramide Riconosciuta* (1748), *La Contesa de' Numi* (1749), *Ezio* (1750), *La clemenza de Tito* (1752), *Le Cinesi* (1754), *Antigono* (1756), *Il rè pastore* (1756), *Il Telemacco* (1765).
His French *opéras-comiques* include:
L'Isle de Merlin (1758), *La Cythère Assiégée* (1759, Paris version 1777), *L'Arbre Enchanté* (1759, Versailles version 1777), *L'Ivrogne Corrigé* (1760), *La Cadi Dupé* (1761), *La Rencontre Imprévue* (1764).
His French operas for Paris were:
Iphigénie en Aulide (1744), *Orphée et Eurydice* (1774, Vienna version 1762), *Alceste* (1776, Italian version 1767), *Armide* (1777), *Iphigénie en Tauride* (1779), *Echo et Narcisse* (1779).
His 'reform' operas were:
Orfeo (1762), *Alceste* (1767), *Paride ed Elena* (1770).
H. BERLIOZ: *Gluck and his Operas* (English edition, 1914)
M. COOPER: *Gluck* (1936)
A. EINSTEIN: *Gluck* (1937)
P. HOWARD: *Gluck and the Birth of Modern Opera* (1963)
E. NEWMAN: *Gluck and the Opera* (1895)

Glückliche Hand, Die (Ger., *The Fortunate Hand*), monodrama in one act by Schoenberg, published in 1913, though not performed until eleven years later, in Vienna. The libretto, by the composer himself, concerns the artist's quest for happiness. The principal part is sung by a baritone, supported by a chorus who comment on the action.

Gobbi, Tito (born 1915), Italian baritone, who studied law at Padua University before deciding to make singing his career. A pupil of the tenor, Giulio Crimi, he was awarded a scholarship by La Scala, Milan, in 1937, and the following year won first prize for baritone at the International Competition in Vienna. He made his début in *La Traviata* in Rome, and soon established himself as one of the world's great singing actors, particularly impressive in such works as *Tosca*, *Gianni Schicchi* and *Falstaff*.

Godard, Benjamin Louis Paul (1849–95), French composer and violinist. He was the founder and conductor of the Concerts Modernes (1885) and winner, with Dubois, of the Prix de la Ville de Paris (1878). He composed several operas (the most famous being *Jocelyn*), *Le Tasse* for soloists, chorus and orchestra, a symphony, symphonic poems, two violin concertos, a piano concerto, chamber music, incidental music for plays, piano pieces and over one hundred songs.

Godfrey, Daniel (Dan) Eyers (1868–1939), English conductor. His principal achievement was the creation of a symphony orchestra at Bournemouth in 1893, where he was appointed director of music at the Winter Gardens. Before he retired in 1934 he had introduced several hundred works by British composers. He was knighted in 1922.

Godowsky, Leopold (1870–1938), pianist and composer, Polish by birth, U.S. by naturalization. He showed great gifts as a child and first appeared as a soloist in Vilna in 1879. Subsequently he studied at the Berlin Hochschule. From 1884 onwards he toured widely. He taught in Philadelphia, Chicago, Berlin and Vienna, and from 1914 lived regularly in the United States. His published works include a number of transcriptions, a series of studies on études by Chopin, and numerous smaller pieces including *Triakontameron* (a series of thirty piano pieces, each composed on a different day).

God save the King, the earliest known version of the British national anthem, a tune in galliard rhythm of uncertain origin, appeared in the collection *Thesaurus Musicus* (c. 1744) in the following form:

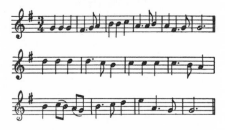

In the second edition (1745) the first four bars are altered to:

Its popularity dates from 1745, when it was sung in London theatres as a loyal demonstration on the occasion of the Rebellion of the Young Pretender. The earliest known arrangement for four voices was made by Arne for Drury Lane Theatre in that year.

In the course of its history, alternative verses and alternative words have frequently been written for the tune; frequent attempts have been made to suppress or tone down the verse attacking the enemies of the

'God save the King': an early version of Arne's famous tune, as performed at Drury Lane in 1745, when the Scottish Jacobites looked as if they would overrun England. It can be seen that the melody differs in certain details from the final version.

monarch. The tune was also adopted in several Continental countries and started the fashion for national anthems all over the world. In the United States it is used for the national song 'My country, 'tis of thee' (1831), and Charles Ives's *America* variations are based on it. Among other composers who have written variations on the tune are Beethoven, Cramer, Dussek, Glazunov, Kalkbrenner, Liszt, Paganini and Reger. It has also been introduced into compositions by Beethoven, Brahms, Meyerbeer, Spontini, Verdi and Weber.

P. A. SCHOLES: *God save the Queen* (1954).

Goehr, Alexander (born 1932), English composer of German origin (his father was the conductor Walter Goehr). He studied at the Royal Manchester College of Music and, in Paris, under Messiaen. A member of the so-called Manchester School (along with Peter Maxwell Davies, Harrison Birtwistle and John Ogdon), he has established himself as one of the leading English composers of his generation. His works include an opera, *Arden Must Die*, to a text by Erich Fried; and several pieces of 'music theatre', including *Naboth's Vineyard*, for the performance of which he formed his own Music Theatre Ensemble. He has also written a symphony (modestly entitled *Little Symphony*) in memory of his father, a violin concerto, several cantatas (among them *The Deluge*, *Sutter's Gold*, *Hecuba's Lament*, and *A Little Cantata of Proverbs*), chamber music and songs. He was professor of music at Leeds University from 1971, later at Cambridge.

Goetz, Hermann (1840–76), German composer. After studying in Berlin he became organist at Winterthur (1863) and settled in Zurich (1867). He composed two operas, a symphony, an overture, a piano concerto, a violin concerto, choral works with orchestra, chamber music, piano pieces, songs and partsongs. His first opera, *Der Widerspänstigen Zähmung* (after Shakespeare's *The Taming of the Shrew*; Mannheim, 1874) had some success in Germany and was given in London, where it was admired by Bernard Shaw.

Goldberg Variations, the fourth part of Bach's *Clavierübung* (1742), described by him as 'an aria with different variations for harpsichord with two manuals, designed for the refreshment of music-lovers.' According to Forkel, Bach's first biographer, the variations were written for J. T. Goldberg, a pupil of Bach's, to play to Count Kaiserling, formerly Russian Ambassador at the Court of Saxony, who suffered from insomnia (*see* H. T. David & A. Mendel, *The Bach Reader*, pages 338–9). The aria itself is in chaconne rhythm, with a highly ornamented melody:

The thirty variations include nine canons, at different intervals, two of which (at the fourth and at the fifth) are in contrary motion. The last variation is a *quodlibet*, i.e. a piece incorporating the melodies of popular songs.

Golden Cockerel, The (Russ., *Zolotoy Petushok*; Fr., *Le Coq d'or*), opera in three acts by Rimsky-Korsakov, to a libretto by Vladimir Ivanovich Bielsky (after Pushkin), first performed in Moscow in 1909.

King Dodon, lazy, gluttonous and worried about affairs of state, is offered by an astrologer a golden cockerel which will warn him of danger. When the alarm is sounded, Dodon sends his sons out to battle. The alarm sounds again, and Dodon himself has to go. He finds his sons dead, but meets the beautiful Queen of Shemaka, whom he takes home to be his bride. The astrologer demands her as his reward. Dodon kills him and is himself killed by the cockerel. The queen disappears in the darkness which covers the sky.

This, the last of Rimsky-Korsakov's fourteen operas, was banned during the composer's lifetime, because of the vein of political satire. Its première took place months after his death, and has only gradually gained the reputation it deserves. The work is sometimes known as *Le Coq d'Or*, but the use of the French title in countries other than France is unnecessary.

Goldmark, Karl (1830–1915), Hungarian composer and teacher. He studied privately and at the Conservatorium in Vienna, where he spent most of his life, as teacher and critic. His compositions include *The Queen of Sheba* (Vienna, 1875) and five other operas, two symphonies (one of them known as the *Rustic Wedding*), the overtures *Sakuntala* and *Im Frühling* (In Spring), two violin concertos, choral works, chamber music, piano pieces and songs. His memoirs were published in 1922.

Rubin Goldmark (1872–1936), was a nephew of Karl, also a composer and teacher. He studied in Vienna and New York, where he was a pupil of Dvořák. He was director of Colorado College Conservatory (1895–1901) and was director of composition department, Juilliard Graduate School, New York, (1924). His pupils included Abram Chasins, Aaron Copland and George Gershwin.

Gombert, Nicolas (c. 1500–c. 1560), Flemish composer. He was in the service of the emperor Charles V from 1526 to 1540. Hermann Finck called him in 1556 'he who shows the way to composers'. In his polyphonic writing he adopted the method of continuous imitation, which was to become the chief feature of the style of Palestrina, and avoided both homophonic writing and the use of alternating pairs of voices, which were characteristic of Josquin's style. Finck observed that his music was *plena cum concordantiarum tum fugarum* (imitations). He composed more than 160 motets, ten Masses, eight Magnificats, and some sixty *chansons*. A complete edition by J. Schmidt-Görg of his works was begun in 1951.

J. SCHMIDT-GÖRG: *Nicolas Gombert – Kapellmeister . . . Karls V* (1938)

Gombosi, Otto (1902–55) Hungarian musicologist, who went to the United States in 1939. He studied at the Budapest Academy and in Berlin. He was music critic in Berlin from 1929–35. After moving to the United States, he held professorships at Washington University (Seattle), 1940; Chicago, 1946; Harvard, 1951. He published a study of Obrecht and edited the hymns and psalms of Thomas Stoltzer (with H. Albrecht).

Gondoliers, The, operetta in two acts by Gilbert and Sullivan, first performed in London in 1889.

The heroes of the piece are two Venetian boatmen (supposed brothers). In spite of holding socialist views, they find themselves reigning jointly after it is revealed that one of them (which is not clear) is actually the King of Barataria. It also appears that the King (who was stolen in infancy) was married by proxy to Casilda, the daughter of the Duke of Plaza-Toro. Unfortunately, the gondoliers have married two Venetian girls, and Casilda is in love with her father's attendant, Luiz. Eventually, it is all cleared up: Luiz is discovered to be the real king, marries Casilda, and the two gondoliers return to their simple lives.

The operetta is one of the most popular of Gilbert and Sullivan's, and includes the song 'Take a pair of sparkling eyes', often performed separately.

gong, a percussion instrument of oriental origin. As used in the orchestra it consists of a piece of circular metal with a rim several inches deep and is hit either by a wooden mallet covered with leather or felt or by a stick similar to that used for the bass drum. If it is played softly, the sound is sinister; a loud stroke produces a menacing and terrifying effect. The pitch of the instrument is indeterminate.

Goossens, Eugene (1893–1962), English conductor and composer, whose father and grandfather were both conductors of the Carl Rosa Opera Company. He studied at Bruges Conservatoire, Liverpool College of Music and the Royal College of Music, London. He was violinist in the Queen's Hall Orchestra (1911–15), and assistant conductor to Beecham (until 1920). He founded and conducted his own orchestra (1921) and conducted Russian opera and ballet at Covent Garden. After holding posts with the Rochester Philharmonic Orchestra (1923) and Cincinnati Symphony Orchestra (1931) he became director of the Conservatory of New South Wales and conductor of the Sydney Symphony Orchestra (1947–56). He was a champion of new music, and himself wrote two operas – *Judith* (London, 1929) and *Don Juan de Manara* (London, 1937), a ballet, two symphonies and other orchestral works, an oboe concerto, chamber music, incidental music for plays, songs, piano pieces and a volume of memoirs entitled *Overture and Beginners*.

gopack (also known as *hopak*), a Russian folk dance in a lively 2-4 time, occasionally used by Russian composers, e.g. by Mussorgsky in his unfinished opera *Sorochintsy Fair*.

gorgia (It.), literally 'throat'. The name given to the improvised embellishments employed by solo singers in the 16th and 17th centuries. Examples are given in Caccini's *Nuove musiche* (1602; facsimile edition, 1934; modern edition by H. W. Hitchcock, 1970).

Gossec, François Joseph (1734–1829), Belgian composer who moved to Paris in 1751. Through the good offices of Rameau he became conductor of the concerts organized by La Pouplinière and later director of music to the Prince of Condé. In a large number of compositions, many on a grand scale, he showed his sympathy with the ideals of the French Revolution, and was one of the first teachers at the Paris Conservatoire (founded, 1795). His compositions include symphonies, oratorios, and choral works in celebration of the Revolution. Long before Berlioz he experimented with elaborate instrumentation in his *Messe des morts* (Requiem Mass), and in general exercised a stimulating influence on orchestral composition in Paris.

    J. G. PROD'HOMME: *Gossec* (1949)

Gothic music, in the 18th century this would have meant barbarous, primitive music. As used by modern historians it means music in northern Europe contemporary with Gothic architecture – roughly the 13th, 14th and early 15th centuries. Some later music with qualities of 'Gothic' spirituality and transcendentalism (e.g. the 'transcendental' organ toccatas of Bach and Buxtehude) has been called Gothic, while modern works in a similar vein (e.g. some of Hindemith's and Kaminski's) are termed 'neo-gothic'.

Götterdämmerung (*Twilight of the Gods*, i.e. the end of the world in German mythology), opera in three acts (with prologue) by Wagner, the fourth and last part of the cycle the RING DES NIEBELUNGEN. The first performance took place at Bayreuth in 1876.

Gottschalk, Louis Moreau (1829–69), U.S. composer and pianist, born in New Orleans, the son of an English Jew and a French Creole. At the age of fifteen he performed in Paris, and thereafter toured the world as a virtuoso pianist. His piano pieces (including *The Aeolian Harp* and *The Dying Poet*) at one time dropped from the repertory, but have recently been undergoing revival. He also wrote two operas and orchestral works.

Goudimel, Claude (c. 1514–72), French composer, first known from his contributions to an anthology of *chansons* published (in eleven volumes) between 1549 and 1554. Originally a Catholic, he turned Protestant and published a number of settings of Huguenot melodies. A modern edition of his collected works in fourteen volumes was begun by the Institute of Mediaeval Music in 1967.

    M. BRENET: *Claude Goudimel* (1898)

    W. S. PRATT: *The Music of the French Psalter of 1562* (1939)

Gould, Glenn (born 1932), Canadian pianist. After studying at the Toronto Royal Conservatory (where he graduated at the age of twelve), he rose quickly to fame and made his U.S. début in 1955. He is one of the few performers today to have 'made a case' for playing Bach on the piano; and though many of his interpretations have been deemed eccentric (e.g. use of exceptionally fast tempi and of staccato effects), they

are nevertheless fascinating, obviously carefully thought out, and often remarkably convincing. With Bach as its pivot, his repertory extends back to 16th century keyboard music and forward to serial compositions. He has stated that he now prefers the atmosphere of the recording studio (where he almost exclusively performs) to that of the concert hall.

Gould, Morton (born 1913), U.S. composer, conductor and pianist. His works, often in a popular idiom, include a concerto for tap dancer and orchestra, three symphonies, four *American Symphonettes*, *Spirituals* for string choir and orchestra, *Cowboy Rhapsody*, *Homespun Overture*, *Lincoln Legend*, *Foster Gallery*, *Jekyll and Hyde Variations*, etc. His *Fall River Legend* (1947) has established itself as a classic of U.S. dance. He has also written several Broadway musicals, in one of which (*Delightfully Dangerous*) he made a personal appearance.

Charles François Gounod. Was *Faust* the most popular opera ever? It was performed by the Paris Opéra alone no less than 2000 times in the years up to 1935, following its first production in 1859.

Gounod, Charles François (1818–1893), French composer. He studied at the Paris Conservatoire and won the *Prix de Rome* in 1839. After visiting Austria and Germany he became organist and choirmaster at the Eglise des Missions Etrangères in Paris. He studied for the priesthood but decided not to be ordained, began composing operas in 1851, was conductor of the Orpheon (united choral societies), from 1852 until 1860, and lived in Britain from 1870 until 1875, forming a choir which later became the Royal Choral Society.

    His work is unequal in quality. Even in *Faust* (Paris, 1859), the most famous of his operas, the level is not consistently maintained: the enchantment of the garden scene is not always matched by a similar inspiration in the rest of the work. Gounod was primarily a lyrical composer, most successful when a light touch was required; in this respect, *Mireille* (1864) is among the most successful of his operas. When he attempted to be impressive, as in the oratorio *La Rédemption*, he merely became self-conscious: the intended mysticism of this work is wholly artificial. His principal compositions are:

(1) Operas: *Sappho* (1851); *La Nonne sanglante* (1854); *Le Médecin malgré lui* (1895); *Faust* (1859); *Philémon et Baucis* (1860); *La Reine de Saba* (1862); *Mireille* (1864); *La Colombe* (1866); *Roméo et Juliette* (1867); *Cinq-Mars* (1877); *Polyeucte* (1878); *Le Tribut de Zamora* (1881)

(2) Oratorios: *La Rédemption* (1882); *Mors et Vita* (1885)

(3) Cantatas: *Marie Stuart* (1837); *Gallia* (1871)

(4) Church Music: nine Masses (including *Messe solennelle*, 1849); three Requiems; *Stabat Mater*; *Te Deum*; motets, etc.

(5) Orchestra: three symphonies

P. LANDORMY: *Charles Gounod* (1942)

Goyescas, (1) two sets of piano pieces by Granados, inspired by Goya's pictures of Spain, composed in 1911 and first performed in 1914. There are seven pieces in all;

(2) opera in three acts by the same composer, incorporating material from the piano pieces, and first performed in 1916 in New York. The work, concerning love and death in Spain, has a libretto by Periquet.

Grabu, Louis, French violinist composer of the late 17th century who spent some years in London. He was composer to Charles II in 1665, and Master of the King's music from 1666 to 1674. He returned to France in 1679, but was back in England a few years later and composed the music for Dryden's patriotic opera *Albion and Albanius* (1685).

grace, an ornament, whether vocal or instrumental. Grace notes are ornamental notes used to decorate or embellish a melody and normally printed in smaller type.

gradevole (It.), pleasing.

gradual (Lat. *graduale*): (1) a responsorial chant forming part of the Proper of the Roman Mass and sung between the Epistle and the Gospel. Apparently so called because it was sung from the steps (Lat. *gradus*) of the ambo (or pulpit). The plainsong melodies, designed for alternations of soloist and chorus, are elaborate.

(2) originally a book containing graduals and hence, by a natural extension, one containing all the music of the Mass to be sung by the choir.

Gradualia (Lat.), the title of two sets of Latin motets by Byrd, published in 1605 and 1607 and designed for

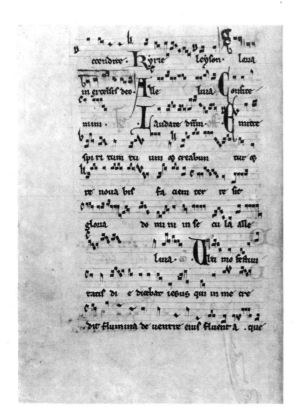

An opening from the 'Crowland Gradual' (second quarter of the 13th century) showing part of the plainsong masses for Whitsun Eve and Whit Sunday. The use of 'square notation' for the music is the earliest known in Britain.

liturgical use in the Roman church. The motets form a complete cycle of Mass PROPERS for the principal festivals of the church year.

> J. L. JACKMAN: 'Liturgical Aspects of Byrd's *Gradualia*', *Musical Quarterly*, xlix (1963)

Gradus ad Parnassum (Lat.), literally 'steps to Parnassus' (home of the Muses):

(1) the title of a treatise on counterpoint by Fux (1725);

(2) the title of a collection of piano studies by Clementi (1817);

(3) *Doctor Gradus ad Parnassum*, a parody of a piano study, is the first piece in Debussy's suite *Children's Corner* (1908).

Graener, Paul (1872–1944), German composer, conductor and teacher. He held appointments in London, Vienna, Salzburg, Leipzig and Berlin. His compositions, romantic in style, include an opera about W. F. Bach (*Friedemann Bach*, 1931), orchestral and choral works, chamber music and songs.

> G. GRAENER: *Paul Graener* (1922)

Grainger, Percy Aldridge (originally George Percy) (1882–1961), Australian born composer and pianist. He played the piano in public at the age of ten, studied in Melbourne and Frankfurt, and rapidly made a reputation as a recitalist, particularly in Britain, where he lived from 1900. Having met Grieg in Norway in 1907 he became interested in folk songs and actively collected them. He settled in the United States in 1914 and became naturalized in 1919. For some years he was head of the music department at Washington Square College, New York University. His arrangements of traditional tunes for a wide variety of resources have won him great popularity. There is in his music, whether original works or transcriptions, no pretensiousness: there is much rhythmical energy and a simple delight in sentiment and jollity. His passion for using colourful English (instead of Italian) for indications of speed and dynamics (e.g. 'louden', *crescendo*) caused amusement but not emulation. His most famous pieces are *Country Gardens* and *Handel in the Strand*; he also wrote a *Rosenkavalier Ramble* for piano, based on music from Strauss's opera. In recent years his music has retained (and even increased) its popularity, and was greatly admired by – among others – Benjamin Britten.

Granados, Enrique (1867–1916), Spanish composer, pianist and conductor. A pupil of Pedrell, he studied in Barcelona and Paris, returned to Barcelona (1890), gave many concerts, founded (1900) the Society of Classical Concerts which he conducted, and founded (1901) and directed (until his death) a music school (Academia Granados). His music was written in a Spanish 'nationalist' idiom. He composed seven operas, two symphonic poems, three suites and other orchestral works, a choral work with organ and piano accompaniment, chamber music, songs and a collection of *tonadillas*, *Goyescas* (two volumes based on the paintings and tapestries of Goya) and other piano pieces. The music of *Goyescas* was used to form the material of an opera with the same title (New York, 1916). The ship in which he was returning from this performance was torpedoed in the English Channel, 1916.

Grand Duke, The, operetta in two acts by Gilbert and Sullivan, first performed in 1896. This was the last work in which Gilbert and Sullivan collaborated as librettist and composer. It was a failure.

Grande Messe des Morts (Fr.), a setting of the Requiem Mass by Berlioz, op 5 (1837), commissioned by the French Minister of the Interior and performed as a memorial service for French soldiers who had fallen at the siege of Constantine in Algeria. It is scored for an exceptionally large orchestra, including four brass bands, though to describe it as a 'mammoth' work (as many commentators do) would be misleading: many of its most characteristic moments make use of delicate, imaginative sonorities.

grandezza (It.), grandeur. *Con grandezza*, with grandeur.

Grandi, Alessandro (died 1630), Italian composer of church music, madrigals (with accompaniment) and solo cantatas. Among his appointments were: second *maestro di cappella* at St. Mark's, Venice (1620), and *maestro di cappella* at Santa Maria Maggiore, Bergamo. He was one of the most important composers of solo cantatas, and church music in the *stile concertato*, with considerable influence in his day.

grandioso (It.), in an imposing manner.

grand opéra, the term *grand opéra* (opera on a large scale) grew up in France in the 19th century to distinguish serious operas set to music throughout from *opéra-comique*, which had dialogue. Works of this kind, by Meyerbeer and his contemporaries, were often on a lavish scale. Hence 'grand opéra' came to be used not simply of a form but of the elaborate performances to be heard in a large opera house attended by the aristocracy.

grand piano, *see* PIANO

Graner Messe (Ger.), a Mass for soloists, chorus and orchestra by Liszt, composed for the dedication of the cathedral at Esztergom (Ger., Gran, hence the name Graner) in Hungary, in 1856.

Grassineau, James (c. 1715–67), London born secretary to Pepusch and author of *A Musical Dictionary . . . of Terms and Characters* (1740), which was to a large extent a translation of Brossard's *Dictionnaire de musique* (1703).

Grassini, Josephina (1773–1850), Italian operatic contralto. She studied in Milan, where she made her first appearance in 1794. She sang subsequently in various Italian opera houses, in Paris and in London, where she arrived in 1804 and was the rival of Mrs. Billington. Her dramatic as well as her singing ability made a great impression. Sir Charles Bell (1805) said that 'she *died* not only without being ridiculous, but with an effect equal to Mrs. Siddons.' The title role of Paër's *Didone abbandonata* was written for her.

Graun, Johann Gottlieb (c. 1702/3–71), German composer and violinist, pupil of Pisendel and Tartini. He was in the service of Crown Prince Frederick at Rheinsberg (1732) and leader of the royal orchestra at Berlin (1740). He composed about 100 symphonies, twenty violin concertos, church cantatas, string quartets and other chamber music.

His brother, **Karl Heinrich Graun** (1704–59), was a singer as well as a composer. He was in the service of Crown Prince Frederick at Rheinsberg and became court *Kapellmeister* (1740). He composed thirty operas (the most famous being *Montezuma*, 1755), dramatic cantatas, a Passion Cantata (*Der Tod*

Jesu, 1755) and other church music, piano concertos and trios.

Graupner, Christoph (1683–1760), German composer, a pupil of Kuhnau at St. Thomas's, Leipzig. He was harpsichordist at the Hamburg Opera under Keiser (1706), vice-*Kapellmeister* at Darmstadt (1709) and *Kapellmeister* (1712). He was elected cantor of St. Thomas's, Leipzig in 1723, but was unable to obtain his dismissal from Darmstadt: the post went instead to Bach. He wrote a few operas, six of which were produced at Hamburg, and a vast quantity of church music and instrumental compositions.

grave (It.), solemn and slow.

grazioso (It.), graceful.

Grechaninov, Alexander Tikhonovich (1864–1956), Russian composer. He studied in Moscow under Rimsky-Korsakov at the St. Petersburg Conservatory. He made a European tour (1922), lived in Paris from 1925 and settled in New York in 1941. He composed five symphonies and other orchestral works, choral works, Catholic church music including Masses and motets, Russian church music including two complete liturgies, string quartets and other chamber music, incidental music for plays, piano pieces, songs and music for children (including children's operas). His *Missa Oecumenica* (1944) was intended to encompass both Eastern and Western Christianity.

Greek music, the surviving fragments of ancient Greek music are very few and widely separated in time. There exists a substantial body of theoretical writings of different periods, but the authors of them frequently disagree and it is obvious that both the theory and the practice of Greek music were considerably modified as time went on. We know, however, that the Greeks used modal patterns, though the names of these sometimes changed from one period to another. We know also that they used intervals smaller than a semitone (*see* ENHARMONIC) – one of the striking evidences of the influence of Asiatic music. So far as our evidence goes they did not employ harmony, though they used the word *harmonia*, which means properly a fitting together and hence a consistent pattern (in their case of melodic material). We know from Plato that the modes had non-musical associations according to the order in which the intervals occurred: thus one was considered martial, another languorous, and so on.

The Roman theorist Boethius derived a good deal of his material from Greek writers, but he does not seem to have understood clearly what they wrote; and the medieval theorists who used Boethius as a text book often added to the confusion by further misunderstandings. Greek names, for example, were assigned to the medieval modes but the medieval nomenclature did not correspond with the Greek.

Greek theory may be said to have made two important contributions to medieval and modern theory: (1) it supplied a terminology (words like *tonic, diatonic, melody, harmony, diapason* are only a few of the many still in use which were originally employed by Greek theorists); (2) it provided the basis of medieval and modern acoustics by establishing the mathematical basis of musical sounds (here again the medieval writers, though appreciating the principles, sometimes went sadly astray in their calculations).

There was also one indirect result of Greek music – the creation of opera at the end of the 16th century. From the mistaken belief that Greek drama was sung throughout came the attempt to provide a modern equivalent by clothing dialogue with a form of musical declamation which came to be known as RECITATIVE. It is a striking example of the fact that an intellectual error can produce results of high aesthetic value.

See also CHROMATIC, DIATONIC, DIESIS, MODE

Greenberg, Noah (1919–66), U.S. choral conductor and musicologist. He founded the New York Pro Musica in 1952, and did much to develop U.S. interest in medieval and Renaissance music.

Greene, Harry Plunket (1865–1936), Irish born baritone, who excelled particularly in the interpretation of English songs. He also made a few appearances in opera. His book, *Interpretation of Song*, is a standard work (1912).

Greene, Maurice (1695–1755), English composer and organist. He was a chorister at St Paul's Cathedral in London, where he was organist from 1718. He became organist and composer to the Chapel Royal in 1727; professor, Cambridge, 1730; Master of the King's music, 1735. He inherited an estate in Essex (1750) and began a collection of English church music for publication which was completed by his pupil Boyce. He was a close friend of Handel. He composed an opera, oratorios, *Forty Select Anthems* (1743) and other church music, works for organ and for harpsichord, songs, odes for festal occasions, duets, trios, catches and canons.

Greensleeves, traditional English tune, at least as old as Shakespeare (who referred to it). A modern *Fantasia on Greensleeves* was written by Vaughan Williams, who combined it with another English tune, *Lovely Joan*. Vaughan Williams also made use of *Greensleeves* in his opera, *Sir John in Love* (1929).

Greeting, Thomas, author of *The Pleasant Companion; or new Lessons and Instructions for the Flagelet* (1673). He was also a member of Charles II's private music, and one of the 24 violins. Among his pupils for the flageolet were Samuel Pepys and his wife. There are several references to him in Pepys's diary.

Gregorian Chant, the term 'Gregorian Chant' refers to a large collection of ancient monophonic melodies, preserved, and until recently widely performed, within the Roman Catholic Church. Most of the chants belong within two liturgical rites: the MASS (modern edition in the *Graduale Romanum*, 1961), based on texts commemorating Christ's Last Supper and Sacrifice, and central among the ceremonies of the church; and the OFFICE (modern editions in the *Antiphonale pro Diurnis Horis*, 1934, and the *Liber Responsorialis*, 1895), eight monastic rites chanted daily, based primarily on the psalms (selected chants from both the Mass and the Office are printed in the *Liber Usualis*, 1961).

The earliest manuscripts containing the musical repertory of Gregorian chant are of Frankish provenance and were written in the 9th, 10th and 11th centuries (facsimiles of the most important are in *Paléographie Musicale*, iv, vii, viii, x, xi, and series, ii). Before the 9th century the chants were probably not written down, but disseminated orally. Modern knowledge of the origins of Gregorian chant and its possible connection with Pope Gregory (590–604) is therefore sketchy, and theories are controversial.

Jewish influence is prevalent in the general liturgical form and texts of the Roman Catholic rites. The Office, for example, originated from the psalmodic Prayer Hours of the Jews, and the Christian Mass replaced the Passover Feast. Textual fragments, the simplest examples of which are the Amen, Alleluia, Sanctus and Hosannah, were also part of the Jewish service. More interesting from the musical point of view are similarities found between: (1) the eight Gregorian psalm tones and their equivalent in synagogic chant, and (2) Gregorian psalmodic recitations and ancient chants sung among Yemenite and Persian Jews. Comparative studies between the oldest Gregorian and Byzantine chants (see BYZANTINE MUSIC) also suggest that both repertories partly derive from a common source – the early Christian liturgies of Antioch and Jerusalem.

According to the earliest surviving *Ordo Romanus* (c. 700), St. Jerome (c. 347–420) obtained the Jerusalem liturgy, and under the auspices of Pope Damasus (366–384) the first recorded reorganization of Roman liturgy and chant was undertaken, using the Jerusalem liturgy as a model. Pope Gregory is reputed to have compiled a cycle of chants for the church year, and an antiphoner, perhaps intended for universal use throughout western Christendom, but the belief that he was personally responsible for the codification of what is now known as 'Gregorian' chant is no longer seriously upheld. There is some evidence that a distinct but related version of the 'Gregorian' melodies, sung in Rome up to about 950 (modern edition by B. Stäblein in *Monumenta Monodica Medii Aevi*, ii), was completed under Pope Vitalian (657–672). This old Roman repertory appears to have been spread to France during the next 200 years: thus in 753 Bishop Shrodegang introduced Gregorian chant into the cathedral at Metz, having been sent by Pepin to Rome, and seven years later Pepin received a gradual and an antiphoner from Pope Paul I. Subsequently Pepin's son Charlemagne (742–814) issued decrees for the promotion and protection of the chant. It is impossible to speculate concerning the melodic changes which inevitably took place in France, but it seems likely that the chant was modified by French influences, and probably reached its final form in about 850, after which it returned to Rome, and replaced the local Roman chant currently in use.

See AMBROSE, BYZANTINE MUSIC, PLAINSONG, PSALMODY, SOLESMES

W. APEL: *Gregorian Chant* (1958)

J. BRYDEN and D. HUGHES: *An Index to Gregorian Chant* (two volumes, 1969)

J. W. A. VOLLAERTS: *Rhythmic Proportions in Early Medieval Ecclesiastical Chant* (1958)

P. WAGNER: *Einführung in die gregorianischen Melodien* (three volumes, latest edition, 1911–21; English translation of volume i, 1910)

Grenon, Nicolas, 15th century French singer and composer. Examples of his work are in J. Marix, *Les musiciens de la cour de Bourgogne* (1937) and C. van den Borren, *Polyphonia Sacra* (1932).

Grétry, André Ernest Modeste (1741–1813), Belgian composer. He was born in Liège, where he became a chorister at St Denis's Church. He studied in Rome (1759–66), taught singing at Geneva (1767) and produced operas in Paris from 1768. He was made one of the original members of the Institut (1795), an inspector of the new Conservatoire (1795), a member of the new Legion d'Honneur (1802), and received a pension from Napoleon. He composed many operas (mostly comic), six small symphonies (1758), a Requiem, motets and other church music, two piano quartets with flute, and piano sonatas. The most successful of his operas was *Richard Coeur-de-Lion* (Paris, 1784), an excellent example of the late 18th century *opéra-comique*, which was given all over Europe. He also composed *Zémire et Azor* on the subject of Beauty and the Beast. Of his literary works the most important is *Mémoires ou essais sur la musique* (three volumes, 1789–97): for an extract in translation, see O. Strunk, *Source Readings in Music History*, pages 711–27.

Edvard Grieg: in spite of the popularity of his piano concerto, he revealed his musical skills to best effect as a miniaturist in his piano pieces and songs

Grieg, Edvard Hagerup (1843–1907), Norwegian composer. He began composing at the age of nine and his parents were persuaded by Ole Bull to send him to study in Leipzig (1858), where he entered the Conservatorium, from which he graduated in 1862, gave his first concert in Bergen, settled in Copenhagen (1863), where he studied under Niels Gade, and after his return to Norway became a close friend of Richard Nordraak, who was working to produce a national Norwegian school of music. He founded (1867) and conducted (until 1880) a musical society in Christiania (now Oslo), married his cousin Nina Hagerup (1867), who sang many of his songs and with whom he later gave concerts, visited Italy (1865 and 1870), and became acquainted with Liszt in Rome. He made several visits to England but spent most of his later life at his country home near Bergen.

The individual charm of his music lies in the combination of national idioms, which he used constantly, with the romanticism which he had imbibed at Leipzig. He was not, however, content merely to accept the harmonic conventions of German romanticism, and evolved for himself a practice of modulation and a use of dissonance, bold for its time, which has no exact parallel in the work of any other contemporary composer. Primarily a lyrical composer, he was most successful in short pieces of a tender and lively character. In longer works, such as the piano concerto, the tendency to repeat short phrases can become wearisome, and the attempt to create a formal structure in the German tradition results in artificiality. Liszt nevertheless admired the piano concerto, which continues to be one of the most popular of all concertos today. The popularity of his music to *Peer Gynt* is due to the qualities which won success for his other works in the shorter forms. It shows, however, little understanding of the irony and bitter characterization of Ibsen's play.

His principal compositions are:

(1) Orchestra: overture, *I Höst* (In Autumn, 1866); piano concerto (1868; revised 1907); two suites from *Peer Gynt* (1888, 1891); three pieces from *Sigurd Jorsalfar* (1892); symphonic dances (1898); suite for strings, *Fra Holbergs Tid* (From Holberg's Time, 1885);

(2) Chamber music: string quartet; three violin sonatas; cello sonata.

(3) Piano: Sonata in E minor; *Lyriske Stykker* (Lyric Pieces, ten books); *Ballads*; many collections of folk songs and dances;

(4) Choral works: *Foran Sydens Kloster* (At a Southern Convent Gate, 1871); *Landjaenning* (Recognition of Land, 1872; revised, 1881);

(5) Incidental music: *Sigurd Jorsalfar* (1872); *Peer Gynt* (1875; revised orchestration, 1886).

Also the melodrama *Bergljot*, numerous songs (including the *Haugtussa* cycle) and part-songs.

G. ABRAHAM (editor): *Grieg* (1948)

Griffes, Charles Tomlinson (1884–1920), U.S. composer. Though he studied in Berlin (under Humperdinck) his musical leanings were towards French impressionism. A schoolmaster by profession, he found time to write some striking instrumental and vocal works, including the symphonic poem *The Pleasure Dome of Kubla Khan*. He also produced a dance drama (*The Kairn of Koridwen*) and a string quartet entitled *Sketches on Indian Themes*. Ill health and overwork brought about his death from pneumonia before he was able to realise his full potential.

Grigny, Nicolas de (1672–1703), French composer and organist of Rheims Cathedral. Bach made a copy of his *Livre d'orgue* (1711; modern edition in A. Guilmant, *Archives des maîtres de l'orgue*, v).

Grisi, Giulia (1811–69), Italian operatic soprano. She sang Adalgisa in the first performance of Bellini's *Norma* (Milan, 1831). She had an outstanding success in Paris, where she sang Norina in the first performance of Donizetti's *Don Pasquale* (Paris, 1843) and in London. Her second husband was the tenor Giovanni Matteo Mario, with whom she frequently sang in opera.

Her elder sister was Giuditta Grisi, a mezzo-

soprano. Together they appeared in the première of Bellini's *I Capuletti ed i Montecchi*, Giuditta singing Romeo to Giulia's Juliet.

Grocheo, Johannes de, theorist active in Paris around 1300. His treatise, *De musica*, is especially valuable for its information about the musical forms, sacred and secular, and musical instruments of his time. It has been edited, with a German translation, by E. Rohloff (1943). An English translation was published by A. Seay in 1967.

groppo, *see* GRUPPO

grosse caisse (Fr.), bass drum.

Grosse Fuge (Ger., *Great Fugue*), fugue by Beethoven for string quartet, originally intended as the finale of his B flat major quartet, op 130. Because it was so long and complex, however, Beethoven published it separately as op 133 (1825) and wrote a new finale for the B flat quartet. Today some performers like to reinstate the fugue in its proper place, though it does tend to shift the emotional focus of the work from the cavatina (where it usually lies) to the finale.

Grosse Orgelmesse (Ger., *Grand Organ Mass*), the name given to Haydn's *Missa in honorem Beatissimae Virginis Mariae* in E flat, composed c. 1766 (no 2 in the Haydn Society's edition, no 12 in Novello's edition). So called on account of the part for organ *obbligato*. See KLEINE ORGELMESSE

grosse Trommel (Ger.), bass drum.

Grossi, Ludovico, *see* VIADANA

ground, (1) = GROUND BASS.

(2) a composition built on a ground bass.

ground bass (It., *basso ostinato*), a bass line, whether simple or complex, long or short, which is constantly repeated throughout a vocal or instrumental composition and forms the foundation for varied melodic, harmonic or contrapuntal treatment. Its origin is presumably to be found in the dance. The effect of a ground bass, which was widely cultivated in the 17th and early 18th centuries, was to substitute a formal and unifying symmetry for the polyphonic development characteristic of 16th century music. Instrumental improvisation above a ground bass was also common in the 17th century, particularly in Britain, for the bass viol: *see* DIVISION (2), DIVISION VIOL. Among the forms related to the use of a ground bass are CHACONNE, FOLÍA, PASSACAGLIA.

Grove, George (1820–1900), English scholar, editor, and writer on music. Originally a civil engineer by profession, he became secretary of the Crystal Palace, 1852–73, and for many years wrote programme notes for the concerts given there. He also devoted himself to biblical studies and helped to establish the Palestine Exploration Fund. With Sullivan he visited Vienna in 1867 and discovered the parts of Schubert's *Rosamunde* music. He edited the *Dictionary of Music and Musicians* which still bears his name (first edition, 1879–89; second edition, J. A. Fuller-Maitland, 1904–10; third edition, H. C. Colles, 1927–8; fourth edition, H. C. Colles, 1940; fifth edition, E. Blom, 1954; sixth edition, S. Sadie). He was the first director of the Royal College of Music (1882–94) and was knighted in 1883. He wrote *Beethoven and his Nine Symphonies* in 1896.

C. L. GRAVES: *The Life and Letters of Sir Charles Grove, C.B.* (1904)

Grovlez, Gabriel (1879–1944), French conductor and composer. He studied at the Paris Conservatoire, taught piano at the Schola Cantorum and conducted at the Paris Opera (1914–33). His compositions include symphonic poems, ballets and the comic opera *Le Marquis de Carabas*. He also edited examples of old French keyboard music.

Gruenberg, Louis (1884–1964), Russian born composer and pianist. He lived in the United States from early childhood, apart from his musical education in Europe. He was a pupil of Busoni in Berlin and Vienna, and toured as a pianist (1912–19). His compositions, which show the influence of Negro spirituals and jazz, include the operas *Jack and the Beanstalk* (commissioned by the Juilliard School, 1931) and *Emperor Jones*, based on O'Neill's play (New York, 1933), five symphonies, concertos, chamber music, songs and piano pieces, including 'Jazzberries'.

Grumiaux, Arthur (born 1921), Belgian violinist who has established himself as one of the finest living exponents of the classical repertory from Bach to Bartók, Berg and Stravinsky.

gruppetto (It.), diminutive of *gruppo*.

gruppo or **groppo** (It.), literally 'group'. A generic term for various ornaments consisting of the association of one or more decorative notes with a melody note, in particular:

(1) a shake or trill employing both the upper and the lower accessory notes, e.g.:

is to be played

PRAETORIUS, *Syntagma Musicum*, iii (1618–19)

(Note that *trillo* in 17th century usage denoted something quite different – a tremolo or vibrato on a single note.)

(2) a turn (represented also by the diminutive *gruppetto*), e.g.:

is to be played

MATTHESON, *Der volkommene Capellmeister* (1739)

Guadagni, Gaetano (c. 1725–92), Italian castrato contralto (and later soprano). He sang in Italy, England, Ireland, France, Portugal, Austria and Germany. In London he sang also solos in Handel's *Messiah* and *Samson*.

Guadagnini, a family of Italian violin makers, active throughout the 18th century.

Guarneri, Guarnerius, family of Italian violin makers in Cremona, the first of whom was Andrea (died 1698), a pupil (like Stradivari) of Nicola Amati. The most celebrated was Giuseppe (1687–1744), known as Giuseppe del Gesù from the letters IHS (Jesu hominum salvator) which appear after his name on his labels.

Guédron, Pierre (c. 1565–1621), French composer, in the service of Henri IV and Louis XIII. He composed ballets for the court and published collections of *airs de cour*, of which seventeen are published in A. Verchaly, *Airs de cour pour voix et luth* (1961). His *Ballet de la délivrance de Renaud* (1617) is printed in H. Prunières, *Le Ballet de cour en France* (1914), pages 251–65.

Guerre des Bouffons, La (Fr., The War of the Comedians), name given to the violent controversy which arose in Paris as the result of a series of performances of comic opera given there by an Italian company (the comedians) in 1752–4. The subject of the controversy was a familiar theme – the rival merits of French and Italian music; but on this occasion it was pursued with unusual intensity. The arguments for either side were presented in a host of pamphlets: for two examples in translation (by Baron von Grimm and Jean-Jacques Rousseau).

O. STRUNK: *Source Readings in Music History*, pages 619–54.

Guerrero, Francisco (1527 or 1528–1599), Spanish composer. He was a chorister at Seville Cathedral. After an appointment at Jaén Cathedral he was successively director of the choir school and eventually (1574) *maestro de capilla* at Seville Cathedral. He twice visited Rome and also made a pilgrimage to Palestine, of which he published an account.

He was one of the outstanding Spanish composers of church music in the 16th century; a modern edition of selected works is in F. Pedrell, *Hispaniae schola musica sacra*, ii. His non-liturgical works include a collection of *Canciones y villanescas espirituales* (1589) which have been edited by V. García as the first two volumes (*Monumentos de la Música Espanola*, xvi and xix) of a projected complete edition of his music.

He was first taught by his elder brother, **Pedro Guerrero,** examples of whose compositions are preserved in printed lute-tablatures and also in manuscript part-books.

R. MITJANA: *Francisco Guerrero: estudio critico-biographica* (1922)

Guglielmi, Pietro (1728–1804), Italian composer. After studying under Durante at the Conservatorio Santa Maria di Loreto, Naples, he composed a large number of operas, winning his first outstanding success with the production of *Il ratto della sposa* at Venice in 1765. He also visited Dresden, Brunswick and London. He became *maestro di cappella* at St Peter's, Rome in 1793. In addition to some one hundred operas he also wrote nine oratorios, motets and chamber music.

Gui, Vittorio (1885–1975), Italian conductor and composer. After studying at the Liceo di S. Cecilia, Rome, he conducted at a number of Italian opera houses (including San Carlo, Naples, and La Scala, Milan), and in Britain at Covent Garden, Glyndebourne and the Edinburgh Festival. In 1928 he founded an orchestra in Florence, and was subsequently closely

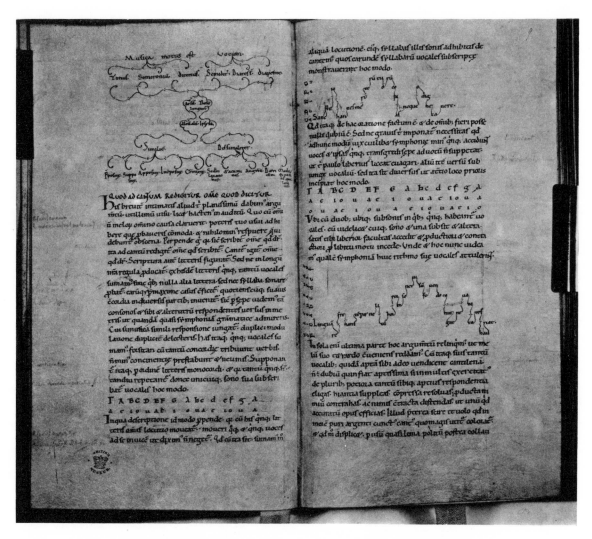

An opening of an 11th century copy of Guido d'Arezzo's treatise *Micrologus*

involved with the creation of the Florence Maggio Musicale – at which he revived many important Italian operas, especially works by Rossini. His own compositions include the opera *La fata malerba* (Turin, 1927).

Guido d'Arezzo or **Guido Aretinus** (end of the 10th century–c. 1050), French theorist and teacher, a Benedictine monk. His name derived from the fact that for some time he was in charge of the choir school at Arezzo in Italy. He simplified the teaching of choirboys by getting them to associate each note of a HEXACHORD with a particular syllable. These syllables – *ut, re, mi, fa, sol, la* – begin the successive lines of the hymn 'Ut queant laxis', which was chosen because the initial notes of each line are successively C, D, E, F, G, A. This system, known as SOLMIZATION, created the names for the notes still used in France and Italy, and was the basis of TONIC SOL-FA in the 19th century. He also extended the principle of using horizontal lines to indicate the pitch of notes, recommending the use of three or four lines for this purpose. This recommendation, once adopted, proved invaluable: the STAFF of four or more lines became indispensable to composers and copyists. Guido's theoretical works are printed in Gerbert, *Scriptores*, ii. A new edition of his *Micrologus* was published by J. Smits van Waesberghe in 1955. An English translation of his *Prologus antiphonarii sui* and *Epistola de ignoto cantu* is in O. Strunk, *Source Readings in Music History*, pages 117–125.

Guildhall School of Music and Drama, founded in 1880 by the Corporation of the City of London. Its principals have included Thomas Henry Weist-Hill, Joseph Barnby, William Hayman Cummings, Landon Ronald and Edric Cundell. Its present principal is Allen Percival.

Guilielmus Monachus, late 15th century theorist, probably Italian, whose treatise *De praeceptis artis musicae et practicae* contains useful information about

Guitars: (1) ornate 17th century Italian guitar (2) *bandurria*
(3) *cittern* (4) banjo (5) guitar

the practice of FAUXBOURDON. A modern edition by
Albert Seay was published in 1965.

Guillaume de Machaut (Machault) (1300–77), poet
and composer. He was ordained and became secretary
to John, Duke of Luxembourg and King of Bohemia,
with whom he travelled. He later served Charles V of
France and became canon of Rheims. The dominant
French composer of the 14th century, he composed the
first known setting of the Ordinary of the Mass by a
single composer (*Messe Notre Dame*). In his *Remède de
Fortune* he explained the seven forms of lyric poetry
and wrote a composition to illustrate each one. Of his
twenty-three motets all but three are isorhythmic. His
secular compositions form the first great repertory of
the polyphonic *chanson*, and comprise *ballades*, *rondeaux*, and *virelais*. He also composed monophonic
lais and *virelais*. The edition of his musical works by
Friedrich Ludwig comprises two volumes (1926, 1929)
containing respectively the *ballades*, *rondeaux* and *virelais*, and the motets, a volume of commentary (1928)
and a volume containing the Mass and the *lais* (1943;
reprinted, 1954). Another edition by Leo Schrade is in
Polyphonic Music of the Fourteenth Century, ii–iii.
There are several modern editions of the Mass.

> A. MACHABEY: *Guillaume de Machault*, two volumes
> (1955)
> G. REESE: *Music in the Middle Ages* (1940), chapter
> 12

Guillaume Tell, *see* WILLIAM TELL

Guilmant, Félix Alexandre (1837–1911), French
organist and composer. He settled in Paris in 1871,
where he was organist at the Trinité until 1901. A
founder (with Bordes and Vincent d'Indy) of the
Schola Cantorum, he taught the organ there and at the
Conservatoire (from 1896). He inaugurated many new
organs and toured in Britain, the United States and
on the Continent. He composed two symphonies for
organ and orchestra, sonatas and other works for organ.
He also edited ten volumes of old organ music, under
the title *Archives des maîtres de l'orgue* (1898–1910).

Guiraud, Ernest (1837–92), U.S. composer, son of a
French composer and music teacher. He studied at
the Paris Conservatoire, won the *Prix de Rome* in
1859, and taught at the Paris Conservatoire from
1876 until his death. He wrote several operas, of which
the most successful was *Piccolino* (Paris, 1876), and
composed the recitatives for Bizet's *Carmen* (in place
of the spoken dialogue) on the occasion of its production at Vienna in 1875 (the first production outside
Paris). These recitatives, though still widely used
today, distort and dilute the opera and are condemned
by purists. Guiraud's well-intentioned interest in
Bizet also led him to arrange the second suite from
L'Arlésienne (a more praiseworthy project). He also
revised Offenbach's *The Tales of Hoffmann*, left unfinished by the composer; but, as with Carmen, the
results proved controversial.

guiro, a scraper consisting of a notched gourd, played
by scraping a stick over the notches. It is used to
emphasize the beat in rhythmic music.

guitar (Fr., *guitare*; Ger., *Guitarre*; It., *chitarra*;
Sp., *guitarra*), a plucked string instrument, originally
brought to Spain by the Moors in the middle ages. It
differs from the lute in having a flat back. The modern
instrument has six strings, tuned:

The earliest known compositions (for a four-stringed instrument) were printed in Fuenllana's *Orphenica lyra* (1554). Related instruments are the BALALAIKA, BANDURRIA, CITTERN and GITTERN.

Guntram, opera in three acts by Strauss, to a libretto by the composer. It was first performed at Weimar in 1894. This was Strauss's first opera, now overshadowed by his later works.

Gurlitt, Cornelius (1820–1901), German organist, composer and teacher. He wrote nearly 250 works, including two operettas and an opera. Today he is best known for his educational piano music.

Wilibald Gurlitt (1889–1963), the musicologist, was Cornelius's grand nephew. He played an important part in the revival of old instruments (including the organ) for the performance of the music of the past. He edited a volume of the complete edition of the works of Praetorius, published a facsimile edition of part II of Praetorius's *Syntagma Musicum*, and wrote a concise but valuable study of Bach (second edition 1949).

Gurlitt, Manfred (1890–1972), German composer and conductor, a pupil of Humperdinck. His compositions include the opera *Wozzeck* (Bremen, 1926), a setting of Büchner's play (previously set by Alban Berg, 1922, produced in Berlin, 1925).

Gurney, Ivor Bertie (1890–1937), English composer and poet. He was a chorister at Gloucester Cathedral, where he became assistant organist, 1906. He studied at the Royal College of Music under Vaughan Williams, Stanford and others and served in the army (from 1915). After he was discharged because of unfitness resulting from being gassed and wounded, he suffered continually from bad health and poverty and was sent to a mental hospital in 1922, where he remained until his death. He composed songs (some to his own poetry), *Ludlow and Teme* (a song-cycle for tenor and string quartet, to words by A. E. Housman) and two other song cycles, piano pieces and two works for violin and piano.

Gurrelieder (Ger., *Songs of Gurra*), large scale vocal work by Schoenberg, completed in 1911 and scored for soloists, three male choruses, one mixed chorus, narrator and a lavish orchestra incorporating eight flutes and a set of iron chains. The work is based on a German translation of Danish poems by J. P. Jacobsen. Gurra is the castle occupied by Tove, who is loved by a 14th century Danish king, Waldemar IV. *Gurrelieder* is one of the high points of late romantic music.

Guttoveggio, Joseph, *see* CRESTON

Gwendoline, opera in two acts by Chabrier, to a libretto by Catulle Mendès, first performed in Brussels in 1886. The story concerns the Viking King Harald, who falls in love with Gwendoline, the daughter of his enemy, Armel the Saxon. The music shows Chabrier's admiration for Wagner.

gymel (derived from the Lat. *cantus gemellus*, 'twin song'), term first occurring in the 15th century to denote a characteristically English method of singing in two parts with the same range. The practice may be traced as far back as the 13th century, earlier examples making liberal use of parallel thirds.

M. BUKOFZER: 'The Gymel, the Earliest Form of English Polyphony', *Music and Letters*, xvi (1935)

Gyrowetz, Adalbert (Czech name: Jirovec) (1763–1850), Bohemian composer. He studied law in Prague and music in Vienna (where one of his symphonies was performed by Mozart, 1786), Naples and Milan. On visiting Paris, he discovered that several of his symphonies were being performed under Haydn's name. From 1789 until 1792 he lived in London and was *Kapellmeister* and *Intendant* of the two court theatres in Vienna from 1804 until 1831. He composed about thirty operas (German and Italian), among which was *Hans Sachs*, an early treatment of the subject of Wagner's *Mastersingers*. He also wrote prolifically in other forms, his output including melodramas, forty ballets, sixty symphonies, serenades, overtures and other orchestral works, nineteen Masses, cantatas and other choral works, sixty quartets, quintets, trios, forty piano sonatas and songs. He published his autobiography under the title *Biographie des Adalbert Gyrowetz* (1848; new edition by A. Einstein in *Lebensläufe deutscher Musiker*, iii–iv, 1915).

H (Ger.), B natural.

Haas, Joseph (1879–1960), German composer. He was a pupil and disciple of Max Reger. He taught at the Munich Academy of Music from 1921, and was President there from 1945 until 1949. He composed operas, oratorios, orchestral works, chamber music, piano pieces, and songs.

Haas, Robert Maria (1886–1960), Austrian historian, composer, and conductor, editor of seven volumes of the series *Denkmäler der Tonkunst in Osterreich*, and contributor to Adler's *Handbuch*. He wrote a number of books on music of the 17th and 18th centuries, including *Die Musik des Barocks* and *Aufführungspraxis der Musik* in Bücken's *Handbuch der Musikwissenschaft*. In 1929 he initiated the publication of the original versions of Bruckner's works and wrote (1934) a biography of that composer.

Hába, Alois (1893–1973), Czech composer, pupil of Novak and Schreter. In 1921 he became a protagonist of music written in quarter- and sixth-tones, which he has used in piano music, string quartets, and works for violin and for cello. A quarter-tone piano, clarinets, and trumpets were specially made for the first performance of his quarter-tone opera *The Mother* (Czech, *Matka*), first performed in Munich in 1931. In a subsequent opera (*Thy Kingdom Come*, 1934) he required his singers to master sixth-tones. Until 1948 he directed a microtone class at Prague University. His pioneering activities in this field of music have influenced a number of present-day composers.

habanera (Sp.), a Cuban dance adopted in (or re-imported into) Spain in the 19th century. It is usually written in 2/4 time and its characteristic rhythm is

The name is believed to derive from Habana (Havana). A *habanera* by Sebastian Yradier, 'El Arreglito', was adapted by Bizet in *Carmen*, and later examples were written by Chabrier (1885), Ravel (1895) and Debussy.

Habeneck, François Antoine (1781–1849), French conductor, violinist and composer. He founded the Société des Concerts du Conservatoire in Paris in 1828, and introduced many of the works of Beethoven into France.

    A. CARSE: *The Orchestra from Beethoven to Berlioz* (1948)

    L. SCHRADE: *Beethoven in France* (1942)

Haberl, Franz Xaver (1840–1910), German priest, organist and historian of the church music of the 15th, 16th and early 17th centuries. In his *Bausteine zur Musikgeschichte* (1885–8) he laid the foundation for later research on Dufay, on the history of the Papal choir, and on the music in the Vatican Library. He edited the works of Palestrina.

Hacomplaynt (Hacomblene), Robert (died 1528), English composer. He was educated at Eton (King's Scholar, 1469–72) and King's College, Cambridge. He was provost of King's College from 1509 to 1528. His five-part 'Salve regina' in the Eton choirbook is printed in *Musica Britannica*, xi.

Hadley, Henry Kemball (1871–1937), U.S. composer and conductor. He studied composition in Boston and Vienna, and conducted the San Francisco Symphony Orchestra from 1911 to 1916. He was one of the founders of the National Association of American Composers and Conductors. His works include operas (*Safie*; *Azora*; *Bianca*; *Cleopatra's Night*; *A Night in Old Paris*; *The Garden of Allah*; *Nancy Brown*) orchestral, choral and chamber music, and numerous songs.

Hadley, Patrick Arthur Sheldon (1899–1973), English composer and teacher. He was educated at Winchester, Cambridge, and the Royal College of Music. He became lecturer at Cambridge (1938) and succeeded E. J. Dent as professor in 1946, holding the appointment until 1963. Most of his compositions are for voices and instruments, and include *The Trees so High* (1931), freely based on a ballad of that name, *La Belle Dame Sans Merci* (1935), *My Beloved Spake* (1938), *The Hills* (1946) and *The Cenci* (1951).

Hadow, William Henry (1859–1937), English historian, composer, writer on musical criticism and authority on musical and general education. He lectured on music at Oxford from 1890 until 1899. He was principal of Armstrong College, Newcastle-on-Tyne (1909–19) and vice-chancellor of Sheffield University (1919–30). His *Studies in Modern Music* (two volumes, 1894–5) contain extended essays on six 19th century composers. He was general editor of the *Oxford History of Music* and author of the fifth volume, *The Viennese Period* (1904). His position as administrator and as chairman of the Committee which published the Hadow report, *The Education of the Adolescent* (1927), gave weight to his claim 'that we should admit musical history to the same place in our annals which we now accord to the history of literature' (Rice Institute Lectures, Houston, Texas, 1926; published in *Collected Essays*, 1928).

He was knighted in 1918 and became a C.B.E. in 1920.

Haffner, the title given to two compositions by Mozart: (1) serenade in D major (1776, K250) composed together with a March (K249) for the marriage of Elizabeth Haffner at Salzburg on June 22, 1776;

    (2) symphony in D major (1782, K385) composed for the Haffner family and based on a serenade (though a different one from K250). In transforming the work into a symphony for his Viennese concerts, Mozart

was obliged to drop the first of the two minuets it originally contained.

Hahn, Reynaldo (1875–1947), Venezuelan born composer and conductor. He was brought up in Paris, where he studied under Dubois, Lavignac and Massenet at the Conservatoire. His works, beginning with *L'Ile de rêve* (1898) are almost entirely for the stage, and include the operas *La Carmélite* (1902), *La Colombe de Bouddha* (1921), *Le Marchand de Venise* (after Shakespeare's *Merchant of Venice*, 1935), operettas, ballets, and incidental music. He also composed chamber music, piano pieces, and songs to poems of Verlaine (*Chansons grises*) and Leconte de Lisle (*Études latines*). He was director of the Paris Opéra (1945–6). Mozart was one of his specialities; he composed incidental music for Sacha Guitry's play, *Mozart*.

Haieff, Alexei (born 1914), Siberian born composer who settled in the United States in 1932. He studied at the Juilliard School of Music and under Nadia Boulanger in Paris. His works include orchestral and chamber music, and a ballet, 'Beauty and the Beast'.

Haitink, Bernard (born 1929), Dutch conductor. He studied at the Amsterdam Conservatory, and in 1957 became conductor of the Netherlands Radio Philharmonic. In 1959, he was appointed joint conductor (with Eugen Jochum) of the Concertgebouw Orchestra, Amsterdam, and five years later became principal conductor of that orchestra. In 1967 he became conductor of the London Philharmonic, an appointment he held simultaneously with his Dutch one. From one of his Dutch predecessors, Eduard van Beinum, he has inherited a taste for the music of Bruckner, and from another, Willem Mengelberg, a taste for Mahler, though his interpretations of the works of these composers have their own individual (and exceptionally musical) stamp.

Halbe (Ger.), minim.

Halbton (Ger.), semitone.

Hale (Halle), *see* ADAM DE LA HALE

Halévy, Jacques François (originally Fromental Elias Lévy) (1799–1862), French-Jewish composer. He was a pupil of Berton and Cherubini at the Paris Conservatoire and winner of the *Prix de Rome* in 1819. He wrote more than thirty operas, of which only *La Juive* (1835) gained permanent fame. He also wrote several ballets, one of them after Prévost's *Manon Lescaut*. He taught at the Conservatoire, where he became professor of composition in 1840. Among his pupils were Gounod and Bizet, who married his daughter.

half cadence or **half close**, imperfect CADENCE.

Halffter, Christobal (born 1930), Spanish composer, nephew of ERNESTO and RODOLFO HALFFTER. He studied with Conrado del Campo and Alexandre Tansman, and in 1962 became professor of composition at Madrid Conservatory. His works include a sinfonia for three orchestral groups, a concertino for strings, *Cinco microformas* for orchestra, *Dos movimientos* for timpani and strings, *Espejos* for four percussionists and tape, *Antifona pascual* for soloists, chorus and orchestra, *Cantata in Expectatione Resurrectionis Domini*, and *Trespiezas* for solo flute.

Halffter, Ernesto (born 1905), Spanish composer and conductor of partly German descent (his full surname is Halffter Escriche). After the Spanish Civil War he settled in Portugal. His works include an opera (*The Death of Carmen*), a sinfonietta and other orchestral pieces, a *Suite ancienne* for wind instruments, two string quartets and other chamber music.

Rodolfo Halffter (born 1900), his elder brother, was a composer who was also a writer on music. After the Spanish Civil War he settled in Mexico. His works include ballets (*Don Lindo de Almeria* and *The Baker's Morning*), a violin concerto, an *Overtura concertante* for piano and orchestra and a number of piano pieces.

half note (U.S.), minim.

half step (U.S.), semitone.

Hälfte, die (Ger.), literally 'the half' – a direction indicating that a passage is to be performed by only half the usual number of instruments or voices.

half tone (U.S.), semitone.

Hallé, Charles (originally Carl Hallé) (1819–95), German-English pianist and conductor. After studying with Rinck and Gottfried Weber in Darmstadt (1836), he settled in Manchester in 1848 where he founded the Hallé Orchestra (1857). He became a prominent figure in British musical life, notably as a conductor of the works of Berlioz. He was knighted in 1888 and became first Principal of the Royal Manchester College of Music in 1893.

C. E. and M. HALLÉ: *Life and Letters of Charles Hallé* (1896)

Hallé Orchestra, English Manchester-based symphony orchestra founded in 1857 by Sir Charles Hallé. Hans Richter was its conductor from 1899 until 1911 (when the orchestra's close relationship with the music of Elgar began to develop), Sir Hamilton Harty from 1920 until 1933, and Sir John Barbirolli from 1945 until 1970. The orchestra's present conductor is James Loughran.

hallelujah, basically, a Biblical word for the joyous praise of God. In chant (Gregorian or Ambrosian) it is spelt *Alleluia*. In the 17th and 18th centuries, choral compositions often incorporated substantial *Hallelujah* choruses in fugal style. Handel's, in the Messiah, is the most famous example.

Hallen, Johan Andreas (1846–1925), Swedish composer, conductor and critic. He studied in Leipzig, Munich and Dresden and was conductor of the Stockholm Philharmonic from 1884 until 1895, and of the Royal Swedish Opera from 1892 until 1897. He composed operas, symphonic poems, suites and other orchestral works, choral works with orchestra, a piano quartet, theatre music and songs.

halling (Norw.), a popular Norwegian dance, moderately fast in tempo and generally in 2/4 time. The dance is performed by men, with a good deal of dramatic action, including sudden leaps into the air. The music is properly played on the Hardanger fiddle, a violin with four sympathetic strings in addition to the normal four. There are several examples of the dance in Grieg's works.

Hallström, Ivar (1826–1901), Swedish composer and pianist. He became librarian to Prince Oscar (later King Oscar II) and settled in Stockholm, where he was appointed director of Lindblad's Music School in 1861. He composed operas (one with Prince Gustav, 1847), operettas, ballets, cantatas, piano pieces and songs. His operas, whose use of folk material made them popular in their time, include *The Enchanted Cat* (1869) and *The Bewitched One* (1874).

Halvorsen, Johan (1864–1935), Norwegian violinist, composer and conductor. He studied in Stockholm, Leipzig, Liège, and Berlin, and also lived in Bergen, Aberdeen and Helsinki. He became conductor of the symphony concerts at Bergen in 1893, and of the National Theatre, Oslo, in 1899. He composed two symphonies, a violin concerto, nine suites and other orchestral works, a coronation cantata for King Haakon, incidental music for plays, three suites for violin and piano, choral works, and songs. He married a niece of Grieg.

Hambacher, Josepha, *see* DUŠEK (3)

Hamboys, *see* HANBOYS

Hambraeus, Bengt (born 1928), Swedish composer, organist and musicologist. He studied at Uppsala University (where he later became a teacher) and has worked in Germany. One of Sweden's most progressive composers, he was an early champion of Boulez, Stockhausen and Nono, and a pioneer of electronic music. His works include *Rota* for three orchestras, percussion and tape, and a series of pieces entitled *Constellation* for varying instrumental and electronic forces.

Hamerik (originally Hammerich), **Asger** (1843–1923), Danish composer, brother of ANGUL HAMMERICH, and pupil of Gade and Berlioz. His compositions include seven symphonies (the sixth being the *Symphonie Spirituelle*), two choral trilogies and a Requiem, four operas, five suites for orchestra, cantatas and chamber music. From 1872 until 1898 he worked in the United States as director of the Conservatory of the Peabody Institute, Baltimore.

His son **Ebbe Hamerik** (1898–1951) was a composer and conductor. He was conductor at the Royal Theatre, Copenhagen, from 1919 until 1922. Later he moved to Austria, but in 1934 returned home. He wrote several operas, including *Leonardo da Vinci* and *The Travelling Companion* (after Hans Andersen). Among his other works are five symphonies, *Variations on an Old Danish Folk Tune* for orchestra, a suite for contralto and small orchestra, chamber music, piano pieces and songs. He died through drowning in the Kattegat.

Hamilton, Iain (born 1922), Scottish composer, pianist and teacher. Born in Glasgow, he studied engineering before becoming a pupil of William Alwyn and Harold Craxton in London. In 1951 he won the *prix d'honneur* at the Royal Academy of Music, the Royal Philharmonic Prize and the Koussevitsky Foundation Award. Since 1962 he has been professor of music at Duke University, North Carolina, in the United States. With Thea Musgrave, he is one of Scotland's two most internationally renowned composers. Early in his career, his adoption of an outward-looking musical idiom (twelve-note, as opposed to nationalistic) aroused controversy in his native Scotland and possibly prompted his decision to work elsewhere. His *Sinfonia* for two orchestras, commissioned by the Robert Burns Federation to commemorate the poet's bicentenary, caused a scandal when it was presented at the 1959 Edinburgh Festival – it was a thoroughly abstract, uncompromising

score, not the string of song arrangements that was presumably expected. In the 1970s, however, at a time of Scottish musical renaissance, Hamilton's importance is recognised in his homeland as well as abroad. His opera, *The Catiline Conspiracy*, revealed the tautness of his dramatic sense when Scottish Opera staged it in 1974. The rest of his substantial output includes another opera (*The Royal Hunt of the Sun*, based on Peter Shaffer's play), two violin concertos, a piano concerto, two symphonies, two orchestral pieces (*Alastor* and *Aurora*), *Arias* for small orchestra, and *Cantos* for orchestra. The most important of his choral works are *The Bermudas* (based on Marvell) and a war cantata, *Pharsalia*. Among his chamber and orchestral works are *Dialogues* for coloratura and instrumental ensemble (written for Lukas Foss's group from Buffalo), a flute sonata for Severino Gazzelloni, *Nocturnes* and *Cadenzas* for piano and *Threnos: In Time of War*, a powerful work for solo organ inspired by events in Vietnam.

Hammerklavier (Ger.), literally 'hammer keyboard' – an obsolete German name for the piano. Beethoven used it in the published titles of his piano sonatas op 101 in A major and op 106 in B flat major; it was also his original intention to use it for op 109 in E major (*see* A. C. Kalischer, *Beethoven's Letters*, translated by J. S. Shedlock, ii, pages 3–4, 181–2) and op 110 in A flat major. The habit of referring to op 106 as the "Hammerklavier" sonata' is pointless. *Sonate für das Hammerklavier* means simply 'piano sonata'.

Hammerich, Angul (1848–1931), Danish critic and historian, brother of ASGER HAMERIK. From 1896 to 1922 he was professor of musical history at the University of Copenhagen. He wrote *Mediaeval Musical Relics of Denmark* (Danish and English, 1912) and *Dansk Musik Historie indtil c. 1700* (1921).

Hammerschmidt, Andreas (1611 or 1612–1675), Bohemian organist and composer. He was an important figure in the history of Lutheran music. He was organist at Freiburg from 1635 to 1639, and at Zittau from 1639 until his death. In his *Dialogi oder Gespräche zwischen Gott und einer gläubigen Seele*, (*Dialogues between God and a faithful Soul*: two parts, Dresden, 1645) he applied the method of dramatic dialogue to settings of Biblical words for two, three or four voices with figured bass, in some cases with an introductory *sinfonia* for instruments (modern edition of Part I in *Denkmäler der Tonkunst in Osterreich*, xvi, Jg. viii, 1). His *Musikalische Andachten* (*Musical Devotions*: five parts, 1638–53) contain more than 150 pieces for one to twelve voices with figured bass, with or without instruments. A selection was printed in *Denkmäler deutscher Tonkunst*, xl, with a list of published works. He also wrote instrumental chamber music and secular songs, modern editions of which are in *Das Erbe deutscher Musik*, Reichsdenkmale, volumes xlix and xliii, respectively.

Hammerstein, Oscar (1848–1919), German–U.S. impresario, who built and managed theatres and opera houses in New York from 1890. From 1906 to 1910, when his interests were bought by the Metropolitan Opera, his Manhattan Opera House presented many famous singers, and gave first U.S. performances of Debussy's *Pelléas et Mélisande* (1908), and Richard Strauss's *Salome* (1907) and *Elektra* (1910).

Hammond organ, a brand of electronic organ.

Hampel, Anton Joseph (died 1771), Czech horn-player, a member of the Dresden orchestra from 1737. He is said to have invented the practice of using the hand to produce stopped notes on the horn. He wrote a tutor for the horn which was revised by his pupil Giovanni Punto.

Hampton, John, English musician, who was master of the choristers at Worcester Cathedral from 1484 to 1522. The Eton College choirbook (c. 1500) contains a five-part setting of 'Salve Regina' by him, printed in *Musica Britannica*, xi.

Handel Variations, a set of twenty variations and fugue for piano by Brahms, op 24, composed in 1861. The work is based on the Air from Handel's harpsichord suite in B flat.

Handschin, Jacques (1886–1955), Swiss musicologist, who studied at Basle and Munich, and became professor of musical history, University of Basle, in 1935. He wrote extensively on medieval music.

Hanboys (Hamboys), John, 15th century theorist. His treatise *Summa super musicam continuam et discretam* is printed in Coussemaker's *Scriptores*, i, page 416.

Handel, George Frideric (originally Händel, Georg Friedrich) 1685–1759), German born, English naturalised composer. Though he showed early musical leanings, he did not come of a musical family, unlike his exact contemporary, J. S. Bach. His father was a barber-surgeon, who (unwillingly) allowed him to study music under Zachau, the local organist in Handel's hometown of Halle. But when the court of Berlin offered to further the boy's musical education, his father refused to accept and insisted that he study law instead. After a year, however, Handel left Halle University and became a violinist in Keiser's opera house in Hamburg, where he had his first operas, *Almira* and *Nero*, produced in 1705. In Italy (1706–9) he gained a knowledge of Italian styles in opera, oratorio, serenata, concerto, and chamber music, had a success with his opera *Agrippina* (Venice, 1709), and composed the oratorios *La Resurrezione* and *Trionfo del Tempo*, the serenata *Aci, Galatea e Polifemo*, solo cantatas, and chamber duets. In 1710 he was appointed *Kapellmeister* to the Elector of Hanover, accepted an invitation to write a new opera for London, and in 1711 produced *Rinaldo* there with great success. In 1712 he returned to London on leave of absence from his Hanover post, which he never resumed, and produced *Il Pastor fido* (1712), *Teseo* (1712), *Silla* (1714) *and Amadigi* (1715). He received a life pension from Queen Anne, and wrote for her a Birthday Ode and a *Te Deum* on the Peace of Utrecht (1713). The at first embarrassing accession of his former master as George I did not long affect his position adversely, and he was soon in favour with an increased pension, an event which (in spite of popular theory) does not appear to have been due to the charms of the *Water Music*.

No Italian operas were given in London between 1717 and 1720 and Handel became musical director to the Duke of Chandos, for whom he composed the *Chandos Anthems*, *Acis and Galatea* (1720), and the masque *Haman and Mordecai* (1720) which was revised in 1732 as his first English oratorio, *Esther*. Between 1720 and 1733 he produced twenty new operas at the

Royal Academy of Music (King's Theatre, Haymarket) and published fifteen *sonate da camera* (1724), nine trio sonatas (1733), and eight suites for harpsichord (1720). The difficulties of maintaining the Italian opera were complicated by Handel's differences with Bononcini, by the ostentatious rivalry of Faustina and Cuzzoni, and by the great success of *The Beggar's Opera* (1728). After the favourable reception of *Esther* he turned to oratorio for performances in Lent, and wrote *Deborah* (1733), *Athaliah* (1733), *Saul* (1739), *Israel in Egypt* (1739), and *Messiah* (Dublin, 1742), besides producing fifteen new operas and a revised version of *Il Pastor fido* with an added prologue *Terpsichore* (1734). He composed his last opera, *Deidamia*, in 1741, and between 1743 and 1745 the oratorios *Samson*, *Joseph*, and *Belshazzar* and the secular choral works *Semele* and *Hercules*, which did not, however, bring him financial success. *Judas Maccabaeus* (1746, to mark the suppression of the rebellion of 1745) was well received, and the last eleven years of his life, during which he wrote six further oratorios and *The Triumph of Time and Truth* (1757), the third version of an oratorio of 1708, brought him acceptance and comparative serenity, though clouded by blindness from 1753. He was buried in Westminster Abbey.

Handel's writing, though not seldom perfunctory and at times shallow in expression, is at its greatest a brilliant and infallibly effective combination of the Italian traditions of solo and instrumental style, the English choral tradition, and the German contrapuntal style in which he was trained. These qualities are clear in the well-known works, but his remarkable versatility and quickness of response to a really dramatic situation produced many little masterpieces in the course of larger compositions which must be sought to be found, and some of the comparatively neglected oratorios keep this high level of inspiration almost throughout. Likewise the instrumental compositions are, at their best, delightful for their surety of writing and felicity of expression. Handel's borrowings from other composers, though reprehensible from a modern point of view, are in large part due to the 18th century custom of concocting pasticcios, to inadvertence, and possibly to a keen but unconscious memory, rather than to deliberate appropriation.

In recent years there has been a move towards a more 'authentic' style of Handel performance, using smaller, lighter-toned forces than were once fashionable for a work such as *Messiah*, and adding appropriate embellishments to the musical line. As a result, *Messiah* has emerged as the intimate work it really is, though massive, grandiose performances still have a following among a less discerning public. Many of Handel's operas, long thought to have been killed by the cramping conventions of opera seria, have likewise gained a fresh lease of life in sympathetic performances by such groups as the Handel Opera Society of London. His principal compositions are:

(1) Operas: *Almira* (1705); *Rodrigo* (1707); *Agrippina* (1709); *Rinaldo* (1711); *Il Pastor fido* (1712); *Teseo* (1712); *Silla* (1714); *Amadigi* (1715); *Radamisto* (1720); *Muzio Scevola* (1721); *Floridante* (1721); *Ottone* (1723); *Flavio* (1723); *Giulio Cesare* (1724); *Tamerlano* (1724); *Rodelinda* (1725); *Scipione* (1726); *Alessandro* (1726); *Admeto* (1727); *Riccardo Primo*

George Frideric Handel, whose magistral influence changed the course of music in 18th century England by ensuring the dominance of the Italian style

Complete works (with a few omissions) were published by the German Handel Society, 96 volumes (1859–1902). A new edition of the complete works (*Hallische Händel-Ausgabe*) under the auspices of the German Handel Society was begun in 1955.

G. ABRAHAM (editor): *Handel: a Symposium* (1954)

W. DEAN: *Handel's Dramatic Oratorios and Masques* (1959); *Handel and the Opera Seria* (1970)

E. J. DENT: *Handel* (1934)

O. E. DEUTSCH: *Handel, a Documentary Biography* (1955)

N. FLOWER: *George Frideric Handel* (1947, revised 1959)

P. H. LANG: *Handel* (1966)

H. LEICHENTRITT: *Handel* (1924)

E. H. MULLER *The Letters and Writings of George Frideric Handel* (1935)

P. ROBINSON: *Handel and his Orbit* (1908)

R. ROLLAND (translated by A. E. Hull): *Handel* (1916)

W. C. SMITH: *Concerning Handel* (1948)

R. A. STREATFIELD: *Handel* (1910)

S. TAYLOR: *The Indebtedness of Handel to Works by Other Composers* (1906)

P. M. YOUNG: *Handel* (1947); *The Oratorios of Handel* (1949)

Handl, Jakob (Latin, Jacobus Gallus) (1550–1591), Austrian or Slovenian composer. He was master of the chapel of the Bishop of Olmütz from 1579, and cantor at St. Johann's, Prague, from 1585 until his death. He composed nineteen Masses and numerous motets, both sacred and secular. Modern editions of the Masses are in *Denkmäler der Tonkunst in Osterreich*, lxxviii, Jg. xlii (1); xciv/xcv; cxvii; cxix. His *Opus Musicum* (four volumes, 1586–90), containing motets for the liturgical year, is reprinted in the following volumes of the same series: xii, Jg. vi (1); xxiv, Jg. xii (1); xxx, Jg. xv (1); xl, Jg. xx (1); xlviii, Jg. xxiv; li/lii, Jg. xxvi. This work ranges from short four-part pieces to settings for two, three, and four choirs in the Venetian polychoral style, of which he is one of the great masters. His secular motets were published in four books entitled *Moralia* (1589–96; modern edition by D. Cvetko and L. Zepič of the four-part motets, 1966; by A. B. Skei of the motets in five and more parts, 1970).

D. CVETKO: *Jacobus Gallus: Sein Leben und Werk* (Munich, 1972)

Handlo, Robert de, 14th century English theorist. His *Regulae cum maximis Magistri Franconis cum additionibus aliorum musicorum*, dated 1326, was reprinted in Coussemaker's *Scriptores* i, page 383. It consists of the rules of mensural notation by Franco of Cologne, Jean de Garlande and others, with comments and additions by Handlo.

Hans Heiling, opera in three acts, with a prologue, by Marschner, to a libretto by Eduard Devrient, first performed in Berlin in 1833. The story concerns the son of the Queen of the Spirits and his unhappy love for a human. The work was a milestone in the development of German romantic opera between Weber and Wagner.

Hansel and Gretel (Ger., *Hänsel und Gretel*), opera in three acts by Humperdinck, to a libretto by Adelheid Wette (sister of the composer) from a tale by the

(1727); *Siroe* (1728); *Tolomeo* (1728); *Lotario* (1729); *Partenope* (1730); *Poro* (1731); *Ezio* (1732); *Sosarme* (1732); *Orlando* (1733); *Arianna* (1734); *Ariodante* (1735); *Alcina* (1735); *Atalanta* (1736); *Arminio* (1737); *Giustino* (1737); *Berenice* (1737); *Faramondo* (1738); *Serse* (1738); *Imeneo* (1740); *Deidamia* (1741);

(2) Passions: *St. John Passion* (1704); *Der für die Sünden der Welt gemarterte und sterbende Jesus* (1716);

(3) Oratorios: *La Resurrezione* (1708); *Esther* (1720, 1732); *Deborah* (1733); *Athaliah* (1733); *Saul* (1739); *Israel in Egypt* (1739); *Messiah* (1742); *Samson* (1743); *Semele* (1743); *Joseph and his Brethren* (1743); *Belshazzar* (1744); *Hercules* (1744); *Occasional Oratorio* (1746); *Judas Maccabaeus* (1746); *Alexander Balus* (1747); *Joshua* (1747); *Solomon* (1748); *Susanna* (1748); *Theodora* (1749); *Jephtha* (1751); *The Triumph of Time and Truth* (1757);

(4) Secular choral works: *Acis and Galatea* (1720); *Alexander's Feast* (1736); *Ode for St. Cecilia's Day* (1739); *L'Allegro, il Penseroso ed il Moderato* (1740);

(5) Church music: Utrecht *Te Deum* (1713); Chandos *Te Deum* (c. 1718); eleven Chandos anthems (1716–19); three coronation anthems (1727); funeral anthem for the death of Queen Caroline (1737); Dettingen *Te Deum* (1743);

(6) Orchestra: *Water Music* (1715–17); six concertos ('Oboe Concertos', 1729); twelve organ concertos (1738–40); twelve *concerti grossi* (1739); *Fireworks Music* (1749);

(7) Chamber music: sonatas for flute, recorder, one and two violins, two oboes, with keyboard accompaniment;

(8) Harpsichord: seventeen suites (1720, 1733);

(9) Songs: numerous Italian cantatas for one and two voices.

Brothers Grimm. First performed at Weimar in 1893, it established itself as Humperdinck's most important work, its qualities being recognized (enthusiastically) by Richard Strauss and (somewhat grudgingly) by Eduard Hanslick. In this operatic treatment of the story, the two children, Hänsel and Gretel, are sent to pick berries in the woods, where they lose their way. They lie down to rest and are protected by angels during the night but in the morning they are captured by the witch of the forest, who loves to eat children. They succeed in locking her in the oven which had been prepared for them, and her death brings to life all the children who had been turned into gingerbread figures. The parents of Hansel and Gretel arrive and the opera closes with the merry dances of the children.

Humperdinck's Wagnerian style enhances the story, instead of overwhelming it, as one might think. Comparisons have been drawn, not unconvincingly, between *Hänsel and Gretel* and Act 1 of *Die Walküre*, Hansel, Gretel and the Witch having their equivalent in the Walsung twins and Hunding.

Hanslick, Eduard (1825–1904), Austrian (though Prague born) critic and writer on the aesthetics of music. He lectured at Vienna University from 1856 until 1895. As critic of the *Presse* and *Neue freie Presse* he was one of the most influential writers on the music of his day. In *Vom Musikalisch-Schönen* (1854: seventh edition of 1885 translated as *The Beautiful in Music*, 1891) he maintained the autonomy of music ('the ideas which a composer expresses are mainly and primarily of a *purely musical* nature'). In his articles he opposed the 'New Music' of Liszt and Wagner and praised Schumann and Brahms. Though Wagner pilloried him as Beckmesser in the Meistersingers, Hanslick's attacks on Wagner were not as consistent as they are often made out to be. He recognised the importance of Wagner's music, while admitting his dislike for it.

Hanson, Howard (born 1896), U.S. composer and conductor, of Swedish parentage. After winning the U.S. *Prix de Rome*, he studied in Italy from 1921 until 1924. From then until 1964 he was director of the Eastman School of Music, Rochester, New York State. His opera *Merry-Mount* was produced at the Metropolitan, New York, in 1934. He has written five symphonies (no 1, *Nordic*; no 2, *Romantic*; no 3, 'conceived as a tribute to the epic qualities of the Swedish pioneers in America'; no 4, *Requiem*; no 5, *Sacra*), symphonic poems, works for chorus and orchestra, piano music, chamber music, and songs.

Hanuš, Jan (born 1915), Czechoslovak composer. He has written several operas, including *The Servant of Two Masters* (after Goldoni) and *The Torch of Prometheus*, and other works, among which are four symphonies and some chamber music.

Harfenquartett, see HARP QUARTET

harmonic flute (Fr., *flûte harmonique*), an organ stop first regularly used by Cavaillé-Col of Paris from 1841. A hole is bored mid-way in an open cylindrical metal pipe, making the predominant pitch the first harmonic, or octave (four foot pitch).

harmonic piccolo, an organ stop similar to the HARMONIC FLUTE, but sounding an octave higher (two foot pitch).

harmonica, (1) (musical glasses, glass harmonica;

Ger., *Glasharmonika*), an instrument in which sounds are produced by the application of the moist fingers to drinking glasses (in the earlier form played by Richard Pockrich from 1734 and by Gluck in London in 1746), or to glass bowls (in the form perfected by Benjamin Franklin, c. 1761). Its most famous exponents were Marianne Davies (for whom, with her sister Cecilia, Hasse wrote in 1769 an ode for voice and harmonica to words by Metastasio) and Marianne Kirchgessner, the blind player for whom Mozart wrote the *Adagio and Rondo* for harmonica, flute, oboe, viola and cello (K617) in 1791.

A. HYATT KING: 'The Musical Glasses and Glass Harmonica' (*Proceedings of the Royal Musical Association*, 1945–6, pages 97–120)

(2) (Ger., *Mundharmonika*), mouth organ.

harmonics (Fr., *sons harmoniques*; Ger., *Flageolett-Töne*; It., *flautato*, *flautando*), sounds produced on a string instrument or harp by touching the string lightly at one of its nodes, i.e., exact fractional points. They correspond to the upper partials of the string, and have a soft, flute-like quality. On bowed instruments harmonics played on an open string are called natural, those played on a stopped string are called artificial. The natural harmonics played on the G string of the violin, for example, are:

The black notes indicate at what point the string is touched.

Harmonics are indicated by writing either a small circle over the sound to be produced or a diamond-shaped note corresponding to the point to be touched.

harmonic series, the composite series of notes produced by a vibrating substance or air column. If the principal note (or 'fundamental') is:

the first sixteen notes of the series will be:

Of these nos 7, 11, 13 and 14 are not in tune with our normal scale. Nos 2–16 (and upwards) are called 'overtones' or 'upper partials'. The actual sound of the overtones is faint. Their effect in practice is to enrich the sound of the principal note. The individual tone-quality of instruments results from the presence or absence of particular overtones, and from their relative intensity. Thus the clarinet (a cylindrical tube, stopped at one end) produces only the alternate overtones – 3, 5, 7 etc. Individual overtones can be isolated from the principal note: this is done on string instruments by touching the string lightly at sectional points (*see*

HARMONICS), and on wind instruments (particularly brass instruments) by overblowing. By this means a brass instrument without VALVES is able to produce a complete series of notes, the upward limit being determined by the capacity of the lips to increase the tension. The addition of valves makes available several such series of notes, and so provides a complete chromatic compass. The same result is achieved on the TROMBONE by the slide, which progressively lengthens the tube and so lowers the pitch of the instrument.

See ACOUSTICS, HORN, TRUMPET

Harmonie (Fr., Ger.), an ensemble of wind instruments.

Harmonie der Welt, Die (Ger., *The Harmony of the World*), opera in five acts by Hindemith, to a libretto by the composer (based on the life of Kepler), first performed in Munich in 1957.

Harmoniemesse, (Ger., *Wind-Band Mass*), the name given to Haydn's Mass in B flat, composed in 1802 (no 12 in the Haydn's Society edition, no 6 in Novello's edition). It owes its name to the importance of wind instruments in the score.

Harmonious Blacksmith, The, the nickname given to the air and variations (E major) in the fifth suite of Handel's first book of harpsichord suites (published 1720) from a story (erroneous) that he had composed it after listening to a blacksmith at work. The name was first given to the piece c. 1822, long after the composer's death, and the story was concocted during the following years.

harmony, (1) until the 17th century the term was used in the general sense of the sound of music. Zarlino used it in the sense of the comprehensive science of music (*Institutioni harmoniche*, 1558) and Thomas Morley (1597), discussing the sound of music in two parts, says: 'But withal you must take this caveat, that you take no note above one minim rest (or three upon the greatest extremity of your point) in two parts, for in that long resting the harmony seemeth bare.' In the medieval period, chords were viewed as resulting from the addition of intervals to an original part. Although a HOMOPHONIC style of writing was regularly used in the 16th century, e.g. in *frottole*, balletts, and the music of the metrical PSALTERS, the same view persisted. The chromatic 'harmony' of such composers as Gesualdo is not based on a theory of harmony in the modern sense, but results from the free alteration of the notes of normal chords, which could go to such extremes as:

GESUALDO, *Moro lasso*

(2) in the modern sense harmony means the structure, functions and relationships of chords. It was used by Mersenne (1636) in the sense of the physical and mathematical nature of sound, and this remained its meaning until Rameau founded the modern theory of

harmony (1722) by combining the point of view of a rational scientist with that of a practising composer.

The unit of harmony is the CHORD. The smallest element of harmonic 'progression', or movement, consists of two chords. A pair of chords which marks off a period or phrase is called a CADENCE. The perfect, imperfect, and plagal cadences show in the simplest form the relation of the dominant and subdominant chords of a KEY to each other and to the tonic chord. The harmonic relationships between the chords of a key are true for every key, since all keys are transpositions of the same two MODES, major and minor. The modern theory of harmony is based on the chords of the major scale. Those of the minor scale, though different in quality, are treated as having the same functions in relation to each other and to the tonic.

The tonic chord, the centre of the harmony of a key, is clearly defined as the tonic when it is preceded by the dominant chord, as in the perfect cadence. The chord which most strongly reinforces that definition by preceding and following a perfect cadence is the subdominant chord, e.g.:

These three chords are the primary chords of the key, and since they contain between them all the notes of the scale, they may suffice to harmonise any melody which remains in the key, in the form of spontaneous accompaniment known as 'vamping'.

Two of the most important parts of Rameau's theory of harmony are (*a*) the theory of INVERSION, in which all chords which do not consist of superimposed thirds (i.e. are not in ROOT position) are held to be inverted positions of, and to derive their harmonic function from, chords which do; and (*b*) the theory of the FUNDAMENTAL BASS, in which the successive roots of a series of chords, represented as notes on a staff or, as is now more usual, by Roman numerals, are held, as a consequence of the theory of inversion, to give the clearest picture of the harmonic functions of the chords. In the following phrase the figures (*see* FIGURED BASS) show the position of a chord ($\frac{5}{3}$ is a root position; $\frac{6}{3}$ is the first inversion; $\frac{6}{5}$ is the first inversion of a seventh chord), the Roman numerals represent the fundamental bass (b denotes first inversion) according to the degree of the scale, and the notes on the staff are the notes of the fundamental bass:

The progression, or movement, in the example is from the tonic to the dominant. Of the chords within a key, the tonic is a point of rest, the dominant and sub-dominant play the most important parts in harmonic movement, and the other chords, except the LEADING-NOTE CHORD, have subsidiary functions. The leading-chord acquires from its bass-note the tendency to 'lead' to the tonic. In addition it has two notes in common with the dominant, so that it may precede the tonic in a cadence in the same way as does a dominant, though with less finality. The sense of movement arising from chord-relations within a key is the most important property of harmony. Since key-relations arise from chord-relations, the sense of movement is carried over with enhanced quality into modulation. In a larger context it becomes the sense of movement arising from the key-design of forms as wholes.

Harmonic relations between different keys, and the possibility and functioning of MODULATION, depend on the fact that a chord may exist in several keys and can assume the function appropriate to it in each of those keys. For example

is the dominant in C and the tonic in G, and

is the submediant in C and the supertonic in G. The further fact that the relationships of keys retain the same functions as the relationships of the corresponding chords within the key makes us hear a modulation to the dominant of C:

as merely a more emphasised form of a progression to the dominant in C:

A dominant or a leading-note chord used in this way can not only supply emphasis to a cadence in a short form such as a hymn-tune, but also precede a chord on any degree of the scale, and so enable a simple harmonic progression to become the basis of an extended passage:

In the larger context of forms as a whole such harmonic relationships of keys are the basis of the harmonic design of all 18th and 19th century forms, however extended the scope of the keys involved, and however numerous the incidental modulations. The key-design of SONATA FORM, which may be represented thus: Tonic —— Dominant ‖ Free modulations —— Tonic ‖ is the same, in an enlarged version, as that of the earlier BINARY FORM, and its principle is still valid in, for example, the first movement of Hindemith's second sonata for piano, which has this harmonic plan:

	Exposition	Development	Recapitulation	Coda
Keys:	G F	Modulation	G B C G	G

Another important property of harmony, which is primarily a property of single chords, is the sense of movement caused by the use of discords. The movement from (comparative) discord to (comparative) concord is a movement from tension to relaxation. Since only an octave or a unison is completely consonant, the progression involves this kind of movement just as does the progression:

since both are movements towards relative consonance. The principles and effects of the movement from relaxation to tension to relaxation are the same whether the general level of dissonance is relatively low, as in the 18th century, or high, as in the 20th.

The richness of colour in 19th century harmony, with its increasing complexity of detail, resulted from the extension of the function of chromatic chords (such as the Neapolitan sixth and augmented sixth chord) within a key to their relations to other keys, from the growing chromaticism of melody, which suggested and necessitated new forms of harmonic relations, and from a more continuous use of dissonance to achieve dramatic tension.

E. C. BAIRSTOW: *Counterpoint and Harmony* (1937)

P. C. BUCK: *Unfigured Harmony* (second edition 1920)

M. CARNER: *A Study of Twentieth-Century Harmony*, volume II (1942)

P. HINDEMITH: *A Concentrated Course in Traditional Harmony*, two volumes (1943, 1953)

R. LENORMAND: *A Study of Twentieth-Century Harmony*, volume I (second edition, 1940)

R. O. MORRIS: *Foundations of Practical Harmony and Counterpoint* (1931)

W. PISTON: *Harmony* (1941)

A. SCHOENBERG: *Theory of Harmony* (1948; abridged translation of *Harmonielehre*, third edition, 1921)

M. SHIRLAW: *The Theory of Harmony* (1917)

P. WISHART: *Harmony* (1956)

Harold in Italy (Fr., *Harold en Italie*), symphony with viola *obbligato* by Berlioz, op 16 (1834). The titles of the four movements are:

(1) *Harold aux montagnes: scènes de mélancolie, de bonheur et de joie* (Harold in the mountains: scenes of melancholy, happiness and joy);

(2) *Marche de pèlerins, chantant la prière du soir* (March of pilgrims, singing the evening prayer);

(3) *Sérénade d'un montagnard des Abruzzes à sa maîtresse* (Serenade of a highlander in the Abruzzi to his mistress);

(4) *Orgie de brigands: souvenirs de scènes précédentes* (Brigands' orgy: recollections of earlier scenes).

Harold is represented by the solo viola and by a recurring theme borrowed from Berlioz's *Rob Roy* overture. The use of a solo viola, unusual at this period, is due indirectly to Paganini, who had asked Berlioz to write a piece for this instrument. In spite of the title the work has only a remote connection with Byron's *Childe Harold's Pilgrimage*. Berlioz says that it is in part a recollection of his own wanderings in the Abruzzi and that his intention was that the viola should represent 'a sort of poetic dreamer of a similar type to Byron's Childe Harold'.

harp (Fr., *harpe*; Ger., *Harfe*; It., *arpa*), an instrument which has a long recorded history from the Sum-

erians and Babylonians to the present day. In the tomb of Rameses III (c. 1200 B.C.) are depicted two decorated vertical harps each about seven feet high. In the West the harp was played in Ireland in the early middle ages, and is frequently mentioned and depicted in Europe in the centuries before the Renaissance. Harpers were attached to royal courts from the 15th century.

An Egyptian wooden five-stringed harp, with a crowned head as terminal of the body (from Thebes, XIXth Dynasty, c. 1250 B.C.)

The Bavarians Hochbrucker and Vetter devised about 1720 the first pedal mechanism, enabling the harp to be played in sharp keys as well as diatonically. The modern double action harp with seven pedals dates from 1820, and is due to Sébastien Érard. Its normal key is C flat, and each pedal raises its strings a semitone when pressed half-way down, and a whole tone when pressed down fully. The compass is from

Since then the harp has been used both as a solo instrument and as an occasional member of the symphony orchestra. The harp was used by Monteverdi in *Orfeo* (1607) and by Handel in *Esther* (1720). The last of Handel's *Six Concertos for the Harpsichord or Organ* (Walsh, 1738) is marked *Concerto per la Harpa* in a manuscript in the King's Library at the British Museum. Mozart composed a concerto for flute and harp, K299, and it has been included in chamber music pieces by Debussy, Ravel, Roussel, Bax, and Hindemith.

H. J. ZINGEL: *Harfe und Harfenspiel* (1932)

harp-guitar, harp-lute-guitar, harp-lute, instruments made by E. Light of London, c. 1800.

'Harp' Quartet, the nickname commonly given to Beethoven's string quartet in E flat, op 74 (1809), from the *pizzicato* arpeggios in the first movement.

harpsichord (Fr., *clavecin*; Ger., *Flügel, Kielflügel, Klavicimbal*; It., *arpicordo, clavicembalo, gravicembalo, cembalo*), a keyboard instrument of horizontal harp- or trapezoid-shape in which the strings are plucked by a

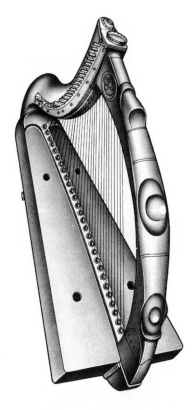

Harps: (left) small 14th or 15th century Irish harp, with a thick solid soundbox, heavy neck, curved fore-pillar, and brass strings; (right) early 19th century English pedal harp, a drawing room instrument

quill or leather tongue attached to a jack, an upright piece of wood set in motion by the inner end of the key. References to such an instrument are found in the 14th century. In the 16th century it was made occasionally in an upright form (depicted in Sebastian Virdung's *Musica getutscht*, 1511, as *clavicyterium*), more often in 'grand' or 'square' (virginal or spinet) form. The leading makers of the 17th century were the Ruckers family of Antwerp. In its developed form it had one or two (exceptionally three) keyboards (the second being used either for ease of transposing or for contrast of tone) and up to four stops, for eight feet and four feet pitch and for producing special effects such as that of the lute. In the 18th century harpsichords were made in London by Tabel, a Fleming, and his pupils Schudi (Tschudi) and Kirkman (Kirchmann), and in Germany by the Silbermann family.

In the baroque period the harpsichord was used as a solo instrument, in all forms of chamber and ensemble music (except the English viol music of the 17th century), and to accompany the voice in opera, cantata and oratorio. As an accompanying instrument its main function was to realise the harmonies indicated by the composer in the form of FIGURED BASS. During the second half of the 18th century it was dropped from the orchestra, and its place in solo and chamber music was taken by the piano. In the present century the use of the harpsichord has been revived for the performance of music of the baroque period, and some modern composers (e.g. Poulenc, de Falla) have written concertos for it. Some contemporary makers are Dolmetsch, Goff and Goble in England, Pleyel and Gaveau in Paris, and Chickering and Challis in the United States.

> D. BOALCH: *Makers of the Harpsichord and Clavichord, 1440–1840* (1956)
> W. LANDOWSKA: *Music of the Past* (1926)
> P. JAMES: *Early Keyboard Instruments* (1930)

Harris, Renatus (1652–1724), the most famous member of a family of organ builders. He built a number of cathedral organs and rebuilt the organ in Magdalen College, Oxford, originally built by his grandfather. His sons, Renatus and John, carried on the family tradition to the middle of the 18th century.

Harris, Roy (born 1898), U.S. composer. Born in Oklahoma, the son of a farmer, he went to Paris in 1926 to study with Nadia Boulanger. On returning to the United States he held posts at the Westminster Choir School at Princeton, New Jersey, Cornell University, Colorado, Logan (Utah), Nashville and Pittsburgh. One of the most prolific of contemporary U.S. composers, he has written twelve symphonies, works for chorus and orchestra and for unaccompanied chorus, chamber music and piano music. His work is distinguished by its use of U.S. folksong (*Folksong Symphony*, *When Johnny Comes Marching Home* overture, etc.), asymmetrical rhythm, angular melody, and modal and polytonal harmony.

Harrison, Julius (1885–1963). English composer and conductor. studied under Bantock in Birmingham, and conducted the Beecham Opera Company, the British National Opera Company, and the Hastings Municipal Orchestra. His compositions include suites for orchestra, chamber music, piano pieces, a Mass, and songs.

Harrison, Lou (born 1917), U.S. composer, pupil of Cowell and Schoenberg. He has worked in many musical forms, and experimented with new sonorities. His works include an opera (*Rapunzel*) and several ballets (e.g. *Almanac of the Seasons, Changing World, Johnny Appleseed, The Perilous Chapel* and *Solstice*). He has also written a series of harpsichord sonatas and many works for percussion (employed, for the most part, quietly), a violin concerto with percussion orchestra, and *Four Strict Songs* for eight baritones and orchestra in pure intonation. He has edited a number of works by Charles Ives, including the third symphony, of which he conducted the première in 1946. His interest in Ives inspired him to compose an orchestral tribute, *At the Tomb of Charles Ives*. In addition to his work as a composer, he has taught music at various colleges and has been a playwright, poet, dancer and maker of musical instruments. His range of interests is in fact exceptionally wide: some of his works have been inspired by Indian, Indonesian and Korean music, and others (e.g. his choral pieces) by Elizabethan music.

Harsányi, Tibor (1898–1954), Hungarian composer. He studied at the Budapest Academy of Music and in 1923 settled in Paris, where he died. He composed operas, ballets, orchestral works, *Divertimento* no 1 for two violins and chamber orchestra, *Divertimento* no 2 for string orchestra and trumpet, chamber music, and piano pieces.

Hart, Fritz Dennicke (1874–1949), English born composer and conductor, who studied at the Royal College of Music and settled in Melbourne in 1912, where he became director of the Conservatory and conductor of the Symphony Orchestra. He was conductor of the Honolulu University from 1937 until 1946. He composed more than twenty operas, choral and orchestral works, piano pieces and songs.

Hartmann, Karl Amadeus (1905–63), German composer. He studied at the Munich Academy of Music and privately with Scherchen and Webern. In 1945 in Munich he founded Musica Viva, an organisation (of pioneering importance) for promoting performances of contemporary music. His compositions, which reflect his admiration for the work of Alban Berg, include eight symphonies, concertos for various combinations of instruments, two string quartets, and the chamber opera *Des Simplicius Simplicissimus Jugend* (1934; performed, Cologne, 1949; revised, 1955).

Harty, Herbert Hamilton (1879–1941), Irish conductor and composer. After working as an organist in Belfast and Dublin he settled in London in 1900, and in 1920 became conductor of the Hallé Orchestra in Manchester. His compositions include a symphony, a violin concerto and works for voices and orchestra, though he is more famous for his orchestral arrangements of movements from Handel's *Water Music* and *Fireworks Music* – very popular in their time, though now regarded as stylistically dubious. He was knighted in 1925.

Harwood, Basil (1859–1949), English organist and composer of church music, organ works, and cantatas. He was organist at Ely Cathedral (1887) and Christ Church, Oxford (1892–1909).

Háry János, ballad opera by Kodály, founded on Hungarian melodies, in five parts with prologue and epilogue. The libretto by Béla Paulini and Zsolt Harsányi is based on a poem by J. Garay. The story concerns the exploits of a Hungarian folk hero. The work was first performed in Budapest in 1926. Later the composer made a suite for orchestra in six sections: *The Tale Begins, Viennese Musical Clock, Song, The Battle and Defeat of Napoleon, Intermezzo, Entrance of the Emperor and his Court.*

Hasse, Faustina Bordoni, *see* BORDONI

Hasse, Johann Adolph (1699–1783), German composer. He sang tenor at the Hamburg Opera under Keiser (1718–1719), then at Brunswick (1719–1722). He went to Naples in 1722, and studied opera composition with Porpora and A. Scarlatti. Thereafter he was at Venice from 1727, at Dresden as *Kapellmeister* from 1734, at Vienna from 1764, and again at Venice from 1773 until his death.

He was in his time the most popular composer of Italian opera in the Neapolitan style. Burney wrote of him (*The Present State of Music in Germany*, ii, pages 349–50) after his visit to Vienna in 1772, when the work of Metastasio and Hasse was being compared with the new innovations of Calzabigi and Gluck, that he

> succeeds better perhaps in expressing, with clearness and propriety, whatever is graceful, elegant, and tender, than what is boisterous and violent; whereas Gluck's genius seems more calculated for exciting terror in painting difficult situations, occasioned by complicated misery, and the tempestuous fury of unbridled passions.

Hasse also composed Masses and other church music, oratorios, and instrumental music.

Hassler, Hans Leo (1564–1612), German composer and organist. He was taught by his father and, in 1584 and 1585, by Andrea Gabrieli in Venice. From 1585 he was organist to Octavian Fugger in Augsburg, from 1601 to 1604 in Nuremberg, and from 1608 to his death at the Electoral chapel at Dresden. An accomplished master of polyphony and of the Venetian polychoral style, he also wrote secular choral music and compositions for organ. A complete edition by C. Russell Crosby of his works was begun in 1961.

Hassler's song 'Mein G'müt ist mir verwirret', published in his *Lustgarten neuer teutscher Gesäng* (1601) was adapted in 1613 to the words of the hymn 'Herzlich thut mir verlangen' and subsequently to those used by Bach in his settings in the *St Matthew Passion*, 'O Haupt voll Blut und Wunden'; (O Sacred Head, surrounded).

See CHORALE

Hans Leo's elder brother **Jakob Hassler** (1569–1622), was also an organist and composer. He composed Italian madrigals and church music. Two organ compositions are printed in *Denkmäler deutscher Tonkunst*, iv (2), pages 127–33.

The youngest of the brothers, **Kaspar Hassler** (1562–1618), an organist, edited collections of *Sacrae symphoniae*, including works of Hans Leo.

Hatton, John Liptrott (1809–1886), English composer of operas, cantatas, church music, incidental music for Shakespeare plays, and songs, for which 'To Anthea', and 'Simon the Cellarer' are the most famous.

Haubiel, Charles (born 1892), U.S. composer, piano teacher at the Institute of Musical Art, New York, and subsequently (1923) assistant professor of composition and theory at New York University. He founded the Composers Press (1935) for the publication of contemporary U.S. music. He composed a musical satire, incidental music, orchestral works, choral and chamber music.

Hauer, Josef Matthias (1883–1959), Austrian composer and theorist. He developed and expounded in a series of pamphlets (and uninfluenced by Schoenberg) a technique of atonal composition based on groups of notes ('tropes') chosen from the twelve notes of the chromatic scale. In this system he composed an oratorio, orchestral works, chamber music, piano pieces, and songs, mainly to poems of Hölderlin.

Haugtussa (Norw., *Troll Maiden*), a cycle of eight songs by Grieg, op 67 (1896–8), words from a collection of poems by Arne Garborg. 'Haugtussa' is the name given to a girl who had the gift of seeing and hearing the trolls. The titles of the songs are:

(1) *Det syng* (The singing).
(2) *Veslemöy* (Little maiden).
(3) *Blaabaerli* (Bilberry slopes).
(4) *Möte* (Meeting).
(5) *Elsk* (Love).
(6) *Killingdans* (Kidlings' Dance).
(7) *Vond Dag* (Evil day).
(8) *Ved Gjaetle-Bekken* (By the brook).

Hauk, Minnie (1852–1929), U.S. operatic soprano. She performed in the United States, Covent Garden, London (1868), and subsequently in many cities of Europe. In 1876 she introduced Carmen (her most famous role) to the United States in a performance at the New York Academy of Music. She was also the first U.S. Manon, and the first London Carmen. She retired in 1896, at the height of her powers, and went to live in Wagner's villa at Triebschen, Lucerne. Her autobiography, *Memoirs of a Singer*, was published in 1925.

haupt (Ger.), principal, chief. Thus *Hauptstimme*, principal part; *Hauptsatz*, main section (or theme); *Haupttonart*, principal key; *Hauptwerk*, great organ.

Hauptmann, Moritz (1792–1868), German theorist, composer and violinist. He taught counterpoint at Leipzig Conservatory from 1842, where his pupils included Ferdinand David, von Bülow, Joachim, Sullivan and Cowen. His chief work on theory was translated into English as *The Nature of Harmony and Metre* (1888); and a selection of his letters as *Letters of a Leipzig Cantor* (translated by A. D. Coleridge, 1892). He also composed an opera (*Mathilde*), chamber music, and choral works.

Hausegger, Siegmund von (1872–1948), Austrian composer and conductor. He studied at the Styrian Musikverein and Graz University. He conducted in Graz (from 1895), Bayreuth, Munich, Frankfurt (1903–6), Glasgow, Edinburgh, the Hamburg Philharmonic Concerts (1910–20) and the Munich Konzertverein (1920–36). He was director of the Munich Adacemy of Music from 1920 until 1934. He composed

two operas, symphonic poems, programme symphonies, choral works and songs.

Hausmusik (Ger.), literally, 'house music', i.e. music for domestic performance, as opposed to music for public performance.

Haussmann (Hausmann), Valentin, late 16th century German composer and organist at Gerbstädt (Saxony). He wrote secular songs and instrumental dances (a selection is published in *Denkmäler deutscher Tonkunst*, xvi) and published works of Marenzio, Vecchi, Gastoldi, and Morley with German texts.

hautbois (Fr.), OBOE. From Elizabethan times to the 18th century, the English equivalent was 'hautboy' (also 'hoeboy', 'hoboy', etc.).

haut-dessus (Fr.), soprano.

haute-contre (Fr.), alto.

Hawaiian guitar, a style of guitar playing in which a steel bar is used to stop the strings instead of the fingers. In this way, the pitch is made to slide between the notes.

Hawkins, Coleman (1904–69), U.S. tenor saxophonist, one of the most important in the history of jazz. He was famous for his juicy, full-bodied tone, whose qualities have been handsomely preserved on disc. An exceptionally romantic player, he was associated during the 1920s and 1930s with Fletcher Henderson. Later he was sympathetic to the bop revolution, and was the progenitor of many of the saxophonists (e.g. Sonny Rollins) of that school.

Hawkins, John (1719–1789), English attorney, historian of music, writer, and editor. He was a member (from 1740) and historian (1770) of the Academy of Ancient Music, and member (from 1752) of the Madrigal Society. He edited the *Compleat Angler* and the works of Samuel Johnson, and wrote lives of Johnson and Walton. He was knighted in 1772. His *General History of the Science and Practice of Music* in five volumes appeared in 1776, the same year as the first volume of Burney's history. The two were the first, and for many years the only works of their kind in English. Hawkins's *History* was reprinted in 1853 and in 1875 by Novello (London).

P. A. SCHOLES: *The Life and Activities of Sir John Hawkins* (1953)

Haydn, Franz Joseph (1732–1809), Austrian composer. Born at Rohrau, he was the son of a wheelwright and was accepted at eight as a choir boy in St. Stephen's Cathedral, Vienna, on account of his good singing voice. There he revealed a sense of mischief that was to reappear later in some of his music. When his voice broke he left the choir school and taught, played, acted as assistant to Niccolo Porpora, and received some help from Count Fürnberg, for whom he wrote his first quartets (1755). In 1759 he became musical director to Count Morzin and wrote his first symphony, and in 1761 began his long period of service in the household of the Esterházy family. The greater part of each year was spent at the palace of Esterház, which Prince Nicolaus built in 1766, and there Haydn wrote most of his compositions. His friendship with Mozart began in 1781. In 1784 he wrote *The Seven Words of the Saviour on the Cross* (originally for orchestra; arranged for string quartet, 1787; for voices, 1796) for the Cathedral of Cadiz, and in 1786 six symphonies (nos 82–87) for the Concert Spirituel in Paris.

On the death of Prince Nicolaus in 1790 the musical establishment at Esterház was disbanded, but Haydn retained his title and salary, without duties. In 1791 he went to London with a contract from J. P. Salomon to write an opera, six new symphonies (nos 93–98), and twenty other pieces, and stayed in England for more than a year. There his music was warmly received. He attended the Handel Festival at Westminster Abbey, and became an honorary D. Mus. of Oxford. For his second visit, in 1794–5, he wrote the second set of six 'Salomon' symphonies (nos 99–104). In 1795 Prince Nicolaus II reconstituted the household music, but Haydn's duties were light and consisted principally of the composition of a mass each year – the series of six great masses (1796–1802) whose full importance has only recently begun to be widely recognised. During this period he was also able to complete the composition of the two big choral works, *The Creation* (1798) and *The Seasons* (1801). During the last few years of his life he lived quietly in Vienna, composing little and only dimly aware of the important place he would hold in history.

Of his work at the Esterházy court Haydn wrote: 'There was no one about me to confuse and torment me, and I was compelled to become original.' His originality and mastery of technical means are apparent in the symphonies, quartets, and stage works of the years 1761–80, after a decade in which his work was modelled on that of the Viennese composers Reutter, Monn, and Wagenseil, and, especially in the keyboard works, on C. P. E. Bach. In the next decade (1781–90), partly under the influence of Mozart, his music achieved the maturity of expression and the balance between the harmonic and the contrapuntal elements in design and texture which are the marks of the classical style, while retaining its individual traits of energy, warmth, and humour. His unflagging vitality and fertility of imagination enabled him to write in the final period of his life (from 1791) the twelve symphonies which are his best-known works in that form, and, inspired by his English experience of Handel, the two oratorios and six great settings of the Mass composed between 1796 and 1802.

Though Tovey wrote of 'Haydn the inaccessible' (but at the same time praised him as 'matchless and admirable'), more and more of Haydn's music has been performed in recent years. Thanks in the first place to the collected edition begun by Breitkopf and Härtel in 1907 (but suspended in 1914), then to the activities of the Haydn Society of Boston and of Haydn's greatest modern champion, the musicologist Robbins Landon, we now have access to the enormous body of his output, from his cycle of London symphonies (in authentic editions) back to his earliest works in the form. His operas, though of unequal importance, with a streak of provinciality about them which place them on a lower plane than Mozart's, have also been explored. They include *Lo Speziale* (1768), *Il Mondo della Luna* (1777), *La Vera Constanza* (1779), *L'Isola Disabitata* (1770), *La Fedelta Premiata* (1780), *Armide* (1784) and *L'Anima del Filosofo* (1791). His symphonies and string quartets, remarkable for their tightness of construction (whole movements often grow out of the cells of a single theme), richness, harmonic and rhythmic verve, form the foundation of

Franz Joseph Haydn: This wax bust gives a lifelike if un-flattering likeness, even down to the scars left by small-pox. The score is a sketch of part of the chorus 'The heav'ns are telling' from *The Creation* (1798). The signature is appended from another manuscript.

what we have come to call the classical style. More recently his keyboard sonatas and piano trios, once thought to be of lesser importance, have established themselves as works with their own personality, shedding fresh light on the character of their composer. Indeed, among Haydn's orchestral and instrumental works, only the concertos could be said to lack consistent interest. Though Haydn wrote numerous concertos – a second cello concerto, in C major, turned up in the 1960s to join the familiar but not very typical piece in D major – they were not central to his output, the way Mozart's were. Possibly this was because Haydn's musical background was different. He was not a distinguished public soloist; his main medium was the orchestra, for which he wrote with unstoppable inspiration.

His principal compositions are:

(1) Orchestra: 104 symphonies; about thirteen keyboard concertos; three violin concertos; two cello concertos; two horn concertos; one trumpet concerto; five concertos for two *lire organizzate*; *Sinfonia concertante* for violin, cello, oboe, and bassoon with orchestra;

(2) Stage works: about eighteen operas, of which five are lost, and four marionette operas;

(3) Oratorios and church music: eight oratorios and cantatas; two solo cantatas; twelve Masses; two settings of the *Te Deum*; three of *Salve Regina*; one of *Stabat Mater*;

(4) Chamber music: 84 string quartets, the last unfinished; 31 piano trios; 125 *divertimenti* for baryton, viola, and cello; about 56 string trios; *divertimenti*, *cassations*, and *notturni* for various instruments.

(5) Keyboard music: 52 sonatas, of which five have been published with a violin part; five sets of variations; a fantasia;

(6) Songs: 47 songs, 377 arrangements of Scottish and Welsh airs for the Scottish publishers Napier, Thomson, and Whyte.

R. BARRETT-AYRES: *Haydn's String Quartets*
M. BRENET: *Haydn* (translated by C. L. Leese, 1926)
K. GEIRINGER: *Haydn* (1947)
R. HUGHES: *Haydn* (1950)
H. R. C. LANDON: *The Symphonies of Joseph Haydn* (1956)
J. P. LARSEN: *Die Haydn-Uberlieferung* (1939); *Drei Haydn-Kataloge* (1941)
H. C. ROBBINS-LANDON: *Haydn Symphonies* (1966)
C. ROSEN: *The Classical Style* (1969)
E. F. SCHMID: *Joseph Haydn: ein Buch von Vorfahren und Heimat des Meisters* (1934)

Haydn, Johann Michael (1737–1806), Austrian composer, brother of Joseph. He was a chorister at St. Stephen's, Vienna (1745–55), episcopal choirmaster, Grosswardein (1757), director of the orchestra of the Archbishop of Salzburg (1762), and later organist at the Cathedral. Weber, Neukomm and Reicha were among his pupils. He composed twenty-four Masses, two Requiem Masses, four German Masses, and other church music, operas, oratorios and cantatas, fifty-two symphonies, serenades, divertimenti, five concertos, quintets, and other instrumental pieces.

H. JANCIK: *Michael Haydn* (1952)

Haydn Variations (Variations on a Theme by Haydn), a set of variations by Brahms on a theme ('St Anthony Chorale') taken from a *divertimento* for wind instruments by Haydn. The theme, as has now been established, was not Haydn's own – which is why the title *St. Anthony Variations* is nowadays preferred for Brahms's work. Brahms wrote in two forms: (1) for orchestra, op 56a; (2) for two pianos, op 56b (both composed in 1873).

Haydon, Glen (born 1896), U.S. musicologist, educated at the University of California and the University of Vienna. In 1934 he became head of the department of music at the University of North Carolina. He wrote *The Evolution of the Six-four Chord* (1933) and *Introduction to Musicology* (1941).

Hayes, Philip (1738–97), English organist and composer. Son of William Hayes, whom he succeeded as professor at Oxford and organist of Magdalen College. He composed anthems, an oratorio, a masque, and an ode.

Hayes, William (1705–77), English organist and composer, father of Philip Hayes. He was organist at Worcester Cathedral (1731) and Magdalen College, Oxford (1734). In 1741 he became professor of music at Oxford. He composed church music, odes and glees.

Haym, Nicola Francesco (c. 1679–1729), Italian musician, of German extraction. He went to England in 1704, and took part in Italian opera as a cellist and arranger in collaboration with Clayton and Dieupart. From 1713 he acted as librettist for Handel, Ariosti, and Bononcini. He wrote two sets of trio sonatas, a serenata, and church music.

head voice, the upper 'register' of the voice, as distinct from the lower register ('chest voice').

Heart of Oak, a song in David Garrick's play *Harlequin's Invasion* (1759), set to music by William Boyce. It commemorates the British victories of that year, the *annus mirabilis*.

Heather (Heyther), William (c. 1563–1627), English musician. He was a gentleman of the Chapel Royal and lay-vicar of Westminster Abbey. In 1627 he founded the chair of music at Oxford which is still called by his name.

Hebenstreit, see PANTALEON, DULCIMER

Hebrides, The, overture by Mendelssohn, op 26 (1832), also known as *Fingal's Cave*. It was inspired, like the Scottish Symphony (no 3 in A major and minor), by a visit to Scotland in 1829. The original version of the work (1830) was entitled *The Lonely Island*. In its revised version, the overture was first performed in London in 1832.

Heckelclarina (Ger.), wooden instrument of the saxophone type made by the firm of Heckel of Biebrich. It is in B flat and has a single reed. Its compass corresponds to that of the soprano saxophone.

Heckelphone, a double reed instrument corresponding to the French baritone oboe, with a range an octave below that of the OBOE. Used for the first time by Strauss in *Salome* (1905).

Heckelphone-clarinet, wooden instrument of the saxophone type designed for use in military bands. It has a single reed, and its compass corresponds to that of the alto saxophone.

heftig (Ger.), violent.

Heger, Robert (born 1886), German conductor and composer, born in Strasbourg. He studied in Zürich and under Max von Schillings in Munich. Later he conducted opera in Vienna, Munich, Berlin and London. In 1950 he became president of the Munich Academy of Music. His works include operas, two symphonies, a violin concerto, and other instrumental works.

Heifetz, Jascha (born 1901), Russian born violinist, a pupil of his father until he entered the Music School of Vina at the age of five. Subsequently he studied with Leopold Auer in St. Petersburg. From 1912 onwards he toured as a soloist with remarkable success. He became a U.S. citizen in 1925. Among works written for him are violin concertos by Walton, Gruenberg and Achron.

Heiller, Anton (born 1923), Austrian composer and organist. In 1945 he was appointed professor of organ at the Vienna Academy of Music, and in 1952 won first prize in the international organ competition at Haarlem in Holland. His works include a *Symphonie Nordique*, a *Psalm Cantata*, *Te Deum* and other choral pieces, and much organ music.

Heimkehr aus der Fremde, Die *see* SON AND STRANGER

Heinichen, Johann David (1683–1729), German composer and theorist. He was a pupil of Schelle and Kuhnau in Leipzig, where, after practising law for a short time in Weissenfels, he began the composition of operas. After six years in Italy, he was from 1717 until 1720 *Kapellmeister* at Dresden, where he lived until his death. Besides operas he wrote church music and published a treatise on figured bass (first form as *Neu erfundene und gründliche Anweisung*, 1711; second and greatly enlarged form as *Der General-Bass in der Composition*, 1728).

F. T. ARNOLD: *The Art of Accompaniment from a Thorough-Bass* (1931)

Heintz, Wolff (c. 1490–c. 1555), German organist in 1516 at Magdeburg, and from 1523 in Halle. Two four-part settings of chorales by him were printed in Georg Rhau's collection of 1544 (modern edition by J. Wolf in *Denkmäler deutscher Tonkunst*, xxxiv).

Heinze, Bernard Thomas (born 1894), Australian conductor. He studied at Melbourne University, in London, in Paris under d'Indy and in Berlin, and conducted in various European cities. He returned to Australia in 1923 and was appointed to the staff of Melbourne University. He was conductor of the Melbourne Symphony Orchestra from 1933 until 1949. He was knighted in 1949 and became director of the New South Wales Conservatorium in 1956.

Heise, Peter Arnold (1830–1879), Danish composer. He studied with Gade and at the Leipzig Conservatorium. His opera *Drot og Marsk* (King and Marshal; Copenhagen, 1878) was successful in Denmark, where it was revived in 1909 and 1922. He also wrote incidental music, choral music and songs.

heiter (Ger.), cheerful.

Heldenleben, Ein (Ger., *A Hero's Life*), autobiographical symphonic poem by Richard Strauss, composed in 1898 and first performed the following year in Frankfurt. In the section entitled 'The Hero's Works of Peace', Strauss quotes from some of his own previous compositions.

Heldentenor (Ger., heroic tenor), tenor with a voice 'heroic' enough to sustain the heavier operatic roles, i.e. the principal tenor parts in Wagner's operas (Tristan, Siegfried, etc.). The Italian equivalent of a *Heldentenor* is a *tenore robusto*.

helicon, a name given to the tuba when made in the circular form used in marching bands.

Hellendaall, Pieter (1721–99), Dutch violinist and composer. He studied the violin with Tartini in Padua, appeared in London in 1752, and lived in England thereafter, becoming organist of Pembroke College, Cambridge, in 1762 and of St. Peter's College in 1777. Instrumental works, glees and psalms by him were published in Amsterdam, London and Cambridge between 1744 and 1780.

Heller, Stephen (1813–88), Hungarian pianist and composer. He studied in Vienna and toured Europe extensively, meeting Chopin and Liszt in Paris in 1838. He composed about one hundred and fifty pieces for piano.

Hellinck, Lupus (c. 1495–1541), Netherlands composer. He belonged to the choir of St. Donatian's, Bruges, in 1511, and was its choirmaster from 1523 until his death. Eleven four-part settings of chorales by him were printed in Georg Rhau's collection of 1544 (modern edition by J. Wolf in *Denkmäler deutscher Tonkunst*, xxxiv) and at least fourteen Masses by him survive in manuscript. He was for some time confused with Johannes Lupi.

J. GRAZIANO: 'Lupus Hellinck: a Survey of Fourteen Masses', in *Musical Quarterly*, lvi (1970)

Helmholtz, Hermann Ludwig Ferdinand von (1821–94), German physiologist and physicist. While professor of physiology at Heidelberg he published in 1862 his *Die Lehre von dem Tonempfindung* (translated by A. J. Ellis as *On the Sensations of Tone as a Physiological Basis for the Theory of Music*, 1875, second edition, 1885). This work is the basis of modern theories of consonance, tone-quality, and resultant tones.

Helmore, Thomas (1811–90), English writer on church music. He became Master of the choristers, Chapel Royal, in 1846 and priest in ordinary in 1847. He edited a number of collections of plainsong melodies, hymns, and carols, including *A Manual of Plainsong*.

Hely-Hutchinson, Victor (1901–47), South African born pianist, composer, and conductor. He was educated at Eton and Oxford, and became a lecturer at Cape Town University (1922–25). He was on the staff of the B.B.C. (1926–34), then became professor at Birmingham University (1934–44). He returned to the B.B.C. where he was director of music from 1944 until his death. He composed a *Carol Symphony*, a symphony for small orchestra, a piano quintet, a string quartet, choral works and songs.

hemiola (Gr., meaning the ratio of one and a half to one, or $\frac{3}{2}$: Fr., *hémiole*; Ger., *Hemiole*; It., *emiolia*; Lat., *sesquialtera*), in medieval and Renaissance theory the proportion of $\frac{3}{2}$ in two senses:

(1) the interval of a perfect fifth, which has the vibration ratio 3:2, e.g.:

96   144

(2) the rhythmic relation of three notes in the time of two, e.g. of

In the baroque period the idiom was stylised in an instrumental form in the COURANTE, and in a vocal form exemplified in a favourite cadence of Handel (*see* ACCENT). In the 19th century it was exploited most persistently by Chopin, e.g.:

CHOPIN, *Etude no 27*

and by Schumann and Brahms.

Hempel, Frieda (1885–1955), German soprano whose début, at Schwerin, resulted in the Kaiser ordering the Schwerin authorities to release her to sing in Berlin. She was a famous Marschallin in *Der Rosenkavalier*, and her uncommonly wide repertory included Euryanthe (in Weber's opera of that title), Eva in *The Mastersingers*, the Queen of Night in *The Magic Flute* and Rosina in *The Barber of Seville*. Later in her career she gave Jenny Lind recitals in costume.

Hen, The (Fr., *La Poule*), the nickname given to Haydn's symphony no 83 in G minor (1786), one of the six symphonies commissioned by the Concert de la Loge Olympique in Paris and known as the 'Paris' symphonies. The nickname is usually thought to refer to the 'clucking' notes of the oboe in the first movement, although there is an alternative theory that the slow movement bears a slight resemblance to Rameau's harpsichord piece, *La Poule*.

Henkemans, Hans (born 1913), Dutch composer and pianist, pupil of Pijper and authority on Debussy. He made his début at the age of nineteen playing the first of his two piano concertos. He has also written concertos for flute, violin, viola and harp, a symphony, three string quartets and piano music.

Henderson, William James (1855–1937), U.S. critic and writer. He was music critic of the *New York Times* in 1887 and of the *New York Sun* in 1902. His writings include *Some Forerunners of Italian Opera* (1907) and *The Early History of Singing* (1921).

Henry, Pierre (born 1927), French composer who carried out experimental work for the music section of the French Radio with Henri Barraud and Pierre Schaeffer in the years after World War II. He is a noted exponent of electronic music.

Henry IV (1367–1413), King of England from 1399 to 1413. A *Gloria* and *Sanctus* in the OLD HALL MANUSCRIPT, ascribed to 'Roy Henry', may be by either Henry IV or Henry V.

Henry V (1387–1422), King of England from 1413 to 1422. He had a 'complete chapel full of singers' which he sent for during his French campaigns to celebrate Easter at Bayeux. He also maintained a large company of minstrels. An 'Alleluya' by him survives and he may be the composer of a *Gloria* and *Sanctus* in the OLD HALL MANUSCRIPT (*see* HENRY IV).

Henry VIII (1491–1547), king of England from 1509 to 1547. He is said to have played well on the recorder, lute, and virginals, and was a composer, though of no great distinction. Apart from an antiphon setting, 'Quam pulchra es', his compositions are contained in a manuscript connected with the royal court in the early years of his reign (modern edition by J. E. Stevens in *Musica Britannica*, xviii) and consist of three- and four-part secular songs and instrumental pieces.

'Green groweth the holly', by Henry VIII, from a manuscript which was probably used at his court.

Henry VIII, opera in four acts by Saint-Saëns, to a libretto by Léonie Détroyat and Paul Armand Silvestre, first performed in Paris in 1883. Six years later it was reduced to three acts. The work deals with the English king's relationship with Anne Boleyn.

Henschel, George (originally Isidor Georg) (1850–1934), German born baritone, composer and conductor, educated in Leipzig and Berlin. He first sang in London in 1877, and was the first conductor of the Boston Symphony Orchestra from 1881 until 1884. He then settled in London as singer and conductor, and was in charge of the Scottish Orchestra in Glasgow from 1893 until 1895. He retired and was knighted in 1914. His compositions include choral works and songs, two operas and instrumental works. His *Musings and Memories of a Musician* was published in 1918.

Hensel, Fanny Cäcilla (1805–47), German pianist and composer, Mendelssohn's elder sister. She wrote songs, part-songs, piano pieces, and a piano trio.

Henselt, Adolf von (1814–89), German pianist and composer. He studied piano with Hummel in Weimar and theory with Sechter in Vienna, and became one of the greatest players of his age. From 1838 he lived in St. Petersburg as court pianist. His compositions include a piano concerto, concert studies and other piano works.

Henze, Hans Werner (born 1926), German composer. Born in Westphalia, he grew up during the Nazi years and was conscripted into the German Army during World War II. Towards the end of the war he deserted and (at the risk of being shot by the Gestapo) escaped to Denmark, where he lived incognito as a church organist at Esbjerg. On returning to his homeland he became a repetiteur at the Bielefeld Opera and artistic director of the Wiesbaden Ballet (a period that yielded his ballet *Ondine*) but his love-hate relationship with Germany resulted in his spending long periods in other countries, especially Italy. A pupil of Fortner (in Heidelberg) and Leibowitz (in Paris), he established himself as the leading German operatic composer of the day, and the only one to have enjoyed an international success equivalent to that of Britten. His first important work was *Boulevard Solitude* (1952), a modern version of *Manon Lescaut*, employing ballet as well as singing. In his early works the influence of Stravinsky and Schoenberg can be discerned, but during his Italian years his style softened and gained a feeling of Mediterranean romance. His opera *König Hirsch* (King Stag) (1952–55) is a large-scale treatment of a fable by Gozzi, filled with some of his most ravishing music, some of which he reworked in orchestral terms to form the fifth of his six symphonies. An Italian lyricism also stamps such vocal works as *Ariosi* and *Being Beauteous*, the latter written for an idyllic combination of high soprano, harp and four cellos. His next operas were *Der Prinz von Homburg* (1960), inspired by Kleist's soldier-dreamer, and *Elegy for Young Lovers* (1961), written to a libretto by Auden and Kallman for the Schwetzingen Festival and dealing (wittily) with a great but egotistical poet who uses those around him as fodder for his art, destroying them in the process. Germany again beckoned Henze, and when he returned there he was feted, given the most lavish commissions, and performed by the best orchestras and opera companies. Showing his willingness to bite the hand that fed him, he wrote *The Young Lord* (1965), a brilliant satire on the bourgeois conventions of life in a small German town. Its target was obviously West Germany; significantly, the sharpest productions it has received have been in East Germany. Then in 1966 came *Die Bassariden* (*The Bassarids*), based on Euripides, again with a libretto by Auden and Kallman, a grand opera in one (large) act, written for the Salzburg Festival. His second piano concerto, one of the few successful big-scale piano concertos since the time of Brahms, was commissioned for the opening of a new Kunsthaus in Bielefeld – but the 'Bielefeld affair' caused a minor scandal, because the man who commissioned it wanted to name the building after an early member of the Nazi party. Henze riposted with the declaration: 'Unnecessary are museums, opera houses and world premières – necessary is the creation of mankind's greatest work of art: the world revolution.' Since then, politics have gone hand in hand with Henze's music. He became associated with the Socialist German Student League and joined the East Berlin Academy. The Hamburg première of his oratorio *The Raft of the Medusa*, commissioned by the North German Radio, was broken up by a riot during which a red flag was hoisted in the hall and the (West) German chorus chanted 'We will not sing under the red flag.' Later performances revealed it as a powerful, large-scale music drama, describing a pernicious event in French history (also depicted in Géricault's famous painting) whereby the officers of a foundering frigate in 1816 made their escape in the lifeboats, leaving the other

ranks to their fate on a raft. When the raft was picked up nine days later, only fourteen of the 145 people on board were still alive. Henze treated the subject spatially, using one side of the platform to represent the living and the other side the dead – to which all but fourteen of the singers eventually cross. The work was dedicated to Che Guevara, and it ends with the rhythms of 'Ho! Ho! Ho-Chi-Minh!' pounded out by the percussion.

Henze's most recent period – his Cuban one – has resulted in *El Cimarrón* (*The Runaway Slave*) (1967), a 'recital for four performers' inspired by the autobiography of a 104-year-old slave (as dictated to Miguel Barnet). Inspired also by the remarkable talents of the Negro baritone, William Pearson, and the Japanese percussionist, Stomu Yamashta, lyrically supported by flute and guitar, the music is a tour de force – not quite an opera, not quite a concert piece. Again the work preached revolution, though by the time his next piece of music theatre was written in 1970, an element of questioning appeared to have entered Henze's politics. This was *The Long and Weary Journey to the Flat of Natasha Ungeheur*, produced amid much controversy in West Berlin, and again making use of the vocal and percussive potentialities of Pearson and Yamashta. A modern 'quest opera' with symbolic elements, it suggests Natasha Ungeheur to be a political ideal but disillusion sets in when she turns out to be nothing but a frousy old whore.

heptachord (Gr., seven string), a scale of seven notes, e.g. the modern major or minor scale.

Herbert, Victor (1859–1924), Irish born composer, conductor and cellist. He was educated in Germany and in 1886 went to New York, where he was active as cellist and conductor. From 1898 until 1904 he was in charge of the Pittsburgh Symphony Orchestra. Between 1894 and 1917 he composed a series of some thirty highly successful operettas, of which the most popular were *Naughty Marietta* and *Babes in Toyland*. He also wrote a cello concerto, a symphonic poem (*Hero and Leander*), and other orchestral music.

Herbst, Johann Andreas (1588–1666), German composer and theorist. Some of his choral compositions were published in 1613 (*Theatrum Amoris*) and 1619 (*Meletemata sacra Davidis*). He was probably the first to disapprove explicitly of 'hidden' fifths and octaves, in his *Musica poetica* (1643). Other theoretical works were *Musica practica* (1641) and *Arte prattica e poetica* (1653).

Hercules, oratorio by Handel, to a libretto by Thomas Broughton (after Ovid's *Metamorphoses*, ix, and Sophocles's *Trachiniae*), first performed in 1745 in London.

Heredia, Pedro (d. 1648), Spanish composer of Masses and motets. He was *maestro di cappella* at St. Peter's, Rome, from 1630 until his death.

Heredia, Sebastian Aguilera de, *see* AGUILERA

Héritier, Jean L', *see* L'HERITIER

Hermannus Contractus (1013–54), Swiss (or possibly German) composer and theorist. He trained at Reichenau and became a monk there. His theoretical treatises were printed in Gerbert, *Scriptores*, ii, pages 124 on. He composed the antiphon 'Alma redemptoris mater', but not the 'Salve regina', which was long attributed to him. His treatise *Musica* has been edited with an

English translation (1936) by L. Ellinwood.

hermeneutics, term usually meaning interpretation of the Scriptures, applied by H. Kretzschmar (about 1900) to his method for interpreting musical motifs as the expression of human feeling. The method differs from AFFEKTENLEHRE of the 18th century in that it places greater emphasis on a scientific approach to intervals, rhythms and so forth.

Hero's Life, A, *see* HELDENLEBEN

Hérodiade, opera by Massenet, to a libretto by Paul Milliet and Henri Grémont (i.e. Georges Hartmann), founded on a story by Flaubert. It was first performed in 1881 in Brussels. In this version of the Salome story, John the Baptist confesses his love for Herodias' daughter, who pleads for his life and ultimately stabs herself after Herod has had the prophet killed.

Hérold, Louis Joseph Ferdinand (1791–1833), French composer. He studied at the Paris Conservatoire, where he won the *Prix de Rome* in 1812. His first opera was produced in Naples in 1815. From 1816 to his death he composed operas and ballets in Paris. He is chiefly remembered by *Zampa* (1831) and *Le Pré aux clercs* (1832), both first performed at the Opéra-Comique. From 1820 until 1827 he was répétiteur at the Théâtre Italien in Paris, and was later chorus master at the Paris Opéra.

Herrmann, Bernard (born 1911), U.S. composer and conductor. After studying in New York under Bernard Wagenaar and Percy Grainger, he established himself as a composer of film and radio music. His opera, *Wuthering Heights* (1965), was based on Emily Bronte's novel. He has also written two Christmas operas, a dramatic cantata (*Moby Dick*), and film scores for *Citizen Kane* and *The Devil and Daniel Webster*. From 1940 until 1955 he was conductor of the C.B.S. Symphony Orchestra.

Herrmann, Hugo (1896–1967), German composer and organist. He studied at Stuttgart and Berlin and became choral conductor at Reutlingen and director of the Donaueschingen Festival. He composed operas, works for chorus and for orchestra, and instrumental music.

Hervé (real name Florimond Ronger) (1825–92), French composer of operettas. He wrote about 100 works for the stage, of which *L'Oeil crevé* (1867), *Childéric* (1868), and *Le Petit Faust* (1869) were the most successful. He was also a theatre manager, librettist, and conductor.

Hervelois, *see* CAIX D'HERVELOIS

hervorgehoben (Ger.), emphasised.

Hesdin, Nicolle des Celliers d' (died 1538), French composer. He was master of the choristers at Beauvais Cathedral, where he was buried. He has often been wrongly identified as 'Pierre' Hesdin, a singer in the chapel of Henry II of France from 1547 to 1559. Masses, motets and *chansons* by him were published in collections of the time. A *chanson* of his was reprinted in F. Lesure, *Anthologie de la chanson parisienne au XVIᵉ siècle* (1953). Motets and a Magnificat by him were reprinted in *Treize livres de motets parus chez P. Attaingnant*, iii, iv, v, vii and viii (edited by A. Smijers and A. Tillman Merritt, 1936–62).

Heseltine, Philip, *see* WARLOCK

Hess, Myra (1890–1965), English pianist. She studied at the Guildhall School of Music and the Royal Academy of Music, appeared in 1907 at the Queen's Hall, toured extensively in Europe, the United States and Canada and gave daily lunch-hour concerts at the London National Gallery during the war. A pupil of Matthay, she was a notable exponent of Beethoven. She was made a D.B.E. in 1941.

heterophony (Gr., difference of sound), the simultaneous playing by two or more performers of differently treated forms of the same melody. The principle may have been used in Greek music, and is the basis of ensemble playing in China, Japan, and Java, e.g.:

Heugel, a firm of music publishers in Paris, founded in 1812 by Jean-Antoine Meissonnier (1783–1857). It takes its name from Jacques Léopold Heugel (1815–83), who became a partner of Meissonnier in 1839.

Heure Espagnole, L' (Fr., *The Spanish Hour*) opera in one act by Ravel, first performed in 1911 in Paris. Based on a comedy by 'Franc-Nohain' (Maurice Legrand) the story concerns the amorous exploits of a clockmaker's wife in her husband's shop.

Heward, Leslie Hays (1897–1943), English conductor and composer. In 1920 he became director of music at Westminster School, London. After conducting with the British National Opera Company, he went to South Africa in 1924 as director of music of the Broadcasting Corporation and conductor of the Cape Town Orchestra. On returning to Britain, he was conductor of the Birmingham Orchestra from 1930 until his death. Compositions include an unfinished opera, works for orchestra, a string quartet, and songs.

E. BLOM (editor): *Leslie Heward* (1944)

hexachord (Gr., six string), a scale of six notes, adopted by Guido d'Arezzo and incorporated in medieval musical theory. There were three hexachords:

   (1) *Hexachordum durum* (hard hexachord, requiring *B durum* or *quadratum,* the square B, otherwise B natural): G, A, B natural, C, D, E.

   (2) *Hexachordum naturale* (natural hexachord, in which neither B flat nor B natural occurred): C, D, E, F, G, A.

   (3) *Hexachordum molle* (soft hexachord, requiring *B molle* or *rotundum,* the rounded B, otherwise B flat): F, G, A, B flat, C, D.

(From *durum* is derived the German *dur* (major), from *molle* the German *moll* (minor), and from *B molle* the French *bémol* (flat). The French *bécarre* (natural) is a translation of *B quadratum.*) Each hexachord had the same succession of intervals: two tones, a semitone, and two tones. The range of notes in ordinary use was divided into seven overlapping hexachords:

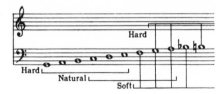

In teaching, the notes of the system could be indicated by their position on the 'Guidonian' hand. The application of syllables to the notes of the hexachords was called SOLMIZATION.

In the 16th and 17th centuries many compositions used the hexachord as a *cantus firmus*. The idea was applied to the Mass (e.g. Avery Burton), to the madrigal (e.g. John Farmer, 'Take time while time doth last', *The English Madrigal School*, viii, page 59), and especially to instrumental music (examples by Byrd, Bull and Sweelinck in the *Fitzwilliam Virginal Book*).

G. G. ALLAIRE: *The Theory of Hexachords, Solmization and the Modal System* (1972)

Heyborne, Ferdinando, *see* RICHARDSON

Heyden, Sebald (1499–1561), German theorist and composer. He was cantor at the Spitalschule, Nuremberg, in 1519. From 1537 he was rector of St. Sebaldus school. His theoretical treatises include *Ars canendi* (1537) and *De arte canendi* (1540; modern edition and translation by C. A. Miller, 1972). He also composed church music.

Heyther, William, *see* HEATHER

Hiawatha, cantata in three sections by Coleridge-Taylor, op 30, with words from Longfellow's *Song of Hiawatha*. The three sections are *Hiawatha's Wedding-Feast*, *The Death of Minnehaha* and *Hiawatha's Departure*. The first complete performance was in 1900 in London.

Hidalgo, Juan (died 1685), composer of the earliest Spanish opera to have partly survived, *Celos aun del ayre matan* ('Jealousy, even of air, is fatal'), libretto by Calderón, first performed, Madrid, December 5, 1660. An edition was published by J. Subirá in 1933.

hidden fifths and **octaves,** *see* SIMILAR MOTION

hi-hat cymbal, a pair of cymbals mounted face to face on a stand. The lower one is fixed but the upper one can be moved by a foot pedal and made to strike the lower one. The hi-hat cymbal is an essential part of a drum kit, and is principally used to keep time by striking the upper cymbal with a stick and then closing the pair to stop the sound with a characteristic clunk. It is also known as the choke cymbal.

Hill, Edward Burlinghame (1872–1960), U.S. composer and teacher. He studied at Harvard University and under Widor in Paris. From 1908 he was a member of the faculty of music at Harvard. He composed works for orchestra, ballets, choral music, chamber music, piano pieces, and songs, and wrote *Modern French Music* (1924).

Hiller, Ferdinand (1811–85), German pianist, composer and conductor. After studying with Hummel (1825–27), he gave concerts in Paris (1828–35) and was soloist in the Paris performance of Beethoven's fifth concerto. In 1850 he founded the Cologne Conservatorium. His compositions include six operas, three piano concertos, three symphonies, and numer-

ous works in other forms. He published a number of books of criticism.

Hiller, Johann Adam (1728–1804), German composer and conductor. From 1758 he was conductor in Leipzig of various musical societies which he incorporated into the Gewandhaus Concerts, founded by him in 1781. He conducted the concerts until 1785, and from 1789–1801 was at the Thomasschule, where he became cantor in 1797. He was one of the originators of the SINGSPIEL, of which he wrote a series of successful examples for the Leipzig theatre. His first, *Der Teufel ist los* (1766), to a text by C. F. Weisse, was derived from Coffey's *The Devil to Pay*, which was performed in Leipzig in 1750. In these scores Hiller followed English, French and Italian models in adopting and developing the native *Lied* for stage purposes. His writings include a volume of musical biographies and textbooks on singing and the violin.

Hilton, John (died 1608), English organist and composer. He was a lay clerk at Lincoln Cathedral in about 1584, and organist at Trinity College, Cambridge, in 1594. He composed anthems, and a five-part madrigal, 'Fair Oriana, beauty's queen', which was included in *The Triumphes of Oriana* (*The English Madrigal School*, xxxii, page 49).

Hilton, John (1599–1657), English organist and composer, possibly a son of the preceding. He was parish clerk and organist at St. Margaret's, Westminster, in 1628. He composed some church music and fancies for viols. Seven songs by him are included in *Musica Britannica*, xxxiii. He was editor and part-composer of *Catch that catch can* (1652), a collection of catches, rounds and canons which initiated a long period of popularity for the catch in Britain.

Himmel, Friedrich Heinrich (1765–1814), German composer. He was court *Kapellmeister* in Berlin (1795–1806) and produced operas in Venice, Naples, and St. Petersburg. His 'Liederspiel' *Frohsinn und Schwärmerei* (1801) and his opera *Fanchon, das Leiermädchen* (1804) were popular in Germany in the first half of the 19th century.

Hindemith, Paul (1895–1963), German composer. He studied under Arnold Mendelssohn and Bernard Sekles at the Hoch Conservatorium in Frankfurt, paying his fees by performing in café bands. From 1915 until 1925 he was leader of the Frankfurt Opera Orchestra, from which he resigned to travel as viola player with the Amar-Hindemith Quartet (which he founded with Licco Amar). He was one of the leading figures in the Donaueschingen Festivals of contemporary music (1921–6) and taught at the Berlin Hochschule from 1927 to 1935. In 1934 a projected performance of his opera *Mathis der Maler* was banned by the Nazis, who considered his music degenerate – though he was not Jewish. After spending some time in Ankara as musical adviser to the Turkish government, he went to the United States in 1939 and became professor of theory at Yale in 1942. In 1946 he returned to Europe and became professor of composition at Zürich University.

One of the most versatile musicians of his day, Hindemith achieved eminence as a composer, theorist, performer, teacher and conductor. The compositions written in the 1920s, which include several operas – e.g. *Mörder, Hoffnung der Frauen* (Murder,

Hope of Women), 1921; *Sancta Susanna*, 1921; *Cardillac*, 1926; *Neues vom Tage* (NEWS OF THE DAY), 1929 – on bizarre subjects reflecting the expressionist movement of the period, as well as many instrumental works (e.g., six chamber concertos, four string quartets, two violin sonatas, a viola sonata, and a cello sonata, solo sonatas for violin, viola, and cello, *Konzertmusik* for wind orchestra and for piano, brass, and two harps, and *Kammermusik* for five wind instruments) showed a free and highly resourceful treatment of traditional form and tonality. After 1927, when he observed that 'a composer should write today only if he knows for what purpose he is writing', he was one of those associated with the idea of *Gebrauchsmusik* ('music for use', also known as 'utility music'), and wrote compositions for player-piano and mechanical organ and pieces intended especially for amateur performance.

From about 1931 his style entered a new phase, marked by increased clarity of tonality and form and greater expressiveness of melody, which came to maturity in the opera *Mathis der Maler* (completed 1935; first performed, Zürich, 1938), the ballets *Nobilissima Visione* (1938) and *The Four Temperaments* (1940), the three piano sonatas (1936), the three sonatas for organ (1937–40), the violin concerto (1939), and a series of sonatas for solo wind instrument and

Paul Hindemith playing the viola. He wrote a great deal of music for solo instruments whose possibilities had been neglected by other composers

piano. The new and more comprehensive theory of tonality on which these works were based was expounded in *Unterweisung im Tonsatz* (two volumes, 1937 and 1939; translated into English as *The Craft of Musical Composition*, 1941–2), and further exemplified in a set of preludes and fugues for piano (*Ludus Tonalis*, 1942) which were described as 'Studies in Counterpoint, Tonal Organisation and Piano Playing'.

As Charles Eliot Norton professor at Harvard (1949–50) he gave a series of lectures which have been published as *A Composer's World* (1952). He has also published the text-books *A Concentrated Course in Traditional Harmony*, two volumes (1943, 1953), and *Elementary Training for Musicians* (1946). His principal compositions since 1931 are:

(1) Orchestra: Concert Music for strings and brass (1930); *Philharmonic Concerto* (variations, 1932); symphony from the opera *Mathis der Maler* (1934); ballet, *Nobilissima Visione* (1938); *Symphonic Dances* (1937); symphony in E flat (1940); overture, *Cupid and Psyche* (1943); *Symphonic Metamorphosis* on themes by Weber (1943); *Sinfonia serena* (1946); *Hériodiade* (after Mallarmé's poem, 1944) for chamber orchestra; symphony, *Die Harmonie der Welt* (1951), from the opera (1957).

(2) Solo instruments and orchestra: *Der Schwanendreher* for viola and small orchestra (1935); *Trauermusik* for viola and strings (1936); violin concerto (1939); cello concerto (1940); piano concerto (1945); clarinet concerto (1947); horn concerto (1949); *The Four Temperaments* for piano and strings (1940); concerto for trumpet, bassoon and orchestra (1949); concerto for wood-wind, harp and orchestra (1949).

(3) Voices and orchestra: oratorio, *Das Unaufhörliche* (1931); *Plöner Musiktag* (1932); operas: *Cardillac* (1926; revised 1952), *Neues vom Tage* (1929; revised 1953), *Mathis der Maler* (1935), *Die Harmonie der Welt* (1957); 'When lilacs last in the dooryard bloom'd' (Whitman, 1946); *Apparebit repentina dies* for chorus and brass (1947); *In Praise of Music* (revised version of *Frau Musica*, originally composed 1928).

(4) Chamber music: three pieces for clarinet, trumpet, violin, double bass and piano; two string trios; quartet for clarinet, violin, cello and piano; six string quartets; sonatas with piano for violin (four), viola, cello, double bass, flute, oboe, cor anglais, clarinet, bassoon, horn, trumpet, trombone; septet for wind instruments; sonatas for piano duet and for two pianos.

(4) Solo instruments: three sonatas and *Ludus Tonalis* for piano; three organ sonatas; harp sonata.

(5) Unaccompanied chorus: *Six chansons*; *Five Songs on Old Texts*.

(6) Songs: *Das Marienleben* (fifteen songs, 1922–3; revised 1948); *Nine English Songs*; *La Belle dame sans merci*.

I. KEMP: *Hindemith* (1971)

Hine, William (1687–1730), English organist and composer. He was a chorister and clerk of Magdalen College, Oxford, and became organist of Gloucester Cathedral in 1710. Anthems and a voluntary for organ by him were published posthumously.

Hines, Earl (born 1905), U.S. jazz pianist. He has been called the founder not only of the modern piano style but of almost every other from the early 1920s, when he was associated with such musicians as Louis Armstrong and Jimmie Noone.

Hingston (Hingeston), John (died 1683), English organist and composer, a pupil of Orlando Gibbons. He was in the service of Charles I, Cromwell and Charles II. His compositions include fancies with organ accompaniment. In 1657 he and William Howes signed a petition for the founding of a national college of music.

Hipkins, Alfred James (1826–1903), English pianist and writer on musical instruments. He cultivated an interest in the harpsichord and clavichord, and in problems of tuning and pitch. He wrote *Musical Instruments, Historic, Rare, and Unique* (1888), with coloured illustrations by William Gibb, and *The Standard of Musical Pitch* (1896).

Hippolyte et Arcite, opera with a prologue and five acts by Rameau, to a libretto by Simon Joseph de Pellegrin, first performed in 1733 in Paris.

history of music, some chief works in English:
GENERAL: C. BURNEY, *General History of Music* (four volumes, 1776–89; modern edition by F. Mercer, two volumes, 1935). J. HAWKINS, *A General History of Music* (five volumes, 1776; reprinted 1853, 1875). C. H. H. PARRY, *The Evolution of the Art of Music* (1897). *The Oxford History of Music* (seven volumes, 1929–34). C. V. STANFORD and C. FORSYTH, *A History of Music* (1916). P. LANDORMY, *A History of Music* (1923). P. A. SCHOLES, *Listener's History of Music*, (three volumes 1923–29). W. H. HADOW, *Music* (1924). C. GRAY, *The History of Music* (1928). G. DYSON, *The Progress of Music* (1932). K. NEF, *An Outline of the History of Music* (1935). D. N. FERGUSON, *A History of Musical Thought* (1935). T. M. FINNEY, *A History of Music* (1935). A. EINSTEIN, *A Short History of Music* (1938; illustrated edition, 1953). H. LEICHTENTRITT, *Music, History, and Ideas* (1938). P. LANG, *Music in Western Civilisation* (1941). C. SACHS, *Our Musical Heritage* (1948; published in the U.K. as *A Short History of World Music*, 1950). *The New Oxford History of Music* (eleven volumes, 1954 onwards). D. J. GROUT, *A History of Western Music* (1960). D. STEVENS (editor), *A History of Song* (1960). A. ROBERTSON and D. STEVENS (editors), *The Pelican History of Music* (two volumes, 1960, 1963). A WARMAN and W. MELLERS, *Man and his Music* (1962). P. H. LANG and N. BRODER, *Contemporary Music in Europe* (1965). W. STERNFIELD, *A History of Western Music* (five volumes). A. KALLIN and N. NABOKOV: *Twentieth-century Composers* (five volumes). H. SCHONBERG, *Lives of the Great Composers* (1971).
PERIODS: C. SACHS, *The Rise of Music in the Ancient World* (1943). E. WELLESZ, *A History of Byzantine Music and Hymnography* (1949). H. G. FARMER, *A History of Arabian Music to the 13th Century* (1929). G. REESE, *Music in the Middle Ages* (1940); *Music in the Renaissance* (1954). M. BUKOFZER, *Studies in Mediaeval and Renaissance Music* (1950); *Music in the Baroque Era* (1947). G. ABRAHAM, *A Hundred Years of Music* (1938; new edition 1949). A. EINSTEIN, *Music in the Romantic Era* (1947). G. DYSON, *The New Music* (1924). C. GRAY, *Contemporary Music* (1924). A. SALAZAR, *Music in Our Time* (1948). H. J. FOSS (editor), *The Heritage of Music* (studies of particular composers, 1550–1950), three volumes. (1927, 1934, 1951). N. SLONIMSKY, *Music Since 1900* (1949).

COUNTRIES:
The United States: F. R. BURTON, *American Primitive Music* (1909). J. T. HOWARD, *Our American Music* (1931). A. COPLAND, *Our New Music* (1941). W. MELLERS, *Music in a New Found Land* (1964).
China: J. H. LEWIS, *Foundations of Chinese Musical Art* (1936).
Czechoslovakia: R. NEWMARCH, *The Music of Czechoslovakia* (1942).
Britain: H. DAVEY, *History of English Music* (1921). P. A. SCHOLES, *The Puritans and Music* (1934); *The Mirror of Music, 1844–1944* (two volumes, 1947). R. NETTEL, *Music in the Five Towns, 1840–1914* (1944). H. G. FARMER, *History of Scottish Music*. E. WALKER, *A History of Music in England*, revised and enlarged by J. A. WESTRUP (1952). PERCY M. YOUNG, *A History of British Music* (1967)
France: G. JEAN-AUBRY, *French Music of Today* (1919). E. B. HILL, *Modern French Music* (1924). M. COOPER, *French Music from the Death of Berlioz to the Death of Fauré* (1951).
Hungary: G. CALDY, *A History of Hungarian Music* (1903).
INDIA: A. H. FOX STRANGWAYS, *Music of Hindostan* (1914). A. B. FYZEE-RAHAMIN, *The Music of India* (1925).
Ireland: W. H. GRATTAN FLOOD, *A History of Irish Music* (1905).
JAPAN: F. T. PIGGOTT, *The Music of the Japanese* (1909).
Java: J. KUNST, *The Music of Java* (two volumes, 1949),
Jews: A. Z. IDELSOHN, *Jewish Music in its Historical Development* (1929).
Latin America: C. SEEGER, *Music in Latin America* (1942). N. SLONIMSKY, *Music of Latin America* (1945).
Mexico: R. STEVENSON, *Music in Mexico* (1952).
Norway: B. QVAMME, *Norwegian Music and Composers* (1949).
Russia: M. MONTAGUE-NATHAN, *A History of Russian Music* (1914). L. SABANEIEV, *Modern Russian Composers* (1927). G. ABRAHAM, *Studies in Russian Music* (1935); *On Russian Music* (1939); *Eight Soviet Composers* (1943).
Spain and Portugal: G. CHASE, *The Music of Spain* (1941). J. B. TREND, *The Music of Spanish History to 1600* (1926).

DICTIONARIES: E. BLOM (ed.), *Grove's Dictionary of Music and Musicians* (nine volumes, 1954). W. APEL, *Harvard Dictionary of Music* (1969). A. E. HULL, *Dictionary of Modern Music and Musicians* (1924). P. A. SCHOLES, *The Oxford Companion to Music* (ninth edition, 1955). E. BLOM, *Everyman's Dictionary of Music* (second edition, 1956). O. THOMPSON and N. SLONIMSKY (editors), *The International Cyclopedia of Music and Musicians* (1946). H. ROSENTHAL and J. WARRACK, *Concise Oxford Dictionary of Opera* (1964). K. THOMPSON, *A Dictionary of Twentieth-century Composers* (1973).
PERIODICALS (wholly or partly in English): *Acta Musicologica* (1931 foll.). *Journal of the American Musicological Society* (1948 foll.). *Journal of the Galpin Society* (for the history of musical instruments) (1948 foll.). *Journal of Renaissance and Baroque Music*

(1946–7). *Modern Music* (1924–40). *Monthly Musical Record* (1873 foll.). *Musica Disciplina* (1948 foll.). *Musical Antiquary* (1909–13). *Musical Quarterly* (1915 foll.). *Musical Times* (1844 foll.). *Music and Letters* (1920 foll.). *Music Review* (1940 foll.). *Notes of The Music Library Association* (1944 foll.). *Proceedings of the Royal Musical Association* (1874 foll.).

ANTHOLOGIES: (a) Music: A. SCHERING, *History of Music in Examples* (1931; reprinted, 1950). A. T. DAVISON and W. APEL, *Historical Anthology of Music* (volume one, to 1600, 1946; volume two to c. 1780, 1950). J. WOLF, *Music of Earlier Times* (1930; reprinted New York c. 1948). C. PARRISH and J. F. OHL, *Masterpieces of Music before* 1750 (1952).

(b) Writings: O. STRUNK, *Source Readings in Music History* (1950).

(c) Pictures: G. KINSKY, *History of Music in Pictures* (1930).

BIBLIOGRAPHY: W. D. ALLEN, *Philosophies of Music History* (1939; contains a list of histories of music from 1600–1930). E. KROHN, *The History of Music; An Index to a Selected Group of Publications* (1952: an index of the contents of periodicals).

H.M.S. Pinafore, operetta in two acts by Gilbert and Sullivan, first performed in 1878 in London. The work is subtitled *The Lass that loved a Sailor*, and the story unfolds on an English warship.

Hobrecht, Jakob, *see* OBRECHT

Hochzeit des Camacho, Die (Ger., *Camacho's Wedding*), opera in two acts by Mendelssohn, to a libretto by Carl August von Lichtenstein, first performed in 1827 in Berlin. The work is based on an episode from Cervantes's *Don Quixote*.

hocket (Fr., *hocquet, hoquet*; It., *ochetto*; Lat., *hoquetus, ochetus*), the breaking of a melody into single notes or very short phrases by means of rests, particularly as used by composers and discussed by theorists in the 13th and 14th centuries. It is found in parts for instruments (e.g. P. Aubry, *Cent Motets du XIIIe siècle*, ii, page 221) and for voices (e.g. in the motets of Machaut). Most often it is used in two parts at a time, so that one sings while the other has a rest. In some cases it may be based on a single melody which is shared by two voices. A *Credo* by Pennard of about 1400 (*The Old Hall Manuscript*, edited by A. Hughes and M. Bent, i, page 293) treats this melody:

as a hocket in the final section:

Hoddinott, Alun (born 1929), Welsh composer. He studied in Cardiff, at the University College of South Wales, where he was appointed professor in 1968. His works include four symphonies, a sinfonietta, concertos for piano and other instruments, an oratorio (*Job*) and chamber and instrumental music.

Hofer, Josepha, *see* WEBER (5)

Høffding, Finn (born 1899), Danish composer and teacher. After studying in Copenhagen and Vienna, he became professor at the Royal Danish Conservatory in 1931 and founded the Copenhagen Folk Music School with Jørgen Bentzon. His works include an opera, *The Emperor's New Clothes* (after Hans Andersen), orchestral and chamber music, piano pieces and songs.

Hoffmann, Eduard, *see* REMENYI

Hoffmann, Ernst Theodor Amadeus (1776–1822), German author and composer, who changed his third name from Wilhelm in honour of Mozart. He studied music and law, and was a civil servant until 1806. He conducted at the theatre in Bamberg in 1806 and in Leipzig and Dresden from 1813 until 1816, when he re-entered the civil service in Berlin. He composed eleven operas (of which *Undine* (1816) was the most successful), a symphony, piano sonatas, and other works. His essays on music were collected in *Fantasiestücke in Callot's Manier* (1814) where appears the character Johannes Kreisler who inspired Schumann's *Kreisleriana*. The style of his essays had considerable influence on the musical criticism of the romantic period, and his stories were used as material for a number of operas' libretti, including Offenbach's *Tales of Hoffmann* (1881) and Hindemith's *Cardillac*.

Hofhaimer, Paul (1459–1537), Austrian organist and composer. He was organist at Innsbruck in 1479, Augsburg in 1507, and Salzburg in 1519. He was one of the leading organists of his day and the founder of an important school of players and composers. Three- and four-part songs by him have been published in *Denkmäler der Tonkunst in Osterreich*, lxxii, Jugend xxxvii (2), together with instrumental arrangements of them by later composers.

H. J. MOSER: *Paul Hofhaimer* (1929)

Hofmann, Josef Casimir (1876–1957), Polish born pianist and composer (original name, Józef Kazimierz Hofmann), who played in public at six, toured Europe at nine, and made his first appearance in the United States in 1887. He studied with Anton Rubinstein (1892–4) and toured extensively thereafter. From 1926–38 he was director of the Curtis Institute of Music at Philadelphia. He composed a number of works for the piano, and a symphony and a 'symphonic narrative' for orchestra.

Hogarth, George (1783–1870), Scottish writer on music. After studying law and music in Edinburgh, he settled in London and became critic of the *Morning Chronicle* in 1830. Six years later his daughter married Charles Dickens, who was appointed editor of the *Daily News* in 1846 and hired Hogarth as his music critic. His books include *Musical History, Biography, and Criticism* (1835) and *Memoirs of the Opera*.

Hohane, an anonymous keyboard piece called *The Irish Hohane* (Gaelic *ochone*, alas!) in the *Fitzwilliam Virginal Book*, no 26.

Holborne, Antony (died 1602), English composer. He is described as 'servant of her most excellent Majestie' on the title of his *Cittharn Schoole* (1597). He also published *Pavans, Galliards, Almains and other short Aeirs* in 1599, four dances in five parts were printed in Füllsack and Hildebrand's *Ausserlesener Paduanen . . .* (Hamburg, 1607). Other compositions are in John Dowland's *Varietie of Lute Lessons* (1610), which refers to him as Gentleman Usher of Queen Elizabeth. A complete edition of his works was begun in 1967 by M. Kanazawa; the first volume contains lute and pandora music, the second cittern music. Four consort-dances from the 1599 publication are reprinted in *Musica Britannica*, ix.

His brother, William Holborne, composed six 'aers' for three voices which were included in Antony's *Cittharn Schoole* (1597). They are reprinted in the second volume of Kanazawa's edition of Antony Holborne's *Complete Works* (1973).

B. JEFFERY: 'Anthony Holborne', in *Musica Disciplina*, xxii (1968)

Holbrooke, Joseph (1878–1958), English composer, conductor and pianist. He studied at the Royal Academy of Music in London and composed symphonic poems for orchestra, including *The Raven* (1900) and *Byron* (1906). He also composed a setting of Poe's *The Bells* for chorus and orchestra, and an operatic trilogy entitled *The Cauldron of Annwen*, consisting of *The Children of Don* (1912), *Dylan* (1914) and *Bronwen* (1929). Among his other works are orchestral variations on *Three Blind Mice*, *Auld Lang Syne* and *The Girl I Left Behind Me*.

Holiday, Billie (1915–1959), U.S. jazz singer, whose voice may have been rough-edged but whose eloquence was equalled only by that of Bessie Smith. Her recordings, of which there are fortunately many, give a good impression of her qualities. Her style is heard at its best in such numbers as 'If dreams come true', 'A fine romance', 'What shall I say?', 'It's easy to blame the weather', 'Nice work if you can get it', 'Am I blue?' and the searing 'Gloomy Sunday' and 'Strange Fruit'. Though she used pop music rather than the blues as her inspiration, she had the knack of raising all the songs she sang by an uncommon subtlety of nuance and inflection. Among the instrumentalists with whom she was most closely associated was the tenor saxophonist, Lester Young, and the pianist, Teddy Wilson, who took part in several important recordings with her. The wretchedness of her life – which progressed from childhood rape to drink and drugs – is described in her autobiography, *Lady Sings the Blues*. After her death she became a cult figure, but her qualities seem strong enough to survive it.

Holliger, Heinz (born 1939), Swiss oboist and composer. He studied at the Berne Conservatory, and later with Pierre Boulez at Basel. In 1959 he won first prize in the international music competition at Geneva, and in 1961 he won the Munich Competition. Today his repertory includes oboe music of all periods, and he has done much to extend the technique of the instrument,

Billie Holiday, whose contribution to jazz in the 1930s equalled that of her great predecessor, Bessie Smith, in the 1920s. But whereas Bessie Smith sang the blues, Billie Holiday used mainly the pop songs of the day as the source of her inspiration, transforming them into bitter-sweet vehicles for her artistry. Towards the end of her career, her voice was irreparably damaged by the life she led; yet this made her performances, if anything, even more moving.

inspiring such composers as Amy, Berio, Castiglioni, Globokar, Henze, Kelemen, Křenek, Martin, Penderecki and Stockhausen to write works for him. His own compositions have revealed him to be an avid experimenter, not only with the oboe but also in other mediums. His most important work so far has been *Siebengesang*, which is a kind of oboe concerto with a vocal postlude. In the course of it the oboist has to add an electronic attachment to the inside of his instrument, which amplifies and distorts the tone.

Holmboe, Vagn (born 1909), Danish composer, pupil of Jeppessen and (in Berlin) of Ernst Toch. One of the most important Danish composers in the wake of Nielsen, he has produced ten symphonies, thirteen chamber concertos, ten string quartets and other chamber music. A period spent in Romania, collecting folk music, has had some influence on his otherwise Nordic style.

Holmes, John, 16–17th century composer who was organist of Winchester Cathedral. His five-part madrigal 'Thus Bonny-Boots the birthday celebrated' was printed in *The Triumphes of Oriana* (*The English Madrigal School*, xxxii, page 77).

Holmès (originally Holmes), **Augusta Mary Anne** (1847–1903), Irish composer and pianist who was born in Paris and later took French nationality, A pupil of César Franck from 1875, she wrote four operas, of which one, *La Montagne noire* (1895), was staged at the Paris Opéra, and a series of symphonic poems or dramatic symphonies, including *Irlande* (1882), *Pologne* (1883), and *Au Pays Bleu* (1891).

Holst (originally von Holst), **Gustav Theodore** (1874–1934), English composer of Swedish descent. Born in Cheltenham of musical parents, he gained early experience as organist, pianist and conductor. In 1893 he moved to London, studying composition at the Royal College of Music under Stanford. On leaving, he played the trombone in the Carl Rosa Opera Orchestra. In 1907 he became director of music at Morley College and from 1919 until 1924 he was teacher of composition at the Royal College of Music. He was also, from 1905, music master at St. Paul's Girls' School in London, for which he wrote his *St. Paul's Suite* for strings, and where he remained until his death. His integrity of ideal and singleness of purpose enabled him to assimilate diverse elements into a style which fused vitality, clarity, and austere mysticism. His early interests were in folk-song (*Somerset Rhapsody*, 1907), and in Sanskrit literature and Hindu scales (*Hymns from the Rig-Veda* for voices and instruments, published 1911, and chamber-opera *Savitri*, composed 1908, produced 1916). The use of five- and seven-beat bars in this period is continued in the next, and is allied with greater harmonic tension (e.g. clashes of unrelated triads) and larger orchestral and choral resources (*The Planets*, completed 1916, and *The Hymn of Jesus* for two choruses, semi-chorus and orchestra, 1917). In the later music Holst pursued his experiments in harmony (*Choral Symphony*, performed 1925; *Egdon Heath* for orchestra, 1927; and the *Choral Fantasia*, 1930), leading to polytonality (*Hammersmith* for orchestra, 1930, *Six Canons for equal voices*, 1932), and showed leanings towards neo-Baroque forms (*Fugal Overture* and *Fugal Concerto*, both completed in 1923) and parody (opera-ballet *The Perfect Fool*, staged in 1923). His principal compositions are:

(1) Operas: *Savitri; The Perfect Fool; At the Boar's Head.*
(2) Orchestra: *Somerset Rhapsody; St. Paul's Suite* for strings; *The Planets; Fugal Overture; Fugal Concerto; Egdon Heath; Hammersmith.*
(3) Choral works: *Hymns from the Rig-Veda; The Cloud Messenger; The Hymn of Jesus; Ode to Death;* Choral Symphony; Choral Fantasia.
(4) Songs: Nine hymns from the *Rig-Veda;* twelve songs to words by Humbert Wolfe.

I. HOLST: *Gustav Holst* (1938); *The Music of Gustav Holst* (1951)
E. RUBBRA: *Gustav Holst* (1947)

Holst, Imogen (born 1907), English composer, conductor, writer and teacher. She is the daughter of Gustav Holst, on whom she has written two important books. She has also written studies of Purcell and Britten, and in recent years has been closely associated with the Aldeburgh Festival. Her compositions include an orchestral overture, piano pieces and folk song arrangements.

Holzbauer, Ignaz (1711–93), Austrian composer. He was director of music at the Vienna court theatre from 1745 until 1747, and became court *Kapellmeister* at Stuttgart in 1750. In 1753 he moved to Mannheim, where he directed the orchestra in the period of its greatest fame, and wrote 65 symphonies in the style of Stamitz. He composed eleven Italian operas and one German, *Günther von Schwartzburg* (Mannheim, 1777).

Home, Sweet Home, a song in the opera *Clari, or the Maid of Milan* (London, 1823); words by John Howard Payne (1791–1852), music by Sir Henry Bishop. Its popularity led to the production of another opera by Bishop with the title *Home, Sweet Home* (London, 1829).

Gustav Holst in his study

Homme armé, L', the title of a 15th century *chanson* which was more frequently used than any other as a *cantus firmus* for Masses. It was so used from the 15th century to the 17th in more than thirty Masses by various composers, including Dufay, Busnois, Caron, Faugues, Regis, Ockeghem, de Orto, Basiron, Tinctoris, Vaqueras (these ten have been published as Tomus i in the series *Monumenta Polyphoniae Liturgicae Sanctae Ecclesiae Romane*, 1948), Obrecht, Josquin (two settings), Brumel, La Rue, Pipelare, Senfl, Morales, Palestrina, and Carissimi. The tune and its words (first discovered in 1925) were:

L'ho-me, l'ho-me, l'home ar - mé. (L'home ar-mé)

L'home ar-mé doibt on doub - ter. On a

fait par tout cri - er Que chas-cun se

viegne ar-mer D'un hau-bre-gon de fer.

A setting of the tune, without words, as a four-part *chanson* by Robert Morton is printed in J. Marix, *Les Musiciens de la cour de Bourgogne au XVe siècle* (1937).

Honegger, Arthur (1892–1955), Swiss composer. Born at Le Havre in France, he studied at the Zürich Conservatory (1909–11) and at the Paris Conservatoire (1911–13). Later he became a private pupil of d'Indy and Widor. With Satie, Milhaud, and Jean Cocteau he formed the group *Les Nouveaux Jeunes* which later became *Les Six*. A prolific composer in many forms, he became known chiefly for his portrait of a railway engine, *Pacific 231*, for orchestra (1923), the oratorio *Le Roi David* (completed 1921), and his setting of Claudel's *Jeanne d'Arc au Bûcher* (completed 1935). He composed an opera on *Antigone* (after Sophocles) and collaborated with Ibert on *L'Aiglon* (*The Eaglet*). Of his five symphonies, the second is scored for strings (plus optional trumpet), the third is entitled *Symphonie Liturgique* (*Liturgical Symphony*), and the fifth subtitled *di tre re* – i.e., 'of the three D's', referring to the fact that each of its three movements ends on the note D. Other orchestral works include *Rugby* (a 'symphonic movement' similar to *Pacific 231*) and *Pastorale d'été*. He also composed film music, chamber and instrumental works, and songs.

Hongroise, *see* ALL'ONGARESE

Hook, James (1746–1827), English composer and organist. He worked at Marylebone Gardens in London from 1769 to 1773 and at Vauxhall Gardens from 1774 until 1820. He wrote music for a number of stage pieces, concertos, sonatas, choral works and some two thousand songs, including 'The Lass of Richmond Hill' and 'The Blackbird'.

Hooper, Edmund (c. 1553–1621), English organist and composer. He was master of the children at Westminster Abbey in 1588, a gentleman of the Chapel Royal in 1604, and organist at Westminster Abbey in 1606. Two pieces by him were printed in Sir William Leighton's *Teares or Lamentacions of a Sorrowful Soule* (1614; modern edition by Cecil Hill, 1970), and three of his anthems in Barnard's *Selected Church Music* (1641). An *almaine* and a *coranto* by him are in the *Fitzwilliam Virginal Book* (nos 222 and 228).

Hopkinson, Francis (1737–91), statesman and poet, generally regarded as the first U.S. composer. He composed songs, such as 'My days have been so wondrous free' (the first published composition by a U.S. born composer); also *The Temple of Minerva* (1781) – an 'oratorical entertainment', of which the music has not survived, and published *A Collection of Psalm Tunes with a few Anthems* (1770).

hoquetus, *see* HOCKET

Horenstein, Jascha (1898–1973), Russian born conductor, pupil of Adolf Busch in Vienna and Schrecker in Berlin. He was appointed conductor of the Dusseldorf Opera in 1926, but for most of his life he worked as a guest conductor of orchestras and opera companies all over the world. He was noted for his interpretations of Bruckner, Mahler and Schoenberg.

horn (Fr., *cor*; Ger., *Horn*; It., *corno*), brass instrument with a conical tube wound into a spiral, ending in a bell, and played with a funnel-shaped mouthpiece; known in England since the early 18th century as the French horn, since it was in France that it was perfected as an orchestral instrument. In its modern form it is built in F (*see* TRANSPOSING INSTRUMENTS) and equipped with three valves which progressively lower the pitch of the instrument's natural harmonic series and so make available a complete chromatic compass of:

(written a fifth higher in the score).

A particular type of instrument much favoured by players today has a switch which instantaneously turns it into a horn in B flat alto. This facilitates the playing of the high notes. The low notes were formerly written in the bass clef an octave below their written pitch, i.e. a fourth below their sounding pitch. The modern practice is to write all the notes – in the bass clef as in the treble – a fifth higher than the sounding pitch. Stopped notes are played by bringing the hand into the bell: the sound produced is a semitone higher than the open note, and the tone is muffled. A similar effect is obtained by inserting a pear-shaped MUTE into the bell, except that the pitch remains unaltered. 'Brassy' notes, whether stopped or open, are indicated by the terms *cuivré* (brassed) or *schmetternd* (blaring) and are played with increased lip pressure. The sign + over a note indicates that it is to be stopped; if the note is to be played *forte* it will automatically be brassy, since considerable pressure is necessary to play stopped notes loud.

The valve horn described above (Fr., *cor à pistons*; Ger., *Ventilhorn*; It., *cornoventile*) came into use towards the middle of the 19th century: the earliest parts written for it appear to be in Halévy's opera *La Juive* (1835). It was some time, however, before it was generally adopted. Its predecessor, which survived for several years after this date, was the natural horn without valves. It first came into use at the end of the 17th century as an improved form of the earlier hunting horn (*Jagdhorn*). 18th century nomenclature was not always consistent. The following terms (respectively French, German and Italian) were, however, in regular use: *cor de chasse*, *Waldhorn* and *corno da caccia*. *Waldhorn* continued in use in Germany in the 19th century to distinguish the natural instrument from the one with valves (*Ventilhorn*). Bach wrote both for *corno* and for *corno da caccia*: attempts have been made (*see* C. S. Terry, *Bach's Orchestra*, pages 41-7) to show that he intended two different types of instrument, but the arguments advanced are not wholly convincing. The origin of the horn as a hunting instrument was not merely commemorated by the names *cor de chasse* and *corno da caccia*: it also influenced the practice of composers and the style of music written for it. Among early examples of its use are Carlo Badia's opera *Diana rappacificata* (1700), various concertos by Vivaldi, Bach's first Brandenburg concerto (1721), and Handel's *Water Music* (1715–17) and *Giulio Cesare* (1724), which employs four horns.

In the classical symphony of the later 18th century two horns were used as subsidiary instruments, frequently employed to sustain notes of the harmony but occasionally coming into the foreground, e.g.:

Horns in G (sounding a fourth lower)

MOZART, *Symphony in G minor*, K 550

The characteristic open fifth (a), called 'horn fifth', resulted from the fact that the instrument was virtually restricted to the notes of the harmonic series. It remained an idiom even after the introduction of a third horn by Beethoven in the *Eroica* symphony (1804) and after the invention of valves in 1813. In order to be able to play in more than one key players used a series of 'crooks' – additional pieces of tubing of varying lengths – to change the pitch of the instrument. The practice of writing the parts as if the players still used crooks persisted in scores until the end of the 19th century, long after the valve horn in F had become the standard instrument. The modern practice of writing for the horn as a transposing instrument is a survival of this practice. The only means of playing notes other than those of the harmonic series on the natural horn was by 'stopping' with the hand, which altered the pitch of the open notes but at the same time changed the tone-quality.

Concertos for the horn have been composed by Haydn, Mozart, Strauss and Hindemith, and chamber music including the horn by Haydn, Mozart, Beethoven, Schubert, Schumann, Brahms, Hindemith and Wellesz.

The name 'horn' is also used, misleadingly, for two woodwind instruments – the BASSET HORN, which is an alto clarinet, and the English horn or *cor anglais*, which is an alto oboe.

A. CARSE: *Musical Wind Instruments* (1939)

F. PIERSIG: *Die Einführung des Hornes in die Kunstmusik* (1927)

horn, basset, *see* BASSET HORN

Horn, Charles Edward (1786–1849), English composer and singer, son of Karl Friedrich Horn. He sang in and composed operas in London and Dublin (1809–33). He went to the United States in 1833 and produced English operas in New York, four of which he composed himself. From 1843 until 1847 he was in England again, and then in Boston until his death. He is now remembered by his song 'Cherry Ripe'.

horn, English, *see* OBOE

Horn, Karl Friedrich (1762–1830), German composer and pianist. He went to London in 1782 and became music master to Queen Charlotte and her daughters, and in 1824 organist of St. George's Chapel, Windsor. He composed some instrumental music and edited, in collaboration with Samuel Wesley, Bach's *Well-tempered Clavier*.

hornpipe, (1) a wind instrument with a single reed and a horn attached to each end, played in Celtic countries, and in Wales, where it was called pibgorn, until the 19th century;

(2) by the beginning of the 16th century applied to a dance in triple time and to its music. Hugh Aston's 'Hornpipe' of that time is an early example of English secular keyboard music (printed in J. Wolf, *Music of Earlier Times*, no 24).

Several hornpipes from the end of the century are built on a GROUND, the same as that adopted in contemporary *bergamasca* settings (see the example in A. Holborne, *Complete Works*, edited by M. Kanazawa, ii, 1973, no 33). The following is the first section of a 17th century hornpipe from Purcell's *The Married Beau*:

Allegro

About the middle of the 18th century the hornpipe's rhythm changed to 4-4 time and it seems to have acquired an association with sailors.

Horn Signal, Symphony with the, nickname for Haydn's Symphony no 31 in D major (1765), so called because of the work's striking fanfares for four horns (most works at this period required only two horns).

Horowitz, Vladimir (born 1904), Russian born pianist, a pupil of Felix Blumenfeld. He played in Berlin (1924) and rapidly acquired an international reputation. In 1928 he settled in the United States, where in 1937 he married Toscanini's daughter, Wanda. For some years his career was interrupted by illness, but from the 1960s he again appeared in public, revealing once more his qualities as an exponent of Chopin, Scarlatti and other composers.

'Horseman' Quartet, nickname for Haydn's string quartet in G minor, op 74, no 3 (1793), presumably inspired by the 'riding' rhythms of the first movement and finale. The work is also known as the 'Rider' Quartet.

Horsley, William (1774–1858), English organist. He was organist at several churches in London, and one of the founders of the Philharmonic Society. He composed glees, hymn tunes, and piano music, and wrote *An Explanation of Major and Minor Scales* (1825).

Horwood, William (died 1484), English composer. He was appointed in 1477 to instruct the choristers of Lincoln Cathedral. The Eton choirbook (c. 1500) contains a Magnificat and three antiphons (one now incomplete) by him.

Hothby, John (died 1487), English theorist. He lectured at Oxford in 1435, visited Spain, France and Germany, and in about 1440 settled in Florence. Later he was at Lucca, but he was recalled to England in 1486, and died there. His surviving compositions and his three theoretical treatises have been edited in two volumes by A. Seay (1964).

Hotter, Hans (born 1909), German baritone, Austrian by naturalization. He studied at the Munich Academy of Music, and began his career as an opera singer in his twenties. One of the most renowned Wagner exponents of the century, he has appeared as Wotan at Covent Garden and produced one of the company's *Ring* cycles. He is also known as a recitalist, performing such works as Schubert's *Winterreise* and Brahms's *Four Serious Songs*.

Hotteterre (Hotteterre-le-Romain), Jacques (died c. 1760), French flautist, author, composer and member of a numerous family of wind instrument makers and players many of whom played in Louis XIV's orchestra. He is sometimes confused with Louis Hotteterre who was royal flute-player at the Court in 1664. He spent part of his early life in Rome. He is believed to have been the first to play the transverse flute in the opera at Paris, c. 1697. He wrote *Principes de la Flûte traversière* (1707, and many later editions) and composed flute pieces, sonatas and suites for two flutes and continuo, and a tutor and pieces for the musette.

Howells, Herbert (born 1892), English composer. He studied under Brewer at Gloucester and under Stanford in London. He was teacher of composition at the Royal College of Music from 1920 and director of music at St. Paul's Girls' School (where he succeeded Holst) from 1936. In 1954 he became professor at London University. He wrote works for orchestra, a concerto and a suite for strings, two piano concertos, a *Requiem*, *Hymnus Paradisi*, and *Missa Sabrinensis* for soloists, chorus and orchestra, organ and piano pieces, chamber music and songs.

Howes, Frank Stewart (born 1891), English music critic and author. He studied at St. John's College, Oxford, and at the Royal College of Music where he was appointed lecturer in 1938. He joined the staff of *The Times* in 1925, and became chief music critic in 1943. He wrote *The Borderland of Music and Psychology* (1926), *William Byrd* (1928), *The Appreciation of Music* (1929), *Beethoven: Orchestral Works* (1933), *A Key to the Art of Music* (1935), *The Music of William Walton* (two volumes, 1943) and *The Music of Ralph Vaughan Williams* (1954).

Hubay, Jenö (originally Eugen Huber) (1858–1937), Hungarian violinist and composer. He studied under Joachim in Berlin, and later became teacher at the Brussels Conservatoire (1882) and in Budapest in 1886. He composed operas, orchestral works, and concertos and other pieces for violin. His pupils included Szigeti and Jelly d'Aranyi.

Huber, Hans (1852–1921), Swiss composer. He studied at the Leipzig Conservatorium and was director of the Basel Conservatory from 1896 until 1918. He wrote nine symphonies, five operas, chamber music, and works for chorus and for piano.

Huberman, Bronislaw (1882–1947), Polish violinist, who studied in Warsaw, Paris and Berlin (where he was a pupil of Joachim). He made his first public appearance at the age of ten in Vienna, and four years later performed Brahms's violin concerto in the composer's presence. He was the founder of the Israel Philharmonic Orchestra.

Hucbald (c. 840–930), theorist and monk of St. Amand. He wrote *De institutione harmonica* (published in Gerbert, *Scriptores*, i, page 104), but not *Musica enchiriadis* nor certain other treatises formerly thought to be by him.

> R. WEAKLAND: 'Hucbald as Musician and Theorist', in *Musical Quarterly*, xlii (1956)

Hudson, George, 17th century English violinist and composer. He was a member of the King's orchestra in 1661, and composer to the court, with Matthew Locke, in 1668. He composed music (with Henry Lawes, Charles Colman and Cooke) for Davenant's *The First Dayes Entertainment at Rutland-House by Declamations and Musick: after the manner of the Ancients* (1656) and (with Colman, Cooke, Lawes and Locke) for Davenant's *Siege of Rhodes* (1656), the first English opera.

Hüe, Georges Adolphe (1858–1948), French composer. He studied at the Paris Conservatoire, winning the *Prix de Rome* in 1879. He succeeded Saint-Saëns as a member of the Academie des Beaux-Arts in 1922. His works include operas, ballets, a pantomime, a *Romance* for violin and orchestra, symphonic poems and other orchestral works, incidental music for plays, choral works and songs.

Hufnagelschrift (Ger.), literally 'hobnail script'. A type of plainsong notation used in medieval Germany, so called from the shape of the notes.

Hugh the Drover, ballad opera in two acts by Vaughan Williams, to a libretto by Harold Child, first performed in 1924 in London. The action takes place in a Cotswold village at the time of the Napoleonic wars. Mary's father (the Constable) has chosen John the Butcher for her husband, but she falls in love with Hugh the Drover who offers to fight with John for the prize of Mary. When John loses the fight he charges Hugh with being in Napoleon's pay as a spy and Hugh is put in the stocks. Mary comes to free him during the night, but being frightened by the sound of people approaching she gets into the stocks with him and is discovered there in the morning. She refuses to leave Hugh, her outraged father and John both disown her, and a fight follows between the supporters of Hugh and those of John, interrupted by the sergeant who has come to arrest the supposed spy. He recognizes Hugh as a loyal servant to the King and demands John for the army, thus leaving Hugh free to take Mary as his bride.

Hugo von Reutlingen (Hugo Spechtshart) (1285–

1359 or 1360), German theorist. He was school cantor in Reutlingen, and in 1332 wrote a treatise entitled *Flores musicae omnis cantus Gregoriani* (published in 1488; reprinted in 1868). His *Chronikon* contained the words and melodies of songs of the flagellants (*Geisslerlieder*) such as were sung during the plague of 1349; a modern edition by P. Runge is in *Die Lieder und Melodien der Geissler des Jahres 1349* (1900).

See also LAUDA

Huguenots, Les, opera in five acts by Meyerbeer, to a libretto by Auguste Eugene Scribe. It was first performed in 1836 in Paris. The story of Meyerbeer's most famous opera has as its climax the St. Bartholomew Massacre of 1572.

Hullah, John Pyke (1812–1884), English composer and teacher. In 1839–40 he studied in Paris G. L. Wilhelm's method of teaching singing in classes, which he followed with great success in England. He wrote on the system (*A Grammar of Vocal Music*, 1843) and on other musical topics, and composed three operas (one of them, *The Village Coquettes*, with a libretto by Charles Dickens) and many other vocal works.

Hume, Tobias (died 1645), English composer and performer on the *viola da gamba*. He published *The First Part of Ayres* (1605) which contained some pieces for the lyra viol, and *Captain Hume's Poeticall Musicke* (1607). Facsimile editions by F. Traficante of both works were published in 1969. Four songs to the viol have been reprinted in D. Greer, *Twenty Songs from Printed Sources* (1969), and twelve instrumental pieces by him are in *Musica Britannica*, ix.

Humfrey, Pelham (1647–74), English composer. He began to compose when a chorister at the Chapel Royal. He was sent to study in France and Italy by Charles II. In 1667 he was a gentleman of the Chapel Royal, becoming master of the choristers in 1672. He wrote anthems, odes, and songs. His complete church music has been edited by P. Dennison in *Musica Britannica*, xxxiv and xxxv.

Hummel, Johann Nepomuk (1778–1837), Austrian composer and pianist. As a boy he was a pupil of Mozart, gave concerts in Germany, Holland, and England, studied with Clementi in London, and from 1793 with Albrechtsberger and Salieri in Vienna. He was *Kapellmeister* to Prince Esterházy from 1804 until 1811, and later worked in Stuttgart and Weimar, where he died. The most important of his many works are the seven concertos and other compositions for piano. He wrote nine operas, chamber music, and choral music.

humoresque (Fr.), **Humoreske** (Ger.), occasionally used as the title of a capricious piece of music, e.g. Schumann's *Humoreske*, op 20, and Dvořák's *Humoresque*, op 101, both for piano.

Humperdinck, Engelbert (1854–1921), German composer. He studied in Cologne under Hiller, in Munich under Lachner and Rheinberger, and assisted Wagner at Bayreuth from 1880–1. Later he taught in Barcelona, Frankfurt, and Berlin. His six operas – of which *Hansel and Gretel* (1893) is the most famous – show Wagner's influence. He also wrote much incidental music, a pantomime (*The Miracle*), choral works and songs.

Huneker, James Gibbons (1860–1921), U.S. critic and writer. He studied the piano in Philadelphia, Paris, and New York, and taught in New York from 1881 until 1891, thereafter writing on music, drama and art for various newspapers. His books include *Mezzotints in Modern Music* (1899) and studies of Chopin and Liszt.

Hungarian Dances, a collection of 21 dances by Brahms, originally written for piano (four hands) and published in four volumes between 1852 and 1869. Brahms also wrote orchestral arrangements of nos 1, 3 and 10. Though he never claimed to have invented the melodies of the *Hungarian Dances*, some of them were almost certainly his own.

Engelbert Humperdinck seen by Oscar Garvens in company with his two best-known creations.

Hungarian Rhapsody, the title given by Liszt to nineteen piano pieces which he composed in Hungarian gypsy style. Several of them were later published in orchestral arrangements.

Hungarian String Quartet, an ensemble formed in 1935 with the following players: Zoltán Székely, Sándor Végh, Dénes Koromzay and Vilmos Palotai.

Hunnenschlacht (Ger., *Battle of the Huns*), symphonic poem by Liszt (after a painting by Wilhelm von Kaulbach, representing the defeat of the Huns under Attila in 451), first performed in 1857 at Weimar.

'Hunt' Quartet, nickname for Mozart's string quartet in B flat major, K 458, so called because the opening theme resembles the sound of hunting horns.

hupf auf (Ger.), literally 'hopping up' – one of the names given to the NACHTANZ.

hurdy-gurdy, a medieval stringed instrument in which the tone was produced by the friction of a wooden wheel and the pitch was determined by stopping a string with rods actuated by keys. Instructions for making such an instrument were given by Odo of Cluny in the 10th century, when it was called *organistrum*. It was still made in the 18th century, especially in France. The *lira organizzata* for which Haydn wrote five concertos and seven *Notturni* was an 18th century form of the instrument. As a street instrument it was replaced by the street organ, to which the name was transferred.

Huré, Jean (1877–1930), French organist and composer, appointed to St. Augustin, Paris in 1925. He composed three symphonies, Masses, motets and instrumental music. His books on music include *L'Esthetique de l'orgue* (1917) and *Saint-Augustin, musicien* (1924).

Hurlebusch, Konrad (1696–1765), German organist and composer. He lived in Hamburg, Vienna, Munich, Stockholm, and from 1737 in Amsterdam as organist. He composed operas, cantatas, overtures, and works for harpsichord.

Hurlstone, William Yeates (1876–1906), English composer and pianist. He studied with Stanford at the Royal College of Music in London, where he became teacher of counterpoint in 1905. His works include *Fantasie-Variations on a Swedish Air* for orchestra, much chamber music, piano pieces, songs and part-songs.

Husa, Karel (born 1921), Czech composer, pupil of Honegger and Nadia Boulanger, and now resident in the United States. He has written orchestral and chamber works, including a trio for clarinet, violin and cello entitled *Evocations of Slovakia*.

Hutchings, Arthur (born 1906), English musicologist and teacher. He has held professorships at Durham and Exeter, and has written important studies of Mozart's piano concertos and the baroque concerto. He has also written books on Schubert and Delius.

hydraulis, an organ described in writings of the 2nd century B.C. and used in the Roman circus. The wind pressure was maintained by a water compressor.

Hygons, Richard (c. 1450–c. 1508), English composer. He was a vicar-choral of Wells Cathedral from 1459, one of the organists there in 1461 and 1462, and master of the choristers from 1479 to 1508. His five-part 'Salve regina' in the Eton choirbook is printed in *Musica Britannica*, xi.

hymn, the Christian hymn is a poem sung to the praise of God. The modern hymn-book is a collection of hymns drawn from various times and places. Among the more important groups are:

(1) early Eastern hymns: one of the oldest hymns still in use is the evening hymn 'Hail, gladdening Light' (translated by John Keble), now sung to a tune by John Stainer. The greatest hymn-writer of the Syrian church was St. Ephraim (c. 307–373) whose hymns were written to counteract the doctrines of the earlier gnostic hymns of Bardesanes (died 223). Many later Eastern hymns were translated and adapted by J. M. Neale in *Hymns of the Eastern Church* (1862), and are sung to modern tunes;

(2) Latin hymns: the foundation of Western hymn-writing was laid by St. Ambrose (died 397), and the iambic metre of the few hymns still attributed to him was adopted for the many hymns sung to plainsong tunes in the cycle of Offices in the Western church. In the later middle ages the most important development in hymn-writing was the rise of the SEQUENCE. Polyphonic settings of hymns and sequences, either free or based on the plainsong tunes (e.g. Dufay's settings in *fauxbourdon*) were written by many composers from the 13th to the 16th centuries.

(3) Lutheran chorales: the earliest collections of Lutheran hymns were edited by Johann Walther in 1524. Some were set to new tunes and others to tunes adapted from plainsong or from secular songs. Their number grew rapidly, especially in the 17th century, and they were used for polyphonic treatment in a great variety of ways by German composers from Walther to Bach;

(4) English hymns: the hymns sung in the English church in the 16th and 17th centuries were metrical translations of the psalms (*see* PSALTER). The history of the modern English and American hymn began with the *Hymns and Spiritual Songs* (1707) of Isaac Watts, whose *Psalms and Hymns* was adopted as the hymn-book of the Congregationalists, and with the Methodist hymns of John Wesley, who published his *Collection of Psalms and Hymns* at Charlestown, Georgia, in 1737. In the 19th century new hymns were written by Bishop Heber, Keble, H. F. Lyte and others, and new tunes by Crotch, Elvey, Goss, Dykes, Stainer, Ouseley and others, and in America by Lowell Mason. Among the representative modern collections are *Hymns Ancient and Modern* (1861; revised, 1875; new edition, 1904; latest edition, 1950), *The English Hymnal* (1906; 2nd edition, 1933), *The Oxford Hymnbook* (1908), *Hymns of Western Europe* (1927), and *Songs of Praise* (1931).

M. FROST: *English and Scottish Psalm and Hymn Tunes, 1543–1677* (1953)

M. FROST: *Historical Companion to Hymns Ancient and Modern*, a revision of Frere's 'Historical Edition' (1962)

J. JULIAN: *Dictionary of Hymnology* (1915)

E. WELLESZ: *History of Byzantine Music and Hymnography* (1949)

Hymn of Praise (Ger., *Lobgesang*), Symphony-Cantata by Mendelssohn, composed in 1840. The setting of the text for chorus and soloists is preceded by three symphonic movements.

Hypoaeolian, Hypodorian, etc., *see* AEOLIAN MODE, DORIAN MODE, etc.

Iberia, (1) four sets of piano pieces by Albéniz, characterized by the use of the rhythms, harmonies and melodic idioms of Spanish popular music. The four sets – comprising twelve pieces – were first performed complete in 1909. Five of the pieces were later orchestrated by Arbos;

(2) the second of Debussy's three IMAGES for orchestra.

Ibert, Jacques François Antoine (1890–1962), French composer who studied at the Paris Conservatoire, won the *Prix de Rome* in 1919, and became director of the Académie de France in Rome in 1937. His witty *Divertissement* for chamber orchestra – arranged from his incidental music to *The Italian Straw Hat* – is often performed. He wrote several operas, ballets, a symphonic poem after Wilde's *The Ballad of Reading Jail*, an orchestral suite entitled *Escales (Ports of Call)*, as well as a *concertino da camera* for saxophone and eleven other instruments, film and radio music, and some melodious piano pieces including *Le petit âne blanc* (the little white donkey).

idée fixe (Fr., fixed idea), term used by Berlioz for what is usually called a motto theme, i.e. a theme which recurs (sometimes transformed) in the course of a piece of music. The most famous example of an *idée fixe* is in Berlioz's *Fantastic Symphony*, where the *idée fixe* is stated in the opening movement and dramatically metamorphosed in the four succeeding movements.

idiophone, any instrument in which a solid mass of material (often the whole instrument) vibrates to make a sound. There are four classes. Struck idiophones include such instruments as gongs, bells, chimes, the triangle, vibraphone, xylophone, and castanets. Shaken idiophones include rattles and maracas. Plucked idiophones include the jew's harp and music box; and rubbed idiophones include the glass harmonica.

Idomeneo, Rè di Creta (It., *Idomeneus, King of Crete*), opera in three acts by Mozart, to a libretto by Giovanni Battista Varesco, first performed in Munich in 1781. Idomeneo, on his journey home from the Trojan War, vows that if he is delivered safely over the stormy seas he will sacrifice to Poseidon the first living creature he meets after his arrival. When he lands he is greeted by his own son Idamante. Horror-struck, he tells him to fly with Electra (Agamemnon's daughter) to Argos. Since Electra is in love with Idamante, she readily agrees to go with him (though in fact he is secretly in love with Ilia, Priam's daughter, who is captive in Crete). The impatient Poseidon, however, sends a sea monster to remind Idomeneo of his vow. Idamante slays the monster, and in the end – after Ilia has offered to sacrifice herself in Idamante's stead – Poseidon withdraws his demand.

Idomeneo, Mozart's first major work for the stage,

is arguably the greatest *opera seria* ever written. The accompaniments, composed for the finest orchestra in Europe, are of a richness unsurpassed by Mozart's later operas, and the choral writing is equally remarkable. In the 20th century, *Idomeneo* was overshadowed for many years by Mozart's great comedies, but it has now rightly emerged from its period of neglect. The role of Idamante, originally written for castrato, is today usually sung an octave lower than intended – by a tenor. But a more satisfactory solution musically is to cast the part for female voice.

Illuminations, Les, cycle of nine songs by Britten for high voice and strings, op 18. Composed in 1939, the songs are based on poems by Rimbaud.

Images, (1) the collective title of three symphonic poems by Debussy, 1909:

(a) *Gigues*;

(b) *Iberia* (Spain), in three sections: *Par les rues et par les chemins* (In the Streets and By-ways), *Les Parfums de la nuit* (The Fragrance of the Night) and *Le Matin d'un jour de fête* (The Morning of a Festival Day);

(c) *Rondes de Printemps* (Spring Roundelays);

(2) also the title of two sets of piano pieces by Debussy (1905 and 1907).

imitation, contrapuntal device whereby a motif or phrase is presented successively by different voices. If the imitation is exact or governed by a stated rule (canon), e.g. of AUGMENTATION or DIMINUTION, it is called CANON. Imitation, as the term is generally used, is less strict and may extend over less than a complete phrase. It first came into wide use in the church style of the 16th century, and thence became the basis of the *canzona*, the *ricercar* for instruments, and the English fancy (fantasia), e.g.:

BYRD, *Fantasia a 3*

FUGUE results from the systematic organization of imitation with regard to key relationship. In the Classical and Romantic periods imitation was an occasional device, usually treated with some freedom (*see also* INVERSION, RETROGRADE MOTION).

Immortal Hour, The, opera in two acts by Rutland

Boughton, to a libretto adapted from the works of Fiona Macleod (pen name of William Sharp), first performed at Glastonbury in 1914. King Eochaidh, led by Dalua, the shadow-god, meets the fairy Etain and marries her. A year later a fairy prince, Midor, visits the court. Etain is impelled to follow him back to fairyland. Dalua touches Eochaidh, who falls dead. The work was a considerable success when first performed (Elgar admired it greatly), but its atmosphere of Celtic twilight soon caused it to fall from favour.

imperfect, (1) the INTERVALS of the third and sixth are imperfect consonances;

(2) in mensural NOTATION an imperfect note-value contains two of the next lower note-value, e.g., an imperfect breve = two semibreves. In the imperfect mode in that notation a long contains two breves; in imperfect time, shown by the sign C, a breve contains two semibreves; in imperfect prolation, shown by the absence of a dot in the circle or semicircle, a semibreve contains two minims (*see also* PERFECT).

'Imperial' Symphony, nickname for Haydn's symphony no 53 in D major, composed about 1780. It is not known how the name came about.

Impresario, L', *see* SCHAUSPIELDIREKTOR, DER

impressionism, a term used, by analogy with impressionist painting, for the musical style of Debussy, Delius, Ravel and other composers contemporaneous with the impressionist movement. This style might with more aptness be called 'symbolist', for Debussy, with whom it originated, developed his aesthetic ideas in the circle of Mallarmé, who regarded music as the symbolist art *par excellence* and his music shows rather more evidence of suggestions from the work of the symbolist poets than from that of the impressionist painters. Paul Dukas wrote: 'Verlaine, Mallarmé and Laforgue provided us with new sounds and sonorities. They cast a light on words such as had never been seen before . . . It was the writers, not the musicians, who exercised the strongest influence on Debussy'. Debussy's first important essay in the style was the *Prélude à l'après-midi d'un faune* (1892), originally planned as a prelude, interlude and finale expressive of the imagery of Mallarmé's poem.

impromptu, a title applied by early romantic composers, e.g. Schubert, Chopin, to a short piece for piano which was thought to have something of the character of an extemporization, or an air of delicacy and casualness.

Improperia (Lat.), 'reproaches'. Part of the Roman liturgy for Good Friday; sung in plainchant, and from the 16th century set also in homophonic style for choral singing. Since 1560 they have been sung in the Sistine Chapel to Palestrina's setting.

improvisation, the improvising or extemporizing of music is the art of spontaneous composition, variation or ornamentation. Its chief forms are the improvisation of one or more counterpoints on a given theme or CANTUS FIRMUS, of variations on a given theme or harmonic framework, of ornamentation which embellishes a given melody, and of a part of a movement, e.g. a CADENZA, or of a complete movement or set of movements on original or given themes. Since it is the nature of improvisation to be a creation of the moment, not recorded in notation, the style and content of improvisations of the past can only be inferred from the

equivalent forms of written composition, from descriptions, and from the few examples given from time to time for instruction and emulation.

It may be assumed that plainsong melodies which existed before the use of NEUMES were improvised by the rearrangement, ornamentation and extension of the melodic idioms of a given MODE. In the medieval period the usual form of improvisation was the addition of a part or parts to a plainsong, often by a simple rule of thumb, as in ORGANUM (parallel fifths and fourths) and in 'English descant' and FAUXBOURDON (parallel sixths with or without parallel thirds). Elementary composition was taught through improvising a part on a plainsong (*see* SIGHT). Morley's *Plaine and Easie Introduction* (1597) was a development of this method. The melodies of BASSES DANSES were used in this period in a similar fashion, being treated as 'tenors' on which one of the players improvised a running part in triple rhythm (*see* M. BUKOFZER, *Studies in Medieval and Renaissance Music*, 1950, chapter vi).

With the increased use of instruments in the 16th century this form of improvisation was further developed in the extempore playing of variations (in Spanish, *glosas*, as in Ortiz's *Tratado de glosas* of 1553; in English 'divisions', as in Simpson's *Division-Violist* of 1659) on basses which became common property (e.g. PASSAMEZZO, RUGGIERO, ROMANESCA) and on basses which were continuously repeated ('divisions on a GROUND'). At the same time the improvising of more extended polyphonic pieces became a recognised test of the musicianship of a keyboard player, and in the 17th century the ability to improvise an accompaniment on a FIGURED BASS became an essential part of a keyboard player's qualifications. When Matthias Weckmann competed for the post of organist in Hamburg in 1654 he was required to improvise on a *cantus firmus* and on its inversion, to improvise a motet on a given bass and a chorale prelude on 'An Wasserflüssen Babylon', and to accompany a violin sonata from figured bass. The fame of J. S. Bach in his lifetime rested chiefly on the powers of improvisation which he showed in the well-known instances of the variations on 'An Wasserflüssen Babylon' he improvised for Reinken and the fugue he improvised for Frederick the Great on the King's theme which became the basis of the *Musical Offering*. Handel used improvisation freely in playing his organ concertos, and Mozart and Beethoven were renowned for their improvising of cadenzas and of complete movements.

During the baroque and classical periods performers customarily embellished the composer's melody, especially in slow movements. Examples of the style in which Corelli is said to have ornamented his own music are printed in the edition of his *sonate da chiesa* by Joachim and Chrysander. The custom of inserting extempore cadenzas in operatic arias was adopted in the classical concerto, and became one of its most characteristic features. In the romantic period the art of improvisation was cultivated by some pianists (e.g. Hummel, Liszt) and organists (e.g. S. S. Wesley, Franck, Bruckner). In modern times its display in performance of classical music has become the almost exclusive preserve of French organists, notably Marcel Dupré and André Marchal, while JAZZ instrumentalists and singers make great use of improvisation.

M. Dupré: *Cours complet d'Improvisation à l'Orgue* (1937)

E. Ferand: *Die Improvisation in der Musik* (1938)

F. J. Sawyer: *Extemporization*

G. P. Wollner: *Improvisation in Music* (1963)

In Nomine (Lat.), 'in the name [of the Lord]'. A title used by English composers of the 16th and 17th centuries for an instrumental composition based on a plainsong theme. The origin of the term was an instrumental arrangement (found in the Mulliner Book, *Musica Britannica*, i, page 30) of that part of the *Benedictus* of Taverner's Mass *Gloria tibi Trinitas* (printed in *Tudor Church Music*, i, page 148) which was set to the words 'in nomine Domini'. Other composers of the time wrote new instrumental pieces on the same *cantus firmus* which begins:

Words in original plainsong   Glo-ri-a ti - bi tri-ni-tas
Words in Taverner's Benedictus   In no-mi-ne

and the name was applied to the large number of such pieces written by various composers until Purcell.

In the South, concert overture by Elgar, op 50, also known as *Alassio*, in tribute to the Italian city where he composed it in 1904.

In the Steppes of Central Asia, 'orchestral picture' by Borodin describing the gradual approach and passing of a caravan. It was composed in 1880 as accompaniment to a *tableau vivant*.

incidental music, strictly speaking, music for performance during the action of a play. Commonly used to denote a group of pieces written for a play, including overture and interludes, e.g. Beethoven's music for *Egmont* and Grieg's for *Peer Gynt*.

Incognita, opera in three acts by Wellesz, to a libretto by Elizabeth Mackenzie (after Congreve's novel). It was first performed at Oxford in 1951.

Incoronazione di Poppea, L' (It., *The Coronation of Poppaea*), opera with a prologue and three acts by Monteverdi to a libretto by Giovanni Francesco Busenello, first performed in Venice in 1642. The plot concerns the infatuation of the Roman emperor, Nero, for Poppaea, the wife of Nero's general Otho, and of Poppaea's ambition to be crowned empress. Poppaea achieves her desire by persuading Nero to banish Otho and divorce his own wife Ottavia. Monteverdi's insight into human character and passions is abundantly evident in this his last and greatest dramatic work.

incudine, (*It.*), ancudine.

Indes Galantes, Les, opera-ballet in a prologue and three entrées by Rameau, to a text by Louis Fuzelier, first performed in Paris in 1735; a further entrée was added the following year. This was Rameau's most successful opera and, with its exotic story of love in four different parts of the world, is still the most viable of all his works for the stage. Its most triumphant modern revival was at the Paris Opéra in 1952 in a production by Maurice Lehmann.

Indy, (Paul Marie Théodore) Vincent d' (1851–1931), French composer. From 1862 until 1865 he studied piano with Diémer and harmony with

L'Incoronazione de Poppea: the years following World War II saw a revival of interest in early opera, previously considered virtually unstageable in modern terms. Now their dramatic potential was realised on productions like this one by the English National Opera in 1971, with Janet Baker as Poppaea and Robert Ferguson as Nero.

Lavignac, and after serving in the Franco-Prussian war became a pupil of César Franck in 1872. Franck, Liszt and Wagner were the most important influences on his musical style, which also sometimes shows his interest in folk song and in plainsong. In 1894 he joined with Charles Bordes and Guilmant in founding the Schola Cantorum (a Paris musical academy), where he taught composition until his death. He published a *Cours de composition musicale* in two volumes, and biographies of Beethoven (1906) and César Franck (1911). His compositions include the operas *Fervaal* (Brussels, 1897), *L'Etranger* (Brussels, 1903) and *La Légende de St. Christophe* (Paris, 1920), symphonies, tone-poems – e.g. *Wallenstein*, a trilogy completed in 1882, *Istar* (1896), and *Jour d'été à la montagne* (1905) – a *Symphonie sur un chant montagnard français* for orchestra and piano (1886), chamber music, piano music, and songs.

M. Cooper: *French Music* (1951)

L. Vallas: *Vincent d'Indy*, two volumes (1946–50)

inflection, *see* PSALMODY

Ingegneri, Marc Antonio (c. 1547–92), Italian composer. From 1568 he lived in Cremona, where Monteverdi was his pupil. He composed Masses, motets, a set of Responsories for Holy Week which were until 1897 attributed to Palestrina, other church music, and madrigals (modern edition of Book i in *Istituzioni e monumenti dell' arte musicale italiana*, vi).

Inghelbrecht, Désiré-Emile (1880–1965), French conductor and composer. From 1908 he was associated with the Pasdeloup concerts as conductor, and from 1932 with the Opéra-Comique. He wrote operas and operettas, symphonic poems and other orchestral works, ballets (including *El Greco*), chamber music, and piano pieces. He was author of *The Conductor's World* (1953) and *The Composer's World* (1954).

Inglot, William (1554–1621), English composer. He was organist of Norwich Cathedral in 1608. The *Fitzwilliam Virginal Book* contains two pieces by him (nos 250–1) entitled 'A Galliard Ground' and 'The leaves bee greene'.

innig (Ger.), 'heartfelt', a term used by Beethoven and Schumann, in particular, to suggest a quietly intense manner of performance.

instrumentation, *see* ORCHESTRATION

instruments, the instruments used in Western music may for general purposes be divided into five types: (1) *Woodwind*: recorder, transverse flute, and instruments using a single or double reed, even if sometimes made of metal, e.g. oboe, clarinet, bassoon, saxophone; (2) *Brass*: trumpet, cornet, bugle, French horn, trombone, and other lip-reed instruments; (3) *Percussion*: drum, cymbal, triangle, etc.; (4) *Keyboard*: harpsichord, virginal, clavichord, pianoforte, organ, celesta; (5) *String*: viol, violin, harp, lute, guitar. For the study and classification of instruments of various times and cultures according to acoustical principles Sachs and Hornbostel devised in 1914 a system of terminology using five main categories: (1) *Idiophones*: instruments made of naturally sonorous material; (2) *Membranophones*: instruments using a stretched membrane; (3) *Aerophones*: woodwinds, brass, and instruments using a free reed; (4) *Chordophones*: instruments using strings; (5) *Electrophones*: e.g. etherophone and electronic organ.

The history of musical instruments is closely related to the history of musical styles and forms. In the 15th century instruments and voices were judiciously mixed to produce contrast of tone-quality and line. In the Renaissance families of instruments of similar qualities were developed, and were used interchangeably with voices of corresponding range. In the baroque period string instruments were made in great variety, and compositions for instruments alone or in combination with voices were the most important musical forms. In the classical period definite instruments from each type were combined to form a relatively unvarying orchestra. In the romantic period the expressive possibilities of these and additional instruments of the same types were explored by the methods subsumed under the term ORCHESTRATION.

See also ELECTRONIC INSTRUMENTS, MECHANICAL MUSICAL INSTRUMENTS

N. BESSARABOFF: *Ancient European Musical Instruments* (1940)

A. BUCHNER: *Musical Instruments through the Ages* (1956)

A. CARSE: *Musical Wind Instruments* (1939); *The Galpin Society Journal* (1948 onwards)

F. W. GALPIN: *Old English Instruments of Music* (third edition, 1932); *A Textbook of European Musical Instruments* (1937)

K. GEIRINGER: *Musical Instruments* (1943)

G. R. HAYES: *Musical Instruments and their Music, 1500–1750*, two volumes (1930)

A. J. HIPKINS: *Musical Instruments* (1921)

C. SACHS: *The History of Musical Instruments* (1940)

C. S. TERRY: *Bach's Orchestra* (1932)

R. WRIGHT: *Dictionnaire des instruments de musique* (1941)

interlude, the term is occasionally used as the title for part of a complete composition, as by Paul Dukas for his *Variations, Interlude et Finale* on a theme of Rameau (1903). It is applied in the sense of the German *Zwischenspiel* to an instrumental phrase between the lines of a song (Luis Milán, 'Durandarte', song with lute, 1536) or of a chorale (Bach, 'Gelobet seist du'). English organists were formerly in the habit of improvising interludes between the verses of a hymn. In a more general sense, an interlude is a piece of incidental music for performance during a play.

See ACT TUNE, ENTR'ACTE

interpretation, the activity of the performer in communicating the intentions of the composer, especially those that are not explicitly given by the notation. In the 19th century notation tended to become more explicit as to tempo, phrasing and dynamics, and there would appear to be much less left than formerly to the interpretative ability of the performer or conductor. There will always be, however, some parts of the composer's intention, over and above those expressed in the notation, which it must remain the responsibility of the performer to supply by dint of study and insight. Some special problems of certain periods have been made subjects of particular study, such as ornamentation in the 18th century and the rendering of continuo parts in the baroque style. There are peculiar difficulties facing the interpreter of medieval music, both because the notation is very reticent about media of performances and other practical matters, and because tradition supplies no guiding principles.

See CONDUCTING

F. T. ARNOLD: *The Art of Accompaniment from a Thorough-Bass* (1931)

R. T. DART: *The Interpretation of Music* (1954)

A. DOLMETSCH: *The Interpretation of the Music of the 17th and 18th centuries* (1946)

interrupted cadence, *see* CADENCE

intermezzo (Fr., *intermède*; Lat., *intermedium*), a play with music performed between the acts of a drama or opera. There are examples in the 16th century, and the custom became general in the 17th century, especially in Italy and France. In the first half of the 18th century the comic *intermezzi* of Neapolitan opera began to be performed as separate entertainments. The most famous is Pergolesi's *La serva padrona* which was first performed as two *intermezzi* in the composer's opera *Il Prigionier superbo* (1733). It was soon widely performed on its own and gave the impulse to the cultivation of *opera buffa*, and indirectly of the French *opéra comique*. Later the term came to stand for an instrumental interlude in the course of an opera or other dramatic work, e.g. the *intermezzo* in Mascagni's *Cavalleria Rusticana*.

interval, the distance in pitch between two notes, which is expressed in terms of the number of notes of the diatonic scale which they comprise (e.g. third, fifth, ninth), along with a qualifying word (perfect, imperfect, major, minor, augmented or diminished). The number is determined by the position of the notes on the staff, the qualifying word by the number of tones and semitones in the interval. Thus

is always a third, while

is a major third, being a distance of two tones, and

is a minor third, being a distance of a tone and a half. Intervals of an octave or less are called simple intervals, those of more than an octave compound intervals. For the purposes of the theory of harmony, compound intervals are regarded as the equivalent of the corresponding simple intervals (e.g. the tenth as the equivalent of the third), except in the cases of chords of the ninth, and the dominant eleventh and dominant thirteenth chords.

The terms 'perfect' and 'imperfect' are applied only to the octave, fifth and fourth, other intervals being major or minor. The terms 'diminished' and 'augmented' are applied to all intervals. The following table shows the intervals in normal use within and including the octave, reckoned from C, from F sharp, and from G flat. The curved bracket indicates intervals which have the same sound, i.e. enharmonic intervals. Intervals in square brackets would not normally appear in the form shown, but in the enharmonic equivalent (see next column).

In the theory of harmony, octaves, fifths, thirds and sixths, when perfect, major or minor, are counted as consonances; seconds, sevenths and all diminished and augmented intervals are counted as dissonances. An older terminology, based on the mathematical ratios of the intervals arrived at by exact divisions of the single string of the monochord, called the octave, fifth and fourth perfect consonances (having the simple ratios $1:2$, $2:3$, $3:4$) and the third and sixth imperfect consonances (having less simple ratios). In so far as the theory of harmony is based on the triad, i.e. on the superimposition of thirds (*see* CHORD), the fourth is in an anomalous position, being a perfect interval in physical structure and when used melodically, a consonance when used between the upper notes of a chord, i.e. as the inversion of a fifth, and a dissonance, i.e. requiring resolution, when used between an upper part and the bass, as in the second inversion of a triad.

See also ACOUSTICS, INVERSION

Intolleranza, 1960, opera in two acts by Luigi Nono, to a libretto by the composer, first performed at Venice in 1961. The work attacks a variety of modern social

Name	Distance in tones	Examples
Unison	0	
Augmented unison	½	
Minor second	½	
Major second	1	
Diminished third	1	
Augmented second	1½	
Minor third	1½	
Major third	2	
Diminished fourth	2	
Perfect fourth	2½	
Augmented fourth	3	
Diminished fifth	3	
Perfect fifth	3½	
Augmented fifth	4	
Minor sixth	4	
Major sixth	4½	
Diminished seventh	4½	
Augmented sixth	5	
Minor seventh	5	
Major seventh	5½	
Octave	6	

evils, including fascism, the atom bomb and racial segregation; it ends with the annihilation of the world. The first performance caused an uproar, more on account of the composer's politics (he is a declared Communist) than his musical progressiveness, which here incorporates serial and electronic techniques and cinematic effects. The U.S. première, at Boston in 1965, was attended by the composer, but only after he had received special permission to enter the country from the U.S. State Department.

intonation, (1) the true or false judgement of pitch by a performer is referred to as good or bad intonation;

(2) the opening phrase (sung by the precentor, celebrant, or other person) of a plainsong melody, such as that of the Creed:

Cre-do in u-num De-um

used by Bach in the first part of the *Credo* of the B Minor Mass.

intrada (It.; Fr., *entrée*), a term regularly used by German composers in the 17th century for the opening movement of a suite, and occasionally used later, e.g. by Mozart for the overture ('Intrade') to *Bastien und Bastienne* (K 50).

introduction, a section (usually in slow time) often

found at the start of a symphony, string quartet, sonata or overture. Famous examples of slow introductions are those which begin Brahms's first symphony, Mozart's 'Dissonance' string quartet, K 465, and Weber's *Der Freischütz* overture. Composers usually write slow introductions for both structural and dramatic reasons – the music creates a feeling of expectation, and may contain material which is developed in some way later in the work.

Introit, liturgical music at the beginning of the Mass, being the first part of the Proper of the Mass. Originally an antiphon and psalm, it now consists of an antiphon, a verse of a psalm, the *Gloria Patri* and the repeat of the antiphon.

invention, a title used by Bonporti for violin partitas (*Invenzioni a violino solo*, Bologna, 1712) and by Bach for two-part pieces in contrapuntal style for clavier. The three-part pieces in the same style he called *sinfonie*, though these, too, have come to be called 'inventions'. They were designed to help 'lovers of the clavier . . . not alone to have good *inventiones* but to develop them well.'

inversion, (1) of an interval: an interval is inverted when the lower note is sounded above the upper note, e.g.:

inversion:

The number of an interval when inverted is found by subtracting it from nine. The inversion of a fifth is a fourth, of a third a sixth. The qualifying term of a perfect interval is unchanged by inversion, e.g. the inversion of a perfect fifth is a perfect fourth. A major interval when inverted becomes minor, a diminished becomes augmented, and vice versa;

(2) of a melody: a melody is inverted when the intervals through which it proceeds are replaced by their inversions (also called contrary motion, and *per arsin et thesin*). Such an inversion may be inexact, as in Brahms's 'How lovely is they dwelling-place' from the *German Requiem*:

where the inversion follows the statement. In this particular case the second form was probably written first. Where the statement overlaps the inversion we have imitation by contrary motion, also called canon by inversion, as in four of the pieces in Bach's *Musical Offering* and in the Trio in double canon *al rovescio* (this term is used both for inversion and RETROGRADE MOTION) in Mozart's Serenade for wind instruments, K388:

This kind of canon is sometimes called 'mirror' canon;

(3) of a chord: a chord is commonly said to be inverted when its 'root' is in an upper part instead of in the bass. A triad, e.g.:

has two inversions:

A seventh chord, e.g.:

has three inversions:

The theory of inversions, although generally accepted in the teaching of harmony and convenient as a means of describing chords, is however open to the objection that it ignores the functions of chords. A triad in 'root position' is at rest. Its 'inversions' are not; and the directions in which they are likely to move are not necessarily the same as those that would be taken by the chord in 'root position'. The theory becomes even more illogical when it is extended to more complex chords, e.g. when a diminished seventh chord is analysed as the inversion of a minor ninth with the 'root' missing. If the 'root' is missing, it is clearly not part of the chord. The theory of inversions is not only illogical: it is also historically unsound, since it ignores the fact that chords other than triads in 'root position' derive for the most part from the use of passing notes and appoggiaturas.

See CHORD, FIGURED BASS, MODULATION

(4) of counterpoint: a piece of counterpoint is inverted when the melody which was originally in the bass is put in one of the upper parts. Counterpoint which is designed so that any one of its parts will make a good bass to the others is called 'invertible counterpoint'. If it is in two parts, it is in DOUBLE COUNTERPOINT, if in three parts, in TRIPLE COUNTERPOINT;

(5) of the page. For example of pieces so made as to

be playable upside down, *see* RETROGRADE MOTION.

inverted mordent, *see* MORDENT

Invitation to the Dance (Ger., *Aufforderung zum Tanz*), piano piece by Weber, op 65 (1819). It consists of a slow introduction, an extended dance and a reminiscent coda. The music is familiarly (but erroneously) known in Britain as 'Invitation to the Waltz'. Orchestrations of the piece have been made by Berlioz and Felix Weingartner.

Iolanthe or The Peer and the Peri, comic opera by Gilbert and Sullivan, first performed in London and New York in 1882.

Iphigénie en Aulide (Fr., *Iphigenia in Aulis*), opera in three acts by Gluck, to a libretto by François Louis Lebland du Roullet, first performed in Paris in 1774. The goddess Artemis, who has been angered by Agamemnon, sends winds to prevent the Greek fleet leaving for Troy. Agamemnon offers to sacrifice Iphigenia (his daughter). When she arrives unexpectedly with Clytemnestra (Agamemnon's wife), Calchas (the high priest) declares this to be a sign from the goddess. Clytemnestra claims that Achilles (Iphigenia's bridegroom-to-be) has been unfaithful, but he denies it and is about to lead her to the altar when he is told that Agamemnon is going to sacrifice her. Achilles decides to try to save her from the Greeks by force, but the goddess appears and declares herself appeased and thus Iphigenia is free. Achilles bids farewell to his bride before his departure for Troy.

Iphigénie en Aulide, inspired by Racine and Euripides, was Gluck's first work for the French stage. It was an immediate success, was much admired by Marie Antoinette and (later) by Wagner, who revised it in 1846. Apart from Gluck's opera, some thirty other works have been inspired by the story of Iphigenia in Aulis, the most famous being Cherubini's Italian opera, *Ifigenia in Aulide* (1788).

Iphigénie en Tauride (Fr., *Iphigenia in Tauris*), opera in four acts by Gluck, to a libretto by Nicolas François Guillard, first performed in Paris in 1779. The plot is a sequel to *Iphigénie en Aulide*. After Agamemnon returned from Troy he was slain by Clytemnestra, who was later murdered by her son Orestes. Orestes, pursued by the Furies, consults the oracle of Apollo and is promised safety if he delivers his sister (Iphigenia) from Tauris (where she is a priestess of the temple against her will and longs to see her brother again). Orestes, however, not knowing that his sister is at Tauris, interprets the oracle to mean that he is to carry off the statue of Diana. The Scythians capture Orestes and his friend Pylades and bring them as prisoners to the temple where Thoas (King of Scythia) orders that they should be sacrificed to Diana. Iphigenia, although she does not recognise Orestes, declares that she will save him in order that he may take a message to her sister Electra, but he threatens to kill himself if she does not save Pylades instead. When Thoas discovers that Pylades has escaped he is furious and demands that Iphigenia and Orestes shall die together on the altar. Pylades, however, returns with an armed band and stabs Thoas. Diana then tells the Scythians to give her statue to Orestes, promises him her protection and releases Iphigenia so that she may return to Greece with her brother and Pylades.

Piccinni's opera on the same subject was produced in Paris two years after Gluck's. The supporters of the two composers clashed over the performances.

Ippolitov-Ivanov, Mikhail (1859–1935), Russian composer. Pupil of Rimsky-Korsakov in St. Petersburg, he taught in the Conservatory at Tiflis from 1882, and was director of the Moscow Conservatory from 1906 until 1922. He wrote several operas (including *Ruth, Treachery,* and *The Last Barricade*) and completed Mussorgsky's *The Marriage*. Today he is remembered mainly for his picturesque orchestral pieces, particularly the *Caucasian Sketches*. He made a special study of Russian folk music, reflected in many of his works. His substantial output included choral music, *An Evening in Georgia* for harp and wind instruments, and more than a hundred songs.

Ireland, John (1879–1962) English composer, born in Cheshire. He studied under Stanford at the Royal College of Music in London, where he later became teacher of composition. Ireland destroyed all the music he wrote prior to 1908. Thereafter his output included a number of picturesque orchestral works, the most famous being *The Forgotten Rite* (1913), *Mai-Dun* (1921), *A London Overture* and *Satyricon*. His piano concerto, in a backward-looking romantic idiom, dates from 1930, and a choral work, *These Things Shall be*, from 1937. He wrote numerous piano pieces and songs.

Irmelin, opera in three acts by Delius to a libretto by the composer, first performed under Sir Thomas Beecham at Oxford in 1953, though composed sixty years earlier. The story concerns a princess who is loved by a prince disguised as a swineherd. The so-called 'Prelude' to *Irmelin*, sometimes heard in the concert hall, was written 39 years after the opera.

Isaac, Heinrich (Isaak, Hendryk) (c. 1450–1517), composer, who was probably a Netherlander from Brabant, although the Italians called him 'Arrigo tedesco' (Harry the German). He entered the service of Lorenzo de' Medici in Florence in 1480, and of the Emperor Maximilian in 1497. During the remainder of his life he lived at Innsbruck, Constance, Ferrara, and Florence. He composed secular works to German, French, Italian, and Latin texts (modern edition in *Denkmäler der Tonkunst in Osterreich*, xxviii, Jg. xiv, 1), and a number of Masses (modern edition by F. Fano, 1962, and H. Birtner, 1970, 1973) and motets. His greatest work is the *Choralis Constantinus* (posthumously published in Nuremberg, 1550–55), containing polyphonic settings of the parts of the Proper of the Mass for the whole liturgical year; a modern edition is in *Denkmäler der Tonkunst in Osterreich*, x, Jg. v (1), and xxxii, Jg. xvi (1) (Books 1 and 2) and by L. Cuyler (1950) (Book 3). One of his most well-known compositions, 'Innsbruch ich muss dich lassen', is a four-part vocal setting of a melody probably not by him. His setting was adapted in 1598 to Johann Hesse's hymn, 'O Welt, ich muss dich lassen'. A complete edition of his works by E. R. Lerner is in progress.

isorhythm, a principle of construction used by composers, most often in motets, from about 1300 to about 1450, in which the same rhythmic pattern is applied to successive divisions or to successive repetitions of a melody. In his motet 'Veni Sancte Spiritus' (*Musica Britannica*, viii, p. 88) John Dunstable (died

1453), for example, gives the same rhythm to two phrases of the hymn 'Veni Creator Spiritus':

The principle is generally, as here, applied to the tenor, which is usually a plainsong melody. The tenor is normally repeated several times in diminishing note values, governed by the system of proportions, to serve as the basis for the complete composition. The section of tenor quoted above is the last of three such statements. (For a tenor by Dunstable which is repeated in inversion and in retrograde motion, *see* RETROGRADE MOTION). As in Dunstable's motet, the parts written above the tenor may also be treated isorhythmically, with more or less strictness. For the purpose of analysis the term *talea* is used for a rhythmic pattern, *color* for a melody. In the example quoted the relation between rhythm and melody may be expressed as *color = two taleae*; if the same rhythm is applied to successive statements of the same melody (with diminishing note-values in the second and subsequent statements) then *color = talea*.

Isouard, Nicolò (1775–1818), Maltese composer, sometimes known as Nicolò di Malta. Of French descent, he was educated at a military academy in Paris, but left France during the Revolution and studied music in Naples and Palermo. His first opera, *L'avviso ai maritat*, was produced at Florence in 1794. The following year he became organist to the Order of John at Valetta, and in 1799 returned to Paris, where he wrote many operas and other vocal music, some in collaboration with other composers, e.g. Méhul, Cherubini, Boieldieu.

Israel in Egypt, oratorio by Handel, with words from the Book of Exodus, first performed in London in 1739.

Israel Philharmonic Orchestra, Israel's leading orchestra, founded by Bronislaw Huberman with refugees who had played for many famous European orchestras. Toscanini conducted its inaugural concerts, but the orchestra as a matter of policy has never had a permanent musical director. It is run as a co-operative. Its home is the Mann Auditorium in Tel Aviv, though it also performs regularly in Jerusalem and Haifa.

Israel Symphony, work by Bloch for five solo voices and orchestra, first performed in New York in 1916 and inspired by Jewish religious festivals.

Istar, symphonic variations for orchestra by d'Indy, op 42, first performed in Brussels in 1897. The work concerns the Babylonian legend of Istar's descent into limbo. The seven stations of her progress are depicted by a series of variations of diminishing complexity; only at the end is the theme itself performed, in its simplest form.

istesso tempo, l' (It.), 'In the same time', an indication to the performer that the beat is to remain the same, even though the time-signature changes. In Beethoven's piano sonata op 111, for example, the theme of the second movement is in 9/16; the second variation, in 6/16, is marked *L'istesso tempo*, and is to be played in the same three in a bar, as is the third variation, in 12/32, also so marked. Also used to refer to a previous beat, as by Beethoven in the third movement of the sonata op 110, where he indicates *L'istesso tempo di Arioso*.

Istomin, Eugene (born 1925), U.S. pianist. After studying at the Mannes School and the Curtis Institute of Music, he won the Philadelphia Youth Contest and Leventritt Award in 1943. Apart from appearing as a soloist, he is a member of the Istomin-Stern-Rose Trio, in which he is partnered by Isaac Stern and Leonard Rose in performances of piano trios.

Italiana in Algeri, L' (It., *The Italian Girl in Algiers*), comic opera in two acts by Rossini, to a libretto by Angelo Anelli, first performed in Venice in 1813. The 'Italiana' of the title is Isabella, who has been searching for her lover, Lindoro, a slave of the Mustapha, Bey of Algiers. In the end they are reunited, though not before the Bey, too, has fallen for Isabella.

L'Italiana was Rossini's first major comic opera, written in just over three weeks when he was 21.

Italian Concerto (Ger., *Concerto nach Italienischen Gusto*, concerto in the Italian style), a work in three movements for harpsichord solo by Bach, published in the second part of his *Clavierübung* (1735). It imitates the style of the contemporary Italian concerto with orchestra, reproducing on the keyboard the contrast between soloist and *tutti*.

Italian Serenade (Ger., *Italienische Serenade*), a single movement by Hugo Wolf which exists in two forms: (1) for string quartet (1887), (2) arranged for small orchestra (1892). The orchestral version was intended by the composer to be the first movement of a longer work.

Italian sixth, *see* AUGMENTED SIXTH

Italian Songbook (Ger., *Italienisches Liederbuch*), settings by Hugo Wolf (1890–6) of 46 Italian poems in a German translation by Heyse.

Italian Symphony, Mendelssohn's symphony no 4, op 90, in A major and minor. Inspired by a visit to Italy, the work had its première in London in 1833, with the composer conducting.

Italian overture, type of overture which evolved during the 17th and 18th centuries. Characterised by its three-movement layout – quick/slow/quick – it was the precursor of the classical symphony.

Ivanhoe, opera in three acts by Sullivan – his only 'serious' opera. The libretto, by Julian Sturgis, is based on Scott's novel. The first performance took place in London in 1891, but the work failed to hold its place in the repertory.

Ivan Sussanin, the originally-intended title (revived in recent years) of Glinka's opera *A Life for the Tsar*. The work, in four acts with an epilogue, has a libretto by Baron Georgy Fedorovich Rosen and was first performed at St. Petersburg in 1836. The alternative title, *A Life for the Tsar*, was chosen in honour of Nicholas I, to whom the opera was dedicated. The story is set in Russia and Poland in the winter of 1612. The Poles, on hearing that Romanov has been made Tsar, decide to advance on the Russians. They order Sussanin, a Russian peasant, to act as guide, but he leads them on a false trail and pays for this with his life.

Ivan Sussanin is the foundation-stone of the Russian nationalist school of opera. Until the time of the Revolution, it was used to open every new season in Moscow and St. Petersburg. Today it is given with an amended plot, the Tsar being replaced by the nationalist hero Minin.

Ivan the Terrible, the name given by Sergei Diaghilev in 1909 to Rimsky-Korsakov's opera *Pskovitianka* (*The Maid of Pskov*). Also the title of an opera by Bizet, to a libretto by Leroy and Trianon, about the Russian Tsar. Composed in 1865, it was subsequently withdrawn, was believed to be lost, but turned up in 1944 and was produced in Württemburg in 1946.

Ives, Charles Edward (1874–1954), U.S. composer. Born at Danbury, Connecticut, he received his basic musical training from his father, who taught him the value of 'manly' classical composers like Handel, Beethoven and Brahms, and encouraged him to 'stretch his ears' by exposing him to polytonal performances of 'Swanee River' and to contraptions that played quarter-tones. This left its mark on his son's musical personality. Although (after studying under Horatio Parker at Yale) Ives went into business in New York, he became the most advanced and adventurous U.S. composer of his day, often anticipating ideas which other composers were to hit upon years later.

Ives experimented successfully with polytonality, polyrhythms, quarter-tones, chord clusters, musical autobiography and the spatial presentation of music. His *Concord Sonata* for piano – written between 1908 and 1915 and thereafter continually revised – was dedicated to the New England transcendentalists (Emerson, Hawthorne, Thoreau and the Alcott family) who lived at Concord between 1840 and 1860. His second string quartet (1907–13) incorporates linear and rhythmic independence between the instruments and introduces a character called Rollo, a 'lillypad' academic who is unwilling to allow his viola to enjoy the freedom of the other instruments; Rollo was to make a comic reappearance later in a work by another composer, Thea Musgrave's second chamber concerto. Ives also pioneered the use of the multiple orchestra, a stock-in-trade of many living composers, but used in a fresh and almost autobiographic sense by Ives, who tried to recreate in his music the sights and sounds of his hometown, particularly the bands which, at carnival time, used to play different music simultaneously in all four corners of the town square.

'The main group in the bandstand at the centre usually played the main themes', Ives was later to write, 'while the others, from the neighbouring roofs and verandahs, played the variations, refrains and so forth. The bandmaster told of a man who, living nearer the variations, insisted that they were the real music and that it was more beautiful to hear the tune come sifting through them than the other way round. Others, walking round the square were surprised at the different and interesting effects they got as they changed positions.'

These memories, of changing perspectives, of

Charles Ives, the prophet of new American music, whose ideas were years ahead of his time. A very private man, he was neglected and misunderstood for most of his life, and only at the end did he begin to receive the recognition he deserved

traditional U.S. tunes played simultaneously (sometimes in different keys), fill Ives's music, and can be heard at their most invigorating in such pieces as *Putnam's Camp* (no 2 of the *Three Places in New England*, 1903–14) and *Washington's Birthday* (1913) and at their most complex and experimental in the great fourth symphony, which can need as many as four conductors to hold it together. But conflicting bands, while important to Ives, are not entirely what his music is about – though this method of composition is one of the bases of his style. Perhaps the essence of Ives is to be found in his short philosophical orchestral piece, *The Unanswered Question* (1908), in which the two instrumental groups represent the Real and the Transcendental, and in which the performers have to bring a degree of improvisation to the music. Needless to say, Ives's music was largely neglected and misunderstood during his lifetime, and not widely performed until after his death. Today he is recognised not only as the United States' first great composer, but as one of the pioneers of modern music in all its most progressive aspects. Apart from his orchestral works, including five symphonies, and *Central Park in the Dark* (1898–1970), he wrote two string quartets, five sonatas for violin and piano, choral and more than 200 songs.

C. IVES: *Essays Before a Sonata* (1961)

C. IVES: *Memos* (edited by J. Kirkpatrick) (1972)

W. MELLERS: *Music in a New Found Land*, chapter 2 (1964)

Ives, Simon (1600–62), English composer. He was vicar-choral of St. Paul's and organist of Christ Church, Newgate. In 1633 he collaborated with William Lawes in composing the music for Shirley's masque *The Triumph of Peace*. His surviving compositions include an elegy on the death of William Lawes, catches and rounds, and fancies and an *In nomine* for viols. Three of his songs are printed in *Musica Britannica*, xxxiii.

Jachet of Mantua (died 1559), French composer. Masses, motets, and other church music by him appeared in various publications in Italy between 1539 and 1567. A complete edition was begun in 1971 by P. Jackson and G. Nugent.

jack, *see* HARPSICHORD

Jackson, William (1730–1803), English composer. Organist of Exeter Cathedral, he was known as 'Jackson of Exeter'. He composed church music, odes and canzonets.

Jacob, Gordon Percival Spetimus (born 1895), English composer. He was a pupil of Stanford and Charles Wood at the Royal College of Music, London, where he became teacher of orchestration in 1926. As a composer his main interest was in instrumental music; he wrote music for ballets and films, numerous orchestral works, traditional in style but of expert craftsmanship including *Passacaglia on a Well-known Theme* ('Oranges and Lemons'), symphonies, suites, concertos for piano, violin, viola, oboe, bassoon and horn – also a three-handed piano concerto written for Cyril Smith and Phyllis Sellick. Among his chamber works are a serenade for wind instruments and a divertimento for wind octet. His books include *Orchestral Technique* (1931), a standard work, and *The Composer and His Art* (1956).

Jacobi, Frederick (1891–1952), U.S. composer and conductor. A pupil of Bloch and others, he went on to study the music of Pueblo Indians in Arizona and Mexico, and made use of it in some of his works. He wrote an opera, *The Prodigal Son*, orchestral music (including *Indian Dances* and a series of concertos), Jewish liturgical music, and chamber works. In 1936 he was appointed teacher of composition at the Juilliard School of Music.

Jacobus de Bononia, *see* JACOPO DA BOLOGNA

Jacobus de Leodio or **Jacques de Liège,** (c. 1260–c. 1330), Walloon author of the treatise *Speculum musicae* (c. 1330) in seven books, divided into 518 chapters, in which he shows a strong preference for the music of the 13th century over the innovations of the *Ars nova* (*see* VITRY) of the early 14th century. His treatise was long attributed to Johannes de Muris who took the opposite view. Books six and seven are printed in Coussemaker's *Scriptores*, ii, and an English translation of part of the seventh book in O. Strunk, *Source Readings in Music History* (1950). The first volume of a complete edition by R. Bragard appeared in 1955.

Jacopo da Bologna or **Jacobus de Bononia,** Italian composer and harpist of the mid-14th century. He wrote secular songs, mainly madrigals, which have been printed in two modern editions: *Polyphonic Music of the Fourteenth Century*, vi, edited by W. T. Marrocco (1967), and *Music of Fourteenth Century Italy*, edited by N. Pirrotta, iv (1963).

Jacotin or **Jacques Godebrie, Jacobus Godefridus** (died 1529), Flemish composer. He was a singer in Antwerp Cathedral from 1479 to 1528. Examples of his *chansons* are printed in H. Expert, *Les Maîtres musiciens de la Renaissance française*, v, and in F. Lesure, *Anthologie de la chanson parisienne au XVIᵉ siècle* (1953).

Jacotin or **Jacobus Picardus,** a musician at the court of Milan from 1473 to 1494. He was probably the composer of motets under this name in Petrucci's *Motetti della corona* (1519).

Jacques de Liége, *see* JACOBUS DE LEODIO

Jacquet, Elisabeth-Claude (c. 1659–1729), French composer and clavecinist. She showed early promise as a player and became a *protégée* of Mme. de Montespan. In 1687 she married the composer Marin La Guerre. Her compositions include an opera *Céphale et Procris* and other music for the stage, cantatas, harpsichord pieces, chamber sonatas, and church music.

Jadassohn, Salomon (1831–1902), German theorist and composer. He studied at the Leipzig Conservatorium and under Liszt at Weimar. In 1871 he became teacher of theoretical subjects at the Leipzig Conservatorium. Of his many works on harmony, counterpoint and instrumentation, the *Harmonielehre* (1883) was published in an English edition in 1893. He composed four symphonies and other works for orchestra, chamber music and choral music.

Jagd (Ger.), hunt (*Jagdhorn*, hunting horn; *Jagdquartett*, 'Hunt Quartet' – Haydn). Also the title of an opera, *Die Jagd*, by J. A. Hiller (1770).

Jahn, Otto (1813–69), German archaeologist, philologist, and writer on music and art. He wrote an important biography of Mozart (1856–9; English translation, 1882), which was subsequently remodelled and rewritten by Abert, and prepared material on the lives of Haydn and Beethoven which he passed on to C. F. Pohl and A. W. Thayer respectively.

Jahreszeiten, Die, *see* SEASONS

James, Philip (born 1890), U.S. composer and conductor. He studied in New York, and became professor at New York and Columbia universities. His music, which contains elements of satire, includes *Station WGZBX* for orchestra, two symphonies, overtures on French *noëls* and *Bret Harte*, *Missa Imaginum* and other choral music, chamber and instrumental works.

Janáček, Leoš (1854–1928), Czech composer. The son of a poor Moravian schoolmaster, he became a choirboy at the Augustine Monastery at Brno and subsequently studied at the Prague Organ School. After a few restless years as conductor of the Brno Philharmonic Society and as a student in Leipzig and Vienna, he founded his own organ school in Brno in 1881 and directed it until the state took it over in 1920. He was then appointed professor at the Prague Conservatory.

In 1926, two years before his death, he visited Britain. Always fascinated by the rhythms and intonations of folk song and speech, he is said to have jotted down the 'notes' voiced by a pageboy calling a room-number in his hotel. This interest in the natural sound of the human voice helped to give Janáček's operas their special character. *Jenufa* (1894–1903) was his first important work in the form, though its worth was not widely recognised until the famous Prague production of 1916. A comparatively late developer, Janáček wrote many of his greatest works in his old age. His international reputation rests mainly on his operas, which include *The Excursions of Mr Brouček* (1920), *Kátya Kabanová* (1921), *The Cunning Little Vixen* (1924), *The Makropoulos Case* (1926) and *From the House of the Dead* – the last of these a setting of Dostoyevsky's autobiographical novel which Janáček was in the process of completing at the time of his death. Each of these reveal his lyrical genius, and his ability to build a powerful score from short-breathed phrases of piercing beauty. Like Bartók, he was a naturalist as well as a composer; he wrote his woodland opera, *The Cunning Little Vixen*, while living in a cottage situated in a game reserve. His *Sinfonietta* (1926), with its fanfares of trumpets, tubas and drums, is also a work of great personality, and so are his two autobiographical string quartets, which are about his love for Kamila Stosslova, a married woman nearly forty years younger than himself. 'Wherever there is warmth of pure sentiment, sincerity, truth, and ardent love in my compositions,' he wrote to her, 'you are the source of it.' It was while searching for Kamila's eleven-year-old son, who had got lost in the forest of Hukvaldy, that Janáček caught a cold which developed into fatal pneumonia. Among his other works are a *Glagolitic Mass* for solo voices, chorus and orchestra; a symphonic poem, *Taras Bulba*; a wind sextet entitled *Mladi* (Youth); a capriccio for chamber ensemble and other chamber music; piano pieces, including the sonata subtitled '1.X.1905' (in memory of a Czech martyr), *In the Mist*, and *On an Overgrown Path*; and *The Diary of One Who Vanished* for voice and piano.

J. VOGEL: *Leoš Janáček* (1962)

Janequin, Clement (c. 1474–c. 1560), French composer, who lived in Bordeaux, Angers, and Paris. A large number of his *chansons*, mostly for four voices, were published during his lifetime by Attaingnant. He is best known for the long 'pictorial' *chansons*, such as *Le Chant des Oiseaux*, *La Guerre*, and *La Chasse*, which have been published by Expert in *Les Maîtres musiciens de la Renaissance française*, vii. Five of the shorter chansons have been reprinted in volume v of the same work, an edition of Attaingnant's *Trente et une chansons musicales* (1529). He also composed two Masses, a volume of motets, and settings of the *Proverbes de Salomon* and 82 *Psaumes de David*. A bibliography and alphabetical list of his chansons have been published by F. Lesure in *Musica Disciplina*, v (1951). A complete edition of the polyphonic *chansons* was begun by A. Tillman Merritt and F. Lesure in 1965.

Janissary music, in the 18th century, European MILITARY BANDS adopted some instruments in imitation of those used by the Janissary, the imperial guards of the Turkish sultan. Among them were the triangle, cym-

bals, bass drum, and crescent (called in Britain 'Jingling Johnny', in France *chapeau chinois*; a pole with a crescent-shaped top hung with bells and jingles). The sounds of Janissary music were also imitated in opera (e.g. in Mozart's *Die Entführung*) and in instrumental music (e.g. in the rondo of Mozart's piano sonata in A, K 331, and in the section for tenor solo and male chorus in the last movement of Beethoven's ninth symphony). The combination of bass drum, cymbals, and triangle, as in Haydn's Military Symphony, was called 'Turkish music'. Michael Haydn's 'Turkish March', dated 1795, is written for wind band, with *piatelli* (little cymbals) and *tamburo turchese* (bass drum).

Jaques-Dalcroze, Emile (1865–1950), Swiss composer and teacher. He had his musical training in Geneva and Hellerau. In 1915 he founded the Jaques-Dalcroze Institute in Geneva, where he taught and developed the principles of training through rhythm known as 'eurhythmics'. He composed five operas (including *Sancho Panza*, after Cervantes), choral works, two violin concertos, orchestral works, chamber music, piano pieces, and songs. An English version of his book *Rhythm, Music and Education* was published in 1921.

Jarnach, Phillipp (born 1892), Spanish composer, born in France; son of a Catalan sculptor and German mother. He studied in Paris, and in Berlin under Busoni, whose unfinished opera, *Doktor Faust*, he completed. He taught in Zurich and in Germany. His music includes a *Sinfonia Brevis* and other orchestral works, a fine string quintet and other chamber music, two sonatas for solo violin, and various instrumental pieces and songs.

Järnefelt, Armas (1869–1958), Finnish composer and conductor. He studied in Helsinki, Berlin, and Paris, and conducted the Royal Opera, Stockholm from 1907 until 1932; in 1910 he took Swedish nationality. Later he directed the Helsinki Orchestra and in 1940 was appointed professor at Helsinki University. His *Praeludium* and *Berceuse* for orchestra have long been popular small pieces. He also wrote choral music, piano pieces and songs. His sister married Sibelius.

jazz, a style of music marked by improvisation, inspired by the uplift of intensely rhythmic playing, and by an individual approach to instrumental and vocal tone and to rhythmic articulation. Improvisation may be total, but to give it a basis a simple framework is often adhered to. Some jazz works are entirely scored but still remain within the idiom when performed by jazz players with their particular intensity of expression. Jazz may be played solo or by any combination of players, although ensembles larger than about twenty players seldom succeed because of the problems in attaining rhythmic cohesion. Most groups consist of a rhythm section of drums, double bass or bass guitar, and piano or guitar, usually amplified, to produce a rhythmic springboard for the other instruments: usually called the horns, these are mostly wind instruments, predominantly trumpet, trombone and saxophone. The rhythm section may improvise completely or with only the sketchiest of frameworks while the horns may play short composed passages and interludes around and sometimes behind improvised sections – often solo improvisations, backed

Charlie Parker, the principal figure of the jazz revolution of 1945, when many performers believed 'swing' had played itself out and needed to be replaced by a fresher and more potent form of jazz. The result was bepop, harmonically and rhythmically more adventurous, with a neurotic quality about it, felt by many to reflect the times. Parker's influence was enormous, but he burned himself out and died young

John Coltrane, one of the major figures of the post-Parker years, who played tenor and soprano saxophone with a jagged fervour. He rose to fame as a member of the Miles Davies Quintet but later directed his own group

Dizzy Gillespie, one of the leading exponents of modern jazz, seen at full pressure playing his special elevated trumpet

The Modern Jazz Quartet, who brought a new delicacy and restraint to the performance of jazz, creating their own cool sound quality — based particularly on the timbres of piano and vibraphone

by the rhythm section. The music should be enjoyed for its rhythmic uplift and for the inventiveness and ingenuity of the improvisation.

Jazz has its origins in the poor quarters of New Orleans, where a unique fusion of Black and European cultures gave rise to the music at the turn of the century. It began in the street bands that played in the city's frequent parades as well as in bars and brothels. Musically, the light syncopation of RAGTIME gave way to a driving beat, to which the flattened notes of the BLUES added characteristic melodic lines. Form and harmony were simple, often being derived from march tunes, but the instruments – mostly military instruments left over from the Civil War – improvised collectively around them in a freewheeling counterpoint. This traditional jazz is associated with New Orleans, although it rapidly spread north. With it went the first great jazz soloist, the trumpeter Louis Armstrong. An awesome virtuoso, Armstrong created a solo style for himself in the late 1920s that contrasted strongly with the collective playing of the New Orleans bands. He also made a fundamental advance in that he based his improvised solos on the harmonic sequence of tunes rather than the melodies themselves.

Bands grew bigger as the popularity of jazz spread, and a style known as swing dominated the 1930s. Big bands made up of brass and reed sections roaring against each other over a solid beat produced a sound that echoed round the world. The clarinet player Benny Goodman created the sound, in which the routine character of the arrangements was often only compensated for by the excitement that they generated. However, some fine soloists emerged, notably the tenor saxophone player Lester Young in Count Basie's band, and one great composer – Duke Ellington. Ellington cannot be tied to any particular era of jazz because his music is so personal. The form of each of his many pieces, including his use of improvisation, follows no set dictum – each develops naturally and inevitably from beginning to end. His other great virtue was the way he wrote music for particular musicians to play; every piece was a synthesis of the individual voices of his musicians and captured a moment of time in the way that inspired improvisation does.

The mid 1940s saw a reaction against the routines of swing in a return to improvisation. The reaction was extreme – from the easy bravado of swing to great but introspective virtuosity and a consequent loss of popularity that jazz has never really recovered. The new music was called bebop, rebop or simply BOP. Its chief exponent was a soloist to rival Armstrong in quality – the alto saxophone player Charlie 'Bird' Parker – but Dizzy Gillespie (trumpeter), Art Tatum (pianist), and Miles Davis (trumpeter), also dominated the new jazz. The music was often frenetic, but made up of complex harmonies, convoluted and totally original melodic lines, and involved rhythms; it sounds breathtaking still, even today. But formally, little had changed; pieces still used repeating harmonic sequences as a basis for improvisation.

Consolidation after this near revolution marked the 1950s. A cool style centred on the west coast of the United States and a hard bop style based on New York vied in popularity among jazz enthusiasts. Then from 1960, the break with the past was really made – not by a new face but a man who emerged with Charlie Parker: the trumpeter Miles Davis. He began to base his improvisations on modes – on scales of notes rather than harmonies. The harmonic basis was simplified, leading to a greater freedom in the structure of improvisation. Two divergent schools then appeared. One continued along the path towards total freedom and eschewed all organization in performance, even that of a regular and vital pulse, hitherto a mainstay of jazz. Ornette Coleman, who principally plays the alto saxophone, is often considered the founder of this free school. The other school, spearheaded by Miles Davis, took up the propulsive rhythms and electric sounds of rock music. Formally, there are no particular rules but common to both schools is an emphasis on collective improvisation. One other remarkable feature of the late 1960s and early 1970s is the way that creative playing spread beyond the United States to Europe and Japan, as the United States lost its long domination of the music. As it progresses today, jazz approaches the avant-garde on one hand and the rock and pop world on the other. The movements of yesteryear (at least until the advent of bop) have become part of today's light music.

The origin and development of jazz by the poorer people of the United States gave it a raw vitality still present today, but the music has consequently suffered an unjustly disreputable image. It is still seldom realized that a good jazz musician has a rare talent, and one that takes as much perseverance (and considerably more creative ability) to achieve as does that of a good performer of classical music. For this reason, and also because jazz music has become intertwined with other movements in modern music, new musicians from the jazz tradition seldom like the term 'jazz' to be applied to them. As a label, jazz music is therefore a disappearing art but its qualities will live on in much new music.

jazz band, an instrumental ensemble which has no fixed constitution. There is usually a percussion section to supply a rhythmic background. This function may be shared by a plucked double bass and by a piano, which is also used as a solo instrument. The proportion of woodwind and brass varies considerably. The favoured solo instruments have tended to be clarinet, saxophone, trumpet and trombone, although the clarinet is not currently so important a jazz instrument as it once was. A jazz trio (piano, bass and percussion) and quintet (trumpet, saxophone, piano bass and percussion) are typical modern combinations, but the possibilities are wide.

Jean de Garlande, *see* GARLANDE

Jeffreys or **Jeffries, George** (died 1685), English composer. He was organist to Charles I when the king went to Oxford in 1643. After the siege of Oxford in 1646 he retired from professional musical life and became steward to Lord Hatton of Kirby, Northamptonshire, where he remained till his death. A considerable number of compositions survive in manuscript, including anthems and services, motets, incidental music, and fancies for strings. Three of his songs are printed in *Musica Britannica*, xxxiii.

P. ASTON: 'George Jeffreys', *Musical Times*, cx (1969)

Jemnitz, Sándor (1890–1963), Hungarian composer

and critic, known as Alexander Jemnitz. He studied at the Budapest Academy of Music, at Leipzig with Reger and in Berlin with Schoenberg (1921–4). Apart from a few orchestral works, his compositions consist mainly of chamber music, keyboard works and songs. He concentrated on the composition of sonatas for solo instruments without accompaniment: violin, cello, harp, double bass, trumpet, flute and viola. He also wrote a ballet, *Divertimento*, and seven *Miniatures* for orchestra.

Jenkins, John (1592–1678), English composer. He lived in the household of his patrons Sir Hamon L'Estrange, Lord North (1660–66 or 7), and Sir Philip Wodehouse of Kimberley. Anthony Wood called him 'the mirrour and wonder of his age for musick' and Roger North, whom he taught, described him as an innovator who 'superinduced a more airy sort of composition, wherein he has a fluent and happy fancy'. He was a prolific writer of instrumental music, including fancies and dances for two to six viols with organ, airs and fantasia-suites for one or more violins with bass and organ, and lyra-viol pieces. There is a smaller quantity of songs and anthems, including an Elegy on the death of William Lawes. Modern editions of his music include the consort music of four and five parts (edited by A. Ashbee in *Musica Britannica*, xxvi, and by R. Nicholson, 1971, respectively), selected fancies and airs (edited by H. J. Sleeper, 1950), selected fancies and airs for two trebles, bass and organ (edited by R. A. Warner, 1966), and two songs in *Musica Britannica*, xxxiii.

Jensen, Adolf (1837–79), German composer. He studied with Ehlert and Liszt, taught in Russia in 1856 and was in Copenhagen, where he became a friend of Gade, from 1858–60; later he taught in Königsberg and Berlin. Jensen's numerous songs show the influence of Schumann, whom he greatly admired. He also composed an opera, cantatas, part-songs, and piano pieces. His grandfather, Wilhelm Gottlieb Martin (died 1842), and his brother and pupil, Gustav (1843–95), were also composers.

Jenůfa, opera in three acts by Janáček, to a libretto by the composer, based on a story by Gabriela Preissová; the first performance was at Brno in 1904. The original Czech title was *Její Pastorkyna (Her Foster-daughter).* The work is Janáček's first major opera, a human drama of intense lyrical beauty, depicting Bohemian village life at the end of the 19th century with love and insight. Jenůfa, the heroine of the piece, is loved by two step-brothers and has an illegitimate child by one of them. Jenůfa's foster-mother, the puritanical local sextoness (Kostelnicka), is unable to face the situation and drowns the baby.

Jephtha, (1) Latin oratorio – one of the earliest examples of the form – by Carissimi with a text mainly form Judges, xi. It was composed in 1650;
(2) oratorio by Handel, to a libretto by Thomas Morell, first performed at Covent Garden, London, in 1752.

Jeppesen, Knud (born 1892), Danish musicologist and composer. He studied in Copenhagen under Carl Nielsen and later in Vienna. From 1934 he was director of the Royal Conservatory at Copenhagen and, later, professor at the university of Aarhus. His *The Style of Palestrina and the Dissonance* (1927) and *Counterpoint*

(1939) have been published in English. His compositions include an opera, *Rosaura*, after Goldoni; also a symphony, horn concerto, choral music, and songs.

jeu (Fr.), organ stop. *Jeux de fonds*, foundation stops. *Jeux d'anches*, reed stops.

jeu de clochettes, jeu de timbres (Fr.), glockenspiel.

Jeune, Claude le, *see* LE JEUNE

Jeune France, La, literally, Young France. The name of a group of four French composers – Baudrier, Jolivet, Lesur and Messiaen – who united in 1936 with the aim of championing 'sincerity, generosity and artistic good faith'. Music, they claimed, should carry a 'personal message', which was not generally the aim of other composers of the period.

Jewess, The, *see* JUIVE

Jew's harp, a simple instrument consisting of a metal frame to which a strip of metal is fixed. The frame is placed loosely between the teeth and the strip twanged. It produces several harmonics, which can be made to resonate individually in the mouth cavity. The Jew's harp originated in Asia and was a popular instrument in Europe until the last century, when it was supplanted by the mouth organ. It has no connection with Jews and the name is not a corruption of jaws harp, but derives from the Dutch *jeugdtromp*, meaning child's trumpet.

jig, *see* GIGUE

Jig Fugue, *see* GIGUE FUGUE

jingling johnny, a percussion instrument consisting of a rod surmounted by a cone beneath which a crescent is attached, the whole being adorned with bells and jingles and sometimes decorative tails of horsehair. It came to Europe from Turkey, and is also known as the Turkish crescent. It is still sometimes played in military bands.

Joachim, Amalie, *nee* Schneeweiss (1839–98), Austrian contralto. She sang under the name of Amalie Weiss until her marriage in 1863 to Joseph Joachim, from whom she separated in 1884. She first appeared on stage at Troppau in 1853 and in the 1860s was at the Hanover Opera. Later she devoted herself to concert work. She taught for a time in the United States, and subsequently at the Klindworth-Scharwenka Conservatorium, Berlin. She excelled in the interpretation of Schumann's songs.

Joachim, Joseph (1831–1907), Hungarian violinist and composer. Joachim studied in Pest, Vienna, and from 1843 with Mendelssohn and Schumann in Leipzig. He was leader under Liszt of the Ducal Orchestra at Weimar from 1849 until 1853, and became director of the new Hochschule für Musik in Berlin in 1869. In the same year he founded the quartet which became famous for its interpretation of Beethoven and Brahms. As a soloist he was most admired for his performances of Bach, Beethoven, Mendelssohn, and Brahms, who dedicated his violin concerto to him. His own compositions include a *Hungarian Concerto* and other works for violin and orchestra, overtures to *Hamlet* and *Henry IV*, and songs and cadenzas for violin concertos by Mozart, Beethoven and Brahms. He also made an orchestration of Schubert's *Grand Duo*.

Johannes Affligemensis, *see* COTTON

Johannes de Florentia, *see* GIOVANNI DA CASCIA

Johannes de Garlandia, *see* GARLANDE

Johannes de Grocheo, *see* GROCHEO

Johannes de Limburgia or **John of Limburg,** Netherlands composer of the early part of the 15th century who probably lived in Italy. The manuscript Q 15 in the Liceo Musicale in Bologna, which came from Piacenza, contains 46 sacred compositions by him.

Johannes de Muris, *see* MURIS

Johnny Strikes Up, *see* JONNY SPIELT AUF

John IV of Portugal (1604–56), King of Portugal who was trained in music and composed a Magnificat and several motets, and wrote a *Defensa de la musica moderna*, published in Lisbon in 1649. He collected a large library in Lisbon which was lost in the earthquake of 1755.

Johnson, Edward, English composer of the late 16th and early 17th centuries. One of his vocal pieces is a setting of a song performed at the entertainment for Queen Elizabeth I on her visit to Lord Hertford at Elvetham in September, 1591 (modern edition in *Musica Britannica*, xxii). He contributed a six-part madrigal 'Come, blessed byrd' to *The Triumphes of Oriana* (1601; reprinted in *The English Madrigal School*, xxxii), and instrumental ensemble music by him was printed in Füllsack and Hildebrand's *Ausserlesener Paduanen und Galliarden* (Hamburg, 1607), and Simpson's *Taffel Consort* (Hamburg, 1621).

Johnson, John (died ?1595), English lutenist and composer. His name appears among the musicians of Sir Thomas Kitson at Hengrave Hall, Suffolk, in 1572, as a participant in entertainments given by Leicester at Kenilworth Castle in 1575, and as one of the Queen's musicians from 1581 to his death. He wrote compositions for the lute, some of which have been printed in D. Lumsden, *An Anthology of English Lute Music* (1954).

His son **Robert Johnson** (c. 1583–1633) was also a composer, and was lutenist to James I and Charles I. He composed music for the stage, including two songs from *The Tempest*, and contributed two pieces to Sir William Leighton's *Teares or Lamentacions* of 1614 (modern edition by C. Hill, 1970). Pieces by him for instrumental ensemble were printed in the collections of Brade (Lübeck, 1617) and Simpson (Hamburg, 1621). The *Fitzwilliam Virginal Book* contains several dances by him (nos 39, 145–7). His lute music has been edited by A. Sundermann (1972). Two compositions for instrumental ensemble are in *Musica Britannica*, ix.

Johnson, Robert (c. 1485–c. 1560), Scottish priest and composer, said in a manuscript containing his music to have fled to England 'before the Reformation . . . for accusation of heresy'. He composed music for the Latin and English services, and secular songs. Examples of his works are in *Musica Britannica*, xv.

Jolie Fille de Perth, La, *see* FAIR MAID OF PERTH

Jolivet, André (1905–74), French composer. A pupil of Le Flem and Varese, Jolivet was associated with Messiaen, Daniel Lesur and Yves Baudrier in the group known as 'La Jeune France'. He became musical director of the Comédie-Française in 1945. His compositions include a one-act comic opera *Dolores*, two ballets and other stage music, miscellaneous orchestral works, an oratorio (*La Verité de Jeanne*), concertos for piano, trumpet, flute, harp, bassoon, and ondes martenot, chamber music, piano works, and songs.

Jomelli, Niccolò (1714–74), Italian composer. Trained

in the Neapolitan operatic tradition, he wrote his first opera *L'Errore Amorosa* for Naples in 1737, and *Ricimero* for Rome in 1740. After producing operas in Bologna, Naples, Venice and Vienna, he served the Duke of Wurttemberg at Stuttgart as *Kapellmeister* from 1753 until 1769. In the later operas written for Stuttgart, *Vologeso* (1766) and *Fetonte* (1768), he paid greater attention than did earlier Neapolitan composers to dramatic expression and to instrumentation, and increased the amount of accompanied recitative (as compared with *recitativo secco*). He anticipated Gluck in his dislike for the *da capo* aria, and Rossini in his affection for the orchestral crescendo. Writing to his sister from Naples in June, 1770, Mozart described Jomelli's style as 'beautiful, but too clever and old-fashioned for the theatre'. Besides some seventy operas, he wrote church music, including Passion music, Masses and a *Miserere*.

H. ABERT: *Niccolò Jomelli als Opernkomponist* (1908)

Jones, Robert (born c. 1577), English composer and lutenist. His six-part madrigal 'Fair Oriana, seeming to wink at folly' was included in *The Triumphes of Oriana* (1601; *The English Madrigal School*, xxxii) and he published a book of madrigals in 1607 (*The English Madrigal School*, xxxv). His lute songs, which are among the most attractive of the period, were published in five sets: *First Booke*, 1600; *Second Booke*, 1601; *Ultimum Vale, or the Third Booke*, 1605; *A Musicall Dreame, or the Fourth Booke*, 1606; *The Muses Gardin for Delights, or the fift Booke*, 1611. Modern editions are in *The English School of Lutenist Songwriters*, second series; facsimile editions were published in 1970. Three pieces by Jones were printed in Leighton's *Teares or Lamentacions* (1614; modern edition by C. Hill, 1970).

Jongen, Joseph (1873–1953), Belgian composer, teacher, organist and pianist. A student at the Liège Conservatoire, he won the Belgian Prix de Rome in 1897. Later, he was director of the Brussels Conservatoire (1925–39). He composed a ballet, *S'Arka*, a *Symphonie concertante* for organ and orchestra, a suite for viola and orchestra, a *Pièce symphonique* for piano and wind orchestra, concertos for violin, for piano and for cello, a symphony, symphonic poems and other orchestral works, chamber music, choral music, keyboard pieces and songs.

jongleur, medieval minstrel and entertainer.

See TROUBADOUR

Jongleur de Notre Dame, Le (Fr., *Our Lady's Juggler*), opera in three acts by Massenet, to a libretto by Maurice Léna; first performed in Monte Carlo in 1902. Based on a story by Anatole France, which in turn was based on a medieval miracle play, the work concerns a juggler who has nothing to offer the Virgin Mary but his own talents. His tribute is accepted, and the image of the Virgin miraculously wipes his brow. In a New York production in 1908, the title role – previously sung by a tenor – was taken by the soprano Mary Garden. Although Massenet had intended the opera to have an all-male cast (on the lines of a mystery play), he approved of Mary Garden's portrayal, and the work thereafter became closely associated with her.

Jonny spielt auf (Ger., *Johnny Strikes Up*), opera in two parts (eleven scenes) by Křenek, to a libretto by the composer; first performed in Leipzig in 1927. Johnny is a Negro jazz band musician who steals a violin from a colleague and rises to stardom. With its (then) novel use of jazz idioms, the opera caused a sensation when first performed and was soon translated into eighteen languages. Though still regarded (in textbooks) as a milestone in 20th century opera, it has failed to retain its place in the international repertory.

Joseph, opera in three acts by Méhul, to a libretto by Alexandre Duval; first performed in Paris in 1807. The work is based on the Bible story, but the action opens after Joseph has been sold to the Egyptians by his brothers. The title role is scored for a contralto. Weber composed a set of piano variations, op 28, on a theme from the opera.

Joseph and his Brethren, oratorio by Handel, to a libretto by James Miller; first performed in London in 1744.

Joshua, oratorio by Handel, to a libretto by Thomas Morell; first performed in London in 1748.

Josquin des Prés (Deprez; Lat., Jodocus Pratensis) (c.1440–1521), Flemish composer, the most celebrated of his day. He was a singer in Milan Cathedral from 1459 to 1472. From 1474 until after 1479 he was in the service of Duke Galeazzo Maria Sforza of Milan. He was a member of the Papal Chapel until 1494, and choirmaster at Cambrai from 1495 till 1499. From about 1500 he was in Paris in the service of Louis XII, and in 1503 he was in Ferrara in the chapel of Duke Hercules d'Este, on whose name he wrote the Mass *Hercules dux Ferrariae* (see SOGGETTO). Towards the end of his life he became Provost of Condé. He was called '*princeps musicorum*' by his pupil Coclico and admired by Luther for his technical mastery. He composed over thirty Masses, more than fifty motets, and some seventy chansons. In his style he developed some of the features which chiefly distinguish the music of the Renaissance from that of the later middle ages: use of imitation, the momentary division of the choir into contrasting groups, and a more expressive treatment of words. His music combines a consummate use of artifice with the widest range of expression and feeling. His complete works have been edited by A. Smijers (1925–69).

> H. OSTHOFF: *Josquin Desprez* (German text, two volumes, 1962–5)

Josten, Werner (1885–1963), U.S. composer and conductor in Germany. He studied in Munich, Geneva, and Paris, later settling in the United States. (1921), where he was appointed professor of music at Smith College, Massachusetts (1923). He composed ballets, two *concerti sacri* for strings and piano (based on Grunewald's altar-painting at Isenheim which also inspired Hindemith's *Mathis der Maler*), a symphony and other orchestral works, vocal music and chamber music. His symphonic movement entitled *Jungle* – also the name of one of his ballets – derives from Henri Rousseau's painting, *Forêt exotique*.

jota, a Spanish dance from Aragon (*jota Aragonesa*) in a moderately fast 3/4 time, often accompanied by castanets. The best known example is the tune used by Liszt in his *Spanish Rhapsody* for piano and by Glinka in his overture *Jota Aragonesa*:

Other examples can be found in Falla's *Three-cornered Hat* and in the music of Saint-Saëns and Albéniz.

Jour d'Eté à la Montagne (Fr., *Summer Day on the Mountain*), suite of three orchestral pieces by d'Indy, op 61; first performed in Paris in 1905.

Judas Maccabaeus, oratorio by Handel, to a libretto by Thomas Morell; first performed in London in 1747.

Juive, La (Fr., *The Jewess*), opera in five acts by Halévy, to a libretto by Augustin Eugène Scribe; first performed in Paris in 1835. The fate of the 'Jewess' is execution by order of the 15th century Cardinal Brogni of Constance. While being immersed in a vat of boiling water, she reveals that she is in fact the cardinal's own daughter. Pauline Viardet and Rosa Ponselle were famous exponents of the role.

Julius Caesar (in Egypt) (It., *Giulio Cesare in Egitto*), opera in three acts by Handel, to a libretto by Nicola Francesco Haym; first performed in London in 1724. Today it remains one of the most frequently performed of Handel's operas, especially in Germany. The title role was originally scored for a castrato, but is now frequently transposed down for a baritone. The plot concerns Caesar's relationship with Cleopatra.

Jullien, Gilles (c. 1650–1703), French organist and composer. He was organist at Chartres Cathedral in 1668. His *Livre d'orgue*, published in Paris in 1690, was reprinted, with an introduction by N. Dufourcq, in 1952.

Junge Lord, Der, *see* YOUNG LORD

Jungfernquartette, *see* RUSSIAN QUARTETS

Juon, Paul (1872–1940), Russian composer. A pupil of Taneyev and Arensky at the Moscow Conservatory, he later settled in Germany where he taught composition at the Berlin Hochschule. He wrote two symphonies, three violin concertos and chamber music, among other works.

Jupiter Symphony, name given to Mozart's symphony no 41 in C major, K 551, written with the two preceding symphonies in just seven weeks in 1788.

just intonation, system of tuning to the pure 'natural' scale (see TEMPERAMENT) theoretically possible in singing, or playing bowed string instruments, but not those with fixed pitches and a limited keyboard, which use EQUAL TEMPERAMENT.

K, with a number following refers to (1) the catalogue of Mozart's works compiled by Ludwig von Köchel (third edition by Alfred Einstein, 1937, reprinted with supplement, 1947); and (2) to the catalogue of Domenico Scarlatti's works compiled by Ralph Kirkpatrick.

Kabalevsky, Dmitri Borisovich (born 1904), Russian composer. He studied at Moscow Conservatoire under Myaskovsky (composition) and Skryabin (piano), and subsequently himself became a professor there. His compositions, mainly in a popular diatonic idiom, include four symphonies (no 1 in commemoration of the 15th anniversary of the Revolution; no 3 with chorus, a Requiem for Lenin; no 4 with chorus, *Shchors*, after a Red Army commander), three piano concertos, ballets, and the operas *The Master of Clamecy* (1937), after Romain Rolland's *Colas Breugnon*) and *Invincible* (1948), also piano music and songs.

G. ABRAHAM: *Eight Soviet Composers* (1943)

Kade, Otto (1819–1900), German writer on music. He was director of music to the Grand Duke of Mecklenburg-Schwerin from 1860 until 1893. His most important publications were a volume of musical examples, issued as a supplement to Ambros' *Geschichte der Musik*, and *Die altere Passionskomposition bis zum Jahre 1631* (1892).

Kadosa, Pal (born 1903), Hungarian pianist and composer, pupil of Kodály and Arnold Szekely at the Budapest Academy of Music. He taught at the Fodor School of Music, Budapest, from 1927 until 1943, and at the Budapest Academy of Music, from 1945. By his piano recitals and his activity as a composer he has done much to further the cause of contemporary music. His compositions include orchestral, choral and piano works.

Kaiserlied (Ger.), *see* EMPEROR'S HYMN

Kaiserquartett (Ger.), *see* EMPEROR QUARTET

Kajanus, Robert (1856–1933), Finnish conductor and composer. He studied at the Helsinki Conservatoire and in Leipzig, and with Svendsen in Paris. He founded the Philharmonic Society Orchestra, Helsinki, in 1882, and taught at Helsinki University from 1897. He was a close friend of Sibelius and devoted much of his life to making Finnish music better known abroad. His compositions include several orchestral and choral works.

Kalbeck, Max (1850–1921), German music critic and poet. He is best known for his four-volume biography of Brahms (1904–14).

Kalevala, *see* LEGENDS

Kalinnikov, Vassily Sergeyevich (1866–1901), Russian composer. After studying at the Philharmonic Music School, Moscow, he was assistant conductor of the Italian Opera, Moscow (1893–4). For the rest of his life consumption compelled him to abandon an active career. Of his compositions the best-known is the first symphony in G minor, which was not only successful in Russia but was performed in several European cities.

Kalischer, Alfred Christlieb Salomo Ludwig (1842–1909), German poet, critic and teacher, who devoted much of his life to the study of Beethoven. His complete edition of Beethoven's letters (English translations by J. S. Shedlock, two volumes, 1909) is a standard work.

Kalkbrenner, Friedrich Wilhelm Michael (1785–1849), German pianist and composer, son of the composer Christian Kalkbrenner. He studied at the Paris Conservatoire and lived from 1814 until 1823 in London, where he was in great demand as a teacher. He joined the firm of Pleyel, piano manufacturers, in Paris in 1824. He had a great reputation as a pianist and was admired by Chopin, who dedicated his E minor piano concerto (op 11) to him. His compositions were numerous and many of them purely ephemeral. He is known today only for his *Etudes*.

Kalliwoda, Johan Václav (1801–66), Czech violinist and composer, born Bohemia. After studying at the Prague Conservatoire, he became Kapellmeister to Prince von Fürstenberg, Donaueschingen in 1822. His numerous compositions include seven symphonies, the fifth of which was admired by Schumann, who dedicated to him his *Intermezzi* (op 4).

Kamieński, Lucjan (born 1885), Polish composer and critic who was professor at Poznan University from 1922 until 1939. His compositions, written under the name Dolega-Kamienski, include the comic opera *Damy i Huzary* (Ladies and Hussars, 1932), *Symphonia paschalis* for chorus and orchestra, and a large number of songs, to German and Polish words. He lived in Canada after 1957.

Kamieński, Maciej (1734–1821), the first Polish opera composer. His *Nedza Uszczesliwiona* (Misery Contended, Warsaw, 1778) was followed by seven others (two unperformed). He also wrote church music and a cantata for the unveiling of the monument to Sobieski.

Kaminski, Heinrich (1886–1946), German composer. After studying in Heidelberg and Berlin, he taught composition at Berlin Academy from 1930 until 1932. His compositions, serious in character and polyphonic in style, include several large-scale choral works, chamber music, organ works, and the operas *Jürg Jenatsch* (Dresden, 1929) and *Das Spiel vom König Aphelios* (Gottingen, 1950).

Kammenyi Gost, *see* STONE GUEST.

Kammer (Ger.), chamber, room.

Kammermusik (Ger.), chamber music.

Kammersymphonie (Ger.), chamber symphony.

Kammerton (Ger.), 'chamber pitch': (1) the PITCH of

orchestral instruments in the 17th and 18th century in Germany. By the early 18th century it was substantially lower (by a tone or a minor third or more) than CHORTON (choir pitch) to which the older organs were tuned. As *Chorton* varied considerably, it is impossible to define the relationship more precisely. A tuning-fork which belonged to Handel gives a pitch which is approximately a semitone flatter than the standard pitch today, and this may be taken as a general pointer to the pitch of *Kammerton* in the middle of the 18th century. The practical advantages of *Kammerton* (particularly for woodwind instruments) were such that it came to be adopted for the performance of choral works with organ and orchestra. This involved transposing down the organ parts, which was Bach's practice at Leipzig.

C. S. TERRY: *Bach's Orchestra* (1932)

(2) used exceptionally by Praetorius in his *Syntagma Musicum*, vol. ii (1719) to indicate the highest *Chorton* in general use in North Germany at the time, approximately a minor third higher than our standard pitch today. Though he calls this *Kammerton* he recognizes that it was generally known as *Chorton*. He reserves the name *Chorton* for a pitch a tone lower than this, i.e. approximately a semitone higher than our standard pitch today.

(3) in modern German=standard pitch (Fr., *diapason normal*), according to which the note is

established, by international agreement, at 440 cycles a second.

Kapellmeister (Ger.; Fr., *maître de chapelle*; It., *maestro di cappella*; Sp., *maestro di capilla*), literally 'master of the chapel', i.e. director of music to a prince, king, bishop or nobleman. The term *Kapellmeistermusik* is used contemptuously by German writers to describe music which is correct but lacking in invention.

Karajan, Herbert von (born 1908), Austrian conductor, a pupil of Franz Schalk. One of the foremost conductors of the day, he held minor posts in Ulm and Aachen before World War II. His international career began in the 1950s, when he worked with the Philharmonia Orchestra in London; in 1955 he became conductor of the Berlin Philharmonic–an appointment he has held ever since. From 1957 until 1964 he was also musical director of the Vienna State Opera, and later founded the Salzburg Easter Festival, where his Wagner performances have been particularly admired. Although sometimes blamed rather than praised for the high technical polish of his conducting, nevertheless he is an outstanding exponent of Beethoven, Brahms, Schumann, Wagner, Verdi, Bruckner and Richard Strauss.

Karel, Rudolf (1880–1945), Czech composer, a pupil of Dvořák, with whom he studied at the Prague Conservatoire. He was interned in Russia in 1914, but appointed to teaching posts at Taganrog and Rostov. He escaped from Russia after the 1917 Revolution and joined the staff of the Prague Conservatoire. War again caught up with him, however, and he died in a concentration camp. His compositions include several large-scale orchestral works, chamber music, piano works, and the operas *Ilseino Srdce* (Ilse's Heart, Prague, 1924) and *Smrt Kmotřička* (Godmother Death, Brno, 1933).

Karelia, overture, op 10, and orchestral suite, op 11, by Sibelius, composed in 1893. The suite is in three movements: 1 Intermezzo; 2 Ballade; 3 Alla Marcia. A tribute to the province of Karelia in southern Finland, the suite is one of the most popular of Sibelius' early works.

Karg-Elert, originally **Karg, Sigfrid** (1877–1933), German composer, organist and pianist. He studied at the Leipzig Conservatorium, where he was appointed teacher of piano and composition in 1919. His works include a large number of songs, chamber music and piano works, but he is best known for his organ works, often extremely elaborate and characterized by an overlush chromaticism. They include sixty-six *Choral Improvisationen*, twenty preludes and postludes on chorales, three *Sinfonische Chorale*, and other pieces of an impressionistic character. His experience as an organist was limited, and he was singularly unsuccessful as a recitalist in the United States.

Kastagnetten (Ger.), castanets.

Kastner, Jean Georges (1810–67), Alsatian composer, a pupil of Reicha at the Paris Conservatoire. His compositions include nine operas and a large amount of music of a popular character. Extremely active as a writer on music, his published works include *Traité général d'instrumentation* (1837, the first work of its kind in France), *Manuel général de musique militaire* (1848), books on harmony and counterpoint, methods for saxophone and timpani, and elementary tutors for a large number of other instruments.

Kastner, Macario Santiago (born 1908), Portuguese pianist, harpsichordist and musicologist, born in England. He studied in Amsterdam, Leipzig, Berlin and Barcelona, and became teacher of harpsichord and clavichord at Lisbon Conservatory in 1933. He has travelled widely as a recitalist and published editions of old Spanish and Portuguese keyboard music, as well as *Música Hispánica* (1936), *Contribución al estudio de la música española y portuguesa* (1941), and other historical works.

Katchen, Julius (1926–69), U.S. pianist, born in Russia. Katchen, who settled in Paris, was especially associated with the music of Brahms, whose complete piano works he recorded. With Josef Suk (violin) and Janos Starker (cello) he formed a trio; although his last years were dogged by illness, he toured widely as a soloist and chamber music performer until the end.

Katerina Ismailova, opera in four acts by Shostakovich, originally entitled *Lady Macbeth Mtsenskago Uyesda* (Lady Macbeth of Mzensk). Libretto by A. Preiss and the composer (after a novel by Nikolai Leskov). First performed, Moscow, January 22, 1934. It was condemned in *Pravda*, January 28, 1936, as a 'leftist mess instead of human music', but has now won acceptance.

Katya Kabanová, opera in three acts by Janáček, to a libretto by Vincenc Cervinka, first performed at Brno in 1921. Based on Ostrovsky's play, *The Storm*, the work is one of the great series of operas which Janáček produced towards the end of his life. The story is a domestic tragedy: Katya, unhappily married to a weakling and hated by her mother-in-law, falls in love with another man, who turns out to be as feeble as her husband; lonely and guilt-ridden, she drowns herself in the Volga.

Kaun, Hugo (1863–1932), German composer. Kaun held various academic posts in Germany and worked between 1884 and 1901 in the U.S., where he conducted male-voice choirs at Milwaukee. He wrote a number of works for male-voice choirs, and also three symphonies, a piano concerto, four string quartets, a piano quintet, two piano trios and four operas.

kazoo, *see* MIRLITON.

Keilberth, Joseph (1908–68), German conductor. He acquired experience at the Karlsruhe Opera, conducted at Dresden and Bayreuth after World War II, and ultimately became musical director of the Bavarian State Opera, Munich. There he became famous for his performance of Richard Strauss.

Keiser, Reinhard (1674–1739), German composer, son of an organist. He was a pupil at St. Thomas' School, Leipzig. He became associated with Johann Kusser in the production of operas in Brunswick and Hamburg, and succeeded him in 1695 as chief composer to the Hamburg Opera. For many years he was active in Hamburg as director and organizer of orchestral concerts, with famous soloists. He became director of music to the King of Denmark, Copenhagen in 1723; cantor of Hamburg Cathedral in 1728.

He wrote nearly 120 operas, as well as a great quantity of church music – Passions, oratorios, cantatas, motets – and other vocal and instrumental works. Keiser's private life was marked by gross self-indulgence. His music, melodious and expressive, was extremely popular. Handel was employed at the Hamburg opera under Keiser, whose jealousy was so strongly aroused by the success of the younger composer's *Almira* (Hamburg, 1705) that he set the same libretto himself in the following year.

Keller, Hermann (born 1885), German organist, editor and teacher, a pupil of Reger and Straube. He held teaching posts at Weimar and Stuttgart, and was appointed director of the Württemberg Hochschule für Musik in 1945. In addition to publishing books on organ music and organ-playing, he edited several of Bach's keyboard works, Buxtehude's organ works, Frescobaldi's *Fiori musicali,* and miscellaneous organ works by old composers.

Kelley, Edgar Stillman (1857–1944), U.S. composer and critic. He studied in Chicago and Stuttgart and taught piano and composition in Berlin and at Cincinnati Conservatory. His compositions include the comic opera *Puritania* (Boston, 1892), two symphonies (*Gulliver* and *New England*), incidental music to *Macbeth* and *Ben Hur,* chamber music, and songs.

Kellner, Johann Peter (1705–72), German organist and composer. Kellner was an admirer of Bach and Handel, whom he knew personally, and he became better known for the copies he made of Bach's works than for his own compositions. These included keyboard works, a complete set of church cantatas and an oratorio.

Kelly, Michael (1762–1826), Irish tenor and composer. He studied singing with Italian masters, and went to Naples in 1779 for further study. He made his first appearance there in 1781, subsequently visiting various Italian cities. From 1784 until 1787 he was at the Court Theatre, Vienna, where he sang Basilio and Curzio in the first performance of Mozart's *Figaro* (1786). In 1787 he returned to Britain, and from that time sang frequently in opera and concerts. He also wrote the music for more than sixty stage productions. His *Reminiscences* (two volumes, 1826) are valuable, not for the evidence they afford of his own vanity, but for their references to his contemporaries, particularly Mozart, whom he knew well and admired.

Kelway, Joseph (c. 1702–82), English organist, successively of St. Michael's, Cornhill and St. Martin's in the Fields. A pupil of Geminiani, he had a reputation as a harpsichordist and gave lessons to Queen Charlotte. He was described by Burney as 'at the head of the Scarlatti sect in England'. His elder brother, Thomas Kelway (c. 1695–1744), was organist of Chichester Cathedral in 1726, and composed anthems and services.

Kempe, Rudolf (1910–76), German conductor, born in Dresden. At one time oboist with the Leipzig Gewandhaus Orchestra, from 1949 until 1952 he was musical director of the Dresden State Opera, and from then until 1954 of the Bavarian State Opera in Munich. He was famed as an opera conductor, with a flair for the music of Richard Strauss, but he also had a solidly established reputation in the concert hall. In Germany he was conductor of the Munich Philharmonic, and in Britain he was Sir Thomas Beecham's successor with the Royal Philharmonic, an appointment from which he resigned in 1974 to become conductor of the BBC Symphony Orchestra.

Kempff, Wilhelm (born 1895), German pianist who was born in Jüterborg. Kempff took up a concert career in 1917 after twice winning the Mendelssohn Prize. From 1924 until 1929 he was head of the Hochschule für Musik in Stuttgart. He has also composed a number of works, including two operas (*King Midas* and *The Gozzi Family*), ballets, symphonies, concertos for piano and for violin, but it is as a pianist that he is internationally renowned. He is an especially sensitive interpreter of the music of Beethoven, Schubert and Schumann.

Kennedy-Fraser, Marjorie (1857–1930), Scottish singer and collector of Hebridean songs. She was the daughter of the popular singer David Kennedy, and wife of A. J. Fraser. Her publications include three volumes of *Songs of the Hebrides* (1909–21). She wrote the libretto for Bantock's opera *The Seal Woman* (Birmingham, 1924), which introduces Hebridean melodies.

Kentner, Louis (born 1905), British pianist, born in Hungary. He studied at the Budapest Academy of Music, and settled in Britain in 1935. He was soloist in the first performance of Bartók's second piano concerto in 1933, and with Menuhin gave the first performance of Walton's violin sonata in 1949. He is a distinguished exponent of the music of Liszt, and is president of the Liszt Society.

Kerle, Jacob van (1532–91), Flemish organist and composer. He held various church and court appointments in Italy, Germany and Flanders, and from 1582 was in the service of the Emperor Rudolf II in Prague. His work as cathedral organist at Augsburg (1568–75) was of particular importance. His compositions consist of polyphonic church music (Masses, motets, Magnificats, etc.) and include a setting of special prayers (*Preces speciales*) for the Council of Trent in 1562 (modern edition in *Denkmäler der Tonkunst in Bayern*, xxvi).

Kerll, Johann Caspar (1627–93), German organist and composer. He studied in Vienna and Rome, was vice-*Kapellmeister* to the Bavarian court at Munich in 1656, and *Kapellmeister* there from 1659 to 1674. Subsequently he was organist of St. Stephen's and court organist in Vienna. His compositions include several operas, church music and keyboard works. A modern edition of two of his Masses is in *Denkmäler der Tonkunst in Osterreich*, xlix, Jg. xxv (1), and a third, the *Missa superba*, has been edited by A. C. Giebler (1967). His Requiem is printed in *Denkmäler der Tonkunst in Osterreich*, lix, Jg. xxx (1), and miscellaneous vocal and instrumental works are in *Denkmäler der Tonkunst in Bayern*, ii (2). One of his organ canzonas was adapted by Handel for the chorus 'Egypt was glad when they departed' in *Israel in Egypt*.

Kertesz, István (1929–73), Hungarian conductor. Educated in Budapest and Rome, he held appointments with the London Symphony Orchestra and the Cologne Opera. He was a gifted exponent of the music of Bartók, Kodály and Dvořák, but his career was cut short when he was accidentally drowned during a conducting tour of Israel.

key (1) on the piano, harpsichord, clavichord, organ, harmonium and similar instruments one of a series of balanced levers operated by the fingers which control the mechanism for producing sound (Fr., *touche*; Ger., *Taste*; It., *tasto*); *see* KEYBOARD;

(2) on woodwind instruments a metal lever operated by the finger which opens or closes one or more soundholes (Fr., *clef*; Ger., *Klappe*; It., *chiave*). The purpose of such keys is to bring under control sound-holes which the fingers could not reach or cover unaided;

(3) a term used to indicate the precise tonality of music which uses as its basic material one of the major or minor scales and accepts certain relationships between the notes of the scale and the chords built on them (Fr., *ton, tonalité*; Ger., *Tonart*; It., *tonalità*). These relationships have not remained constant, but the acceptance of the tonic chord (the triad on the first note of the scale) as the base or centre is fundamental to the conception of key. Keys are of two kinds – *major* and *minor* – according to whether they are based on the notes of the major or minor scale. In all major keys the relationships between the notes of the scale and the chords built on them are exactly the same, e.g.:

C major:

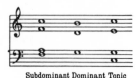

Subdominant Dominant Tonic

D major:

Subdominant Dominant Tonic

A flat major:

Subdominant Dominant Tonic

The only difference is one of pitch. Similarly with minor keys:

C minor:

Subdominant Dominant Tonic

D minor:

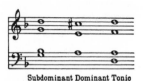

Subdominant Dominant Tonic

A flat minor:

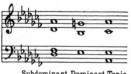

Subdominant Dominant Tonic

In spite of this identity keys appear to have associations for composers, who frequently use the same key to express a similar mood. The reasons for this have never been satisfactorily established. A contributing factor in orchestral music is undoubtedly the fact that some keys appear brighter than others because they employ the open notes of string instruments: even if the open notes are not actually played they vibrate in sympathy and so contribute resonance. On keyboard instruments, on the other hand, there can be no such difference.

The key of a piece of music is partly indicated to the performer by the KEY SIGNATURE, indicating which notes, if any, are to be consistently sharpened or flattened, unless there is any indication to the contrary, i.e. unless the sharps or flats in the key are neutralized by ACCIDENTALS. For the listener, however, the key has to be established by the harmony. In most 18th century works this is done unequivocally by a clear statement of the tonic chord and one or more of the chords most nearly associated with it (particularly the dominant), or by a simple assertion in unison or octaves of the tonic and dominant notes of the scale:

MOZART, Overture, *Die Zauberflöte*

HAYDN, *Symphony no 104*

In the latter case, however, it is not immediately clear whether the key is major or minor: the third of the tonic chord (in this case F natural) must be heard before the listener can be certain. Later composers often used deliberately ambiguous openings. In the following example:

BEETHOVEN, *Symphony no 1*

the first two chords suggest to the ear the key of F major: it is not until the end of the passage that the key is clearly heard to be C major.

Structural unity makes it desirable that a piece or movement should end in the key in which it began. To emphasize this unity Beethoven, in particular, often reiterates the tonic chord at the end of a movement. The common exceptions to this principle are: (i) a piece which begins in the minor key may end in the major key with the same tonic (e.g. C major instead of C minor), or even vice versa; (ii) a movement which is going to lead directly to another movement may end in a key other than the tonic in order to provide a satisfactory transition.

The relationship between keys varies: some are closely related, others distantly. Examples of close relationship are:

(i) major and minor keys having the same tonic, e.g. C major and C minor. The relationship is strengthened by the fact that both keys may have the same dominant chord, through the sharpening of the seventh degree of the minor scale:

C major:

C minor:

C major is said to be the *tonic major* of C minor; C minor is the *tonic minor* of C major.

(ii) major and minor keys using the same series of notes but with a different tonic, e.g. C major and A minor:

C major:

A minor:

C major is said to be the *relative major* of A minor; A minor is the *relative minor* of C major.

(iii) keys whose tonic chords have a close association, e.g. in the key of C major the chords of F major (subdominant) and G major (dominant) are closely related to the tonic chord – a relationship particularly evident in progressions like the following:

F   G   C

Hence the keys of F major and G major are closely related to the key of C major: in the former the chord of C major is the dominant chord:

F major:

Dominant Tonic

in the latter it is the subdominant:

G major:

Subdominant Tonic

Relationships between keys facilitate MODULATION from one key to another. Such modulation is normal in any but the simplest and shortest pieces. If the composer announces that he has written a prelude in G minor, he takes it for granted that listeners will not be surprised to find that he has modulated to other keys in the course of the piece. It is, in fact, quite normal to have one or more sections in such a piece which are wholly in keys different from the principal key. The establishment of different key centres for the sake of contrast is the basic principle of what is known as

SONATA FORM. In all such divergences the principal key of the piece is thought of as the home base to which the music must return at the end. Key contrast is also used between the several movements of a suite, sonata or symphony; e.g. in Brahms' second symphony in D major, the first and last movements are in this key, while the second movement is in B major and the third in G major.

keyboard (Fr., *clavier*; Ger., *Klaviatur*; It., *tastatura*), a horizontal series of keys which enable the performer, by means of intervening mechanism, to produce sound on the piano, organ, harpsichord, clavichord and similar instruments. Its origin was the series of sliders on the early medieval ORGAN which were used to admit air to the pipes. A series of levers which could be pressed down was found preferable to the labour of pushing and pulling the sliders, and these were the foundation of the modern keyboard, which dates probably from the 13th century. By the 15th century the levers, or keys, had been reduced to manageable size. The earliest keyboards were diatonic (i.e. corresponding to the white notes of the modern keyboard), but chromatic notes had certainly been introduced by the early 14th century. The fact that they were an addition to the original keyboard explains why the black notes on the modern keyboard are inserted between the white notes, each black note occupying part of the space properly belonging to the two adjacent white notes.

This arrangement, which enables a large number of notes to lie within the stretch of a normal hand, has certain inconveniences: scales require different fingering, according to the number and position of the black notes involved, and melodic progressions and chords which are comfortable in one key may be awkward if transposed to another. A further inconvenience results from the fact that the keyboard is straight: this means that the notes at either end are further away from the performer than those in the middle, and the angle of approach is different for every note on the keyboard. Attempts have been made to neutralize these inconveniences: they have been defeated, not by argument but by tradition and custom. Keyboard technique is a discipline involving many years' study, since the human hand was not designed by nature to deal with such a mechanism, and it is only natural that systems of technique should be founded on the practice of the past.

In the 14th century the keyboard was adopted for instruments with vibrating strings, whether plucked or pressed, resulting in the HARPSICHORD and CLAVICHORD. On the organ the keyboard played by the fingers is known as a manual. For the sake of greater variety and contrast in tone colour organs came to be equipped with two manuals, and this practice was also adopted for the harpsichord. On large organs the number of manuals was increased still further; at the present day four is the largest number normally found, though instruments exist with five or even seven. The piano, having no facilities for contrasts of tone colour, has remained content with a single manual; the Duplex Coupler piano, invented by Emanuel Moór (1863–1931), with an upper manual tuned an octave higher than the lower, has not been generally adopted. A pedal keyboard, to be played by the feet, was in use for the organ by the 15th century, and was later adopted for the harpsichord and, less frequently, the clavichord. A pedal keyboard has also been added to the piano, to facilitate the practice of organ music at home.

The compass of keyboard instruments, originally small, has gradually increased up to the present day. The standard keyboard of the modern piano has a range from

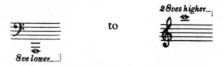

The maximum range of the organ manual keyboard is:

and of the pedal keyboard:

(the black notes indicate the upper limit on less up-to-date instruments). The smaller range of the organ manual keyboard, as compared with the piano, is due to the fact that it is automatically extended by the use of 2 foot, 4 foot and 16 foot stops, and by the pedal keyboard. In the 16th and early 17th century space was often saved by the use of the so-called SHORT OCTAVE at the lower end of the keyboard. Since sharps and flats were not normally required in this register, the black notes were used to fill up the diatonic octave.

The increasing use of chromaticism in the 16th century created problems of tuning, since the black notes had to do double duty, e.g. the note E flat had to serve also as D sharp (for an example see the fantasia on 'Ut re mi fa sol la' by John Bull, *Fitzwilliam Virginal Book*, no 51). One solution was to increase the number of keys, i.e. to have separate keys for D sharp and E flat and so on, but such instruments created fresh problems for the performer and they did not survive. The only practical solution was to retain the existing keyboard and make the tuning of all the semitones equal. This practice came into use in the 18th century and is now universal (*see* EQUAL TEMPERAMENT). It has not been affected by 20th century experiments in constructing keyboards capable of playing quartertones.

Reference has been made above to 'black' and 'white' notes, in accordance with the normal practice today. On many old instruments, however, the white notes of the modern keyboard are black, and the black notes white or ivory. Some modern manufacturers of harpsichords and clavichords have adopted this method, though without any obvious justification other than elegant workmanship.

keyboard music, a generic term for all music written for keyboard instruments, applicable particularly to music up to and including the time of Bach and Handel, much of which was not designed specifically for a particular keyboard instrument but could be played equally well on harpsichord, clavichord or organ.

key bugle (Fr., *bugle à clefs*; Ger., *Klappenhorn*; It., *cornetta a chiavi*), a bugle with holes pierced in the tube (like a woodwind instrument) and controlled by keys, patented by Joseph Halliday, 1810; also called the Kent bugle (after the Duke of Kent). In the course of the 19th century it was superseded by brass instruments with valves – the *Flügelhorn* and the cornet.

key note, the first note of the scale of a key, also known as the tonic. It gives its name to the key, e.g. the note E is the key note of the keys of E major and E minor.
See KEY (3)

key signature, sharps or flats placed at the beginning of a composition to indicate the key. Thus the key of A major employs the following scale:

Since F sharp, G sharp and C sharp are normal notes in the key, the key signature for A major is:

The same key signature is used for the relative minor of A major–F sharp minor. Since the seventh degree of the scale in a minor key is frequently sharpened, it has been suggested that the key signature of a minor key should incorporate this sharpening. If this suggestion were adopted, the key signature of F sharp minor would be:

The objections to this suggestion are (i) that a key signature should indicate a consistent sharpening or flattening, apart from incidental divergences; (ii) that in flat keys there would be illogical or confusing key signatures, e.g. the key signature of C minor would be:

(the B remaining natural) and the key signature of G minor would be:

Modulation and the temporary employment of another key do not necessarily involve a change of key signature. Any alterations that are needed can be indicated by ACCIDENTALS. An extended passage in a new key however, is best given a new key signature, to avoid

the persistent use of accidentals. The key signature of a piece is repeated at the beginning of each stave of the compostion and remains in force until a new key signature is indicated. It was formerly the practice to use the natural sign (♮) to cancel any sharp or flat that was to be omitted in the new key signature, but this is quite unnecessary (except where the new key is C major or A minor). A double bar preceding the new key signature is normally quite sufficient, e.g.:

The key signature of the major keys are:

and of the minor keys:

Keys with one or more sharps in the signature are called *sharp keys*; those with one or more flats are called *flat keys*. In the 17th and 18th centuries these terms had a different significance: a 'sharp key' was a major key, and a 'flat key' a minor key, since in a major key the third above the key note was 'sharp' (major third), while in a minor key it was 'flat' (minor third) – see FLAT.

The following pairs of keys are identical on a keyboard instrument: B major and C flat major; F sharp major and G flat major; C sharp major and D sharp major; G sharp minor and A flat minor; D sharp minor and E flat minor; A sharp minor and B flat minor. A further extension of key signatures is theoretically possible, but not practical, as this would involve the use of the double sharp (×) and the double flat ($\flat\flat$), e.g. the key of G sharp major would require the following key signature:

Beethoven's third symphony (*Eroica*) in E flat was described at the first performance as in D sharp, but this was merely a peculiarity of nomenclature, not a description of the key signature.

A sharp or flat in a key signature is assumed to govern not only the notes occurring on the same line or space but also all notes of the same name, in whichever octave they may occur. Thus the key signature of F major:

indicates that all Bs are to be flattened, not merely those directly governed by the $\flat$ in the signature. This was not always the case; e.g. in 15th and 16th century sources it is quite common to find two Bs flattened at the beginning of the line:

Key signatures originated in the practice of transposing plainsong melodies up a fourth: the result of this was that every F in the original melody became B flat in the transposed version. To save the trouble of marking every B in the melody the rounded B (*B molle* or *B rotundum*), which was the original form of the $\flat$, was placed at the beginning of the stave to remind the performer to sing B flat and not B natural (*see* FLAT, NATURAL). This labour-saving device was adopted in the secular songs of the troubadours and trouvères and in polyphonic music. In the latter it was reserved for the parts in which it was essential. From the 13th to the early 16th century it is quite common to find one or more of the lower parts with a flat in the signature and one or more of the upper parts without any flat. This represents a fundamental difference of tonality between the parts, which may be weakened, however, by the use of the flat as an accidental in the upper part (or parts), and of the natural in the lower. Key signatures with two flats (B flat and E flat) appear in the 15th century, but the use of more than two flats, and of sharps, in key signatures did not become general

until the 17th century. This might suggest a rather limited range of tonalities in 16th century music, but accidentals were by this time freely employed (particularly in secular music) and transposition of the written notation could be implied by the clefs used for the voice-parts (*see* CHIAVETTE). The tradition of limited key signatures was so strong that as late as the early 18th century it was normal to omit one of the flats in the signature of flat minor keys, e.g. C minor had the signature:

instead of

Khachaturian, Aram Ilich (1903–78), Russian composer, born in Armenia. He was a pupil of Gnessin and Myaskovsky. His compositions, which show the influence of Armenian folk music, include symphonies, piano concerto, violin concerto, cello concerto, ballets (*Gayaneh* and *Spartacus*), chamber music, *Song of Stalin* for chorus and orchestra, piano pieces and stage music. His music is written in the direct and comprehensible style favoured by the Soviet authorities.

Khovanshchina, opera in five acts by Mussorgsky to a libretto by the composer and Vladimir Vassilyevich Stassov, first performed in St. Petersburg in 1886. The complex story tells of the fortunes of the Khovansky family in 17th century Russia. Mussorgsky left the work unfinished; Rimsky-Korsakov completed and orchestrated it for the 1886 première; a more recent, and stylistically more authentic, version, has been prepared by Shostakovich.

Khrennikov, Tikhon Nikolayevich (born 1913), Russian composer. A pupil of Shebalin at the Moscow Conservatory in 1932. His works include an opera, *The Brothers*, incidental music for *Much Ado About Nothing*, two symphonies, two piano concertos, solo piano music and many songs – some of them to words by Robert Burns. Outside the Soviet Union, Khrennikov gained notoriety when, as secretary general of the Union of Soviet Composers, he denounced Prokofiev and other composers in 1948 for 'formalism'.

Kidson, Frank (1855–1926), English antiquarian, who collected and published a large number of English folk songs and dances. His other publications include *British Music Publishers, Printers and Engravers* (1900) and *The Beggar's Opera, its Predecessors and Successors* (1922).

Kielflügel (Ger.), harpsichord.

Kiene, Marie, *see* BIGOT DE MOROGUES

Kienzl, Wilhelm (1857–1941), Austrian composer. He studied in Graz, Prague and Munich. A strong admirer of Wagner, Kienzl devoted himself extensively to the composition of operas, of which he wrote nine, the most important being *Der Evangelimann* (The Preacher; Berlin, 1895), which had an enormous success. He also wrote a large number of songs, chamber music and piano works, and published volumes of collected criticisms and essays, an autobiography entitled *Meine Lebenswanderung* (1926) and studies of Wagner and Richter.

Kiesewetter, Raphael Georg (1773–1850), German civil servant and music historian. His publications include works on Greek music, Arab music, Guido d'Arezzo and Palestrina.

Kilpinen, Yrjö (1892–1959), Finnish composer. He studied at the Helsinki Conservatory, and in Vienna and Berlin. Kilpinen wrote chamber music and orchestral works, but is best known for his very imaginative songs in a romantic idiom, of which there are more than 500. He received a government grant, as Sibelius did, which enabled him to devote himself wholly to composition.

Kindermann, Johann Erasmus (1616–55), German organist and composer. After spending two years in Venice he returned to Nuremberg as organist, first at the Marienkirche, 1636, and then at St. Agidien, 1640. His published works include sacred and secular songs for one or more voices with instrumental accompaniment, suites for wind instruments, *canzoni* for strings, and preludes, fugues and Magnificats for organ. Modern editions of selected works are in *Denkmäler der Tonkunst in Bayern*, xiii and xxi–xxiv.

Kinderscenen (Ger., Scenes of Childhood), suite of thirteen easy pieces for piano solo by Schumann, op 15 (1838). Each piece has a descriptive title. According to the composer, 'The superscriptions came into existence afterwards and are, indeed, nothing more than delicate directions for the rendering and understanding of the music.'

Kindertotenlieder (Ger., Songs on the death of children), cycle of five songs with orchestral accompaniment by Mahler. Words by Friedrich Rückert.

King Arthur, 'dramatick opera' with a prologue, five acts and an epilogue by Purcell, to a libretto by John Dryden, first performed in London in 1691. The story takes place during the contest between the Britons (under King Arthur) and the Saxon invaders (under Oswald) who had settled in Kent. Arthur, who is betrothed to Emmeline (the blind daughter of the Duke of Cornwall), bids her farewell before making an attack on the enemy. The Saxons employ Osmond (a magician) and his attendant sprites to lead the Britons astray, but Philidel (one of the attendants) is persuaded by Merlin (a British magician) to help the Britons. Emmeline is captured by Oswald but Merlin sends Philidel to her with a magic liquid to restore her sight. Later Osmond imprisons Oswald and makes love to Emmeline, but when his magic spells fail to overcome the approaching Arthur (who is helped to resist him by Philidel), he releases Oswald. Oswald then challenges Arthur but is defeated by him and promises to return to his native land. Emmeline is rescued, Osmond is imprisoned, and Merlin predicts the future greatness of Britain.

King Christian II, incidental music by Sibelius (1898) for Adolf Paul's play about the 16th century Danish king.

King Stephen (Ger., *König Stephan*), incidental music by Beethoven, op 117, for A. von Kotzebue's play about Stephen I of Hungary. The play was written for the opening of the German Theatre at Pest (now part of Budapest) and was performed there in 1812.

It served as the first half of a double-bill of which the second half was *The Ruins of Athens* (for which Beethoven also wrote incidental music). Beethoven referred affectionately to these works as 'my little operas'.

Kingdom, The, oratorio by Elgar, op 51, dealing with the activities of the apostles after Christ's ascension. The text is from the Bible and the first performance was at the Birmingham Festival in 1906. The work forms the second part of a trilogy which began with *The Apostles* but was never completed.

Kinkeldey, Otto (1878–1966), U.S. musicologist. He studied at the College of the City of New York, Columbia University and Berlin University. After holding teaching appointments in New York and Breslau, he became chief of the Music Division, New York Public Library in 1915 – an appointment he held in alternation with a professorship at Cornell University. His most important publication is *Orgel und Klavier in der Musik des XVI Jahrhunderts* (1910), which is still a standard work. He was first president of the American Musicological Society (1934–6).

Kinsky, Georg Ludwig (1882–1951), German musicologist, self-taught musician. He was curator from 1909 until 1927 of the Heyer Museum, Cologne; the collection included instruments and musical autographs, of which he published a catalogue. From 1921 until 1932 he taught at Cologne University. His most widely known, and perhaps his most valuable publication is *Geschichte der Musik in Bildern* (1929; English edition, *History of Music in Pictures*, 1930), containing illustrations of instruments, title pages, manuscripts, printed music, musical activities of every kind, and portraits, from the earliest times down to the present day. His other works include *Die Originalausgaben der Werke J. S. Bach* (1937), and *Die Erstausgaben und Handschriften der Sinfonien* on Beethoven's works.

Kipnis, Alexander (born 1896), Russian born bassbaritone. He studied in Warsaw and Berlin and sang widely in Europe and the U.S., before becoming an American citizen in 1934. His interpretations of Wolf's songs became familiar from the gramophone records made for the Hugo Wolf Society. He was also a noted interpreter of Russian song.

Kirbye, George (c. 1565–1634), English composer of a volume of madrigals (1597; modern edition in *The English Madrigal School*, xxiv) which show a sensitive imagination, particularly in the treatment of dissonance. He also contributed to East's *The Whole Booke of Psalmes* (1592) and *The Triumphes of Oriana* (1601). Other works survive incomplete in manuscript.

Kirchenkantate (Ger.), church CANTATA.

Kircher, Athanasius (1602–80), Jesuit professor of natural science at Würzburg University, who left Germany in 1633 on account of the Thirty Years War and settled first in Avignon and finally in Rome in 1637. His principal work on music is *Musurgia universalis sive ars magna consoni et dissoni* (two vols., 1650; reprinted, 1969), which is often interesting but thoroughly unreliable, particularly the section on Greek music.

Kirchgessner, Marianne (1770–1809), blind German musician, who made her reputation as a performer on the glass harmonica. Mozart wrote for her a quintet for harmonica, flute, viola, oboe and cello, K617, and an Adagio for harmonica solo, K356 (1791).

Kirchner, Theodor (1823–1903), German composer, mainly of works for piano solo or piano duet. Kirchner studied in Leipzig and Dresden. In 1843 he went to Switzerland to become an organist at Winterthur. From 1862 until 1872 he conducted in Zürich, and later taught in Würzburg and Dresden.

Kirkman, a firm of harpsichord and piano manufacturers in London, founded by Jacob Kirkman (originally Kirchmann), a German who settled there some time before 1739. They began to make pianos c. 1775. The firm was amalgamated with COLLARD in 1896.

Kirkpatrick, Ralph (born 1911), U.S. harpsichordist and musicologist. He studied at Harvard and in Paris. In addition to his work as a recitalist he has devoted a good deal of research to the problems of performance and has edited Bach's Goldberg Variations.

Kirnberger, Johann Philipp (1721–83), German composer, violinist and teacher. A pupil of Bach in Leipzig from 1739 until 1741. He became violinist in the service of Frederick the Great in 1751 and *Kapellmeister* to Princess Amalie in 1758. He composed a large number of instrumental and vocal works (keyboard pieces, trio sonatas, orchestral symphonies and suites, motets, songs, etc.) and published a number of technical works, including *Die Kunst des reinen Satzes* (two volumes, 1771) which was several times reprinted. His manuscript copy of Bach's *St. Matthew Passion* preserves the earliest form of that work.

Kistler, Cyrill (1848–1907), German opera composer. Originally a schoolmaster, he entered the Munich Conservatorium, where he was a pupil of Rheinberger, in 1876. He taught at the Sonderhausen Conservatorium from 1883 until 1885, and subsequently at Kissingen. His first opera, strongly influenced by Wagner, was *Kunhild* (Sonderhausen, 1884). His later works include the comic opera *Eulenspiegel* (Würzburg, 1889), whose hero was the same as that of Strauss's *Till Eulenspiegel*. He also wrote technical works, critical essays and a dictionary of composers, which reached a third edition.

Kistner, a Leipzig firm of music publishers, originally founded by Heinrich Albert Probst in 1823 and taken over by Karl Friedrich Kistner (1797–1844) in 1831. The business was bought by Carl and Richard Linnemann in 1919, and amalgamated with the firm of Siegel in 1923, under the title Fr. Kistner and C. F. W. Siegel.

kit (Fr., *pochette*; Ger., *Taschengeige*), a miniature violin, formerly used by dancing-masters and carried in their pockets (hence the French and German names). It was made either in the ordinary shape of a violin (from the late 17th century), or long and narrow like a REBEC (the earlier form). It is known to have been in use in the early 16th century and may very well be considerably older.

Kitezh, opera in four acts by Rimsky-Korsakov to a libretto by Vladimir Ivanovich Bielsky, first performed at St. Petersburg in 1907. The translation of the complete title is: *The Legend of the Invisible City of Kitezh and the Maiden Fevronia*. Nicknamed 'The Russian Parsifal', the opera tells (in mystical and symbolic terms) how Fevronia escapes from the Tartars and is led to the safety of Kitezh by the spirit of her husband, Prince Vsevolod.

kithara, the LYRE of ancient Greece. The *kithara*

Kithara carried by the god Dionysos as he escorts Ariadne from Naxos. A red-figure cup painting of the early 4th century B.C.

originated in Mesopotamia, but was adopted by the Greeks to such an extent that it became their national instrument. In pre-classical times, bards accompanied themselves on the *kithara* but it later became more highly regarded as a solo instrument. The *kithara* had a square box resonator and up to eleven gut strings. It was held upright and supported against the body. The Romans took over the *kithara* from the Greeks, and it may have descended into Europe. The name certainly was influential; from *kithara* are derived both the name of the guitar and the zither, and possibly the sitar.

Kitson, Charles Herbert (1874–1944), English organist, teacher and theorist. Educated at Cambridge, he was organist of Christ Church Cathedral, Dublin, from 1913 until 1920, professor at the National University of Ireland from 1916 until 1920, and at Trinity College, Dublin, from 1920 until 1935. He also taught at the Royal College of Music, London. He was author of several books on counterpoint, harmony, fugue and allied subjects.

Kittel, Bruno (1870–1948), German conductor. He studied in Berlin, where he held various conducting and academic appointments. He founded (1902) and conducted the Bruno Kittel Choir.

Kittel, Johann Christian (1732–1809), German organist and composer. A pupil of Bach in Leipzig, and an exact contemporary of Haydn. He held organ appointments at Langensalze and Erfurt, and had a considerable reputation as a performer and teacher. His published works include preludes for organ, piano sonatas, an instruction book *Der angehende praktische Organist* (three volumes, 1801–8), and *Neues Choralbuch* for Schleswig-Holstein (1803).

Kittl, Emmy, see DESTINN.

Kittl, Johann Friedrich (1806–68), Czech composer. A pupil of Tomašek, in 1843 he became director of the Prague Conservatoire. Of his three operas the most successful was *Bianca und Giuseppe oder die Franzosen vor Nizza* (Prague, 1848). The libretto (after Heinrich König's novel *Die hohe Braut*) is by Wagner, who had originally written it in the form of a sketch which he submitted in a French translation (unsuccessfully) to the librettist Augustin Eugene Scribe in Paris. Later he wrote the complete libretto in verse and offered it to Reissiger, who declined it. It was then offered to Kittl.

Kjellstrom, Sven (1875–1951), Swedish violinist. After studying in Stockholm and Paris, he joined the Colonne Orchestra, Paris, in 1900, and founded the Kjellstrom Quartet in 1911. From 1929 until 1940 he was director of the Stockholm Conservatoire. Kjellstrom toured widely as a soloist, often with his daughter, Ingrid, a noted pianist and harpsichordist.

Kjerulf, Halfdan (1815–68), Norwegian composer. He took law at Christiania University, then turned to music in 1840, and studied in Christiania and in Leipzig under E. F. E. Richter. Apart from founding a series of subscription concerts in Christiania, he took little part in public activities. His compositions include songs and part-songs, which have enjoyed considerable popularity in Norway, and piano pieces.

Klafsky, Katharina (1855–96), Hungarian operatic soprano. A pupil of Mathilde Marchesi, she began her career as a chorus singer in Vienna and Salzburg, but began to make her name as a soloist in Leipzig, from 1876 onwards. She soon established herself as an outstanding Wagnerian singer, and was principal soprano at the Hamburg Opera from 1886 until 1895. She also appeared in St. Petersburg, London and the United States, where she was principal soprano of the Damrosch company from 1895 until her death.

Klang (Ger.), sound, sonority.

Klangfarbenmelodie (Ger.), term coined by Schoenberg in his *Harmonielehre* (1911) to describe a form of composition in which varying tone colours are applied to a single level of pitch, or to different pitches. The procedure had been used by Schoenberg in his *Five Orchestral Pieces* (1909), and was also to become a feature of the music of Webern, Berg and other Schoenberg disciples who aimed to establish timbre as a structural element in their work. Famous examples of *Klangfarbenmelodie* can be found in Berg's *Wozzeck* and (using notes of different pitch) in Webern's *Five Pieces for Orchestra*, op 10 (1913):

Klavier (Ger., also *Clavier*), (1) keyboard;

(2) keyboard instruments with strings, i.e. clavichord, harpsichord or piano (see CLAVIER, HAMMERKLAVIER);

(3) specifically, in modern German, the piano.

Klavierauszug (Ger.), piano reduction, piano arrangement.

Kleber, Leonhard (c. 1490–1556), German organist. He studied in Heidelberg, and was successively organist at Horb, Esslingen and Pforzheim. He was the compiler of an early 16th century manuscript collection of organ music in TABLATURE (for example *see* H. J. Moser and F. Heitmann, *Frühmeister der deutschen Orgelkunst*).

Kleiber, Erich (1890–1956), Austrian conductor. He studied at Prague Conservatoire and University, and

held appointments in Darmstadt, Dusseldorf and other German cities before becoming director of the Berlin State Opera in 1923. With that company, he gave the world première of Berg's *Wozzeck* in 1925 (heavily censured by the German critics) and of Milhaud's *Christophe Colombe* in 1930. Five years later he was expelled from Germany by the Nazis, and in 1938 became a citizen of Argentina. During this period he conducted frequently in the United States, but after World War II he returned to Europe, working in Germany, Austria and London, where he conducted the British première of *Wozzeck* at Covent Garden in 1952. He was a fine, unmannered conductor of the orchestral classics, and an outstanding exponent of the operas of Mozart and Strauss. A biography of him was written by John Russell in 1958. His son, Carlos Kleiber, has established himself as one of the foremost conductors of the present day.

Kleine Nachtmusik, Eine (Ger., A Little Serenade), work for string orchestra, or string quintet, in four movements by Mozart, K 525 (1787). According to Mozart's own catalogue there were originally five movements: Allegro, Minuet and Trio, Romance, Minuet and Trio, Finale, but the first minuet and trio is now lost. The Mozart scholar, Alfred Einstein, has suggested that the minuet of the piano sonata, K Anh 136, was originally written for this serenade.

Kleine Orgelmesse (Ger., Little Organ Mass), the name given to Haydn's *Missa brevis Sti. Joannis de Deo* in B, composed c. 1775 (no 5 in the complete edition, no 8 in Novello's edition). So called on account of the part for organ *obbligato*. The adjective distinguishes it from the GROSSE ORGELMESSE.

Kleinmichel, Richard (1846–1901), German pianist and composer. After studying at the Leipzig Conservatorium, he worked as an opera conductor in Hamburg, Danzig and Magdeburg. He composed two operas, two symphonies, chamber music and piano works, but is chiefly remembered for his simplified piano scores of Wagner's operas.

Klemperer, Otto (1885–1973), German conductor and composer. After studying in Frankfurt and Berlin, where he was a composition pupil of Pfitzner, he became conductor of the German Opera in Prague in 1907. Subsequently he held posts in Hamburg, Strasbourg, Cologne and Wiesbaden, before becoming musical director of the Kroll Opera, Berlin, in 1927. There he specialised in presenting important modern works by Janáček, Stravinsky, Schoenberg, Hindemith and other composers, until the Kroll was forced to close in 1931. In that year he joined the Berlin State Opera, but in 1933 was compelled by the Nazis to leave Germany. From then until 1939 he conducted the Los Angeles Philharmonic, and he remained in the U.S. during World War II.

After the war, and after suffering serious illness which left him permanently crippled, he entered a new phase in his career when he returned to Europe and devoted his attention almost exclusively to the classics. During this remarkable Indian summer, he became permanent conductor of the Philharmonia (subsequently New Philharmonia) Orchestra in London, establishing himself as an unsurpassed interpreter of Beethoven and Brahms. His special quality as a conductor was his magisterial sense of structure, which served him in good stead in his performances of Mahler and Bruckner. At Covent Garden, his performances of *Fidelio* were especially admired. He wrote a tantalizingly brief book of reminiscences, *Minor Recollections*, in 1964. *Conversations with Klemperer*, a collection of interviews with Peter Heyworth of the London Sunday newspaper the *Observer*, usefully amplified the earlier book.

Klenau, Paul von (1883–1946), Danish composer and conductor. He studied at the Berlin Hochschule, and in Munich and Stuttgart. After establishing himself as an opera conductor at Freiburg and Stuttgart, he founded the Philharmonic concerts, Copenhagen, in 1920 and became conductor of the Wiener Singakademie and Konzerthausgesellschaft, Vienna, in 1926. As a conductor he devoted particular attention to contemporary composers, and frequently performed works by Delius. His own works included seven operas, the most famous being *Gudrun auf Island* (1924), six symphonies and other orchestral pieces, a ballet, vocal music, chamber music, piano pieces and songs.

Klengel, August Alexander (1783–1852), German composer, a pupil of Clementi with whom he visited Russia. In 1816 he was appointed court organist in Dresden. His compositions include two piano concertos and several works for piano. He is chiefly remembered, however, for his *Canons et Fugues dans tous les tons majeurs et mineurs*, published posthumously in 1854 by Moritz Hauptmann.

Klengel, Julius (1859–1933), German cellist and composer. He was principal cello of the Gewandhaus Orchestra, Leipzig, from 1881 until 1924, and was a teacher at the Leipzig Conservatorium. Among his pupils were Guilhermina Suggia and Emanuel Feuermann. His compositions include three cello concertos, and a double concerto for violin and cello. His brother, **Paul Klengel** (1854–1935), was a conductor and composer. He studied at the Leipzig Conservatorium and held conducting posts in Leipzig, Stuttgart, New York and other cities. His compositions include songs and chamber music.

Klindworth, Karl (1830–1916), German pianist and conductor, a pupil of Liszt. He lived in London from 1854 until 1868, as pianist and conductor of orchestral concerts. From then until 1884 he taught at the Moscow Conservatory. Subsequently he settled in Berlin, where he conducted the Philharmonic Concerts and founded a music school. He made piano scores of Wagner's *Ring* and edited the complete piano works of Chopin. His adopted daughter Winifred married Siegfried Wagner.

Klose, Friedrich (1862–1942), German composer. He studied in Karlsruhe and Geneva, and in Vienna with Bruckner. He taught in Basle and Munich. His compositions, showing the influence of Bruckner, include a Mass in D minor, a 'dramatic symphony' *Ilsebill*, choral music, chamber music and songs. He wrote a book of reminiscences, *Meine Lehrjahre bei Bruckner* (1927).

Klose, Hyacinthe Eleonore (1808–80), French clarinettist, born in Corfu. He taught at the Paris Conservatoire from 1839 until 1868, and successfully adapted to the clarinet the Boehm system originally designed for the flute. He wrote a number of works for his instrument, as well as instruction books for clarinet and for saxophone.

Klotz, a family of violin makers active in Mittenwald, in Bavaria, in the 17th and 18th centuries.

Klughardt, August Friedrich Martin (1847–1902), German conductor and composer. He became director of music to the court at Weimar in 1869; at Neustrelitz in 1873; and at Dessau in 1882. His compositions include four operas, three oratorios – *Die Grablegung Christi, Die Zerstörung Jerusalem* and *Judith* – and other choral works, four symphonies, six overtures, concertos for oboe, violin and cello, and chamber music.

Knab, Armin (1881–1951), German composer. For many years he combined composition with a legal career, until he became teacher of composition at the Berlin church music Hochscule in 1934. His enthusiasm for Nazism found expression in a number of unaccompanied choral works. More important are his solo songs, which combine simplicity of structure with extreme sensibility.

Knaben Wunderhorn, Des (Ger., Youth's Magic Horn), a collection of German folk poems, several of which were set by Mahler as solo songs, nine with piano accompaniment and thirteen with orchestra. Settings of poems from his collection also appear in Mahler's second, third and fourth symphonies.

Knarre (Ger.), rattle.

Knecht, Justin Heinrich (1752–1817), German composer and organist. He was court *Kapellmeister* at Stuttgart from 1807 until 1809. His numerous compositions include a symphony entitled *Le Portrait musical de la nature*, which successively represents a cheerful woodland scene, the approach of a storm, its full fury and gradual subsidence, and a concluding hymn of thanksgiving. It is possible that this programme suggested to Beethoven the composition of his Pastoral Symphony, which has a very similar scheme.

Knipper, Lev Konstantinovich (born 1898), Russian composer. He took up music at the age of 24, studying at Berlin, Freiburg and Moscow. His early works show an attempt to follow modern European developments, but in course of time he came to accept the Soviet conception of music which would appeal to the masses, without however satisfying the authorities that his work was ideologically sound. An important influence on his work has been his study of folk song in the Caucasus and Tadzhikstan. His compositions include three operas (one on Voltaire's *Candide*), several symphonies – among them the *Far Eastern Symphony*, for orchestra, military band, soloists and male-voice chorus, and *Poem about Komsomols*, in praise of Communist Youth – orchestral suites on folk melodies, chamber music and songs.

G. ABRAHAM: *Eight Soviet Composers* (1943)

Knorr, Iwan (1853–1916), German composer and teacher. After studying at the Leipzig Conservatorium, and spending some years in Russia as a teacher he returned to Germany to work at the Hoch Conservatorium, Frankfurt, where he was appointed director in 1908. His pupils included several British musicians, among them Cyril Scott, Balfour Gardiner and Roger Quilter. Apart from songs and piano pieces, his published compositions are few in number. He was the author of books on harmony and fugue and also wrote a biography of Chaikovsky.

Koanga, opera with a prologue, three acts and an epilogue by Delius. The English libretto by Charles Francis Keary was based on George Washington Cable's novel *The Grandissimes.* The first performance (in German) took place at Elberfeld in 1904. The opera concerns an African chief named Koanga, transported as a slave to America. After the composer's death, the work was revised by Sir Thomas Beecham and Edward Agate, in which form it was given its London première in 1935. The orchestra interlude, *La Calinda,* is sometimes performed separately in the concert hall.

Köchel, Ludwig Alois Friedrich, Ritter von (1800–77), Austrian musical bibliographer. Imperial councillor until 1852, he devoted years of his retirement to the pursuit of studies in botany, mineralogy and music. His most important publication was the *Chronologisch-thematisches Verzeichnis sämtlicher Tonwerke W. A. Mozarts* (1862; second edition by P. Waldersee, 1905; third edition by Alfred Einstein, 1937, reissued with supplement, 1947), the first attempt to make a systematic list of Mozart's compositions. His numbering, though revised by recent research, is still retained as a means of identification, preceded by the letter K, or by KV – Köchel-Verzeichnis (Köchel Index).

Zoltán Kodály: he and Bartók were the two most influential figures in Hungarian musical life in the first half of this century

Kodály, Zoltán (1882–1967), Hungarian composer, one of the three major figures of Hungarian music this century (the others being Bartók and Ligeti). He studied at the Budapest Conservatory, where he taught composition from 1907 and was appointed deputy director in 1919. In 1930 he became a lecturer at Budapest University. Like Bartók, he was active in collecting and publishing Hungarian folk songs, which had a decided influence on his work. There is in his work no striking break with tradition. Its dominant characteristics are a passionate sincerity, and a willingness to incorporate elements from folksong. He was

therefore, in some ways a Hungarian counterpart to Vaughan Williams, although there is no actual resemblance between the idioms they employ. His principal compositions are:

(1) ballad operas: *Háry János* (Budapest, 1926); *Székely Fonó* (The Spinning Room of the Szekelys; Budapest, 1932); *Czinka Panna* (Budapest, 1948);

(2) choral works: *Psalmus Hungaricus* (1923); *Budavári Te Deum* (1936); *Missa brevis* (1945); miscellaneous works for mixed voices, male voices, and children's choirs;

(3) orchestra: Suite from *Háry János; Dances of Marosszék* (1930); *Dances of Galánta* (1933); *Peacock Variations* (1939); concertos for orchestra (1943), viola (1947) and string quartet (1947);

(4) chamber music: two string quartets (1908, 1917); cello sonata (1910); duo for violin and cello (1914); sonata for cello solo (1917).

He also wrote piano pieces, songs, arrangements of folk songs, and music for children. His book, *The Pentatonic Scale in Hungarian Folk Music,* was published in 1917.

Koechlin, Charles (1867–1950), French composer. He studied at the Paris Conservatoire and was a pupil of Fauré and Massenet. His compositions were numerous and often very original, but owing to his horror of publicity many of them were for long unknown outside the circle of his friends. They include three string quartets, a piano quintet, sonatas for violin, viola, cello, flute, oboe, clarinet, bassoon and horn, many piano pieces and songs, ballets, and a small group of orchestral works, some of them inspired by Kipling's *Jungle Book.* The influence of his refined, austere and disciplined style on his pupils, who included Poulenc, Tailleferre, Désormière and Sauguet, was very marked. He showed his devotion to his master, Fauré, by orchestrating his suite *Pelléas et Mélisande* and by devoting to him a critical study (1927). His other publications include a *Traité d'harmonie* (three volumes, 1929–33) and *Traité d'orchestration* (four volumes, 1949 ff.).

Köhler, Christian Louis Heinrich (1820–86), German composer, conductor and teacher. He studied in Brunswick and Vienna, and held various posts as conductor at Marienburg, Elbing and Königsberg. From 1847 he lived in Königsberg as teacher and critic. He composed three operas and a ballet, but is best known for his numerous piano works, including studies and other educational music.

Kolisch, Rudolf (born 1896), Austrian violinist. A pupil of Sevcik, and also of Schreker and Schoenberg, he founded the Kolisch Quartet (1922–39). It rapidly acquired an international reputation, not only for its extensive repertory of modern works, many of which it performed for the first time, but also for its practice (unusual in ensembles) of playing without the music. In 1942 he became leader of the Pro Arte Quartet.

Koloratur (Ger.), *see* COLORATURA.

Königin von Saba, Die, *see* QUEEN OF SHEBA.

Königskinder (Children of the King), opera in three acts by Humperdinck, to a libretto by 'Ernst Rosmer' (i.e. Elsa Bernstein Porges), first performed in New York in 1910. (Originally a play with musical accompaniment; in this form first performed, Munich, January 23, 1897.)

Kontakte, a 'dramatic structure' by Stockhausen for electronic sounds, piano and percussion, first presented in London at an Albert Hall prom. in 1968.

Kontrabass (Ger.), double bass. Also used as a prefix to denote instruments an octave lower than the normal bass members of a family, e.g. *Kontrabassposaune*, double bass trombone.

Kontrafagott (Ger.), double bassoon.

Kontretanz (Ger.), country dance. The term, used by Mozart, Beethoven and other composers, derives from the French *contredanse* (counter-dance), derived in turn from the English country dance.

Konzert (Ger.), (1) concert; (2) concerto.

Konzertmeister (Ger.), the principal first violin in an orchestra. The American term, concertmaster, derives from this, though in Britain the term 'leader' is preferred.

Konzertstück (Ger.; It., *concertino*), a work for one or more solo instruments with orchestra, less formal in structure and often shorter than an ordinary concerto, e.g. Weber's *Konzertstück* for piano and orchestra (op 79).

Koppel, Herman (born 1908), Danish composer. Koppel established his reputation with *The Psalms of David* (1949), one of a series of choral works written in the wake of World War II. In these he declared a wish to 'compose music immediately deriving from knowledge of evil done to others'. The rest of his output, written in a vigorous, traditional idiom, includes an opera, *Macbeth*, five symphonies, four piano concertos and other orchestral works, chamber music and instrumental pieces.

Kornett (Ger.), the modern cornet (the German for the obsolete cornet is *Zink*).

Korngold, Erich Wolfgang (1897–1957), Austrian composer, born in Moravia. He was the son of Julius Korngold, music critic of the *Neue Freie Presse* in Vienna. As a child, he showed enormous precocity. His music to the pantomime *Der Schneemann* (The Snow Man) was composed in 1908, was orchestrated by Zemlinsky and performed at the Vienna Opera in 1910. In that year also his piano sonata was performed by Artur Schnabel. His *Schauspiel-Ouvertüre*, performed in Leipzig in 1911, prompted an American critic to remark: 'If Master Korngold could make such a noise at fourteen, what will he not do when he is 28? The thought is appalling.' A prolific composer of chamber and orchestral music, he also wrote the following operas: *Violanta* (one act, Munich, 1916), *Die tote Stadt* (The Dead City; Hamburg and Cologne, 1920 – his most successful opera), *Der Ring des Polycrates* (one act, Munich, 1916), and *Das Wunder der Heliane* (Hamburg, 1927). He was for a short time conductor in Hamburg and also taught in Vienna. In 1938 he emigrated to the U.S., where his natural facility assured him a successful career in Hollywood as a composer of film music. For a time he worked with Max Reinhardt at his Hollywood Theatre School. In recent years there has been a revival of interest in Korngold's music, his violin concerto and symphony in F sharp enjoying a new success.

Köselitz, Johann Heinrich, see GAST.

Kosleck, Julius (1835–1905), German trumpeter. Originally an army bandsman, he became a member of the court orchestra in Berlin. In 1871 he discovered a medieval trumpet which he reconstructed to enable him to play the high trumpet parts in the works of Bach and Handel. In 1884, he introduced a modern trumpet in A, with two valves, on which he performed with considerable success. In the following year he played in Britain, and a similar instrument was used by British players until in 1894 the Belgian firm of Mahillon produced a trumpet in high D, which superseded it.

Kotter, Hans (1485–1541), Alsatian organist, a pupil of Paul Hofhaimer. He was organist at Freiburg (Switzerland) from 1514 to 1530. His collection of organ pieces in TABLATURE is an important source for the early history of organ music: examples are in W. Apel, *Musik aus früher Zeit*, i., and H. J. Moser and F. Heitmann, *Frühmeister der deutschen Orgelkunst*.

Kotzeluch, Leopold Anton, see KOZELUCH.

Koussevitsky, Serge, spelling of name used by Sergey Alexandrovich Kussevitsky (1874–1951), Russian conductor. He studied at the Philharmonic Music School, Moscow, and began his career as a double-bass player. After establishing himself as a conductor in Russia and France, he was appointed conductor of the Boston Symphony Orchestra in 1924 and emigrated to the United States. He held this post until 1949, bringing the orchestra to a peak of excellence and presenting many first performances of important works by Stravinsky, Prokofiev, Ravel and others. He encouraged younger composers – also the emigré Bartók, whose Concerto for Orchestra he commissioned – and established the Koussevitsky Music Foundation, which continues to play an important role in U.S. musical sponsorship.

H. LEICHTENTRITT: *Serge Koussevitsky* (1946)

Koven, Henry Louis Reginald de (1859–1920), American composer, educated at Oxford and elsewhere in Europe. He was a successful composer of operettas – particularly *Robin Hood* (Chicago, 1890) – but less so with his serious operas *The Canterbury Pilgrims* (New York, 1917) and *Rip van Winkle* (Chicago, 1920).

Kox, Hans (born 1926), Dutch composer. He was a pupil of Henk Badings. His works include *Concertante Music* for horn, trumpet, trombone and orchestra, commissioned by the Concertgebouw Orchestra in 1956. He has also written concertos (for violin, for two violins, and for piano) and a song cycle entitled *Chansons cruelles*.

Kozeluch, Leopold Anton (1752–1818), Czech composer. He taught in Vienna from 1778 and Germanised his name from Koželuh. He succeeded Mozart as composer to the Imperial Court in 1792. His works include operas, an oratorio, symphonies, piano concertos (including one for two pianos), cello concertos, two clarinet concertos, two basset horn concertos, chamber music and piano works.

Kraft, Anton (1752–1820), Austrian cellist and composer, born in Bohemia. He was a member of the Esterházy Orchestra (under Haydn) from 1778 until 1790, and subsequently in the service of Prince Grassalkovich (1790), and Prince Lobkowitz (1795) until his death. Most of his compositions were written for cello, though the theory that he composed Haydn's cello concerto in D major is now discredited.

kräftig (Ger.), vigorously.

Krakowiak (Fr., *cracovienne*), Polish dance (so called after the town of Cracow) in a lively 2/4 time with syncopated accents. Chopin wrote a *Rondo à la Krakowiak*, op 14 (1828), for piano and orchestra.

Kramer, Arthur Walter (born 1890), U.S. composer and critic. He was editor of *Musical America* from 1929 until 1936, and managing director of Galaxy Music Corporation (music publishers). His compositions are numerous, for a wide variety of vocal and instrumental resources.

Kraus, Joseph Martin (1756–92), German composer and conductor. He studied philosophy and law at Mainz, Erfurt and Göttingen, and was also a pupil of Vogler. He migrated to Sweden, where he became conductor at the Stockholm Opera in 1778. He travelled extensively in Germany, Italy, France and England, and became court *Kapellmeister* in Stockholm in 1788. His compositions include four symphonies, overtures, chamber music and vocal works (sacred and secular). He attacked Forkel in the anonymous essay *Etwas von und über Musik* (1777). His autobiography (in Swedish), together with fifty letters, was published in 1833.

Kraus, Lili (born 1908), Hungarian pianist. She was a pupil of Bartók and Artur Schnabel. During World War II she was interned in a Japanese prison camp; later, during a tour of New Zealand, she took out British citizenship. She is noted for performances of Mozart and Schubert, and of modern music; at one time she worked in duo with the Polish-Dutch violinist, Szymon Goldberg.

Krauss, Clemens (1893–1954), Austrian conductor. After studying at the Vienna Conservatorium, he held various provincial appointments until becoming director of the Frankfurt Opera in 1924. From there he moved to the Vienna State Opera (1929), the Berlin State Opera (1934) and Munich (1938–45). He was a friend of Richard Strauss, with whose music he was closely associated. He conducted the first performances of Richard Strauss's *Arabella* (Dresden, 1933) and *Friedenstag* (Munich, 1938). He was married to the soprano Viorica Ursuleac.

Krauss, Marie Gabrielle (1842–1906), Austrian operatic soprano. She studied at the Vienna Conservatorium and first appeared in opera in Vienna in 1859. After some years at the Vienna Opera she appeared in Paris, Naples, Milan and St. Petersburg. She was the great-aunt of the conductor Clemens Krauss.

Krebs, Johann Ludwig (1713–80), German composer and organist. A pupil of Bach at the Thomasschule, Leipzig. He held organ appointments at Zwickau (1737), Zeitz (1744) and Altenburg (1756). His compositions include *Klavierübungen* for organ (modern edition by K. Soldan), trio sonatas for flute, violin and continuo, flute sonatas, a harpsichord concerto and preludes for harpsichord. A modern edition of his organ trios has been made by H. Keller.

Krebs, Karl August (1804–80), German composer and conductor. He studied in Vienna and from 1850 until 1872 was Court *Kapellmeister* in Dresden. He wrote several operas, of which *Agnes Bernauer* (Hamburg, 1833) was the most successful.

Krebskanon, see CRAB CANON

Krehbiel, Henry Edward (1854–1923), U.S. music critic. He worked for the *Cincinnati Gazette* (1874) and the *New York Tribune* (1880). His published works include the revised edition of Thayer's *Life of Beethoven* (three volumes, 1921), *Studies in Wagnerian Drama* (1891), *How to Listen to Music* (1897), *Music and Manners in the Classical Period* (1898), *Chapters of Opera* (1908, with two further volumes in 1917 and 1919) and *Afro-American Folksongs* (1914).

Kreisler, Fritz (1875–1962), Austrian violinist and composer. He entered the Vienna Conservatorium at the age of seven, and won the gold medal after only three years. He studied also at the Paris Conservatoire where he won the Grand Prix de Rome (violin) at the age of twelve. After a successful tour of the United States in 1889 he temporarily abandoned music, studying medicine and art and becoming an army officer. He returned to the concert platform in 1899 and acquired a world-wide reputation by the brilliance and sophistication of his playing. He gave the first performance of Elgar's violin concerto in 1910. Later he settled in the United States. He was the foremost violinist of his day, but also found time to compose operettas, a string quartet and a series of pastiche violin pieces which (for a time) he successfully passed off as the works of various 17th and 18th century composers. Among these were the famous *Praeludium* and *Allegro*, which he claimed to have arranged from Pugnani (1731–98) but all of which he admitted to be his own work in 1935.

Kreisleriana (Ger.), a suite of eight piano pieces by Schumann, op 16 (1838). The name derives from the eccentric 'Kapellmeister Johannes Kreisler', the name under which E. T. A. Hoffmann contributed articles to the Leipzig *Allgemeine Musikalische Zeitung*, subsequently republished, with additions, in *Fantasiestücke in Calotts Manier* (two vols., 1814). Schumann's work was dedicated to Chopin. A revised edition appeared in 1850.

Krejči, Iša (1904–68), Czech composer, pupil of Novák and Jirák. His comic opera, *The Revolt at Ephesus* (1943), is based on Shakespeare's *The Comedy of Errors*. He also wrote three symphonies and other orchestral works, and three string quartets, in a style which has been likened to that of his compatriot, Martinů.

Křenek, Ernst (born 1900), Austrian composer, conductor and pianist, of Czech origin. He studied with Schreker in Vienna and Berlin. After holding conducting posts in Cassel and Wiesbaden, he lived from 1928 until 1937 in Vienna, from where he toured as a pianist. In 1938 he emigrated to the United States, where he taught at various colleges and universities, eventually settling in Los Angeles. His first wife was Mahler's daughter Anna. His compositions show several varieties of style. In the 1920s he became interested in jazz idioms, which he employed with remarkable success in the opera *Jonny spielt auf* (Johnny strikes up; Leipzig, 1927). In the 1930s he adopted seriously the twelve-note method of composition employed by Schoenberg, and his book, *Uber neue Musik*, is a defence of the twelve-note system. His opera *Karl V* (1938) incorporates cinema effects, speech and pantomime with an atonal framework. At heart he is probably a romantic, as the song-cycle *Reisebuch aus den österreichischen Alpen* (Travel Book from the

Austrian Alps) would suggest. Latterly he made use of electronic music, and of aleatory ideas. Throughout his career he consistently sought to express his ideas in an up-to-date musical style. His principal compositions are:

(1) operas: *Zwingburg* (Berlin, 1924); *Der Sprung über den Schatten* (Frankfurt, 1924); *Orpheus und Eurydike* (Cassel, 1926); *Jonny spielt auf* (Leipzig, 1927); *Schwergewicht* (*Die Ehre der Nation*, Wiesbaden, 1928): *Der Diktator* (Wiesbaden, 1928); *Das geheime Königreich* (Wiesbaden, 1928); *Leben des Orest* (Leipzig, 1930); *Karl V* (Prague, 1938); *Tarquin* (Vienna, 1950); *Dark Waters* (Darmstadt, 1954);

(2) choral works: *Die Jahreszeiten* (four unaccompanied choruses); four choruses to words by Goethe; three choruses to words by Keller; *Kantate von der Vergänglichkeit des Irdischen*; *Lamentatio Jeremiae*; *Cantata for Wartime*.

(3) ballets: *Mammon*; *Der vertauschte Cupido*; *Eight Column Line*;

(4) orchestra: five symphonies; two *concerti grossi*; *Kleine Symphonie*; four piano concertos; violin concerto; *concertino* for flute, violin, harpsichord and strings; *Pot-pourri*; *Theme and thirteen variations*; *Brazilian Sinfonietta* for strings; *Exercises for a Late Hour*;

(5) chamber music: *Symphonic Music* (nine solo instruments); seven string quartets; two violin sonatas; viola sonata; unaccompanied sonatas for violin (two) and viola; unaccompanied suite for cello;

(6) piano: six sonatas; five sonatinas; two suites;

(7) song cycles: *Reisebuch aus den österreichischen Alpen*; *Fiedellieder*; *Durch die Nacht*; *Gesänge des späten Jahres*.

He has also produced a modernized version of Monteverdi's opera *L'Incoronazione di Poppea* and a book on Johannes Ockeghem.

Kretzschmar, August Ferdinand Hermann (1848–1924), German conductor and writer on music. He held academic posts in Leipzig and Berlin, and wrote *Führer durch den Konzertsaal* (1887–90) – a series of analytical programme notes, *Geschichte des neuen deutschen Liedes* (1912), *Geschichte der Oper* (1919), and *Einführung in die Musikgeschichte* (1920).

Kreutzer, Konradin (1780–1849), German composer and conductor. He began to study law at Freiburg, but turned to music and studied in Vienna with Albrechtsberger from 1804. He held conducting appointments in Stuttgart, Cologne and Vienna. Kreutzer wrote thirty operas, of which *Das Nachtlager von Granada* (Vienna, 1834) enjoyed an international success. His other compositions include an oratorio, three piano concertos, chamber music, songs, and male-voice choruses.

Kreutzer, Rodolphe (1766–1831), French violinist and composer, who served Louis XVI, Napoleon and Louis XVIII. He taught the violin at the Paris Conservatoire from its foundation in 1795 till 1825, conducted at the Paris Opéra, toured successfully as a soloist in Italy, Germany, Austria (where he met Beethoven) and Holland. His compositions include forty operas, nineteen violin concertos, two concertos for two violins, a concerto for violin and cello, fifteen string quartets, fifteen string trios, several violin

sonatas, and other chamber works. His forty *Études ou caprices* for solo violin has remained a standard work.

Kreutzer Sonata, nickname for Beethoven's sonata for violin and piano in A major (1802–3). Described by the composer as written in a highly concerted style, almost as it were a concerto, it was composed for the mulatto violinist George Augustus Polgreen Bridgetower, and first performed by him with Beethoven as pianist in 1803. The sonata was published in 1805 with a dedication to the French violinist Rodolphe Kreutzer. The finale was originally intended for an earlier sonata in A major, op 3 no 1.

Kreuz (Ger.), sharp (literally 'cross', so called because this was an earlier form of the sign).

Křička, Jaroslav (1882–1969), Czech composer. He studied at the Prague Conservatory, joining the teaching staff there in 1918; he eventually became its director (1942). His compositions include the operas *Hypolita*, after Maurice Hewlett (Prague, 1917), and *Bílý pan* (The Gentleman in White, after Oscar Wilde's *The Canterville Ghost*).

Krieger, Adam (1634–66), German organist and composer, a pupil of Scheidt. He was organist at St. Nicolas, Leipzig, in 1655, and court organist at Dresden in 1657. He published a collection of songs (to his own words) for one, two and three voices for continuo and *ritornelli* for two violins and continuo (1657). A second collection, for one, two, three and five voices with five-part *ritornelli* for strings, appeared posthumously (1667; enlarged edition, 1676). Until recently no copy of the first collection (*Arien*) was known to have survived, but the text was reconstructed from manuscript sources by H. Osthoff in *Adam Krieger* (1929). A modern edition of the second collection (*Neue Arien*) is in *Denkmäler deutscher Tonkunst*, xix.

Krieger, Johann Phillipp (1649–1725), German composer. He studied in Copenhagen and later (1673) in Venice with Rosenmüller and in Rome with Paquini. He was chamber organist at Bayreuth from 1670 to 1672, court organist and vice-*Kapellmeister* at Halle in 1677, and court *Kapellmeister* at Weissenfels in 1680. He wrote a large number of operas (some fifty for Weissenfels), trio sonatas, sonatas for violin, viola da gamba and continuo, *Lustige Feldmusik* for wind instruments, and *Musikalischer Seelenfriede* (sacred songs). Selections from his church music are in *Denkmäler deutscher Tonkunst*, liii–liv. Some of his organ pieces are in *Denkmäler der Tonkunst in Bayern*, xviii.

His brother, **Johann Krieger** (1651–1735), was also a composer. He was court organist at Bayreuth from 1672 to 1677, court *Kapellmeister* at Greiz and Eisenberg in 1678, and director of music at Zittau in 1681. He published *Neue musicalische Ergetzlichkeit* (1684, in three parts: *Geistliche Andachten*, *Politische Tugendlieder*, and *Theatralische Sachen*), *Sechs musicalische Partien* (1697, suites for harpsichord) and *Anmuthige Clavierübung* (1699). The last of these publications, consisting of preludes, fugues and other pieces for organ, was much admired by Handel. A modern edition of his harpsichord and organ works is in *Denkmäler der Tonkunst in Bayern*, xviii. Motets and Masses by him survive in manuscript.

Krips, Josef (1902–74), Austrian conductor. He studied in Vienna with Weingartner and Mandyczewski, and began his career as a violinist at the Volks-oper. Later, he held conducting appointments in Dortmund (1925), Karlsruhe (1926) and at the Vienna State Opera (1933–8, 1945–50). From 1950 until 1954 he was conductor of the London Symphony Orchestra. In the United States he held posts in Buffalo and San Francisco. In his later years he divided his time be-tween opera house and concert hall, and was an admired exponent of Mozart, Beethoven, Bruckner and Richard Strauss.

Krohn, Ilmari Henrik Reinhold (1867–1960), Fin-nish musicologist and composer. He was professor at Helsinki University from 1918 until 1935. He pub-lished a collection of some 7000 Finnish folksongs and theoretical works. His compositions include the opera *Tuhotulva* (Deluge; Helsinki, 1928), church music and songs.

Krönungskonzert (Ger.), *see* CORONATION CONCERTO

Krönungsmesse (Ger.), *see* CORONATION MASS

Kroyer, Theodor (1873–1945), German musicologist. A pupil of Sandberger and Rheinberger, he held academic appointments in Munich, Heidelberg, Leip-zig and Cologne, and founded the series *Publikaţionen älterer Musik* (1926–41). He wrote books on the Italian madrigal and on Rheinberger, and edited music by Ockeghem, Marenzio and other composers.

Krummhorn (Ger.; Fr., *cromorne*; It., *storto, corn-amuto torto*), a double reed instrument, current in the middle ages and at the Renaissance. Its tube was curved at the end, rather like a hockey stick, and the reed was enclosed in a sort of capsule, through which the player directed his breath without having direct contact with the reed. It was made in several sizes.

Kubelik, Jan (1880–1940), Czech violinist and com-poser. He studied at the Prague Conservatoire, where he was a pupil of Sevčík. He rapidly made his name as a soloist and toured widely in Europe and America. Kubelík became a naturalized Hungarian in 1903. His works include three violin concertos. His son **(Jeronym) Rafael Kubelík** (born 1914), is a con-ductor and composer. He studied at the Prague Con-servatoire and was conductor of the Czech Philhar-monic from 1942 until 1948. He then emigrated to Britain and in 1950 went to the U.S. as conductor of the Chicago Symphony Orchestra. From 1955 until 1958 he was musical director of the Royal Opera, Cov-ent Garden, and in 1961 was appointed conductor of the Bavarian Radio Orchestra. In 1972 he became musical director of the New York Metropolitan – a strife-ridden appointment from which he almost immediately resigned. As a conductor, he is particu-larly associated with the music of Dvořák, Janáček, Smetana and Mahler. As a composer, he has written an opera, *Veronika*, a choral symphony, concertos and other orchestral works.

Kuhlau, Daniel Friedrich (1786–1832), German composer and flautist who settled in Copenhagen in 1810 and established himself as court composer. In 1825 he visited Vienna, where he met Beethoven who composed a punning canon on his name. His works include operas, instrumental music – much of it for flute, but some also for piano and for violin – and numerous songs.

Kuhnau, Johann (1660–1722), German organist and composer. He was a chorister at the Kreuzschule,

Dresden, and studied law in Leipzig, where he became organist of St. Thomas's in 1684. In 1701 he was university director of music and cantor of St. Thomas's (Bach's immediate predecessor). His compositions include church cantatas (modern edition of four in *Denkmäler deutscher Tonkunst*, lviii-lix) and the fol-lowing keyboard works (modern edition in *Denkmäler deutscher Tonkunst*, iv): *Neue Clavier Ubung* (two volumes, each containing seven suites, 1689 and 1692), *Firsche Clavier-Früchte oder sieben Sonaten von guter Invention* (1696), and *Musicalische Vorstellung einiger biblischer Historien in sechs Sonaten, auff dem Claviere zu spielen* (1700). He also published literary works on music. His keyboard compositions have an important place in the music of the 18th century: in particular, the *Biblische Historien* are interesting as early examples of programme music.

Kühnel, August (1645–c. 1700), German *viola da gamba* player. He was active as a soloist in Germany and France, and also gave concerts in London in 1685. He was *Kapellmeister* at Cassel in 1695. In 1698 he published *Sonate o Partite ad una o due Viole da gamba con il basso continuo*. Selected works by him have been edited by A. Einstein in *Zur deutschen Literatur für Viola da Gamba im 16. und 17. Jahrhundert* (1905), and by F. Bennat and C. Döbereiner.

Kuhreigen (Ger.), *see* RANZ DES VACHES

Kulenkampff, George (1898–1948), German violinist. He was a pupil of Willy Hess at the Berlin Hochschule. Well known as a soloist, he taught at the Berlin Hoch-schule from 1923 until 1926. Kulenkampff lived in Switzerland from 1943.

Kullervo, symphonic poem for soprano, baritone, male chorus and orchestra by Sibelius, op 7. The largest of Sibelius' early works, *Kullervo* is based on episodes in the *Kalevala*, the Finnish national mythology. Its five movements are entitled: 1, Introduction; 2, Kullervo's Youth; 3, Kullervo and his Sister; 4, Kullervo goes to Battle; 5, Kullervo's Death.

Kunst der Fuge, Die, *see* ART OF FUGUE

Kurth, Ernst (1886–1946), Austrian musicologist. A pupil of Adler in Vienna, he moved to Switzerland in 1912 and became a professor at Berne University in 1920. His books include studies of Gluck's operas and of Bruckner; he also produced several books on harmonic theory.

Kusser or **Cousser, Johann Siegmund** (1660–1727), Austrian or Hungarian composer, who spent his formative years (1674–82) in Paris, where he was a close friend of Lully. Subsequently he was court *Kapellmeister* at Brunswick, director of Hamburg Opera from 1694 to 1695, and conductor of Stuttgart Opera from 1698 to 1704. He then came to England and settled in Dublin, where he was appointed master of the King's band and master of the choristers, Christ Church Cathedral, 1710. He published a number of orchestral suites expressly modelled on the French style (four sets, 1682 and 1700). He also wrote several operas for Brunswick, Hamburg and Stuttgart; a modern edition of the surviving arias of *Erindo* (Ham-burg, 1693) is in *Das Erbe deutscher Musik, Land-schaftsdenkmale, Schleswig-Holstein*, iii. The composi-tions of his Irish period include a *serenata teatrale* in honour of Queen Anne and a birthday serenade for George I (1724).

Kussevitsky, Serge, *see* KOUSSEVITSKY

Kutchka, literally 'handful'. The name given in Russia to a group of five musicians who were active in the 19th century in proclaiming the virtues of a national style based on folk music, and in practising (in varying degrees) what they preached. The leader of the group, known outside Russia as the 'Five', was Balakirev. The original members were Borodin, Cui, Mussorgsky and Rimsky-Korsakov.

Kylisma, *see* QUILISMA

Kyrie, short for 'Kyrie eleison' (Gr.), 'Lord, have mercy'. The first part of the Ordinary of the Mass, consisting of three sections: 'Kyrie eleison', 'Christe eleison', and 'Kyrie eleison' – the only part of the Mass in which Greek words survive. The text of each petition is sung three times. Three types of musical setting are found in Gregorian chant: (*a*) with the repetitions in each section sung to the same music, and the third section ('Kyrie eleison') sung to the same music as the first; (*b*) with the repetitions in each section sung to the same music, but different music for sections one and three; (*c*) with independent music for each section, as in (*b*), but with the music of each section cast in the basic form *A B A*. These three types may be expressed diagrammatically as: (*a*) *A A A, B B B, A A A*; (*b*) *A A A, B B B, C C C*; (*c*) *A B A, C D C, E F E* (the third part of the third section being slightly amplified – a feature which also occurs in several examples of the second type). The following *Kyrie* from Mass VIII (known as the *Missa de angelis*) is an example of type (*b*), in which the three sections, though independent, may also be regarded as variants of a single melody:

The custom arose of interpolating into the more elaborate settings additional words, which were sung syllabically to the notes of the melody, or to a portion of it (for an example, *see Historical Anthology of Music*, edited by A. T. Davison and W. Apel, no 15). A *Kyrie* treated in this way was known as a 'farced *Kyrie*' (*Kyrie cum farsura*, literally '*Kyrie* with stuffing') and was a form of PROSULA. The initial words of these interpolations were used as titles for the *Kyries* to which they were added, and these titles survived after the use of the added words was abolished by the Council of Trent in the 16th century.

Polyphonic settings of the *Kyrie* (whether plain or farced) appeared as early as the 13th century. The *Kyrie* naturally had its place in the complete polyphonic settings of the Ordinary of the Mass which came into use on the Continent in the 15th century. In England, however, it was the practice of pre-Reformation composers to omit it from their Masses.

After the Reformation the first Prayer-Book of Edward VI (1549) translated the nine-fold *Kyrie* into English as:

> Lord, have mercy upon us (three times);
> Christ, have mercy upon us (three times);
> Lord, have mercy upon us (three times).

The Second Prayer-Book of 1552 introduced the practice of the recitation of the ten commandments by the Priest. After the first nine the people had the petition:

> Lord, have mercy upon us, and incline our hearts to keep this law.

After the tenth:

> Lord, have mercy upon us, and write all these thy laws in our hearts, we beseech thee.

In this extended form the petition was set polyphonically by English composers: examples will be found in Byrd's 'Short Service' and 'Great Service' (*Tudor Church Music*, ii, pages 72, 81, 175).

l, in TONIC SOL-FA = lah, the sixth note (or submediant) of the major scale.

L, abbreviation for 'Longo' – the identification tag used for the numbering of Domenico Scarlatti's keyboard works (thus L.100, L. 125, etc.). Alessandro Longo (1864–1945) was an Italian pianist who catalogued Scarlatti's music, but his catalogue, while valuable in its day, has now been superseded by that of Ralph Kirkpatrick, whose numbering is preceded by the letter K.

la (Fr., It.), the note A; also the sixth note of the Guidonian hexachord.

See SOLMIZATION

Labarre, Théodore (1805–70), French harpist and composer. He wrote operas, ballets and a *Méthode* for harp.

L'Abbé, *see* ABBÉ

Labey, Marcel (1875–1968), French composer, conductor and teacher. Studied with Lenormand and d'Indy, on whose style he modelled his compositions, which include an opera, orchestral works and chamber music.

Lablache, Luigi (1794–1858), Italian born bass singer, of French and Irish parentage. Trained in the Conservatorio at Naples, he made his début at the San Carlino theatre there in 1812, and thereafter sang with great success all over Europe. He made his first appearance in London in 1830, and in Paris in the same year. Leporello was one of his most famous roles. He was a torch bearer at the burial of Beethoven, and in 1836–7 was Queen Victoria's singing-master.

Lachner, Franz (1803–90), German composer and conductor. He studied in Munich and with the Abbé Stadler in Vienna, where he became *Kapellmeister* at the Kärntnertor Theatre in 1826, and was a friend of Schubert. He conducted at Mannheim from 1834 and at Munich from 1836 until 1865. His numerous compositions in many forms, including eight suites for orchestra, are now forgotten.

Lacombe, Louis Trouillon (1818–84), French pianist and composer, who studied in Paris under Zimmerman and Vienna under Czerny. He composed operas, dramatic symphonies, chamber music and piano pieces. His *Philosophie et Musique* was published in 1895.

Lacrimosa ('Ah what weeping'), traditional movement of the Latin Requiem Mass.

lacrimoso (It.), sad, mournful.

Lady Macbeth of Mzensk, original title of Shostakovich's opera KATERINA ISMAILOVA.

L'Africaine, *see* AFRICAINE

Lage (Ger.), (1) position, e.g. on a stringed instrument or of a chord (*see* INVERSION);
   (2) the range of instruments or voices.

La Guerre, *see* JACQUET, ELISABETH-CLAUDE

lah, anglicized form of the Italian *la* (A). In TONIC SOL-FA the sixth note (or submediant) of the major scale.

La Hale (Halle), Adam de, *see* ADAM

lai (Fr.), a type of *trouvère* song closely related in form to the SEQUENCE, consisting of sections of irregular length, each with melodic repetition. A single stanza of the poem could comprise one or more sections. Machaut's eighteen *lais*, of which sixteen are monodic, were more regular in form than those of the 13th century; each stanza falls, with few exceptions, into two parts, each sung to the same melody. In the *Leich*, the equivalent form adopted by the *Minnesinger* in the 14th century, complete regularity in the setting of each pair of stanzas to one melody is observed, as in the sequence. Examples of *trouvère lais* are printed in A. Jeanroy, L. Brandin, and P. Aubry, *Lais et descorts français* (1901).

laissez vibrer (Fr.), 'let it vibrate'. This direction, when given to the players of plucked or struck instruments (e.g. harp, piano, cymbal, tom-tom), indicates that the sound should not be damped but allowed to die away slowly. The opposite is *étouffez*.

Lakmé, opera in three acts by Delibes, to a libretto by Edmond Gondinet and Philippe Gille, first performed in Paris in 1883. The story, based on Gondinet's poem *Le Mariage de Loti*, concerns the daughter of a Brahmin priest, and her ill-fated love for a British army officer on duty in India. Lakmé's Bell Song, a coloratura test-piece, is the opera's most famous aria.

Lalande, Michel Richard de (1657–1726), the most significant French composer of church music of his time. In 1683 he became one of the superintendents, and later sole superintendent, of the music of Louis XIV's chapel, for which he wrote 42 motets for chorus and instruments. A complete copy is in the Fitzwilliam Museum at Cambridge. He also composed three *Leçons de Ténèbres* for solo voice, cantatas, ballets and chamber music.

L'Allegro, *see* ALLEGRO, IL PENSEROSO

Lalo, Victor Antoine Edouard (1823–92), French composer of Spanish origin. He studied at Lille and at the Paris Conservatoire under Habeneck and Crevecoeur. His most successful work is the *Symphonie espagnole* for violin and orchestra, first played by Sarasate in Paris in 1875. The most famous of his three operas is *Le Roi d'Ys* (1888). His other works include a ballet, *Namouna*, concertos, chamber music and songs.

Lambe, English composer of the early 15th century. His only surviving composition is a three-part Sanctus in the Old Hall manuscript (edited by A. Hughes and M. Bent, i/2, page 318).

Lambe, Walter (1451–about 1500), English composer. He was elected King's Scholar at Eton on July 8, 1467 (at the age of fifteen), and was later a member of the choir of St. George's, Windsor, where he was Master of the Choristers, with William Edmonds, in 1480.

He was one of the most accomplished composers of his generation. Apart from fragments, his existing compositions comprise six antiphons and a Magnificat, and are printed in *Musica Britannica*, x-xii.

lambeg drum, large double-headed bass drum. It is found in Northern Ireland where it is associated with the functions of the Orange Lodges.

Lambert, Constant (1905–51), English composer, conductor, and critic. While he was still a student at the Royal College of Music, Diaghilev commissioned from him the music for the ballet *Romeo and Juliet*, produced at Monte Carlo in 1926. The great success of his setting for chorus, solo piano, and orchestra without woodwind of Sacheverell Sitwell's *Rio Grande* (1929), which makes effective use of jazz idioms, was not repeated by his later works, which did not achieve a consistent style. They include *Music for Orchestra* (1931), the masque *Summer's Last Will and Testament* (1936), the ballet *Horoscope* (1938), a piano concerto, a piano sonata, and songs. He conducted the Sadler's Wells ballet from 1937, and published a book *Music Ho!* (1934), containing witty though now somewhat dated observations on contemporary music.

lament. There are examples of early medieval laments (Lat. *planctus*) with music which may date from the 7th century. A transcription of a lament on the death of Charlemagne (814) is printed in Naumann's *History of Music*, (English ed., 1880), vol. i, p. 199. A *Planctus Mariae Virginis* in the form of a sequence by Godefrid of Breteuil (*d.* 1196) is printed in F. Gennrich, *Grundriss einer Formenlehre des mittelalterlichen Liedes* (1932), p. 143. The troubadour Gaucelm Faidit wrote a lament (*planh*) on the death (1199) of Richard Lion-Heart (J. Beck, *La Musique des troubadours*, 1910, p. 92).

In Irish and Scottish folk music the lament is a type of song or piece for bagpipes. Examples will be found in Bunting's *Ancient Music of Ireland* (1840) and in the standard collections of Irish and Scottish folk music.

The earliest and one of the most famous of the laments in 17th-century opera is Monteverdi's 'Lamento d'Arianna', the only surviving fragment of the opera *Arianna* (1608). Later examples in opera and oratorio were conventionally written on a falling chromatic GROUND BASS, as is the lament of Dido in Purcell's *Dido and Aeneas* (1689).

There are three laments for harpsichord by J. J. Froberger, which have been published in *D.T.O.*, x (2). They are a Lamentation on the death of the Emperor Ferdinand III (1657), a *Plainte* in the form of an Allemande composed in London 'to purge Melancoly', and a *Tombeau* on the death of M. Blancrocher. Ravel copied the idea of the 17th-century *tombeau* in his *Tombeau de Couperin* (for piano 1914–17; transcribed for orchestra, 1919). *See also* TOMBEAU.

Lamentations, at Matins (*Tenebrae*) on Thursday, Friday, and Saturday of Holy Week the first three lessons, from the Lamentations of Jeremiah, are sung to a chant, including their initial Hebrew letters (*Aleph, Beth*, etc.). The first polyphonic setting is that of Ockeghem (1474); Palestrina's setting (1588) has continued to be sung ever since in the Sistine Chapel. A collection of settings from the first half of the 16th century has been edited by G. Massenkeil (1965). Settings by three English composers of the 16th century, Tallis, White and Byrd, have been published in *Tudor Church Music*, vi, v and ix.

'Lamentation' Symphony, nickname for Haydn's symphony no 26 in D minor, so called because it contains thematic resemblances to plainsong melodies sung in Roman Catholic churches during the week before Easter.

L'Amico Fritz, *see* AMICO FRITZ

Lamond, Frederic (1868–1948), Scottish pianist, pupil of von Bülow and Liszt – with whose style he was one of the last and most famous links. From 1885 he gave recitals in many countries and became known for his fine playing of Beethoven. He taught in Berlin from 1904 and at The Hague for several years after 1917. He composed a symphony and some chamber music and piano pieces.

L'Amore dei Tre Re, *see* LOVE OF THE THREE KINGS

L'Amour des Trois Oranges, *see* LOVE FOR THREE ORANGES

Lamoureux, Charles (1834–99), French violinist and conductor. In 1881 he founded the Concerts Lamoureux in Paris at which he conducted extracts from Wagner's operas and compositions by the younger French composers of the day.

Lampe, John Frederick (1703–51), German born composer who went to Dublin in 1748 and two years later settled in Edinburgh, where he died. He composed music for plays and burlesque operas, including *Pyramus and Thisbe*.

Lampugnani, Giovanni Battista (1706–81), Italian composer who lived in London from 1743 as opera composer and conductor. His opera *Semiramide* (Rome, 1741), songs from other operas, and two sets of trio sonatas were published in Britain by Walsh.

Landi, Stefano (c. 1590–c. 1655), Italian composer. He was *maestro di cappella* in Padua from about 1619 and a member of the Papal chapel from 1629. He composed madrigals, monodies, church music and instrumental canzonas. Of special importance in the history of opera is his *Sant' Alessio* (Rome, 1632), on a sacred subject with comic scenes and dance songs.

Landini, Francesco (c. 1335–97), Italian composer and organist, the most famous musician of his age. He became blind in childhood. His surviving compositions number 154, of which all but 13 are *ballate*. Most of them are contained in a 15th century manuscript which belonged to the organist Antonio Squarcialupi (died 1480) and which depicts him with his *organetto*. He was celebrated for his playing on this and other instruments. His complete works are edited and discussed by Leo Schrade in *Polyphonic Music of the Fourteenth Century*, iv (1959).

Landini Cadence, Landini Sixth, a cadential formula, called after the composer Francesco Landini, in which the cadence note is preceded by notes a second and a third below it, i.e., by the seventh and sixth degrees of its scale. It appears in the music of Landini's contemporaries, and was widely used by French and English composers of the 15th century.

DUNSTABLE, *Veni sancte Spiritus*

Ländler, an Austrian dance in what we would now

call slow waltz-time, though it was in fact a precursor of the waltz. It was popular in the late 18th and early 19th century. Collections of *Ländler* (the word is either singular or plural) can be found in the works of Mozart, Beethoven and Schubert. The 'trio' sections of some of Haydn's and Schubert's symphonies are in Ländler-style.

Landon, H. C. Robbins (born 1926), U.S. musicologist and leading authority on the music of Haydn, whose works he has edited. He studied musicology with Karl Geiringer at Boston University, graduating in 1947. He has lived in Europe since 1947. He is founder of the Haydn Society and an editor of the Mozart *Gesamtausgabe*. He is a member of the Zentralinstitut fur Mozartforschung, Salzburg, and has written books on Haydn and on the Viennese classical style. His wife, **Christa Landon-Fuhrmann**, is a harpsichordist and musicologist.

Landowska, Wanda (1877–1959), Polish born harpsichordist and pianist. After studying in Warsaw and Berlin, she opened a school and centre for concerts at Saint-Leu-la-Forêt, near Paris, in 1919. From 1940 onwards, she lived in New York. By her performances, teaching, and writing she played an important part in the revival of the harpsichord and its music. Her books include *Bach et ses interprètes* (1906) and *La Musique ancienne* (1908). Manuel de Falla and Francis Poulenc composed harpsichord concertos specially for her.

Landre, Guillaume (1905–68), Dutch composer of French descent, pupil of Pijper. His opera *Jean Levecq* was based on Maupassant's *The Return*. He also wrote symphonies, a violin concerto and chamber music.

Lang, Paul Henry (born 1901), U.S. musicologist of Hungarian parentage – he was born in Budapest. In 1943 he became Professor of Musicology at Columbia University, New York, and in 1945 editor of the *Musical Quarterly*. His books include *Music in Western Civilisation* (1941, revised 1963) and *Handel* (1966).

Lange, Aloysia, see WEBER, JOSEPHA

Lange, Gregor (c. 1540–87), German composer. He was cantor at Frankfort-on-the-Oder from 1574 to 1584. He wrote Latin and German motets and German songs. A selection of motets for four to eight voices from his *Cantiones sacrae* (1580) was printed in *Publikationen der Gesellschaft für Musikforschung*, xxv. His 'Vae misero mihi' (page 6) is remarkable for its chromaticism. The song books of the years 1584–86 have been edited by F. Bose (1968).

Langlais, Jean (born 1907), blind French born organist and composer. He was a pupil of Dupré and Dukas at the Paris Conservatoire, where he won the *premier prix* for organ in 1930. In 1953 he became organist at St. Clotilde, Paris.

langsam (Ger.), slow.

Laniere (Lanier), a family of English musicians of French descent in the 16th and 17th centuries. The most famous member, Nicholas, lived from 1588 to 1666. He may have been the first to write recitative in England when in 1617 Ben Jonson's *Lovers made Men* 'was sung (after the Italian manner) *Stylo recitativo*, by Master Nicholas Lanier; who ordered and made both the Scene, and the Musicke'. A reconstruction of the music for this masque was published by A. J. Sabol in 1963. He wrote music for other

masques, besides a cantata, songs, and dialogues. In 1625 he was sent to Italy to buy pictures for Charles I, and in the following year became Master of the King's Music. During the Commonwealth he was in the Netherlands, and returned at the Restoration and resumed his positions at Court. A self-portrait is in the School of Music at Oxford. Eleven of his songs have been edited by Ian Spink in *Musica Britannica*, xxxiii.

McD. EMSLIE: 'Nicholas Lanier's Innovations in English Song', in *Music and Letters*, xli (1960)
I. SPINK: 'Lanier in Italy', in *Music and Letters*, xl (1959)

Lanner, Joseph Franz Karl (1801–43), Austrian composer, the first to produce Viennese dance music on a large scale. After teaching himself the violin, he formed his own quintet which he expanded into a famous dance orchestra in partnership with Johann Strauss the Elder. Later the partnership broke up, and the two men became rivals. Lanner's output as a composer included more than 200 waltzes, polkas, and other pieces.

Lantins, Arnold de, Flemish composer. He was born in the province of Liège and became a singer in the Papal chapel in 1431. Of his thirteen sacred compositions, which include a complete Mass, four have been published by Charles van den Borren in *Polyphonia Sacra* (1932). The same editor has published the fourteen surviving three-part *chansons* in *Pièces polyphoniques profanes de provenance liégeoise* (1950).

Lantins, Hugh de, Flemish composer of the first half of the 15th century, born in the province of Liège. His compositions show that he spent some time in Italy. Charles van den Borren has edited four of his twelve liturgical compositions in *Polyphonia Sacra* (1932), and four Italian *canzoni* and fourteen French *chansons* in *Pièces polyphoniques profanes de provenance liégeoise* (1950). The latter make, for their time, remarkably constant use of imitation.

L'Apprenti Sorcier, see SORCERER'S APPRENTICE

L'Après–Midi d'un Faune, see PRÉLUDE À L'APRÈS-MIDI D'UN FAUNE

largamente (It.), broadly.

largando, see ALLARGANDO

large, the longest note (Lat. *maxima*) in the medieval system of MENSURAL NOTATION. It had virtually disappeared from practical use by the beginning of the 16th century.

larghetto (It.), slow and broad, but less so than *largo*.

largo, (It.), slow and broad.

larigot (Fr.), an organ stop. Its pipes are open cylindrical metal pipes which sound at the 19th, i.e. two octaves and a fifth above normal (8 ft.) pitch.

Lark Ascending, The, 'romance' for violin and orchestra by Vaughan Williams, composed in 1914 as a musical evocation of a poem by Meredith.

'Lark' Quartet, nickname of Haydn's string quartet in D, op 64, no 5, composed in 1789; so called because of the first violin's high, birdlike notes at the start of the first movement.

L'Arlésienne, see ARLESIENNE

Larsson, Lars–Erik (born 1908), Swedish composer. He studied in Stockholm, Leipzig and Vienna, where he was a pupil of Berg but remained uninfluenced by atonalism. In 1929–30 he was chorus master at the

Stockholm Opera and in 1937 became conductor in the State Radio. His works include symphonies, overtures and other orchestral music, a popular serenade for strings, chamber music, choral works, film music and songs.

La Rue, Pierre de (c. 1460–1518), Flemish composer. A disciple of Ockeghem, he was in the service of Maximilian from 1492, of Philip of Burgundy in Brussels from 1496 to 1506, and subsequently of Margaret of Austria, Regent of the Netherlands. He held a canonry at Courtrai, and retired there in 1516. Some of his 31 Masses were published by Petrucci and other early printers, but there are few modern editions. The Mass *Ave Maria* was published by H. Expert in *Maîtres musiciens de la Renaissance française*, *Kyries* I and II from the *L'Homme armé* Mass in *Historical Anthology of Music*, edited by A. T. Davison and W. Apel, no 92, and the *Kyrie* from the Mass *De Sancto Antonio* in Schering's *Geschichte der Musik in Beispielen*, no 65. Four of his 23 motets were edited by Nigel Davison in 1962. He also wrote more than thirty *chansons*, seventeen of which are printed in *The Chanson Albums of Marguerite of Austria*, edited by M. Picker (1965).

lasciare vibrare, *see* LAISSEZ VIBRER

lassú, the slow section of a CSARDAS.

Lassus, Roland de (Orlando di Lasso) (1532–94), Netherlands composer. He was the most famous contemporary of Palestrina, remarkable for the wide range of his forms and the versatility of his expression. He was a choir boy at the church of St. Nicholas at Mons, the town of his birth, but was taken to Italy at an early age. From 1553 to 1554 he was choirmaster at St. John Lateran in Rome. In 1554 he is reported to have travelled with Giulio Cesare Brancaccio to England and then to Antwerp. In 1556 he became a member of the chapel of the Duke of Bavaria at Munich, which he directed from 1560 until his death.

Among his very numerous compositions are Masses, motets, Magnificats, Passions, psalms, Italian madrigals and *villanelles*, French *chansons*, and German choral *Lieder* and chorale-motets. His style encompasses every resource of 16th century choral technique. About a third of his works were printed in a projected complete edition by F. X. Haberl and A. Sandberger (21 volumes, 1894–1926). A new series was begun by Bärenreiter in 1956.

> W. BOETTICHER: *Orlando di Lasso und seine Zeit* (1958)
>
> C. VAN DEN BORREN: *Orlande de Lassus* (fourth edition, 1943)

Last Rose of Summer, The, Irish air, originally called 'The Groves of Blarney' (1790), but with new words written by Thomas Moore in 1813. Beethoven and Mendelssohn both made arrangements of the air (Mendelssohn's taking the form of a piano fantasia) and Flotow employed it, somewhat over-repetitively, in his opera *Martha*.

Last Savage, The, comic opera in three acts by Menotti, to a text by the composer, first produced at the Paris Opéra-Comique in 1963. The work is a satire on the pretensions of modern living, its targets ranging from cocktail parties to abstract art and twelve-note music.

La Tombelle, Fernand de (Antoine Louis Joseph Gueyrand Fernand Fouant) (1854–1928), French organist and composer, pupil of Saint-Saëns. He gave organ concerts at the Trocadero with Guilmant (from 1878) and was appointed professor at the Schola Cantorum. He composed theatre music, orchestral and choral works, music for organ and harmonium, chamber music, and songs.

L'Attaque du Moulin, *see* ATTAQUE DU MOULIN

Lattuada, Felice (1882–1926), Italian opera composer, whose works include a latter-day *Don Giovanni*.

lauda (It.), *laude* were songs of popular devotion in Italy which probably date from the time of St. Francis (1182–1226). The 14th century examples which survive with their melodies, numbering about 150, are associated with the flagellants of Northern Italy, who sang *laude spirituali* in their processions (*see also* HUGO VON REUTLINGEN). In later centuries the singing of *laude* was fostered by local fraternities of *Laudisti*. Throughout the 16th century polyphonic *laude* in the style of the simpler secular forms were published, and the addition of the dramatic element to their performance in the oratory of Filippo Neri in Florence after 1560 provided one of the points of departure for the ORATORIO. Examples of monophonic *laude* are published in F. Liuzzi, *La Lauda* (two volumes, 1934), of polyphonic in K. Jeppesen, *Die mehrstimmige italienische Lauda* (1935).

Laudon, nickname for Haydn's symphony no 69 in C, composed in 1778 in honour of the Austrian field marshal Ernst von Laudon.

Laute (Ger.), lute.

Lautenclavicymbel (Ger.), lute-harpsichord, i.e. a harpsichord with gut strings instead of metal strings. The instrument existed in the sixteenth century, and Bach had one made in 1740.

Lavallée, Calixa (1842–91), French-Canadian pianist and composer, who studied at the Paris Conservatoire, and settled in Boston as a teacher. He is best known as the composer of the Canadian national anthem *O Canada*.

Lawes, Henry (1596–1662), English composer. He became a member of the Chapel Royal in 1626. At the Restoration in 1660 he resumed his position there and wrote a coronation anthem for Charles II. Milton and Herrick wrote poems in praise of his music. His compositions include songs, music for masques, including that for the performance of Milton's *Comus* at Ludlow Castle (1634), part of the music for Davenant's *The Siege of Rhodes* (1656), psalm tunes, and anthems. 28 of his songs have been edited by Ian Spink in *Musica Britannica*, xxxiii.

His brother **William Lawes** (1602–45) was also a composer. He was a pupil of Coprario, and became one of the musicians of Charles I after his accession in 1625. Like his brother, he became a Gentleman of the Chapel Royal in 1626. He joined the Royalist army in the Civil War, and was killed at the siege of Chester. He was an accomplished composer of consort suites, and wrote anthems, psalms, songs (including 'Gather ye rosebuds while ye may'), catches, and masque music. His *Select Consort Music* has been edited by Murray Lefkowitz in *Musica Britannica*, xxi. Nine of his songs have been edited by Ian Spink in *Musica Britannica*, xxxiii.

W. McC. Evans: *Henry Lawes* (1941)

M. Lefkowitz: *William Lawes* (1960)

Lazarus, or the Feast, of the Resurrection, unfinished cantata by Schubert, based on a sacred drama in three parts by August Niemeyer, a pastor, theologian and poet from Halle. Though Schubert called the work an Easter cantata, it is really a hybrid – half oratorio, half opera. Perhaps because he was dissatisfied with the form, he failed to write part three of the work. A performance of the unfinished score was nevertheless given after the composer's death, though the music was not published (in full score) until 1892 as part of the collected edition of Schubert's works. In recent years it has been championed by Raymond Leppard and Pierre Boulez, among other conductors.

leader, (1) British name for the principal first violin of an orchestra (U.S., concertmaster, Fr., *chef d'attaque*, Ger., *Konzertmeister*).

(2) The first violin of a string quartet or other ensemble.

(3) Alternative term (in the United States) for conductor.

leading motif, *see* Leitmotiv

leading-note (Fr., *note sensible*; Ger., *Leitton*), the seventh degree of the scale (e.g. B in the scale of C), so-called because of its tendency to rise to ('lead to') the tonic. It is a semitone below the tonic in the major and in both forms of the minor scale. In the medieval modes this was true only of the modes with the finals F and C, whereas in the modes with the finals D, G, and A the seventh degree was a whole tone below the final. It is generally held that in these modes the singers were accustomed to sharpening the leading note in certain contexts before it became usual to mark such sharpening in manuscript and prints. Editors of music written before 1600 have usually supplied such accidentals, but the evidence is not at all clear, and the practice probably varied according to period and place. In any event, the term implies that the rise of a semitone tends to support the tonic as the key-note, and is thus essentially bound up with post-Renaissance theories of harmony and tonality. The fall of a semitone to the tonic has a similar function of supporting the tonic in chromatic harmony, as in Hindemith's theory of tonality, in which both D flat and B in the key of C, for example, are leading-notes.

leading-note chord, the chord on the leading note contains a diminished fifth, and is therefore a discord, which is usually resolved on the tonic chord, e.g., in the key of C:

It is much more often used in the first inversion than in the root position:

The second inversion normally occurs only in three-part writing:

See Chord, Harmony, Inversion

Le Bègue, Nicolas Antoine (1631–1702), French organist and composer. He was organist to Louis XIV in 1678. His organ works are reprinted in Guilmant's *Archives des maîtres de l'orgue*, ix. He left a manuscript *Méthode pour toucher l'orgue*.

N. Dufourcq: *Nicolas Lebègue* (1955)

Lebewohl, Das (Ger.), title of Beethoven's piano sonata in E flat, op 81a, familiarly (but erroneously) known as *Les Adieux* – at the time of writing it, Beethoven would have been appalled by the use of the French name. The work was dedicated to the Archduke Rudolph on his departure in 1809 from Vienna during the French occupation. The three movements were headed 'Das Lebewohl', 'Die Abwesenheit' and 'Das Wiedersehen' by Beethoven ('Farewell', 'Absence', and 'Return').

lebhaft (Ger.), lively.

Lechner, Leonhard (c. 1553–1606), Austrian composer. He was a choirboy under Lassus in Munich, and from 1575 was a teacher in Nuremberg. He was *Kapellmeister* at Hechingen from 1584, and at Stuttgart from 1595 to his death. One of the most important and capable German composers of his time, he wrote Masses, motets, Magnificats, a St. John Passion, sacred and secular songs to German words, and edited works of Lassus. A collected edition of Lechner's works is being published by Bärenreiter (1954–onwards).

Leclair, Jean Marie (1697-1764), French composer and violinist. In 1722 he was a dancing-master in Turin where he studied the violin under Somis. From 1729 he lived in Paris as a violinist. He was the first to adapt the French instrumental style to the concerto form of Vivaldi. In his chamber music he shows both a progressive technique and a mature command of expression in writing for the violin. Besides concertos and solo and trio sonatas he composed an opera and ballets. At the age of 67 he was murdered near his home in Paris.

Lecocq, Alexandre Charles (1832–1918), French composer, pupil of Halévy at the Paris Conservatoire. His first successful operetta was *Fleur de Thé*, and with *La Fille de Madame Angot* (1872) and *Giroflé-Girofla* (1874) his position was established. He wrote a series of operettas until 1911, and in 1877 edited a vocal score of Rameau's *Castor et Pollux*.

ledger lines, *see* Leger lines

Leeuw, Ton de (born 1926), Dutch composer, pianist and critic, pupil of Messiaen and Henk Badings. His works include an opera (*The Dream*), an oratorio (*Job*), orchestral music and chamber music.

Lefébure-Wély, Louis James Alfred (1817–69), French organist and composer. He began publicly performing at the age of eight. He was organist at the Madeleine from 1847–58 and at St. Sulpice from 1863 and gained a reputation as a lively and inventive player and composer. His works include music for the organ and harmonium, an opera, symphonies, church music, and chamber music.

Lefebvre, Charles Edouard (1843–1917), French composer, who was awarded the *Prix de Rome* in 1870. In 1895 he became professor in charge of the ensemble class at the Conservatoire. He composed operas, a symphony, and other orchestral music, church music and chamber music.

legatissimo (It.), as smooth as possible.

legato (It.), smooth.

legatura (It.), slur.

légature (Fr.), slur.

Legend of St. Elizabeth, The, oratorio with a prologue and four scenes by Liszt, to a text by Otto Roquette. It was first performed, in Hungarian, at Budapest in 1865, and was subsequently produced as an opera at the Weimar Court Theatre in 1881.

Legend of the Czar Saltan, The, opera with a prologue and four acts by Rimsky-Korsakov, to a libretto by Vladimir Ivanovich Belsky (from a tale by Pushkin). Its first performance was in Moscow in 1900.

Legend of the Invisible City of Kitezh, The, opera in four acts by Rimsky-Korsakov, to a libretto by Vladimir Ivanovich Belsky, first performed at St. Petersburg in 1907. The full title of the work is *The Legend of the Invisible City of Kitezh and of the Maid Fevronia*. The subject matter is based on two Russian legends, one of them concerning the miraculous rescue of Kitezh from the Tartars.

Legends, the title given to a set of four symphonic poems by Sibelius (op 22) which are based on the Finnish national epic *Kalevala*. They are entitled:

(1) *Lemminkäinen and the Maidens* (1895; final form, 1900).

(2) *Lemminkäinen in Tuonela* (1895; final form, 1900).

(3) *The Swan of Tuonela* (1893, as prelude to the unfinished opera *The Building of the Boat*; final form, 1900).

(4) *Lemminkäinen's Homecoming* (1895; final form, 1900).

leger lines, short lines above or below the staff, used to indicate the pitch of notes which lie outside it, e.g.

légèrement, Fr., lightly.

leggero (It.), = LEGGIERO.

leggiero (It.), light.

legno (It.), wood. In certain scores the term indicates a wood-block. *Col legno* (literally 'with the wood') is a direction to string players to use the back of the bow instead of the hair. *Bacchetta di legno* is a direction to percussion players to use a wood-headed stick.

Legrenzi, Giovanni (1626–90), Italian composer. He was director of the *Conservatorio dei Mendicanti* at Venice, and from 1685 was choirmaster at St. Mark's. His work has an important place in the history both of opera and of instrumental music in the 17th century. In the arias of his seventeen operas he makes some use of a short *da capo* form. He was an early practitioner of the TRIO SONATA, and also wrote

oratorios, cantatas, ensemble sonatas and church music. Bach wrote a fugue for organ on a theme by Legrenzi (*Neue Bach-Ausgabe*, iv/6, page 19). Ten *sonate da chiesa* have been edited by A. Seay (1968). An ensemble sonata is printed in Apel and Davison's *Historical Anthology of Music* (no 220), and an aria in Schering's *Geschichte der Musik in Beispielen* (no 231).

Lehár, Franz (1870–1948), Hungarian born composer, whose Christian name, Ferencz, was subsequently Germanised as Franz. After studying at the Prague Conservatoire, he conducted military bands in various cities. He settled in Vienna in 1902, and became famous as a composer of operettas, of which the earliest and most successful was *The Merry Widow* (1905). His later works included *The Count of Luxembourg* (1909), *Gipsy Love* (1910), *Frasquita* (1922), *The Land of Smiles* (1923) and *Giuditta* (1924).

Lehmann, Lilli (1848–1929), German soprano who sang at the Berlin Opera from 1870, and at the New York Metropolitan from 1885 until 1889. She first appeared in London in 1880, and was associated with the Mozart Festivals in Salzburg from 1905. Her performances in Wagner and Mozart were especially notable. In 1876 she appeared in the first production of Wagner's *Ring* at Bayreuth. Her books *Meine Gesangkunst* and *Mein Weg* were translated into English as *How to Sing* (1903) and *My Path through Life* (1914).

Lehmann, Liza (1862–1918), English born soprano and composer, of English and German parentage (her full name was Elizabetta Nina Mary Frederika Lehmann). Her large-scale works included operas on *The Vicar of Wakefield* and *Everyman* (the latter conducted by Beecham in 1916) but it is for such pieces as *In a Persian Garden*, with words from *Omar Khayyam*, that she is remembered.

Lehmann, Lotte (born 1888), German born soprano, equally at home in opera house and concert hall. Her qualities were quickly recognised by Richard Strauss, who wrote *Arabella* for her and invited her to sing the role of Christine (a study of his own wife) in *Intermezzo*. She also sang the Composer in the first production of *Ariadne auf Naxos* and Barak's wife in *Die Frau ohne Schatten* in the Vienna premieres of these operas. She was a famous Sieglinde in *Die Walkure*, Leonore in *Fidelio*, and the Marschallin in *Der Rosenkavalier*. During the Nazi regime she settled in the United States, and became a U.S. citizen. She has written several books, including a novel and a series of autobiographical volumes.

Lehrstück (Ger.), literally 'educational play', a kind of musical drama. It was used by certain German composers and writers in the 1920s and early 1930s to reach the working class. Eisler, Hindemith and Weill were the chief composers in the movement, with Brecht as the leading writer. They used documentary material and ideological argument in their works, typical of which are Hindemith's *Wir bauen eine Stadt* (We build a town) and Weill's *Der Jasager* (The Yes-Sayer). For a time the plays were used to counter Nazism, until 1933 when Hindemith's music was proscribed and Weill driven out of Germany.

See GEBRAUCHSMUSIK

Leibowitz, René (1913–72), Franco-Polish composer, conductor and writer, pupil of Ravel, Schoenberg and

Webern. A champion of twelve-note music, he wrote orchestral works, chamber music (including a chamber symphony), choral music, and piano pieces, but was more distinguished as a theoretician than as a composer.

Leich, *see* LAI

leicht (Ger.), lightly.

Leichtentritt, Hugo (1874–1951), German born musicologist and composer. He studied at Harvard, Paris, and Berlin, and wrote a history of the motet (1908), *Musikalische Formenlehre* (1911, published in English as *Musical Form*, 1952), *Music, History and Ideas* (1938) and *Serge Koussevitzky* (1946).

Leidenschaft (Ger.), passion, **leidenschaftlich**, passionately.

Leider, Frieda (born 1888), German operatic soprano, who excelled in performances of Wagner's works. She sang for many years at the Berlin State Opera, as well as at Covent Garden, the Vienna State Opera, and other European opera houses.

Leier (Ger.), hurdy-gurdy.

Leigh, Walter (1905–42), English composer, pupil of Dent at Cambridge and Hindemith in Berlin. His works include two comic operas, a concertino for harpsichord and strings, and other pieces. He was killed in action in Libya.

Leighton, Kenneth (born 1929), English composer and pianist, pupil of Petrassi in Rome and now professor of music at Edinburgh University. His works include symphonies, violin concerto, viola concerto, cello concerto, organ concerto, chamber music, and piano music.

Leighton, William (died 1616), English composer, publisher and poet. He was one of the Gentlemen Pensioners of the court under Elizabeth I and James I, and was knighted in 1603. He was, however, conspicuously unsuccessful in managing his financial affairs, and towards the end of his life served a number of terms of imprisonment for debt. In 1613 he published *Tears or Lamentations of a Sorrowful Soul*, a large collection of metrical psalms and hymns written by himself. In the following year he published, under the same title, musical settings of 55 of these poems (modern edition by Cecil Hill, 1970). Eight were set by himself and the remainder by contemporary composers including Byrd, Bull, Dowland, Gibbons, Peerson, Weelkes, Wilbye, and a mysterious 'Timolphus Thopul' (perhaps Thomas or Theopilus Lupo, or both). Eighteen of the pieces are described as 'consort songs' in which three of the four vocal parts are doubled by treble viol, flute, and bass viol, and harmonic support is provided by lute, cittern, and bandora. The other pieces are for four and five parts without accompaniment.

Leinsdorf, Erich (born 1912), Vienna born conductor who settled in the United States and held appointments with the New York Metropolitan and (from 1962 until 1969) the Boston Symphony Orchestra.

leise (Ger.), soft, gentle; thus *leiser*, softer.

Leitmotiv (Ger.), 'leading theme'. Term used in 1887 by H. von Wolzogen in a discussion of Wagner's *Götterdämmerung* for the numerous recurring themes symbolising characters, objects, ideas, and emotions which Wagner used in the *Ring*. Two reasons in particular contributed to the extensive use of 'leading themes' in the *Ring* cycle: the fact that the thematic substance of the music is contained in the orchestral part, and the large symphonic scale of the drama. Recurring themes had been used in earlier operas, e.g. in Mozart's *Don Giovanni* and *Così fan tutte*, Grétry's *Richard Coeur-de-Lion* and Weber's *Der Freischütz*, and the idea of the recurrence and transformation of themes had been developed in orchestral music by Berlioz, who used the term *idée fixe* for it, Schumann, and Liszt, who called it 'metamorphosis of themes'. From Wagner's later operas the principle was adopted by a number of opera composers, notably by Richard Strauss.

Leitton (Ger.), leading note.

Le Jeune, Claude (1528–1600), French composer. From 1564, when he published *Dix Pseaumes de David*, he probably lived in Paris under the protection of noblemen of Protestant sympathies. From 1570 he was associated with the *Académie de Poésie et de Musique* of Jean-Antoine de Baïf in the composition of *musique mesurée à l'antique*. His *chansons* were published in *Livre de mélanges* (1585) and a volume of *Airs* in 1594. A number of works appeared shortly after his death, among them the *Cinquante Pseaumes de David* (1602, 1608), and the *Pseaumes en vers mesurés* (1606). A selection of his works has been republished by Henry Expert in his *Les Maîtres musiciens de la Renaissance française* and *Monuments de la musique française*. His *Missa ad placitum* (first published in 1607) has been edited by M. Sanvoisin (1967).

D. P. WALKER and F. LESURE: 'Claude Le Jeune and musique mesurée', *Musica Disciplina*, iii (1949)

Lekeu, Guillaume (1870–94), Belgian composer, pupil of Franck and d'Indy. He composed orchestral works (including a symphonic study after *Hamlet*), a *Chant Lyrique* for chorus and orchestra, a piano quartet, and other chamber music. His works showed great promise, but some had to be completed by d'Indy as Lekeu died from typhoid the day after his twenty-fourth birthday.

Lélio, ou le Retour à la Vie, monodrama by Berlioz for narrator, solo voices, chorus, piano, and orchestra, op 14b. This work was composed as a sequel to the *Symphonie Fantastique* with which it was first performed in Paris in 1832; but its awkward choice of forces has prevented it from establishing itself in the musical repertory.

Le Maistre (Le Maître), **Mattheus** (died 1577), Dutch composer. He was appointed court *Kapellmeister* at Dresden in 1554 and retired in 1567. He composed Magnificats (1577), five-part motets (1570), Latin and German sacred music (1563, 1574), German secular songs, and quodlibets.

Lemminkäinen, *see* LEGENDS

L'Enfance du Christ, *see* CHILDHOOD OF CHRIST

Leningrad Symphony, nickname of Shostakovich's symphony no 7, in which the German siege of the Russian city during World War II is portrayed in musical terms. Begun (in Leningrad) in 1941, the work glorifies Russian heroism.

lent (Fr.), slow, so *lentement*, slowly.

lento (It.), slow.

Lenz, Wilhelm von (1809–83), musical historian. He was Russian councillor at St. Petersburg and wrote two books on Beethoven (1852 and 1855–60), a book on contemporary piano-playing (1872) and a collection of essays on Liszt, Chopin and other musicians. In his first book on Beethoven, *Beethoven et ses trois styles*, he analysed Beethoven's development according to the three periods first suggested by Fétis and generally adopted after Lenz's time.

Leo, Leonardo (Lionardo Oronzo Salvatore de Leo) (1694–1744), Italian composer. He studied at the Conservatorio della Pietà dei Turchini in Naples (1703–15), where he became second master (1715) and first master (1741). He was appointed organist (1717) and first organist (1725) of the Royal Chapel and teacher at the Conservatorio di S. Onofrio (1725). His pupils included Pergolesi, Piccinni and Jommelli. He composed many operas, oratorios, Masses, motets, psalms and other church music, 6 concertos for cello with two violins and continuo, a concerto for four violins, and pieces for organ and for harpsichord. The most successful of his serious operas was *Demofoonte* (Naples, 1733), of his comic operas *Amor vuol sofferenza* (Naples, 1739).

Ruggiero Leoncavallo

Leoncavallo, Ruggiero (1858–1919), Italian composer. After studying at Naples Conservatorio, he became a café pianist and travelled in England, France, Holland, Germany and Egypt. He returned to Italy and in 1892 his most successful opera *Pagliacci* – a classic example of the Italian *verismo* style – was produced in Milan. In 1906, he toured the United States with an opera company. He composed operas to librettos by himself, including *La Bohème*, produced fifteen months after Puccini's opera with the same title. He also wrote a ballet and a symphonic poem, *Serafita*.

Leonel, *see* POWER

Leoni or **Leone** (c. 1560–1627), Italian composer who was choirmaster of Vicenza Cathedral from about 1588. He composed Masses, motets (some for double choir), Magnificats, psalms, *Sacrae cantiones* (1608) and other church music, five books of madrigals (1588–1602), a book of sacred madrigals (1596) and concertos in the style of Giovanni Gabrieli for four voices and six instruments (1615).

Leoni, Franco (1865–1938), Italian composer. His operas *Ib and Little Christina* (1901) and *L'Oracolo* (1905), the latter his most successful work, were produced in London, where he lived for 22 years. He also composed three oratorios and some songs.

Leoninus or **Léonin,** late 12th century composer at Notre Dame, Paris, where he was succeeded by Perotinus. A late 13th century theorist (known as Anonymous IV after Coussemaker, *Scriptores*, i) described him as *optimus organista* (a very excellent composer of *organa*) and as the composer of a *Magnus Liber Organi de Gradali et Antiphonario pro servitio divino multiplicando* (a great book of *organum* music on melodies from the Gradual and Antiphoner, designed to augment and enrich divine service). A transcription of the *Magnus Liber* from the so-called St. Andrews manuscript facsimile in *An Old St. Andrews Music Book*, edited by J. H. Baxter, 1931) is in W. G. Waite, *The Rhythm of Twelfth-Century Polyphony* (1954).

Leonore, (1) the title of three overtures written by Beethoven for his opera *Fidelio*, first produced at Vienna in 1805. The name is that of the heroine, who disguises herself as a man in order to rescue her husband Florestan from prison. The history of the three overtures is as follows:

Leonore no 1: never used (now thought to have been the original overture, though Thayer maintained that it was written for a performance at Prague in 1807 which never took place; *see* A. W. Thayer, *The Life of Ludwig van Beethoven*, volume iii, pages 24–5).

Leonore no 2: played at the first performance in 1805.

Leonore no 3: replaced *Leonore no 2* when a revised version of the opera was produced in 1806.

For the third and final version of the opera, produced in 1814, Beethoven wrote a fourth overture, called *Fidelio*. *Leonore no 2* and *Leonore no 3* are closely related to each other. *Leonore no 1* and the *Fidelio* overture are independent works. The reason for discarding *Leonore no 3* was that its powerfully dramatic character and preoccupation with the heroic climax of the opera made it unsuitable as an introduction to the homely comedy of the opening scene. It survives in the concert room, its proper home, though some conductors (without the composer's authority) incorporate it as a prelude to the last scene of the opera.

D. F. TOVEY: *Essays in Musical Analysis*, volume iv (1936), pages 28–43

(2) as well as being the title of three Beethoven overtures, and the name of the heroine of *Fidelio*, *Leonore* was also the title of an opera by Gaveaux (1798) with a plot anticipating Beethoven's. Rolf Liebermann's *Leonore 40/45* (1952) offers a modern adaptation of the same story, set during World War II.

Leopold I (1640–1705), Austrian emperor and composer. He composed music for the opera *Apollo deluso* (1669) by Sances and for many operas by his court musician Antonio Draghi. He also wrote Masses, offices and ballet suites.

L'Epine, Françoise Marguerite de (died 1746), soprano who arrived in England in the early years of the 18th century and appeared in association with the composer Jakob Greber, earning in consequence the contemptuous nickname 'Greber's Peg'. She rapidly acquired a reputation and sang frequently in operas and other dramatic representations between 1703 and 1716. Some time after her retirement from the stage she married J. C. Pepusch.

Leppard, Raymond (born 1927), English conductor, musicologist and harpsichordist, who studied at Trinity College, Cambridge, and returned there as a member of the music staff. In 1968 he resigned so as to have more time for conducting and for preparing modern editions of neglected 17th century Italian masterpieces. His realisation of *The Coronation of Poppaea* at Glyndebourne in 1963 was a major contribution to the Monteverdi revival; and though purists objected to his arguably over-glossy treatment of the music, he did much to popularise (in Britain and the United States) this and other works of the period. His other realisations have included Monteverdi's *Orfeo*, and Cavalli's *Ormindo* and *Calisto*.

Leroux, Xavier Henri Napoléon (1863–1919), Italian composer, pupil of Massenet at the Paris Conservatoire, where he won the *Prix de Rome* (1885) and was teacher of harmony from 1896 until his death. He composed operas, incidental music for plays, an overture, cantatas, a Mass with orchestra, motets and numerous songs. His most successful opera was *Le Chemineau* (Paris, 1907).

Le Roy, Adrien, 16th century French lutenist, composer, and music printer in partnership with his brother-in-law Robert Ballard. From 1551 to 1571 he published over twenty volumes containing original compositions and arrangements of *chansons*, psalms and dances for lute, cittern and guitar with or without voice. They include a collection of *airs de cour* for lute published in 1571 (modern edition in *Chansons au luth et airs de cour français*, edited by L. de la Laurencie, A. Mairy and G. Thibault, 1934). He also wrote instruction books for the guitar (1551), cittern (1565) and lute (1567?), but the first of these has not survived and the lute-book is known only through the English translations printed in 1568 and 1574. A bibliography by F. Lesure and G. Thibault of the publications of Le Roy and Ballard appeared in 1955.

Les Adieux, see LEBEWOHL

Leschetizky, Theodor (1830–1915), Polish-born teacher, pianist and composer. He studied under Czerny, began teaching at a young age and made concert tours from 1842–48 and in 1852. He taught at St. Petersburg Conservatory (1852–78), gave concerts in England, Holland and Germany and settled in Vienna, where he founded his own (exceptionally famous), school of piano playing and his own 'method'. His pupils included Paderewski and Schnabel. He composed many piano pieces and an opera.

A. HULLAH: *Theodor Leschetizky* (1906)

Lescurel, Jehan de (d. c. 1304), French composer of 34 songs, all but one monophonic. He is probably to be identified with the Lescurel who was a student cleric at Notre Dame, Paris, and who was executed for debauchery in 1304. He was one of the first to use the FORMES FIXES in the patterns which remained established throughout the fourteenth and for most of the fifteenth centuries. A complete edition of his works by N. Wilkins was published in 1966.

Les Six, see SIX

lesson, term for a piece of music used in England in the seventeenth and eighteenth centuries. It was used by Morley as a title for ensemble music (*First Booke of Consort Lessons,* 1611), but later was usually applied only to pieces for harpsichord or other solo instrument which would now be called suites (e.g., Purcell's posthumous *A Choice Collection of Lessons for the Harpsichord or Spinet,* 1696) or sonatas (e.g. Thomas Roseingrave's edition of *Forty-two Suites of Lessons for the Harpsichord by Domenico Scarlatti*) or studies (e.g., the various collections of *Select Lessons* for flute, solo violin, and bass viol published by John Walsh).

Lesueur, Jean François (1760–1837), French composer. He was a chorister at Abbeville and from 1779 held important church appointments at Séez, Paris, Dijon, Le Mans and Tours. He returned to Paris (1784) and was appointed music director at Notre Dame (1786), where he introduced a full orchestra during the Mass, causing a controversy which finally forced him to resign (1788). He was professor at the École de la Garde Nationale (from 1793) and professor of composition (1818 until his death) at the Paris Conservatoire. He was also Paisiello's successor as *maître de chapelle* to Napoleon (from 1804) and held the post under Louis XVIII. His pupils included Berlioz and Gounod. He composed operas, oratorios, cantatas, a *Te Deum* and Mass for Napoleon's coronation, about thirty Masses, psalms, motets and other church music and wrote an essay on Paisiello. His *La Caverne* (1793) was one of the earliest examples of the type called 'bandit' opera, fashionable at the time. His *Le Triomphe de Trajan* (1807) was written, with Persuis, to celebrate Napoleon's return from Prussia. He anticipated his pupil Berlioz in using a large orchestra, and in giving the audience illustrative notes for his orchestral compositions.

Lesur, Daniel (Daniel-Lesur) (born 1908), French composer and organist. He became organist of the Benedictine Abbey in Paris and professor of counterpoint at the Schola Cantorum (from 1938) and with Jolivet, Baudrier and Messiaen formed the group called *La Jeune France.* He has composed an orchestral suite, Passacaille for piano and orchestra, chamber music, piano and organ pieces, and songs. With Jolivet he collaborated on a ballet, *The Child and the. Monster.*

Let's Make an Opera, entertainment for children by Britten, to a text by Eric Crozier, produced at Aldeburgh in 1949. The work, which involves audience participation, shows the planning, rehearsal and finally the performance of a children's opera, *The Little Sweep.*

Leveridge, Richard (c. 1670–1758), English composer and bass singer who appeared in London operas, plays, masques, etc., from about 1695–1751. He composed incidental music for plays, a masque, songs and a 'new Entertainment of Vocal and Instrumental Musick (after the manner of an Opera)' called *Britain's Happiness* (1704). The most famous of his songs is 'The Roast Beef of Old England'.

Levi, Hermann (1839–1900), German conductor famous in his day for his interpretations of opera. He studied in Mannheim and Leipzig. From 1872 until 1896 he was conductor at the Munich Court Theatre. In 1882 he conducted the première of Wagner's *Parsifal* at Bayreuth. He was especially famous for his conducting of Wagner at Bayreuth and elsewhere. He composed a piano concerto and songs among other works.

Lévy, Roland Alexis Manuel, *see* ROLAND-MANUEL

Lewis, Anthony (born 1915), English musicologist, conductor and composer. He became professor of music at Birmingham University in 1947, and since 1968 has been principal of the Royal Academy of Music in London. He is an authority on the music of the 17th and 18th centuries, and is founder and general editor of *Musica Britannica*. As conductor, he has helped to rehabilitate a number of neglected operas, including works by Handel and Rameau's *Hippolyte et Aricie*. He was knighted in 1972.

Lewis, Richard (born 1914), English tenor, notable in opera house and concert hall. He originated the role of Troilus in Walton's *Troilus and Cressida* at Covent Garden in 1954, and has sung principal parts in many other first productions, including Tippett's *A Midsummer Marriage* and the British première of Schoenberg's *Moses and Aaron*.

Ley, Henry George (1887–1962), English organist and composer who was director of music at Eton College from 1926 until 1945. He composed orchestral variations on a Handel theme, chamber music, church music, works for organ and songs.

L'Héritier, Jean, French composer of the first half of the 16th century, a pupil of Josquin. In 1521 he became *maestro di cappella* at the French church of St. Louis in Rome. By 1540 he was *maître de chapelle* to the Cardinal of Clermont at Avignon. Motets, a Magnificat and a Mass by him were published in contemporary collections. His works have been edited by L. Perkins (two volumes, 1969).

L'Heure Espagnole, *see* HEURE ESPAGNOLE

L'Homme Armé, *see* HOMME ARME

Liadov, Anatol Konstantinovich (1855–1914), Russian composer, teacher and conductor. He studied at the St. Petersburg Conservatory under Rimsky-Korsakov until 1877 and from 1878 taught at the Conservatory and at the Imperial Chapel. He was commissioned by the Imperial Geographical Society to study and collect Russian folksongs. His most famous works are his symphonic poems, *Baba Yaga* (1904), *The Enchanted Lake* (1909), and *Kikimora* (1910). He also wrote two orchestral scherzos, choral music, piano pieces and songs. As a composer, however, he lacked drive. When he was invited to write the *Firebird* ballet by Diaghilev he threw away his opportunity and the commission went to Stravinsky instead.

Liapunov, Sergey Mikhailovich (1859–1924), Russian composer. He studied at the Moscow Conservatory (1878–83) under Chaikovsky and Taneyev, and taught at the St. Petersburg Conservatory from 1910 until 1918. He was commissioned (with Liadov and Balakirev) by the Imperial Geographical Society to study and collect Russian folksongs, went to Paris during the Revolution and appeared as pianist and conductor in Germany and Austria. His works include two symphonies, two concertos and a *Rhapsody* for piano and orchestra, settings of folksongs, mazurkas and numerous other piano pieces.

libretto (It.), literally 'booklet'. The text of an opera or oratorio. The ideas and work of a librettist have at times had an important influence on the style and character of opera, e.g. those of Rinuccini on the early Florentine operas, of Metastasio on 18th century opera and of Scribe on French grand opera of the 1830's. Librettists and composers have often formed long-lasting working relationships, such as Calzabigi and Gluck, Hofmannsthal and Strauss, and, of course, Gilbert and Sullivan. Wagner is the most famous composer-librettist; other composers who have written some or all of their own libretti are Berlioz, Busoni, Rimsky-Korsakov, Delius, Holst, Hindemith and Tippett.

Libuše, opera in three acts by Smetana, to a text by Joseph Wenzig (Czech translation by Erwin Spindler). This work was written for the inauguration of the Czech National Theatre in Prague in 1881, and concerns two brothers who are rivals in love. They are brought to trial before Libuše, Queen of Bohemia, and are ultimately reconciled.

licenza (It.), licence, freedom. Thus *andante cantabile, con alcuna licenza* (Chaikovsky's marking of the slow movement of his fifth symphony) means 'slowly and in a singing manner, with some freedom in its manner of performance'.

Lichfield (Lichfild), Henry, English composer who was probably in the service of Lord and later Lady Cheney (Cheyney) at Toddington House near Luton. He published a book of five-part madrigals in 1613 (modern edition in *The English Madrigal School*, xvii).

Liebe der Danae, Die (The Love of Danae), opera in three acts by Richard Strauss.

Liebermann, Rolf (born 1910), Swiss composer and opera administrator. His works, whose style ranges from twelve-note music to jazz, include several operas (including *Leonore 40/45*, *Penelope* and *The School for Wives*) and a concerto for jazz band and symphony orchestra. Later his activities as an administrator curbed his output as a composer. Between 1959 and 1972 he developed the Hamburg State Opera as the most progressive company in Europe, with an enviable list of commissions and first performances to its credit. He later redeveloped the Paris Opéra.

Liebesflöte (Ger.), a flute built a minor third below the normal size, now obsolete.

Liebeslieder (Ger., Songs of Love), a set of eighteen waltzes for vocal quartet and piano duet by Brahms, op 52 (also published for piano duet only as op 52a). The words are from Georg Friedrich Daumer's *Polydora*. A second set of fifteen was issued under the title *Neue Liebeslieder*, op 65. Brahms also made a version of nine of the *Liebeslieder* for voices and small orchestra, with the addition of a tenth waltz which was later revised for incorporation in the *Neue Liebeslieder*.

Liebesoboe (Ger.), oboe d'amore.

Liebestod (Ger., love-death), title commonly used for Isolde's death scene at the end of *Tristan and Isolde*. Wagner himself, however, applied the title, significantly, to the love duet in Act 2 of the opera.

Liebestraum (Ger., dream of love), title chosen by Liszt for the piano arrangements he made of three of his songs. The most famous of these is *Liebestraum* no 3.

Liebesverbot, Das (Ger., *The Love Ban*), opera in two acts by Wagner. The libretto, by the composer himself, is based on Shakespeare's *Measure for Measure*. The first performance was at Magdeburg in

1836. The music dates from Wagner's formative years. His first major opera, *Tannhäuser*, followed in 1845.

lieblich (Ger.), 'sweet'. Applied to a family of sweet-toned stops on the organ which have stopped pipes, e.g. to the Lieblichflöte, Lieblich Gedeckt (*gedeckt* or *gedackt* = 'stopped'), and Lieblich Bourdon.

Lied (Ger.), 'song'. The term has come to be particularly applied to the German romantic songs of Schubert, Schumann, Brahms, Wolf, Strauss and others but has also been used since the Middle Ages in the more general sense. Special features of the *Lied* (plural *Lieder*) are the attention paid to the mood of the words and the importance of the piano part.

Liederbuch (Ger.), songbook. Term applied to many early collections of German songs, as well as to Wolf's Italian and Spanish Songbooks.

Lieder eines fahrenden Gesellen (Ger., *Songs of a Wayfarer*), a set of four songs with orchestral accompaniment by Mahler (1884). The words, by the composer himself, tell of a young man who has been forsaken by his sweetheart. Material from the first, second and fourth songs reappeared later in Mahler's first symphony (1888).

Liederkreis (Ger.), song cycle, established as a definite form during the great *Lied* period. The songs in the cycle are linked by meaning and musical style. Schumann used the term for two of his sets of songs.

Liederspiel (Ger.), 'song play': (1) the German equivalent of ballad opera and of the French *vaudeville*, in which the songs are folk songs or in folk-song style. It was originated by J. F. Reichardt, whose *Lieb' und Treue*, first performed in Berlin in 1800, was the first example;

(2) also applied to a song cycle of which the text involves some element of action, e.g., to Schumann's *Spanisches Liederspiel*, op 74, for quartet and piano, and Brahms's *Liebeslieder* Waltzes, op 52, for quartet and piano duet, and *Zigeunerlieder*, op 103, for quartet and piano.

Liedertafel (Ger.), song table, name given to male-voice choral societies in parts of Germany or in German-descended parts of the United States.

Lied von der Erde, *see* SONG OF THE EARTH

Lieutenant Kizhe, Russian film with incidental music by Prokofiev (1933). The composer later arranged a five-movement concert suite, op 60, from the music for the film.

Life for the Tsar, A, *see* IVAN SUSSANIN.

ligature, (1) form used for the writing of a group of notes in plainsong notation from about 1150. In modal notation the arrangement and order of the ligatures indicated a particular RHYTHMIC MODE, which was maintained more or less throughout the part. In MENSURAL NOTATION ligatures were used for writing successions of longs and breves, and their rhythm was interpreted according to the principles of perfection (*see* PERFECT) and PROPRIETY, and in the single form in which semibreves appeared, by the principle of opposite propriety. In vocal performance a ligature was sung to one syllable. Because they were derived originally from the NEUMES of plainsong notation, their forms differed in descending and ascending. Ligatures of two notes had the following meanings:

Descending	Ascending		Rhythm
♭	♮ or ♪	With propriety and perfection	Breve-Long
♮	♮ or ♪	Without propriety and with perfection	Long-Long
♩	♪	With propriety and without perfection	Breve-Breve
◻	♪	Without propriety and without perfection	Long-Breve
♮ or ♭	♮ or ♭	With opposite propriety (used only at the beginning of a ligature or separately)	Semibreve-Semibreve

In ligatures of more than two notes, all but the first and last, whose values were determined by the two-note forms, were breves unless shown as long or large, and except in the case of a ligature beginning with two semibreves in opposite propriety, e.g.:

= Semibreve-semibreve-breve-breve-long-breve-long

Like single notes, notes in a ligature could be dotted, to increase their value by one-half, or coloured (red in black notation, black in white notation) to decrease their value by one-third:

= dotted semibreve-dotted semibreve

W. APEL: *The Notation of Polyphonic Music* (fifth edition, 1961)

Ligeti, György (born 1923), Hungarian composer who left his homeland in 1956 to settle in Austria and Germany. The most important Hungarian composer since Bartók, he makes imaginative use of sliding string textures and strands of wind tone. Such works as *Atmospheres*, *Lontano* and *Ramifications* reveal a fastidious ear for detail, and though their idiom is 'advanced' they are by no means hard to listen to. The rest of his output includes a concerto for flute and oboe, chamber music, and a Requiem which shows his choral music to be just as original and fascinating as his instrumental works.

Lilliburlero, the words of a topical satire, beginning 'Ho! broder Teague, dost hear de decree, Lilliburlero, bullen a la', on Irish Roman Catholics and on the appointment of General Talbot as Lord Lieutenant of Ireland in 1687 were set to a tune called 'Quick Step' in *The Delightful Companion* (second edition, 1686):

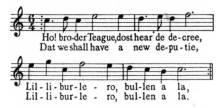

and became the most popular political ballad of the day. It appeared as 'A New Irish Tune' in the second part of *Musick's Hand-Maid . . . for the Virginal and Spinet* (1689) in a setting by Purcell, who also used it as the bass of the Jig in the *Gordian Knot unty'd* (1691).

Lily of Killarney, The, opera in three acts by Benedict, to a libretto by John Oxenford and Dion Boucicault (founded on Boucicault's *Colleen Bawn*), first performed in London in 1862.

Limburgia, Johannes de, *see* JOHANNES DE LIM-BURGIA

Limma, remainder.
See DIESIS (1)

Lincoln Portrait, A, work for narrator and orchestra by Copland, with a text based on Lincoln's letters and speeches. First performed in 1942, the work quotes Stephen Foster's 'Camptown Races' and a traditional ballad, 'Springfield Mountain'.

Lind, Jenny (1820–87), Swedish soprano whose exceptional range, purity and flexibility of voice earned her the nickname of 'The Swedish Nightingale'. She made her debut as Agatha in Weber's *Der Freischütz* in Stockholm in 1838. Nine years later she moved to London, from where she toured extensively. She visited the United States (1850–52) and was appointed singing teacher at the Royal College of Music, 1883. She sang the soprano part which had been written for her in Meyerbeer's *Feldlager in Schlesien* (1844) and the role of Amalia in the first performance of Verdi's *I Masnadieri* (1847). Her last operatic appearance was in 1849 but she continued to sing in oratorios and concerts until 1870. She married Otto Goldschmidt.

Linda di Chamounix (Fr., *Linda of Chamonix*), opera in three acts by Donizetti, to a libretto by Gaetano Rossi, first performed in Vienna in 1842.

lingual stops, *see* REED STOPS

Liniensystem (Ger.), staff, stave. Commonly abbreviated to *System*.

lining out, the practice of having the lines of a hymn or psalm read or sung out by the minister or preacher before being sung by the congregation. The aim was to familiarise the congregation with the text. In Britain the practice was also known as 'deaconing'.

Linley, Thomas, (1733–95), English composer and singing teacher. He studied in Bath and London and lived in Bath, where he taught singing and produced concerts. He was appointed manager of the oratorios (with Stanley from 1774 and with Arnold from 1786) at the London Drury Lane Theatre, where he became part owner (succeeding Garrick) and music director in 1776. He composed an opera, incidental music (with his son Thomas) for *The Duenna* by Sheridan (his son-in-law) and many other stage works, cantatas, six elegies for three voices and piano, part-songs and ballads. His children were all musicians and included **Thomas** (1756–78) a violinist, composer and friend of Mozart, and **Elizabeth Ann** (1754–92) a famous soprano and wife of Sheridan.

'Linz' Symphony, nickname for Mozart's symphony no 36 in C, K 425, so called because it was composed and first performed at the house of Count Thun in Linz, during a visit made by Mozart in 1783.

lion's roar, a type of friction drum. The drum head is vibrated by a piece of rosined string that is attached to it. Varèse, in *Hyperprism* and *Ionisation*, both written in 1924, was probably the first significant composer to use the instrument.

Lipatti, Dinu (1917–50), Romanian pianist and composer, pupil of Cortot and Nadia Boulanger. One of the most gifted pianists of the century, with a special flair for Mozart, Chopin and Schumann, he died too soon (of leukaemia, in Switzerland) to fulfil his great potential. His compositions, of considerable pianistic interest, include a concertino for piano and orchestra, a *symphonie concertante* for two pianos and strings, and a sonatina for left hand.

lira (It.), a stringed instrument played with a bow. In use between about 1580 and 1650, it was made in two sizes, the smaller (*lira da braccio*) being played on the arm, and the larger (*lira da gamba*) between the knees.
See LYRA

lira organizzata, *see* VIELLE ORGANISEE

Lisley, John (16th–17th centuries), English composer who contributed a six-part madrigal to *The Triumphes of Oriana* (1601). Nothing more is known of his life or works.

Listenius, Magister Nikolaus (born c. 1500), German theorist. He studied in Wittenberg in 1529 and was in Salzwedel in 1535, perhaps as cantor. He wrote an elementary treatise *Rudimenta musicae* which was published at Wittenberg in 1533, was revised under the title *Musica* in 1537, and appeared in many editions until 1583. A facsimile of the 1549 edition by G. Schünemann was published in 1927.

l'istesso tempo (It.), the same tempo.

Liszt, Ferencz (German, **Franz**) (1811–86), Hungarian composer and pianist. Born at Raiding, he received his first piano lessons from his father, a steward on the Esterházy estate and devoted amateur musician. His first recital, at the age of nine, attracted the attention of various rich Hungarians, who subsidised his studies for the next six years. His progress was so rapid that in 1823 his father took him to Vienna, where he became a pupil of Czerny and Salieri and gave a recital attended by Beethoven (who was impressed). From 1823 until 1835 he lived in Paris, became famous as a pianist, and absorbed the many musical influences of the city, including those of Chopin, Berlioz and Paganini. In 1835 he eloped to Switzerland with the Countess d'Agoult (later known as Daniel Stern, the novelist); their second daughter, Cosima, was born at Como in 1837. At the age of 33 she became Wagner's second wife. During the years in Paris he wrote many compositions for piano, including the first two parts of the *Années de Pèlerinage* (Years of Pilgrimage) and studies based on the caprices of Paganini. From 1838 until 1847 he gave concerts in all parts of Europe, and was acknowledged as the greatest virtuoso of the day, enjoying the kind of adulation which now is reserved for pop groups. In 1847, in Kiev, he met Princess Caroline Sayn-Wittgenstein, the wife of a rich Russian landowner, who fell in love with him and for whom he temporarily forsook the life of a travelling virtuoso in favour of a more settled appointment at Weimar. There he was appointed court conductor and musical director, encouraging progressive fellow-composers and performing their latest works. Wagner's *Lohengrin* had its première at Weimar, which, through Liszt's presence, re-established itself as the great cultural centre it had been in Goethe's time. Liszt's own music also flourished during this period; while at Weimar he composed his symphonic poems and Hungarian Rhapsodies. From 1861 (after a disagreement over an operatic production) he lived in Rome, composed his two oratorios and other works and took minor orders, which enabled him to call himself Abbé but did not interfere with his musical career or private life. From 1869 until his death he divided his time between Rome, Budapest and Weimar, and in his later

Franz Liszt in 1838, on his way to Italy. This portrait by Kriehuber shows that Liszt's romantic image was well established at the age of 27

years received as pupils many musicians who later became famous, including Busoni, Siloti, Rosenthal, Lamond, Sauer and Weingartner. He died while visiting his daughter Cosima at Bayreuth, where he was buried.

One of the most stimulating musical personalities of the 19th century, Liszt was the first of the great piano recitalists, and in sheer virtuosity he was unmatched. His symphonies, symphonic poems (a title he invented), concertos, and piano music, though sometimes weakened by an over-rhetorical style, have great importance in the history of PROGRAMME MUSIC, and for their adoption and development of the idea of the *idée fixe* and of thematic metamorphosis. Some of his later piano pieces, e.g. *Nuages gris*, were to prove far-reaching in their harmonic innovations. He published books on Wagner's *Lohengrin* and *Tannhäuser*, on Chopin, on the nocturnes of Field, on *The Gypsy in Music* (English translation by E. Evans), and an essay on Robert Franz. Apart from the many transcriptions of orchestral works, operas, songs, and other compositions, his more important works are:

(1) Orchestra: *Faust* Symphony (1853–61), *Dante* Symphony (1856), twelve symphonic poems, piano concertos in E flat (1857) and A (1863).

(2) Piano: *Années de Pèlerinage*: *Suisse* (1852), *Italie* (1848), *Troisième année* (posthumously collected, 1890); twelve *Études d'Exécution Transcendante* (final form, 1854); three *Études de Concert* (1849); *Deux Études de Concert*: *Waldesrauchen, Gnomenreigen* (1849–63); *Deux Légendes* (1866); twenty Hungarian Rhapsodies (1851–86).

(3) Choral works: Two oratorios: *The Legend of St. Elizabeth* (1862), *Christus* (1866); *Psalm XIII* (1863); Hungarian Coronation Mass (1867).

(4) Songs: Fifty-five songs (collected edition, 1860).

A selection from the letters of Liszt was published in two volumes in 1894, and the letters of Liszt and Von Bülow in 1896, both translated by C. Bache.

W. BECKETT: *Liszt* (1956)

F. CORDER: *Franz Liszt* (1933)

E. NEWMAN: *The Man Liszt* (1934, reissued 1969)

H. SEARLE: *The Music of Liszt* (1954)

S. SITWELL: *Franz Liszt* (1934)

A. WALKER (editor): *Franz Liszt: The Man and His Music* (1970)

litany, a series of invocations to God, the Blessed Virgin, and the Saints sung by the priest and responded to by the people with *Kyrie eleison* ('Lord, have mercy') or a similar response, both to a simple plainsong formula. Polyphonic settings of one such litany, the *Litaniae Lauretanae* ('Litanies of Loreto') were written by Palestrina, Lassus, and Mozart (K 109 for choir, strings, and organ; K 195 for choir, orchestra, and organ). Mozart also set the *Litaniae de venerabili altaris sacramento* (K 243 for choir, orchestra, and organ).

At the command of Henry VIII, Archbishop Cranmer made and adapted to the plainsong an English version of the litany which was printed in 1544. There is evidence that a five-part setting was printed in the same year. Cranmer's litany (facsimile edition in J. E. Hunt, *Cranmer's First Litany, 1544 and Merbecke's Book of Common Prayer Noted 1550*, (1939)) became, with few changes, the litany of the English Prayer Book, and its music was the basis of settings in four and five parts composed by Tallis.

lithophones, ancient group of instruments on which tuned sounds are produced by striking stone surfaces. They may be regarded as forerunners of the xylophone.

Litolff, Henry Charles (1818–1891), French composer, pianist and music publisher, born in London of Anglo-Alsatian parentage. A pupil of Moscheles, he composed operas, works for piano and orchestra (on several of which he bestowed the title *concerto symphonique*) and piano pieces. Though the bulk of his output has fallen by the wayside, he achieved immortality with the scherzo from the fourth of his symphonic concertos – a movement nowadays almost invariably performed out of context.

'Little Russian' Symphony, nickname for Chaikovsky's symphony no 2 in C minor, op 17, first performed in 1873. The name refers not to the size of the work, but to the fact that it makes use of Little Russian (or, in modern nomenclature, Ukrainian) folk tunes.

liturgical drama, *see* TROPE

lituus (Lat.), an ancient type of trumpet used in the Roman army. Being similar in shape to a krummhorn it was later confused with that instrument. Two instruments are marked *lituus* by Bach in his cantata no 118, but what he intended is uncertain.

liuto, *see* LUTE

Liuzzi, Fernando (1884–1940), Italian musicologist and composer, pupil of Reger and Mottl. From 1927 he was professor of musical history at Rome University. In 1939 he moved to the United States. He composed a chamber opera for puppets, three oratorios, an orchestral work, five sets of songs, organ pieces and works for piano and violin.

Lloyd, John (died 1523), English composer. He was a gentleman of the Chapel Royal from 1511 or earlier. His five-part Mass *O quam suavis*, which is remarkable for the 'canons' or riddles used for the notation of the tenor, has been edited by H. B. Collins (1927). The composer's name is hidden in the enigmatic inscription 'Hoc fecit Johannes maris', i.e. 'This is the work of

John of the Sea' (he interpreted Lloyd to mean 'flood' or 'sea').

Lobgesang, *see* HYMN OF PRAISE

Locatelli, Pietro (1695–1764), Italian violinist and composer. After studying in Rome under Corelli, he toured extensively and settled in Amsterdam where he produced concerts. He was a great innovatory violinist. He composed twelve *concerti grossi* (1721), flute sonatas (1732), twelve violin concertos with twenty-four caprices to serve as cadenzas (1733), concertos and caprices for four-part strings, trio sonatas, and solo sonatas, many of which are played by violinists, violin cellists and flautists nowadays.

Locke, Matthew (?1622–77), English composer. He was a chorister at Exeter Cathedral under Edward Gibbons, and has left his name carved in the organ-screen. When cathedral services stopped during the Interregnum, he continued his studies, and became composer in ordinary to Charles II in 1660. He composed the music for the king's procession to his coronation in 1661. Later he was organist to Queen Catherine. He was the cause of several controversies, both in his innovatory settings of music and in his writing in defence of 'modern music'. With Christopher Gibbons he composed music for Shirley's masque *Cupid and Death* (1653, edited by E. J. Dent in *Musica Britannica*, ii). Subsequently he contributed music to the earliest English operas, Davenant's *Siege of Rhodes* (1653; lost) and Shadwell's *Psyche* (1673), the latter being an imitation of a *comédie-ballet* with the same title by Molière and Lully (1671). Locke's music for *Psyche* was published together with his instrumental incidental music to *The Tempest* as *The English Opera* (1675). He also composed incidental music for other plays, consort music for strings and for 'sagbutts and cornetts', a *Kyrie*, a *Credo*, anthems, and songs. His *Melothesia* (1673) is the earliest extant printed English treatise on playing from figured bass. The chamber music has been edited by Michael Tilmouth in *Musica Britannica*, xxxi–xxxii.

Purcell wrote an elegy when he died, 'On the death of his Worthy Friend, Mr. Matthew Locke'.

Lockwood, Normand (born 1906), U.S. composer. He won the U.S. *Prix de Rome* (1929), studied under Boulanger and Respighi, was appointed associate professor of theory and composition at Oberlin College (1933) and later taught at Columbia University. He has composed choral works (some with orchestra), a chamber opera *The Scarecrow*, string quartets and other chamber music and piano pieces.

loco (It.), place, i.e. in the normal place. Used (1) to contradict a previous indication 8*va* or *all'ottava*, by indicating that the music is to be played at the normal pitch, not an octave higher or lower; (2) also in string music to indicate that a passage is to be played in the normal position, after a previous contrary indication.

Locrian mode, (1) in ancient Greek music:

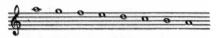

(2) in modern usage applied to:

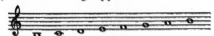

This mode was called Hyperaeolian by Glareanus in his *Dodecachordon* (1547) and its plagal form (F to F, with B as final) Hyperphrygian. He points out, however, that it is of no practical use, since the interval between the first and fifth notes is not a perfect fifth, as in all the other modes, but a diminished fifth. For this reason it had virtually only a theoretical existence. For an apparent attempt at writing in the Locrian mode see the three-part instrumental piece by Cornyshe printed in *Musica Britannica*, xviii (page 46).

See also GREEK MUSIC, MODE

Loder, Edward James (1813–65), English composer and conductor. He was the son of a music publisher, studied in Frankfurt under Ferdinand Ries and was a theatre conductor in London and Manchester, but due to a brain disease he was forced to retire in 1856. The new English Opera House (Lyceum Theatre) opened with his first opera, *Nourjahad*, in 1834. He composed *The Night Dancers* (1846) and other operas which were very popular during the middle decades of the last century. He also wrote stage works, a cantata, string quartets, and sacred and secular songs, by which he is remembered.

Loeffler, Charles Martin (1861–1935), Alsatian born composer and violinist, pupil of Joachim in Berlin and Massart and Ernest Guiraud in Paris. He played in orchestras in Europe, in New York (1881–2) and in the Boston Symphony Orchestra (1882–1903). His compositions, written in a delicate and evocative style resembling in some respects that of Debussy, include *La Mort de Tintagiles* for orchestra and viola d'amore (1905), *A Pagan Poem* (after Virgil) for orchestra (1905–6), *The Canticle of the Sun* for solo voice and orchestra (1925), *Five Irish Fantasies* for voice and orchestra (1922), choral works, chamber music, and songs.

Loeillet, Jean-Baptiste (1680–1730), Belgian composer, flautist and oboist. He lived in Paris from 1702 and in London from 1705, where he became a member of the King's Theatre orchestra. In one of his publications he calls himself chamber musician to the elector of Bavaria and concert-master to Duke Ferdinand. He composed sonatas for one to three flutes and a set for flute, oboe or violin, and gave concerts in his own house in 1710 at which some of Corelli's works received their first London performance. He also composed sonatas for flute, oboe or violin and flute trios and published a set of six lessons for harpsichord. He helped to popularise the flute in London.

Loewe or **Loew, Johann Jakob** (1629–1703), German composer and organist. He studied under Heinrich Schütz at Dresden (1652), was *Kapellmeister* at Wolfenbüttel (from 1655), went to Zeitz (1663) and was organist of St. Nicholas's Church at Lüneburg (from 1682). He composed two operas, ballets, instrumental suites (with introductory movements called *Synfonia*), and songs for solo voice.

Loewe, Johann Karl Gottfried (1796–1869), German composer, conductor, pianist and singer. He was a chorister at Cöthen (1807–9), studied in Halle and later taught at the Singakademie there. He settled in Stettin where he was appointed professor at the Gymnasium, municipal music director, and organist of St. Jacob's (1821). He travelled extensively, visiting Vienna (1844), London (1847), Scandinavia (1851) and France (1857), and retired to Kiel in 1866, where he died after going into a trance. He composed five operas (one produced), oratorios, a cantata, a ballad, *Die Walpurgisnacht*, for soloists, chorus and orchestra, string quartets and other chamber music, numerous solo songs, part-songs, piano solos and duets, and orchestral works (unpublished). He is most notable as the composer and populariser of the dramatic type of *Lied* known as 'ballad', of which he wrote about 150. Among the most famous of these are 'Der Erlkönig' (composed three years after Schubert's setting of the same Goethe poem – Wagner considered Loewe's song to be superior), 'Tom der Reimer' and 'Edward', well known today. Several of Loewe's ballads, including two of the above, are of Scottish origin.

Loewenberg, Alfred (1902–49) German musicologist. He studied at Jena University, left Germany in 1934 and settled in London. His *Annals of Opera* (1943, revised edition 1955) is a valuable chronological tabulation of first and subsequent performances of some 4000 operas from 1597 to 1940.

log drum, made of wood and usually cylindrical, log drums are hollow and sealed off at the two ends, but they have a slit that runs almost their entire length. They are made in various sizes and produce notes of precise pitch. Ginastera and Henze, among others, have written for them.

Logier, Johann Bernhard (1777–1846), German born inventor of the Chiroplast (mechanism to train hands for piano-playing); also a flautist, piano teacher, bandmaster and organist. He travelled to Britain when he was ten and later settled in Dublin (1809) where he opened a music shop (1811). He patented the Chiroplast (1814), gave lectures on its use and lived in Berlin for three years. He wrote a *Thoroughbass* (which was the first musical textbook used by Wagner) and books on his piano-teaching system, and composed a piano concerto, trios, ode on the fiftieth year of George III's reign (1809), and piano sonatas.

Logroscino or **Lo Groscino, Nicola** (1698–1765), Italian composer. He studied at the Conservatorio di Loreto in Naples (1714–27), was an organist in Conza, later lived in Naples and from 1747 was teacher of counterpoint at the Conservatorio in Palermo. He composed more than 25 operas, some of them in collaboration with Piccinni, but few of his works have survived.

Lohengrin, opera in three acts by Wagner, to a libretto by the composer. The first performance at Weimar in 1850 was conducted by Liszt. The opera opens with the discovery that Gottfried, Duke of Brabent, has mysteriously disappeared, and that Count Frederick of Telramund has claimed the throne. He accuses Elsa, Gottfried's sister, of having murdered her brother. An unknown champion appears in a boat drawn by a swan. He agrees to espouse Elsa's cause on condition that she does not ask his name. He defeats Telramund in combat and marries Elsa. Her curiosity having been aroused by Ortrud, Telramund's wife, she asks her husband's name, but he refuses to tell her. Telramund rushes in to attack him, but is instantly killed. The next morning, before the king, the knight reveals that his name is Lohengrin: he is the son of Parsifal and a knight of the Holy Grail. Only as long as he remains unknown is he invincible, and so he must now leave. Ortrud reveals that the swan is Gottfried, whom she has transformed by enchantment. As the dove of the Holy Grail descends, the swan changes into the young Duke Gottfried. Lohengrin departs in the boat, now drawn by the dove of the Holy Grail, and Elsa falls dead.

Lombardi alla prima corciata, I (It., *The Lombards at the First Crusade*), opera in four acts by Verdi, to a libretto by Temistocle Solera, first performed at Milan in 1843. This was the first Verdi opera performed in the United States (in 1847). A second version, entitled *Jérusalem*, with a French libretto by Royer and Vaëz, was presented at the Paris opera in 1847. The plot concerns two rival brothers, one of whom becomes a hermit in the Holy Land after accidentally killing his father in mistake for his brother. Ultimately they are reconciled during the First Crusade, though not before there has been considerable intervening bloodshed.

Lombardic rhythm, *see* SCOTCH SNAP

Londonderry Air, Irish folk tune, first printed in the Petrie collection in 1855. It has been arranged by composers all over the world, including Percy Grainger. The words frequently sung to it now ('Danny Boy') were not the first: two poems by Alfred Perceval Graves had previously been set to it.

As a powerfully emotive melody, it has appealed, among others, to Parry, who called it 'the most beautiful tune in the world', and to Plunket Greene, who claimed that only the violin could do it justice – it was beyond the range of the human voice.

London Philharmonic Orchestra, one of London's five principal symphony orchestras, founded in 1932 by Sir Thomas Beecham. Until World War II, it played regularly for the concerts of the Royal Philharmonic Society, for the Courtauld-Sargent concerts and for the summer season of opera at Covent Garden. When war broke out it became self-governing, with a chairman and board of directors elected from among its own members. Since 1945 its principal conductors have included Eduard van Beinum, Sir Adrian Boult, John Pritchard and Bernard Haitink.

London Symphony, (1) nickname for Haydn's last symphony, no 104 in D, first performed in 1795 during the composer's second visit to London. The name is somewhat misleading, since Haydn's last twelve symphonies (the 'Salomon' symphonies) were all written for London.

(2) Vaughan Williams's second symphony (composed 1914, revised 1920), which incorporates sounds of London life such as street cries and the chimes of Big Ben.

London Symphony Orchestra, one of London's five principal symphony orchestras. It was founded in 1904 by a group of players who resigned from the Queen's Hall Orchestra because they refused to accept Wood's ruling that deputies should not be employed. From its inception it has managed its own affairs, and has chosen its own conductors. In recent years, these have included Pierre Monteux, István Kertesz and Andre Previn.

long (Lat., *longa*), in modal notation and mensural notation the note written ꟼ (later ꟼ) which had the value of three breves if perfect and of two breves if imperfect. A perfect large (Lat. *maxima*) contained three longs and an imperfect large two longs.

Long, Marguérite (1874–1966), French pianist and lifelong champion of French music. Ravel dedicated his G major piano concerto to her. She was a teacher for many years at the Paris Conservatoire.

lontano (It.), distant. The term was used by Berlioz at the start of the slow movement of his *Symphonie Fantastique* where the oboist (in emulation of a distant shepherd) plays off-stage. *Lontano* is also the title of an orchestral work by Ligeti.

Loosemore, Henry (died 1670), English composer and organist of King's College Chapel, Cambridge, from 1627 until his death. He composed a service, anthems, two Latin litanies and a fantasia for three viols and organ. His son George, who was organist of Trinity College (1660–82), composed anthems.

Lopatnikov, Nicolai Lvovich (born 1903), Russian composer and pianist. He studied at the St. Petersburg Conservatory (1914–17), went to Helsinki during the 1917 revolution, studied in Heidelberg, lived in Berlin (from 1929) and in 1933 returned to Finland where he received advice from Sibelius. He visited London (1934) and settled in the United States (1939), where he taught at the Carnegie Institute in Pittsburgh. He has composed an opera (*Danton*), two symphonies and other orchestral works, two piano concertos, a violin concerto, string quartets and other chamber music and piano pieces.

Lorenzani, Paolo (1640–1713), Italian composer. He studied in Rome under Benevoli, was choirmaster at Messina Cathedral (from 1675) and went to France (1678), where he was *maître de musique* to the Queen (1679 to 1683) and afterwards *maître de chapelle* at the Theatine monastery in Paris. In 1694 he returned to Rome as choirmaster at St. Peter's. He composed operas, Magnificats, cantatas, motets, Italian and French airs, and serenades. His *Nicandro e Fileno* (Fontainebleau, 1681) was the only Italian opera given in France between 1662 (Cavalli's *Ercole amante*) and 1729.

Loriod, Yvonne (born 1924), French pianist, wife of the composer Messiaen and leading exponent of his keyboard works. Especially associated with 20th century music, she has given first performances of works by Bartók and Schoenberg as well as by her husband.

Loris, Heinrich, *see* GLAREANUS

Lortzing, Gustav Albert (1801–51), German composer, singer, conductor and librettist. He was the son of wandering actors, learnt to play the piano, violin and cello and was a member of a travelling opera company. He was first tenor at the Stadt Theater in Leipzig (1833–43), an unsuccessful conductor for short periods at the Leipzig theatre (1844) and at the Theater an der Wien in Vienna (1848). From 1850 he was conductor of the suburban Friedrich-Wilhelmstadt Theater in Berlin. He composed romantic and comic operas to his own libretti, incidental music for plays, two oratorios, partsongs and songs. His most important opera, *Zar und Zimmermann* (1837), is still performed; others which had some success were *Die beiden Schützen* (1837), *Hans Sachs* (1840; the subject anticipated Wagner's *Die Meistersinger*), *Der Wildschütz* (1842), *Undine* (1845), *Der Waffenschmied*

(1846), and *Die vornehmen Dilettanten* (1851). His *Regina* was first produced in 1899 – its 'revolutionary' subject having been deemed too liberal during the composer's lifetime.

Lossius, Lucas (1508–82), German theorist. He was rector of St. John's School in Lüneburg from 1533 until his death. He published the theoretical treatise *Erotemata musicae practicae* (1563) and *Psalmodia sacra veteris ecclesiae* (1553), a collection of Latin texts and their plainsong melodies for use in the Lutheran liturgy.

Lotti, Antonio (1667–1740), Italian composer. He studied under Legrenzi in Venice where he produced his first opera in 1683, and was at St. Mark's Cathedral as chorister (1687), deputy organist (1690), second organist (1692), first organist (1704) and choirmaster (1736). He visited Dresden (1717–19) with his own opera company from Venice, and produced there his *Giove in Argo* (1717) and his last opera *Teofane* (1719). In addition to operas, he composed oratorios, a Requiem, Misereres, Masses, motets and other church music, cantatas and madrigals.

loud pedal, name often used wrongly to describe the sustaining pedal of the piano.

Louise, opera in four acts by Gustave Charpentier, to a libretto by the composer, first performed in Paris in 1900. Louise, a dressmaker's employee, is in love with Julian, an artist, in spite of the opposition of her parents. She goes to live with her lover in Montmartre. She responds to her mother's appeal to go home and see her father, who is seriously ill, but she refuses to stay with her parents and rejoins her lover. The most famous aria of this *roman musical* is 'Depuis le jour', sung by the heroine in Act 3. The work, very popular during the first half of the present century, was closely associated with Mary Garden, who appeared in its first American performance (1908).

Louis Ferdinand of Prussia, Prince (1772–1806), nephew of Frederick the Great, amateur composer and pianist. He was a friend of Beethoven (who praised his playing and dedicated to him the C minor piano concerto) and of Dussek (who was in his service teaching him piano and composition). He composed two rondos for piano and orchestra, piano trios, piano quartets and quintets and other chamber music, and piano pieces. He died in battle at Saalfeld.

loure, a type of bagpipe once used in Normandy. The word came to mean a rustic dance the bagpipe accompanied, adopted into the ballet (e.g. Lully's *Alceste*, 1677) and into instrumental music. Bach's fifth French suite shows the best known example of *loure* rhythm and style, the sixth movement of which begins:

The French term for legato-bowing, *louré*, is possibly derived from *loure* playing and dancing. Each note, although played with several others by one stroke of the bow, is distinct and emphasised, indicated thus:

Lourié, Arthur Vincent (1892–1966), Russian born composer who studied at St. Petersburg Conservatory, was appointed director of the music department of the Ministry of Education (1918), became disaffected and left Russia (1922), lived in France, where he met Stravinsky, and settled in the United States (1941). He composed *Feast During the Plague*, a symphonic suite with chorus and soloist (1945, originally a short opera, 1933), ballets, *Symphonie dialectique* (1930) and other orchestral works, church music, a cantata and other choral works, chamber music, song cycles and piano pieces.

Love for Three Oranges, The, comic opera in four acts by Prokofiev. The libretto, written in Russian by the composer himself, was based on an Italian comedy by Gozzi. Prokofiev himself conducted the première at Chicago in 1921 – when for arbitrary reasons it was performed in French translation. The story concerns a prince who takes three oranges with him into the desert. Each contains a princess. Two die of thirst but the third survives and marries the prince. An orchestral suite drawn from the opera includes a famous march, very characteristic of the composer.

Love of the Three Kings, The (It., *L'Amore dei tre re*), opera in three acts by Montemezzi, to a text by Sen Benelli, first performed at Milan in 1913 under Toscanini. The medieval story concerns an old king who poisons his son, his daughter-in-law and his daughter-in-law's lover.

Love, the Magician (Spanish, *El Amor Brujo*), ballet by Falla, first performed in Madrid in 1915. The work requires a ballerina who can sing as well as dance. The story concerns a girl who is haunted by the spirit of her dead lover.

Lowe, Edward (c. 1610–82), English organist and composer. He was a chorister at Salisbury Cathedral and became organist of Christ Church, Oxford in about 1630. In 1660 he became organist of the Chapel Royal, and in 1662 was appointed professor of music at Oxford. He published *A Short Direction for the Performance of Cathedrall Service* (1661) and composed anthems.

Lualdi, Adriano (born 1887), Italian composer and critic, pupil of Wolf-Ferrari. He was appointed director of the Conservatorio di S. Pietro e Maiella in Naples, and later the Florence Conservatory. He was one of the founders of the International Music Festivals in Venice (1932). He has composed operas, including *The Moon of the Caribbees* (after Eugene O'Neill).

Lübeck, Vincent (1654–1740), German organist and composer. A pupil of Buxtehude, he was organist in Stade from 1673 and at St. Nicholas Church in Hamburg from 1702 until his death. He composed cantatas, chorale preludes and other organ works.

Lucas, Charles (1808–69), English conductor, composer, cellist and organist. He studied at the Royal Academy of Music where he was conductor from 1832 and principal (succeeding Potter) from 1859–66. He became a member of Queen Adelaide's private orchestra (1830) and cellist at the opera (1832) and was active as a music publisher (1856–65).

Lucas, Leighton (born 1903), English composer and conductor. Without a teacher, he studied music while working as a ballet dancer and began conducting at the age of nineteen. He has composed works for orchestra, for chorus and orchestra, a *Sonatina concertante* for saxophone and orchestra, ballets, masques, film music, a string quartet, and songs.

Lucia di Lammermoor (It., *Lucy of Lammermoor*), opera in three acts by Donizetti, to a libretto by Salvatore Cammarano (based on Scott's novel *The Bride of Lammermoor*). The first performance was at Naples in 1835, with Fanny Persiani (for whom Donizetti composed it) in the title role. The work contains the most famous of all operatic mad scenes.

Lucio Silla (It. *Lucius Sulla*), opera in three acts by Mozart, to a libretto by Giovanni de Gamerra (altered by Metastasio). The first performance of this *drama per musica* took place at Milan in 1772. Other operas on the same subject were composed by Anfossi and J. C. Bach.

Lucrezia Borgia, opera with a prologue and two acts by Donizetti, to a libretto by Felice Romani (after Hugo), first performed at Milan in 1833. In the course of poisoning her adversaries, Lucrezia finds that she has killed her own son.

Ludford, Nicholas (c. 1485–c. 1557), English composer. In 1521 he became a member of the Fraternity of St. Nicholas (the City of London Guild of Parish Clerks). He was a member of St. Stephen's Chapel, Westminster, at its dissolution in 1547–8. He composed Masses, a Magnificat, and antiphons. A modern edition of his collected works was begun in 1963 by John Bergsagel.

H. BAILLIE: 'Nicholas Ludford', in *Musical Quarterly*, xliv (1958)

J. D. BERGSAGEL: 'An Introduction to Ludford', in *Musica Disciplina*, xiv (1960)

Ludus Tonalis (Lat., play of tones), work for piano by Hindemith consisting of twelve fugues and eleven interludes, with a prelude and postlude (the postlude being an inverted version of the prelude). The composer described *Ludus Tonalis* as 'studies in counterpoint, tonal organisation and piano technique', intending it to be a kind of modern equivalent of Bach's *Well-Tempered Clavier*. The first performance took place in 1944, but the cerebral quality of the writing has limited the work's success.

Ludwig, Christa (born 1924), German mezzo-soprano, successful in opera house and concert hall. She made her operatic début in *Die Fledermaus* at Frankfurt in 1946. Since then she has been specially associated with operas by Mozart and Richard Strauss, and has appeared memorably as Leonore in Beethoven's *Fidelio*.

Luening, Otto (born 1900), U.S. composer, conductor, and flautist. He studied in Munich and Zürich and was a pupil of Busoni. In 1920 he founded the American Opera in Chicago. Later he was attached to the Eastman Music School and the Opera in Rochester (1925–28) and won a Guggenheim Fellowship (1930). He has also taught at the University of Arizona, Bennington College in Vermont, and Columbia University. He has composed an opera, a symphony, symphonic poems and other orchestral works, choral works, string quartets, and other chamber music, songs and pieces for piano and organ.

Luftpause (Ger.), breathing rest.

Lugge (Luge, Lugg), John (born c. 1587), English composer and organist. He was organist at Exeter Cathedral in 1603 and was vicar choral there from 1606 till at least 1647. He was also for some time organist of St. Peter's in Exeter. He composed services (some of which may be by Robert Lugge), anthems, and organ and harpsichord pieces. A canon by him was published in Hilton's *Catch that catch can* (second edition, 1658). Three voluntaries for 'double organ' (i.e. organ with two manuals) were published in 1956 (edited by Susi Jeans and John Steele).

His son, **Robert Lugge,** was also an organist. He was appointed organist of St. John's College, Oxford, at the age of 15, and received a B. Mus. in 1638. He later became a Roman Catholic and went abroad. Some vocal compositions ascribed to 'Lugge' may be by either Robert or John.

Luisa Miller, opera in three acts by Verdi, to a libretto by Salvatore Cammarano (based on Schiller's drama *Kabale und Liebe*). The first performance was at Naples in 1849. A special feature of the opera was that it was about 'ordinary' people rather than obscure royalty. The action takes place in the Tyrol in the 18th century. Luisa is the daughter of an old soldier, and the opera exploits the father-daughter relationship which Verdi was to use again, to popular effect, in some of his later works.

lujon, percussion instrument. Its metal plates, mounted above resonators, are usually beaten by soft-headed sticks. The resulting sounds, although of the indefinite pitch, have an affinity with the low notes of the vibraphone.

Lully, Jean-Baptiste (originally **Giambattista Lulli**) (1632–87), French composer of Italian origin. At the age of fourteen he was brought to Paris by the Chevalier de Guise, and placed in the service of Louis XIV's cousin, Mademoiselle d'Orleans, some say as a kitchen boy. She soon discovered his talent, and made him the leader of her group of string players. At the age of twenty, he passed into the young king's service, becoming a dancer, a player in *Les Vingt-quatre Violons du Roi* and a composer. He formed and directed a smaller group, *Les Petits Violons*, which became famous for the perfection of its ensemble, and became court composer and music-master to the royal family. From 1664 he composed music for the comedy-ballets of Molière, including *Le Mariage forcé* (1664), *L'Amour médecin* (1665), *Le Sicilien* (1667), *Monsieur de Pourceaugnac* (1669), *Les Amants magnifiques* (1670), and *Le Bourgeois Gentilhomme* (1670), in which he appeared, as he often did, as actor and dancer. By 1673 he had intrigued Perrin and Cambert out of their patent to establish opera in Paris, and became, with the collaboration of the poet Quinault, the founder of French opera, then called *tragédie lyrique*. As the king's favourite, he amassed privileges and wealth. His grand house in Paris can still be seen. He was a full member of Louis's corrupt and vicious court. He died in 1687 of blood-poisoning, having become infected after he struck his foot with his baton while conducting a Te Deum.

The chief characteristics of French opera which he established were: (1) the overture in the form of a slow section in dotted rhythm followed by a fugal

Jean-Baptiste Lully, father of French opera. The court dress, complete with sword, reflects his social position: a composer was either accepted as a gentleman or remained (like Mozart) below the salt

quick section; (2) extensive use of the ballet; (3) the important place given to choruses; and (4) the development of a rhetorical style of recitative closely related to the rhythms of the language. His arias, save in a few cases, are of minor importance.

Besides operas and comedy-ballets, Lully composed music for court ballets and *divertissements*, some church music, and two instrumental suites. Ten volumes of his complete works, edited by H. Prunières, have been published (1930–9). Vocal scores of many of the operas have been published in the series *Chefs d'oeuvres classiques de l'opéra français*.

Operas: *Cadmus et Hermione* (1673), *Alceste* (1674), *Thésée* (1675), *Atys* (1676), *Isis* (1677), *Psyché* (1678), *Bellérophon* (1679), *Proserpine* (1680), *Persée* (1682), *Phaëton* (1683), *Amadis de Gaule* (1684), *Roland* (1685), *Armide et Renaud* (1686), *Acis et Galatée* (1686), *Achille et Polyxène* (with Colasse, 1687).

R. H. F. SCOTT: *Jean-Baptiste Lully* (1973)

Lulu, unfinished opera in three acts by Berg, to a libretto by the composer (from Wedekind's plays *Erdgeist* and *Die Büchse der Pandora*). Written in the wake of *Wozzeck*, the work was not staged until 1937 in Zürich – two years after the composer's death. The story concerns a sexual *femme fatale* who destroys all her lovers – until in the end she herself is destroyed by Jack the Ripper. The first two acts of the opera were completed by Berg, but the unfinished Act 3 can only be staged in skeletal form. Even incomplete however, *Lulu* is one of the few real operatic masterpieces of the 20th century.

Lumbye, Hans Christian (1810–74), Danish conductor and composer of ballet music, galops, and other dances. His most important music has been preserved in the repertory of the Royal Danish Ballet. His sons, **Carl Christian Lumbye** (1841–1911) and **Georg August Lumbye** (1843–1922) were also composers and conductors.

lunga pausa (It.), long pause, long rest.

Lupi, Johannes (Jennet Leleu) (c. 1506–39), Flemish composer. He studied at Louvain from 1522 to 1527, and became choirmaster at the Cathedral in Cambrai. He composed motets and *chansons* which were published by Attaingnant and others. Ten *chansons* have been published in a modern edition by H. Albrecht (*Das Chorwerk*, xv).

> B. J. BLACKBURN: 'Johannes Lupi and Lupus Hellinck: a double portrait', *Musical Quarterly*, lix (1973)

Lupo, the name of a family of musicians of Italian origin who were active at the English court between 1540 and 1640. They included Ambros (died 1594), Thomas I (died 1628), Thomas II (died before 1660), and Theophilus (died before 1660). Compositions under the name Thomas Lupo include pieces in Leighton's *Teares or Lamentacions* of 1614 (one by 'Timolphus Thopul', who may be Thomas or Theophilus or both), 25 three-part fantasies, thirteen in four parts, 28 in five parts, thirteen in six parts, and a *Miserere* for strings in five parts. Modern editions of eight fantasies are in *Musica Britannica*, ix.

Lupus Hellinck, *see* HELLINCK

lur, primitive horn of bronze found in Denmark and Sweden.

> H. C. BROHOLM: *The Lures of the Bronze Age* (1949)

Luscinius (Ger. **Nacht(i)gall**), **Ottomar (Othmar)** (1487–1537), Alsatian organist, theorist, theologian, and composer. He studied under Hofhaimer, became organist at Strasbourg (1517), cathedral preacher at Augsburg (1523) and at Basle (1526), and later lived at Freiburg-im-Breisgau. He published two treatises, *Musicae Institutiones* (1515) and *Musurgia seu praxis musicae* (1536), and composed pieces for organ.

lusingando (It.), literally flattering. Hence, in a tender manner.

Lusitano, Vicente (died after 1553), Portuguese composer and theorist. He settled in Rome in about 1550 and was involved in a controversy on music with Vicentino. He published a treatise, *Introductione facilissima et novissima di canto fermo* (1553), and a book of motets (1551).

lustig (Ger.), merry, cheerful.

Lustigen Weiber von Windsor, Die, *see* MERRY WIVES OF WINDSOR

lute (Fr., *luth*; Ger., *Laute*; It., *liuto*), plucked stringed instrument with a body shaped like a half-pear, fretted finger-board, and peg-box bent back. It was one of the most popular instruments for solo-playing and song accompaniment in the 16th and early 17th centuries, although its history stretches back to 2000 B.C., when short lutes were depicted on Mesopotamian figurines.

16th and early 17th century lutes had eleven strings in six course, i.e. five pairs in double courses at the octave and a single string, tuned thus:

About the middle of the 17th century the French lutenist Denis Gaultier introduced a new tuning:

which was generally adopted.

Lute music was written in the various forms of lute TABLATURE. The music for lute solo consisted of dance pieces, variations, preludes, ricercars, and arrangements of sacred and secular choral music and of folk and popular songs. The instrument for which such music and song-accompaniments were written in Spain was the *vihuela da mano* which, having a flat back, was actually a member of the guitar family, but was in other respects equivalent to the lute. Large quantities of lute music, both printed and manuscript, exist, dating from Petrucci's first collection of 1507 to the middle of the 18th century. Among the more important are the compositions of Luis Milan (*El Maestro*, 1535; modern edition by L. Schrade, 1927), Francesco da Milano (four publications between 1536 and 1563), Adrien le Roy (three publications between 1551 and 1562 and a treatise, 1557, which was published in English translations in 1568 and 1574), the English school of lutenist song composers (including Dowland, Ford, Pilkington, Campion, Jones, Danyel, and others; modern editions by E. H. Fellowes), Denis Gaultier (*Pièces de luth*, 1669; *Rhétorique des Dieux* in manuscript; facsimile edition by A. Tessier, 1932), and Esaias Rousner (*Deliciae testitudinis*, 1667; *Neue Lautenfrüchte*, 1676). The second part of Thomas Mace's *Musick's Monument* (1676) contained a detailed discussion of the lute, its playing, and its music. Two volumes of lute music from the 16th century to 1720 have been printed in *Denkmäler der Tonkunst in Osterreich*, xviii (2) and xxv (2). J. S. Bach wrote some pieces for lute and wrote a part for it in the accompaniment to the arioso 'Consider, O my soul' in the *St. John Passion*. Among Haydn's works are a *Cassazione* for lute, violin, viola, and cello. The chief varieties of the lute used in the same period were the ARCHLUTE, THEORBO, CHITARRONE, MANDOLA and MANDOLINE. *See illustration on* p. 332.

lute-harpsichord, *see* LAUTENCLAVICYMBEL

luth, *see* LUTE

Luther, Martin (1483–1546), German reformer and

Martin Luther. His creative interest in music had a strongly beneficial influence on the tradition of music in the Reformed Church in Germany, which culminated in the music of Bach

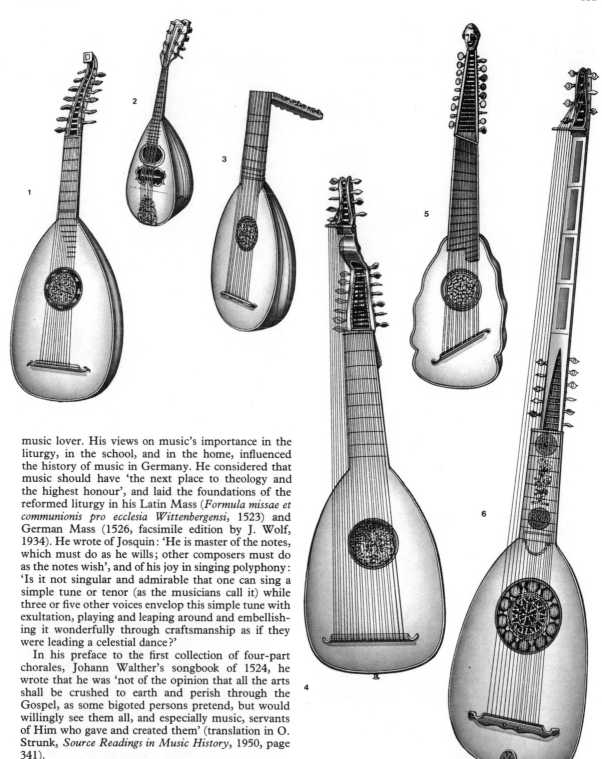

music lover. His views on music's importance in the liturgy, in the school, and in the home, influenced the history of music in Germany. He considered that music should have 'the next place to theology and the highest honour', and laid the foundations of the reformed liturgy in his Latin Mass (*Formula missae et communionis pro ecclesia Wittenbergensi*, 1523) and German Mass (1526, facsimile edition by J. Wolf, 1934). He wrote of Josquin: 'He is master of the notes, which must do as he wills; other composers must do as the notes wish', and of his joy in singing polyphony: 'Is it not singular and admirable that one can sing a simple tune or tenor (as the musicians call it) while three or five other voices envelop this simple tune with exultation, playing and leaping around and embellishing it wonderfully through craftsmanship as if they were leading a celestial dance?'

In his preface to the first collection of four-part chorales, Johann Walther's songbook of 1524, he wrote that he was 'not of the opinion that all the arts shall be crushed to earth and perish through the Gospel, as some bigoted persons pretend, but would willingly see them all, and especially music, servants of Him who gave and created them' (translation in O. Strunk, *Source Readings in Music History*, 1950, page 341).

The thoroughness with which music was taught in the Lutheran schools may be seen in the theory-books of Rhau, Listenius, Henry Faber, and others. Luther composed a motet 'Non moriar sed vivam' for Joachim Greff's play *Lazarus*, and may have written the music of the *Sanctus* in his German Mass and of the chorales

Lutes: (1) mandola (2) mandolin (3) lute (4) theorbo (5) orpharion (6) chitarrone

'Ein' feste Burg' and 'Mit Fried und Freud'. He wrote the words to hymns which are sung nowadays all over the world.

W. E. BUSZIN: 'Luther on Music', in *Musical Quarterly*, xxxii (1946)

P. NETTL: *Luther and Music* (1948)

Lutoslawski, Witold (born 1913), Polish composer who studied at Warsaw Conservatoire with Maliszewski (a pupil of Rimsky-Korsakov). His *Concerto for Orchestra* (1954) brought him international fame, and his *Funeral Music* in memory of Bartók (1958) and *Venetian Games* (1961) helped to consolidate his position as Poland's most important modern composer. His other works include symphonies, *Livre pour orchestre*, *Trois Poèmes d'Henri Michaux* for chorus and orchestra, and *Paroles Tissées*, written for Peter Pears, who performed it for the first time at the 1965 Aldeburgh Festival. His music is remarkable for its technical and its emotional content and for the wide range of styles encompassed.

Lutyens, Elisabeth (born 1906), English composer, daughter of Sir Edward Lutyens, the architect. She studied at the Royal College of Music and at the Paris Conservatoire. Her works include operas (*Infidelio* and *Time Off? – Not a Ghost of a Chance*), a horn concerto, a viola concerto and a series of chamber concertos, vocal music (including *And Suddenly It's Evening* for tenor and eleven instruments), chamber music, and film scores. Her works reveal her as a dedicated exponent of twelve-note music. Her autobiography, *A Goldfish Bowl*, was published in 1972.

Luython, Karel (c. 1557–1620), Netherlands composer. From about 1576 he was court organist in Prague to the Emperor Maximilian II and his successor Rudolf II. He published a volume of madrigals (1582), of motets (1603), of Lamentations (1604), and of Masses (1609). He also wrote organ music which has been edited by J. Watelot in *Monumenta Musicae Belgicae*, iv (1938). He built a harpsichord with separate keys for C sharp and D flat, D sharp and E flat, F sharp and G flat, G sharp and A flat, E sharp and B sharp to overcome the inadequacy of the meantone system to provide a practical tuning for these notes.

Luzzaschi, Luzzasco (1545–1607), Italian composer, organist, and harpsichordist. He was court organist at Ferrara from about 1576 and his organ pupils included Frescobaldi. Of his seven books of madrigals published between about 1575 and 1604 the first and sixth have not survived. He dedicated the fourth book (1594) to Gesualdo, and the style of his later madrigals, especially those in the posthumous collection *Seconda scelta delli madrigali* (1613), resembles that of Gesualdo in its texture, though not in the extent of its chromaticism. In 1601 he published a collection of madrigals for one, two, and three sopranos *per cantare et sonare*; an example with a highly ornamented solo part and keyboard accompaniment is printed in Schering's *Geschichte der Musik in Beispielen*, no 166, and one for three sopranos and accompaniment in the third volume of Einstein's *The Italian Madrigal* (1949), which also reprints two madrigals from the 1594 and 1613 sets. Two ricercars and a toccata for organ from Diruta's *Il Transilvano* are reprinted in Torchi's *L'arte musicale in Italia*, volume iii. Luzzaschi also published a volume of motets in 1598.

Lvov, Alexis Feodorovich (1798–1870), Russian composer and violinist, director of music in the Imperial Court Chapel at St. Petersburg under Nicholas I. He was also leader of a distinguished string quartet, and a high-ranking officer in the army. As a composer, he wrote the pre-Revolutionary Russian National Anthem, which (immortalised in Chaikovsky's *1812 Overture*) has stood the test of time rather better than his operas and church music.

Lydian mode, (1) in ancient Greek music:

(2) from the middle ages onwards applied to:

The tonic (or final) and dominant are marked respectively T and D. This mode is often found with flattened B, which makes it identical with the modern major scale.

See also GREEK MUSIC, MODE

lyra, alternative name for the medieval REBEC, which was continued in the Italian LIRA of the 17th and 18th centuries.

Lyraflügel (Ger.), type of upright piano, in the form of a Greek lyre, made in Germany between c. 1825 and c. 1850.

Lyra-glockenspiel, glockenspiel suitable for marching bands. It is also called bell-lyra.

lyra viol, bowed instrument used in Britain in the 17th century. In size it falls between the bass and tenor viol, and therefore was called the *viola bastarda*. In his *Musick's Recreation on the Viol, Lyra way* (1661) Playford observes that Daniel Farrant, Alphonso Ferrabosco and Giovanni Coprario were the first composers to write for the instrument, and that Daniel Farrant had invented a lyra viol with wire sympathetic strings under the playing strings.

lyre (Gr., *lyra*), instrument of the ancient Greeks, Assyrians, and Hebrews and so on. It was a simpler form of kithara, having a body made of tortoise shell or wood, and two horns or wooden arms joined by a cross bar; it had the same number of strings, varying from three to twelve, as the kithara. The ancient Greek instrument was shaped like a small harp, and can be seen depicted on vases and so on.

Lyric Suite, string quartet in six movements by Berg, composed in 1926. Part of the work was later arranged by the composer for string orchestra.

lyzarden (also **lyzardyne, lysard,** and **lizard**), medieval English name for the largest member of the cornett or zinke family of instruments. It was the forerunner of the serpent.

M., as an abbreviation M. = *medius*, the middle voice (in polyphonic music). M.M. = Maelzel's metronome (*see* METRONOME). M.-S. = mezzo-soprano. *m.d.* = *mano destra* or *main droite*, right hand (in keyboard music); *mf* = *mezzo forte*, moderately loud; *m.g.* = *main gauche*, left hand; *mp* = *mezzo piano*, moderately soft; *m.s.* = *mano sinistra*, left hand; *m.v.* = *mezza voce*, with a moderate volume of tone. In TONIC SOLFA **m** = *me*, the third note (or mediant) of the major scale.

ma (It.), but. *Allegro ma non troppo*, quickly but not too quickly.

Macbeth, (1) opera in four acts by Verdi, to a libretto by Francesco Maria Piave (after Shakespeare), first performed in Florence in 1847. The 'Paris' version, prepared by Verdi in 1865, contains some extra music.

(2) symphonic poem by Richard Strauss (op 23) based on Shakespeare's play. A precursor of Strauss's more famous symphonic poems, this work was first performed at Weimar in 1890.

(3) opera with a prologue and three acts by Bloch, to a libretto by Edmond Fleg, first performed in Paris in 1910. Lawrance Collingwood also based an opera on Shakespeare's play.

McCormack, John (1884–1945), Irish-born tenor who studied in Italy under Sabbatini and first appeared in opera in *Cavalleria rusticana* at Covent Garden in 1907. He sang with the Boston Opera Company (1910–11) and the Chicago Opera Company (1912–14) and became a U.S. citizen in 1917; later he was made a papal count. He excelled in Mozart and Verdi, and was also widely known as a concert singer. In Britain his reputation with the general public was based largely on his interpretation of popular ballads and drawing-room songs.

MacCunn, Hamish (1868–1916), Scottish composer and conductor. He was one of the first students to attend the newly-formed Royal College of Music in London (1883), where he was a pupil of Parry. At the age of nineteen he wrote the concert overture *The Land of the Mountain and the Flood*, which remains his best-known work, even though some of his later music (such as the opera *Jeannie Deans*, based on Scott's *The Heart of Midlothian*) was more ambitious.

MacDowell, Edward Alexander (1861–1908), U.S. composer. He studied piano in New York and Paris and composition in Frankfurt under Joachim Raff. With Liszt's encouragement, he was already an active composer in Europe (and an important teacher at Darmstadt) before returning to the United States permanently in 1888. In 1896 he became head of the newly-founded Department of Music at Columbia University, New York. He resigned in 1904 and became mentally ill in the following year.

His most characteristic works are those for piano,
which include four sonatas, twelve studies, six *Idylls after Goethe*, six *Poems after Heine*, *Woodland Sketches*, *Sea Pieces*, *New England Idylls*, *Fireside Tales* and other lyrical pieces. For orchestra he wrote symphonic poems (one of them entitled *Hamlet and Ophelia*) and two suites, of which the second uses melodies of the North American Indians. He also composed two piano concertos, and more than fifty songs. In New Hampshire a 'MacDowell Colony' was founded in his memory as a refuge for composers and other artists.

L. GILMAN: *Edward MacDowell* (1905)

Mace, Thomas (c. 1613–c. 1709), English writer and instrumentalist, chiefly known for his *Musick's Monument; or A Remembrancer of the best Practical Musick, both Divine and Civil, that has ever been known to have been in the world* (1676), which deals with the lute, viol and musical affairs in general. A facsimile edition was published in 1966 together with a commentary by J. Jacquot and transcriptions by A. Souris of pieces in the book for lute, theorbo and viol. This edition also contains pieces for the viol and an anthem, 'I heard a voice', which have survived in manuscript.

McEwen, John Blackwood (1868–1948), Scottish composer and teacher, educated in Glasgow and at the Royal Academy of Music in London, where he later became principal (1924–36). He composed five symphonies, three 'Border Ballades' and other orchestral works, seventeen string quartets (including no 6, *Biscay*), concertos, cantatas and piano music. He was knighted in 1931. An endowment left by him to Glasgow University enables a piece of Scottish chamber music to be commissioned and performed each year, and a series of programmes of new or recent Scottish music to be given triennially.

Macfarren, George Alexander (1813–87), English composer and teacher. He was educated at the Royal Academy of Music in London, where he became a professor in 1834 and principal in 1876. He was also professor of music at Cambridge. His compositions include operas (on Don Quixote, Robin Hood, Charles II and other subjects), oratorios, cantatas, orchestral works, chamber music and songs.

His brother **Walter Cecil Macfarren** (1826–1905) was also a composer and a conductor. He taught piano at the Royal Academy of Music from 1846 until 1903. His works include a symphony and Shakespearian overtures for orchestra, piano compositions, church music, songs and part-songs.

Machaut, Guillaume de, *see* GUILLAUME DE MACHAUT

machine drums, TIMPANI fitted with a mechanism, such as a foot-pedal, capable of making rapid and accurate changes of pitch.

Mackenzie, Alexander Campbell (1847–1935), Scottish composer and teacher. He was educated in Germany and at the Royal Academy of Music in

London, of which he was appointed principal in 1888. Though he spent most of his life outside Scotland, he poured his love for his homeland into his music, which includes operas, incidental music after Sir Walter Scott and James Barrie, a cantata on *The Cottar's Saturday Night* (Burns), Scottish rhapsodies, a Scottish piano concerto (premiered in London by Paderewski) and a *Pibroch* suite for violin and orchestra. He was knighted in 1895.

A. C. MACKENZIE: *A Musician's Narrative* (1927)

Mackerras, Charles (born 1925), Australian conductor. Born in the United States, he was, however, educated in Sydney, where later he became principal oboist of the Sydney Symphony Orchestra. In 1946 he went to Europe, where he studied under Vaclav Talich in Prague and subsequently settled in Britain, becoming musical director of the English National Opera (formerly Sadler's Wells Opera). Though a conductor of wide sympathies, he is especially associated with Czech music (above all, the operas of Janáček) and with Mozart. His performances of *The Marriage of Figaro* in the 1960s set a stylistic standard through their use of appoggiaturas, and of properly-observed 18th century graces. As an arranger, Mackerras made a witty adaptation of music by Sullivan for the ballet *Pineapple Poll*.

Maconchy, Elizabeth (born 1907), English composer of Irish parentage. She studied at the Royal College of Music under Vaughan Williams, and later in Prague. Her compositions, in which she developed an individual treatment of contemporary idioms within the traditional forms, include orchestral works, operas, ballet music, concertos for piano, viola and clarinet, nine string quartets and other chamber music. A number of her works have been successfully performed at the International Society for Contemporary Music festivals abroad.

Macpherson, Stewart (1865–1941), English teacher, writer and composer. He was educated at the Royal Academy of Music in London where he taught harmony from 1887. He wrote a number of textbooks on harmony, counterpoint, form and musical history, and composed a symphony and other orchestral works, a Mass, songs and piano pieces.

Macque, Giovanni (Jean) de (c. 1551–1614) Flemish composer. A pupil of Philippe de Monte, he was in Rome from 1576 to 1582 and in Naples from 1586 until after 1610. He composed some motets and published a number of books of madrigals, of which one appeared with English words in Nicholas Yonge's *Musica Transalpina* (1588) and another in Morley's collection of Italian madrigals (1598).

Madama Butterfly, opera originally in two acts, later in three acts, by Puccini, to a libretto by Giuseppe Giacosa and Luigi Illica. The first performance, in Milan in 1904, was a failure; but the revised version, conducted by Toscanini in the same year, was so successful that the work has held its place in the repertory ever since. The text is based on a drama by the American playwright David Belasco, which itself is based on a story by John Luther Long. Lieutenant Pinkerton, a United States naval officer stationed in Japan, marries a Japanese girl, Cio-Cio-San, who renounces the faith of her ancestors to show her trust in him and thus can never return to her own people. After Pinkerton leaves for the United States she bears his son and is befriended by Sharpless (the U.S. consul). Pinkerton later returns with a U.S.

Madama Butterfly: Left: Zenatello (Pinkerton) and De Luca (Sharpless) in the disastrous first performance at La Scala in 1904. *Right:* a famous American Cio-Cio-San, Geraldine Farrar.

wife, who wishes to adopt the child. Cio-Cio-San, having agreed to hand over the child, commits suicide. The music represents the high watermark of Puccini's characteristic Italian lyricism, shot through with Japanese touches, including adaptations of Japanese melodies. The United States national anthem is also quoted.

Maderna, Bruno (1920–73), Italian composer and conductor. He studied the violin and piano at the Accademia di Santa Cecilia in Rome, then took composition and conducting lessons under Malipiero and Scherchen. One of the most interesting and musically most sensitive figures of modern Italian music, he concentrated more on instrumental music than on the traditional Italian art of opera (though he was an impressive operatic conductor). His works include concertos for piano, two pianos, flute and oboe, and other orchestral music; *Musica du due Dimensioni* for flute, percussion and electronic tape; studies on Kafka's *The Trial* for speaker, soprano and chamber orchestra; other chamber pieces, including *Composizione in tre tempi, Improvisizione I and II, Serenata I* for eleven instruments and *Serenata II* for thirteen instruments. He also produced a number of electronic works, among them *Notturno, Syntaxis, Continuo,* and *Dimensioni*. As a conductor, he had a natural flair for modern music.

madrigal. The name may connote a poem in the mother tongue (*matricale*) or a pastoral poem (*mandriale*). Musical settings first appeared in the 14th century in Italy, in two or three parts, by such composers as Jacopo da Bologna, Giovanni da Cascia and Francesco Landini. Examples are printed in *Historical Anthology of Music*, edited by A. T. Davison and W. Apel (nos 49, 50, 54) and in Schering's *Geschichte der Musik in Beispielen* (no 22). Each of the two or three verses of the poem has three lines in iambic pentameters, sung to the same music, and there is a final *ritornello* of two lines, sung to different music.

The madrigal poem of the 16th century was a free form, and the musical style of the earliest published collection entitled *Madrigali* (1533) was derived from the *frottola*. The work of Verdelot, Festa and Arcahelt in this style was followed by that of Willaert and his pupil Cipriano de Rore, who widened the scope of the madrigal in the expression of the words and the use of technical resources. The 'classic' Italian madrigal of the second half of the century was written in imitative polyphony, most often in five parts, and made a moderate use of word-painting and word-symbolism (A. Gabrieli, Palestrina, Lassus, Philippe de Monte). The mannered style of the late madrigal (Marenzio, Gesualdo, Monteverdi) used less restrained forms of word-painting, chromaticism, and dramatic effects of melodic line and choral texture. The transition from the imitative madrigal to the madrigal for solo, duet or trio accompanied by continuo, which resulted from the pursuit of dramatic expression, can be traced in the seven books published by Monteverdi from 1587 to 1619.

Italian madrigals were sung in England before 1588 when Nicholas Yonge's *Musica Transalpina* appeared containing madrigals translated from the Italian. About forty publications containing madrigals by some thirty composers appeared in England between 1593 and 1627 (modern editions in *The English Madrigal School*, edited by E. H. Fellowes). Morley's collection of 1594 was the first to use the term madrigal in the title. Although Italian in origin, the English madrigal tradition quickly assumed its own characteristics in the hands of Morley, Weelkes, Wilbye, and others. This was partly due to the influence of a distinct native tradition of secular song exemplified in the work of Byrd and Gibbons. A notable feature of the English madrigal school, when compared with the Italian, is the lack of a suitable literary tradition and the presence of a greater feeling for tonality and purely musical organization.

A. EINSTEIN: *The Italian Madrigal* (3 volumes, 1949)
E. H. FELLOWES: *English Madrigal Composers* (1921)
J. KERMAN: *The Elizabethan Madrigal* (1962)
J. ROCHE: *The Madrigal* (1972)

Maelzel, Johann Nepomuk (1772–1838), German born inventor and constructor of mechanical musical instruments. He made a Panharmonicon, or mechanical orchestra, a mechanical trumpeter, a chronometer about which Beethoven wrote a canon (*Ta, ta, ta, lieber Mälzel*), which is musically related to the Allegretto of the eighth symphony. He patented the metronome which still bears his name, and which Beethoven was the first composer to use to indicate the tempi of his composition (although in fact the invention was filched by Maelzel from D. N. Winkel). Maelzel spent the later part of his life in America.

maestoso (It.), majestic, dignified.

maestro al cembalo (It.), musician who, during the 18th century, directed performances of concertos, etc., while seated at the harpsichord.

maestro di cappella (It.), literally, master of the chapel, i.e. director of music to a prince, king, bishop or nobleman; (Fr., *maître de chapelle*; Ger., *Kapellmeister*; Sp., *maestro de capilla*).

Maggini, Giovanni Paolo (1580–after 1630), celebrated Italian violin-maker. He was an apprentice to Gasparo da Salò in 1602, and later improved on Salò's designs and methods in several respects.

M. L. HUGGINS: *Gio. Paolo Maggini* (1892)

maggiore (It.), major mode.

Magic Flute, The (Ger., *Die Zauberflöte*), *Singspiel* (opera with dialogue) in two acts by Mozart, to a libretto by Emanuel Schikaneder, first performed in Vienna on September 30th, 1791, two months before the composer's death. The work is a mixture of allegory, fantasy and pantomime which conceals several references to freemasonry and the political situation in Austria at the time. The prince Tamino, having fallen in love with a picture of Pamina, daughter of the Queen of Night, sets out to rescue her from the clutches of Sarastro, High Priest of Isis and Osiris. He is given a magic flute as a protection against evil, and Papageno, a bird-catcher, who accompanies him, is given a chime of magic bells. When Tamino reaches the temple he discovers that Sarastro is wise and good and that it is the Queen of Night who is evil. Tamino and Pamina, having passed through several mysterious ordeals (culminating in the trial by fire and water) are finally united, the Queen of Night being powerless to injure them. Papageno is also rewarded with a bride, Papagena.

Magnard, Albéric (1865–1914). French composer, pupil of Massenet and d'Indy. The son of the editor of *Le Figaro*, Magnard taught counterpoint at the Schola Cantorum in Paris and was a composer of notable originality. Martin Cooper, in his book on French music, praises Magnard's 'passionate earnestness'. His works include four symphonies, chamber music and three operas, of which *Bérénice* is the most important. In 1931 the Paris Opéra presented his *Guercoeur* in a reconstruction by Ropartz from the original score, which was partly destroyed when the Germans burned down his house during their advance on Paris in 1914. Magnard himself was killed (or committed suicide – no one is quite sure) during this incident, in the course of which he shot at the advancing troops from an upper window, killing one and wounding another.

Magnificat, canticle of the Virgin sung at Vespers in the Roman rite and at Evensong in the English rite. In plainsong it is sung antiphonally to one of its eight tones. Polyphonic settings first appeared as early as the 14th century and many were written for the Latin and Lutheran liturgies thereafter. Most often the even-numbered verses were set, for voices or organ, the other verses being sung in plainsong, which was commonly used as the basis of the polyphony. Bach set the Magnificat in the form of an elaborate cantata. In its English translation the Magnificat has been set as part of the Evening Service by English composers from the Reformation to the present.

Mahillon, Charles Victor (1841–1924), Belgian writer on musical instruments. In 1865 he entered the wind instrument firm founded by his father and in 1876 became curator of the museum of the Brussels Conservatoire. He published a catalogue of the museum and *Les Éléments d'acoustique musicale et instrumentale* (1874).

Mahler, Gustav (1860–1911), Austrian (Bohemian born) composer and conductor, who rose from humble origins to become director of the Vienna State Opera and to be the last of the great Vienna-based symphonists. Born at Kališt, he was the second of a family of fourteen children, his father being a Jewish publican, his mother the daughter of a soap manufacturer. Though his father was a coarse and brutal man, he nevertheless recognized and encouraged Gustav's talents. The boy was sent to the Vienna Conservatory at the age of fifteen to study piano under Epstein and theory under Fuchs and Krenn; he also attended Bruckner's lectures at Vienna University and came to admire Bruckner's music deeply. He served his apprenticeship as an opera conductor in various provincial houses, and climbed the ladder to Cassel, Prague, Leipzig, Budapest, and Hamburg before winning his Vienna appointment in 1897. His period with that company was one of the most brilliant in its history, and also one of the most tempestuous. In 1907 he was dismissed, and in that same ill-fated year his adored elder daughter died at the age of four and his own incurable heart disease was diagnosed. The death of his daughter was commemorated in the composition of *Das Lied von der Erde*, whose last movement (*Abschied*) addressed itself to life's sweetness and transitoriness: a pervading theme of Mahler's music.

Gustav Mahler

Leaving Europe for the United States, he conducted the New York Metropolitan Opera and the New York Philharmonic Symphony Orchestra. His relationship with the former soon became strained, but between 1908 and 1911 he enjoyed conducting the latter (it gave U.S. premières of several of his works). In that year, however, failing health precipitated his return to Europe and he died in a Vienna sanatorium on May 18th – a few years later his disease would have been easily cured. In his memory, Bruno Walter conducted the première of *Das Lied von der Erde*, which had lain unperformed from 1908.

Though Mahler's importance as a musician was soon recognized, his importance as a composer took longer to establish itself widely. In Britain there was initial resistance to the self-indulgent emotionalism of his music; Mahler's symphonies, written during summer holidays between his busy concert and opera seasons, were reckoned to be the price that had to be paid for his greatness as a conductor. Vaughan Williams, in a notorious gibe, called him a 'tolerable imitation of a composer'. In 1937 Eric Blom declared that it was 'too late to champion Mahler very fervently'.

Yet Mahler already had champions in Bruno Walter and Willem Mengelberg, and by the 1960s he was to have many more, among them Bernstein, Boulez, Haitink, Kubelik, and Solti. Indeed, during the past 25 years, at a time of world unrest and nervous tension, he was a composer with whom more and more performers and listeners developed a bond of sympathy. His importance as the main musical link between the 19th and 20th centuries, between the Vienna of Siegmund Freud and the present, was fully recognized. Though Schoenberg called him a 'classical' composer, he also hailed him as a pioneer. Though Mahler's music could seem neurotic and self-pitying, it could also conjure up vistas of the Austrian mountains and countryside with a beauty surpassed by no other composer. Though his style was once dismissed as eclectic, what he had to say was absolutely personal.

Mahler developed and expanded the concept of the

vocal symphony begun by Beethoven. Four of Mahler's symphonies, as well as *Das Lied von der Erde* (a symphony in all but name), use voices. He also developed the concept of the orchestral song cycle begun by Berlioz. His three great song cycles – *Lieder eines fahrenden Gesellen*, *Des Knaben Wunderhorn*, and *Kindertotenlieder* – contain the essence of Mahler, as do the five Rückert songs he composed during the same period as the *Kindertotenlieder* (by the same poet). His use of the human voice, whether solo or chorally, and of the orchestra is individual, exceptionally lucid, and instantly recognizable.

His tenth symphony, left unfinished, was completed from the composer's sketches by Deryck Cooke and publicly performed in 1964. Though the results reveal elements of plastic surgery, the completed work is nevertheless a valuable and psychologically revealing addition to the Mahler canon.

Mahler's principal compositions are:

(1) SYMPHONIES:

No 1 in D major (1884–8, first performed 1889, later revised)

No 2 in C minor ('Resurrection') for soprano, contralto, mixed chorus, and orchestra (1884–94, firs performed 1895, later revised)

No 3 in D minor, for contralto, women's chorus, boys' chorus, and orchestra (1895–6, first performed 1902)

No 4 in G major, for soprano and orchestra (1899–1900, first performed 1901, later revised)

No 5 in C sharp minor (1901–2, first performed 1904, later revised)

No 6 in A minor (1903–5, first performed 1906, later revised)

No 7 in B minor (1904–5, first performed 1908, later revised)

No 8 in E flat major, for eight soloists, mixed chorus, boys' chorus, and orchestra (1906–7, first performed 1910)

No 9 in D major (1909–10, first performed 1912)

No 10 in F sharp major (unfinished) (1910); Deryck Cooke 'performing version' first performed 1964.

(2) SONGS AND OTHER WORKS:

Lieder eines fahrenden Gesellen for voice and orchestra (1884, later revised; first performed 1896)

Des Knaben Wunderhorn for voice and orchestra (1888–9)

Kindertotenlieder for voice and orchestra (1901–4, first performed 1905)

Five Rückert songs for voice and orchestra (1901–2)

Das Lied von der Erde for alto (or baritone), tenor, and orchestra (1907–9, first performed 1911)

Also cantata, *Das klagende Lied*, for four soloists, chorus, and orchestra. Original version in three parts completed 1880: I Waldmärchen, II Der Spielmann, III Hochzeitstück.

P. BARFORD: *Mahler Symphonies and Songs* (1970)

N. BAVER-LECHNER: *Erinnerungen an Gustav Mahler* (1923)

N. CARDUS: *Gustav Mahler: his Mind and his Music: The First Five Symphonies* (1965)

H. L. DE LA GRANGE: *Mahler* (volume 1, New York, 1973; London, 1974)

M. KENNEDY: *Mahler* (1974)

A. MAHLER: *Gustav Mahler: Memories and Letters*, edited by Donald Mitchell (London, 1968)

D. MITCHELL: *Gustav Mahler: the Early Years* (1958); *Gustav Mahler: The Wunderhorn Years* (1975)

H. REDLICH: *Bruckner and Mahler* (1955, revised 1963)

B. WALTER: *Gustav Mahler* (1936, English translation, 1937 and 1958)

Maid of Pskov, The (Russ., *Pskovitianka*), opera in four acts by Rimsky-Korsakov, to a libretto by the composer (after a play by Lev Alexandrovich Mei). The work was first produced in St. Petersburg in 1873, and revived with a new prologue in Moscow in 1898. An alternative title is *Ivan the Terrible*, the Czar being one of the principal characters.

main (Fr.), hand. So *main droite*, right hand; *main gauche*, left hand; *deux mains*, two hands; *quatre mains*, four hands. These terms apply mainly to piano music.

Maiskaya Noch, *see* MAY NIGHT.

Maistre, Mattheus Le, *see* LE MAISTRE

maître de chapelle, *see* MAESTRO DI CAPPELLA

maîtrise (Fr.), a choir school of a French church. Such institutions have a history dating back as far as the 15th century, though the term *maîtrise* today has come to mean simply 'church choir'.

majeur (Fr.), major.

major, minor, the two predominant scales of the western tonal system. A major key is one based on a major scale, a minor key on a minor. *See* CHORD, INTERVAL, KEY, SCALE.

Majorano, Gaetano, *see* CAFFARELLI

malagueña, Andalusian folk-dance originating in Malaga, in southern Spain. Such dances are often sung, but can also be instrumental pieces. The music is said to be improvised in parallel chords on a repeated bass of the pattern AGFE with a G flat (major third) in the last chord. However, the examples with words printed in Subirá's *Antología Musical de Cantos Populares Españoles* (1930) follow that formula rather freely, e.g.:

Cuan-do sa-li de Mar-be-ya

Maldeghem, Robert Jullien van (1810–93), Flemish organist. He was editor of a pioneer collection of *chansons* and motets by composers of the early 16th century, *Trésor musical* (1865–93).

Malherbe, Charles Théodore (1853–1911), French writer and composer, who became curator of archives at the Paris Opéra in 1898. His publications include *L'œuvre dramatique de R. Wagner* (1886), *Précis de l'histoire de l'Opéra-Comique* (1887), and a biography of Auber (1911).

Malibran, Maria Felicita (1808–36), Spanish operatic singer, who combined a natural contralto with a soprano range. She was taught by her father Manuel Garcia and by Hérold in Paris and made her official operatic début as Rosina in *The Barber of Seville* in

The romantic Maria Malibran in 1829

London in 1825. She sang with great success in London, Paris, New York and Italy. Her marriage with Malibran was annulled in 1836 and she married the Belgian violinist Charles de Bériot. Her triumphant career was cut short when she fell from a horse in the spring of 1836. In spite of her injuries, she insisted on singing at a festival in Manchester that autumn, but died during her visit to the English city. Several books have been written about her, the most famous being Musset's *Stances*. She is also the subject of Robert Russell Bennett's three-act opera, *Maria Malibran* (1935).

malinconia (It.), melancholy (noun). The adjective is *malinconico*.

Malipiero, Gian Francesco (1882–1973), Italian composer. He studied under Enrico Bossi in Bologna, and was also a pupil of Ravel and Casella. He taught composition at the Parma Conservatorio (1921–3) and in 1939 became director of the Liceo Benedetto Marcello, Venice. He edited the complete works of Monteverdi and music by Frescobaldi and Stradella, and as a composer is representative of the neo-baroque in modern Italian music. His first work to gain general notice was *Pause del Silenzio* (1917), consisting of seven 'impressions' for orchestra portraying states of mind. The first of his seven string quartets, called *Rispetti e Strambotti*, was awarded the Coolidge Prize in 1920. Among the orchestral works are a series of descriptive symphonies (on such subjects as the sea, silence and death, a bell, and the zodiac) and he wrote numerous operas and other stage works, oratorios, chamber music, piano music and songs. His operas include two imposing trilogies, *L'Orfeide* (1925) and *Il Mistero di Venezia* (1932), and two works after Shakespeare, *Julius Caesar* (1936) and *Anthony and Cleopatra* (1938). Several of his operas have been staged outside Italy. *Sette Canzoni*, a series of sharp little sketches of life and death forming part two of *L'Orfeide*, scored a deserved success when staged at the Edinburgh Festival in 1970.

Mamelles de Tirésias, Les (Fr., *The Breasts of Tiresias*), *opéra burlesque* in a prologue and two acts by Poulenc, to a libretto by Guillaume Apollinaire, first performed at the Paris Opéra-Comique in 1947. The work concerns a bored wife who rids herself of her breasts and becomes a man, while her husband also changes his sex and gives birth to 40,000 children.

Ma Mère l'Oye, *see* MOTHER GOOSE

Manchester Group, name for a group (now dispersed) of young English composers, all of whom studied at the Royal Manchester College of Music in the 1950s and shared progressive musical ideals. The major figures of the group were Harrison Birtwistle, Peter Maxwell Davies, Alexander Goehr, and John Ogdon.

Manchicourt, Pierre de (c. 1510–64). Flemish composer. From 1539 he held positions at the cathedrals of Tours, Tournai, and Arras, becoming *maestro de capilla* in the royal chapel, Madrid, in 1560. His motets were published by Attaingnant (1539) and by Phalèse at Louvain (1554). A collection of 29 *chansons* by him was published by Susato at Antwerp in 1545 (facsimile edition, 1970; modern edition by M. A. Baird, 1972). The Attaingnant motets have been edited by J. D. Wicks in the first volume of a projected complete edition of Manchicourt's works (1971).

Mancinelli, Luigi (1848–1921), Italian conductor and composer. He studied the cello in Florence, and from 1874 was conductor in Rome, Bologna, London, New York (Metropolitan Opera, 1894–1903), and Buenos Aires (Teatro Colon, 1906–12). He composed several operas, including *Paolo e Francesca* (after Dante) and *A Midsummer Night's Dream* (after Shakespeare).

Mancinus, *see* MENCKEN

mandola, also **mandora, mandore** (It.), tenor mandolin.

mandolin, a member of the lute family. Its eight wire strings are tuned as four pairs (G, D, A, E) as on the violin, and it is played with a plectrum. The stringing makes possible rapid alternations of the same note, which is the instrument's most characteristic feature. The best known instance of its use is probably in the accompaniment to 'Deh vieni' from Mozart's *Don Giovanni*, but many 20th century composers (including Mahler, Schoenberg, and Gerhard) have incorporated the mandolin into their scores.

mandora, *see* MANDOLA

Mandyczewski, Eusebius (1857–1929), Austrian historian and editor. Educated in Vienna, he became keeper of the archives of the Gesellschaft der Musikfreunde in 1887 and teacher at the Vienna Conservatorium in 1897. He co-edited the complete works of Schubert and Brahms and began an unfinished edition of the works of Haydn published by Breitkopf and Härtel.

Manfred, (1) incidental music to Byron's poem by Schumann, op 115 (composed in 1848–9). It consists of an overture, solos, choruses, and other pieces, fifteen numbers in all. Schumann composed it for stage performance, some of the music being intended to accompany the spoken words.

(2) symphony by Chaikovsky, op 58 (1885), inspired by the same poem. The work was written between the fourth and fifth of Chaikovsky's numbered symphonies, but does not itself carry a number. The music has a specific programme, portraying various events in Byron's poem.

manicorde (Fr.), 16th century term for the clavichord.

Manieren (Ger.), 18th century term for musical ornaments or grace notes.

Mannheim, a town in western Germany, famous in the mid 18th century for its orchestra. The reputation of this ensemble was due to its excellent discipline, the individual skill of its players and a lively style of performance which included boldly contrasted dynamics, a calculated use of crescendo and dimenuendo, and early use of the clarinet as an orchestral instrument. A number of composers wrote symphonies for this orchestra, among them Johann Stamitz, Franz Xaver Richter, Ignaz Holzbauer and Christian Cannabich, who in the present century have come to be known collectively as the 'Mannheim School', with Stamitz as their founder. The fame of the orchestra ensured that the composers also became well-known and so helped to extend the demand for this type of composition, in which the main elements were pregnant themes, bold contrasts and the minimum of contrapuntal elaboration. The Mannheim School played an important role in the development of the symphony, paving the way for Haydn and Mozart.

See SYMPHONY

Manns, August Friedrich (1825–1907), German conductor. He played in and conducted various bands and orchestras in Germany before going to England in 1854. He became conductor of the Crystal Palace band in 1855, and was in charge of the Crystal Palace Saturday Concerts until 1901. He also conducted the Handel Festival there from 1883 until 1900, his performances being reviewed frequently by George Bernard Shaw. He was knighted, 1903.

    H. S. WYNDHAM: *August Manns and the Saturday Concerts* (1909)

mano (It.), hand; *mani*, hands.

Manon, opera in five acts by Massenet, to a libretto by Henri Meilhac and Philippe Gille, first performed in Paris in 1884. Like several other operas (see below), it was based on the Abbé Prévost's novel about the ill-fated relationship between the young Chevalier Des Grieux and the pleasure-loving Manon Lescaut. Act 2 contains Manon's famous (soprano) aria, '*Adieu notre petite table*', and the tenor-hero's '*Rêve*'. Ten years after completing his lyric masterpiece, Massenet wrote a less successful one-act sequel, *Le Portrait de Manon.*

Manon Lescaut, opera in four acts by Puccini, to a libretto by Marco Praga, Domenico Oliva and Luigi Illica, first performed in Turin in 1893. Like Massenet's French opera, Puccini's Italian one is based on the Abbé Prévost's novel. Unlike Massenet's version, in which Manon dies on the road to Le Havre, Puccini's has a geographically correct death scene in the desolate plain of New Orleans, where Manon has been exiled for immorality. The work was Puccini's third opera, and his first major success.

    Other operas on the subject have been written by Auber (1856) Balfe (*The Maid of Artois*; 1836) and Henze (*Boulevard Solitude*, a modernized version of the story; 1952).

manual (Lat. *manus*, 'hand'), a keyboard; in particular one of the keyboards of an organ or harpsicord. A small organ may have only one manual; larger instruments have two or more, each of which controls its own set of pipes. The manuals normally found on English organs are: Solo, Swell, Great, Choir in this order, beginning from the top. A three-manual organ will have Swell, Great, and Choir; a two-manual organ, Swell, and Great. By using a COUPLER it is possible to play on the pipes of two manuals simultaneously.

    See CHOIR ORGAN, GREAT ORGAN, ORGAN, SOLO ORGAN, SWELL ORGAN.

Manuel, Roland, *see* ROLAND-MANUEL

Manzoni Requiem, title sometimes given to Verdi's Requiem, written in memory of the Italian novelist and poet Alessandro Manzoni, who died a year before the Requiem was performed.

Maometto II, opera in two acts by Rossini, to a libretto by Cesare della Valle, Duke of Ventignano, first performed in Naples in 1820. The music was subsequently adapted to a new French libretto in three acts by Louis Alexandre Soumet and Giuseppe Luigi Balochi (with additional numbers) and performed as *Le Siège de Corinthe* in Paris in 1826.

maraca, a Latin American instrument, essential in rumba bands. It consists of a gourd containing dried seeds and a handle to shake it. Maracas are made in various sizes and always in pairs. They often find a place in scores that have no Latin American associations.

Marais, Marin (1656–1728), French composer and viol player. He studied the viol with Hottemann, and composition with Lully. From 1685 to 1727 he was solo violist to Louis XIV. He played on a bass viol with seven strings instead of the usual six, and published five books of pieces for his instrument, besides other chamber music. Among his programmatic pieces is a curiosity describing an operation for the removal of gallstones. He also composed operas and some church music.

Marazzoli, Marco (?1619–62), Italian singer and composer. He was a member of the papal chapel in Rome in about 1637. In collaboration with Virgilio Mazzocchi, he wrote the music of the first comic opera, *Chi soffre, speri* (Rome, 1637). He also composed the music for the second act of another comic opera, *Dal male il bene* (Rome, 1653), the music of the first and third acts being by Abbatini.

Marbeck or **Merbecke, John** (c. 1510–85), English singer, organist and composer. He was a chorister and later organist of St. George's Chapel, Windsor. He was arrested as a Protestant heretic in 1543 and narrowly escaped burning. In 1550 he issued his well-known *Booke of Common Praier noted* (facsimile edition with commentary by J. Eric Hunt, 1939) and, having escaped persecution under Mary, produced in the following reign several vigorously Protestant theological books. His *Booke of Common Praier noted* was the first setting to music of the English liturgy as authorized by the 1549 Act of Uniformity. A Mass, two motets (one lacking the tenor part) and a carol have been published in *Tudor Church Music*, x.

marcato (It.), marked, emphatic.

Marcello, Benedetto (1686–1739), Italian composer. He was educated in law, and combined its profession with those of composer, librettist, and writer on music. His most famous composition is *Estro poetico-armonico* (eight volumes, Venice, 1724–27), consisting of settings of fifty paraphrases of psalms by G. A. Giustiniani. He also composed cantatas, oratorios, concertos and sonatas. His *Il teatro alla moda* is a satirical commentary on early 18th century opera. He wrote the libretto for Ruggeri's *Arato in Sparta* in 1709.

His elder brother, **Alessandro Marcello** (c. 1684–c. 1750), was also a composer of cantatas, solo sonatas and concertos. Some of his music has been falsely ascribed to his more famous brother.

march (Fr., *marche*; Ger., *Marsch*; It., *marcia*), basically, a piece for marching. Music for a procession or parade must necessarily be in duple time (2/4 or 6/8 for a quick march)ᶜ or in quadruple time – common time for a regular march and a slow common time for a funeral march, though Schumann's 'March of the Davidsbündler against the Philistines' (*Carnaval*) is eccentrically in 3/4 time. In form, a march (Schubert, Sousa, Elgar, Walton) consists of a main section alternating with one or more trios. Marches to accompany a stage procession appear in some operas, for example those of Lully, Handel, Mozart, Meyerbeer, Verdi, and Wagner, and in incidental music, e.g. Mendelssohn's *Wedding March*. In the form of instrumental music not intended to accompany action, marches are found for example in English virginal music of the 16th century, in suites in the Baroque period, and in Beethoven's piano sonata, op 101. Examples of funeral marches are in Beethoven's sonata, op 26, and third symphony, and in Chopin's B flat minor sonata.

Marchal, André (born 1894), French organist who was blind from birth. He studied at the Paris Conservatoire, where he won several prizes. He became organist at St. Germain-des-Prés in 1915, and at St. Eustache in 1945. A master of improvisation, he toured as a recitalist in Europe, the United States, and Australia.

Marchand, Louis (1669–1732), French organist and composer. He lived in Paris from about 1698, becoming court organist at Versailles and from 1708 to 1714 organist of the Royal Chapel. Exiled in 1717, he went to Dresden. At a concert there, Bach and Marchand improvised variations on the same theme; Marchand (according to legend) avoided a further contest and returned to Paris.

He composed organ music and an opera, and published two books of harpsichord pieces. Two volumes of his organ music have been edited by A. Guilmant in *Archives des maîtres de l'orgue*, iii and v.

G. B. SHARP: 'Louis Marchand . . . a Forgotten Virtuoso', *Musical Times*, CX, page 1134 (1969)

Marchesi (de Castrone), Italian family of singers, the most famous of whom were **Salvatore Marchesi** (1822–1908), and his wife **Mathilde Marchesi** (née Graumann, 1821–1913). During the 1848 revolutions Salvatore fled to the United States as a political refugee, and made his first stage appearance in New York. He soon returned to Europe, settling in London, and married Mathilde in 1852.

Mathilde Marchesi was a mezzo-soprano, who began teaching in Paris after Garcia, her teacher, suffered an accident. She went to London in 1849, singing at many concerts. Soon after marrying Salvatore, she became professor of singing at the Vienna Conservatorium; later she held posts in Cologne and Paris. Her pupils included Emma Calve, Mary Garden and Nelly Melba.

She wrote a book on singing techniques, 24 books of exercises, and a volume of memoirs, *Marchesi and Music* (1897). Their daughter Blanche Marchesi (1863–1940) was also a noted singer and teacher, especially successful in Britain.

Marchetto or **Marchettus de Padua,** early 14th century Italian theorist. He expounded the use of imperfect as well as perfect time and the Italian method of notation of the various divisions of the breve and semibreve. He wrote two treatises on notation, *Lucidarium in arte musicae planae* and *Pomerium in arte musicae mensuratae* (1318) which aroused much opposition. They were published in Gerbert's *Scriptores*, iii, (pages 64 and 123). The *Pomerium* has been edited more recently by G. Vecchi (1961) and partially translated in O. Strunk's *Source Readings in Music History* (1950).

N. PIRROTTA: 'Marchettus de Padua and the Italian Ars Nova', *Musica Disciplina*, ix (1955).

marcia (It.), march, *tempo di marcia*, march time.

Marenzio, Luca (1553–99), Italian composer. He was in the service of the Cardinal d'Este from 1578 to 1587, and at the Polish court from 1596 to 1598. Finally he became a member of the papal chapel. He was one of the greatest composers of madrigals, and perhaps the most resourceful in expression and technical command. Several of his madrigals were reprinted in Yonge's *Musica Transalpina* (1588, 1597) and in Watson's *Italian Madrigals Englished* (1590), and his style had a strong influence on madrigal composition in England. Morley recommended him as a model of 'good air and fine invention', and Peacham (1622) goes further: 'For delicious Aire and sweet Invention in Madrigals, Luca Marenzio excelleth all other whatsoever.' He published sixteen books of madrigals and one book of *Madrigali spirituali*, besides other volumes of sacred and secular music. The first six books of five-part madrigals have been edited by Alfred Einstein (*Publikationen älterer Musik*, iv/1 and vi). A selection of ten madrigals was reprinted in 1966 by Denis Arnold who has also edited Marenzio's madrigal cycle *Giovane Donna* (1967). A complete edition of his works was begun in 1974 by Les Editions Renaissantes.

D. ARNOLD: *Marenzio* (1965)

H. ENGEL: *Luca Marenzio* (1956, in Italian)

mariachi (Sp.), a Mexican folk group, of varying size, but usually incorporating two violins, guitar (*jarana*), harp (*arpón*), and large guitar (*guitarron*). The word can also apply to a solo folk singer.

Maria Theresia, nickname for Haydn's symphony no 48 in C major, supposedly performed on the occasion of a visit of the Empress Maria Theresa (Theresia is a misspelling) to the Esterhazy Castle in the autumn of 1773. On being introduced to the Empress, Haydn reminded her that she had once had him thrashed for climbing the scaffolding of Schönbrunn Castle with some school friends. 'That thrashing,' replied the Empress, 'yielded good fruit.' Though the anecdote is authentic, the symphony which the Empress heard in 1773 was not no 48. According to the Haydn scholar, Robbins Lardon, the real Maria Theresia symphony was probably no 50 – also in C major.

Mariazell Mass (Ger., *Mariazellermesse*), title of a Mass in C major by Haydn, composed in 1782 (no 6 in the modern complete edition, no 15 in Novello's edition). It owes its name to a shrine of Our Lady at Mariazell in the Styrian Alps and was commissioned by a government official, Anton Liebe von Kreutzner, who (on his ennoblement) wished to make a votive offering there. The work is also known as the *Missa Cellensis*.

Marienleben, Das (Ger., *The Life of Mary*), cycle of fifteen songs for soprano and piano by Hindemith, to a text by Rainer Maria Rilke. The work was composed in 1922 and revised in 1948.

marimba, Latin American (of African origin) instrument, similar to the XYLOPHONE in construction but with larger resonators and usually made of metal. The marimba is pitched an octave lower and is more mellow in tone. The usual compass is four octaves starting from one octave below middle C, although some manufacturers have extended the range. There is also a bass marimba. Since hard-headed sticks are not used, only a limited amount of volume can be produced, but four-note chords, played with two sticks in each hand, are very effective. Sometimes two to five players perform on one instrument. Concertos have been written for it by Milhaud, Creston and others.

marine trumpet, *see* TROMBA MARINA

Marini, Biagio (c. 1597–1665), Italian composer and violinist. He was a player in St. Mark's, Venice, from 1615 to 1618. Marini and Farina, who may have taught him, were the earliest composers of sonatas for solo violin and continuo. Two examples are printed in Schering's *Geschichte der Musik in Beispielen* (nos 182 and 183), and one in *Historical Anthology of Music* (no 199), A. T. Davison and W. Apel. Marini's many published compositions also include music for a wide variety of instrumental and vocal combinations, but little is available in modern editions.

Mario, Giovanni Matteo (1810–83), Italian tenor. After a military education, he became an officer in the Piedmontese guard and an excellent amateur singer. In Paris he was persuaded to embark on an operatic career and made his first appearance there in 1838 in *Robert le diable*. For nearly thirty years he sang regularly in opera in Paris and London, and also visited St. Petersburg. He married the soprano Giula Grisi, and appeared with her, along with Tamburini and Lablache, in the première of Donizetti's *Don Pasquale* (1843). A biography of him, *The Romance of a Great Singer*, was written by his daughter, Mrs. Godfrey Pearce, in collaboration with F. Hird (1910).

Maritana, opera in three acts by Vincent Wallace, to a libretto by Edward Fitzball, first performed in London in 1845. The work is based on a French play, *Don César de Bazan* by Adolphe Philippe d'Ennery and Philippe François Pinel Dumanoir, on the subject of a Spanish gypsy girl.

Markevitch, Igor (born 1912), Russian born conductor, composer, and teacher whose earliest works date from 1926 when he went to Paris to study under Nadia Boulanger. His ballet, *Rebus*, (1931), was dedicated to the memory of Diaghilev, who had encouraged his work. He has written another ballet, *L'Envoi d'Icare*, a cantata on Milton's *Paradise Lost*, a concerto grosso and sinfonietta for orchestra, and chamber music. He was appointed conductor of the Lamoureux Orchestra in Paris in 1958, after which he held conducting appointments in Madrid and Monte

Carlo; he is conductor emeritus of the Philharmonic Orchestra of Japan.

Marpurg, Friedrich Wilhelm (1718–95), German theorist and writer on music. In Paris in 1746 he became acquainted with Rameau's theory of harmony, on which he based his *Handbuch dem Generalbasse* (1755–62). Later he lived in Berlin, Hamburg and from 1763 again in Berlin. Among his other writings are treatises on keyboard playing, fugue, and musical history, and the preface to the second edition of Bach's *Art of Fugue*. He composed sonatas and other keyboard pieces, organ works, and songs.

Marriage of Figaro, The (It., *Le Nozze di Figaro*), opera in four acts by Mozart, to a libretto by Lorenzo da Ponte, first perfomed in Vienna in 1786. The work is based on the Beaumarchais comedy *La Folle Journée ou le mariage de Figaro*.

Figaro, valet to Count Almaviva, is going to marry Susanna, the Countess's maid. The plot is concerned with his successful frustration of the Count's designs on his bride. In the process he discovers himself to have a father, Dr. Bartolo, and a mother, Marcellina, who – not knowing herself to be his parent – has been trying to marry him (using, as a lever, the fact he owes her money). The situation is further complicated by the behaviour of the page Cherubino, who is ready to fall in love with any woman he meets and imagines himself in love with the Countess. The Countess also has her problems. Weary of her husband's infidelities, she impersonates Susanna and meets him in the garden. When all the misunderstandings have been sorted out, Figaro wins his bride and the Countess shows herself ready to forgive her husband.

Figaro is an opera that explores love in all its aspects, from the puppy love of Cherubino (a role given by Mozart to a female soprano) for the Countess, to the Countess's melancholy love for her husband. At the same time, the work is a social critique, attacking the aristocracy and the '*droit de seigneur*' as exercised by the Count. Three years after the opera's first performance, the French Revolution took place.

Marsch (Ger.), march

Marschner, Heinrich August (1795–1861), German composer and conductor. He was sent to Leipzig to study law, but by 1824 had become musical director of the Dresden Opera. Three years later he became *Kapellmeister* in Leipzig, and from 1831 until 1859 he held a similar post in Hanover. Marschner was the most successful composer of German romantic opera between Weber (whose disciple he was) and Wagner. His *Heinrich IV und Aubigne* was produced by Weber at Dresden in 1820. *Der Vampyr* (The Vampire, 1828) successfully reflected his taste for the macabre, and *Der Templer und die Jüdin* (The Templar and the Jewess, 1829) was based on Scott's *Ivanhoe*. His most representative opera, *Hans Heiling* (Berlin, 1833), has kept its place in the repertory of German opera houses. He also composed songs and choral music.

Marseillaise, La (Fr.), French national hymn. The words and music were written by Rouget de Lisle on the night of April 24, 1792. It acquired the name because it was sung in Paris by troops from Marseilles on their entry into the city in July of that year. It was used by Salieri in the opera *Palmira* (1795) and by

Schumann in his *Faschingsschwank aus Wien* for piano
and the song 'Die beiden Grenadiere' (The Two
Grenadiers).

Marson, George (c. 1573–1632), English composer.
He was organist at Canterbury from about 1599 until
his death. His five-part madrigal 'The nymphs and
shepherds danced lavoltas' was published in *The
Triumphes of Oriana* (*The English Madrigal School*,
xxxii). He also composed church music.

Marteau sans Maître, Le (Fr., *The Hammer without
a Master*), work in nine movements for contralto and
chamber ensemble by Boulez, first performed in 1955
at the Baden Festival and revised in 1957. The music
is based on René Char's surrealist poems of the same
title, written in 1934. With its subtle scoring (incorporating G-flute, vibraphone, viola, guitar and
xylorimba), the work established Boulez as a major
figure of modern music.

martelé, *see* MARTELLATO

martellato, (It.; Fr., *martelé*), literally 'hammered'.
A term used in string-playing, indicating heavy,
detached up-and-down strokes, played with the point
of the bow, without taking the bow from the string, and
in piano-playing, indicating a forceful, detached touch.
Use of the heel of the bow is indicated by the term
'martelé au talon'.

Martenot (Fr.), *see* ONDES MARTENOT

Martha, opera in four acts by Flotow, to a libretto by
W. Friedrich (i.e. Friedrich Wilhelm Riese). It was
first performed in Vienna in 1847. The story tells how
Lady Harriet, Queen Anne's maid of honour, visits
Richmond Fair disguised as a country girl and falls in
love with a young farmer. The opera makes use of the
Irish song, 'The Last Rose of Summer.'

Martin, Frank (1890–1974), Swiss composer who later
settled in Holland. He studied in Geneva (his birthplace) under Joseph Lauber, and taught there for a
while at the Jaques-Dalcroze school. He has been
widely recognized as a composer of originality and
power. His works, which incorporate a very personal
use of twelve-note technique, include two operas (*The
Tempest* after Shakespeare, and *Monsieur Pourceaugnac*)
and incidental music for *Oedipus Rex, Oedipus at
Colonus* and *Romeo and Juliet*. He has also composed
oratorios (*In Terra Pax* and *Golgotha*) and other choral
music, *Le Vin Herbé* for twelve voices, strings and
piano (on the subject of Tristan and Isolde), and
orchestral music including the fastidiously-written
Petite Symphonie Concertante for harp, harpsichord,
piano and strings.

Martinelli, Giovanni (1885–1969), Italian tenor who
studied in Milan, where he made his debut in 1910 as
Ernani in Verdi's opera. Puccini, who heard his
performance, engaged him the following year for the
European premiere of *La Fanciulla del West*. In the
1920s he was regarded as Caruso's natural successor at
the New York Metropolitan, where he sang more than
fifty principal tenor roles before he retired in 1945. He
was particularly renowned for his portrayals of Otello
and Radamès (in *Aida*).

Martini, Giovanni Battista (also known as
Giambattista) (1706–84), Italian priest, theorist, historian and composer, the most renowned musical
savant of his day. He studied the harpsichord, violin
and counterpoint. He was ordained in 1722 (hence

called 'Padre'), and became *maestro di capella* at S.
Francesco, Bologna, in 1725. He corresponded with a
wide circle of professional and amateur musicians, and
gave advice on technical points to many celebrated
composers, among them Mozart and J. C. Bach. His
most important works are the unfinished history of
music (*Storia della musica*, three volumes, 1757–81)
and a treatise on counterpoint (*Esemplare . . . di
contrappunto*, two volumes, 1774–5). His compositions
include church music, oratorios and keyboard sonatas.

Martini il Tedesco (i.e. Martini the German), Italian
nickname for Johann Paul Aegidius Schwartzendorf
(1741–1816), German composer and organist who
settled in France and called himself by the Italian name
of Giovanni Paolo Martini. Today he is known mainly
for his song, 'Plaisir d'Amour', but he also wrote
operas, church music and other works. After the
French Revolution, he joined the staff of the Paris
Conservatoire, and in 1814 was appointed superintendent of the court music.

Martinon, Jean (1909–76), French conductor and
composer. He studied the violin at Lyons Conservatoire
and composition under Roussel at the Paris Conservatoire. After working with various French
orchestras, he became conductor of the Chicago
Symphony Orchestra in 1963; later he returned to
Europe. As a composer, he has written an opera,
Hecube (after Euripides), symphonies, concertos and
other orchestral works, choral music and chamber
music.

Martinů, Bohuslav (1890–1959), Czech composer.
He was a pupil of Suk in Prague and Roussel in Paris,
where he lived from 1932 until 1940. When France was
invaded by the Germans, he took refuge in the United
States. After World War II he continued wandering,
dividing his time between the United States,
Czechoslovakia and Switzerland, where he died.
During his U.S. years he taught at Princeton and the
Berkshire Music Center.

He was a prolific, somewhat eclectic composer,
whose works, according to his biographer, Miloš
Safránek, combined the form of concerto grosso and
the melody of Czechoslovakia. He wrote thirteen
operas, including *Julietta, Comedy on a Bridge, The
Marriage* (after Gogol) and *The Greek Passion* (after
Kazantzakis' novel, *Christ Recrucified*). Among his
other works are several ballets, six symphonies,
numerous concertos and other orchestral works,
choral music, seven string quartets and other chamber
music, sonatas and other instrumental pieces.

M. SAFRÁNEK: *Bohuslav Martinů* (1944, revised
1961)

Martín y Soler, Vicente (1754–1806), Spanish composer. Chorister at Valencia and organist at Alicante, he
produced his first Italian opera at Florence in 1781. A
melody from his most successful opera *Una cosa rara*,
written to a libretto by Da Ponte and produced in
Vienna in 1786, was used by Mozart in the banquet
music in the finale of the second act of *Don Giovanni*
(1787). He produced two operas in St. Petersburg (the
second with Pashkeievich) to libretti by the Empress
Catherine II (1789, 1791) and two in London to
Italian texts by Da Ponte (1795).

Martucci, Giuseppe (1856–1909), Italian pianist,
conductor and composer who studied at Naples

Conservatory and became a professor there in 1874. In 1886 he was appointed director of the Liceo Musicale at Bologna, where he produced the Italian première of Wagner's *Tristan and Isolde* in 1888. As well as being a devoted Wagnerian, he did much to encourage the performance of instrumental music in Italy and was founder of the Quartetto Napoletano. He composed an oratorio, *Samuele,* two symphonies, a piano concerto in B flat minor and other orchestral works, chamber and instrumental music, and arrangements of old Italian music.

Martyre de Saint Sébastien, Le (Fr., *The Martyrdom of St. Sebastian*), a mystery play (written in French) by Gabriele d'Annunzio for which Debussy wrote incidental music for solo voices, chorus and orchestra (1911).

Marx, Adolph Bernhard (1795–1866), German theorist and writer on music. In 1820 he became professor of music at Berlin University, and in 1850 he founded, with Kullak and Stern, the school of music which afterwards became the Stern Conservatorium. He founded the *Berliner allgemeine musikalische Zeitung* (1824), and wrote a four-volume treatise on composition and books on Handel, Gluck and Beethoven. His own compositions included operas and oratorios.

Marx, Joseph (1882–1964), Austrian composer who studied in Vienna and in 1924 succeeded Ferdinand Löwe as director of the Academy of Music there. His compositions, in a late romantic style, include symphonic poems, choral works with orchestra, chamber music and many songs.

Marxsen, Eduard (1806–87), German composer and pianist. He studied in Hamburg and Vienna, and later became a teacher in Hamburg, where Brahms was one of his pupils.

marziale (It.), martial, war-like.

Masaniello, Italian title for five-act opera by Auber, also known – more correctly – as *La Muette de Portici* (The Dumb Girl of Portici). The libretto, by Augustin Eugène Scribe and Germain Delavigne, concerns the Italian revolutionary hero, Masaniello, and his sister Fanella, a mute (the role in the opera is taken by a dancer). In the course of the work, Masaniello captures Naples, is given poison, loses his reason, and is finally killed; Fanella commits suicide by jumping from her window into the crater of Vesuvius. The opera, first performed in Paris in 1828, was enormously successful in its day and struck Wagner with its dramatic intensity. When presented in Belgium in 1830 its impact was so powerful that it precipitated the Belgian revolt against the Dutch which established an independent Belgium. Today *Masaniello* is remembered mainly for its overture.

Mascagni, Pietro (1863–1945), Italian composer. He was the son of a baker, who wanted him to study law, not music, but a sympathetic aristocrat, Count Florestano de Larderel, paid for him to attend Milan Conservatorio under Ponchielli – an opportunity Mascagni soon abandoned in favour of joining a touring opera company as a conductor. At the age of 26 he made his name with *Cavalleria Rusticana*, which won first prize in a competition, and gained him a fortune, taking Europe by storm. Though he wrote many other operas, including *L'Amico Fritz* (1891),

Pietro Mascagni

Iris (1898), *Le Maschere* (1901), *Isabeau* (based on the story of Lady Godiva, 1911) and *Il Piccolo Marat* (1921), none of these equalled the success of *Cavalleria*. Nor, in 1935, did *Nerone* (Nero), with which he hoped to curry favour with Mussolini. As a convinced fascist, Mascagni lost the friendship of Toscanini and other musicians. Three months after the end of World War II, he died, dishonoured, in a Rome hotel.

Maskarade (Dan., masquerade), comic opera in one act by Carl Nielsen, to a libretto by Vilhelm Anderson, first performed in Copenhagen in 1906. The story (based on a comedy by Ludvig Holberg) concerns a pair of young lovers at an 18th century masked ball. The overture is often performed in the concert hall, but the rest of the work is equally worthwhile, though it has yet to receive the international exposure it deserves.

Masked Ball, A (It., *Un Ballo in Maschera*), opera in three acts by Verdi, to a libretto by Antonio Somma, first performed in Rome in 1859. Founded on Scribe's text for Auber's *Gustav III*, the opera suffered initially from censorship trouble. An attempt on the life of Napoleon III, not long before the opera's proposed first performance, made Verdi's portrayal of the assassination of a Swedish king hardly seem tactful. So, for political reasons, the action was transferred to New England and King Gustav became Count Riccardo, governor of Boston. Similarly, Counts Ribbing and Horn, the leaders of the conspiracy, were renamed Sam and Tom.

Because it contains some of Verdi's finest music, the opera triumphed over its change of locale. Nevertheless, a number of modern productions (especially one by the Royal Stockholm Opera, a company which naturally has a special interest in the subject) has restored the action to Sweden and given the characters their original names.

Mason, Lowell (1792–1872), U.S. organist and teacher who compiled a collection of psalm tunes which were published in Boston in 1822 under the auspices of the Handel and Haydn Society. He was one of the pioneers of musical education in schools in New England, where his work left a lasting impression.

His son **William Mason** (1829–1908) became a pianist. His autobiography, *Memories of a Musical Life* (1902), contains an account of his studies in Leipzig under Moscheles and Moritz Hauptmann and in Weimar under Liszt.

Daniel Gregory Mason (1873–1953), William's son, is the most famous of the family, both as a composer and a writer on music. He studied at Harvard, and later under Arthur Whiting in New York and d'Indy in Paris. From 1919 he taught at Columbia University, becoming professor in 1929. He composed three symphonies (the third is called *A Lincoln Symphony*) and other orchestral works, choral music, chamber music, songs and other piano pieces. One of his string quartets is based on Negro themes, and his piano variations on 'Yankee Doodle' are parodies of various composers. His books include: *From Greig to Brahms* (1902), *The Romantic Composers* (1906), *The Chamber Music of Brahms* (1932) and *The Quartets of Beethoven* (1947).

masque, the English masque (mask, maske) inherited the tradition of the choirboy plays with music of the first half of the 16th century, and by the early 17th century had become an elaborate court entertainment combining poetry and dancing with vocal and instrumental music, and with scenery, machinery and costume. Among the writers of pre-Commonwealth masques were Ben Jonson, Beaumont, Campion, Dekker, and Shirley; among the composers, Campion, Robert Johnson, the younger Ferrabosco, Laniere (who 'ordered and made both the scene and the music' of Jonson's *Lovers made Men* in 1617), and the brothers Lawes. Inigo Jones designed the scenery and machines of some of Jonson's masques. The most extravagant and expensive masque of the period was Shirley's *The Triumph of Peace* (1633) for which some music of William Lawes has survived (*see* M. Lefkowitz, *Trois masques à la cour de Charles 1er d'Angleterre*, 1970). Henry Lawes wrote the music for Milton's *Comus*, produced at Ludlow Castle in 1634. The masque came closer to the opera with the increasing use of recitative instead of spoken dialogue, as in the fifth entry of Shirley's *Cupid and Death* (1653), with music by Matthew Locke and Christopher Gibbons (modern edition by E. J. Dent in *Musica Britannica*, ii). After the Restoration the masque was still popular; but its artistic importance was much less, if we except Blow's *Venus and Adonis* (edited by A. Lewis, 1949), actually a miniature opera, and the masque which forms part of Purcell's incidental music to *Dioclesian*. The 18th century masques of Arne, Hayes, and others were light and elegant entertainments.

J. P. CUTTS: 'Jacobean Masque and Stage Music', *Music and Letters*, xxxv (1954)

P. REYHER: *Les masques anglais* (1909)

A. SABOL: *Songs and Dances for the Stuart Masque* (1959)

Mass, in the musical sense, a setting of the Ordinary, or invariable parts (*Kyrie, Gloria, Credo, Sanctus* with *Benedictus, Agnus Dei*) of the Mass. From the 11th to the 13th centuries the original plainsong melodies were used as a basis for polyphonic settings of some parts of the Ordinary, particularly the *Kyrie, Sanctus,* and *Agnus Dei*. The practice of setting single movements, and later also pairs of movements (e.g. *Gloria-Credo, Sanctus-Agnus*) was continued in the 14th and 15th centuries. Settings of the Ordinary as a musical whole, such as Machaut's *Messe de Nostre Dame*, were uncommon in the 14th century, but became usual after about 1430. A frequent method of establishing musical unity was the use of a *cantus firmus*, taken either from plainsong (e.g. Leonel Power's *Alma redemptoris* Mass and Dufay's *Ave Regina caelorum* Mass) or from secular song (e.g. Dufay's *Se la face ay pale* Mass, and the *L'Homme armé* Masses by Dufay, Ockeghem, Obrecht and others). Another unifying device was the use of a common opening for each movement. 16th century settings in imitative polyphony more commonly derived their material from a motet or *chanson* (*see* PARODY MASS) or were independent compositions (*sine nomine*). From the 15th to the 17th centuries the Mass was often performed in plainsong alternating with organ: there exists a number of ORGAN MASSES written for this purpose.

Lutheran composers in the 17th century wrote Masses for combinations of voices and instruments: the final stage of this tradition is seen in Bach's Mass in B Minor. The Masses of the classical and romantic periods reflect the dominant styles of those periods in other forms. Beethoven's *Missa Solemnis*, like Bach's Mass in B Minor, ignores the practical requirements of liturgical performance to attain its grandeur of conception. In the present century there have been some notable examples of settings of the Mass, e.g. those by Stravinsky and Vaughan Williams. For the individual items of the Mass (*Kyrie, Gloria,* etc.), *see* under those headings.

Massenet, Jules Emile Frederic (1842–1912), French composer. He studied composition under Ambroise Thomas at the Paris Conservatoire, where he won the *Prix de Rome* at the age of 21. He taught composition there from 1878 to 1896. The lyrical beauty of his music, and his smooth, voluptuous style helped to establish him as one of the favourite composers of the period. Though he had his detractors – and still does – who dismiss him as a feminine Wagner, he has held his place in the repertory. *Manon* (1884), *Werther* (1892) and *Thais* (1894) were the milestones of his career. The last of these, in particular, exploited the mixture of religion and sin at which he was so adept. His tally of 27 operas also includes his earliest major success, *Le Roi de Lahore* (1877), *Hérodiade* (1881), *Le Jongleur de Notre Dame* (1902) and *Don Quichotte* (1910). Among his other works are ballets, orchestral and choral music, a piano concerto, cantatas (one of them entitled *David Rizzio*), a cello fantasy and some 200 songs.

mässig (Ger.), moderate.

Mass of Life, A, Delius' setting of passages from Nietzsche's *Also sprach Zarathustra* for soloists, chorus and orchestra, composed in 1905. The first complete performance took place in London four years later.

Masson, Paul Marie (1882–1954), French musical

historian. He studied history of music with Rolland at the Ecole Normale Supérieure, Paris, and composition at the Schola Cantorum with d'Indy and Koechlin. He held academic appointments in Florence and Naples, before becoming professor at the Sorbonne in 1931. His books include studies of Florentine carnival songs, Rameau's operas, and Berlioz.

mastersingers, see MEISTERSINGER

Mastersingers of Nuremberg, The (Ger., *Die Meistersinger von Nürnberg*), opera in three acts by Wagner, to a libretto by the composer, first performed in Munich in 1868. Walther von Stolzing (a knight) sees Eva Pogner (daughter of a rich goldsmith) in a church and falls in love with her. He discovers that her father has promised her hand to the winner of the singing contest on St. John's day and applies to the Mastersingers to take part in the competition. Beckmesser (the marker and a rival for Eva's hand) attempts to discredit Walther by noisily noting one error after another during his singing. At night Eva agrees to elope with Walther but they are forced to take shelter when Hans Sachs (the cobbler at whose house Walther has been staying) opens a window and throws a light on the street. Beckmesser, who arrives to serenade Eva, is constantly interrupted by Hans Sachs, who marks his errors by loudly hammering a nail into a shoe. Walther dreams of a prize song and sings it to Sachs who writes it down; but it is later stolen by Beckmesser, who is greeted with laughter when he tries to sing it at the contest. He claims that it was written by Sachs, but Sachs denies this and asks Walther to sing. Walther then sings his song successfully, is asked to become a member of the guild and receives the hand of Eva.

The role of Beckmesser is a caricature of the anti-Wagner critic Eduard Hanslick. But, though the portrait is malicious, the work as a whole has a tenderness, humour and humanity that make it the one Wagner opera which even non-Wagnerians find themselves able to love. For the historical background to Wagner's plot, see MEISTERSINGER.

Mathis der Maler (Ger., *Mathis the Painter*), opera in seven scenes by Hindemith, to a libretto by the composer, first performed in Zürich in 1938. A performance scheduled by the Berlin Opera four years earlier was banned by the Nazis and resulted in the resignation of the conductor Wilhelm Furtwängler from his post. The story is based on the life of the 16th century painter Matthias Grünewald and deals with the conflict between a creative artist's duty to himself and his obligations to society. A 'symphony' in three movements with the same title, based on music from the opera, was first performed in 1934. The prelude to the opera, subtitled *Engelkonzert* (concert of angels) forms the first movement of the symphony.

Matin, Le Midi, Le Soir et La Tempête, Le (Fr., *Morning, Midday, Evening and Storm*), the titles of three symphonies by Haydn (no 6 in D major, no 7 in C major, and no 8 in G major), composed in 1761. The music was clearly meant to be programmatic, though no authentic description of its programme has survived. Composed for Prince Paul Anton Esterházy, this symphonic trilogy was an early milestone in Haydn's career, and revealed to the Esterházy family his potential as a composer.

Matrimonio Segreto, see SECRET MARRIAGE

Matteis, Nicola, 17th century Italian violinist who came to London in 1672. His playing is praised in Evelyn's *Diary* under the date of November 19th, 1674. He published three books of 'ayres' for violin (between 1685 and 1688) and a book entitled *The False Consonances of Musick*. In 1696 he published a collection of songs in two books and composed an *Ode on St. Cecilia's Day* for the annual celebration in London. Burney studied French and the violin under his son, Nicholas Matteis.

M. TILMOUTH: 'Nicola Matteis', in *Musical Quarterly*, xlvi (1960)

Matthay, Tobias (1858–1945), English pianist, teacher and composer. He studied at the Royal Academy of Music in London, where he was appointed teacher of piano in 1880. In 1900 he founded his own piano school, evolving a method of his own (the Matthay System), and became one of the leading teachers of Europe. His pupils included Harriet Cohen, Myra Hess and Ray Lev. He is well known for his books on piano technique, which include *The Art of Touch* (1926) and *The First Principles of Pianoforte Playing* (1905).

Mattheson, Johann (1681–1764), German composer, theorist and organist. He was versatile in many fields. From the age of nine he sang in the Hamburg opera and in 1699 he produced his first opera, *Die Pleyaden*. In 1703 he went with Handel to Lübeck, where both had applied to be Buxtehude's successor; on hearing that marriage to Buxtehude's daughter was a condition of the post, each withdrew his application. In 1704 he made his last appearance in Handel's *Nero* and then retired from the stage. He later became tutor-secretary to the English envoy and ambassador. In 1715 he was appointed canon and cantor of Hamburg Cathedral, where he took an active part in the development of the church cantata. Among his compositions are eight operas, 24 oratorios and cantatas, a Passion and twelve sonatas for flute and violin. His books include *Der musikalische Patriot* (1728), *Grundlage einer Ehrenpforte* (1740, modern edition by M. Schneider, 1910), *Der vollkommene Kapellmeister* (1739, facsimile edition 1954), and *Kleine General-Bass-Schule* (1735).

F. T. ARNOLD: *The Art of Accompaniment from a Thorough-Bass* (1931)

B. C. CANNON: *Johann Mattheson* (1947)

Matthews, Denis (born 1919), English pianist and teacher. He studied under Harold Craxton and William Alwyn at the Royal Academy of Music, London, before making his début in 1939. A noted exponent of Mozart and Beethoven, he became professor of music at Newcastle University in 1971.

Matton, Roger (born 1929), French Canadian composer. He studied at the Provincial Conservatory in Montreal and later in Paris under Nadia Boulanger. In 1957 he joined the staff of the Archives de Folklore at Laval University in Quebec as ethnomusicologist. Among his orchestral works are a series of *Mouvements Symphoniques*, the second of which, written in 1962 for the Montreal Symphony Orchestra, has been performed internationally.

Mauduit, Jacques (1557–1627), French composer. He was associated with Antoine de Baïf's Academy in the setting of poetry to music on the basis of the classical metres (*musique mesurée à l'antique*). His volume of *Chansonnettes mesurées de Jean-Antoine de Baïf mises en musique à quatre parties* (Paris, 1586) has been reprinted by H. Expert in *Les Maîtres musiciens de la Renaissance française*, x.

Maurel, Victor (1848–1923), French baritone. He studied at the Paris Conservatoire, and first appeared at the Paris Opera in *Les Huguenots* in 1867. He was the first Iago in Verdi's *Otello* (Milan, 1887) and the first Falstaff (Milan, 1893). He repeated his success in both works in performances in Paris, London and New York, where he eventually settled as a teacher in 1909. He published four books on singing and an autobiography, and was also active as a painter and stage designer.

Má Vlast (*My Country*), a cycle of six symphonic poems by Smetana inspired by the Czech countryside and by episodes in Czech history. The works were composed between 1874 and 1879, and have the following titles:

(1) *Vyšehrad* (The citadel of Prague);
(2) *Vltava* (The Moldau River);
(3) *Šárka* (Leader of the Bohemian Amazons);
(4) *Z Českych Luhův a Hájův* (From Bohemia's Fields and Groves);
(5) *Tábor* (Stronghold of the blind leader of the Hussites);
(6) *Blaník* (Mountain in southern Bohemia).

Mavra, comic opera in one act by Stravinsky, to a libretto by Boris Kochno, first performed at the Paris Opera in 1922. Scored for four solo singers and orchestra, the work is based on Pushkin's story, *The Little House of Kolomna*, and was written in reaction to what the composer described as Wagner's 'inflated arrogance'. The music makes humorous use of the vocal style and conventions of 'the old Russo-Italian opera'.

Maw, Nicholas (born 1935), English composer, pupil of Lennox Berkeley and Nadia Boulanger. His lyrical, post-Straussian style is heard at its best in his vocal music, which includes two operas (*One Man Show* and *The Rising of the Moon*) and *Scenes and Arias*, a concert work for three female voices and orchestra, based on old French texts. He has also written a *Nocturne* for mezzo-soprano and orchestra, and *Chamber Music* for piano and wind instruments.

maxima (Lat.), the note of the greatest time value in the medieval system of MENSURAL NOTATION, written ⌐. It was called a 'large' in England.

Maynard, John (16th–17th centuries), English lutenist and composer. In 1611 he published *The XII wonders of the world, Set and composed for the Violl de Gambo, the Lute and the Voyce to sing the Verse, all three jointly and none severall* (facsimile edition, 1970), which contains twelve songs describing character-types and twelve pavans and galliards for the lute, and refers to the composer as 'Lutenist at the most famous Schoole of St. Julian's in Hartfordshire'.

I. HARWOOD: 'John Maynard and *The XII Wonders of the World*', in *Lute Society Journal*, iv (1962)

May Night, A (Rus., *Maiskaya Noch*), opera in three acts by Rimsky-Korsakov, to a libretto by the composer, first performed in St. Petersburg in 1880. Based on a story by Gogol, the work is the earliest of Rimsky-Korsakov's 'magic' operas. It tells how a water nymph helps a young man to win the girl he loves.

Mayr, Johann Simon (also known as Giovanni Simone Mayr) (1763–1845), German-Italian composer, born in Bavaria. He was educated at the Jesuit Seminary in Ingolstadt, and later studied with Lenzi in Bergamo and Bertoni in Venice. In 1805 he became teacher of composition at the newly-founded Institute of Music in Bergamo, where Donizetti was one of his pupils. He composed about seventy operas, among which *Medea in Corinto* (1813) has been successfully revived; it contains some striking foretastes of Verdi. In addition to operas, he wrote a variety of church music and a book on Haydn.

Mayuzumi, Toshiro (born 1929), Japanese composer who studied in Tokyo and Paris. His works include an orchestral *Bacchanal*, a divertimento for chamber ensemble, and *Tonepleromas 55* for wind, percussion and musical saw. He has also written electronic music.

Mazeppa, (1) opera in three acts by Chaikovsky, with a libretto by the composer and 'Viktor Petrovich Burenin' (i.e. Count Alexei Zhasminov), after Pushkin's *Poltava*. First performed in Moscow in 1884, the work concerns Mazeppa's plot against Peter the Great in the 17th century. A number of operas have been written on the subject.

(2) symphonic poem by Liszt, first performed at Weimar in 1854, and based on a piano study in *Etudes d'exécution transcendante*. The music was inspired by Victor Hugo's poem and describes how Mazeppa, after surviving the rigour of being tied naked to a wild horse, becomes a cossack chief.

mazurka, a Polish folk dance in a moderate to fast triple time with the second or third beat often strongly accented. It was first adapted as a stylized piece for piano by Chopin, who wrote more than fifty mazurkas, and later used by other composers, e.g. Chaikovsky and Szymanowski. Its most characteristic rhythm is

e.g.:

CHOPIN, *Mazurkas*, op 33, no 2

Mazzocchi, Domenico (1592–1665), Italian composer. His book of madrigals of 1638 contained works in both the old and new (continuo) styles, and used signs for *crescendo* and *diminuendo* for the first time. He composed the opera *La Catena d'Adone* (Rome, 1626;

extracts in H. Goldschmidt, *Studien zur Geschichte der italienischen Oper im 17. Jahrhundert*, i), motets, and monodic *laude*. His monody *Planctus matris Euryali* was quoted by Kircher (*Musurgia universalis*, 1650) as an example of the mixture of diatonic, chromatic and enharmonic genera. It is printed in Schering's *Geschichte der Musik in Beispielen*, no 197.

His brother **Virgilio Mazzocchi** (1597–1646) was also a composer. He was *maestro di cappella* at St. John Lateran in 1628, and at St. Peter's in 1629. With Marazzoli he composed the earliest comic opera, *Chi soffre, speri* (Rome, 1637, extracts in H. Goldschmidt, *Studien zur Geschichte der italienischen Oper im 17 Jahrhundert*, i), and wrote choral music and monodic *laude*.

me, anglicized form of the Italian *mi* (E). In TONIC SOL-FA the third note (or mediant) of the major scale.

meane, mene, a term used in England in the 15th and early 16th centuries for the voice between the treble and tenor (*Lat. medius*) in a choral composition. In the method of extemporizing a part above a plainsong used at that time (*see* SIGHT) the meane sight was the fifth above the tenor. The term was also used for the middle part of a three-part keyboard piece.

mean-tone tuning, *see* TEMPERAMENT

measure, U.S. term for bar. The word is also applied, more widely, to rhythm or time.

mechanical musical instruments, the principal of the revolving cylinder with protruding pins was applied in the 15th and 16th centuries to the carillon, and to keyboard instruments. The addition of a clockwork mechanism made it possible to apply it to a number of contrivances, such as musical clocks, mechanical organs and orchestras, and musical boxes, which were very popular in the 18th century. Mozart wrote three pieces for a mechanical organ (K 594, 608, 616) of which the first two are major compositions. Beethoven's *Wellington's Victory* or *The Battle of Vittoria* (1813) was originally written for Maelzel's Panharmonicon, a mechanical orchestra.

See also BARREL ORGAN, PIANOLA, STREET PIANO

J. E. T. CLARK: *Musical Boxes* (1948)

medesimo tempo (It.), in the same tempo.

mediant, the third degree of the diatonic scale, e.g. E in the scale of C.

Medium, The, opera in two acts by Menotti, to a libretto by the composer, first performed in New York in 1946. The story concerns a fraudulent spiritual medium, who shoots dead one of the inmates of her house. With music palatable to the point of seeming predigested, the opera scored an enormous success in its early years and was filmed in 1951. Today its colours seem somewhat faded, and it has failed to hold its place in the international repertory.

medley, mixture, miscellany, potpourri. An operatic medley is therefore a selection of excerpts performed non-stop. The term has a long musical history, and was used in 16th century keyboard music.

Medtner, Nikolai Karlovich (real name, Nikolay Karlovich) (1880–1951), Russian composer and pianist, of German descent. He studied in Moscow under Arensky, Taneyev and Safonov. From 1921 he lived successively in Berlin, France, and England. His most important compositions, which are in a traditional style, are for piano, and include concertos, a sonata-

trilogy and a series of *Fairy Tales*. A Medtner Society, sponsored by the Maharajah of Mysore, was founded in 1948.

R. HOLT: *Medtner and his Music* (1948)

Mefistofele (*Mephistopheles*), opera with a prologue, four acts and an epilogue by Boito, to a libretto by the composer, first performed in Milan in 1868. Like Gounod, Boito based his opera on Goethe's *Faust*, with dramatically more faithful (though less popular) results.

Megli (Melio, Melli), **Domenico** (16th–17th centuries), Italian composer. He was one of the earliest composers of monodic solos and dialogues, published between 1602 and 1609. His first book probably came out about two months before Caccini's *Le nuove musiche*. A monody with lute was included in Robert Dowland's *Musicall Banquet* (1610).

mehr (Ger.), more.

Mehrstimmigkeit (Ger.), polyphony.

Méhul, Etienne Henri Nicolas (1763–1817), French composer. An organist from the age of ten, he studied and taught in Paris from 1778. Encouraged by Gluck, he wrote several operas, of which the first to be staged was *Euphrosine et Coradin* (1790). His later operas developed the style of Grétry, and he became one of the most prominent composers of the period of the Revolution. The most mature of his works are *Uthal* (1806), which has no violins in the orchestra, and *Joseph* (1807).

Meibom (Meibomius), **Marcus** (1626–1711), German or Danish philologist. In 1652 he printed the texts, with Latin translations and commentary, of treatises on music by Aristoxenus, Aristeides Quintilianus, Nichomachus, Cleonides, Gaudentius, Alypius and Baccheius the Elder. Some were re-edited by Karl von Jan in *Musici Scriptores Graeci* (1895).

Meissen, Heinrich von, *see* FRAUENLOB

Meistersinger (Ger.), mastersinger, member of literary and musical guilds which were founded in certain German cities in the 15th and 16th centuries. The guilds, whose members were traders and craftsmen, grew up as the aristocratic *Minnesinger* declined. The *Meistersinger* thought of themselves as the *Minnesinger's* heirs, and Heinrich Frauenlob, regarded as the last of the *Minnesinger*, founded the first guild in Mainz in 1311. The movement spread throughout Germany in the 16th century, but declined rapidly in the 17th. The *Meistersinger* held weekly meetings with very rigid rules, and members of the guild were divided into equally rigid grades, with promotion by examination. The highest grade was that of *Meister*, and was awarded to the inventor of a new melody (*ton* or *weise*). The other grades were *Dichter* (who wrote words to existing melodies), *Singer*, *Schulfreund* (school-friend, one who had mastered the guild's rules), and *Schuler* (pupil, the lowest grade). The guilds held competitions in which compositions were rigorously judged and prizes given. The organization of the guilds and the contests they held are vividly brought to life by Wagner in *The Mastersingers of Nuremberg*, who drew heavily on the account of the *Meistersinger* by J. G. Wagenseil, printed in 1697. Hans Sachs was the most famous *Meistersinger* of the 16th century and all but one of the names of Wagner's

Mastersingers (Fritz Zorn was changed to Balthazar Zorn) were listed by Wagenseil as distinguished masters of Nuremberg.

Songs composed by masters became part of the repertory of the guild. Each verse or *Bar* (the traditional form of the *Minnesinger*) consisted of two *Stollen* and an *Abgesang*, in the form of AAB. Wagner used some of the original tunes in his opera.

Meistersinger von Nürnberg, Die *see* MASTER-SINGERS OF NUREMBERG

Mel, Rinaldo del (?1554–c. 1600), Flemish composer. He was in the service of the King of Portugal and, from 1580, Archdeacon Carolo Valigano in Rome. From about 1588 he was employed by the Duke of Bavaria, and from 1591 he served Cardinal Paleotto, Archbishop of Bologna who made him *maestro di capella* to Magliano Cathedral. Between 1581 and 1595 he published six books of motets and fifteen books of madrigals.

Melba as Rosina in *The Barber of Seville* at Covent Garden in 1898

Melba, Nellie (originally Helen Mitchell) (1859–1931), Australian operatic soprano who came to Europe in 1886 and studied in Paris under Mathilde Marchesi. She made her début in Brussels the following year, as Gilda in *Rigoletto*. She was one of the greatest singers of her day in lyric and coloratura roles including Lucia di Lammermoor, Marguérite (in *Faust*), Violetta (in *Traviata*), Mimi (in *Bohème*) and Rosina (in *The Barber of Seville*). The title-role in Saint-Saëns's *Hélène* (1904) was written for her. An ice-cream dessert and a kind of toast were named after her. Her autobiography, *Melodies and Memories*, was published in 1925, one year before she retired.

melisma (Gr., *melisma* = song; plural, *melismata*), a unit of melody which is sung to one syllable, especially in plainsong. Today the term is also applied, more widely, to any florid vocal passage. One modern composer noted for melismatic vocal writing is Benjamin Britten.

Mellers, Wilfrid Howard (born 1914), English musical historian and composer. He studied at Cambridge, and since 1964 has been professor of music at York University, where he has built up the most progressive music department in Britain. He has composed an opera (*The Tragicall History of Christopher Marlowe*), orchestral music, vocal music (including a cantata, *Yggdrasil*), chamber and instrumental music, but is more noted for his books, among which are *Music and Society* (1946), *Studies in Contemporary Music* (1948), *François Couperin* (1950), *Man and his Music* (1962, in collaboration with Alec Harman), *Caliban Reborn* (1967), and *The Twilight of the Gods*, a study of the Beatles (1973).

mellophone, resembling in appearance (and also to some extent in tone quality) a horn, this instrument was invented primarily for use in jazz or dance bands. Although inferior to the horn, it is much easier to play and is suitable as a doubling instrument for trumpet players. Very few musicians have specialized in it.

mélodie (Fr.), (1) in general, melody;

(2) in particular, a song with piano accompaniment, the French equivalent of the German *Lied*.

melodrama, spoken words with musical accompaniment, either as a complete work (also called monodrama or duodrama) or as part of an opera. Complete plays in this style were written by J. J. Rousseau (*Pygmalion*, 1762) and Georg Benda (*Ariadne auf Naxos*, 1775; *Medea*, 1778). 'Melodramatic' scenes in opera were used by Cherubini in *Les Deux Journées* (1800), Beethoven in the grave-digging scene in *Fidelio* (1805), and Weber in *Der Freischütz* (1820). Modern works in this form include Fibich's trilogy *Hippodamia* (1889–91). The modern use of the term, to denote a violent or otherwise sensational play or film, is a development from its original meaning.

melody, a succession of sounds which achieve a distinctive musical shape. The factors which determine the character and effect of a melody are its MODE, its RHYTHM, and its design in relation to pitch, which may for convenience be referred to as its 'contour'. The only one of these factors which has in the past been the subject of more or less clear and consistent theories is mode. Since the melodies of any given period are composed by the manipulation of a set of idioms comprised within a system of modes, and only for special expressive purposes come to their final end on a note other than the final or key-note, their mode or key is always determinable. The differences of effect which result from differences of mode may be illustrated by a comparison of a melody in the eighth ecclesiastical mode:

with one in the modern minor mode:

MOZART, *Symphony in G minor*, K 550

and one in the Hindu rāga (mode) called Bhairau:

The composer determines the rhythmic character of a melody by writing it down, but a good performer can vary this to an important degree by rubato, and by slight delay and anticipation. The most obvious varieties of effect in rhythm may be exemplified in the gentle accumulation of movement of:

PALESTRINA, *Tribulationes civitatum*

in the exuberant onrush of:

R. STRAUSS, *Don Juan*

and in the placid gait of:

BEETHOVEN, *Piano Sonata*, op 90

Melodic contour is the subject of a section of Hindemith's *Craft of Musical Composition* (volume ii) in which he plots on a graph the higher and lower points of a melodic line, and the extent to which the idioms of the melody group themselves around notes which tend to become momentary key-notes. The possible range of melody depends on the voice or instrument for which it is written: hence the range of a

plainsong melody seldom exceeds a tenth, while the pitch range of an organ is greater than that of any other instrument. The examples from Palestrina and Strauss above show the extremes of effect resulting from melodic contour.

The theory that modern composers cannot write melodies is a widespread one, but it has existed in previous eras also. *Rigoletto* was once criticized for its tunelessness. So, too, in the present century was Bartók's second violin concerto. Yet the slow movement of this work unquestionably opens with a melody, one of the most remarkable of our time:

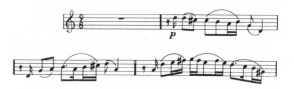

A melody is not necessarily a 'tune' which can be instantly remembered, hummed or whistled. Especially in modern music, it may contain very wide leaps. But familiarity breeds understanding, and the patient listener will find that many 'unmelodic' modern melodies turn out in the end to be melodic after all.

See also METRE, SEQUENCE

membranophone, the generic name for all percussion instruments, whether tuned (e.g. timpani) or untuned (e.g. side drum), producing sounds by means of a vibrating skin or similar substance.

Mencken (Mancinus), Thomas (1550–1611/12), German composer. From 1587 to 1604 he was *Kapellmeister* at Wolfenbüttel, being succeeded by Michael Praetorius. He composed a setting of the Passion (1608), motets and madrigals.

Mendelssohn, (Jakob Ludwig) Felix (1809–47), German composer. Born in Hamburg, he was the grandson of the Jewish philosopher, Moses Mendelssohn, and the son of a successful banker. Felix was brought up in an atmosphere of culture and domestic comfort. His mother, a pianist, gave him his first piano lessons; his sister, Fanny Cäcilie (1805–1847), was also to develop as a pianist and composer, and proved a valuable confidante for her brother. His remarkable gifts as composer, conductor and pianist were encouraged by teachers including Marie Bigot (in Paris), Ludwig Berger, and Moscheles for piano, and Zelter for composition (in Berlin in 1817). In 1821 he visited Zelter's friend Goethe in Weimar. By the age of nine he was performing in public, by twelve he had written his piano quartet (op 1), by fourteen he had his own private orchestra, by sixteen he had produced his first masterpiece (the octet for strings) and by seventeen his second (the overture to Shakespeare's *A Midsummer Night's Dream*). He also worked on behalf of other composers, in particular J. S. Bach, whose cause he championed by conducting – at the age of twenty – the first public performance of the St. Matthew Passion since Bach's death. This took place at the Berlin Singakademie in 1829, and in the same year he made the first of his ten visits to England, where he conducted the Philharmonic Society in London. He also holidayed in Scotland, for which his feelings were expressed in his Hebrides overture and 'Scottish' symphony (no 3 in A minor and major) – though he did not start work on them until his visit to Italy (1830–31). There he met Berlioz in Rome and made a start on his 'Italian' symphony (no 4 in A major and minor). His next major stopping-point was Paris (1831–32), where he met Liszt and Chopin, but by 1833 he was back in Germany, completing his Italian Symphony and being appointed musical director at Düsseldorf. In 1835 he became conductor of the famous Gewandhaus concerts in Leipzig, in 1837 he married Cécile Jeanrenaud, the descendant of a French Huguenot family, and in 1842 he founded, with Schumann and others, the Leipzig Conservatorium. He still managed to visit England, however, where he conducted his oratorio, *Elijah*, at the 1846 Birmingham Festival, one of his greatest triumphs. By now his health was weakening. The death of his beloved sister the following year upset him deeply and hastened his own death six months later.

Mendelssohn's earliest 'mature' works, the overtures *A Midsummer Night's Dream* (1826) and *The Hebrides* (1830–32), showed superb craftsmanship and an individual melodic style, and marked an important stage in the history of the programmatic or pictorial concert overture. In later compositions his range was greatly extended (symphonies, concertos, oratorios, choral music, chamber music, piano works, organ sonatas, songs), but there was little development in 'technique or expression. The polish, beauty and harmonic harmlessness of much of his music, crowned by the Birmingham première of *Elijah*, set the canons of mid-Victorian musical taste; but he could be adventurous, too, as the unusual structure and Wagnerian foretastes of the underrated 'Reformation' symphony (no 5 in D minor) demonstrate. His *Songs without Words* for solo piano are exquisite miniatures, too bland to be listened to in bulk, but full of delightful invention. His famous performance of the *St. Matthew Passion* gave a strong impulse to the revival of Bach's music, and his conducting of the Gewandhaus Orchestra initiated its great reputation and set new standards in orchestral performance.

His principal compositions are:

(1) Orchestra: five symphonies (no 2, *Lobgesang* (Hymn of Praise), symphony-cantata, 1840; no 3, *Scottish*, 1842; no 4, *Italian*, 1833; no 5, *Reformation*, 1830); overtures: *A Midsummer Night's Dream* (1826); *The Hebrides* (1830–2; also known as *Fingal's Cave*), *Meeresstille und glückliche Fahrt* (Calm Sea and Prosperous Voyage, 1828), *Märchen von der schönen Melusine* (The Legend of the Fair Melusina, 1833), *Ruy Blas* (1839); piano concertos: G minor (1831), D minor (1837); violin concerto (1844).

(2) Choral works: Oratorios: *St. Paul* (1834–6), *Elijah* (1846–7), *Christus* (unfinished, 1847); symphony-cantata, *Lobgesang* (Hymn of Praise, 1840; also known as symphony no 2); nine psalms; nine motets.

(3) Stage music: Operas: *Die Hochzeit des Camacho* (Camacho's Wedding, 1825), *Die Heimkehr aus der*

Mendelssohn aged 22, two years after his momentous performance of the Bach St. Matthew Passion at Berlin

Fremde (Son and Stranger, 1829), *Lorelei* (unfinished, 1847); incidental music: *Antigone* (1841), *Die erste Walpurgisnacht* (The First Witches' Sabbath, 1831, 1842), *A Midsummer Night's Dream* (1843), *Athalie* (1843–5), *Oedipus at Colonus* (1845).

(4) Chamber music: six string quartets; three piano quartets (1822–25); two string quintets (1831, 1845); string sextet (1824); string octet (1825); two trios (D minor, 1839; C minor, 1845); violin sonata; two cello sonatas (1838, 1843).

(5) Piano: *Capriccio* in F sharp minor (1825); *Rondo capriccioso* in E minor; six preludes and fugues (1832–7); eight books of *Lieder ohne Worte* (Songs without words).

(6) Organ: three preludes and fugues (1833–37); six sonatas (1839–44).

(7) Songs and part-songs: ten sets of songs with piano; eleven sets of part-songs.

T. ARMSTRONG: *Mendelssohn's 'Elijah'* (1931)

R. B. GOTCH: *Mendelssohn and his Friends in Kensington* (1934)

J. HORTON: *Mendelssohn Chamber Music* (1972)

S. KAUFMAN: *Mendelssohn* (1934)

P. RADCLIFFE: *Mendelssohn* (1954, revised 1967)

G. SELDEN-GOTH (editor): *Mendelssohn's Letters* (1946).

mene, *see* MEANE

Mengelberg, Willem (1871–1951), Dutch conductor. He studied at the Cologne Conservatorium and in 1895 became conductor of the Concertgebouw Orchestra, Amsterdam, a post he held until 1941. He developed this orchestra into one of the finest in Europe, especially in the performance of Mahler, Richard Strauss and French composers. During World War II he sympathized with the Nazi rule, and thereafter his career went into decline. He died in exile in Switzerland.

Mennin, Peter (born 1923), U.S. composer and conductor, pupil of Howard Hanson and Serge

Koussevitsky. From 1947 he taught composition at the Juilliard School of Music, from 1959 until 1963 he was director of the Peabody Conservatory, Baltimore, and in 1963 he became president of the Juilliard. His compositions, largely orchestral, include seven symphonies, concertos for violin, cello, and piano, a 'concertato' for orchestra (inspired by Melville's *Moby Dick*), and *Canto* for orchestra. He has also written a *Christmas Cantata*, chamber music and instrumental pieces.

meno mosso, (It.), with less movement, i.e. less quickly. *Meno* by itself is used in the same sense.

Menotti, Gian Carlo (born 1911), Italian born composer who lived in the United States from 1928. He studied at the Curtis Institute of Music, Philadelphia, with Scalero. His comic opera *Amelia goes to the Ball*, to his own libretto, was produced at the Curtis Institute and in New York in 1937 and again in New York by the Metropolitan Opera House in 1938. His works include the operas *The Island God, The Old Maid and the Thief, The Medium, The Telephone, The Consul, Amahl and the Night Visitors, The Saint of Bleecker Street, The Last Savage* and *Help, help, the Globolinks!* Most of these, *The Consul* especially, show a strong sense of theatre but are musically marred by their watery post-Puccini idiom. His piano concerto, for all its fluency, is similarly flawed. In 1958, Menotti founded the Festival of Two Worlds at Spoleto in Italy, with the aim of developing new musical and theatrical talent. He himself has worked as a stage producer, and has directed a film version of *The Medium*.

mensural music (Lat., *musica mensurata*), a medieval term for music with definite relative note-values, as distinct from plainsong (*musica plana*).

mensural notation, a system of notation formulated by Franco of Cologne in his *Ars cantus mensurabilis* (c. 1260) and used, with various additions, refinements and modifications, until the gradual adoption of metrical rhythm with bar-lines during the 17th century. In the course of the 15th century black notes began to be written as white and red as black (*see* NOTATION). In white notation the notes and corresponding rests were:

Their relations were governed by a time-signature at the beginning of a part, and by signs of PROPORTION and the use of black (imperfect, i.e. duple subdivision) notes instead of white (perfect, i.e. triple subdivision) in the course of a part. The relation of the long to the breve was called mode (or 'mood') and was normally imperfect; of the breve to the semibreve, time; of the semibreve to the minim, prolation. The time signatures were:

⊙ perfect time and perfect prolation; ○ perfect time and imperfect prolation; ₵ imperfect time and perfect prolation; ₵ imperfect time and imperfect

prolation. Under ⊙ a breve = three semibreves = nine minims; under ○ a breve = three semibreves = six minims; under ₵ a breve = two semibreves = six minims; and under ₵ a breve = two semibreves = four minims.

A dot was used both to add to a note half its value, making an imperfect note perfect (*punctus additionis*), and to mark off a group of three notes (*punctus divisionis*). A perfect note followed by one of the next lower value became imperfect by position, whether marked off by a *punctus divisionis* or not. Thus a breve followed by a minim followed by a *punctus divisionis* was sung within the value of a perfect breve (i.e. two perfect or three imperfect semibreves). The *punctus additionis* was also used with notes written in LIGATURE. The principle of alteration, adopted in the pre-mensural system of the RHYTHMIC MODES, whereby the second of the two breves preceding a long was doubled in length, was extended in mensural notation to semibreves preceding a breve and minims preceding a semibreve.

These general principles may be seen in the opening of the *cantus* part of Dufay's four-part *chanson* 'Ma belle dame souverainne'. The signature ₵, though not indicated, is understood:

which, transcribed in its original note-values, would read:

or, as is more usual, in one-quarter of the original values (crotchet = semibreve):

W. APEL: *The Notation of Polyphonic Music* (fifth edition 1961)

menuet, (Fr.; Ger., *Menuett*), minuet. The form *menuetto*, frequently used by German composers, is a corruption of the Italian *minuetto*.

Menuhin, Yehudi (born 1916), U.S. born violinist and conductor. He began violin lessons at the age of four with Sigmund Anker in San Francisco, and also took lessons from Louis Persinger. At seven he made his first public appearance in San Francisco, at eleven made his European début playing concertos by Bach, Beethoven and Brahms in Paris, and soon became internationally famous. He was taught by George Enescu and Adolph Busch. He gave a Carnegie Hall recital in 1927, and made his London debut in 1929 with the Brahms concerto. At the age of twenty he went into retirement for eighteen months for intensive study. In 1944 he commissioned Bartók's solo violin sonata – he was a champion of Bartók's violin music at a time when it was less popular than it is now. He is also closely associated with Elgar's violin concerto (a work in which he was coached by the composer). Today he remains the world's best-loved violinist, though in recent years he has become known as a conductor, mainly of chamber music. As a player, he is notable now for the warmth of his interpretations than for his technical precision, which is too often erratic. In 1963 he founded a school in England for exceptionally musical children. He now lives in London, where in 1965 he received the K.B.E. His sisters, Hephzibah, and Yaltah, are both pianists, as is his son Jeremy, who also conducts. He has given sonata recitals with his sister Hephzibah.

Mer, La (Fr., the sea), three symphonic sketches by Debussy (1905) expressing his musical reactions to the moods of the sea. The titles of the movement are:

(1) *De l'aube à midi sur la mer* (From dawn to midday on the sea);

(2) *Jeux de vagues* (Play of the waves);

(3) *Dialogue du vent et de la mer* (Dialogue of the wind and the sea).

The original titles of nos 1 and 2 were *Mer belle aux Iles Sanguinaires* and *Le vent fait danser la mer*.

Merbecke, John, see MARBECK

Mercadante, Giuseppe Saverio Raffaele (1795–1870), Italian composer, pupil of Zingarelli at the Collegio di San Sebastiano, Naples. In 1833 he became *maestro di cappella* at Novara Cathedral, in 1839 he was music director of Lanciano Cathedral and in 1840 was appointed director of Naples Conservatorio. He lost an eye while at Novara and became totally blind in 1862. He wrote almost 60 operas, of which *Elisa e Claudio* (1821) and *Il Giuramento* (his chief work, 1827) were the most successful. His other works included 21 Masses, four funeral symphonies, instrumental pieces, and songs.

Mercure, Pierre (1927–66), French Canadian composer who studied at the Provincial Conservatory in Montreal and later in Europe and the United States under a distinguished list of teachers including Nadia Boulanger, Luigi Dallapiccola, Henri Pousseur, Luigi Nono, and Luciano Berio. His orchestral *Triptyque*, composed for the Vancouver Festival in 1959, has been internationally performed, and so has *Lignes et Points* (lines and dots), commissioned by the Montreal Symphony Orchestra in 1965. In the latter work, electronic sound effects are achieved by purely orchestral means. Mercure also wrote electronic music and *musique concrète*, but his promising career was cut short when he was killed in a car accident at the age of 39.

'Mercury' Symphony, nickname for Haydn's symphony no 43 in E flat major (c. 1771). The reason for the name is unknown.

Merlo, Alessandro (Alessandro Romano or **Alessandro della Viola)** (born c. 1530), Italian singer, violinist and composer, a pupil of Willaert and Rore. He was a bass-tenor with a range of three octaves. In 1594 he became a singer in the Papal Chapel. His compositions include *canzoni*, madrigals, a book of *villanelle*, and a book of motets.

Merlotti, Claudio, see MERULO

Merry Mount, opera in three acts by Howard Hanson, to a libretto by Richard Stokes, staged in New York in 1934. The work is based on Hawthorne's story, *The Maypole of Merry Mount*.

Merry Widow, The (Ger., *Die lustige Witwe*), operetta in three acts by Lehár, to a libretto by Viktor Léon and Leo Stein, first performed in Vienna in 1905. Along with Johann Strauss's *Die Fledermaus*, this is the most popular of all Viennese operettas. Though he wrote numerous other operettas after it, Lehár failed to produce another work with such staying power and charm. The story, based on Meilhac's comedy *L'Attaché*, is a light-hearted piece of amorous and diplomatic intrigue, revolving round the merry (and rich) widow Hanna Glawari, whose Act 2 aria, 'Vilja', remains the best-loved passage of the work.

Merry Wives of Windsor, The (Ger., *Die Lustigen Weiber von Windsor*) opera in three acts by Nicolai, to a libretto by S. H. Mosenthal, first performed in Berlin in 1849. Nicolai based his last and most successful opera on Shakespeare's play of the same title.

Mersenne (Mersennus), Marin (1588–1648), French theorist. He taught philosophy at Neves and later studied mathematics and music in Paris, where he made the acquaintance of Descartes and the elder Pascal. He corresponded with scholars in England, Holland and Italy, and visited Italy three times. From 1613 he was a member of the Franciscan order. His works include *De la nature des sons* (1635) and *Harmonie universelle* (1636; facsimile edition, 1963). The latter is a comprehensive and scientific study of music theory which includes particularly informative sections on musical instruments (translated by Roger E. Chapman, 1957).

Merula, Tarquinio (c. 1590–1665), Italian composer. He held appointments alternately at Bergamo and Cremona, except in 1624 when he was court organist at Warsaw. He also held a court appointment at Florence. His compositions include canzonas, madrigals, motets, sonatas for solo violin and continuo, and keyboard music. A complete edition of his work was begun in 1974 by A. Sutkowski, beginning with the first book of canzonas (1615). His keyboard music has been edited by A. Curtis (1962).

Merulo, Claudio (Claudio da Correggio, Merlotti) (1533–1604), Italian organist and composer. He was organist at Brescia in 1556, second organist at St. Mark's, Venice, in 1557, and first organist there in 1566. In 1566 he became a publisher, editing madrigals by Verdelot and Porta, and printing his own book of five-part madrigals. In 1574 he produced an opera in madrigal style, *La Tragedia*. From 1586 till his death he was organist of the ducal chapel at Parma. His compositions include two books of *Sacrae Cantiones* (1578), madrigals, four Masses, and organ pieces. His organ toccatas (examples in Schering's *Geschichte der Musik in Beispielen*, no 149, in Davison and Apel's

Historical Anthology of Music, no 153, and in Torchi's *L'arte musicale in Italia*, iii) are the most developed works in this form in the 16th century. An edition of his sacred works was begun in 1970 by J. Bastian.

messa di voce (It.), 'placing of the voice'. The term is used to indicate a *crescendo* and *diminuendo* on a long note in singing.

Messager, André Charles Prosper (1853–1929), French composer and conductor, pupil of Gigout and Saint-Saëns. Though he composed a number of serious operas, and conducted the premiere of Debussy's *Pelléas and Melisande* (which was dedicated to him), his reputation rests on his operettas, such as *Véronique* and *Monsieur Beaucaive*, and on his ballet music (e.g. *Les Deux Pigeons*). Apart from being conductor at the Opéra-Comique in Paris, he was artistic director at Covent Garden from 1901 until 1907.

Messa per i Defunti (It.); **Messe des Morts** (Fr.), Requiem Mass.

Messiaen, Olivier Eugène Prosper Charles (born 1908), French composer and organist; son of the poetess Cécile Sauvage and of a French professor of literature. He studied at the Paris Conservatoire under Dukas (composition) and Dupré (organ) and himself became a teacher at the École Normale de Musique and the Schola Cantorum. Since 1931 he has been organist at La Trinité, Paris. In 1936 with Baudrier, Lesur and Jolivet he formed the group known as *La Jeune France*. In 1940 he was imprisoned by the Nazis (his *Quartet for the End of Time* reflects his period in a concentration camp) but he was subsequently repatriated and in 1942 he became teacher of harmony at the Conservatoire. Though his musical roots seem to lie in César Franck and to some extent in Berlioz, Messiaen is one of the most original of modern composers, and one of the most influential. His musical language makes use of diverse but (in his case) surprisingly compatible sound sources – birdsong, Indian music, plainsong, the timbres of oriental percussion, Franckian harmony, Bartokian night-music – which he employs to immensely spacious and powerful effect. A lifelong Catholic, he uses nature (birds, mountains etc.) as symbols of divinity in works such as *Oiseaux exotiques* (Exotic Birds) (1956) for piano and wind instruments, the vast *Catalogue d'oiseaux* (1956–58) for piano, and *Et expecto resurrectionem mortuorum* (1964) for woodwind, brass and percussion – a work designed (hopefully) to be performed in the open air, on mountain slopes, where its great gong-strokes and silences would surely find the surroundings they deserve. The early *Turangalila* symphony (1949), described by the composer as a 'love song', shows him responding to Indian rhythms, and *Chronochromie* (1960) to the sound of oriental percussion. His *Vingt Regards Sur l'Enfant Jesus* (1944) in twenty movements for solo piano, shows his religious ecstasy at its most grandly extended, and the more recent *Transfiguration de Notre Seigneur Jesus Christ* (1969) for seven instrumental soloists, chorus and orchestra, in fourteen movements, shows no slackening of intensity in the composer's approach to his subject. Among his works for organ, *La Nativité du Seigneur* (1935), a set of nine meditations, has established itself as one of the few 20th century masterpieces for the instrument.

Messiah, oratorio by Handel, to a text selected from the Bible by the composer and Charles Jennens. The work, composed in less than a month, continues to be in Britain the most popular of Handel's oratorios. The première, performed by chamber-sized forces, took place in Dublin in 1742. The first British performance – at the Covent Garden theatre – took place the following year. The title given to the work by Handel was *Messiah*, not *The Messiah*.

mesto (It.), sad.

mesure (Fr.), (1) bar; (2) time. *Battre de mesure*, to beat time.

metalallophone, instrument of the xylophone family but made of bronze. Its history goes back for more than 1000 years. Carl Orff has used metalallophones in several scores.

metal block, similar to a wood-block or small anvil, this instrument is of very recent origin and produces sounds of indefinite pitch. Boulez has written for metal blocks, directing that they should be played with soft xylophone beaters.

Metamorphosen (Ger., *Metamorphoses*), work for 23 solo strings by Richard Strauss, composed in 1945 and believed to express the composer's sense of loss after the destruction of Munich. Inscribed 'In Memoriam', the music in its closing section quotes the funeral march from Beethoven's *Eroica* symphony.

Metastasio (originally **Trapassi**), **Pietro Antonio Domenico Bonaventura** (1698–1782), Italian poet and librettist. He was court poet at Vienna, succeeding Apostolo Zeno, from 1730 till his death. He inherited from Zeno the three act plan of the opera libretto, and stabilised it as an alternation of recitatives with arias in a consistent order and form. His libretti remained the basis of the form of classical opera from Alessandro Scarlatti to Mozart's *La clemenza di Tito* (1791), and many were set over and over again – some of them as often as sixty or seventy times. The form and style of his libretti for serious opera held complete sway until questioned by Calzabigi and Gluck, who objected to the formality of Metastasio's texts, with the opportunities they provided for vocal display at the expense of dramatic credibility.

metre, the scheme of regularly recurring accents, indicated by a time signature, which underlies the particular rhythm of a melody or harmonic progression. The time signatures in mensural notation (13th – 16th centuries) did not imply metrical accents in performance. Music in which the rhythm was directly related to the metre of poetry was written in the early 16th century by Tritonius and in the late 16th century by the members of the French Academy of de Baïf (*see* MUSIQUE MESURÉE À L'ANTIQUE). Bar-lines to show metrical schemes were used in the lute and keyboard music of the 16th century, and first came into general use in the early 17th century. Since then the rhythmic design of melodies and harmonies has been contained in and related to the underlying metrical scheme of each composition, which is indicated by its TIME SIGNATURE. For example, 3/4 time means that the basic values are quarter notes and that every third quarter note is accented. A new metrical scheme may replace or be imposed upon the original one, either momentarily, as in HEMIOLA, and in this passage from the scherzo of Beethoven's *Eroica* symphony:

or for a complete section, as in the last movement of Schumann's piano concerto:

Two or more metrical schemes are occasionally combined in one piece, as in Brahm's *Intermezzo*, op 76, no 6, in which 2/4, 6/8 and 3/4 are combined in various ways throughout:

More frequent and more extended use of combined metres has been made by contemporary composers, both in succession, e.g. in Stravinsky's *Rite of Spring*, and in Constant Lambert's piano concerto:

and in combination, as in the second movement of Hindemith's third sonata for piano:

An interesting example of the use of combined metres as the rhythmic scheme of a movement is the *Scherzo polimetrico* of Rubbra's second string quartet (1951).

metrical psalter, *see* PSALTER

metronome, a device which produces regular beats. The model in general use was patented by MAELZEL in 1816 and adopted in the following year by Beethoven to indicate the tempo of his compositions. ♩ = M.M. (i.e., Maelzel Metronome) 60, for example, indicates sixty crotchet beats per minute.

R. E. M. HARDING: *Origins of Musical Time and Expression* (1938)

Meyerbeer, (originally Jakob Liebmann Beer) **Giacomo** (1791–1864), German born composer, who studied with Clementi, Zelter and Vogler and wrote his first opera in 1813. In 1816 he went to Venice, and in Italy wrote operas in the style of Rossini. After 1830 he became the dominant composer in the most brilliant period of French grand opera in Paris under Scribe, who wrote his libretti. In this elaborate and spectacular style he found his métier in such works as *Robert le Diable* (1831), *Les Huguenots* (1836) and *Le Prophète* (1849). The style of Wagner's *Rienzi* (1842) owes much to Meyerbeer.

mezzo (It.), half. *Mezzo forte*, moderately loud (abbreviated *mf*); *mezzo piano*, moderately soft (abbreviated *mp*). *Mezzo-soprano*, the voice between a soprano and a contralto in range. *Mezza voce*, with a moderate volume of tone.

mi (Fr., It.), the note E. Also the third note of the Guidonian hexachord (*see* SOLMIZATION).

Miaskovsky, Nikolai Yakovlevich (1881–1950), Russian composer. He trained for a military career but studied music with Glière in Moscow and in 1906 entered the St. Petersburg Conservatory as a pupil of Rimsky-Korsakov and Liadov. He became teacher of composition at the Moscow Conservatory in 1921. In 1948 he was one of the composers (Prokofiev and Shostakovich were others) denounced by the Central Committee of the Communist Party as inculcators of inharmonious music in the educational institutions of the Soviet Union. His compositions include 27 symphonies, an oratorio (*Kirov is with us*), nine string quartets, piano works and songs, few of which can be deemed to be inharmonious.

Michael, Rogier (c. 1554–c. 1619), Flemish singer and composer. He was a tenor in the Electoral Chapel, Dresden, in 1575, and *Kapellmeister* there in 1587. He was succeeded by Heinrich Schütz in 1619. His compositions include introits in motet style, four-part chorales, and other church music. His son **Tobias Michael** was born in Germany in 1592, and became a composer. He was *Kapellmeister* at Sondershausen in 1619, and cantor at St. Thomas's, Leipzig, in 1631. His works include the *Musikalischer Seelenlust* (1634–7), which is a collection of sacred concertos, and other church music. He died in 1657.

Michelangeli, Arturo Benedetti (born 1920), Italian pianist. He studied in Brescia and at the Milan Conservatory, and in 1939 won the international piano competition at Geneva. One of the foremost pianists of the age, he brings exceptional clarity of timbres and textures to everything he touches, whether it be the Bach-Busoni chaconne or Debussy's *Images*. Unfortunately, his concert appearances are very infrequent and even when a recital by him is promised there is no guarantee that he will actually turn up.

Micheli, Romano (c. 1575 – c. 1659), Italian composer. He studied under Soriano. He became *maestro di cappella* at the Church of Concordia, Modena, in 1616, and at San Luigi de' Francesi, Rome, in 1625. His compositions include psalms, motets, canons and madrigals.

microtones, intervals which are fractions of a semitone. Such intervals have always been a part of the theory and practice of tuning (*see* TEMPERAMENT), but only in modern times have they been introduced by some composers into notation and performance. Alois Hába has written a string quartet in a system of sixth-tones, and the Mexican composer Julián Carrillo has written some works in a system which divides the octave into 96 parts. More recently, György Ligeti has been another composer who has put microtones to productive use, for example in his double concerto for flute and oboe.

middle C, the note C at (approximately) the middle of the piano keyboard.

See PITCH

middle fiddle, viola. The term was invented by Percy Grainger who used it in his scores.

Midi, Le, *see* MATIN

Midsummer Marriage, The, opera in three acts by Tippett, to a libretto by the composer, first performed at Covent Garden in 1955. Tippett's 'quest opera', the first of his four operas so far, was consciously modelled on Mozart's *The Magic Flute*, of which it is a modern equivalent. The story concerns Mark and Jennifer who quarrel on their wedding day but are reconciled after undergoing a series of tests and trials. These characters are the Tamino and Pamina of Tippett's opera; but, as in *The Magic Flute*, there is another couple (Jack and Bella) on a lower social level. The complex symbolism and philosophy of the plot at first interfered with the success of the work, but a second Covent Garden production (in 1968) established it as a major modern opera. The four *Ritual Dances* – three from Act 2 and one from Act 3 – are sometimes performed out of context in the concert hall.

Midsummer Night's Dream, A, incidental music by Mendelssohn, to Shakespeare's play of that title. The overture (op 21) was written in 1826 when the composer was seventeen; the rest of the music (op 61), including vocal as well as orchestral movements, followed sixteen years later in 1842, and was used for a stage performance in Potsdam in 1843. Other incidental music to the play has been written by Carl Orff, and a three-act opera (using an abbreviation of Shakespeare's text) has been written by Britten. The latter, with the role of Oberon cast for counter-tenor and Puck for spoken voice, had its première at Aldeburgh in 1960.

Mighty Handful, The, name coined by the Russian critic Vladimir Stassov for the group of Russian composers otherwise known as 'The Five'. They were Balakirev, Borodin, Cui, Mussorgsky, and Rimsky-Korsakov, who together formed a Russian nationalist 'school', as opposed to, say, Chaikovsky, who was considered to have musical leanings towards Western Europe.

Mignon, opera in three acts by Ambroise Thomas, to a libretto by Jules Barbier and Michel Carré, first performed in Paris in 1866. The work is based on Goethe's *Wilhelm Meister*. Mignon is a gypsy girl with whom the rich Wilhelm Meister falls in love; in the end she turns out to be the daughter of a count. The famous aria, 'Je suis Titania' (I am Titania), is sung by Mignon during a performance (within the context of the opera) of *A Midsummer Night's Dream*.

Migot, Georges Elbert (born 1891), French composer, painter and writer on aesthetics, pupil of Widor at the Paris Conservatoire. His compositions include operas, ballets, large-scale choral works, symphonies and other orchestral music (including *La Jungle* for organ and orchestra), mainly in a personal, polyphonic idiom. His independence of any fashionable school of French composition won him the nickname of the 'Group of One'. His books include *Essais pour une esthétique générale* (1919).

Mihalovici, Marcel (born 1898), Rumanian composer, pupil of d'Indy in Paris where he settled. His compositions include an opera (*L'Intransigeant Pluton*), several ballets, a fantasia for orchestra, *Symphonie du temps présent* (1943), and chamber music. He married the pianist Monique Haas.

Mikado, The, operetta in two acts by Gilbert and Sullivan, first performed in London in 1885. With its Japanese setting, this remains the most popular of all the Gilbert and Sullivan operettas, and has even won an audience outside Britain. Film versions were made in 1938 and 1966.

Mikrokosmos (Gr., microcosm), a collection of 153 short piano pieces by Bartók, intended as a complete course of instruction in technique and also illustrating a rich variety of invention. The six progressively graded volumes offer young pianists a fascinating introduction to the sound world of Bartók, and, through him, to modern music in general. But the *Mikrokosmos* are not merely good teaching pieces, exploring Bartokian rhythms, harmonies and time signatures: volume six, in particular, contains music that can stand on its own feet in the concert hall (such as *From the Diary of a Fly* and the *Six Bulgarian Rhythms*) and even in the earlier volumes there are pieces (e.g. *Wrestling* and *From the Island of Bali*) which express the essence of Bartók.

Milán, Luis de (c. 1500 – after 1561), Spanish composer and *vihuela* player. His *Libro de música de vihuela de mano, intitulado El Maestro* (1536; edited and translated by C. Jacobs, 1971) contained the earliest collection of accompanied solo songs of the Renaissance period, together with fantasias and pavanes for the *vihuela*. He also published *El Cortesano* (1561), an account of life and music at the court of Germaine de Foix at Valencia.

J. B. TREND: *Luis Milan and the Vihuelistas* (1925)

Milanov, Zinka (born 1906), Yugoslav soprano who studied in Zagreb, Prague and New York, and made her début in 1927 as Leonora in *Il Trovatore*. In 1937 she sang in Verdi's Requiem under Toscanini at the Salzburg Festival, and in the same year appeared in *Trovatore* at the New York Metropolitan. She was one of the leading Verdi sopranos of her generation.

Milford, Robin Humphrey (1903–59), English composer, pupil of Holst, Vaughan Williams and R. O. Morris. His compositions include two oratorios (*A Prophet in the Land* and *The Pilgrim's Progress*), orchestral works, a violin concerto, and songs.

Milhaud, Darius (1892–1974), French composer of Jewish ancestry, born at Aix-en-Provence. He studied violin and composition from 1909 at the Paris Conservatoire, where his teachers included Gédalge, Widor, d'Indy, and (later) Dukas. From 1917 until 1919 he was attaché to the French legation in Rio de Janeiro, where he met Paul Claudel – future librettist of several of his works. On returning to France he became a member of the group of French composers known as 'LES SIX'. In 1940 he emigrated to California, but in 1947 again returned to France to teach at the Paris Conservatoire. His prolific output of works reflected his varied career. Between 1919 and 1923, under the spell of Les Six, he produced such works as the jazz-inspired *La Creation du Monde* (*The Creation of the World*), the ballet *Le Boeuf sur le Toit* (*The Ox on the Roof*) with a scenario by Jean Cocteau, and works with texts drawn from agricultural and horti-cultural catalogues (*Machines Agricoles* and *Catalogue des Fleurs*). His collaboration with Claudel resulted in one of his most important works, the opera *Christophe Colomb* (1930) which uses film effects and a Greek chorus. His Provençal boyhood is reflected in a number of pieces, including the orchestral *Suite Provençale*, the *Carnaval d'Aix* for piano and orchestra (1927), based on his *Salade* ballet music of three years earlier, and the wind quartet *La Cheminée du Roi René* (*King René's Chimney* – called after a street in Aix). His Latin-American period is commemorated by his orchestral *Saudades do Brazil* and two volumes of piano pieces of the same title. His other works include an opera, *David* (1954), written for the 3000th anniversary of Israel, numerous symphonies for large and small orchestras, eighteen string quartets (of which nos 14 and 15 can be performed separately or together). He also wrote a version, in French, of *The Beggar's Opera*. His autobiographical *Notes sans Musique* (1949) has been published in English translation.

military band, originally applied only to regimental bands, the term has, in Britain, come to mean the same as 'concert' or 'symphonic' band in the United States. The inclusion of woodwind instruments distinguishes a military from a brass band. The instrumentation of military bands varies considerably in different countries and even within the same one. A typical British band might well play from the following parts: piccolo, two flutes, two oboes, two clarinets in E flat, four clarinets in B flat, alto saxophone, tenor saxophone, two bassoons, four horns in F or E flat, two cornets in B flat, two trumpets in B flat, two tenor trombones and bass trombone, euphonium, tubas in E flat and B flat, timpani, side drum, bass drum, and other percussion instruments. The number of players to a part will depend on the size of the band, e.g. there may be as many as sixteen B flat clarinet players, divided as follows: six solo clarinets, four firsts, three seconds, and three thirds.

H. E. ADKIN: *Treatise on the Military Band*, three volumes (1931)

military music, since ancient times, music has been used for military purposes, for signalling, marching etc. As armies became organized during the 15th and 16th centuries, certain instruments and practices became standardized, such as trumpets and kettledrums for cavalry, and fifes and drums for the infantry. Military music widened its scope during the 18th century, when Louis XIV and Frederick the Great established bands including hautboys, bassoons and drums. Later in the same century, the fashion for things Turkish (*see* JANISSARY MUSIC) introduced instruments such as cymbals, triangles and other percussion instruments. Modern military music has grown from early 19th century French developments. During the 19th century military bands containing all the usual wind and percussion instruments were established in most countries.

Composition of music for military purposes, or using military effects, dates from the 15th and 16th centuries, when composers occasionally imitated the sounds of trumpets and drums to symbolize an amorous assault or depict a battle, as in Dufay's *chanson* 'Donnez l'assaut', Jannequin's *chanson* 'La Guerre' (1529), and Alessandro Striggio's madrigal 'Non rumor di tamburi' (1571). Similar effects, suggested by the words of psalms, are found in the motets of Byrd and of Lutheran composers in the 17th century (*see* BATTLE MUSIC). The 18th century Turkish influence can be heard in the Turkish March of Mozart's piano sonata in A, in some passages in his *Die Entführung*, and in the finale of Beethoven's ninth symphony.

H. G. FARMER: *Military Music and its Story* (1912)

'Military' Symphony, Haydn's symphony no 100 in G major (1794), the eighth of the 'Salomon' symphonies written for performance in London. It derives its nickname from the fact that a trumpet call is introduced into the second movement, which also has parts for triangle, bass drum and cymbals (instruments which were not a normal part of the 18th century orchestra).

Millöcker, Karl (1842–99), Austrian composer and conductor who studied in Vienna and worked at the Theater an der Wien from 1869. He wrote numerous operettas, the best known being *Der Bettelstudent* (*The Beggar Student*) and *Gasparone*.

Milner, Anthony (born 1925), English composer, pupil of R. O. Morris and Matyas Seiber. He has written orchestral and chamber music, though it is for his vocal output (including a Mass and several cantatas) that he is most famous. He has held several academic posts in London.

Milstein, Nathan (born 1904), Russian born violinist who later settled in the United States. He studied first at the Odessa School of Music, then in St. Petersburg under Auer. He was also a pupil of Ysaye. His qualities were quickly recognized when he appeared with the pianist Horowitz, and his subsequent international career confirmed this early promise.

Milton, John (c. 1563–1647), English composer, father of the poet. His musical abilities are alluded to in the poem 'Ad Patrem' by his more famous son. His compositions include a madrigal in *The Triumphes of Oriana* (modern edition in *The English Madrigal School*, xxxii), four pieces in Leighton's *Teares or Lamentacions* (1614; modern edition by C. Hill, 1970) two psalms in Ravenscroft's *Psalter* (1621) and five fancies for viols, one of which is printed in *Musica Britannica*, ix.

E. BRENNECKE: *John Milton the Elder and his Music* (1938)

minacciando, minaccevole (It.), in a menacing fashion.

Mines of Sulphur, The, opera in three acts by Richard Rodney Bennett, to a libretto by Beverly Cross, first performed at Sadler's Wells, London, in 1965. The work is a ghost story, set in an 18th century English manor house whose owner is murdered by his mistress and her criminal accomplice. The supernatural element arises when a group of strolling players seek refuge in the house, with fateful results.

miniature score, a score containing all the voice and/ or instrumental parts of a piece of music, but in smaller type and page-size than a full score. Also known (for self-explanatory reasons) as a pocket score or study score. A score of this size is obviously of more value to a concert-goer than it would be to a conductor, who in general uses a full score.

minim (U.S., half-note; Fr., *blanche*; Ger., *Halbe*; It., *minima*), from the Latin *minima* (*nota*), smallest (note). Introduced in the early 14th century as a subdivision of the semibreve, and then the shortest note value in mensural notation. In modern notation it is one half of a semibreve (whole-note) and is represented by the sign ♩. The minim rest is ▬. See CROTCHET.

Minnesinger (Ger., *Minne* = chivalrous love, Fr., *amour courtois*), a German poet and musician of the period of chivalry, corresponding to the TROUBADOUR and *trouvère* of Provence and France. The period of the *Minnesinger* lasted from about 1150 to 1450, when their traditions were taken over by the guilds of MEISTERSINGER, a transference from the aristocracy to the merchant class. The *Minnesinger* period includes the names of Walther von der Vogelweide (died c.

1230), Neidhart von Reuenthal (died c. 1240), Heinrich Frauenlob (died 1318), and Oswald von Wolkenstein (died 1445) who departed from the monophonic tradition by writing songs in two, three and four parts. Wagner's opera *Tannhäuser* is founded on an actual 'contest of singers' (*Sängerkrieg*) held at Wartburg by the Landgrave Hermann of Thuringia in 1207, in which the *Minnesinger* Tannhäuser and Wolfram von Eschenbach took part.

The chief form of the *Minnesinger* songs, the *Bar* form consisting of two *Stollen* and an *Abgesang*, was adopted from the troubadours. R. J. Taylor's *The Art of the Minnesinger* (two volumes, 1968) is a collected edition of the 12th and 13th century *Minnesinger* melodies, excepting those of Neidhart, which were edited by A. T. Hatto and R. J. Taylor in 1958.

Minnesinger fiddle, an instrument that appeared in the 13th century; it was one of the forerunners of the violin.

minor, *see* MAJOR

minore, (It.), minor mode.

minstrel, name given to the professional entertainer, and in particular to the performing musician, of the middle ages, whether attached to a household or court, or self-employed. In the 12th and 13th centuries the French word *menestrel* had a similar meaning to *jongleur*, expect that the former was an expression of respect while the latter carried a pejorative connotation. During the 16th century the term 'minstrel' became debased; in England, for example, it was used for wandering ballad singers, and was eventually incorporated into the vagrancy laws. The respectable performer, who tended to specialize in music alone, now termed himself 'musician'.

minuet (Fr., *menuet*; Ger., *Menuett*; It., *minuetto*), a French dance, of popular origin, in 3/4 time at a moderate pace. It was first introduced in a stylized form by Lully about 1650, and thereafter appeared in many instrumental suites and ballets during the baroque period. It remained to be one of the regular movements in the classical sonata and symphony, always in ternary form (minuet-trio-minuet). In Beethoven's music, by taking on a much quicker tempo and a boisterously playful style, it was transformed into the SCHERZO.

'Minute' Waltz, nickname for Chopin's waltz in D flat major, op 64, no 1 (1847). Only bad pianists, however, play it in a minute. Performed with proper sensitivity, the music should last longer. The piece is also sometimes known as the *Dog Waltz*, because Chopin is thought to have composed it while watching a dog chasing its tail.

Miracle, The, the name popularly given to Haydn's symphony no 96 in D major (1791). It derives its name from the story that at the first performance a chandelier fell from the ceiling and missed the audience by a miracle. In actual fact this accident occurred at the first performance of Haydn's symphony no 102 in B flat major (1794); *see* H. C. ROBBINS LANDON, *The Symphonies of Joseph Haydn*, pages 534–5.

miracle play, *see* TROPE

Mireille, opera in five acts by Gounod, to a libretto by Michel Carré, first performed in Paris in 1864. Inspired by Mistral's poem, *Mirèio*, the work tells of a Provençal love affair. In Gounod's first version, it had a tragic ending; later he supplied an alternative happy one.

mirliton (Fr.), a wind instrument consisting of a pipe with one end closed by thin parchment or skin and a hole in the side into which the performer sings. The tone produced is similar to the bleating of a sheep. An instrument of this type was known in the 17th century under the name *flûte-eunuque* (eunuch flute) and is described by Mersenne in his *Harmonie universelle* (1636). At the present day it is merely a toy, known in England and America as the 'kazoo'. The passage for brass instruments in the *Danse des mirlitons* in Chaikovsky's ballet *Casse-Noisette* appears to be intended as a grotesque imitation of the sound of this instrument.

Missa (Lat., Mass), name presumably derived from the concluding words of the MASS: 'Ite, missa est.' (Go, (the congregation) is dismissed). A *Missa brevis* is a short Mass. *Missa Cellensis, see* MARIAZELL MASS; *Missa in angustiis, see* NELSON MASS; *Missa in tempore belli, see* PAUKENMESSE; *Misa pro defunctis*, REQUIEM MASS; *Missa sine nomine,* a Mass which is not founded on any pre-existing melody (or *canto fermo*) and hence has no title; *Missa solennis* or *Missa solemnis, see* next entry. *Missa supra voces musicales,* a Mass which uses a *canto fermo,* the notes of the HEXACHORD.

Other titles fall into the following categories:

(1) those which indicate the plainsong on which the Mass is built, or the motet from which it borrows material;

(2) those which indicate a particular saint's day or festival for which the Mass is intended;

(3) those which indicate the mode in which the Mass is written, e.g. *Missa quarti toni,* a Mass in the fourth (Hypophrygian) mode.

Missa solemnis (or **solennis**) (Lat.), solemn Mass. The title is usually reserved for a Mass of specially exalted character, such as Beethoven's in D major – the most famous work to bear this name.

misterioso (It.), mysteriously.

misura (It.), measure, a term which can be used in the English sense of 'bar', but is more usually applied to regularity. Thus *alla misura,* in strict time; *senza misura,* not in strict time (i.e. the bar-lines are usually omitted); *misurato,* measured.

mit (Ger.), with.

Mitridate, Rè di Ponte, (It., *Mithridates, King of Pontus*), opera seria, K 87, by Mozart, to a libretto by Vittorio Amadeo Cigna-Santi, first performed in Milan in 1770 when the composer was fourteen. The work is based on a tragedy by Racine.

Mitropoulos, Dimitri (1896–1960), Greek born conductor, pianist, and composer. He studied in Athens, and under Busoni in Berlin. After holding various European posts, he became conductor of the Minneapolis Symphony Orchestra in 1937 and of the New York Symphony Orchestra in 1950. He was noted for his conducting of 20th century music. His own works included an opera (*Sister Beatrice*), a concerto grosso, chamber and instrumental music, and songs.

mixed voices, a chorus comprising male and female voices.

Mixolydian mode, (1) in ancient Greek music:

(2) from the Middle Ages onwards applied to:

The tonic (or final) and dominant are marked respectively T and D. The sharpening of the seventh note of this mode makes it identical with the modern major scale.

See GREEK MUSIC, MODE

mixture, organ stop which produces three or four sounds higher than the pitch corresponding to the key which is depressed. A three-rank mixture sounds the fifteenth, nineteenth, and twenty-second, which are the fourth, sixth, and eighth notes of the harmonic series, above the foundation note.

mock trumpet, early English name for the *chalumeau* or early clarinet.

mode (Fr., *ton*; Ger., *Tonart*; It., *tuono*), a set of notes which form the material of melodic idioms used in composition. Medieval theorists commonly illustrated the characteristics of modes by giving the NEUMA of the mode and quoting from plainsong melodies; this had a practical value in classifying the antiphons of plainsong and the psalm-tones and endings which were used with them. For the purposes of theoretical discussion the notes of a mode may be arranged in scalewise order. The medieval (also called ecclesiastical) modes may thus be represented by scales of white notes on the modern keyboard. They bear names derived from the Greek musical system, though neither this concept of mode nor the application of the names corresponds to Greek theory:

Early numbering	Later numbering	Name	Compass	Final	Dominant
Protus (authentic)	I	Dorian	D-D	D	A
„ (plagal)	II	Hypodorian	A-A	D	F
Deuterus (authentic)	III	Phrygian	E-E	E	C
„ (plagal)	IV	Hypophrygian	B-B	E	A
Tritus (authentic)	V	Lydian	F-F	F	C
„ (plagal)	VI	Hypolydian	C-C	F	A
Tetrardus (authentic)	VII	Mixolydian	G-G	G	D
„ (plagal)	VIII	Hypomixolydian	D-D	G	C

The *final* of the mode is the note on which its melodies end; for the meaning of *dominant* see PSALM-ODY. The distinction between authentic and plagal is in the range of the melody; they have the same final, or note of ending. Modes on A and C (Aeolian and Ionian) were first theoretically recognized in the *Dodecachordon* (system of twelve modes) of Glareanus in 1547. He also gave the name Hyperaeolian to the mode on B, and Hyperphrygian to its plagal form, but rejected both as impractical on account of the diminished fifth between B and F. These modes are now generally known as Locrian and Hypolocrian. Glareanus's additions to the medieval modal system are therefore as follows:

Numbering	Name	Compass	Final	Dominant
IX	Aeolian	A-A	A	E
X	Hypoaeolian	E-E	A	C
XI	Ionian	C-C	C	G
XII	Hypoionian	G-G	C	E

Until the end of the 16th century the medieval modal theory and the medieval interval theory were the bases of polyphonic composition. By the end of the 17th century the exclusive use of the two modern modes, major and minor (*see* SCALE) was established. The first of these was, melodically, of great antiquity, though it was not officially recognized by medieval theorists. It occurs frequently in plainsong melodies and in the secular songs of the Middle Ages, in the form of the F mode with flattened B. The intervals are thus identical with those of Glareanus's Ionian mode. The practice of sharpening the seventh in the Mixolydian mode resulted in a similar identity. The minor mode was a conflation of the Dorian and Aeolian modes, with the seventh sharpened as required.

Modal idioms, generally derived from folksong, reappeared in the 19th century (e.g. the Lydian mode in Chopin's *Rondeau à la Mazurka*, op 5), and are an element of some importance in the style of Debussy, Ravel, Sibelius and Vaughan Williams, among others. For the use of the term in the rhythmic sense, *see* RHYTHMIC MODES.

moderato (It.), **modéré** (Fr.), moderate (with reference to speed).

modes, rhythmic, *see* RHYTHMIC MODES

modulation, basically a change of key, the process being achieved by logical harmonic progressions. At its simplest, the establishment of a new key is effected by a perfect cadence in that key, e.g.:

In this bald modulation from C to D minor, three of the notes (A, E, G) in the second chord, the dominant seventh of D, belong to both keys, and the other note moves chromatically from C to C sharp.

In modulating from C to F sharp, there are no notes common to the first two chords, and three of the notes move chromatically. Modulations which involve chromatic movement in one or more of the parts are sometimes called 'direct' modulations.

Modulation is often effected by passing through a chord, called a 'pivot' chord, in which two or more of the notes belong to both of the keys concerned, on the way to the dominant of the new key. In this modulation from C to E minor:

the second chord acts as a pivot chord, being the sub-mediant chord (VI) in C, and the sub-dominant chord (IV) in E minor. Such pivot chords exist, and may be similarly used for modulation, between every major key and the key of its supertonic minor, mediant minor, sub-dominant, dominant, relative minor, and leading-note minor, e.g. between C and D minor, E minor, F, G, A minor, and B minor.

Chords of which the root and fifth are common to the two keys concerned are equally effective as pivot chords, e.g.:

where the second chord is the sub-dominant of C with the third flattened and also the supertonic of E flat. Chords in which the root and fifth are common exist between every two major keys, except those of which the key-notes are a tritone apart. Modulation which takes its departure from a minor key may be effected along similar lines.

Modulation may also be effected by using as the intermediate:

(1) chords which, since they divide the octave into equal parts, are inherently capable of assuming as many key-contexts as they have notes (e.g., the augmented triad and the diminished seventh chord), and

(2) chromatic chords which have by historical usage established themselves within the key (e.g., the Neapolitan sixth and augmented sixth chords). In the mediant chord of the minor mode with sharpened fifth, which is an augmented triad, any one of the three notes may be used as a dominant.

In

for example, G sharp in the mediant chord of A minor is used as the dominant to lead to C sharp minor, and in

C is used as the dominant to lead to F minor. In the seventh chord on the leading-note of the minor mode, which is a diminished seventh chord, any one of the four notes may be used as a leading-note. In

for example, D is used as the leading-note in modulating to E flat, in

F (E sharp) as the leading-note to modulate to F sharp minor, and in

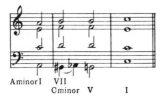

B as the leading-note to modulate to C. In modulations in this group the chord through which the modulation is made is, in fact, a pivot chord, since it belongs to both keys, and an enharmonic change, shown in the examples by a tie, is always expressed or implied.

The Neapolitan sixth chord, the root of which is a semitone above the tonic (e.g. D flat in C), can effect a modulation either up or down a semitone from the key, for example from C to B minor:

or from C to D flat:

The augmented sixth chord, which in its most usual form ('German' sixth chord) is based on the flattened sub-mediant of the key, e.g.

in C, is identical in sound with the dominant seventh of the key a semitone above, and may be used to modulate to that key:

An enharmonic change is always involved.

If a modulation is repeated from the new key as a starting point, i.e. transposed into that key, the result is a modulating or 'real' sequence. A special case of such a sequence is the canon *per tonos* in Bach's *Musical Offering*, which modulates up a tone with each repetition of the theme until it arrives at the original key an octave higher.

Such formulae as are given in these examples may be the basis of modulations which are momentary (sometimes called 'transitions') and are soon followed by a return to the original key, or are modulations (or 'transitions') on the way to a further modulation, or are part of a large tonal design. The question of their terminology is unimportant, so long as they are heard and understood in relation to the time-scale of the complete composition, be it hymn tune, symphony, or opera. The technique and art of modulation is fundamental to the artistic use of the effects of tonality, to the control of tonal design, and thus to the art of composition. *See also* HARMONY

Moeran, Ernest John (1894–1950), English composer of Irish descent. He entered the Royal College of Music in 1913, and was later a pupil of John Ireland. In 1924 his first orchestral *Rhapsody* was performed in Manchester and the second at the Norwich Festival. After a period of retirement for further study he composed a sonata for two unaccompanied violins (1930) and a second piano trio (1931). Some of his works show the influence of Delius, Vaughan Williams, and Bernard van Vieren. His compositions include a symphony in G minor (his most important work; 1937), violin concerto (1942), cello concerto (1945), many songs, choral works, church music, and chamber music.

Moeschinger, Albert (born 1897), Swiss composer and teacher. He studied in Berne, Leipzig, and Munich, and taught theory and piano in Berne until his retirement in 1943. Though he has written several fine chamber works, he has also been prolific in other fields and has composed three symphonies, three piano concertos, orchestral variations and fugue on a theme of Purcell, works for piano and organ, choral music and songs.

Moiseiwitsch, Benno (1890–1963), Russian born pianist, pupil of Leschetizky in Vienna. He first appeared in Britain in 1908, and took British nationality in 1937. He was famed especially for his performances of Rakhmaninov.

moll (Ger.), 'minor', as opposed to 'major' (*dur*). The word derives from the Latin *B molle* (soft B), the name given to the rounded B used in medieval times to indicate B flat, and hence adopted as the symbol for flattening.

See B, DUR

Molteni, Benedetta Emilia, *see* AGRICOLA (2)

molto (It.), very. *Allegro molto* (or *Allegro di molto*), very fast.

Moments Musicaux (singular, *Moment Musical*), set of six short piano pieces by Schubert, op 94, published in the spring of 1828 (and at least four of them written that year). Schubert called them *Moments Musicals*, but it is customary, if pedantic, to correct his faulty French.

Mompou, Federico (born 1893), Spanish (Catalan) composer and pianist. He studied at the Barcelona Conservatory and from 1911 in Paris under Philipp and Lacroix (piano) and Samuel Rousseau (harmony). From 1914–21 he lived in Barcelona, subsequently in Paris. He developed an individual style of composition called *primitivista*, which has no bar-divisions, key-signatures or cadences. His compositions are chiefly piano music and songs. His best-known piano pieces are the exquisite series of *Songs and Dances*, based on popular airs.

Mondonville, Jean Joseph Cassanéa De (1711–72), French violinist and composer who became director of the Royal Chapel in Paris in 1744, and of the Concert Spirituel in 1755. He composed operas, including *Titon et l'Aurore* (1753), three oratorios, and motets. His violin sonatas *Les sons harmoniques* (c. 1738) made the first extended use of harmonics. He was active on the French side during the musical *Guerre des Bouffons*.

Mondo della Luna, Il (It., *The World of the Moon*),

comic opera in three acts by Haydn, to a libretto by Goldoni, first performed at Eszterhazy in 1777. The story concerns a Venetian astronomer who becomes so obsessed with life on the Moon that he imagines himself to have been transported there. His obsession enables his daughter, whom hitherto he has closely guarded, to marry her suitor. A modern edition of the score was prepared by the Haydn scholar, H. C. Robbins Landon, in 1958, and in this form the work has been fairly frequently revived.

Moniuszko, Stanislaw (1819–72), Polish composer who studied in Warsaw and (1837–39) under Rungenhagen in Berlin. He was organist of St. John's Church, Wilno, 1840–58. Later he was conductor at the Warsaw Opera and teacher at the Conservatory. His opera *Halka*, the first Polish opera on a national theme (1847), was given more than a thousand performances in Warsaw alone. He composed more than twenty other operas, including *Straszny Dwór* (*The Haunted Manor*) and *Flis* (*The Raftsman*). He also composed songs, choral works, incidental music for plays, church music and a symphonic poem, *Bajka* (*The Fairy Tale*). After Chopin, he was the leading Polish composer of the 19th century.

Monn, Georg Matthias (1717–50), Austrian organist and composer. Organist, Karlskirche, Vienna. His compositions, which are sometimes confused with works by a younger composer (Johann Matthias Monn or Mann), include symphonies, quartets, and trio sonatas. He is one of the composers whose symphonies were being played in Vienna when Haydn was growing up. His symphony in D major of 1840 is the earliest known symphony to have four movements, with a minuet in third place.

monochord, instrument consisting of a single string stretched over a wooden resonator, with a movable bridge. It was used, especially in the middle ages, to demonstrate the relation between musical intervals and the division of the string.

monodrama, (1) a dramatic work involving only one character, e.g. Schoenberg's one-act opera *Erwartung* (*Expectation*) (1909);

(2) in particular a work for speaking voice with instrumental accompaniment.

See MELODRAMA

monody, solo song with accompaniment. Solo songs with lute, for example in Luis Milán's collection of 1536, and arrangements of madrigals for solo voice and lute, were common in the 16th century. The term is particularly applied to the Italian monody (for solo voice and continuo) in the new style, exploiting the dramatic and expressive possibilities of the solo singer, written in the early 17th century. This style appeared in solo monodies, e.g. Caccini's *Le nuove musiche* (1602), and in opera. For a summary, *see* N. Fortune, 'Italian Secular Monody from 1600 to 1635', in *Musical Quarterly*, (1953).

monophony (Gr., single sound), music which consists of melody only, without independent or supporting accompaniment, as in plainsong, folk song, troubadour and *trouvère chansons* and in most non-European music.

monotone, the recitation of words on a single note.

Monsigny, Pierre Alexandre (1729–1817), French composer. He studied the violin in his youth and went to Paris in 1749. On hearing Pergolesi's *La serva padrona* he was inspired to compose a comic opera of his own. The result, *Les Aveux indiscrets,* was produced at the Théâtre de la Foire in 1759. Thereafter he wrote several other comic operas, but in 1777 he stopped composing although he was then at the height of his success. He lost his fortune during the Revolution but in 1798 he was granted a pension by the Opéra-Comique. His most important operas were *Rose et Colas* (1764), *Le Deserteur* (his most famous work, 1769), and *La belle Arsène* (1773).

Monte, Philippe de (1521–1603), Flemish composer, who spent his early years in Italy. He became a member of the chapel of Philip II of Spain in about 1555, and with him visited England. He returned to Italy shortly after this and eventually succeeded Jakob Vaet as *Kapellmeister* to the Emperor Maximilian II in 1568. He continued to hold this office under Maximilian's successor, Rudolf II. With Palestrina, Lassus and Victoria he is one of the great masters of 16th century polyphony and one of the most prolific. He published 36 books of secular madrigals and five books of *madrigali spirituali*. He also composed French *chansons,* Masses and an enormous number of motets. 32 volumes of a projected edition of his works were published between 1927 and 1939 by C. van den Borren and J. van Nuffel. They contain some of the Masses and motets, the first book of *Madrigali spirituali, chansons* and lute songs.

  G. VAN DOORSLAER: *La Vie et les oeuvres de Philippe de Monte* (1921)

Montéclair, Michel Pinolet de (1667–1737), French composer and teacher. After some time as a chorister in the cathedral of Langres, he went to Italy in the service of the Prince de Vaudémont, and later settled in Paris, becoming in 1707 a double-bass player in the Opéra orchestra. He also became a distinguished teacher of the violin. He composed operas, cantatas, chamber music and church music, and published textbooks, among them *Méthode pour apprendre la musique* (1700) and *Méthode pour apprendre à jouer le Violon* (1712). The latter is one of the earliest on its subject.

Montemezzi, Italo (1875–1952), Italian composer. He was sent to a technical school to study engineering but later decided to study music. After being rejected twice, he was admitted to the Milan Conservatorio and obtained a diploma in composition in 1900. His first opera, *Giovanni Gallurese,* was produced at Turin in 1905, and at the Metropolitan Opera House, New York, in 1925. His best-known opera is *L'Amore dei Tre Re* (The Love of the Three Kings), a setting of Sem Benelli's drama, which he composed in 1913. He also wrote a symphonic poem, *Paolo e Virginia,* and an elegy for cello and piano.

monter (Fr.), to tune (an instrument) up in pitch.

Monteux, Pierre (1875–1964), French conductor. He studied at the Paris Conservatoire and won first prize for violin in 1896. In 1912 he became conductor of Diaghilev's Ballet Russe, with which he gave the premières of Stravinsky's *Petrushka, The Rite of Spring,* and *The Nightingale,* Debussy's *Jeux* and Ravel's *Daphnis and Chloe.* From 1917–19 he conducted at the Metropolitan Opera House, New York, from 1919–24 the Boston Symphony Orchestra, and from 1929–38 the Orchestre Symphonique de Paris. He conducted the San Francisco Symphony Orchestra from 1936–54, and was principal conductor of the London Symphony Orchestra from 1961 until his death.

Monteverdi (Monteverde), Claudio Giovanni Antonio (1567–1643), Italian composer. He was born in Cremona, the eldest son of a doctor, and studied with Ingegneri. His first published work was a collection of *Cantiunculae sacrae* (1582). He was in the service of the Duke of Mantua, firstly as a violist (c. 1590), and later as *maestro di cappella* (c. 1602). He was dismissed in 1612, but became *maestro di cappella* at St. Mark's, Venice, in the following year. He was ordained a priest in 1632. His church music includes three Masses (the earliest of which is founded on Gombert's motet 'In illo tempore'), Vespers, Magnificats and numerous motets. Among his secular vocal music are nine books of madrigals (the last posthumous), a book of *canzonette* and two books of *Scherzi musicali*. For the stage he wrote at least twelve operas (of which only three survive complete) and ballets.

Monteverdi's madrigals show an increasing tendency to break away from tradition by the use of new forms of dissonance for the sake of pathetic expression, and by the writing of melodic lines akin to the declamatory style of recitative. The fifth book (1605) was published with a *basso continuo* part, which is obligatory for the last six pieces in the collection. In the sixth book (1614) there are also six pieces which require a harpsichord accompaniment. In the seventh book (1619) none of the pieces are madrigals in the traditional sense: most of them are solos, duets and trios with accompaniment. The eighth book (1638), divided into *madrigali guerrieri* (warlike madrigals) and *madrigali amorosi* (amorous madrigals), is on similar lines. The seventh and eighth books also include shorter stage works. The church music may be divided into two contrasted groups, one of which accepts the traditional polyphonic style while the other adopts the new baroque methods of brilliant and expressive writing for solo voices and chorus, together with an effective use of instrumental resources.

The earliest of the three surviving operas, *Orfeo,* was performed at Mantua in 1607. It is clearly modelled to some extent on the earlier *Euridice* by Peri and also includes a substantial amount of choral writing in the style of the madrigal and motet; but it is also a landmark in the history of opera on account of its remarkable understanding of the contribution that music can make to dramatic representation. Of the music of *Arianna* (Mantua, 1608) only the heroine's lament survives – an expressive piece of extended recitative which had a great vogue in the 17th century. The two Venetian operas – *Il ritorno d'Ulisse in patria* (1641) and *L'incoronazione di Poppea* (1642) – are no less expressive in their declamation but incorporate also a rich variety of symmetrical songs and duets.

A complete edition of Monteverdi's works has been published by Malipiero.

  A. ABERT: *Claudio Monteverdi und das musikalische Drama* (1954)

  D. ARNOLD: *Monteverdi* (1963)

  D. ARNOLD and N. FORTUNE (editors): *The Monte-*

verdi Companion (1968)

G. E. MALIPIERO: *Claudio Monteverdi* (1930, including all the composer's letters)

H. PRUNIÈRES: *Claudio Monteverdi* (1924; English translation, 1926)

H. F. REDLICH: *Claudio Monteverdi: Life and Works* (1952)

L. SCHRADE: *Monteverdi: Creator of Modern Music* (1950)

Montezuma, opera in three acts by Roger Sessions, to a libretto by G. A. Borgese, first performed at the Deutsche Oper, Berlin, in 1964; the U.S. première followed five years later, at Boston. The story concerns the Spanish invasion of Mexico in the 16th century, and its bloody aftermath.

montre (Fr.), one of the names for an 8 ft. open diapason stop on the organ.

mood, English term of the 16th and early 17th centuries, used, for example, by Morley in his *Plaine and Easie Introduction* (1597), for the note relationships (mode, time, prolation) of MENSURAL NOTATION.

moog synthesizer, *see* SYNTHESIZER

'Moonlight' Sonata, name given (though not by the composer) to Beethoven's *Sonata quasi una fantasia* in C sharp minor for piano, op 27, no 2 (1801). Its origin seems to be due to H. F. L. Rellstab (1799–1860), who thought that the first movement suggested moonlight on Lake Lucerne.

Moór, Emanuel (1863–1931), Hungarian composer and pianist. He studied in Budapest and Vienna and from 1885 until 1887 toured Europe and the United States as conductor and pianist. He invented the Duplex-Coupler piano, with two manuals which can be coupled to simplify the playing of octaves. His compositions include operas, symphonies, piano, cello and violin concertos, violin and cello sonatas, many piano pieces and songs.

Moore, Douglas Stuart (1893–1969), U.S. composer and teacher. He graduated from Yale in 1915 and studied composition with Parker, Bloch and d'Indy. He received a Guggenheim Fellowship, the Pulitzer Scholarship and the Eastman School Publication award. In 1926 he became associate professor (later professor) of Columbia University. His compositions include the operas *The Devil and Daniel Webster*, with text by Stephen Vincent Benét (1938) and *The Ballad of Baby Doe*. He also wrote an operetta, *The Headless Horseman*, with text by Benét (1937), orchestral works, choral works, and chamber music. Among his books are *Listening to Music* (1931) and *From Madrigal to Modern Music* (1942).

Moore, Gerald (born 1899), English pianist, specially noted as a song accompanist, the greatest of his day. With Moore on the platform, singer and pianist were invariably equal partners. Elisabeth Schwarzkopf, Victoria de los Angeles and Dietrich Fischer-Dieskau are three of the many singers who have benefited from this partnership; and though Moore retired in 1967, his art can continue to be savoured on disc and through reading his three illuminating books, *The Unashamed Accompanist*, *Singer and Accompanist* and *Am I too Loud?*.

Moore, Thomas (1779–1852), Irish poet and musician. He studied at Trinity College, Dublin, and was musically largely self-taught. From about 1802 he published songs for which he composed the music as well as the words. In 1807–8 he published the first set of *Irish Melodies*, for which he wrote the poems and Sir John Stevenson edited traditional folk melodies, many from the collections of Edward Bunting. In 1816 he published the first number of *Sacred Songs* and from 1818–28 six sets of a *Selection of Popular National Airs*. He produced an opera *M.P., or The Blue Stocking* with text by himself and music by himself and Charles Edward Horn. His songs became very popular, and he had a singular gift for writing new poems which very aptly caught the spirit of traditional tunes.

Morales, Cristóbal de (c. 1500–53), Spanish composer. He studied under the Seville Cathedral choirmaster, Fernández de Castilleja. In 1526 he became *maestro de capilla* at Avila. Later he went to Rome, where he was ordained a priest, and in 1535 became a singer in the Papal chapel. He was *maestro de capilla* at Toledo from 1545 to 1547, was in the service of the Duke of Arcos at Marchena in 1550, and was *maestro de capilla* at Málaga in 1551. He was the first important Spanish composer of polyphonic church music, and published two books of Masses, Magnificats and motets. His compositions also include Lamentations, a motet for the peace conference at Nice (1538) and a few madrigals. His motet 'Emendemus in melius' is printed in the *Historical Anthology of Music*, edited by A. T. Davison and W. Apel, no 128. A complete edition of his works by H. Anglès was begun in 1952.

morceau (Fr., plural *morceaux*), piece. Satie used the term wittily for his *Morceaux en forme de poire* (pieces in the shape of a pear).

mordent, lower (Fr., *pincé*; It., *mordente*), ornament played by alternating rapidly once or twice the written note with the note below it. The speed and number of alternations depend on the length of the written note, having regard to the tempo in which it occurs. It is indicated thus:

and performed thus:

mordent, upper, or **inverted,** common English term for the ornament introduced about 1750 by C. P. E. Bach and called *Schneller* until c. 1800, and *Pralltriller* since. It generally occurs on the upper of two notes in a descending second, and is indicated thus:

and played thus:

Moreau, Jean-Baptiste (1656–1733), French church musician and composer. He was a chorister at Angers Cathedral, *maître de chapelle* at Langres Cathedral, and later at Dijon. From about 1686 he was in Paris where he wrote incidental music for Racine's *Esther* (1688) and *Athalie* (1691), and also for plays by Abbé Boyer and Duché. He set to music a large number of poems by Laînez. He taught singing and composition, and his pupils included Montéclair and Clérambault.

morendo (It.), 'dying', i.e. decreasing in volume (and also possibly speed) at the end of a phrase or the end of a composition.

moresca (It.), a dance of the 15th and 16th centuries, most often a sword dance in which a fight between Christians and Mohammedans was represented. The English morris dance is related to it. It appeared as a dance in Venetian operas and Viennese operas in the 17th century. Though originally in triple time, it was more often in march rhythm in the ballets of opera, as in this example from a ballet suite by J. H. Schmelzer (from E. Wellesz, *Die Ballettsuiten von J. H. und A. A. Schmelzer*, 1914):

Morhange, Charles Henri Valentin, *see* ALKAN

Morin, Jean Baptiste (1677–1745), musician to the Duke of Orléans and one of the first French composers of cantatas. He also wrote motets and songs.

Morlacchi, Francesco (1784–1841), Italian composer and conductor, pupil of Zingarelli at Loreto and Mattei at Bologna. He was commissioned in 1805 to write a cantata for the coronation of Napoleon as King of Italy. In 1807 his first comic opera, *Il ritratto*, was produced at Verona. He was conductor of the Dresden Opera (where Weber became his rival) from 1810 until his death, being succeeded there by Wagner. His works include operas, ten Masses, oratorios and cantatas.

Morley, Thomas (1557–c. 1602), English composer and theorist, a pupil of Byrd. He was organist at St. Paul's Cathedral in 1591, and a gentleman of the Chapel Royal in 1592. In 1598 he was granted a monopoly of music printing which he assigned to East in 1600. He published canzonets, madrigals, balletts, consort lessons for six instruments, and ayres, and edited *The Triumphes of Oriana* (reprinted in *The English Madrigal School*, xxxii). His *Plaine and Easie Introduction to Practicall Musicke* (1597; modern edition by R. A. Harman, 1952; facsimile edition, 1971) was the first comprehensive treatise on composition printed in England. He introduced the ballett, modelled on the *balletti* of Gastoldi, into England. E. H. Fellowes has edited the canzonets, balletts, and madrigals in *The English Madrigal School*, i–iv, and the *First Book of Ayres* (1600) in *The English School of Lutenist Songwriters*, first series, xvi.

J. KERMAN: *The Elizabethan Madrigal* (1962), chapter five.

Morning Heroes, symphony by Arthur Bliss (1930) for orator, chorus and orchestra with words selected from Homer, Li-Tai-Po, Walt Whitman, Robert Nichols and Wilfred Owen. It was written in memory of the composer's brother and others killed in World War I.

Mornington, Garrett Colley Wellesley, Earl of (1735–81), Irish-born violinist, organist and composer, largely self-taught. In 1757 he founded the Academy of Music in Dublin and in 1764 was elected the first professor of music at Dublin University. A complete collection of his glees and madrigals was published in 1846, edited by Sir H. R. Bishop. He was the father of the Duke of Wellington.

morris dance, traditional English folk dance, believed to originate about the 15th century and to derive its name from the Moorish *moresca*, a popular dance of that period. An element of the *moresca* – the bells or jingles which were tied to the dancers' legs – was carried over into the morris dance. The music, using a wide variety of tunes, was usually played on pipe and tabor.

Morris, R(eginald) O(wen) (1886–1948), English teacher, composer and theorist. He was educated at Harrow, New College, Oxford, and the Royal College of Music in London, where he was appointed teacher of counterpoint and composition in 1920. From 1926–28 he taught at the Curtis Institute of Music in Philadelphia and then rejoined the R.C.M. His books include *Contrapuntal Technique in the 16th Century* (1922), *Foundations of Practical Harmony and Counterpoint* (1925), and *The Structure of Music* (1935). He composed a symphony in D major (1935), a violin concerto, chamber music and songs, but these were less important than his work as writer and teacher.

Mortaro, Antonio, Italian composer. He entered the Minorite monastery at Brescia in 1595 and in 1598 was in the Franciscan monastery at Milan. From 1602 he was organist at Novara Cathedral and from 1606 to 1608 he was again at Brescia. His compositions are written in the elaborate polychoral style of which Giovanni Gabrieli was the greatest exponent.

Moscaglia, Giovanni Battista, late 16th century Italian madrigal composer, and an associate of Luca Marenzio in Rome. In 1585 he published a book of settings of his own madrigal poems by himself and other Roman composers, including Marenzio. He published other books of madrigals and a volume of villanellas *alla Napolitana*.

Moscheles, Ignaz (1794–1870), Bohemian pianist, teacher and composer. He studied under Dionys Weber at the Prague Conservatorium, and later in Vienna under Albrechtsberger and Salieri. In 1814 he arranged the piano score of *Fidelio* under Beethoven's supervision. He toured throughout Europe for ten years and in 1824 gave piano lessons to Mendelssohn in Paris. After 1826 he settled in London and in 1846 he became teacher of piano at the new Leipzig Conservatorium founded by Mendelssohn. His compositions include eight piano concertos, many piano sonatas and studies, and chamber music. His memoirs (English translation by A. D. Coleridge, 1873) give an interesting picture of the musical life of his day.

Mosè in Egitto (It., *Moses in Egypt*), opera in three acts by Rossini, to a libretto by Andrea Leone Tottola, first performed in Naples in 1818. An enlarged French four-act version by Giuseppe Luigi Balochi and Victor Joseph Étienne de Jouy was performed in Paris in 1872.

Moser, Hans Joachim (1889–1967), German historian, composer and singer. Studied under his father, Andreas Moser, and in Berlin, Marburg and Leipzig. He held academic posts in Halle, Heidelberg and Berlin. His numerous books include a three volume history of German music, and studies of Bach, Schütz, Handel, Gluck, and Weber – whose work he has edited.

Moses and Aaron (Ger., *Moses und Aron*), unfinished opera in two acts by Schoenberg, to a libretto by the composer, performed in a radio version in Germany in 1954, three years after the composer's death, but not staged until 1957 in Zürich. Schoenberg completed the first two acts in 1932, but did not begin Act 3 until 1951 – he died too soon to finish it. The role of Moses is cast for a baritone and that of Aaron for a speaker. Though some of the opera is sensational, such as the orgy round the Golden Calf, it is otherwise a penetrating study of the relationship between God and humanity.

Mosonyi, Mihály (originally Michael Brand) (1815–70), Austrian born composer, double-bass player, and critic. As a composer he was largely self-taught. Beginning in the German tradition, he became more and more aware of the Hungarian heritage of folk music, changed his name to a Hungarian one after he settled in Budapest, and was honoured after his death as a pioneer in the development of a national style. His compositions include operas, symphonies, string quartets, church music, piano music and songs.

mosso (It.), literally 'moved', i.e. lively. *Più mosso*, faster; *meno mosso*, slower. Also used as a warning against dragging, e.g. *Andante mosso*, not too slow.

Mossolov, Alexander Vassilievich (born 1900), Russian pianist and composer, pupil of Glière and Prokofiev. Several of his compositions have been influenced by his studies of the folk music of Turkmenia and other central Asian republics. In 1936 he was suspended by the Union of Soviet Composers for drunkenness, but was later re-admitted. His works include three operas (*The Dam, The Hero* and *The Signal*), symphonies and concertos.

Moszkowski, Moritz (1854–1925), German born pianist and composer of Polish origin. He studied in Dresden and Berlin, where he subsequently taught the piano. Though he wrote a number of large-scale works (e.g. a *Joan of Arc* symphony, a piano concerto, and a violin concerto), his reputation rests mainly on his lighter pieces, particularly his *Spanish Dances* for piano duet.

Mosto, Giovanni Battista (died c. 1596), Italian composer, a native of Udine. He studied under Merulo and from 1580 to 1589 was *maestro di cappella* of Padua Cathedral. With Merulo he published an anthology (*Il primo fiore della ghirlanda musicale*, Venice, 1577) which contained the first published madrigal by Marenzio. He also published books of madrigals and a second anthology (1579).

motet, the term first arose in the early 13th century by the addition of words (Fr., *mot*, therefore the diminutive 'motet') to the hitherto vocalized upper part of a two-part *clausula*. The motet became an independent composition, and flourished throughout the 13th century. It was most frequently in three parts. The lowest part, the tenor, was the basis; it was normally taken from plainsong, and was disposed in a regularly recurring rhythmic pattern. The other parts, called *duplum* and *triplum*, had different words, sacred or secular. In the latter case, they sometimes quoted the words and music of a well known REFRAIN, e.g.:

One of the most important sources of 13th century motets, the Montpellier Codex, has been published in facsimile together with transcription and commentary (Y. Rokseth, *Polyphonies du XIIIe siècle*, 1935–9). A selection of motets from this period has been edited by Hans Tischler (*A Medieval Motet Book*, 1973).

The isorhythmic motet of the period from 1300 to 1450 (Machaut, Dunstable, Dufay) represented an expansion of the 13th century motet. The tenor was still the basis, and was disposed in two or more sections, each with the same rhythm in successively diminished note values. For an example using inversion, retrograde motion, and diminution *see* RETROGRADE MOTION. Motets of this time could be secular, sacred, or written to mark a notable occasion.

From about 1450 to 1600 the term motet denoted a setting for unaccompanied voices of sacred Latin text, all the parts having the same words. The use of a tenor taken from plainsong continued in some cases until after 1500, but after about 1530 the imitative style with original themes was generally adopted.

In the following centuries a motet was a setting of a sacred text in the current style of the period, for solo voices or choir or both, with or without instrumental accompaniment. In the *Psalmen Davids* (1619) Schütz used the term for two pieces written for voices and instruments without distinction of style between their parts. A *Motetto concertato* written in about 1663 by Matthias Weckmann has all the appearance of a cantata. Bach's motets are for unaccompanied double chorus, for five-part chorus, and for four-part chorus with organ continuo. Schubert and Mendelssohn wrote both accompanied and unaccompanied motets;

those of Brahms are unaccompanied and in polyphonic style.

H. LEICHTENTRITT: *Geschichte der Motette* (1908)

Mother Goose (Fr., *Ma Mère l'Oye*), a suite of five children's pieces for piano duet by Ravel (1908; published, 1910) based on fairytales by Perrault and entitled:

(1) *Pavane de la Belle au Bois Dormant* (Pavan of the Sleeping Beauty).
(2) *Petit Poucet* (Tom Thumb).
(3) *Laideronette Impératrice des Pagodes* (Little Ugly, Empress of the Pagodas).
(4) *Les entretiens de la Belle et de la Bête* (Colloquy between Beauty and the Beast).
(5) *Le Jardin Féerique* (The Fairy Garden).

Ravel scored the work for orchestra (1912) and it was produced as a ballet, with added linking passages between the movements.

motif, motive, *see* SUBJECT

moto (It.), motion. *Con moto*, with motion, i.e. quickly.

moto perpetuo (It.), *see* perpetuum mobile.

Mottl, Felix (1856–1911), Austrian conductor and composer. He studied at the Vienna Conservatorium, where his teachers included Bruckner. In 1876 he was a stage conductor for Wagner at Bayreuth, and was court *Kapellmeister* at the Karlsruhe Opera, where he presented many important modern works including the complete operas of Berlioz and Wagner. He was chief conductor at Bayreuth in 1886, director of the Munich Opera (1903), co-director of the Berlin Royal Academy and director of Court Opera in 1907. He composed three operas, a string quartet and songs, but is today better known for his arrangements of Gluck, Wagner and other composers.

motto, motto theme, a recurring theme, which a composer uses to special dramatic purpose in the course of a piece of music. Sometimes the theme will have a pictorial or symbolic significance, sometimes it will be metamorphosed on each of its appearances, sometimes it will have the effect of a self-quotation. Important examples of the device can be found in Chaikovsky's fifth symphony and Berlioz's *Symphonie Fantastique* (though Berlioz preferred to call it an *idée fixe*). *See also* LEITMOTIV

Motu Proprio (Lat.), instruction on sacred music given by Pope Pius X (1903), in which Gregorian melodies 'which the most recent studies [i.e., those of the monks of Solesmes] have so happily restored to their integrity and purity' were affirmed to be its supreme models, and requiring the classic polyphony of the Roman school, especially of Palestrina, to be used in ecclesiastical functions.

Mount of Olives, *see* CHRIST ON THE MOUNT OF OLIVES

'Mourning' Symphony (Ger., *Trauersinfonie*), nickname for Haydn's symphony no 44 in E minor (c. 1771). The title is believed to have come from Haydn himself, who wanted the slow movement performed at his own funeral. The story may be apocryphal, but at least it fits the character of the symphony, one of the finest examples of the composer's *Sturm und Drang* style at this period in his career.

mouth organ, small wind instrument also known (confusingly) as a HARMONICA. The mouth organ, which comes in various sizes, is blown from the side, one of the

pair of metal reeds for each note being operated by blowing, the other by sucking. Chromatic notes are produced by a slide. Though very much a domestic instrument, it found a virtuoso exponent in Larry Adler; composers such as Milhaud and Vaughan Williams composed works for him.

Mouton, Jean (c. 1459–1522), French composer. He was a pupil of Josquin des Prés, the teacher of Willaert, and musician to Louis XII and François I. He was also canon of Thérouanne and later of Saint-Quentin. His compositions include Masses, motets, psalms, and *chansons*. A complete edition of his works was begun in 1967 by Andrew C. Minor.

mouvement, (Fr.), (1) time, speed. *Au mouvement*, in time (It., *a tempo*). *Premier* (or *1er*) *mouvement*, at the original speed (It., *tempo primo*).
See TEMPO
(2) movement (of a sonata, symphony, etc.).

movement (Fr., *mouvement*; Ger., *Satz*; It., *movimento, tempo*), a section, self-contained but not necessarily wholly independent, of an extended instrumental composition such as a symphony, sonata, string quartet, suite, etc. The movements of the 17th century trio sonata grew out of the contrasts of mood, metre and tempo to be found in the 16th century *capriccio, canzona* and *ricercar* (which in turn developed from the contrasts of mood to be found in the madrigal and the motet). The structure of the trio sonata was also influenced by the suite, consisting of a series of contrasted dances – a development of the 16th century practice of pairing a slow dance with a quick one (*see* PAVANE, GALLIARD).

The 18th century symphony normally consisted of three or four movements. The three-movement symphony consisted of two quick movements with a slow movement in between. If there were four movements, a minuet was generally included before or after the slow movement. Beethoven, in his fifth symphony, combined the scherzo (successor of the minuet) and the finale into a single movement. Later composers have gone further in relating movements together, e.g. Schumann in his fourth symphony, and Sibelius in his seventh symphony, where the various movements are linked into a continuous whole.
See SONATA, SONATA FORM, SYMPHONY

movimento (It.), (1) speed. *Lo stesso movimento*, at the same speed;
(2) movement (of a sonata, symphony, etc.)

Mozart, Wolfgang Amadeus (1756–91), Austrian composer, born in Salzburg. His father, **Leopold Mozart**, was a violinist and composer, and author of an important violin tutor. Leopold encouraged Wolfgang, who gave clavier recitals in Munich and Vienna at the age of six. In 1763 he began a long tour with his father and sister Maria Anna ('Nannerl'), who as a player was also a prodigy. Together they visited Germany, Belgium, Paris, London (1764–65) and Holland. All these places made their imprint on his subsequent musical style. By the time of his return to Salzburg in November 1766 he had composed his first symphonies and some thirty other works, and had arranged several piano concertos from sonatas by J. C. Bach – Johann Sebastian's 'English' son, who was the most important of Mozart's early influences (Mozart's great series of piano concertos grew out of his ex-

Wolfgang Amadeus Mozart

perience of Johann Christian's works). In 1768, at the age of twelve, he composed his first operas, *La finta semplice*, commissioned by the Emperor Joseph II, and *Bastien und Bastienne*, a *Singspiel* composed for performance in Dr. Mesmer's private theatre. Between 1769 and 1771 he went with his father to Italy, where he took lessons from Martini, copied Allegri's *Miserere* from memory, and showed enough knowledge of counterpoint to be elected a member of the Philharmonic Society of Bologna. During this time his opera seria, *Mitridate*, was acclaimed in Milan, and the Pope awarded him the honour of the Golden Spur. In spite of his tremendous international success as a child prodigy, Mozart found it singularly difficult to make his way as a young man and to achieve the kind of patronage his genius deserved. His father's efforts to secure him a court position in Vienna failed, and he remained in the household of the Archbishop of Salzburg, composing prolifically, until he was abruptly discharged in 1781. Mozart did not suffer fools gladly, and his open contempt for his noble employer resulted in his being shown the door – three months after his *Idomeneo*, the greatest *opera seria* ever written, had been successfully premiered in Munich, during a productive period which Mozart had spent in Germany and Paris. After his dismissal, he decided to set himself up as a freelance composer in Vienna. He was the first composer ever to attempt independence, away from the shelter of a menial court appointment, and he paid the penalty for being ahead of his time by ending in a pauper's grave (not until Beethoven established himself in Vienna did the risk of being a freelance begin to diminish). Vienna remained his home until the end of his short life. During that period he taught the piano (mainly to the daughters of the rich), gave concerts (for which he composed some of his greatest piano concertos) and married Constanze Weber; the minor appointment of

chamber musician to the Viennese court (1787) merely involved him in the composition of quantities of dances – not entirely to be disparaged, however, for they are exquisite examples of their kind. In 1789 he visited and played in Dresden, Leipzig (where he discussed Bach's music with Bach's successor, Doles) and Berlin, and in 1787 and 1791 he made two successful journeys to Prague (where he was much admired) for the first performances of *Don Giovanni* and *La Clemenza di Tito*. However, he never found the major musical appointment he was always hoping for and deserved. Unfortunately there were many lesser men who could hold such appointments perfectly efficiently, and (it was presumably believed) with less trouble than the genius, whose music, to quote one royal patron, contained 'too many notes'. In 1790 he was disappointed in his hope of being made *Kapellmeister* by the new Emperor Leopold II. Towards the end of his life he became interested in Freemasonry, a subject which inspired *The Magic Flute* and other works, and some of his financial worries were temporarily alleviated by a friend and fellow-mason, Michael Puchberg (though Mozart's begging letters to the latter make harrowing reading). His death seemed to be foreshadowed in a peculiar way by the appearance in July 1791 of a mysterious stranger – actually the steward of a nobleman who needed a composition in order to announce himself as a composer, and who wanted Mozart to ghost-write a *Requiem*. Mozart was deeply perturbed by the appearance of this mysterious man in grey. He died before the work was finished and the *Requiem* was completed by his pupil Sussmayr. The theory that he was poisoned, possibly by a rival composer, Salieri, has never yielded any convincing evidence, though it is true that his last illness was never satisfactorily diagnosed. His funeral was without honour, or even mourners, who turned back before a storm; they left Mozart to be buried in an unmarked pauper's grave.

Music flowed from Mozart unceasingly. He was in the habit of composing complete movements in his mind in all their detail before writing them down, as in the case of the overture to *Don Giovanni*, written two nights before the performance, and of the last three symphonies, written in the space of a fortnight. With his innate liveliness of imagination went the ability to seize immediately on the essence of another composer's style and to possess it as part of his own. He was influenced all his life by the music of others, including J. C. Bach, C. P. E. Bach, Handel, Haydn, Johann Stamitz, and Gluck, yet he is the composer above all others to whose style the word 'influence' is least appropriate. The endowments of surety of technique, infallible command of design, and keen dramatic sense made him the supreme master of the classical style in all the forms of the period. His six greatest operas – *Idomeneo* (1781), *Die Entführung aus dem Serail* (1782), *The Marriage of Figaro* (1786), *Don Giovanni* (1787), *Così fan tutte* (1790), and *The Magic Flute* (1791) – explore, in music of unsurpassed beauty, aptness and wit, the full range of human emotion. His piano concertos are the greatest ever written. Beethoven, Brahms and Chaikovsky may later have developed the form, and provided a more powerful cut and thrust between soloist and orchestra, but none of them succeeded in striking more sharply to the heart, with woodwind parts often as eloquent as that of the soloist.. The Mozart scholar, Alfred Einstein, considered them the most characteristic of all his works, though that is not to say that the chamber music (including the series of 'Haydn' quartets composed in tribute to the senior master, the string quintets and the clarinet quintet), the symphonies (not only the tremendous emotional contrasts of the last three but also the powerful *Prague* symphony, no 38), the great wind serenades, the springlike violin concertos (Mozart, as well as being a pianist whose playing 'flowed like oil', was also an accomplished violinist and viola player) and autumnal clarinet concerto, are in any way uncharacteristic.

Mozart's works were catalogued by Ludwig Köchel (1862) and are referred to by their numbers in Köchel ('K' numbers). The most recent edition of Köchel's catalogue is that by Einstein (1937). His principal compositions are:

(1) Operas: *Bastien und Bastienne* (K50, 1788); *Mitridate* (K87, 1770); *Lucio Silla* (K135; 1772), *Il Re pastore* (K208, 1775); *Idomeneo* (K366, 1781); *Die Entführung aus dem Serail* (K384, 1782); *Der Schauspieldirektor* (K486, 1786); *The Marriage of Figaro* (K492, 1786); *Don Giovanni* (K527, 1787); *Così fan tutte* (K588, 1790); *The Magic Flute* (K620, 1791); *La clemenza di Tito* (K621, 1791).

(2) Orchestra: 41 symphonies which have acquired numbers, including *Paris* (no 31, K297, 1778), *Haffner* (no 35, K385, 1782), *Linz* (no 36, K425, 1783), *Prague* (no 38, K 504, 1786), E flat (no 39, K543, 1788), G minor (no 40, K550, 1788), *Jupiter* (no 41, K551, 1788), and about eight other symphonies. Numerous *divertimenti*, serenades, marches, etc., including *Eine kleine Nachtmusik*, for strings (K525, 1787).

Detail of a contemporary painting said to represent Mozart going to a pauper's grave

(3) Concertos: 21 for piano; one for two pianos; one for three pianos; five violin concertos; two for flute; one for clarinet; four for horn; one for flute and harp; *Sinfonia concertante* for violin and viola (K364, 1779); *Sinfonia concertante* for oboe, clarinet, horn, and bassoon (K App. 9, 1778); fourteen sonatas for organ and strings; three sonatas for organ and orchestra.

(4) Chamber music: six string quintets; 23 string quartets; *Adagio and Fugue* in C minor (K546, 1788) for string quartet; two piano quartets; seven piano trios; trio for clarinet, viola and piano (K498, 1786); clarinet quintet; horn quintet; quintet for piano and wind; two flute quartets; oboe quartet; 37 violin sonatas (two unfinished).

(5) Piano: seventeen sonatas; two Fantasias; fifteen sets of variations; sonata for two pianos (K448, 1781); six sonatas for piano duet (one unpublished); *Adagio* and *Allegro* in F minor (K594, 1790) and *Fantasia* in F minor (K608, 1791) for piano duet (both originally for a mechanical organ).

(6) Church music: eighteen Masses; four litanies; *Requiem* (K626, 1791).

    H. ABERT: *W. A. Mozart* (enlarged edition of Jahn), two volumes (seventh edition, 1955–56)

    E. ANDERSON: *The Letters of Mozart and his Family* three volumes (1938)

    E. BLOM: *Mozart* (1935)

    B. BROPHY: *Mozart the Dramatist* (1964)

    E. J. DENT: *Mozart's Operas* (second edition, 1947)

    A. E. F. DICKINSON: *Mozart's Last Three Symphonies* (1927)

    T. DUNHILL: *Mozart's String Quartets* (1927)

    A. EINSTEIN: *Mozart* (1945)

    C. M. GIRDLESTONE: *Mozart and his Piano Concertos* (1948)

    A. HUTCHINGS: *A Companion to Mozart's Piano Concertos* (1948)

    A. H. KING: *Mozart Chamber Music* (1968)

    O. JAHN: *The Life of Mozart*, translated by P. D. Townsend, three volumes (1891)

    A. H. KING: *Mozart in Retrospect* (1956)

    H. C. R. LANDON and D. MITCHELL: *The Mozart Companion* (1956)

    T. DE WYZEWA and G. DE SAINT-FOIX: *W. A. Mozart: sa vie musicale et son oeuvre*, five volumes (1912–46)

Mozart and Salieri, opera in two acts by Rimsky-Korsakov, based on Pushkin's dramatic poem about the (conjectural) poisoning of Mozart by his rival, Antonio Salieri. The work was first performed in 1898 in Moscow.

Mozartiana, title of Chaikovsky's fourth orchestral suite, op 61, composed in 1887. It comprises orchestrations of three Mozart keyboard works and of the choral motet, *Ave verum corpus*, K 618. The keyboard works are the gigue, K 475, the minuet, K 355, and the variations on a theme of Gluck, K 455.

Mudd, Thomas (born c. 1560), English composer who studied at Cambridge and was a fellow of Pembroke until 1590. His anthems are confused with those of John Mudd (died 1639) who was organist of Peterborough Cathedral from 1583 to 1630, and possibly with a younger Thomas Mudd (died 1667) who was organist at Peterborough from 1631. A set of nine dances in manuscript at the British Library is by the younger Thomas. There was also a Henry Mudd (died c. 1588) whose compositions include an *In nomine*.

Muette de Portici, *see* MASANIELLO

Muffat, Georg (1653–1704), German composer and organist. He studied for six years with Lully in Paris. He was appointed organist at Molsheim in 1671, and in about 1678 became organist to the Bishop of Salzburg. He was organist in 1690, and *Kapellmeister* in 1695, to the Bishop of Passau. He published many organ works, including *Apparatus musico-organisticus* (1690). His *Florilegium* (1695–6), consisting of orchestral suites (*ouvertures*) in the style of Lully has been reprinted in *Denkmäler der Tonkunst in Osterreich*, ii, Jg. i (2) and iv, Jg. ii (2). Other instrumental music by him has been reprinted in volumes 23 (Jg. xi/2), 50 (Jg. xxv/2), and 89 of the same series. The prefaces to three of his publications have been published in an English translation by O. Strunk in *Source Readings in Music History* (1950). The preface to the *Auserlesene Instrumental-Musik* (1701) tells us that he met Corelli and heard his concertos in Rome about 1682, and gives some interesting observations on the performance of concertos.

His son **Gottlieb,** or **Theophil Muffat** (1690–1770), also became a composer. He was a pupil of Fux, and from 1717 was court organist in Vienna. Organ and harpsichord works by him have been published in *Denkmäler der Tonkunst in Osterreich*, lviii, Jg. xxix (2), and vii, Jg. iii (3).

muffle, drums are occasionally required to be 'muffled' by placing a piece of cloth or similar material on their vibrating surfaces. The resulting tone quality is sombre, an effect often associated with funereal music.

Mulliner, Thomas, English organist. In the only contemporary record of his life he was entered in 1563 as *modulator organorum* at Corpus Christi College, Oxford. He compiled, probably in the 1560s, a manuscript containing keyboard compositions and arrangements by Redford, Blitheman, Allwood, Shepherd, Tallis, Johnson, and others, to which were added before 1587 some pieces for the cittern and gittern. A modern edition is in *Musica Britannica*, i.

    D. STEVENS: *The Mulliner Book* (1952)

    J. M. WARD: 'Les sources de la musique pour le clavier en Angleterre,' in *La musique instrumentale de la Renaissance*, edited by J. Jacquot (1955)

Munch, Charles (1891–1968), French (Alsatian) conductor. After studying the violin in Strasbourg and Berlin, he became leader of the Leipzig Gewandhaus Orchestra in 1926. His career as a conductor began in Paris in 1933. He conducted the Société des Concerts du Conservatoire, from 1938 until 1945, and the Boston Symphony Orchestra from 1948 until 1962. He was a distinguished conductor of Berlioz and other French composers.

Mundharmonica (Ger.), mouth harmonica or MOUTH ORGAN.

Mundy, John (died 1630), English organist and composer. He was educated by his father, William Mundy, and like him became a gentleman of the Chapel Royal. He was also organist of Eton College and afterwards JOHN MARBECK's successor at St. George's Chapel, Windsor. He published *Songs and Psalms* (1594), a collection of madrigals and airs (modern edition in *The English Madrigal School*, xxxv), and contributed a madrigal to *The Triumphes of Oriana* (reprinted in *The English Madrigal School*, xxxii). Several of his keyboard compositions are in the *Fitzwilliam Virginal Book*.

His father, **William Mundy,** was a chorister at Westminster Abbey, vicar-choral of St. Paul's Cathedral, and a gentleman of the Chapel Royal for nearly 30 years under Elizabeth. He died about 1591. His compositions include services, anthems, and motets. His Latin antiphons and psalms have been edited by F. Ll. Harrison (1963).

Muris, Johannes (Jean) de (before 1300–c. 1351), theorist, mathematician, and philosopher for whom Welsh, English, French and (possibly) Swiss nationality have been proposed. A friend of Philippe de Vitry, he supported the style and principles of notation of the *ars nova*. The *Speculum musicae* of Jacobus of Liège, formerly attributed to de Muris, takes the opposite view. His writings have been printed in Gerbert's *Scriptores*, iii and in Coussemaker's *Scriptores*, iii. His earliest two treatises, *Notitia artis musicae* and *Compendium musicae practicae* (both 1321), have also been printed in an edition by U. Michels (1972). An English translation of his *Ars novae musicae* is in O. Strunk, *Source Readings in Music History* (1950).

    U. MICHELS: *Die Musiktraktate des Johannes de Muris* (1970)

Murrill, Herbert Henry John (1909–52), English composer. He studied at the Royal Academy of Music in London and at Worcester College, Oxford. He joined the music staff of the B.B.C. in 1936, and in 1950 became B.B.C. Head of Music. His compositions include two concertos for cello and orchestra, *Man in Cage* (a jazz opera, 1929), and incidental music for films, ballets, and plays.

musette (Fr.), a type of bagpipe popular in French aristocratic circles during the 17th and 18th centuries. The name was also given to dance movements incorporating drone bass notes suggestive of the instrument. An eight foot reed stop on an organ approximating to the tone of bagpipes is called *musette*.

Musgrave, Thea (born 1928), Scottish composer, pupil of Hans Gal at Edinburgh University and Nadia Boulanger in Paris (where she was the first British composer to win the Lili Boulanger prize). Though her early works reveal a fastidious musical mind, it was not until the 1960s that she began to reveal her real potential in an important series of orchestral and instrumental works. In these, as she put it, she wanted to 'find a vivid dramatic form for abstract instrumental music'. Thus the soloists in her clarinet concerto (written for Gervase de Peyer) and horn concerto (for Barry Tuckwell) are given specific 'roles'. In the clarinet work, the soloist moves around the platform, forming splinter groups with members of the orchestra in opposition to the conductor; in the horn work, it is the orchestral horns who move around, answering the soloist like Hunding's vassals responding to his horn calls. In the second of her three chamber concertos there is a comic part for a viola player in opposition to the rest of the ensemble. But the composer's dramatic sense is not confined to her concert music.

Her operas, including *The Decision* (1967, about a Scottish mining disaster), *The Voice of Ariadne* (1974, based on a story by Henry James), and *Mary, Queen of Scots* (1977) are an important part of her compositions. She has also written a full-length ballet, *Beauty and the Beast*, and a dramatic choral work, *The Five Ages of Man*.

Musica Britannica, a collection of British music published by the Royal Musical Association with the support of the Arts Council of Great Britain. The series was begun in 1951 and to date (1975) 37 volumes have appeared.

musica da camera (It.), chamber music.

Musica Enchiriadis, a treatise of disputed authorship (formerly thought to be by Hucbald), written around 900. With the contemporary treatise, *Scholia enchiriadis*, it gives some of the earliest examples of ORGANUM. The two treatises are printed in Gerbert's *Scriptores*, i, pages 152 and 173; an English translation of the *Scholia enchiriadis* is in O. Strunk, *Source Readings in Music History* (1950).

musica falsa, musica ficta, (Lat.), the former term used by theorists in the early middle ages in discussing the use of accidentals which lay outside the Guidonian hexachord system. Later medieval theorists applied the latter term to transpositions of the hexachord whereby (in addition to B flat), E flat, A flat, and D flat became necessary. In modern times this term is also used in referring to the accidentals which, it is presumed, singers in the 15th and early 16th centuries supplied to provide a B flat for the mode on F and leading notes for the modes on D, G, and A. In modern editions these are indicated above the staff. No convincing basis for the presumption has been proposed, and there is no general agreement about the extent of its application.

musical box, *see* MECHANICAL MUSICAL INSTRUMENTS

musical comedy, U.S. (and to some extent British) equivalent of operetta, popular during the late 19th and early 20th centuries, and using music interspersed with spoken dialogue. Though it rarely reached the heights of the best Viennese specimens of its kind, it yielded a substantial repertory of pieces, some of which (e.g. Romberg's *The Desert Song*) are still performed today. Its slicker and more sophisticated offspring – including such pieces as Cole Porter's *Anything Goes*, Richard Rodger's *Pal Joey*, Leonard Bernstein's *West Side Story* and *Wonderful Town*, and Stephen Sondheim's *A Little Night Music* – have come to be called simply 'musicals', 'American musicals', or 'Broadway musicals'.

musical glasses, *see* HARMONICA

Musical Joke, A (Ger., *Ein Musikalischer Spass*), a miniature symphony in F by Mozart, K 522 (1787), for two horns and strings. There are four movements. The work is a caricature of the work of any third-rate composer of the period. It imitates remorselessly all the most threadbare conventions – melodic, harmonic and rhythmic – and provides each movement with a form as rigid as a strait-jacket. For good measure the slow movement includes a pretentious cadenza for solo violin. The alternative title *Dorfmusikanten-Sextett* (sextet for village musicians), which it has inherited from a 19th century publisher, has neither authority nor justification. The work is not chamber music, and it is not incompetent performers who are parodied but incompetent composers.

Musical Offering (Ger., *Musikalisches Opfer*), a set of pieces, including two *ricercari* (fugues), several canons and a sonata for flute, violin and harpsichord, written by Bach (1747) on a theme by Frederick the Great. It originated in an improvisation which Bach was invited to give when he visited Potsdam. The work was printed and dedicated to Frederick the Great. The initial letters of the inscription 'Regis Iussu Cantio Et Reliqua Canonica Arte Resoluta' (a theme and other things worked out in canon by the king's command) make the word *ricercar*. Bach's delight in acrostics, evident from this inscription, finds expression also in the directions given for solving the canons.

musical saw, *see* SAW

musica mensurata, *see* MENSURAL MUSIC

musica plana (Lat.), medieval term for PLAINSONG.

musica reservata (Lat.), a term used in the latter part of the 16th century, supposedly to indicate music suitable for connoisseurs and private occasions, and more particularly music which gave vivid and faithful expression to the spirit of the words. The first known reference to it is in the work of Adrianus Petit Coclicus, author of a *Compendium musices* and a collection of psalm settings entitled *Musica reservata*, both published in 1552.

> E. LOWINSKY: *Secret Chromatic Art in the Netherlands Motet* (1946)
>
> G. REESE: *Music in the Renaissance* (1954), pages 511ff

Musica Transalpina, title of the first printed collection of Italian madrigals with English words, published by Nicholas Yonge in 1588, shortly after Byrd's *Psalmes, Sonets and Songs*. It contained 55 madrigals by Italian composers and two by Byrd, and was the first of a series of anthologies of Italian madrigals published in England in the latter part of the 16th century. Yonge published a second collection with the same title in 1597. Facsimiles of both prints were published in 1972.

Music for strings, percussion and celesta, work by Bartók, commissioned for the tenth anniversary of the Basel Chamber Orchestra and first performed by them in 1947 under Paul Sacher.

Music Makers, The, ode for contralto solo, chorus and orchestra by Elgar, op 69, to words by Arthur O'Shaughnessy, first performed in Birmingham in 1912. The music includes quotations from the following earlier works by the composer: *The Dream of Gerontius*, *Sea Pictures*, *Enigma* Variations, violin concerto, first and second symphonies. Fragments of 'Rule Britannia' and the 'Marseillaise' are also introduced.

musicology (Fr., *musicologie*; Ger., *Musikwissenschaft*), the systematic study of musical composition and its history. The English term is a fairly recent one, and is sometimes used pretentiously by people who deem themselves to be 'musicologists', i.e. intellectually superior beings to critics or researchers. The German term *musikalische Wissenschaft* (musical science), implying the application of scientific methods to the investigation of the nature and history of music, was first used in 1863 by Friedrich Chrysander, and was adopted in the title of the periodical *Vierteljahrschrift* *für Musikwissenschaft* (1885). In its first volume Guido Adler divided the subject of musicology into a *historical* part (comprising musical palaeography, the grouping of musical forms, the norms of composition in practice and theory, and musical instruments) and a *systematic* part (including canons of harmony, rhythm, and melody, musical aesthetics, musical pedagogics, and musical ethnography), and enumerated the general and particular studies auxiliary to each part (e.g. liturgiology, history of the dance, acoustics). As both the value and the limitations of a 'scientific' approach to the explanation of the historical development of musical styles have become apparent, the term has more recently been applied to the study of musical history, and in particular to the transcribing and editing of manuscripts and early prints, and the discovery and interpretation of new knowledge about composers, institutions, instruments, forms, and methods of performance. Besides compositions, modern editions extend to the treatises of theorists, text books on performance, dictionaries, and the writings of critics. The central object of musicology remains the search for fuller understanding of the art of the composer as it concerns the performer, the listener and the historian.

G. HAYDON: *Introduction to Musicology* (1941)

music printing, *see* PRINTING OF MUSIC

music theatre, name for musical-dramatic works, produced (usually) more economically than operas, and employing smaller forces. Such pieces, increasingly composed from the 1960s onwards, can be produced often just as easily in concert halls or drama theatres as in opera houses, and indeed their composers in general have striven consciously to shake off not only the name 'opera' but also many of its conventions. Examples of music theatres are *Naboth's Vineyard* by Alexander Goehr (who founded his own Music Theatre Ensemble to perform such pieces as this), Iain Hamilton's *Pharsalia*, Peter Maxwell Davies's *Songs for a Mad King* and Hans Werner Henze's *The Long and Weary Journey to the Flat of Natasha Ungeheuer.*

Musikalisches Opfer, *see* MUSICAL OFFERING

Musikalischer Spass, *see* MUSICAL JOKE

musique concrète (Fr., concrete music), a type of music made possible by developments in tape recording. The sounds required by the composer are recorded and may then be manipulated, combined or distorted by him according to his imagination or ingenuity. The first person to experiment with this process, or at any rate to give a name to it, was the French engineer-composer Pierre Schaeffer (born 1910) who 'invented' *musique concrète* at the Paris radio station in 1948. The sound effects, or 'objets sonores', could come from any source to which the composer was attracted. How inventively (or otherwise) he treated the sounds determined whether the results were worth listening to as 'music' – as in the case of the *Symphonie pour un homme seul* (1950) by Schaeffer and Pierre Henry, a classic of its kind – or remained merely sound effects suitable for use in the theatre, cinema or radio. The term *musique concrète* has now been largely superseded by ELECTRONIC MUSIC.

F. C. JUDD: *Electronic Music and Musique concrète* (1961)

A. MOLES: *Les Musiques expérimentales* (1960)

P. SCHAEFFER: *A la Recherche d'une Musique concrète* (1952); *Traité de objects Musicaux* (1966); *Incontri Musicali* nos 1–4 (1956–60); 'Musique concrète et connaissance de l'objet musical', *Revue belge de musicologie* xiii

G.–W. BARUCH: 'Was ist Musique concrète?', *Melos* (1953)

musique de chambre (Fr.), chamber music

musique de table, *see* TABLE

musique mesurée à l'antique, (Fr.), music in which the rhythm was rigidly governed by the metre of the poetry which it set, practised by the composers and poets of the *Académie de Poésie et de Musique* founded by de Baïf and de Courville in Paris in 1570. Costeley, Mauduit, Claude le Jeune and Caurroy were the chief composers concerned. A long syllable in the metre was always set to a minim or its equivalent and a short syllable to a crotchet or its equivalent, and all the parts moved in syllabic homophony. Le Jeune's *Pseaumes en vers mesurés* (1606) have been reprinted by H. Expert in *Les Maîtres musiciens de la Renaissance française*, xx–xxii, and Mauduit's *Chansonettes mesurées de Jean-Antoine de Baïf* (1586) in the same series, x.

F. A. YATES: *The French Academies of the Sixteenth Century* (1947)

Mussorgsky, Modest Petrovich (1839–81), Russian composer. Born well-to-do, Mussorgsky spent much of his life in poverty – partly because his family income dwindled after the serfs' emancipation in 1861 (a case he strongly supported) and partly because of his own instability of character. He was intended for a military career and joined a regiment in 1856; but, after he met Balakirev and Dargomizhsky in 1858, music increasingly commanded his attention and he resigned his commission. Though studying under Balakirev, he was too unsystematic to make a full-time career of music. Instead he took a minor post in the civil service, but soon sank into drunkenness and degradation. He died of alcoholic epilepsy in a hospital in St. Petersburg, one week after his 42nd birthday.

Mussorgsky composed as erratically as he lived. Much of his music was left unfinished and in disorder, but it is a wonder that he wrote as much as he did. In many ways, he was Russia's most individual and human genius. As a vivid and moving portrait of the Russian people, his opera *Boris Godunov* (completed in the first of several versions in 1870) has never been surpassed. The series of genre pieces that form *Pictures at an Exhibition* (1874) were the first real masterpiece for solo piano by a Russian composer. In both these works, Mussorgsky's harmonic and rhythmic audacity was mistaken by pedantic minds for musical ineptitude: it was assumed that he did not know what he was doing. Thus Rimsky-Korsakov, in revising *Boris Godunov*, 'corrected' Mussorgsky's errors, inflated the sharp, telling colours of the original orchestration, and turned the opera into a much more conventional work. Yet his efforts on Mussorgsky's behalf were well intentioned and not wholly to be despised. He helped to popularise *Boris* and, more than anyone else, was responsible for tidying up and completing Mussorgsky's unfinished music. Similarly Ravel's orchestration of *Pictures at an Exhibition*, though it alters the character

Modest Petrovich Mussorgsky

singing the scale the change was usually made by substituting *re* for *sol* or *la* in ascending and *la* for *re* or *mi* in descending, *ut* being used for the lowest note only, e.g. (from N. Listenius, *Musica*, 1549):

Morley's examples in his *Plaine and Easie Introduction* dispense with *ut* and *re*, e.g.

The use of *fa* on E sharp is an example of MUSICA FICTA, by which hexachords on notes other than C, G, and F had gradually been brought into use.

mutation stops, organ stops which produce a sound other than the pitch corresponding to the key which is depressed or to its octaves. Quint stops (e.g. the twelfth, $2\frac{2}{3}$ ft.) sound the twelfth (the third note of the HARMONIC SERIES), and Tierce stops (e.g., Tierce, Larigot $1\frac{3}{5}$ ft.) the seventeenth (the fifth note of the harmonic series), above the foundation note or one of its octaves.

See MIXTURE, ORGAN

mute (Fr., *sourdine*; Ger., *Dämpfer*; It., *sordino*), any device used to soften or alter the normal tone colour of an instrument. On bowed instruments it is a small fork-shaped clamp that fits onto the bridge, thereby reducing the vibrations; on brass instruments, it is often made of wood or metal and pear-shaped, but a wide variety of mutes are available for trumpets and trombones, all of them producing distinctive tone colours. On rare occasions this type of muting has been applied to woodwind instruments but without much success. Drums, particularly timpani, were formerly muted placing a cloth over the drum head; nowadays sponge-headed drumsticks are used. In all these cases the usual indication to play mutes is *con sordino*, but this is often abbreviated to *con sord*, or simply *sord*. On a piano muting is effected by depressing the soft pedal and in this case the usual indication is *una corda*.

My Country, *see* MA VLAST.

mystery play, *see* TROPE

mystic chord, term for a chord invented by Skryabin. It consists of a series of ascending fourths, C – F sharp – B flat – E – A – D, and forms the basis of *Prometheus*, op 60, composed in 1910, and the seventh piano sonata, op 64. Similar chords can be found in other Skryabin works.

of the original, has helped to introduce this work to a far wider public than would otherwise have heard it. After *Boris*, Mussorgsky's most viable works for the stage are his comedy, Gogol-inspired *Sorochintsy Fair* (1874–80, completed by Tcherepnin), and *Khovanshchina* (1872–80, completed by Rimsky-Korsakov). At various stages in his career he also embarked on operas on Flaubert's *Salammbô* (1863–66, unfinished) and Gogol's *The Marriage* (unfinished). With Rimsky-Korsakov, Borodin and Cui, he produced a communal ballet-opera, *Mlada* (1872), to which he contributed his *Night on the Bare Mountain* (well known in its own right as an orchestral tone poem, adapted by Rimsky-Korsakov) and other material. His feeling for the Russian people and their language is heard to powerful effect in his songs, of which he managed to produce about sixty, including the three great cycles, *The Nursery* (1868–72), *Songs and Dances of Death* (1875–77), and *Sunless* (1874).

> M. D. CALVOCORESSI: *Mussorgsky* (1946); *Modest Mussorgsky – his Life and Works* (1956)
> J. LEYDA and S. BERTENSON: *The Mussorgsky Reader* (1947)

Mustel Organ, invented by Victor Mustel (1815–90) of Paris, this instrument is a development of the HARMONIUM.

muta, (It.), imperative of *mutare* (to change). A direction to the performer found in parts for wind instruments and timpani, indicating either a change of instrument (e.g. flute to piccolo, oboe to cor anglais, B flat clarinet to A clarinet), or a change of crook (e.g. horn in F to horn in E), or a change of tuning (for timpani). *Muta in flauto grande* (in a piccolo part) = change from piccolo to flute. *Muta in mi* (in a horn part) = change to horn in E. *Mutano* (third person plural of the present indicative) also occurs where more than one instrument is concerned.

mutano, *see* MUTA

mutation, the change from the syllables of one HEXACHORD to those of another in SOLMIZATION. In

Nabokov, Nicholas (born 1903), Russian born composer, author, and administrator, who studied in Berlin and Stuttgart, worked with Diaghilev's ballet during the 1920s and later settled in the United States. His works include operas (*The Death of Rasputin* and *Love's Labours Lost*), ballets, a *Sinfonia Biblica*, and other music for the concert hall.

Nabucco or **Nabucodonosor** (It., *Nebuchadnezzar*), opera in four acts by Verdi to a libretto by Temistocle Solera, first performed at La Scala, Milan in 1842. This was Verdi's third opera, and first major success. Its story of the Babylonian captivity of the Jews became symbolic of Italy's desire for independence – voiced above all in the chorus, 'Va, pensiero'. The soprano Giuseppina Strepponi, who played one of the leading roles in the first performance, later became Verdi's wife. The full title of the opera is seldom used.

nacchera (It.), kettledrum. *Nacchere* (the plural) usually refers to drums designed for military use, especially by cavalry, as opposed to timpani which are used in orchestra. *See* NAKER

naccherone (It.), large kettledrum.

nach (Ger.), in the manner of, after, towards. Thus '*nach* E' would be an instruction to a performer to tune his instrument to E.

Nachdruck (Ger.), emphasis.

nachgehend (Ger.), following.

nachlassend (Ger.), relaxing (literally 'leaving behind').

Nachschlag (Ger.; Eng., springer, acute; Fr., *accent*, *aspiration*, *plainte*), ornament in German music of the 17th and 18th centuries. In its most usual form it was played as a short passing note between two notes a third apart (the French called this *couler les tierces*), as in this example from the opening of Bach's choral prelude 'Allein Gott in der Höh' sei Ehr' ':

In another form the *Nachschlag* is an equivalent to the English SPRINGER.

In later music the term denotes the two notes which end a trill:

notation   played

Nachtanz, (Ger.), 'following dance'. A dance in quick triple time following a dance in duple time, in German instrumental music of the 16th and 17th centuries. It was also called *Proportz* (i.e., in *proportio tripla*), *Hupf auff* (hopping up) as in Hans Neusiedler's *Hoftanz* for lute printed in the *Historical Anthology* (no 105), and *tripla*, as in the suites in J. H. Schein's *Banchetto musicale* of 1617 (modern edition by A. H. Prufer, 1901). Dances most often paired in this way were PAVANE and GALLIARD in the 16th century and the ALLEMANDE and COURANTE in the 17th century. The second dance of the pair was commonly a rhythmically altered form of the first, as in Posch's *Musikalische Tafelfreudt* of 1621, reprinted in *D.T.Ö.*, xxv (2). The allemande-courante sequence was incorporated into the SUITE.

Nachstück (Ger.), night piece. The title was used by Schumann for a set of four piano pieces (op 23).

Nachtmusik (Ger.), literally 'night music', music of serenade-like character, often in several movements, e.g. Mozart's *Eine kleine Nachtmusik*, K 525. Mahler also used the term for two of the central movements of his seventh symphony.

Nagel, Willibald (1863–1929), German musical historian, who studied in Berlin under Spitta and Bellermann. He taught music history at Zurich and from 1893–6 lived in London doing research in early English music. He published the results of his researches in a history of English music (two volumes, 1891, 1897) and also wrote on the piano sonatas of Beethoven.

Nagelclavier, Nagelgeige, *see* NAIL VIOLIN

Nägeli, Hans Georg (1773–1836), Swiss musician and publisher. He established himself in Zurich and was acquainted with contemporary composers including Beethoven. He produced the first authentic edition of Bach's 48 preludes and fugues. He also published first editions of some of Beethoven's works, and was an active supporter of educational music.

nail violin (also nail fiddle and nail harmonica), instrument devised by Johann Wilde in St. Petersburg in 1740. It consisted of a semicircular resonator of wood into which were driven U-shaped nails of graduated lengths. The sound was produced by a bow. In 1791 Träger of Bernburg extended the idea to the nail piano (*Nagelclavier*) in which the sound was produced by the friction of a wheel.

naker (Arabic, *naqqara*; It., *nacchera*; Fr., *nacaire*), early English name for small, high-pitched kettledrum of Arabic origin which found its way into Europe during the 13th century. Nakers were used in pairs and their tuning could not be altered.

Namensfeier (Ger., *Name Day*), overture by Beethoven, op 115, performed in 1815 in honour of the name day festivities of the Emperor Francis II.

naqqara, *see* NAKER

Nardini, Pietro (1722–93), Italian violinist and composer, who studied at Leghorn and later at Padua under Tartini. He was appointed solo violinist at the ducal court of Württemberg at Stuttgart and in 1771 musical director at the court in Florence. His violin-playing was praised by Leopold Mozart. His compositions include six violin concertos, sonatas, string quartets, and keyboard sonatas.

Nares, James (1715–83), English organist and composer. He studied with Pepusch as a chorister at the Chapel Royal in London. He became deputy organist at St. George's Chapel, Windsor, and in 1734 was appointed organist of York Minster. From 1756 he was Greene's successor at the Chapel Royal and from 1757–80 master of the children. His works include church music, harpsichord lessons (a sonata in D, which has been edited by H. G. Ley, is one of his best works), glees and catches. He also wrote treatises on singing and keyboard playing.

Narváez, Luis de, 16th century Spanish composer and *vihuela*-player. His book of *vihuela* music of 1538 (*Los seys libros del Delphin de música*) contains some of the earliest examples of variation form (modern edition by E. Pujol in *Monumentos de la Música Española*, iii). An example is printed in the *Historical Anthology of Music*, edited by A. T. Davison and W. Apel, no 122.

Nash, Heddle (1896–1961), English tenor who studied in London and Milan and made his début in Milan in 1924 as Almaviva in *The Barber of Seville*. A lyrical singer of rare sensitivity, he was at his best in Mozart roles, especially Ottavio in *Don Giovanni*. During his career he sang for all the leading British opera companies.

national anthem, the song or hymn chosen by a country to represent it on official occasions, either nationally or internationally. Thus the British national anthem is 'God Save the Queen' (the same tune is used by Switzerland under the title of 'Rufst Du, mein Vaterland'), the French anthem is the *Marseillaise* ('Allons, enfants de la patrie'), the U.S. one is 'The Star-Spangled Banner', and so forth.

national music, in addition to those traits of national character in music which can be described only in the most general terms, the more concrete differences of practice in composition and performance, of musical forms and their social functions, and of idioms in folk music have always had their effects on the course of musical history. In the 15th century Tinctoris remarked on the conservatism of the English, who in contrast to the French persisted in using the same way of composing, 'which is a sign of a very poor talent'; and the Italian theorist Guilielmus explained to his fellow countrymen how some of the English methods (*regulae contrapuncti Anglicorum*) worked. The English madrigal and ballett were at first imitations of the 'kinds of songs which the Italians make'. Both J. H. Schein in his *Opella Nova* (1618) and Heinrich Schütz in his *Psalms* (1619) mentioned the Italian composers to whom they owed their knowledge of the new styles they introduced to Lutheran music, Schein to Viadana and Schütz to Giovanni Gabrieli. Italian opera and Italian instrumental music led the way in the 17th century, as Dryden observed:

> The wise *Italians* first invented show;
> Thence, into *France* the noble Pageant past;
> 'Tis *England's* Credit to be cozen'd last.
>> (Prologue to *Albion and Albanius*).

Both Purcell (Preface to *Sonatas of Three Parts*, 1683) and Couperin (Preface to *Les Goûts réunis*, 1724) acknowledged Italian influence. Couperin essayed the union of French and Italian styles (*Les Goûts réunis* and *Les Nations*, 1726), while J. S. Bach and Georg Muffat united both with traditions of North and South Germany. The differences between the French and Italian styles in opera were the issues in the *guerre des bouffons*.

The object of the nationalist movement in the music of the romantic period was to accentuate these differences rather than to absorb them, and folk music and folk stories were the obvious means of doing so. Glinka wrote from Berlin in 1833 about the opera (*A Life for the Tsar*) which was taking shape in his mind; 'In every way it will be absolutely national – and not only the subject but the music.' In the past hundred years every country has had its national music and its folksong revival, manifested in the works of Bartók and Kodály in Hungary, Sibelius in Finland and Vaughan Williams in Britain. More recently, however, national differences have again been absorbed and overriden in the cosmopolitan styles of many present-day composers.

R. VAUGHAN WILLIAMS: *National Music* (1934)

natural, note which is neither sharp nor flat. The sign ♮ is used to indicate it where this has been made necessary by the presence of a sharp or flat in the key-signature or of an 'accidental' earlier in the same bar.

See also B

natural horn, natural trumpet, horn or trumpet not furnished with valves or other means of altering the length of tubing in use. Except where hand-stopping can be used, such instruments are limited to the notes of the harmonic series.

See HORN, TRUMPET

Naumann, Johann Gottlieb (1741–1801), German composer who travelled to Padua, where he had lessons from Tartini and met Hasse. He went to Naples in 1761 and later studied counterpoint under Padre Martini at Bologna. He produced his first opera in Venice and in 1764 became court composer of church music at Dresden. From 1765–68 he lived in Italy, producing operas, and in 1776 became *Kapellmeister* at Dresden. His works include about 26 operas, oratorios, church music, chamber music, and songs.

Naylor, Edward Woodall (1867–1934), English writer and composer, who in 1908 became lecturer at Emmanuel College, Cambridge. His compositions include an opera *The Angelus* (1909), which won the Ricordi prize for an English work, services and other church music, songs, and part-songs. He wrote *Shakespeare and Music* (1896, revised 1931), and *An Elizabethan Virginal Book* (1905), a discussion of the Fitzwilliam Virginal Book.

His son, **Bernard Naylor** (born 1907), also became a composer. He was a pupil of Vaughan Williams, Holst and Ireland. His works include a setting of Elizabeth Barrett Browning's *Sonnets from the Portuguese* for voice and string quartet.

Neapolitan sixth, the name given to a 6/3 chord with a minor sixth and minor third on the fourth degree of the scale, e.g. in the key of A minor:

It derives from the following cadential progression:

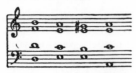

If the B in the first chord is flattened, the chord becomes a Neapolitan sixth:

The progression can be made more concise by eliminating the second chord:

Though the chord occurs more frequently in minor keys, it was also used in a similar way in major keys. Its name seems to be due to the use made of it, for pathetic effect, by opera-composers at Naples in the 17th century.

neben (Ger.), secondary. Thus *Nebenthema*, second theme (of a symphony or sonata).

neck, the part of a stringed instrument that supports the finger board.

Neefe, Christian Gottlob (1748–98), German conductor and composer. He studied under Hiller and succeeded him as conductor of a travelling opera company in 1776. He conducted the Grossman-Hellmuth Society in Bonn in 1779 and became organist at the court of the Elector in 1781. Beethoven became his pupil at the age of eleven. He wrote eight *Singspiele*, and his *Adelheit von Veltheim* (1780), produced two years before Mozart's *Entführung*, was one of the earliest German operas on a Turkish subject.

Neel, Louis Boyd (born 1905), English composer and founder in 1932 of the Boyd Neel Orchestra (renamed Philomusica of London in 1957, after Neel had become Dean of the Royal Conservatory of Music, Toronto).

Negro spiritual, see SPIRITUAL

nei (Rom.), panpipes, pandean pipes or syrinx. An ancient instrument, commonly associated with Greece, although its use today is confined almost entirely to Romania. It consists of a number of pipes of the whistle-type made of wood or from reeds and bound together in a row. On larger instruments there may be twenty or more such pipes, which are graduated in size so as to produce scales when they are blown in sequence. Romanian folk musicians can perform extraordinary feats of virtuosity on a full-sized nei, but it is a much smaller variety, often no more than a toy, that usually appears in illustrations and is used by Papageno in *The Magic Flute*.

'Nelson' Mass, (Ger., *Nelsonmesse*), nickname given to Haydn's Mass in D minor, composed in 1798 (no 9 in the new complete edition, no 3 in Novello's edition). The dramatic entry of trumpets and timpani in the *Benedictus* is said to commemorate Nelson's victory at the Battle of the Nile. Haydn's own title for the work was *Missa in Angustiis* (Mass in time of need). In Britain the work is sometimes called the *Imperial Mass*.

Nenna, Pomponio (c. 1555–1617), Italian composer. He published his first book of madrigals in 1582, and eight books thereafter. Some of his settings bear a close resemblance to madrigals by Gesualdo who may have been his pupil. He also wrote a set of Holy Week responses (1607). His first and fourth books of five-part madrigals have been edited by E. Dagnino (Rome, 1942), and selections from the remaining books by Glenn Watkins (1973).

neo-Bechstein piano, electronic piano invented by Vierling in Berlin between 1928 and 1933, and later further developed. It is played, and strings are struck, in the normal way, but the sound is modified electronically. The neo-Bechstein piano is similar to an ELECTROCHORD.

neo-classicism, term for 20th century musical movement which (especially in the 1920s) revolted against the lush, emotional, chromatic romanticism of music written towards the end of the 19th century and at the beginning of the 20th. Aspects of neo-classical music were the emphasis on clarity of texture, lightness of orchestration, coolness of approach, and a back-to-the-18th-century (especially back-to-Bach) respect for counterpoint and close-knit musical forms. The most famous exponent of neo-classicism has been Stravinsky who, during one period in his career, produced a neo-Bachian piano concerto, a neo-Pergolesian suite (*Pulcinella*), and a neo-Mozartian opera (*The Rake's Progress*). Other composers attracted to neo-classicism have included Hindemith, Auric, Poulenc, Casella, and Malipiero.

neo-modalism, the use by some 20th century composers of harmony based on old modes rather than on the major or minor scales. The device, now somewhat out of date, was at its most effective when used sparingly rather than throughout a composition. Among composers who used it productively were Vaughan Williams and, to a lesser extent, E. J. Moeran.

neo-romanticism, term for the reaction by some 20th century composers against the wave of neo-classicism which sprang up during the 1920s. The term, however, is not a very specific one.

Neri, Massimiliano, 17th century Italian organist and composer. He was first organist at St. Mark's, Venice, in 1644, and was court organist to the Elector of Cologne in 1664. His compositions include a book of motets (1664), *Sonate e canzone in chiesa et in camera* (1644) and sonatas for three to twelve instruments (1951). He continued the tradition of the ensemble *canzona* of Giovanni Gabrieli and was also a practitioner of the new style of the sonata.

Nerone (It., *Nero*), opera in four acts by Boito, to a libretto by the composer. Though left unfinished at the time of Boito's death, the music was completed by Tommasini and Toscanini, and the première was conducted by Toscanini at La Scala, Milan, in 1924. Among several other composers who wrote operas about the Roman emperor was Pietro Mascagni, whose *Nerone*, also produced at La Scala, had its première in 1935.

Netherlands Chamber Orchestra, ensemble founded in 1955 with Szymon Goldberg as its musical director. Though particularly esteemed for its Bach performances, the orchestra has a wide and interesting repertory.

Neue Liebeslieder (Ger., *New Songs of Love*), a set of fourteen waltzes with an epilogue (Zum Schluss) for vocal quartet and piano by Brahms, op 65 – a sequel to the earlier set entitled *Liebeslieder* op 52. Words of the waltzes by Georg Friedrich Daumer; words of the epilogue by Goethe.

Neues vom Tage, see NEWS OF THE DAY

Neukomm, Sigismund, Chevalier von (1778–1858), Austrian composer. He was a chorister at Salzburg Cathedral where he studied under Michael Haydn. Later he went to Vienna to study under Joseph Haydn. In 1809 he settled in Paris and made the acquaintance of Grétry, Cherubini and Cuvier. In 1812 he succeeded Dussek as pianist to Talleyrand. He accompanied the Duke of Luxembourg to Rio de Janeiro in 1816 and stayed there as *maître de chapelle* to Dom Pedro until the revolution in 1821. The last years of his life he lived alternately in Paris and London. His compositions include operas, over 200 songs, piano and organ pieces, choral and chamber music, oratorios, Masses, and a Requiem for Louis XVI (1815).

neuma (from the Greek for breath), phrase of melody used by medieval theorists to illustrate the characteristics and range of a MODE. The following is the neuma of the first mode in the Salisbury rite (W. H. Frere, *The Use of Sarum*, ii, Appendix page lxvii):

A neuma was occasionally used as the tenor in a 13th century MOTET, e.g. the neuma given above is the tenor of the motet 'Salve virgo Ave lux' (Y. Rokseth, *Polyphonies du XIIIe siècle*, ii, page 131).

neume (from the Greek for sign), individual sign in the notation used for eastern chant, and for western plainsong. By the end of the 12th century the neumes had evolved into the square and diamond-shaped forms of note which are still used in the printing of plainsong.

See NOTATION

Neusiedler, Hans (c. 1509–63), German lutenist and composer. He lived in Nuremberg from about 1530 and published collections of lute music in German tablature in 1536 (facsimile edition by *Institutio pro arte testudinis*, Neuss, 1974), 1540 and 1544. Some compositions have been published in *Denkmäler der*

Tonkunst in Osterreich, xxxvii, Jg. xviii (2). A *Jew's Dance* by him (printed in Davison and Apel's *Historical Anthology of Music*, no 105) has achieved fame as a curious example of bitonality, but unfortunately its jarring tones are due solely to a wrong transcription of the tablature in modern times owing to a misunderstanding of the lute tuning (see M. Morrow, 'Ayre on the F sharp String', in *Lute Society Journal*, ii, 1960).

Melchior Neusiedler (1531–90), German lutenist and composer, was probably related to Hans. He lived in Augsburg from 1552 to 1561, in Italy for some time after 1565, and in Innsbruck from 1580. He published two collections of lute music in Italian tablature at Venice in 1566, and a *Teutsch Lautenbuch* in 1574.

Newman, Ernest (1868–1959), English music critic, biographer and writer on music. He was successively critic of the *Manchester Guardian*, (1905), *Birmingham Post* (1906), *Observer* (1919) and *Sunday Times* (1920–58). He was guest critic on the New York *Evening Post* (1924–5). His main contribution to musical history was his exhaustive study of Wagner as man and composer. This resulted in several books – first *Wagner as Man and Artist* (1924), then *The Life of Richard Wagner* (four volumes, 1933–47) and *Wagner Nights* (1949). His other works include *Gluck and the Opera* (1895), *Hugo Wolf* (1907), *A Musical Critic's Holiday* (1925), *Opera Nights* (1943) and *More Opera Nights* (1955).

Newmarch, Rosa Harriet (1857–1940), English writer on music. In 1897 she went to Russia, studied at the Imperial Public Library under Vladimir Stasov and came into contact with most of the composers of the day. Later she helped to introduce important Russian and Czech music to the British public. She wrote many articles and lectures on Russian music and art, and from 1908–27 supplied programme notes for the Queen's Hall concerts – these were later published in book form. Her other works include *Chaikovsky* (1900) and *The Music of Czechoslovakia* (1942).

New Philharmonia Orchestra, London based symphony orchestra, formed in 1964 after its predecessor (called, simply, the Philharmonia Orchestra) had been disbanded. Originally, the orchestra had been privately run, by Walter Legge, with gramophone recording as one of its main activities. Today the players are self-governing. Otto Klemperer, towards the end of his life, was closely associated with the orchestra, and was its honorary president.

News of the Day (Ger., *Neues vom Tage*), opera in three parts by Hindemith, to a libretto by Marcellus Schiffer, first performed at Berlin 1929, in revised version, 1953. The opening of the work includes parts for two typewriters, and the music as a whole adopts a humorous idiom to describe the marital conflicts of a young couple, Laura and Eduard. Among the features of the score are the bathtub aria and a hymn to hot water – the libretto extols the virtues of electricity (so much so that a gas company once attempted to sue).

New World Symphony, see FROM THE NEW WORLD

New York Philharmonic-Symphony Orchestra, founded by U. C. Hill in 1842 as the Philharmonic Society of New York. It is the oldest symphony orchestra in the United States. The New York Symphony Society (founded in 1878 and conducted until

1885 by Leopold Damrosch, then by his son Walter) was absorbed by the New York Philharmonic in 1928, resulting in the double-barrelled name now employed. Permanent conductors have been: A. Seidl, 1892–8; E. Paur, 1898–1902; Safanov, 1906–9; Mahler, 1909–11; Stransky, 1911–20; Mengelberg, 1921–30; Toscanini, 1930–36; Barbirolli, 1937–40; Rodzinsky, 1943–7; Bruno Walter, 1947–9; Dmitri Mitropoulos, 1950. Leonard Bernstein, who became conductor in 1958, is now the orchestra's 'laureate conductor'.

Nibelung's Ring, The, see RING

Nicolò, see ISOUARD

Nichelmann, Christophe (1717–62), German composer. He studied under J. S. Bach at Leipzig and counterpoint under Quantz in Berlin. In 1744 he was appointed second cembalist under C.P.E. Bach at the Court of Frederick the Great. His output includes a treatise on melody (1755), as well as harpsichord concertos and sonatas.

Nicholson, Richard (c. 1570–1639), English organist and composer. He was probably organist and choirmaster at Magdalen College, Oxford, in 1595. In 1627 he became the first professor of music at Oxford under Dr. William Heather's foundation. His compositions include anthems, a motet, a madrigal in *The Triumphes of Oriana* (1601, reprinted in *The English Madrigal School*, xxxii), consort songs (printed in *Musica Britannica*, xxii) and music for instrumental ensemble.

Nicholson, Sydney Hugo (1875–1947), English organist and teacher. He was organist at Westminster Abbey from 1918–27, then founded the School of English Church Music in 1945, and directed it until his death.

nicht (Ger.), not.

Nicolai, Carl Otto Ehrenfried (1810–49), German composer and conductor. After running away from home, where he was unhappy, he studied in Berlin and Rome. In 1833 he became organist of the chapel of the Prussian Embassy at Rome. In 1837–8 he was *Kappelmeister* of the Kärntnertortheater in Vienna, returned to Rome in 1838 and composed a series of operas, and from 1841–47 was first *Kappelmeister* of the court opera in Vienna. He founded the Vienna Philharmonic concerts in 1842. In 1847 he became director of the court opera in Berlin. His most famous work, the lively comic opera *The Merry Wives of Windsor* was first produced there two months before his death from apoplexy. He also wrote two symphonies, chamber music, and some church music.

Nicolai, Philipp (1556–1608), Lutheran pastor, poet and amateur musician. His *Freudenspiegel des ewigen Lebens* (Frankfurt, 1599) contained the melodies of two chorales which were frequently used by Lutheran composers down to J. S. Bach. They are known in English collections as 'Sleepers, wake' and 'How brightly shines the morning star'.

Niecks, Friedrich (1845–1924), German born violinist and musical historian. He studied under his father and later under Langhans, Grunewald, Auer and Tausch. At thirteen he made his debut as a violinist in Dusseldorf. In 1868 A. C. Mackenzie invited him to be violinist in his string quartet in Edinburgh. He was appointed Reid Professor of Music at Edinburgh University in 1891. His books include *Frederick*

Chopin (1888), *A History of Programme Music* (1907) and a biography of Schumann which was published posthumously in 1925.

Niedt, Friedrich Erhard (1674–c. 1717), notary-public of Jena. He published a *Musicalische Handleitung*, of which the first part (Hamburg, 1700) gives rules for playing from figured bass, contained in a story which has interesting particulars on the teaching practices of German organists. Bach borrowed from it in compiling rules and examples for use in teaching. The second part appeared in 1706, and the third, edited by Mattheson, posthumously in 1717.

F. T. ARNOLD: *The Art of Accompaniment from a Thorough-Bass* (1931)

Nielsen, Carl August (1865–1931), Danish composer who became – with Sibelius, born in the same year – one of Northern Europe's most important and individual musical voices. He was born at Odense (also the hometown of Hans Andersen) on the island of Funen, studied at the Copenhagen Conservatory under Gade, and joined the Royal Orchestra as a violinist in 1891 (earlier he had played the bugle in the Odense military band). He was conductor of the orchestra from 1908–14, and was director of the Conservatory and the conductor of the Musical Society from 1915 until 1927. Though he soon established himself as Denmark's leading composer, it was not until the 1950s that his qualities, especially as a symphonist, began to win international recognition. His first symphony, completed in 1892, made history by beginning in one key and ending in another – not through eccentricity or clumsiness but through convincing tonal and structural principles which subsequently came to be referred to as 'progressive tonality'. These ideas stamped much of Nielsen's symphonic thinking, and were cogently worked out in many of his later works.

Each of his six symphonies is a work of character, strongly felt and powerfully argued, reflecting a musical personality which can be both bitter and humorous, thoughtful and breezy, and filled with inimitable dramatic strokes – as when a side drum marches starkly into the fifth symphony, disrupting its pastoral spirit. This represents Nielsen at his fiercest, but optimism is usually allowed to break through – most notably in the grandly sonorous but in no way superficial ending to the fourth symphony (known as *The Inextinguishable*). Nor in his concertos, especially those for clarinet and for violin, is there anything glib about Nielsen's inspiration. His operas, *Saul and David* (1902) and *Maskarade* (1906), deserve a wider circulation than they have so far achieved outside the composer's homeland. His chamber music, including a fine wind quintet, and his songs are characteristic of his warm-hearted personality. Two of his books have been published in English: *My Childhood* (1953) and *Living Music* (1953).

Nielsen, Ricardo (born 1908), Italian composer. He studied at the Liceo Musicale of Bologna, at Salzburg and under Carlo Gatti in Milan. His compositions include an opera, *The Incubus*, a *Sinfonia concertante* for piano and orchestra, psalms for male voices and orchestra, chamber music, piano works and songs.

niente (It.), nothing. Thus *quasi niente*, an instruction to a performer to refine the tone of his instrument or voice almost to a whisper.

Nightingale, The, opera in three acts by Stravinsky, to a libretto by the composer and Stepan Mitusov after the fairy tale by Hans Andersen. The first performance, at the Paris Opéra in 1914, was conducted by Pierre Monteux. Stravinsky later wrote a symphonic poem, *The Song of the Nightingale*, based on material from the opera, which was used as the music for a ballet, with choreography by Leonid Massine, at the Paris Opéra in 1920.

Night in May, A, *see* MAY NIGHT

Night on the Bare Mountain, orchestral work by Mussorgsky. He seems to have planned it originally as part of the music for Mengden's play *The Witch*. Later he turned it into a symphonic fantasia (1886–7), used it in the third act of the opera *Mlada* (1872), and when he died left it as part of his unfinished opera *Sorochintsy Fair* (1875). A more accurate title for the concert piece would be *St. John's Night on the Bare Mountain*. Rimsky-Korsakov later re-orchestrated the music and directed the first performance in St. Petersburg. There is a verbal description attached to the score:

'Subterranean sounds of unearthly voices. Appearance of the spirits of darkness followed by that of the god Chernobog. Chernobog's glorification and the Black Mass. The Revels. At the height of the orgies is heard from afar the bell of a little church, which causes the spirits to disperse. Dawn.'

Nights in the Gardens of Spain (Span., *Noches en los Jardines de España*), three symphonic impressions for piano and orchestra by Falla, composed 1909–15, and first performed in Madrid in 1916. Their titles are: *En el Generalife, Danza lejana* (distant dance), *En los jardines de la Sierra de Córdoba*.

Nikisch, Arthur (1855–1922), Hungarian-German conductor. He studied at the Vienna Conservatorium under Dessof and Hellmesberger. He started his career as a violinist in the Vienna Hofkappelle, then in 1882 became first conductor of the Leipzig opera. He was conductor of the Boston Symphony Orchestra, 1889–93; of the Royal Opera, Budapest, until 1895; and of the Leipzig Gewandhaus and Berlin Philharmonic Orchestra (with which he made many tours) until his death. In 1912 he toured the United States with the London Symphony Orchestra. He was one of the greatest and most influential conductors of his time, notably of Bruckner and Chaikovsky, and was renowned for the precision and intensity of his performances achieved with a clear but unostentatious conducting technique.

Nilsson, Birgit (born 1918), Swedish soprano. She studied at the Royal Academy in Stockholm and made her operatic debut in that city in 1946 as Agathe in *Der Freischutz*. After singing Lady Macbeth in Verdi's opera the following year, she went on to one success after another until she established herself as the leading Wagner soprano of the day. She appeared as Brünnhilde in the *Ring* at Munich in 1954 and 1955, thereafter becoming closely associated with this role, singing it in London and the United States, and recording it with Sir Georg Solti. She is also a noted exponent of the title-roles in Strauss's *Salome* and *Elektra* and Puccini's *Turandot*.

Nilsson, Bo (born 1938), Swedish composer, self-taught and sometimes referred to as the *enfant terrible* of modern Scandinavian music. His works include

Quantitaten (1958) for solo piano, *Madchentotenlieder* (1959) for soprano and chamber ensemble and *Reaktionen* (1960) for four percussionists.

Nin, Joaquín (Nin y Castellano) (1879–1949), Spanish-Cuban pianist and composer, father of Nin-Culmell. He studied piano under Carlos Vidiella in Barcelona and under Moszowski and d'Indy in Paris. He also studied at the Schola Cantorum, where he became teacher of piano in 1906. He lived for short periods in Berlin, Cuba, Brussels and Paris, and in 1939 returned to Havana, his birthplace. He edited collections of Spanish music and composed piano pieces, works for violin and piano, a ballet and songs for voice and orchestra.

His son, **Joaquín Maria Nin-Culmell** (born 1908), also a composer, was born in Berlin and now lives in the United States. He studied in New York, in Paris under Paul Braud and Dukas and in Granada under Manuel de Falla; later he became professor at the University of California. His works include a sonata and a concerto for piano, a quintet for piano and strings, and songs.

ninth, The interval of an octave and a second, totalling nine steps, e.g.:

For the so-called 'chord of the ninth' *see* CHORD.

Nivers, Guillaume Gabriel (1632–1714), French composer and theorist. From 1654 till his death he was organist of St. Sulpice. He was also organist to the King and music-master to the Queen. His three books of organ music, published between 1665 and 1675, had a considerable influence on French style in the second half of the 17th century (modern editions by N. Dufourcq, 1963, 1956 and 1958, respectively). He also published motets, editions of Gregorian chant, a *Traité de la composition* (1667), and other treatises.

G. BEECHEY: 'Guillaume Gabriel Nivers . . . his Organ Music and his Traité de la Composition', in *The Consort*, xxv (1968–9)

W. PRUITT: 'Bibliographie des oeuvres de Guillaume Gabriel Nivers', in *Recherches sur la musique française classique*, xiii (1973)

Nobilissima Visione (Lat., *Noblest Vision*), orchestral suite by Hindemith, first performed at Venice in 1938. It is based on a ballet of the same title (dealing with St. Francis of Assisi) which Hindemith had produced earlier that year.

nobilmente (It.), nobly. A term often used by Elgar. It refers to the method of performance and not, as has sometimes been supposed, to the composer's estimate of his music.

Noble, Dennis (1899–1966), English baritone, who was educated as a chorister at Bristol Cathedral and appeared regularly at Covent Garden, also in the United States and Italy. In addition he sang frequently as a soloist in choral works, and was especially notable in the first performance of Walton's *Belshazzar's Feast*.

Noces, Les, *see* WEDDING

noch (Ger.), still, yet. Thus *noch lebhaft*, still lively; *noch lebhafter*, even livelier.

Noches en los Jardines de España, *see* NIGHTS IN THE GARDENS OF SPAIN

nocturne, night-piece. A name introduced by John Field – from whom Chopin adopted it – for piano pieces which had a *cantabile* melody, often elaborately ornamented, over an arpeggiated or chordal accompaniment. Earlier, in its Italian form (*notturno*), the name was used to describe a type of serenade, usually scored for chamber ensemble and laid out in several movements. Haydn composed a series of *Notturni* for instrumental nonet.

Nocturnes, apart from the numerous pieces with this title by Field and Chopin, Debussy composed a set of three orchestral *Nocturnes* between 1893 and 1899. Their titles are *Nuages* (Clouds), *Fêtes* and *Sirenes*, and they were first performed as an entity in 1901. The third nocturne makes use of a wordless female chorus.

node, *see* HARMONICS

noël (Fr.), a Christmas carol or song. Many collections of noëls have been published in vocal form since the 16th century and as arrangements and variations for organ since the 17th century. A modern example is Marcel Dupré's *Variations sur un noël*.

noire (Fr.), British crotchet, U.S. quarter-note (literally 'black note').

Nola, Giovanni Domenico del Giovane da (c. 1510–1592), Italian composer. He was *maestro di cappella* at the Church of the Annunziata, Naples, from 1563 to 1588. His compositions, which were published between 1541 and 1564, include motets, madrigals, and villanellas *alla Napolitana*, of which he was one of the earliest composers.

non (It.), not.

nonet, combination of nine instruments or piece for such a combination, e.g. Schubert's *Eine kleine Trauermusik*, for two clarinets, two bassoons and double bassoon, two horns, and two trombones (1812).

non-harmonic note (U.S., non-harmonic tone), note which is not part of the chord with which it sounds, i.e. a passing note or appoggiatura.

Nonnengeige (Ger.), literally 'nun's fiddle'. One of the alternative names for the TROMBA MARINA.

Nono, Luigi (born 1924), Italian composer, pupil of Maderna and Scherchen. He began his career as a follower of Webern and quickly won attention outside Italy with his orchestral variations on a note series by Schoenberg, performed at Darmstadt in 1950. By the time he completed his opera, *Intolleranza* (1960), which mixed live and recorded performances, using actors and film sequences, he was recognised as one of Italy's major progressive composers. His other works include *Epitaph for Federico Garcia Lorca* for speaker, singers and orchestra, *Incontri* (Encounters) for chamber ensemble, and *Sul ponte di Hiroshima* (On the bridge of Hiroshima) for soprano, tenor and orchestra. In recent years he has used his music increasingly as a vehicle for his left-wing political views, sometimes to the point of seeming dauntingly dry and didactic.

Non più andrai, Figaro's aria at the end of Act 1 of Mozart's *The Marriage of Figaro*, in which he tells Cherubino what life will be like in the army.

Norcombe, Norcome, Daniel (c. 1576–before 1626), English composer and violinist. He was at the Danish court in 1599, but fled from Copenhagen, travelling through Germany and Hungary to Venice. He was later appointed a minor canon at St. George's Chapel, Windsor. The madrigal 'With angel's face and brightness' in *The Triumphes of Oriana* (1601, modern edition in *English Madrigal School*, xxxii) is probably by him, while the pieces for viol in Simpson's *The Division Violist* (1659) are probably by a relation with the same name.

Nørgård, Per (born 1932), Danish composer, pupil of Vagn Holmboe and Nadia Boulanger. In 1961 his *Fragment VI* for six orchestra groups won the international first prize at the Dutch music week, 'Gaudeamus', where the judges were Krenek, Ligeti and Stockhausen. His other works include a two-act opera, *The Labyrinth*; a ballet after Ionesco, *Le Jeune Homme à Marier*; an oratorio, *Babel*; and numerous orchestral pieces, chamber music and songs.

Norma, opera in two acts by Bellini, libretto by Felice Romani, first performed in Milan in 1831. One of the most famous and musically perfect examples of *bel canto* opera, *Norma* was greatly admired by Wagner, who considered that it had the dignity of a Greek tragedy. The story concerns a Druidic priestess torn between love and duty. The most famous aria is 'Casta Diva' in Act 1, in which Norma prays to the moon for peace between Gaul and Rome.

North, Roger (1653–1734), English lawyer and amateur musician, attorney-general to James II. His *Memoires of Musick* (edited by E. Rimbault, 1846) and *The Musicall Gramarian* (edited by Hilda Andrews, 1926) contain an interesting account of the music of his time and of the immediate past. His brother Francis North, Lord Guilford, published *A Philisophical Essay on Musick* (1677).

Nose, The, opera in two acts by Shostakovich, based on a satirical story by Gogol. First performed in Leningrad in 1930, this was Shostakovich's first opera and its progressiveness of outlook alarmed the Soviet authorities, giving advance warning of the furore caused a few years later by the composer's next opera, *Lady Macbeth of Mzensk*.

nota cambiata, *see* CAMBIATA

notation, the writing down of music so as to indicate its pitch and rhythm. From the early middle ages, letters were used to designate notes (*see* ODO), as at present. By the 6th and 7th centuries signs (neumes) over the words of plainsong were in use, both in the eastern and western churches. They had a common origin in the Greek prosodic signs, of which there were three which affected pitch—*oxeia* / (rise in pitch), *bareia* \ (fall in pitch), and *perispomene* ∧ (rise and fall). In evolving these signs into groups representing two or more notes, eastern (*see* BYZANTINE MUSIC) and western notation followed different paths. In their early stages both were mnemonic notations, inexact as to pitch, and serving to remind singers of music they had already memorised.

The first step towards a more exact notation of pitch was the use of a red line, drawn through the neumes, to represent the pitch of F, the next the addition of a yellow or green line for C. In the preface to his Antiphoner of c. 1025 Guido of Arezzo pointed out that the writing of neumes on three, four or more lines, marked at the beginning with letters of the monochord, made it possible for singers to read the music for themselves. By the 13th century the four line staff was accepted for plainsong and monophonic chansons, and the five line staff for polyphonic music. There have been only occasional or periodic exceptions, such as the six or seven line staff in English keyboard music in the 16th century. Theoretically, any one of the three or more CLEFS may be placed on any line of the staff. The variety of positions in use until the 17th century has been progressively reduced in practice to one position each for the G and F clefs, and two for the C clef.

ACCIDENTALS are a device for changing the pitch of a line or space by a semitone, or two successive semitones. Their use has developed from the flat as a clef in plainsong to the KEY SIGNATURES of the complete key-system of the 18th century. The complications which arise from the notation of music in a completely chromatic (or even microtonal) system on a staff devised for diatonic music have given rise to some attempts to 'reform' the notation of pitch, without practical result.

For the writing of music for string instruments on which chords and arpeggios were normally played, and of organ music in polyphonic style, various forms of TABLATURE notation were used in the 16th and 17th centuries. The advantage of tablature lies in its closer relation to the actual fingering of the string instrument, and to the style of organ music, as well as in its greater compactness.

The notation of rhythm has had a more varied history. The rhythm of neumes was not shown in their notation, but was established by their relation to the words, and by tradition and usage. Some manuscripts shortly before the 10th century had letters above the neumes (e.g. x = *expectare*, to wait; c = *celeriter*, quickly) which affected the rhythm, and *ad hoc* rhythmic signs were an important part of Byzantine notation. In the first period of mensurable music (c. 1150–c. 1250) the note-forms which had been evolved from the neumes were used in rhythmic patterns involving the relation: long = 3 breves. The long ⸲ and breve ■ were used both singly and in combinations, called LIGATURES, which had developed from compound neumes, and the arrangement and order of the ligatures indicated a particular rhythmic mode (*see* RHYTHMIC MODES), which was maintained more or less throughout the part.

By the middle of the 13th century the rhythm of the upper parts in a MOTET had become more varied than modal notation could intelligibly comprise, and a notation more adequate to the newer motets was formulated by Franco of Cologne. His *Ars cantus mensurabilis* (c. 1260), which was the basis of all subsequent developments in the notation of rhythm, was based on the four note-values: duplex long ▬, long, breve, and semibreve ◆, and their corresponding rests, and laid the foundation of the system of MENSURAL NOTATION.

The differences in the 14th century between French notation as outlined by Philippe de Vitry (*Ars nova*, c. 1320) and Italian notation as expounded by Marchetto of Padua (*Pomerium*, 1318) were mainly concerned with the method of writing groups of semibreves and minims (*semibreves minimae*). Both recognised duple (imperfect) time as having equal standing with triple (perfect), and both used time signatures to indicate the relations of note-values in a composition. By the end of the century the French signatures were generally accepted, and one (C) is still in use. To represent more complex rhythms the use of red for imperfect notes was introduced, and the degree of complication possible with the combination of colour and signs of PROPORTION reached its highest point c. 1400 (*see* the facsimiles in W. Apel, *French Secular Music of the Late Fourteenth Century*, 1950, and in *The Old Hall Manuscripts*, edited by A. Ramsbottom, iii, 1938, where there were black, red and blue notes).

In the course of the 15th century the writing of notes changed, so that black became white and red became black. This was a change of convenience, largely due to writing on paper instead of parchment, and not a change of system. The gradual change during the course of the 16th and 17th centuries from the concept of measured rhythm to that of metrical rhythm caused more than the usual number of anomalies and of differences of local practice in the notation of rhythm. The change involved the introduction of BAR lines, of TIME SIGNATURES, of TEMPO marks, of the TIE, and of the grouping of notes smaller than the crotchet (called in Britain 'the new tied-note'). By the middle of the 18th century all these devices had settled down into their modern usages.

Among the chief accessories to modern notation are the various marks of expression, which multiplied enormously during the 19th century. They may affect rhythm (e.g. *accelerando*, *rallentando*), intensity (e.g. *piano*, *forte*, *crescendo*, *diminuendo*), phrasing (e.g. the slur, the *staccato* dot), accentuation (e.g. *sforzando*, *marcato*), touch (e.g. *martellato*), or a mental attitude to be conveyed (e.g. *innig*, *nobilmente*).

Today, though traditional composers accept the system of notation more or less as it stands, the quantity of notational innovations has been tantamount to a musical revolution. New symbols and modifications have been introduced to fulfil the needs of more advanced forms of modern music. In some scores the composer's explanatory notes on how to interpret his symbols occupy more pages than the music itself. But though these symbols and diagrams sometimes seem merely eccentric or wilful, at other times they are of real value.

W. APEL: *The Notation of Polyphonic Music, 900–1600* (fifth edition, 1961)

H. COLE: *Sounds and Signs* (1974)

C. G. PARRISH: *The Notation of Medieval Music* (1958)

H. RISATTI: *New Music Vocabulary* (1975)

E. WELLESZ: *History of Byzantine Music and Hymnography* (1949)

J. WOLF: *Handbuch der Notationskunde*, two volumes (1913–19)

note cluster (U.S., tone cluster), term coined by Henry Cowell for a dissonant group of notes, lying close together and played usually on a piano. Cowell pioneered the effect, which can be obtained by applying the fist or forearm, or even a strip of wood of suitable length, to the piano keyboard. Charles Ives also employed note clusters in his *Concord Sonata* (completed 1915) – an early example of a device which today has become commonplace. Note clusters can be played on instruments other than the piano; in Britten's church opera, *Curlew River*, an organ is used.

note row, the order of notes chosen by a composer as the basis, or gravitational force, of a composition. In twelve-note music, a note row would consist of twelve chromatic notes, from which the rest of the work derives through the development and mutation of those notes. A note row need not, however, consist of twelve notes only; nor, except in the strictest form of twelve-note music, need the repetition of a note be forbidden until the other eleven have been sounded. In the United States the expression twelve-tone row is preferred to twelve-note row, though British authorities regard this as sloppy – an octave contains twelve semitones, not twelve tones, and twelve-note row is thus a more precise definition.

note sensible *see* LEADING NOTE

notes égales (Fr., equal notes), indication found in French music of the 17th and early 18th centuries. Its purpose is to warn the player that where there is a group of short notes of the same value (e.g. a group of quavers) he is to make all the notes of the group equal, as written, and not to follow the conventions of the period by making them alternately long and short. A series of dots, one over each note of a group, is sometimes used to convey the same warning. In such cases the modern performer needs a further warning that the dots do not mean *staccato*. *See* DOT (2.iv), NOTES INÉGALES.

notes inégales (Fr., unequal notes). In French music of the 17th and early 18th centuries it was the custom to vary the monotony of a succession of short notes (e.g. quavers) of the same value by making them unequal in length. Normally no instruction to this effect was given by the composer: the practice was taken for granted. The commonest treatment was to lengthen the odd-numbered notes and shorten the even-numbered notes in compensation. *See* DOT, NOTES EGALES.

Notker (called Balbulus, i.e. the stammerer) (c. 840–912), the most famous member of the Music School of St. Gall, who wrote poems to the melodies of the Alleluia of the Mass to form SEQUENCES. He also wrote the poems, and probably the music, of new sequences. From his time until the Council of Trent in the 16th century the sequence was the most widely cultivated form of liturgical poetry. A guide to modern editions of melodies attributed to Notker is in B. Stäblein's 'Notkeriana', *Archiv für Musikwissenschaft*, xix-xx (1962–3), page 84.

W. VON DEN STEINEN: *Notker der Dichter* (1948)

Notre Dame (Fr., Our Lady), the cathedral church of Paris, the construction of which began in 1163. During the late 12th and early 13th centuries it was an important centre for church music and particularly for the development of church polyphony in the form known as ORGANUM. The two leading composers associated with Notre Dame at this period were LEONINUS and PEROTINUS. Because of its reputation as a musical centre the term 'Notre Dame school' is generally applied to all the polyphonic music of this period which appears to be of French or Anglo-French origin.

Nottebohm, Martin Gustav (1817–82), German musical historian. He studied in Berlin under Berger and Dehn, and in Leipzig where he became a friend of Mendelssohn and Schumann. From 1845 he lived in Vienna. He edited Beethoven's sketch-books, and compiled thematic catalogues of Beethoven's and Schubert's works.

notturno (It.), night piece: (1) a title given by the 18th century composers to music for evening entertainment, e.g. Mozart's *Notturno*, K 286, for four small orchestras, each composed of a string quartet and two horns, and Haydn's eight *Notturni* for nine instruments, written in 1790 for the king of Naples;

(2) in the nineteenth century, the Italian equivalent of the NOCTURNE.

novachord, electronic domestic six-octave keyboard instrument, akin to a small organ. It has stops for varying the tone colour and pedals for controlling and sustaining the volume.

Novák, Vitězslav (1870–1949), Czech composer and teacher. While at Prague University reading law, he studied music at the Prague Conservatory under Jiránek (piano) and Dvořák (composition). Dvořák's influence made Novák take up music professionally, and Brahms helped him publish his first works. He taught as a professor at the Prague Conservatory for many years. His music was influenced at first by the German romantic composers, but later developed a distinctly Czech style. His operas include *The Imp of Zvikov* (1915), *The Lantern* (1923) and *The Grandfather's Heritage* (1926). He also wrote symphonic poems, a cantata entitled *The Spectre's Bride* (same subject as Dvořák's), string quartets, piano pieces and songs.

Noveletten (Ger.), 'short stories'. Title given to short instrumental pieces, usually of descriptive character. It was first used by Schumann, who wrote a set of eight piano pieces, op 21, under that title (1838).

Novello, Vincent (1781–1861), London publisher, editor, organist and composer. He was organist of the chapel at the Portuguese Embassy from 1797–1822, and founded the music publishing firm of Novello in 1811. He edited many collections of music including anthems by Boyce, Croft, and Greene, Masses by Mozart, Haydn, and Beethoven, and Purcell's church music.

His son, **Joseph Alfred Novello** (1810–96), succeeded to the family business, and instituted cheap editions of standard works. He also produced concerts, and introduced Mendelssohn's works to England.

Clara Anastasia Novello (1818–1908), Vincent's daughter, became one of the most famous sopranos of her time, earning the praise of Mendelssohn and Schumann.

Noye's Fludde, opera in one act by Britten, to a libretto taken from the Chester Miracle Plays. The title is early English for 'Noah's Flood', and the music is intended principally (though not necessarily) for performance in church (with the audience joining in traditional hymns. It was first performed at the 1958 Aldeburgh Festival.

Nozze di Figaro, Le, *see* MARRIAGE OF FIGARO, THE

Nuits d'Été (Fr. *Summer Nights*), song cycle, op 7, by Berlioz, to poems from Théophile Gautier's *La comédie de la mort*. Though they are usually sung by a soprano or mezzo-soprano, the character of these six songs, and the wide vocal compass demanded by them, really necessitates their being divided (as Berlioz originally intended) between different voices. A special feature of the cycle is that in its definitive version it has an orchestral, not a piano, accompaniment. Dating from 1841 (though not completely orchestrated until fifteen years later) it was the first important orchestral song cycle ever written. In this respect it anticipated Mahler, as it did also in its concentration on a single subject (in this case, aspects of love). The six songs are:

(1) *Villanelle*;
(2) *Le spectre de la rose* (spectre of the rose);
(3) *Sur les lagunes* (on the lagoons);
(4) *Absence*;
(5) *Au cimetière* (in the cemetery);
(6) *L'île inconnue* (the unknown island).

number opera (Ger., *Nummeroper*), opera consisting of 'numbers', i.e. arias, duets, ensembles, etc., separated by recitative or spoken dialogue. Number operas were prevalent until the eighteenth century and even later, until composers (especially Wagner and Verdi) began to react against them and to advocate a more continuous form of opera. In the present century, some composers have deliberately reverted to number operas if they think the form is appropriate to the work they are writing (e.g. Stravinsky's *The Rake's Progress* and Hindemith's *Cardillac*).

nun's fiddle, *see* TROMBA MARINA

Nuove Musiche, Le (It.), collection of monodies published in 1602 by Giulio Caccini. In the foreward he discusses the new style of singing, his own part in developing it, and the use of such ornaments as the *trillo* and the *gruppo*. A modern translation by H. Wiley Hitchcock, with an English translation of the foreword, was published in 1970.

nut, (1) the part of a bow which is held by the player of a stringed instrument. It incorporates a screw device by which the tension of the hairs can be adjusted;

(2) a strip of ebony at the peg-box end of the finger-board of a stringed instrument which keeps the strings raised slightly above the level of the finger-board and marks off the sounding length at that end.

Nutcracker, The (Russ., *Shchelkunchik*), ballet by Chaikovsky. Ivanov's choreography was based on a fairy-tale by E. T. A. Hoffmann. The first performance was at St. Petersburg in 1892. Though often known by a French title (*Casse-Noisette*), the use of this nomenclature is merely an affectation outside France. Chaikovsky also prepared a concert suite from the ballet, containing the following numbers:

(1) Miniature overture.

(2) Characteristic dances.
  (a) March.
  (b) Dance of the Sugar-Plum Fairy.
  (c) Russian dance – Trepak.
  (d) Arab dance.
  (e) Chinese dance.
  (f) Reed-pipe dance.

(3) Waltz of the Flowers.

Nystroem, Gösta (1890–1966), Swedish composer, pupil of d'Indy. His works include a *Sea Symphony* and other orchestral works, stage music and songs. He was also a painter of some distinction.

obbligato (It.), literally 'essential' or 'obligatory'. The term refers to a part, usually instrumental, which cannot be dispensed with in performance, as distinct from a part which is optional, or *ad libitum*. An obbligato part, therefore, is usually an important one – like the part for clarinet in Schubert's song 'The Shepherd on the Rock'. Earlier, obbligato parts had been much used during the baroque period. Muffat pointed out that the concertos in his *Auserlesene . . . Instrumental-Musik* (1701), which were modelled on those of Corelli, could be played by the solo instruments of the *concertina* alone; hence these were *obbligato* instruments. The term came to be applied particularly in this sense, as in Vivaldi's *L'Estro Armonico*, for example, where the first concerto is *con quattro violini obbligati*. In some music in the 19th century the term was applied in the opposite sense to an additional part which is optional.

Oberon, opera in three acts by Weber, to a libretto by James Robinson Planché (founded on William Sotheby's translation of Wièland's poem *Oberon*). Weber's last opera was commissioned by Covent Garden where it was conducted by the composer in 1826 – less than a month before his death. The score (which has no connection with Shakespeare's *A Midsummer Night's Dream*) contains a wealth of beautiful music, unfortunately hamstrung by a maladroit text – in Tovey's famous phrase, Weber poured his last and finest music into a pigtrough. Nevertheless, the work is still performed from time to time, especially in Germany, though whether German translation disguises the weaknesses of the English libretto is debatable. The overture and the soprano aria, 'Ocean, thou mighty monster' (with its fore-tastes of Wagner), are familiar concert-hall excerpts. The action ranges from the court of Charlemagne to that of Harun al Rashid.

obertas, Polish round dance in fast triple time, also known as the *oberek*. Chopin's mazurka, op 56, no 2, is in the style of an *obertas*.

Oberto, Conte di San Bonifacio, opera in two acts by Verdi, to a libretto by Piazza, revised by Merelli and Solera. This was Verdi's first opera, and its production at La Scala, Milan, in 1839 led to a contract for three more operas for that theatre. The principal soprano role in this 13th century drama of seduction and death was originally played by Giuseppina Strepponi, who eventually became Verdi's second wife. Though obviously immature, the music reveals a number of characteristically Verdian traits and was hugely successful at its first performance.

Oberwerk (Ger.), swell organ.

oblique motion, term describing two melodic lines or parts, one of which moves while the other stays on the same note:

oboe, woodwind instrument with a conical bore and a double reed. It is non-transposing, and has a natural scale of D. Although still higher notes are attainable, its generally accepted range is from:

Oboe-type instruments have a long history, stretching back to Sumer and Ancient Egypt. The modern oboe is a descendant of the medieval and Renaissance instruments called shawms. Shawms were made in various sizes: in Germany the small, high ones were called *Schalmei*, and the large *Pommern* (Fr., *bombarde*). The family provided the principal reed instruments for medieval wind bands.

Out of these developed, during the 16th and 17th centuries, the *hautbois*, or 'high-wood' instruments, and from them developed the hautboys and bassoons of the 17th and 18th centuries. Early hautboys were harsh and powerful, and could compete with brass. Present day oboes date from about the period of Mozart and Haydn, although many improvements were made during the later 18th and 19th centuries.

During the late baroque period the oboe was used frequently as a solo instrument in chamber music, concertos, and cantatas. With the advent of the classical era, a pair of oboes was essential for every symphony orchestra, and later composers, such as Wagner, sometimes required three or more.

Modern oboes have a wider scope than their forebears, since recent technical discoveries, most of them attributable to the Swiss oboist Heinz Holliger, have opened up new possibilities, including the playing of two or more notes simultaneously.

The oboe family now includes:

(1) **E flat oboe**, rare instrument pitched a minor third above the normal oboe. It is unknown in the symphony orchestra, its use being confined to certain continental military bands.

(2) **oboe d'amore** (It.; Fr., *hautbois d'amore*; Ger., *Liebesoboe*), slightly larger than the normal oboe and with a pear-shaped bell, this instrument originated in Germany about 1720. As its name suggests its tone quality is more tender than the oboe's. It is pitched a minor third lower and treated as a transposing instrument. However, it lacks the key for producing the written low B flat, and consequently its lowest sounding note is A flat. It became obsolete with the advent

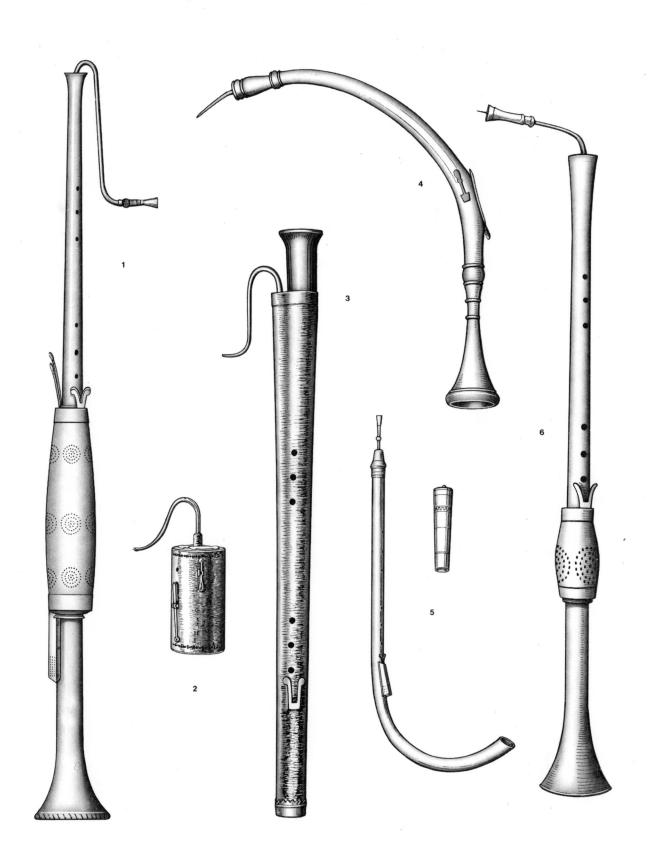

Oboe family: (1) shawm (bass) (2) racket (3) curtal (double) (4) *oboe da caccia* (5) crumhorn (tenor) (6) shawm (tenor)

Oboe family: (7) double bassoon or contra bassoon (8) bassoon (9) *cor anglais* (10) oboe (11) sarusophone

of the classical period, only to be revived in the twentieth century by such composers as Strauss in his *Sinfonia Domestica* and Debussy in *Iberia*.

(3) **cor anglais** (Fr.; Ger., *Englisch horn*; It., *corno Inglese*), the custom of referring to this instrument as an English horn has almost died out; it is neither English nor a horn, but a large oboe with a bulb-shaped bell. It was developed from the *oboe da caccia* (see below) and is a transposing instrument in F. Like the *oboe d'amore* it lacks a key for the written low B flat, although at one time this seems to have existed. Consequently its sounding range for general purposes is from

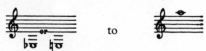

Higher notes are obtainable, but they are of better quality on the oboe. Although Haydn, Beethoven, and Antonin Rejcha wrote for the *cor anglais*, it was not until Berlioz exploited it in his *Symphonie Fantastique* that it really began to come into its own. Romantic and modern composers have favoured it greatly, with the result that orchestras have a player who specializes on it, while also doubling for third (or fourth) oboe.

(4) **oboe da caccia** (It., literally 'hunting oboe'; Fr., *taille*; early Eng., tenor hautboy), developed from the alto *Pommer*. It was much used by Bach and is an early form of the *cor anglais*.

(5) **Heckelphone** (Fr., *hautbois baryton*), rarely used instrument aptly described by its French name. It is pitched an octave below the oboe, but lacks a key for the low B flat. Strauss wrote for it in his opera *Salome*.

A. CARSE: *Musical Wind Instruments* (1939)

Obrecht or **Hobrecht, Jacob** (1450–1505), Flemish composer. He was choirmaster to the Guild of our Lady at his probable home-town, Berg-op-Zoom, from 1480 to 1484. Subsequently he was Master of the Children at Cambrai Cathedral (1484–5) and succentor at St. Donatian, Bruges (1485–91), spending some time on leave at Ferrara during the years 1487 to 1488. He succeeded Barbireau at Notre Dame, Antwerp, in 1492. From 1496 to 1498 he was back at Berg-op-Zoom, and returned to Italy in 1504.

Obrecht was one of the leading composers of his period. As compared with Ockeghem's works in the same forms, his 24 Masses (a much larger number than any of his contemporaries) and 22 motets show their slightly later style in their more frequent use of sequence in the melodies, of imitation between the parts and of definite cadences. He also composed *chansons* to Dutch, French and Italian words. A complete edition of his works has been edited by Johannes Wolf (1908–21). It is not certain that the setting of the *St. Matthew Passion* published in volume xxviii is actually by Obrecht; it may be by Longueval. A new edition of Obrecht's works, begun by Albert Smijers in 1953, is being continued by Maurice van Crevel.

L. G. VAN HOORN: *Jacob Obrecht* (1968) [in French]

Oca del Cairo, L' (It., *The Goose of Cairo*), unfinished opera by Mozart, to a libretto by Varesco. Composed in 1783, between *Die Entführung* and *Figaro*, it is a work of minor importance by Mozartian standards.

Nevertheless, various hands have seen fit to complete it. In Paris in 1867 there was a performance eked out with other music by Mozart; more recent versions have been made by Mortari and Redlich.

ocarina, a small pear-shaped wind instrument of the recorder type and with a similar tone quality. With its limited range it is hardly more than a toy, but a few composers, notably Janáček, have found it of use.

O'Carolan, Turlough (1670–1738), Irish harper and composer, blinded by smallpox in his youth. Many of his airs were well-known in the 18th century and appear in the Bunting and Petrie collections, while some were set to new words by Thomas Moore. Shield adapted one as 'The Arethusa'. 220 of his tunes, edited by Donal O'Sullivan, have been published.

Occasional Oratorio, work by Handel, composed in 1746 to celebrate the suppression of the Jacobite rebellion. The text was compiled from various sources including Milton's Psalms. The first performance was given in London in 1746.

Oceanides, The, symphonic poem, op 73, by Sibelius. Composed in 1914, the music portrays the Aallottaret – the Finnish equivalent of the sea nymphs of Greek mythology.

Ocean, thou mighty monster, aria in Act 2 of Weber's *Oberon* in which the heroine, Reiza, hails the ocean and the boat which she hopes is coming to her rescue. This large-scale aria, which uses material also to be found in the *Oberon* overture, is one of Weber's grandest conceptions, pointing the way towards Wagnerian music drama.

ochetto, *see* HOCKET

Ochsenmenuette, Die, *see* OX MINUET

Ockeghem (Okeghem, Ockenheim), Johannes (Jan) (c. 1430–c. 1495), Flemish composer. He was a chorister at Antwerp Cathedral from 1443 to 1444 and was in the chapel of the Duke of Bourbon from 1446 to 1468. He joined the chapel of the King of France in Paris in 1453 and was in the royal service until his death. In 1459, he became treasurer of St. Martin's Abbey in Tours, and in 1465 the king's *maître de chapelle*. He composed some sixteen Masses, motets, and *chansons*. He was the first in the long succession of famous Flemish composers. The characteristics of his style are continuity of flow, achieved by long overlapping phrases and infrequent use of cadences, and independence of the parts, which implies, of course, absence of imitation. Two volumes, containing sixteen Masses, of the projected complete edition of his works have been edited (second edition, 1959) by D. Plamenac; two *chansons* were printed in Petrucci's *Odhecaton* (1501; modern edition by H. Hewitt, 1942).

E. KŘENEK: *Johannes Ockeghem* (1953)

Octandre, work by Varèse for seven wind instruments and double bass, composed in 1924.

octave, (1) the INTERVAL between the first and eighth notes of the diatonic SCALE, e.g.:

Notes which are an octave apart are called by the same letter name (thus a note an octave above C is also called C). The upper note has exactly twice the number of vibrations of the lower one (see ACOUSTICS) and the two notes have the effect of mutual duplication and reinforcement. To play in octaves means that each note is doubled one or more octaves above or below.

(2) A 4 foot diapason stop on the organ, also known as the principal.

octave coupler, a mechanical device on the organ which automatically doubles at the octave above any note which is played. A sub-octave coupler similarly doubles at the octave below.

octave fiddle (Ger., *Oktargeige*), an obsolete, small, four-stringed instrument, tuned an octave below the violin.

octet, a piece for eight solo instruments, e.g. Beethoven's octet in E flat, op 103, for two oboes, two clarinets, two horns and two bassoons, and Schubert's in F for two violins, viola, cello, double bass, clarinet, bassoon, and horn. Mendelssohn's octet in E flat, op 20, is for a double string quartet of four violins, two violas, and two cellos. Octets can also be composed for eight voices. At one time in the United States there was an eight piano octet (one of whose specialities was an arrangement of Rakhmaninov's prelude in C sharp minor).

octobass (Fr., *octo basse*), a three-stringed double-bass of vast proportions invented in 1849 by J. B. Vuillaume in Paris. Levers were needed to stop the strings because of their thickness. The octobass could descend an octave below the lowest note of the cello, a downward compass that can be obtained on the modern five-stringed double-bass or on a four-stringed one equipped with an extension mechanism. Although considered usable by Berlioz, the instrument failed to establish itself.

ode, (1) a form of strophic poetry. Odes of Horace were set in the first half of the 16th century for solo voice and lute in the note-values corresponding to their metrical feet;

(2) a vocal composition in honour of some person or occasion, e.g. in the 17th century Purcell's *Welcome Songs* and *Birthday Odes* and his three *Odes for St. Cecilia's Day*. In musical form these works are cantatas, as are the odes of John Blow and Handel's *St. Cecilia's Day* and *Alexander's Feast*. Following this tradition, later odes, e.g. Parry's setting of A. C. Benson's *Ode to Music* (1901) and Holst's of Whitman's *Ode to Death* (1919) are usually written for chorus, with or without soloists, and orchestra. On the other hand, Stravinsky's *Ode* (in spite of being subtitled 'Elegiacal Chant') is an orchestral work. It was composed in 1943 in memory of Koussevitsky's wife.

Ode to Napoleon, work by Schoenberg (op 41) for speaker, strings and piano, to a text by Byron. Composed in 1942, the piece is an attack on despotism, drawing parallels between Napoleon and Hitler. The spoken part is rhythmically set down in the score, though the actual pitch of the words is left to the performer's discretion.

Odhecaton (from the Greek for song and hundred), the *Harmonice musices Odhecaton A*, published in Venice by Petrucci in 1501, was the first printed collection of polyphonic music. It contained 96 chansons written in the latter part of the 15th century by Agricola, Compère, Busnois, Isaac, Josquin, Ockeghem, Obrecht and other composers. A modern edition by Helen

Jacques Offenbach, at once the inventor and supreme exponent of modern *opéra bouffe*

Hewitt was published in 1942, and a facsimile of the 1504 edition in 1973. Two further collections (labelled *B* and *C*) were published in 1502 and 1503.

Odington, Walter de (Walter of Evesham) (before 1278–after 1316), Benedictine monk, musical theorist, and astronomer who spent some time at the monastery at Evesham and also at Oxford. His treatise, *De Speculatione Musicae* (c. 1300; edited by Frederick F. Hammond, 1970), is one of the most informative of the period.

Odo of Cluny (c. 879–942), French musical theorist and composer. He was a canon of St. Martin's, Tours, in 899, and subsequently studied under Rémy d'Auxerre in Paris. In 909 he entered the monastery at Beaune, and became abbot of Cluny in 927. His *Dialogus de Musica*, c. 935 (printed in Gerbert's *Scriptores*, i, p. 251; translated in O. Strunk, *Source Readings in Music History*, p. 103) contains a discussion of the MONO-CHORD which is the earliest to give a complete set of letters for the notes of the scale from *L*:

to *aa*:

Odysseus (It., *Ulisse*), opera by Dallapiccola, inspired by Homer, first performed in Berlin in 1968.

Oedipus at Colonus (Ger., *Oedipus auf Kolonos*), incidental music, op 93, by Mendelssohn for the tragedy by Sophocles. Scored for male chorus and orchestra, the music was first performed at Potsdam in 1845.

Oedipus Rex, 'opera-oratorio' in two acts by Stravinsky. The *libretto* is a Latin translation by Jean Daniélou of a French play by Cocteau based on the Greek tragedy by Sophocles. The composer chose a Latin text for the sake of impersonality, though the intensity of the music tends to act against this aim. The work, in which the characters are asked to wear masks as in a Greek play, was first performed in Paris in 1927.

oeuvre (Fr.), opus

Offenbach, Jacques (1819–80), German-French composer. He was born in Cologne (the son of a cantor in a synagogue) but educated in Paris, where he spent most of his life. In 1849 he became conductor at the Théâtre Français. From 1855–61 he was manager of the Bouffes Parisiens, and from 1873–5 of the Théâtre de la Gaîté. Of his ninety operettas the exhilaratingly sparkling and satirical *Orpheus in the Underworld* (1858), *La Belle Hélène* (1864) and *La Vie Parisienne* (1866) achieved very great popularity. His most important work, *The Tales of Hoffmann*, was unfinished at the time of his death, but was completed by Guiraud and produced in 1881. He published in 1877 *Notes d'un musicien en voyage* – an account of his visit to the United States in the previous year.

> S. SITWELL: *La Vie Parisienne: A Tribute to Offenbach* (1937)

offertory (Lat., *offertorium*, Fr., *offertoire*), part of the Proper of the Mass, sung after the Credo while the priest is preparing and offering the oblation of bread and wine. It was originally a psalm with an antiphon but now consists simply of an antiphon. Polyphonic settings of the offertory were composed during the 15th and 16th centuries, and in the 17th century instrumental *offertoria* were written for performance at this point in the service, e.g. Frescobaldi's organ ricercars *dopo il Credo* in the *Fiori Musicali* (1635).

Office, the 'Hour Services' of the Roman Catholic Church, also used by the Church of England for Matins and Evensong. In Roman Catholic liturgy, Divine Office occurs eight times daily, as follows:-

    (1) Matins, between midnight and dawn;
    (2) Lauds, immediately after Matins;
    (3) Prime, about 6 a.m.;
    (4) Terce, about 9 a.m.;
    (5) Sext, about noon;
    (6) None, about 3 p.m.;
    (7) Vespers, at sunset;
    (8) Compline, between Vespers and retiring.

Offrandes, work by Varèse for soprano and chamber orchestra, based on poems by Vicente Huidobro and José Juan Tablada. Composed in 1922, it was the first of Varèse's works to gain a performance in the United States.

Ogdon, John (born 1937), English pianist and composer, joint winner (with Vladimir Ashkenazy) of the International Chaikovsky Competition in Moscow in 1962. His repertory is unusually large and adventurous, with special emphasis on music written in the second half of the 19th century and first half of the 20th, e.g. Busoni's piano concerto, with which he is particularly associated. His own compositions, including a piano concerto, a sonata and preludes for piano, reflect his tastes as a performer.

ohne (Ger.), without.

Oiseau de Feu, L', *see* FIREBIRD

Oiseaux Exotiques (exotic birds), work by Messiaen for piano, wind instruments and percussion, composed in 1956.

Oistrakh, David (1908–74), Russian violinist, pupil of Pyotr Stoliarsky. Though he won the Ysaye Prize in Brussels in 1937, he did not travel extensively in the West until the 1950s – before that, listeners had to rely on his gramophone records as evidence of his superb qualities as a musician and of his pure sweetness of tone. Numerous Russian composers have written works for him. His son, Igor Oistrakh (born 1931), is also a noted violinist.

Okeghem, *see* OCKEGHEM

Okeover (Okar, Oker), John, English organist and composer. He studied at Oxford and was organist at Wells Cathedral (1619–39 and 1660–62) and Gloucester Cathedral (1640–44). He composed anthems and three- and five-part fancies for viols. A fancy and a pavan are printed in *Musica Britannica*, ix.

Oktargeige, *see* OCTAVE FIDDLE

Oktave (Ger.), octave.

Old Hall Manuscript, manuscript collection of English polyphonic music of the late 14th and early 15th centuries, which was acquired by John Stafford Smith (1750–1836) and given by his descendants to the library of St. Edmund's College, Old Hall, near Ware. In 1974 it passed to the British Library.

The manuscript was originally planned as a well-organized selection of settings of the movements of the

Old Hall MS: the 'Roy Henry' Gloria

Ordinary of the Mass (excepting the Kyrie, together with Mary-antiphons and five motets. The compositions which form part of this plan were all copied by the same hand, probably between 1410 and 1415. They include at least 23 pieces by Leonel Power, as well as pieces by Byttering, Chirbury, Cooke, Olyver, Pycard and Typp. Two of the selections are headed by pieces attributed to 'Roy Henry', but it has yet to be established whether they were composed by Henry IV (1399–1413) or Henry V (1413–22). The provenance of this earlier 'layer' of the Old Hall Manuscript is not known, but it seems that around 1415 the book came to be used in the Royal Household chapel, and that in the next five years various hands added new pieces by composers such as Damett, Dunstable, Forest and Sturgeon. A modern edition of the entire collection by Andrew Hughes and Margaret Bent was published in 1969.

 M. BENT: 'Sources of the Old Hall Music,' in *Proceedings of the Royal Musical Association*, xciv (1968)

 A. HUGHES: 'The Old Hall Manuscript; a Re-appraisal,' in *Musica Disciplina*, xxi (1967)

Old Hundredth, the hymn-tune known by this name first appeared in the Genevan Psalter of 1551, set to Psalm 134, in this form:

It was adopted in Thomas Sternhold's 'Anglo-Genevan' Psalter *Four Score and Seven Psalmes of David in English Mitre* (1561), where it was set to Psalm 100 and also to a metrical version of the Lord's Prayer. It was known as the 'Hundredth' in the Psalters of the old version, and became the 'Old Hundredth' after the publication of Tate and Brady's new version of the Psalter in 1696. In the United States it is known as 'Old Hundred'.

oliphant horn, a small medieval horn or bugle made of an elephant's tusk and often elaborately carved.

Oliver, Joe 'King' (1885–1938), U.S. jazz cornet player, who in the 1920s helped to popularize the New Orleans style throughout the United States. During this period he encouraged the young Louis Armstrong (fifteen years his junior) and featured him in his Creole Jazz Band, in which the two players produced some incomparable two-cornet passages (fortunately preserved on disc). In his later years, however, Oliver slid into obscurity.

Olsen, Ole (1850–1927), Norwegian composer. He settled in Christiania (now Oslo) where he conducted and wrote music criticism. He composed four operas to his own libretti, symphonic poems, cantatas, a symphony, and an oratorio. His suite for Rolfson's children's play *Svein Uræd* is still popular in Norway.

Olympians, The, opera in three acts by Bliss, first performed at Covent Garden in 1949. The libretto, by

J. B. Priestley, relates the modern adventures of the Olympian gods, who are reduced to a party of travelling players but are permitted to regain their power once a year.

Ombra mai fu, correct name for Handel's *Largo*, which is not a '*largo*' at all but is marked *larghetto*. Nor does it have the sacred overtones given to it by generations of singers. In fact it is a song to a tree, originally written for male soprano, and is the opening aria of the opera *Serse* (Xerxes).

O mio babbino caro (It., 'Oh my beloved daddy'), Lauretta's aria in Puccini's *Gianni Schicchi* in which she pleads for her father's permission to marry Rinuccio.

O namenlose Freude, the duet in Act 2 of Beethoven's *Fidelio* in which Leonore and Florestan are reunited.

ondeggiando, *see* ONDULÉ

Ondes Martenot or **Ondes Musicales,** electronic musical instrument invented (patented 1922) by Maurice Martenot. Dimitri Levidis wrote a *Poeme Symphonique pour Solo d'Ondes Musicales et Orchestre* for it, which was played at the instrument's first public performance in 1928. The pitch is infinitely variable, and some variety of tone-colour is possible. The instrument has been written for by Olivier Messiaen, notably in his *Turangalila* symphony; other composers who have written for it include Honegger, Milhaud and Koechlin.

ondulé (Fr.), 'undulating'. An effect, indicated by the sign ᴧᴧ, used in violin playing in the baroque period either on a single note, or on several notes in ARPEGGIO, and produced by an undulating motion of the bow.

 The Italian term is *ondeggiando*.

one-step, U.S. dance in quick 2/4 time, popular during the early years of the 20th century, but later ousted by the slow foxtrot (or two-step).

Ongarese, *see* ALL' ONGARESE

On Hearing the First Cuckoo in Spring, orchestral piece by Delius, first performed at Leipzig in 1913. It makes use of the Norwegian folk-song 'I Ola Dalom' (In Ola Valley), also used by Grieg in his *Nineteen Norwegian Folk Tunes*, op 66. The sound of the cuckoo is evoked by a clarinet. The piece is one of a set of two written by Delius for small orchestra, the other being *Summer Night on the River*.

Onslow, André Georges Louis (1784–1853), Franco-British composer, also known as George Onslow. He studied piano under Dussek and Cramer in London, and composition under Reicha in Paris. He settled down as a country squire in central France in early middle age, but suffered an accident while hunting which left him partially deaf. He recorded the progress of the illness caused by the accident in *The Bullet Quartet*, which has parts called 'Fever and Delirium', 'Cure', and so on. He was elected a member of the London Philharmonic Society in 1832, and in 1842 succeeded Cherubini as member of the *Academie Française*. He composed a great deal of chamber music, including 36 string quartets, various works for piano, comic operas and symphonies.

On This Island, cycle of five songs, op 11, by Britten for high voice and piano, to poems by W. H. Auden. They were composed in 1937 and entitled 'Volume One'; the second volume, however, never appeared.

On Wenlock Edge, cycle of six songs by Vaughan

Williams, based on poems from A. E. Housman's *A Shropshire Lad*. Written in 1909, the songs are scored for solo tenor, string quartet and piano. An alternative version was written later for tenor and orchestra. Housman objected strongly to Vaughan Williams's song cycle, claiming (wrongly, posterity would consider) that the composer had mutilated his poetry.

op, abbreviation for Lat. *opus*, 'work'. The term is traditionally used by composers to indicate the numbering of their works in order of composition, e.g. op 95. In the 17th and early 18th centuries, opus numbers were used only occasionally, generally to draw attention to the importance of a collection of pieces, e.g. a set of sonatas or concertos. Some composers (or their publishers) have used opus numbers erratically, so that they do not always accurately indicate the order of composition. This is true of Beethoven. In the case of Schubert the opus numbers are virtually meaningless. If an opus consists of more than one piece, it may be subdivided, e.g. op 59, no 2. The plural abbreviation of 'op' is 'opp'. The abbreviation 'op post' or 'op posth' is used to indicate that the work received its number after the composer's death.

open, not muted. This direction, appearing in brass parts, indicates the removal of a mute or, in the case of horns only, that hand-stopping is to be discontinued.

open diapason, *see* DIAPASON

open fifth, a common chord without a third is said to have an open fifth. In medieval polyphony it was usual to end a composition on a unison, octave or open fifth, in the 16th century on a chord with an open fifth or with a major third (*see also* ACOUSTICS). The open fifth was one of the idioms in the writing for two horns in the 18th century orchestra: for an example *see* HORN.

open notes, on brass or woodwind instruments, notes produced without the use of valves, keys, etc. Unless hand-stopping is used to vary the pitch (*see* HORN) a sequence of such notes must form part of the HARMONIC SERIES. The term is also used to mean ordinary, as opposed to stopped, notes on the horn.

When used of stringed instruments, the term means notes not stopped by finger pressure, a technique also called 'open strings'. The sign ° above a note indicates that it is to be played on an open string when possible, or as a harmonic.

See HARMONICS

open strings, *see* OPEN NOTES

opera, a dramatic work in which the whole, or the greater part, of the text is sung with instrumental accompaniment. The word 'opera', now in universal use (Fr., *opéra*; Ger., *Oper*; It., *opera*; Sp., *opera*), was originally a colloquial abbreviation of the Italian *opera in musica* (a musical work). The early Italian operas of the 17th century were described as *favola in musica* (a story in music), *dramma per musica* (a play for music) or some similar term. In 17th century France, serious opera was entitled *tragedie en musique* (a tragedy set to music).

The association of music with drama is as old as civilization. In western Europe music was an essential part of the liturgical drama of the middle ages, which was therefore in a sense the ancestor of the oratorio, and it also figured prominently in the many dramatic entertainments presented at Italian courts in the 16th century. However, though opera owed much to these entertainments, which were marked by a love of spectacle and a lively interest in classical mythology, it was essentially a new form. The cult of the antique which was a feature of Renaissance humanism induced a group of artists, musicians and scholars in Florence to attempt a revival of Greek drama, which they falsely supposed to have been sung throughout.

The first product of this movement was Rinuccini's *Dafne*, performed privately in 1597, with music by Peri and Jacopo Corsi. A suitable musical formula for setting the text of a dramatic work was found in the new type of declamatory song. It began as a reaction against the madrigal, where the clear enunciation of words often suffered from the complexities of choral polyphony. The declamatory song came to be known as *recitativo* (from *recitare*, to recite). It translated the accents of speech into music and allowed the individual singer the greatest freedom for interpretation. For this reason the accompaniment, assigned primarily to a keyboard instrument or to the lute, was treated as a subordinate harmonic background. *Dafne* was followed in 1600 by *Euridice* (libretto by Rinuccini, music mainly by Peri), which was performed at Florence to celebrate the wedding of Henry IV of France and Maria de' Medici.

The most important opera on the Florentine model was Monteverdi's *Orfeo* (Mantua, 1607), which also included a substantial amount of choral writing. Choruses were also employed extensively at Rome, where the first secular opera to be performed was Landi's *The Death of Orpheus*. The erection of a magnificent theatre by the Barberini family in 1632 encouraged the development of opera as a spectacle, with splendid scenery and elaborate machines. In 1637 the first public opera house was opened at Venice, followed by several others. Opera was no longer an entertainment for invited guests but appealed to a wider audience. For economic reasons the chorus was neglected in favour of solo singing, and the orchestra consisted normally of strings and harpsichord. Already in Rome there had been a tendency to relieve the monotony of continuous recitative by incorporating arias (or songs), and this tendency was continued in the Venetian operas, which also frequently introduced duets. Castrato singers, who had become familiar in opera in Rome, now acquired an even greater vogue, which continued down to the end of the 18th century.

The subject matter of opera was also broadened. Monteverdi's last opera, *The Coronation of Poppaea* (Venice, 1642) was the first to deal with a historical theme, as distinct from mythology; it also introduced comic characters as a relief from the serious tone of the rest of the work. Comic characters had already made their appearance at Rome before this, and a complete comic opera, *Chi soffre, speri*, by Mazzocchi and Marazzoli, had been performed there in 1639. The staple elements of comic opera (or *opera buffa*, as it became known) were rapid recitative, patter songs, and scenes parodying serious opera. Comic opera also contributed the concerted finale for an ensemble of singers, which was not normally used in serious opera before the late 18th century, presumably because it would have been undignified for princely characters to have to struggle to make themselves heard.

In the course of the 17th century Italian opera also

became known abroad, e.g. in Vienna, where the court became a centre for lavish productions, in Brussels and in Warsaw. It was also introduced to Paris in 1645, but the hostility which it aroused, both aesthetic and political, led the French to produce their own operas, which owed much to the traditions of the spoken drama and to the ballet. The earliest French opera dates from 1655, but its success as a national form was due to the Italian-born Lully, whose first opera, *Cadmus et Hermione*, was performed in 1673. Lully was already at this time an experienced composer of ballets, *pastorales* and *comédies-ballets* – the last a form which combined the spoken drama and ballet. Ballet continued to be an integral part of French opera right down to the 19th century. In England, where the masque (a form of ballet with dialogue) was popular at court and in private societies in the early 17th century, an attempt at establishing opera was made by Davenant, whose *Siege of Rhodes*, with music by several composers, was performed in London in 1656. Restoration society, however, rejected opera on the Italian model and preferred a type similar to the French *comedie-ballet*, i.e. an association of music and spoken dialogue. Purcell's *King Arthur* (text by Dryden, 1691) is a work of this kind. His *Dido and Aeneas* (1689), a miniature opera on the Italian model, was written not for the public theatre but for a girls' school at Chelsea.

The traditions of Italian opera were continued by Stradella (died 1682) and Alessandro Scarlatti (1660–1725). In the work of Scarlatti the aria acquired absolute supremacy: recitative became virtually a series of conventional formulas used for essential conversation or simple reflection, except where the dramatic situation justified an outburst with orchestral accompaniment (*recitativo stromentato*). The standard type of aria was in *da capo* form, which may be represented by the formula A B A, the repetition of the first section offering the singer improvised ornamentation. In general ornamentation was freely used to embroider a simple vocal line, particularly in slow arias which offered ample scope for such treatment. The overture also developed into a standard form – two quick movements separated by one in slower tempo. French composers, on the other hand, preferred a slow introduction followed by a quick movement in fugal style.

In Germany Schütz had set a translation of Rinuccini's *Dafne* as early as 1627, but German opera did not become fully established until the opening of the first public opera house at Hamburg in 1678, though Italian opera flourished in the work of Steffani (1654–1728) at Munich, Hanover and Dusseldorf. It was at Hamburg that Handel gained his first operatic experience, which he developed further by a visit to Italy. The great majority of his Italian operas, however, were written between 1711 and 1741 for London, where he took advantage of the nobility's newly awakened enthusiasm for the form.

In the course of the 18th century there was a growing dissatisfaction with the rigidity of operatic conventions. It was felt that vocal virtuosity was exploited at the expense of dramatic expression and that an overture should be an integral part of the work and not merely an instrumental introduction to which nobody listened seriously. These views found expression in the work of several writers, notably Francesco Algarotti in his *Saggio sopra l'opera in musica* (1755). The operas of Jommelli and Traetta show that they were aware of these problems, but it was above all Gluck who demonstrated in his later works, particularly in *Alceste* (Vienna, 1767), *Iphigénie en Aulide* (Paris, 1774) and *Iphigénie en Tauride* (Paris, 1779), that a simple, sincere and direct form of expression could be more truly dramatic than the emphasis on fine singing which counted for so much in earlier 18th century works. Rameau, whose operatic activity in Paris covered the years 1733–64, had already shown what an important contribution the orchestra could make to dramatic intensity. Gluck's imagination went further: he realized that the instruments could speak, as if they were themselves witnesses of the drama. This conception of instrumental writing was to have a powerful effect on the development of the symphony.

Comic opera (*opera buffa*) did not become firmly established in Italy until the early years of the 18th century. It aimed above all at being 'natural' in contrast to the artificiality of *opera seria*. Hence when Pergolesi's *La serva padrona* (originally a comic *intermezzo*) was reintroduced to Paris in 1752 it was seized upon by the critics of French opera, particularly Rousseau, as a stick with which to attack all that was stilted and conventional in the French tradition. The violent controversy which ensued was known as the *guerre des bouffons* (war of the comedians). Hostility was still active when Gluck, who was accepted as the champion of French opera, came to Paris in 1773. The *guerre des bouffons* had the important effect of stimulating the composition of French *opéras comiques*, for which there was a modest precedent in the comedies interspersed with popular songs which had been performed at the Paris fairs from the early years of the 18th century. *Opéra comique*, unlike *opera buffa*, employed spoken dialogue in place of recitative. In the course of time romantic and pathetic elements were introduced into *opera buffa* (as in Mozart's *Don Giovanni*, 1787) and into *opéra comique* – so much so that in the 19th century *opéra comique* came to mean simply opera with dialogue, as opposed to *grand opéra*, which was set to music throughout and produced on a lavish scale.

In Britain comic opera also employed dialogue. It had its forerunners in the Restoration parodies of plays with music, but as an independent form its history began with Gay's *Beggar's Opera* (1728), in which the songs were set to popular tunes, either traditional or by well-known composers like Purcell and Handel. *The Beggar's Opera* was followed by a host of works of a similar kind, known as 'ballad operas'. The term was still retained when later in the century it became the custom to have the songs specially written by living composers, e.g. Arne, Dibdin and Shield. The popularity of opera with dialogue and the example of French *opéra comique* led to the romantic opera of the early 19th century, e.g. Balfe's *The Bohemian Girl* (1845). Ballad opera also had an influence in Germany, where a translation of an English work was performed in 1743. This started the fashion for a German counterpart to *opéra comique*, for which the German name was *Singspiel*. Mozart's *Die Entführung* (1782), which incorporates many of the elements of Italian opera, was an elaborate response to the Emperor Joseph II's desire to found a national *Singspiel* in Vienna – an institution which lasted only a few years. Mozart's *The Magic Flute* (1791), written for a popular theatre in Vienna, is technically a *Singspiel*, but is unique in its combination of pantomime and masonic symbolism.

Mozart's principal activity was in the field of Italian opera – a form which he learned to master by writing operas in Italy while still in his teens. His first mature work in this form was *Idomeneo* (Munich, 1781), which owes much to the influence of Gluck. In Vienna, however, circumstances compelled him to devote himself to *opera buffa*, of which he wrote three outstanding examples – *The Marriage of Figaro* (1786), *Don Giovanni* (1787) and *Cosi fan tutte* (1789). The one exception, *La clemenza di Tito* (1791), was an *opera seria* commissioned to celebrate the coronation of Leopold II as King of Bohemia in Prague.

In France the horrors of the revolution led to the composition of *opéras comiques* dealing with dramatic rescues, e.g. Cherubini's *Les deux journées* (Paris, 1800), known in Britain as *The Water Carrier*. Beethoven, who admired Cherubini, chose a story from the revolution for his only opera, *Fidelio* (Vienna, 1805), which also has spoken dialogue. *Fidelio*, however, had no successors. The impact of romantic literature on German composers led to the composition of works which combined supernatural elements with homely, rustic, sentiment – e.g. Weber's *Der Freischütz* (1821) and Marschner's *Hans Heiling* (1833) – and a romantic interpretation of the pageantry and intrigue of the middle ages, e.g. Weber's *Euryanthe* (1823), in which dialogue was abandoned.

Contemporary with this movement in Germany was the development of the so-called *grand opéra* in Paris – a form which gave scope for the representation of reaction against tyranny, e.g. Rossini's *William Tell* (1829), and spectacular scenes on a large scale. The outstanding practitioner of this type of opera was Meyerbeer, of German-Jewish origin, whose *Les Huguenots* (1836) is a vivid picture of the conflict between Catholics and Protestants in the 16th century. Berlioz's *The Trojans* (1856–9) accepts this tradition, but transmutes it into a wholly individual approach and an intellectual awareness of the dignity of Virgil's epic. Many of the conventions of *opéra comique* came to be incorporated in *grand opéra*, e.g. choruses of soldiers, conspirators, etc., and the building of an organ in the Paris Opéra made possible the inclusion of church scenes.

In Germany, Wagner was familiar with the tradition of *grand opéra* and also of romantic German opera. The former is represented in his work by *Rienzi* (1842), the latter by *The Flying Dutchman* (1843), *Tannhäuser* (1845) and *Lohengrin* (1850) – the dates are those of performance. A growing reaction against tradition, however, led him to expound a new theory of opera, arguing that the form should be a union of all the arts, with dignified (i.e. legendary) subject matter, verse forms which would stimulate by the use of alliteration, and a continuous running commentary (explaining the action by the repeated introduction of significant themes) in the orchestra. This theory was put into practice in the tetralogy of *The Ring*, the composition of which occupied him, with intervals, from 1853 to 1874. Wagner's principles, however, were to some extent relaxed in *Tristan and Isolde* (first performed

1865) and *The Mastersingers* (first performed 1868); the latter work includes not only set songs but also elaborate ensembles – a form of dramatic expression which is specifically condemned in his theoretical works.

In Italy in the 19th century, the traditions of the past were maintained in the work of Rossini (1792–1868), Donizetti (1797–1848) and Bellini (1801–35). Of these three composers Rossini was the most original and the most influential. He assigned to the orchestra more importance than was customary in Italian opera, broke with the convention of recitative accompanied merely by a keyboard instrument, and put an end to the practice of improvised ornamentation for singers. *The Barber of Seville* (Rome, 1816) brought new life into the traditional form of Beethoven.

Verdi, whose first opera, *Oberto*, was performed in 1839, inherited the traditions established by his predecessors. But in the course of the years his art grew steadily in stature. He proved himself to be a superbly equipped musician, with a new mastery of orchestral technique and a remarkable instinct for dramatic effect. The culmination of his development is to be found in *Aida* (Cairo, 1871 – a spectacular work in the tradition of French *grand opéra*), *Otello* (Milan, 1887) and *Falstaff* (Milan, 1893) – the last two a brilliant re-creation of Shakespearian drama in Italian terms.

Simultaneously the growth of nationalism was having stimulating effects in other countries, notably Russia and Czechoslovakia (then a part of the Austro-Hungarian Empire). The foundations of Russian opera, hitherto dependent on Italy, were laid by Glinka in 1836. Among his successors in this field were Mussorgsky, whose *Boris Godunov* (1868) is the most original and the most characteristically Russian work of this period, Borodin and Rimsky-Korsakov. Chaikovsky was more inclined to model his lyrical style on western European music. In Czechoslovakia, Smetana, though attacked by critics as 'Wagnerian', won a striking and enduring popular success with *The Bartered Bride* (Prague, 1866).

In the present century, opera has pursued no consistent path. In Germany, Richard Strauss, using at one stage in his career an orchestra even larger than Wagner's, found that a combination of bourgeois sentiment and wild extravagance could be utilized equally for tragedy – e.g. *Der Rosenkavalier* (1911). In France, Debussy utilized the technique of impressionism to clothe with a tenuous musical fabric Maeterlinck's fantastic drama *Pelleas and Melisande* (1902). The work has influenced many other composers. In Italy, a movement for exploiting realism (*verismo*) already foreshadowed by Bizet's *Carmen* (Paris, 1875) had been inaugurated by Mascagni's *Cavalleria rusticana* (1890) and Leoncavallo's *Pagliacci* (1892). This type of treatment was accepted by the theatrical Puccini in a series of still popular operas, two of which – *Madama Butterfly* (1904) and *Turandot* (1926) – are coloured by a skillful suggestion of an oriental atmosphere.

Realism, of a musically more subtle kind, is also a characteristic of Berg's *Wozzeck* (1925), and *Lulu* (produced 1937), but it is associated with an interpretation of character reminiscent of psychoanalysis, and the musical idiom, based on the twelve note system of composition, is far removed from Puccini's frankly sentimental melody and harmony. In England, Britten's *Peter Grimes* (1945) also presented a psychological study of a personality at odds with society, but without abandoning traditional tonality. Some of his later works, notably *The Turn of the Screw* (1954), have employed a small chamber orchestra to brilliant effect – a practice which has also been used by some continental composers, for aesthetic or economic reasons, or both. His *The Rape of Lucretia* (1946) based on a play by Obey, employs a 'chorus' of two singers, who stand outside the action, as in Greek tragedy, and comment on it.

Symbolism is a not uncommon element in modern opera, no doubt as a reaction against realism; it has also influenced opera production. A further reaction against the continuity of Wagnerian opera has led in some works to a return to the 18th century system of using recitative to link arias, duets, etc., e.g. in Stravinsky's *The Rake's Progress* (1951).

Germany, which has a vested interest in keeping opera alive, has been the source of some of the most important of recent operas, including a series of finely crafted works by Henze. Zimmerman's *The Soldiers* (1958–1964) which requires several stages and orchestral groupings to achieve its desired 'pluralistic' effect, points to one direction in which opera is going, and Kagel's anti-opera, *Staatstheater*, which does not require an orchestra at all, points to another. Economic factors, and a reaction among some composers against the word 'opera' has led to the development of so-called MUSIC THEATRE, a form to which Peter Maxwell Davies, Alexander Goehr and Harrison Birtwistle in Britain have creatively contributed. In France, Pierre Boulez has uttered warnings about the tendency among modern composers to write operas based on plays instead of original material, but he himself has yet to write a work based on his own principles.

W. BROCKWAY and H. WEINSTOCK: *The World of Opera* (1941, revised 1962)

N. DEMUTH: *French Opera: Its Development to the Revolution* (1963)

E. J. DENT: *Foundations of English Opera* (1928); *Opera* (1940)

D. EWEN: *New Encyclopedia of the Opera* (1971)

H. GOLDSCHMIDT: *Studien zur Geschichte der italienischen Oper im 17. Jahrhundert* (2 volumes, 1901–4)

D. J. GROUT: *A Short History of Opera* (2 volumes, 1947)

J. KERMAN: *Opera as Drama* (1952)

C. W. KOBBE: *Complete Opera Book* (1919, revised 1954)

A. LOEWENBERG: *Annals of Opera* (2 volumes, 1947)

F. L. MOORE: *Crowell's Handbook of World Opera* (1941, revised 1962)

E. NEWMAN: *Opera Nights* (1943); *More Opera Nights* (1954)

L. ORREY: *A Concise History of Opera* (1972)

H. PLEASANTS: *The Great Singers* (1967)

H. ROSENTHAL (editor): *The Opera Bedside Book* (1965)

H. ROSENTHAL and J. WARRACK: *Concise Oxford Dictionary of Opera* (1964)

J. WECHSBERG: *The Opera* (1972)

E. WELLESZ: *Essays on Opera* (1950)

S. T. WORSTHORNE: *Venetian Opera in the Seventeenth Century* (1954)

Opera Ball, The (Ger., *Der Opernball*), operetta in three acts by Heuberger, after the farce *Les Dominos Roses* by Delacour and Hennequin. Its first performance was in Vienna in 1898.

opéra-ballet, type of stage work which flourished in France in the 17th and 18th centuries, in which song and dance were given more or less equal prominence. Important exponents of the form included Lully and Rameau.

opéra-bouffe (Fr.), a species of French comic opera. The name derives from the Italian *opera buffa*.

opera buffa (It.), comic opera. This type of opera developed in Italy in the 18th century. In contrast with *opera seria*, which dealt formally with mythological or regal subjects, *opera buffa* used light subject matter and drew its characters from normal life. Traditionally its plots involved master-and-servant relationships, disguises, and amorous intrigues, set generally to simpler, shorter-winded music than is found in *opera seria*.

opéra-comique (Fr.), literally 'comic opera', though the term is applied more widely to include in the 19th century, any French opera containing spoken dialogue. Thus Bizet's *Carmen* (in its authentic version with spoken dialogue) is an *opéra-comique*, even though it has a tragic ending.

opera-oratorio, hybrid stage work, involving elements of opera and oratorio, as in Stravinsky's *Oedipus Rex*, in which the action of the drama is kept as static as possible. Some of Wieland Wagner's productions of his grandfather's operas (e.g. *Lohengrin*) could be said to belong to this genre.

opera semiseria (It.), a serious opera containing comic elements, such as Mozart's *The Marriage of Figaro* and *Don Giovanni* (though the composer preferred to call the latter a *dramma giocoso*, or humorous drama).

opera seria (It.), 'serious' opera. This was the most prevalent operatic form of the 17th and early 18th centuries, and was identified by its noble subjects, its serious, elaborate arias and general air of formality. The libretto was in Italian (the main operatic language of the day) and important roles were often given to castrato singers. Handel was one of the leading exponents of *opera seria*, Gluck attempted to reform its principles by making it more human and dramatic, and by Mozart's time the style was dying – though Mozart himself wrote two masterly works in the form, *Idomeneo* (1781) and *La Clemenza di Tito* (1791).

operetta, originally a diminutive of 'opera'. The term came to be used in the 19th century for a type of opera with dialogue which employed music of a popular character, and used for its subject matter a judicious mixture of romantic sentiment, comedy and parody of serious opera. Another name for operetta is 'light opera'. The outstanding composers of the genre in the 19th century were Offenbach in Paris, Johann Strauss in Vienna and Sullivan in London. The waltz became an indispensable element in Viennese operetta and hence found its way also into the work of composers in other countries. In the 20th century, operetta became known as 'musical comedy', acquiring often a more spectacular mode of production but not losing its essential character. The term 'musical comedy' has in recent years become abbreviated to 'musical', used as a noun. In the United States the art of the musical has been developed to a high polish, notably in the works of Rodgers and Hart (*Pal Joey*), Lerner and Loewe (*Guys and Dolls*), Cole Porter (*Kiss me Kate*) and Leonard Bernstein (*West Side Story*).

ophicleide (Gr. *ophis*, snake; *kleis*, key; hence keyed serpent), despite its name this instrument does not resemble the serpent in appearance, although the method of playing is the same. The ophicleide is the bass of the keyed bugle family, and for a period during the last century it was a regular member of the orchestra. Its range is a little over three octaves and its usual function was to supply a bass to other brass instruments, especially the trombones. One of its earliest appearances is in Spohr's opera *Olympia* (1819), and one of its last is in Verdi's *Requiem* (1874). It was also an important instrument in military bands, but its tone is somewhat coarse, and because of this it was eventually ousted by the smoother toned tuba. Ophicleides were made in various sizes from alto to double bass, but the two in common use were built in C and B flat, and had as their lowest notes

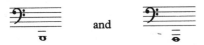

Nowadays all ophicleide parts are played on tubas, almost always with advantage, but in the few cases where a composer deliberately sought a coarse quality something is lost by the transfer. Perhaps the best known instance of this is the clown's passage in Mendelssohn's *A Midsummer Night's Dream* overture.

Opieński, Henryk (1870–1942), Polish composer and conductor. He studied under Paderewski, d'Indy and Nikisch. He taught music history at the Warsaw Conservatory and was the director of the state conservatory in Poznan from 1920 until 1926. He composed operas, choral works, symphonic poems and songs, and published books on Polish music and an edition of Chopin's letters.

opus, *see* OP

oratorio, a setting of a text on a sacred or epic theme for chorus, soloists, and orchestra, for performance in a church or concert hall. The name arose from the Oratory of the church in Vallicella where St. Philip Neri instituted, in the second half of the 16th century, the performance of sacred plays with music. Emilio Cavalieri's *Rappresentazione di anima e di corpo* (*Representation of the Soul and Body*, 1600), sometimes described as the first oratorio, is closely related in style to the early Florentine operas, and was staged. The first important composer of oratorios proper was Carissimi, who adopted the forms of opera with a more extensive use of the chorus, a practice which has always tended to distinguish the form of oratorio from that of opera. The later history of Italian oratorio runs parallel to that of Italian opera: its composers (e.g. Draghi, A. Scarlatti, Caldara) were primarily opera composers, and opera librettists (e.g. Zeno and Metastasio) wrote many of the texts.

In Germany, Schütz's *Historia der fröhlichen und*

siegreichen Auferstehung (*Story of the Joyful and Triumphant Resurrection*, 1623) was the first work in a new style which was later developed by Lutheran composers in their settings of the PASSION. The words of the Evangelist (the *testo* of Italian oratorio) are set in imitation plainsong, accompanied by four viols. In his Passions there is a similar musical declamation, but without any accompaniment. In *Die sieben Worte* (*The Seven Words*, 1645) and the *Christmas Oratorio* (1664) the narration is in accompanied recitative. J. S. Bach used the term *Oratorium* for the set of six cantatas for the season Christmas to Epiphany (*Christmas Oratorio*), for the Easter cantata *Kommt, eilet und lauftet*, and for the Ascensiontide cantata *Lobet Gott in seinen Reichen*. The two oratorios of C. P. E. Bach – *Die Israeliten in der Wüste* (*The Israelites in the Wilderness*, 1775) and *Auferstehung und Himmelfahrt Jesu* (*The Resurrection and Ascension of Jesus*, 1787) – are among his finest and most mature works, and in some of their movements approach the full realization of the classical style in oratorio which was achieved in Haydn's *Creation* (1797). The only oratorios by German composers in the romantic period which have had more than an occasional performance are those of Mendelssohn, although Spohr, Liszt and Max Bruch each wrote more than one work in the form.

Apart from *Messiah* and *Israel in Egypt* (which uses a double choir) Handel's oratorios differ little in style (the choruses excepted) from his operas. It is through those two works that he has exercised his continuous influence on British oratorio until the present century. Mendelssohn's influence, which was also very strong, complemented rather than excluded that of Handel, but no British composer between Arne and Parry was able to equal the largeness of Handel or rise above the suavity of Mendelssohn. Since Parry began his series of oratorios with *Judith* in 1888, the oratorio has been one of the chief forms of the English choral renascence, especially in the work of Elgar (*The Dream of Gerontius*), Vaughan Williams (*Sancta Civitas*) and William Walton (*Belshazzar's Feast*).

In France the oratorio has been cultivated only sporadically. In the second half of the 17th century, M. A. Charpentier composed a series of *Histoires sacrées* which were more than mere imitations of his teacher Carissimi. Berlioz's *L'Enfance du Christ* contains some of his most beautiful music, but the later examples by Franck, Saint-Saëns and d'Indy have not emulated its simplicity of style. Arthur Honegger's dramatic psalm *King David* (1921) and Kodály's *Psalmus Hungaricus* (1923) are two of the more successful modern essays in the oratorio tradition.

A. SCHERING: *Geschichte des Oratoriums* (1911)

A. JACOBS (editor): *Choral Music* (1963)

Orchésographie (Fr.), a treatise on the dance, in the form of a dialogue, by Thoinot Arbeau (an anagram of his real name, Jehan Tabourot), published in 1589. It has a musical interest in that it is the earliest surviving book on the dance which prints the tunes, of which there are some fifty.

orchestra (Gr., place for dancing), the name arose from the position of the orchestra in the opera house, which is the same as that of the semicircle for the dancers and instrumentalists in the ancient Greek theatre, between the audience and the stage. The orchestra as a definite group of instruments grew up in the opera houses of the 17th century. Groups (consorts) of instruments, such as strings, recorders, or trumpets, had earlier played together, and occasionally several consorts had been joined. The first orchestras were temporary and very variable. Montiverdi used a miscellaneous collection of wind, string, and continuo instruments for the performance of *Orfeo* in 1607. The regular opera orchestra of the baroque period consisted of strings, usually with oboes and bassoons, and other instruments were added for solo *obbligati*. The same principle held in the concerto, the chorus instruments being strings and the solo group variable, either strings or wind or both. The standardization of the orchestra took place in the classical period, with the regular use of wind, brass, and timpani, and the division into four groups; strings, woodwind (one or two flutes, two oboes, two bassoons), brass (two horns, two trumpets) and two kettledrums. Clarinets were added later in the course of the 18th century. On this basis the orchestra was expanded in the 19th century to include triple and eventually quadruple woodwind, a complete brass section, harp, and auxiliary percussion. Trombones had been used for special scenes in 18th century opera. Beethoven added them in the fifth symphony and wrote for four horns in the ninth. The composition of the late romantic orchestra may be seen in the score of Strauss's *Ein Heldenleben* (1899):

Woodwind	piccolo 3 flutes 3 oboes English horn (also playing 4th oboe) E flat clarinet 2 B flat clarinets Bass clarinet 3 bassoons Double bassoon
Brass	8 horns 5 trumpets 3 trombones B flat tenor tuba Bass tuba
Percussion	kettledrums (mechanical) bass drum cymbals small side-drum tenor drum
Strings	16 first violins 16 second violins 12 violas 12 cellos 8 double basses 2 harps

Mahler, Skryabin, Stravinsky (in *The Rite of Spring*) and Prokofiev (in his *Scythian Suite*) used equally large forces. A reaction set in (in which economics played a part) at the period of World War 1, and many later composers (including Stravinsky) have been content with orchestras of more modest size.

Many later composers, following Mahler's lead,

have treated the orchestra as a reservoir from which to draw chamber ensembles. Among the most striking examples of this approach are the later works of Stravinsky, among them *Threni*, *Abraham and Isaac*, the *Variations in Memory of Aldous Huxley* and *Requiem Canticles*.

P. BEKKER: *The Story of the Orchestra* (1936)

A. CARSE: *The Orchestra in the Eighteenth Century* (1940); *The Orchestra from Beethoven to Berlioz* (1948)

F. HOWES: *Full Orchestra* (1942)

R. NETTEL: *The Orchestra in England* (1949)

C. S. TERRY: *Bach's Orchestra* (1932)

orchestration, the art of writing for the orchestra is concerned with the tone colour, technical capacity, and effective range of instruments, with their use in combination, and with the setting out of an orchestral SCORE. Though single instruments of contrasting colour played together in 15th century *chansons*, and consorts of instruments were sometimes combined in the 16th century, the basic elements of such an art did not appear until the early 17th century. Between 1600 and 1620 Giovanni Gabrieli indicated specific instruments in his *Sacrae Symphoniae*, Monteverdi used instruments in accordance with the dramatic situation in *Orfeo*, and Praetorius wrote the first comprehensive account of instruments in the *Syntagma Musicum* (1617). The choice of a particular instrument to express a text or a dramatic situation in the baroque period appeared mainly in the essentially chamber-music combinations used in the opera, cantata and Passion; larger combinations were arrived at by superimposition, as with Bach's trumpets and drums, or by doubling.

Contrasts of tone colour and weight were essential elements in the late baroque concerto, but they first became allied to a standardized orchestra in the early classical symphonies of the Mannheim and Viennese composers. In the classical style of Haydn, Mozart, and Beethoven the woodwind, though often used to play a leading melody, is in general subordinated to the strings, who alone can play rapid figuration. The brass provides support for climaxes, though the horns, more versatile than the trumpets, are also used for soft accompaniment and for idiomatic melody. In Beethoven, the section for three horns in the scherzo of the *Eroica* symphony and the variation for solo horn in the finale of the ninth symphony are signs of a new direction, as is Weber's writing for horns in the overture to *Der Freischütz*.

The rise of the romantic idea of orchestration as the art of dramatic expression in music is due largely to Berlioz, both as a composer and as the writer of the first modern textbook of orchestration. Wagner, Strauss (who produced a new edition of Berlioz's treatise) and Mahler developed his methods. The orchestration of Rimsky-Korsakov, who also wrote a treatise, took a new turn, though continuing to develop its individual characteristics, after the performance of Wagner's *Der Ring des Nibelungen* in St. Petersburg in 1889. A more selective and delicate treatment of the orchestra is characteristic of the impressionistic orchestration of Debussy and Ravel. In general the tendency of modern orchestration is to be linear rather than massive, and to exploit the rhythmic and melodic possibilities of all instruments equally.

Except when a piece of music in another medium (usually a piano composition) is being transferred to the orchestra, orchestration is, or should be, a part of the compositional process. Although some people think otherwise, composers do not conceive their music in a vacuum and then find suitable instrumental colours for it. Indeed, they begin by thinking of their music in terms of the medium for which they are writing.

H. BERLIOZ: *Grand Traité d'Instrumentation et d'Orchestration* (1844; English translation by M. C. Clarke, 1858)

A. CARSE: *The History of Orchestration* (1925)

C. FORSYTH: *Orchestration* (second edition, 1935)

G. JACOB: *Orchestral Technique* (second edition, 1940)

W. PISTON: *Orchestration* (1955)

N. RIMSKY-KORSAKOV: *Principles of Orchestration*, two volumes (1922)

E. WELLESZ: *Die neue Instrumentation*, two volumes (1928–9)

C. M. WIDOR: *The Technique of the Modern Orchestra*, translated by E. Suddard (1906)

orchestrion, a mechanical instrument able to imitate the sounds of various orchestral ones. A particularly successful example seems to have been the Panharmonicon, built by MAELZEL.

Ordinary, the parts of the Ordinary of the Mass, i.e. those with invariable texts, are the *Kyrie, Gloria, Credo, Sanctus,* and *Benedictus,* and *Agnus Dei.* These parts of the Mass are distinct from the Proper (whose texts are 'proper to their day or season').

ordre (Fr.), name given by François Couperin to various groups of harpsichord pieces, more usually called SUITE.

Orfeo, L' (It., *The Story of Orpheus*), opera by Monteverdi consisting of a prologue and five acts, to a libretto by Alessandro Striggio. First produced in Mantua in 1607, this is one of the earliest of all operas, a masterpiece still as potent today as it was more than three and a half centuries ago. The plot is similar to that of Gluck's *Orpheus,* but it does not have the same happy ending.

Orfeo ed Euridice (Orpheus and Eurydice), opera in three acts by Gluck, first performed in Vienna in 1762. The first performance of the revised version *Orphée* (translated by Pierre Louis Moline) was given in Paris in 1774. Orpheus, mourning the death of Eurydice, is told by Amor that Zeus has taken pity on him and that he may descend into Hades to search for her. He is warned, however, that if he looks at her before they have left the shores of the Styx, death will reclaim her for ever. He charms the Furies with his singing and succeeds in gaining an entrance to Hades. He reaches the Elysian Fields, where the happy ones bring Eurydice to him. Without looking at her he takes her by the hand and leads her away. She implores him for one look of love; finally unable to resist any longer, he turns around and she immediately disappears. Orpheus in despair declares that he will die also and follow her, but Amor, believing he has suffered enough, decides to restore Eurydice to life.

The role of Orpheus was written originally for a castrato voice – that of the great Gaetano Guadagni (whom Handel had earlier engaged for *Samson* and *Messiah*). Today the part is usually sung by a woman, though Gluck wrote a tenor arrangement for the Paris version. The opera's most famous aria is 'Che Faro', Orpheus' lament for the loss of his wife.

Orff, Carl (born 1895), German composer, born and educated in Munich, where he later became a prominent teacher and educationalist. In 1925 he was one of the founders of the Dorothee Günter School and in the 1930s he produced his *Schulwerk,* a quantity of short pieces for various instruments, suitable for schoolchildren. His other compositions consist mainly of stage works. Some of these are 'scenic cantatas' involving optional action and dance – e.g. *Carmina Burana* (1937) and *Catulli Carmina* (1943). Others are operas, including *Der Mond* (The Moon; 1939), *Die Kluge* (The Clever Girl; 1943), *Antigone* (1949), *Oedipus der Tyrann* (Oedipus the Tyrant; 1959) and *Prometheus* (1968). Whether setting German folk tales or classical Greek tragedy, Orff favours strongly rhythmic, often percussive, non-contrapuntal music, which he uses both to dramatic and comic effect.

A. LIESS: *Carl Orff: His Life and his Music* (1955; English translation 1966)

Orff-Schulwerk, a collection of percussion instruments of simple construction designed by Carl Orff for educational purposes.

organ (Fr., *orgue*; Ger., *Orgel*; It., *organo*), keyboard instrument, played with the hands and feet, in which wind under pressure sounds the notes through a series of pipes. The mechanism of the organ comprises: (1) a supply of wind under constant pressure, by hand pump, or electric blower;

(2) one or more MANUALS (keyboards) and a PEDAL BOARD, connected with the pipes by means of trackers, electro-pneumatic devices, or electric contacts and wires;

(3) pipes, of flue type, and also, in all but the smallest instruments, of reed type;

(4) stops, to admit wind to each register or set of pipes;

(5) couplers, to join the actions of manuals to each other, and to that of the pedal.

Flue pipes are of the whistle (i.e. recorder) type, and may be open or stopped; stopping lowers the pitch an octave. Reed pipes have a beating reed and a cylindrical or conical resonator. Since organ specifications (i.e. number and character of stops) vary widely, the choice of stops (*see* REGISTRATION), apart from general indications, is usually left to the player. Flue stops are of three classes: diapason, flute, and string; reeds are classified as chorus reeds and solo reeds. The range of pitch within which a stop sounds is indicated by reference to the length, which is approximately 8 ft., of an unstopped pipe which sounds the C below the bass stave. Since this is the lowest note of the keyboard, it is taken as a convenient standard of measurement. An 8 ft. stop sounds at a pitch corresponding to the key which is depressed, a 4 ft. stop an octave higher, a 2 ft. stop two octaves higher, and 16 ft. and 32 ft. stops an octave and two octaves lower. A MIXTURE STOP has three or four sets (ranks) of pipes which sound the octave, fifteenth, double octave, etc., above the normal pitch of the key; MUTATION STOPS sound at the twelfth or seventeenth, or their octaves.

The tonal design of each of the three manuals, GREAT, CHOIR, and SWELL, is complete in itself; the

Great includes the most powerful stops, the Swell the softest. In large organs the pedal stops will also have their own tonal design, and the Solo manual will have stops of more individual character. Large instruments may also have an ECHO ORGAN. Designers and makers use a great variety of names for stops, but the following may be regarded as basic: diapasons of 16, 8, 4 and 2 ft. and a mutation stop on the Great and Swell: one or more flute stops on each manual; a flue stop of string quality (gamba) on the Choir, Swell and Solo; chorus reeds (e.g. trumpet, clarion) on the Great and Solo; solo reeds (e.g. clarinet, oboe) on the Choir, Swell and Solo; diapasons and flute stops of 16, 8 and 4 ft., and on large organs a reed of 16 ft., and a double diapason of 32 ft., on the Pedal Organ. The effect of a 32 ft. stop is sometimes simulated, with indifferent results, by combining an open diapason pipe with a stopped pipe a fifth above to produce a difference tone (*see* ACOUSTICS).

The Swell is always enclosed in a box, and usually also the Choir and Solo; this enables a *crescendo*, controlled by a pedal, to be made by opening one side of the box.

The organ is one of the most ancient instruments still in use. It was known to the Greeks and Romans as *hydraulis*. In 757 the Byzantine Emperor Constantinus Copronymus sent an organ as a gift to Pepin. There are accounts of organs in Christian churches all through the Middle Ages, but the earliest surviving manuscript collections of organ music date from the 15th century. The smaller medieval organs were called, according to size, POSITIVE or PORTATIVE. The greatest period of organ music began with Merulo and ended with Bach. In the course of the 19th century the action was completely changed by the use of electricity, and organs increased steadily in size. Organs with as many as seven manuals have been built; the organ in the Royal Festival Hall, London, has four manuals controlling five manual departments, and 102 stops. The most recent tendency in organ designing is towards the revival of the tone qualities of the late baroque organ, either in smaller instruments or as part of the scheme of a larger organ.

> G. A. AUDSLEY: *The Art of Organ Building*, two volumes (1905)
> E. M. SKINNER: *The Modern Organ* (1917)
> W. L. SUMNER: *The Organ* (1951)
> C. F. ABDY WILLIAMS: *The Story of the Organ* (1903)

organ, electronic, an instrument, of which the Hammond organ and the Compton Electrone are examples, with manuals and pedals in which the tone is produced and amplified electrically. By means of controls which select and regulate the intensity of a certain number of overtones the player is able to produce some variety of tone colour.

See ACOUSTICS, ELECTRONIC INSTRUMENTS.

organetto (It.), small medieval PORTATIVE ORGAN.

Organ Mass, from the 15th century it was customary to perform the music of the Ordinary of the Mass by singers and organ in alternating phrases. The singers sang the plainsong and the organist played a polyphonic elaboration of it. In England this was referred to as 'keeping the Mass with organs'. Scheidt composed a complete Organ Mass for the Lutheran rite in Part III of his *Tablatura nova* (1624). The name has

also been given to two Masses by Haydn with orchestral accompaniment which include a part for organ *obbligato*. These are known in English as the 'Great' Organ Mass in E flat major (1766) and the 'Little' Organ Mass in B flat major, written about four years later.

organistrum (Lat.), hurdy-gurdy.

organo, *see* ORGAN

organo di coro (It.), choir organ.

organo di legno (It.), literally wooden organ. A term used in the 16th and 17th centuries for a small organ with flue pipes, as opposed to the REGAL, which was a reed organ.

organo pieno (It.; Lat., *organo pleno*), full organ.

organum (Lat., from Gr. ὄργανον instrument), (1) organ. Thus *pro organo pleno* means 'for full organ', that is, for an instrument of substantial size and adequate resources;

(2) a name (probably of popular origin) for a method of composition used in the several stages of medieval polyphony. The first stage was expounded about 900 in *Musica Enchiriadis* (printed in Gerbert, *Scriptores*, i, page 152). The *Scholia Enchiriadis* (printed in Gerbert, op. cit. i, page 173; English translation in O. Strunk, *Source Readings in Music History*, page 126), of about the same time, gives these examples:

P is the plainsong and O the added part, which follows the plainsong in parallel fifths or fourths, and in the latter case uses thirds and ends on a unison. If either or both of the parts were doubled at the octave above the result was called 'composite' *organum*.

In the next stage (11th–12th centuries) the added part moves in perfect intervals (octaves, fifths and fourths) above the plainsong. This is the earliest form of true polyphony:

In compositions of the middle of the 12th century the added part is much more florid, and the plainsong must have been sung quite slowly:

Léonin, the composer attached to Notre Dame, Paris, in the second half of the 12th century, wrote long liturgical compositions partly in plainsong, partly in florid organum with added parts composed in the RHYTHMIC MODES, and partly in measured descant:

Such measured sections were called *clausulae*. The addition of words to the upper parts of *clausulae* gave rise to the motet of the following century. The tenor of the last example is the same as that of the motet '*Mout me fugriés | In omni fratre | In seculum*', of which the opening is quoted under MOTET.

orgatron, an electronic organ invented in 1934 by Everett of Michigan.

Orgel, *see* ORGAN

Orgelbüchlein (Ger.), 'little organ book'. A collection of 46 short chorale preludes, composed by Bach between 1708 and 1717, 'in which a beginner at the organ is given instruction in developing a chorale in many different ways, and at the same time in acquiring facility in the study of the pedal, since in the chorales contained therein the pedal is treated as wholly *obbligato*.' It was originally intended to include 164 preludes, dealing with the church's year and with the principal articles of the Christian faith, but was never completed.

> H. GRACE: *The Organ Works of Bach* (1922)
> S. DE B. TAYLOR: *The Chorale Preludes of J. S. Bach* (1942)
> P. WILLIAMS: *Bach Organ Music* (1972)

Orgelpunkt (Ger.), pedal point.

Orgelwalze (Ger.), mechanical organ. *See* MECHANICAL MUSICAL INSTRUMENTS.

orgue (Fr.), organ. The plural, *orgues*, is also common.

orgue expressif (Fr.), harmonium.

Orlando, opera in three acts by Handel, inspired by Ariosto's 16th century epic poem *Orlando Furioso*. First performed in London in 1733, this work shows Handel at the height of his power as an opera composer, and contains notably (apart from an imposing mad scene) what is believed to be the earliest use of 5/8 time.

Ormandy, Eugene (born 1899), Hungarian born conductor, who studied the violin at the Budapest Royal Academy of Music from an early age and appeared frequently as a child prodigy – he was a professor of the violin by the time he was seventeen. He settled in the United States after a visit in 1921 and became a U.S. citizen. In 1931 he became conductor of the Minneapolis Symphony Orchestra, a post he held for five years. Thereafter he succeeded Stokowski as conductor of the Philadelphia Symphony Orchestra,

an association which has lasted to this day.

ornaments (Fr., *agrements*; Ger., *Manieren*; It., *abellimenti*), in some periods, ornaments (graces or embellishments) have been an important feature of melodic style, whether added extemporaneously by singers and players, or indicated by the composer in the form of signs, or incorporated in the notation. In the keyboard and lute pieces of the 16th century, some of which were elaborations of choral pieces, conventions of ornamentations arose, and to some extent, as in English virginal music, signs were used to indicate them. In the 17th and 18th centuries the principal types for which signs were used, varying somewhat in different countries, were: TRILL, MORDENT, APPOGGIATURA, ARPEGGIO, TURN, SPRINGER or NACHSCHLAG. In later periods most ornaments have been written out by the composer, though even as early as Bach (particularly in Bach's slow movements) the notation of decorations was often written out in full.

> P. ALDRICH: *Ornamentation in J. S. Bach's Organ Works* (1951)
> E. DANNREUTHER: *Musical Ornamentation* (1893)
> A. DOLMETSCH: *The Interpretation of the Music of the Seventeenth and Eighteenth Centuries* (1946)
> W. EMERY: *Bach's Ornaments* (1953)

Ornithoparcus, Andreas (c. 1485–1535), German theorist. His *Musicae activae micrologus* (1517) was translated into English by John Dowland (1609). A facsimile of both publications appeared in 1973.

orpharion, a type of CITTERN.

Orphée (Fr., *Orpheus*), title of the revised (French) version of Gluck's opera ORFEO ED EURIDICE.

Orpheus (1) symphonic poem by Liszt, originally intended to precede a performance of Gluck's opera at Weimar in 1854, but subsequently revised for the concert hall.

(2) ballet by Stravinsky, with choreography by Balanchine, first performed in New York in 1948.

Orpheus Britannicus, a collection of songs by Purcell (1659–95), published in two volumes in 1698 and 1702 (facsimile edition, 1965). A second edition, enlarged, appeared in 1706 and 1711.

Orpheus in the Underworld (Fr., *Orphée aux Enfers*), operetta in two acts by Offenbach, to a libretto by Crémieux and Halévy, first performed in 1858 at the Bouffes Parisiens. The work is one of the most popular and effervescent of Offenbach's satires, presenting the Second Empire in terms of the Greek gods, and burlesquing the legend, particularly Gluck's treatment of it.

Orr, Robin (born 1909), Scottish composer. After studying at the Royal College of Music and at Cambridge, he became a pupil of Casella in Siena and Nadia Boulanger in Paris. From 1956–1965 he was professor of music at Glasgow University; thereafter professor of music at Cambridge. His compositions include two operas (*Weir of Hermiston* and *Full Circle*), two symphonies and other orchestral works, chamber and instrumental music, song cycles (*From the Book of Philip Sparrow* and *Journeys and Places*), songs and church music.

Ortiz, Diego (born c. 1510), Spanish composer and, from 1553, court *maestro di cappella* in Naples. He wrote a treatise (*Tratado de glosas . . . en la música de Violones*, 1553; modern edition by Max Schneider,

1936) on the extemporising of variations (*glosas, diferencias*) on the viola da gamba in the style originated by Luis de Narvaez for the lute. A volume of his church music was published in 1565.

Orto, Marbriano de (died 1529), Flemish singer and composer. He was a singer in the Papal Chapel at Rome from 1484 to 1494 and, from 1505, at the court of Philip of Burgundy where he was also chaplain. His *Ave Maria* and a *chanson* were printed in Petrucci's *Odhecaton* (1501; modern edition by H. Hewitt, 1942), and Masses and motets in later publications of Petrucci.

Ory, 'Kid' (1889–1973), U.S. jazz trombonist whose heyday was in the 1920s when he appeared with King Oliver, Jelly Roll Morton and Louis Armstrong. His lusty style was also notable in his work with his own ensemble, Kid Ory's Creole Jazz Band. Though his career was unusually long by jazz standards, his playing lost much of its inventiveness in his later years.

Osiander, Lucas (1534–1604), German musician and theologian. His *Fünfzig geistliche Lieder und Psalmen* of 1586 was the first collection of chorales in which the tune was put in the treble; Lutheran composers had previously followed the old tradition of putting it in the tenor. His setting of 'Komm, heiliger Geist' is published in Schering's *Geschichte der Musik in Beispielen*, no 143.

O soave fanciulla (lovely maid in the moonlight), the love duet for Mimi and Rudolfo in Act 1 of Puccini's *La Boheme*.

ossia (It.), or. Used to indicate an alternative, usually simplified, to a passage in a composition.

ostinato (It.), a persistently repeated musical figure which may occur during a section of a composition or even throughout a whole piece. Ostinato patterns very often occur in the bass, so *basso ostinato* = ground bass.

Otello, Italian title for Shakespeare's play, used as the basis of a number of operas of which the most famous are Verdi's and Rossini's. Verdi's opera, in four acts to a libretto by Arrigo Boito, had its première at Milan in 1887. Dating from sixteen years after *Aida* (during which time he wrote no other operas) *Otello* was Verdi's penultimate opera, and reveals a fresh subtlety in his handling of music and text, and a vitality remarkable in a man of 73. To begin with, Verdi thought of calling the opera *Iago*, because of the musical and dramatic importance he gave to that role. Iago's 'Credo' in Act 2, in which he expounds his evil philosophy, is as vivid as any great Shakespearean soliloquy. Most Shakespeare operas debase the plays on which they are based. Verdi's Otello complements Shakespeare's, and at times seems even to surpass it.

Rossini's *Otello*, less profound than Verdi's, is in three acts, with a libretto by Marchese Francesco Berio di Salsa. It was first performed in Naples in 1816.

Othmayr, Caspar (1515–53), German composer. He studied at Heidelberg University under Lemlin and in 1545 was Rector of the school at Heilsbronn, near Ansbach. In 1548 he became Provost in Ansbach. He wrote settings of German songs, and composed motets and settings of Lutheran hymns. His *Symbola* (1547), a collection of five-part pieces each in honour of a notable person of his time, have been printed in a modern edition (1941) by Hans Albrecht.

ôtez, ôter (Fr.), remove (e.g. a violin mute).

ottava (It.), octave. Often abbreviated 8*va.*, *All'ottava* or 8*va*, an octave higher or lower (generally the former); *ottava alta* or *ottava sopra*, an octave higher; *ottava bassa* or *ottava sotto*, an octave lower; *coll'ottava* or *con ottava*, doubled at the octave above or below. The indications are written above the notes when they refer to the higher octave, below when they refer to the lower. A dotted line indicates how long the indication is valid. When the term 8*va* (or its equivalents) ceases to be valid, it is often contradicted by *loco*, '[in the normal] place'.

ottavino (It.), piccolo.

Ottobi, Giovanni, *see* HOTHBY

ottone (It.), brass. *Strumenti d'ottone* (or *ottoni* alone), brass instruments.

Ottone, Rè di Germania (It., *Otho, King of Germany*), opera in three acts by Handel to a libretto by Nicola Francesco Haym, first performed in London in 1723.

Our Hunting Fathers, symphonic song cycle, op 8, by Britten, for high voice and orchestra. Composed in 1936, it has a text (at one time criticised for its irreverence) devised by W. H. Auden.

Ours, L', *see* BEAR, THE

Our Town, music by Copland for the film of Thornton Wilder's drama. Written in 1940, it was later transformed by the composer into an orchestral suite.

Ousely, Frederick Arthur Gore (1825–89), English composer and musical historian. He was something of a prodigy, revealing his keen ear at the age of five when he recognised the key in which his father blew his nose; and at six played a piano duet with Mendelssohn. He was educated at Oxford, where he became professor in 1855 and remained so for 34 years. He edited the sacred music of Orlando Gibbons. His valuable collection of manuscripts, books and scores is now in St. Michael's, Tenbury, which he founded in 1854.

Out of Doors, set of five piano pieces by Bartók, first performed (by Bartók himself) in Budapest in 1926.

ouvert (Fr.; Lat., *apertum*; It., *verto*), open. A medieval term used in dance music, and in vocal pieces similar in structure, to indicate an intermediate cadence at the end of a repeated section when it is performed the first time, in contrast to a final cadence (Fr., *clos*: Lat., *clausum*; It., *chiuso*) used when it is performed the second time. *Ouvert* and *clos* thus correspond to what is now called 'first time' (or 'first ending') and 'second time'. For a 14th century example *see* CLOS.

ouverture (Fr.), overture.

overblowing, the means whereby HARMONICS are produced on woodwind instruments instead of fundamental notes. Normally there is a special key opening a small hole near the mouth piece to assist overblowing, and when it is brought into use the player merely duplicates his fingering in the lower register to produce the same note transposed. Most woodwind instruments produce the first harmonic when overblown and consequently the resulting notes are an octave higher, but clarinets overblow at the second harmonic or twelfth above the fundamental. Other harmonics are brought into use for higher notes.

overstrung, a method of positioning the strings in pianos so that they are on two levels and cross each other diagonally. This allows strings of greater length to be used in small instruments than would otherwise be possible.

overtones, *see* HARMONIC SERIES

overture, introductory music to an opera, oratorio, ballet, play, or other large-scale work. A 'concert overture', on the other hand, is written as an independent concert piece, e.g. *The Hebrides* by Mendelssohn, and Brahms's *Tragic Overture*.

The first established form was the French overture of Lully, which consisted of a slow section in a pompous dotted rhythm followed by a fast section in imitative style, as in his overture to *Thésée* (1675);

followed by

In some cases the Allegro ended with a short section in similar style to the opening. Blow's *Venus and Adonis*, Purcell's *Dido and Aeneas* (1689), Handel's *Rinaldo* (1711) and *Messiah* (1742) have overtures in the French style. The instrumental 'overtures' of German composers such as Muffat, Telemann, and Bach are French overtures followed by dance movements, and are now generally called SUITES.

The Italian opera overture (*sinfonia avanti l'opera*) in three movements, Allegro-Adagio-Allegro, was established by A. Scarlatti after 1680, and its later history merged with that of the symphony. The opera overture of the classical period was a single movement,

usually in sonata form. Gluck's idea that it should prepare the audience for the nature of the action (as in *Alceste*, 1769) was adopted in many later overtures, e.g. Mozart's *Don Giovanni* and *Cosi fan tutte*, by using musical themes from the opera, and was carried a stage further in such overtures as Weber's *Der Freischütz*, Wagner's *Tannhauser* and Verdi's *Force of Destiny*. Beethoven's *Leonore* overtures nos 2 and 3 adopted Gluck's principle so dramatically that they threatened to interfere with the effect of the opera (*Fidelio*) itself. They have been given, therefore, a separate existence as concert hall pieces which are really 'symphonic studies' of *Fidelio*. Similarly, since the time of Beethoven's *Egmont* (1810), overtures to incidental music generally use themes from the following scenes, a process which was carried out in reverse in Mendelssohn's *Midsummer Night's Dream* music.

Following Wagner's Lohengrin (1847), operas and incidental music frequently open with a PRELUDE — often (though not necessarily) shorter than an overture and leading straight into the first act. Sometimes the later acts of an opera also have preludes, e.g. Verdi's *La Traviata* and Bizet's *Carmen*.

The programmatic concert overture of the early romantic period (e.g. Mendelssohn's *Hebrides*) was the ancestor of the symphonic poem. The writing of concert overtures (many of which have a sonata-form basis) has continued to this day. Some of them are works composed originally for a specific occasion (e.g. Britten's *The Building of the House*), others continue the miniature tone-picture idea (e.g. Walton's *Portsmouth Point*).

Owen Wingrave, television opera by Britten, to a libretto by Myfanwy Piper, based on a ghost story by Henry James. First screened in Britain in 1971, it was later revised for stage production at Covent Garden.

Oxford Symphony, the name given to Haydn's symphony no 92 in G major after it was performed at a concert in Oxford (July, 1791) during his visit there to receive an honorary D. Mus. In fact the work was written three years earlier without this occasion in mind.

Ox Minuet, The (Ger., *Ochsenmenuett*), title of a *Singspiel* by Seyfried, first performed in Vienna, 1823. The music is arranged from works by Haydn, and is based on two earlier French works (*Le Menuet du Boeuf, ou Une Leçon de Haydn*, 1805, and *Haydn, ou Le Menuet du Boeuf*, 1812), which also used Haydn's music. The title is often misattributed to one of Haydn's minuets.

p., abbreviation (1) for *piano* (It., soft); in combination used to indicate degrees of softness, e.g. *pf.*, *poco forte*, moderately loud; *pp.*, *pianissimo*, very soft; *mp.*, *mezzo piano*, moderately soft;

(2) in French organ music, for *pédales*, i.e. pedals; or for *positif*.

Pachelbel, Johann (1653–1706), German organist and composer. He studied under Heinrich Schwemmer and in Vienna under Kerll from 1674. In 1677 he was organist at the court at Eisenach where he became a friend of J. S. Bach's father. Subsequently he held appointments at Erfurt (1678), Stuttgart (1690), Gotha (1692), and St. Sebaldus, Nuremberg (1695). As a composer of suites for harpsichord and chorale preludes in fughetta style for organ he was one of the important precursors of J. S. Bach. His harpsichord and organ works are printed in *Denkmäler der Tonkunst in Bayern*, ii (1) and iv (1), respectively. 94 organ verses for the eight tones of the Magnificat in the form of short fugues are printed in *Denkmäler der Tonkunst in Österreich*, viii (2). He also wrote several motets, arias, concertos and cantatas, though many have been lost.

His son **Wilhelm Hieronymous Pachelbel** (1685–1764), was also a composer. He was organist at St. Jacobi, Nuremberg in 1706, and at St. Sebaldus in 1725. Organ works by him are in *Denkmäler der Tonkunst in Bayern*, ii (1) and iv (1).

Pachmann, Vladimir de (1848–1933), Russian pianist who studied with his father in Odessa and at the Vienna Conservatorium. After making his first public appearance in Russia in 1869 he devoted himself to ten years' further study (interrupted by a brief emergence on the concert platform) before he finally embarked on the career of a travelling virtuoso. He excelled in the performance of Chopin, whose works he played with remarkable delicacy. His habit of making remarks to an audience (or to himself) during a performance endeared him to some listeners and infuriated others.

Pacific 231, 'symphonic movement' for orchestra by Honegger (1923) describing the 'visual impression and physical enjoyment' produced by a railway engine. The name is that of a U.S. engine.

Pacini, Giovanni (1796–1867), Italian composer, pupil of Marchesi in Bologna and under Furlanetto in Venice. He wrote his first opera for Milan in 1813. He was appointed *Kappelmeister* to the Empress Marie Louise and in 1834 founded a school of music in Viareggio. His works include more than seventy stage works, Masses, oratorios and cantatas.

Pacius, Fredrik (1809–91), German (naturalised Finnish) composer and violinist who studied under Spohr and Hauptmann in Cassel. He became violinist to the court orchestra at Stockholm in 1828; violin teacher at Helsinki University, 1834; professor 1860. His *Kung Carls Jakt*, generally referred to as the first

Finnish opera, was sung in Swedish on its first production in Helsinki in 1852, and was revived in a Finnish translation in 1905.

Paderewski, Ignacy Jan (1860–1941), Polish pianist and composer. He studied in Warsaw and Berlin, and in Vienna under Leschetizky, and became one of the most renowned pianists of his day, especially in his performances of Chopin. From 1915 he worked and spoke in the cause of Polish independence, and in 1919 became prime minister of his country. He resumed his concert tours in 1922. He composed many works including a piano concerto, an opera (*Manru*), a symphony, and songs.

padiglione, *see* PAVILLON

padiglione cinese, *see* PAVILLON CHINOIS

Padilla, Juan de (1605–73), Spanish composer. He was at the convent of San Pablo, Zamora, in 1660, at Zamora Cathedral in 1661, and at Toledo Cathedral in 1663. Several motets and villancicos by him are in manuscript at Valladolid. Until recently his identity has been confused with that of JUAN GUTIÉRREZ DE PADILLA.

Padilla, Juan Gutiérrez de (c. 1595–1664), Spanish-Mexican composer. He worked at Puebla (Mexico) from about 1620 until his death, becoming *maestro de capilla* at the cathedral there in 1629. A large number of church compositions, including five Masses, are in manuscript at Puebla. Several of his works are for

Niccolò Paganini: a portrait that catches something of the obsessive quality of the man

double choir. He was one of the most important composers in the history of music in Mexico.

R. STEVENSON: 'The "Distinguished Maestro" of New Spain: Juan Gutiérrez de Padilla' in *The Hispanic American Historical Review*, xxxv (1955)

Padmâvatî, opera-ballet in two acts by Roussel, to a libretto by Louis Lalois, first produced in Paris in 1923. The story is based on a violent episode in 13th century Indian history.

Paer, Ferdinando (1771–1839), Italian born composer who settled in France (where he became known as Paër) and was appointed musical director to Napoleon, who admired his music more than anyone else's. He wrote more than forty operas, including *Le Maitre de Chapelle* (1821), a popular *opéra comique*, and a sequel to Mozart's *The Marriage of Figaro* entitled *The New Figaro* (1797). Another of his operas, *Leonora*, had the same plot as Beethoven's *Fidelio* (it pre-dated the Beethoven by a year). He also composed two oratorios, cantatas, church music and some instrumental music. His works, very successful in their day, were performed at Parma, Venice, Vienna and Dresden, as well as in Paris.

Paganini, Niccolò (1782–1840), Italian violinist and composer, one of the most famous executants in musical history. He studied at Genoa and Parma, and made his first concert tour at thirteen. From 1805–13 he was music director at the court of the Princess of Lucca, and in 1828 began a tour which took him to Vienna, Germany, Paris (1831) and the British Isles. He also played the guitar and viola, and commissioned a work for the latter instrument from Berlioz. The result was *Harold in Italy* (1834), but Paganini never played it – reputedly because the solo part was insufficiently brilliant.

It was as an exponent of his own works that Paganini performed his greatest feats. Tall and skeletal, he played the violin with such verve and demonic intensity that many people believed him to be inspired by the Devil. The extraordinary range of his technical mastery can be found in his 24 caprices, op 1, for solo violin – among the few works by him which he allowed to be published during his lifetime. Some of the new technical developments in these pieces were adapted to the piano in the studies of Liszt and Schumann, and used for piano variations by Brahms and Rakhmaninov. He also wrote at least five violin concertos (one of his works in this form came to light only recently), *The Carnival of Venice* and other pieces for violin, and chamber music for guitar and strings. Ill health caused by a life of excess caused him to reduce his public appearances after 1834. His death, in Nice, brought in its wake a legend that he had been buried alive.

J. PULVER: *Paganini: the Romantic Virtuoso* (1936)
H. SPIVACKE: *Paganiniana* (1945)
L. DAY: *Paganini of Genoa* (1929)

Pagliacci, I (The Clowns), opera with a prologue and two acts by Leoncavallo to a libretto by the composer, first performed in Milan in 1892 under Toscanini. The opera, one of the finest examples of the Italian *verismo* style, is founded on a real-life incident in Calabria when an actor murdered his wife after a performance. Leoncavallo's father was the judge at the trial.

The opera concerns a group of travelling players. One of them, Tonio, explains in the prologue that

Pagliacci: Melba as Nedda and De Lucia as Canio at Covent Garden in 1893

actors are only human. The comedians erect their booth and parade in their costumes before the villagers. After the angelus is heard, Nedda (the wife of Canio) and Tonio are left alone but she, annoyed by his attentions, strikes him with a whip. He leaves her, swearing revenge. Silvio (a young peasant) tries to persuade Nedda to fly away with him that night. Tonio, who has been listening to their conversation, fetches Canio and brings him to the scene. Silvio escapes unrecognized, and Nedda will not reveal the name of her lover.

During the play Canio stumbles through his part and finally demands to know her lover's name. When she answers lightly he becomes enraged and stabs her with a knife. Silvio, who leaps on to the stage to try to protect her, is recognised by Canio, who quickly plunges the knife into his heart. Everyone stands irresolute with horror. Canio turns to the audience and announces: 'The comedy is ended.'

Paine, John Knowles (1839–1906), U.S. composer who studied in Portland and Berlin, and in the 1870s built up the music faculty at Harvard University (where he was appointed professor in 1875). He composed two symphonies, symphonic poems, cantatas and other choral works, chamber music, piano and organ works and incidental music for plays.

Paisiello, (Paesiello), Giovanni (1740–1816), Italian

composer, pupil of Durante in Naples. He began as a composer of church music, but from 1763 found his true *métier* in *opera buffa*. In 1776 he became court conductor to Catherine the Great and director of the Italian opera in St. Petersburg. In 1784 he was appointed court conductor at Naples, and in 1802 moved to Paris as director of music in the chapel of Napoléon Bonaparte (of whom he was a supporter). On returning to Naples, he found himself under a cloud, which lasted until his death. His *Barber of Seville* (1782) was the most famous setting of the text before Rossini's. Beethoven wrote a set of variations for piano on his aria 'Nel cor più' from *La Molinara* (1788). His output included about a hundred operas, church music, symphonies, concertos and chamber music.

Paladilhe, Émile (1844–1926), French composer, pupil of Halévy and winner of the *Prix de Rome*, 1860. He composed operas, a symphony, two Masses and songs.

Palestrina, Giovanni Pierluigi da (c. 1525–94), Italian composer, who took his name from his birthplace, Palestrina, near Rome. He was a chorister at Santa Maria Maggiore in Rome in 1537, becoming organist and choirmaster at Palestrina Cathedral in 1544. In 1551 he was summoned to be choirmaster of the Cappella Giulia by Pope Julius III, who in 1555 made him a member of the Papal Choir. With two others, he was dismissed in the same year, apparently because he was married, but nevertheless was appointed musical director at St. John Lateran in succession to Lassus. He resigned in 1560, and from 1561 was choirmaster at Santa Maria Maggiore, from 1567 in the service of Cardinal Ippolito d'Este, and from 1571 director of the Cappella Giulia, succeeding Animuccia. On the death of his wife in 1580 he decided to become a priest and received the tonsure, but three months later married a wealthy widow.

Since the writing of Fux's *Gradus* in 1725 Palestrina's style has been regarded as the exemplar of the greatest age of counterpoint, and since Baini's monograph of 1828 as the purest model of devotional polyphony (*see* MOTU PROPRIO). While his style is noteworthy for its serenity of expression, artistic discipline and thorough consistency (*see* H. K. ANDREWS, *Introduction to the Technique of Palestrina*, 1958; *see also* K. JEPPESEN, *The Style of Palestrina*, 2nd edition, 1946), it is by no means representative of 16th century contrapuntal style as a whole. Nor is there any historical basis for Baini's story that his *Missa Papae Marcelli* influenced decisions of the Council of Trent. The reforms instituted by Pius IV and Pius V forbade the singing of Masses whose counterpoint was so elaborate as to obscure the words, and which contained words foreign to the liturgy of the Mass. Palestrina's later works were in conformity with those decrees, and his position caused him to be entrusted with a 'reformed' version of the plainsong of the mass, published in the 'Medicean' Gradual of 1614, which has been replaced in this century by the Solesmes versions of the medieval chant.

Palestrina's most typical style is a diatonic and modal imitative polyphony, beautifully balanced in rhythm, in melody, and in the use of dissonance. In compositions in six or more parts it leans more often towards the originally Venetian and more homophonic style of antiphonal writing for divided choir, as in the *Stabat Mater*. About three-quarters of his Masses, for four to eight voices, are PARODY MASSES; a few are based on a plainsong *cantus firmus*, e.g. *Ecce sacerdos magnus*, or on a secular song, e.g., *L'homme armé*. His church music includes motets in four to eight and in twelve parts, Lamentations, Magnificats, Litanies and Psalms. He also wrote sacred and secular madrigals.

A complete edition of the works of Palestrina in 33 volumes was published by Breitkopf and Härtel (1862–1907). A new complete edition in 34 volumes, edited by R. Casimiri and L. Bianchi, is nearing completion.

> H. COATES: *Palestrina* (1938)
> Z. K. PYNE: *Palestrina; his Life and Times* (1922)
> J. ROCHE: *Palestrina* (1971)

Palestrina, opera in three acts by Pfitzner, to a libretto by the composer, first performed in Munich in 1917. Though not widely performed outside Germany, the work has an impressive reputation as a milestone of the post-Wagnerian opera. Pfitzner called it *Musikalische Legende* (musical legend) and founded his text on the story that the composer Palestrina had written his *Missa Papae Marcelli* through angelic inspiration, thereby persuading the Council of Trent not to ban polyphonic music.

palindrome, a word, phrase or sentence which reads the same backwards as forwards. Hence also a musical phrase or piece of music of which the second half is the first half in retrograde motion, e.g. the 'crab' canon in Bach's *Musikalisches Opfer*.

Pallavicini (Pallavicino), Carlo (c. 1630–88), Italian composer. He lived in Venice and also (from 1667) in Dresden, where he was appointed court *Kapellmeister*. He contributed greatly to the development of the aria in Venetian opera. The most mature of his 21 operas is *Gerusalemme liberata* (Dresden, 1687; modern edition in *Denkmäler deutscher Tonkunst*, 1v).

Pallavicino, Benedetto (c. 1551–1601), Italian composer. He was at the court of Mantua from 1581, and in 1596 succeeded Giaches de Wert as *maestro di cappella* to the Duke of Mantua. Monteverdi was his successor in this post. Ten books of his madrigals were published between 1579 and 1612. Madrigals by him are printed in Torchi's *L'arte musicale in Italia*, ii, and in *Das Chorwerk*, lxxx.

Palmgren, Selim (1878–1951), Finnish composer, pianist, and conductor, who studied in Helsinki and later in Germany and Italy. In 1923 he became teacher of piano and composition at the Eastman School, Rochester (New York State). In 1930 he returned to Finland, as critic and teacher. He composed piano concertos, choral works and songs, operas and orchestral works, and piano pieces, the latter popular with amateur pianists.

Pammelia, title of Thomas Ravenscroft's collection (1609) of anonymous canons, rounds, and catches, the first such collection to be published in England. A continuation, *Deuteromelia*, was published in the same year. Facsimiles of both were published in 1961.

pancake drum (Fr., *tarole*), a side drum of normal diameter but only about eight centimetres deep. Its tone is crisp and high pitched.

pandora (*pandore, bandora, bandore*). A plucked string

instrument of the CITTERN family, developed in England in the mid 16th century.

pandorina, a small LUTE.

pandoura, an instrument of the LUTE type with a long neck. It is still in use in Balkan countries, and in Turkey, Egypt and the East.

pandura (Gr.), an oriental name (supposedly of Sumerian origin) applied by the Greeks to the three-stringed lute, for which the vernacular term was *trichordon.*

Panharmonicon, a mechanical instrument, invented by Maelzel, which apparently could reproduce orchestral sounds with reasonable success, remembered today largely because Beethoven wrote *The Battle of Victoria* for it.

panpipes, pandean pipes or syrinx, instrument of great antiquity consisting of several PIPES of different lengths bound together in a slight arc. *See* NEI

pantaleon, a type of DULCIMER invented during the 18th century by Pantaleon Hebenstreit, and named after him by Louis XIV.

pantomime, traditionally a play in dumb-show. The name derives from the Greek, 'all imitating'. In England in the 18th century the name was used to refer to a stage entertainment with music similar to the Italian *commedia dell'arte.* This led in turn to the popular stage entertainment, still popular today, in which a fairy-tale or traditional story was enacted on stage at Christmas time, incorporating spoken words interspersed with music.

pantonality, term referring to music not written in any definite key. Schoenberg preferred this term to 'atonality'.

Panufnik, Andrzej (born 1914), Polish composer and conductor, son of a Polish father and an English mother. He studied at the Warsaw Conservatoire and with Weingartner in Vienna. During World War II, which he spent in Nazi occupied Poland, he composed patriotic songs under a pseudonym. In 1945 he became conductor of the Cracow Philharmonic, and in 1946 of the Warsaw Philharmonic. His dislike of post-war politics in Poland led to his move in 1954 to Britain, where for three years he was conductor of the Birmingham Symphony Orchestra. His compositions, mainly for orchestra, include a *Sinfonia rustica* (1948) and a *Sinfonia sacra* (1963).

Papillons, (Fr., *Butterflies*), a set of twelve short piano pieces by Schumann, op 2 (published, 1832). The composer claimed that his inspiration derived from a scene describing a masked ball in Jean Paul's novel *Die Flegeljahre,* though some of the material is in fact derived from a set of eight Polonaises for piano duet, composed in 1828 but not published till 1933. The music also contains thematic and atmospheric links with *Carnaval,* op 9.

paradiddle, a method of executing a repeated pattern of notes (usually four) on the side drum so that successive principal beats are not played by the same hand.

Paradies, (Paradisi), Pietro Domenico (1707–91), Italian composer, who studied under Porpora and in 1747 went to London, where he taught the harpsichord and singing. He composed harpsichord sonatas and operas.

Paradise and the Peri (1) *Das Paradies und die Peri,* a large-scale composition for soloists, chorus and orches-

tra by Schumann, op 50 (1843) with words from a German translation of a poem in Thomas Moore's *Lalla Rookh.* The Peri is an angel who has been cast out of Paradise and who searches the world for a gift which will gain her readmittance. In spite of the sentiment of the story the music contains a good deal of lyrical charm;

(2) fantasia-overture by Sterndale Bennett, op 42 (1862), based on the same poem by Thomas Moore.

Paradisi, *see* PARADIES

parallel intervals, *see* CONSECUTIVE INTERVALS

parallel motion, the movement of two or more parts of the same INTERVAL, whether the interval is major or minor, perfect or imperfect. *See* CONSECUTIVE INTERVALS.

Paray, Paul M. A. Charles (born 1886), French conductor and composer. He studied at the Paris Conservatoire, and won the *Prix de Rome* in 1911. For many years he was conductor of the Colonne Orchestra of Paris, which was one of the first European orchestras to visit Britain after World War II – in 1947 it opened the inaugural Edinburgh Festival with Paray as conductor. In 1952 he took charge of the Detroit Symphony Orchestra, an appointment he held until 1964.

pardessus de viole (Fr.), descant viol made in the 18th century. It was tuned a fourth higher than the treble viol (*dessus de viole*).

Paride e Elena (Paris and Helen), opera in five acts by Gluck, to a libretto by Raniero de' Calzabigi, first performed in Vienna in 1770.

Paris Symphonies, a set of six symphonies by Haydn commissioned by the Concert de la Loge Olympique in Paris:

no 82 in C major, The Bear, 1786;
no 83 in G minor, The Hen, 1785;
no 84 in E flat major, 1786;
no 85 in B flat major, The Queen of France, c. 1786;
no 86 in D major, 1786;
no 87 in A major, 1785.

Paris Symphony, the title given to Mozart's symphony no 31 in D major, K297 (1778), which he composed during his visit to Paris at the age of 22, and which had its first performance at a *Concert Spirituel* in that city. The work contains a number of witty references to the symphonic style in fashion in Paris.

Parker, Charlie 'Bird' (1920–55), black U.S. jazz musician. A brilliant alto saxophonist, he was the principal figure of the 1945 jazz revolution, when swing was replaced by modern jazz. His complex, wriggling, often astoundingly fast improvisations were copied by a multitude of disciples, not only saxophonists. But it was those who learnt from Parker without actually imitating him (e.g., Miles Davis) who enabled modern jazz to progress in the years after Parker's early death.

Parker, Horatio William (1863–1919), U.S. organist and composer, pupil of Chadwick in Boston and Rheinberger in Munich. He was teacher at the National Conservatory, New York (of which Dvořák was the director), and in 1894 became professor at Yale. He composed oratorios (including *Hora Novissima*), orchestral works and keyboard pieces.

parlando (It.), speaking. A style of singing, found particularly in opera, in which the tone approximates to that of speech.

Parody Mass (Lat., *missa parodia*), a term used, since the 19th century, for a polyphonic Mass composed by using the existing music, in more or less complete sections, of a motet or *chanson*, a procedure adopted by many composers from Ockeghem to Palestrina. Nicholas Gombert's Mass *Je suis déshéritée*, for example, begins thus:

The *chanson* by Pierre Cadéac on which it was based begins:

L. LOCKWOOD: 'On "Parody" as Term and Concept in 16th-century Music', in *Aspects of Medieval and Renaissance Music*, editor J. La Rue (1967)

Parry, Charles Hubert Hastings (1848–1918), English composer and musical historian, educated at Eton and Oxford. After further studies with Sterndale Bennett, Macfarren, Henry Hugo Pierson and Dannreuther, he produced a piano concerto in F sharp minor and *Promethus Unbound* for chorus (1880). A series of choral works, including *Ode on St. Cecilia's Day* (1889), *L'Allegro ed il Penseroso* (1890), *Job* (1892), *The Lotus-Eaters* (1892), *Ode to Music* (1901), *The Pied Piper of Hamelin* (1905), and *Songs of Farewell* (1916–18), and his work as director of the Royal College of Music from 1894 established him as the leader, with Stanford, of the so-called English

musical renaissance. Today he is remembered for his setting of Milton's *Blest Pair of Sirens* (1887) and the unison song, *Jerusalem*. He was knighted in 1898, made a baronet in 1903, and was professor of music at Oxford from 1900 until 1908.

Parsifal, opera in three acts by Wagner, to a libretto by the composer himself. First performed at Bayreuth in the summer of 1882, it was described by Wagner as a *Bühnenweihfestspiel* (sacred festival drama) and was his last work for the stage.

The story is based on a medieval legend related to that of Lohengrin, but is earlier in the sequence. It tells how Amfortas, ruler of the Knights of the Holy Grail, has yielded to the charms of the enchantress Kundry. He has been wounded by the spear that pierced the side of Christ. Klingsor, an evil magician, possesses the spear, which was one of the sacred relics guarded by the Knights before Amfortas sinned. Only one who is completely guileless and simple can recapture the spear and with it heal Amfortas' wound. Parsifal, a forest lad, has in ignorance killed a sacred swan and is brought to the castle of the knights where Gurnemanz, an old knight, hopes to find in him the deliverer from sin. He is, however, so simple and ignorant that he fails to understand the celebration of the Eucharist which he is allowed to witness, and is dismissed. Having found his way into Klingsor's magic garden, he resists the enchantment offered him by Kundry, and when Klingsor desperately hurls the spear at him, he catches it and bears it off. After long wanderings, he returns to the castle. He heals Amfortas' wound, and uncovers the Grail. As the knights kneel before their new ruler, Kundry, long since a penitent in the service of the Grail, dies.

Wagner believed that performances of *Parsifal* outside Bayreuth would be detrimental to the character of the work, and consequently he forbade them. His widow, Cosima, compromised by allowing concert performances to be given. In 1903 the New York Metropolitan fought a legal battle to stage the work, and successfully broke copyright. Other companies followed suit, and the opera soon established itself internationally – though it has taken until the 1970s for the Bayreuth practice of listening to it reverentially, without applause, to be broken.

Parsley, Osbert (c. 1511–85), English composer and singer at Norwich Cathedral for fifty years. His church music is printed in *Tudor Church Music*, x.

Parsons, Robert (died 1570), English composer. From 1563 he was a Gentleman of the Chapel Royal. He composed services, anthems, motets, consort songs and pieces for viols. His music had an important influence on the early compositions of Byrd, notably a five part In Nomine which Byrd arranged for keyboard (*Musica Britannica*, xxviii).

part-book, when large CHOIRBOOKS began to go out of use in the early 16th century it became usual to write and print the parts (e.g. *cantus, altus, tenor, bassus*) of a choral work, and later of pieces for instruments, in separate part-books. In some cases it has unfortunately resulted that sets of early manuscript or printed part-books have been dispersed, and one or more of the set has been lost. Since about 1600 SCORE form has been used for orchestral, chamber and choral works, while the various parts of an orchestral or chamber piece, and occasionally the voice parts of a choral work, are published or written separately for performance.

parte (It.), voice-part.

Parthenia (Gr., maidenhood), the title, which continues thus: *or The Maydenhead of the first musicke that ever was printed for the Virginalls*, of a collection of 21 pieces by Byrd, Bull, and Gibbons, published in 1612 or early in 1613 as a present for Frederick V, Elector Palatine of the Rhine, and his wife-to-be, Princess Elizabeth, daughter of James I. It was probably the

Parthenia (c. 1612): the title page

first book of music printed from engraved plates in England. Facsimiles were published in 1942 and 1972, and a modern edition (edited by Thurston Dart) in 1960. A sister volume, *Parthenia Inviolata*, was published later, possibly in 1625 as a wedding present for Prince Charles of England and Princess Henrietta Maria of France. It contains twenty anonymous arrangements for virginals and bass viol. A facsimile (with a substantial introduction by Thurston Dart) and a modern edition (also by Dart) were published in 1961.

partials, tones of the HARMONIC SERIES. The lowest note of the harmonic series is known as the first partial, and the others are upper partials, or overtones.

partial signature, a term used to denote a situation common in music between c. 1350 and c. 1520 in which the key signatures of some parts, usually higher parts, have fewer flats than those of others, usually the lower parts. The theoretical implications of the practice have not been fully explained. From it arose the frequent occurrences of FALSE RELATION, e.g.:

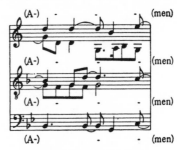

DAVY, *Stabat Mater* (c. 1500)

which was a persistent idiom in English music until Purcell.

> E. E. LOWINSKY: 'Conflicting Views on Conflicting Signatures', in *Journal of the American Musicological Society*, vii (1954); 'The Function of Conflicting Signatures in Early Polyphonic Music', in *Musical Quarterly*, xxxi (1945)

partita (It.), division. The term originally meant variation, and was first used in the early 17th century, e.g. in Frescobaldi's *Toccate e Partite d'Intavolatura di Cembalo* of 1615. It is not clear why German composers at the end of the century began to use it in the sense of SUITE, as Bach did in the six partitas for harpsichord (*Clavierübung*, part 1), in the Suite (*Ouverture*) in the French style (*Clavierübung*, part 2) and in the three partitas for solo violin. The term is still sometimes used by composers today, e.g. Walton, who has written a partita for orchestra, and Penderecki, whose partita is scored for harpsichord and other instruments.

partition (Fr.), score. *Partition d'orchestre*, full score. *Partition chant et piano*, vocal score.

Partitur (Ger.), score.

partitura (It.), score.

partiturophon, one of the group of electronic ether wave instruments using oscillating frequencies. The difference between two electrical frequencies produces the sound which is then amplified.

part song, a term used, especially in the 19th and 20th centuries, for a short unaccompanied piece for choir in HOMOPHONIC style, as distinct from the polyphonic style of the 16th century MADRIGAL.

part writing (Ger., *Stimmführung*), hence U.S. 'voice leading', the writing of the parts of a polyphonic composition in such a way as to produce a good melodic line in each part, which is the chief end of the study of COUNTERPOINT.

pasodoble (or **paso doble**) (Sp.), modern Spanish dance in quick 2/4 time – the name literally means 'double step'. A tongue-in-cheek example of the dance is to be found in Walton's *Façade*.

paspy, 17th century English equivalent of *passepied*.

Pasquali, Nicolò (died 1757), Italian violinist and composer, who lived in Edinburgh from c. 1740, in Dublin 1748–51, and then returned to Edinburgh. He composed songs, overtures, and solo and trio sonatas. He wrote *Thoroughbass made easy* (1757) and *The Art of Fingering the Harpsichord*, published about three years after his death.

Pasquini, Bernardo (1637–1710), Italian composer,

pupil of Vittori and Cesti. He was organist of Santa Maria Maggiore, Rome, and harpsichordist of the opera orchestra, in which Corelli was first violinist. His pupils included Durante, Georg Muffat, Gasparini and Domenico Scarlatti. He composed keyboard music, operas, oratorios, and cantatas.

passacaglia (It., Fr., *passecaille*; both possibly from Sp. *pasacalle*, 'street song'), a dance introduced into keyboard music early in the 17th century; later the term came to mean a piece of music in which a theme is continually repeated. Composers made no effective distinction between the passacaglia and the CHACONNE; both were normally in triple time, were composed in regular phrases of two, four, or eight bars, and had a FULL CLOSE at the end of each phrase. (For a passacaglia in duple time see Handel's harpsichord suite no 7.) French composers wrote the passacaglia in RONDO form (*passecaille en rondeau*) by alternating it with a series of different phrases. In the *Passacaille* in F. Couperin's eighth *ordre* for clavecin the theme:

is repeated after each of eight different *couplets*. German composers usually composed the passacaglia in variation form, over a regular GROUND BASS, as in the passacaglias for organ by Buxtehude:

and Bach. Modern examples, e.g. the finale of Hindemith's fourth string quartet, also exist in this form.

The original dance was slow and stately, and this character is generally preserved in the instrumental examples.

passamezzo (It.), 'half step', a dance in duple time and in fairly quick tempo, which was popular in the second half of the 16th century. The melody (a) is thus given by Nicholaus Ammerbach in his *Orgel oder Instrument Tablatur* (1571):

The bass, of which (b) is the simplest form, was later used as a basis for variations, for example, the *Passamezzo* pavanes and galliards by Byrd and Philips in the *Fitzwilliam Virginal Book* and Scheidt's *Passamezzo* Variations in Part I of the *Tabulatura Nova* (1624). Philips's *Galiarda Passamezzo* begins thus:

The word appears in other English virginal books as 'passinge mesures' and 'passa measures'. New tunes were composed on this or slightly varied forms of the *passamezzo* bass, for example *Quodling's Delight*, used for a set of variations by Giles Farnaby (*Fitzwilliam*

Virginal Book, no 114) and Campion's 'Fain would I wed' in his *Fourth Booke of Ayres* (c. 1617). Some versions of *Greensleeves* make partial use of the *passamezzo* harmonies along with those of the ROMANESCA. The bass known as *passamezzo nuovo* or *moderno*:

was also used in variations as in the *Passameza* for five instruments by Valentin Haussmann in his *Neue Intrade* of 1604, printed in *Denkmäler deutscher Tonkunst*, xvi, page 141.

passecaille (Fr.), passacaglia.

passepied (Fr.), a French dance, said to have come from Brittany, which was introduced into the French ballet c. 1650 and thence into the SUITE, as in Bach's fifth *English Suite*. It is in quick triple time. The *passepied* in Couperin's second *ordre* for clavecin begins thus:

English composers wrote the word as 'paspy'.

passing note (Fr., *note de passage*; Ger., *Durchgangsnote*), a note taken scalewise between two notes consonant with the prevailing harmony, which may itself be dissonant with that harmony, e.g.:

where both the C and A are passing notes. The principle may be extended to two or more notes taken scalewise, as in the penultimate bar of Chopin's Nocturne, op 48, no 2:

If a passing note falls on a weak beat, it is called an unaccented passing note; if on a strong beat, an accented passing note.

Passion, from about the 12th century the plainsong to which the gospel accounts of the Passion were recited on Palm Sunday and the following days was divided between three singers who recited the parts of Christ

(*bassa voce*, in a low range), the Evangelist (*media voce*, in middle range), and the crowd or *turba* (*alta voce*, in a high range). In the 15th century part singing began to be used for the words of the *turba*, the other parts being still sung in plainsong; three of the earliest settings of this kind are English, two by unknown composers (c. 1450), the other by Richard Davy (c. 1500). Another method, that of setting the whole text in polyphony, sometimes using the plainsong as a CANTUS FIRMUS in the tenor, arose about the beginning of the 16th century. During the next century and a half Passions, in one or other of these ways, were written by many composers, among them Lassus, Victoria, Scandello, Byrd, Gallus, Lechner and Schütz. A number of settings of the Passion composed between c. 1500 and 1631 are printed in whole or in part in O. Kade's *Die ältere Passionskomposition* (1893).

The new features in settings of the Passion by Lutheran composers after 1640 were the use of recitative, and the introduction of contemplative poems in the form of chorales and arias. The *St. John* (1723) and *St. Matthew* (1729) Passions by Bach are the final flowering of this development. Thomas Selle used recitative in his *St. John* Passion of 1643, Johann Sebastiani included chorales for solo voice in his *St. Matthew* Passion, composed in 1663, and Johann Theile's *St. Matthew* Passion of 1673 has arias with instrumental ritornelli. C. P. E. Bach composed two Passions in Hamburg (1787 and 1788), but in later times there have been few important works in this form. One of the most recent settings is Penderecki's *St. Luke* Passion (1966).

A list of Passions up to J. S. Bach in modern editions is given in Basil Smallman's study, *The Background of Passion Music* (second edition, 1970).

Passione, La (It., *The Passion*), name given to Haydn's symphony no 49 in F minor (1768). Einstein believed that Haydn composed this symphony for performance in Holy Week; but its title could refer just as easily to the sombre intensity of the music – which dates from the composer's *Stürm und Drang* period.

pasticcio (It.), literally a pie. A work that has been put together by taking items from the works of various composers, as was often the case with 18th century operas. For example, J. C. Bach's first appearance before an English audience was with the comic opera *Il Tutore e la Pupilla*, a *pasticcio* 'selected from various celebrated authors' (i.e. composers) and 'performed under the direction of Mr. John Bach, a Saxon Master of Music', who also composed the overture. A *pasticcio* may be the result of voluntary collaboration, as with the opera *Muzio Scevola* (1721), of which Mattei, Bononcini and Handel each composed one act.

pastiche, a piece in which a composer deliberately apes the style of another (usually well-known) composer.
See also PASTICCIO

pastoral (noun) (1) alternative name for the madrigal, as in F. Pilkington's two sets of *Madrigals and Pastorals* (1614 and 1624);

(2) any work dealing with, or representing, country life, e.g. Bliss's *Lie strewn the white flocks* for mezzo-soprano, chorus, flute, timpani and strings.

pastorale (It.), (1) an instrumental movement, usually in 6/8 or 12/8 time, with long bass notes, giving a drone effect similar to that of the MUSETTE. One of the earliest examples in this style is a *Capriccio pastorale* in Fresco-baldi's *Toccate d'Intavolatura di Cembalo et Organo* of 1614/15. Later instances are the optional last movement of Corelli's *Concerto Grosso No. 8*:

the pastoral symphonies in Handel's *Messiah* and Bach's *Christmas Oratorio*, and Bach's *Pastorale* for organ;

(2) a stage entertainment based on a legendary or rustic subject, originally with little or no music, but during the 18th century more operatic in style, e.g. Handel's *Acis and Galatea*.

'Pastoral' Sonata, (1) the name given to Beethoven's piano sonata in D major, op 28, by the Hamburg publisher August Cranz (1789–1870), probably because the finale has elements of a rustic dance;

(2) Rheinberger's third organ sonata in G major, op 88.

Pastoral Symphony, (1) Beethoven's sixth symphony in F major, op 68 (1808), entitled *Sinfonia pastorale*. The titles of the five movements are:

1. *Erwachen heiterer Empfindungen bei der Ankunft auf dem Lande* (awakening of happy feelings on arriving in the country).
2. *Scene am Bach* (scene by the brook).
3. *Lustiges Zusammensein der Landleute* (merry gathering of peasants), interrupted by
4. *Gewitter. Sturm* (thunderstorm), leading to
5. *Hirtengesang. Frohe und dankbare Gefühle nach dem Sturm* (shepherds' song. Cheerful and thankful feelings after the storm).

The second movement introduces the characteristic calls of the nightingale (flute), quail (oboe) and cuckoo (clarinet). In the programme of the first performance, December 22nd, 1808, the work was described as 'Pastoral Symphonie: mehr Ausdruck der Empfindung als Malerei' (Pastoral symphony: an expression of emotion rather than tone-painting). Beethoven may have got the idea of a work on this subject from J. H. Knecht's symphony *Le Portrait Musical de la Nature* (c. 1785), which has a similar programme.

(2) the title which Vaughan Williams gave to his third symphony. First performed in London in 1922, the music incorporates a wordless soprano voice. The composer revised the score in 1955;

(3) the name given to an instrumental piece in *siciliano* rhythm in Handel's *Messiah* (1742). It occurs immediately before the recitative beginning 'There were shepherds abiding in the field' and was called 'Pifa' by the composer;

(4) also applied to an instrumental piece in the same

rhythm at the beginning of Part 2 of Bach's *Christmas Oratorio* (1734). *See* PASTORALE

Pastor fido, Il, (It. *The Faithful Shepherd*), opera in three acts by Handel, to a libretto by Giacomo Rossi (from Guarini's pastoral play). The first performance was in London in 1712.

'Pathetic' Sonata, Beethoven's piano sonata in C minor, op 13, published in 1799 with the title *Grande sonate pathétique* (one of the few sonata titles chosen by the composer himself). Note, however, that the title was intended to mean 'with emotion' rather than 'with pathos'. The plan of the first movement, with its alternation of slow and quick sections, is similar to that of the first movement of a sonata in F minor dating from 1783, when Beethoven was twelve years old. It is also possible that he was influenced by Dussek's sonata in C minor (c. 1793), the slow movement of which is marked *patetico*.

'Pathetic' Symphony, Tchaikovsky's sixth symphony in B minor, op 74 (1893). The title *Symphonie Pathétique* was authorised by the composer, who died of cholera shortly after conducting the first performance, thus giving this emotional music an additional morbid interest.

Patience, comic opera in two acts by Gilbert and Sullivan, satirising 'aestheticism' and first performed in London in 1881.

Patrick, Nathaniel (died 1595), English organist and master of the choristers at Worcester Cathedral from c. 1590. He composed services and consort songs.

patter song, a kind of song, popular in comic opera, involving the rapid, often tongue-twisting enunciation of syllables. Leporello's 'Catalogue Aria' in *Don Giovanni* was an early example of the style. Other examples are Figaro's 'Largo al factotum' in Rossini's *Barber of Seville* and the duet, 'Cheti, cheti,' for Don Pasquale and Dr. Malatesta in Donizetti's *Don Pasquale*. Patter songs also play an important part in the operettas of Gilbert and Sullivan.

Patti, Adelina (Adela Juana Maria) (1843–1919), Spanish-born soprano of Italian parentage, who studied under Maurice Strakosch and in 1859 made her opera debut in New York as Lucia. She sang in Britain, Europe, North and South America, and in 1914 made her last public appearance. She was the most famous soprano of her time (1860–1906), excelling both in opera and oratorio.

Patzak, Julius (1898–1974), Austrian tenor. He was originally active as a conductor but turned to singing in his twenties and sang at the Munich Opera from 1928 until 1945. Thereafter he was a member of the Vienna State Opera. He was a famed exponent of Florestan in *Fidelio* and Palestrine in Pfitzner's opera. In addition he was a captivating performer of the songs of his native Vienna.

Pauken (Ger.), timpani.

Paukenmesse (Ger., Drum Mass), the nickname given to Haydn's Mass in C major (1796) because of the prominent part played in it by the timpani. Haydn himself entitled the work *Missa in tempore belli* (Mass in time of war).

Paukenschlag, Symphonie mit dem, *see* SURPRISE SYMPHONY

Paukenwirbel, Symphonie mit dem, *see* DRUM ROLL SYMPHONY

Paulus, see ST. PAUL

Paumann, Conrad (c. 1410–1473), German organist and composer. Blind from birth, he was organist at St. Sebaldus in Nuremberg from 1446, and court organist at Munich from 1467. His gravestone in the Frauenkirche in Munich shows him playing a portative organ. His *Fundamentum organisandi* (Foundations of Composition) of 1452 is one of the earliest manuscripts of keyboard tablature. It contains exercises in composing in organ style and arrangements of German songs. A facsimile of the *Lochamer Liederbuch*, which contains the *Fundamentum*, was published by K. Ameln in 1925. Paumann's organ setting of 'Mit ganczem Willen' from this manuscript is printed in *Historical Anthology of Music*, edited by A. T. Davison and W. Apel, no 81.

Paumgartner, Bernhard (1887–1971), Austrian musicologist, conductor and composer, who was director of the Salzburg Mozarteum from 1917 until 1938 and again after 1945. He took a prominent part in the organization of the Salzburg festivals and founded the Salzburg Mozart Orchestra. His studies were devoted principally to the 18th century: he published a biography of Mozart and also edited (with O. E. Deutsch) Leopold Mozart's letters to his daughter. His compositions include operas, ballets and incidental music for an open air production of Goethe's *Faust* at Salzburg.

Paur, Emil (1855–1932), Austrian conductor who studied at the Vienna Conservatorium. After holding posts in Germany, he was appointed conductor of the Boston Symphony Orchestra (succeeding Nikisch) in 1893; New York Philharmonic Orchestra (succeeding Anton Seidl) in 1898; Pittsburgh Orchestra in 1903; and the Berlin Royal Opera in 1912.

pausa (It.), a rest.

pause, (1) (Eng.), a wait of indefinite length on a note or rest, indicated by the sign ⌒ (Fr., *point d'orgue*; Ger., *Fermate*; It., *fermata*).

(2) (Fr.), a rest (in particular, in French, a semibreve rest). *Generalpause* (Ger.), abbreviated *G.P.*, a rest for the complete orchestra for a whole bar (or even several bars in quick tempo).

pavane, a dance, normally in slow duple time, which was introduced into instrumental music early in the 16th century. The name apparently derives from *paduana*, a dance from Padua (the town was also known in dialect as Pava). After about 1550 it was usually followed by a GALLIARD (*see* for an example of both), which often used the same theme. Detailed instructions for dancing the pavane are given in Arbeau's *Orchésographie* (1589; revised edition of M. S. Evans's translation, 1967, pages 57–66), but by this time the musical form was becoming stylized, no longer being written expressly for dancing. In the numerous pavanes (various spellings, e.g. pavan, pavana, paven, pavin) in the English virginal and lute books each of the three sections is followed by a variation. In suites by German composers in the first half of the 17th century, e.g. Schein's *Banchetto musicale* of 1617, the pavane (*paduana*) and galliard (*gagliarda*) are the first two movements.

N. DOLMETSCH: *Dances of England and France, 1450–1600* (1949)

Pavane for a dead Infanta (Fr., *Pavane pour une Infante défunte*), piano piece by Ravel, composed in 1899; the more famous orchestral version of the piece (written by Ravel himself) dates from thirteen years later. The Spanish princess commemorated by the music was an imaginary one. Ravel is said to have chosen the (French) title merely because he liked the sound of the words.

pavillon (Fr.; It., *padiglione*), literally pavilion or tent, hence (from the shape) the bell of a brass instrument. The direction *pavillons en l'air*, usually found in horn parts, instructs the players to raise the bells of their instruments in order to increase the weight of tone that penetrates over the orchestra to the audience.

pavillon Chinois (Fr.; It., *padiglione cinese*), a percussion instrument shaped like a pavilion or tent with little bells hanging from it. In Britain it has been called Turkish crescent and jingling johnny.

Pearl-Fishers, The (Fr., *Les Pecheurs de Perles*), opera in three acts by Bizet, to a libretto by Eugène Cormon and Michel Carré, first performed in Paris in 1863 – twelve years before *Carmen*. The story is set in Ceylon, and concerns a priestess who has vowed chastity but who is in love with a fisherman. The work contains a great tenor/baritone duet – 'Au fond du temple' (Act 1).

Pears, Peter (born 1910), English tenor, pupil of Elena Gerhardt. He has been closely associated with the music of Britten, many of whose works were written with Pears's voice in mind. These include song cycles (the *Serenade, Nocturne, Winter Words*, etc.), and also many leading roles in Britten's operas (Peter Grimes, Albert Herring, Captain Vere in *Billy Budd*, Peter Quint in *The Turn of the Screw*, the Mad Woman in *Curlew River*, Aschenbach in *Death in Venice*, etc.). Pears is also a distinguished Bach singer, specialising in such parts as the Evangelist in the St. Matthew and St. John Passions. As a *lieder* singer he is famed for his interpretations of Schubert's *Winterreise* and Schumann's *Dichterliebe*, with Britten as his accompanist.

Peasant Cantata (*Mer hahn en neue Oberkeet*, we have a new magistracy), secular cantata no 10 (cantata no 212) by J. S. Bach (1742) for solo voices, chorus and orchestra, with words in Saxon dialect. The work represents Bach in light-hearted vein.

pedal, (1) part of the mechanism of an instrument, controlled by the feet.

See HARP, HARPSICHORD, ORGAN, PEDAL BOARD, PIANOFORTE

(2) a sustained note which persists through changes of harmony.

See PEDAL POINT

(3) the fundamental (or first note of the HARMONIC SERIES) on a brass instrument. These notes can be produced by a slack lip on the trombone, the tuba and the B flat section of the double horn. On the trumpet they have no practical value.

pedal board, pedals were added to the organ in the 14th century in the Netherlands, probably from the carillon, and in Germany. They were in use in Italy from the 15th century. The first definite reference to pedals on an English organ is at St. Paul's Cathedral in 1720–21; many English organs did not have pedals until more than a century later. The modern organ has a concave and radiating pedal board with a compass of two octaves and a fifth above:

For the application of pedals to the harpsichord and piano *see* PEDAL HARPSICHORD, PEDAL PIANO.

pedal clarinet, an alternative, though nowadays little-used, name for the CONTRABASS CLARINET.

pedalcoppel (Ger.), pedal coupler (on an organ).

pedale (It.), (1) pedal (of an organ, piano, etc.); (2) pedal point.

Pedalflügel (Ger.), pedal piano.

pedal harp, name sometimes used to distinguish the ordinary harp from the much more recent and little used CHROMATIC HARP, which has no pedals.

pedal harpsichord, Bach owned a *Pedal-Klavizimbel* which was a harpsichord with pedal board for practising organ music. It is not to be assumed that he intended his trio-sonatas for two manuals and pedal for this instrument rather than for the organ.

pedalier (Fr.), pedal board.

pedaliera (It.), pedal board.

pedal notes, *see* PEDAL (3)

Pedalpauken (Ger.), chromatic timpani with pedal mechanisms that allow instant pitch changes, as opposed to the older types of instruments whose pitch can be changed only by means of the tuning screws.

See TIMPANI

pedal piano (Fr., *pédalier pianoforte*; Ger., *Pedalflügel*), piano with pedal board. It made sporadic appearances in the 19th century. Besides Schumann (*Studies for the Pedal Piano*, op 56 and 58, 1845), Alkan and Gounod composed for the instrument.

pedal point (Fr., *point d'orgue*; Ger., *Orgelpunkt*; It., *pedale*), a note, most commonly in the bass, which is held while harmonic progressions, with which it may be discordant, continue above it. It is generally known simply as 'pedal'. A pedal on the tonic frequently comes at the end of a piece, as at the close of Bach's fugue in C minor from the first book of the *Well-tempered Clavier*:

A dominant pedal often precedes the re-establishment of the tonic, after a series of modulations, as at the end of the DEVELOPMENT in sonata form.

Drones, which occur in primitive music and in some branches of Eastern chant, are a form of pedal point. Its earliest forms in Western polyphonic music are the third stage of ORGANUM (from which the alternative term 'organ point', *punctus organicus*, may arise), and the *clausulae* of Perotin (*see above* for an example).

Pedrell, Felipe (1841–1922), Spanish composer and musicologist. Although he studied music at home and was a chorister at Tortosa Cathedral, he was largely self-taught. At the Madrid Conservatorio he was teacher of music, history and aesthetics; later he settled in Barcelona. His pupils included Albéniz, Granados, Manuel de Falla, and Roberto Gerhard – an impressive list, which suggests why he came to be called the founder (or, some say, the midwife) of the 20th century Spanish nationalist school of composition. He edited the complete works of Victoria, and composed operas, symphonic poems, and other orchestral works, chamber music, cantatas, and songs. His most important work was the publication of the results of his researches in collections of Spanish church music, organ music, music for the stage before the 19th century and folksong.

Peer Gynt, (1) incidental music written by Grieg for the original production of Ibsen's drama (1876). For concert-hall purposes, Grieg arranged the music as two orchestral suites:

Peer Gynt Suite no 1 (op 46):
> (1) *Morning Mood*; (2) *The Death of Aase*; (3) *Anitra's Dance*; (4) *In The Hall Of The Mountain King*.

Peer Gynt Suite no 2 (op 55):
> (1) *Abduction of the Bride and Ingrid's Lament*; (2) *Arabian Dance*; (3) *Peer Gynt's Home-Coming*; (4) *Solvejg's Song*.

Incidental music has also been written by the Norwegian composer, Saeverud.

(2) opera in three acts by Egk to a libretto by the composer (after Ibsen's play). It was first performed in Berlin in 1938, and enjoyed the dubious honour of a prize from Adolf Hitler (who greatly admired it, in spite of the German press's initial condemnation of it as 'unfit for Nazi Germany').

Peerson, Martin (c. 1572–1650), English composer, organist and master of the choristers at St. Paul's Cathedral. He published *Private Musicke or the First Booke of Ayres and Dialogues* (1620), and *Mottects or Grave Chamber Musique* (1630) with an organ part. Some of his compositions are in the *Fitzwilliam Virginal Book* and in Leighton's *Teares or Lamentacions* (1614). He also wrote music for viols (modern edition of two pieces in *Musica Britannica*, ix).

> M. WAILES: 'Martin Peerson', in *Proceedings of the Royal Musical Association*, lxxx (1954)

Peeters, Flor (born 1903), Belgian organist, composer, and writer, pupil of Dupré and Tournemire. He became teacher of organ at Ghent Conservatory in 1931, and director of Antwerp Conservatory, 1952. In addition to a large number of organ works (including a concerto with orchestra) he has composed church music and piano pieces. He is the author of an important organ treatise.

Peitsche (Ger.), whip.

See SLAPSTICK

Pelléas and Mélisande (Fr., *Pelléas et Mélisande*), (1) opera in five acts by Debussy, a setting of a play by Maurice Maeterlinck (with minimal alterations). It was first performed in Paris in 1902, with Mary Garden as Mélisande.

At the start of the opera Melisande is found weeping by Golaud, who has lost his way while hunting in a forest. She tells him that she has thrown her crown into the well but will not explain who she is. Nevertheless Golaud marries her. Later Mélisande is attracted to Golaud's half-brother, Pelléas, and Golaud becomes extremely jealous, even using his child by a former marriage to spy on them. Finally he discovers them by a fountain, where they have met for a last farewell, and slays Pelléas with his sword. Mélisande bears a child and lies dying. Golaud begs her forgiveness.

The work, in many ways the obverse of Wagner's TRISTAN AND ISOLDE, is Debussy's only opera. Musically, its fusion of play and opera was achieved with extraordinary subtlety, with restraint in the writing, and an avoidance of operatic 'emotion'. The sheen and delicacy of the orchestration were to have far reaching importance;

(2) incidental music to Maeterlinck's play composed by Fauré (op 80) in 1898 and Sibelius (op 46) in 1905;

(3) symphonic poem (op 5) by Schoenberg, completed in 1903 and first performed in 1905.

Pellegrini, Vincenzo (died c. 1631), Italian composer. He was a canon at Pesaro c. 1603, and from 1611 to 1631 *maestro di cappella* at Milan Cathedral. He composed Masses, canzonets for organ (1599), secular canzonets for voices, and three- and four-part instrumental pieces.

Penderecki, Krzysztof (born 1933), Polish composer, one of the most important and progressive figures to have been produced by that country since World War II. Though he has all the modern techniques at his fingertips – piled-up note clusters, indeterminate pitch, the sound of instruments or voices at the extremes of their register, the use of the orchestra as a vast reservoir from which to extract a variety of colours – he is not a difficult composer and his St. Luke Passion (1965) and its successor *Utrenja* (Morning Service; 1971) have enjoyed a wide and immediate popularity. These and his opera *The Devils of Loudun* (1969) are large-scale works, but some of his smaller pieces are no less impressive. Among these, the most famous is the *Threnody for the Victims of Hiroshima* (1960) for 52 strings, in which the instrumentalists are required to play on a given number of strings behind the bridge as well as across the bridge. His other works include a Dies Irae dedicated to those who died in Auschwitz, a cello concerto, a capriccio for violin and orchestra, a symphony (commissioned in 1973 by Perkins Engines of Peterborough in England) and a partita for harpsichord, five solo instruments and orchestra.

Pénélope, opera in three acts by Fauré, to a libretto by René Fauchois, first performed at Monte Carlo in 1913. The story is based on an episode of the *Odyssey*. Other operas on the subject have been composed by Cimarosa, Galuppi, Puccinni and (in 1954) Rolf Liebermann – whose version was a modernised one, set during World War II.

Penitential Psalms, psalms of a penitential character, i.e., nos 6, 32 (31), 38 (37), 51 (50), 102 (101), 130 (129), and 143 (142). The numbers in brackets are those of the Roman Bible. They were set complete by Lassus (*Psalmi penitentiales,* 1565).

Penna, Lorenzo (1613–93), Italian composer. He was *maestro di cappella* of S. Ilario, Casale Monferrato in 1656. Around 1669 he entered the Carmelite order at Mantua, and became *maestro di cappella* of the Car-

melite church at Parma and at Imola Cathedral. He wrote Masses, psalms and other church music, and 'French Correntes' in four parts (1673). The third part of his *Li Primi Albori Musicali* (1672) is one of the important treatments in the 17th century of the rules for playing the organ from figured bass, with examples of the use of the trill (*see* F. T. ARNOLD, *The Art of Accompaniment from a Thorough-Bass,* pages 133–54).

penny whistle, a rudimentary pipe with a small range and, usually, six finger holes. Also known as a tin whistle, it is hardly more than a toy, but Copland has used it in his ballet score *Billy the Kid.*

penorcon, a type of CITTERN that was used in the 17th century.

pentatonic scale, a scale which has five notes to the octave, e.g.:

It can also be played by striking the black keys of the piano. The scale is used in the traditional music of China and Japan, and also elsewhere in the Far East, and in Africa; but the five-note scale (*slendro*) of the music of Java and Bali consists of five equal divisions of the octave, and cannot be reproduced on the piano. Some Irish and Scottish folksongs are in a pentatonic scale:

Gala Water (Scottish)

U.S. Negro music also makes use of the pentatonic scale (e.g. 'Swing Low, Sweet Chariot'), and 20th century composers have used it for its 'oriental' effect, e.g. Debussy in *Pagodes* in the suite *Estampes* (1903) for piano, and Ravel in *Laideronette Impératrice des Pagodes* from *Mother Goose* (1908):

Pepping, Ernst (born 1901), German composer who studied at the Berlin Hochschule für Musik. His compositions include symphonies, piano sonatas, chamber music, songs and organ works, but his major activity has been in the field of Protestant church music (Masses, motets, choral works for the Church's year, chorale settings, etc.).

Pepusch, Johann Christoph (1667–1752), German born composer and theorist. From fourteen he was in

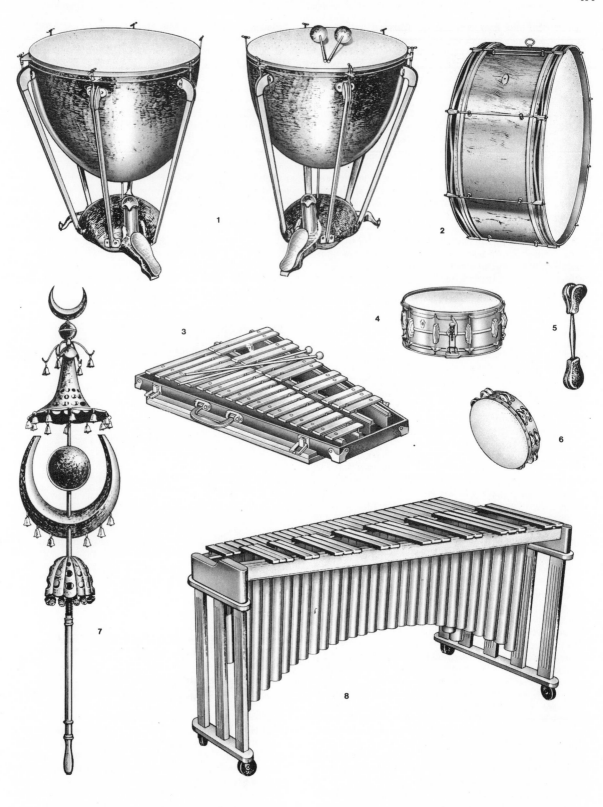

Percussion instruments: (1) timpani (pedal) (2) bass drum (3) Glockenspiel (4) snare drum (5) castanets (6) tambourine (7) Turkish crescent or jingling johnny (8) marimba

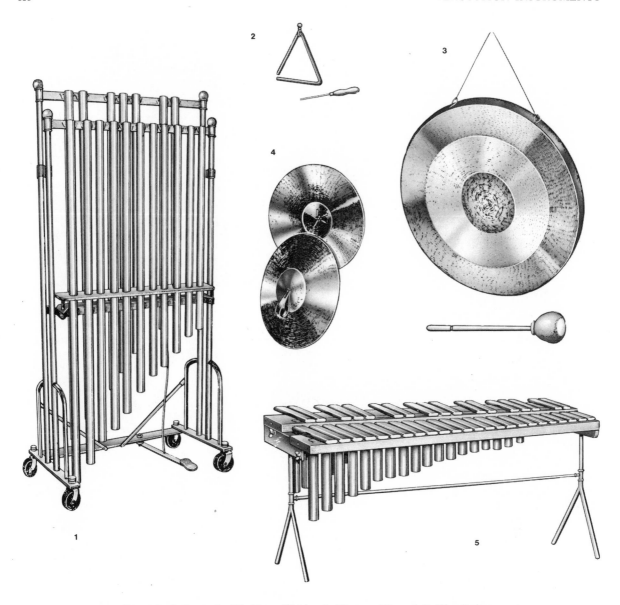

Percussion instruments: (1) chimes (2) triangle (3) gong (4) cymbals (5) xylophone

the service of the Prussian court, but in 1698 went to Holland and in 1700 settled in London. There he was appointed violinist in the Drury Lane Orchestra, and in 1710 was one of the founders of the Academy of Ancient Music. From 1712–18 he was organist and composer to the Duke of Chandos (being succeeded by Handel), from 1713 music director of Lincoln's Inn Fields Theatre, and from 1737–52 organist of the Charterhouse. He composed music for masques, odes, cantatas, motets, and he selected and arranged the tunes for John Gay's *Beggar's Opera* (1728). He published *A Treatise on Harmony* (1730; reprinted, with the addition of musical examples, 1731).

percussion band, normally confined to schools, this ensemble usually consists of the more manageable percussion instruments of indefinite pitch, along with a piano. It should not be confused with a percussion ensemble.

percussion instruments, instruments which produce sound when struck or shaken. Broadly speaking they can be divided into two categories – those with definite pitch, and those with indefinite pitch. For the most part the latter serve a purely rhythmic or colouristic function. A general characteristic of percussion instruments is their inability to sustain sounds, although in some cases rapid repetition can have this effect. Partly because of this (though principally because the notes are struck) the piano is often classified as a percussion rather than a stringed instrument. Perhaps a more general tendency is to regard all instruments played by percussionists as being percussive, but this introduces a few, the WIND MACHINE and WHISTLE among them, which strictly speaking are anomalous. Composers sometimes add to this category utensils that are not thought of as musical instruments. For instance, Ravel introduced a cheese-grater into his opera *L'Enfant et les Sortilèges*.

perdendosi (It.), 'losing itself'. Term indicating that the music should be played softer and softer until it dies away.

perfect, (1) the INTERVALS of the octave, fifth and fourth are called perfect consonances;

(2) a perfect note-value in MENSURAL NOTATION contains three of the next lower note-value, e.g. a perfect breve = three semibreves. In the perfect mode in that notation a long contains three breves; in perfect time, shown by the sign O, a breve contains three semibreves; in perfect prolation, shown by a dot in the circle or semicircle, a semibreve contains three minims. A perfect note-value is made imperfect by being written in red or white in black notation, or black in white notation. An imperfect note-value, which contains two of the next lower value, is made perfect by a dot (*punctus perfectionis* or *additionis*) following it;

(3) in a combination (LIGATURE) of two notes in mensural notation the normal ('proper' and 'perfect') sequence was considered to be that which had the shorter note (*brevis*) followed by the longer (*longa*); the term 'perfection' referred to the latter note, so that a ligature of two or more notes ending with a long, e.g.

$\mathbb{P}_b$ ($= {}^{B\ L}_{\substack{\square\ \square}}$) was defined as a ligature 'with perfection'

(*cum perfectione*), and a ligature ending with a breve,

e.g. $\mathbb{P}$ ($= {}^{B\ B}_{\substack{\square\ \square}}$) was *sine perfectione*;

(4) the word also refers to a type of CADENCE, and to a type of time – 'perfect time' (i.e. triple time in medieval music);

(5) perfect pitch describes a sense of pitch so acute that it can identify any note by name, without reference to a tuning fork or musical instrument.

perfect cadence, type of CADENCE.

Perfect Fool, The, comic opera in one act by Holst, to a libretto by the composer, first performed in London in 1923. This work is a parody of operatic conventions, with an allegorical story about a wizard, a princess and a fool. Today the music is known through Holst's orchestral suite of the same title.

Pergolesi, Giovanni Battista (1710–36), Italian composer who studied at Naples under Durante, Feo and others. His comic intermezzo *La serva padrona* was first performed between the acts of his serious opera *Il prigionier superbo* in 1733, and his other intermezzo *Il maestro di musica* became the prototype of the later form of the *opera buffa*. Its 1752 production of the Opera in Paris made it the centre of the so-called *Guerre des Bouffons* (war of the buffoons) between the supporters of the French and Italian opera.

His renown as a composer of church music, of which he wrote much, has rested mainly on his *Stabat mater*. In his trio sonatas he cultivated the melodious style of allegro movement later adopted by J. S. Bach, and made some contribution to the development of the

Giovanni Battista Pergolesi, who died aged 26

sonata form. His early death from tuberculosis prevented him from achieving his full potential as a composer – though his fame was sufficient for many works to be ascribed to him which were not by him at all.

Peri, Jacopo (1561–1633), Italian composer and singer. He studied under Cristoforo Malvezzi in Lucca. As a member of the *camerata* of Count Giovanni Bardi he composed the music, which has not survived, of the first opera *La Dafne*, to a text by Rinuccini, performed in the palace of Jacopo Corsi in Florence during the Carnival of 1597. His *Euridice*, also to a text by Rinuccini, which was performed in Florence in 1600, is the first opera of which the music is extant. Part of the music was by Caccini, whose complete setting of the same text was produced in Florence in 1602. Peri's score was published in 1601 and in facsimile editions in 1934 and 1973; a modern edition by C. Perinello was published in 1919, and extracts are printed in Schering's *Geschichte der Musik in Beispielen*, no 171, and in Davison and Apel's *Historical Anthology of Music*, no 182.

Péri, La (*The Peri*), dance-poem by Dukas, produced as a ballet in Paris in 1912.

periodicals, *see* HISTORY OF MUSIC

Perosi, Lorenzo (1872–1956), Italian composer and church musician. After studying at the Milan Conservatorio and at Halberl's School of Church Music in Ratisbon, he became *maestro di cappella* at St. Mark's, Venice, in 1895; and at the Sistine Chapel in 1898 (after he had been ordained). His works include oratorios, Masses, cantatas, motets and other church choral works, organ pieces, symphonic poems, suites for orchestra and chamber music.

Perotinus Magnus (Pérotin) (flourished 1180–1210), composer whose existence is known through the late 13th century English theorist Anonymous IV (so called in Coussemaker, *Scriptores*, i, 327) and Jean de Garlande. He appears to have worked at Notre Dame, Paris, where he revised the cycle of two-part *organa* of Leoninus's *Magnus Liber* by the use of substitute *clausulae.* Seven works specifically attributed to Perotinus by Anonymous IV may be identified in surviving manuscripts, and have been edited by E. Thurston (1970). They comprise three *conductus*, two three-part settings of *Alleluia* melodies, and two large scale four-part *organa* (*quadrupla*), *Viderunt omnes* and *Sederunt*, which may have been composed during the period 1197 to 1200. Both these works contain *clausulae* in DESCANT style (Anonymous IV calls him *optimus discantor*) with the rhythm of all voices measured according to the RHYTHMIC MODES (*see* NOTATION). The style may be seen in the following example from *Viderunt omnes*:

Several other anonymous compositions may well be by Perotinus.

    E. H. SANDERS: 'The Question of Perotin's Oeuvre and Dates', in *Festschrift für Walter Wiora*, edited by L. Finscher and C. Mahling (1967)

    H. TISCHLER: 'Perotinus Revisited', in *Aspects of Medieval and Renaissance Music*, edited by J. LaRue (1967)

perpetuum mobile (Lat.), title given to a rapid piece of music in which a repetitive note-pattern is maintained from start to finish. Paganini's *Moto Perpetuo*, op 11, is a classic example of the form, and Johann Strauss's *Perpetuum Mobile* one of the wittiest. Some of Chopin's studies are in fact of this kind and Poulenc's *Mouvements perpétuels* (1918) is a popular piano suite.

Persée (Perseus), opera with a prologue and five acts by Lully, to a libretto by Philippe Quinault, first performed in Paris in 1682.

Persephone, melodrama in three parts by Stravinsky for orchestra, chorus, a tenor and a speaking voice. Based on a poem (after the Greek myth) by André Gide, the work was first performed in Paris in 1934.

pes (Lat.), foot. A term used in English 13th and 14th century music for the tenor of a MOTET (as in Worcester manuscripts; *see* A. Hughes, *Worcester Mediaeval Harmony*, 1928) and for the lowest part or parts of a ROTA, as in the manuscript of *Sumer is icumen in.*

pesante (It.), heavy, ponderous, solid.

Pescetti, Giovanni Battista (1704–66), Italian composer who studied under Lotti in Venice, where he produced his first opera in 1725. He became director of Covent Garden in 1739, and of the King's Theatre, London, in 1740. He composed operas, an oratorio, church music and harpsichord sonatas. On returning to his native Venice, he became second organist at St. Mark's in 1762.

Peter and the Wolf, a 'musical tale for children' by Prokofiev, op 67, first performed in Moscow in 1936. The work is scored for storyteller and orchestra, with each character in the story represented by a different instrument or group of instruments. A kindred work (but without the folk tale element) is Britten's *Young Person's Guide to the Orchestra*, written nine years later.

Peter Grimes, opera by Britten, to a libretto by Montagu Slater (from part of Crabbe's poem *The Borough*). The first performance, in London in 1945, was a milestone in Britten's career as a composer (it was his first published opera) and a milestone also in British musical history (it was the first major British opera since Purcell's *Dido and Aeneas*). At the première, the title role was sung by Peter Pears, and the conductor was Reginald Goodall. The U.S. première, at Tanglewood a year later, was conducted by Leonard Bernstein.

    Grimes, the anti-hero of the story, is a fisherman in a town on the west coast of England. Imaginative and wayward, he fails to come to terms with his neighbours – only the local schoolmistress, Ellen Orford, stands by him. Accused of murdering a boy in his employment, he is acquitted; but the townsfolk still suspect him, and when another boy dies in his service they pursue him. In the thick fog he evades them, puts out to sea in his boat and sinks it. Grimes is an archetypal Britten character, an outcast, victimized by society.

Peters, a firm of publishers founded in Leipzig in 1814 by C. F. Peters, who bought the business of Kühnel and Hoffmeister. Dr. H. Hinrichsen became head of the firm in 1900. Publishing is now carried on under the original name in London and New York by the Hinrichsen family.

Peterson-Berger, Olof Wilhelm (1867–1942), Swedish composer, music critic and poet. In Stockholm he was director of the Royal Opera from 1908 until 1911. His works include operas (some with librettos by himself), five symphonies, festival cantatas, violin sonatas, songs and piano pieces.

petite flûte (Fr.), piccolo.

Petits Riens, Les (Fr., *The Little Nothings*), ballet with music by Mozart, K App. 10; choreography by Jean Noverre; first performed in Paris in 1778.

Petrassi, Goffredo (born 1904), Italian composer who studied at the Santa Cecilia Conservatorio in Rome, where he later became teacher. Though sometimes called the 'elder statesman' of Italian music, he remains a remarkably progressive composer, youthful and adventurous in outlook, very much aware of the latest sounds and styles, and able to use them to his own ends. His output includes two contrasted one-act operas, *The Tapestry* (*Il Cordovano*) and *Death in The Air* (*Morte dell'aria*) – a comedy and tragedy – though Italy's operatic tradition has not otherwise found him to be an eager recruit to its ranks. His major works, indeed, have been written for the concert hall. These include several concertos for orchestra, a *Portrait of*

Don Quixote for orchestra, a Magnificat and other choral music, settings of Edward Lear's nonsense poems, chamber music and piano pieces.

Petri, Egon (1881–1962), German born pianist, son of the Dutch violinist Henri Petri (1856–1914), who settled in Germany in 1877. Egon Petri studied the violin from an early age and was a member of his father's quartet from 1899–1901, but, having decided to become a pianist, he studied with Busoni, of whose works he gave authentic interpretations. He was also joint editor with Busoni of Bach's keyboard music, but it was as a distinguished concert pianist that he was most widely renowned. He taught successively at the Royal Manchester College of Music (1905–11), the Basle Conservatory, the Berlin Hochschule für Musik (1921–6), and at Zakopane (in southern Poland). He migrated to the United States in 1939, becoming residential pianist at Cornell University in 1940 and then at Mills College, Oakland (California) in 1947.

Pétrouchka, *see* PETRUSHKA

Petrucci, Ottaviano dei (1466–1539), Italian music printer. He published the first printed collection of part music, the *Harmonice Musices Odhecaton A*, in 1501. In all he printed 61 volumes of music, sacred and secular, between that date and 1520. A bibliography of his publications by C. Sartori appeared in 1948, the *Bibliografia delle opere musicali stampate da Ottaviano Petrucci*.

Petrushka, ballet with music by Stravinsky (choreography by Fokine) telling of the fate of a Russian puppet who comes to life. The first performance was in Paris in 1911 by Diaghilev's Russian Ballet. In 1914 the composer prepared the concert suite which he revised in 1947. Along with *The Firebird* (which preceded it) and *The Rite of Spring* (which followed it) *Petrushka* is one of the landmarks of Stravinsky's early output, and of 20th century music in general. Its rhythmic vitality is as exhilarating today as ever it was. The music also uses parallel chords to striking effect, and places special emphasis on what has become known as the 'Petrushka chord' – the sound of C against F sharp, much employed by later composers.

Peuerl (Peurl, Bäurl, Beurlin or **Bäwerl), Paul** (c. 1570–after 1625), Austrian composer. He was organist at Horn in 1602 and at Steyr from 1609 until his death. His *Newe Padouan, Intrada, Däntz, und Galliarda* (1611) contains the earliest known examples of the variation SUITE. Pieces from this and his other publications, *Weltspiegel* (1613), which contains secular part-songs, and *Gantz Neue Padouanen* (1625) are printed in *Denkmäler der Tonkunst in Osterreich*, lxx, Jg. xxxvi (2).

Pfeife (Ger.), pipe.

Pfitzner, Hans (1869–1949), German composer, born in Moscow and brought up in Frankfurt, where he studied at the Conservatorium. Between 1892 and 1933 he was teacher and conductor in a number of German cities, including Mainz, Berlin and Munich. During the immediate post war years he lived in an institution for old people in Munich until he finally retired to Salzburg.

Pfitzner was active as a composer from his student days to the end of his life. He was a romantic in an age when romanticism was turning to extravagance, from which he held aloof. His writing for the opera has none of the glitter of Strauss's works; he was in fact closer to the traditions established by Schumann and Brahms. An idealist with a passionate belief in his own integrity, he fought vigorously against what he thought to be corrupting influences in modern music. He was in a sense a visionary who lived in a world of his own creation. In his best known work, the opera *Palestrina* (Munich 1917), he strives to identify himself with a composer whom he does not seem to have fully understood – a fact which does not necessarily weaken the opera, however. Though his music is often said by German writers to express the very spirit of the German race, he was by no means universally appreciated even in his own country. Elsewhere his reputation has been tenuous. He composed several operas, symphonies, concertos, choral music, chamber music and a hundred songs.

Phaéton, opera with a prologue and five acts by Lully, to a libretto by Philippe Quinault, first performed at Versailles in 1683.

phagotus, an extraordinary instrument, long since obsolete, which was developed from the BAGPIPE in the 16th century. It had two pipes with holes for fingering, but the wind was supplied by hand bellows. Because of its name, derived from Italian *fagotto*, it has been confused with the BASSOON to which it is not related.

Phantasie (Ger.), fantasy.

phantasy, a title used for a number of chamber music compositions written between 1906 and 1930 for the competitions instituted by W. W. Cobbett. The first of the series of prizes was won by W. Y. Hurlstone's phantasy string quartet in A minor, and later prizes by compositions of Frank Bridge, John Ireland and Vaughan Williams. Britten's phantasy quartet, op 2, for oboe and strings, was written in 1932.

Philadelphia Orchestra, one of the United States' most famous symphony orchestras, founded in 1900 by Fritz Scheel, who was its conductor until 1907. Later conductors were Karl Pohlig, 1907–12; Leopold Stokowski, 1912–38. Eugene Ormandy took charge of the orchestra in 1938.

Philémon et Baucis, opera in three acts by Gounod, to a libretto by Jules Barbier and Michel Carré, (after Ovid), first performed in Paris in 1860.

Philidor, François André Danican (1726–1795), French composer, chess player and member of a family of musicians whose original name was Danican. He studied music under Campra, played chess in Holland, Germany and England and in 1754 returned to Paris, where he produced his first *opéra comique* in 1759. He composed operas (including *Tom Jones*), motets and a Requiem for Rameau (1766). The Library of St. Michael's College, Tenbury (catalogue by E. H. Fellowes, 1934) contains a collection of manuscript scores of operas, ballets, motets, and instrumental music by French composers of the 17th and early 18th centuries written by Philidor's father, André Philidor *l'aîné*, which formerly formed part of the French Royal Library. His half-brother founded the *Concert Spirituel* in Paris in 1725.

Philips, Peter (c. 1560–1628), English composer and organist who lived abroad from 1582. A Roman Catholic, he gained a post as organist to the English College in Rome. After travels with his patron from 1585, Lord Thomas Paget, he went to Antwerp in 1590.

In 1597 he entered the household of the Archduke Albert, and was organist at the royal chapel at Brussels until his death. In 1591 he edited a collection of Italian madrigals published in Antwerp. Between 1596 and 1603 he published three books of his own madrigals, and from 1612 to 1628 seven books of motets and other sacred music. In style he is closer to his continental than to his English contemporaries; his *Gemmulae Sacrae . . . cum Basso Continuo ad Organum* (1613) seems to be the earliest use of a continuo part by an English composer. Peacham observed that 'he affecteth altogether the *Italian* veine'. A selection of his madrigals has been edited by J. Steele in *Musica Britannica*, xxix. Nineteen keyboard pieces, the earliest dated 1580, are in the *Fitzwilliam Virginal Book*. Among them are keyboard arrangements of vocal pieces by Marenzio, Lassus, Striggio and Caccini. Three pieces for viols are printed in *Musica Britannica*, ix.

> A. G. PETTI: 'New Light on Peter Philips', *Monthly Musical Record*, lxxxvii (1957)
> A. G. PETTI: 'Peter Philips, Composer and Organist', *Recusant History*, iv (1958)

Philosopher, The (Ger., *Der Philosoph*), nickname for Haydn's symphony no 22 in E flat major (1764) – perhaps because of its slow, solemn opening movement. The scoring, unusually, includes two *cors anglais*, which Haydn uses to remarkable effect, especially in conjunction with the horns.

Phinot (Finot), Dominicus, 16th century French musician who composed two books of motets (Lyons, 1547–48), two books of *chansons* (Lyons, 1548), a book of Psalms and Magnificats (Venice, 1555) and other church music. A collected edition of his works by J. Höfler and R. Jacob was begun in 1972.

photona, an electronic instrument with a two-manual keyboard. A photoelectric cell is used to produce sound.

phrase, a unit of melody, of indeterminate length. In the classical period it is most frequently of four bars, and since it usually ends with some form of cadence, is a unit of harmonic progression as well as of melody:

If a smaller unit, such as that marked (a), comes under discussion, as when it is used separately in a later context:

it is more conveniently referred to as a MOTIVE. Though it is not necessary to use the term with complete consistency, shorter or longer units may be called phrases if they form a unit in both melodic design and underlying harmony.

The art of 'phrasing' concerns not only the articulation of complete phrases, but the articulation of their details. The chief marks by which phrasing is indicated are the slur and the *staccato* dot. The player of an instrument will observe these by means of short rests, for example:

BEETHOVEN, *Sonata op 10, no 3*

is played:

Phrygian cadence, the Phrygian mode was the only mode in which the interval between the final and note above it was a semitone. Hence the harmonization of a cadence in this mode presented a peculiar problem to composers of polyphonic music. The seventh note of the scale (D) could not be sharpened because that would have created an augmented sixth, and to have sharpened the note above the final would have destroyed the character of the mode. The following, therefore, came to be adopted as the standard harmonization of the cadence (with a TIERCE DE PICARDIE, or major third) in the final chord:

When the modal system settled down into major and minor in the 17th century this cadence survived in use, but with a changed implication, the final chord now suggesting dominant harmony in a minor key. The cadence was therefore no longer final and was regularly used in the 17th and early 18th centuries as a transition from one movement to another. This became so much a convention that the new movement did not necessarily accept the concluding chord of the previous movement as a dominant but began instead in a related key. This practice was particularly common where the first and third movements of a sonata or concerto were in a major key and the middle movement in a minor key.

Thus in Bach's fourth Brandenburg concerto in G major the slow movement, which is in E minor, ends with a Phrygian cadence on the chord of B major, and this leads to the opening of the last movement in G major. In the third concerto, also in G major, there is no middle movement at all. The two movements in G major are simply separated by the two chords which constitute a Phrygian cadence in E minor (i.e. 6/3 on C and major triad on B).

Phrygian mode, (1) in ancient Greek music:

(2) from the middle ages onwards applied to:

The tonic (or final) and dominant are marked respectively T and D. The dominant was originally B (a fifth above the tonic, as in the other modes) but was changed to C as early as the 11th century, since B was regarded as an ambiguous note: its relation to F was dissonant and it was the one note which was not common to all three hexachords. The change, however, though accepted by theorists, was not always observed in practice.

See GREEK MUSIC, HEXACHORD, MODE

physharmonica, invented in 1818, this instrument paved the way for the HARMONIUM.

piacere (It.), pleasure. So *A piacere* means 'at the performer's pleasure' i.e. strict adherence to tempo and rhythm need not be observed.

piacevole (It), in an agreeable, pleasant manner – a term used by Elgar in his serenade for strings.

pianette, a tiny upright piano, even smaller than the PIANINO.

piangendo (It), crying, i.e. in a plaintive manner.

pianino, a small upright piano.

pianissimo (It.), very soft, abbreviated *pp*.

piano (1) (It.), soft, abbreviated *p*.;
   (2) (Eng., Fr.), standard abbreviation of PIANOFORTE.

piano accordion, *see* ACCORDION

piano duet, a term normally applied to two players at one instrument. The earliest known work of this kind is a 16th century piece by Nicholas Carlton 'for two to play on one Virginal or Organ'. Burney published eight sonatas for piano (or harpsichord) duet in 1777–8. Among the composers who have written original piano duets are Mozart, Beethoven, Schumann and Brahms.

pianoforte, piano, the mechanism of the piano comprises a keyboard, action, hammers, dampers, strings, and pedals. The keyboard of the modern piano has a compass of seven octaves when the highest note is A, or seven octaves and a minor third when the highest note is C. A damper stops the vibration of the strings when the key returns to its normal position. The right (or sustaining) pedal suspends the action of the dampers, allowing the strings to vibrate freely; the left (or soft) pedal mutes the sound by moving the hammers either towards the strings so that their length of travel is shortened or parallel to the strings so that they strike only one or two of the strings which are provided for each note. On some pianos a third pedal

allows notes to continue sounding which have been played before the pedal is depressed, while any other notes remain unaffected.

The piano and its name originated in instruments made in Florence about 1710 by Bartolommeo Cristofori, who called them *gravicembali col pian e forte*, i.e. harpsichords which can produce *piano* and *forte* by touch. Cristoferi devised a hammer action for the instrument, the hammer being hinged to a rail and free to rise independently of the key. By a principle known as escapement, a spring-jack raises the hammer with the help of an under-lever and then, when the hammer strikes the string, allows the hammer to drop away. Cristoferi's hammer action is still, in essence, the one which is used today.

The most important makers in the 18th century were Silbermann and Stein in Germany, Kirkman, Zumpe and Broadwood in Britain; the main developments were the escapement, which allowed the hammer to return for the repetition of a note though the key was still down, the pedal (patented by Broadwood in 1783), and the return to Cristofori's 'grand' shape in addition to the square. The piano was played as a solo instrument for the first time in Britain by J. C. Bach in 1768. Mozart praised Stein's pianos in a letter to his father in 1777.

The chief developments in the nineteenth century were the extension of the compass (the Broadwood presented to Beethoven in 1817 had six octaves from C_1 to c^{1111}), the increase in sonority, the devising of a double escapement which allowed quicker repetition (patented by Érard of Paris in 1821), and the adoption of the upright shape.

The upright piano evolved in the second half of 18th century, as a space-saving up-ended grand, with the strings running vertically instead of horizontally from the keyboard. The first really successful upright was patented in 1800 by John Isaac Hawkins, who hit on the idea of extending the strings below the keyboard, so that the hammers struck nearer the top of the strings, resulting in a more vivid sound quality.

The earliest known publication of music for the piano is a set of sonatas for *cembalo di piano e forte* by Lodovico Giustini (1732). The first English music to mention pianoforte in the title was John Burton's (1730–85) *Ten Sonatas for the Harpsichord, Organ, or Pianoforte*, published by the composer in 1766. Clementi published piano sonatas in 1773, and all but the first set of C. P. E. Bach's sets of sonatas (*für Kenner und Liebhaber*) of 1779–87 are for the 'Forte-piano'. Beethoven's *Waldstein* sonata was one of the first major works to take advantage of the piano's extended compass. The chief landmarks in the later developments of the technique of piano-playing are the studies of Clementi (*Gradus ad Parnassum*, 1817), Hummel (*Ausführliche Anweisung zum Pianofortespiel*, 1828), Czerny, Cramer, Schumann (*VI Études de concert pour le pianoforte, composées d'après les Caprices de Paganini*, 1832), Chopin (*Études*, 1837), Liszt (*Études d'exécution transcendante*, final form, 1854; also inspired by Paganini), and the teaching and methods of Tausig, Leschetizky, Breithaupt, Scharwenka and Matthay.

In the present century, Debussy was one of the most important composers to take advantage of the colour qualities of the piano and so did Bartók (especially in his passages of 'night' music), though he also exploited the instrument's percussiveness – a feature also of Prokofiev's works. Haba explored the possibilities of a quarter tone piano. Stockhausen's series of piano pieces are as comprehensive an examination of modern keyboard possibilities as were Bach's preludes and fugues and Chopin's studies in previous centuries. Stockhausen, moreover, has made creative use of the amplified piano, and many other living composers have revealed a desire – not always successful in its outcome – to extend the sonic range of the instrument. Frequently the performer is asked to grope inside the instrument, in order to pluck, thump or tickle the strings. Sometimes the piano has to be 'prepared' beforehand, through the addition of foreign bodies (nuts, bolts, pieces of wood etc.) to its interior, thus altering its sound quality. In Bussotti's *Passion selon Sade* the long-suffering instrument has to be struck with a whip. On the other hand, in one piece by John Cage (the pioneer of the prepared piano) the notes have to be pressed but not actually sounded, the music nevertheless being written out, so that if the pianist accidentally sounds a note, it is always the right one.

M. BREE: *The Groundwork of the Leschetizky Method* (1905)
R. M. BREITHAUPT: *Natural Piano-Technique* (1909)
E. CLOSSON: *History of the Piano* (1944, revised by Robin Golding 1974)
H. FERGUSON: *Keyboard Interpretation* (1975)
R. E. M. HARDING: *A History of the Pianoforte to 1851* (1933)
P. JAMES: *Early Keyboard Instruments* (1930)
T. A. MATTHAY: *The Act of Touch* (1924)
H. SCHONBERG: *The Great Pianists* (1965)

pianola, a piano played mechanically by means of rolls pierced with openings corresponding to the duration and pitch of the notes, thus allowing air under pressure to act on a device which moves the hammers. It was widely used from the late 19th century until the rise of the gramophone and wireless. It is also known generally as the 'player-piano'.

piano organ, a mechanical instrument similar to the BARREL ORGAN but without pipes. Instead the notes are produced by hammers striking strings.

piano quartet, term usually applied to quartets for piano, violin, viola and cello, of which there are examples by Mozart, Beethoven, Mendelssohn, Schumann, Brahms, Dvořák, and Fauré. But quartets for keyboard and other instruments, e.g. those by J. C. Bach for violin, oboe, flute and keyboard (with cello), have been written from the 18th century onwards. Among 20th century examples are Hindemith's quartet for clarinet, violin, cello and piano (1939), and Messiaen's *Quartet For the End of Time*, written for the same ensemble.

piano quintet, the combination of piano with (usually) a string quartet. Compositions in this medium have been written by Schumann, Brahms, Dvořák, Fauré, Elgar, Shostakovich, Roy Harris and others. Mozart (K 452) and Beethoven (op 16) wrote quintets for piano, oboe, clarinet, horn, and bassoon. Schubert's *Trout* quintet is for piano, violin, viola, cello and double bass.

piano trio, popular term for a piece of chamber music for piano, violin and cello.

Pianotron, an electronic upright piano. It evolved from the NEO-BECHSTEIN PIANO, and was produced by the firm of Selmer in 1938.

piatti (It.), cymbals.

Piatti, Alfredo Carlo (1822–1901), Italian cellist who studied under his great uncle Zanetti and under Merighi in Milan, where he made his first public appearance in 1837. He gave concerts in Munich (with Liszt, 1843), Paris, the British Isles, Italy and Russia, and rose to become the leading solo cellist of the 19th century. He composed cello concertos, songs with cello accompaniment, and sonatas and other works for his instrument.

pibgorn, *see* HORNPIPE

pibroch (Gaelic, *piobaireachd*, 'pipe-tune'), the most important category of bagpipe music. It consists of variations on a theme (*urlar*), played with an increase of tempo in each variation, and with many grace notes.

Picardy third, *see* TIERCE DE PICARDIE

Picchi, Giovanni, 17th century Italian organist and composer. Around 1620 he was organist at the church Della Casa Grande in Venice. He composed a book of harpsichord music (c. 1619), canzonas and sonatas for instruments, and church music. There is a toccata by him in the *Fitzwilliam Virginal Book*.

Piccinni, Niccolò (1728–1800), Italian composer. He studied in Naples under Leo and Durante, and from 1755 produced there and in Rome a number of successful operas, serious and comic. In 1776 he went to Paris, was tutor in singing to Marie Antoinette, and produced Italian operas, and after 1778 operas to French texts. The management of the Opéra took advantage of the feud between his supporters and those of Gluck by commissioning a setting of *Iphigénie en Tauride* from both composers. Piccinni's, produced in 1781, was not unsuccessful, being given more than thirty performances; it was Gluck's, however, which posterity deemed the greater work. During the French Revolution. Piccinni went to Naples and returned to Paris in 1798. In all he wrote some 120 operas. His comic opera *La buona figliola* (*The Good Girl*, Rome 1760), to a libretto by Goldoni (after Samuel Richardson's novel *Pamela, or Virtue Rewarded*), enjoyed an extraordinary popularity. Vocal scores of *Roland* (1778) and *Didon* (1783) are in *Chefs d'oeuvre de l'opéra français*.

piccolo (Fr., *petite flûte*; Ger., *kleine Flöte, Pickelflöte*; It., *flauto piccolo, ottavino*), an abbreviation of *flauto piccolo*, meaning little flute. A small flute, with the natural scale of D and a range of about three octaves, written:

and sounding an octave higher. It was not a regular member of the orchestra before the middle of the 19th century. Among its earlier appearances are Gluck's *Iphigénie en Tauride* (1779), Beethoven's fifth and sixth symphonies (1807–8) and Weber's *Der Freischütz* (1821).

See FLUTE

piccolo timpano (It.), a very small kettledrum capable

of producing a middle C. *See* TIMPANI

picco pipe, an instrument of the recorder type.

Pickelflöte, *see* PICCOLO

Pictures at an Exhibition, a set of piano pieces by Mussorgsky (1874), composed in memory of the painter and architect Victor Alexandrovich Hartmann and containing musical pictures of some of his works. In addition to the following there are also a prelude and interludes (each entitled *Promenade*):

no 1: *Gnomus* (a limping dwarf).
no 2: *Il Vecchio Castello* ('A Medieval Castle').
no 3: *Tuileries* (Children playing and quarrelling).
no 4: *Bydlo* (a Polish ox-cart on enormous wheels).
no 5: *Ballet of the Chickens in their Shells*.
no 6: *Samuel Goldenberg and Schmuyle* (two Polish Jews, rich and poor).
no 7: *Limoges* ('The Market').
no 8: *Catacombae*.
no 9: *The Hut on Fowl's Legs*.
no 10: *The Great Gates of Kiev*.

Orchestral arrangements have been made by Ravel, Henry Wood, Walter Goehr and Tushmalov. Though Ravel's, in particular, has been considered an improvement on the original – being more 'colourful', a more subtle realisation of the composer's ideas, indeed the sort of work Mussorgsky would have written if he had had the technical knowledge – there is now a growing body of opinion that Mussorgsky knew exactly what he was doing and that his own piano version is more potent and natural than any orchestral arrangement.

pieno (It.), full. *Organo pieno*, full organ. *A voce piena*, with full voice.

Pierné, Henri Constant Gabriel (1863–1937), French composer, organist and conductor who studied at the Paris Conservatoire under Franck and Massenet. He won the *Prix de Rome* in 1882. From 1890 until 1898 he was organist of Sainte-Clotilde, Paris, and from 1910 until 1932 first conductor of the Concerts Colonne. He composed operas, ballets, pantomimes, oratorios, suites and other works for orchestra, chamber music, incidental music for plays, piano pieces and songs. Today he is remembered mainly for the *Entry of the Little Fauns* from his ballet *Cydalise and the Satyr*.

Pierrot Lunaire (Fr., *Moonstruck Pierrot*), melodrama by Schoenberg, op 21, first performed in 1912. It consists of 21 settings of poems by Albert Giraud in a German translation by Otto Erich Hartleben, scored for voice and an instrumental ensemble consisting of flute (also piccolo), clarinet (also bass clarinet), violin (also viola), cello and piano. The vocal part has to be voiced in such a way that it is neither sung nor spoken.

Pierson, Heinrich Hugo (originally Henry Hugh Pearson) (1815–73), Oxford born English composer who lived most of his life in Germany. He studied at Cambridge and from 1839 under Rinck, Tomášek and Reissiger in Germany where he met Mendelssohn and Schumann. In 1844 he became Reid professor at Edinburgh but resigned two years later and returned to the continent, where he spent the remainder of his life in Vienna, Hamburg and Leipzig. He composed operas, oratorios, overtures, music to the second part of Goethe's *Faust* (1854), church music, and songs (including 'Ye Mariners of England'). The most interesting of mid Victorian composers, he failed to find appreciation in England, but was highly regarded in Germany.

pietoso (It.), compassionate, sympathetic.

Pifa, Handel's name for the 'Pastoral Symphony' in *Messiah*, indicating that it is intended to represent the sound of music played on *pifferi* by shepherds.

piffero (It.), small flute, or shepherd's pipe, of the 18th century.

Pijper, Willem (1894–1947), Dutch composer, pianist and writer on music. He studied under Johan Wagenaar in Utrecht, where he was music critic from 1918–23. In 1925 he became teacher of composition at the Amsterdam Conservatory, and in 1930 the director of the Rotterdam Conservatory. The father of modern Dutch music, he composed three symphonies and six Symphonic Epigrams, string quartets and other chamber music, concertos for piano, cello and violin, an opera (*Halewijn*), choral works, incidental music for plays, piano pieces and songs, and wrote essays on music and musicians.

Pikovaya Dama, *see* QUEEN OF SPADES

Pilgrims from Mecca, The, *see* RENCONTRE IMPRÉVUE

Pilgrim's Progress, The, opera in four acts, with a prologue and an epilogue by Vaughan Williams, to a libretto by the composer (after Bunyan's allegory). The greater part of the earlier one-act opera *The Shepherds of the Delectable Mountains* (1922) is incorporated in this work as Act 4, Scene 2.

pincé (Fr.), mordent.

Pincherle, Marc (born 1888), Algerian born musicologist. After studying under Roland, Laloy and Pirro, he became teacher at the Ecole Normale in Paris. He has written books on the history of the violin, on Corelli (1934), and on Vivaldi (two volumes, 1948; the second volume contains a thematic catalogue of Vivaldi's works).

Pines of Rome, The (It., *Pini di Roma*), symphonic poem by Respighi, laid out in four linked movements depicting the pine trees in four areas of the city. The work, first performed (in Rome) in 1924, made history by incorporating, as part of its orchestration, a gramophone record of the song of a nightingale. The work was intended as a companion piece to *The Fountains of Rome*, composed seven years earlier.

pipe, a hollow cylinder in which vibrating air produces either a single note, as in the case of an organ pipe, or a series of notes when its effective length can be altered by the player who, with his fingers, opens and closes holes made for this purpose.

pipe and tabor, a combination of two primitive instruments. The player holds a small pipe in one hand while he beats time with the other on the TABOR, which either hangs from his shoulder or is strapped to his waist.

Pique-Dame, *see* QUEEN OF SPADES.

Pirata, Il (It., *The Pirate*), opera in two acts by Bellini, to a libretto by Felice Romani, first performed in Milan in 1827 by a cast including Meric-Lalande, Rubini and Tamburini. In the present century the work was successfully revived for Maria Callas. The heroine, Imogene, loses her reason after her (unloved) husband has been murdered by her pirate-lover.

Pirates of Penzance, The, comic opera in two acts by Gilbert and Sullivan. First performed at Paignton in 1879.

Pirro, André (1869–1943), French musicologist. After studying law, letters, and organ under Franck and Widor at the Paris Conservatoire, he became director and teacher at the Schola Cantorum on its foundation in 1896. He succeeded Romain Rolland as professor of musical history at the Sorbonne in 1912, and became the leading French musicologist of his time. Among his many writings are books on Bach, Buxtehude and Schütz, and a history of music in the 15th and 16th centuries.

Pisendel, Johann Georg (1687–1755), German violinist and composer. He studied as a choirboy under Torelli and Pistocchi, from 1709 at Leipzig University and later under Vivaldi in Venice and Montanari in Rome. From 1714 he travelled with the Prince of Saxony to Paris, Berlin, Italy and Vienna, and was leader of the Dresden court orchestra from 1730. He composed a symphony, two *concerti grossi*, eight violin concertos and other works for violin.

Pistocchi, Francesco Antonio Mamiliano (1659–1726), Sicilian born composer, conductor and singer. His *Cappricci puerili* for keyboard and other instruments was published at Bologna when he was eight years old. He first appeared as an opera singer at Ferrara in 1675, and became *Kapellmeister* to the Margrave of Ansbach in 1696. Later he founded an important school of singing in Bologna. He composed operas, oratorios, cantatas and other church music, vocal duets, trios and arias.

piston, (1) (Fr.), short for *cornet à pistons*, the modern cornet; (2) valve on a brass instrument.

Piston, Walter (1894–1976), U.S. composer who studied at Harvard University from 1914–24 and under Nadia Boulanger in Paris. He taught composition at Harvard from 1932, and in 1944 became professor there. His compositions, written in a direct and vigorously traditional style, include eight symphonies and other orchestral works, a violin concerto, five string quartets, sonatas and other chamber music and a ballet – *The Incredible Flautist*. He has also written several important textbooks, including *Principles of Harmonic Analysis* (1933), *Harmony* (1941), *Counterpoint* (1947) and *Orchestration* (1955).

pistone (It.), a cornet pitched a fourth above the normal instrument.

pitch, the relative height or depth of a sound, determined by the rate of vibration of the medium (*see* ACOUSTICS). During the 17th century three standards of pitch were in common use: the pitch for chamber music was either about a semi-tone lower than our international pitch or identical with it, while that for organ and choir music and for town band music about a tone higher. Instrumental music of the 18th century used the first of these and consequently sounded about a semitone lower than it does today. The standard of pitch rose steadily until a French Commission of 1859 recommended the fixing of *diapason normal* at A.

=435 vibrations a second at a temperature of 59°F., or 439 vibrations at 68°F. (i.e. the average temperature of

a concert hall, hence called 'Concert Pitch'). This was adopted as international pitch at a conference in Vienna in 1889. In 1939 it was amended to an absolute frequency (i.e. independent of temperature) of 440 cycles per second. The pitch of instruments tends to sharpen in a warm room, or (in the case of wind instruments) when the instruments grow warm through blowing. *See* CHORTON, KAMMERTON

pitch pipe, a small pipe with a graduated stopper by which any note of the scale can be produced. It is used for giving the pitch to a choir which is about to sing without accompaniment.

più (It.), more. *Più allegro, più mosso,* faster; *più forte,* louder. *Più andante* is an ambiguous direction: if *andante* is taken in its literal meaning of 'moving', it means 'a little faster'; if it is regarded as meaning moderately slow, *più andante* will mean 'slower'. *Più* by itself = *più mosso. Il più* = the most: *il più piano possibile,* as soft as possible.

piuttosto (It.), rather. *Andante piuttosto allegro,* rather fast than slow, i.e. not too much on the slow side.

    See also TOSTO.

piva (It.), bagpipe.

Pizzetti, Ildebrando (1880–1968), Italian composer and writer on music. After studying at the Parma Conservatorio, he held important academic appointments in Florence, Milan and Rome. He was primarily a composer for the stage and for voice. The libretto of his operas, which he called 'dramas', are on tragic or religious subjects, and were written either wholly or partly by himself for the works composed since 1921. They include *Debora e Jaele* (Milan, 1922), *Fra Gherardo* (Milan, 1928), *Lo Straniero* (Rome, 1930), *Orsèolo* (Florence, 1935), *Vanna Lupa* (Florence, 1949), *Higenia* (Florence, 1951), *Cagliostro* (Milan, 1954) and *Murder in The Cathedral* (on T. S. Eliot's play; Milan, 1958). His choral style is polyphonic, and his songs are for the most part in a serious vein. He also composed some orchestral music, a cello concerto, piano concerto, chamber music and piano music, and wrote books on Bellini, on Paganini, on contemporary composers, and on dramatic music.

    G. M. GATTI: *Ildebrando Pizzetti* (1934; English translation, 1951)

pizzicato (It.), plucked. Used, generally in the abbreviated form *pizz.,* to indicate plucking of the string by the finger on a bowed instrument. Early examples of printed directions to play *pizzicato* occur in Tobias Hume's *Ayres . . . for the Viole de Gambo* (1605) and Monteverdi's *Il Combattimento di Tancredi e Clorinda* (1638; composed in 1624). Paganini introduced *pizzicato* for the left hand, with or without another note bowed. Among more recent innovations is the Bartók *pizzicato,* which allows the string to rebound off the fingerboard with a snap.

    Pizzicato tremolando, term used by Elgar in his violin concerto to indicate that he wanted the orchestral string players to produce a rapid thrumming sound with the fingers across the strings.

plagal cadence, a cadence which has the harmony of the subdominant preceding that of the tonic:

Its most familiar use is for the Amen at end of a hymn or prayer.

See CADENCE.

plagal mode, *see* MODE.

plainsong (Lat., *cantus planus*), the term 'plainsong' is most commonly used for GREGORIAN CHANT. The liturgical melodies of other Western rites, e.g. Gallican, Ambrosian, Mozarabic, as well as those of Eastern rites, e.g. Byzantine, Syrian, are usually referred to simply as 'chant'. The term was first used about the 13th century, when it became desirable to distinguish plainsong from measured song (*cantus mensuratus*).

Plainsong and Mediaeval Music Society, formed in 1888 with the object of cataloguing and publishing the sources for plainsong and medieval music in England and promoting performances of it. The most important publications of the society are:

> *Graduale Sarisburiense* (1894) – facsimile.
> *Bibliotheca Musico-Liturgica* (1894–1932) – catalogue.
> *Early English Harmony* (1897) – facsimiles.
> *Antiphonale Sarisburiense* (1901–25) – facsimile.
> *Piae Cantiones* (1910) – a reprint of a Swedish publication of 1582.
> *Missa 'O quam suavis'* (1927) – transcription.
> *Worcester Mediaeval Harmony* (1928) – transcriptions.
> *Anglo-French Sequelae* (1934) – transcriptions.

plainte (Fr.), an ornament used in French music of the 17th and 18th centuries, equivalent to the German NACHSCHLAG.

Planets, The, suite for orchestra, organ and (in the last movement) female chorus by Holst, op 32 (1915), in seven movements entitled: (1) *Mars, the Bringer of War*; (2) *Venus, the Bringer of Peace*; (3) *Mercury, the Winged Messenger*; (4) *Jupiter, the Bringer of Jollity*; (5) *Saturn, the Bringer of Old Age*; (6) *Uranus, the Magician*; (7) *Neptune, the Mystic*.

player-piano, *see* PIANOLA

Playford, John (1623–86), the first regular music publisher in England and the most active in the 17th century. His first publication was a collection of folk tunes entitled *The English Dancing Master* (1651) which he later reprinted in many editions. Among his other publications were *A Musicall Banquet* (1651), Hilton's *Catch that Catch can* (1652), *Introduction to the Skill of Musick* (1654 and many later editions; written by himself), *Cantica sacra* (1674), *The Whole Book of Psalms* (1677; twenty editions to 1757), and *Choice Ayres* (five books, 1676–84). His son, Henry Playford, continued his business.

plectrum, a small piece of horn, ivory, wood or other suitable substance used for playing such instruments as the PSALTERY (which may be considered a prototype of the harpsichord, but was also played with the fingers), MANDOLINE, GUITAR, and ZITHER.

plein jeu (Fr.), full organ.

pleno (It.), full; hence full organ.

Pleyel, Ignaz Joseph (1757–1831), Austrian piano manufacturer, violinist and composer. He studied under Wanhal and Haydn, and in 1777 became *Kapellmeister* to Count Erdody (who granted him leave to study in Rome). In 1792 he conducted in London several concerts in rivalry to those organised by Salomon for Haydn. On moving to Paris in 1795, he

established himself as a music-dealer, and founded in 1807 the piano factory which still bears his name. His numerous compositions include 29 symphonies, concertos for piano and violin, string quintets and quartets, piano sonatas and songs. Some of his works were much admired by Haydn and Mozart.

plica, medieval Latin (from the classical *plicare*, to fold), literally 'plait'. The *plica* was an ornament in early medieval notation, indicated by a vertical stroke attached to the note. The ornament was a passing note, and the descriptions of the theorists seem to suggest that it was sung with an effect resembling a TREMOLO. By the middle of the 13th century the notation of the *plica* was more or less systematised. If the stroke went up, the *plica* was above the note to which it was attached; if it went down, the *plica* was below. Thus the sign for a breve with a descending *plica* was:

If the next note was a third below the first, this example was sung:

If the succeeding note was the same as the first, the *plica* would descend a second in the same way (or rise, in the case of an ascending *plica*). Where the interval between the two principal notes was other than a third, the pitch of the *plica* had to be decided by the context. The sign for a breve with an ascending *plica* was:

for a long with an ascending *plica*:

for a long with a descending *plica*:

The value of a perfect long (*see* PERFECT) with a *plica* was divided as follows: two-thirds of the normal value to the principal note, one-third to the *plica*. An imperfect long with a *plica* was divided into two equal halves, one half to the principal note and one to the *plica*. It would appear, therefore, that it was the method of performance which properly differentiated the *plica* from other forms of notation. On the other hand copyists seem often to have used it simply as a conveniently rapid way of writing two notes with a single symbol. In modern transcriptions it is generally represented by a note of smaller size. For further information *see* W. Apel, *The Notation of Polyphonic Music, 900–1600*, pages 234–8, 298.

Plunket Greene, Harry, *see* GREENE

pneuma, *see* NEUMA

pochette (Fr.), literally 'little pocket', a miniature

violin formerly used by dancing masters.

See KIT

pochettino (It.), very little, very slightly.

poco (It.), little, i.e. slightly, rather. *Poco più lento*, rather slower. *Poco diminuendo*, getting slightly softer. *Poco a poco*, little by little, gradually.

podium, the dais on which a conductor stands to direct an orchestra. This term is widely used in the United States, though in Britain the word 'rostrum' is preferred.

Poem of Ecstasy, symphonic poem for orchestra by Skryabin, op 54 (1908). The work, which had its première in New York, depicts the artist's joy in creative activity.

poème symphonique (Fr.), symphonic poem.

Poglietti, Alessandro (died 1683). Italian composer. He was organist at the court chapel in Vienna from 1661 until he was killed during the Turkish siege. He composed *ricercari* for organ, suites for harpsichord, and church music. Two suites published in *Denkmäler der Tonkunst in Osterreich*, xxvii, Jg. xiii (2), contain some picturesque items. The second is a musical depiction of the Hungarian rebellion of 1671, with appropriate sub-titles. The first, written for the twenty-second birthday of the third wife of the Emperor Leopold I, contains a German air (*Aria Allemagna*) with 22 variations, some of which illustrate the style of regional dances, e.g. Bohemian *Dudlsackh*, Dutch *Flagolett*, Bavarian *Schalmay*. This movement is printed in part in *Historical Anthology of Music*, edited by A. T. Davison and W. Apel, no 236.

Pohjola's Daughter, symphonic fantasia by Sibelius, op 49, one of a group of orchestral works based on the Finnish epic *Kalevala*. Its première, conducted by the composer, was given in St. Petersburg in 1906.

Pohl, Carl Ferdinand (1819–87), Austrian musicologist and organist. He studied under Sechter in Vienna, where he was a church organist, 1849–55. From 1863 until 1866 he lived in London, doing research on Haydn and Mozart. On returning to Vienna he became librarian of the Gesellschaft der Musikfreunde, and wrote *Mozart and Haydn in London* (two volumes, 1867), *Joseph Haydn* (two volumes, 1875–82, completed by Hugo Botstiber, 1927).

Pohl, Richard (1826–96), German music critic who befriended Liszt at Weimar and wrote a three volume work on Wagner, as well as studies of Liszt and Berlioz.

poi (It.), then. This word is used usually when a section of music is to follow another in a way not made clear by the notation. Thus, a composer who wants to repeat a scherzo and then tack on a coda at the end might write: 'scherzo da capo, poi la coda'.

point, the end of the bow opposite the heel.

See PUNTA D'ARCO

point, a 16th century English term for the theme used in a passage in imitative counterpoint. Thus Morley in *A Plaine and Easie Introduction to Practicall Musicke* (1597) says that in writing a fantasy (i.e. fancy) 'a musician taketh a point at his pleasure and wresteth and turneth it as he list'.

point d'orgue (Fr., organ point), (1) pedal point; (2) pause; (3) cadenza (since the place for it, in a concerto or similar work, is indicated by a pause).

pointé (Fr.), a term used by French composers of the late 17th and early 18th centuries to indicate that a succession of short notes (e.g. quavers) of apparently equal value should actually be played with a marked inequality, the odd numbered notes being lengthened and the even numbered ones being proportionately shortened. If there were already dotted notes in the music (e.g. dotted quaver followed by semiquaver), the dotted note was to be prolonged and the note after it shortened still further.

See DOT (2), NOTES INÉGALES

pointillism, term for the spare, pointed style, with use often of pizzicato effects, adopted by some 20th century composers (e.g. Webern) in some of their works. The sound of such music has been compared with the pointillist school of painting, characterised by the use of dots of colour to convey the artist's ideas.

pointing, *see* ANGLICAN CHANT.

Poisoned Kiss, The, comic opera in three acts by Vaughan Williams, to a libretto by Evelyn Sharp, first performed at Cambridge in 1936. Based on a story by Richard Garnett (*The Poison Maid*) the opera – described as a 'romantic extravaganza' – concerns a sorcerer's daughter who has the power to bestow kisses of death; but when she falls sincerely in love, the magic spell is broken.

polacca (It.), polonaise.

polka, a dance in moderately quick 2/4 time, said to have originated in Bohemia about 1830. After 1835 it spread to other European countries and to the United States and became immensely popular. It was used by Smetana in his string quartet *From my Life* and in *The Bartered Bride*:

and by Dvořák.

Polly, ballad opera with text by John Gay and musical arrangements by Pepusch. The work was a sequel to *The Beggar's Opera*, and was intended to repeat its success. It was published in 1729 but was deemed to be subversive of authority, and banned until 1777 when it was performed with alterations in the text by George Colman the elder and with six new songs by Samuel Arnold. An adaptation by Clifford Bax, with the music arranged and newly composed by Frederic Austin, was first performed in London in 1922.

polo (Sp.), an Andalusian folk dance in a moderately fast 3/8 time, frequently syncopated, and with periodic ornamental phrases on a syllable such as 'Ay!'. Bizet adapted a *polo* by Manuel Garcia in the prelude to the fourth act of *Carmen*. The last of Falla's *Seven Popular Spanish Songs* is entitled 'Polo'.

polonaise (Fr.; It., *polacca*), a Polish dance in moderately fast 3/4 time. Its chief characteristics are its stately rhythm in a persistent pattern:

and its use of a feminine ending:

W. F. BACH, *Polonaise no 6*

It is found in the works of J. S. Bach (e.g. in the first Brandenburg Concerto and the second suite for orchestra), W. F. Bach, Mozart (in the piano sonata K 284), Beethoven, Weber and Schubert. Chopin's great series of polonaises, which may be martial or funereal in expression and in a ternary or free form (e.g. the *Polonaise-Fantaisie*, op 61) represent the romantic concept of its style, poetic and patriotic.

polyphony (Gr., multiplication of sounds; Ger., *Mehrstimmigkeit*), the style of music in the writing of which the composer pays particular attention to the melodic value of each part, as distinct from HOMO-PHONY, the style consisting of melody with chordal accompaniment. The most important polyphonic forms are MOTET, ROTA or ROUND, polyphonic MASS, CANON, polyphonic CHANSON, CANZONA, RICERCAR, and FUGUE. True polyphony was first written in the second stage (11th–12th century) of ORGANUM. Medieval polyphony was written by the method of successive composition, i.e. by the addition of a complete part or parts to the first complete part (MOTET, CANTUS FIRMUS). The imitative polyphony of the 16th century choral music and of the *canzona* and *ricercar* was composed by disposing the same theme in each of the parts successively. The tonal or harmonic polyphony of the 18th century fugue was composed in a similar fashion, but normally used a single theme (subject) throughout, and was organised according to the principles of TONALITY. In modern compositions the employment of polyphonic forms and devices may follow the principles of chromatic tonality, as in Hindemith's *Ludus Tonalis* (1942), or of atonality, as in Schoenberg's *Pierrot Lunaire* (1912).

polytonality, the use of two or more keys simultaneously, generally by superimposing chords, arpeggios, or melodies each of which unequivocally defines a different KEY (tonality). Before the present century deliberate examples, such as in Mozart's *A Musical Joke*, were rare. Pietro Raimondi (1786–1853) composed as a scientific curiosity (*Opera Scientifica*) fugues for four and for six four-part choirs, each in a different key, which could be performed separately or simultaneously. In general, however, polytonality is a twentieth century practice. Among composers who have made important use of it are Stravinsky, Bartók, Milhaud and Holst, e.g.:

BARTÓK, *Bagatelle* op 6, no 1

See also BITONALITY.

pommer, name given to four of the six members of the Schalmey-Pommer family of double-reed instruments, from which the oboe, *cor anglais* and bassoon eventually derived. In pitch the alto pommer was roughly the equivalent of the *cor anglais*, while the double bass pommer, also known as the bombard, corresponded to the bassoon. In between these two came the tenor and bass pommers.

See OBOE

Pomo d'Oro, Il (The Golden Apple), opera with a prologue and five acts by Cesti, to a libretto by Francesco Sbarra, first performed in Vienna in 1667.

Pomone, opera with a prologue and five acts by Cambert, to a libretto by Pierre Perrin, first performed in Paris in 1671.

pomposo (It.), in a pompous manner.

Ponce, Manuel (1882–1948), Mexican composer. He studied at the National Conservatorio in Mexico City, and in Berlin and Bologna. In 1906 he returned to Mexico where he taught and conducted. From 1915–18 he taught at Havana (Cuba). At the age of forty, he studied composition in Paris under Dukas and in 1933 returned again to Mexico. He composed orchestral works, concertos, chamber music, piano works and songs (including the popular 'Estrellita'). One of his works was a guitar concerto composed for Segovia. He collected and arranged Mexican folk songs.

Ponchielli, Amilcare (1834–1886), Italian composer. Of his nine operas only *La Gioconda* (Milan, 1876) – containing the famous *Dance of the Hours* – is today regularly performed. He also composed ballets and cantatas, among which was one in Garibaldi.

Ponte, Lorenzo Da (1749–1838), Italian born poet and librettist, of Jewish parents. He was educated for the church, becoming a priest in 1773, and was appointed a teacher in the seminary in Trieste (1774). His life as a priest was irregular, however, and he was banished from Venice as a result of scandal in 1779. He became poet to the court opera in Vienna (1784), where he met Mozart and wrote librettos for *The Marriage of Figaro*, *Don Giovanni* and *Così fan tutte*. He lived in London as teacher of Italian and poet to the Italian Opera, in Holland and in New York (from 1805, to escape his London creditors) as a businessman, and later as a teacher of Italian at Columbia College. He wrote an autobiography (four volumes, 1823–27; English edition in one volume, 1929).

A. FITZLYON: *The Libertine Librettist* (1955)

ponticello (It.), the bridge of a stringed instrument. *Sul ponticello* is a direction to instrumentalists to bow as near as possible to the bridge, the result being a thin and brittle tone.

Poot, Marcel (born 1901), Belgian composer, son of the director of the Royal Flemish Theatre, Brussels, and pupil of Gilson and Dukas. In 1949 he became director of the Brussels Conservatoire. His compositions include operas, ballets, oratorios, symphonies and other orchestral works, including a symphonic poem, *Charlot*, inspired by Charlie Chaplin.

Popov, Gavryil Nikolaievich (born 1904), Russian composer who studied at Rostov and from 1922 at the Leningrad Conservatory under Steinberg. He composed operas, a symphony, suites for orchestra, film and chamber music, and piano works.

Popper, David (1843–1913), Czech born cellist, who studied at the Prague Conservatory under Goltermann and made his first tour in 1863. From 1868–73 he was cellist of the Hubay Quartet, and in 1896 became cello professor at the National Academy of Music, Budapest. He composed concertos and many other works for cello.

Porgy and Bess, opera in three acts by George Gershwin, to a libretto by Du Bose Hayward and Ira Gershwin, the composer's brother. This was Gershwin's only opera, and made operatic history as it was written for a Negro cast. The story tells how the crippled Porgy falls in love with Bess, who is lured away from him by a character called Sporting Life. Though the music makes use of certain Negro idioms, the songs are genuine Gershwin. Several of them, including 'Summertime' and 'I got plenty o' nuttin', are famous outside their operatic context. The work was first performed at Boston in 1935. Twenty years later it was the first U.S. opera ever to be performed at La Scala, Milan.

Porpora, Niccolò Antonio (1686–1767), Italian composer and singing teacher. He studied in Naples, where he became music director to the Portuguese Ambassador. In 1708 he established a school of singing. He subsequently became singing teacher at the Conservatorio di San Onofrio in 1715 and at the Conservatorio della Pieta in Venice in 1725. He then visited Vienna, Dresden (as conductor of the court opera and rival to Hasse), and London, where from 1729 he was the rival conductor to Handel. In 1745 he returned to Vienna (where Haydn became his pupil and accompanist) and in 1747 he became teacher of the Electoral Princess in Dresden. In 1760 he settled in Naples as *maestro di cappella* of the Cathedral and director of the Conservatorio di San Onofrio. He composed 53 operas, oratorios, Masses, solo cantatas and other church music, violin sonatas and other chamber music, and pieces for harpsichord. He was, however, more famous as a singing teacher, one of the most famous ever.

Porta, Costanzo (c. 1530–1601), Italian composer and Franciscan monk. He studied under Willaert in Venice, and in 1552 was appointed *maestro di cappella* at Osimo Cathedral. Subsequently he moved to S. Antonio, Padua (1564), Ravenna Cathedral (1567) and Loreto Cathedral (1575). Later he returned to Padua. He composed motets, Masses, hymns and other church music, and madrigals. A complete edition of his works by S. Cisilino is in progress.

portamento (It.; Fr., *port de voix*), literally 'carrying'. An effect used in singing or in playing a bowed instrument, obtained by carrying the sound in a continuous glide from one note to the next:

es____ holt Euch doch

rit.
schaurig("horrid") *a tempo*
(Fort) ins Zi - geu - ner-land

The examples are from Alban Berg's *Wozzeck*. The second of them is a *portamento* which is partly defined as to pitch.

portative or **portative organ** (It., *organetto*), a small portable organ, developed in the middle ages.

portato (It.), *mezzo staccato*.
See STACCATO

port de voix (Fr.), (1) a 17th–18th century term for the *appoggiatura*.
(2) PORTAMENTO

portée (Fr.), staff, stave.

Porter, Cole (1893–1964), U.S. composer, pupil of d'Indy, but associated more with the popular song and the American musical than with concert pieces. One of the principal and most evergreen composers in his field, he was not only a subtle melodist, with a keen ear for syncopation, but he also wrote the equally subtle and witty words of his songs, of which 'You're the top' is a superb example. The most famous of his works for the stage are *Anything Goes* and *Kiss Me Kate* – the latter, a modern spoof on *The Taming of the Shrew*, now holds its place in the repertoire of a number of European opera companies.

Porter, Quincy (1897–1966), U.S. composer, who studied at Yale under Horatio Parker and David Stanley Smith, in Paris under d'Indy, and later in the United States under Bloch. He taught theory at Cleveland Institute of Music from 1922, in 1928 went to Paris for two years as a Guggenheim Fellow, was professor of music and conductor at Vassar College from 1932 and was appointed Dean of the Faculty of New England Conservatory, Boston in 1938. In 1946 he became professor of theory at Yale School of Music. He composed two symphonies and other orchestral works (including a symphonic suite, *New England Episodes*), a viola concerto and a concerto for two pianos, ten string quartets and other chamber music, and incidental music for plays.

Porter, Walter (c. 1587 or c. 1595–1659), English composer who studied under Monteverdi. In 1603 he was a choirboy at Westminster Abbey. He became a Gentleman of the Chapel Royal in 1617 and master of the choristers at Westminster Abbey in 1639. After the suppression of the choral service in 1644 he came under the patronage of Sir Edward Spencer. He published *Madrigales and Ayres . . . with Toccatos, Sinfonias and Rittornellos to them after the manner of Consort Musique* (1632; with a continuo part), and *Mottets of Two Voyces . . . with the Continued Bass or Score* (1657). He was one of the earliest English composers to publish a continuo part, and to use the *trillo* in the manner of the Italian monodists.

G. E. P. ARKWRIGHT: 'An English Pupil of Monteverdi', in *The Musical Antiquary*, iv

C. W. HUGHES: 'Porter, Pupil of Monteverdi', in *Musical Quarterly*, xx (1934)

Portsmouth Point, concert overture by Walton, after a drawing by Thomas Rowlandson depicting a bustling 18th century quayside scene. The piece had its première in 1926 at the Festival of the International Society for Contemporary Music, held that year in Zürich.

Posaune (Ger.), trombone.

Posch, Isaak (died before 1623), Austrian or German composer. He was organist at Ljubljana. He published books of instrumental dances in 1618 and 1621. The second of these, his *Musicalische Tafelfreudt* (modern edition in *Denkmäler der Tonkunst in Osterreich*, lxx, Jg. xxxvi, 2), contains a number of Paduana-Gagliarda pairs, each pair being thematically related, followed by a number of Intrada-Couranta pairs, similarly related. A set of sacred concertos for one to four voices with continuo was published in 1623 under the title *Harmonia concertans*.

positif (Fr.), choir organ.

position, (1) on a stringed instrument, the placing of the left hand on the string in relation to the open note of the string. Thus in the first position on the G string the first finger plays A, in the second position it plays B, and so on. The thumb is used in the higher positions on the cello;

    (2) the placing of the slide of the TROMBONE;

    (3) the disposition of a chord in relation to its ROOT. Root position, first inversion, second inversion, etc., of a chord are all said to be positions of that chord, in that they consist of the same notes, though differently arranged.

Positive (Ger.), choir organ.

positive organ, originally the term meant a small chamber organ which, unlike the PORTATIVE, was fixed in position. Later the name was given to part of a large organ controlled by the CHOIR ORGAN manual.

Possenti, Pellegrino, early 17th century Italian composer who published two books of madrigals (1623, 1625), and was one of the earliest composers of sonatas for two, three, and four instruments with continuo (*Concentus armonici*, 1628).

posthorn, a simple brass instrument akin to the bugle but usually straight and therefore much longer. It was used by postillions in the 18th and 19th centuries. As it had no valves it could produce only the notes of the HARMONIC SERIES.

postlude, generally a final piece, or a closing section of a piece of music. The term may also apply to a piece played on the organ at the end of a service.

Poston, Elizabeth (born 1905), English composer and writer about music. She studied at the Royal College of Music in London. Her compositions include vocal and piano pieces, though she is best known for her arrangements of British folk songs. Her compilations include *The Cambridge Hymnal, Folk Songs of Britain for Women's Voices, The Children's Song Book, The Penguin Book of Folk Songs of the British Isles, The Penguin Book of American Folk Songs, An English Kalendar* and *The Faber Book of French Folk Songs*.

Pothier, Dom Joseph (1835–1923), Benedictine authority on plainsong. He entered the Benedictine Order at the Abbey of Solesmes in 1859 and in 1898 became abbot of St. Wandrille monastery which was later moved to Belgium. He continued the study of plainsong begun by his teacher Dom Guéranger, published many works on the subject, and initiated the series *Paleographie musicale* for publishing facsimiles of manuscripts of the 9th–16th centuries. He chaired the committee responsible for the preparation and publication of the Vatican edition of the liturgical chant.

pot-pourri (Fr.), a succession of familiar tunes fashioned, with links, in a continuous composition.

Potter, Philip Cipriani Hambly (1792–1871), English pianist, composer and conductor. He studied under Attwood, Callcott, Crotch, Woelfl, and (after his appearance with the London Philharmonic Society in 1816) under Aloys Förster in Vienna, where he was advised by Beethoven. From 1832 until 1859 he was principal of the Royal Academy of Music in London. His works include sonatas and other piano pieces, a sextet for strings and piano and other chamber music; he also composed nine symphonies, four overtures, piano concertos, and a cantata.

Pougin, Francois Auguste Arthur (1834–1921), French writer on music. He edited *Le Ménestrel* from 1885, and wrote many biographies of composers.

Poule, La, *see* HEN

Poulenc, Francis (1899–1963), French composer and pianist. After studying under Ricardo Vines and Koechlin, he became a member of the group of French composers known as *Les Six*. He was influenced by Satie. He composed ballets (the most famous being *Les Biches*), chamber music, a concerto for two pianos and many piano pieces, a concerto for harpsichord, numerous songs, choral works and a cantata. His style combines classical clarity with an irrepressible talent for satire and caricature, though in the years after World War II his music gained a new vein of seriousness, especially in his opera *Les Dialogues des Carmelites* (*The Carmelites*, 1957) and his concerto for strings and

Francis Poulenc, the most successful of Les Six in realizing their anti-impressionist views

kettledrums. As a pianist he appeared frequently with his partner, the French baritone Pierre Bernac.

Pouplinière, Alexandre Jean Joseph le Riche de la (1693–1762), French amateur and patron of music. He studied under Rameau, who lived in his house for a number of years and conducted his private orchestra. He was the patron of the concerts conducted by Johann Stamitz in Paris in 1754–5, and on the advice of Stamitz added clarinets, horns and harp to his orchestra for the first time in France.

  G. CUCUEL: *La Pouplinière et la musique de chambre au XVIIIe siècle* (1913)

poussez (Fr.), literally, 'push ahead', i.e. quicken the tempo.

Power, Leonel (d. 1445), English composer, the most important contemporary of Dunstable. Like Dunstable many of his compositions survive in continental sources such as the TRENT CODICES. His music, with that of Dunstable and other English composers, had a considerable influence on the style of continental composers. His *Alma redemptoris* Mass (modern edition by L. Feininger) is the earliest complete Mass on a *cantus firmus*. Many of his compositions are in the OLD HALL MANUSCRIPT. He wrote an elementary treatise on descant, which has been printed in M. F. Bukofzer, *Geschichte des englischen Diskants* (1936). A complete edition of his works by Charles Hamm is in progress.

praeludium (Lat.), prelude.

Praetorius, Hieronymous (1560–1629), German organist and composer. He studied with his father (organist of St. James's, Hamburg) and in Cologne. In 1580 he was cantor at Erfurt. In 1582 he was assistant organist at St. James's, Hamburg, and in 1586 he succeeded his father as organist there. His compositions, exclusively for the church and written for as many as twenty voices, were at first published in separate volumes and then reissued in a collected edition in five volumes entitled *Opus musicum novum et perfectum*. The contents include Masses, Magnificats, and motets with Latin and German texts. Sixteen motets appear in *Denkmäler deutscher Tonkunst*, xxiii.

Praetorius, Michael (1571–1621), German composer and theorist who was one of the most versatile and prolific musicians of his time. Among the posts which he held were those of *Kapellmeister* and secretary to the Duke of Brunswick and *Kapellmeister* to the Saxon court. He was one of the foremost German composers to practise the elaborate style of writing for several choirs which was cultivated in Venice. His works for the church include settings of both Latin and German words. Among them are settings of the Magnificat (*Megalynodia Sionia*), Kyries, Glorias, etc. (*Missodia Sionia*) and many settings of Lutheran chorales ranging from simple harmonizations to elaborate contrapuntal treatment. His *Polyhymnia Caduceatrix et Panegyrica* consists of choral works with independent instrumental accompaniment. A few organ settings were printed in *Musae Sioniae*, pt. vii and *Hymnodia Sionia*. The dances for instrumental ensemble in *Terpsichore* include several by French composers. Praetorius's principal publications were:

  Musae Sioniae, 9 pts. (1605–10)
  Musarum Sioniarum Motectae et Psalmi Latini (1607)

  Missodia Sionia (1611)
  Hymnodia Sionia (1611)
  Eulogodia Sionia (1611)
  Megalynodia Sionia (1611)
  Terpsichore (1612)
  Urania (1613)
  Polyhymnia Caduceatrix et Panegyrica (1619)
  Polyhymnia Exercitatrix (1620)
  Puericinium (1621)

A modern edition of his works has been published in 21 volumes under the general editorship of F. Blume (1928–60). The organ works are also published separately in an edition by K. Matthaei (1930).

In addition to his musical compositions Praetorius also published *Syntagma Musicum* in three volumes (1614–20). The first volume deals with the origins and history of liturgical music and also with the secular music of the ancient world. The second volume, subtitled *De Organographia* (facsimile edition, 1929), gives a detailed account of instruments and their function and includes a valuable series of illustrations, drawn to scale. The third volume (modern edition by E. Bernouilli, 1916) deals with notation and the various forms of secular music current in the early 17th century and adds an important section on methods of performance and principles of choir training. The second and third volumes together shed light on a great many details of 17th century music and performance which would otherwise remain obscure. The treatment is systematic and the approach scholarly.

'Prague' Symphony, nickname given to Mozart's symphony no 38 in D major, K 504 (1786), after its première in Prague, 1787, during a visit by the composer for the performance of *The Marriage of Figaro*.

Pralltriller (Ger.), an ornament used in instrumental music in the 18th century. C. P. E. Bach, in his *Versuch über die wahre Art, das Klavier zu spielen* (1753–62), calls it 'Der halbe [i.e. half] oder Prall-Triller' and gives this example:

He points out that it occurs only on the lower of two notes in a descending second played legato, that it must be played very fast and with a 'snap', and that it is doubtful therefore that it can be properly executed on the pianoforte. When it is marked over a pause note preceded by an appoggiatura, the latter is held, and the *Pralltriller* is played immediately before the end of the note:

Since c. 1800 the name has been applied to the ornament formerly called *Schneller*, and commonly called INVERTED MORDENT.

  See also TRILL.

Pré aux Clercs, Le (*The Scholars' Meadow*), opera in three acts by Hérold, to a libretto by François Antoine

Eugène de Planard, first performed in Paris in 1832. The work is based on Mérimée's *Chronique de Règne de Charles IX*.

precentor (Lat., *praecentor, cantor*), (1) the official charged with the supervision of music in a cathedral, college chapel or monastery.

(2) official of the Presbyterian Churches of Scotland and of 17th–18th century Puritan churches of New England who gave out and led the psalm and hymns.

Preciosa, overture and other music written by Weber for P. A. Wolff's German play of that title, based on Cervantes's *La Gitanella*, first produced in 1821 in Berlin.

precipitato, precipitoso (It.), 'precipitately', i.e. impetuously.

preclassical, term, increasingly used today, for music written before the time of Haydn and Mozart (or, if the term is more loosely applied, before Bach).

prelude (Lat., *praeludium*), an introductory movement; also, in Chopin and later composers, a short self-contained piano piece in one movement. The preludes written for organ, lute, and virginals in the 15th and 16th centuries were free pieces in an extemporary style. In Italy such pieces for lute were called *tastar* ('touching') and in Spain *tañer*. Some of the SUITE preludes of the baroque period continued this style, e.g. those of Louis Couperin, which he wrote down without giving the rhythm, a practice which continued to the time of Rameau, as in:

from his first book of clavecin pieces (1706), and in the prelude to Handel's first suite for harpsichord. In others a more regular and extended form was adopted, e.g. the cyclic form of the preludes in Bach's *English Suites*, and of some of his organ preludes. The preludes of the *Well-tempered Clavier* are, with one or two exceptions, short pieces based on a single musical idea, as in the prelude in D minor in the first book:

The 24 preludes of Chopin, while romantic in style and piano technique, have in common with those of Bach's *Forty-eight* the use of a single theme and of the complete cycle of keys, and later sets of preludes, though not always using a complete key sequence, have followed the same plan, e.g. Skryabin's twelve preludes, op 11, Rakhmaninov's ten preludes, op 23, and thirteen preludes, op 32, Debussy's two sets of twelve preludes, and Shostakovich's twenty-four preludes, op 34.

Since about 1840 many composers have written a short orchestral piece as a prelude to, and usually taking its music from, an opera, as in Wagner's *Lohengrin* and *Tristan und Isolde* and Verdi's *La Traviata*, rather than a full-length OVERTURE.

See also CHORALE PRELUDE.

Prélude à l'Après-Midi d'un Faune (Fr., *Prelude to the afternoon of a faun*), orchestral piece by Debussy (1894), designed to illustrate a poem by Mallarmé. One of Debussy's earliest essays in impressionism, it was originally intended to be the first of a set of three pieces. A ballet by Nijinsky was later based on the music.

Préludes, Les, symphonic poem by Liszt, inspired by a poem by Lamartine, and first performed in 1854 at Weimar. Initially, the music was intended to be an overture to *Les quatres éléments*, a choral setting of four poems by Joseph Autran. Not until Liszt rewrote the work as a symphonic poem did Lamartine enter the picture. In its definitive version, *Les Préludes* is prefaced by a printed question: 'What is our life but a series of preludes to that unknown song of which death sounds the first and solemn note?' But these words simply confuse the issue further, since they seem to have no special bearing either on Lamartine or on the music itself.

prepared piano, a piano that has been 'prepared' by having various objects, such as pieces of rubber and screws, placed between selected strings. Not only does this affect the tone greatly, it also can alter the pitch. The U.S. experimental composer, John Cage, and his followers have made much use of this device.

Prés, Josquin des, *see* JOSQUIN

près de la table (Fr.), near the sounding-board. An indication found in harp music, resulting in metallic sounds similar to those of the banjo.

prestant, a four foot open diapason stop on the organ.

presto (It.), originally meant 'lively, brisk', but it came to be used to indicate the fastest speed in normal use. The superlative, *prestissimo*, can only mean the fastest speed of which the performer or performers are capable – though Schumann having marked the coda of his G minor piano sonata *prestissimo* requests the performer to make an *accelerando* in the closing bars.

Previn, André (born 1929), German born conductor, pianist and composer. He received his early musical education in Berlin, but moved with other members of his family to California at the outbreak of World War II. At the age of sixteen he joined the music department of the MGM film company, and later won four Academy Awards for film scores. He studied conducting with Pierre Monteux and composition with Joseph Acron and Mario Castelnuovo-Tedesco. After a period as a jazz pianist of outstanding quality he became conductor of the Houston Symphony Orchestra in 1967 and of the London Symphony Orchestra in 1968. As a composer, he has written a cello concerto, a guitar concerto, two wind quintets and a suite of piano preludes.

prick song, a term derived from 'pricking,' in the sense of writing musical notes, used in England in the first half of the 16th century to distinguish written poly-phonic music from plainsong, and later extended to include all music except plainsong, whether written down or not.

prima (It.), 'first of all, formerly'. *Come prima*, as at first, i.e. resume the original tempo of a piece or movement.

prima donna (It.), 'first lady'. The singer of the most important female part in an opera. The corresponding term in the 18th century for the singer of the most important *castrato* or tenor role was *primo uomo*.

prima prattica, seconda prattica (It.), first and second practice. Terms used by Monteverdi to dis-tinguish between the old contrapuntal style of the 16th century and the new style of the 17th century in which solo instruments or voices were exploited, with figured-bass accompaniment.

See also STILE

Primavera, Giovanni Leonardo (c. 1540–after 1585), Italian composer. In 1573 he was *maestro di cappella* to the Spanish governor of Milan. He wrote madrigals and *canzone napolitane* for three voices, published between 1565 and 1585. Palestrina composed a PARODY MASS on his madrigal 'Nasce la gioia mia.'

prima volta (It.), 'first time', i.e. a first ending when a repeat is indicated. It is usually shown by $\boxed{1\quad\quad}$, and the ending of the repeated section, the second ending (*seconda volta*) by $\boxed{2\quad}$.

See CLOS, OUVERT.

prime, the interval 'zero', or unison. The term also refers to the third of the canonical hours.

primo (It.), 'first': (1) the upper part of a piano duet, the lower part being termed *secondo* (second). In most editions of piano duets the *primo* part is printed on the right-hand page and the *secondo* on the left-hand page. This is in many ways the most convenient arrange-ment for the performers. Some publishers, however, prefer to print the two parts together, in score, which enables each player to see what the other is doing but imposes an inconvenient angle of vision.

(2) the first of two or more players or singers, or of two or more groups of performers. *Violino primo*, the first violin in a string quartet, or the whole body of first violins in an orchestra. *Flauto (oboe, clarinetto,* etc.) *primo*, first flute (oboe, clarinet, etc.). In an orchestral score the parts for two wind instruments of the same kind are generally printed on the same stave. Hence when only one is playing, *primo* (abbreviated *Imo,* or simply *I*) indicates that the first player is intended.

(3) *tempo primo* (abbreviated *tempo Imo* or *tempo I*), 'the original speed'. An indication that the speed of the opening of a movement or piece is to be resumed after one or more sections in a slower or faster tempo.

primo uomo, *see* PRIMA DONNA

Primrose, William (born 1904), Scottish born viola player who has lived in the United States since 1937. The most famous viola player of his day, he has had numerous works written for him – including Bartók's viola concerto.

Prince Igor (Russ., *Kniaz Igor*), opera with a prologue and four acts by Borodin, who wrote his own libretto for it, but left the work unfinished. After his death it was completed by Rimsky-Korsakov and Glazunov, and first performed at St. Petersburg in 1890. The opera deals with the capture of a 12th century Russian hero by the Polovtsians – whose leader, Khan Konchak, treats him with respect and entertains him in Act 2 to a display of Polovtsian dances (often performed out of context).

Prince of the Pagodas, The, ballet in three acts with music by Britten, produced in London in 1957. The choreography and fairy-tale scenario were both by John Cranko.

Princess Ida, comic opera in two acts by Gilbert and Sullivan, first performed in London in 1884 and styled 'a respectful operatic per-version of Tennyson's *Princess*'. The princess is the principal of a woman's university, who, like Turandot, is eventually convinced of the power of love.

principal, (1) in an orchestra, the first player of a particular group of instruments (e.g., 'principal violin');

(2) in an opera company, a singer who takes leading parts, but not the chief ones;

(3) an organ stop: in Britain, the four foot diapason; in Germany (*Prinzipal*) and Italy (*principale*) the eight foot diapason.

See ORGAN

principale, a term used for trumpet parts until about 1750.

printing of music, plainsong books with music were printed in Rome (1476), Venice and Würzburg in the second half of the 15th century, the notes being printed in black and the staves separately in red. Ottaviano dei Petrucci of Venice published the *Harmonice Musices Odhecaton,* the first book of printed part-music, in 1501, and some fifty collections there-after. Pierre Attaingnant began printing in Paris in 1528, and a book of *XX Songes* in three and four parts was published in London in 1530. Engraving of music was practised in Italy in the second half of the 16th century, and *Parthenia,* engraved in 1612 or early 1613, was 'the first musicke that ever was printed for the Virginalls'. Early in the 18th century John Walsh introduced the use of special punches for engraving music, a system which is still in use and has almost entirely superseded the use of type. At the end of the century lithography was invented, and Weber himself lithographed his Variations for Piano, op 2, in 1800. In recent years photolithography has been used to publish scores from the composer's, or a copyist's, manuscript.

W. GAMBLE: *Music Engraving and Printing* (1923)

C. HUMPHRIES AND W. C. SMITH: *Music Publishing in the British Isles* (1954)

O. KINKELDEY: *Music and Music Printing in Incuna-bula* (1932)

. R. R. STEELE: *The Earliest English Music Printing* (1903)

Printz, Wolfgang Kaspar (1641–1717), German composer. He studied theology, and was appointed cantor at Promnitz, and at Triebel. In 1665 he was cantor at Sorau. His *Historische Beschreibung der edlen Sing- und Klingkunst . . . von Anfang der Welt bis auf* *unserer Zeit* (Dresden, 1690) was the first history of music written in German.

Prise de Troie, La, *see* TROJANS

Pritchard, John (born 1921), English conductor, principally associated with Glyndebourne Festival Opera, where he began his career as repetiteur and chorus master under Fritz Busch in 1947 and subsequently became musical director and artistic counsellor. He is specially associated with the operas of Mozart and Richard Strauss. In the concert hall, he has been musical director of the Royal Liverpool Philharmonic and the London Philharmonic.

Prix de Rome (Fr.), a prize given by the French Government for excellence in each of the following fields: painting, sculpture, engraving, architecture and music. The prizes are awarded by the Académie des Beaux-Arts, a branch of the Institut de France, on the results of examinations. The winners are required to reside for three years at the Villa Medici (headquarters of the Académie de France) in Rome, and to submit for inspection the work completed during their period of residence.

The prize for music was first awarded in 1803. It has on occasion been divided. Among the composers who have won it are Hérold (1812), Halévy (1819), Berlioz (1830), Thomas (1832), Gounod (1839), Bizet (1857), Guiraud (1859), Paladilhe (1860), Dubois (1861), Bourgault-Ducoudray (1862), Massenet (1863), Lenepveu (1865), Wormser (1875), P. Hillemacher (1876), Huë (1879), L. Hillemacher (1880), Pierné (1882), Debussy (1884), Charpentier (1887), Büsser (1893), Rabaud (1894), Schmitt (1900), Caplet (1901), Paray (1911), L. Boulanger (1913), Delvincourt (1913), Dupré (1914), Ibert (1919), Fourestier (1925), Barraine (1929).

The prize, as the above list suggests, has not invariably been a gauge of musical inspiration. Ravel was one composer who failed to win it.

Prodaná Nevěsta, *see* BARTERED BRIDE

Prodigal Son, The, church parable by Britten, to a libretto by William Plomer. The third of three such works (the others being *Curlew River* and *The Burning Fiery Furnace*, each of them being really a short opera for church performance) it had its première at the Aldeburgh Festival in 1968.

programme music, music in which sound is used to depict the concrete elements of, and whose form is governed by, a story or image, as distinct from ABSOLUTE MUSIC. A few pictorial passages may be found in plainsong, in 16th century Masses and motets, in English virginal music, and in French harpsichord music of the 17th century, and many in the madrigals of the 16th century, and in the operas, oratorios and cantatas of the 17th and 18th centuries. In all of these they are incidental factors in compositions which have an orthodox musical design. Only in rare instances, such as some of the Italian *caccie* of the 14th century, the bird and battle *chansons* of Janequin, the battle piece for virginals by Byrd, and the *Biblical Sonatas* of Johann Kuhnau, are both the form and the themes directly related to a programme.

Beethoven affirmed that his *Pastoral Symphony* was 'an expression of emotion rather than tone-painting'; nevertheless the fourth movement, like all storm scenes in music, is programme music. Berlioz, on the other hand, introduced the written programme of his *Symphonie Fantastique* in terms which show that he regarded the symphony as an instrumental drama 'deprived of the resource of words'. There is an even stronger contrast of attitude between Mendelssohn, who kept the pictorial elements in his concert overtures well within the limits of the traditional form, and Liszt, whose SYMPHONIC POEMS were in form and expression so closely related to their subject that he thought it desirable to provide a programme or preface 'to guard the listener against a wrong poetical interpretation'.

The difference between the tone-poet, as Liszt preferred to call the composer of programme music, and the 'mere musician' was that, in his view, the former 'reproduces his impression and the adventures of his soul in order to communicate them, while the latter manipulates, groups and connects the tones according to certain established rules, and, thus playfully conquering difficulties, attains at best to novel, bold, unusual and complex combinations' (English version of the essay on *Berlioz and his Harold Symphony* of 1855 printed in O. Strunk's *Source Readings in Music History*, 1950).

In the series of symphonic poems which culminated in *Ein Heldenleben* (1898) and the *Domestic Symphony* (1903) Richard Strauss brought the pictorial possibilities of orchestral music with an accompanying programme to their final point. The idea that all music is by its nature an expression of such a 'programme', avowed or implied, had been vigorously attacked many years earlier by Hanslick in his *Vom Musikalisch-Schönen* (1854). The question is no longer a burning one, but Hanslick's view, though put in an extreme form, is much closer to the generally accepted view in this century: that any judgment of the value of a programme to music must ultimately be a judgment of the musical qualities of the result.

F. NIECKS: *Programme Music* (1907)

Prokofiev, Sergey Sergeyevich (1891–1953), Russian composer. Born at Sontsovka, in the Ekaterinoslav region, his pianist mother ensured that his precocious gifts, both as composer and pianist, were speedily encouraged. He began to compose before he could write properly, and at the age of nine he wrote an opera (*The Giant*) for performance by members of his family. His first major teacher was Glière; then, at the St. Petersburg Conservatory, he studied under Rimsky-Korsakov, Liadov and Tcherepnin, and won the Rubinstein Prize for the first of his five piano concertos. His *Scythian Suite* (1916), with its bludgeoning rhythms, established him as one of Russia's most progressive composers, and his *Classical Symphony* (1917) revealed his talent for pastiche. During the Russian Revolution – an event he was to commemorate later in his powerful *Cantata for the 20th Anniversary of the October Revolution* – he absented himself from his homeland and travelled the world. He lived in London for a time, and then went to Japan. In 1921, during a spell in the United States, he conducted the première of his opera, *The Love for Three Oranges*, in Chicago. In 1922 he moved to Paris, where he wrote music for Diaghilev's Russian Ballet, which put on several of his works. In 1934, cured of his wanderlust, he returned to Russia, where he voluntarily adopted Soviet citizenship and where his previously astringent musical style gradually

Serge Sergeievitch Prokofiev: a study that reflects the precision of his technique but not the boldness of his imagination

mellowed. Nevertheless his outlook was still sufficiently uncompromising for him to rouse the wrath of the Soviet authorities, who insisted on getting readily comprehensible music from their resident composers. In 1948 he was criticised in a resolution of the Central Committee of the Communist Party. In his reply he affirmed his intention of using 'lucid melody and, as far as possible, a simple harmonic language' in his next opera. In fact, he continued to compose more or less exactly as he liked. The next opera failed to please, and was described (by Khrennikov) as 'modernistic and anti-melodic'. The resolution is printed, along with Prokofiev's letter, in Slominsky's *Music since 1900* (1949). Prokofiev was awarded a Stalin Prize in 1951. He died in 1953, three hours before Stalin himself – an irony the composer would surely have savoured.

Prokofiev composed important works in most musical forms. Of his operas, *War and Peace, The Fiery Angel, The Gambler* and *The Love for Three Oranges* hold their place in the (by no means bulky) repertory of 20th century opera. Of his ballets, *Romeo and Juliet* still seems the greatest work of its kind since Chaikovsky's *Sleeeping Beauty*. Of his seven symphonies, the fifth remains the most glamorous (though the sixth, a darker, more disturbing work, is preferred by connoisseurs). His five piano concertos (especially the third) and two violin concertos continue to be played. His cantata, *Alexander Nevsky*, easily keeps its reputation as one of the greatest and most picturesque choral works of our time (in its original form it is also a superlative example of film music). The wit and pugnacity of the piano music seem as sharp as ever, and the lyricism just as sweet.

Prokofiev's principal works are:

(1) Stage works: operas: *Magdalen* (1913); *The Gambler* (1915–16, first performed 1927); *Love for Three Oranges* (1919); *The Fiery Angel* (1919–26, first performed 1955); *Semyon Kotko* (1939); *Betrothal in a Monastery* (1940); *War and Peace* (1941–52); *The Story of a Real Man* (1947–48, first performed 1961); six ballets, including *Romeo and Juliet* (1936) and *Cinderella* (1946).

(2) Orchestra: seven symphonies; sinfonietta; overtures; symphonic suites; film music for *Lieutenant Kizhe, The Queen of Spades, Ivan the Terrible*, etc.; five piano concertos; two violin concertos; cello concerto.

(3) Chamber works: quintet for wind and strings; string quintet; two string quartets.

(4) Piano: nine sonatas; two sonatinas; suites; studies. Also choral cantatas, songs, and *Peter and the Wolf* (1936) for speaker and orchestra.

G. ABRAHAM: *Eight Soviet Composers* (1943)

L. and E. HANSON: *Prokofiev, the Prodigal Son* (1964)

I. W. NESTYEV: *Serge Prokofiev* (1946)

C. SAMUEL: *Prokofiev* (1960, English translation 1971)

V. SEROFF: *Sergei Prokofiev – a Soviet Tragedy* (1968)

prolation, in mensural NOTATION prolation is the relation of the semibreve to the minim, and is either perfect or imperfect. In perfect prolation, shown by a dot in the circle or semicircle which indicates the time (*tempus*, i.e. the relation of the breve to the semibreve), thus: ⊙, ℭ, the semibreve has three minims. In imperfect prolation, shown by the absence of a dot, the semibreve has two minims.

See MENSURAL NOTATION

Promenade Concerts, in 1838 a series of concerts called the 'Promenade Concerts à la Musard' was given in London. The idea was imported from Paris, where Musard, a composer of popular quadrilles, had conducted promenade concerts from 1833. Occasional series of promenade concerts were organised during the nineteenth century, conducted by Musard, Jullien, Balfe and others. The present London 'Proms', held in the summer, were instituted in 1895 by Robert Newman. The character of the programmes, which always include a number of new works, was the creation of Sir Henry Wood, who conducted the concerts from their beginning until his death in 1944. In 1927 the responsibility for the organization of the London concerts was assumed by the B.B.C.

Among Sir Henry Wood's successors, the most popular was Sir Malcolm Sargent, who attracted a young and enormously enthusiastic public to the Royal Albert Hall. But equally important has been the contribution made, as an administrator, by Sir William Glock, who brought a new sense of adventure to the programmes of the London proms. Other cities also, in Britain and elsewhere, now hold regular seasons of proms – though the word itself is now almost everywhere a misnomer. By tradition there is always standing room at a prom, but people do not walk about at these events.

Prometheus, hero of Greek myth about whom several musical works have been written, including: (1) *Die Geschöpfe des Prometheus* (Ger., *The Creatures of Prometheus*), ballet with music by Beethoven, op 43 (1800). It consists of an overture and eighteen numbers. The finale contains the theme, used about the same time for a *contredanse*, which he subsequently used for the Variations and Fugue in E flat, op 35, for piano, and for the variations in the finale of the EROICA SYMPHONY.

(2) *Prometheus*, symphonic poem by Liszt (1850).

(3) *Prometheus: the Poem of Fire*, tone poem for orchestra by Skryabin, op 60 (1819). The score calls for a *tastiera per luce*, a keyboard instrument which projects colours on a screen.

(4) Song settings of Goethe's poem, 'Prometheus', made by Schubert and Wolf among others.

Proper, the parts of the Proper of the MASS, i.e. those with texts and music which are proper to their day or season, as distinct from the Ordinary (the parts with invariable texts), are the Introit, Gradual, Alleluia (Tract in penitential seasons), Offertory, and Communion.

Prophète, Le (*The Prophet*), opera in five acts by Meyerbeer, to a libretto by Augustin Eugène Scribe, first performed in Paris in 1849. The plot concerns the Anabaptist rising in Holland in the 16th century, ending in the burning of the Palace of Münster. Though now rarely staged, the work has had Jean de Reszke, Caruso and Martinelli among leading exponents of the title role.

proportion, the rhythmic system of all part-music is based on proportion. Our present TIME-SIGNATURES are derived from signs of proportion which were used in mensural NOTATION to show the relation between a new note-value and an immediately preceding one. This relation could be one of AUGMENTATION, or more frequently, of DIMINUTION, and was shown by a fraction or ratio, as in this example by Richard Davy (c. 1500):

(called *sesquialtera* proportion or HEMIOLA) where the proportion 3:2 is the equivalent of the modern triplet. In his *Plaine and Easie Introduction* (ed. R. A. Harman, 1952) Morley gives a table of the usual proportions, copied from Gafori, for the benefit of those who 'would be curious in Proportions', and a song 'Christ's Cross be my speed' for practice in performing them. Some signs were still used in the 17th century in the proportional rather than the time-signature sense, as in the following:

in which 3/1 means that three semibreves following are to be sung in the time of one preceding. In more modern notation:

Proporz, *see* NACHTANZ

propriety (Lat., *proprietas*), in a combination (LIGATURE) of two notes in mensural NOTATION the normal ('proper' and 'perfect') sequence was considered to be that which had the shorter note (*brevis*) followed by the longer (*longa*). The term propriety referred to the first note, so that a ligature of two or more notes beginning with a breve, e.g. ⬛ = B L , was defined as a ligature 'with propriety' (*cum proprietate*), and a ligature beginning with a long, e.g. ⬛ = L B was *sine proprietate*. A ligature beginning with two semibreves, shown by upward stem, e.g. ⬛ = S S B was defined as a ligature 'with opposite propriety' (*cum opposita proprietate*).

Prosa, *see* SEQUENCE (2).

Proske, Karl (1794–1861), Silesian editor of church music. He practised medicine until 1823 and then studied theology at Ratisbon where he was ordained in 1826 and became canon and *Kapellmeister* of the Cathedral in 1830. He visited Italy, collected and published choral church music of the 16th and 17th centuries in *Musica divina* (four volumes, 1853–62) and *Selectus novus missarum* (1855–59), which contributed greatly to the revival of the music of Palestrina and his contempories. His valuable collection is now in the Episcopal Library at Ratisbon.

prosula, *see* TROPE

Prout, Ebenezer (1835–1909), English composer, organist and theorist who taught in London at the Royal Academy of Music (1879) and Guildhall School of Music (1884). He wrote *Harmony, its Theory and Practice* (1889) and other textbooks which had very wide use.

Provençal tambourine, *see* TABOR

Provenzale, Francesco (c. 1627–1704), Italian composer. He lived in Naples as teacher at the Conservatorio S. Maria di Loreto (1663) and as director there (1673–1701). He was also *maestro di cappella* at S. Gennaro from 1686 to 1699. He composed operas, cantatas, oratorios, motets and other church music, and was the first of a line of Neapolitan opera composers who assumed the leadership in the development of opera in the late baroque period. His aria on an *ostinato* bass 'Lasciatemi morir' is published in *Historical Anthology of Music*, edited by A. T. Davison and W. Apel, no 222.

Prunières, Henry (1886–1942), French musicologist, who studied under Romain Rolland at the Sorbonne, founded and became editor of *La Revue Musicale* (1920) and edited the works of Lully. His writings include books on opera in the 17th century, and on Lully, Monteverdi, and Cavalli. His *Monteverdi* (1924) and *New History of Music* (1945) have been published in English.

Prussian Quartets, nickname for a set of three string quartets by Mozart, composed in 1789–90 for King Frederick William of Prussia, who was an amateur cellist. His original intention was to write six. The three quartets are: no 1 in D major, K575; no 2 in B flat major, K589; no 3 in F major, K590. All three works have a prominent part for the cello.

Psalmody, the oldest part of Christian liturgical music. The verses of a complete psalm are normally sung in alternation by the two sides of the choir to an ANGLICAN CHANT, or to one of the eight psalm tones of plainsong:

The example is the first tone; I is the opening (*initium*), D the dominant or reciting note (*tenor*), M the half-verse ending (*mediatio*), and T the verse-ending (*terminatio*). Originally an ANTIPHON, which varied with the church calendar, was sung after each verse, later before and after the psalm only. The psalm-tone is chosen to agree with the MODE of the antiphon. Each psalm-tone has a series of verse-endings, called 'differences', to agree with the opening notes of the antiphon. A verse of a psalm is sung in more elaborate plainsong as part of a RESPOND.

See also TONUS PEREGRINUS, TRACT

Psalmus Hungaricus (Lat., Hungarian Psalm), a setting by Kodály, op 13, of Psalm 55 in a translation by the 16th century poet, Michael Vég. Scored for solo tenor, chorus and orchestra, the work was commissioned by the Hungarian government in 1923 for the fiftieth anniversary of the union of the cities Buda and Pest (as was Bartók's *Dance Suite*).

psalter, metrical, in the 16th century the Reformed churches in the Netherlands, England, Scotland, and Switzerland decided to replace the singing of psalms to plainsong by the singing of metrical translations of the psalms to tunes suitable for congregational use. The tunes were set in imitative style, as in Goudimel's *Les CL pseaumes de David* of 1564 (published from the 1580 edition by H. Expert in *Les Maîtres musiciens de la Renaissance française*, ii, iv, vi, 1895–97), or more frequently in HOMOPHONIC style with the tune in the tenor or treble:

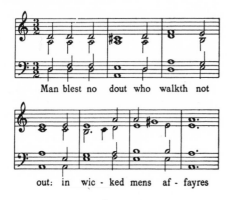

The example, from the first of Tallis's eight tunes for Archbishop Parker's Psalter of 1567/8, has the tune in the tenor. The psalter of Sternhold and Hopkins was published (with four-part music) by Day in 1563, and later English psalters by East (1592), Ravenscroft (1621) and Playford (1677). The first complete form of the Genevan Psalter was published in 1562, with music composed and arranged by Louis Bourgeois, and the Scottish Psalter, which adopted a number of the French tunes, in 1564–5. The first Netherlands psalter, the *Souterliedekens* of 1540, used secular tunes; it was replaced by the French Psalter in 1566. Some tunes contained in the psalters of the 16th and 17th centuries were included in later hymn books, and are still in use.

> M. FROST: *English and Scottish Psalm and Hymn Tunes, 1543–1677* (1953)
> W. S. PRATT: *The Music of the French Psalter of 1562* (1939)
> R. R. TERRY: *Calvin's First Psalter* (1932); *The Scottish Psalter of 1635* (1935)

psalterion, *see* PSALTERY

psaltery (Fr., *psalterion*; It., *salterio*), a medieval instrument of the zither type with plucked strings, of similar shape to the DULCIMER, the strings of which were struck. It usually had the shape of a symmetrical trapezoid; a half-psaltery had a wing shape, which was kept when it was developed into the harpsichord by the addition of a keyboard.

Pskovitianka, *see* MAID OF PSKOV

Puccini, Giacomo Antonio Domenico Michele Secondo Maria (1858–1924), Italian opera composer. Of a musical family, he studied in Lucca and at the Milan Conservatorio, where he was a pupil of Pon-

Giacomo Puccini. Early poverty made him keenly appreciative of the good things success can bring

chielli. He entered his first opera *Le Villi* (1884) for a competition which was won by Mascagni's *Cavalleria rusticana*, and had a success with *Manon Lescaut* in 1893. *La Bohème* was first performed with Toscanini conducting in 1896, *Tosca* in 1900, *Madama Butterfly*, which initially was a failure, in 1904. The success of these three was not equalled by *La Fancuilla del West* (*The Girl of The Golden West*), produced in New York in 1910, nor by *Il Trittico*, the triptych of one-act operas (*Il Tabarro, Suor Angelica, Gianni Schicchi*) on which he worked during the 1914–18 war, although the latter contains some of his best music. The final duet of *Turandot*, left unfinished at his death, was completed by Alfano. Gifted with a vivid sense of the stage and a strong and natural melodic talent, Puccini developed with them an impressive resource in harmony and orchestration which have made his operas among the most successful of the past century, even though he was a more superficial and more limited composer than his predecessor, Verdi. In a nutshell, Verdi was a great dramatic composer, Puccini an expert theatrical one.

W. ASHBROOK: *The Operas of Puccini* (1968)

M. CARNER: *Puccini, a Critical Biography* (1958)

DANTE DEL FIORENTINO: *Immortal Bohemian: An Intimate Memoir of Giacomo Puccini* (1952)

G. R. MAREK: *Puccini* (1952)

R. SPECHT: *Puccini* (1933)

Pugnani, Gaetano (1731–98), Italian violinist and teacher. After studying under Sonis and Tartini, he became leader of the court orchestra in Turin, travelled as a violinist from 1754–70, spending some time in London as leader of the Italian Opera orchestra, and then returned to Turin where he was leader, conductor and teacher. His pupils included Viotti, Bruni, and Conforti. He composed operas, ballets, cantatas, violin concertos and sonatas, quintets, quartets and other chamber music, but not, however, the famous 'Praeludium and Allegro' once ascribed to him, which was in fact a pastiche by Kreisler.

Pujol, Juan Pablo (1573–1626), Spanish composer. He was *maestro di cappilla* at Tarragona in 1593, at Saragossa in 1595, and at Barcelona from 1612 until his death. In 1600 he was ordained as a priest. He composed Masses and other church music and secular songs. Two volumes of his church music have been published by H. Anglès (1926, 1932).

Pulcinella, ballet with music by Stravinsky (after Pergolesi), composed in 1919 and later arranged as an orchestral suite. The ballet (incorporating songs) was first produced in Paris in 1920, with choreography by Massine and décor by Picasso. The music was initially criticised for its 'distortion' of 18th century music – Constant Lambert in *Music Ho!* likened it to the adding of false moustaches and beards to a book of old engravings – but today *Pulcinella* is admired more for the Stravinsky it contains than for the Pergolesi which inspired it.

Pult (Ger.), desk. In the orchestra two string players sharing the same music-stand constitute a desk.

Punch and Judy, opera in one (long) act by Harrison Birtwistle, to a libretto by Stephen Pruslin, first performed at the Aldeburgh Festival in 1968. The work uses the familiar fairground puppet-play as the basis of what the librettist has described as 'a source opera after the events'. The combination of ancient (dra-

matic) ritual and modern (musical) ritual here combined to give Britain its first truly modern opera.

punctum or **punctus** (Lat.), 'point'. (1) a note, as in *contrapunctus*, counterpoint.

(2) in MENSURAL NOTATION a point after a note (*punctus additionis*) adds one half of its value, a point placed between two notes or beside the stem of a note (*punctus divisionis*) marks off a group of three notes in PERFECT time or perfect PROLATION.

(3) each of the repeated sections in the ESTAMPIE, a medieval dance, was called a *punctus*.

(4) the theorist Anonymus IV uses *punctum* as an alternative for *clausula* (*clausulae sive puncta*) in discussing the composition of Perotin.

punta d'arco (It.), the point of the bow, or the opposite end to the heel. *A punta d'arco* is a direction to the player to use only the last few inches of the bow on the strings.

Henry Purcell. His successful blending of the Italian and native English traditions made him the most successful composer of his day and one of England's greatest.

Purcell, Henry (1659–95), English organist and composer, the son of a Gentleman of the Chapel Royal. He was a chorister of the Chapel Royal from about 1668 till 1673. He became composer for the violins in 1677. From 1679 he was organist at Westminster Abbey, and from 1682 organist at the Chapel Royal. In 1683 he was appointed keeper of the king's instruments..

Henry Purcell was the most original and most gifted English composer of his time; he was active in every field – theatre music, church music, court odes, secular and sacred songs, odes for various occasions and instrumental music. His early work shows a certain attachment to the past combined with an awareness of newer harmonic resources. As he developed he came to accept the conventions of baroque music – its clear-cut outlines, its brilliance and its inclination to pathetic expression – without ever sacrificing his own personality. His theatre music includes six operas, only one of which (*Dido and Aeneas*) is set to continuous music; the others all contain a substantial amount of dialogue. His church music includes both full anthems in traditional style and up to date verse anthems with solos for counter tenor, tenor and bass. His odes are rich in contrasts between solo voices, chorus and orchestra. As a writer of solo songs he has never been surpassed, either for imagination, technical adroitness or skill in catching the accents of English words. The most remarkable of his instrumental works are the fantasias for viols composed in 1680, which handle a traditional form in a curiously individual way. His trio sonatas are the most striking evidence of his capacity for mastering the Italian style, for which he had a confessed admiration. His contributions to the twelfth edition of Playford's *Introduction to the Skill of Music* (1694) show more than a conventional interest in technical procedures.

His principal compositions are:

(1) stage music: *Dido and Aeneas* (1689); *Dioclesian* (1690); *King Arthur* (1691); *The Fairy Queen* (1692); *The Indian Queen* (1695); *The Tempest* (1695); and music for more than forty plays.

(2) odes: seventeen for the king and other members of the royal family; four for St. Cecilia's day; three for other occasions.

(3) songs and cantatas: nine cantatas for two or more voices with instruments; 41 secular duets; more than 100 secular songs; sacred songs, duets, trios and quartets; numerous catches.

(4) church music: twelve complete full anthems; more than forty verse anthems; three services.

(5) chamber music: Fantasias in three, four, and five parts; two In Nomines; twelve *Sonatas of III Parts* (1683); ten *Sonatas of IV Parts* (1697).

(6) keyboard works: various pieces printed in *Musick's Hand-Maid*, ii (1689) and *A Choice Collection of Lessons* (1696); others in MS.

His complete works have been edited in 32 volumes under the auspices of the Purcell Society (1878–1962). A revision programme for the earlier volumes is in progress.

D. ARUNDELL: *Henry Purcell* (1927)

H. C. COLLES: *Voice and Verse: a Study in English Song* (1928)

E. J. DENT: *Foundations of English Opera* (1928)

A. K. HOLLAND: *Henry Purcell: the English Musical Tradition* (1932)

J. A. WESTRUP: *Purcell* (1937; 6th edition, 1968)

F. B. ZIMMERMAN: *Henry Purcell: his Life and Times* (1967)

His brother, **Daniel Purcell** (c. 1663–1717), was an English organist and composer. Like his brother, Henry, he was a chorister of the Chapel Royal. From 1688 to 1695 he was organist at Magdalen College, Oxford, and from 1713 to 1717 organist at St. Andrew's, Holborn. In 1700 he won the third prize for a setting of Congreve's *The Judgment of Paris*. In 1695 he completed his brother's music for *The Indian Queen* by writing a masque for the fifth act. From that time until c. 1707 he was active as a composer for the theatre. He also set several odes for St. Cecilia's day and an ode in honour of Princess Anne's birthday (1700). His published works include the music in *The Indian Queen* (in *Deliciae Musicae*, ii, 1, 1696), *The Judgment of Paris*, sacred and secular songs in various collections, six cantatas for solo voice, flute sonatas, violin sonatas and *The Psalms set full for the Organ or Harpsichord*. Some anthems survive in manuscript.

Puritani, I (It., *The Puritans*), opera in three acts by Bellini, to a libretto by Carlo Pepoli founded on a play by François Ancelot and Xavier Boniface Saintine, *Têtes Rondes et Cavaliers*, which in turn was derived from Walter Scott's *Old Mortality*. Though the full title of Bellini's last opera is *I Puritani di Scozia* (The Puritans of Scotland) the story is set in Plymouth and tells how Lord Arthur Talbot, a cavalier, helps Queen Henrietta, widow of Charles I, to escape from prison, while at the same time he is engaged to marry the daughter of the fortress's Puritan warden. In the end, the daughter loses, then regains, her reason, and Arthur is pardoned by Oliver Cromwell. The Paris première, in 1835, starred Grisi, Rubini, Tamburini, and Lablanche.

Q, as an abbreviation Q. = *quintus, quinto* or *quinta pars,* the fifth part in a 16th century composition for five or more voices or instruments; *see* QUINTUS.

quadratum, *see* B

quadrille, a fashionable French dance in the early 19th century, introduced into Britain in 1815 and Germany in 1821. Danced by two or four couples, it had five parts (*Le Pantalon, L'Été, La Poule, La Tremise, La Pastourelle*) in 6/8 and 2/4 time alternately. Its name is said to have originated with the introduction of *contredanses* performed by an even number of couples (*Quadrille de contredanse*) in the fifth act of Rousseau's *Fêtes de Polymnie* in 1745. Very often operatic music was arranged for performance as a quadrille – the French composer Chabrier even going so far as to write a *Tristan* quadrille.

quadrivium (Lat.), the division of the seven liberal arts, which formed the course of studies in the medieval university, in which music was included. It comprised the four mathematical arts of arithmetic, geometry, music, and astronomy. The other division, the *trivium,* consisted of the rhetorical arts of grammar, dialectics, and rhetoric. The material of the musical part was chiefly the study of the proportions of intervals as contained in Boethius's *De Musica.* In England it was replaced during the 16th century by DEGREES IN MUSIC.

quadruple counterpoint, the combination of four melodies or voices so designed that when the positions of the parts are inverted (i.e. the upper parts becoming the lower, and vice versa) the results still make sense.

quadruple croche (Fr.), hemidemisemiquaver.

quadruple fugue, fugue with four different subjects, e.g. the final (unfinished) movement of Bach's *Art of Fugue.*

quadruple stop, chord of four notes played on a bowed stringed instrument. The term applies even if one or more notes are not stopped by the fingers but played on open strings.

quadruplet, group of four notes to be performed in the time of three, e.g.:

CHOPIN, *Scherzo* op 39, no 3

quadruplum (Lat.), the fourth part above the tenor, counting the tenor itself as the first part, of the ORGANUM and CLAUSULA of the period c. 1200. Hence the term is also applied to the whole composition, e.g. those of Perotin.

Quagliati, Paolo (c. 1555–1628), Italian composer who was organist at Santa Maria Maggiore, Rome, from 1606. His work stands between the old and the new styles of the early 17th century. His pageant with monodic and polyphonic music, *Il carro di fedeltà d'amore* (modern edition by V. D. Gotwals and P. Keppler, 1957), was performed in Rome in 1606. His four-part madrigals of 1608 could be sung either as monodies or as madrigals with continuo. His *Sfera armoniosa* (1623; also edited by Gotwals and Keppler) contains duets with obbligato instrumental solos. A toccata for keyboard is printed in Torchi's *L'arte musicale in Italia,* iii.

quail, a toy instrument that imitates the sound of the quail. It appears in Haydn's *Toy Symphony.*

Quantz, Johann Joachim (1697–1773), German flautist and composer. As a young boy he learned to play several instruments. He was appointed assistant to the Town Musician of Radeburg in 1714, and became a member of the Dresden orchestra in 1716. He studied counterpoint under Fux and Zelenka in Vienna and from 1718 played in Dresden and Warsaw as oboist to the King of Poland. Having studied flute under Buffardin in Paris and counterpoint under Gasparini in Rome in 1724, he visited Paris and London and then returned to Dresden. From 1728 he taught the flute to the Crown Prince Frederick, who after he became King of Prussia in 1741 appointed him as chamber musician and court composer. He composed about 300 flute concertos, sonatas and about 200 other works for flute. His *Versuch einer Anweisung die Flöte traversiere zu spielen* (1752) is more than a treatise on flute-playing; it has a place beside the treatises of C. P. E. Bach and Leopold Mozart as an important source of information on the performance of 18th-century music.

 J. J. QUANTZ: *On Playing the Flute* (edited and translated by Edward R. Reilly, 1966)

quarter note, U.S. for 'crochet'.

quarter tone, half a semitone, which is the smallest interval traditionally used in Western music. Quarter tones had a place in the enharmonic tetrachord of Greek music, and were discussed in that connection by some medieval and Renaissance theorists, e.g. Guido and Vicentino. They have been used by some modern composers as an occasional effect or as a complete system. Alois Hába has written a number of compositions using a complete quarter tone scale for strings, for quarter tone piano, and for quarter tone harmonium, as well as in a complete opera (*Die Mütter,* 1931). The notes are indicated by modified forms of the usual signs for accidentals. Ernest Bloch used occasional quarter tones, marked with an 'x', in the string parts of his piano quintet (1923–4). More recently, quarter tones have been put to important use by Boulez, Stockhausen, and Ligeti, among other composers.

The quarter tone piano for which Hába wrote was devised by A. Förster in Prague in 1923, and has two manuals, of which one is tuned a quarter tone higher than the other. A patent for a quarter tone piano had earlier been taken out by G. A. Behrens-Senegalden in Berlin (1892).

See ENHARMONIC, MICROTONES

quartet (Fr., *quatuor*, Ger., *Quartett*, It., *quartetto*), a composition, vocal or instrumental, for four performers. Since the mid 18th century, its most frequent forms are the STRING QUARTET, PIANO QUARTET, quartets for mixed instruments, e.g. Mozart's quartet, K370, for oboe and strings, and the solo vocal quartets of opera, oratorio, glee and partsong. Mozart composed a *Sinfonia concertante* for wind quartet and orchestra (1778) and Rossini wrote six quartets for flute, clarinet, horn and bassoon.

Quartet for the End of Time (Fr., *Quatuor pour la fin du Temps*), work in eight movements for violin, clarinet, cello and piano by Messiaen. It was composed while Messiaen was a prisoner of war in Silesia. The reason for the unusual choice of instruments was that Messiaen's fellow prisoners included a violinist, clarinettist, and cellist – the composer himself being the pianist. Following Messiaen's example, several other composers (including, in Scotland, Thomas Wilson and Martin Dalby) have written works for these instruments.

Quartettsatz (Ger., quartet movement), a single allegro movement in C minor for string quartet by Schubert (1820). It was clearly intended to be the first movement of a complete quartet, since it is followed in the autograph manuscript by 41 bars of andante in A flat.

Quartfagott (Ger.), large bassoon pitched a fourth below the normal instrument. Obsolete since the beginning of the 19th century, its manufacture and use appear to have been confined to Germany.

Quartgeige (Ger.), violin tuned a fourth higher than the usual pitch; *see* VIOLINO PICCOLO.

Quartposaune (Ger.), TROMBONE pitched a fourth below the tenor trombone in B flat. It is, therefore, a bass trombone in F.

quatreble, term used in the 15th and early 16th centuries as the equivalent of the Latin *quadruplex*, for the highest voice in a choir, being the fourth part above the tenor (counting the tenor itself as the first part, as with the QUADRUPLUM, of c. 1200). The parts between quatreble and tenor were the meane and the treble. In the method of extemporizing a part above a plainsong used at that time (*see* SIGHT) the quatreble sight was a twelfth above the tenor.

quasi (It., 'as if', 'nearly'), e.g. in the tempo mark *Andante quasi allegretto*, or in the expression mark *quasi niente*, 'almost nothing', i.e. as softly as possible.

Quatorze Juillet, Le (Fr., The Fourteenth of July), incidental music to a play by Romain Rolland, composed in combination by Auric, Honegger, Ibert, Koechlin, Lazarus, Milhaud, and Roussel. It was first performed in Paris in 1936.

Quattro Rusteghi, I (Ger., *Die Vier Grobiane*; Eng., *School for Fathers*), comic opera in four acts by Wolf-Ferrari, to a libretto by Giuseppe Pizzolato after

Goldoni. It was first performed (in German) at Munich in 1906. The Italian version followed eight years later at Milan. The story concerns four boorish Venetians who treat their women harshly, but are finally outwitted.

quatuor (Fr.), quartet.

quaver (U.S., eighth note; Fr., *croche*; Ger., *Achtel*; It., *croma*), the note

♪ grouped ♫

which is half the length of a crotchet (quarter note) and an eighth of the length of a semibreve (whole note). The word meant originally a shake or trill and hence was applied in the 16th century to the short notes of which a shake is composed.

Queen of France, The, name given to Haydn's 85th symphony in B flat major (1785), one of the six symphonies commissioned by the Concert de la Loge Olympique in Paris and familiarly known as the 'Paris' Symphonies. The 85th symphony was reputed to be the favourite of Queen Marie Antoinette – hence the nickname.

Queen of Sheba, The (Ger., *Die Königin von Saba*), opera in four acts by Goldmark, to a libretto by Salomon Hermann Mosenthal. It was first performed in Vienna in 1875. The story concerns the wooing of the Queen of Sheba by Assad, King Solomon's favourite courtier, who ends by being banished.

Queen of Spades, The (Russ., *Pikovaya Dama*; Fr., *Pique-Dame*), opera in three acts by Chaikovsky, to a libretto by Modest Chaikovsky, the composer's brother. The work was first performed at St. Petersburg in 1890. The story, based on Pushkin's novel, concerns the love of Herman, a young officer, for Lisa, granddaughter of an elderly Countess said to possess the secret of winning at cards. Herman, in trying to extract the secret from the Countess, frightens her to death. Later her ghost gives him what he supposes to be the winning combination, but his downfall is brought about when he stakes all on the ace instead of the Queen of Spades. The opera is one of the few by Chaikovsky to have gained a place in the repertory outside Russia.

Quercu, Simon de (or **van Eycken**), late 15th century Flemish theorist, and cantor at the court of Milan. He went to Vienna, where he was still living in 1513. He published a treatise on elementary theory, *Opusculum musices* (1509), and a volume of motets (1513).

Querflöte (Ger.), cross or transverse flute. This is the modern flute as distinct from the RECORDER or *Blockflöte*.

Querstand (Ger.), false relation.

Questa o quella (the one or the other), flirtatious aria sung by the Duke of Mantua in Act 1 of *Rigoletto* in which he proclaims that all women please him equally.

quest opera, opera in which the principal character (or characters) undergoes various hardships, tests, or difficult journeys before reaching his goal. A famous example of the form is *The Magic Flute*.

quickstep, a march in quick steps, or the music for such a march. The same name is used for a modern ballroom dance, also notable for its quick beat.

Quiet City, work by Copland, for trumpet, cor anglais and strings, first performed in 1941 and based on incidental music which the composer had written for a play of the same title.

Quiet Flows the Don, opera in four acts by Dzerjinsky, to a libretto by the composer, based on the novel by Sholokhov. First performed in Leningrad in 1935, the work was dedicated to Shostakovich and was proclaimed in Russia as an outstanding example of Soviet opera. The story concerns a Cossack who, on returning from war in 1914, discovers that his wife has fallen in love with an aristocrat. He thereupon kills his rival, and then leads the peasants in revolt.

quilisma, NEUME used in the notation of plainsong, written thus ᷈. It usually came between two notes a third apart, and was probably sung with a trill or tremolo in the same way as the later PLICA. It occurs in Byzantine chant as the *kylisma*, where it indicated a 'rolling and rotating of the voice'.

Quilter, Roger (1877–1953), English composer who was educated at Eton and later studied composition under Iwan Knorr at Frankfurt. He composed song settings of Shakespeare, Herrick and other distinguished poets, small orchestral works (including *A Children's Overture*), incidental music for plays, and pieces for piano and violin.

Quinet, Fernand (born 1898), Belgium composer and cellist who studied at the Brussels Conservatoire, where he won the Prix de Rome in 1921. He was a member of the Pro Arte String Quartet and became director of the Charleroi Conservatoire and the Liège Conservatoire. He has composed string quartets and other chamber music and songs.

quint, five-stringed tenor VIOL.

Quintadena, *see* QUINTATON

Quintatön (Ger.), an organ STOP of the stopped flue type in which the twelfth, i.e. the third note of the HARMONIC SERIES, is present as well as the fundamental. The smaller size is called Quintadena.

quinte (Fr.), term used in France in the 17th and early 18th centuries for the fifth part (Lat., *quinta pars*) in a five-part instrumental piece and applied specifically to the viola.

Quintenquartett (Ger., 'Fifths Quartet'), name given in Germany to Haydn's string quartet in D minor, op 76, no 2, composed in 1797–8. Its principal theme begins with two falling fifths, thus:

quintet (Fr., *quintette*, *quintuor*; Ger., *Quintett*; It., *quintetto*), a composition, vocal or instrumental, for five performers. A string quintet is usually for two violins, two violas and cello, as in those of Mozart, Beethoven, Mendelssohn, Brahms, and the *Fantasy Quintet* by Vaughan Williams; Boccherini wrote quintets for two violins, viola and two cellos and Schubert wrote a great C major work for the same

instruments. The combination of piano with string quartet is called a PIANO QUINTET. Similarly a work for clarinet and string quartet is known as a clarinet quintet, e.g. Mozart's K 581 and Brahms's op 115. Mozart's horn quintet, K 407, is for violin, two violas, horn and cello. The term is usually applied to vocal pieces only in opera, e.g. the quintet in the third act of Wagner's *Mastersingers*.

quinto (It.), a specific type of trumpet, prescribed by Monteverdi in his opera *Orfeo*.

quinton, a violin with five strings used in France in the 18th century. Its tuning was:

Quintposaune (Ger.), a trombone pitched a fifth below the tenor trombone in B flat. This rare instrument is, therefore, a bass trombone in E flat. *See* TROMBONE.

Quintsaite (Ger.), a misleading name for the E or first string of the violin.

quintuor (Fr.), quintet.

quintuple time, five beats, usually crochets, in a bar, i.e. 5/4 time. In practice it usually resolves into the alternation, regular or irregular, of 3/4 and 2/4, occasionally into 4/4 plus 1/4. It was quite uncommon before the 20th century. There are earlier examples in Act 2, Scene xi of Handel's *Orlando* (1732), where occasional bars of 5/8 express mental confusion, in the third movement of Chopin's sonata in C minor, op 4 and the second movement of Chaikovsky's sixth symphony (a complete movement in both cases), and in the recurring interludes in Moussorgsky's *Pictures at an Exhibition*:

quintuplet, a group of five notes which is to be performed, in equal lengths, in the time of 4, e.g.:

CHOPIN, *Nocturne* op 48, no 2

quiterne, *see* CITTERN

quodlibet (Lat.), 'what you will.' (1) A composition, extemporized or written down, in which two or more well-known tunes are sung or played simultaneously. It was practised in the 16th and 17th centuries, especially by German composers, and was a favourite amusement in family gatherings of the Bach households. A *quodlibet* of c. 1460, in which the melody of Dunstable's 'O rosa bella' is accompanied by snatches of a number of German songs, is printed in the *Historical Anthology*, no 82. Other examples are in the German songs of Ludwig Senfl, e.g.:

A well-known instance is the last of Bach's *Goldberg Variations*, in which he combines two popular songs thus:

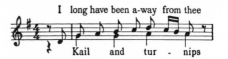

(2) The term is also used for a succession of pieces or songs spontaneously strung together.

r, in TONIC SOL-FA symbol for the second note (or supertonic) of the major scale, pronounced *ray*. R (abbreviation of Lat. responsorium)=Respond.

Rabaud, Henri Benjamin (1873–1949), French composer, pupil of Massenet and Gedalge at the Paris Conservatoire, where he won the Prix de Rome (1894) and later taught harmony. He was conductor at the Paris Opéra, 1908; and of the Boston Symphony Orchestra, 1918–19. In 1920 he succeeded Fauré as director of the Paris Conservatoire, a post he held until 1940. He composed operas, two symphonies and other orchestral works, chamber music, an oratorio and songs. His opera *Marouf, savetier du Caire* (Paris, 1914) was very successful in its day. Another of his works was based on Synge's *Riders to the Sea*. Fauré's *Dolly* suite was orchestrated by Rabaud.

rabbia (It.), 'rage'.

Rachmaninoff, Rachmaninov, *see* RAKHMANINOV

racket, rackett or **ranket,** a woodwind instrument in use from the late 16th to the early 18th century. The body was solid; in it were pierced a number of vertical channels, parallel to each other and connected alternately at the top and the bottom so as to form a continuous tube.

Holes pierced in the side made available a limited scale. The instrument was played with a double reed, which at first was partly enclosed in a kind of cup and later was inserted into a crook similar to that used for the bassoon. In consequence of its shape it was popularly known in France as *Cervelas* (saveloy) and in Germany as *Wurstfagott* (Sausage bassoon).

Radamisto (Rhadamistus), opera in three acts by Handel, to a libretto by Nicola Francesco Haym, first performed in London in 1720.

raddoppiamento (It.), 'doubling', usually to indicate the doubling of the bass at the octave below.

Radetzky March, march by Johann Strauss the elder, written in 1848, and named after an Austrian field-marshal. The music has come to be regarded as a symbol of the Hapsburg monarchy.

radio-synthetic organ, an electronic organ in which electrical waves are converted to sound. It was invented by Abbé Puget in 1934.

Radziwill, Prince Antoni Henryk (1775–1833), German cellist, singer and composer. Governor of Posen, and a friend of Beethoven and Chopin, he composed incidental music to Goethe's *Faust* (published 1835), vocal duets, part songs, and songs with guitar and cello. Beethoven dedicated to him his *Namensfeier* (name-day) overture, op 115.

Raff, Joseph Joachim (1822–82), Swiss composer, teacher and music critic. As a schoolmaster he taught himself piano, violin and composition, and later became a friend of Liszt and Mendelssohn. He lived in Cologne, Stuttgart, Weimar from 1850, Wiesbaden from 1856 as a piano teacher, and in Frankfurt from 1877 until his death as director of the Hoch Conservatorium. He composed operas, eleven symphonies, concertos, overtures and other orchestral works, choral works, chamber music, incidental music for plays, songs and piano pieces.

Raft of the Medusa, The (Ger., *Das Floss der Medusa*), oratorio for speaker, solo voices, chorus and orchestra by Henze, written for the Hamburg Radio in 1968; its first performance was broken up by the police, after noisy demonstrations. Described by the composer as an *oratorio volgare e militare*, the work is dedicated to Che Guevara and was inspired by Gericault's famous picture (1819), now in the Louvre, of an infamous incident in French naval history. When the French frigate *Medusa* foundered on a reef in 1816, the officers escaped in the boats and towed the crew behind them on a huge raft; but because this impeded progress, it was cut adrift. The officers soon reached port. Of the 154 people on the raft, only fifteen were still alive when picked up thirteen days later.

Henze's oratorio, to a text by Ernst Schnabel, casts a soprano in the role of Death and a baritone as the spokesman of the crew. In the course of the performance, the chorus, attracted by Death's voice, move from one side of the platform to the other, until only fifteen are left.

rāga, basically an Indian scale, but the term refers more widely to a piece of music which has a *rāga* as its basis, and whose mood or atmosphere is determined by the constant use of certain notes of the *rāga*. Each piece has its own, fixed scale material, which is used without modulation throughout the performance.

ragtime, a style of dance music popular from the late 19th century until the early years of the jazz age. It used such rhythms as

and various kinds of syncopation against a regular rhythmic background in 2/4 or 4/4 time. Stravinsky composed *Ragtime* for eleven instruments in 1918, and *Piano Rag-Music* in 1920. In recent years a new enthusiasm for ragtime has sprung up through the revival of the piano rags of Scott Joplin and his contemporaries.

Raimondi, Pietro (1786–1853), Italian composer and conductor. He studied at the Naples Conservatorio, and from 1807 produced operas at Genoa, Rome, Milan, Naples and in Sicily. He became director of the Royal Theatre, Naples, 1824; teacher of composition, Palermo Conservatorio, 1832; *maestro di cappella*, St. Peter's, Rome, 1852. He composed 62 operas, 21 ballets, eight oratorios, Masses, Requiems, psalms and

443

RAMEAU

other church music. He was famed as a deviser of multiple counterpoint, and wrote three opera-oratorios – *Potiphar*, *Joseph* and *Jacob* – which were staged separately and then simultaneously in Rome in 1852.

'Raindrop' Prelude, nickname for Chopin's prelude in D flat major for piano, op 28, no 15 (1839) – so called because its repeated note A flat (G sharp) was thought to resemble raindrops dripping from the roof of the composer's (temporary) residence in Majorca.

Rainier, Priaulx (born 1903), South African composer, now resident in Britain. She studied at the South African College of Music, in Paris under Nadia Boulanger, and at the Royal Academy of Music in London – where she became a teacher in 1942. Her compositions include a cello concerto, a *Sinfonia da camera* for strings, three string quartets, a viola sonata, and songs (including settings of Donne for unaccompanied voice).

Raison, André (17th–18th century), organist of Sainte-Geneviève and of the Jacobin Church in Paris. He composed two books of organ works. Bach used the theme of a passacaglia in G minor from the first book as the first four bars of his passacaglia in C minor for organ.

Rake's Progress, The, opera in three acts by Stravinsky, to a libretto by W. H. Auden and Chester Kallman, first performed at Venice in 1951. Inspired (fairly distantly) by Hogarth's series of 18th century pictures, the work is one of the masterpieces of Stravinsky's neo-classical period. It relates how Tom Rakewell is lured by Nick Shadow to London, where he forgets his true love (Ann Trulove), visits Mother Goose's brothel, and marries a bearded woman (Baba the Turk). In the end – when Nick Shadow tries to claim his soul – Rakewell contrives to beat him at cards, but loses his reason in the process and dies in Bedlam.

Rakhmaninov, Sergey Vassilievich (1873–1943), Russian composer and pianist. He studied in St. Petersburg and at the Moscow Conservatory under Zverev and Arensky. His early compositions were influenced by his warm admiration for Chaikovsky, and the fame of the prelude in C minor brought him an invitation to conduct in London in 1898. He lived in Dresden for several years, gave concerts in the United States in 1909–10, and then returned to Moscow, where he conducted the Philharmonic concerts from 1911–13. He left Russia in 1917, because he disliked the Soviet regime, and later settled in the United States. He composed three operas, three symphonies, a tone poem *The Isle of the Dead* (1907) and other works for orchestra, four concertos and a *Rhapsody on a Theme by Paganini* (the same as that used by Brahms for his Variations) for piano and orchestra, piano music (including an important series of preludes and *etudes-tableaux*), choral works, chamber music, and songs. At one time it was fashionable to disparage Rakhmaninov as a romantic born out of his period, to condemn many of his large-scale works because of their 'structural weaknesses', and to claim that his inspiration dwindled as he grew older. But now that his music has come more fully into focus, it is easy to refute these accusations. His largest orchestral work – the second symphony – is probably also his best. It is a work of great emotional

Sergey Vassilievich Rakhmaninov. An early portrait, before his cataclysmic nervous crisis.

power and melodic intensity, and it is structurally sound – provided that performers do not attempt to 'improve' it by cutting it. His romanticism was an asset rather than a liability, and in any case was irrelevant to works like the third piano concerto and the *Rhapsody on a Theme of Paganini* – finely integrated scores, in which style and content are perfectly suited to each other. As for the loss of inspiration, one need only point out that one of his most progressive and compelling works, the *Symphonic Dances* for orchestra, dates from the very end of his career.

S. BERTENSSON and J. LEYDA: *Sergei Rachmaninov* (1956)

J. CULSHAW: *Sergei Rachmaninov* (1949)

Rákóczi March, the title of the Hungarian national tune which is called after Prince Ferencz Rákóczi (leader of the revolt against Austria, 1703–11). It has been used by Berlioz (the Hungarian March in *Damnation of Faust*), Liszt (the Hungarian Rhapsody for piano and *Rákóczi March* for orchestra), Johann Strauss in *The Gipsy Baron*, and other composers.

rallentando (It.), becoming gradually slower. Abbreviation *rall.*

Rameau, Jean Philippe (1683–1764), French composer and theorist. The first part of his life was spent as an organist in Clermont-Ferrand (1702–6), Paris, Lyons, and from 1722 again at Clermont. In 1706 he published his first book of *Pieces de Clavecin*, modelled on those of Couperin, and in 1722 his *Traité de l'Harmonie reduite à ses Principes naturels*, in which he laid the foundation of the modern theory of harmony by setting forth the principles of key-centre, of fundamental bass, and of the roots and inversions of chords. This and further treatises laid the foundation for modern musical theory. He settled in Paris in 1732 and was introduced to Voltaire, who was several times his librettist. With *Hippolyte et Aricie* (1733) he began, at the age of fifty, a new and distinguished career as the most important composer of French opera since Lully. His chief stage works were the operas *Castor et Pollux* (1737) and *Dardanus* (1739), the opera-ballets *Les Indes galantes* (1735) and *Les Fêtes d'Hébé* (1739), and the ballet-bouffon *Platée* (1745). The revival of *Platée* in 1754 sealed the fate of the Italian *intermezzo* in Paris, Rameau leading the French faction against Pergolesi's champions in the so-called 'Guerre des Bouffons' (war of the buffoons). Rameau published in 1741 a book of *Pièces de clavecin en concert* which contained trio-sonatas, and in 1750 a *Démonstration du principe de l'harmonie*. His complete works were edited by Saint-Saëns (1895–1924).

C. GIRDLESTONE: *Jean-Philippe Rameau* (1957)

L. LALOY: *Rameau* (1908)

L. DE LA LAURENCIE: *Rameau* (1908)

P. M. MASSON: *L'Opéra de Rameau* (second edition, 1943)

G. MIGOT: *J. P. Rameau et le génie de la musique francaise* (1930)

Ramis (Ramos) de Pareja, Bartolomé (c. 1440–1521?), Spanish theorist and composer. He taught in Salamanca, lived in Bologna from 1480 to 1482 and was in Rome in 1491. In his *Musica practica* of 1482 (English translation in O. Strunk, *Source Readings in Music History*, page 201) he set forth a simpler method of dividing a string than the Pythagorean tuning given by Boethius and taught throughout the Middle Ages. This system was disputed by Gafori and developed by Zarlino.

Ranelagh Gardens, gardens on the bank of the Thames in London in which a Rotunda was built for concerts and to which it was fashionable to resort for entertainment for some years after its opening in 1742. Arne and other English composers wrote music and arranged concerts for Ranelagh; Mozart played the harpsichord and organ there, at the age of eight. The gardens were closed in 1803.

M. SANDS: *Invitation to Ranelagh* (1946)

Rangström, Anders Johan Türe (1884–1947), Swedish composer and conductor, pupil of Lindegren in Stockholm and Pfitzner in Munich. He worked as music critic in Stockholm from 1907 until 1921, conducted the Gothenburg Symphony Orchestra from 1922 until 1925, and was attached to the Stockholm Royal Opera from 1930 until 1936. He composed numerous songs, operas, symphonic poems and symphonies (one of them in memory of Strindberg), suites and other works for orchestra, cantatas, choral works with orchestra, incidental music for plays, chamber music and piano pieces.

rank, the set of pipes belonging to one stop on the ORGAN. The word is most often used in connection with MUTATION STOPS; thus a mixture is referred to as three-rank or four-rank according to the number of pipes which sound for each note.

ranket, *see* RACKET

Rankl, Karl (1898–1968), Austrian born conductor and composer, pupil of Schoenberg and Webern. After holding various conducting posts in opera houses in Germany, Austria and Czechoslovakia, he travelled to Britain and was Covent Garden's first post-war musical director (1946–1951). He was conductor of the Scottish National Orchestra from 1952 until 1957, then left for Australia to direct the Elizabethan Trust Opera Company (1957–60). His output as a composer includes an opera (*Deirdre of the Sorrows*, based on Synge's play), eight symphonies, chamber music and songs.

ranks, two strings tuned to the same note on instruments of the LUTE family.

Ranz des Vaches (Fr.; Ger., *Kuhreigen*), a melody sung or played on the Alpine horn by Swiss cowherds to call their cattle. It exists in a number of forms. Common idioms are:

in which the F is about a quarter of a tone higher than normal. It has been used by composers in various versions, e.g. by Rossini in the overture to William Tell:

Other examples can be found in Beethoven's *Pastoral Symphony* (finale), Berlioz's *Fantastic Symphony* (third movement) and Walton's *Facade*.

rape, *see* GUERO

Rape of Lucretia, The, opera in two acts by Benjamin Britten, to a libretto by Ronald Duncan (after André Obey's play *Le Viol de Lucrèce* – though Shakespeare's poem was the original source). First performed at Glyndebourne in 1946, this was the first of Britten's chamber operas using only a small team of singers and instrumentalists. The original cast included Kathleen Ferrier (in the title-role), Joan Cross and Peter Pears.

rappresentativo, *see* STILE (3)

Rappresentazione di Anima e di Corpo (*Representation of Soul and Body*), a morality play set to music by Emilio de'Cavalieri and staged in Rome, February 1600. It has often been described as 'the first oratorio', though most performances today treat it as an opera.

Rapsodie Espagnole (Fr., *Spanish Rhapsody*), an orchestral composition by Ravel (1907) in four movements: *Prélude à la Nuit*, *Malagueña*, *Habanera* and *Feria*. It is unusual among Ravel's works in having been conceived in the first place as a piece of orchestral concert music, rather than being an arrangement of a piano work or ballet score.

Rasch (Ger.), quick.

Raselius (Rasel), Andreas (c. 1563–1602), German composer. He studied at the Lutheran University in Heidelberg. In 1584 he was cantor and teacher at the

Gymnasium, Ratisbon. From 1600 until his death he was court *Kapellmeister* to Friedrich IV in Heidelberg. In *Denkmäler der Tonkunst in Bayern*, xxix-xxx, there have been published nine Latin motets from the *Dodecachordum vivum*, a manuscript collection of 1589, 53 German motets from Teutscher Sprüche (1594) and 22 German motets from Neue Teutscher Sprüche (1595). He also wrote a theoretical treatise, *Hexachordum seu quaestiones musicae practicae* (1589).

Rasiermesserquartett, *see* RAZOR QUARTET

Rasumovsky, Count (from 1815 **Prince) Andreas Kyrillovich** (1752–1836), Russian ambassador in Vienna, patron of music and amateur musician. From 1808 he played the violin in his own string quartet (leader Schuppanzigh, violist Weiss, and cellist Lincke), which played new quartets by Beethoven. The latter dedicated three quartets, op 59 (1806) to Rasumovsky, and the fifth and sixth symphonies (published in 1809) to him and Prince Lobkowitz jointly. In 1816 he pensioned the members of his quartet, but they continued to play, with Sina, and later Holz, as second violinist.

Rasumovsky Quartets, three string quartets by Beethoven, op 59 (1806) – no 1 in F major, no 2 in E minor, no 3 in C major – dedicated to COUNT ANDREAS KYRILLOVICH RASUMOVSKY. As a compliment to him, the finale of no 1 has a tune marked *theme russe*; so has the third movement of no 2 (in this case the tune which Mussorgsky used in the coronation scene of *Boris Godunov*). It has been suggested that the slow movement of no 3 is also based on a Russian folksong, though there is no indication of this in the score.

rataplan, term for solos or ensembles in operas which have the character of a military march (the word is onomatopoeic for the sound of a drum). The most famous operatic rataplan is sung by the gypsy girl, Preziosilla, in Verdi's *The Force of Destiny*. Other examples are in Donizetti's *The Daughter of the Regiment* and Meyerbeer's *The Huguenots*.

Rathaus, Karol (1895–1954), Polish born composer who studied under Schreker in Vienna and Berlin where he was teacher at the Hochschule from 1925 until 1934. Later lived in Paris, London and the United States, where he became attached to Queen's College, Flushing (New York), in 1940. He composed symphonies, an opera, ballets, string quartets and other chamber music, choral works, incidental music for plays, songs, and pieces for piano and organ.

Ratsche (Ger.), rattle

rattle (Fr., *crécelle*; Ger., *Knarre, Ratsche*), more in evidence in football matches than in the concert hall, the sound of the rattle produced by a piece of hard but flexible wood striking against a ratchet-toothed cogwheel. Its best known musical use occurs in Richard Strauss's *Till Eulenspiegel*.

Rauzzini, Venanzio (1746–1810), Italian castrato singer and composer. He sang in opera in Rome, Munich and other cities, and settled in England in 1774. He appeared in the premiere of Mozart's *Lucio Silla* in Milan; Mozart's motet, *Exsultate, jubilate*, was written for him. Of some ten operas which he produced in Munich and London the most successful was *Piramo e Tisbe* (London, 1775). In 1780 he settled in Bath, where he remained until his death.

Ravanello, Oreste (1871–1938), Italian organist and composer. He was organist, St. Mark's, Venice, 1893; director, Istituto Musicale, Padua, 1914. He composed Masses and other church music, and wrote a method for the organ and a treatise on the rhythm of Gregorian chant.

Ravel, Maurice (1875–1937), French composer, of Swiss and Basque descent. He entered the Paris Conservatoire at the age of fourteen, studying the piano with Beriot, counterpoint with Gédalge and composition with Fauré. His progressive outlook as a composer resulted in his losing the Prix de Rome three times, and being forbidden to try for it a fourth time. During the 1914–18 war he served as an ambulance driver at the front. In 1920 he refused to accept the Légion d'Honneur, but eight years later accepted an honorary doctorate from Oxford University. He died in Paris, after an unsuccessful operation for a brain tumour.

Maurice Ravel. His clouded closing years were a melancholy contrast to the gay clarity of his music

Ravel's first mature works – *Jeux d'eau* for piano and the string quartet – showed the virtuosity of means and compact clarity of form which were characteristic of his style. Like Debussy, he was strongly influenced by Chabrier and Satie, but his interest in French harpsichord music, in the orchestration of Rimsky-Korsakov, and in the piano writing of Liszt led his development away from impressionism to a precise and often wittily ironic style based on traditional harmonies and forms. The source of his inspiration, however, was more often poetic than abstract, and only two of his orchestral works, *Rapsodie espagnole* and *La Valse*, were not originally written for the theatre or as piano pieces. He was a masterfully lucid orchestrator. Of his ballet scores the most important and successful was *Daphnis et Chloé*. The later works, such as the sonata for violin and cello, the opera-ballet *L'Enfant et les sortilèges*, the two piano concertos, and *Don Quichotte à Dulcinée* for baritone and chamber orchestra, tended towards more economy of means without losing in deftness of expression and versatility of technique. His principal compositions are:

(1) Ballets: *Daphnis et Chloé* (1912); *Ma Mère l'Oye* (from the suite for piano duet, 1915).

(2) Operas: *L'Heure espagnole* (1907); *L'Enfant et les sortilèges* (1925).

(3) Orchestra: *Rapsodie espagnole* (1907); *La Valse* (1920); *Bolero* (1928); concerto for piano (left hand only) and orchestra (1931); concerto for piano and orchestra (1931).

(4) Chamber music: string quartet (1903); *Introduction and Allegro* for harp, string quartet, flute, clarinet (1906); piano trio (1915); cello sonata (1922); violin sonata (1927).

(5) Piano: *Jeux d'eau* (1901); *Miroirs* (1905); *Sonatine* (1905); *Gaspard de la Nuit* (1908); *Ma Mère l'Oye* (piano duet, 1908); *Valses nobles et sentimentales* (1911); *Le Tombeau de Couperin* (1917).

(6) Songs: *Shéhérazade* (1903; the accompaniment was later orchestrated); *Histoires naturelles* (1906); *Deux Mélodies hébraïques* (1914); *Ronsard à son âme* (1924); *Chansons madécasses* (for voice, flute, cello, piano, 1926); *Don Quichotte à Dulcinée* (baritone and chamber orchestra. 1932).

V. JANKELÉVITCH: *Maurice Ravel* (1939)

ROLAND-MANUEL: *Maurice Ravel*, translated by C. Jolly (1947)

F. H. SHERA: *Debussy and Ravel* (1925)

H. H. STUCKENSCHMIDT: *Ravel*

Ravenscroft, Thomas (c. 1590–c. 1633), English composer and editor. He was a chorister at St. Paul's Cathedral and studied at Cambridge. From 1618 to 1622 he was music master at Christ's Hospital. He published collections of rounds, catches and arrangements of popular songs entitled *Pammelia* (1609), *Deuteromelia* (1609) and *Melismata* (1611); a facsimile edition of all three was published in 1961. His compositions include anthems and instrumental works. His *Briefe Discourse of the true (but neglected) use of Charact'ring the Degrees . . . in Measurable Musicke* (1614) drew some of its material from Morley's *Plaine and Easie Introduction*, and included songs by various composers for 'Hunting, Hawking, Dauncing, Drinking, and Enamouring'.

Rawsthorne, Alan (1905–71), English composer who initially studied dentistry but turned to music at the age of twenty. He studied at the Royal Manchester College of Music and later under Egon Petri, was appointed teacher at Dartington Hall and in 1935 settled in London. His compositions, written usually in a vigorously contrapuntal style, include *Symphonic Studies* (1938), three symphonies, *Street Corner* overture, two piano concertos, two violin concertos, a clarinet concerto and other orchestral works, three string quartets and other chamber music, piano pieces and songs.

ray, Anglicized form of the Italian *re* (D). In TONIC SOL-FA the second note (or supertonic) of the major scale.

Raymond, opera by Ambroise Thomas, to a libretto by A. de Leuven and J. B. Rosier, after *The Man in the Iron Mask*. The work had its première in Paris in 1851.

Razor Quartet (Ger., *Rasiermesserquartett*), the name given to Haydn's string quartet in F minor and major, op 55, no 2 (published in 1789). The story is that when Haydn told John Bland (a London music publisher who happened to visit him while he was shaving) that he would give his 'best quartet for a good razor' Bland presented him with his own set of razors and Haydn later produced the promised quartet. However, the set of quartets to which this belongs was not published by Bland but by Longman and Broderip.

re (1) second note of the hexachord (*see* SOLMIZATION). (2) (It., Fr.), the note D.

Read, Gardner (born 1913), U.S. composer, who studied at the Northwestern University School of Music and at the Eastman School in Rochester. He has composed symphonies and other orchestral works, chamber music, vocal music and keyboard pieces.

Reading, John (died 1692), English organist. He was junior vicar-choral (1667) and master of the choristers (1670) of Lincoln Cathedral. From 1675 he was organist of Winchester Cathedral, and from 1681 of Winchester College, for which he composed Latin Graces and the Winchester School song, *Dulce domum*.

His namesake, who lived from 1677–1774, was probably his son or otherwise related. He was also an English organist. He was a chorister of the Chapel Royal. From 1696 to 1698 he was junior vicar-choral (1702), master (1703) and instructor (1704) of the choristers at Lincoln Cathedral. After 1707 he was organist of several London churches. He published a book of *New Songs (after the Italian manner)* and a book of anthems.

Reading rota, *see* SUMER IS ICUMEN IN

real answer, *see* FUGUE

realization, the act of completing the harmony of a 17th or 18th century work by providing a keyboard accompaniment based on the indications afforded by the FIGURED BASS. In a broader sense, the word is applied to, say, Raymond Leppard's realisations of operas by Monteverdi and Cavalli, though in these cases 'arrangement' might be a more appropriate term.

rebec or **rebeck** (It., *ribeca*); also rebab, rebibe, ribibe, ribible, rubible, rubybe and rybibe, a small bowed instrument of an elongated pear-shape, adopted from the Arabian *rebâb*, used in Europe from the 16th century. As described by Agricola in *Musica instrumentalis deudsch* (1528) the treble size had three strings tuned as are the three lower strings of the violin; it is one of the instruments from which the violin was developed in the course of the 16th century. In a form with four strings of which the lowest was:

It survived into the 17th and 18th centuries as the KIT (or pochette) used by dancing masters.

Rebikov, Vladimir (1866–1920), Russian composer. He studied at the Moscow Conservatory and in Berlin and Vienna, where he also taught. He composed operas, ballets, suites and other works for orchestra, church music, vocal works and pieces for piano. In his time he was considered an advanced composer because of his occasional use of the whole-tone scale and of parallel fifths.

rebop, *see* BOP

rebute, French form of JEW'S HARP.

recapitulation, *see* SONATA FORM

récit (Fr.), (1) recitative; (2) swell organ.

recital, a public programme of solo music, or music for two performers – where more performers are involved, the term is usually 'concert'. The term 'recital' was probably used for the first time in the announcement of Liszt's appearance at the Hanover Square Rooms, London, on June 9, 1840, which read: 'M. Liszt will give Recitals on the Pianoforte of the following pieces.'

recitative (Fr., *récit, récitatif,* Ger., *Rezitativ, Sprechgesang,* It., *recitativo*), a style of singing which is more closely related in pitch and rhythm to dramatic speech than to song. It originated c. 1590 in the works of the Florentine composers, e.g. Jacopo Peri, and was adopted also in operas, oratorios, cantatas and some forms of church music during the first half of the 17th century. With few exceptions, it was accompanied by a harpsichord, organ or other CONTINUO instrument, with or without a string bass, e.g. in the Prologue to Monteverdi's *Orfeo*:

The earliest operas are largely recitative, but the technique was soon used especially for the narrative and less lyrical sections of operas and oratorios, where information has to be conveyed.

The principle of recitative had long been used in the less ornate forms of plainsong, and its relation to plainsong can be observed in the work of Schütz, who wrote it both in the free rhythm of the chant, unaccompanied in the *Passions*, accompanied by four viols in the *Resurrection History*, and in the usual style, accompanied by the continuo, in the *Christmas Oratorio*.

In England Nicholas Laniere wrote recitative in his music for Ben Jonson's *Lovers made Men* in 1617. Purcell's recitative shows a finer application of the style to the characteristics of the language than that of any composer before the present century, e.g.:

from *Dido and Aeneas*. Similarly, Lully developed special idioms in his treatment of recitative in French opera, where the language imposed a distinctive style.

In the 18th century the accepted style of recitative, that of Italian opera, sung in the quick free rhythm of stage dialogue, the composer's notation merely indicating approximate note-values, was called *recitativo secco*. Recitative in a more expressive style accompanied by the orchestra, as in Bach's setting of the words of Christ in the *St. Matthew Passion*, was called *recitativo stromentato* or *accompagnato*. The style of recitative was at times transferred to instruments, as in the second movement, marked *Recitativo*, of Haydn's symphony no 7 (*Le Midi*), in one of the variations, marked *Recitativo, senza rigor di tempo*, in the fourth movement of Michael Haydn's divertimento in B flat, in Beethoven's piano sonatas op 31, no 2 and op 110, and in the introduction to the finale of his ninth symphony.

In Wagner's later operas neither recitative nor aria was used in the distinct and formal manner of previous operas; both styles were absorbed into the vocal line and used freely as the dramatic situation required. Opera since Wagner has tended to use the style of recitative to an even greater extent, to the exclusion of all but the shortest passages in aria style. At the same time the orchestral part, as in Wagner, has assumed the function of providing thematic continuity and development. Stravinsky has used recitative in the earlier sense, accompanied by harpsichord or piano, in *The Rake's Progress* (1951).

recitativo (It.), recitative. *Recitativo secco*, recitative accompanied only by continuo and largely made up of conventional formulas. *Recitativo stromentato* (or *accompagnato*), dramatic or expressive recitative accompanied by the orchestra.

See RECITATIVE

reciting note (Lat., *repercussio, tuba*), the note on which the intermediate words of each verse of a psalm are sung in plainsong. It is the dominant of the MODE in which the psalm-tone is written.

See PSALMODY

recorder (Fr., *flûte douce, flûte à bec*; Ger., *Blockflöte*; It., *flauto dolce*), a straight or end-blown flute, as distinct from the transverse or side-blown flute, which was used from the Middle Ages until the 18th century and has been revived in modern times. In the 16th century recorders were made in sets, or consorts, and the most usual sizes were the descant (in Germany, soprano or treble), treble (in Germany, alto), tenor and bass, of which the lowest notes were normally:

Bass Tenor Treble Descant

Praetorius, in the *Syntagma musicum* (1619), lists also a *Kleines Flötlein*, a fourth or fifth above the descant, a bass with

as its lowest note, and a double bass a fourth lower than the bass. When Bach writes for the recorder, as in the accompaniment to the aria known as 'Sheep may safely graze' in the secular cantata *Was mir behagt*, or in Brandenburg Concertos nos 2 and 4, he designates it as *flauto*; where the transverse flute is intended he calls it *traversa*. He occasionally uses one of the smaller sizes of descant recorder, calling it *flauto piccolo*, as in the opening chorus of Cantata no 96 (*Herr Christ, der ein'ge Gottessohn*), where it has an important part to play, in unison with a *violino piccolo*. The recorder has a sweet and gentle tone – hence the French name *flûte douce*; its English name seems to be derived from the verb 'record', to practise a song or tune – a term used particularly of birds. There are a number of modern instruction-books for the instrument.

    A. CARSE: 'Fingering the Recorder', in *The Music Review*, i (1940), page 96
    C. WELCH: *Six Lectures on the Recorder* (1911)

reco-reco or **reso-reso**, similar to a GUERO, but made of bamboo or, less often, a cow horn. The sound is somewhat hollow and more woody than that of a guero.

recte et rectro, per, *see* RETROGRADE MOTION

recueilli (Fr.), meditative, collected.

Redford, John (died 1547), English organist, composer and dramatist. He was organist and master of the choristers at St. Paul's Cathedral from about 1530. He was one of the most important English composers of liturgical organ music before the Reformation. Apart from a few short 'points' all his keyboard pieces are based on plainsong themes. Several pieces are contained in the 'Mulliner' book and are printed in *Musica Britannica*, i. His music for the Office and Mass is printed in *Early Tudor Organ Music*, edited by J. Caldwell (volume i, 1966) and D. Stevens (volume ii, 1969), respectively. He was concerned with the production of plays, probably acted (as many were throughout the 16th century) by the St. Paul's choristers. One play by him, *Wyt and Science* (printed by the Shakespeare Society, 1848), has survived.

reduction (Fr., *réduction*), an arrangement of a piece of music whereby the composer's original scoring is in some way reduced, or simplified. Thus a piano version of an orchestral work could be called a piano 'reduction', and similarly the vocal score of an opera, where again the orchestra is replaced by a piano.

reed (Fr., *anche*; Ger., *Zunge*; It., *ancia*), the vibrating element in many musical instruments usually made of cane or metal. A single beating reed, i.e. one which vibrates against the material of the instrument, is used in the reed stops of the organ (metal reed) and in the

clarinet and saxophone (cane reed). Double beating reeds, i.e. two reeds of cane which vibrate against each other, are used in the instruments of the oboe family, e.g. cor anglais and bassoon. Free, as distinct from beating, reeds – i.e. reeds of metal which vibrate freely in a slot – are used in the harmonium and concertina. The pitch of a metal reed, being determined by its length and thickness, is fixed; that of a cane reed is variable, being determined by the length of the pipe to which it is attached.

Reed, William Henry (1876–1942), English violinist, composer and author. He studied at the Royal Academy of Music, and was a founder-member of the London Symphony Orchestra. He composed orchestral and chamber music, and wrote two books on the life and work of Elgar.

reed-organ, name covering the many instruments, both old and modern, which have no pipes and use free-beating reeds (one for each note) to produce their notes. *See* ACCORDION, AMERICAN ORGAN, CONCERTINA, HARMONIUM, MOUTH ORGAN, REGAL

reed pipe, *see* ORGAN, REED

reed stops, organ stops controlling reed pipes.

reel, a dance, probably of Celtic origin, practised in northern countries of Europe, in which the dancers stand face to face and perform figures of eight. The music is usually in a quick 4/4 time and in regular 4-bar phrases. The Scottish strathspey is related to the reel, but is danced in a slower tempo. The rhythms:

        ♪.♪   and   ♪♪.

occur constantly in its music. 'Symphonic' reels have been written by the Scottish composer, Ian Whyte.

Reese, Gustave (born 1899), U.S. musicologist. He studied at New York University, where he was lecturer from 1927 until 1937, and professor of musicology there from 1945. He was associate editor (1933) and editor (1944–45) of *The Musical Quarterly*, and one of the founders of the American Musicological Society (1934). His *Music in the Middle Ages* (1940) and *Music in the Renaissance* (1954) are standard works on their respective periods.

'Reformation' Symphony (Ger., *Reformationssinfonie*), the title given by Mendelssohn to his symphony no 5 in D major, op 107 (1830), which was composed for the tercentenary of the Augsburg Conference but (because of Catholic opposition) not performed there. It uses the 'Dresden Amen' in its first movement, and the chorale 'Ein' feste Burg' (A Stronghold Sure) in its finale – Catholic musical quotation being counterbalanced by Protestant one.

refrain, recurring lines in a poem, which are usually set to the same music, as in the monophonic and polyphonic settings of such forms as the BALLADE, RONDEAU and VIRELAI from the 12th to the 15th century. In trouvère *chansons* the melody and words of well-known refrains were sometimes quoted in new songs, as in the *chanson avec des refrains*, in which, paradoxically, each refrain was different, since it consisted of a quotation. Similarly, refrains were frequently quoted in the upper parts of 13th century MOTETS. A motet which quotes the first part of a refrain at the beginning and the second part at the end is called a *motet enté*. The prototypes of the refrain are the plainsong RESPOND and the original use of the ANTIPHON between the verses of a psalm; its related forms are the burden of the CAROL and the recurring section of the instrumental RONDO.

regal, a portable reed organ used in the 16th and 17th centuries. It had beating reeds, and unlike the portable organ with flue pipes, was capable of *crescendo* and *diminuendo*. The Bible-regal could be folded up and packed into the bellows. When flue stops and reed stops were combined in the same instrument, the word was used both for the instrument and for a reed stop. The regal was commonly used in the music of plays and mysteries; the office of keeper of the King's Regals existed in England until the 18th century. Monteverdi specified the regal to accompany the recitative of Charon in the third act of *Orfeo* (1607).

Reger, Max (1873–1916), German composer, pianist, organist, conductor and teacher. He studied under Hugo Riemann in Sondershausen and Wiesbaden, and became teacher at the Wiesbaden Conservatorium (1895–6), Munich Academy of Music (1905–6), director of music, Leipzig University (1907–8), and teacher of composition, Leipzig Conservatorium (from 1907 until his death). Though a musical conservative, Reger claimed to be a progressive and had a habit of making enemies in both camps, especially during his Munich period. From 1911 until 1914 he was conductor of the Meiningen Court Orchestra, and after 1915 lived in Jena, travelling each week to the Leipzig Conservatorium. He gave concerts in Germany, Switzerland, Russia, Holland and Britain.

Through Riemann's influence he early became attached to the music of Bach and Brahms, and acquired a mastery of counterpoint as well as of the complete resources of late romantic harmony. In his instrumental music he avoided using any kind of programme, building up large structures on the basis of classical and pre-classical forms to a degree of harmonic complexity that at its best is splendidly massive but too often tends to become turgid and cumbersome. He did not live to develop the discipline over his prodigious gifts which began to appear in his later works. His organ music, which includes chorale preludes, preludes and fugues, passacaglias, and many shorter pieces, has an important place in the literature of the instrument, especially in Germany. His opus numbers run to 147 and comprise, besides orchestral and organ works, chamber music, choral works, concertos, two large works for two pianos, piano pieces in many forms, and songs. His orchestral *Variations on a theme of Mozart* (the theme being the opening one of the A major piano sonata, K 331) are still occasionally performed. He also wrote a textbook on modulation.

A. LINDNER: *Max Reger* (1923)

Regino (of Prüm) (died 915), Benedictine monk and musical theorist. He was abbot of the monastery at Prüm (near Trier) in 892 and was at St. Maximin in Trier from about 899. His *De harmonica institutione*, which discusses music as one of the seven liberal arts, is published in Gerbert's *Scriptores*, i, page 230, and his *Tonarius*, one of the earliest examples of the classification of plainsong melodies according to MODE, in Coussemaker's *Scriptores*, ii, page 1.

Regis, Johannes (c. 1430–c. 1485), Flemish composer. He was master of the choristers at Notre Dame, Antwerp, in 1463, and later was secretary to Dufay. He went to Mons in 1474, and in 1481 was at Soignies, where he became canon. His surviving works, which comprise Masses, motets and *chansons*, have been published by C. W. H. Lindenburg (two volumes, 1956).

régisseur (Fr.), a term used in France and Germany for the person in charge of the artistic and technical parts of the production of opera.

register, (1) a set of pipes, which may consist of one or more RANKS, controlled by a single stop on an organ.

(2) A division in the compass of a singer's voice, e.g. head register, chest register. The word is also applied to an instrument's compass, e.g. the Chalumeau register of a clarinet.

registration, the art of choosing and combining stops in organ playing. Indications given by the composer may include changes of manual, a particular type of solo stop, or the relative weight of sound. Indications of any kind are infrequent before the 19th century, though Scheidt gave general directions and suggested some specific stops for the registration of the chorales, Magnificats, and hymns in his *Tabulatura nova* (1624), and French composers in the baroque period commonly gave some information about registration, either in the title, as in Couperin's *Fugue sur les jeux d'anches* and *Dialogue sur la Trompette et le Cromhorne* in the *Kyrie* of his first Organ Mass, or in the course of the piece. Details of Bach's registration of a few of his organ pieces have been recorded, but his own markings are rare, and concern changes of manual, as in the 'Dorian' toccata, or a particular stop, as in the second prelude in the *Orgelbüchlein*. In the 19th century the practices of registration tended to approach those of orchestration; more recently they have been considered in connection with the revival of the tonal design of the Baroque organ.

G. A. AUDSLEY: *Organ Stops and their Artistic Registration* (1921)

W. L. SUMNER: *The Organ* (1952)

Regnart, François (c. 1530–c. 1600), Flemish composer. He studied at the Cathedral of Tournai and the University of Douai. He composed motets which were published by Augustin Regnart in 1590 in a collection of 39 motets by the brothers François, Jacques, Paschaise and Charles. A volume of chansons, *Poésies de P. Ronsard et autre poètes* (1575), has been published by Henri Expert in *Les Maîtres musiciens de la Renaissance française*, xv.

His brother **Jacques Regnart** (c. 1540–99), was a singer and composer. He was a tenor in the Imperial Chapel at Vienna and Prague from 1564, and deputy choirmaster from 1576. He held a similar post in Innsbruck from 1582 to 1595, and again in Prague from 1595 to his death. Some of his motets appeared in his brother Augustin's publication of 1590; others and his 29 Masses were published after his death. A volume of five-part German songs was printed in 1580, three volumes of three-part songs to German words after the style of the Neapolitan or Italian villanellas between 1576 and 1579. The latter was published in *Publikationen der Gesellschaft für Musikforschung*, xix (1895), and two pieces from this volume were reprinted in Schering's *Geschichte der Musik in Beispielen*, no 139.

Regnault, Pierre, *see* SANDRIN

Reichardt, Johann Friedrich (1752–1814), German composer, who became musical director at the Prussian court in 1776. He lived in Berlin and Potsdam, writing operas, plays with music, and incidental music, but in 1793 he was dismissed after revealing his sympathy for the French Revolution. His works include *Hansel and Gretel, Cephalus and Procris* and *L'Olimpiade*, though today he is best known for his songs – he was a notable forerunner of Schubert. He wrote several books on music.

Reid (originally **Robertson**), **John** (1721–1807), Scottish born army general who left his fortune to Edinburgh University where he had studied, mainly for the foundation of a chair of music and an annual Reid concert to be given on the anniversary of his birth. Among those who have held the Reid professorship are Henry Bishop, Frederick Niecks, and Donald Tovey, who organised and conducted the Reid orchestral concerts for which his *Essays in Musical Analysis* were written. Tovey was succeeded by Sidney Newman, and the present Reid professor is Kenneth Leighton.

Reimann, Aribert (born 1936), German composer and pianist, pupil of Blacher at the Berlin Academy of Music. His most important work so far has been *Melusine* (an opera containing elements of Debussy's *Pelléas et Mélisande* and Berg's *Lulu*) written for the Deutsche Oper, Berlin, in 1971. He has also written *Ein Totentanz* (Dance of Death) for baritone and orchestra, *Reflexionen* for seven instruments, and a ballet, *Die Vogelscheuchen* (The Scarecrows).

Reinagle, Alexander (1756–1809), English pianist, composer and conductor. He settled in the United States and from 1786 gave concerts and taught in New York and in Philadelphia, where, in 1793, in partnership with Thomas Wignell he built a theatre for which he directed the music. He composed incidental music for plays, songs, quartets and a concerto for 'the Improved Pianoforte with Additional Keys'.

Reinecke, Carl Heinrich Carsten (1824–1910), German pianist, violinist, composer and conductor. He was court pianist in Copenhagen from 1846 until 1848; teacher at the Cologne Conservatorium, 1851; conductor of the Gewandhaus Orchestra and teacher at the Leipzig Conservatorium, 1860. He composed operas, canons and fairy tale cantatas for female voices, choral works, symphonies, overtures, four piano concertos, chamber music, songs and wrote books on musical subjects and two volumes of memoirs.

Reiner, Fritz (1888–1963), Hungarian born conductor who settled in the United States after holding various European appointments. From 1938 until 1948 he conducted the Pittsburgh Symphony Orchestra, but his most famous post was his conductorship of the Chicago Symphony Orchestra, from 1953.

Reinken (Reincken), Johann (Jan) Adam (1623–1722), German (possibly of Dutch extraction) organist and composer. He studied under Scheidemann in 1654 and 1657, and in 1663 succeeded him as organist of St. Catherine's in Hamburg, where J. S. Bach made several visits to hear him play. His chorale preludes for organ are in the extended fantasia style practised by North German organists of the period; in 1720, at the age of 97, on hearing Bach extemporise in that style on 'Am Wasserflüssen Babylons', he said: 'I thought this art was dead, but I see that it lives still in you.' His *Hortus musicus* (1687), a set of pieces for two violins, gamba and continuo, each consisting of a sonata followed by several dance movements, has been reprinted (1886) in *Vereeniging voor Nederlandsche Muziekgeschiedenis*, xiii, and his eighteen variations on 'Schweiget mir vom Weiber nehmen' in volume xiv of the same series and in part in Schering's *Geschichte der Musik in Beispielen*, no 207. Bach transcribed two sonatas and a fugue from the *Hortus musicus* for harpsichord (*Bach Gesellschaft*, xlii, pages 29, 42 and 50).

Reissiger, Karl Gottlieb (1798–1859), German composer and conductor. He succeeded Marschner as director of the Dresden opera, and from 1856–9 was director of the Dresden Conservatorium. He composed operas, church music, a symphony, 27 piano trios and other chamber music, many works for piano, and songs.

Reizenstein, Franz (1911–68), German born composer and pianist, pupil of Hindemith and Vaughan Williams. In 1934 he settled in England, and took British nationality. His works, which show influences of both his teachers, include a radio opera, *Anna Kraus*, concertos, a cantata (*Voices of Night*) based on English poems, chamber music and piano pieces.

Rejcha, Antonin (1770–1836), Bohemian composer and theorist. At the age of eighteen he went to Bonn, where he became a friend of Beethoven, while working as a flautist in the Electoral orchestra. He lived in Hamburg from 1795, Paris from 1799 and Vienna from 1802 to 1808, when he returned to Paris and became teacher of composition at the Conservatoire in 1818. His pupils included Berlioz, Liszt, Gounod and César Franck. He composed operas, two symphonies and other orchestral works, 24 quintets for woodwind and horn, twenty string quartets, 24 horn trios and other chamber music, duets for flutes and for violins, violin and piano sonatas and pieces for piano, and wrote treatises on harmony, melody and composition.

M. EMMANUEL: *Antonin Rejcha* (1937)

réjouissance (Fr.), literally 'enjoyment'. Title of a spirited movement sometimes found in suites of the Bach–Handel era.

Relâché, two-act surrealist ballet by Satie, composed in 1924, with choreography by Jean Borlin and a film episode directed by René Clair. The title refers to the term employed in France to indicate that a theatre is closed and that there will be no performance. On the 'official' first night of Satie's ballet, the fashionable audience found the Théâtre des Champs-Elysées in darkness. They were the victims of a characteristic hoax; the première took place three days later, with mixed success. The film episode, which shows the composer firing a canon on the roof of the theatre and surmounting the gargoyles on Notre Dame, is now a collectors' piece. The ballet score, Satie's last important work, has also been performed successfully as a concert suite.

related, term describing the harmonic relationship between one key and another. Thus D major and A

Renaissance music-making a lutenist accompanied by two singers, in a painting by Lorenzo Costa; on the table are a rebec with its bow, a recorder, and two part-books

major are closely related, because A major is the dominant of D major and there is a difference of only one sharp between their key-signatures. On the other hand, the relationship between B major and E flat major is more distant, and thus a modulation between them would be harder to achieve – though Beethoven achieved it, with memorable brevity, in the passage linking the slow movement and finale of his *Emperor* concerto.

relative major, relative minor, terms used to indicate the relation between two keys, one major and the other minor, which have the same key-signature, e.g. A minor is the relative minor of C major, and C major is the relative major of A minor.

Reményi, Eduard (1830–98), Hungarian violinist, whose real name was Hoffmann. He studied at the Vienna Conservatorium, but was forced to flee to the United States after taking part in the 1848 Revolution. Later he toured Germany with Brahms (1852–53) and introduced him to Hungarian gypsy music. He made friends with Liszt in Weimar, was appointed violinist to Queen Victoria (1854) and at the Austrian Court (1860). He gave many concerts and made a world tour in 1887. He composed a violin concerto and other works for violin.

Renaissance music, term flexibly used to refer to music composed from about the middle of the 15th century to the end of the 16th century. The word Renaissance, meaning literally 'rebirth', is borrowed from the fields of literature and art, where even in the 15th century itself it stood for a feeling of renewal, of

being 'born again', or a 'reawakening' after a prolonged period of sleep (the middle ages). The word also referred particularly to the revival of the ideas of antiquity, but in music this aspect did not become important until towards the end of the period, mainly because of the lack of examples of Greek music.

The beginning of the Renaissance period in music saw Dufay at the height of his career, and Ockeghem and Busnois at the threshold of their creative lives. It was marked by some important changes, for example: the replacement of isolated settings of individual Mass movements by cyclic settings of the five-section Ordinary of the Mass unified by a single tenor melody, or by common headmotifs, or both; the abandonment of ISORHYTHM and other medieval structures in MOTET composition in favour of free forms which took their inspiration from the text, itself no longer tied to the liturgy; the disappearance of the old FORMES FIXES in song writing, again in the interests of greater freedom and flexibility, and a shift in emphasis from courtly to popular types of song. Associated with these changes was a move away from successive composition (the medieval tendency to work out one voice at a time) to a simultaneous method of composition. The central sonority became a four-part texture with each part corresponding to one of the four principal ranges of the human voice. Mixtures of voices and instruments were eschewed in the writing (though not necessarily the performance) of music in favour of a homogenous texture, which displayed a steadily evolving feeling for harmony.

In the forefront of these developments were the composers of the Flemish School, and their successors, Obrecht, La Rue, and above all Josquin des Prés. Writers on music throughout the 16th century considered that Josquin had brought music to perfection, and eulogised him for the supreme skill and suavity of his music. This view epitomizes both the new self-awareness of the Renaissance, and its presumption. Josquin and his generation refined the technique of imitation, which became the established method of polyphonic writing in the first half of the 16th century, whether on original or derived themes (*see* PARODY MASS), and caused the method of *cantus firmus* treatment to be regarded as old-fashioned.

The chief characteristic of imitative polyphony was the direct relation of the themes to the words, which, in the secular forms, was carried further into details of word-painting and word-symbolism (*see* MADRIGAL). In conformity with the more expressive treatment of words the melodic style of Renaissance music was less florid than that of the 15th century, the rhythms were simpler and more controlled, and the use of dissonance was more clearly regulated. Other accomplishments of the early 16th century were the emergence of instrumental music and writings about instruments (*see* SCHLICK, VIRDUNG), and the displacement of the modes by major and minor.

Attempts to revive the musical practices of antiquity were a feature of the latter part of the Renaissance. Notable were the experiments in relating poetic metres to musical rhythm, as in the odes of Tritonius and in MUSIQUE MESURÉE À L'ANTIQUE, in what was conceived to be the modern equivalent of Greek tragedy; and in the theory and practice of chromatic and enharmonic intervals, as in the writings of Vicentino and Zarlino and in Luython's chromatic harpsichord. More far reaching, however, was the criticism of the polyphonic style by Galilei and others, and the appearance of MONODY, which, though founded on a false Renaissance concept of the nature of Greek music, and allied to the lute-songs of the 16th century, became one of the chief embodiments of the baroque style. Other late Renaissance styles which were maintained and developed in the early baroque period were the divided-choir style (*see* CORI SPEZZATI), the styles of the keyboard toccata, fantasia and variations, of the homophonic dance-piece, and of the English fantasia for viols.

F. BLUME: *Renaissance and Baroque Music* (1968)

E. E. LOWINSKY: 'Music in the Culture of the Renaissance', *Journal of the History of Ideas*, xv (1954)

Renard, burlesque by Stravinsky, to a text by the composer adapted from Russian folk tales about a fox, a cock, a cat and a goat (or ram). The premiere was given by the Russian Ballet at the Paris Opéra in 1922. The score includes a part for cimbalom, a dulcimer-type instrument used in Hungarian gypsy orchestras.

Rencontre Imprévue, La (Fr., *The Unforeseen Encounter*), comic opera in three acts by Gluck, to a libretto by L. H. Dancourt (from an earlier French *vaudeville* by Alain René Lesage and d'Orneval). The first performance was in Vienna in 1764. The German version – *Die unvermuthete Zusammenkunft oder Die Pilgrimme von Mecca*, now generally known simply as

Die Pilger von Mekka (*The Pilgrims from Mecca*) – was first performed at Frankfurt in 1771.

Re Pastore, Il (It., *The King as Shepherd*), (1) opera in three acts by Gluck, to a libretto by Pietro Metastasio, first performed in Vienna in 1756;

(2) opera in two acts by Mozart, a setting of the same libretto, first performed in Salzburg in 1775. Metastasio's story was set to music by at least twelve composers. Mozart's youthful *opera seria* has little dramatic force, but is rich in beautiful arias (one of which, 'L'amerò, sarò costante', is for soprano with violin obbligato) and recitatives which, according to Edward J. Dent, should be 'sipped like imperial Tokay'.

repeat, the exact restatement of a section of a composition. The passage to be repeated is indicated by the sign ‖: at the beginning and :‖ at the end. These are called 'repeat marks'. If the repeat is from the very beginning of a composition, the first repeat mark is unnecessary. A repeat of a first section after a middle section has been performed, as in the aria and in the minuet and trio, is marked *Da capo* (from the beginning); a repeat from the sign .$. in such a case is marked *Dal segno* (from the sign). In classical music – up to the time of Brahms and even beyond – the exposition of movements in sonata-form were generally repeated, and marked accordingly. Sometimes this was merely a formality, but sometimes the repeats were of structural importance. Impatient performers, who today omit the repeats from symphonies by Haydn, Mozart, Beethoven, Schubert, Mendelssohn, Brahms and Schumann (to mention seven regular victims), damage the music in the process.

See also OUVERT

repercussio, *see* RECITING NOTE

répétiteur (Fr.), a coach, generally in an opera house, who teaches singers their parts. Many great conductors have served as repetiteurs during their prentice years.

répétition (Fr.), rehearsal; *répétition generale*, dress rehearsal.

reports, a term used in England and Scotland in the 17th century for entries in IMITATION, especially in connection with psalm-tunes, as in the title of the Scottish Psalter of 1635: *The Psalmes of David in Prose and Meeter. With their whole Tunes in four or more parts, and some Psalmes in Reports.* Modern editions of psalms in reports are in M. Frost, *English and Scottish Psalm and Hymn Tunes* (1953), *Musica Britannica*, xv, and *Fourteen Psalm-settings*, edited by K. Elliott (1960).

reprise (Fr.), (1) REPEAT. In C. P. E. Bach's Sonatas *mit veränderten Reprisen* (with varied *reprises*) of 1760 the repeat of the exposition is varied.

(2) recapitulation (*see* SONATA FORM).

(3) the recurrence of the first section as the latter part of the second section of a binary form, as commonly in the classical minuet.

Requiem (Fr., *messe des morts*, Ger., *Totenmesse*, It., *messa per i defunti*), accusative case of Lat. *requies*, 'rest'.

(1) A Mass for the dead (Lat. *missa pro defunctis*) in the Roman Catholic church, so called from the opening words of the introit, '*Requiem aeternam dona eis, Domine*' (Lord, grant them eternal rest). It consists normally of the following sections:

(1) *Introit*: '*Requiem aeternam*' (Grant them eternal rest);

(2) *Kyrie* (Lord, have mercy upon us);

(3) *Sequence*: '*Dies irae*' (Day of wrath);

(4) *Offertorium*: '*Domine Jesu*' (Lord Jesus Christ, King of glory);

(5) *Sanctus* (Holy, holy, holy);

(6) *Benedictus* (Blessed is he that cometh);

(7) *Agnus Dei* (O Lamb of God);

(8) *Communion*: '*Lux aeterna*' (Light eternal shine on them).

To these may be added at the end the *Responsorium*: '*Libera me Domine*' (Deliver me, O Lord). It will be noticed that the *Gloria* and *Credo* of the ordinary Mass are not included.

The three great continental masters of the 16th century – Palestrina, Lassus and Victoria – all wrote Requiem Masses. Later settings, with solos and orchestral accompaniment, include those by Mozart, Berlioz (*Grande Messe des Morts*), Dvořák, Verdi and Fauré. Delius's Requiem is based on a pagan text compiled from Nietzsche, and Britten's *War Requiem* interweaves the Latin words with poems by Wilfred Owen on the subject of World War I.

    ALEC ROBERTSON: *Requiem – Music of Mourning and Consolation* (1967)

(2) Brahms gave the name *Ein deutsches Requiem* (*A GERMAN REQUIEM*) to a setting for soloists, chorus and orchestra of passages chosen from the German Bible, op 45 (1868). It is a sacred cantata, not a Mass.

Requiem Canticles, Stravinsky's pocket requiem, composed for Princeton University in 1966, and scored for contralto, bass, chorus and orchestra. This was Stravinsky's last major work. Though only some fifteen minutes long, its nine densely-packed sections (making use of six short passages from the Latin Requiem Mass) successfully compress the whole spirit of a vast 19th century Requiem into the sparse, sharply-etched idiom adopted by this composer in his old age.

reservata, musica, *see* MUSICA RESERVATA

resolution, a term used in harmony for the process by which a discord progresses to a concord. For example the dissonant *appoggiatura* of the seventh in:

is resolved on an octave, a consonance; the dissonant *appoggiatura* of the augmented unison in:

is resolved on a less dissonant major second. The regular resolution of a diminished fifth is a major or minor third, e.g.

that of an augmented fourth is a major or minor sixth:

See DISSONANCE, HARMONY, SUSPENSION

resonance, the creation by a vibrating body of vibrations in another body. It occurs in the form of:

(1) *sympathetic vibrations* in such cases as those of two tuning forks of the same pitch;

(2) of a sung note acting on the free strings of a piano;

(3) of a stopped string on a violin acting on an open string of the same pitch;

(4) of the overtones of a vibrating string on the piano acting on the corresponding higher strings when the sustaining pedal is held down.

In a wind instrument played with a reed, the column of air which determines the pitch causes the need to vibrate in its period. Resonance occurs in the form of *forced vibrations* in the sounding board of the piano and the belly of the violin, which do not naturally vibrate in the same period as the notes of the strings.

    See ACOUSTICS

reso-reso, *see* RECO-RECO

Ottorino Respighi

Respighi, Ottorino (1879–1936), Italian composer. He became leading viola in the opera orchestra at St. Petersburg and there studied composition and orchestration with Rimsky-Korsakov. He became teacher of composition at the Liceo Musicale, St. Cecilia Academy in Rome, in 1913. In 1923 he was appointed director of the Conservatorio Regio, Rome, and taught composition there from 1925 to his death. He was a composer of considerable talent who lacked a decided musical personality. Nevertheless some of his orchestral works are so strikingly written and so colourful that they have remained in the repertory. These include his suites, *The Fountains of Rome* and *The Pines of Rome* (which incorporates a gramophone record of a nightingale). Among his numerous effective arrangements are *La Boutique Fantasque* (*The Fantastic Toyshop* – ballet music based on Rossini), *The Birds* (bird pieces by old masters), and *Ancient Airs and Dances for Lute*. He also made a transcription of

Monteverdi's *Orfeo*. Of his nine operas, *La Fiamma* (Rome, 1934) was the most successful. He also composed tone-poems and other works for orchestra, concertos, chamber music, choral music and songs.

R. DE RENSIS: *Ottorino Respighi* (1935)

respond, responsory, a plainsong chant sung by a chorus alternating with one or more solo verses. This method of performance, which is used, e.g. for the Responds between the lessons at Matins and for the Gradual and Alleluia in the Mass, is called 'responsorial psalmody'. In the 12th and 13th centuries it was customary, as in the ORGANUM of Léonin, to set the solo parts in polyphony for two or more soloists, leaving the other sections to be sung by the choir in plainsong as before. Instances of this practice recur until the 16th century. An example by Tallis, a four part setting of the solo parts of 'Audivi vocem', the eighth respond at Matins on All Saints Day in the Sarum rite, is printed with the plainsong sung by the choir in the *Historical Anthology*, no 127. The editors include the plainsong of the *Gloria patri*, which, however, was not sung with the eighth respond and should be omitted.

rest (Fr., *pause*; Ger., *Pause*; It., *pausa*), a silence.

See NOTATION

resultant tone, *see* COMBINATION TONE

'Resurrection' symphony, nickname for Mahler's symphony no 2, composed in 1894, which ends with a choral setting of Klopstock's poem *Auferstehen* (Resurrection).

Reszke, Édouard de (1853–1917), Polish operatic bass, brother of Jean de Reszke, with whom (among others) he studied. He first appeared in *Aida* in a performance conducted by the composer in Paris in 1876, and subsequently sang there frequently at the Opéra. He appeared as Méphistophélès in the 500th performance of Gounod's *Faust* at the Opéra with his brother Jean in the title-role.

His brother **Jean (Jan Mieczyslaw) de Reszke** (1850–1925), was an operatic tenor (originally a baritone). He first appeared in Donizetti's *La Favorite* in Venice in 1874, and subsequently in London (1874) and Paris (1876). His first appearance as a tenor was in Madrid in 1879. Just as his brother was one of the greatest operatic basses, so he was one of the greatest tenors.

retenu (Fr.), held back (reference to the speed of a piece).

Reti, Rudolph (1885–1957), Serbo-Austrian critic, composer and pianist, who became a U.S. citizen. He studied in Vienna, where he was music critic of *Das Echo*, 1930–8. A champion of modern music, he was a founder of the International Society for Contemporary Music in 1922. His theories about thematic unity have come to seem increasingly valuable, and are expounded in his book, *The Thematic Process in Music*, (1950). He also wrote *Tonality, Atonality and Pantonality* (1958). His compositions include an opera, *Ivan and the Drum* (after Tolstoy), and an opera-ballet, *David and Goliath*; also orchestral works, choral music and songs.

retrograde motion (It., *al rovescio*; Lat., *cancrizans*, *per recte et retro*), the use of retrograde, i.e. backwards, motion has been applied in composition both to melodies, as a contrapuntal device, and to entire

textures, as a formal device. Examples of the former are found in the tenors of 15th century motets, as in that of Dunstable's three-part setting of *Veni Sancte Spiritus*, which is first sung thus:

then in its inversion, thus:

and finally in retrograde motion a fifth lower in notes of two-thirds of the original value:

Later examples occur in Bach's *Musical Offering*, in the fugue in the last movement of Beethoven's *Hammerklavier* sonata, op 106, and in modern compositions written in the twelve-note technique by Schoenberg and others. Among examples of the second type are Machaut's *rondeau* 'Ma fin est mon commencement', Byrd's eight-part motet 'Diliges Dominum', the two-part crab canon in Bach's *Musical Offering*, the minuet of Haydn's fourth violin sonata, and the fugue in F in Hindemith's *Ludus Tonalis*.

A special kind of retrograde motion, combined with inversion, is produced when the music is performed with the page turned upside down. The Prelude and Postlude of Hindemith's *Ludus Tonalis* are related in this fashion.

In the following example by Johann Schobert, the second half of the minuet will be found by turning the first half upside down:

Return of Lemminkäinen, The, see LEGENDS

Reubke, Julius (1834–58), German pianist and composer, pupil of Liszt at Weimar. He is known only for his programme-sonata for organ *The Ninety-fourth Psalm*, published posthumously, as were some piano pieces and songs. His early death cut short an obviously promising career.

Reusner, Esajas (1636–79), German lutenist and composer. After studying under a French lutenist at the court of the Polish Princess Radziwill he became court lutenist at Liegnitz and Berg (1655) and in Berlin (1674). He composed three books of dance suites for the lute and published several books of lute arrangements. A Courante, Sarabande, and Gigue from his *Deliciae testudinis* (1667) are printed in Schering's *Geschichte der Musik in Beispielen*, no 216.

Reutlingen, Hugo von, see HUGO VON REUTLINGEN

Reutter, Hermann (born 1900), German composer and pianist, who became teacher of composition in the High School for Music in Württemberg in 1932; director of the High School for Music in Frankfurt in 1936, and of the Stuttgart State Conservatory in 1956. He has composed operas, oratorios and other choral works, a ballet, chamber music, piano works and songs.

Reutter, Johann Adam Karl Georg (1708–72), Austrian composer, son of Georg Reutter. He succeeded his father as *Kapellmeister* of St. Stephen's in 1738, and became court *Kapellmeister* in 1747. He was ennobled (thus becoming von Reutter) in 1740. He was *Kapellmeister* at St. Stephen's when Haydn was a choirboy there, but took little interest in Haydn's efforts at composition and expelled him from the choir-school in 1749. Haydn must have been familiar in his youth with Reutter's symphonies. Immensely prolific, he also wrote some forty operas, eighty Masses, six Requiems and one hundred and twenty motets.

Revolutionary Study, nickname for Chopin's study in C minor – the last of his set of twelve studies, op 10 (1831). The music is believed to represent Chopin's patriotic feelings on hearing that the Russians had invaded Warsaw.

Revueltas, Silvestre (1899–1940), Mexican composer, violinist and pianist. He studied in the United States and was violinist in Mexico City from 1920. He gave recitals of contemporary music with Chávez as pianist, assisted him in conducting the Mexico Symphony Orchestra and became professor at the Conservatoire. He worked for the Republican side during the Spanish Civil War. His compositions, strongly Mexican in character, include symphonic poems on Mexican subjects, string quartets and other chamber music, songs and numerous film scores.

Reyer, Ernest (real name: **Louis Ernest Etienne Rey**) (1823–1909), French composer and critic. In 1848 he settled in Paris where he met Gautier, Flaubert and Méry, who provided texts for his compositions, and in 1871 became music critic for the *Journal des Débats*. He succeeded Berlioz as librarian of the Conservatoire and was a staunch Wagnerian. His compositions include operas, of which *Sigurd* (Brussels, 1884) and *Salammbô* (Brussels, 1890) were the most notable, a ballet-pantomime, choral music and songs.

Rezitativ (Ger.), recitative.

Reznicek, Emil Nikolaus von (1860–1945), Austrian composer and conductor. Born in Vienna, he studied at the Leipzig Conservatorium under Reinecke and Jadassohn. Later he held conducting and academic appointments in Berlin and Mannheim. He was director of the Warsaw Opera and Philharmonic from 1907 until 1909. Today he is remembered mainly for the vivacious overture to his opera *Donna Diana*. His numerous other operas include *The Maid of Orleans* (after Schiller) and *Till Eulenspiegel*. He also composed four symphonies, choral and chamber music, keyboard pieces and songs.

rhapsody (from Gr., *rhapsōidia* – an epic poem), a title given by composers in the 19th and early 20th centuries to instrumental compositions of a heroic, national, or rhetorical character, e.g. Liszt's *Hungarian Rhapsodies* and Brahms's two rhapsodies, op 79 for piano, Delius's *Brigg Fair* (an 'English rhapsody'), Rakhmaninov's *Rhapsody on a theme of Paganini*, Ravel's *Rapsodie Espagnole*.

Rhapsody in Blue, work for piano and orchestra by Gershwin, first performed in New York in 1924 by Paul Whiteman's Orchestra with the composer as soloist. This was the first important 'concert' work to bridge the gap between jazz band and symphony orchestra, and it remains one of the few successful works of its kind. Gershwin left the task of orchestrating it to the U.S. composer, Ferde Grofé, though in his later concert music he undertook this responsibility himself.

Rhau (**Rhaw**), **Georg** (1488–1548), German composer and publisher. He published many of the early collections of Lutheran church music, including *Newe deudsche geistliche Gesenge* (1544; facsimile edition, 1969), which contains polyphonic settings of chorales by various composers. In 1542 he published a volume of polyphonic settings of Latin hymns for the Lutheran liturgy by Heinrich Finck, Thomas Stoltzer, Ludwig Senfl and others (modern edition in *Das Erbe deutscher Musik*, 1 Reihe, xxi and xxv). A modern edition of all his music prints for the years 1538 to 1545 was begun in 1954 under the general editorship of H. Albrecht (Bärenreiter and Concordia). Rhau's handbook of elementary theory, *Enchiridion utriusque musicae practicae*, was published in a facsimile edition in 1951.

Rheinberger, Joseph Gabriel (1839–1901), Liechtenstein-born organist and composer. He was appointed an organist at the age of seven, and studied at the Munich Royal Conservatorium, where he taught from 1859 almost continuously until his death. From 1865 until 1867 he conducted the Munich Court Opera, and from 1877 was director of court church music. He composed operas, orchestral works, church music, secular choral works, two organ concertos, twenty sonatas and other works for organ, piano pieces and songs.

H. GRACE: *The Organ Works of Rheinberger* (1925)

Rheingold, Das (*The Rhine Gold*), opera in one act by Wagner, the first part of his RING cycle. The first performance took place at Munich in 1869.

Rheinische Sinfonie, see RHENISH SYMPHONY

Rhené-Baton (real name: **René Baton**) (1879–1940), French conductor and composer. He worked at the Opéra-Comique and from 1918 until 1932 was conductor of the Concerts Pasdeloup. He composed a lyric drama, a ballet, orchestral works, piano pieces and songs.

'Rhenish' Symphony (Ger., *Rheinische Sinfonie*), the name given to Schumann's symphony no 3 in E major, op 97 (1850), which incorporated the impressions he received during a visit to Cologne.

Rhine Gold, The, *see* RHEINGOLD

rhythm, the organisation of music in respect to time. Rhythm may be:

(1) free, as in some types of Oriental music;

(2) flexible, as in plainsong, where each note is regarded as having approximately the same length;

(3) measured, either in rhythmic modes (*See* MENSURAL NOTATION) as in the 11th–12th centuries, or in a complete system of duple and triple note-values, as in the 13th to the 16th centuries;

(4) metrical, i.e. accentual, as from the 16th century to the present.

Within each of these systems the rhythmic character of a phrase, period, section or movement of a composition is a fundamental element in its style, and the chief criterion for distinctions of style, e.g. between the plainsong hymn, psalm and antiphon, between the 13th-century motet and *conductus*, between the isorhythmic motet and non-isorhythmic *chanson* in the 14th and 15th centuries, between the motet and madrigal in the 16th, between the movements of a suite in the baroque period, and between the movements and themes of a movement in the modern symphony and sonata. The effect of good polyphonic writing is caused by apt combinations of rhythm as much as by melodic independence, as in the measured rhythm of:

from a *Credo* by Leonel Power, or the metrical rhythm of:

from the fugue in C sharp minor in the first book of Bach's *Forty-eight*.

The effect of the metrical rhythm of homophonic writing arises from both the melodic and the harmonic rhythm, as well as from the relation between them,

since they may be contrasted, as in the opening of John Blow's anthem, 'How doth the city sit solitary':

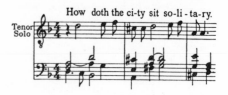

or combined, as in the Allegretto of Beethoven's seventh symphony:

In the present century composers have extended the possibilities of metrical rhythm by the use of different metres in succession and in combination, of more complex melodic rhythms, and of more varied relations between melodic and harmonic rhythm by syncopation and other methods.

See ACCENT, BAR, METRE, SYNCOPATION, TIMESIGNATURE

C. SACHS: *Rhythm and Tempo* (1953)

rhythmic modes, the term mode had a rhythmic meaning in the NOTATION of c. 1150 to c. 1250, and denoted a rhythmic pattern used more or less consistently in each part of a polyphonic composition. These patterns were arrangements of the long and the breve, which were used in the following combinations: Mode I: long-breve; Mode II: breve-long; Mode III: long-breve-breve; Mode IV: breve-breve-long; Mode V: successive longs; Mode VI: successive breves. Since the relation of long to breve was considered to be always perfect, i.e. long=three breves, the principles of imperfection, whereby a long followed by a breve became imperfect (two breves), and alteration, whereby a breve preceding a long was doubled (*brevis altera*), were applied in the first four modes, in order to keep them within perfect (triple) units. The equivalent patterns in modern notation, i.e. reduced to one-sixteenth of the original values, would be:

Mode I: etc.;

Mode II: etc.;

Mode III: etc.;

Mode IV: etc.;

Mode V: etc.;

Mode VI: etc.;

Music composed in the rhythmic modes was written in LIGATURES and the form of the opening ligatures showed in what mode the part was to be interpreted. In practice it was not possible to use ligatures throughout, for example in the case of repeated notes, which cannot be written in ligature. The term mode continued to be used for the relation of the long to the breve in the period of MENSURAL NOTATION.

rhythmicon, an electrical instrument incorporating a photoelectric cell invented by THEREMIN and the U.S. composer Henry Cowell. Although possessing a keyboard it is concerned not with pitch but with producing cross-rhythms, particularly complex ones. It has, therefore, the character of a percussion instrument.

ribeca, ribibe, ribible, *see* REBEC

ributhe, Scottish form of JEW'S HARP.

Riccardo I, Re d'Inghilterra (*Richard I, King of England*), opera in three acts by Handel, to a libretto by Paolo Antonio Rolli, first performed in London in 1727.

Ricci, Luigi (1805–59), Italian composer. He studied under Zingarelli at Naples Conservatorio where he became teacher in 1819. Later he went to Trieste as conductor of the Opera and director of music at the Cathedral. He composed about thirty operas, some with his brother Federico (1809–77), who was also an opera composer. Their most successful collaboration was in the comic opera *Crispino e la Comare* (Venice, 1850).

Riccio, Antonio Teodoro (c. 1540–c. 1603), Italian composer. After being *maestro di cappella* in Brescia he was appointed in 1564 *Kapellmeister* to Georg Friedrich at Ansbach, and in 1579 moved with him to Königsberg. He composed Masses, motets and Magnificats, madrigals and *Canzoni alla napolitana*.

ricercar (It., from *ricercare*, to seek out), a term used in the general sense of essay or study as the title of certain compositions in the 16th and 17th centuries.

The earliest ricercars for organ in Marco Antonio Cavazzoni's *Recerchari, motetti, canzoni* (1523), were in free style, but the later examples by Girolamo Cavazzoni (1542), Andrea Gabrieli, Frescobaldi, and Lutheran composers up to Bach are in imitative polyphonic style. A ricercar is based on one or a succession of themes of a rather abstract character, is usually in 4/2 time throughout, and is not clearly distinguishable in style from a contrapuntal FANTASIA, the term which German composers preferred for pieces in this style until late in the seventeenth century. Froberger used both titles, without effective distinction, for pieces in contrapuntal style in 2/2 time, with or without changes of metre. Themes with solmization titles were frequently used, as in Frescobaldi's *Recercar sopra Mi, Re, Fa, Mi* in his first book of *Capricci, Canzon francese e Recercari* (1626). The same collection contains a *Recercar obligo di non uscir mai di grado*, i.e. without using stepwise motion, in which no part uses the interval of a second. It begins:

Later ricercars on one theme are fugues, which is the sense in which Bach uses the term in his *Musical Offering*. The first published collection of contrapuntal ricercars for instrumental ensemble was *Musica Nova* (1540; modern edition by Colin H. Slim, 1964), containing compositions by Willaert, Julio da Modena and others. Ganassi's *Regola Rubertina* (1542–3) and Ortiz's *Tratado de glosas* (1553) contain studies entitled ricercar for solo viol. Domenico Gabrielli's ricercars of 1689 are for cello both unaccompanied and with continuo. The two-part ricercars by Metallo (1605; twelve editions to 1685) are *per sonare et cantare* ('to play and sing'), while those of Giovanni Gentile (1642) are for singers.

The earliest ricercars for lute, in Petrucci's publications (1507–11), were in free style. Later examples, such as those of Vincenzo Galilei (edited by F. Fano in *Istituzioni e Monumenti*, iv, pages 8–11), were in pseudo-contrapuntal or in homophonic style.

Richafort, Jean (c. 1480–c. 1547), Flemish composer. He studied under Josquin des Prés and from 1543 to 1547 was choirmaster of St. Gilles at Bruges. He composed a Requiem, Masses, motets and *chansons*. The *chanson* 'Sur tous regrets' was printed in volume two of Ott's *Liederbuch* of 1544 (reprinted in *Publikationen der Gesellschaft für Musikforschung*, ii) and the motet 'Christus resurgens', on which Willaert wrote a Mass, was printed by Glareanus in the *Dodecachordon* (1547) as an example of the Ionian mode, and reprinted in C. A. Miller's translation of the *Dodecachordon* (1965), ii, page 364.

Richard Coeur-de-Lion, opera in three acts by Grétry, to a libretto by Jean Michel Sedaine, first performed in Paris in 1784. Beethoven composed a set of piano variations on a song from it.

Richardson (originally **Heyborne**), **Ferdinando** (c. 1558–1618), English composer and poet. He studied under Tallis and was groom of the Privy Chamber from 1587 till 1611. Two pavanes and two galliards, each with a variation, were included in the *Fitzwilliam Virginal Book*.

　　R. MARLOW: 'Sir Ferdinando Heyborne alias Richardson', in *Musical Times*, cxv (1974)

Richter, Ernst Friedrich Eduard (1808–79), German theorist and organist. Studied in Leipzig, where he taught at the Conservatorium (1843), conducted at the Singakademie (1843–47), was organist of various churches and cantor of the Thomasschule (1868). Three of his books were translated into English by Franklin Taylor: *Harmony* (1864), *Simple and Double Counterpoint* (1874) and *Fugue* (1878). He composed church music, chamber music, organ pieces and songs.

Richter, Franz Xaver (1709–89), Moravian composer, violinist and singer. He was choirmaster of the abbey at Kempten, Swabia, from 1740, singer and violinist at Mannheim Electoral Court from 1747 and choirmaster of Strasbourg Cathedral from 1769 until his death. He composed 69 symphonies, six harpsi-

chord concertos with string orchestra, twelve trio sonatas for two violins and continuo and other chamber music, 28 Masses, two Requiems, motets and other church music, and wrote a textbook on harmony. He was a leading member of the group of composers connected with the Mannheim orchestra whose work contributed much to the early history of the symphony.

Richter, Hans (1843–1916), Austrian-Hungarian conductor. He studied at the Vienna Conservatorium (1860–5), was horn player in the Kärntnertor Theatre Orchestra (1862–5) and chorus master of the Munich Court Opera (1868–9). He was conductor of the Budapest National Opera (1871–5), Court Opera and Philharmonic Concerts, Vienna (1875) and the Hallé Orchestra in Manchester (1900–11). He conducted at the Bayreuth Festivals and the Birmingham triennial festivals, and from 1879 gave an annual series of Richter concerts in London. He worked with Wagner preparing for publication the score of *The Mastersingers* and of the *Ring*, of which he conducted the first performance in 1876 at Bayreuth. One of the great conductors of his age, he did much to improve the standards of conducting and of orchestral playing, and to further the knowledge of Wagner's works both in Vienna and in England. He conducted the first British performances of *The Mastersingers* and of *Tristan and Isolde* in 1882 and 1884.

Richter, Sviatoslav (born 1914), Russian pianist who studied at the Moscow Conservatory and became one of the most outstanding musicians in the Soviet Union. His first appearance in the United States was not until 1960 (and in Britain 1961) but his reputation preceded him by way of his recordings. Beethoven and Schubert are among the composers with whom his name is specially associated, and he has appeared many times in sonata recitals with the equally famous Russian cellist, Mstislav Rostropovich. Prokofiev's ninth piano sonata was dedicated to him. His intensely self-critical temperament as a musician (rather than restrictions placed on him by the Soviet authorities) sometimes resulted in his cancelling performances at short notice, but in Britain he made memorable appearances at the Aldeburgh and Edinburgh festivals. He has been given annual leave of absence from the Soviet Union to run his own music festival in a converted barn near Tours in France.

riddle canon, term for a canon in which the composer deliberately supplies only one part, leaving it to the performer to decide where and at what pitch the other voices enter.

Riders to the Sea, opera in one act by Vaughan Williams, a setting (nearly word-for-word) of Synge's play about a doom-laden Irish fishing family. The first performance was in London in 1937.

Riegger, Wallingford (1885–1961), U.S. composer who studied at the Institute of Musical Art in New York and at the Berlin Hochschule. He conducted for a few years in Germany before returning to the United States, where he held various academic appointments. He composed numerous works for modern dancers, including Martha Graham, Charles Weidman and Doris Humphrey, symphonies and other orchestral works, and chamber music, including a *Study in Sonority* for ten violins.

Riemann, Karl Wilhelm Julius Hugo (1849–1919),

German musicologist and theorist. Studied at the Leipzig Conservatorium and at Göttingen (1873) and held various academic appointments in Germany. He wrote many books on musical history and theory, and edited collections of music. A number of his textbooks have been translated into English, as has his *Musiklexicon* (1882, revised by W. Gurlitt, 1959).

Rienzi, der Letzte der Tribunen (Ger.; *Rienzi, the Last of the Tribunes*), opera in five acts by Wagner, to a libretto by the composer (founded on Bulwer Lytton's novel about a 14th century Italian patriot). The first performance was in Dresden in 1842. The music is written in the conventional Meyerbeer-like idiom employed by Wagner before he began to forge his own style in *Tannhäuser* and *The Flying Dutchman*.

Ries, Ferdinand (1784–1838), German pianist, composer and conductor, member of a family of musicians. He studied under Beethoven in Vienna, toured as a pianist, and lived in London as pianist and teacher from 1813 until 1824. Later he held musical appointments at Aix-la-Chapelle and Frankfurt. He published a biographical work on Beethoven with Wegeler (1838) and composed three operas, two oratorios, six symphonies, chamber music, and many works for piano.

Riesco, Carlos (born 1925), Chilean composer, pupil of Copland, David Diamond and Nadia Boulanger. His works, in which Latin-American idioms are discernible, include a ballet, *Candelaria*, a violin concerto and other orchestral music.

Rieti, Vittorio (born 1898) Italian (Egyptian born) composer, pupil of Respighi in Rome. He settled in New York in 1939. He has composed ballets (one of them on Robinson Crusoe), an opera (based on Lorca's play, *Don Perlimplin*), five symphonies, concertos, chamber music and piano pieces.

Rietz, Julius (1812–77), German cellist, conductor and composer. He was assistant conductor to Mendelssohn at the Düsseldorf Opera from 1834; succeeded him in 1835; and became municipal music director there in 1836. In Leipzig he was conductor of the Opera and director of Gewandhaus Concerts. He worked in Dresden from 1860 as Court conductor and director of the Conservatorium.

rigaudon (Fr.; Eng., rigadoon), a Provençal dance in lively 2/2 time which was adopted into the suite and into the ballet of French opera in the late 17th century. There is a 'rigadoon' for harpsichord by Purcell in the second part of Playford's *Musick's Handmaid*. The *rigaudon* in Couperin's second *ordre* for harpsichord begins thus:

rigo (It.), staff, stave.

Rigoletto, opera in three acts by Verdi, to a libretto by Francesco Maria Piave (based on Victor Hugo's *Le Roi s'amuse*), first performed at Venice in 1851. Rigoletto (the humpbacked jester of the Duke of Mantua) mocks the court noblemen and advises the duke to get rid of them. The noblemen in turn resolve to take vengeance on him, and Count Monterone (whose daughter the duke has dishonoured) curses both the jester and the duke. Meanwhile the duke, disguised as a student, has been courting Gilda (Rigoletto's concealed daughter). The noblemen, believing Gilda to be the mistress of Rigoletto, abduct her, telling him that they are abducting the Countess Ceprano (one of the duke's favourites), so that unawares he assists them with their plans.

Rigoletto later finds Gilda with the duke at the palace. Admitting that she is his daughter, he takes her away, cursing his master. Gilda is taken by her father to spy on the duke, who is at the house of Sparafucile (a professional assassin) where he has an amorous rendezvous with Maddalena (Sparafucile's sister). Rigoletto pays Sparafucile to kill his guest. When Maddalena begs her brother not to do the deed, he promises that he will spare the duke if he can find another to take the duke's place by midnight.

Gilda, having overheard this conversation, enters the house disguised as a man. When the jester returns with the money he is given a body tied in a bag and is about to throw it into the river when he hears in the distance the voice of the duke singing. He quickly opens the bag and discovers his dying daughter, who declares that she is happy to die for her lover. In horror Rigoletto realises that the curse of Count Monterone is fulfilled.

Rigoletto was Verdi's first mature opera, dramatically stronger and more boldly characterised than anything he had produced up to that time. Its most famous aria is 'La donna è mobile', sung by the Duke (tenor) in Act 3.

Riisager, Knudåge (born 1897), Danish composer, educated at Copenhagen University and in Paris with Roussel. He won the Wilhelm Hansen prize for composition in 1925. His compositions include an opera (*Susanne*), four symphonies, and other orchestral works, ballet music, choral works, chamber music, piano pieces and songs.

Rimbault, Edward Francis (1816–76), English musical historian and organist. He was one of the founders of the Musical Antiquarian Society and of the Percy Society, and editor of the Motet Society publications. He edited many collections of early English music and wrote books on music history.

Rimsky-Korsakov, Nikolay Andreyevich (1844–1908), Russian composer. At twelve he entered the Corps of Naval Cadets at St. Petersburg, and five years later met Balakirev, Cui and Mussorgsky, and began the serious study of music under Balakirev. He sailed to London and New York as a petty officer in 1862, returning in 1865, and in 1871 was appointed professor of composition at St. Petersburg Conservatory. In 1874 he became director of the New Free School of Music in St. Petersburg and soon became the leader of a new group of composers, including Liadov, Glazunov, and Arensky. After the perform-

Nikolay Andreyevitch Rimsky-Korsakov. In view of his flair for brilliant orchestration it is fitting that Serov's portrait shows him at work on a full score

ance of Wagner's *Ring* in St. Petersburg in 1888 he began to write for a larger orchestra and to develop the ideas on orchestration which were published in *Principles of Orchestration* (English translation by E. Agate, 1912). In 1902 he met Stravinsky, who became his pupil. He showed sympathy with the cause of the revolution of 1905 and was dismissed from the Conservatory, but was later reinstated. The element of satire on government in his last work, the opera based on Pushkin's *The Golden Cockerel* (1907), caused its performance to be forbidden until 1910.

Like other members of Balakirev's circle of composers known as 'The Mighty Handful', Rimsky-Korsakov was strongly influenced by national ideas in his early work. His later development acquired a solid foundation through concentrated work on technical matters after 1871, through his work on the collection of folk songs, published as op 24, and through the experience of editing Glinka's operas. After 1887–8 when he wrote his most mature orchestral pieces, *Spanish Capriccio*, *Sheherazade*, and the *Russian Easter Festival* overture, he re-orchestrated many of his earlier works, but gave his main creative effort to the composition of the operas – *Mlada*, 1890; *Christmas Eve*, 1895; *Sadko*, 1896; *Czar Saltan*, 1898; *Kitezh*, 1904; and *The Golden Cockerel* – which are his greatest achievement. He also edited and arranged (some would now say disarranged) operas by other Russian composers, including Mussorgsky's *Boris Godunov* and Borodin's *Prince Igor*. His clear and brilliant orchestrations had a marked effect on Stravinsky, and through Stravinsky on the orchestral writing of many contemporary composers. His memoirs were published in English in 1924 as *My Musical Life*.

> G. ABRAHAM: *On Russian Music* (1939); *Rimsky-Korsakov* (1945); *Studies in Russian Music* (1935)
> M. MONTAGU-NATHAN: *Rimsky-Korsakov* (1916)

Rinaldo, opera in three acts by Handel, to a libretto by Giacomo Rossi (from a sketch by Aaron Hill, after Tasso's *Jerusalem Delivered*). This was the first opera written by Handel for London, where it had its première in 1711.

Rinck, Johann Christian Heinrich (1770–1846), German organist and composer. He studied under Kittel, a pupil of Bach, and held posts at Giessen and Darmstadt. He wrote a *Practical Organ School* and other organ works, church and chamber music.

Ring des Nibelungen, Der (Ger., *The Ring of the Nibelung*), cycle of four operas by Wagner, described by him as 'Ein Bühnenfestspiel für drei Tage und einen Vorabend' (a festival drama for three days and a preliminary evening) and dedicated to Ludwig II, King of Bavaria. Libretto by the composer:

> (1) *Das Rheingold* (The Rhine Gold), first performed, Munich, September 22nd, 1869;
> (2) *Die Walküre* (The Valkyrie), first performed, Munich, June 26th, 1870;
> (3) *Siegfried*, first performed Bayreuth, August 16th, 1876;
> (4) *Götterdämmerung* (Twilight of the Gods), first performed, Bayreuth, August 17th, 1876.

The first performance of the complete cycle was given by Wagner at Bayreuth between August 13th and 17th, 1876.

(1) *Das Rheingold*. The Rhine gold is stolen from the Rhine maidens by the Nibelung dwarf Alberich, who makes from it the ring that gives mastery of the world – but at the cost of the renunciation of love. The gods, led by Wotan, steal both gold and ring, to ransom the goddess Freia, who has been taken by the giants as payment for their building of Valhalla. The curse placed on the ring by Alberich operates immediately. The giants Fasolt and Fafner quarrel over the ring, and Fasolt is slain. The gods enter Valhalla.

(2) *Die Walküre*. Wotan has nine daughters by the earth goddess Erda (The Valkyries) and also others by a human mother (Siegmund and Sieglinde). Wotan hopes that his human progeny will recover the ring (now guarded by Fafner who has become a dragon). The human children are under the same curse. Without realising they are brother and sister, Siegmund and Sieglinde fall in love. Brünnhilde, one of the Valkyries, disobeys Wotan's commandment by protecting Siegmund against Hunding, but Wotan intervenes and Hunding kills the defenceless Siegmund. Brünnhilde rescues Sieglinde, and tells her she will bear a son, Siegfried. Wotan punishes Brünnhilde by removing her godhead. She falls into a trance, and lies surrounded by fire, which only a fearless hero can penetrate.

(3) *Siegfried*. Siegfried, child of the incestuous union of Siegmund and Sieglinde (who died in giving birth), has been brought up in the forest by Alberich's brother, the dwarf Mime. He forges a sword from fragments of his father's weapon, broken by Hunding's attack,

Ring of the Nibelungs. Left: Josef Hoffmann's design for the third act of *Rhinegold*, for the first complete *Ring* cycle at Bayreuth in 1876, realistic and heavily romantic in what was to become the early Bayreuth tradition. *Right:* Amalie Materna made a suitably athletic figure as the first Bayreuth Brünnhilde, without the faintly ridiculous appearance of some later interpreters

kills Fafner, possesses the ring and the magic helm (which Alberich had also made from the gold), and wins Brünnhilde.

(4) *Götterdämmerung*. Hagen, son of Alberich, plots to recover the ring. Siegfried, made to lose his memory by a potion, falls in love with Gutrune. He captures Brünnhilde for Gunther, Hagen's half-brother. Siegfried then marries Guntrune who is Gunther's sister. Brünnhilde, with Hagen and Gunther, plots Siegfried's destruction. Siegfried is killed by Hagen and so is Gunther. Brünnhilde, now aware of the truth, builds a funeral pyre for Siegfried and rides into it with the ring on her finger. The Rhine overwhelms the stage. The ring, vainly pursued by Hagen, returns to the Rhine maidens, and Valhalla is seen in flames. The curse is complete.

Wagner based *The Ring* on the Nordic Nibelung saga. The work is timeless moral drama on the subject of power and corruption, as topical today as a century ago, and is the most complete embodiment of Wagner's musical and ethical beliefs.

Rio Grande, The, work by Constant Lambert for piano, contralto, chorus and orchestra, to words by Sacheverell Sitwell, first performed in 1929. The music incorporates jazz percussion instruments as part of its orchestration, and is one of the few successful attempts by a 'classical' composer to merge the worlds of concert hall and jazz band.

ripieno (It.), literally 'full'. The term refers – particularly in the *concerto grosso* of the baroque period – to the full body of the orchestra, as distinct from the soloist or group of soloists (*concertino*). *Senza ripieni* indicates that the first desks only of the accompanying orchestra are to play.

Rippe, Albert de (Alberto da Ripa, Alberto Mantovano) (c. 1500–51), Italian lutenist, who spent most of his career at the court of Francis I of France. He was one of the most famous lutenists of his time. His lute compositions were published posthumously in six volumes by his pupil, Guillaume Morlaye, and consist of *fantasies*, dances, and transcriptions of *chansons* and motets. A complete edition was begun in 1972 by J.-M. Vaccaro.

ripresa (It.), 'repeat': (1) the REFRAIN in the Italian BALLATA of the 14th century.

(2) a dance movement for lute in the form of a variation in the 16th century.

(3) in later music any REPEAT or recapitulation.

See SONATA FORM

Rise and Fall of the City of Mahagonny, The (Ger., *Aufstieg und Fall der Stadt Mahagonny*), opera in three acts by Kurt Weill, to a libretto by Bertolt Brecht, first produced in Leipzig in 1930. The work, a ferocious political satire on capitalist morality, quickly achieved notoriety in the Germany of the period (Weill, a Jew, settled in the United States five years later). When the hero, Jimmy Mahoney, cannot pay for his drinks, he is brought to trial; his sentence is two days' imprisonment for indirect murder, four years for seduction by means of money, and death for inability to pay his whisky bill. Though the work makes use of Weill's characteristic bitter-sweet, cabaret-style idiom, it is operatically more ambitious than his other pieces of this kind. Among the most famous songs from *Mahagonny* are the 'Havanna Lied' and the 'Alabama Song'. An earlier, simpler version of the work was produced at Baden-Baden in 1927.

risoluto (It.), in a resolute manner.

rispetto, Italian improvised folk-poem with inter-rhyming lines, sung to popular tunes.

risposta (It.), (1) the answer in a FUGUE or IMITATION. (2) The *comes* in a CANON.

risvegliato (It.), in an animated (or re-animated) manner.

ritardando (It.), becoming gradually slower – the equivalent of *rallentando*. Commonly abbreviated *rit.*

ritenuto (It.), held back in tempo, i.e. slower, though sometimes used as the equivalent of *ritardando*.

Rite of Spring, The, ballet with music by Stravinsky, first performed at the Théâtre des Champs-Elysées, Paris, in 1913 – when it resulted in the most famous riot in musical history. The work is in two parts, *The Adoration of the Earth* and *The Sacrifice*, and is a milestone in 20th century music. Its grinding discords and rhythms were of an uncompromising ferocity never previously attempted by a composer, and never again attempted by Stravinsky – after *The Rite* came his neo-classical period, which at the time seemed a musical *volte face* but which now seems an integral part of his musical personality. Because it was first performed in Paris, *The Rite* was initially known as *Le Sacre du Printemps*.

ritmo (It.), rhythm. Beethoven's indication, *ritmo di tre battute*, in the scherzo of his ninth symphony, means that the music is to be performed in groups of three bars – i.e. the tempo is so fast that there is only one beat per bar, and each group of three bars forms a rhythmical unit. Similarly, *ritmo di quattro battute*, also indicated in Beethoven's scherzo, refers to groups of four bars.

ritornello (It.), return. (1) The last section of an Italian MADRIGAL of the 14th century which is thus a conclusion, not a return.

(2) an instrumental piece in early opera. In Monteverdi's *Orfeo*, for example, the *ritornello* of four bars before the Prologue returns four times with the first bar omitted during the Prologue, and is played complete between the Prologue and the first act.

(3) the orchestral prelude, interludes, and postlude in an aria of the 17th and 18th centuries, and the recurrences of the *tutti* theme in the main movements of a *concerto grosso* of the baroque period. In both cases the intermediate *ritornelli* are in nearly-related keys, and the final *ritornello* is in the tonic.

(4) an interlude for instrumental ensemble played after each verse of German songs in the 17th century, as in Adam Krieger's *Neue Arien* of 1676.

(5) passage for full orchestra in a concerto, during which the soloist is silent.

Ritorno d'Ulisse in Patria, Il (It., *The Return of Ulysses to his Fatherland*), opera with a prologue and five acts by Monteverdi, to a libretto by Giacomo Badoaro, first performed in Venice in 1641. Modern arrangements of this opera have been made by Dallapiccola and Raymond Leppard.

Rivier, Jean (born 1896), French composer, prolific in output and accessible in idiom. His works include seven symphonies, concertos, chamber music and songs.

Roberday, François (1624–80), French composer

who was attached to the courts of Queen Anne of Austria and Queen Marie-Thérèse. He was one of the teachers of Lully and organist at the Church of the Petits-pères in Paris. He published *Fugues et caprices* for organ (1660), reprinted in an edition by Jean Ferrard (1972).

P. HARDOUIN: 'François Roberday', in *Revue de Musicologie*, xlv (1960)

Robert le Diable (*Robert the Devil*), opera in five acts by Meyerbeer, to a libretto by Augustin Eugène Scribe, first performed in Paris in 1831. With its midnight orgy, ghostly nuns and a hero (Robert, Duke of Normandy) who is the son of a mortal and a devil, this opera was a sure fire success in the 19th century. Jenny Lind made her London debut in it in 1847.

Robeson, Paul (1898–1976), U.S. black bass, world-renowned for his performance of Negro songs and spirituals.

rococo, *see* STYLE GALANT

Rode, Jacques Pierre Joseph (1774–1830), French violinist and composer, pupil of Viotti in Paris. He taught violin at the Paris Conservatoire in 1795, and became court violinist in St. Petersburg under Boïeldieu in 1803. He was a fine player in his early years, but his powers had declined when he played Beethoven's sonata in G, op 96, for the composer in Vienna. Besides studies and caprices for violin, he wrote thirteen concertos, quartets, duets for violins, and other short pieces.

Rodelinda, opera in three acts by Handel, to a libretto by Antonio Salvi (altered by Nicola Francesco Haym). The first performance was in London in 1725. With its emphasis on marital love, and its dungeon scene in which the hero escapes death at the hands of the villain, *Rodelinda* is a notable precursor of Beethoven's *Fidelio*.

Rodeo, ballet music by Copland, composed for Agnes de Mille and first produced by the Ballet Russe de Monte Carlo in New York in 1942. The action takes place in the Wild West, and the music quotes traditional U.S. songs. A four-movement concert suite (*Buckaroo Holiday*; *Corral Nocturne*; *Saturday Night Waltz*; *Hoedown*) was later prepared by the composer with the subtitle of *Four Dance Episodes*.

Rodgers, Richard (born 1902), U.S. composer of successful musicals, including *Oklahoma!* and *South Pacific*. In these and other pieces the words were written by Oscar Hammerstein II, though it has been suggested that Hammerstein brought out a sentimental streak in Rodgers's music which was absent from the more pungent scores (e.g. *Pal Joey*) which he composed with a previous partner, Lorenz Hart.

Rodrigo, Joaquin (born 1902), Spanish composer, blind from the age of three. A pupil of Dukas, he has produced a number of sensitively-written works of Spanish character, the most famous being his *Concerto de Aranjuez* for guitar and orchestra.

Rodzinski, Artur (1892–1958), Polish-Yugoslavian conductor who studied in Vienna and was conductor at the Warsaw Opera from 1920 until 1924. Later he emigrated to the United States and took U.S. citizenship. He held conducting posts in various U.S. cities (Los Angeles, Cleveland, New York, Chicago) but ultimately worked as a freelance.

Roger-Ducasse, Jean Jules Amable (1873–1954), French composer, pupil of Fauré at the Paris Conservatoire, where he won the second *Prix de Rome* in 1902. He succeeded Dukas as teacher of composition at the Conservatoire in 1935. He composed an opera (*Cantegril*) and a mimed drama (*Orphée*), orchestral works, choral music, chamber music, songs and piano pieces.

Rogers, Bernard (1893–1968), U.S. composer, pupil of Ernest Bloch in Cleveland, Frank Bridge in London, and Nadia Boulanger in Paris. In 1938 he was appointed teacher of composition at the Eastman School of Music in Rochester. He received a Pulitzer Scholarship and a Guggenheim Fellowship. He composed four operas, four symphonies and other orchestral works, choral music, chamber music and songs.

Rohrflöte (Ger.; Fr., *flûte à cheminée*), 'chimney flute'. An organ stop of the flute type. The pipe is stopped at one end, but the stopper is pierced by a hole, in which is inserted a metal tube or chimney.

Rohrwerk (Ger.), the reed stops on an organ.

Roi de Lahore, Le (Fr., *The King of Lahore*), opera in five acts by Massenet, to a libretto by Louis Gallet, first performed in Paris in 1877. The story tells how King Alim is murdered by a treacherous minister of state, but is allowed by the gods to return to earth as a beggar.

Roi d'Ys, Le (Fr., *The King of Ys*), opera in three acts by Lalo, to a libretto by Edouard Blau, first performed in Paris in 1888. The story is based on the legend of the submerged city off the Breton coast – also the subject of Debussy's piano prelude, *La Cathédrale Engloutie*.

Roi l'a Dit, Le (Fr., *The King has said it*), opera in three acts by Delibes, to a libretto by Edmond Gondinet, first performed in Paris in 1873. The story concerns a marquis who claims to have a son, and who recruits a peasant boy as a pretender. The boy makes the most of the situation.

Roi Malgré Lui, Le (It., *The King in spite of himself*), opera in three acts by Chabrier, to a libretto by Émile de Najac and Paul Burani (based on a comedy by François Ancelot). The first performance was in Paris in 1887.

Roland, opera by Lully with a prologue and five acts, to a libretto by Philippe Quinault. The first performance was at Versailles in 1685.

Roland-Manuel (real name: **Roland Alexis Manuel Lévy**) (1891–1966), French composer and writer on music, pupil of Roussel and Ravel. He composed operas, ballets, chamber music (including a *Suite dans le goût espagnol* for oboe, bassoon, trumpet, and harpsichord), orchestral works and film music. He also wrote musical criticism, a book on Falla (1930) and three works on Ravel: *Maurice Ravel et son oeuvre* (1914), *Maurice Ravel et son oeuvre dramatique* (1928) and *Maurice Ravel* (1938; English edition, 1947).

roll, a succession of notes on a drum or other percussion instrument so rapid that it approximates to a continuous sound.

Rolland, Romain (1866–1944), French writer and musical historian. He became president of the musical division of the Ecole des Hautes-Études Sociales in 1901, and lectured on musical history at the Sorbonne from 1903 till 1913, when he retired to Switzerland. He returned to France in 1938 and was put in a concentration camp by the Germans and released only when mortally ill. He wrote a valuable work on the opera of the 17th century (*Histoire de l'opéra en Europe avant Lulli et Scarlatti*, 1895), biographies of Handel and Beethoven, and shorter studies of other composers. Among the works which have been translated into English are *Beethoven* (1917), *Beethoven the Creator* (1929), *Goethe and Beethoven* (1931), *Musicians of Former Days* (1933) and *Musicians of To-day* (1933). The subject of his ten-volume novel *Jean-Christophe* (1904–12) is a musician.

Rolle, Johann Heinrich (1718–85), German composer and organist. He held various musical appointments at Magdeburg, and was viola player in the orchestra of Frederick the Great from 1741 until 1746. He composed twenty oratorios, sets of cantatas, five Passions, motets and organ works.

Rolltrommel, *see* TENOR DRUM

Roman, Johan Helmich (1694–1758), Swedish composer. He studied under Ariosti and Pepusch in London, was in the service of the Duke of Newcastle, and was influenced by Handel. He returned to Stockholm (1720) where he was appointed *Kapellmeister* (1729). In 1740 he became a member of the Swedish Academy. He composed a Mass, motets, and psalms, 21 symphonies, overtures, concertos, sonatas for violin and for flute and vocal works.

romance (Ger., *Romanze*, It., *romanza*), a title used occasionally – and often somewhat vaguely – for a piece of instrumental or vocal music. Examples are the second movement of Mozart's piano concerto in D minor, K466, Beethoven's two romances for violin and orchestra, op 40 and op 50, Schumann's three romances, op 94, for oboe and piano, the second movement of his fourth symphony, and his four sets of *Romanzen und Balladen* for mixed voices, Brahms's fifteen romances from Tieck's *Magelone* for voice and piano, op 33, and Fauré's romance for violin and orchestra, op 28.

Roman de Fauvel (Fr.), a poem written from 1310 to 1314 by Gervais du Bus, in which he attacked abuses prevalent in the Church at the time. The subject of the poem, a fawn-coloured stallion, symbolises the vices whose initial letters spell *Fauvel*, i.e. *Flatterie, Avarice, Vilenie, Variété, Envie* and *Lâcheté*. One of the manuscripts of the poem, now in the Bibliothèque Nationale, Paris (facsimile edition by P. Aubry, 1907), contains several musical pieces copied by Chaillou de Pesstain in 1316, consisting of motets, monophonic pieces, and plainsong pieces. The motets, many of which are adaptations of pieces written up to a century earlier, are printed in *Polyphonic Music of the Fourteenth Century*, i, edited by L. Schrade (1956).

romanesca (Sp.), the earliest settings of this song ('O guardame las vacas') occur in Spanish lute-books about 1540, e.g. in Alonso Mudarra's *Tres libros de música en cifras para vihuela* (1546; modern edition by E. Pujol, 1949). A version used in a set of variations by A. de Valderravano in 1547 is printed in the *Historical Anthology of Music*, edited by A. T. Davison and W. Apel, no 124. The simplest form of its bass:

became known as the *romanesca* bass, and was used as a basis for variations in the same fashion as was the PASSAMEZZO bass, which differs from the *romanesca* only in its first note. Many early versions of *Greensleeves* employ *romanesca* harmonies, but the tune is better known today as one whose two halves are based on the *passamezzo* and *romanesca*, respectively. Frescobaldi wrote a set of variations, entitled *Partite sopra l'aria della Romanesca* in the *Toccate d'Involatura* of 1614, and his *Arie Musicali per Cantarsi* of 1630 contains an *Aria di romanesca* which begins thus:

Romano, Alessandro, *see* MERLO, ALESSANDRO

romantic music, the romantic era in music may be dated c. 1820 (Weber's *Der Freischütz* was produced in 1821; Schubert scored the *Unfinished* Symphony in 1822 and wrote *Die schöne Mullerin* in 1823) to c. 1920 (Schoenberg arrived at the principles of 'twelve-note composition' in 1921; Stravinsky composed *The Soldier's Tale* in 1918). In the broadest terms, the change from the classical age to the romantic may be described as a change of emphasis from the universal to the individual (Rousseau: 'I am different from all men I have seen'); from the conservative to the liberal (Hugo: '[Romanticism is] Liberalism in literature'); from the abstract to the poetic (Schumann: 'Romanticism is not a question of figures and forms, but of the composer's being a poet or not').

In such a period music, because its symbols are more remote than those of the other arts, is considered the ideal of the arts (E. T. A. Hoffmann: 'Music is the most romantic of all the arts'; Schopenhauer: 'Music is the direct manifestation of the original nature of the world, of the will'), music and poetry are more intimately allied (Baudelaire: 'La poésie touche à la musique par une prosodie dont les racines plongent plus avant dans l'âme humaine que ne l'indique aucune théorie classique'; Mallarmé: 'La musique rejoint le vers pour former, depuis Wagner, la poésie'), and a union of the arts becomes the highest form of art. There is a clear relation between these ideas and the chief forms which were developed in the 19th century, the *Lied*, the poetic piano-piece, the symphonic poem, and the music-drama.

Within the broad unifying ideas of romantic music there developed such apparent contradictions as those between the musician's remoteness from society, in that he regarded himself as essentially different from his fellows and was no longer, with them, a member of a patron's household, and his closeness to it, expressed in his use of folksong and national idioms and in the development of virtuosos and of public concerts: between the 'modernist' and more conservative elements in the movement itself, which led to the controversy between the supporters of the 'New Music' and those of Brahms; and between the cultivation of the smaller and more intimate forms and the creation of the largest and most spectacular. The attitude of the romantic musician to the past, which is chiefly, as in most periods, a rejection of the immediate past, may take the form of valuing it for its remoteness (e.g. the use of exotic and medieval subjects for operas), adopting its methods (e.g. Brahms's use of fugue and variations), and investigating and publishing its productions (e.g. the editions of the Tudor composers, and of Palestrina, Schütz, Purcell, Bach, Handel).

The changes in style and in technical matters which took place during the romantic period can be most clearly seen in (1) harmony, which went through a very rapid development of chromaticism (valuable to the romantic composer because of its ambiguity, sense of remoteness, and tension) to its extreme forms in *Tristan* and in the writing of Strauss and Schoenberg between 1900 and 1910; (2) the orchestra, which grew rapidly from the time of Berlioz's new conception of its possibilities of dramatic and poetic expression to the monster orchestras of 1900–1910 in Strauss's *Ein Heldenleben*, Schoenberg's *Gurrelieder* and Mahler's eighth symphony; and (3) the technique of instruments, which from the invention of the valve mechanism in 1813 kept pace with the development of chromatic harmony and the growth of the orchestra, and in the extension of the capacities of the piano and organ provided solo players with media of greatly increased power and range.

Of less importance were the changes in melodic style, which tended to become more lyrical in the small forms and more rhetorical in the large, in rhythmic style, which in some composers tended to become more diffused by the use of conflicting metres and of rubato, and in form, in which the romantic composers aimed at a greater continuity of texture, a more 'organic' unfolding and development of themes, and a closer relation to the programme in a symphonic poem or to the dramatic conflict in a music-drama.

In the two decades 1890–1910 a new conflict in the working out of the romantic ideal in music appeared between the two forms of the association of music and poetry, one represented by the extreme realism of Strauss's later tone-poems and the other by the Impressionist (or symbolist) style developed by Debussy under the influence of Mallarmé and his circle.

See IMPRESSIONISM

Romberg, Andreas Jakob (1767–1821), German violinist and composer. He played at the Concert Spirituel in Paris at the age of seventeen, toured with his cousin Bernhard from 1784 until 1796 and played with him in the Electoral Court Orchestra in Bonn from 1790 until 1793. He settled in Hamburg in 1801 until appointed court conductor in Gotha in 1815. He composed operas, choral works, symphonies, numerous violin concertos, string quartets and other chamber music, part-songs and pieces for violin.

Romberg, Bernhard (1767–1841), German cellist and composer. He toured with his cousin Andreas from 1784 until 1796 and played with him in the Electoral Court Orchestra in Bonn from 1790 until 1793. He taught at the Paris Conservatoire from 1800 until 1803, was first cellist and conductor (1815–19) of the Berlin Court Orchestra, and in 1819 retired to Hamburg. He also gave concerts in Britain, France, Spain, Austria, Sweden and Russia. He composed operas, ten cello concertos and other works for cello, incidental music for plays and chamber music.

Romberg, Sigmund (1887–1951), Hungarian born composer, who studied in Bucharest and Vienna before settling in the United States in 1909. Though originally an engineer, he established himself successfully in the world of operetta, where his successes included *The Student Prince*, *The Desert Song*, *The Rose of Stamboul*, *Blossom Time* and *New Moon*.

Romeo and Juliet, (1) dramatic symphony in seven movements for soloists, chorus and orchestra by Berlioz, op 17 (1839), described as 'after Shakespeare's tragedy'. The work is dedicated to Paganini, who had given Berlioz 20,000 francs. Some of the orchestral movements – especially the love music, the *Queen Mab* scherzo, and the music depicting the feast of the Capulets – are sometimes performed as a concert suite, usually in the wrong dramatic order and with damaging effect on the music.

(2) opera in five acts by Gounod, to a libretto by Barbier and Carré, based on Shakespeare's tragedy and first performed in Paris in 1867.

(3) orchestral piece by Chaikovsky, originally (1869) described as 'overture'. It was twice revised, in 1870 and 1880, and after the second revision called 'overture-fantasia.'

(4) ballet by Prokofiev, produced at the Bolshoi Theatre, Moscow, in 1935. Two orchestral suites have been drawn from it. Originally the work was given a happy ending, but this proved so unpopular with Russian audiences that the Shakespearian ending was restored.

Many other works have been written on the theme of Romeo and Juliet, including operas by Bellini, Steibelt, Zandonai, Sutermeister, Delius and Barkworth. The earliest known opera on the subject was by Benda (1776).

Rome Prize, *see* PRIX DE ROME

ronde (Fr.), semibreve.

rondeau (Fr.), (1) a form of medieval French poetry, written and set to music from the 13th to the 15th centuries. The poems have a REFRAIN which occurs two or three times in a single strophe. The music of a *rondeau* is composed of two sections, which serve both for the refrain and the verses. The simplest type with six lines is illustrated by the following 13th century example which has the form *aAabAB* (capital letters indicate the refrain which is italicized in the example):

In the more elaborate type the complete refrain was sung at the beginning as well as at the end, giving the form *ABaAabAB*; the first section of the refrain, and of each verse, had either two or three lines, and the second section two lines. The earlier musical settings of *rondeaux*, including those by Lescurel and the above anonymous example, were monophonic. Polyphonic *rondeaux* were composed by Adam de la Hale, by Machaut to his own poems, and by Grenon, Binchois, Dufay and many other composers in the 15th century. A representative selection of *rondeaux* is printed in Nigel Wilkins's *One Hundred Ballades, Rondeaux and Virelais* (1969);

(2) a form of French instrumental music in the baroque period, e.g., the *Rondeau* and the *Passacaille en rondeau* in François Couperin's eighth *ordre* for harpsichord, in which the opening section recurs after each of two (as in the former) or more (as in the latter) different sections, called *couplets*.

Rondes de Printemps, *see* IMAGES

Rondine, La (Fr., The Swallow), opera in two acts by Puccini, to a libretto by Giuseppe Adami (adapted from a German libretto by Alfred Maria Willner and Heinrich Reichert). The first performance was at Monte Carlo in 1917. In this lyric comedy, Puccini attempted to write the Italian equivalent of a Viennese operetta – the work was actually intended for Viennese performance, but the First World War intervened. The story is reminiscent of *La Traviata* (except that the heroine does not suffer from consumption), but the work for all its charm has never held a regular place in the Puccini repertory.

rondo, a form of instrumental music with a recurring section. It may occur as a single piece, e.g. Mozart's rondo for piano in A minor, K 511, or more often as the last movement of a sonata, symphony or concerto. The chief varieties of the form are: (a) the simple rondo, in which the opening section alternates with a number of different sections, or 'episodes', in the form *ABACADA* . . ., as in the third movement of Bach's violin concerto in E; (b) the symmetrical rondo, in which the first episode, initially in the dominant key, returns at a later stage in the tonic, as in the last movement of Beethoven's piano sonata in E flat, op 7, in the form *A B* (in the dominant) *A C* (in the relative minor) *A B* (in the tonic) *A*; or the last movement of Mozart's piano sonata in B flat, K 281, in the form *A B* (dominant) *A C* (relative minor) *A D* (subdominant) *A B* (tonic) *A*. In this variety, as in the 'sonata-rondo', there are commonly transitions between the sections and a coda, and the recurring section is varied and shortened, though always in the tonic key; (c) the sonata-rondo, having three sections, corresponding to the exposition, development and recapitulation of a sonata movement, and two episodes, of which the

first returns in the dominant and the second is actually a development. Instances are frequent in Beethoven, e.g. the last movement of the piano sonata in G, op 31, no 1, in the form *A B* (dominant) *A C* (development) *A B* (tonic) *A*. A variety of (b) and (c) is the short-circuited rondo, in which the third appearance of *A* is omitted, so that the form is *A B A C B A*. Examples are frequent in Mozart, Schubert and Brahms, e.g., the finale of Mozart's string quintet in G minor, K 516.

Ronger, Florimond, *see* HERVÉ

Röntgen, Julius (1855–1932), German composer of Dutch descent – he was the son of Engelbert Röntgen, Dutch violinist who was leader of the Leipzig Gewandhaus Orchestra from 1873. He studied at the Leipzig Conservatorium and from 1878 taught at the Amsterdam Music School. In 1885 he was one of the founders of the new Amsterdam Conservatory, which he directed from 1918 until 1924. He was a friend of Brahms and Grieg and edited Brahms's correspondence with Theodor Engelmann (1918). His compositions include two operas, a symphony, concertos for piano and violin, chamber music, and arrangements of Dutch folksongs. Donald Tovey called him 'one of the greatest musical scholars within the orbit of Brahms', and wrote analyses of several of his works.

root, a term used by 19th century theorists to indicate the 'fundamental' or 'generating' note of a chord. According to this theory the chords:

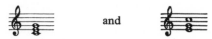

have the same 'root' C; the former is said to be in root position, i.e. having the 'root' in the lowest part, and the latter the first INVERSION. Likewise

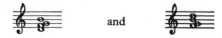

are respectively the second and third 'inversions' of the dominant seventh chord:

of which the 'root' is G.

See HARMONY, INVERSION

Rootham, Cyril Bradley (1875–1938), English organist and composer, pupil of Parratt and Stanford at the Royal College of Music, and at St. John's College, Cambridge, where he became organist in 1901. He composed an opera – *The Two Sisters* (Cambridge, 1922), two symphonies, choral and chamber music, songs and instrumental pieces.

Ropartz, Joseph Guy Marie (1864–1955), French composer, pupil of Dubois, Massenet and Franck. He became director of Nancy Conservatoire in 1894; Strasbourg Conservatoire, 1919–29. Later he retired to Brittany. He composed five symphonies and other orchestral works, two operas, chamber music, choral works, incidental music for plays, songs and instrumental music.

Rore, Cipriano de (1516–65), Flemish composer. He studied under Willaert in Venice, and in about 1547 went to Ferrara, where he was appointed court *maestro di cappella* about 1549. He was in Flanders from 1558 to 1561, then at Parma. He succeeded Willaert as *maestro di cappella* of St, Mark's, Venice, in 1563, but in the following year returned to the court at Parma. He published five books of five-part and three books of four-part madrigals, motets, Masses, a St. John Passion (1557) and other church music, and a volume of three-part fantasies and *ricercari* (with Willaert, 1549). The greatest madrigal writer of his time, he established the five-part madrigal in imitative polyphony as the norm, and after 1550 added to his style the expressive chromaticism and harmonic experiments which were developed by later composers, such as Marenzio and Gesualdo. A complete edition of his works by B. Meier was begun in 1959.

Rorem, Ned (born 1923), U.S. composer and author, pupil of Copland and Virgil Thomson. After studying in Philadelphia and New York, he won various awards and moved to Paris for six years. From 1959 until 1961 he was professor at Buffalo University, and from 1965 until 1967 at Utah. His works include several operas – one of them based on Strindberg's *Miss Julie* (1964) – song cycles, three symphonies and other orchestral music, a piano concerto in six movements, a *Paris Journal* and *Letters from Paris* for chorus and orchestra. His numerous songs have so far been the most successful side of his output – Virgil Thomson has compared them with those of Poulenc. His books include *The Paris Diary of Ned Rorem* (1966), *Music from Inside Out* (1967), *The New York Diary of Ned Rorem* (1967) and *Critical Affairs: A Composer's Journal* (1970).

Rosamunde, Fürstin von Cypern (Ger., *Rosamund, Princess of Cyprus*), play in four acts by Helmine von Chézy, produced, with incidental music by Schubert, at the Theater an der Wien, Vienna, 1823. The overture played at that performance had in fact been written for *Alfonso und Estrella*. The overture now known as *Rosamunde* was originally the overture to *Die Zauberharfe* (*The Magic Harp*) produced in 1820, and was published in a piano duet arrangement under the title *Ouvertüre zum Drama Rosamunde* about 1827.

The rest of the music consists of three entr'actes, two ballet movements, a romance for contralto, a chorus of spirits, a shepherd's song and shepherds' chorus, and a hunting chorus. Some authorities believe that one of the entr'actes (in B minor) is the 'lost' finale of the *Unfinished* symphony.

Rosbaud, Hans (1895–1962), Austrian conductor, famous for his performances of 20th century music. He held posts in Mainz, Munster, Strasbourg and Munich, and in 1948 became chief conductor of the Baden-Baden Radio. Among his numerous contributions to modern music was the première of Schoenberg's *Moses and Aaron* in Hamburg in 1954; he conducted the performance, in a concert version, at a few days' notice.

Roseingrave, English family of musicians. **Daniel Roseingrave** (c. 1650–1727), was an organist and composer, and a chorister of the Chapel Royal. He was organist, Gloucester Cathedral, 1679; Winchester, 1682; Salisbury, 1692; St. Patrick's and Christ Church,

Dublin, 1698. He composed services, anthems and other church music.

His son, **Ralph Roseingrave** (1695–1747), was also an organist and composer. He studied under his father, whom he succeeded as vicar-choral (1719) and organist (1726) of St. Patrick's Cathedral, Dublin, and as organist of Christ Church Cathedral (1727). He composed services and anthems.

The most important member of the family is **Thomas Roseingrave** (1690–1766), organist and composer, son of Daniel Roseingrave, and brother of Ralph. He studied under his father and at Trinity College, Dublin, travelled to Italy in 1710 and became a friend of Domenico Scarlatti. He settled in London, was appointed organist of St. George's, Hanover Square, in 1725 and later returned to Dublin. He composed an opera, six Italian cantatas, services and other church music, *Fifteen Voluntarys and Fugues* for organ or harpsichord, lessons for harpsichord or spinet, pieces for German flute with continuo, and additional songs for Scarlatti's opera *Narciso*, which he produced in London (1720). He edited a collection of sonatas by Scarlatti.

Rosenberg, Hilding (born 1892), Swedish composer and conductor, who studied in Stockholm, Germany, Austria and France. His output includes a series of dramatic oratorios based on Thomas Mann's *Joseph and his Brethren*, six symphonies (one of them an oratorio-symphony entitled *The Revelation of St John*), concertos and other orchestral works, twelve string quartets and instrumental pieces. Rosenberg is a composer of Jewish parentage, and his music has been described as possessing an 'Old Testament dignity'. The Schoenberg school shows its influence in his string quartets, but his period in Paris also had its effect – discernible in his witty ballet music, *Orpheus in Town*.

Rosenkavalier, Der (Ger., *The Knight of the Rose*), opera in three acts by Richard Strauss, to a libretto by Hugo von Hofmannsthal, first performed in Dresden in 1911. The Marschallin (Princess von Werdenberg) is entertaining her lover Octavian (a youth of seventeen) in the absence of her husband (a Field-Marshal), when Baron Ochs (a cousin of the Princess) is announced and Octavian is forced to disguise himself hastily as a chamber maid. The Baron, who is seeking a messenger to be the bearer of a silver rose (his betrothal token) to Sophie (daughter of a wealthy noble), is charmed by the supposed chambermaid. After his departure the Marschallin, who is cynical about her growing age, delivers the rose to Octavian in order that he may take it to Sophie. When Octavian visits Sophie to bring her the rose they fall in love, but her father is determined that she shall marry the Baron. In order to thwart this scheme Octavian returns to his maid's disguise to keep an appointment which he had made with the Baron to meet him at a country tavern. Here the Baron is made an object of ridicule. He calls for the police, who in turn demand an explanation of his presence there with a young woman. The Marschallin arrives and intervenes to settle the confusion. Sophie now receives her outraged father's permission not to marry the Baron. The Marschallin, now resigned to the loss of Octavian, induces Sophie's father to give his blessing to the young pair.

Rosenmüller, Johann (c. 1620–1684), German composer. He studied at Leipzig University, becoming assistant master at the Tomasschule in 1642 and organist at the Nikolaikirche in 1651. He was imprisoned for an offence against morals in 1655, but later escaped and went to Hamburg and to Venice until 1674, when he returned to Germany as court conductor at Wolfenbüttel. He composed sonatas and dance suites for instruments, Masses, Latin and German motets with instruments and continuo, cantatas, psalms and other church music. He was one of the most important composers of Lutheran church music between Schütz and Buxtehude. Part of his setting of the *Lamentations* for solo voice and continuo is printed in *Historical Anthology of Music*, edited by A. T. Davison and W. Apel, no 218. Eleven suites from his *Sonate da camera* for five instruments, first printed in Venice in 1670, are in *Denkmäler deutscher Tonkunst*, xviii.

Rosenthal, Manuel (born 1904), French composer and conductor, pupil of Ravel (from whose style his music derives). As a conductor he has worked principally in France and the United States. His compositions include operas and operettas (one of them entitled *The Bootleggers*), an oratorio (*St. Francis of Assisi*), a symphonic suite (*Joan of Arc*) and other orchestral works, songs and piano pieces. He has orchestrated some of Ravel's music.

Roslavetz, Nikolay Andreivich (1881–1944), Russian composer, who studied at the Moscow Conservatory and was notable for his forward-looking style. He wrote a cantata, *Heaven and Earth* (after Byron), a symphony, two symphonic poems, chamber music, piano pieces and songs.

Rosseter, Philip (1570–1623), English composer. In 1601 he published jointly with his friend Thomas Campion *A Booke of Ayres* in which his contribution of 21 lute songs formed the second part (modern edition by E. H. Fellowes, 1923). His *Lessons for Consort* (1609) comprise pieces 'made by sundry excellent authors and set to . . . the treble lute, treble viol, bass viol, bandora, cittern and the flute'.

Rossi, Lauro (1812–85), Italian composer and conductor. He studied in Naples and produced operas from the age of eighteen. He went to Milan in 1834, to Mexico in 1835 and later to Havana, New Orleans and Madras. On returning to Italy, he became director of the Milan Conservatorio (1850) and Naples Conservatorio (1870). He composed 29 operas, cantatas, an oratorio and a Mass, six fugues for string quartet, and songs, and wrote a textbook on harmony.

Rossi, Luigi (c. 1598–1653), Italian composer. He was a prolific writer of cantatas in monodic style, of which about 250 have survived. His arias are generally in binary form, but occasionally, as in the solo cantata 'Io lo vedo' (printed in the *Historical Anthology of Music*, edited by A. T. Davison and W. Apel, no 203), there is a short *da capo*. His longer cantatas show a clear distinction between recitative, aria and arioso. The opera *Palazzo d'Atlante incantato* was staged in the Barberini Palace in Rome in 1642, and *Orfeo*, the first Italian opera commissioned for performance in Paris though not the first to be played there, was produced at the Palais Royal in 1647. Extracts from *Orfeo* are printed in H. Goldschmidt, *Studien zur Geschichte der italienischen Oper im 17. Jahrhundert*, pages 295–311.

Rossi, Michelangelo, early 17th century Italian organist and composer who studied under Frescobaldi in Rome. He composed operas and a book of *Toccate e Correnti* (second edition, 1657) for organ or harpsichord. A well-known toccata in A has been attributed variously to M. Rossi, Purcell (improbable) and J. S. Bach (see G. Rose in *Acta Musicologica*, xl, 1968, page 203). Extracts from his opera *Erminia sul Giordano*, staged in the Barberini Palace, Rome, in 1633, are printed in H. Goldschmidt's *Studien zur Geschichte der italienischen Oper im 17. Jahrhundert*, pages 258–72. His collected keyboard works have been edited by John R. White (1966).

Rossi, Salomone (c. 1570–c. 1630), Jewish composer, who was at the court of Mantua from 1587 to 1628. He published five books of five-part madrigals between 1600 and 1622. The second book (1602) was probably the earliest book of madrigals to be published with a continuo part (*basso continuo per sonare in Concerto*). In 1628 he published a set of *Madrigaletti a due*. That he was one of the modernists of his time is also shown by his early use of the medium of the trio sonata in his two volumes of *Sinfonie e gagliarde* for three to five instruments (1607–8; modern ed. in 3 vols. by Fritz Rikko and Joel Newman). He published two further volumes of instrumental music, and in 1623 a volume of psalms, songs and hymns for the synagogue (modern edition by Fritz Rikko, 1967).

rossignol, *see* NIGHTINGALE

Gioacchino Antonio Rossini, the complete professional

Rossini, Gioacchino Antonio (1792–1868), Italian composer. The son of musical parents (his father was town trumpeter in Pesaro, his mother a singer), he studied at the Liceo Musicale in Bologna, and produced his first comic opera, *La cambiale di matrimonio*, in 1810, and *Tancredi*, his first *opera seria* and first great success, in 1813, both in Venice. Under the title

Almaviva, his *Il barbiere di Siviglia* had an unfortunate first night at Rome in 1816, but later became his greatest triumph, and today still represents the high watermark of brilliant *opera buffa*. Between 1816 and 1824, when he became director of the Théâtre Italien in Paris, *Otello* and *Mosè in Egitto* were produced in Naples, *La Cenerentola* in Rome, and *Semiramide* in Venice; in Paris were staged *Moïse* (a revised version of *Mosé in Egitto*), *Le Comte Ory*, and *Guillaume Tell*, apart from *Il barbiere di Siviglia*, his most renowned and greatest work. As a result of the revolution of 1830 his contract with the government to write five operas in the following ten years was broken; his claim to an annuity was, however, granted in 1835. He had composed forty operas in fifteen years, and during the remainder of his life he perplexed not only his admirers but also posterity by writing only the *Stabat mater* (1842), the *Petite Messe solennelle* (1864) and numerous short pieces. After living in Italy from 1830 to 1855, Rossini settled in Paris, where his house was famous as a meeting place and he as a wit. Besides opera, he composed cantatas, songs and piano pieces (*Péchés de vieillesse*, 1857–68), and six instrumental quartets. When he died, on Friday, 13 November 1868, he was buried in Paris near Cherubini, Chopin and Bellini. Nine years later his body was taken to Florence for reburial, when 6000 mourners, four military bands and 300 choristers attended the ceremony, during which the Prayer from *Mosè* was performed and encored.

> LORD DERWENT: *Rossini and some Forgotten Nightingales* (1934)
> F. TOYE: *Rossini; a study in Tragicomedy* (1934)
> F. BONAVIA: *Rossini* (1941)
> G. RADICIOTTI: *Gioacchino Rossini* (1927–29)
> H. WEINSTOCK: *Rossini*

Rostropovich, Mstislav Leopoldovich (born 1927), Russian cellist, pianist and conductor, one of the most renowned performers of the century. He studied at the Moscow Conservatory, where he later became a professor. His first appearance in western Europe was at Florence in 1951, and he made his U.S. debut five years later, playing Prokofiev's cello concerto (one of many works dedicated to him) at Carnegie Hall. Since that time he has also been a frequent visitor to Britain, where his friendship with Britten has resulted in many appearances at the Aldeburgh Festival and in several works written for him by Britten – including the cello symphony, a sonata for cello and piano, and two suites for solo cello. He is married to the soprano, Galina Vishnevskaya, with whom he frequently appears in the role of pianist (in which capacity he is also an impressive musician). As conductor, he has built up a further distinguished career at the Bolshoi Theatre. In 1974 he was given extended leave of absence from the Soviet Union to work in Britain.

rota, *see* ROTE

Rota, Nino (born 1911), Italian composer, pupil of Pizzetti and Casella. His works include operas (one of them, *Il Principe Porcaro*, being based on a Hans Andersen story), music for broadcasting, orchestral works, church music, instrumental music and songs, some to Tagore's poems. As a composer of film music, he achieved fame outside Italy with a score entitled *The Legend of the Glass Mountain*.

rotary valve, a special type of brass instrument valve. In Britain and the United States its use is largely confined to horns, but in many European countries it is equally common on trumpets.

rote (also **rotte, rota,** or **rotta**), a medieval instrument of the LYRE type, similar to the CRWTH.

Rouget de Lisle, Claude Joseph (1760–1836), French royalist soldier, poet, violinist, and composer. He settled in Strasbourg in 1791, wrote the words and music of the *Marseillaise* in 1792 and was imprisoned during the Revolution. After the violence subsided, he was released and re-entered the army. He went on to write patriotic hymns, romances with violin obbligato, *Chants français* with piano and libretti for operas.

roulade, ornamental vocal phrase, usually quite extended and traditionally (though not invariably) consisting of a descending scale with intermediate notes rising by one degree.

Rousseau, Jean-Jacques (1712–1778), French philosopher. Apart from his observations on music and musical education, his direct interventions in the musical life of his time are of some interest. His own education in music was slight, and his opera-ballet *Les Muses galantes*, privately produced in 1747, was a failure. His one-act *intermède*, *Le Devin du village*, was an immediate and lasting success, as were both the French and German versions of Favart's parody *Les Amours de Bastien et Bastienne* (the latter set by Mozart). Paradoxically, however, Rousseau took the side of Italian opera in the *guerre des bouffons*, declaring in his *Lettre sur la musique française* that 'the French have no music, and never will have any'.

Rousseau composed two pieces for the melodrama *Pygmalion* (Lyons, 1770), the rest of the music being by Coignet; some music for an opera *Daphnis et Chloé* and a volume of songs with the title *Consolations des misères de ma vie* were published after his death. In 1743 he proposed a new system of musical notation by numbers in a *Dissertation sur la musique moderne*. His articles on music in Diderót's *Encyclopédie* were severely criticised by Rameau, but his *Dictionnaire de musique* (1767) has valuable information on the musical terminology and ideas of the period. He wrote two pamphlets in support of Gluck, one being a commentary on *Alceste*, written at the request of the composer, in the form of a letter to Burney.

> A. R. OLIVER: *The Encyclopedists as Critics of Music* (1947)
> A. POUGIN: *Jean-Jacques Rousseau musicien* (1901)
> J. TIERSOT: *Jean-Jacques Rousseau* (1912)

Roussel, Albert (1869–1937), French composer. He was a marine officer in Indo-China from 1887 to 1893, then studied under Gigout and Vincent d'Indy at the Schola Cantorum, where he was appointed teacher of counterpoint in 1902. His visit to Cochin China and India in 1909 inspired his orchestral *Évocations* (1911) and his opera-ballet *Padmâvati* (1914–18). While composing the latter, he did war service with the Red Cross, which seriously damaged his health. He composed operas, ballets (including *Bacchus and Ariadne* and *The Spider's Banquet*), four symphonies, chamber music, songs and piano pieces. Taking its departure from the late romatic style of Franck and d'Indy, as in his first symphony (*Le Poème de la forêt*) of 1908, his music developed through a period of impressionism to the mature and impressive writing of the *Eightieth Psalm* for chorus and orchestra (1928) and the third symphony (1930).

> N. DEMUTH: *Albert Roussel* (1947)
> A. HOÉRÉE: *Albert Roussel* (1937)
> L. VUILLEMIN: *Albert Roussel et son oeuvre* (1924)

rovescio, al (It.), 'in reverse'. (1) melodic INVERSION; (2) RETROGRADE MOTION.

Rowley, Alec (1892–1958), English composer, pianist, organist and teacher. He composed two piano concertos, a suite and other works for orchestra, a ballet (Carnegie award, 1927), choral works, chamber music, instrumental pieces, and songs, mostly in a traditional British idiom.

Roxolane, La, name of Haydn's symphony no 63 in C (c. 1780). Haydn himself applied the name to the slow movement of this work, a set of variations which owes its name to the heroine of a play that had recently been a success, *Eszterházá.*

Royal Philharmonic Orchestra, one of London's five major symphony orchestras, founded by Sir Thomas Beecham in 1946. It takes its name from the Royal Philharmonic Society, though it has no official link with that organisation. In 1961, Rudolf Kempe succeeded Beecham as conductor.

Royal Philharmonic Society, a society for the encouragement of orchestral and instrumental music, founded in London in 1813. The title 'Royal' was granted on its centenary. The first series of concerts in 1813 were conducted at the piano by Clementi, and Salomon was the leader. Spohr conducted with a baton on his first visit to the society in 1820, and the term 'conductor' was used thereafter instead of 'at the pianoforte'. Many works were introduced to Britain at concerts of the society; among new works commissioned by it were Beethoven's ninth symphony (1825), Mendelssohn's *Italian* symphony (1833), Dvořák's *Husitzka* overture (1884), Saint-Saëns's symphony in C minor (1886), and Stanford's symphony in D minor (1911–12).

> R. ELKIN: *Royal Philharmonic* (1946)
> M. B. FOSTER: *History of the Philharmonic Society of London* (1912)
> T. RUSSELL: *Philharmonic Decade* (1945)

Rozsa, Miklos (born 1907), Hungarian born composer, who studied in Leipzig and later settled in the United States, working in the film industry from 1939. His works include a *Ballet Hungarica*, a symphony and other orchestral pieces, chamber music and many film scores.

rubato (It.), literally 'robbed', controlled flexibility of tempo by which notes are deprived of part of their length by slight quickening of the tempo, or given more than their strict length by slight slowing. Such 'expressive' variation of tempo may have been practised by solo performers in the 16th and 17th centuries; J. J. Froberger's lament (*Tombeau*) on the death of M. Blancrocher, for example, was marked by the composer to be played very slowly, and 'without observing any beat'. The use of *rubato* is referred to in the 18th century writings of C. P. E. Bach, Leopold Mozart and others. There are contemporary accounts of Chopin's style of *rubato*, and it is commonly applied to the performance of both solo and orchestral music of the 19th century.

In so far as *rubato*, which is at its best when least obtrusive and least susceptible to analysis, can be defined, it may affect: (1) an ornamental group of notes in a melody over a standing harmony; or (2) a phrase of melody, while the accompaniment keeps a strict rhythm; this is said to have been characteristic of Chopin's *rubato*, and Leopold Mozart observed that 'when a true virtuoso who is worthy of the title is to be accompanied, then one must not allow oneself to be beguiled by the postponing or anticipating of the notes which he knows how to shape so adroitly and touchingly, into hesitating or hurrying, but must continue to play throughout in the same manner' (translation by Editha Knocker); or (3) the melody and harmony of a phrase, period, or section of a composition.

> J. B. MCEWEN: *Tempo Rubato or Time-variation in Musical Performance* (1928)

Rubbra, Charles Edmund (born 1901), English composer, pupil of Vaughan Williams, Holst and R. O. Morris. His interest in the music of the 16th century has resulted in an acute awareness of melody and in the use of every kind of contrapuntal elaboration. He has, on the whole, been less successful in vocal music than in instrumental works, where his instinct for thematic development has had more scope. His orchestration, which at first was almost excessively austere, has shown a greater interest in colour in his later works. His compositions include nine symphonies, concertos for viola and piano, *Festival Overture*, Masses, motets, madrigals, string quartets, piano trio sonatas and songs. As pianist, he has directed his own piano trio; he was lecturer in composition at Oxford University from 1947 until 1968.

rubible, rubybe, *see* REBEC

Rubinstein, Anton Gregoryevich (1821–94), Russian composer who toured as a pianist from 1840 to 1843, studied with Dehn in Berlin (1844–46), and after other tours settled in 1858 in St. Petersburg, where he founded the Conservatory and was its director from 1862 until 1867 and again from 1887 until 1890. As a composer and teacher he represented the traditional western and anti-national ideas in Russian music. He adopted the methods of Liszt (whom he met in Paris) in such works as the three *Musical Portraits* (*Faust, Ivan the Terrible, Don Quixote*) for orchestra, but his numerous compositions had not enough individual qualities to take any lasting place in musical history. Among his shorter piano pieces is the celebrated Melody in F. His autobiography was translated into English by A. Delano (1890).

Nicholas Rubinstein (1835–81), Anton's brother, was a conductor and composer. He studied under Kullak (piano) and Dehn (composition) in Berlin from 1844 until 1846, and settled in Moscow, where he founded the Russian Musical Society in 1860 and the Conservatory in 1866. His pupils included Sauer, Siloti and Taneyev. He introduced the early works of Chaikovsky, who dedicated to him the piano trio in A minor, op 50.

Rubinstein, Artur (born 1887), Polish born pianist, pupil of Paderewski, among others. He made his debut at the age of twelve in a concert conducted by Joachim in Berlin. In 1905 he made his first appearances in Paris and London, and in 1906 toured the United States. In 1946 he became a U.S. citizen. One of the greatest (as well as one of the most enduring) pianists today, he is specially associated with the music of Chopin, Beethoven, Schubert, Schumann and Brahms. His performances are notable for their exceptional clarity of line, as well as for intelligence and warmth. A substantial autobiography, *My Young Years*, was published in 1973 and takes his career up to World War I. Today he chooses to call himself Arthur rather than Artur. Reference books disagree about his date of birth, some saying 1886 and others 1889; Rubinstein himself, in his autobiography, opts for 1887.

Ruckers, Hans (c. 1550–c. 1623), the first member of a family of harpsichord makers who lived in Antwerp, and whose instruments were famous for their quality and tone. They were made from c. 1580 to c. 1670, and many were still in use late in the 18th century. After Hans the chief members of the family were his sons Hans the younger, also called Jean (born 1578), and Andries (born 1579), and the latter's son Andries the younger (born 1607).

Rückpositif, *see* CHAIR ORGAN

Ruddigore, or **The Witch's Curse,** comic opera in two acts by Gilbert and Sullivan, first performed in London in 1887. The plot is a parody of Victorian melodrama.

Rue, *see* LA RUE

Ruffo, Vincenzo (c. 1510–87), Italian composer. He was *maestro di cappella* at Verona Cathedral (1554), Milan Cathedral (1563), Pistoia (1574) and at Sacile (1580). He published Masses, motets, Magnificats (1578) and five-part Psalms (1574) written 'in conformity with the decree of the Council of Trent'. Though he was a church musician, his madrigals, of which he published nine books, are more numerous than his sacred works. Without reaching great depth of expression, the madrigals have considerable variety of style, at times approaching the later *canzonetta* in lightness of touch. He also published a volume of three-part ensemble music entitled *Capricci in Musica* (1564). Three madrigals are printed in A. Einstein, *The Italian Madrigal*, volume iii, and three sacred and two secular pieces in L. Torchi, *L'arte musicale in Italia*, volume i.

> L. H. LOCKWOOD: 'Vincenzo Ruffo and Musical Reform after the Council of Trent', *Musical Quarterly*, xliii (1957)

Rugby, a symphonic movement by Honegger (1928) depicting a game of rugby football. It is the second of a group of three pieces, the first being *Pacific 231* and the third, *Mouvement Symphonique*.

ruggiero, an internationally known ballad and dance tune of the late 16th and early 17th centuries. It probably originated as a setting of lines from Ariosto's *Orlando furioso* beginning, 'Ruggier, qual sempre fui, tal' esser voglio'. The bass was used as the pattern for variations and for new melodies in the same way as were the PASSAMEZZO and the ROMANESCA:

Frescobaldi, for example, published in his *Toccate d'Intavolatura* ... (1614) a set of twelve variations on it, and a set of six variations on the tune of *Fra Jacopino*:

combined with it, which begins:

In addition, his *Primo Libro di Capricci* (1624) contains a *Capriccio sopra l'Aria di Ruggiero* which uses the phrases of the bass as points of imitation:

In England the title 'rogero' signified a ballad tune to which the same bass could be added, although it is not always present.

Ruggles, Carl (1876–1971), U.S. composer and painter, colleague of Edgard Varese in the International Composers' Guild and the Pan-American Association of Composers. Born of a whaling family from Cape Cod, Ruggles had a practical musical training as violinist and conductor. As a composer he developed a fiercely dissonant and personal idiom, with Schoenbergian leanings. Like Ives, he was one of the important questing figures of U.S. music – though in Europe his output was smaller and he has yet to achieve anything resembling Ives's popularity. But his *Angels*, for seven muted trumpets and trombones, caused a sensation at one of the early International Society for Contemporary Music festivals. His other works include *Marching Mountains* for chamber orchestra (1924, revised 1936), *Portals* for string orchestra (1926), *The Sun-Treader* for orchestra (1933), *Organum* for orchestra (1945) and *Vox Clamans in Deserto*, a song cycle for mezzo-soprano and chamber orchestra. In his later years he turned increasingly towards painting, and exhibited in museums.

Rührtrommel, *see* TENOR DRUM

Ruins of Athens, The (Ger., *Die Ruinen von Athen*), a play by August Friedrich Ferdinand von Kotzebue for which Beethoven composed incidental music, op 113, first produced in 1812, comprising an overture and eight pieces for chorus and orchestra. The music was composed for the opening of the German Theatre at Pest, in Hungary.

Rule Britannia, song with words probably by James Thomson and music by Thomas Arne, first performed in the masque *Alfred* (1740). It is generally sung today in a garbled version. There is a modern edition of the original score by Adam Carse. Beethoven wrote a set of variations for piano on the tune (1804) and also introduced it into the orchestral piece *Wellington's Sieg oder die Schlacht bei Vittoria* (Wellington's Victory or the Battle of Vittoria), op 91 (1813).

rule of the octave, a simple formula for harmonising a bass rising and descending stepwise through an octave, used in teaching harmony in the 18th century.

rumba, a fast Afro-Cuban dance in syncopated 2/4 time, often divided into eight beats in the pattern 3+3+2. It was introduced into ballroom dancing and jazz in the 1930s.

Russian bassoon (Fr., *basson russe*; Ger., *Russiches Fagott*), far from being a kind of bassoon this instrument, which paved the way for and was then ousted by the OPHICLEIDE, was made of brass and had a cup mouthpiece like a trombone. Its fingering was similar to that of the SERPENT. Its compass extended from about D below the bass clef upwards for two and a half octaves, but many of its notes apparently left much to be desired both in tone quality and accuracy of pitch.

Russian Easter Festival, overture by Rimsky-Korsakov, composed in 1888 and making use of melodies associated with the Russian Orthodox Church.

Russian Quartets (Ger., *Russische Quartette*), the title given to a set of six string quartets by Haydn, op 33 (1781) dedicated to the Grand Duke Paul of Russia. The set, also called *Gli Scherzi* (as Haydn gave the name of *scherzo* to the minuet movements) or *Jungfernquartette* (according to the title page of an old edition), includes: no 1 in B minor, no 2 in E major (*The Joke*), no 3 in C major (*The Bird* or *Birds*), no 4 in B major, no 5 in G major (*How do you do?*), and no 6 in D major.

Russlan and Ludmilla, opera in five acts by Glinka, to a libretto by Valeryan Fedorovich Shirkov and Konstantin Alexandrovich Bakhturin (founded on Pushkin's poem). It was first performed at St. Petersburg in 1842. The story concerns two lovers, one of whom is stolen by a dwarf but is rescued when the other succeeds in cutting off the dwarf's magic beard. Pushkin himself had hoped to write the libretto, but was killed in a duel before being able to do so.

Rust, Wilhelm (1822–92), German pianist, violinist and composer. He studied under Friedrich Schneider, and settled in Berlin as teacher. He went to Leipzig where he became organist (1878) and cantor (1880) at St. Thomas's Church and teacher at the Conservatorium. He edited eighteen volumes of the *Bach Gesellschaft* and the piano sonatas of his grandfather, Friedrich Wilhelm Rust (with additions of his own), and composed vocal works and pieces for piano.

Rustle of Spring, piano piece by Sinding, one of many he composed for that instrument, but the only one now widely played. It is the third of a set of six, published in 1909.

Ruthe (Ger.), a kind of birch occasionally used on the bass drum, often while an ordinary stick beats on the other head.

Ruy Blas, a play by Victor Hugo for which Mendelssohn composed an overture (C minor, op 95) and a two-part song (*Lied aus Ruy Blas*, op 77, no 3) for a production at Leipzig in 1839.

rybibe, *see* REBEC

S., abbreviation for SCHMIEDER, in the catalogue of Bach's works.

s. abbreviation for (1) *superius*, the highest part in 16th century vocal and instrumental compositions, i.e. *soprano*.

(2) *segno*, as in *d.s.*, *dal segno* (see REPEAT);

(3) *sinistra*, as in *m.s.* (in keyboard music) *mano sinistra*, left hand;

(4) *soh*, in TONIC SOL-FA, the fifth note (or dominant) of the major scale.

Sabaneyev, Leonid Leonidovich (born 1881), Russian music critic and writer. He studied under Taneyev at the Moscow Conservatory, and after the revolution was attached to the State Institute for Musical Science; in 1924 he left Russia. He has written *Modern Russian Composers* (1927), *Music for the Films* (1935), books on Wagner, Medtner and Skryabin and a history of Russian music. He has also composed songs and piano pieces.

Sabata, Victor de (1892–1967), Italian conductor and composer. He studied at the Milan Conservatory under Orefice from 1902–10 and later was appointed conductor at La Scala. He also conducted frequently in Europe and the United States. He composed operas, a ballet, orchestral works and chamber music.

Sacchini, Antonio Maria Gasparo (1730–86), Italian composer. He studied in Naples under Durante, lived in Rome (1762–69), Venice, Munich, Stuttgart, London (1772–82) and Paris, where he was under the patronage of Marie Antoinette and produced his best opera, *Oedipe à Colone* (1786). He composed about sixty operas, two symphonies, an intermezzo, oratorios, Masses, motets and other church music, chamber music, and sonatas for harpsichord and for violin.

Sacher, Paul (born 1906), Swiss conductor. He studied at the Basel Conservatorium under R. Moser and Weingartner, and at the University under Karl Nef. He founded the Basel Chamber Orchestra in 1926, the Chamber Choir in 1928 and the Schola Cantorum Basiliensis in 1933. He was appointed president of the Swiss section of the International Society for Contemporary Music in 1935 and conductor at the Collegium Musicum in Zurich in 1941. He has conducted many first performances of works by contemporary composers, and has been associated with the music of Bartók, among others.

Sachs, Hans (1494–1576), German shoemaker, poet and composer; the most famous personality amongst the Mastersingers of the 16th century. He is the hero of operas by Lortzing, Gyrowetz and Wagner (*Die Meistersinger*). Two of his songs are published in anthologies, one in Schering's *Geschichte der Musik in Beispielen*, no 78, and one in *Historical Anthology of Music*, edited by A. T. Davison and W. Apel, no 24. Facsimiles of his early songs (1514–18) are included in

F. H. Ellis's *The Early Meisterlieder of Hans Sachs* (1974).

Sachs, Kurt (1881–1959), German musicologist, who studied at Berlin University and under Fleischer, Kretzschmar and Wolf. In Berlin he was appointed professor of musicology at the University, teacher at the Hochschule and at the Academy for Church and School Music and curator of the State Collection of ancient instruments (1919). In 1938 he became professor of musicology at New York University. He has published in English *The Rise of Music in the Ancient World* (1943), *History of Musical Instruments* (1943), *The Commonwealth of Art* (1946), and *Our Musical Heritage* (1948; published in Britain as *A Short History of World Music*, 1950).

sackbut, although often said to be merely the early name for the TROMBONE, the sackbut was smaller in both bell and bore. Largely as a consequence of the latter it was lighter in tone, and this made it eminently suited to chamber music playing. Singly or paired it was often used in small combinations with woodwind instruments and strings.

Sackpfeife, *see* BAGPIPE

Sacre du Printemps, Le, *see* RITE OF SPRING

Sadko, opera in seven scenes by Rimsky-Korsakov, with a libretto by the composer and Vladimir Ivanovich Belsky. First performed in Moscow in 1898, the work concerns the wanderings, on sea and land, of the minstrel Sadko, and of his betrothal to Volkhova, the daughter of the Sea-King. Rimsky-Korsakov also composed a symphonic poem on the same subject.

Sadler's Wells, London theatre with origins dating back to the 17th century, though the present building was constructed as recently as 1931. It owes its name to medicinal wells discovered in the area by Sadler. In the present century it owes its existence to Lilian Baylis, who was responsible for its reopening as a home for opera, ballet and drama in conjunction with the Old Vic. The Sadler's Wells opera company resided there until 1968, when it moved into larger premises (the Coliseum) in central London. In 1974 the company changed its name to the English National Opera.

Saeverud, Harald (born 1897), Norwegian composer of nine symphonies, including a *Sinfonia Dolorosa* written in 1942. Though he has composed numerous large scale works, and incidental music for Ibsen's *Peer Gynt* (1947), he is at his most characteristic in writing for the piano. In this field he has produced a stirring *Ballad of Revolt* and other aphoristic pieces which have established him as one of the leading Scandinavian composers of the century, as important to Norway as Sibelius to Finland.

Saga, En (Fin., *A Tale*), symphonic poem by Sibelius (op 9, 1892; revised, 1901), the earliest of his works in this form. The music has a narrative quality, though the composer appears not to have had any specific story in mind.

Sagittarius, Henricus, *see* SCHÜTZ

St. Anne, the name of a hymn-tune, probably by Croft, first published in 1708. It begins:

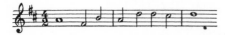

Coincidentally, Bach's Fugue in E flat at the end of the *Clavierübung*, Part III, has the same theme, and for that reason is sometimes called the 'St. Anne' fugue.

'St. Anthony' Variations, work by Brahms which exists in two forms – for orchestra, op 56a, and for two pianos, op 56b (in spite of the numbering, the piano version was written first). The theme on which the variations are based is known as the 'St. Anthony' Chorale. It comes from a partita for wind instruments in B flat by Haydn, though Haydn is now thought to have borrowed it from someone else. For this reason, Brahms's work should be referred to as the '*St. Anthony' Variations* rather than (as used to be the case) the 'Variations on a theme of Haydn'. There are eight variations in the set, and an extended finale. The first performance took place in Vienna in 1873.

St. Cecilia, patron saint of music – though for reasons which are obscure. The saint was martyred about A.D. 176 in Sicily for professing Christianity, and her association with music does not appear to have come about until the 16th century, evidently through the misreading of a Latin text. Nevertheless various works have been composed in tribute to her (by Purcell and Gounod, among others), an Italian orchestra and academy have been named after her, and she is commemorated annually on November 22nd.

Saint-Foix, Georges de (1874–1954), French musicologist, author of a famous study of Mozart in five volumes (the first two volumes written in collaboration with Théodore de Wyzéwa).

St. John Passion, accepted name for Bach's *Passion according to St. John*. It was first performed at St. Thomas's Church, Leipzig, in 1723, and is scored for solo voices, chorus and orchestra. Though the main source of the work was the gospel of St. John, Bach interpolated episodes from elsewhere, such as the tearing of the temple veil from St. Matthew's version of the Passion.

St. Martial School, an important school located in the vicinity of the Abbey of St. Martial, Limoges, which produced sequences, tropes and *prosulae* in the 10th and 11th centuries, and polyphonic settings of sacred songs, sequences and Benedicamus *prosulae* in the 12th century. The latter employ the style of both melismatic ORGANUM and note-for-note DISCANT, overlapping with the repertory of the NOTRE DAME school.

> J. CHAILLEY: *L'École musicale de Saint Martial de Limoges* (1960)
>
> P. EVANS: *The Early Trope Repertory of Saint Martial de Limoges* (1970)
>
> L. TREITLER: 'The Polyphony of St. Martial', *Journal of the American Musicological Society*, xvii (1964)

St. Matthew Passion, accepted name for Bach's *Passion according to St. Matthew*. It was first performed at St. Thomas's Church, Leipzig, in 1729, and like the St. John Passion it is scored for solo voices, chorus and orchestra. It is, however, written on a much grander scale than the earlier work. Again the text includes interpolations.

St. Nicolas, cantata, op 43, by Britten for tenor solo, mixed voices, string orchestra, piano duet, percussion and organ. It was composed in 1948, and has a text by Eric Crozier.

Saint of Bleecker Street, The, opera in three acts by Menotti, with a libretto by the composer. First performed in New York in 1954, the work is an attempt to recapture the blood-and-thunder *verismo* style of Puccini. The story, a religious melodrama, takes place in New York's Italian quarter.

St. Paul (Ger., *Paulus*), oratorio by Mendelssohn (op 36), completed in 1836 and first performed at the Düsseldorf Lower Rhine Festival in the spring of that year. The text is drawn from the Bible.

St. Paul's Suite, work for strings by Holst, written in 1913 for the orchestra of St. Paul's Girls School in London, where the composer was teacher of music.

Saint-Saëns, Charles Camille (1835–1921), French composer and pianist. He gave his first concert at the age of ten, and from 1848 studied organ under Benoist and composition under Halévy at the Conservatoire. He became organist at the Madeleine in 1857. The influence of Liszt, whom he met in 1852, turned him towards a 'cyclic' design in his symphonies and concertos – the third symphony is based on a single theme – and towards the symphonic poem (*Le Rouet d'Omphale*, 1871; *Phaëton*, 1873; *Danse macabre*, 1874; *La Jeunesse d'Hercule*, 1877). But Liszt had no effect on the rather shallow elegance of Saint-Saëns' style or the natural lucidity of his form. His first opera, *Le Timbre d'argent*, composed in 1864–5, was produced in 1877,

Charles Camille Saint-Saëns, pianist, organist, composer, and critic, dominant figure in Paris musical life at the turn of the century.

Salome: the first performance in Dresden in 1905. The photograph shows Frau Wittich as if about to launch into her dance. In fact in the first performance the dance was performed by a ballerina. Subsequently Frau Wittich insisted on doing it herself, much to the composer's distress.

and the first performance of *Samson et Dalila*, which was refused by the Paris Opera until 1892, was given (in German) by Liszt at Weimar in the same year. It is his most lasting work. He was an extremely prolific composer (his opus numbers run to 169 and his compositions to the last year of his life), but his music, though meticulously crafted, suffers from superficiality and lack of adventurousness. His *Carnival of the Animals*, a 'zoological fantasy' for two pianists and orchestra, retains its wit and charm, however; and his G minor piano concerto (no 2) remains popular with soloists – not many works, after all, have the attraction of 'beginning like Bach and ending like Offenbach'.

Saint-Saëns edited the works of Rameau and wrote essays on music and philosophy, and some plays and poems. Two volumes of his essays have been translated into English: *Musical Memories* (1921) and *Outspoken Essays* (1922).

A. DANDELOT: *La Vie et l'oeuvre de Saint-Saëns* (1930)

A. HERVEY: *Saint-Saëns* (1921)

L. WATSON: *Camille Saint-Saëns* (1923)

J. HARDING: *Saint-Saëns and his Circle* (1965)

Saite (Ger.), string; *Saiteninstrument*, string instrument.

salicional, salicet, salcional, a soft eight foot metal organ stop producing a tone bearing some resemblance to that of stringed instruments.

Salieri, Antonio (1750–1825), Italian composer, conductor and teacher. He studied at the San Marco singing school in Venice and under Florian Gassmann, who took him to Vienna (1766), where he conducted at the Court Opera as Gassmann's deputy (1770) and succeeded him as chamber composer and conductor of the Italian Opera (1774). His intrigues against Mozart were inflated into the story that he poisoned Mozart, used in a dramatic poem by Pushkin (1830); this became the libretto of Rimsky-Korsakov's opera *Mozart and Salieri* (1898).

Salieri composed operas for several Italian cities 1778–79) and one for Paris, *Les Danaides* (1784), announced as written in collaboration with Gluck (who was then his teacher) but actually entirely by Salieri. He succeeded Bonno as court musical director in Vienna (1788), conducted the Tonkünstler Society until 1818, and in 1824 retired from court service. He was a teacher of Beethoven, Schubert and Liszt. His works include about forty operas, four oratorios, cantatas, Masses, a Passion, a Requiem, motets and other church music, a symphony, concertos for organ, for two pianos, and for flute and oboe, odes, canons and other vocal works.

Salinas, Francisco de (1513–90), Spanish musical theorist and organist. Blind from the age of ten, he went to Italy in 1538 and lived in Rome and in Naples until 1561 as organist to the Spanish Viceroy. He returned to Spain and became organist of León in 1563. From 1567 to 1587 he was a professor at the University of Salamanca. In his theoretical treatise *De musica libri septem* (1577) he expounded the theories of Zarlino and quoted a number of Spanish folk songs of the time.

J. B. TREND: 'Salinas', in *Music and Letters*, viii (1927), page 13

Salò, (originally **di Bertolotti**), **Gasparo, da** (1540–1609), Italian violin maker and grandson of the lute maker, Santino di Bertolotti. He was one of the first to use the form of the violin instead of the viol.

Salome, opera in one act by Richard Strauss, a setting of Oscar Wilde's drama, translated into German by Hedwig Lachmann. It was first performed in Dresden in 1905.

The Tetrarch, Herod, has imprisoned Jokanaan (John the Baptist) in a cistern as punishment for his words against Herod's marriage to his brother's wife Herodias. Salome (daughter of Herodias), hearing the voice of the prophet, becomes fascinated by him and demands to be allowed to see him. Narraboth (the captain of the guard, who loves Salome) against strict orders gives in to her and Jokanaan is brought forth. He denounces Herodias and begs Salome to turn to a virtuous life; when she pleads for a kiss from his lips he rebukes her. Narraboth, in despair, kills himself. Jokanaan, appalled by Salome, returns to his prison. Herod, Herodias and their suite arrive. Herodias demands that the prophet be given to the Jews for punishment but Herod replies that he is holy and must not be injured. Herod, disturbed by the prophet's voice and by two Nazarenes who announce that the Messiah has already come, asks Salome to dance for him. She finally consents after he swears an oath to grant anything she demands. She dances the dance of the seven veils and then asks for the head of Jokanaan as her reward. Herod begs her to ask for anything else but when she refuses he reluctantly orders the execution of the prophet. Salome is presented with his head, addresses ecstatic words of love to it and kisses the mouth. Herodias is triumphant but Herod is revolted by the scene and, unable to bear it any longer, commands his soldiers to kill Salome.

In its early days, Strauss's one-act shocker caused a scandal almost everywhere it was performed. Its Vienna première was cancelled by the censors; in New York it caused such a storm of protest in 1907 that it was quickly dropped from the repertory of the Metropolitan; in Berlin, the Kaiser tried to prevent its performance, and in London in 1910 the Lord Chamberlain asked for certain lines to be deleted. In due course, however, the piece established itself. Famous exponents of the title role have included Ljuba Welitsch, Birgit Nilsson and Anja Silja.

Salomon, Johann Peter (1745–1815), German born violinist, composer, and concert promoter. He studied in Bonn, where he became a member of the Electoral orchestra in 1758. After a concert tour in 1765 he was appointed orchestra leader and composer to Prince Heinrich of Prussia in Rheinsberg. In 1781 he visited Paris and then settled in London where he played symphonies by Haydn and Mozart in his concerts (1786). He arranged Haydn's visits to England (1791–2 and 1794–5); hence the twelve symphonies written for those visits are known as the 'Salomon' symphonies. He gave Haydn the text which Lidley had adapted from *Paradise Lost*, and which became, in a translation by van Swieten, the text of *The Creation*.

Salón México, El, orchestral work by Copland, first performed in 1937 in Mexico City. The music, an evocation of a Mexican dance hall, incorporates folk song material.

saltando (It.), leaping. In string-playing indicates that the bow is to be allowed to bounce lightly on the string. The French term for this is '*sautillé*'.

saltarello (It., from *saltare*, to jump), an Italian dance in quick tempo, most often in 6/8 time with a jumping effect in the rhythm, as in the first theme of the last movement of Mendelssohn's *Italian* symphony:

An example dating from as long ago as the 14th century is printed in Schering's *History of Music in Examples*, no 28. The saltarello also occurs in the 16th and early 17th century as the second dance (see NACHTANZ) of a pair of which the first is a passamezzo. Peter Philips follows the seven variations of his *Galiarda Passamezzo* (of which the opening is quoted under PASSAMEZZO) with a *Saltarella* which begins thus:

In general the dance is like a somewhat jerky version of a tarantella. The modern Italian spelling of the word is '*salterello*'.

salterio (It.), psaltery. *Salterio tedesco*, dulcimer.

Salve Regina (Lat.), 'hail Queen', an antiphon to the Blessed Virgin Mary sung at the end of Compline, the last service of the day, in the Latin liturgy. It has long been attributed to Hermannus Contractus, but the words are most probably by Aymar, Bishop of Puy (died 1098), who may or may not have written the music. The Sarum form began thus:

Settings of the words are very numerous from early in the 15th century to Haydn, who wrote four. Those in polyphonic style sometimes made use of the plainsong melody, as can be seen in this example by Walter Lambe, c. 1490:

Salzédo, Carlos (1885–1961), French born harpist and composer. He studied at the Paris Conservatoire, and settled in New York where he became first harpist at the Metropolitan Opera (1909) and teacher at the Juilliard School. He also became head of the harp department at the Curtis Institute in Philadelphia, and with Varèse founded the International Composer's Guild (1921). His works include music for harp and orchestra, a concerto for harp and seven wind instruments and other works for harp and groups of instruments, and pieces for harp solo and for harp ensemble. He published *Modern Study of the Harp* (1921).

Salzman, Eric (born 1933), U.S. composer and critic, pupil of Sessions and Babbitt. Many of his works are for voice, instruments and prerecorded tape, including *Foxes and Hedgehogs* (1967), a piece of music theatre with words by John Ashbery. He also wrote a series of *Verses* (1967) for voice, guitar and multitrack tape; *The Peloponnesian War* (1968), a ballet with Daniel Negrin; and *The Nude Paper Sermon* for speaker, Renaissance consort, chorus and electronics. He is the author of *Twentieth-Century Music: an Introduction* (1967).

samba, dance of Portuguese-Brazilian origins, basically in 2/4 time, but with syncopated rhythmic patterns. In Brazil it is a traditional form of carnival music, and in its authentic form is danced by groups of people forming a circle. It has also been popularized in ballrooms all over the world, in a form danced by couples at a more moderate tempo.

Saminsky, Lazare (1882–1959), Russian born composer and writer on music. He studied at the Moscow Conservatory and the Petrograd Conservatory under Rimsky-Korsakov and Glazunov. He visited London and Paris and in 1920 settled in the United States, where he became director of music at the Temple Emanu-El, New York. He was one of the founders of the American League of Composers (1932). His works include an opera-ballet, *Jephtha's Daughter*, five symphonies (one with chorus), symphonic poems, a Requiem, chamber music, choral works, songs and piano pieces. He was author of *Music of Our Day* (1923) and *Music of the Ghetto and the Bible* (1934).

Sammartini (San Martini), Giovanni Battista (c. 1698–1775), Italian composer and organist. He studied in Milan, where from 1725 he held several posts as organist and was also *maestro di cappella* at various churches and at the Convent of Santa Maria Maddalena (1730–70). He taught Gluck from 1737 until 1741. His prolific output, believed to run to more than 2,000 works, includes operas, serenatas, more than 23 symphonies, overtures, many Masses, motets and other church music, *concerti grossi*, trio sonatas and other chamber music, violin concertos and other works for violin. He was the most important Italian composer of symphonies of his day, and his instrumental style contains notable foretastes of Haydn and Mozart.

Giuseppe Sammartini (1693–1750), his brother, was an oboist and composer. He settled in London (c. 1727) where he gave concerts with Arrigoni in 1732 and later was appointed musical director of chamber concerts for the Prince of Wales. He composed twelve *concerti grossi*, overtures, concertos for violin and for harpsichord, an oratorio, trio sonatas and other chamber music, violin sonatas and flute solos and duets.

Samson, oratorio by Handel. The text by Newburgh Hamilton is based on poems by Milton (*Samson Agonistes*, *Ode on the Morning of Christ's Nativity* and *At a Solemn Musick*). The first performance was in London in 1743. Handel declared this to be his favourite of all his oratorios.

Samson and Delilah (Fr., *Samson et Dalila*), opera in three acts by Saint-Saëns, with a libretto by Ferdinand Lemaire based on the biblical story about the betrayal of the Hebrew hero Samson by the seductress Delilah. The work was first performed (in Germany) at Weimar in 1877. The first French performance was at Rouen in 1890, but it was not staged in Britain until 1909 because of its biblical subject.

San Carlo, Naples, Teatro di, one of Italy's leading opera houses, built in 270 days and opened in 1737 with Sarro's *Achille in Sciro*. In 1816 it was destroyed by fire, but was rebuilt. Rossini composed several operas for this theatre, and Donizetti his *Lucia di Lammermoor* (1835).

Sances, Giovanni Felice (c. 1600–1679), Italian composer and singer. He was a tenor (1636), assistant *Kapellmeister* (1649) and *Kapellmeister* (1669) at the Vienna Court Chapel. He composed operas (one with Emperor Leopold I), oratorios, and monodies and duets with continuo.

Sancta Civitas (*The Holy City*), oratorio by Vaughan Williams for solo voices, chorus and orchestra, with a text from the Bible and other sources. Its first performance was at Oxford in 1926.

Sanctus (Lat.), 'holy, holy.' One of the parts of the Ordinary of the MASS and the Communion SERVICE. The text usually comprises three sections: *Sanctus, Pleni sunt coeli*, and *Benedictus qui venit*.

Sandrin (originally **Regnault**), **Pierre** (died after 1561), French composer. From about 1540 he was a singer at the King's Chapel at Paris. He also spent some time in the service of Ippolyte d'Este, Cardinal of Ferrara, and in 1554 was a singer in the Cardinal's chapel at Sienna. A modern edition by Albert Seay of his complete works, consisting of fifty *chansons* and possibly one Italian madrigal, was published in 1968.

His 'Doulce memoire' became one of the most popular *chansons* of the 16th century.

sanft (Ger.), soft, gentle.

San Martini, *see* SAMMARTINI

Sappho (Fr., *Sapho*), opera in two, three or four acts by Gounod, to a libretto by Emile Augier, produced at the Paris Opéra in 1851. Composed for the prima donna, Pauline Viardot, this was Gounod's first opera which he revised several times. The heroine is the Greek poetess.

Massenet's five act opera of the same title (1897) was based on a novel by Alphonse Daudet whose hero falls in love with an artist's model of Sappho.

sarabande (Fr.), a dance in slow 3/2 or 3/4 time which was one of the four dances (allemande, courante, sarabande, gigue) regularly included in the SUITE between c. 1650 and c. 1750. In Bach and Handel it often has a predominating rhythm which emphasizes the second beat:

as in Handel's harpsichord suite no 11:

The dance seems to have been originally introduced from the East into Spain, where it was ordered to be suppressed in the 16th century because of its lascivious character. Orlando Gibbons's *Sarabande* with variations is an innocuous tune in folksong style in moderately quick 6/8 time. Later in the century it frequently appears as a slow and rather pensive movement, as in Blow's *Sarabande for the Graces* in *Venus and Adonis* (c. 1682):

Sarasate (Sarasate y Navascues), Pablo Martin Melitón (1844–1908), Spanish violinist and composer.

After studying at the Paris Conservatoire, he rapidly made a reputation as a soloist and toured widely, both in Europe and the United States. Among the works written for him were Lalo's first violin concerto and Bruch's second violin concerto. He wrote a number of works for the violin, as well as transcriptions of Spanish dances.

sardana (Sp.), national dance of Catalonia, often in fast 6/8 time and performed in a circle to an accompaniment of pipe and drum.

Sargent, (Harold) Malcolm (Watts) (1895–1967), English conductor, one of the most popular of his day. He began his career as an organist, and was also a pianist (trained by Moiseiwitsch) and at one time a composer. He directed his own *Impressions on a Windy Day* at a promenade concert in London in 1921. Thereafter he turned increasingly to conducting, working with the British National Opera Company, the D'Oyly Carte Opera (1926), Robert Mayer's children's concerts, the Courtauld-Sargent concerts (from 1929), The Royal Choral Society at the Albert Hall (from 1928), the Leeds Festivals and the B.B.C. Symphony Orchestra (1951–7). He was knighted in 1947. During the last sixteen years of his life he was conductor-in-chief of the London Proms, an activity into which he flung himself with relish, winning the enthusiasm of a huge young audience. He arranged many traditional songs and carols, and championed an authentic version of Arne's 'Rule, Britannia'. As a conductor he was associated particularly with British music.

Sarro (Sarri), Domenico (1678–1744), Italian composer. He studied under Provenzale at the Conservatorio de' Turchini in Naples, where he became assistant *maestro di cappella* in 1712 and later *maestro di cappella* of the court chapel. His works include about fifty operas, oratorios, cantatas, Masses and other church music, a concerto for strings and flute, serenades and arias. Sarro helped to bring fame to the librettist Metastasio by setting *Dido abbandonata* in 1724 – it was Metastasio's first libretto.

sarrusophone, a family of double reed instruments with a wide conical bore and made of brass, invented in the latter part of the last century by a French bandmaster named Sarrus. They were constructed on the basis of a bassoon and have the same fingering. Primarily intended for use in military bands as substitutes for oboes and bassoons, they have been made in eight sizes ranging from the high sopranino in E flat to the low contrabass, also in E flat. These two seem to have been very little used, but separating them are five instruments that correspond in both name and pitch to the members of SAXOPHONE family – that is the soprano in B flat, alto in E flat, tenor in B flat, baritone in E flat and bass in B flat. It is, however, the contrabass sarrusophone in C, made specially for symphonic work, that has captured the attention of composers, particularly, but by no means only, French ones. It might have become a formidable rival to the double-bassoon had not that instrument been much improved during the last century. Even today it is not quite obsolete, for it occasionally appears in modern scores, among the Stravinsky's *Threni* and Elisabeth Lutyens's *Music for Orchestra II*. Holbrooke in *Apollo and the seaman* wrote for both the alto sarrusophone, which he misleading called a soprano, and the contrabass in E flat.

Sarti, Giuseppe (1729–1802), Italian composer and conductor, who studied under Martini in Bologna. He was organist at Faenza Cathedral in 1748; opera conductor under Mingotti in 1752; director of Italian opera (1753) and court conductor (1755) in Copenhagen. He visited Italy from 1765–8 and returned to Copenhagen as court composer (1768) and court opera conductor (1770). He was director of the Ospedaletto Conservatorio, Venice (1775); *maestro di cappella* at Milan Cathedral (1779); court conductor to Catherine II of Russia (1784); founder-director of a music school in the Ukraine (1787), and director of the new conservatory in St. Petersburg, 1793. Sarti invented a machine for counting sound vibrations. He was a teacher of Cherubini. His works include some seventy operas to Italian, Danish and Russian texts, an oratorio, Requiem, Te Deum, Masses, motets and other church music, choral works, two concerti, and harpsichord sonatas. Mozart used the aria 'Come un agnello' from his opera *Fra due litiganti* (1782) in the banquet music in the finale of the second act of *Don Giovanni* (1787) and wrote variations on it for piano solo, K 460.

Sarum Rite, the liturgy, with its plainsong, of the cathedral church of Salisbury, which was the most widely used rite in England until the Reformation. Its origins are traced back to the work of St. Osmund (died 1099), and its earliest surviving complete form is contained in a manuscript *Consuetudinarium* dating from c. 1210.

> W. H. FRERE: *The Use of Sarum* (two volumes 1898, 1901); *The Sarum Gradual*, facsimile edition (1894); *The Sarum Antiphonary*, facsimile edition (1901–24)

sassophone (It.), SAXOPHONE.

Satie, Erik Alfred Leslie (1866–1925), French composer, of partly Scottish descent. He studied at the Paris Conservatoire from 1879 and at the Schola Cantorum under d'Indy and Roussel from 1905–8. He became friends with Debussy in 1890 and had some influence on his style. He composed three ballets (including *Parade*, produced by Satie, Cocteau, Picasso and Diaghilev in Paris, 1917), operettas, a symphonic drama *Socrate*, *Messe des pauvres* for voice and organ, four sets of songs and many piano pieces. The ironically humorous character of his style, which is in strong contrast with the impressionism of his period, is indicated in the satirical titles of his piano pieces, e.g. *Pièces froides*, *Pièces en forme de poire*, *Choses vues à droite et à gauche (sans lunettes)*, *Aperçus désagréables*, *Croquis et agaceries d'un gros bonhomme en bois*. He worked for a period as a café pianist, and this had its effect on the personality of his music. At one time he was regarded merely as a talented eccentric, but today his importance is more widely recognized. He inspired not only LES SIX and the ÉCOLE D' ARCUEIL, but his musical surrealism also made him the father-figure of a number of more recent composers, including John Cage and Maurizio Kagel.

> R. MYERS: *Erik Satie* (1948)
> P.-D. TEMPLIER: *Erik Satie* (1932)

Satz (Ger.), (1) a movement of a sonata, symphony, suite, etc., e.g., *erster Satz*, 'first movement'. Schubert's *Quartettsatz* is an isolated quartet movement intended by the composer to be the first movement of an extended work;

(2) composition or musical setting (in full *Tonsatz*, 'musical composition');

(3) style in composition, e.g. *freier Satz*, 'free style'; *strenger Satz*, 'strict style';

(4) theme or subject, e.g. *Hauptsatz* and *Seitensatz*, 'first subject' and 'second subject'.

saudades, Portuguese word, usually used in the plural, evoking 'nostalgia' and 'wistful yearning'. It was used as the title of a set of three songs by Peter Warlock (1917) comprising 'Along the Stream' (Li Po, translated by L. Cranmer-Byng), 'Take, O take those lips away' (Shakespeare) and 'Heracleitus' (Callimachus, translated by W. Cory).

Saudades do Brasil (*Nostalgia for Brazil*), two volumes of piano pieces by Milhaud composed 1920–1. The music was the outcome of the composer's spell in Rio de Janeiro as an attaché to the French legation. He also wrote an orchestral suite of the same title.

Sauguet, Henri (born 1901), French composer and critic, pupil of Koechlin and disciple of Satie. His music is notable for its clarity and wit, and includes several operas and ballets (*Les Caprices de Marianne*, *La Chartreuse de Parme*, *Les Forains*, etc.), three symphonies and other orchestral works, cantatas, songs and chamber music.

Saul, oratorio by Handel, with a text by Charles Jennens based on the Bible. Its first performance was in London in 1739. The so-called 'Dead March' from *Saul* has long enjoyed a separate popularity. The oratorio was first performed in London on January 16th, 1739.

Saul and David, opera in four acts by Nielsen, with a libretto by Einar Christiansen, based on the Old Testament. This was the first of the Danish composer's two operas, and had its première in Copenhagen in 1902.

sausage bassoon, *see* RACKET

sautillé, Fr., 'leaping'.

> *See* SALTANDO

Sauveur, Joseph (1653–1716), French scholar. Though a deaf-mute from birth, he studied and wrote about the science of sounds, which he was the first to call 'acoustics'. He was elected a member of the Académie in 1696.

Savitri, chamber opera in one act by Holst, composed in 1908 but not performed until 1916 (in London). The libretto, by the composer, is based on an episode in the *Mahabharata* (Hindu scriptures). It tells how Death comes to claim a woodman, Satyavan, but changes his mind when the woodman's wife, Savitri, placates him with love and reason. Scored for three singers, off-stage female chorus and chamber ensemble, *Savitri* was written in the wake of (and was to some extent a distillation of) a much larger and more powerful opera, *Sita*, the manuscript of which is in the British Museum.

Savoy Operas, *see* SULLIVAN

saw, musical, a hand-saw held between the knees and played with a bow while the left hand alters the pitch by bending the blade.

> *See* FLEXATONE

Sax, Adolphe (1814–94), real name was Antoine Joseph Sax, the inventor of the saxhorn and saxophone and the most distinguished member of a Belgian family of instrument makers.

saxhorn, family of brass instruments, invented by Adolphe Sax and patented by him in 1845. His invention resulted from the application of valves instead of keys to the BUGLE family. The instrument was made in at least seven sizes, the highest of which are virtually cornets in E flat and B flat, and the lowest tubas, also in E flat and B flat. The great confusion about these instruments is due to the variety of names they were given in different countries. In particular, they have often been referred to as FLUGELHORNS, but although similar in most respects they have a smaller bore and consequently a different tone quality.

saxophone (It. *sassophone*; Ger. *Saxophon*). In 1846, Adolphe Sax patented the saxophone, an instrument that, although made of brass, belongs rather to the woodwind group. A single reed type set in a clarinet-type mouthpiece is used, while the conical shape of the bore as well as the fingering relate the instrument to the OBOE. Of the seven members of the family the little used soprano in E flat is straight like a clarinet, while the alto in E flat, tenor in B flat, baritone in E flat, bass in B flat, and the rarely to be found contrabass in E flat all have an upturned bell like a bass-clarinet. The soprano in B flat is made in both shapes. For practical purposes today the family can be reduced to four instruments – soprano, alto, tenor and baritone. These all have a normal written compass from the B flat below middle C to the F above the stave, although higher notes can be produced by means of a harmonic technique using unorthodox fingerings. On the soprano saxophone, the notes sound a tone lower; on the alto a major sixth lower; on the tenor a major ninth lower; and one the baritone a major thirteenth lower. Consequently middle C written for each of the seven instruments would sound:

Sections of saxophones – usually made up of two altos, two tenors and a baritone, sometimes with one player doubling on a soprano – form an essential part of larger jazz and dance bands, but in symphony orchestras they are usually found singly. There are, however, many exceptions, among them d'Indy's *Fervaal* and Strauss's *Sinfonia Domestica*, both of which have parts for four saxophones. Ravel in *Bolero* asks for, but rarely gets, a sopranino in addition to a soprano and a tenor, while in several works Penderecki favours a trio made up of two altos and a baritone. Among the best known uses of a single saxophone are Bizet's *L'Arlesienne*, Prokofiev's *Romeo and Juliet* and Vaughan Williams's Sixth Symphony. Saxophone concertos and other works featuring the instrument as a soloist, most of them for the alto, have been written by many composers, including Debussy and Glazunov.

Scacchi, Marco (c. 1600–before 1685), Italian composer. He studied under Anerio. From 1623 to 1648 he was composer at the Polish Court in Warsaw, after

which he returned to Italy. He composed an opera, an oratorio, Masses, motets and madrigals. He published in two books (1643, 1644) a critical examination of the style of the Psalms of Paul Siefert of Danzig, and proposed a division of styles into those appropriate to the church, to the chamber, and to the theatre.

Scala, La, (Teatro alla Scala) Milan, Italy's leading opera house, opened in 1778 with Salieri's *Europa Riconosciuta*. Among the many important works written for this theatre have been Rossini's *La Pietra di Paragone* and *Il Turco in Italia*, Donizetti's *Lucrezia Borgia*, Bellini's *Norma*, Verdi's *Nabucco*, *Otello* and *Falstaff*, and Puccini's *Madama Butterfly*. Artistically, perhaps the theatre's greatest era was when Toscanini reigned as its conductor between 1898 and 1903 and again between 1921 and 1929.

Scala di Seta, La, see SILKEN LADDER

scale (Fr., *gamme*; Ger., *Tonleiter*; It., *scala*), a progression of notes in ascending or descending order, so arranged for theoretical purposes, for vocal or instrumental exercise, or as part of a composition. In composition scales are used in a great variety of ways, e.g. in transitional passage work, in ornamentation (*see* PASSING NOTE), and as the whole or part of a theme, as in:

from the third movement of Mozart's piano concerto in A, K 488.

A scale consists of a certain number of divisions of a fourth (TETRACHORD) or of an OCTAVE. The manner of such division is a MODE, though scale is commonly used in the sense of mode in referring to a PENTATONIC SCALE, a major or minor scale, a CHROMATIC scale, and a WHOLE-TONE scale. The medieval HEXACHORD was a six-note scale in which the order of intervals was TTSTT, where T = tone and S = semitone.

The modern DIATONIC scale has two modes: major (TTSTTTS):

and minor (TSTTSTT):

The latter has only a theoretical existence; in practice

it has two forms, both of which involve an element of chromaticism in the treatment of the LEADING NOTE. They are the harmonic minor scale:

and the melodic minor scale, in which the ascending and descending forms differ:

In the system of EQUAL TEMPERAMENT each of the two modes may begin on any of the twelve notes from C upwards to B by using sharps or flats, usually shown by a KEY-SIGNATURE, thus giving rise to the twelve scales in the major mode and twelve in the minor mode, on which music has been based since the early eighteenth century. The notes of the scale are designated in both modes and in all positions by name which express their function in relation to their KEY, viz., tonic, supertonic, mediant, subdominant, dominant, submediant, leading note. A pentatonic scale consists of five notes corresponding to the succession of black notes on a piano. A chromatic scale consists of the stepwise succession of all black notes and white notes – in other words the twelve adjacent semitones within an octave. In the whole-time scale, on the other hand, no semitones at all are presented. This scale, associated particularly with the music of Debussy, has two forms – one beginning on C (and consisting of C–D–E–F sharp–G sharp–A sharp), the other beginning on D flat.

See also QUARTER-TONE

scale degrees, the name and numbers used in harmonic analysis for the notes of the scale, as follows: tonic (I), supertonic (II), mediant (III), subdominant (IV), dominant (V), submediant (VI), leading note (VII).

Scandello (Scandellus), Antonio (1517–80), Italian composer and cornett-player. He was cornett-player in Bergamo (1541) and in Trent (1547). From about 1553 he was at the Dresden Court, becoming assistant *Kapellmeister* to Le Maistre in 1566, and *Kapellmeister* from 1568 until his death. He composed Masses, motets, a Passion and other church music, two books of *Canzoni napolitane* (1566, 1577), and sacred and secular choral songs to German words. His *St. John Passion* c. 1560; printed in O. Kade, *Die ältere Passionskomposition,* 1893), was intermediate in method between those with plainsong narrative and polyphonic choruses and those which were set in polyphony throughout. He used Johann Walther's monophonic music for the Evangelist, and wrote in five parts for the people (*Turba*), four for Christ, and two or three for other persons. A modern edition of his 'Missa super Epitaphium Mauritii' by L. Hoffmann-Erbrecht was published in 1957. His 'Vorria che tu cantass' una canzon' from the first book of *Canzoni* (1566) is printed in Schering's *Geschichte der Musik in Beispielen,* no 132.

Scapino, comedy overture by Walton, inspired by an etching from Jacques Callot's *Les Trois Pantalons* (1619) – Scapino being the rascally servant of Commedia dell'Arte. The work was composed in 1940 to commemorate the fiftieth anniversary of the foundation of the Chicago Symphony Orchestra, who gave it its first performance the following year. Walton revised it in 1950.

Scarlatti, Alessandro, (1660–1725), Italian composer. He was conductor at the private theatre of Queen Christina of Sweden in Rome, 1684–1702, lived at Florence, 1702–3, and composed operas for Ferdinando (III) de' Medici (until 1707). He was appointed deputy choirmaster (1703) and choirmaster (1707) of S. Maria Maggiore in Rome and music director to Cardinal Pietro Ottoboni. He returned to Naples (1709) as

Alessandro Scarlatti, founder of the famous Neapolitan school of opera and father of Domenico, the harpsichordist

musical director to the Austrian Viceroy and was later director of the Conservatorio S. Onofrio. His pupils included Logroscino, Durante and Hasse. He was the greatest and most prolific of the composers of Italian opera in a period when its forms were assuming their most lasting characteristics. In his mature works are found the fully developed *da capo* aria with instrumental accompaniment and *ritornelli*, the rapid style and special cadence formulas of *secco* recitative, and the use of accompanied recitative for more intense dramatic effects. In his later operas he used the three-movement form which became the distinguishing mark of the Italian overture. Besides 115 operas, by his own count, he composed 150 oratorios, some 600 cantatas with continuo and 61 with instrumental accompaniment, Masses, a Passion, motets and other church music, concertos, chamber music and pieces for harpsichord. The cantatas contain music in a more intimate and a more deeply expressive style than was appropriate to that of the operas. Few of the latter have survived in the repertory, in spite of their immense historical importance. *Mitridate Eupatore* (1707) shows his style at its grandest. *Il Trionfo dell' Onore* (1718) is a work in lighter vein, in which he pokes fun at the dignified classical style of which he himself was a leading exponent.

E. J. DENT: *Alessandro Scarlatti, his Life and Works* (1905)

Alessandro's son, **(Giuseppe) Domenico Scarlatti** (1685–1757), became a composer and harpsichordist. He studied under his father, under Gasparini, and Pasquini. In 1705 he went to Florence with a singer Nicolino and is said to have had a contest in 1709 with Handel in Rome which was arranged by Cardinal Ottoboni. He was attached to the court of the Polish Queen Maria Casimira from 1709 and wrote eight operas for her private theatre in Rome where he was also musical director of St Peter's, 1715–19. He was in the service of the King of Portugal in Lisbon, c. 1721–5, lived in Italy, 1725–9, and from then until 1757 was at the Madrid Court (his pupil, the Infanta Barbara, had married the heir to the Spanish throne, and Scarlatti had settled into her service).

Scarlatti was the greatest Italian writer for the harpsichord of his time. He composed about 600 pieces in one movement, now generally called sonatas, though some printed in his lifetime were called *Esercizi*. Within the binary form in which most of them are written there is inexhaustible variety in the character of the themes and continuous flexibility in their texture and treatment. Among the most original and characteristic technical devices which appear in them are wide skips, crossing of hands, rapidly repeated notes, and repeated dissonant chords which suggest, and were presumably suggested by, the strumming of the guitar. The complete edition in ten volumes by A. Longo (1906 onwards) contains 545 pieces. A more up to date catalogue of Scarlatti's works has been compiled by Ralph Kirkpatrick, the U.S. harpsichordist. This has now become standard, the 'L' prefix of the Longo numbering being replaced by 'K' for Kirkpatrick. Scarlatti's other compositions, besides operas, include concertos, cantatas, Masses, a *Stabat Mater* and two *Salve regina*'s.

R. KIRKPATRICK: *Domenico Scarlatti* (1953)

S. SITWELL: *A Background for Domenico Scarlatti* (1935)

scat singing, jazz term for the use of nonsense syllables and other wordless effects in the course of a vocal number. The technique has been employed in a rapid and virtuoso way by Ella Fitzgerald amongst others.

scena (It.), 'scene': (1) stage (of a theatre). *Sulla scena,* on the stage (as opposed to 'in the orchestra');

(2) a dramatic scene in an opera, consisting often of an extended aria, usually of dramatic character, e.g. Leonore's monologue, 'Abscheulicher', in Act 1 of Beethoven's *Fidelio*;

(3) a concert piece for solo voice with accompaniment, similar in character to an operatic *scena*. An example of such a piece is Beethoven's 'Ah, perfido' for soprano and orchestra (1796);

(4) Spohr's violin concerto no 8 in A minor is described as '*in modo d'una scena cantante*' (in the style of a vocal *scena*).

Schallbecken (Ger.), CYMBALS

Schalmei, *see* OBOE

Scharwenka, Franz Xaver (1850–1924), German born piano virtuoso, composer and teacher. He studied at the Kullak Academy in Berlin where he taught from 1868–73, and gave chamber concerts and conducted. He founded a conservatory in 1881 (which joined the Klindworth Conservatorium, in 1893). With Walter Petzet he founded a new Master School in 1914. He toured extensively as a pianist in Europe and the United States, where he lived from 1891–98 and founded a conservatory in New York. He composed an opera, a symphony, four piano concertos, piano trios, church music, songs, sonatas and other piano pieces, edited the piano works of Schumann and wrote (with A. Spanuth) *Methodik des Klavierspiels* (1908).

His brother, **Ludwig Philipp Scharwenka** (1847–1917), also became a composer and teacher. He studied at the Kullak Academy in Berlin where he taught from 1870. He worked at his brother's conservatory as composition teacher from 1881 and was director in 1892 and co-director from 1893, when it amalgamated with the Klindworth Conservatorium. He composed an opera, two symphonies, symphonic poems and other works for orchestra, works for solo voices, chorus and orchestra, a violin concerto, piano music, chamber music and songs.

Schat, Piet (born 1935), Dutch composer, one of his country's most progressive musicians. His most imposing work is his opera, *Labyrinth*, which he wrote for the 1966 Holland Festival. It is a piece of 'total theatre' in which Schat collaborated creatively with a film maker, a choreographer, a writer and other Dutch artists. His other works include *Signalement* (1962) for six percussion instruments and three double basses; *On Escalation* (1968), a continuous crescendo for percussion and other instruments, involving controlled improvization and quotations ranging from Palestrina to Ravel's *Bolero*; and *The Fifth Season* (1973), a piece of political music theatre about the Vietnam War, written for outdoor performance by the Netherlands Wind Ensemble and the composer's own group known as the Amsterdam Electric Circus.

Schauspieldirektor, Der (Ger., *The Impresario*, It., *L'Impresario*), 'comedy with music' in one act by Mozart, first performed in Vienna in 1786.

Scheherazade, *see* SHÉHÉRAZADE

Scheibe, Johann Adolph (1708–76), German composer and writer. He taught at Hamburg from 1736, was conductor to the Margrave of Brandenburg-Kulmbach from 1740, of Court Opera in Copenhagen from 1745, and director of a music school in Sonderburg (Holstein), from 1758. He published a periodical entitled *Der critische Musicus* (1737–40) in which he denounced Italian operatic conventions and also the style of J. S. Bach (though he withdrew the latter attack in the second edition of his paper, 1745). His works include an opera, choral music, 150 flute concertos, thirty violin concertos, seventy quartet-symphonies, incidental music for plays, trios, flute sonatas and songs.

Scheidemann, Heinrich (c. 1596–1663), German organist and composer. He studied under his father, Hans, and Sweelinck in Amsterdam. He succeeded his father as organist of St. Catherine's, Hamburg, in 1625 and was in turn succeeded by his pupil J. A. Reinken. His organ music is of some historical importance. Of two organ preludes by him printed in Davison and Apel's *Historical Anthology of Music* (no 195), the second is a brief prelude and fugue, an early example of that form. He wrote ten chorale melodies for Rist's fifth book of chorales (1651), and published a volume of sacred dialogues (1658).

W. Breig: *Die Orgelwerke von Heinrich Scheidemann* (1967)

Scheidt, Samuel (1587–1654), German organist and composer. He was appointed organist of the Moritz-kirche in Halle, studied under Sweelinck in Amsterdam, and returned to Halle, where he became court organist in 1609 and archiepiscopal *Kapellmeister* in 1619. He published *Cantiones sacrae* (1620) for eight voices, *Paduana, Galliarda* . . . (1621) for four and five instruments with continuo, *Concerti sacri* (1621–22) for two to twelve voices with instruments, *Tabulatura nova* for organ (three volumes, 1624), *Ludi musici* (two volumes, 1621–2) containing dance pieces for instruments, *Newe geistliche Concerten* (four volumes, 1631–40; volumes v and vi are lost) for two and three voices with continuo, *Liebliche Kraftblümlein* (1635) for two voices and instruments, seventy *Symphonien auf Concerten-Manier* (1644) for three voices and continuo, and a *Tabulaturbuch* (1650) containing 100 harmonised chorales for organ. The *Tabulatura nova*, so called because the music was written in score with five lines for each part, and not in TABLATURE as was the German custom, nor on two staves of six lines, as was usual in England and Holland, marked the beginning of a new era in German organ music. The first and second volumes contain variations on sacred and secular melodies, fantasies, and a few dance movements, the third volume a complete set of liturgical organ music for the Lutheran Mass and Vespers. A projected complete edition of Scheidt's works was begun in 1923 by G. Harms and is being continued by C. Mahrenholz. The collected keyboard works were separately edited by Hermann Keller in 1939.

Schein, Johann Hermann (1586–1630), German composer. He was a choirboy in the Dresden court chapel, studied at the University of Leipzig (1607), and from 1613 was a teacher in the household of von Wolffersdorf in Weissenfels. From 1615 he was at the Weimar court chapel, and from 1616 he was cantor at St. Thomas's, Leipzig, succeeding Seth Calvisius. Schütz wrote a lament on his death. He was the first Lutheran composer to adapt the Italian monodic style to the treatment of the chorale melodies. His first publication, *Venuskränzlein* (1609) contained five-part choral songs and some instrumental dances and canzonas. His *Cymbalum Sionium* (1615) was in the Venetian polychoral style which Hassler and Praetorius had used before him. The two parts of his *Opella nova* (1618–26) contained settings of chorales for three, four, and five voices with continuo. His *Musica boscareccia* (1621) contained songs in villanella style for three voices and continuo, and his *Diletti pastorali* (1624) five-part choral pieces in madrigal style with continuo. The instrumental suites of his *Banchetta musicale* (1617) are among the earliest in which some or all of the movements use the same theme ('variation-suite'). Schein's works have been edited in seven

volumes by A. Prüfer (1901–23). A new collected edition was begun under the editorship of A. Adrio in 1963.

Schelle, Johann (1648–1701), German singer and composer. He sang under Schütz in Dresden from 1655 to 1657, lived in Wolfenbüttel until 1664, and studied under Knüpfer in Leipzig. He was appointed cantor in 1670 at Eilenburg and in 1676 at St. Thomas's Church, Leipzig. He composed cantatas and motets to German words, and Latin motets, Magnificats, and a Mass. Four of his cantatas are printed in *Denkmäler deutscher Tonkunst*, lviii–lix, which also contains a list of his compositions.

Schellen (Ger.), jingles, sleigh-bells.

Schellenbaum, *see* PAVILLON CHINOIS

Schellengeläute, *see* SLEIGH-BELLS

Schellentrommel (Ger.), tambourine.

Schelling, Ernest (1876–1939), U.S. composer and pianist, who established himself as a boy prodigy at Philadelphia at the age of four. Later he studied in Europe, where his teachers included Bruckner, Leschetizky, Paderewski and Moszkowski. His orchestral works include a symphony, a *Symphonic Legend* and fantasies entitled *A Victory Ball* and *Morocco*. He also wrote *Fantastic Impressions from an Artist's Life* for piano and orchestra, chamber music, piano pieces and songs.

Schemelli, Georg Christian (c. 1676–1762), German musician. He studied in Leipzig under Schelle at the Thomasschule (1695–1700) and in Wittenberg. He later became cantor at the castle of Zeitz. In 1736 he published a collection of songs entitled *Musicalisches Gesangbuch* edited, and in part composed, by J. S. Bach.

Schemelli Hymnbook, collection of hymns, edited by Bach, published in 1736. The collection owes its name to Georg Christian Schemelli (1678–1762), whose *Musicalisches Gesangbuch* was the source of Bach's adaptations. Bach also composed chorale preludes on some of the hymns.

Schenk (Schenck), Johann (?1656–after 1712), German *viola da gamba* player at the electoral court in Düsseldorf (c. 1690). Later he lived in Amsterdam. He composed suites and sonatas for bass viol, chamber sonatas for two violins, bass viol and continuo, sonatas for violin and continuo, an opera, and a setting of the *Song of Solomon* for voice and continuo. His *Scherzi musicali*, a book of suites for viola da gamba and continuo published in Amsterdam as op 6, is reprinted as volume xxviii (1907) of *Vereniging voor Nederlandsche Muziekgeschiedenis*. A fugue from that volume is in Schering's *Geschichte der Musik in Beispielen*, no 245. His *Le Nymphe del Rheno*, op 8, for two bass viols, and *L'Écho du Danube*, op 9, for bass viol (both solo and with continuo) are reprinted as volumes xliv and lxvii, respectively, of *Das Erbe deutscher Musik*.

Schenker, Heinrich (1868–1935), Austrian theorist and teacher. He studied under Bruckner in Vienna, where he settled and taught music privately. He is best known for the methods of detailed analysis of form, harmony and tonality in the music of the 18th and 19th centuries, which he taught and discussed in his writings.

A. Katz: *Challenge to Musical Tradition* (1945)

F. Salzer: *Structural Hearing*, two volumes (1952)

Schenker system, a form of musical analysis which

attempts to prove that every composition can be reduced to a few simple patterns or simple tone structure, from which grow its continuity and coherence. The system was developed by Heinrich Schenker.

Scherchen, Hermann (1891–1966), German born conductor who later settled in Switzerland. He was a specialist in modern music, having lectured on the subject in Berlin and founded a periodical called *Melos*. During the 1920s he conducted at Leipzig, Frankfurt and at festivals of modern music. He left Germany in 1932, and thereafter held courses and conducted in various cities, showing a special interest in the performance of new compositions, especially music using twelve-note technique. He conducted the première of Dallapiccola's *The Prisoner* (Florence, 1950) and Henze's *King Stag* (Berlin, 1956). As an author, he wrote *A Handbook of Conducting* and *The Nature of Music*.

Scherer, Sebastian Anton (1631–1712), German composer. He was deputy organist to Tobias Everlin at the cathedral of Ulm in 1653, director of the Collegium Musicum there in 1662 and organist of the cathedral in 1671. He became organist of St. Thomas's in Strasbourg in 1684 and returned to the cathedral at Ulm in the following year. He published a volume of Masses, psalms and motets in 1657, a volume of *Tabulatura in cymbalo et organo* containing Intonations in the eight modes, with a second part (*Partitura*) containing Toccatas in the eight modes in 1664 (both parts edited by Guilmant, 1907), and a set of fourteen trio sonatas in 1680.

scherzando (It.), playfully, in a light-hearted fashion.

Scherzi, Gli, *see* RUSSIAN QUARTETS

scherzo (It.), literally a joke. The term was occasionally used for both vocal and instrumental compositions before 1750, as in Monteverdi's *Scherzi musicali* (1607), Antonio Brunelli's *Scherzi, Arie, Canzonette, e Madrigali* (1616) for voices and instruments, Johann Schenk's *Scherzi musicali* (c. 1700), consisting of fourteen suites for gamba and continuo, Steffani's *Scherzi* for solo voice with two violins and continuo and the scherzo in Bach's third partita for harpsichord. The scherzo (and trio) after 1750 is almost always in quick triple time, and is generally a movement in a sonata, symphony, etc., where it takes the place of the minuet. Haydn wrote a scherzo and trio in each of the six quartets of his op 33 without making any effective distinction between their style and that of his minuets. The minuet in Beethoven's first symphony is marked *Allegro molto e vivace* with a metronome mark of 108 bars to the minute, so that it is actually a scherzo, and all the later symphonies except the eighth, which has a classical minuet, have a scherzo and trio. With Beethoven the style of the scherzo becomes boisterous –

(Molto vivace)

– or on occasion eerie, as in the fifth symphony. Brahms wrote no scherzos in his symphonies (at least none conforming with traditional pattern), though his first orchestral work, the *Serenade* op 11, includes a scherzo *Allegro non troppo*. He has an *Allegro appassionato* in his B flat piano concerto, op 83, in quick 3/4 time. Other composers since the mid-19th century have incorporated scherzos in their symphonies, e.g. Bruckner, Mahler, Sibelius and Walton. Scherzos also exist outside the symphonic repertory, as in the case of Chopin's four scherzos for piano, and Dukas's orchestral scherzo, *The Sorcerer's Apprentice*.

Schicksalslied, *see* SONG OF DESTINY

Schikaneder, (Johann) Emanuel (1751–1812), German librettist, singer and theatre manager. He was singer, actor and later manager for a group of travelling players. In 1784 he settled in Vienna, where he was manager of several theatres including the suburban Theater auf der Wieden. It was for this house that Mozart in 1791 composed *The Magic Flute*, with Schikaneder as librettist, producer and exponent of the comic role of Papageno. In 1801 he opened the Theater an der Wien, placing a statue of himself as Papageno on the roof and in due course commissioning *Fidelio* from Beethoven. In this case, however, Schikaneder did not supply the libretto. Composers who did use Schikaneder librettos included Schack (the original Tamino in *The Magic Flute*), Süssmayr and Paisiello.

E. VON KOMORZYNSKI: *Emanuel Schikaneder* (1951)

Schildt, Melchior (c. 1593–1667), German organist and composer. He studied under Sweelinck in Amsterdam (1609) and was appointed organist at Wolfenbüttel (1623), at the Copenhagen Court (1626) and of the Market Church in Hanover (1629). His published compositions include two sets of harpsichord variations, two preludes and two chorales for organ.

Schillinger, Joseph (1895–1943), Russian born composer and theorist, who studied at St. Petersburg Conservatory and later taught at Kharkov and Leningrad. In 1929 he settled in the United States, where he taught a mathematical musical method invented by himself. For a time Gershwin was one of his pupils. His works include a *March of the Orient*, and a *First Airphonic Suite* for THEREMIN, orchestra and piano.

Schillings, Max von (1868–1933), German composer and conductor. In 1908 he settled in Stuttgart and worked at the Court Opera where he became music director in 1911. He was director of the Berlin State Opera from 1919 to 1925 and in 1932 became president of the Prussian Academy of Arts. Of his four operas, Wagnerian in style, the last, *Mona Lisa* (Stuttgart, 1915), was one of the most successful German operas of its time.

Schindler, Anton (1794–1864), Austrian violinist and conductor, friend and biographer of Beethoven. He studied in Vienna where he was appointed leader and

BEETHOVEN, *Symphony no 9*

conductor at Josephstadt Theater (1822) and Kärn-trertor Theater (1825). He became choirmaster of Münster Cathedral (1831), city music director in Aix-la-Chapelle (1835) and settled in Frankfurt (1848). He met Beethoven in 1814, became his secretary in 1816, lived in his house from 1822 to 1824 and returned in December 1826 to care for him until his death. He wrote a famous biography of Beethoven (1840), but its accuracy unfortunately leaves something to be desired. A freshly annotated edition of this biography, translated into English as *Beethoven as I knew him*, was made by Donald MacArdle in the 1960s and published in 1966.

Schiötz, Aksel (1906–74), Danish tenor, who appeared in opera at Glyndebourne and in the United States, has been a notable lieder singer, and has written a book about the art of singing.

Schipa, Tito (1890–1965), Italian tenor, who made his stage début in *La Traviata* at Vercelli in 1911. Later he appeared frequently in Chicago and New York, and gave recitals all over the world – even when he was in his seventies.

Schirmer, famous firm of publishers founded in New York in 1861 by Gustav Schirmer and B. Beer. Since 1866, when Schirmer assumed sole control, the business has been carried on under its present name. Its catalogue is a particularly large and important one. In 1915 the firm founded the periodical, *Musical Quarterly*.

Schlag (Ger.), beat.

Schlägel (Ger.), drumstick.

Schlaginstrumente (Ger.), percussion instruments.

Schlagobers (Ger., whipped cream confection), ballet by Richard Strauss, with choreography by Kröller, first performed in Vienna in 1924.

Schlagzither (Ger.), a type of ZITHER in which the strings, instead of being plucked, are struck with hammers. Despite its name it is more of a dulcimer than a zither.

Schlangenrohr (Ger.), serpent.

Schleifer (Ger.), a slide or slur, i.e. an appoggiatura consisting of two grace notes.

Schleppen (Ger.), 'to drag'. *Nicht schleppen*, do not drag. The term, in one or another of its forms, was much favoured by Mahler.

Schlick, Arnolt (before 1460-after 1517), blind organist and composer. He played in Germany and Holland, and was in Strasbourg in 1492 and Worms in 1495. He became organist at the court in Heidelberg sometime before 1496. His book on organs and methods of constructing them, *Spiegel der Orgelmacher und Organisten* (1511), has been reprinted by E. Flade (1951). Two organ settings, one of 'Salve regina' and one of 'Maria zart', from his *Tabulaturen etlicher Lobgesang und Lidlein* (1512; modern edition by G. Harms, 1924), are printed in *Historical Anthology of Music*, edited by A. T. Davison and W. Apel, nos 100, 101.

Schluss (Ger.), end, conclusion.

Schlüssel (Ger.), clef.

Schmelzer, Johann Heinrich (c. 1623–80), Austrian composer. He was at the court in Vienna as chamber musician (1649), assistant *Kapellmeister* (1671) and *Kapellmeister* (1679). He published three volumes of chamber music (modern editions in *Denkmäler der Tonkunst in Osterreich*, xciii, cv and cxi-cxii) and com-posed a number of ballets for the Viennese court opera. One of his ballets has been printed in *Denkmäler der Tonkunst in Osterreich*, volume lvi, Jg. xxviii (2). His *Nuptial Mass* is in volume xlix, Jg. xxv (1) of the same series. His son, **Andreas Anton Schmelzer** (1653–1701) also composed music for ballets.

schmetternd (Ger.), 'blaring', an indication to horn players to use a harsh, brassy tone. The French term for this effect is '*cuivré*'.

Schmidt, Franz (1874–1939), Austrian composer, cellist, organist and pianist. He studied at the Vienna Conservatorium, and was cellist in the Vienna Court Opera orchestra, 1896–1910; teacher of the piano, Vienna Music Academy, 1910; director, 1925–37. His compositions include two operas, the oratorio *The Book of the Seven Seals*, four symphonies, orchestral variations on a Hungarian Hussar song, two piano concertos (originally for left hand only), two string quartets and other chamber music, and several works for organ, all written in the Viennese style of the period.

Schmidt-Isserstedt, Hans (1900–73), German conductor and composer. He studied in Berlin and became conductor of the Hamburg State Opera and of the Deutsche Oper Berlin. In 1945 he founded the Hamburg Radio Symphony Orchestra, with which he toured the world.

Schmidt, Bernhard (Bernard Smith) (c. 1630–1708), German organ builder, known in England as 'Father Smith'. He settled in England in 1660 with two nephews, Christian and Gerard, as his assistants. He built his first English organ at the Chapel Royal in London and was appointed Organmaker in Ordinary to the King and later court organ-builder to Queen Anne. In 1676 he became organist at St. Margaret's Church, Westminster, where he had built the organ (1675).

A. FREEMAN: *Father Smith* (1926)

Schmieder, Wolfgang (1900–73), German musicologist, whose thematic index of Bach's works is the basis of the present numbering system. The numbers bear the prefix BWV, which stands for *Bach Werke-Verzeichnis* (Index to Bach's Works).

Schmitt, Florent (1870–1958), French composer, pupil of Massenet and Fauré at the Paris Conservatoire from 1889. He won the *Prix de Rome* in 1900 and was director of the Lyons Conservatoire from 1922–24, when he settled in St. Cloud, near Paris. He wrote many articles on music criticism for periodicals, and composed ballets, orchestral works, choral works with orchestra, pieces for piano, for piano duet, and for two pianos, chamber music and songs. Though his style was based on French impressionism, his music had a distinctive personality of its own, notably so in his ballet *The Tragedy of Salome* and in his meaty, not to say sumptuous, choral setting of Psalm 47 (1904).

Schnabel, Artur (1882–1951), Austrian pianist, teacher composer. He studied under Leschetizky in Vienna (1888–97) and settled in Berlin where he was teacher at the Hochschule (1925–33). He toured extensively in Europe and the United States and, exiled when the Nazis came to power in Germany, he settled in New York. In his later years he composed a symphony, an orchestral rhapsody, and other works in an advanced tonal idiom that seemed out of keeping with his personality as a pianist. In the latter role, he was renowned for his intellectually authoritative performances of the Viennese classics, especially Beethoven, but also Mozart and Schubert. His pupils included Clifford Curzon, to whom he passed on many of his finest qualities as a musician. He published *Music and The Line of Most Resistance* (1942).

K. WOLFF: *The Teaching of Artur Schnabel* (1972)

Schnabelflöte (Ger.), 'beaked flute', obsolete name for the RECORDER.

Schnarre (Ger.), rattle; *Schnarretrommel*, snare drum; *Schnarrsaite*, 'rattle string', i.e. the snare. The *Schnarrwerk* of an organ, however, is the reed section.

schnell (Ger.), quick.

Schneller (Ger.), an ornament used in the 18th century. It was indicated thus:

and performed thus:

Since c. 1800 it has been called PRALLTRILLER or INVERTED MORDENT.

Schobert, Johann (c. 1720–67), German harpsichordist and composer, who taught at Strasbourg and became organist at Versailles. In 1760 he settled in Paris as chamber cembalist to the Prince of Conti. A selection of his compositions, comprising five sonatas for harpsichord and violin, two trios, two quartets for harpsichord, two violins and cello, and two harpsichord concertos is published in *Denkmäler deutscher Tonkunst*, xxxix, which also contains a thematic catalogue of his compositions. The keyboard instrument is designated as *clavecin* or *cembalo*; in the chamber music Schobert's style is quite pianistic and the violin part of the sonatas is either subsidiary or optional, as was customary in the early part of the classical period. His keyboard style had some influence on Mozart; the second movement of Mozart's concerto K 39 (1767) is an arrangement of a movement from a sonata by Schobert. He died, along with most of his family (as well as a servant and friend), of eating toadstools in mistake for mushrooms.

Schoeck, Othmar (1886–1957), Swiss composer and conductor. He studied at the Zürich Conservatorium, and at Leipzig with Reger. He was for many years active as a choral and orchestral conductor in Zurich. His compositions include six operas and other stage works, several choral works, concertos for violin, cello and horn, chamber music and nearly 400 songs.

Schoenberg, Arnold (1874–1951), Austrian composer, one of the major figures of 20th century music. Largely self-taught, he made some study of counterpoint under Alexander von Zemlinsky, composed *Verklärte Nacht* ('Transfigured Night') in 1899 and in 1900 began work on the *Gurrelieder*, which was not completed until 1911. Between then and the 1920s he taught in Berlin and Vienna; but in 1933, having been condemned by the Nazis for his musical 'decadence' (he was a Jew), he moved to the United States and settled in California,

where he changed the spelling of his name from Schönberg to Schoenberg. From the early works which showed a complete command of the late romantic style, Schoenberg turned about 1907, under a self-confessed 'inner compulsion', to a period of experimentation in such music as the *Three Piano Pieces*, op 11 (1909), the fifteen songs from Stefan George's *The Book of The Hanging Gardens*, op 15 (1907–9), the *Five Pieces for Orchestra*, op 16 (1909), the monodrama *Erwartung* ('Expectation'), op 17 (1909), the drama with music *Die glückliche Hand* (The Lucky Hand), op 18 (1913), and the 21 songs from Albert Giraud's *Pierrot Lunaire* for *Sprechgesang* and instruments, op 21 (1912). The technique towards which these very controversial works had been moving was

Arnold Schoenberg, a portrait study which admirably catches the singlemindedness that characterized his musical thought

formulated about 1921 in the principle of 'composition with twelve notes' (*see* TWELVE-NOTE SYSTEM), essentially a return to polyphony, which the composer regarded as an ascent to 'higher and better order'. The working of this order is exemplified particularly in the compositions written between 1921 and 1933, which include the *Five Pieces*, op 23, and *Suite*, op 25, for piano, the *Serenade* for seven instruments and bass-baritone, op 24, and the quintet for wind instruments, op 26, the third string quartet, op 30, and the *Variations for Orchestra*, op 31.

In many of the compositions written in the United States, Schoenberg returned to more traditional principles of form and tonality – he had, in fact, always regarded 'atonality' as a misnomer – and the string suite in G major (1935) was the first work since the second quartet (1907) to have a key-signature, the second to do so was the *Theme and Variations for Band*, op 43 (1943), which was arranged for orchestra as op 43b in the following year. The most notable works of this last period were the violin concerto, op 36 (1936), the fourth string quartet, op 37 (1936), the *Ode to Napoleon*, a setting of Byron's poem for piano, strings and narrator, op 41 (1943), the piano concerto, op 42 (1943), the string trio, op 45 (1946), and *A Survivor from Warsaw*, for narrator, male chorus, and orchestra, op 46 (1947). The opera *Moses and Aaron* was left unfinished at his death.

Schoenberg's most distinguished pupils were Alban Berg, Anton von Webern, and Egon Wellesz. His *Harmonielehre* (1911, English translation by D. Adams, 1948) is one of the most important modern treatises on harmony. He also published a book of essays, *Style and Idea* (1949), and *Models for Beginners in Composition*, (1942). He was also an able painter, and between 1907 and 1910 he painted a considerable number of pictures, many of them self-portraits. He died in Los Angeles.

D. NEWLIN: *Bruckner, Mahler, Schoenberg* (1947)
E. WELLESZ: *Arnold Schoenberg* (1925)
W. REICH: *Schoenberg, a critical biography* (1968)
E. STEIN (editor): *Arnold Schoenberg's Letters* (1958)
H. H. STUCKENSCHMIDT: *Arnold Schoenberg* (1977)

schola cantorum, the papal choir and song school, first mentioned in the 8th century, but probably originating many centuries earlier. From the *schola* singers were sent to other churches and monasteries, carrying with them the repertory of Gregorian chant which in the early years was not written down but disseminated orally.

Scholes, Percy Alfred (1877–1958), English music critic, author and lexicographer. He founded and edited the *Musical Student* (1908) and *Music and Youth*, was appointed music critic for the London *Evening Standard* (1913) and the *Observer*, was music consultant to the B.B.C. (1923), and extension lecturer for Oxford, Cambridge and London Universities. He settled in Montreux, Switzerland until 1939, and after living in Oxford for several years returned to Switzerland in 1957. His books include the *Listener's History of Music* (three volumes, 1923–8), *The Oxford Companion to Music* (1938; tenth edition, 1970), *The Mirror of Music*, 1844–1944 (two volumes, 1947), *The Great Dr. Burney* (two volumes, 1948), *The Concise Oxford Dictionary of Music* (1952), and *Sir John Hawkins* (1953).

Schöne Melusine, Die (Ger., *The Fair Melusina*), overture by Mendelssohn, op 32 (1833), composed after a performance of the opera *Melusina* (by Kreutzer to a libretto by Grillparzer) with its water-nymph heroine.

Schöne Müllerin, Die (*The Fair Maid Of The Mill*), a cycle of twenty songs composed by Schubert in 1823, with songs selected from the *Müllerlieder* of Wilhelm Müller, who also wrote *Die Winterreise*. The cycle, intended to be performed in sequence, tells the story of an initially happy but finally tragic courtship. The titles of the songs are:

(1) *Das Wandern* (Wandering)
(2) *Wohin?* (Whither)
(3) *Halt!* (Stop!)
(4) *Danksagung an den Bach* (Giving thanks to the brook)
(5) *Am Feierabend* (Evening rest)
(6) *Der Neugierige* (The inquisitive one)
(7) *Ungeduld* (Impatience)
(8) *Morgengruss* (Morning greeting)
(9) *Des Müllers Blumen* (The miller's flowers)
(10) *Thranenregen* (Shower of tears)
(11) *Mein* (Mine)
(12) *Pause* (Break)
(13) *Mit dem grünen Lautenbande* (With the green lute-ribbon)
(14) *Der Jäger* (The hunter)
(15) *Eifersucht und Stolz* (Jealousy and pride)
(16) *Die liebe Farbe* (The favourite colour)
(17) *Die böse Farbe* (The hateful colour)
(18) *Trockne Blumen* (Dead flowers)
(19) *Der Müller und der Bach* (The miller and the brook)
(20) *Des Baches Wiegenlied* (The brook's cradle-song)

School for Fathers, the title of an English version by E. J. Dent of Wolf-Ferrari's opera *I quattro rusteghi*, which was first performed in German as *Die vier Grobiane* (Munich, 1906).

Schoolmaster, The (Ger., *Der Schulmeister*), The nickname given to Haydn's symphony no 55 in E flat (1774). The source of the names is believed to be the serious character of the slow movement. The Haydn scholar, Robbins Landon, has suggested that the dotted figure of the main theme represents the teacher's wagging forefinger.

Schop (Schopp), Johann (c. 1590–1667), German composer, violinist, lutenist and trombonist. He studied under Brade in Hamburg, and was court musician at Wolfenbüttel and at Copenhagen. In 1621 he settled in Hamburg, where he became director of the city music and organist of St. James. He composed sacred concertos (1643–44), sacred songs (1654) and instrumental music, of which little has survived, and was one of the musical editors of Rist's collections of sacred and secular songs.

Schöpfung, Die, *see* CREATION

Schottische (Ger.), literally 'Scottish', a round polka dance similar to, but slower than, the polka danced in the 19th century. In spite of the similarity in name, this dance is not to be confused with the *Écossaise*.

Schott und Söhne, firm of music publishers, founded in Mainz in 1773 by Bernhard Schott. Later it opened branches in Belgium, Paris and London, and became one of the most famous publishing houses in the world. Today it retains its importance, publishing many modern scores, including works by Henze, Tippett and Orff.

Schrammel quartet, a Viennese ensemble usually consisting of two violins, guitar and accordion or clarinet. It owes its name to Joseph Schrammel (1850–93), who led such a quartet. Such an ensemble is often heard accompanying a singer in the light-hearted ditties extolling the 'new wine', usually performed in Viennese dialect in the bars of the Grinzing district.

Schreker, Franz (1878–1934), German composer and conductor. He studied under Fuchs in Vienna, where he founded and conducted the Philharmonic Chorus (1911) and was teacher of composition at the Royal Academy. He was director of the Berlin Hochschule from 1920–32, but was harrassed and sacked by the Nazis, and died in Berlin soon after. Schreker's first major work was his opera *Der ferne Klang* (*The Distant Sound*), which he wrote in 1912 and which influenced other composers of the period – Schoenberg referred to it in his *Harmonielehre*, and Berg adapted its layout of set symphonic forms when he came to write *Wozzeck* twelve years later. Schreker's eight other operas included *Der Schatzgräber* (*The Digger for Treasure*) produced at Frankfurt in 1920. His chamber symphony (1916) also helped to establish him as an avant garde leader, but his music lacks sustaining power – in recent years it has been neglected, outside Germany at least, and stands in need of reappraisal.

Schröder-Devrient, Wilhelmine (1804–60), German soprano. She was the daughter of the baritone Friedrich Schröder and the actress Antoinette Sophie Bürger. She studied in Vienna, where she made her début as Pamina in *The Magic Flute* at the Hofburg Theater (1821) and sang the role of Leonore in *Fidelio* (1822) in the famous revival in Beethoven's presence. From 1823–47 she was at the court opera in Dresden and made appearances in other cities including Paris, London and Berlin. The performances of Wagner's early operas owed much to her great dramatic and musical ability. She was Adriano in the first performance of *Rienzi*, Senta in *The Flying Dutchman* (in which her performance averted a fiasco), and Venus in *Tannhäuser*. She was the wife of the baritone Eduard Devrient.

Schröter, Corona (1751–1802), German singer, composer and actress. After learning music from her father, the oboist Johann Friedrich Schröter, she was invited by Goethe in 1776 to Weimar, where she wrote the music for his play *Die Fischerin*. This included a setting by her of 'Erl King', which Goethe was said to prefer to Schubert's. She also acted in Goethe's plays.

Schröter, Leonhart (c. 1532–c. 1601), German composer. He was cantor at Saalfeld in 1561 and at Magdeburg from 1576 to 1595. He published a number of collections of music for the Lutheran service, including settings of Latin and German hymns, psalms, an eight-part German Te Deum, and a Latin Te Deum.

Schubart, Christian Friedrich Daniel (1739–91), German musician, poet and editor. In 1774 he founded his *Deutsche Chronik* in Augsburg. He moved with his paper to Ulm and was imprisoned at Hohenasperg from 1777–87 for various misdeeds. On his release he became director of the Stuttgart Court Opera. He wrote the words for three songs by Schubert, an autobiography (1791–3) and a book on musical aesthetics (published in 1806), and composed songs and piano pieces.

Schubert, Franz (1808–78), German composer and violinist who lived in Dresden. His violin solo, *L'Abeille* (Fr., *The Bee*), has sometimes been mistaken for the work of his great Viennese namesake.

Schubert, Franz Peter (1797–1828), Austrian composer. Born in Vienna, the son of a music-loving schoolmaster, he began at the age of eight to learn the violin from his father and the piano from his elder brother Ignaz. He soon progressed to organ and counterpoint lessons from Michael Holzer. In 1808 he was admitted as a chorister at the Imperial Chapel in Vienna and as a pupil at the Imperial Seminary (or *Konvikt*). In due course he became leader of the chapel orchestra, and often acted as conductor. At the age of fourteen he composed his first song, 'Hagars Klage' (Hagar's Lament). Salieri, the Court *Kapellmeister*, was impressed with Schubert's talents, and gave him extra music lessons after he left school at the age of sixteen. From this period dated Schubert's first symphony (1813) and first three string quartets – usually deemed 'immature', but good enough to be known and loved by concert-goers today. 'Maturity' was reached at seventeen with the song 'Gretchen am Spinnrade' (Gretchen at the spinning wheel), to Goethe's words. This was soon followed by two more Goethe settings, 'Heidenröslein' and 'Erlkönig', by the second and third symphonies (1815), and by several operettas and melodramas. Thereafter, Schubert's production of a rapid stream of masterpieces continued almost unabated until the end of his short life. Fortunately he was spared military service because of his lack of height, but his work as an assistant master at his father's suburban school must have been scarcely less frustrating for someone who wanted to do nothing more than write, perform and listen to music. At nineteen he applied for the directorship of the Ljubljana music school, but was turned down. Ten years later he was refused a court appointment in Vienna. Between 1818 and 1824, however, he made visits to the Esterházy family's country estate to work as part-time music teacher, which gave variety from Vienna. His many friends also helped him. He made walking-tours with Johann Vogl (the famous baritone and one of the first to recognise Schubert's genius as a song-writer) and during this period the *Trout* quintet (1819) was composed. In Vienna itself, the poet, Schober, gave Schubert a room in his house. Schubert enjoyed the poet's Bohemian life with fellow-writers, artists and musicians.

For most of his short career, Schubert lived on casual earnings and the generosity of friends and his brother Ferdinand. As a freelance composer in Vienna he was even less successful than Mozart, but he did not seem to desire fame. When the Graz *Musikverein* (music society) elected him as an honorary member in 1822 he was delighted to receive this recognition, but characteristically sent Graz an unfinished work as his gesture of thanks. That it was to become the most famous unfinished work in musical history would doubtless have astonished Schubert just as much as Anselm Huttenbrenner, the director at Graz, who seems simply to have tossed the manuscript into a drawer and forgotten about it. Not until 1865, nearly forty years after the composer's death, did the 'Unfinished' Symphony receive its first performance. Fortunately for posterity, he did finish his 'Great' C major symphony (so-called to differentiate it from his 'little' C major symphony), his great C major string quintet, several great string quartets and piano sonatas, and two of the greatest song cycles ever written – *Die schöne Müllerin* (1823) and *Winterreise* (1827). The almost morbid loneliness of the latter work reflects Schubert's personal loneliness at this time. Though he did not lack women friends, he remained unmarried; his Bohemian existence had begun to go stale; and not only was he short of money, he was increasingly unwell. In 1827 he was a torch-bearer at Beethoven's funeral, little knowing that he would travel the same road the following year, after dying from typhus at the age of 31. Towards the end of his life, in an attempt to 'improve' himself as a composer, he contemplated taking a refresher course in counterpoint – a touching example of his modesty and unawareness of his greatness.

At the centre of Schubert's art are his songs, the sheer number of which – more than six hundred –

testifies to his immediate and spontaneous response to early romantic poetry. It is usually said that he read poetry voraciously but uncritically, choosing Goethe or Heine for one song and some piece of doggerel for the next. In fact he set whatever caught his imagination as a composer, and could create a masterpiece out of mediocre verse as easily as out of good. Schubert's songs are duets for singer and pianist, who are partners on equal terms, and in the range of their musical resources they form a compendium, as well as a foundation, of the whole vocabulary of romantic musical speech. Up to 1823 he made strenuous but unsuccessful efforts to achieve a practicable opera, as distinct from *Singspiel*; but the characterisation he

Franz Peter Schubert. This well-known lithograph by Kriehuber was not executed till 20 years after Schubert's death – eloquent witness to the posthumous nature of his fame.

could bring to a three-minute song eluded him when it came to pacing a three-hour work for the stage, and though valiant attempts have been made to breathe new life into some of these works in recent years, none have had more than curiosity value. On the other hand, the choral works of Schubert's last years show a breadth and consistency of choral style which might have developed into something very impressive, if he had lived a little longer. It was in the 'Unfinished' Symphony and the 'Great' C major (1828), the chamber music, notably the A minor (1824), D minor (*Death and the Maiden*, 1824–26) and G major (1826) string quartets, the piano trios in B flat (1826) and E flat (1827), the *Trout* quintet (1819), the C major string quintet (1828), the octet for wind and strings (1824) and the piano sonatas and duets that his lyrical melodic style is most perfectly allied to largeness of conception and form and to a consummate sense of key-design

and harmonic detail.

The chronological thematic catalogue of Schubert's works by O. E. Deutsch lists 998 works. The main divisions, arranged according to their publication in the complete edition (1884–97) are: I. eight symphonies; II. ten overtures and other orchestral works; III. three octets; IV. one string quintet; V. fifteen string quartets; VI. one string trio; VII. three piano trios, one piano quartet, one piano quintet; VIII. eight works for piano and one instrument; IX. 32 works for piano duet; X. fifteen piano sonatas; XI. sixteen other works for piano; XII. 31 dances for piano; XIII. seven Masses; XIV. 22 sacred works; XV. fifteen stage works; XVI. 46 works for male choir; XVII. nineteen works for mixed choir; XVIII. six works for female choir; XIX. 36 vocal trios and duets; XX. 567 songs with piano and 36 other solo vocal pieces; XXI. Supplement of 31 instrumental pieces and thirteen vocal pieces.

Deutsch's numbering of Schubert's works should always be used in preference to the opus numbers, which are chronologically inaccurate. The latter, however, remain popular – op 99 and op 100 for the two piano trios, for instance – and, because of their familiarity, are proving hard to dislodge.

G. ABRAHAM (editor): *Schubert: a Symposium* (1946)
A. BRENT-SMITH: *Schubert: Quartet in D minor and Octet* (1927); *Schubert: the Symphonies* (C major and B minor) (1926)
M. J. E. BROWN: *Schubert: a critical biography* (1958); *Essays on Schubert* (1966); *Schubert Songs* (1967); *Schubert Symphonies* (1970)
R. CAPELL: *Schubert's Songs* (1928)
O. E. DEUTSCH: *Schubert: a Documentary Biography* (1946); *Schubert: Thematic Catalogue* (1951)
A. EINSTEIN: *Schubert* (1951)
N. FLOWER: *Franz Schubert* (1928)
H. GAL: *Franz Schubert and the Essence of Melody* (1974)
A. HUTCHINGS: *Schubert* (1945)
K. KOBALD: *Franz Schubert and his Time* (1928)
G. MOORE: *The Schubert Song Cycles* (1975)
P. RADCLIFFE: *Schubert Piano Sonatas* (1967)
J. READ: *Schubert: the Final Years* (1972)
J. A. WESTRUP: *Schubert Chamber Music* (1969)

Schübler Chorales, set of six chorale preludes by Bach, so called because they were published (about 1747) by Schübler.

Schuhplattler (Ger.), Bavarian dance, usually in 3/4 time, in which the performers slap their knees and the soles of their feet with their hands.

Schuller, Gunther (born 1925), U.S. composer and horn player. He studied at the Manhattan School of Music and his style is an interesting compound of jazz and serialism. His most substantial work is his opera, *The Visitation*, which he composed for Hamburg in 1966, but his international reputation rests mainly on his *Seven Studies on Themes of Paul Klee* for orchestra (1959). He has also written a horn concerto and other orchestral works; *Variants*, a ballet with George Balanchine (1961); and chamber music including a concertino for jazz quartet (1959) and a double quintet (1961). He has written two important books, both standard works: *Horn Technique* (1962) and *Early Jazz: its Roots and Musical Development* (1968).

Schulmeister, Der, *see* SCHOOLMASTER

Schulwerk, Das (Ger., *Schoolwork*), educational work by Orff, composed between 1930 and 1933. It consists of numerous short pieces using different types of instrument, including recorders and percussion, such as are likely to be found in schools.

Schulz, Johann Abraham Peter (1747–1800), German conductor, author and composer. He studied under Kirnberger in Berlin, travelled widely, and became conductor at the theatre of Prince Henry of Prussia in Rheinsberg, 1780 and at the Danish court at Copenhagen, 1787–95. His songs with piano in folk song style, of which he published three books (1782–90), were the first of their kind, and some are still well known in Germany. He composed five operas to French texts, including *Le Barbier de Séville* (1786) and *Aline, reine de Golconde* (1787), which afterwards became popular in a Danish adaptation, and three operas in Danish text.

Schuman, William Howard (born 1910), U.S. composer. He studied at Columbia University, at the Salzburg Mozarteum and with Roy Harris, before teaching at the Sarah Lawrence College (1938) and becoming music editor of Schirmer's. From 1945 to 1961 he was head of the Juilliard School of Music, New York. His music, often distinctively U.S. in flavour, includes eight symphonies, an *American Festival* overture, a *William Billings* overture and a *New England Triptych*, a piano concerto and a violin concerto. He has written a ballet, *Undertow*, and an opera about a baseball player, *The Mighty Casey*; also choral works and chamber music.

Schumann, Clara Josephine (née **Wieck**) (1819–96), German pianist and composer, daughter of Friedrich Wieck (who taught her) and wife of Robert Schumann (see below). She gave her first recital in 1830 at Leipzig, and subsequently appeared in other German towns, and in Paris and Vienna. After considerable opposition from her father she married Robert Schumann in 1840. After her husband's death in 1856 she played frequently in Britain. One of the outstanding interpreters of her time, particularly of her husband's music, she was also influential as a teacher – between 1878 and 1892 she worked at the Hoch Conservatorium, Frankfurt. Her compositions include a piano concerto, a piano trio, piano solos and songs. Themes of some of her works were used by Schumann in his own compositions.

> B. LITZMANN: *Clara Schumann – An Artist's Life*, two volumes (1913); *Letters of Clara Schumann and Johannes Brahms, 1853–96*, two volumes (1927)

> F. MAY: *The girlhood of Clara Schumann* (1912)

Schumann, Elisabeth (1888–1952), German soprano. She was at home both in opera and in *Lieder*, and famous for the silvery delicacy of her voice. From 1919 until 1937 she was a member of the Vienna State Opera, but she left Austria before World War II and settled in New York, where she died. Her portrayals of Mozart roles were specially admired, and so was her Sophie in *Der Rosenkavalier*. She was an unsurpassed exponent of Schubert's songs, many of which she recorded.

Schumann, Robert (1810–56), German composer. Born at Zwickau, he was encouraged by his father – a bookseller, publisher and writer who died when Schumann was sixteen – to develop both musical and literary interests, which were concentrated in his late teens in a burning admiration for the extravagantly romantic sentiment of Jean Paul Richter. Earlier, he had received piano lessons from a local organist and had shown such promise that in 1825 his father applied (unsuccessfully) to Weber to give the boy further tuition. After his father's death, Schumann's mother insisted that he enroll as a law student at Leipzig University – she did not share the young composer's musical or literary tastes. Once installed at Leipzig, however, Schumann neglected his legal studies and in 1829 began to study piano and harmony with Friedrich Wieck, his future (unwilling) father-in-law. At the end of the following year he gave up law for music and wrote his opus one, the piano variations on the name *Abegg* (that of a person, giving the theme A – B flat – E – G – G: Schumann's use of musical anagrams as a source of inspiration was to continue throughout his career, and has recently been the subject of considerable musicological research). During this period he also studied briefly under Weinlig, the St. Thomas cantor, and Dorn, the director of the Opera. In 1832 his aspirations to become a concert pianist ended when his right hand became crippled – tradition tells us that this was the result of using a bad, self-designed contrivance for developing his finger technique, though modern medical knowledge points to disease as a possible source. This infirmity, however, had the advantage of making him devote more time to composition, and it was during the 1830s that he wrote the bulk of his piano works, including the *Symphonic Studies* (1834), *Carnaval* (1834), the *Davidsbündlertanze* (1837), *Phantasiestücke* (1837), *Kinderscenen* (1838), *Kreisleriana* (1838), *Arabeske* (1838), *Novelletten* (1838), C major *Fantasy* (1838), *Blumenstück* (1839) and *Faschingsschwank aus Wien* (1839). In 1833 he founded the *Neue Zeitschrift für Musik* (first issue, 3 April 1834), a journal to champion the cause of the new romantic style, and in 1840 he married Clara Wieck, daughter of his former teacher, who became the most renowned interpreter of his piano music. All his compositions up to 1839 were for piano. In 1840 he turned, equally obsessively, to the art of song and in that year wrote fifteen sets, including the cycles *Myrten*, *Frauenliebe und Leben* and *Dichterliebe*, comprising some 120 songs. In 1841 he wrote his first symphony, which marked the start of his orchestral phase. Also in that year he produced the first movement of his piano concerto (then called *Phantasie* in A minor) and began the D minor symphony (later no 4). In 1842 came chamber music, including the three string quartets, the piano quartet and the piano quintet. These fanatical bursts of activity were largely inspired by the period of domestic bliss which Schumann had entered, in spite of Friedrich Wieck's violent opposition to his daughter's marriage – at one time he forbade the young couple to meet, and in the end Schumann had to apply to the Court of Appeal before getting permission for the wedding. On the founding of the Leipzig Conservatorium in 1843 he was appointed teacher of composition, but moved in 1844 to Dresden, and in 1850 to Düsseldorf as a conductor. From 1843 his work had been disturbed by periodic crises of mental instability, which his Düsseldorf appointment did nothing to alleviate.

Robert and Clara Schumann about the time of his appointment to Düsseldorf and the onset of his final mental deterioration.

In 1854 he threw himself into the Rhine and was taken to a private asylum at Endenich, near Bonn, where he ended his days. During that time he continued to compose, but fitfully; such works as the violin concerto suggest that his inspiration had deteriorated along with his mental state.

His piano music embodies many of the traits which became the idioms of the piano style of the romantic period, such as the impetuous waywardness of rhythm expressed in syncopations and in combinations of different metres, and the new effects of tonal distance resulting from sudden changes of harmony and of sonority and fusion from the use of the pedal. The subjective and literary element in his music takes the themes from names (e.g. from Abegg in the Variations, op 1, from Asch, the birthplace of his beloved in 1834, Ernestine von Fricken, in *Carnaval*, from Bach in the Six Fugues, op 60) and of relating musical styles to personalities (e.g. to the extrovert and introvert aspects of his own personality, symbolised as *Eusebius* and *Florestan*, and to Chopin, Paganini and Clara Wieck – *Chiarina* – in *Carnaval*, to his imaginary society of anti-philistines, the *Davidsbund*, in the *Davidsbündlertänze* and *Carnaval*, and to a character in E. T. A. Hoffmann's *Phantasiestücke nach Callots Manier* in *Kreisleriana*, rather than of dramatic musical narrative, as with Berlioz.

His quick and intuitive insight into romantic poetry shows itself in the varied forms and intimate expression of his songs, although he occasionally upsets the perfect balance which Schubert had achieved between singer and pianist in favour of the piano – not necessarily to the detriment of the music, however, as the marvellous piano introductions and postludes in *Frauenliebe und Leben* and *Dichterliebe* confirm. Apart from the first symphony, which was inspired by a poem of Adolf Böttger and has some thematic cross-references in the first three movements,

the third (*Rhenish*) symphony, written after a visit to Cologne in 1850 and three concert overtures, the orchestral and chamber music is without programmatic titles. The D minor symphony, published in its revised form as no 4 in 1851, is a remarkable pioneering example of thematic transformation, being based almost entirely on two motives; others are the first movements of the piano concerto and of the second quartet. The so-called ineptitude which at times mars his scoring for orchestra is due to his lack of orchestral training and experience, and his inherently 'pianistic' way of thinking; but the weaknesses were greatly exaggerated by an older generation of musicians, and are no excuse for bad performances of these important works today. His only opera *Genoveva* (Leipzig, 1850) did not achieve a real success, and his other dramatic works and choral works, although containing some of the finest of his later music, are rarely performed. In his writings Schumann deprecated the prevalent taste of the 1830s for superficial salon music and was enthusiastic about Bach and Beethoven and the new music of his more significant contemporaries; his first article saluted the genius of Chopin ('Hats off gentlemen, a genius'), his last the promise of Brahms. His articles on *Music and Musicians* were published in English in two volumes in 1877, and a selection in one volume in 1947. His principal compositions are:

(1) Piano solo: three sonatas; three 'sonatas for the Young'; a *Fantasie* in three movements; twelve studies on Caprices by Paganini; Variations on *Abegg*; Impromptus on a Theme by Clara Wieck; twelve Studies in the form of Variations (*Études symphoniques*); three Romances; four Fugues and seven 'Little Fugues' (*Clavierstücke in Fughettenform*); four Marches; sets of pieces with the titles *Papillons, Intermezzi, Davidsbündlertänze, Carnaval, Fantasiestücke* (two), *Kinderscenen* (Scenes from Childhood); *Kreisleriana, Novelletten, Nachtstücke* (Nightpieces), *Faschingsschwank aus Wien* (Carnival Jest from Vienna), *Clavierstücke, Album für die Jugend* (Album for the Young), *Waldscenen* (Woodland Scenes), *Bunte Blätter* (Motley Leaves), *Albumblätter, Gesänge der Frühe* (Songs of the Early Morning); Toccata; Allegro in B minor; *Arabeske; Blumenstücke* (Flower-Pieces); *Humoreske*.

(2) Piano duet: eight Polonaises; six Impromptus (*Bilder aus Osten*); twelve pieces for 'small and big children'; nine dances (*Ball-Scenen*); Six Easy Dances (*Kinderball*).

(3) Two pianos: Andante and Variations; eight Polonaises.

(4) Pedal-piano: six studies and four sketches.

(5) Organ or pedal-piano: six Fugues on the name of Bach.

(6) Orchestra: four symphonies; Overture, Scherzo and Finale; overtures to Schiller's *Braut von Messina* (Bride of Messina), Shakespeare's *Julius Caesar*, Goethe's *Hermann und Dorothea*; concerto in A minor; Introduction and Allegro Appassionato in G, and *Concert Allegro* in D for piano and orchestra; violin concerto; *Phantasie* for violin and orchestra; cello concerto; and *Concertstücke* for four horns and orchestra.

(7) Chamber music: three quartets; three trios; four

Fantasiestücke for trio; piano quartet; piano quintet; *Märchenerzählungen* for piano, clarinet (or violin) and viola; two violin sonatas; *Märchenbilder* for viola and piano; five pieces 'in folk song style' for cello and piano; three Romances for oboe and piano; *Fantasiestücke* for clarinet and piano; Adagio and Allegro for horn and piano.

(8) Vocal works: 33 sets or cycles and fourteen single songs with piano; three ballads for declamation to piano; four sets of vocal duets, one of vocal trios, and four of vocal quartets with piano; seven sets of part-songs for mixed voices, four for male voices and two for female voices; fifteen choral works with orchestra.

(9) Stage works: *Genoveva* (opera); incidental music to Byron's *Manfred* (intended for performance in a version adapted by Schumann).

G. Abraham (editor): *Schumann: a Symposium* (1952)

V. Basch: *Schumann* (1932)

H. Bedford: *Schumann* (1933)

J. Chissell: *Schumann* (1948); *Schumann Piano Music* (1972)

A. Desmond: *Schumann Songs* (1972)

J. A. Fuller-Maitland: *Schumann's Concerted Chamber Music* (1929); *Schumann's Pianoforte Works* (1927)

G. Jansen: *The Life of Robert Schumann told in his Letters*, translated M. Herbert (1890)

F. Niecks: *Robert Schumann* (1925)

R. H. Schauffler: *Florestan: The Life and Work of Robert Schumann* (1945)

C. Schumann: *Robert Schumanns Jugendbriefe* (1885; English translation 1888)

E. Schumann: *Memoirs*, translated by M. Bush (1930)

K. Storck: *The Letters of Robert Schumann*, translated by H. Bryant (1907)

D. Walker: *Schumann* (1975)

S. Walsh: *The* Lieder *of Schumann* (1971)

Schumann-Heink, Ernestine (1861–1936), German–American contralto. She made her operatic debut at Dresden in 1878, appeared regularly at Bayreuth between 1896 and 1906, and played Klytemnestra in the première of Richard Strauss's *Elektra* at Dresden in 1909. After making her U.S. debut at Chicago, she joined the New York Metropolitan, where she played numerous roles.

Schuppanzigh, Ignaz (1776–1830), Austrian violinist; a friend and teacher of Beethoven. He lived in Vienna, where he was a member of Prince Lichnowsky's quartet (1794–95), conductor of the Augarten concerts (1798–99) and founder and leader of the Rasumovsky Quartet (1808), which toured Germany, Russia and Poland (1815–24) and gave first performances of quartets by Beethoven and Schubert. He was a member of the Vienna court orchestra from 1824 and conductor of the court opera from 1828.

Schürmann, Georg Caspar (c. 1672–1751), German composer and singer. He was in the service of the Duke of Brunswick at Wolfenbüttel from 1697, and of the Duke of Meiningen from 1703–6, before returning to Wolfenbüttel in 1707 as court opera conductor. After Keiser (died 1739) he was the most important composer for the German stage in the baroque period, and wrote some forty operas.

Schütz, Heinrich (Lat., **Henricus Sagittarius**) (1585–1672), German composer. He was a chorister at the Court Chapel in Cassel from 1599, and studied law at Marburg University from 1607 and later music under G. Gabrieli in Venice, where he lived from 1609 to 1612. He was court organist at Cassel in 1613 and *Kapellmeister* to the Electoral Court in Dresden in 1617. He visited Venice again from 1628 to 1629. He worked in Copenhagen 1633 to 1635, in 1637 and from 1642 to 1644, and then remained in Dresden until his death. The greatest German composer of his century, his first published compositions were Italian madrigals (1611). In a series of compositions written for the Lutheran church (*Psalms of David*, 1619; *Resurrection Story*, 1623; *Cantiones Sacrae*, 1625; *Symphoniae Sacrae*, three volumes, 1629, 1647, 1650; *Kleine geistliche Konzerte*, two volumes, 1636, 1639) he adopted the elaborate polychoral style of Gabrieli, the continuo madrigal style and some elements of the opera style of Monteverdi, and the *concertante* style for voices and instruments of his Italian contemporaries. In the preface to the German motets in the *Musicalia ad Chorum Sacrum* (1648), which are for five, six, and seven voices with continuo, he deprecated the tendency of younger German composers to write in the Italian style without a thorough grounding in counterpoint. In the *Twelve Sacred Songs* (1657) and the *Christmas Oratorio* he achieved a perfect balance between the Italian style and the Lutheran polyphonic tradition, and in the three Passions (St. Matthew, St. Luke, St. John, 1665–66) he refined his style even further by composing the words of the Evangelist in unaccompanied chant modelled on that of the earliest Lutheran Passions. He made much less use of chorale melodies than did Lutheran composers before him and after him. His complete works were edited, mainly by Philipp Spitta, in eighteen volumes (1885–1927). A new series, known as the *Stuttgart Complete Edition*, was begun in 1967 under the editorial supervision of G. Graulich and P. Horn (36 volumes projected). Yet another collected edition in forty volumes was begun in 1955 under the auspices of the *Neuen Schütz-Gesellschaft*.

H. J. Moser: *Heinrich Schütz, his Life and Work*, translated by C. F. Pfatteicher (1959)

schwach (Ger.), weak, soft; *schwachen*, to weaken.

Schwanda the Bagpiper, *see* SVANDA THE BAGPIPER

Schwanengesang (*Swan Song*), set of fourteen songs by Schubert, composed in 1828 and published after his death. The title was supplied by the publisher. Seven of the songs are based on poems by Heine and one (*Die Taubenpost*) by Seidl. These are among the last songs Schubert wrote (thus the publisher's choice of title) but they do not form a narrative unity as do *Die schöne Müllerin* or *Winterreise*. The titles of the songs are:

(1) *Liebesbotschaft* (Love's message)

(2) *Kriegers Ahnung* (Warrior's foreboding)

(3) *Frühlingssehnsucht* (Spring longing)

(4) *Ständchen* (Serenade)

(5) *Aufenthalt* (Resting place)

(6) *In der Ferne* (In the distance)

(7) *Abschied* (Farewell)

(8) *Der Atlas* (Atlas)

(9) *Ihr Bild* (Her picture)
(10) *Das Fischermädchen* (The fisher girl)
(11) *Die Stadt* (The Town)
(12) *Am Meer* (By the sea)
(13) *Der Doppelgänger* (The spectral self)
(14) *Die Taubenpost* (Pigeon post)

Schwarz, Rudolf (born 1905), Austrian born conductor, who began his career as a viola player in the Vienna Philharmonic. After gaining conducting experience in Dusseldorf and Karlsruhe, he was musical director of the Jewish Cultural Union in Berlin until 1941, when he was sent by the Nazis to Belsen concentration camp. Having survived this, he went to Britain in 1947 as conductor of The Bournemouth Municipal Orchestra. From 1951 until 1957 he conducted the City of Birmingham Orchestra, and from 1957 until 1962 the B.B.C. Symphony Orchestra.

Schwarzkopf, Elisabeth (born 1915), German soprano. She studied in Berlin, made her Vienna début in 1942 as Zerbinetta in Strauss's *Ariadne auf Naxos*, and first appeared at Covent Garden in 1947 as Donna Elvira in *Don Giovanni*. In her prime, she was an outstanding exponent of Mozart and Strauss roles, and an incomparable Hanna in *The Merry Widow*. As a *Lieder* singer, one of the most sensitive and communicative artists this century has produced, she has built up a substantial repertory ranging from Mozart to Wolf and beyond. Many of her performances have been recorded.

Schweigsame, Frau (Ger., *The Silent Woman*), comic opera in three acts by Richard Strauss, to a libretto by Stefan Zweig after Ben Jonson's *Epicoene*. First performed in Dresden in 1935, it soon ran into Nazi disapproval (Zweig was a Jew) and was withdrawn after a few performances. The story, similar to that of Donizetti's *Don Pasquale*, has a heroine who changes from tender young girl to shrieking shrew after a mock marriage to a rich old man.

Schweitzer, Albert (1875–1965), French-Alsatian theologian, medical missionary, organist and musical historian. He studied at Strasbourg, Paris and Berlin universities, and was an organ pupil of Eugen Münch, Ernst Münch and Widor. He was organist of the Strasbourg Bach concerts from 1896 and of the Paris Bach Society concerts from 1906. Thereafter he became a medical missionary in the French Congo but made visits to Europe to give lectures and recitals. In his book on J. S. Bach (English translation by E. Newman, 1911), he expounded his view of Bach as a 'poet-musician' who conceived his musical ideas as expressions of various kinds of emotion suggested by his texts. While his ideas have been contested and may not be valid in all their details, the general soundness has become apparent as Bach's methods have come to be seen as a particular example of the established theory of his period concerning the nature of musical expression. Schweitzer's discussion of the relation of the music of the cantatas to their texts and of Bach's treatment of the melodies of the chorales to their words contributed much to the deeper understanding of Bach's sacred music. His autobiography has been published in an English translation as *My Life and Thought* (1933). He was awarded the Nobel Prize in 1952.

G. SEAVER: *Albert Schweitzer, The Man and His Mind* (1947)

Schweitzer, Anton (1735–87), German conductor and composer. He studied in Bayreuth and in Italy, 1764–66, and from 1772 lived in Weimar, and later in Gotha, as court conductor. He composed a number of successful *Singspiele*, including *Die Dorfgala* (1772). His *Alceste* (Weimar, 1773), to a libretto by C. M. Wieland, was a major step towards the creation of serious German opera. His setting of J. J. Rousseau's *Pygmalion* (1772) was the first important melodrama written by a German composer.

schwindend (Ger.), dying away.

Schwirrholz, *see* THUNDERSTICK

Schwung (Ger.), swing. So *schwungvol*, spirited.

sciolto (It.), free and easy.

Scipione (*Scipio*), opera in three acts by Handel, with a libretto by Paolo Antonio Rolli (based on Zeno's *Scipione nelle Spagne*), first performed in London in 1726.

scoop, a fault found among inexpert singers, whereby they tentatively slide up to a note instead of hitting it accurately.

scordatura (It.), 'mis-tuning'. Term used for the tuning of a stringed instrument to abnormal notes, for the sake of effect. An eighteenth-century example of *scordatura* can be found in Mozart's *Sinfonia Concertante* for violin and viola, K 364, where the viola is tuned a semitone sharp. A later and more grotesque example is in the scherzo of Mahler's fourth symphony, where a solo violinist has to tune his instrument up a tone – an uncanny effect compared by Neville Cardus to the shadows cast by nursery candlelight (*see Gustav Mahler: His Mind and Music*; 1965).

score (Fr., *partition*, Ger., *Partitur*, It., *partitura*), music written down so that the parts for different performers appear vertically above one another. Score form was used for writing down the earliest polyphony, but was replaced by the choirbook form in the 13th century. In Britain however, score form was still used for simpler church music and for carols until late in the 15th century. Since c. 1600 the modern method of writing in score with bar-lines has been used.

A 'full' orchestral score comprises all the parts of an orchestral composition; or of an opera or a work for chorus and orchestra; a 'short' score (piano score, piano reduction) is a reduction of the essential parts of an orchestral or choral work to two staves; a vocal score contains the separate vocal parts of an opera or other composition for voices and orchestra together with a reduction of the orchestral part to two staves for use with piano and organ. A 'miniature' score contains the same material as a full score, but reduces it in size to make it easily transportable (and cheaper to buy).

A modern full score is set down in the following vertical order:

Woodwind (for details *see* ORCHESTRA)
Brass (for details *see* ORCHESTRA)
Percussion
Harp and Keyboard instruments
Solo instrument(s) in a concerto
Voices
First and second violins
Violas
Cellos and double basses

(The older method was to place the voices between the violas and the cellos)

As a part of musical education, score-reading means playing on the piano the essentials of the full score or all the parts of a choral piece, e.g. Mass or motet, written in score. It involves reading the various clefs and restoring to their true pitch the sounds of transposing instruments. Many modern scores are highly complex, and require knowledge of the elaborate new notation used by many composers today (details often being supplied in a printed preface which in some cases is longer than the piece itself).

H. GAL: *Directions for Score-Reading* (1924)

R. O. MORRIS and H. FERGUSON: *Preparatory Exercises in Score-Reading* (1931)

G. JACOB: *Orchestral Technique* (1940)

scorrevole (It.), scurrying, gliding.

Scotch snap, name for a rhythm consisting of a short note on the beat, followed by a longer note:

♫.

This rhythm is one of the idioms of Scottish folk music, and is found in particular in the strathspey. But it is not peculiar to Scotland: J. J. Quantz discussed it as a fashion of the Lombardic violinists, e.g. Vivaldi and Tartini, and it is more often called 'Lombardic' rhythm on the Continent.

'Scotch' Symphony, the third of Mendelssohn's mature symphonies, which he began during a visit to Scotland in 1830 and completed in 1842 as his op 56 in A minor. Though the scherzo, in particular, has certain Scottish characteristics, the work is no more programmatic than the same composer's Italian symphony. The music was dedicated to Queen Victoria, and received its first performance in Leipzig, in 1842.

Scott, Cyril Meir (1879–1970), English composer and poet. He studied in Frankfurt under Uzielli and Iwan Knorr, and lived from 1898 in Liverpool and later in London. He became interested in spiritualism and Oriental philosophy and wrote *The Philosophy of Modernism in its connection with music* (1926), *The Influence of Music on History and Morals* (1929) and *Music: its Secret Influence through the Ages* (1933). His music includes many works for the piano, notably a sonata (1909), *Five poems* (1912) and a concerto (1915). These helped to earn him the label 'the English Debussy', though his music was more original than that implies. He also composed orchestral works, choral works, including a setting of Crashaw's *Nativity Hymn* (1914), a violin concerto, chamber music and songs. His opera *The Alchemist* was performed at Essen (in a German translation) in 1925.

Scott, Francis George (1880–1958), Scottish composer, pupil of Roger-Ducasse in Paris. He was a sensitive and prolific composer of songs, producing five volumes of 'Scottish Lyrics' and a further volume containing 'Thirty-five Scottish Lyrics and other Poems' between 1921 and 1949. These comprise settings of poetry from the 16th to the 20th centuries, and recreate in musical terms the speech rhythms and inflections of Scottish folk poetry.

Scriabin, *see* SKRYABIN

Scriptores, *see* COUSSEMAKER, GERBERT, MEIBOM.

Sculthorpe, Peter (born 1929), Australian composer, whose output includes a series of vivid orchestral works each entitled *Sun Music*; also seven string quartets.

Scythian Suite (also known as *Ala and Lolli*), work by Prokofiev, originally intended to be a ballet on the subject of the Scythians, primeval inhabitants of Southern Russia. Though the ballet never materialized, the composer released the music in 1916 in the form of a concert suite, somewhat reminiscent in its orchestral ferocity of Stravinsky's *Rite of Spring* (which had had its première three years earlier).

Sea Drift, a setting of a poem by Walt Whitman for baritone solo, chorus and orchestra by Delius. It was completed in 1903 and was first performed three years later at Essen, in Germany. Its first British performances were in Sheffield and London in 1908.

Searle, Humphrey (born 1915), English composer, educated at Winchester College and Oxford. He was a pupil of Ireland at the Royal College of Music in London and of Webern in Vienna. One of the first and leading British exponents of twelve-note technique, he has written operas on *The Diary of a Madman* (after Gogol), *The Photo of the Colonel* (after Ionesco) and *Hamlet*, all of which had their first performances in Germany (where Searle is widely admired) rather than Britain. His other works include a trilogy for speakers and orchestra – *Gold Coast Customs* and *The Shadows of Cain* (to texts by Edith Sitwell), and *The Riverrun* (James Joyce). He has written five symphonies, two piano concertos, a ballet (*Noctambules*), a setting of Edward Lear's *The Owl and the Pussy Cat* for speaker and chamber ensemble, a piano sonata and songs. He is a leading authority on the music of Liszt, on which he has written a book.

Seasons, The, (1) secular oratorio by Haydn (Ger., *Die Jahreszeiten*), with words translated and adapted from James Thomson's poem by Baron van Swieten. The English text usually used is a translation of van Swieten's original German. The first performance was in Vienna in 1801. There are four parts: *Spring* (*Die Frühling*), *Summer* (*Der Sommer*), *Autumn* (*Der Herbst*) and *Winter* (*Der Winter*). The work calls for soprano, tenor and bass soloists as well as chorus and orchestra;

(2) a ballet of the same title was composed by Glazunov with choreography by Petipa (1900). For Vivaldi's four concertos on the same subject *see* FOUR SEASONS.

Sea Symphony, A, title of Vaughan Williams's first symphony, which is a setting, for solo singers, chorus and orchestra, of poems by Walt Whitman about the sea. Its first performance was at the Leeds Festival in 1910.

Sebastiani, Johann (1622–83), German composer. He lived in Königsberg from 1650, where he was cantor of the Cathedral church from 1661, choirmaster of the Electoral church from 1663, and retired in 1679. His *St. Matthew Passion* (composed 1663, published 1672; modern edition in *Denkmäler deutscher Tonkunst*, xvii), which includes chorales for solo voice accompanied by four *viole da gamba*, illustrates one of the steps in the development of the Lutheran Passion between the 16th century and J. S. Bach. He also published two volumes of sacred and secular songs, *Parnassblumen* (1672, 1675).

secco, *see* RECITATIVE

Sechzehntel (Ger.), semiquaver.

second, the INTERVAL of a semitone (minor second), of a tone (major second), or of a tone and a half (augmented second) when the two notes concerned have adjacent letter names. For example,

is a minor second formed by G and A flat

is a major second formed by G and A, and

is an augmented second, formed by G and A sharp.

　　　See also TONE, SEMITONE, INTERVAL

seconda prattica, *see* PRIMA PRATTICA

seconda volta (It.), 'second time', i.e. the second ending when a repeat has been indicated.

　　　See VOLTA (1)

secondary dominant, *see* DOMINANT

secondo (It.), 'second'. (1) the lower part of the piano duet, the upper part being termed *primo* (first).

　　　(2) the second of two or more players or singers, or of two or more groups of performers. *Violino secondo*, the second violin in a string quartet, or the whole body of second violins in an orchestra.

　　　See PRIMO

Secret, The (Cz., *Tajemství*), opera in three acts by Smetana, to a libretto by Eliška Krásnohorská, first performed at Prague in 1878. Though less famous outside Czechoslovakia as *The Bartered Bride*, this is one of Smetana's most distinguished operas, dealing with the separation and eventual reunion of two lovers.

Secret Marriage, The (It., *Il Matrimonio Segreto*), comic opera in two acts by Cimarosa, to a libretto by Giovanni Bertati, first performed in Vienna in 1792. This superficial comedy of intrigue was based on the English play, The *Clandestine Marriage*, by David Garrick and George Colman. The first performance was so successful that the Emperor Leopold II ordered it to be repeated after a break for supper. Today, though still popular, it sounds like Mozart without the genius, but at one time it was considered superior to *The Marriage of Figaro*.

segno, dal (It.), 'from the sign', i.e., repeat from the sign.

Segovia, Andrés (born 1893), Spanish guitarist, the most famous in the world. By technique and artistry, he extended the expressive range of his instrument, and inspired numerous composers (including Villa-Lobos and Castelnuovo-Tedesco) to write music for him.

Segreto di Susanna, Il, *see* SUSANNA'S SECRET

segue (It.), 'follows'. Used as a direction (1) to proceed to the following movement without a break;

　　　(2) to continue a formula which has been indicated, such as arpeggiating of chords or doubling in octaves.

Seguidilla (Sp.), a Spanish dance in 3/8 or 3/4 time in the style of, and faster than, the Bolero, with *coplas* sung by the players. It often has a castanet accompaniment. Carmen's 'Séguidille' in the first act of Bizet's opera is modelled on the *seguidilla*:

sehr (Ger.), very.

Seiber, Mátyás György (1905–60), Hungarian born composer, cellist and conductor who took up residence in Britain in 1935. He studied at the Budapest Academy of Music, where he was a pupil of Kodály, and taught at the Hoch Conservatorium, Frankfurt, 1928–33 before joining the staff of Morley College in London. He was founder (1945) and conductor of the Dorian Singers. His interests ranged from 16th century music to jazz and twelve-note music. His compositions include several choral works (among them the cantata *Ulysses*, a setting of extracts from James Joyce's book), stage and film music, a clarinet concerto, four string quartets and other chamber works, piano music, educational music and songs. He was killed in a car crash in South Africa.

Seidl, Anton (1850–98) Hungarian born conductor. He studied at the Leipzig Conservatorium from 1870–72, when he went to Bayreuth as Wagner's assistant and made the first copy of the score of *Der Ring des Nibelungen*. He was conductor of the Leipzig opera (1879–82) and toured Germany, Holland, England and other countries as conductor of A. Neumann's 'Nibelungen' opera company. He was appointed conductor of the Bremen Opera in 1883, of German opera at the Metropolitan Opera in New York in 1885, and of the New York Philharmonic Orchestra in 1891. He conducted the first performances in the United States of *Tristan und Isolde* (1886), of the complete *Ring* (1889), and of Dvořák's *New World* symphony (1893).

Seiffert, Max (1868–1948), German musicologist. His numerous publications include *Geschichte der Klaviermusik* (1899). He edited the complete works of Sweelinck and completed Chrysander's edition of *Messiah*. He was also responsible for practical editions of a large number of works by Bach, Handel and other 18th century composers, and edited a series of editions of old music entitled *Organum*.

Seikilos song, one of the few surviving examples of Greek music. It is inscribed on the tomb of Seikilos

(2nd or 1st century B.C.) at Tralles in Asia Minor. A transcription is in *Historical Anthology of Music*, edited by A. T. Davison and W. Apel, no 7c.

Seiten (Ger.), side. So *Seitenthema*, the second theme of a movement in sonata form, etc.

Selle, Thomas (1599–1663), German composer. He was rector and cantor at various churches, and in 1641 cantor at the Johanneum and musical director at the five principal churches in Hamburg. He published several sets of solo songs with continuo, of sacred concertos, and of secular choral pieces, and contributed melodies to Johann Rist's collections of chorale texts. He was one of the first composers to introduce settings of other words into the Passion; his *St. John Passion* of 1643 (modern edition by R. Gerber, 1933) contained choruses to words from Isaiah and from Psalm 22.

Semele, secular oratorio by Handel, with a text adapted from an opera libretto written some years previously by William Congreve. Its first performance was in London in 1744. The story concerns Semele's love for Jupiter. Today the work is often staged as an opera, as well as performed in the concert hall. Its most famous aria is 'Where e'er you walk'.

semibreve (U.S., whole-note, Fr., *ronde*, Ger., *ganze Note*, It., *semibreve*), 'half a breve'. This is the longest note-value normally used in modern notation, and is written ○. In the 13th century it was the shortest note, and the breve could be divided into from two to nine semibreves. In the 15th century it became the normal beat (tactus), and in the 18th century became the theoretical term of reference for all time-signatures and for all other note-values.

semicrona (It.), semiquaver.

semiminima (It.), 'half a minim', i.e. a crotchet.

semiquaver (U.S., sixteenth-note, Fr., *double croche*, Ger., *Sechzehntel*, It., *semicroma*). The note

grouped

which is half the length of a quaver (eighth-note) and a sixteenth of the length of a semibreve (whole-note).

Semiramide (It., *Semiramis*), opera in two acts by Rossini, with a libretto by Gaetano Rossi (based on Voltaire's tragedy). Its first performance was in Venice in 1823. The legendary Queen of Babylon – who kills her husband and falls in love with her son – attracted many composers, besides Rossini, to write opera about her. Porpora, Vivaldi, Gluck, Paisiello, Salieri, Cimarosa, Meyerbeer and Respighi were some of the most famous. Rossini's version has been sung by Patti, Grisi, Melba and, in our own time, Joan Sutherland. Its success has always depended on an outstanding exponent of the title role. Even when none has been available, its thrilling overture, at least, has remained a concert hall favourite.

semiseria (It.), 'half-serious'. 18th century term for *opera seria* (serious opera) containing some comic scenes or interludes.

semitone, half a tone – the smallest interval in regular use in western music. It can be written either as an augmented unison:

or as a minor second:

according to context. In EQUAL TEMPERAMENT there are twelve equal semitones in an octave.

semplice (It.), in a simple manner.

sempre (It.), 'always', 'still', as in *sempre piano*, still softly.

Semyon Kotko, the first of Prokofiev's Soviet operas, composed in 1939–40 after his return to Russia from his travels. The opera, too, concerns a returning hero – a Ukrainian soldier who has been fighting for the Revolution, but whose fiancée's father is unfortunately an anti-revolutionary. The work is based on Katayev's novel, *I, Son of the Working Class*.

Senallié, Jean Baptiste (1687–1730), French violinist and composer. He was a pupil of Vitali in Modena, where he became attached to the ducal court. From 1720 he was a member of the royal string orchestra in Paris. He introduced Italian violin techniques into France, and was one of the first French composers of solo sonatas for violin, of which he published five books between 1710 and 1727.

Senfl (**Senffl, Sänftli, Senfel**), **Ludwig** (c. 1489–1543), Swiss composer. He studied under Isaac and in 1517 was his successor as court *Kapellmeister* at Vienna. In 1520 he was in Augsburg, and in 1523 became director of the court chapel at Munich. Although attached to a Roman Catholic court he corresponded with Luther and composed polyphonic choral settings of Lutheran chorales, of which eleven were published in Rhau's collection of 1544 (modern edition in *Denkmäler deutscher Tonkunst*, xxxiv). In 1530 and 1531 he completed an unfinished section in Isaac's *Choralis Constantinus* and supervised the copying of the whole work. He was a prolific and versatile composer. The range of his choral compositions extends from settings of German secular songs, printed in such collections as those of Georg Forster (1540) and Johann Ott (1544) to settings of Latin hymns in Georg Rhau's collection of 1542 (reprinted in *Das Erbe deutscher Musik*, xxi and xxv), Magnificats in the eight tones and motets (eight Magnificats and twelve motets were printed in *Denkmäler der Tonkunst in Bayern*, iii, 2), and Masses. A complete edition of his works was begun in 1937 and is still in progress.

sennet (**synnet, cynet, signet**), a direction in Elizabethan plays that instrumental music is to be played. It is probably a corruption of *sonata* as TUCKET is of *toccata*.

sensible (Fr.; It., *sensibilita*), 'sensitive' (the *nota sensibile* is the leading note).

senza (It.), 'without', as in *senza rall.*, without slowing down; *senza sordino*, without the mute.

septet (Fr., *septuor*, It., *settimino*), a group of seven performers, or a composition, usually instrumental, for such a group. Beethoven wrote a septet (op 20) for violin, viola, horn, clarinet, bassoon, cello and double bass, and there are later examples by Saint-

Säens (piano, strings and trumpet, op 65), d'Indy (suite for trumpet, two flutes, and a string quartet, op 24), and Ravel (introduction and Allegro for harp, string quartet, flute and clarinet, 1906).

septuor (Fr.), septet.

septuplet, group of seven notes to be played in the time of four or six.

sequence, (1) repetition of the same melodic pattern at a different pitch, e.g.:

from the fugue in B flat in the first book of Bach's *Forty-eight*. The repetition may be ornamented, as in the subject of the same fugue:

Sequential melody, if it is based on more than one chord, is usually accompanied by sequential harmony. If such a sequence is an exact transposition, involving modulation, it is called a 'real' or modulating sequence, if not, 'tonal' or diatonic.

(2) a form of Latin poetry which was widely used in the Middle Ages, especially in France and England, as an accretion to the liturgy. It probably originated in northern France where, in the 9th century, words were added to the extended melisma (called *sequentia*) which followed the Alleluia of the Mass on festivals and important Saints' days. These early texts were usually in prose; hence the normal Latin term in the manuscripts, '*prosa*', and the present-day French '*prose*'. The sequences of Notker Balbulus of St. Gall (d. 912), however, have poetic texts, and sometimes use the melodies of the Alleluia proper. In form the sequence normally consisted of a series of pairs of lines, each pair being sung to the same melody, thus:

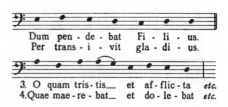

The text of the *Stabat Mater* has been frequently set by composers from the late 15th century to modern times. After the reforms of the Council of Trent only four sequences remained in the Roman liturgy: *Dies irae* (Requiem Mass), *Lauda Sion Salvatorem* (Corpus Christi), *Veni Sancte Spiritus* (Whitsunday), and *Victimae paschali laudes* (Easter). The *Stabat Mater* was admitted to the Roman Missal in 1727.

See also DIES IRAE, STABAT MATER

Seraglio, Il, *see* ENTFUHRUNG

serenade, (1) a song of amorous devotion, e.g. Don Giovanni's 'Deh vieni alla finestra' in Mozart's opera, and Schubert's *Ständchen*. Traditionally a serenade is sung in the evening by a lover beneath his beloved's window, often with a guitar or mandolin accompaniment. A classical composer, in writing a serenade, would try to create this atmosphere in some way – Mozart actually uses a mandolin in the above example, and the piano part of the Schubert imitates a plucked instrument.

(2) a set of movements for chamber orchestra or for wind instruments similar in style to the cassation and divertimento, composed for evening entertainment in the 18th century. Mozart's serenades usually have two minuets and a varying number of sonata movements. Beethoven wrote a serenade for string trio op 8 (afterwards revised as op 41 for flute, violin, and viola, op 25 (arranged as a Notturno, op 42, for piano and viola. Brahm's first works for orchestra were two serenades op 11 for orchestra with four horns and op 16 for small orchestra without violins. Schoenberg wrote a serenade (op 24, 1924) in seven movements, for clarinet, bass clarinet, mandolin, guitar, violin, viola, cello, with a bass voice in the fourth movement.

Serenade to Music, work by Vaughan Williams for sixteen solo voices and orchestra, based on Lorenzo's speech from Act 5 of *The Merchant of Venice*. It was composed in honour of Sir Henry Wood's jubilee as a conductor in 1938, and performed on that occasion by the cream of British singers (including Isobel Baillie, Eva Turner, Astra Desmond, Heddle Nash, Walter Widdop and Roy Henderson). Today it is often performed by larger choral forces.

serenata (It.), a title used in the early 18th century for a secular cantata or short opera composed to do homage to a patron. Bach used the term for his cantata *Durchlaucht'ster Leopold*, written for the birthday of Prince Leopold of Anhalt-Cöthen in 1717, and Handel for his *Aci, Galatea e Polifemo* (Naples, 1709) and his masque *Acis and Galatea*, composed at Cannons in 1720.

See SERENADE

serialism, the method of composition deriving from Schoenberg's twelve-note style. At one time it was believed that Schoenberg's musical principles would be too constricting, but Stravinsky (in his last years),

Boulez, Stockhausen and Dallapiccola, to mention just four, have shown how widely these principles can be applied.

series, a succession of notes presented in a certain order, not necessarily to create a melody, but to establish a relationship between them. Thus the note-row in twelve-note music is a 'series', which can be treated in various ways – played backwards, turned upside down, etc. – once the original order has been established.

serio, seria (It.), serious (also *serioso, seriosa*).

Serkin, Rudolf (born 1903), Austrian born pianist who has lived in the United States since 1939. He is one of today's most distinguished exponents of the classics, especially of works by Mozart, Beethoven, Schubert and Brahms.

serpent (Fr., Ger., *serpent*, It. *serpentone*), an obsolete wind instrument, the name of which was suggested by the shape, and which was the bass of the cornett family. It was made of wood covered with leather, and though in the opinion of Cecil Forsyth it 'presented the appearance of a dishevelled drainpipe which was suffering internally' it pursued a versatile career for some 300 years. As the *serpent d'église* it was used in France from the 16th century to support the singing of plainsong. It was adopted by English church bands in the 19th century. Handel wrote for it, as bass to a large wind group, in the *Fireworks* music. Having changed its name to the *serpent droit* it appeared in the scores of Rossini (*Le Siège de Corinthe*), Mendelssohn (*St. Paul*), Wagner (*Rienzi*), and Verdi (*Les Vêpres Siciliennes*). *See* BASS HORN, RUSSIAN BASSOON, illus. p. 87.

Serov, Alexander Nikolayevich (1820–71), Russian composer and music critic.

serpent droit, *see* BASS HORN, SERPENT

serpentone, *see* SERPENT

serré (Fr.), tightened, i.e. an indication that the music is to be performed more tensely and quickly. The Italian equivalent, more commonly used, is *stringendo*.

Serse, *see* XERXES

Serva Padrona, La (*The Maid as Mistress*), comic opera in two parts by Pergolesi, with a libretto by Gennaro Antonio Federico. It was first performed as two *intermezzi* in the composer's serious opera *Il prigionier superbo* in Naples in 1733. It was soon widely performed on its own and gave the impulse to the cultivation of *opera buffa*, and indirectly of the French *opéra-comique* (first performance in Paris, 1746).

service, the musical setting of the canticles at Morning and Evening Prayer and of the congregational part of the Communion service in the Anglican liturgy. In the Morning Service are the *Te Deum* and *Benedictus* (or *Jubilate*); in the Evening Service the *Magnificat* (or *Cantate domino*) and *Nunc dimittis* (or *Deus misereatur*); in the Communion Service the *Kyrie*, *Sanctus* and *Gloria in excelsis*, and also, in modern times, the *Benedictus* and *Agnus Dei*. A full service includes settings of all these parts, which are sung in English, although they have retained their Latin names.

16th century composers were accustomed to distinguish between a 'short' service, set in simple style, and a 'great' service, set in a more elaborate polyphonic style or in antiphonal style for the two sides of the choir, *Decani* and *Cantoris*, in alternation and combination. Among the best examples of the early period are the services of Tallis, Byrd and Tomkins. Byrd's Second

Service 'with verses to the organs' initiated a style of service corresponding to that of the Verse Anthem, but after Tomkins and Gibbons the composition of services became rather perfunctory, and those of post-Restoration composers are much inferior to their best anthems, with the exception of Purcell's *Te Deum* and *Jubilate* in D and his full service in B flat. The services of S. S. Wesley and Walmisley suggest higher artistic aims than those of their 18th century predecessors, but few services of the past hundred years, with the possible exception of those of C. V. Stanford, have succeeded in fulfilling them or in rising above the general level of the church music of the period.

sesquialtera (Lat.), short for *pars sesquialtera*, a quantity one and a half times as much. In the theory of PROPORTIONS, which had its musical application in the rhythmic practice and in the theory of intervals of medieval and Renaissance music, the prefix *sesqui-* denoted a proportion in which one term was greater than the other by one, e.g. 3:2 (*sesquialtera*), 4:3 (*sesquitertia*), etc.. In connection with rhythm and interval *sesquialtera* was commonly called HEMIOLA. The organ stop *sesquialtera* is a MUTATION stop normally having two ranks of $2\frac{2}{3}$ ft. and $1\frac{3}{5}$ ft. giving the intervals of the twelfth and the seventeenth from the fundamental.

Sessions, Roger (born 1896), U.S. composer. He studied at Harvard University, under Horatio Parker at Yale University, and under Ernest Bloch at Cleveland and New York. In 1921 he became head of the theory department at Cleveland Institute of Music. From 1925–33 he lived in Florence, Rome and Berlin. He taught at Boston University, at Princeton University from 1937, at the University of California from 1945, and again at Princeton from 1953. He composed *The Trial of Lucullus*, a one-act opera after Brecht in 1947. His full-length opera, *Montezuma*, had its première in Berlin in 1954. His other works include five symphonies, a violin concerto, a piano concerto, chamber music, and songs. He is the author of *The Musical Experience of Composer, Performer and Listener* (1950), *Harmonic Practice* (1951), and *Reflections on the Musical Life in the United States* (1956).

sestetto, *see* SEXTET

settimino, *see* SEPTET

seventh, the INTERVAL comprised by the first and last of any series of seven notes in a diatonic scale, e.g.:

Seven Last Words of the Saviour on The Cross, The (Ger., *Die Sieben Worte des Erlösers am Kreuze*), an orchestral work by Haydn (1785) commissioned by the Cathedral of Cadiz and composed in seven slow movements which the composer later arranged for string quartet (op 51, 1787) and as a choral work (1796). An oratorio on the same subject was composed by Schütz (1645) with a text compiled from the four gospels.

A major seventh is a semitone less than an octave:

a minor seventh is a tone less than an octave:

a diminished seventh is a tone and a half less than an octave:

Since the seventh is a dissonance, a CHORD containing a seventh required resolution in traditional harmony. The most important chords containing sevenths are the DOMINANT seventh chord and the DIMINISHED SEVENTH chord.

sextet (Fr., *sextette*, *sextuor*, It., *sestetto*), a composition, instrumental or vocal, for six performers. The instruments normally in a string sextet are two violins, two violas, and two cellos, as in Brahms's two string sextets, op 18 and 36, and Schoenberg's *Verklärte Nacht* (1899). Haydn wrote an *Echo* for four violins and two cellos. Beethoven's wind sextet, op 71, is for two clarinets, two horns and two bassoons, and his op 81b is for two violins, viola, cello and two horns. In vocal music the term is usually applied only to operatic ensembles.

sextolet, sextuplet, a group of six notes to be performed in the time of four of the same kind in the prevailing metre, thus:

It is most often the equivalent of two successive triplets, and is therefore more properly written with that grouping:

Where it is not so grouped and is not accompanied by another rhythm, it should be played evenly, without subsidiary accent, as in:

CHOPIN, *Nocturne* op 48, no 2

sextuor, *see* SEXTET

sfogato (It.), 'evaporated'. The term was used by Chopin, amongst others, to indicate an airy quality of playing.

sforzando, sforzato (It.), 'forcing', i.e. giving a strong accent on a single note or chord. It is usually abbreviated to *sfz* or *sf*.

Sgambati, Giovanni (1841–1914), Italian pianist, conductor and composer, pupil of Liszt. He appeared as pianist and as conductor at the age of six and later toured widely. He was a disciple of Liszt and Wagner, and wrote two symphonies, an *Epitalamio sinfonico* (1887) and two overtures for orchestra, a *Requiem*, chamber music and songs.

shake, alternative name for trill.

shanty, a work-song sung by sailors in the days of sailing ships. Shanties usually have a decided rhythm, and are in the form of solo verses and chorus. Collections of shanties have been published by J. Bradford and A. Fagge (1904), Cecil Sharp (1914), H. Kemp (1922), W. B. Whall (1912) and R. R. Terry (two volumes, 1921 and 1926).

Shapero, Harold (born 1920), U.S. composer, pupil of Hindemith, Křenek, Piston and Nadia Boulanger. His orchestral works include a symphony and a *Nine-minute Overture*. He has also written chamber music and piano pieces.

Shaporin, Yuri Alexandrovich (1889–1966) Russian composer, pupil of Sokolov, Steinberg and Cherepnin. He composed a great deal of incidental music for plays, besides piano sonatas and songs. His three major works are a symphony for orchestra, brass band and chorus, completed in 1932, in which he attempts 'to show the development of the fate of a human being in a great historical upheaval', a setting for chorus, soloists and orchestra of Blok's poem *On the Field of Kulikovo* (1939), and a oratorio *The Battle on Russian Soil* (1944). Parts of an opera *The Decembrists* (dealing with a Russian political conspiracy) were privately performed in Moscow in 1938; the work was completed in 1941.

G. ABRAHAM: *Eight Soviet Composers* (1943)

sharp (Fr., *dièse*, Ger., *Kreuz*, It., *diesis*), the sign ♯ which raises by a semitone the pitch of the line or space on which it stands. Thus the note C sharp would be a semitone higher than C natural.

Sharp, Cecil James (1859–1924), collector of English folk music. He was director of Hampstead Conservatory in London from 1896–1905 and in 1911 founded the English Folk Dance Society and became director of The School of Folksong and Dance, Stratford-on-Avon. He also collected folk music in the Appalachian Mountains in the United States. His collections, which laid the foundation of the English folk song and folk dance revival, include *Folk songs from Somerset* (1904–19), *Country Dance Tunes* (1909 onwards), *The Morris Book* (1907–13), *The Sword Dances of Northern England* (1911), *English Folk chanteys* (1914) and *English Folk songs from the Southern Appalachians* (1917; later edition by Maud Karpeles, two volumes, 1932). He also published *English Folk song; some Conclusions* (1907).

sharp mixture, an organ stop sounding high harmonics in addition to the fundamental note, thereby giving a bright tone. The word 'sharp' refers to the sound quality and not to the pitch.

Shaw, George Bernard (1856–1950), Irish born dramatist and critic whose musical writings, though peripheral to his career, offer an unsurpassed picture of music in London at the end of the 19th century. So witty and penetrating were his weekly reviews for the *Star* and the *World* (many of them under the pseudonym of Corno di Bassetto) that their moments of wrong-headedness are a small price to pay for their vitality.

shawm, shawn (Ger., *Schalmei*), a primitive and coarse sounding instrument that gave rise to the OBOE. It was, and still is, sometimes confused with the CHALUMEAU, the forerunner of the clarinet, since this name was often loosely used to describe any member of the woodwind family. Shawms were made in various sizes and, since the larger ones have tubes curved back to their mouthpieces, they resemble a bassoon rather than an oboe.

Shchedrin, Rodion (born 1932), Russian composer whose output includes a ballet, *The Little Hump-Backed Horse*, several symphonies and other orchestral works, songs and piano music.

Shebalin, Vissarion Yakovlevich (1902–63), Russian composer. He studied at the Moscow Conservatory, where he was a pupil of Miaskovsky and subsequently became teacher and director. In 1948 he was cited by the Communist Party as one of the 'inculcators of inharmonious music in the educational institutions' (at other times however, his works won official approval). His compositions include an opera (*The Embassy Bridegroom*), five symphonies (the third, *Lenin*, with chorus), cantatas, overtures, *concertino* for violin and strings, a violin concerto, a cello concerto, chamber music, instrumental music, and songs.

G. ABRAHAM: *Eight Soviet Composers* (1943)

Sheep may safely graze, an English translation of 'Schafe können sicher weiden', an aria for soprano with two recorders and figured bass from Bach's earliest secular cantata *Was mir behagt* (1716), composed to celebrate the birthday of Duke Christian of Sachsen-Weissenfels. The cantata, the words of which are by Salomo Franck, is in praise of hunting. The text of the aria compares the sense of security felt by a people governed by a wise ruler to that of sheep in the care of a reliable shepherd.

Sheherazade, symphonic suite by Rimsky-Korsakov, op 35 (1888), based on stories from the *Arabian Nights*. Fokine's ballet based on the music was first performed in Paris in 1910.

Shéhérazade (Fr.), a set of three songs (*Asie, La Flûte enchantée* and *L'Indifférente*) by Ravel (1903) for voice and orchestra (originally piano accompaniment) with words from poems by Tristan Klingsor. The work is based on an unpublished overture (1898) with the same title. The subject matter has no connection with Rimsky-Korsakov's suite of the same title.

Shelomo, rhapsody for cello and orchestra by Bloch, composed in 1915 and first performed in New York. This is one of Bloch's most interesting Jewish works, the title being a Hebrew form of the name Solomon. The German spelling, 'Schelomo', is often used, but there seems little point in employing it outside Germany.

Shepherd, Arthur (1880–1958), U. S. composer and conductor. He studied in Boston, where he later became professor at the New England Conservatory. *Horizons* (the first of his two symphonies) includes traditional cowboy music. He also wrote a violin concerto, a fantasy for piano and orchestra, three string quartets, instrumental music and songs.

Shepherds of the Delectable Mountain, The, opera in one act by Vaughan Williams, with a libretto from Bunyan's *The Pilgrim's Progress*. Its first performance was in London in 1922. The greater part of the work was later incorporated in the opera *The Pilgrim's Progress* (London, 1951)

shepherd's pipe, a primitive wind instrument, in which the sound is produced by means of a double reed. It resembles a bagpipe's chanter detached from the rest of the instrument.

Shield, William (1748–1829), English composer. He was apprenticed to a boat-builder and studied under Avison in Newcastle, where he became leader of the subscription concerts. He was appointed leader of the Scarborough theatre orchestra, first viola of the London Opera (1773–91), and composer to Covent Garden from 1782–91. In 1791 he met Haydn in London and visited France and Italy. He returned to Covent Garden as composer (1792–7) and in 1817 became Master of the King's Music. He 'composed and selected' the music for many stage works, of which the opera *Rosina* (1782) was one of the most successful, and published collections of songs, ballads, rounds and glees, a set of six string trios, a set of duets for violins, and two theoretical works: *An Introduction to Harmony* (1800) and *Rudiments of Thorough Bass* (c. 1815). The song, 'The Arethusa', generally attributed to Shield, was adapted from a country dance tune, 'The Princess Royal', first published in 1730.

shift, (1) change of POSITION of the left hand in playing a stringed instrument.

(2) change of position of the slide of a trombone.

shofar, ancient Jewish wind instrument still in use in the synagogue. Made from the horn of a ram, the notes are produced in the same manner as on a bugle. Elgar asked for its sound or something approximating to it in *The Apostles*.

short octave, the lowest notes on keyboard instruments in the 16th and 17th centuries were often arranged so as to provide within the compass of a sixth (short octave) the bass notes normally required, leaving out those which did not occur on account of the restricted range of keys used in the music. In one such arrangement the lowest keys appeared to be from E to C, but the notes they actually played ran thus:

As a further result, left-hand chords occasionally appear in the music which seem to involve the stretch of a tenth, but actually do not. The chord:

for example, in the last bar of a piece by Peter Philips in *The Fitzwilliam Virginal Book* (no 72) was played as if the notes were:

In order to produce a fully chromatic bass down to E some instruments with short octaves were designed with the lowest two 'black' keys split, the fore-parts sounding D and E, the rear-parts sounding F sharp and A flat. Philips's *Pavana dolorosa* (*Fitzwilliam Virgininal Book*, no 80) is an example of a piece requiring such an instrument.

short score, a reduction of all the essential parts of an orchestral or choral score to two staves.

See SCORE.

Dmitri Shostakovich, who dominated the Russian musical scene after the death of Prokofiev.

Shostakovich, Dmitri (1906–75), Russian composer, the most important of the day. He was born in St. Petersburg, where he studied composition under Steinberg and piano under Nikolaiev. He wrote a Scherzo for orchestra at thirteen, and his first symphony – a work of striking precocity – was performed in Leningrad in 1926. The works of the next few years were either political, as in the second symphony (1927), dedicated to the October Revolution of 1917, and the third, *May the First* (1930); or else satirical, as in the opera *The Nose* (1927–8), and the ballet *The Golden Age* (1930). Unfortunately for Shostakovich, official disfavour fell on the more extreme forms of social caricature in music, and his opera *Lady Macbeth of Mzensk* (*Katerina Ismailova*) was denounced in 1936, although it had been performed for two years in Russia and elsewhere. It was criticised as 'the negation of the very principles of opera', and as a 'thoroughly non-political concoction'. The fourth symphony was withdrawn (1936) in rehearsal, and the fifth (1937), in more serious vein and in traditional form without a programme, was described by the composer as 'a Soviet artist's practical reply to criticism' which depicted

'the re-education of the human mind . . . under the influence of the new ideals'. The seventh symphony was composed during the seige of Leningrad in 1941, and depicts peace, struggle and victory. In acknowledging renewed criticism of his music by the Central Committee of The Communist Party in 1948 Shostakovich admitted that his 'artistic reconstruction' had not been complete, and undertook to bring his work closer to 'folk art'. Nevertheless he succeeded in producing some of the most internationally impressive music of our time, and proved himself a composer of remarkable staying power. His symphonies are fifteen in number, of which no 10 is perhaps the finest of all his works; nos 13 (a song-symphony based on poems by Yevtushenko), 14 (a symphony inspired by poems about death) and 15 reveal a vein of pessimism unusual in Soviet music. His string quartets, almost as numerous as his symphonies, are among the finest modern examples of music in this form. Besides these he wrote violin, cello and piano concertos, a piano quintet and piano trio, duo sonatas and solo piano music (including sets of preludes and fugues). In most of his works he replenished the traditional classical forms with fresh vitality and meaning.

Shropshire Lad, A, orchestral rhapsody by Butterworth (1912), inspired by Housman's poems. Butterworth also composed a song-cycle on some of the Housman poems, incorporating some of the same musical material.

shoulder-viol (It., *viola da spalla*), a viol midway in size between that of the *viola da braccio* (arm viol) and the *viola da gamba* (leg viol). As it was too large to play in the violin position and too small for the normal cello position, it was merely held in front of the body and sometimes fastened to it. This made the instrument suitable for playing while walking, and because of this it was much used in Italy for church processions.

Shudi, Burkat (**Burkhardt Tschudi**) (1702–73), Swiss harpsichord maker. He became apprentice to Tabel, a London harpsichord maker, in 1718 and founded his own business in 1742. His son-in-law John Broadwood succeeded him and was in turn succeeded by his own sons. He patented a 'Venetian swell' for the harpsichord in 1769.

Si (Fr.; It.), the note B.

Sibelius, Jean (1865–1957), Finnish composer, the most famous ever produced by that country. He studied at Helsinki Conservatory under Wegelius, in Berlin under Albert Becker, and in Vienna under Robert Fuchs and Carl Goldmark. The works of 1890–1900 expressed the aspirations of Finland towards a national musical culture, and included the tone-poems *En Saga* (1892) and *Finlandia* (1899) and four *Legends* (*Lemminkäinen and the Maidens*, 1895; *Lemminkäinen in Tuonela*, 1895; *The Swan of Tuonela*, 1893; *The Return of the Lemminkäinen*, 1895) based on the Finnish epic, the *Kalevala*. These works showed an individual approach to the treatment of the orchestra and of thematic material which is further developed in seven symphonies (1899–1924). In the exposition of the first movement of the second symphony a number of short motifs are presented, in the development they are built into long phrases, and in the recapitulation they are combined and compressed. The fourth symphony is concise in form and is mainly based on the melodic and harmonic relation of the tritone. In the seventh symphony the normal scheme is compressed into one movement, the final section being a partial recapitulation of the first section. Other notable works of Sibelius are the symphonic *Ride and Sunrise* (1909), *The Bard* (1913), *The Oceanides* (written after his visit to the United States in 1914), *Tapiola* (1925), the incidental music to Shakespeare's *The Tempest* (1926), the violin concerto (1903–5), and the string quartet *Voces intimae* (1909). He also composed a great many pieces for

Jean Sibelius in his ninetieth year. He died two years later.

violin and piano, cello and piano, voice and piano, piano and solo, and chorus – these, however, being of minor importance. In 1897, Finland granted him an annual stipend to enable him to compose without distraction. In 1904 he retired to a country house at Järvenpää to compose in seclusion. In 1926 he ceased to compose, and, though the eighth symphony was long mooted, it never appeared. Yet Sibelius' output up to that time was large enough and imposing enough to establish himself (especially in Britain) as a major composer, even though he was less influential than was at one time hoped. His symphonies and symphonic poems, without being revolutionary works, speak with a taut, decisive and individual voice.

R. LAYTON: Sibelius

siciliano (It.; Fr., *Sicilienne*, Eng., *Siciliana*), a type of Sicilian dance used in the baroque period in instrumental music and in arias, written in a moderately slow 6/8 or 12/8 time, and often in a minor key. In style and in its frequent use of the rhythm

it is similar to the PASTORALE. For example, the second movement of J. S. Bach's Sonata in E flat for flute and harpsichord is a *siciliano* which begins thus:

Sicilian Vespers, The (Fr., *Les Vêpres Siciliennes*), opera in five acts by Verdi with a libretto by Augustin Eugène Scribe and Charles Duveyrier. It was composed for the Paris Opéra where it was first performed in 1855, in honour of the Great Exhibition that year. The story takes place in Sicily in the 13th century. Monforte (the French governor of Sicily) offers to take Arrigo (a commoner who is really the son of Monforte) into the service of the French, but Arrigo refuses. Procida (a Sicilian patriot) tells Elena (a noblewoman) and Arrigo that foreign support awaits the Sicilians, and Elena promises to wed Arrigo if he will avenge her brother who has been executed by Monforte. Arrigo is taken away by Monforte's soldiers and Monforte reveals to him that they are father and son. Arrigo, fearing for Elena, is horrified by the news. Elena, Procida and others plan to assassinate Monforte; Arrigo warns him and the conspirators are arrested. Arrigo persuades Monforte to spare Procida and Elena on condition that he will publicly recognize Monforte as his father. Arrigo and Elena are to be married with Monforte's blessing, but the Sicilians plan to massacre the Frenchmen when the wedding bells ring. Elena, knowing this, declares that she cannot go through with the ceremony, but Monforte forcibly places her hand in Arrigo's and orders that the wedding bells be rung. In the massacre that follows Monforte and all the French are slain.

Though often performed in Italian (under the title of *I Vespri Siciliani*), this work was composed by Verdi in French. It was his first French opera, obedient to the grandiose aspects of the Meyerbeer tradition in Paris, yet an important milestone on the road to Verdi's greater and more characteristic French opera, *Don Carlos*.

side drum (Fr., *tambour*, *tambour militaire* or *caisse claire*; It., *tamburo militaire*; Ger., *Kleine Trommel*), drum, also know as the snare drum, cylindrically shaped and across the lower of its two parchment heads snares made of gut or metal are stretched. It is these that give the drum, the smallest of those normally used in the orchestra, its characteristic rattling sound. When the snares are thrown out of action, which they can be instantly, the tone is utterly different. The technique for playing the instrument, particularly the roll, is difficult to acquire. Although best know as a military band instrument, many symphonic and operatic composers, Rossini and Auber among them, have used the side drum completely solo, while Nielsen in his Fifth Symphony brought it forward as a principal protagonist.

Sieben Worte, Die (Ger., The Seven Words), (1) *Die sieben Worte unsers lieben Erlösers und Seligmachers Jesu Christi* (The Seven Words of our beloved Redeemer and Savious Jesus Christ), short oratorio by Schütz (1645) with a text compiled from the four gospels.

(2) *Die sieben Worte des Erlösers am Kreuze, see* SEVEN WORDS

Siefert, Paul (1586–1666), German composer and organist. He studied under Sweelinck at Amsterdam, was attached to the chapel of Sigismund III in Warsaw, and in 1623 was appointed organist of St. Mary's in Danzig. The style of his *Psalmen Davids* of 1640 was criticised by Marco Scacchi in his *Cribrum musicum* (1643), to which Siefert replied in his *Anticribratio* (1645), which called forth Scacchi's *Judicium Cribri musici*. He also composed fantasies for organ, and a second volume of Psalms which was published in 1651.

Siege of Corinth, The (Fr., *Le Siège de Corinthe*), opera in three acts by Rossini, presented in Paris in 1826. This was the first of Rossini's three French grand operas. It was based on a work entitled *Maometto II* which he had written six years earlier for Naples, with a libretto by Cesare della Valle after Voltaire's *Mahomet, ou le Fanatisme*. In 1828 the work was translated back into Italian (as *L'Assiedo di Corinto*) for performance in Parma and elsewhere.

The story concerns the love of a Greek girl, the daughter of the Christian governor of Corinth, for a Mohammedan prince who leads an attack on the city. In 1949 it was revived in Florence for Renata Tebaldi, and in 1969 at La Scala, Milan, for Beverley Sills.

Siegfried, opera in three acts by Wagner, the third part of the RING cycle. It was first performed at Bayreuth in 1876.

Siegfried Idyll, a work for small orchestra by Wagner (1870), celebrating the birth of his son, Siegfried, in which he used themes from his opera *Siegfried*. It was called at first *Triebschener Idyll*, as it had been performed on the staircase of the Wagner villa in Triebschen on Cosima's birthday.

sight, a system used in England in the 15th and 16th centuries for teaching choristers to descant, i.e. to extemporize a simple part to go with a plainsong melody. The singer imagined his notes to be on the same staff as the plainsong (tenor) but sang them at a pitch suitable to the compass of his voice. Thus, to a treble descanter, who sang an octave above his 'sight' pitch, a third below the plainsong in 'sight' actually sounded a sixth above the plainsong. In place of

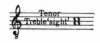

in sight was

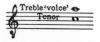

in 'voice', that is, in sound. When the method was applied to singing in two parts the descanting voice was free to vary the interval between it and the plainsong, provided only consonant intervals were used. However, when the sights were used for the performance of FABURDEN by three voices, the permissible intervals were circumscribed: the lowest voice sang only a fifth or third below the plainsong, the highest voice only a fourth above. According to one 15th century theorist, faburden was considered the simplest application of the sight method.

See DESCANT.

sight reading, the act of playing or singing a piece of music at first sight.

signature, *see* KEY-SIGNATURE, TIME-SIGNATURE

Signor Bruschino, Il, comic opera in one act by Rossini, to a libretto by Foppa. The story, a typical 18th century marital tangle, is based on a French comedy by de Chazy and Ourry. The work was first performed at Venice in 1813. The overture, often performed as a separate concert piece, is the one in which the violinists have to tap their music stands with their bows.

Sigurd Jorsalfar (Norw., *Sigurd the Crusader*), incidental music by Grieg for a play by Bjørnson. Grieg's three incidental pieces include the well-known *Homage March*.

Si j'étais Roi (Fr., *If I were King*), opera in three acts by Adam, libretto by Adolphe Philippe d'Ennery and Jules Brésil. It was first performed in Paris in 1852.

Silbermann, Gottfried (1683–1753), the most celebrated member of a German family of organ builders and harpsichord makers. He was apprenticed to a bookbinder, from 1703 lived with his brother Andreas in Strasbourg, and in 1707 returned to Frauenstein where he built his first organ. He settled in Freiberg in 1709 and built the cathedral organ there in 1714. He built 47 organs in Saxony and died while building the organ at the Dresden court. He made clavichords and harpsichords and was the first German to make pianos. C. P. E. Bach wrote a piece entitled *Farewell to my Silbermann Clavichord* in 1781. His nephews **Johann Daniel Silbermann** (who finished his Dresden organ) and **Johann Andreas Silbermann** built organs, and **Johann Heinrich Silbermann** made harpsichords and pianos.

Silken Ladder, The (It., *La Scala di Seta*), opera in one act by Rossini. The libretto, inspired by a French comedy by Francois Antoine Eugene de Planard, concerns a secret marriage – the silken ladder is used by the husband to reach the wife's room, which is guarded by her jealous father. This was Rossini's sixth opera, first performed in Venice in 1812. It has had few productions outside Italy, but its sparkling overture is a concert hall favourite.

Siloti, Alexander Ilyich (1863–1945), Russian pianist who studied at the Moscow Conservatory under Chaikovsky and N. Rubinstein, and later with Liszt and others. Later he settled in the United States, where he taught at the Juilliard School of Music from 1925 to 1942. His edition of Chaikovsky's second piano

503 SINFONIA

concerto is still widely performed, though it incorporates reprehensible cuts.

silver band, a common description of brass bands in the days when instruments were silver rather than gold plated.

similar motion, the movement of two or more parts or melodies in the same direction, either up or down, e.g.,

When the parts move by the same interval, parallel or CONSECUTIVE INTERVALS result. When two parts rise to a fifth, e.g.,

or to an octave, e.g.,

the effect is referred to as 'hidden' fifths or octaves, and is usually avoided between the outer parts in contrapuntal writing, unless the higher part moves by step, e.g.,

simile (It.), 'like, similar', used as a direction to continue a formula which has been indicated, such as arpeggiating of chords. It is abbreviated as *sim*.

Simon Boccanegra, opera with a prologue and three acts by Verdi. The libretto by Francesco Maria Piave is based on a Spanish drama by Antonio Garcia Gutierrez. The work was first performed at Venice in 1857, where it was a failure. A revised version, with a libretto altered by Arrigo Boito, was successfully staged at Milan in 1881. Since then the opera has established itself internationally as one of Verdi's major masterpieces, making the transition from his middle period style to the subtleties of his final period.

The story takes place in Genoa during the 14th century. Paolo and Pietro are plotting to place Boccanegra (a popular corsair) on the Doge's throne. When Boccanegra goes to visit his mistress, Maria, he is confronted by her father, Fiesco, the present Doge, who demands that he should relinquish the daughter born of their love affair. Boccanegra confesses that the child has been lost and when he manages to gain entrance to Fiesco's palace he discovers that Maria is dead. As he leaves the palace he is greeted by a cheering crowd who announce that he is the Doge of Genoa. Twenty-five years pass. Boccanegra discovers his lost daughter (Amelia Grimaldi) living with an old man who is known as Andrea (in reality Fiesco, who does not know that she is his granddaughter). She is in love with Gabriele Adorno who has entered into a conspiracy with Andrea to overthrow the Doge. Paolo kidnaps Amelia in order to be revenged against her father who

has refused to consent to his marriage with her. Andrea and Gabriele accuse Boccanegra of being the kidnapper and when Gabriele attacks Boccanegra Amelia comes between them and saves her father. Paolo, still desiring revenge on Boccanegra, plays on the jealous feelings of Gabriele who does not know the true relationship between Boccanegra and his beloved Amelia. Again Amelia saves her father when he attempts to murder him, and when they explain to him that they are father and daughter he begs for pardon. Paolo as the leader of an uprising against the Doge is condemned to death, but in the meantime Boccanegra has drunk some wine which was poisoned by him. As he is dying he tells Fiesco that Amelia is the lost child, gives his consent and blessing to her marriage with Gabriele, and names Gabriele as his successor as Doge.

simple time, a time-division in which each beat in the bar is divisible into two, e.g.:

as opposed to COMPOUND TIME, in which each beat is divisible into three, e.g.:

Simpson, Robert (born 1921), English composer and writer on music, pupil of Herbert Howells. His works include three symphonies, two concertos and chamber music. As an author, he has written important studies of the music of Carl Nielsen and the symphonies of Bruckner.

Sinding, Christian (1856–1941), Norwegian composer and pianist who studied in Leipzig, Berlin, Dresden and Munich. He settled in Oslo in 1882 and lived there and in Berlin from 1909. He was also given an annual allowance (from 1890) and life pension (from 1915) by the Norwegian government. He taught at the Eastman School in Rochester, New York, 1921–22. His compositions include an opera (*Der heilige Berg*, Dessau, 1914), three symphonies, a violin concerto, and other large-scale works, but today he is remembered solely for his miniatures, such as his piano piece, *Rustle of Spring*.

sinfonia (It.), symphony – but the word has wider meanings than this would suggest. Originally it meant, simply, an instrumental piece, and the title was used thus by Bach among others. Then it could also mean prelude or overture, to an opera, cantata or suite. The so-called 'Italian *sinfonia*', which introduced the operas of Alessandro Scarlatti and other composers, consisted of three short movements (quick-slow-quick) and this layout played its part in the evolution of the classical symphony. Mozart's 32nd symphony, K 318, is a throwback to the form of Italian symphony or overture, and is quite unlike his full-scale symphonies of the period. His overture to *Die Entführung aus dem Serail*, with its slow middle section, also follows the above pattern, and the overture to *The Marriage of Figaro* was nearly destined to do so – though in the end Mozart cut the slow middle section.

The term *sinfonia* is also used nowadays as the performing name of a small orchestra, e.g. The Northern Sinfonia, a leading chamber orchestra in the north of England.

Sinfonia Antartica (It., *Antarctic Symphony*), Vaughan William's seventh symphony, based on the music written for the film *Scott of the Antarctic*. It was first performed in Manchester in 1953. The scoring incorporates a wind machine, vibraphone and wordless soprano voice.

sinfonia concertante (It.), an orchestral work, normally in several movements, in which there are parts for solo instruments, generally two or more, as in Mozart's *sinfonia concertante* for violin and viola, K 364. Usually, in such work, there is less emphasis on display than in a solo concerto – even when the sinfonia concertante, too, is written for a solo instrument, e.g. Walton's *sinfonia concertante* for piano and orchestra.

Sinfonia da Requiem, symphony by Britten, composed in 1940 in memory of his parents. Its three movements – called after sections of the Requiem Mass – are entitled *Lacrymosa, Dies Irae* and *Requiem Aeternam*.

Sinfonia Domestica, *see* DOMESTIC SYMPHONY

Sinfonia Espansiva, Nielsen's third symphony, op 27, first performed in Copenhagen in 1912. The music is 'expansive' both in its picture of the Danish landscape and in its attitude to humanity. The slow movement contains wordless parts for a solo soprano and baritone.

Sinfonie (Ger.), symphony. An alternative spelling is *Symphonie.*

sinfonietta (It.), a short, small-scale symphony. Some 'sinfoniettas', however, may seem self-contradictory (Janáček's *Sinfonietta*, for instance, requires a chorus of nine trumpets). The term is also used nowadays as the performing name for a small orchestra e.g. the Bournemouth Sinfonietta, an offshoot of the Bournemouth Symphony Orchestra.

Sinfonische Dichtung (Ger.), symphonic poem.

Singakademie (Ger.), society for concert giving founded by K. F. C. Fasch in Berlin in 1791. Today the name (which simply means 'singing academy') is used by many choirs in German-speaking countries.

Singspiel (Ger.), German comic opera with spoken dialogue. The earliest examples were written in imitation of English ballad operas, and were in fact settings of translations of ballad opera libretti. The text of Johann Standfuss's *Der Teufel ist los* (Leipzig, 1752, also set by J. A. Hiller, 1766) was translated from Coffey's *The Devil to Pay* (1728) and that of his

Der lustige Schuster (Lübeck, 1759) from Coffey's *The Merry Cobbler* (1735). The music of Haydn's *Singspiel, Der krumme Teufel*, which was produced with some success in Vienna in 1752, has been lost (1752 was also the year of J. J. Rousseau's *Le Devin du Village*). A special company for the performing of *Singspiele* was established in Vienna by the Emperor Joseph II in 1778, and it was for this national *Singspiel* that Mozart's *Die Entführung* was commissioned. This transcended all other *Singspiele* up to that time, and was itself transcended in 1791 by another Mozart work, *The Magic Flute*. The history of the *Singspiel* merges with that of German romantic opera in the early 19th century; one of the latest examples is Schubert's *Die Zwillingsbruder* (1819). Later the term *Singspiel* came to be used in Germany as the equivalent of musical comedy.

Sinigaglia, Leone (1868–1944), Italian composer whose output – unusually – concentrated on the concert hall rather than the opera house. His works include a set of Piedmontese dances (conducted by Toscanini), a *Piedmontese Rhapsody* for violin and orchestra, and a collection of Piedmontese popular songs for voice and piano. His interest in the folk music of his native region was aroused, it seems, by Dvořák, under whom he studied. He also wrote a quantity of chamber and instrumental music.

sinistra (It.), left hand.

sink-a-pace, *see* CINQUE-PACE

sino, sin' (It.), until, e.g. *sin' al segno*, go on until the sign.

Sins of My Old Age (Fr., *Péchés de vieillesse*), title given by Rossini to several sets of songs and instrumental pieces which he wrote after abandoning his career as an opera composer (with *William Tell*, in 1829). The music is characterized by its wit, and by the comic titles chosen by Rossini, in which he anticipated the works of Erik Satie.

Sir John in Love, opera in four acts by Vaughan Williams, the hero being Sir John Falstaff and the libretto being drawn from Shakespeare's *The Merry Wives of Windsor*. The work was first performed in London in 1929.

Siroe, re di Persia (It., *Siroes, King of Persia*), opera in three acts by Handel, with a libretto adapted from Metastasio. It was first performed in London in 1728.

sistema (It.), staff.

sistrum, ancient percussion instrument that probably originated in Egypt. In its long history it has assumed a variety of forms, but the best known are those in which wooden discs or metal bars are strung onto a frame. When the instrument is shaken these strike against each other, producing a rattling sound. A more developed and very different version has sets of tuned bells that can be played with a beater; the compass is about two octaves. Recently this type has been improved by the addition of a keyboard.

sitar, the most internationally famous of Indian instruments – a long-necked lute with movable frets and from three to seven strings, below which are about twelve other sympathetic strings. A distinguished modern exponent of the sitar is Ravi Shankar. Pop groups (e.g. The Beatles) have made use of the hauntingly jangly tones of the sitar as an accompanying instrument, but Western performers on the whole use it at their peril: in India it is considered to require a lifetime of study.

Sitzprobe (Ger.), term used in opera for a 'sitting rehearsal', i.e. a rehearsal in which the singers play their roles sitting down, with the accompaniments played by the orchestra.

Six, Les (Fr.), 'The Six.' The name was given by Henri Collet in 1920 to a group of six young French composers who were influenced by Erik Satie's emphasis on simplicity and by the artistic ideals of Jean Cocteau. Their association was inaugurated by the joint publication of an album of six pieces. The name *Les Six* was imitated from the title 'The Five' given to the group of Russian composers consisting of Balakirev, Cui, Borodin, Mussorgsky and Rimsky-Korsakov. The members of the French group, who soon ceased to be six, were Darius Milhaud, Louis Durey, Georges Auric, Arthur Honegger, Francis Poulenc and Germaine Tailleferre.

six-four chord, a chord containing a sixth and a fourth from its bass note. It is the second INVERSION of the chord based on the note which is the fourth from its bass, e.g.

is the second inversion of

Since it contains a fourth from the bass its use in traditional harmony is usually restricted to those progressions which correspond to the treatment of the fourth in two-part counterpoint. They are (1) the appoggiatura or 'cadential' six-four, e.g.:

(2) the passing six-four, e.g.:

and (3) the auxiliary six-four, e.g.:

See CHORD

sixte ajoutée, *see* ADDED SIXTH

sixteenth-note (U.S.), semiquaver.

sixth, the interval comprised by the first and last of any six notes in a diatonic scale, e.g.

A sixth may be minor:

major:

or augmented:

The sixth, like the third, of which it is the INVERSION, is an imperfect consonance. The term 'sixth chord' is sometimes used in referring to the SIX-THREE chord.
      See AUGMENTED SIXTH, CHORD, INTERVAL.

sixth, added, *see* ADDED SIXTH

six-three chord, a chord containing a sixth and a third from its bass note. It is the first INVERSION of the chord based on the note which is the sixth from its bass, e.g.

is the first inversion of

The chord has an interesting early history, in which it is generally associated with the affection of the English, not fully shared by other nations in the middle ages, for the sweetness of imperfect consonances. A 13th century English treatment of part of the *Te Deum* shows how wholeheartedly it was beloved:

Perhaps in imitation of this English practice, it became the working chord of FAUXBOURDON in the 15th century. It is, in fact, the only position of the common chord, which, in traditional harmony, can be used in continuous parallels, as by Beethoven in the fourth movement of his piano sonata, op 3, no 2:

See CHORD

Skalkottas, Nikos (1904–49), Greek composer, who studied the violin at Athens Conservatory then moved to Berlin in 1921 to work under Schoenberg and Kurt Weill. His earlier works reveal the influence of Schoenberg, but later he developed his own style, in which Greek folk music played a part. His works include *Greek Dances* for orchestra, concertos, music for strings, and four string quartets. On returning to Greece from Germany, he was misunderstood as a composer and earned his living as an orchestral violinist. It was only after his death that his music began to be published, and to win international acclaim.

Skazka o Tsare Saltane, *see* LEGEND OF THE CZAR SALTAN

Alexander Skryabin. He injured his hand trying to write a more difficult piano piece than Balakirev's *Islamey* and turned to composition.

Skryabin, Alexander Nikolaievich (1872–1915), Russian composer and pianist. He studied piano under Safonov and composition under Taneyev and Arensky at the Moscow Conservatory. In 1896 he toured Europe, giving concerts of his own works in Berlin, Paris, Brussels, Amsterdam and The Hague. He was piano teacher at the Moscow Conservatory from 1898–1903, lived in Switzerland until 1905 and in Brussels from 1908–10. His early works (two symphonies, piano concerto, three sonatas, seven sets of preludes,

and other works for piano) had little relation to the Russian music of their time (1890–1903) but was written under the influence of Chopin, Liszt and Wagner, coupled with a subtle sense of harmony. In succeeding compositions (*The Divine Poem* and *Poem of Ecstasy* for orchestra, seven further sonatas, eight further sets of preludes, six *Poems*, *Vers la flamme* and other piano works) he embarked on experiments with esoteric harmonies, which were connected in his mind with his ideas on theosophy. As a basis for his harmonies he devised a so-called 'mystic' chord in which the eighth and the fourteenth notes of the Harmonic Series were disposed in fourths, thus:

In his last works (*Prometheus* and an unfinished *Mystery*) he was moving towards his conception of a synthesis of the arts. The score of the *Prometheus* includes a 'colour organ', invented by Rimington.

A. E. HULL: *A Russian Tone-Poet* (1922)

A. J. Swan: *Scriabin* (1923)

slancio (It.), impetus.

slapstick or **whip** (Fr., *foeut*; It., *frustra*; Ger., *Peitsche*), percussion instrument consisting of two strips of hardboard hinged together but with a spring that normally keeps them at an angle. The sound of the strips striking each other resembles the crack of a whip. The opening of Ravel's G major piano concerto provides an example of the instrument's use.

slått (plural *slåtter*), type of piece, often in march rhythm, played by Norwegian folk musicians on the Hardanger fiddle. Several of Grieg's piano pieces were inspired by *slåtter*, and other Norwegian composers have also been attracted to this native music.

Slavonic Dances, two sets of dances by Dvořák, the first composed in 1878, the second in 1886. Both were originally for piano duet, but the composer later orchestrated them. Though the tunes are suggestive of folk music, they were in fact written by Dvořák himself.

Slavonic Rhapsodies, three orchestral works by Dvořák, in D major, G minor and A flat major, all written in 1878. Like the *Slavonic Dances*, the music sounds as if it were inspired by folk songs, but the tunes are all by Dvořák himself.

Sleeping Beauty, The, ballet by Chaikovsky, with choreography by Petipa, first produced at St. Petersburg in 1890.

sleigh-bells (It., *sonagli*; Fr., *grélots*; Ger., *Schellen* or *Schellengeläute*), small metal bells containing a steel ball. Normally they are fastened to a leather strap, but for orchestral purposes they are fixed to a steel frame connected to a wooden handle. This method of mounting allows a high degree of rhythmic precision when the hand taps the frame or *vice versa*. The earliest use of sleigh bells in the orchestra seems to have been in Cherubini's opera *Elise*, but the best known use is probably Mahler's Fourth Symphony.

slentando (It.), becoming gradually slower.

slide (Fr., *coulé, flatté*; Ger., *Schleifer*), (1) an ornament used in the music of the 17th and early 18th centuries, also called 'elevation' or 'wholefall', consisting of two grace notes moving up by step to the principal note. It was indicated thus:

by Playford and

or

by Marpurg, and played

and

Purcell, who calls it a 'slur', gives

played

and Chambonnières gives

played

Later composers have usually written out the grace notes, as do most editors of Bach, e.g. in the *St. Matthew Passion*:

(2) movement of the left hand on the violin which effects a quick change of POSITION, at the same time producing a slight *portamento*. Paganini extended the use of the slide to the rapid playing of chromatic scale passages;

(3) a device which alters the length of the air column in the TROMBONE.

slide trumpet, *see* TRUMPET

slughorn, slughorne, although mentioned by Browning and Chatterton no such musical instrument has ever existed.

slur (Fr., *légature*; Ger., *Bindungszeichen*; It., *legatura*), (1) a curved line over or under a group of notes which indicates that they are to be played or sung smoothly, or, on a stringed instrument, in one bow. If the slur is combined with staccato marks, it indicates that the phrase should be performed semi-staccato;

(2) Purcell used the term as the equivalent of SLIDE.

Smalley, Roger (born 1943), English composer and pianist, pupil of Stockhausen. He is one of Britain's leading exponents of electronic music, though he also has an interest in the sixteenth century, as reflected in his *Missa Parodia* (1967), in which the material of the Mass is distorted, disintegrated and finally reformed. His *Beat Music* for orchestra and electronic instruments was commissioned for the B.B.C.'s London Proms in 1971. Smalley has founded his own group, Intermodulation, for the performance of music by himself and others.

Smetana, Bedřich (1824–84) Czech composer. The son of a brewer, he studied composition in Prague under Proksch, where until 1856 he taught and wrote his first compositions. He lived as a conductor and teacher in Göteborg in Sweden from 1857–9 and in the winter of 1860–61. He visited Liszt in Weimar, and between

Bedřich Smetana, the composer from Bohemia who made musical nationalism respectable.

1858 and 1861 wrote three symphonic poems for orchestra, *Richard III*, *Wallenstein's Camp* and *Hakon Jarl*. Returning to Prague in 1863, he went on to write his most famous opera, *The Bartered Bride*, in 1866, and three other operas on national subjects by 1874, in which year he suddenly became stone deaf. Nevertheless, he composed in the following years his best instrumental works, *Má vlast* ('My Country'), a set of six musical landscapes, and the first string quartet, *From my Life*, in four movements with an autobiographical programme – in the last movement we actually hear deafness attacking him. Though he very seldom used actual folk songs in his music (his only folk song settings are the *Czech Dances* for piano of 1878), his Czech operas are thoroughly national in subject and feeling. He also composed a trio, a second string quartet, piano pieces, choruses and songs. His operas are: *The Brandenburgers in Bohemia*, 1866; *The Bartered Bride*, 1866; *Dalibor*, 1868; *Libuše*, composed in 1871–2, produced in 1881; *The Two Widows*, 1874; *The Kiss*, 1876; *The Secret*, 1878; *The Devil's Wall*, 1882; and an unfinished work, *Viola*. Smetana was Czechoslovakia's first great nationalist composer (he lived during the period of his country's resurgence after the collapse of the Austrian tyranny) and his patriotism is strongly reflected in his operas – most heroically in *Dalibor*. But his comedies are equally characteristic of him, and just as deeply Czech, *The Two Widows* being a delightful Czech equivalent of Mozart's *Cosi fan tutte*.

> F. BARTOS (editor): *Bedřich Smetana: Letters and Reminiscences* (1955)
> J. CLAPHAM: *Smetana* (1972)
> B. LARGE: *Smetana* (1970)
> Z. NEJEDLY: *Frederick Smetana* (1924)
> W. RITTER: *Smetana* (1907)
> J. TIERSOT: *Smetana* (1926)

Smith, Bernard ('Father Smith'), *see* SCHMIDT, BERNHARD.

Smith, Bessie (1895–1937), U.S. Negro singer, known deservedly as the 'Empress of the Blues'. Born in Chattanooga, Tennessee, she was the greatest of all exponents of what has become known as the 'classic' blues form. Fortunately many of her performances have been preserved on tape, providing vivid evidence of the majesty of her style and the intensity of her response to the songs she sang – many of them about loneliness and wretchedness. Her death could have been the subject of one of her own songs. Having been injured in a car crash, she was turned away from the segregated hospital for whites which could have saved her, and died from loss of blood while being driven to an all-Negro one.

Smith, John Stafford (1750–1836), English organist, composer and editor, pupil of Boyce. He became Gentleman of the Chapel Royal, 1784; lay-vicar, Westminster Abbey, 1785; organist (1802) and master of the children (1805) at the Chapel Royal. He collected and published early English music, including *A Collection of English Songs* (1779) and *Musica Antiqua* (1812), and worked with Hawkins on his *History of Music*. His works include glees (five books), catches, canons, madrigals, anthems, part-songs and songs. The tune of his 'Anacreon in Heaven' was adopted for 'The Star-Spangled Banner'.

smorzando (It.), dying away.

Smyth, Ethel Mary (1858–1944), English composer and author. She studied in Leipzig at the Conservatorium and under Herzogenberg. Back in Britain she became a leader of the women's suffrage movement, and was jailed in 1911. Nine years later she became a Dame of the British Empire. She composed the following operas: *Fantasio* (1898), *The Wood* (1902), *The Wreckers* (first produced as *Strandrecht*, Leipzig, 1906), *The Boatswain's Mate* (1916), *Fête galante* (1923) and *Entente cordiale* (1926). She also wrote a Mass, *The Prison* (1930) and other choral works.

snare drum, *see* SIDE DRUM

snares, *see* SIDE DRUM

Snegourochka, *see* SNOW MAIDEN

Snow Maiden, The (Rus., *Snegourochka*), opera by Rimsky-Korsakov with a prologue and four acts. The libretto by the composer is based on a play by Alexander Ostrovsky, in which the legendary Snow Maiden, the daughter of King Frost, is sought by the Sun-God. It was first performed at St. Petersburg in 1882, and includes the *Dance of the Tumblers*, well known out of context.

soave (It.), in a smooth and gentle manner.

soft pedal, the pedal on the PIANO operated by the left foot. It reduces the volume, either by causing the hammers to strike only one instead of the usual two or three strings, or by bringing the hammers closer to the strings so that the impact is lessened.

soggetto (It.), 'subject', 'theme', (1) the subject of a fugue or other contrapuntal piece which is short and of an abstract or stock type, e.g. that of the fugue in E major in the second book of Bach's *Forty-eight*:

It is thus distinguished from an *andamento*, a longer subject of a more individual character, and from an *attacco*, which is a POINT of imitation.

(2) The term *soggetto cavato* ('carved-out' or derived subject) was used by 16th-century theorists for a theme derived from words by using the SOLMIZATION syllables corresponding to their vowels. Thus the theme

on which Josquin composed a Mass in honour of his patron, Duke Hercules of Ferrara, was derived from the words

re   ut re ut   re   fa mire
Her-cu-les dux Fer-ra-ri-e

soh, anglicized form of the Italian *sol* (G). In TONIC SOL-FA the fifth note (or dominant) of the major scale.

Soirées Musicales (Fr., musical evenings), a collection of songs and other pieces by Rossini, published in 1835 and later quarried by other composers – Respighi's ballet, *La Boutique Fantasque*, is an orchestration of some of Rossini's music, and so is Britten's *Soirées Musicales*.

Soir et la Tempête, Le, *see* MATIN

sol (Fr., It.), the note G. Also the fifth note of the hexachord. *See* SOLMIZATION

Soldier's Tale, The, a work by Igor Stravinsky to be 'read, played and danced', based on a text by Charles Ferdinand Ramuz. The tale, inspired by Russian folk lore, concerns a soldier, a violin, the Devil and a princess. The score calls for a narrator, two actors, a dancer and an instrumental ensemble consisting of clarinet, bassoon, cornet, trombone, violin, double bass and percussion. No singers are needed, and in a sense the work is an anti-opera. It was first performed in Lausanne in 1918, and its French title (*L'Histoire du Soldat*) is still used, though it is hardly relevant outside French-speaking countries. The work is divided into the following sections: *The Soldier's March, Scenes I, II and III, The Soldier's March, The Royal March, Little Concert, Tango, Waltz, Ragtime, The Devil's Dance, Little Chorale, The Devil's Song, Great Chorale, Triumphal March of the Devil.* The music also exists in the form of a concert hall suite, without speakers.

solenne (It.), solemn.

Soler, Padre Antonio (1729–83), Spanish composer and monk. He studied at the Escalonia of Monserrat, was appointed choirmaster at Lérida Cathedral, and entered the Monastery of the Escorial (1753), where he was organist. He composed a Requiem and other church music, sonatas for harpsichord, incidental music for plays, six quintets for strings and keyboard, and other chamber music, and wrote a theoretical treatise, *Llave de la Modulación* (1762). His harpsichord sonatas show in influence of Domenico Scarlatti, who spent much time in Madrid between 1729 and 1754. Modern edition of six quintets by R. Gerhard (1933). Not to be confused with Martin y Soler, composer of *Una Cosa Rara*.

Solesmes, the Benedictine monastery of Solesmes, near Le Mans, has been since the abbacy of Dom Guéranger (died 1875) the chief centre of the study of plainsong. Under Dom Guéranger's successors Dom Pothier and Dom Mocquereau the work of restoring plainsong melodies to their earliest written form (9th–10th centuries) was begun, and since 1904 the Solesmes editions of liturgical chant have been the official Vatican editions.

In preparing their editions the monks studied all the available early manuscripts, some of which have been published in facsimile in the series *Paléographie Musicale,* and evolved a new theory concerning the treatment of rhythm in the performance of plainsong. In this theory each note of the melody is given approximately the same length, and the first of a group of notes is given an *ictus,* which is a 'rhythmic step' of varying strength 'felt and intimated by tone of voice rather than expressed by any material emphasis'.

Though the rhythmic theories and methods of performance of Solesmes have not been everywhere accepted, the research which has been carried out there is universally recognised as the most valuable of all modern studies in the history of medieval plainsong. The results of these studies, which are now under the direction of Dom Gajard, are still being published both in the *Paléographie Musicale* and in the periodical *Revue Grégorienne.*

A short summary of the rules for the interpretation of plainsong according to Solesmes principles will be found in the edition with English rubrics of the *Liber Usualis* (1950).

J. GAJARD: *The Solesmes Method* (1960)

sol-fa, *see* TONIC SOL-FA

solfeggio (It.; Fr., *solfège*), the study of ear-training through the singing of exercises to the syllables of sol-fa, the modern form of SOLMIZATION. Many volumes of *solfeggi* have been published in Italy and France since the eighteenth century. In their more advanced forms such exercises are sung to vowels, and are then more properly called vocalises (*vocalizzi*), as in the collection *Repertoire moderne de vocalises-études* by Fauré, Dukas, d'Indy, Ravel and other composers. In Italy the term *solfeggi* is still used for exercises and studies for singers, whether sung to sol-fa syllables or vocalized. In France the term 'solfège' is applied to a course of ear-training and general musicianship. C. P. E. Bach used the term 'solfeggio' for a short keyboard piece, e.g. in his *Clavierstücke verschiedener Art* (1765).

solmization, the use of syllables to designate the notes of the hexachord. Those adopted by Guido d'Arezzo were used in medieval theory as a system of reference and as a means of ear-training. He derived them from a plainsong hymn to St. John the Baptist, in which the first syllable of each line was sung to a note of the hexachord in rising succession:

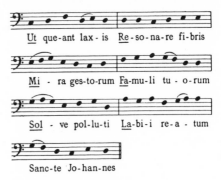

Ut que-ant lax-is Re-so-na-re fi-bris

Mi - ra ges-to-rum Fa-mu-li tu - o-rum

Sol - ve pol-lu-ti La-bi-i re-a - tum

Sanc-te Jo-han-nes

and applied them to the hexachords:

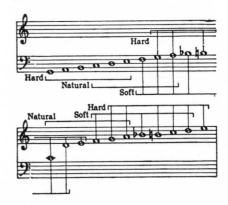

In teaching and discussion the notes were referred to by combining their appropriate syllables. The lowest note was called *Gamma ut* or *Gamut,* a term later applied to the whole system. The designations of the other notes may be found by reading the syllables upwards:

Middle C, for example, is C sol fa ut, the D next above it is D la sol re. Hortensio declared his love for Bianca (*Taming of the Shrew*, iii, 1) through the notes of the first hexachord. In singing, the change of syllable when changing from one hexachord to another was called MUTATION.

In the 16th and 17th centuries a composition which used the hexachord as a *cantus firmus* was usually called 'Ut Re Mi Fa Sol La'. There are examples of keyboard pieces of this kind by Byrd, Bull and Sweelinck in the *Fitzwilliam Virginal Book*. The syllables were also used to indicate the theme of a piece by its title, as in Byrd's fantasia on 'Ut Mi Re' (*Fitzwilliam Virginal Book*, no 102), and to derive a theme from words (*soggetto cavato*), as in Josquin's Mass *Hercules dux Ferrariae* (see SOGGETTO).

G. G. ALLAIRE: *The Theory of Hexachords, Solmization of the Model System* (1972)

solo (It.), alone. Piece to be performed by one person, e.g. Bach's sonatas for solo violin (the term solo violin being preferable to unaccompanied violin, which implies that a violin usually needs an accompaniment).

Solomon, secular oratorio by Handel, first performed in London in 1749. The text, based on the Bible, has been attributed to Thomas Morell (without sufficient authority).

solo organ, the manual on an organ which includes stops intended for solo, rather than combined, use. It is found on organs of four or more manuals and is placed above the swell. Its stops are enclosed in a swell-box. It normally contains a set of loud reeds, and such other stops as viola da gamba, concert flute, clarinet, orchestral oboe and French horn. More recently sets of mutation stops have also been included, as in the solo division of the organ in the Royal Festival Hall, London, which has a Rauschquint sounding the twelfth and fifteenth, a Tertian sounding the seventeenth and nineteenth, and a six rank mixture.

See ORGAN

solovox, electronic instrument usually attached to a piano but with its own keyboard. It imitates sounds of various instruments but can produce only one note at a time.

soltanto (It.), solely.

Solti, Georg (born 1912), Hungarian born conductor, pupil of Dohnányi and Kodály. During his prentice years he was invited by Toscanini to assist at the

Salzburg Festival in 1936 and 1937. After spending the war years in Switzerland, he became director of the Munich Opera (1946) and the Frankfurt Opera (1952). For ten years (1961–1971) he was musical director at Covent Garden, where he was specially associated with the operas of Wagner and Strauss. Later, with the intention of expanding his concert work, he became conductor of the Chicago Symphony Orchestra. He was knighted in 1972.

Sombrero de Tres Picos, El, *see* THREE-CORNERED HAT

Somervell, Arthur (1863–1937), English composer, pupil of Stanford and Parry. He composed a symphony and other orchestral works, choral music, chamber music and songs. He edited *Songs of Four Nations*, a collection of folksongs of the British Isles. He was knighted in 1929.

Somis, Giovanni Battista (1686–1763), Italian violinist and composer. A pupil of Corelli and Vivaldi, he was appointed violinist in the Turin Court Orchestra, played at the Concert Spirituel in Paris in 1733 and became director of the court music at Turin. His pupils included Leclair, Giardini and Pugnani. He composed two violin concertos, solo sonatas, trio sonatas, and other music.

Sommernachtstraum, *see* MIDSUMMER NIGHT'S DREAM

Son and Stranger (Ger., *Die Heimker aus der Fremde*), one-act operetta by Mendelssohn, first performed privately in Berlin in 1829. The first public performance was given at Leipzig in 1851, and the first London performance, translated by Chorley as *Son and Stranger*, also took place that year.

sonata, term derived from the Italian *suonare*, to sound, i.e. to play on (originally) non-keyed instruments. The year 1750 may be taken as a rough dividing line in its history. Before that date it was a composition for a single instrument, e.g. harpsichord or clavichord (after c. 1700), violin, or for one or more solo instrument accompanied by continuo. Since that date, it denotes a composition in several movements for a keyboard instrument, or for a solo instrument and pianoforte. At the beginning of its history it was used as the equivalent of canzona (*canzon da sonar*), as in Giovanni Gabrieli's *Sonata Pian e Forte*, but was soon applied to pieces for violin and continuo, e.g. in Biagio Marini's *Affetti musicali* (1617), and for two violins and continuo, as in Salomone Rossi's *Varie Sonate* (1623). Later in the century these became the two chief media for the sonata.

The sonata for solo instrument and continuo (*sonata a due*) was called a solo sonata, although the composer wrote two parts, solo part and bass; a sonata for two solo instruments and continuo (*sonata a tre*) was called a TRIO SONATA because the composer wrote three parts, although four players usually took part in its performance. In addition, many collections of sonatas for instrumental ensemble were published in the second half of the 17th century, e.g. Rosenmüller's *Sonate da camera a cinque* of 1677, Giovanni Legrenzi's *Sonate a due, trè, cinque, sei* of 1671, and Reinken's *Hortus musicus* of 1687. Rosenmüller's set was apparently the first to apply the term *sonata da camera* to a series of dance movements preceded by a prelude (*sinfonia*), and it was adopted by Corelli in his two sets of trio sonatas, op 2 (1685) and op 4 (1694). Corelli also adopted the term *sonata da chiesa* for his trio sonatas of 1683 and 1689, which have four movements in the order slow-fast-slow-fast. This scheme had appeared in the earliest published sonatas written by an English composer, William Young's collection published at Innsbruck in 1653, and is the general basis of Purcell's sonatas of three and four parts (1783, 1697), though in these, as in many sonatas before 1750, the actual number of movements varies considerably. While movements of a dance type, e.g. sarabande, gavotte, gigue, often appear (though not so entitled) in a *sonata da chiesa*, its historical connection with the canzona is clear in the frequent use of imitative style in the Allegro movements. Both Bach and Handel used the four-movement scheme consistently for solo sonatas and trio sonatas.

Sonatas for an unaccompanied string instrument were comparatively rare. The most notable examples before Bach's set of three sonatas and three partitas (he does not use the term *sonata da camera*) for solo violin are those of J. J. Walther and Heinrich Biber. As a term for keyboard works sonata was hardly known before D. Scarlatti's one-movement pieces (also called *Esercizi* or Lessons). The earliest appear to be the single sonata in Johann Kuhnau's *Clavierübung*, Part II (1692), the seven 'suonaten' in his *Frisch Clavierfrüchte* (1696) and his *Biblical Sonatas* of 1700.

The modern convention which restricts the use of the term sonata to instrumental solos and duets is not based on a distinction of form except as to number of movements, but of medium. The three-movement form (I. Allegro in SONATA FORM; II. Slow movement; III. Allegro in sonata or rondo form) of the classical and romantic duet-sonata is shared by the corresponding movements of the TRIO, STRING QUARTET, quintet, sextet, etc., as well as by the SYMPHONY. The early keyboard and violin sonatas of Mozart are keyboard sonatas with an optional violin part, and have three movements, Allegro-Adagio-Minuet. All of J. C. Bach's pieces in this medium are described as Sonatas for Harpsichord or Pianoforte, accompanied by Violin (or German flute). Haydn wrote practically no duets, and it was in Mozart's mature violin sonatas that a true duet style was developed. His three-movement scheme, Allegro-Adagio-Allegro, was continued by Beethoven, who included a Scherzo in his violin sonata, op 24 (1801) and in his cello sonata, op 69 (1809), but not always thereafter, and three movements became the normal number for duet sonatas. As with Mozart, the second or third movement could be in the form of theme and variations. While the composers of the romantic and modern periods have effected some changes in the style of the sonata, the classical basis of its form has remained relatively stable until the present. Among the noteworthy examples of sonatas for a wind instrument and piano are the two clarinet sonatas of Brahms, op 120, and the series of sonatas for flute, oboe, English horn, clarinet, bassoon, horn, trumpet and trombone by Hindemith.

The modern keyboard sonata takes its departure from the works of C. P. E. Bach for clavichord and harpsichord, and after 1780 for piano. Three movements are normal in the piano sonatas of Haydn, Mozart and Clementi, four in the earlier sonatas of Beethoven. The remarkable development of Beethoven's pianoforte style after the two sonatas *quasi una fantasia*, op 27, affected both the number and form of the movements, and two of the later sonatas, op 90 and 111, have two movements only (though this is not unknown in Haydn and Clementi). Liszt's attempt at a more fluid form in the Sonata in B minor (1854) had little effect on the later history of the form which includes works by Brahms, Stravinsky, Prokofiev, Berg, Hindemith, Boulez, Barraqué, to mention seven composers of piano sonatas. Tippett, in the second of his three sonatas, wrote a work in one movement, as other modern composers have done.

Mozart used the term in an earlier sense in his fourteen sonatas for organ and strings and three for organ and orchestra, all in one movement, written for Salzburg Cathedral between 1767 and 1780. The later history of the sonata for organ solo was begun by Mendelssohn's six sonatas (1839–44) and continued in the sonatas of Rheinberger and Guilmant, in the so-called 'symphonies' of Widow and Vierne, and in the sonatas of Reger, Elgar and Hindemith.

sonata form, a term for the design most often used since c. 1750 for the first movement, and on occasions for the slow movement and finale, of a symphony, sonata, TRIO, quartet, etc., and often for an OVERTURE. The procedures denoted by the names of its three sections – exposition (i.e. presentation), DEVELOPMENT (i.e. discursive treatment), and recapitulation (i.e. return) – were present in earlier music, and both these and the basis of its scheme of TONALITY were developed from its immediate ancestor, the BINARY FORM of the late baroque period. Its special characteristics are the definite distinction between the part which these procedures play in the design, and the complete coordination of thematic character, thematic treatment, and tonality in making that design clear, logical, and symmetrical. Its basic plan in the late 18th century is shown in the table on page 512.

The introduction may be unrelated to the exposition, as is usual before Beethoven, or related, as in the first movement of Beethoven's piano sonata, op 81a (*Lebewohl*) and in the first and fourth movements of Brahms's first symphony. It is frequently dispensed with. The leading theme of the first group and that of the second group are commonly called 'first subject' and 'second subject'. The first group frequently contains one theme only, the second group seldom less than two, and in Beethoven's longer movements as many as six, as in the first movement of the *Eroica* symphony. The latter part of the first group in the exposition has normally the function of making a transition to a related key; hence, the corresponding part of the first group in the recapitulation differs from it, not having that function. The recapitulation may differ from the exposition in details, e.g. in orchestration and in the use of new accompaniments to themes. The latter part of the development has the function of preparing for the return of the tonic. The coda, which in the classical sonata was usually a short addendum by way of 'rounding off,' was extended by Beethoven in many cases to the length of the other sections, and treated as a second development.

The interest which this design has had for composers over a period of more than 200 years arises from its

	(Introduction) Exposition		Development	Recapitulation (Coda)	
TONALITY	1st group (In major mode) Tonic (In minor mode) Tonic	2nd group Dominant Relative major	Varying Varying	1st group Tonic Tonic	2nd group Tonic Tonic major
THEMATIC CHARACTER	Leading theme is direct and concise.	Leading theme is *cantabile*.	Varying	As exposition	
THEMATIC TREATMENT	Complete and successive presentation.		Discursive, e.g. by dismemberment, transposition, contrapuntal treatment, combination.	Re-presentation	

capacity for expansion and contraction, its scope for inter-relations between the sections and for varieties of treatment of the development and coda, and its cheerful submission to those departures from its inherent principles, such as the appearance of the same thematic material in the first and second groups, the use of new themes in the development, and the return of a theme in the recapitulation in a key other than the tonic, which depend for their effect on the strength and clarity of the basic scheme. Since a calculated plan of tonality is essential to its working, its development in the late romantic and modern periods has chiefly been in the direction of greater flexibility in the proportions and relations of the sections, e.g. by the use of discursive treatment in the exposition and recapitulation and by abbreviating the recapitulation, and by extending the range of key-relations used in all the sections. The object in many cases has been to give a form which was originally sectional and symmetrical the effect of continuous and organic growth.

W. H. HADON: *Sonata Form* (1896)

Sonate Pathétique, *see* PATHETIC SONATA

sonata-rondo form, a combination of SONATA FORM and RONDO form.

sonatina, a short sonata. It is usually elementary in its technical requirements, e.g. Clementi's sonatinas and Beethoven's op 79, but not always so, Ravel's *Sonatine* and Busoni's six sonatinas being much more challenging, technically and interpretatively.

song, a short composition for voice. Song as a form of musical expression is of indeterminate antiquity. The earliest recorded examples in Western Europe, however, date from the 10th century. These songs are in Latin, which continued in use as a popular medium for lyrical expression down to the end of the 13th century. The relatively few melodies which are decipherable show a simple symmetrical structure similar to that found in folksong. This symmetry is characteristic also of the vernacular songs of the TROUBADOURS in Provence (11th–13th centuries), the trouvères in northern France (12th–13th centuries) and the MINNESINGER in Germany and Austria (12th–14th centuries), the Spanish *cantigas* in honour of the Virgin (13th century; *see* ALFONSO EL SABIO) and the Italian *laudi spirituali* (13th century). Neither in form nor in tonality is there

any valid distinction between secular and religious songs: melodies are found both in the church modes and in the major key. Common to all these songs is the absence of any written accompaniment.

Though the traditions of this type of song died hard in Germany and were in fact continued in the 15th and 16th centuries by the MEISTERSINGER, elsewhere the 14th century saw a considerable change. Songs (and also duets) of a highly sophisticated character, with accompaniment for one or more instruments, were composed in France and Italy by men like Machaut and Landini. The simple structure of the earlier songs has now been largely replaced by a greater subtlety of rhythm and form. Elaborate ornamentation, particularly in the late 14th century, is often found in these songs, and also an intimate relationship between two voices or between voice and accompaniment (e.g. imitation, canon). With the temporary decline of Italian music in the 15th century the French song (or *chanson*) became the dominant form of secular vocal music, so much so that we find many examples recorded in Italian and German sources. At the same time German composers were developing a characteristic type of song with the melody in an inner part.

Both at this period and in the 16th century there were no hard and fast conditions for performance. Words could be, and often were, applied to the accompanying instrumental parts, so that it is often impossible to make a clear-cut distinction between solo songs and part songs. On the other hand there are numerous examples where the melodic shape of the accompanying parts makes them unsuitable, though not impossible, for vocal performance. This easy-going attitude towards the medium persists in the 16th century – in the Italian *frottole* of the early part of the century, in the French *airs de cour*, and in many of the songs of the English lutenists of the late 16th and early 17th centuries. Many 16th century madrigals (as well as church motets) were arranged for performance by solo and lute, which by this time was the accompanying instrument most in favour. The old tradition of solo song accompanied by an instrumental ensemble survives in English music of the late 16th century, e.g. in Byrd's *Psalms, Sonets, and Songs of sadness and pietie* (1588), most of which were originally written for this medium. The lute-song, as opposed to transcriptions of madrigals, had its origin in Spain with the publication of Milan's *El maestro* in 1535.

A significant development in Italy in the late 16th century was the cultivation of a new form of declamatory song, soon known as RECITATIVE, by Caccini, Peri and others. Here the accompaniment was designed for figured bass and was made completely subordinate to the voice. Accurate declamation, intense expression and ornamentation were among the characteristics of this type of song, as well as the striking effect of original harmonic progressions. It proved to be the ideal medium for the new opera, created about the same time, but it did not kill the instinct for rhythmical song-writing, which also found encouragement in the popularity of court dances. Both in opera and in the chamber CANTATA the ARIA became in the course of the 17th century an indispensable element. Similar developments took place in England, France and Germany, though with differences resulting from the nature of the language. The distinction between songs from operas and songs for concert use is a narrow one at this period, though it is often true that songs published for domestic use have a greater simplicity.

The domination of opera continued through the 18th century, relieved however by the popular style of the songs in the English BALLAD OPERA, which were imitated in Germany and became a staple element in the SINGSPIEL. But songs of this kind, whether designed for the stage or for private music-making, received little attention from serious composers. The songs with keyboard accompaniment written by Haydn and Mozart form a minor (though very attractive) part of their output. Nor did Beethoven, in spite of having written the earliest known song cycle (*An die ferne Geliebte*, 1817), contribute enormously to the form. It was Schubert who showed how the traditional simplicity of German popular song could be combined with a romantic awareness of the text and how an imaginative accompaniment could serve to illuminate the words. Indeed many of his songs are even more subtle than this generalization would suggest; at his best he shows an extraordinary capacity for translating the mood of a poem into sound.

Schubert's example had a powerful influence on romantic composers of the 19th century, notably Schumann and Brahms. Schumann's songs often seem designed for a single performer, and the accompaniment not infrequently suggests a piano solo, to which a voice part has been added (a characteristic which has a parallel in his chamber music with piano). Brahms's accompaniments are generally on more traditional lines, and the vocal melodies in many cases show the influence of the traditions of popular song. The songs of Wolf, on the other hand, are strongly influenced by Wagner. The accompaniments are often orchestral in character, and the vocal line avoids symmetry in favour of precise accentuation of the words. The influence of Wolf is apparent in Strauss's songs; Mahler, on the other hand, follows more closely in the footsteps of Brahms.

In France the language, which lacks a tonic accent, resulted in a refinement which finds its most remarkable expression in the songs of Fauré. England, which in Purcell had had one of the most remarkable song-writers of the 17th century, made little serious contribution to the form after his death until the end of the 19th century. The folk song revival proved both a stimulus and a snare to English composers of the 20th century. Its influence was for the most part resisted by Warlock, who drew his inspiration rather from Elizabethan and Jacobean composers, and it has fortunately had little effect on Britten or Tippett; and by the time Peter Maxwell Davies arrived on the scene, the danger had passed. Russian song found a purely national expression in the picturesque and often very dramatic songs of Mussorgsky. In Norway Grieg was in his element as a song-writer, often combining the melodic idioms of folk song with an individual harmony.

The tendency among the more advanced composers of the 20th century has been to ignore the tradition that a vocal line should be naturally flowing. Some composers, e.g. Schoenberg, substituted for pure singing a form of declamation known as *Sprechgesang*, which is half-way between speech and song. The abandonment of anything like a traditional vocal *cantilena* has not been without its effect on instrumental composition.

song cycle (Ger., *Liederkreis*), a set of songs to words by a single poet, or which have some other form of unity. In most cases a song cycle is intended to be performed complete, but single songs from Schubert's and Schumann's cycles are commonly sung separately. The first use of the term was in Beethoven's *An die ferne Geliebte* (*To the distant Beloved*), to poems by A. Jeitteles. Other examples are Schubert's *Die schöne Müllerin* (*The Fair Maid of the Mill*; words by W. Müller) and *Winterreise* (*Winter Journey*; also by Müller), Schumann's *Dichterliebe* (*Poet's Love*; words by Heine) and *Frauenliebe und Leben* (*Woman's Love and Life*; words by Chamisso), Brahms's *Magelone* (words by Tieck), Debussy's *Chansons de Bilitis* (words by Pierre Louÿs), Vaughan Williams's *On Wenlock Edge* (words by Housman), Britten's *Songs and Proverbs of William Blake* and Tippett's *Songs for Dov* (words by the composer).

song form (Ger., *Liedform*), the basis form A-B-A, which is employed also in many instrumental pieces, e.g. a minuet or trio.

Song of Destiny (Ger., *Schicksalslied*), work for chorus and orchestra by Brahms, op 54 (1871), with words from a poem in Hölderlin's *Hyperion*.

Song of the Earth, The (Ger., *Das Lied von der Erde*), song-symphony by Mahler, scored for two solo voices and orchestra, with words from a German translation of six 8th century Chinese poems (in Hans Bethge's anthology, *The Chinese Flute*). Though Mahler called the work a symphony, he did not bestow a number on it – mainly for superstitious reasons: it would have been his ninth, and Mahler was aware that Beethoven and other composers had died after producing nine symphonies. In fact Mahler lived long enough to produce a (numbered) ninth and part of a tenth though he did not live long enough to hear the *Song of the Earth* publicly performed. He completed it in 1908, but it did not receive its première until three years later, just after the composer's death. The six songs comprising the symphony are as follows:

(1) *Das Trinklied vom Jammer der Erde* (The Drinking song of Earthly Woe);

(2) *Der Einsame im Herbst* (The Solitary Soul in Autumn);

(3) *Von der Jugend* (Of Youth);

(4) *Von der Schönheit* (Of Beauty);

(5) *Der Trunkene im Frühling* (The Drunkard in Spring);

(6) *Der Abschied* (The Farewell).

Song of the Flea, The, setting by Mussorgsky (1879) of Mephistopheles' song from Goethe's *Faust*.

Song of the High Hills, work for chorus and orchestra by Delius, completed in 1912. The chorus plays a wordless role in this composition, singing only vowel sounds.

Songs and Dances of Death, four songs by Mussorgsky, to poems by Golenishchev-Kutuzov, dealing with different aspects of death. They were composed between 1875 and 1877.

Songs of a Wayfarer (Ger., *Lieder eines Fahrenden Gesellen*), set of four songs for voice and orchestra by Mahler, composed in 1884. The texts, by the composer himself, reflect the moods of a young man spurned in love. Mahler re-used some of the musical material later in his first symphony.

Songs without Words (Ger., *Lieder ohne Worte*), the title given by Mendelssohn to eight books of piano pieces which he composed between 1830 and 1845. Each book contains six pieces. He also wrote one *Lied ohne Worte* in D major for cello and piano (op 109, 1845).

La Sonnambula: the Swedish nightingale, Jenny Lind in the title role.

Sonnambula, La (It., *The Girl who Walked in her Sleep*), opera in two acts by Bellini, libretto by Felice Romani. The story concerns a mill-owner's daughter whose somnambulism leads her into a Count's bedroom, where she is discovered in a potentially compromising situation. The work was first performed in Milan in 1831, and was long a vehicle for Tetrazzini,

and for Jenny Lind – who admired it above all other operas. In recent times it was revived (at the 1957 Edinburgh Festival) for Maria Callas.

Sonneck, Oscar George Theodore (1873–1928), U.S. author and musical historian. After studying in Germany, he became the earliest chief music librarian at the Library of Congress (1902–17), where he produced important musical catalogues. He was the earliest editor of the publication department of Schirmer's.

Sonnenquartetten, *see* SUN QUARTETS

sonore (Fr.), sonorous, with full tone – an indication frequently applied to individual parts in an orchestral score. British composers appear to use the word in the mistaken belief that it is Italian. The Italian word, however, is *sonoro*.

sons bouchés (Fr.; Ger., *Gestopft*), stopped notes on the horn produced by inserting the hand far into the bell. If they are played quietly the sound is remote and mysterious; if loudly, it is harsh.

sons étouffés (Fr.), literally 'damped sound'. This indication, which appears most frequently in harp parts, means that the vibrations should be damped by the hand immediately after the string or strings have been plucked, thereby producing a dry sound. An alternative is *sec* (Fr.) or *secco* (It.), and the opposite is *laissez vibrer*.

sons harmoniques (Fr.), harmonics.

sons près de la table, *see* PRES DE LA TABLE

sopra (It.), 'above'. In piano music the term is used to indicate that one hand has to pass above the other.

sopranino flügelhorn, *see* FLÜGELHORN

sopranino saxophone, *see* SAXOPHONE

soprano, the female voice of the highest register with a range extending (approximately) from middle C upwards for two octaves. The term is also applied occasionally to instruments, e.g. soprano saxophone. Boys whose voices have not yet changed can achieve the soprano range, as could *castrati*. The 15th century English term for a boy soprano was 'quatreble', which became 'treble' later.

soprano saxophone, *see* SAXOPHONE

Sor, Fernando or **Ferdinand** (1778–1839), Spanish composer and guitarist, whose real name was Ferdinando Sors. He was educated at the Escalonia in Montserrat, and later taught in Paris and London. He composed several operas (the earliest at the age of nineteen), ballets and guitar music. His guitar tutor was published in 1830.

Sorabji, Kaikhosru Shapurji (born 1892), English born composer, pianist and author, son of a Parsee father and a Spanish mother. His works include two symphonies for orchestra with chorus, piano and organ, five piano concertos, symphonic variations for piano and orchestra, piano quintets, piano sonatas, an elaborate two-hour work for piano entitled *Opus Clavicembalisticum* organ symphonies, five Michelangelo sonnets for baritone and chamber orchestra, and songs. Much of his music is of exceptional complexity, and all of it has until recently been banned by the composer from public performance. He has also written a book of critical essays, *Around Music* (1932).

Sorcerer, The, comic opera in two acts by Sullivan, libretto by W. S. Gilbert. It was first performed in London in 1877.

Sorcerer's Apprentice, The (Fr., *L'Apprenti Sorcier*), symphonic scherzo (1897) by Dukas, inspired by Goethe's ballad about the apprentice who learns how to cast a spell but not how to stop it.

sordino, sordina (It.; Fr., *sourdine*; Ger., *Dampfer*), (1) mute (of a string or wind instrument). *Con sordino*, with the mute; *senza sordino*, without the mute;

(2) damper (in the piano). The indication *senza sordini* in the first movement of Beethoven's piano sonata in C sharp minor, op 27, no 2, means that the dampers are to be raised, i.e. the strings are to be left free to vibrate. This was originally done by means of stops (similar to those used on the harpsichord). When later on a pedal was introduced to perform the same function the abbreviation *Ped.* came to replace the indication *senza sordini*;

(3) also applied in the late 18th and 19th centuries to a strip of leather (later felt) used to mute the strings of a piano and controlled by a pedal. For an example of its use see the slow movement of Schubert's piano sonata in A minor, op 143.

See also CORDA

Sordun (Ger.; It., *sordone*), an instrument of the bassoon family, current in the late 16th and early 17th centuries. It had a cylindrical bore and was played with a double reed. As the name suggests, the sound was muffled. It was made in several sizes.

Sore, *see* AGRICOLA

Soriano (**Suriano, Surianus, Suriani**), **Francesco** (1549–1620), Italian singer and composer. He was a chorister at St. John Lateran in Rome (1564) and a pupil of G. B. Nanini and Palestrina. In 1581 he was *maestro di cappella* at St. Ludovico dei Francesi, and from 1583 to 1586 he was attached to the court in Mantua. In Rome he was *maestro di cappella* at Santa Maria Maggiore (1587), at St. John Lateran (1599) and at St. Peter's (1603). He composed Masses, motets, psalms, 110 canons on *Ave maris stella*, Magnificats, a Passion and other church music, madrigals and *villanelle*.

S. P. KNISELEY: *The Masses of Francesco Soriano* (1967)

Sorochintsy Fair (Rus., *Sorochinskaya Yamarka*), opera in three acts by Mussorgsky. The libretto, by the composer, is based on an episode from Gogol's *Evenings on a Farm near Dekanka*. The work was left incomplete by the composer, and without orchestration. Among the versions which have been performed are those by Cui (Petrograd, 1917), Cherepnin (Monte Carlo, 1923) and Schebalin (Leningrad, 1931).

Sosarme, Ré di Media (It., *Sosarmes, King of Media*), opera in three acts by Handel, libretto adapted from *Alfonso Primo* by Matteo Noris. It was first performed in London in 1732.

sospiro (It.), crotchet rest (literally 'sigh').

sostenuto (It.), 'sustained'. A direction to sustain the tone, which is usually equivalent to slowing the tempo.

sostenuto pedal, whereas the sustaining pedal on a piano removes all the dampers from the strings, the sostenuto pedal, which is only fitted to certain more expensive instruments, enables the player to pre-select specific notes he wishes to be sustained.

sotto (It.), under. In piano music this term is used to indicate that one hand has to pass under the other.

sotto voce (It.), in an under tone, quietly.

soubrette (Fr.), 'cunning, shrewd'. Term used in opera to describe a soprano comedienne who sings the role of cunning servant girl, e.g. Despina in Mozart's *Cosi fan tutte*.

sound board, the resonant wooden part of certain instruments, including the piano, organ and dulcimer, over which the strings are stretched. It vibrates sympathetically and so amplifies the notes sounded.

sound hole, variously shaped opening in the table of stringed instruments. In bowed stringed instruments the *f* shape is usual, while earlier instruments, e.g. viols, had 'c' shapes, and guitars' and lutes' sound holes are circular. The hole allows the table more flexibility, and freer passage of air vibrations from the body of the instrument.

soundpost, the piece of wood, usually pine, that connects the two surfaces (the table and the back) of stringed instruments. Its purposes are to strengthen and, more important, to distribute the vibrations.

soupir (Fr.), crotchet rest (lit. 'sigh'). A quaver rest is *demi-soupir*, a semiquaver rest *quart de soupir*, a demi-semiquaver rest *huitième de soupir*, and a hemidemi-semiquaver rest *seizième de soupir*.

sourdine, *see* SORDINO

Sousa, John Philip (1854–1932), U.S. bandmaster and composer. He was leader of the United States Marine Corps Band, 1880. In 1892 he organized his own band which later made European tours and a world tour (1910–11). He composed many marches, including *The Stars and Stripes Forever* and *Washington Post*; also light operas, orchestral suites and songs. He wrote an autobiography, *Marching Along* (1928), and edited *National Patriotic and Typical Airs* (1890).

sousaphone, type of TUBA first made in 1899 specially for Sousa's band. The tubing encircled the player's body and ended in a large bell above his head and facing forwards instead of upwards. The instrument was much in evidence in early jazz bands and is still occasionally used today.

soutenu (Fr.), sustained, smoothly flowing (French equivalent of *sostenuto*).

Souterliedekens (Flem.), *Psalter Songs*, the title of a Flemish PSALTER which contained the earliest metrical translations of all the Psalms, with their melodies (which were folk songs), first published in Antwerp in 1540. Clemens non Papa made three-part settings of the tunes, with the melodies in the tenor, which were published in four volumes by Susato in 1556 and 1557 (facsimile of volumes i–iii by Editions Culture et Civilisation, Brussels; all four volumes were edited by K. P. Bernet Kempers in volume ii of his complete edition of Clemens's works).

Sowerby, Leo (1895–1968), U.S. composer, pianist and organist. He studied at the American Conservatory in Chicago, was appointed teacher at the American Conservatory and organist at St. James's Church, Chicago, and received the first fellowship at the American Academy in Rome (1922). He composed symphonies and other orchestral works, choral works, chamber music for organ and for piano, and songs.

Spanish Caprice, orchestral work by Rimsky-Korsakov, composed in 1887 and using themes and rhythms of Spanish folk song character. The work is familiarly known in English-speaking countries as the *Capriccio*

Espagnol – a pointless snobbism, since the first word is Italian, the second is French and the work itself is Russian.

Spanish Songbook (Ger., *Spanisches Liederbuch*), settings by Hugo Wolf of 44 Spanish poems of the 16th and 17th centuries, translated into German by Emanuel Geibel and Paul Heyse. The songs – ten sacred and thirty-four secular – were completed in 1890. They can be sung singly or as an entity, usually divided between two singers.

Spanish Rhapsody, *see* RAPSODIE ESPAGNOLE

spassapensieri (It.), JEW'S HARP.

Spataro (Spadaro, Spadarius), Giovanni (c. 1458–1541), Italian musical theorist and composer. He was *maestro di cappella* of San Petronio from 1512 until his death. He defended the system of tuning of the monochord advocated by Ramis de Pareja against the criticisms of Burzio (*Musices opusculum*, 1487) and Gafori (*Apologia*, 1520). His compositions include Masses, motets and secular works. Four of the motets have been printed in L. Torchi's *L'arte musicale in Italia*, i, and K. Jeppesen's *Italia sacra musica*, i.

speaker-key, a key on a reed instrument, e.g. oboe or clarinet, which opens a hole at such a point as to facilitate the playing of notes which are sounded by overblowing at the octave, twelfth or fifteenth.

Specht, Richard (1870–1932), Austrian music critic and writer, associated especially with the music of Mahler, but also with Brahms and Richard Strauss.

species, method of teaching strict counterpoint formulated by Fux in his *Gradus ad Parnassum* (1725). Fux listed five processes, or species, of counterpoint whereby one voice part (i.e. melody) could be set against another. These species are as follows:
(1) the added voice part moves at the same speed as the given one (i.e. note for note);
(2) the added voice part moves at two or three times the speed of the given one (i.e. with two or three notes for each given note);
(3) the added voice part moves at four or six times the speed of the given one (i.e. with four or six notes for each given note);
(4) the notes of the added voice part are in syncopated positions;
(5) the added voice part contains a mixture of the above processes (this species is called Florid Counterpoint).

Spectre's Bride, The (Cz., *Svatební košile*), cantata for three solo singers, chorus and orchestra by Dvořák, based on a supernatural ballad by K. J. Erben. It was first performed (in an English translation) at the Birmingham Festival in 1885. A later setting of the same ballad was made by another Czech composer, Vítězslav Novák, in 1913.

speech-song, *see* SPRECHGESANG.

spezzato (It.), 'divided', as in CORI SPEZZATI.

spherophone, an electrical instrument built in 1924 and producing sounds by means of ether waves.

spianato (It.), smooth, even.

spiccato (It.), 'clearly articulated'. The term is used in string playing for a light staccato played with the middle of the bow and a loose wrist.

Spieltenor (Ger.), term for a light operatic tenor voice, such as that of David in *The Mastersingers*.

spinet (Fr., *épinette*; It., *spinetta*: from Lat. *spina*, a thorn, referring to the quill which plucks the strings),

a term which replaced the word 'virginals' in the course of the 17th century in England for a small, one-manual harpsichord. In the 16th century the Italian spinet was made in a pentagonal shape; the Flemish spinet, like the virginals, was rectangular. The octave or 4-ft. spinet was triangular, with the strings at an angle of 45 degrees to the keyboard, and English makers adopted an enlarged version of this shape for the 8-ft. or normal pitch spinet towards the end of the 17th century.

See HARPSICHORD

spinto (It.), 'pushed', urged on.

Spiral, work by Stockhausen for one soloist with a short-wave receiver. Composed in 1968, it has been closely associated with the Swiss oboist, Heinz Holliger, who in a sense 'creates' each performance himself – its success or failure depends on the soloist's response to sounds obtained at random from the receiver.

spirito (It.), spirit. *Con spirito*, with spirit, lively.

spiritoso (It.), in a spirited manner.

spiritual, religious song of the North American Negro. Its melodic style is simple, with occasional use of modes or of a pentatonic scale, its rhythms are frequently syncopated, and its harmonies are similar to, and possibly modelled on, those of the hymns of the early Baptist and Methodists. It often makes use of call-and-response patterns, and may be partly and wholly extemporized. As the first indigenous music of the North American continent to come to notice, the spirituals attracted much attention in the 19th century through the choirs from educational institutions of Negroes.

    G. P. JACKSON: *White and Negro Spirituals* (1943)
    H. E. KREHBIEL: *Afro-American Folk Songs* (1914)

Spitta, Julius August Philipp (1841–94), German musicologist. He studied at Göttingen, was appointed Secretary to the Academy of Arts and Professor of Musical History at the University of Berlin (1875), where he also taught, and was a director, from 1882, of the Hochschule für Musik. His *Life of Bach* (in German, two volumes, 1873, 1880; English translation, three volumes, 1884–5) was the first comprehensive work on the life and music of Bach, the Lutheran tradition which he inherited, and the Italian and other influences on his music. Spitta edited the complete works of Schütz, the organ works of Buxtehude, and a selection of pieces by Frederick the Great.

Spitze (Ger.), point; hence the direction to string players *an der Spitze*, indicating that they should use the point of the bow.

Spohr, Ludwig (Louis) (1784–1859), German violinist, composer, conductor and teacher. He studied in Brunswick under Franz Eck, with whom he went on a tour of Russia (1802). He played with Meyerbeer in Berlin (1804), became orchestra leader to the Duke of Gotha (1805), toured with his wife (the harpist Dorette Scheidler) and met Weber in Stuttgart (1807). He was leader of the orchestra at the new Theater an der Wien in Vienna from 1812–16, conductor at the Frankfurt Opera from 1817–20 and in 1822, on the recommendation of Weber was appointed *Kapellmeister* to the Elector of Hesse-Cassel. Spohr gave concerts in Switzerland, Italy, Holland, Paris and London (where he caused a sensation by using a baton to conduct with – he was one of the first ever to do so). He conducted music festivals at Frankenhausen (1810–11, the first one in Germany), Aix-la-Chapelle (1840) and Bonn, and presented Wagner's *The Flying Dutchman* in Cassel in 1843 and *Tannhäuser* in 1853. He was a violinist of great ability, a capable conductor, and a prolific composer. His nine symphonies (three with titles: no 4, *The Consecration of Sound*; no 6, *The Historic*, illustrating the musical style of four periods, dated 1720, 1780, 1810, and 1840; no 7, *The Worldly and Divine in Man's Life*, for double orchestra) and fifteen violin concertos were highly regarded in their time. The most successful of his ten operas were *Faust* (1816), *Zemire und Azor* (1819) and *Jessonda* (1823), the last his chief work in this form. His chamber music includes a mellow and still popular nonet, 36 quartets and two double quartets, trios, fifteen duets for two violins and other compositions, and he also wrote choral music, piano pieces, and pieces for harp. His autobiography was published in the English translation in 1865 and reprinted in 1874.

Spontini, Gasparo Luigi Pacifico (1774–1851), Italian composer, pupil of Piccinni. In 1798 he went to Palermo as music director to the Neapolitan court. He settled in Paris in 1803 and became composer to Empress Josephine and director of the Italian Opera (1810–12). He was appointed director of music to the Prussian court in Berlin (1820) but was dismissed (1841) after the death of Friedrich Wilhelm III. He visited Paris and Dresden (1844), returning to Italy in 1848 and founded a music school at Jesi. His most famous and successful operas, *La Vestale* (1807) and *Fernand Cortez* (1809), were written for Paris, and were the first to reflect the Napoleonic era for operas with sumptuous production and plots with historical and political significance. *Nurmahal* (Berlin, 1822) and *Agnes von Hohenstaufen* (Berlin, 1929) were less successful.

   C. BOUVET: *Spontini* (1930)

Sprechgesang (Ger.), speech-song, i.e. a type of voice production midway between song and speech. Humperdinck used the technique as early as his *Königskinder* (1897), but the most famous example is Schoenberg's song cycle *Pierrot Lunaire*. In this the approximate pitch of the voice is indicated by musical notation.

Sprechstimme (Ger.), 'speaking part'.

   See MELODRAMA, SPRECHGESANG

springer, an ornament used in 17th century English music. It is equivalent to one of the forms of the German NACHSCHLAG. According to Christopher Simpson in *The Division Violist* it 'concludes the Sound of a Note more acute by clapping down another Finger just at the expiring of it'.

Notation:

Played:

Spring Sonata (Ger., *Frühlingssonate*), the title given – though not by the composer – to Beethoven's violin and piano sonata in F major, op 24 (1801).

Spring Symphony, (1) (Ger., *Frühlingssymphonie*),

the title, authorized by the composer, of Schumann's symphony no 1 in B flat major, op 38 (1841). He wrote in a letter to Spohr:

> It was inspired, if I may say so, by the spirit of spring which seems to possess us all anew every year, irrespective of age. The music is not intended to describe or paint anything definite, but I believe the season did much to shape the particular form it took.

The four movements were to have been called *Frühlingsbeginn* (Spring's Coming), *Abend* (Evening), *Frohe Gespielen* (Merry Playmates) and *Voller Frühling* (Full Spring), but Schumann suppressed these movement headings when he completed the work.

(2) a song-symphony in four main sections for three solo singers, mixed chorus, boys' chorus and orchestra by Britten, op 44. The work is based on poems to do with spring, the authors of texts being (in alphabetical order) Auden, Barnefield, Beaumont and Fletcher, Blake, Clare, Herrick, Milton, Nashe, Peele, Spenser, Vaughan, and Anon. It was first performed in Amsterdam in 1949.

Squarcialupi, Antonio (1416–80), Italian musician who was organist of Santa Maria, Florence, from 1436 till his death. He is known chiefly through a fine manuscript of which he was the first owner, commonly called the Squarcialupi manuscript, now in the Laurentian Library in Florence, which is the largest surviving collection of 14th century Italian music. It contains pieces by twelve composers, including 145 compositions by Francesco Landini. A modern edition by J. Wolf was published in 1955.

square piano, an early form of piano, oblong in shape and with the strings strung horizontally.

   See PIANO

Squire, William Barclay (1855–1927), English music librarian and editor. He joined the staff of the British Museum and became superintendent of printed music, retiring in 1920. He edited the *Catalogue of Printed Music 1487–1800*, now in the British Museum, a catalogue of music in Westminster Abbey chapter library, *Catalogue of the King's Music Library*, volumes i and iii, *Catalogue of the Printed Music in the Royal College of Music*. He was joint editor, with J. A. Fuller-Maitland, of the *Fitzwilliam Virginal Book*. He also edited Purcell's harpsichord music and works by Byrd and Palestrina, as well as an anthology of madrigals.

Staatsoper (Ger.), state opera house and/or company.

Stabat Mater (Lat.), 'the Mother was standing'. The initial words of a sequence probably written by Jacopone da Todi. The opening is quoted under SEQUENCE. The earliest polyphonic settings (c. 1500) were by English composers (John Browne, William Cornyshe, Richard Davy) and by Josquin des Prés. Later settings occur in all periods; among the most notable are those of Palestrina, Caldara, Pergolesi, Haydn, Schubert, Rossini, Verdi, Dvořák and Stanford.

Stabreim (Ger.), alliteration (term for the alliterative verse used by Wagner in his music dramas).

staccado-pastorole, a type of XYLOPHONE used in the 18th century.

staccato (It.), 'detached'. It may be indicated either by a pointed dash (▼), which was the standard notation in the baroque period, or by a DOT over each note to be detached. The dash indicates that the note is to be as short as possible, the dot that it is to be short. In *mezzo-staccato*, also called *portato*, indicated by a combination of slur and dots, the notes are to be slightly detached.

Stadler, Anton (1753–1812), Austrian clarinettist, whose virtuosity and beauty of tone encouraged the composition of several works by Mozart including the trio in E flat for clarinet, viola and piano, K 498, the clarinet quintet, K 581, and the clarinet concerto, K 622. The obbligatos for clarinet and for basset horn in *La clemenza di Tito* (1791) were also written for him; the low notes in the clarinet obbligato were specially designed for Stadler's instrument, which had a compass extending a major third below the normal.

Stadler, Maximilian (1748–1833), Austrian composer and organist. He studied at the Jesuit College in Vienna, entered the Benedictine order at the monastery of Melk in 1776, and was appointed abbot of Lilienfeld in 1786 and of Kremsmünster in 1798. He later settled in Vienna, where he made friends with Haydn and Mozart. He completed Mozart's piano sonata in A, K 402, and his trio in D, K 442 and wrote two pamphlets in defense of his Requiem. His own compositions included two Requiems and other church music, instrumental works and songs.

Städtische Oper (Ger.), civic opera house and/or company.

Stadtpfeifer (Ger.), a performer on a wind instrument, employed by a municipality, and the equivalent of the English WAIT. Several members of Bach's family belonged to this profession.

staff (or **stave**) (Fr., *portée*, Ger., *Liniensystem, System*, It., *rigo, sistema*), the set of lines, each representing a pitch (as do the spaces between them), on which music is written. Five lines are now used for all music except plainsong, which is written on four lines. LEGER LINES are used for notes above and below the staff, and a CLEF indicates the pitch of one of the lines and hence the particular pitch-position of a staff.

One or two lines, coloured red for F and yellow for C, were used in NEUME notation shortly before the 11th century. Guido d' Arezzo's proposal (c. 1000) that four lines be used was adopted for plainsong, and five lines became the usual for polyphonic music after 1200. Six or more lines were used for the writing of keyboard music in the 16th and 17th centuries.

Music for the harp, piano, harpsichord, clavichord and celesta is normally written on two staves, joined together by a BRACE. Organ music normally uses three, except when there is no pedal part. For the combination of several staves required for an ensemble of voices or instruments or both, *see* SCORE.

Stahlspiel (Ger.), a percussion instrument with steel bars and played with hammers. It is virtually a GLOCKENSPIEL designed for military bands. Because it is manufactured in the shape of a lyre for British military bands, it has acquired the misleading name of lyra.

Stainer, John (1840–1901), English organist and composer. He was organist at Magdalen College, Oxford; and later to St. Paul's Cathedral. He was knighted in 1888 and became professor at Oxford the following year. He composed numerous choral works, the most famous of which was *The Crucifixion* (1887), still occasionally performed.

Stamitz, Carl (1745–1801), German born violinist and composer, of Czech parentage (his real name was Karel Stamic). A member of the 'Mannheim School', he was the son of Johann Stamitz (or Jan Stamic). He was second violinist in the Mannheim orchestra from 1762–70 when he went to Strasbourg, Paris and London (1778) as a viola and viola d'amore player. He returned to Germany in 1785, and lived in Cassel, St. Petersburg and in Jena from 1794 as music director to the university. He composed seventy symphonies (some with two *concertante* violin parts), a symphony for two orchestras, concertos for piano, for viola, and for viola d'amore, string quartets, trio sonatas and other chamber music, and two operas.

His father, **Johann Wenzl Anton Stamitz** (1717–57), was born in Czechoslovakia (his original name was Jan Vaclav Stamic). He was solo violinist at the coronation of Emperor Karl VII (1742). Invited to the electoral court of Mannheim, he became leading violinist and chamber music director in 1745 and is regarded as the founder of the 'Mannheim School'. He himself composed about fifty symphonies, 100 orchestral trios, harpsichord, violin sonatas and other chamber music. He was the most important of the group of composers attached to the Mannheim orchestra who developed some of the chief traits in the style of the symphony, such as marked contrast between *forte* and *piano*, the *crescendo* for full orchestra, contrast of styles between themes, the dropping of the continuo, and the fuller use of wind instruments.

Ständchen (Ger.), serenade.

Stanford, Charles Villiers (1852–1924), Irish born composer. He studied in Dublin, and in 1870 became choral scholar at Queen's College, Cambridge, and in 1873 organist of Trinity College. He was teacher of composition at the Royal College of Music from its opening in 1883; professor, Cambridge, 1887 to his death. He was knighted in 1901. One of the leaders of the English musical renaissance, he taught Vaughan Williams and Arthur Bliss, among other composers, but little of his own prolific musical output has survived. Some of his works are coloured by Irish folk song, particularly the opera *Shamus O'Brien* (1896), the choral ballad *Phaudrig Crohoore* (1896), and the *Irish Rhapsodies* and third symphony (*Irish*, 1887), and there are continental influences in the opera *The Veiled Prophet of Khorassan* (1881), in the Requiem (1897), and in the chamber music. He published, with C. Forsyth, a *History of Music* (1916), a treatise on *Musical Composition* (1911), and three volumes of essays and memoirs.

Stanley, John (1713–86), English composer and organist who was blind from the age of two. He was a pupil of Maurice Greene, and from 1726 was organist of several London churches. He conducted oratorio performances, formerly directed by Handel, from 1760 with J. C. Smith and from 1774 with T. Linley, and in 1779 succeeded Boyce as Master of the King's Musick. His works include cantatas and songs for solo voice and instruments, oratorios, six concertos for strings, a dramatic pastoral, pieces for German flute, violin or harpsichord and organ voluntaries.

stantipes, form of ESTAMPIE

stark (Ger.), strong, loud; *stark blasend*, strongly blown.

Starker, János (born 1924), Hungarian born cellist, who studied at the Budapest Academy of Music. In 1946 he settled in the United States, establishing himself there as performer and professor (at Indiana University, Bloomington). He is internationally renowned for his performances of Bach.

Starokadomsky, Mikhail (1901–54). Russian composer, pupil of Miaskovsky. His works include an opera (*Sot*), an oratorio (*Simon Proshakov*), a concerto for orchestra, two suites for orchestra, an organ concerto, a violin concerto, two string quartets and other chamber music.

Star-spangled Banner, The, the national anthem of the United States, though the tune appears to have been written by an Englishman, John Stafford Smith (c. 1750–1836), who composed it for a poem entitled 'To Anacreon in Heaven'. The words of the national anthem were the work of Francis Scott Key (1779–1843), who is said to have jotted them down in 1814 while observing the British bombardment of Fort McHenry, near Baltimore. The anthem was officially adopted in a bill passed on March 3rd, 1931, though it was in unofficial use long before that – Puccini, for example, quoted it in Act 1 of *Madama Butterfly* in 1904, associating it with one of the principal characters in the opera, Lieutenant Pinkerton of the U.S. Navy.

Stasov, Vladimir (1824–1906), Russian critic and writer on music. He was a friend of the Five, for whom he coined the name 'the mighty handful'. His writings offer a vivid picture of musical life in 19th century Russia, not only of Russian composers themselves, but also of such important visitors as Berlioz, Schumann, Wagner and Liszt.

> V. STASOV: *Essays on Music*, translated by Florence Jonas (1968)

stave, see STAFF

Steffani, Agostino (1654–1728), Italian composer and diplomat who was ordained as a priest in 1680, becoming Abbot of Lepsing in 1682. In 1688 he went to Hanover where he became court music director and held several diplomatic posts, and from 1703 was in the service of the Elector Palatine at Düsseldorf. During a visit to Italy (1708–09) he met Handel, for whom he obtained the post of *Kapellmeister* at the Hanoverian Court. He lived at Padua from 1722 to 1725. His most noteworthy compositions were operas and chamber duets with continuo. In his sixteen operas he combined features of the Italian, French and German styles in a manner afterwards developed by Handel, and his chamber duets also served Handel as models. His opera *Alarico* (Munich, 1687) and extracts from thirteen other operas are published in volumes xi (2) and xii (2), respectively, of *Denkmäler der Tonkunst in Bayern*. Volume vi (2) in the same series contains sixteen chamber duets, two Scherzi for voice, two violins, and continuo, and two cantatas to Latin words for three voices and continuo. His six-part *Stabat Mater* with accompaniment for strings and organ was published in London in 1935. Eight songs with woodwind and continuo are in *Smith College Archives*, xi.

Steg (Ger.; Fr., *chevalet*; It., *ponticello*), bridge of a stringed instrument. Although it means literally 'on the bridge', *Am Steg* is a direction to play as near as possible to it, thereby producing a thin, brittle tone.

Steibelt, Daniel (1765–1823), German pianist and composer. He studied harpsichord and composition under Kirnberger, lived in Paris as pianist, teacher and composer, toured Germany and Austria (1799) and played in a contest with Beethoven. He spent the next few years moving between Paris and London to avoid his creditors, and settled in St. Petersburg (1808) where he became *Kapellmeister* to the Emperor Alexander (1810) and director of the French Opera. He composed operas, ballets, concertos and instrumental pieces (including music for harp).

Stein, Erwin (1886–1958), Austrian music critic and writer who settled in Britain. He was an authority on Mahler and succeeding Viennese composers, on whom his book, *Orpheus in New Guises*, provides a valuable commentary.

Steinberg, Maximilian Osseievich (1883–1946), Russian composer. He studied under Liadov, Glazunov and Rimsky-Korsakov, whose daughter he married in 1908. He taught at St. Petersburg (Leningrad) Conservatory from 1908; director 1934. His pupils included Shostakovich and Shaporin. He composed four symphonies and other orchestral works, ballets, choral music, piano concertos and sonatas, string quartets, and songs.

Steinberg, William (born 1899), German born conductor (original name: Hans Wilhelm), who settled in America and took charge of the Pittsburgh Symphony Orchestra in 1952. From 1958 until 1960 he was conductor of the London Philharmonic, and from 1969 until 1972 of the Boston Symphony Orchestra.

Steinway, a New York firm of piano manufacturers, founded in 1853 by Henry Engelhard Steinway (originally Steinweg), who was previously established in Brunswick. The London branch of the firm opened in 1875.

Stenhammar, Karl Vilhelm Eugen (1871–1927), Swedish composer, conductor and pianist. He studied in Stockholm and Berlin, spent several years touring as a pianist and became conductor of the Stockholm Opera in 1925. His compositions include operas, two symphonies, two piano concertos and other orchestral works, chamber music, piano works and songs.

stentando (It.), 'labouring', i.e. holding back each note in a passage. Hence equivalent to *molto ritenuto*. Often abbreviated *stent*.

Stern, Isaac (born 1920), Russian born violinist who was taken to the United States as a child and made his debut at San Francisco at the age of thirteen. He is one of the most distinguished violinists of the age, with a repertory including modern works as well as classics. In the field of chamber music, he is a member of the Istomin-Stern-Rose Trio.

Sterndale Bennett, William, see BENNETT

Stevens, Bernard (born 1916), English composer, pupil of Dent and Morris. His output includes a *Symphony of Liberation* (1946), other orchestral music, choral works, and chamber and instrumental pieces.

Stevens, Denis (born 1922), English musicologist and conductor, specializing in medieval and renaissance music. In 1964 he became professor of music at Columbia University, U. S.. He has edited many works by Monteverdi, including *Orfeo*, *Vespers* of 1610, *Il Ballo delle Ingrate* and *Il Combattimento di Tancredi e Clorinda*. His edition of the 16th century pieces which form the Mulliner Book has been an important contribution to English music. As conductor, he has been closely associated with the Accademia Monteverdiana and the Ambrosian Singers. As author, he has written *A History of Song* and *Tudor Church Music*.

Stierhorn (Ger.), a primitive instrument made from the horn of a bull or cow. Despite its coarse tone quality and being limited to a single note, it is familiar to opera-goers as the instrument used by the nightwatchman in Wagner's *Die Meistersinger*.

Stiffelio, opera in three acts by Verdi, to a libretto by Francesco Piave, after a play by Souvestre and Bourgeois. After its unsuccessful première at Trieste in 1850, the work was revised and reintroduced under the title of *Aroldo* at Rimini seven years later. The story concerns the matrimonial problems of the 16th century Protestant pastor Stiffelius. Since the work incorporates a divorce scene, among other controversial features, its initial failure in Italy is easy to understand.

stile (It.), style. In particular: (1) *stile antico*: the contrapuntal style of the 16th century as practised by Italian composers and formulated by Italian theorists in the 17th and early 18th centuries. Its principles were expounded by J. J. Fux in his *Gradus ad Parnassum* (1725) and thereafter became the rules of 'strict' COUNTERPOINT;

(2) *stile (genere) concitato*: a style fitted to express anger or agitation. The term was first used by Moneverdi in his preface to *Madrigali guerrieri et amorosi* (1638). He points out that there should be three types of music – *concitato, molle* and *temperato* – to correspond to the three principal passions – anger, temperance and humility – and avers, not quite correctly, that earlier composers had not written in a *genere concitato*;

(3) *stile rappresentativo*: the style of dramatic RECITATIVE practised in the earliest operas and in shorter works such as Monteverdi's *Combattimento di Tancredi e Clorinda*, composed in 1624;

(4) *stile moderno (concertato)*: the 'modern' style of the early 17th century, in which (a) the continuo, with or without other instruments with independent parts, was used to accompany a voice or voices, as distinct from the older practice of doubling or replacing voices by instruments, or (b) the parts in an instrumental composition were written for specific instruments and accompanied by continuo, as in Merula's *Canzoni, overo Sonate concertate per chiesa e camera* (1637).

See also PRIMA PRATTICA

Still, William Grant (born 1895), U.S. composer, the world's first Negro symphonist – his Afro-American Symphony was written in 1931. He studied at Oberlin Conservatory of Music and elsewhere; later he became an orchestral violinist, cellist and oboist, also conductor. His music, much of which has a distinctive Negro stamp, includes six operas, of which *Troubled Island* (namely Haiti; 1938) is perhaps the most important. Other works bear titles like *Darker America* (1927), *Dismal Swamp* (1936), *And They Lynched him on a Tree* (1940), *A Southern Interlude* (1942) and *Highway no 1, USA* (1963).

Stimme (Ger.), (1) voice;

(2) a separate part, vocal or instrumental, in a composition. Hence *Stimmbuch*, part-book; *Stimmführung*, part-writing.

Stimmflöte, Stimmhorn, Stimmpfeife (Ger.), pitchpipe.

Stimmführung (Ger.), part-writing (U.S. usage, voice-leading).

Stimmgabel (Ger.), tuning fork.

Stimmung, large-scale work by Stockhausen composed in 1968 for six vocalists from the 'Collegium Vocale' of Rhenish Music Schools in Cologne. First performed in Paris, it was subsequently toured all over the world and at the 1970 World Fair in Osaka it received 72 performances. The composer has declared that the title has many meanings, among which he suggests 'intonation' (because the vocalists have to sing the second, third, fourth, fifth, seventh and ninth harmonics of a low B flat fundamental), as well as 'tuning in' and 'attuning'. The performers sit on the floor in a circle, and the music, though it makes use of amplification, is mostly very quiet and mesmeric in its effect.

stock and horn, a primitive Scottish instrument, sometimes called a stockhorn or stock in horn. It was fitted with a single reed and played in the same way as the chanter of a bagpipe. As was the PIBGORN it was made of either wood or bone and fitted a cowhorn.

Stockflöte, *see* CZAKAN

Stockhausen, Karlheinz (born 1928), German composer. Born at Modrath, near Cologne, he studied at the Cologne Music High School and then in Paris under Messiaen and Milhaud. During the 1950s he became associated with the electronic studios of West German Radio at Cologne, and, through such works as *Mikrophonie I* and *II*, soon established himself as the world's leading electronic composer. At the same time, however, he was no laggard when it came to composing music for more conventional forces (employed, very often, in an unconventional way). His *Gruppen* (Groups) for three orchestras and conductors (1955–57), with its exploration of spatial effects, has proved to be one of the milestones of 20th century orchestral music, just as his eleven *Klavierstücke* (1952–57) have come to seem the modern equivalent of such earlier masterpieces as Chopin's preludes and Bach's preludes and fugues. Other important works of the period include *Kontra-Punkte* for ten instruments (1952–53), *Zeitmasse* ('Tempi') for woodwind quintet (1955–56), *Carré* for four orchestras and choruses (1959–60) and *Zyklus* (Cycle) for one percussion player (1959). In the last of these the percussionist is allowed to vary the performance by beginning on any page and working his way round to his starting-point. Elements of indeterminacy have become increasingly a feature of Stockhausen's music, to such an extent that in some of his works almost nothing is predetermined: instead of printed notes, the performers simply receive advice from the composer. Thus in *Goldstaub* (Gold Dust), one of the huge cycle of pieces forming *Aus den Sieben Tagen* (From the Seven Days), the performers are asked to starve themselves for four days, living alone and in complete silence. Then, to quote the composer's directions, 'late at night, without conversation beforehand, play single sounds, without thinking which you are playing, close your eyes, just listen'. Though much of Stockhausen's recent music arrives wrapped in mystical philosophy, it can nevertheless be a compelling experience so long as the com-

Karlheinz Stockhausen rehearses one of his works (*Momente*) on stage in Paris.

poser himself is in charge of the performers, directly communicating his ideas to them; performances in which the composer is not present are not always so convincing, but that is the price which Stockhausen pays for leaving so much to a performer's ingenuity and perceptiveness. If a question-mark still hangs over the philosophy behind Stockhausen's latest music, however, the rest of his output undeniably includes some of the most important works of our time, from the richness of *Gruppen* to the hypnotic murmuring of *Stimmung* (Attuning) for six voices (1968), the sweep of *Mantra* for two pianists (1970), the exuberance of *Prozession* (Procession) for mixed instrumental and electronic forces, and the pure electronics of *Hymnen* (Anthems) (1967), which has been described as a 'political drama' and builds elements of various National Anthems into a remarkable dramatic whole.

    K. H. WORNER: *Stockhausen: Life and Work* (1963, revised 1973)

Stokowski, Leopold Anton Stanislaw (1882–1977), English born conductor, son of a Polish father and a British mother. He became a U.S. citizen. He studied at the Royal College of Music under Stanford, and also in Germany and at the Paris Conservatoire; organist of St. James, Piccadilly, 1900; St. Bartholomew's, New York, 1905; conductor, Cincinnati Orchestra, 1909–12; Philadelphia Orchestra, 1913–36; City Symphony Orchestra, New York, 1942–45; New York Philharmonic, 1946, and with Mitropoulos, in 1949–50. He organized the All American Youth Orchestra in 1939. He made orchestral transcriptions of many works by J. S. Bach and appeared in Walt Disney's *Fantasia* and other films. As a conductor, apart from presenting many important premières, he devised an original and remarkably successful seating plan for the orchestra.

Stollen (Ger.), the first portion of a stanza of a MINNE-SINGER or MEISTERSINGER song commonly consisted of two *Stollen* (literally 'props'), the music of the first being repeated for the second. *See* BAR (3)

Stoltzer, Thomas (c. 1480–1526), German composer who was *Kapellmeister* to King Louis of Hungary and Bohemia. He composed Masses, Latin motets, psalms and hymns, German psalms and secular songs. His four-part Easter Mass has been published in *Das Chorwerk*, lxxiv; other Masses, and some motets, are in *Das Erbe deutscher Musik*, xxii. His Latin hymns and psalms are published in *Denkmäler deutscher Tonkunst*, volume lxv; some Latin hymns were also contained in Rhau's *Sacrorum Hymnorum Liber Primus* (modern edition in *Das Erbe deutscher Musik*, xxi and xxv). Twelve German part-songs are printed in *Denkmäler der Tonkunst in Osterreich*, lxxii, Jg. xxxvii (2). Others were included in Georg Forster's collection of 1539, reprinted in *Das Erbe deutscher Musik*, xx.

Stolzel, Gottfried Heinrich (1690–1749), German composer. He studied in Schneeberg and Leipzig, taught in Breslau (1710–12), visited Italy (1713), lived in Prague, Bayreuth and Gera, and in 1719 was appointed *Kapellmeister* to the Duke of Gotha. He composed twenty-two operas, fourteen oratorios, Masses, eight sets of cantatas and motets for the church year, chamber cantatas with piano, concertos and trio sonatas and wrote two theoretical treatises. He was the composer of the song 'Bist du bei mir', generally attributed to J. S. Bach on the basis of a copy made by his second wife, Anna Magdalena.

Stone Flower, The, ballet by Prokofiev, composed between 1948 and 1950. The story, based on folk tales, tells of a potter who leaves his village and his fiancée in order to seek a legendary stone flower which will enable him to perfect his art. This, Prokofiev's last ballet, failed to win the success of *Romeo and Juliet* and *Cinderella*.

Stone Guest, The (Rus., *Kamennyi Gost*), opera in three acts by Dargomizhsky, based (word for word) on Pushkin's play, on the same subject as Mozart's *Don Giovanni*. The score is notable for its natural setting of word rhythms, but the composer died too soon to complete it. This task was undertaken (as so often in the case of unfinished Russian music of this period) by the firm of Cui and Rimsky-Korsakov, and the work had its première at St. Petersburg in 1872, three years after Dargomizhsky's death.

stop, (1) on an organ, the handle or draw-stop which controls the admission of wind to a particular register, or set of pipes. The term is also applied to the register itself. On a harpsichord, stops were formerly used to produce variations of tone or pitch; their function is now generally performed by pedals;

    (2) a stopped pipe on an organ is one in which the upper end is closed. The effect of stopping is to lower the pitch by an octave;

    (3) a string is said to be stopped when its playing length is shortened by the finger. The term 'double stopping' is applied to the playing of two notes simultaneously on a stringed instrument even though this may involve the use of an OPEN STRING;

    (4) a stopped note on the horn is produced by inserting the hand into the bell and so modifying the pitch of an open note.

    See HORN

stopped notes, notes produced on a horn with the aid of the hand inside the bell of the instrument. This affects both the pitch and the tone. On stringed instruments the term applies to all notes except those played on an open string.

See HORN, STOP

stopping, on stringed instruments the placing of the fingers of the left hand on the strings, thereby shortening their effective vibrating length and, therefore, raising the pitch. Two, three, and four notes played simultaneously this way are referred to as double, treble and quadruple stopping respectively, even when one or more open strings are used. For stopping as part of horn technique see STOPPED NOTES and HORN.

Storace, Stephen (1763–96), English composer. He studied in Naples, made the acquaintance of Mozart in Vienna, and returned to England in 1787 with his sister Nancy (Anna Selina), who was the original Susanna in Mozart's *The Marriage of Figaro*. He composed operas, a ballet, chamber music, harpsichord sonatas and songs. The most successful for which he 'selected, adapted, and composed' the music were *The Haunted Tower* (1789), *No Song, no Supper* (1790), *The Pirates* (1792) and *The Cherokee* (1794). He died young, of gout.

stornello, Tuscan folk song, each verse of which has three lines.

storto (It.), Krummhorn.

Story of a Real Man, The, opera in three acts by Prokofiev, with a libretto by the composer's wife. The work, first performed in Leningrad in 1948, was Prokofiev's reply to a severe criticism of him which had been made by the General Committee of the Communist Party. But though the music was intended to be more readily comprehensible, with 'trios, duets and contrapuntally developed choruses', and though the hero was to be a legless Russian pilot, Prokofiev did not escape censure with this work either. It was condemned for its 'negative and repulsive usages' and its 'infatuation with modernist trickery'. Nevertheless it achieved a further performance, at the Bolshoi in Moscow in 1960, but so far it has failed to establish itself in the West.

Stradella, Alessandro (1644–82), Italian composer, violinist and singer. He taught singing at Venice and later visited Vienna and Turin. The story told by the Abbé Bourdelot (*Histoire de la musique*, 1715) of his attempted murder following his elopement with the mistress of a Venetian nobleman is the basis of Flotow's opera *Alessandro Stradella* (1844). He composed six oratorios, sacred and secular cantatas, operas, serenatas, concertos for strings, and trio sonatas. He considered his oratorio *S. Giovanni Battista* (1676) to be his best work. There is a modern edition by Alberto Gentili of the opera *La forza dell' amor paterno* (1678). An aria with instrumental *ritornelli* at the beginning and the end, *Tra cruci funeste*, from the opera *Il Corispero* (about 1665) is printed in *Historical Anthology of Music*, A. T. Davision and W. Apel, no 241. His work is important both in the history of vocal forms and in the early history of the concerto; in his *Sinfonie a più stromenti* of about 1680 he separated the solo instruments from the *concerto grosso*. One of his serenatas, *Qual prodigio*, was used by Handel in the chorus 'He spake the word, and there came all manner of flies' in *Israel in Egypt*, and is printed by Chrysander as the third supplement to his complete edition of Handel.

E. ALLAM: 'Alessandro Stradella', *Proceedings of the Royal Musical Association*, lxxx (1953–4)

R. GIAZOTTO: *Vita di Alessandro Stradella* (1962)

Stradivari (**Stradivarius**), **Antonio** (1644–1737), Italian violin maker. He was apprenticed to Nicolo Amati and founded his own workshop at Cremona. He began to use his own labels about 1667 and made his best instruments between 1700 and 1720. He was assisted by two of his sons, Francesco and Omobono, who carried on their father's work after his death. Among his other pupils were Guadagnini and Gagliano. Although later makers have carried on the methods he evolved, none has surpassed his instruments in craftsmanship and quality of tone.

W., A. F. and A. HILL: *Antonio Stradivari, his Life and Work* (1909)

E. N. DORING: *How many Strads?* (1945)

strambotto (It.), (1) a form of Italian poetry of the 15th and 16th centuries. It has a verse of eight lines with the rhyme scheme *abababcc*, or less frequently *abababab*. The musical settings published in the fourth of Petrucci's collections of *frottole* (1505) have music for the first pair of lines, which is to be repeated for the other three pairs. Two examples from that collection are printed in the third volume of Einstein's *The Italian Madrigal* (1949);

(2) Malipiero used the term in his *Rispetti e Strambotti* for string quartet, in which he wished to evoke 'the character of old Italian poetry'. The work is in the form of twenty instrumental 'stanzas' each preceded by a recurring 'ritornello'.

Strandrecht, *see* WRECKERS

Strangways, *see* FOX STRANGWAYS

Straniera, La (It., *The Stranger*), opera in two acts by Bellini, to a libretto by Felice Romani, first performed at Milan in 1829 by a cast including Meric-Lalande, Rubini and Tamburini. The story of this lakeside romantic drama revolves round various complex problems of identity.

strascinando (It.), dragging.

strathspey, Scottish dance.

See REEL

Straube, Karl (1873–1950), German organist and conductor, son of a German father and an English mother. He studied in Berlin and later moved to Leipzig, where he held a series of important appointments. He excelled in the performance of Reger's works, many of which were written as a tribute to his skill. As a conductor, he was responsible for the performance of a vast amount of music of all periods and all countries, including a complete cycle of Bach's cantatas. His collections, *Alte Orgelmeister* (1904), 45 *Choralvorspiele alter Meister* (1907) and *Alte Meister des Orgelspiels* (two volumes, 1929) are indispensable to organists.

Straus, Oscar (1870–1954), Austrian born composer and conductor who took French nationality in 1939. He was a pupil of Max Bruch, and composed a number of Viennese operettas, including *The Chocolate Soldier* and *A Waltz Dream*. He was a relative neither of Johann nor of Richard Strauss.

Strauss, Christoph (c. 1580–1631), Austrian composer. He was in the service of the imperial court at Vienna from 1594, as conductor from 1617 to 1619. In 1601 he was organist at St. Michael's, Vienna, later becoming *Kapellmeister* at St. Stephen's Cathedral.

He published a collection of 36 motets in five to ten parts (1613) and a set of sixteen Masses in eight to twenty parts with continuo (1631). A modern edition of a Requiem Mass is in *Denkmäler der Tonkunst in Österreich*, lix, Jg. xxx (1).

Strauss, Johann (the younger; 1825–99), Austrian violinist, conductor and prolific composer of waltzes and other Viennese light music. He was son of **Johann Strauss** (the elder; 1804–49), who was also a famous composer of waltzes and other pieces, including the famous *Radetzky March*. The younger Johann studied composition under Drechsler and founded his own orchestra in 1844, joined it with his father's orchestra in 1849 and toured Austria, Poland and

Johann Strauss the younger, glamorous symbol of romantic Vienna, capital of a dying empire.

Germany. He directed summer park concerts in St. Petersburg (1855–65), conducted court balls (from 1863) and visited Paris, London, Italy and the United States. He composed sixteen operettas, a ballet, waltzes, polkas, galops and other dances. The most successful of his operas was *Die Fledermaus* (*The Bat*, 1874) and *Der Zigeunerbaron* (*The Gipsy Baron*, 1885). His waltzes, many of them substantial and picturesque enough to be regarded as Viennese symphonic poems, include *The Blue Danube*, *Tales from the Vienna Woods* and the *Emperor Waltz*. To be savoured to the full, they need to be artisically performed in their correct and often exceptionally delicate orchestration – *Tales from the Vienna Woods*, for instance, requires a zither.

Johann's brother **Joseph Strauss** (1827–70), though trained as a architect, was also a distinguished composer of waltzes – his output running to 283 works, including *Music of the Spheres* and *The Village Swallows in Austria*. Another brother, **Eduard Strauss** (1835–1916), added a further 200 or so pieces to the Strauss family repertory, and was conductor of the Viennese court balls.

Strauss, Richard (1864–1949), German composer. Born in Munich, he was the son of Franz Strauss, a horn player at the Munich Court Opera, who gave him a thoroughly musical upbringing. His earliest compositions, including a *Festival March* for orchestra, op 1, and a short, attractive wind serenade, op 7, were written before he reached his teens. In 1885, after abandoning his studies at Munich University, he became assistant conductor to Hans von Bülow at Meiningen, and within a year succeeded von Bülow as first conductor. Influenced by Alexander Ritter, a violinist in the Meiningen orchestra (and husband of Wagner's niece), he turned from the style of Brahms to that of Liszt and Wagner. With *Aus Italien* (1887) he began the series of daring symphonic poems and illustrative symphonies which helped to bring him fame and fortune and caused much controversy about the merits of programme music. Subsequent works in the form included *Don Juan* (1889), *Death and Transfiguration* (1889), *Till Eulenspiegel* (1895), *Don Quixote* (1898), *Ein Heldenleben* (1898) and the *Domestic Symphony* (1903). Meanwhile his conducting career developed by way of appointments with the Munich Opera and the Weimar Court Opera. In 1891 he was invited by Cosima Wagner to conduct *Tannhäuser* at Bayreuth, and in 1894, with Wagner's music as his principal influence, he completed his first opera, *Guntram*, produced at Weimar with his future wife (Pauline de Ahna) as the heroine. By now he seemed to be Wagner's most successful successor. In 1894 he became conductor of the Berlin Philharmonic, in 1898 conductor of the Berlin Royal Opera, and from 1919 until 1924 was conductor with Schalk of the Vienna Opera. His home, however, was at Garmisch in Upper Bavaria, where he had settled after composing *Salome* (1905) – his first sensational, and very controversial, operatic success. When the Kaiser remarked that this morbid opera would do Strauss no good at all, Strauss is said to have replied that the proceeds of it had enabled him to build his country villa. His next opera, *Elektra* (1909), was almost equally sensational, and in making this adaptation of Sophocles he acquired as his partner the most famous of his librettists – Hugo von Hofmannsthal, the Viennese poet and dramatist who was subsequently to provide Strauss with five more librettos – for *Der Rosenkavalier* (1911), *Ariadne auf Naxos* (1912–16), *Die Frau ohne Schatten* (1919), *Die Aegyptische Helena* (1928) and *Arabella* (1933). While working on the last of these, Hofmannsthal died of a stroke provoked by his son's suicide.

Hofmannsthal is usually credited with having diverted Strauss from the morbid excesses of works like *Salome* and *Elektra* to the more genial style of his later music, with *Der Rosenkavalier* marking the rococo turning-point. Opinion remains divided as to whether this was a good thing. Some authorities claim that, having established himself as a formidable German *enfant terrible*, Strauss began a steady creative decline. Others claim that he had to work *Salome* and *Elektra* out of his system before achieving the more civilised style of his maturity. For the latter, Strauss's last works show his artistry at its purest and most inspired, as in his last opera, *Capriccio* (1942), a polished conversation-piece set in the 18th century. It is possible, and surely preferable, to enjoy both the early and the late Strauss and

Richard Strauss, the anti-romantic who said he looked forward to the day he could describe a teaspoon accurately in music but went on to write one of the most notable of 20th century romantic operas, *Rosenkavalier*

sonata (1883); piano quartet (1884); violin sonata (1887).

(5) Songs: four sets with orchestra (1897–1921); 26 sets with piano (1882–1929); *Four Last Songs* with orchestra.

(6) Piano: sonata in B minor (1881); two sets of short pieces (1881, 1883).

Also editions of Gluck's *Iphigénie en Tauride* (1894), Mozart's *Idomeneo* (1930), Berlioz's *Instrumentation* (1905).

T. ARMSTRONG: *Strauss's Tone-Poems* (1931)

E. BLOM: *Correspondence of Strauss and von Hofmannsthal* (translated by Paul England, 1928; complete edition in German, 1952)

N. DEL MAR: *Richard Strauss: a critical commentary on his life and works* (three volumes, 1962–71)

E. KRAUSE: *Richard Strauss – Gestalt und Werk* (1955)

W. MANN: *Richard Strauss: a critical study of the operas* (1964)

G. R. MAREK: *Richard Strauss: the Life of a Non-hero* (1967)

E. NEWMAN: *Richard Strauss* (1908)

W. SCHUH (editor): *Richard Strauss: Briefe an die Eltern, 1882–1906* (1954); *Richard Strauss: Recollections and Reflections* (1953); *Richard Strauss – Stefan Zweig: Briefwechsel* (1957)

W. SCHUH and F. TRENNER (editors): *Hans von Bülow and Richard Strauss: Correspondence* (1955)

Stravinsky, Igor Feodorovich (1882–1971), Russian composer. Born at Oranienbaum, near St. Petersburg, he was the son of a bass singer at the Imperial Opera. In 1903 he was introduced to Rimsky-Korsakov, whose pupil he became in 1907. His first symphony, op 1, was performed the following year; though conventional in idiom, it is good enough still to merit an occasional performance. *Fireworks* for orchestra (1908), which he wrote for the marriage of Nadia Rimsky-Korsakov and M. Steinberg, is more recognisably Stravinsky, but it was not until he came into contact with Diaghilev and composed his first major ballet, *The Firebird* (Paris, 1910), that his individuality became apparent. In its orchestral colours, it may have had more than a dash of Rimsky-Korsakov about it, but in other respects it looked forward to *Petrushka* (1911) and *The Rite of Spring* (1913), also written for Diaghilev's company. The première of the latter, conducted by Pierre Monteux at the Théâtre de Champs-Elysées, created one of the most famous uproars in the history of music. In contrast with the chromaticism of Wagner, *The Rite* is primarily concerned with rhythm, employed to orgiastic effect – even the harmony, often involving the clash of one tonality against another, is predominantly percussive. In its liberation of rhythm, *The Rite* was to prove an epoch-making score, but was, as far as Stravinsky was concerned, the end of a line. Only rarely thereafter was he to require the heavy orchestral forces which can make *The Rite* still an overwhelming experience. *The Soldier's Tale* (1918), basically an anti-opera in which none of the cast actually sings, involves acting, dancing, a spoken narration and a series of numbers for seven instruments, notable for their nervy economy of style. This economy was to some extent dictated to the composer – the work was written during World War I for a makeshift company

to be thankful that he lived long enough to produce sufficient music of both kinds.

Strauss's activities during the Nazi years are equally contentious. His opera, *Friedenstag* (1938), won Hitler's approval and Strauss did choose to stay in Germany during World War II. However, his comic opera, *Die schweigsame Frau* (1935), had a Jewish librettist, Stefan Zweig, whom Strauss stoutly championed. Again, though the *Metamorphosen* for string orchestra (1945) was widely thought to be a threnody for Hitler – it was banned in Holland after the war – the music may have been simply an expression of grief at the destruction of the Germany he loved.

Strauss's principal works are:

(1) Operas: *Guntram* (Weimar, 1894); *Feuersnot* (Dresden, 1901); *Salome* (Dresden, 1905); *Elektra* (Dresden, 1909); *Der Rosenkavalier* (Dresden, 1911); *Ariadne auf Naxos* (Stuttgart, 1912; revised version, Vienna, 1916); *Die Frau ohne Schatten* (Vienna, 1919); *Intermezzo* (Dresden, 1924); *Die Aegyptische Helena* (Dresden, 1928); *Arabella* (Dresden, 1933); *Die schweigsame Frau* (Dresden, 1935); *Friedenstag* (Munich, 1938); *Daphne* (Dresden, 1938); *Capriccio* (Munich, 1942); *Die Liebe der Danae* (Salzburg, 1952).

(2) Ballets: *Josephslegende* (Paris, 1914); *Schlagobers* (Vienna, 1924).

(3) Orchestra: Tone-poems: *Aus Italien* (1887), *Macbeth* (1887), *Don Juan* (1888), *Tod und Verklärung* (1889), *Till Eulenspiegel* (1895), *Also sprach Zarathustra* (1896), *Don Quixote* (1897), *Ein Heldenleben* (1898), *Symphonia domestica* (1903), *Eine Alpensinfonie* (1915); symphony in F minor (1884); violin concerto (1883); two horn concertos (1884, 1942); oboe concerto (1945); duet-concertino for clarinet and bassoon (1948); *Metamorphosen* for 23 strings (1945); suite for *Le Bourgeois gentilhomme* (1919).

(4) Chamber music: string quartet (1881); cello

in Switzerland – but it obviously suited him.

The main outcome of his prolonged stay in Western Europe was his adoption of neo-classicism in such works as the concerto for piano and wind instruments (1924), the octet for wind instruments, and the ballets *Pulcinella* (after Pergolesi, 1920) and *Apollo* (1928). The climax of this period in his career came with his opera, *The Rake's Progress* (1951) – basically a classical number opera, containing elements of Mozart and Handel, energised by Stravinsky's very personal rhythms and harmonies. By this time Stravinsky had settled in the United States. There, prompted by his friend Robert Craft, he belatedly found inspiration in serialism and (from *Agon* onwards) produced a remarkable series of masterpieces in his old age. Among the most important works of his later years are *Threni* (1957–58), *Movements* for piano and orchestra (1958–59), *The Flood* (1961–62), *Abraham and Isaac* (1962–63) and the *Requiem Canticles* (1965–66), in which the richness of the great 19th century requiems (e.g. Verdi's) seems to have been distilled and compressed into a tight fifteen minute structure. In 1962, Stravinsky made a brief return to Russia, where he was given a hero's welcome. He always remained a Russian at heart, and retained his Orthodox faith (which had its supreme musical reflection in his choral *Psalm Symphony* of 1930). It has been said of him that his works provide a 'map' of 20th century musical developments. No other composer has ranged more widely – consider the violence of *The Rite*, the classical grandeur of *Oedipus Rex*, the poise and polish of the Symphony in C, the wit of the *Dumbarton Oaks* concerto, the laconic beauty of *Movements*. Stravinsky has been the first great composer to provide posterity with recordings of most of his works, with himself as conductor. He has also supplied a valuable autobiography, entitled *Chronicles of my Life* (1936); a volume of essays, *Poetics of Music* (1947); and a series of illuminating conversations with Robert Craft, published in a series of volumes. Craft has also written a portrait of the composer (*Stravinsky: the Chronicle of a Friendship, 1948–1971*).

Stravinsky's principal works are:–

(1) Stage works – Ballets: *The Firebird* (1910); *Petrushka* (1911); *The Rite of Spring* (1913); *The Wedding* (with chorus, 1923); *The Soldier's Tale* (with speaking voice, 1918); *Pulcinella* (after Pergolesi, 1920); *Apollo* (1928); *The Fairy's Kiss* (1928); *Card Game* (1937); *Orpheus* (1948); *Agon* (1957); Operas: *The Nightingale* (1914), *Mavra* (1922), *The Rake's Progress* (1951); Opera-oratorio: *Oedipus Rex* (1927); Melodrama: *Persephone* (1933); *The Flood* (1961–62).

(2) Orchestra: *Fireworks* (1908); *Symphonies for Wind Instruments* (1920); *Dumbarton Oaks* concerto (1938); symphony in C (1940); *Danses Concertantes* (1942); symphony in three movements (1945); concerto for string orchestra (1946); concerto for piano and wind (1924); *Capriccio* for piano and orchestra (1929); violin concerto (1931); *Ebony Concerto* (1945); *Movements* for piano and orchestra (1958–59); *Variations* for orchestra (Aldous Huxley in memoriam, 1963–64).

(3) Choral works: *Symphony of Psalms* (1930); *Mass* (1948); cantata (1951–52); *Canticum sacrum* (1956);

Threni (1957–58); *A Sermon, a Narrative, and a Prayer* (1960–61); *Requiem Canticles* (1965–66).

(4) Other works: *Berceuses du chat* (four songs for female voice and three clarinets, 1916); octet for wind (1923); octet for wind instruments (1922–23, revised 1952); concerto for two pianos (1935); sonata for two pianos (1944); septet for clarinet, bassoon, horn, violin, viola, cello and piano (1954); *In memoriam Dylan Thomas* (tenor, string quartet and four trombones); *Abraham and Isaac* for baritone (or mezzo-soprano) and three clarinets (1964).

M. ARMITAGE: *Igor Stravinsky* (1936)

V. BELAIEV: *Igor Stravinsky's 'Les Noces'* (1928)

R. CRAFT: *Stravinsky: the Chronicle of a Friendship, 1948–1971* (1972)

E. EVANS: *Stravinsky: The Fire-Bird and Petroushka* (1933)

P. HORGAN: *Encounters with Stravinsky* (1972)

L. LIBMAN: *And Music at the Close: Stravinsky's Last Years* (1972)

F. ROUTH: *Stravinsky* (1975)

I. STRAVINSKY: *Themes and Conclusions* (1972)

I. STRAVINSKY and R. CRAFT: *Conversations with*

Igor Stravinsky, rehearsing in 1965 in London's Festival Hall. He was an outstanding interpreter of his own works, many of which he recorded.

Igor Stravinsky (1958; *Dialogues and a Diary* (1961); *Memories and Commentaries*; *Expositions and Developments* (1962); *Themes and Conclusions* (1972)

E. W. WHITE: *Stravinsky's Sacrifice to Apollo* (1930); *Stravinsky: the Composer and his Works* (1966)

straw fiddle (Ger., *Strohfiedel*), a type of XYLOPHONE.

street piano, a mechanical type of piano with a barrel-and-pin action similar to that of a musical box. It is played in the same way as a barrel organ by turning a handle and is thus sometimes called a piano organ. Rarely seen today, it was once a favourite of itinerant performers.

Streich (Ger.), bow (of a bowed instrument). So *Streichinstrumente,* bowed instruments; *Streichquartett,* string quartet, etc.

strepitoso (It.), noisy.

stretto (It.), close, narrow, drawn together, (1) the bringing in of overlapping entries of the subject in a fugue 'closer', i.e. after shorter intervals of time, than those at which they originally came (Ger., *Engführung*). The objects of *stretto* are to show the contrapuntal possibilities of the subject and to increase the cumulative effect of successive sets, or of a final set, of entries. For example, in the exposition of the fugue in E flat in the second book of Bach's *Forty-Eight* the answer comes at the seventh bar:

In bars 30–31 the answer comes at one bar's distance:

(2) the word is also used of a quickening of tempo towards the end of a piece.

Strich (Ger.), bow stroke.

Striggio, Alessandro (c. 1535–c. 1589), Italian composer and player of the *lira da gamba*. A nobleman, he was attached to the court of Cosimo de' Medici in Florence from about 1560 and later went to Mantua. He visited France, Flanders and England in 1567. One of the earliest composers of *intermezzi*, his *Psiche ed Amore* was performed in 1565. He published seven books of madrigals and a set of programme madrigals, 'The Chatter of Women at their Washing' (1567). Five of his madrigals are printed in Torchi's *L'arte musicale in Italia*, i, and his 'naturalistic' madrigal 'The Game of Cards' in the third volume of Einstein's *The Italian Madrigal*. There is a keyboard transcription of his madrigal 'Chi fara fede al cielo' by Peter Philips in the Fitzwilliam Virginal Book (no 78).

His son Alessandro Striggio, a player of the *lira* and a librettist, wrote the libretto of Monteverdi's *Orfeo* (1607).

R. J. TADLOCK: 'Alessandro Striggio, Madrigalist', *Journal of the American Musicological Society*, xi (1958)

string(s), lengths of wire or gut on which the sounds are produced in many diverse instruments, including the piano, harp, violin family, guitar, mandolin and lute; also used to mean stringed instruments, but in this case it usually refers only to violins, violas, cellos, double-basses and their predecessors, and not to such instruments as piano, harp and guitar.

stringed instruments, *see* INSTRUMENTS

stringendo (It.), 'tightening', i.e. increasing the tension and (usually) accelerating the tempo.

string orchestra, strictly, a band consisting of stringed instruments only, distinguished from a wind or brass band.

string quartet, the medium (and music for the medium) of two violins, viola and cello. A string quartet is, in effect, a SONATA in three of four movements for those instruments. Its history began between 1750 and 1760, with the early quartets of Haydn, which were probably written for outdoor performance – hence the absence of a continuo part. The twelve quartets of his op 1 and 2 are in the style of *divertimenti*, and have five movements, including two minuets. From op 3 (c. 1765) onwards Haydn adopted the four-movement form, and with op 9 (1769) he began the development of style, form and texture in quartet writing which continued to the end of his life. Mozart dedicated to Haydn the first six of his ten mature quartets. The concept of the possibilities of this medium at which Beethoven arrived in his last quartets put them for nearly a century outside the main stream of the history both of the string quartet and the sonata form. In their linear style, and in their treatment of thematic development and tonality, they are closer to the quartets written in modern times than to those of the nineteenth century. Between Schubert and Brahms the quartet, an apt medium for lyrical expression but not for rhetoric, has a patchy history. With Debussy's quartet of 1893 it entered a new phase, which later included the remarkable series of six quartets by Bartók and some of the most characteristic compositions of Ravel, Schoenberg, Berg, Webern, Hindemith and Walton. Though Boulez has declared the string quartet to be no longer viable as a musical form, he himself has written some impressive music in that medium, and the U.S. composer, Elliott Carter, has produced three important, progressive quartets. Messiaen's 'Quartet for the End of Time' is not a string quartet, but a work for piano, clarinet, violin and cello.

string quintet, *see* QUINTET

Strogers, Nicholas (flourished 1570–90), English composer. His compositions include services, anthems, motets, consort songs, *In Nomines* for strings, and keyboard music. Three consort songs by him are printed in *Musica Britannica*, xxii. A fantasia by him is in the *Fitzwilliam Virginal Book*.

Strohfiedel, *see* STRAW FIDDLE

Stroh violin, Stroh viola, Stroh cello, Stroh mandolin, Stroh guitar, instruments, invented by Charles Stroh in 1901, in which the normal body is replaced by an amplifying horn. Not to be confused with the *Strohfiedel,* or STRAW FIDDLE.

stromentato (It.), played by instruments. In particular, *recitativo stromentato,* recitative accompanied by the orchestra instead of simply by a keyboard instrument.

    See RECITATIVE.

stromento, *see* STRUMENTO

Strong, George Templeton (1856–1948), U.S. composer who studied in Leipzig and became a disciple of Liszt. In 1892 he settled in Switzerland, where he died. His works include three symphonies (the second and third bearing the titles, *In the Mountains* and *By the Sea*), a symphonic poem (*Undine*), choral music and chamber music.

strophic, term used for a song which uses the same music for each of its verses. Schubert's 'Seligkeit' is thus a strophic song. The opposite of strophic is 'through-composed' (Ger., *durchkomponiert*). An example of a through-composed song is Mozart's 'Abendempfindung'.

strumento (It.), instrument. *Strumenti a corde,* string instruments; *strumenti a fiato,* wind instruments; *strumenti a percossa* (or *percussione*), percussion instruments; *strumenti di legno,* woodwind instruments; *strumenti d'ottone,* brass instruments.

Strungk, Nikolaus Adam (1640–1700), German composer, violinist and organist. At twelve he was assistant organist to his father, the composer Delphin Strungk, at the Magnuskirche in Brunswick. He studied at Helmstedt University and became first violinist in the Celle orchestra (1661). He was in Hanover in 1665, and became music director in Hamburg in 1678. In 1682 he returned to Hanover as chamber composer to the Elector Ernst August, whom he accompanied on a visit to Italy where he received praise from Corelli for his violin playing. He also visited Vienna, where he played for Leopold I. He was appointed chamber organist and assistant *Kapellmeister* (1688) and *Kapellmeister* (1692) of the Dresden Court. He composed about eight operas for Hamburg between 1678 and 1693, when he opened the Leipzig opera, which he founded, with a performance of his *Alceste.* Five of the six *Cappricci* for organ printed in *Denkmäler der Tonkunst in Osterreich,* xxvii, Jg. xiii (2), as by G. Reutter are said by H. J. Moser to be compositions by Strungk.

Stück (Ger.), piece, composition. Thus Schumann's *Fantasiestücke* for piano.

Stuckenschmidt, H. H. (born 1901), German critic and author. During the 1920s he worked as critic and composer in Vienna, Paris, Berlin and Prague, returning in 1929 to Berlin, where he was a close friend of Schoenberg during the latter's last years in Europe. In 1937 he left Berlin because of his opposition to the Hitler regime, and went to Prague where he was later forced to cease his critical activities. Returning to Berlin after World War II, he became president of the German section of the International Society for Contemporary Music, and a professor of musical history at the Berlin Technical University. His books include studies of Schoenberg, Busoni and Ravel.

study (Fr., *étude*), a piece of music designed to give practice in some branch of instrumental technique. There is no intrinsic reason why a piece of this kind should not have artistic merit, as Clementi showed in his *Gradus ad Parnassum* (1817) for piano. The same point was demonstrated even more conclusively by Chopin, whose studies, op 10 and 25, combine the severest technical discipline with a remarkable invention and a characteristic sensitiveness to the tone of the piano. His example has been followed by other composers, without, however, bringing to an end the composition of studies to a purely conventional kind, whose only merit is the opportunity they offer for developing the fingers.

stump, an obsolete and now virtually non-existent type of CITTERN. It was apparently invented in or about 1600 by one Daniel Farrant.

Sturgeon, Nicholas (c. 1390–1454), English composer. He received an annuity from Henry V in 1419, was a canon of Windsor in 1441 and a prebendary of Kentish Town in St. Paul's in 1452. He probably had a part in the writing of the OLD HALL MANUSCRIPT, which contains three *Glorias,* two *Credos* (one incomplete), a *Sanctus* with an incomplete *Benedictus,* and an isorhythmic motet by him.

Sturm und Drang (Ger.), 'storm and stress'. Term for the wave of powerful romantic expressiveness which swept Austrian and German music in the 1760s and 1770s, and which was especially evident in Haydn's symphonies of that time (consequently they became known as his *Sturm und Drang* symphonies). The term, which originated in a play, *Sturm und Drang,* by Friedrich Maximilian von Klinger (1752–1831), was as applicable to German literature of the period as it was to music.

style, the tracing of the history of musical styles, and of the changes in social, technical and aesthetic ideas which accompany and interact with changes in musical style, is one of the chief objects of the study of musical history. The style of a composition is its manner of treating form, melody, rhythm, counterpoint, harmony and tone-colour; it is closely related to and limited by its medium, but not entirely dependent on it, since features of the style appropriate to one medium may be transferred to another. The analysis of compositions written in a particular period, in a particular genre and by a particular composer provides the material for the history of the style of that period, genre or composer.

Musical historians have adopted from historians of painting and sculpture terms for the main periods in the history of style, the use of which is obviously justified by their convenience (gothic, 1150–1475; renaissance, 1475–1600; baroque, 1600–1750; rococo or galant, 1730–1770; classical, 1750–1820; romantic, 1820–90; impressionist, 1890–1910; expressionist, 1910–30), although their implications in terms of musical styles may not have been fully investigated. The history of the style of a genre (more commonly called 'form' in this context, e.g. opera, concerto, etc.) includes changes in its form as well as in its other technical elements.

Among the genres which have been studied in this way are Mass, motet, Italian madrigal, opera, concerto, symphony and suite, and oratorio. The progress of a composer's style assumes a pattern which may be determined by a variety of circumstances, such as his response to outside influences, as in Schütz, his writing in different genres, as in Rameau and Schumann, or an inner development in clearly defined phases, as in Beethoven.

See also NATIONAL MUSIC, STILE

style galant (Fr.; Ger., *galanter Stil*), a term adopted by German writers on music in the 18th century (e.g. Mattheson) for the homophonic and rather elaborately ornamented style of French and Italian music, e.g. that of F. Couperin and D. Scarlatti, as opposed to the contrapuntal style (*gearbeiteter Stil*) of the main German tradition. It is thus the equivalent in music of the rococo style in painting. This style appears in J. S. Bach's music in the variable dances in the suite, which he refers to as 'Menuetten und anderen Galanterien' in the title of the first part of the *Clavierübung*.

Its adoption by such contemporaries of Bach as Telemann and Mattheson led to its becoming an important factor in the marked change of style between Bach and his sons C. P. E. and J. C. Bach, from whom it passed into the early work of Haydn and Mozart. In 1752 J. J. Quantz suggested that a style acceptable to many people might well arise from a mixture of the musical tastes of the three nations, an ideal which was in fact realised some twenty years later on. The period of the *galant* style may be dated c. 1730–c. 1770, overlapping the late baroque and the early classical styles.

subdominant, the fourth degree of the diatonic scale, e.g. F in the scale of C. The subdominant triad is one of the three 'primary' or principal triads – tonic, dominant and subdominant – in a key. The chord of the subdominant followed by the tonic chord forms a plagal CADENCE. The addition of a sixth to the subdominant chord forms the chord of the ADDED SIXTH.

subito (It.), suddenly. *Piano subito*, suddenly soft.

subject, a theme (or group of notes) used as the basis of a musical form, e.g. the subject in a fugue, and the first and second subjects (or group of subjects) in a movement in sonata form.

submediant, the sixth degree of the diatonic scale, e.g. A in the scale of C major.

succentor, the official in charge of the music, under the supervision of the precentor, in a cathedral, college chapel or monastery.

Such Sweet Thunder, Shakespearian suite by Duke Ellington, a work of considerable verve and wit, compiled during the 1950s. Its (literal) high point is its portrait of Hamlet, 'Madness in great ones', featuring the astronomical trumpet playing of Cat Anderson.

Suggia, Guilhermina (1888–1950), cellist of mixed Portuguese and Italian origin. She was a pupil of Casals, to whom she was married for six years. The well-known portrait of her by Augustus John in the Tate Gallery, London, gives a vivid impression of her magnetism.

suite, before c. 1750 a composition consisting of a group of movements which are dance-types and are in the same key; after that date a composition consisting of any group of instrumental movements, frequently drawn from the incidental music to a play or from a ballet. The prototypes of the baroque suite were the pairs (*see* NACHTANZ) or groups of dance pieces in the

keyboard and lute music of the 16th century. Early in the 17th century some German composers published instrumental dances in sets of four or more, as in Peuerl's *Neue Padouan, Intrada, Däntz und Galliarda* (1611) and Schein's *Banchetto musicale* (1617). Some or all of the dances of a set were related thematically, forming what is known as a 'variation suite'.

Later in the century Froberger's keyboard suites had the order allemande-courante-sarabande, with or without a gigue after the allemande or courante, while ballet-suites, such as those written for operas in Vienna by J. H. and A. A. Schmelzer, varied in the number and type of the dances according to the nature of the ballet. When Froberger's suites were published in 1693 they were disposed in the order allemande-courante-sarabande-gigue, which was adopted by Bach and Handel. In addition, Bach's suites and partitas contain one or more dances of French type (*Galanterien*), e.g. bourrée, gavotte, minuet, passepied, after the sarabande, or occasionally, in the partitas, after the courante. The English Suites and Partitas of Bach also contain a prelude, which may be in quite an extended form.

Each of François Couperin's suites for harpsichord (which he called *Ordres*) consists of a considerable number of movements which have the title either of a dance or of a descriptive idea, e.g. *Les Abeilles, L'Enchanteresse*. A second type of French suite, modelled on the overture and set of dances which came at the beginning of the opera and opera-ballet of Lully was adopted by German composers, e.g. Georg Muffat, Telemann (*Musique de Table*) and Bach, and called *Ouverture*. As in Bach's four *Overtures*, now generally called *Orchestral Suites*, the dances are French, and vary in number and type.

The Italian term *sonata da camera* seems to have been first applied to the suite by Rosenmuller, who gave his *sonate* the order sinfonia-allemanda-corrente-ballo–sarabanda. Corelli's trio-sonatas *da camera* have a short prelude followed by allemanda, corrente or sarabanda, and giga or gavotta.

There were dance movements in the *divertimenti* of the mid 18th century and the minuet became one of the movements of the sonata, but the use of the term 'suite' was not resumed until late in the 19th century, and by that time it had become much more generalized in its meaning. It was applied by Bizet to his suites of incidental music to *L'Arlésienne* (1872), to Grieg's *Peer Gynt* and Prokofiev's *Lieutenant Kije*, to a suite abstracted from an opera such as Kodály's *Háry János*, and to ballet suites such as Ravel's *Daphnis et Chloe* and Stravinsky's *Petrushka*.

Suite Bergamasque (Fr.), suite for piano solo by Debussy, published in 1905. The four movements are *Prelude, Menuet, Clair de lune* (frequently performed out of context), and *Passepied*.

See BERGAMASCA

suivez (Fr.), 'follow', (1) begin the next movement or section without a break (*attacca*);

(2) the accompaniment is to follow any modifications of tempo made by the soloist (It., *colla parte*).

Suk, Josef (1874–1935), Czech composer, violinist and viola player, pupil and son-in-law of Dvořák. From 1892 he was a member of the Bohemian String Quartet. He taught at the Prague Conservatory, and composed two symphonies, symphonic poems, overtures, and other orchestral works, a Mass, chamber music, part-songs and many pieces for piano.

sulla scena (It.), on the stage.

sulla tastiera, *see* SUL TASTO

Sullivan, Arthur Seymour (1842–1900), English composer, organist and conductor. He was chorister at the Chapel Royal, and studied at the Royal Academy of Music under Sterndale Bennett and at the Leipzig Conservatorium. In 1867 he went with Sir George Grove to Vienna where they discovered some important Schubert manuscripts. In 1876 he became principal of the National Training School of Music. He was knighted in 1883. His light operas written to libretti by W. S. Gilbert were highly successful in many parts of the world. He also composed a grand opera, *Ivanhoe*, with libretto after Scott (1891), two ballets, oratorios, cantatas, a symphony, overtures, incidental music for plays, anthems, hymns and other church music, songs and piano pieces.

In the operettas, often called the 'Savoy Operas' because they were first performed (by the D'Oyly Carte company) at the Savoy Theatre, London, Sullivan combined tunefulness with neat craftsmanship and a brilliant flair for parody. The more important are:

Cox and Box (1867; libretto by F. C. Burnand; all others except the *Rose of Persia* are by W. S. Gilbert); *Thespis, or The Gods Grown Old* (1871); *Trial by Jury* (1875); *The Sorcerer* (1877); *H.M.S. Pinafore* (1878); *The Pirates of Penzance* (1879); *Patience* (1881); *Iolanthe* (1882); *Princess Ida* (1884); *The Mikado* (1885); *Ruddigore* (1887); *The Yeomen of the Guard* (1888); *The Gondoliers* (1889); *Utopia Limited* (1893); *The Grand Duke* (1896); *The Rose of Persia* (1899; libretto by B. Hood).

Sir Arthur Seymour Sullivan. Unlike his French counterpart, Offenbach, he never achieved his 'great' opera.

Sumer is icumen in, from the Harley MS in the British Library. One voice begins the melody, with each of the others joining when the previous voice has reached the cross between 'in' and 'Lhude'

sul ponticello (It.), on the bridge.
  See PONTICELLO

sul tasto (It.; Fr., *sur la touche*; Ger., *am Griffbrett*), on the fingerboard (of a string instrument), i.e. play near, or actually above, the fingerboard, thus producing a rather colourless tone.

Sumer is icumen in, a *rota* (or round) found in a manuscript written at Reading Abbey c. 1240. In the manuscript it also has Latin words and directions for performance. The melody is sung by four voices with two voices adding a *pes* or ground bass. The result, after all the parts have entered, is:

It is the earliest extant piece in six parts. The complete round is printed in *Historical Anthology of Music*, edited by A. T. Davison and W. Apel, no 42. The manuscript is now in the British Museum.

summation tone, a very faint note resulting from the

sum of the frequencies of two notes sounded simultaneously.

See ACOUSTICS, COMBINATION TONE

Sun Quartets (Ger., *Sonnenquartetten*), the name given to Haydn's six string quartets, op 20, composed in 1772. It derives from the title-page of an old edition.

Suor Angelica (It., *Sister Angelica*), opera in one act by Puccini, with a libretto by Giocacchino Forzano. This is the second of three one-act operas forming *Il trittico* (*The Triptych*), the others being *Il tabarro* and *Gianni Schicchi*. It was first performed in New York in 1918. The story, which brought out the sentimental vein in the composer, concerns Sister Angelica, who entered a convent after giving birth to an illegitimate child. She learns from her aunt, who comes to visit her, that the child is dead. In despair she commits suicide. As she prays for forgiveness a vision appears of the Virgin surrounded by angels, with the child before her.

supertonic, the second degree of the diatonic scale, e.g. D in the scale of C.

Supervia, Conchita (1895–1936), Spanish mezzo-soprano, who studied in Barcelona and made her debut in 1910 in Buenos Aires. Though her career was cut short by her early death, she established herself as one of the leading Rossini exponents of the century, as well as an outstanding Carmen in Bizet's opera. She was particularly associated with the leading roles in *The Barber of Seville*, *The Italian Girl in Algiers*, and *Cenerentola*, which she sang in their original keys. It was in Italy and France that she made her most famous appearances, though she was also heard at Covent Garden (1934). She was a member of the Chicago Civic Opera between 1932 and 1933.

Suppé, Franz von (**Francesco Ezechiele Ermenegildo Cavaliere Suppé-Demelli** (1819–1895), Dalmatian born composer and conductor of Belgian descent, who worked under the German form of his name. He studied at the university of Padua and at the Vienna Conservatorium under Sechter and Seyfried. He conducted at theatres in Vienna, Pressburg, and Baden, at the Theater an der Wien, and from 1865 at Leopoldstadt Theater in Vienna. His works include 31 operattas (including *Light Cavalry* and *The Beautiful Galatea*) farces, ballets, incidental music for plays, a Mass, a Requiem, a symphony, quartets and songs.

sur la touche, *see* SUL TASTO

Suriano, Francesco, *see* SORIANO

Surprise Symphony (Ger., *Symphonie mit dem Paukenschlag*), symphony no 94 in G major by Haydn (1791), so called from the abrupt fortissimo chord for full orchestra which interrupts the quiet opening of the slow movement. Haydn is reputed to have said, 'That will make the women jump.' *Paukenschlag* means 'stroke on the timpani'. It should not be confused with the *Drum Roll Symphony* (no 103), known in Germany as the *Paukenwirbel*.

Survivor from Warsaw, A, cantata by Schoenberg, op 46, for speaker, men's chorus and orchestra, first performed in 1948. Commissioned by the Koussevitsky Foundation, the work has a text describing the atrocities against the Jews in a Nazi concentration camp during World War II. Much of this text is in English, but there are German interpolations and a final prayer in Hebrew.

Susanna, oratorio by Handel, with a text (anonymous) based on the Apocrypha. It was first performed in London in 1749.

Susanna's Secret (It., *Il Segreto di Susanna*), comic opera in one act by Wolf-Ferrari, with a libretto by Enrico Golisciani. It was first performed in a German version by Max Kalbeck (*Susannens Geheimnis*) in Munich in 1909. A sparkling overture sets the atmosphere of the piece. Susanna's secret – which in recent years has begun to regain the point it once seemed in danger of losing – is that she smokes.

Susato, Tylman (**Tielmann, Thielemann**) (end of 15th century – before 1564), Flemish music printer and composer. He settled in Antwerp as a music copyist and transcriber, began printing in 1543 and was a city musician until 1549. His first publication (*Vingt et six chansons*) and his subsequent series of fourteen collections of polyphonic *chansons* (1543–55) have been reprinted in facsimile by Editions Culture et Civilisation (Brussels). He also published many collections of madrigals, motets, Masses and instrumental pieces. Many of these collections contain compositions of his own. A collection of Dutch part-songs which he published in 1551 has been reprinted in *Vereeniging voor Nederlandsche Muziekgeschiedenis*, vol. xxix (1908). His collection of four-part instrumental dances (also 1551) was edited by Franz J. Giesbert in 1936. A rondo and saltarello from this publication is printed in Schering's *Geschichte der Musik in Beispielen*, no 119.

U. MEISSNER: *Der Antwerper Notendrucker Tylman Susato* (1967)

suspension, a harmonic device whereby a note sounded as part of a chord is sustained while a second chord is sounded. The result is a discord, which is then usually resolved by the movement of the dissonant note one step downwards:

The three steps in the process are: (1) preparation by a consonance on a relatively weak beat; (2) suspension on a dissonance on a relatively strong beat; (3) resolution on a consonance on a relatively weak beat. A suspension is a delayed movement in a part, and is therefore as much a rhythmic as a harmonic effect. Hence, it is essential that the point of dissonance should coincide with a metrical accent. Its principle is extended to suspension of two notes:

or of a chord:

A suspended leading note resolves upwards, as the B does in the second example. A suspension may be 'prepared' on a common discord, e.g. a dominant seventh, as in the third example.

Süssmayr (sometimes spelt **Süssmayer**) **Franz Xaver**, (1766–1803), Austrian composer, pupil of Salieri and Mozart in Vienna. He wrote the recitatives for Mozart's *La clemenza di Tito* (1791) and helped to complete Mozart's unfinished Requiem. He also composed operas, two ballets, Masses and other church music, cantatas, a clarinet concerto, serenades and other instrumental pieces.

sustaining pedal, *see* PIANO

Sutermeister, Heinrich (born 1910), Swiss composer. His earlier works show the influence of Orff, with whom he studied in Munich, in their emphasis on simplicity and clear outlines. He has written operas based on *Romeo and Juliet* (Dresden, 1940) and Dostoyevsky's *Crime and Punishment*; also piano concertos and choral music.

Sutherland, Joan (born 1926), Australian soprano who rose to international fame after singing the title-role in Donizetti's *Lucia di Lammermoor* at Covent Garden in 1959. Thereafter she became increasingly associated with the *bel canto* repertory, especially such works as Bellini's *La Sonnambula* and *I Puritani*. Her U.S. début took place at Dallas in 1960 in Handel's *Alcina*, which was followed in 1961 by her New York Metropolitan début as Lucia.

Svanda Dudák, *see* SVANDA THE BAGPIPER

Svanda the Bagpiper (Cz., *Svanda Dudák*), comic opera in two acts by Weinberger, with a libretto by Miloš Kareš, first performed in Prague in 1927. The Brigand Babinsky, in love with Svanda's wife Dorota, persuades him to visit the court of Queen Ice-Heart. Here he is so successful that the Queen wishes to marry him, but the arrival of Dorota makes it clear that he is married already, and the Queen orders his execution. The execution is prevented by a trick of Babinsky's and, having been given back his pipes, he sets everyone dancing. Unfortunately, having uttered a curse, he is taken off to Hell. Dorota will have nothing to do with Babinsky, who is compelled to bring Svanda back to earth by playing cards for him with the devil. The 'Polka and Fugue' from *Svanda the Bagpiper* are sometimes extracted from the opera for concert hall performance. The German spelling (Schwanda) of the hero's name, though long established, seems pointless outside Germany.

Svendsen, Johan Sverin (1840–1911), Norwegian composer, violinist and conductor. He studied at the Leipzig Conservatorium and played in Musard's orchestra in Paris, 1868–9. He conducted the Euterpe Concerts in Leipzig, 1870, the Music Association Concerts in Oslo with Grieg, 1872–83, and at the court in Copenhagen, 1883–1908. His works include two symphonies, concertos for violin and cello and chamber music, but he is remembered mainly for his occasional pieces, like his *Carnival in Paris* for orchestra.

swanee whistle, a whistle with a slide at the opposite end to the mouthpiece that can be pulled in and out by the player, so varying the length of the tube and hence the pitch of the note. Small models are no more than a toy, but Ravel used the more substantial one, which he called *flûte à coulisse*, in his opera *L'Enfant et les Sortilèges*.

Swan Lake, ballet by Chaikovsky, with choreography by Petipa and Ivanov. The music (some of which is played in the form of a concert suite) was composed in 1876. Since the ballet is a Russian one, the use of a French translation of the title (*Lac des Cygnes*) is out of place outside France.

Swan of Tuonela, The, *see* LEGENDS

Swan song, *see* SCHWANENGESANG

Swanson, Howard (born 1909), U.S. Negro composer. As a child he was a manual labourer on the railway. Later he worked as a postal clerk, but his musical aptitude led him to study meanwhile at the Cleveland Institute for Music. He won a scholarship enabling him to study with Nadia Boulanger in Paris, where he lived until 1940. He then returned to the United States, working for a time for the Inland Revenue. Marian Anderson helped to establish him as a composer by singing his songs in New York. In 1952 his *Short Symphony* was played by Mitropoulos and the New York Philharmonic, and won the New York Music Critics' Circle Award. He has written other orchestral works, a cello suite, piano music and songs.

Sweelinck, Jan Pieterszoon (1562–1621), Dutch composer, organist, harpsichordist and teacher. He studied under Zarlino in Venice, and in 1580 succeeded his father as organist of the Old Church, Amsterdam. His most important compositions are for the keyboard, and were much influenced by the music of the English virginalists (four of his pieces are to be found in the Fitzwilliam Virginal Book). He developed their style in his variations on psalm tunes and on secular songs, and in his fantasias, which he constructed on a single subject, anticipating the form of the fugue. His toccatas and 'echo' fantasias, however, are in the Venetian tradition. He handed on these styles to his German pupils, of whom Scheidt and Scheidemann were the most eminent. His vocal music is more conservative in style and includes four published books of metrical psalms for four to eight voices (1604–23), *Cantiones sacrae* for five parts and continuo (1619) and *Rimes françoises et italiennes* (1612). He also wrote a theoretical treatise, *Rules for Composition*. His complete works were edited by Max Seiffert (10 volumes, 1895–1903; second edition of volume i, 1943); a new edition was begun by G. Leonhardt, A. Annegarn, and F. Noske in 1968.

A. CURTIS: *Sweelinck's Keyboard Music* (1969)

swell, a device for producing a *crescendo* or *diminuendo* on an organ or harpsichord. Its most successful form, called Venetian swell for obvious reasons, incorporates a slatted blind, operated by a pedal, which can be opened and closed gradually, so allowing a continuous change of volume.

swell box, a box containing several organ pipes and fitted with a Venetian SWELL.

swell organ (Fr., *recit.*; Ger., *Oberwerk*), the idea of producing an effect of *crescendo* and *diminuendo* by enclosing the source of sound in a box of which one side could be opened and closed by a Venetian shutter arrangement controlled by a pedal was first applied to the harpsichord by Schudi, who patented it in 1769. In 1712 Jordan had made an organ with a swell which acted by the raising of one shutter. When Schudi's patent expired his device was generally adopted for one of the manuals of the organ. The manual so enclosed is called the swell organ, and is placed immediately above the GREAT ORGAN. In most modern organs the CHOIR ORGAN and the SOLO ORGAN are similarly enclosed.

See ORGAN

Swieten, Gottfried, Baron van (1734–1803), Dutch born amateur musician and diplomat. He was ambassador at the court of Frederick II of Prussia (1771) and in Vienna became director of the Royal Library (from which he ordered works used only for the 'fantasy and pedantry' of scholars to be removed) and founded the Musikalische Gesellschaft. He was a patron of Mozart (who wrote accompaniments to Handel oratorios for concerts presented by van Swieten); of Haydn (for whom he translated the *Creation* and *The Seasons* into German); of C. P. E. Bach (from whom he commissioned six string quartets); and of Beethoven (who dedicated to him his first symphony).

swing, (1) basic ingredient of jazz, the quality differentiating a good jazz performance (which should 'swing', i.e. have a rhythmic momentum beyond the actual note values) from a bad one. As Duke Ellington declared, 'It don't mean a thing if it ain't got that swing'.

(2) a specific era and style in jazz history. The swing era began around 1935, and was characterized by the use of big bands – much bigger than those of the previous decade – and by powerful contrasts between the brass and reed (i.e. saxophone and clarinet) sections. The style, whose most famous exponent was a white musician, Benny Goodman, swept America, but in 1945 was itself swept aside by the 'BOP' revolution.

Sylphides, Les, ballet adapted from various piano pieces by Chopin, with choreography by Fokine. Its first performance was in Paris in 1909 (thus the French title which, translated, means simply 'The Sylphs').

Sylvanus, *see* SILVA

Sylvia, ballet by Delibes, with choreography by Merante, dealing with the legendary huntress Diana. Its first performance was in Paris in 1876.

sympathetic resonance, *see* SYMPATHETIC VIBRATIONS

sympathetic vibrations, acoustical phenomenon (also known as sympathetic resonance) that occurs when a resonant body, such as a piano string, glass or tuning fork, vibrates and sounds a note without being touched when the same note is played or sung nearby. Certain old stringed instruments, including the VIOLA D'AMORE, use this effect by having 'free' or sympathetic strings immediately under those played with the bow.

symphonia (Lat.; from the Gr. for simultaneous sound).

(1) in ancient Greek theory (*a*) unison, (*b*) a consonant interval;

(2) according to Isidorus (c. 600 A.D.) the popular name for a kind of drum, the two ends of which produced notes of different pitches;

(3) a 14th century name for the HURDY-GURDY, earlier known as *organistrum*;

(4) in the 16th and early 17th centuries apparently an alternative name for the virginals (Praetorius, *Syntagma musicum*, 1619);

(5) symphony.

Symphonia Domestica, *see* DOMESTIC SYMPHONY

symphonic poem (Fr., *poème symphonique*; Ger.,

Symphonische Dichtung, Tondichtung), the term was applied by Liszt to an orchestral piece in which 'the composer reproduces his impressions and the adventures of his soul in order to communicate with them'. Specific clues to the source of the impressions and the nature of the adventures are given to the listener by the titles and sub-titles, and, if they are somewhat complex, a 'programme' is also provided. The symphonic poem is PROGRAMME MUSIC, since the form becomes a function of the programme. Its immediate ancestors were the concert overture, such as Mendelssohn's *Midsummer Night's Dream*, and the symphony with the programme, such as Berlioz's *Symphonie fantastique*. Liszt wrote his symphonic poems in one movement, and abandoning sonata form, used a more flexible treatment of his thematic material.

After Liszt, symphonic poems (or 'tone pictures' or 'fantasies') were written by composers of various countries, e.g. Borodin, Smetana, Franck, Dukas, Sibelius (in *Tapiola* and several other important works), Delius, Elgar (whose 'symphonic study' *Falstaff*, was perhaps the finest of all his orchestral works). The most famous symphonic poems are the series by Richard Strauss, who used the term 'tone-poem' (*Tondichtung*), and brought the genre to its highest point of circumstantial and realistic depiction. The 'Fantasy Overtures' of Chaikovsky are dramatic concert overtures rather than symphonic poems. The form was an ideal one for the impressionistic style; Debussy's five chief orchestral works are symphonic poems in one or more movements. In recent times the form has been much less cultivated, though it can still be used successfully, as Henze, amongst others, has shown.

symphonic study, somewhat vague musical term, applied by Schumann to his *Symphonic Studies* (a set of piano variations) and by Elgar to *Falstaff* (a large-scale orchestral portrait, subtitled *Symphonic study*). The term has been variously used by other composers, including Alan Rawsthorne.

symphonie (Fr., Ger., also *Sinfonie*), symphony.

Symphonie Cévenole, *see* SYMPHONY ON A FRENCH MOUNTAIN SONG

symphonie concertante (Fr.), *see* SINFONIA CONCERTANTE

Symphonie Espagnole (Fr., *Spanish Symphony*), a composition for violin and orchestra by Edouard Lalo (first performed, 1875). The work is in five movements, one of which is sometimes omitted in performance.

Symphonie Fantastique (Fr., *Fantastic Symphony*), orchestral work in five movements by Berlioz, op 14 (1830), also entitled *Épisode de la vie d'un artiste* (episode in an artist's life). Titles of the movements are:

(1) *Rêveries – Passions* (Daydreams – Passions)

(3) *Un bal* (A ball)

(4) *Scène aux champs* (Scene in the country)

(4) *Marche au supplice* (March to execution)

(5) *Songe d'une nuit de Sabbat* (Dream of a witches' Sabbath).

Berlioz issued a detailed programme for the work, according to which a young and exceptionally sensitive musician (i.e. Berlioz himself), unable to drive from his mind the image of his beloved (i.e. Harriet Smithson), attempts to poison himself with opium. In his delirium he imagines that he has killed his loved one and is led to execution. Finally he dreams that he is present at the witches' sabbath, which includes a parody of the *Dies irae*. His beloved is represented by an *idée fixe*, beginning:

which recurs throughout the work in various forms. In spite of its programme the *Symphonie fantastique* is indebted to earlier works by Berlioz, e.g. the *idée fixe* is borrowed from the cantata *Herminie*, which he submitted unsuccessfully for the *Prix de Rome* in 1828, and the *Marche au supplice* comes from the unfinished opera *Les Francs-Juges*.

Symphonie Funèbre et Triomphale (Fr., *Funeral and Triumphal Symphony*), a symphony by Berlioz, op 15 (1840), for military band, string orchestra and chorus, which was commissioned by the French Government and performed on the tenth anniversary of the 1830 Revolution. The first movement is a vast funeral march, scored for wind only; a second contains a trombone solo representing the 'Panegyric' spoken over the dead; the finale, a hymn of praise, brings in the (optional) chorus. The work was originally intended for performance in the open air.

Symphonie mit dem Paukenschlag, *see* SURPRISE SYMPHONY

Symphonie mit dem Paukenwirbel, *see* DRUM ROLL SYMPHONY

Symphonie Pathétique, *see* PATHETIC SYMPHONY

Symphonie sur un Chant Montagnard Francais, *see* SYMPHONY ON A FRENCH MOUNTAIN SONG

Symphonische Dichtung (Ger.), symphonic poem.

symphony (Fr., *symphonie*; Ger., *Sinfonie, Symphonie*; It., *sinfonia*), in the period of the modern use of the term SONATA, i.e. since c. 1750, a symphony is a sonata for orchestra. Previously the word was used in a variety of ways, usually for instrumental music, but occasionally, as in the *Sacrae symphoniae* of G. Gabrieli and Schütz, for music for instruments and voices. It was applied to instrumental movements in an opera, as in Monteverdi's *Orfeo*, to the prelude to an instrumental suite, as in Rosenmüller's *Sonate da camera*, to the prelude of a cantata, as in Bach's Cantata no 156 (*Ich steh' mit einem Fuss im Grabe*), to the Italian opera overture (*sinfonia avanti l'opera*), to the introduction to a song, and, exceptionally, by Bach to his three-part Inventions.

The modern symphony emerged as an independent piece, modelled on the Italian overture, between 1730 and 1750. A minuet was added to the three movements of the Italian overture in some of the symphonies of the Viennese composers Georg Monn and Georg Wagenseil, and in those of the composers attached to the Mannheim orchestra, e.g. F. X. Richter and Johann Stamitz. All Stamitz's symphonies have four movements. Some of Haydn's first thirty or so symphonies (the first was written in 1759) have three movements, either having no minuet or ending with a minuet, and

some have resemblances to the *concerto grosso* in their use of solo instruments.

In the four-movement form which became normal after c. 1765 the symphony drew the elements of its style from the overture, *concerto grosso* and suite, and from the aria and finale of opera. In the symphonies written after 1780, which include the twelve Salomon symphonies (nos 93–104) composed for London, Haydn absorbed some of the grace and delicacy of Mozart, but kept his characteristic humour and spontaneity in such features as the varying of recapitulations and the unpredictable course of his rondo finales. Mozart's first three symphonies were played when he was eight years old at the J. C. Bach-Abel concerts in London in 1765, the year in which J. C. Bach published his own first set of six symphonies. Besides J. C. Bach's symphonies, those of the Mannheim and Viennese composers, including Haydn, influenced his development, which was crowned by the consummate balance of expression and design of the last three symphonies of 1788.

In writing to his publishers in 1803 about the *Prometheus* Variations for piano, op 35, Beethoven observed that he had 'done nothing in the same manner before'. The first symphony in the 'new manner' was the *Eroica*, the ancestor of all romantic symphonies, and, with the ninth symphony, the largest conception of the form before Mahler. While in the *Eroica*, form is expanded and expression deepened, the only radical departure from tradition is the variation form of the last movement, which may be compared in that respect with the last movement of Brahms's fourth symphony. Wagner saw in Beethoven's ninth symphony the inevitable destiny of dramatic instrumental music to throw off its limitations and use the human voice; nevertheless, its only direct successors before Mahler were Mendelssohn's symphony-cantata *Lobgesang* (*Hymn of Praise*), not one of his best works, in which the cantata over-balances the symphony and fails to achieve unity with it, and Liszt's *Dante* symphony. The choral endings in his *Faust* symphony and in Berlioz's *Symphonie funèbre et triomphale* are optional. The tendency towards a narrative 'programme' in Beethoven's sixth symphony was pursued by Berlioz in the *Symphonie fantastique* and in the 'dramatic symphony' *Romeo et Juliet* for orchestra and voices, and was diverted into a new form by Liszt in the SYMPHONIC POEM.

Schubert's eight extant symphonies encompassed three styles, the classical, the lyrical (in the *Unfinished*) and the 'grand' (in the so-called Great C major). The main tradition goes through Mendelssohn and Schumann (who had some new and progressive ideas on symphonic form) to the four symphonies of Brahms (1875–85), the nine of Bruckner (1866–94), the two of Borodin (1862–76), the six of Chaikovsky (1868–93), the nine of Dvořák (1880–93), the ten of Mahler (1888–1909), and the seven of Sibelius (1898–1924). That its methods were not unaffected by the use of thematic transformation, first applied to a symphony in a comprehensive way by Schumann in his D minor symphony and developed in the symphonic poem, is clear in the first movement of Brahms's first symphony, in Chaikovsky's fourth and in those of Franck and Saint-Säens.

Mahler treated the traditional number and disposition of movements quite flexibly, Sibelius less so; Mahler tended towards expansion, Sibelius to contraction and concentration. Mahler used voices in four of his symphonies, and his all-embracing view of its possibilities culminated in the eighth symphony ('*Symphony of a Thousand*') for large orchestra, eight soloists, two mixed choirs and children's choir. The first part is a setting of the hymn 'Veni creator spiritus', the second, comprising Adagio, Scherzo and Finale, of the closing scene of the second part of Goethe's *Faust*. The tendency to contraction is noticeable in the fourth and sixth symphonies of Sibelius, and his seventh is in one movement. The Danish composer, Carl Nielsen, also brought a strong and individual style to his six works in the form, using (like Mahler) the idea of 'progressive tonality' – the planning of a work (or movement) in such a way that it begins in one key and ends in another

In general, modern composers tend to cast their symphonies in a flexible number of movements, but the advantage of a title to the listener and to the memory of the public is sometimes not overlooked. Notable works composed since 1914 are the symphonies of Vaughan Williams (nine), Prokofiev (seven), Shostakovich (fifteen), Hindemith (two), Stravinsky (three), Walton (two), Gerhard and Roy Harris.

Though the symphony, as a form, has frequently been declared moribund, composers continue to be attracted to it, in some cases with a high measure of success. Among works by living composers, Henze's six symphonies and Tippett's four have all impressively maintained the continuity of the form, and in different ways brought fresh insight to it.

'Symphony of a Thousand', the nickname sometimes misleadingly given to Mahler's eighth symphony (completed in 1906) because of the large number of performers it requires. The work is in two parts entitled:

   (1) *Veni creator spiritus* (based on the ninth century hymn) for two choruses and orchestra.
   (2) *Concluding scene from Faust* – symphonic poem with chorus, eight solo singers and orchestra.

Symphony of Psalms, three-movement symphony for chorus and orchestra by Stravinsky. According to the composer, it was 'composed to the glory of God and dedicated to the Boston Symphony Orchestra' – who gave it its first performance in 1930. The texts, from the Psalms, are sung in Latin.

Symphony on a French Mountain Song (Fr., *Symphonie sur un Chant Montagnard Français*), symphony for orchestra and piano by d'Indy, op 25 (1886), also known as *Symphonie Cévenole* because it uses a theme from the region of the Cévennes mountains.

syncopation, the placing of an accent or accents on parts of a bar which are not usually accented. Syncopation can occur in various ways, e.g. (1) by rhythmic anticipation:

BEETHOVEN, *Piano Sonata* op 31, no 1

(2) by rhythmic suspension, as in the rhythm

SCHUMANN, 'Fast zu ernst', op 15 (*Kinderscenen*) no 10

(3) by an indicated stress on an unaccented beat or on a subdivision of the beat:

MOZART, *Piano Sonata*, K 309

(4) by having a rest on the beat and sound on a subdivision of the beat:

SCHUMANN, *Phantasia* op 17

If, as in these examples, a regularly syncopated rhythm is continued for more than a bar, it has the effect of a displaced metre superimposed on the basic metre.

Syncopation is a characteristic idiom of Negro spirituals, ragtime and jazz. Rhythms made up of different metres in succession, which are not infrequent in modern music, e.g.

CONSTANT LAMBERT, *Piano Concerto*

have an effect similar to, but not identical with, that of syncopation, since there is not a continuous basic metre.

See ACCENT, BAR, METRE, RHYTHM

synthesizer, an integrated array of electronic devices for the generation and modification of sound. Synthesizers were evolved in the 1960s to solve the practical difficulties faced by composers of early electronic music who had to use large quantities of inflexible and bulky equipment designed for quite other purposes. Many individuals (e.g. Robert Moog, Morton Subotnik, Donald Buchla, David Cockcroft, Peter Zinovieff) have contributed to the rapid progress of the 1960s and 70s, but the individuality of their contributions means that the products of different manufacturers vary widely. Modern synthesizers, however, have the following features in common:

(1) signal generators, such as oscillators producing a variety of waveforms and noise generators producing white and pink noise;

(2) signal modifiers, such as filters of various characteristics, reverberation devices, devices for amplitude, frequency, location and ring modulation, and envelope generators which control attack, duration and decay. Signal modifiers may modify 'live', external sound sources as well as the outputs of signal generators.

(3) a system of connecting the various components.

Most devices in the modern synthesizer have two types of control, manual and voltage. Voltage control represents an important development in electronic music, resulting in an enormous range of sounds, enabling fairly extended sequences of electronic sounds to be 'recorded' without using tape recorders and subsequently to be edited and further modified. One of the most effective sequencing devices, however, is incorporated in the RCA Synthesizer and makes use of punched paper tape. The system was evolved by H. F. Olsen in 1954 and the one example of the Mark II version is still in use. But the future lies with control and sequencing by digital computer on the one hand and purely digital synthesis on the other.

Synthesizers come in all shapes and sizes and are used in the production of both live and pre-recorded music by performers and composers of all kinds. Commercial, rock, film and 'art' musicians are commonly using the smaller machines, but the larger, more sophisticated synthesizers are generally to be found only in the better-endowed experimental studios in broadcasting companies or universities.

Syrinx, piece for solo flute by Debussy, originally called *Flûte de Pan* and intended as incidental music to Gabriel Mourey's drama, *Psyché*. The music, dating from 1912, portrays Pan's death song and, in spite of its brevity, is an important contribution to the flute repertory.

System (Ger.), staff (abbreviation of *Liniensystem*).

Székely, Zoltán (born 1903), Hungarian violinist and composer, pupil of Hubay and Kodály. In 1935 he founded the Hungarian String Quartet, of which he is still first violinist. He is closely associated with the music of Bartók, whose second violin concerto and second rhapsody for violin and piano were both written for him.

Szell, George (originally **Georg**) (1896–1970), Hungarian born conductor who studied in Vienna and Leipzig. In his youth he also had considerable success as a pianist and composer. He held the following posts: Strasbourg Opera, 1917; German Theatre, Prague; 1919–21, 1929–37; Darmstadt, 1921; Düsseldorf, 1922; Berlin Staatsoper, 1924–9; Scottish Orchestra, Glasgow, 1937; Residence Orchestra, The Hague (with Frits Schuurman), 1938.

In 1946 he became conductor of the Cleveland Orchestra in the United States, an appointment he held until his death. He was an outstanding exponent of the standard symphonic repertoire, and during his 24 years with the Cleveland Orchestra he transformed it into an ensemble of unsurpassed excellence.

Szigeti, Joseph (1892–1973), Hungarian born violinist, a pupil of Hubay. He made his first appearance as a soloist in Berlin, 1905, then lived in Britain from 1906 until 1913. He gave the first performance of Busoni's violin concerto in 1912, and taught at the Geneva Conservatoire from 1917 until 1924. He travelled extensively as a soloist in Europe, the United States and Asia. Szigeti was especially famous for his interpretations of works by Bartók and Prokofiev. His reminiscences, entitled *With Strings Attached*, were published in 1949.

Szokolay, Sándor (born 1931), Hungarian composer, who studied at the Budapest Academy of Music and wrote some prize-winning instrumental works before turning his attention to dramatic and vocal music. His opera, *Blood Wedding* (based on Lorca's drama), helped to establish his name internationally after its premiere in Budapest in 1964. Among his other major compositions are ballets, oratorios, an opera based on *Hamlet*, a *Negro Cantata* and settings of Negro folk poetry in Hungarian translation.

Szymanowski, Karol (1882–1937), Polish composer, born in the Ukraine. He studied under Noskowski at the Warsaw Conservatory, settled in Berlin in 1905, and from 1908 lived in Russia. He lost his estates in the revolution of 1917, but escaped to Warsaw where he was appointed director of the State Conservatory in 1926. He composed two operas (including the important *King Roger*), ballets, three symphonies (one with men's chorus and tenor solo), works for solo voices, chorus and orchestra, two violin concertos, *Symphonie concertante* for piano and orchestra, works for violin and piano and other chamber music, many piano pieces and songs. Today he is recognized as the father of modern Polish music. Though at first his style was indebted to Chopin, Skryabin and Debussy, it soon became remarkably forward-looking.

T, as an abbreviation T. = tenor, tonic.

t, abbreviation for (1) *corde* in TUTTE LE CORDE or TRE CORDE;

(2) trill (or shake) in 17th century music; the modern sign for a trill is *tr.*;

(3) *tasto*, in the instruction for continuo parts *t.s.* = *tasto solo*, 'only the key'; i.e. the player is to play only the bass notes without filling up chords above them.

(4) *te*, in TONIC SOL-FA, the seventh note (or leading note) of the major scale.

Tabarro, Il (It., *The Cloak*), opera in one act by Puccini with a libretto by Giuseppe Adami (after Didier Gold's *Houppelande*). It is the first of three one-act operas forming *Il trittico* (*The Triptych*), the others being *Suor Angelica* and *Gianni Schicchi*. It was first performed in New York in 1918. Michele, a barge-owner, jealous of his wife's association with the young stevedore Luigi, strangles him and hides the body in his cloak. When his wife comes to him he throws open the cloak and reveals the corpse.

tablas, a type of oriental drum that exists in different forms. The Indian and Arabic forms are the most familiar, as they have been used by Western composers, who sometimes omit to state which type they require. The Indian *tablas* is a single-headed drum resembling a small *timpano*, and the sound produced is similar. As *tablas* have a clearly defined pitch, sets of as many as twelve, providing a complete chromatic scale, have been used. The Arabic *tablas* is normally beaten by the hands and the tone is much drier than that of the Indian instrument.

tablature (Ger., *Tablatur*; It., *intavolatura*), a type of notation used especially in the 16th and 17th centuries for writing music for lute, *vihuela*, organ and other instruments, in which the pitch of the notes is indicated by letters or numbers:

(1) in the two chief varieties of lute and *vihuela* tablature, the Italian-Spanish and the French, lines represented the strings of the instrument, and letters or numbers the frets at which the strings were to be stopped. The rhythm was indicated above the tablature by signs often corresponding to the usual note forms, and each sign held good until another appeared. In Italian and Spanish tablature the highest line represented the lowest string (except in Luis Milan's *El Maestro*, 1535, where the reverse is true; the figure 0 indicated an open string, and the figures 1 to 9 the frets, which marked off semitones. Thus the following passage:

ALONSO MUDARRA, *Fantasia* (1546)

in the tuning:

would be transcribed into staff notation as:

In French lute tablature the highest line or space represented the highest string, the letter a indicated an open string and the letters b, c, d, etc. the frets. A few English tablatures followed the Italian method, but most, including those of the lutenist song composers, were written in the French way, e.g.:

transcribed:

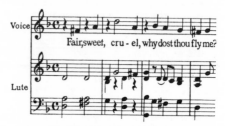

Fair, sweet, cru-el, why dost thou fly me?

THOMAS FORD, *Musicke of Sundrie Kindes* (1607)

In German lute notation a separate number of letter was used to represent the position of each fret with respect to each string. These symbols were written in rows corresponding to the positions of the strings, without, however, using horizontal lines to represent the strings.

The modern notation for the guitar and similar instruments is a tablature in the form of a diagram of the strings and frets on which dots indicate the positions of the fingers;

(2) the principle of tablature for organ (or other keyed instruments) is the representation of the notes of each part of a composition by letters or numbers. In German organ tablature from c. 1450 to c. 1550 the highest part was written in staff notation, the lower parts in letters, which had their normal meaning. After c. 1550 letters were used for all the parts, the rhythm being indicated above each part. Bach was familiar

with this notation, and in one instance used it to fit the last four bars of the chorale prelude *Der Tag, der ist so freudenreich* in the *Orgelbüchlein* in a space that was too small to write them in staff notation. Scheidt's *Tabulatura nova* of 1624 was 'new' to German organists in that it was printed with a separate five-line staff for each part, using the normal note-forms. It was not, therefore, properly called a tablature but was the equivalent of the Italian *partitura* ('score'). Frescobaldi published some of his organ works in this way, e.g. his first keyboard publication the *Fantasie a quattro* (1608), and his *Fiori musicali . . . in partitura a quattro* (1635). Scheidt pointed out that any organist who wished could easily copy from this notation into the German tablature. Italian organ notation (e.g. in Frescobaldi's *Toccate . . . d'intavolatura*, 1614) sometimes used two staves, the upper with six lines and the lower with eight, and normal note-forms. This was a tablature only in the sense that it disposed the notes for each hand on a separate staff, the method best suited to the style of the music. For his organ music published in 1664 S. A. Scherer used this Italian method, engraved by himself, for the first part (entitled *Tabulatura*) and Scheidt's 'new tablature' for the second part (entitled *Partitura*).

In Spanish organ tablature a horizontal line was used to represent each part, and the numbers 1 to 7 on each line to represent the notes of the scale from F up to E, e.g.:

ANTONIO CABEZON, *Tiento in the first Mode* (1557)

in staff notation:

(3) tablature which relates fingering to the notes of the scale has been used to a limited extent for woodwind instruments, generally for teaching purposes.

W. APEL: *The Notation of Polyphonic Music* (fifth edition, 1961)

J. WOLF: *Handbuch der Notationskunde*, two volumes (1913–19)

table (Fr.), (1) the belly, or upper part of the sound box of a string instrument;

(2) the sounding-board of a harp, rising diagonally from the foot of the vertical pillar to the upper end of the neck. *Près de la table*, play near the sounding board, thus producing a metallic sound, similar to that of a banjo;

(3) *musique de table*, music for a banquet (Ger., *Tafelmusik*).

table entertainment, a performance given by a single person seated at a table. It originated in England in the latter part of the 18th century. The performance consisted of songs, stories, recitations, sketches, impersonations, and so on. A prominent figure in this type of entertainment was Dibdin, who also wrote his own songs.

Tábor, the fifth of a cycle of six symphonic poems by Smetana, collectively entitled *Má Vlast* (*My Country*). Composed in 1878, the music is a tribute to the invincible spirit of the Hussites, and quotes the majestic Hussite hymn, 'Ye who are God's warriors'.

tabor, a small drum played with one stick and used in England with a small recorder with three finger holes (hence pipe and tabor) to accompany dancing.

See also TAMBOURIN

taboret, a small TABOR.

tabourin (Fr.), TABOR.

Tabourot, Jehan, *see* ARBEAU

tabrete, an early English word for drum.

tacet (Lat.), 'is silent'. Used in vocal part-books and in the separate instrumental parts of an orchestral or chamber work to indicate that the voice or instrument does not play in a particular movement or section of a movement.

tactus (Lat., from *tangere*, to touch, beat), a term used for 'beat' by theorists of the 15th and 16th centuries. It was a measure of the time-length of the note which was the unit of composition, and was given by the leader to the singers as a regular downward stroke of the finger, hand or arm – a method which was used in England at least until the late 17th century. The semibreve was the normal *tactus* in the 15th century; in the course of the 16th century the minim became the normal, but the semibreve continued to be the theoretical basis of signs of proportion. With the introduction of bar-lines the semibreve became the unit of a bar and the measuring *tactus* was replaced by the metrical beat.

Tafelmusik, *see* TABLE (3)

taille (Fr.), a term used in the 17th and 18th centuries for: (1) the tenor or middle part of a composition;

(2) the tenor member of a family of instruments, e.g. *taille de violon*, viola. *Taille* by itself was often used to indicate the viola, and the *oboe da caccia*.

Tailleferre, Germaine (born 1892), French composer and pianist, one of the group known as *Les Six*. She studied harmony and counterpoint at the Paris Conservatoire and settled in the United States in 1942. She has composed a piano concerto, a Ballade for piano and orchestra, a ballet, *Pastorale* for small orchestra, a quartet and other chamber music, and songs – all in a characteristically lucid style.

Takemitsu, Toru (born 1930), Japanese composer, whose music incorporates both Japanese and European ingredients. Thus *November Steps*, composed for the New York Philharmonic in 1967, makes use of endlessly oscillating rhythms, after the fashion of Noh Theatre, and employs two traditional Japanese instruments (*biwa* and *shakuhachi*) in solo capacity with a symphony orchestra. Takemitsu is internationally the most famous Japanese composer of the day. Born in Tokyo, he is mainly self-taught, but took lessons at the age of eighteen with the Japanese master Kyose, and at the same time discovered the music of Debussy, Messiaen and Varèse, composers who have exerted what could best be described as a discreet influence on his gentle musical style. His works include *Eclipse*, a duet for *biwa* and *shakuhachi*; *Water Music*, for Noh-dancer and tape; *Winter*, a still-life for orchestra; *Seasons* and *Munari by Munari*, percussion pieces closely associated with the Japanese performer Stomu Yamash'ta; and several works for piano, among them *Corona* (for one or more pianists), *For Away*, *Piano Distance* and *Undisturbed Rest*.

Takt (Ger.), (1) bar, (2) beat, (3) time.

Taktstrich (Ger.), bar line.

Tal, Joseph (born 1910), Israeli composer, originally from Poland. His most important work is his opera *Ashmedai*, premièred at Hamburg in 1973. He has also written a choreographic poem, *Exodus*, for baritone and orchestra, and other orchestral works.

talea, *see* ISORHYTHM

Tale of Two Cities, A, opera in three acts, with prologue, by Arthur Benjamin. The libretto, by Cedric Cliffe, is based on the novel by Dickens. The first stage performance was in London in 1957, though a broadcast performance was given four years earlier.

Tales of Hoffmann, The (Fr., *Les Contes d'Hoffmann*), opera in three acts, with a prologue and epilogue, by Offenbach, to a libretto by Jules Barbier and Michel Carré. The composer died before finishing it; the first performance took place in Paris in 1881, four months after his death, the orchestration having been completed by Ernest Guiraud, who also composed recitatives for the piece, and generally revised it. Many performers now discard the recitatives, regarding them as stylistically wrong, and replace them more aptly with spoken dialogue. The opera represents three episodes in the life of E. T. A. Hoffmann (1776–1822), on whose stories the libretto is based. In the first he falls in love with Olympia, a mechanical doll whom he believes to be real. In the second he meets Giulietta in Venice and kills her lover, only to lose her to another. In the third he is in love with Antonia, whose health prevents her from using her beautiful voice. Dr. Miracle induces her to sing and she dies.

Because there is no authorised version of *The Tales of Hoffmann*, there has always been controversy over what order the three acts should be performed in. Today it is widely accepted that Offenbach really wanted the Venetian episode to come last, and a number of productions now place it in that position.

Tálich, Václav (1883–1961), Czech conductor, pupil of Nikisch. He was an outstanding exponent of the music of Dvořák, and was conductor of the Czech Philharmonic from 1919.

Tallis, Thomas (c. 1505–85), English composer and organist. He was organist of Waltham Abbey at its dissolution in 1540, a gentleman of the Chapel Royal from about 1545 until his death, and organist of the Chapel with William Byrd. In 1575 he and Byrd were granted by Queen Elizabeth the sole right to print music and music paper in England. Their first publication was *Cantiones Sacrae* (1575) containing seventeen motets by Tallis and seventeen by Byrd.

Tallis composed two Magnificats, two Masses, Lamentations for five voices, Latin motets (including *Spem in alium* for eight choirs of five parts each),

services, psalms, anthems and other church music, two *In Nomines* for strings, secular vocal works and pieces for keyboard. Such works as the forty-part motet and the seven-part canon 'Miserere nostri' (*Cantiones Sacrae*, no 34) are both technically skilful and artistically satisfying. The deeper aspects of his style are more evident in the Mass *Salve intemerata* (based on the antiphon of that title), in the *Lamentations* and in the motets of the *Cantiones Sacrae*, works which place him among the greatest of the composers of the mid 16th century. Two pieces on the plainsong 'Felix namque' are in the *Fitzwilliam Virginal Book* and eighteen keyboard pieces and arrangements in the *Mulliner Book* (modern edition in *Musica Britannica*, i). His complete keyboard works have been edited by Denis Stevens (1953). His Latin church music is published in *Tudor Church Music*, vi (1928). The English sacred music has been edited by L. Ellinwood (revised by P. Doe, two volumes, 1973–4). It includes nine tunes for Archbishop Parker's Psalter of 1567–8 (*see* PSALTER).

P. DOE: *Tallis* (1968)

talon (Fr.), the nut of a bow. The direction *au talon* means play with the nut-end or heel of the bow.

Tamagno, Francesco (1851–1905), Italian tenor, famous for his creation in 1887 of the role of Otello, written for him by Verdi. He made his début in Palermo in 1873 in *A Masked Ball*, was La Scala's leading tenor by the early 1880s, and died rich as a result of appearances all over the world as Otello.

Francesco Tamagno as Otello, a part created by Verdi to suit Tamagno's unique blend of vocal power and pure *bel canto* technique.

tambour (Fr.), drum. *Tambour militaire*, side drum; *Tambour de basque*, tambourine.

tamboura, an alternative name for the PANDOURA.

tambour de basque (Fr.), TAMBOURINE.

tambouret, *see* TAMBOURINE

tambourin (Fr.), (1) a long narrow drum, played with

one stick when used, especially in Provence (*tambourin de Provence*), with a small, one-handed recorder (*flûtet, galoubet*) to accompany dancing;

(2) the *tambourin du Béarn* (It., *altobasso*) was a DULCIMER with gut strings sounding only the tonic and dominant, and was used similarly with a type of flageolet called *galouvet* to accompany dancing. The term *tambourin* was applied to a dance so accompanied which was introduced by Rameau into his opera-ballet *Les Fêtes d'Hébé* (1739) and into his *Pièces de clavecin*:

tambourine (Fr., *tambour de Basque*; Ger., *Tamburin, Baskische Trommel, Schellentrommel*; It., *tamburino, tamburo basso*; Sp., *panderete*), a small drum with a single head fastened to a narrow circular wooden frame that is slotted to accommodate several pairs of tiny, loosely hanging cymbals, which are known as jingles. The instrument is normally held in one hand and struck by the fingers, knuckles or palm of the other, but on occasion the player strikes it against his knee. In addition there are two methods of bringing the jingles into use without striking the head. The first and simpler is to merely shake it; the second is achieved by rubbing a moistened thumb round the head, thereby setting up vibrations. The tambourine most frequently appears in music of a festive, gipsy or oriental character, Berlioz's *Roman Carnival* overture, Bizet's *Carmen* and the *Arab Dance* from Chaikovsky's *The Nutcracker*, providing an example in each category; but it also appears in contexts that have no such associations and is useful for heightening the rhythmic impact of climaxes. In Italy a type of tambourine without jingles and called *tamburello* is well known. A few composers, Falla among them, have called for it.

tamburello, *see* TAMBOURINE

Tamburini, Antonio (1800–76), Italian baritone, of great technical brilliance, who sang the role of Dr. Malatesta in the première of Donizetti's *Don Pasquale* and Riccardo in Bellini's *I Puritani*. He began his career in Italy, but it was in Paris and London that he was specially famed, and where he appeared in numerous works by Donizetti and other composers.

tamburino, *see* TAMBOURINE

tamburo (It.), drum; *tamburo grande, tamburo grosso,* names sometimes used in old scores for the bass drum; *tamburo rullante,* tenor drum; *tamburo militaire,* snare drum.

tamburo basso, *see* TAMBOURINE

tamburo piccolo, *see* SIDE DRUM

Tamerlano (*Tamburlane*), opera in three acts by Handel, with a libretto by Agostino Pioverne, adapted by Nicola Francesco Haym. The first performance was in London in 1724.

Taming of the Shrew, The (Ger., *Der widerspänstigen Zähmung*), opera in four acts by Goetz, after Shakespeare's comedy. The première was at Mannheim in 1874. The play has been the source of several other operas, as well as of Cole Porter's musical, *Kiss Me, Kate* (1948).

tampon (Fr.), a two-headed drumstick held in the middle and used with an alternating motion of the wrist to produce a roll on the bass drum.

tampur, a three-stringed instrument from the Caucasus, played throughout the Balkans and Near East. It resembles a lute but is played with a bow, and has a variable number of metal strings.

tam-tam (Eng., Fr., Ger., It.), often confused, even on occasion by composers, with the GONG, the tam-tam is significantly different in construction. The metal is thinner and the rim, if any, is very shallow, while there is no protruding boss in the centre; instead the tam-tam is either flat or slightly saucer-shaped. Unlike gongs, which produce a definite fundamental note, the sound of the tam-tam is made up of a dissonant mixture of frequencies spread over a wide range, the overall depth varying according to the size.

Tancredi, opera in two acts by Rossini, with a libretto by Gaetano Rossi. This *melodramma eroica*, based on Tasso's *Gerusalemme liberata* and Voltaire's tragedy, *Tancrède*, had its first performance at Venice in 1813. The work is now a collector's piece, though its brilliant overture remains popular in the concert hall.

tañer, *see* TASTAR

Taneyev, Sergey Ivanovich (1856–1915), Russian composer and pianist, pupil of Chaikovsky and Nicholas Rubinstein. He appeared as a pianist in Moscow (1875), toured Russia with Leopold Auer (1876) and visited Paris (1877–78). He was teacher, Moscow Conservatory, 1880–1906; director, 1885–89. He wrote a treatise on counterpoint and composed symphonies, an overture, string quartets and other chamber music, an operatic trilogy, choral works and songs.

tangent, *see* CLAVICHORD

Tanglewood, *see* BERKSHIRE FESTIVAL

tango, a dance in a moderately slow 2/4 time with syncopated rhythms which originated in urban Argentina about the beginning of this century and appeared in Europe and the United States about 1910. There are a few examples in instrumental suites by contemporary composers.

Tannhäuser, und der Sängerkrieg auf Wartburg (Ger., *Tannhäuser, and the Tournament of Song at Wartburg*), opera in three acts by Wagner (usually known simply as *Tannhäuser*), with a libretto by the composer. The première took place at Dresden in 1845. Tannhäuser, a minstrel knight, weary of the monotony of a year spent with Venus, the goddess of love, decides to return to his earthly friends. At the tournament of song held in the Wartburg he competes for the prize, the hand of the landgrave's niece Elizabeth, but shocks the whole assembly by singing the praises of Venus. In remorse he joins a band of pilgrims and journeys to Rome. Denied absolution by the Pope, he decides, in spite of the remonstrances of his fellow-minstrel Wolfram, to return to Venus. At the last moment, however, he learns that he has been saved by the prayers of Elizabeth, whose funeral procession now appears. As he too dies, the chorus sing of the miracle of God's forgiveness.

In its original form, the opera is an early and somewhat crude example of Wagner's genius. In 1861, however, he made a fascinating revision of the score for a production in Paris, giving the music a new flow and richness, and bringing to it a more obvious maturity of vision. The overture, for example, no longer ends with a grandiose *da capo* of its opening, but proceeds with heightened intensity into the opera itself.

Tansman, Alexandre (born 1897), Polish born composer and pianist who took French nationality after settling in Paris in 1920. Later he toured the world, and spent the war years in the United States, returning to Paris in 1946. His compositions include operas, ballets, seven symphonies and other orchestral works, concertos and a *concertino* for piano and orchestra, string quartets and other chamber music, songs, piano pieces and music for films.

Tans'ur, William (originally **Tanzer**) (1706–83), English composer, teacher and organist. He was organist at Barnes in Surrey, at Ewell (1739), at Stamford in Lincolnshire and St. Neot's. He published books of metrical psalms containing some composed by himself and some with words by himself, and *A New Musical Grammar* (1746–56), later published as *The Elements of Musick Display'd* (1772). This was widely used, and reprinted as late as 1829.

tanto (It.), 'so much'. It has been used as the equivalent of *troppo*, e.g. *allegro non tanto*, not too fast.

Tanz (Ger.), dance.

tap box, *see* WOOD BLOCK

tape music, *see* ELECTRONIC MUSIC

Tapiola, symphonic poem by Sibelius, op 112 (1925). Tapio is the name of the god of the forests in Finnish mythology. The score is prefaced by the following quatrain:

> Wide-spread they stand, the Northland's dusky forests,
> Ancient, mysterious, brooding savage dreams;
> Within them dwells the Forest's mighty God,
> And wood-sprites in the gloom weave magic secrets.

The work, largely monothematic, is one of Sibelius's tersest scores, and one of his greatest. It dates from the very end of his productive career, though he lived for some thirty years after writing it.

Tapissier, Jean, early 15th century composer mentioned in Martin le Franc's poem *Champion des Dames* (c. 1440) as one of the three composers famous in Paris immediately before the rise of Dufay and Binchois:

> Tapissier Carmen Cesaris
> N'a pas longtemps si bien chanterrent
> Qu'ilz esbahirent tout Paris
> Et tous ceulx qui les frequenterrent . . . .

A *Credo* and a *Sanctus* in three parts and a four-part motet, 'Eya dulcis/Vale placens' (printed in J. Stainer, *Dufay and his Contemporaries*, page 187) by him have survived; all three are printed in *Early Fifteenth-Century Music*, edited by G. Reaney, i (*Corpus Mensurabilis Musicae*, xi, i).

tarantella, a very fast Italian dance in 6/8 time, usually with alternating major and minor sections. In the 19th century it attracted such composers as Weber, Chopin and Liszt:

CHOPIN, *Tarantelle*, op 43

An instance by a 20th century composer is the third movement of Rawsthorne's first piano concerto (1945).

There are many accounts from the 15th to the 18th century of the legendary virtue of the *tarantella* as the only cure for the effects of the bite of the tarantula spider. Both dance and spider get their name from Taranto, a town in southern Italy.

C. ENGEL: *Musical Myths and Facts*, volume ii (1876)

Taras Bulba, rhapsody for orchestra by Janáček, inspired by Gogol's novel about the strife in the 15th century between the Poles and the Ukrainian Cossacks. The music, first performed in Leipzig in 1928, depicts three episodes from the story.

tarbouka, a North African drum used by Berlioz in the Slave Dance in *The Trojans*.

tardo (It.), slow. *Tardando,* becoming slower.

tárogató, a Hungarian woodwind instrument with oriental origins. It is still much used by folk musicians in Hungary. Originally it had a double reed, but towards the end of the 19th century this was replaced by a single one set in a clarinet-type mouthpiece. The bore is conical and the instrument, although made of wood, resembles a straight soprano saxophone in both appearance and tone colour. On occasion it has been used to play the shepherd's pipe tune that announces the arrival of the ship in the last act of Wagner's *Tristan and Isolde*.

Tartini, Giuseppe (1692–1770), Italian violinist and composer, teacher and theorist. He studied at Capo d'Istria and at the University of Padua (from 1709), which he was forced to leave after marrying a pupil in 1713. He played as an orchestral violinist in the provinces (1713–16), stayed at the Franciscan Monastery at Assisi, and went to Ancona for further study. He was first violinist at the Basilica di Sant'Antonia in Padua (from 1721) and conductor of Count Kinsky's orchestra in Prague (1723–26). He visited Vienna, and in 1728 established a school of violin-playing in Padua where his pupils included Graun, Nardini and Pugnani. He discovered COMBINATION TONES and advised his pupils to use the 'third sound', as it was then called, to ensure true intonation in double-stopping. He wrote many treatises on violin-playing and on problems in acoustics, and composed over 100 violin concertos, symphonies, numerous sonatas (including *The Devil's Trill*) and some church music.

Tasso, symphonic poem by Liszt, inspired by a poem by Byron. It was first performed at Weimar in 1849 as an overture to Goethe's drama *Torquato Tasso*. In 1850–1 the composer revised and extended the score, which had its second Weimar première in 1854.

tastar (It.; Sp., *taner*), 'touching'. A 16th century term for a prelude in extemporary style for lute, e.g. the *Tastar de corde* followed by a *ricercar* by Joanambrosio Dalza, printed in *Historical Anthology of Music*, edited by A. T. Davison and W. Apel, no 99a.

tastatura (It.), keyboard.

Taste (Ger.), key of a keyboard instrument.

tastiera (It.; Fr., *touche*; Ger., *Griffbrett*), fingerboard of a stringed instrument. The direction *sulla tastiera*, meaning 'on the finger board' is an instruction to play above it, thereby producing a rather veiled tone.

tastiera per luce (It.), literally 'keyboard for light', the instrument invented by Rimington which projected colours. It was prescribed by Skryabin for his *Prometheus*. It had twelve notes, 'tuned' to a 'scale' of colours based on the musical cycle of fifths. The keyboard was used only once for *Prometheus* – at Carnegie Hall in 1915.

tasto (It.), (1) key of a keyboard instrument. In figured bass, *tasto solo* is an instruction to play merely the bass notes without adding harmonies above;

(2) fret on a lute, viol, guitar and other similar instruments;

(3) finger board of a stringed instrument (Fr., *touche*; Ger., *Griffbrett*). The direction *sul tasto*, meaning 'on the finger board' is an instruction to play above it, thereby producing a rather veiled tone.

Tate, Phyllis (born 1911), British composer, whose works include an opera, *The Lodger* (1958), based on the novel by Mrs. Belloc Lowndes. She has also written a saxophone concerto, a sonata for clarinet and cello (performed at the International Society for Contemporary Music Festival, Salzburg, in 1952) and *A Secular Requiem* for voices, organ and orchestra.

tatto (It.), another name (now obsolete) for acciaccatura.

tattoo (Fr., *rappel*; Ger., *Zapfenstreich*; It., *ritirata*; Sp., *retreta*), the bugle-call, or beat of a drum, which recalls soldiers to their quarters at night. Elaborate, as well as rudimentary, versions of these military signals are performed, depending on the occasion.

Tatum, Art (1910–56), U.S. jazz pianist, whose polished, florid style was immensely influential on other performers – though few could match his Lisztian technique. He was heard at his best in solo capacity (he was never a fully satisfactory ensemble player); fortunately many of his most alluring performances, with their breathtaking runs, modulations and changes of tempo, have been preserved on tape. Concert pianists, include Horowitz, have been deep admirers of Tatum, and it is easy to see why.

Tauber, Richard (1892–1948). Austrian born tenor, originally called Ernst Seiffert. He made his début at Chemnitz, where his father was operatic administrator, as Tamino in *The Magic Flute* in 1913. Later he sang in Dresden and Vienna, establishing himself during the 1920s and 1930s as the most famous Mozart tenor of the day. He also appeared frequently at Covent Garden (and, indeed, took British nationality). He had a flair for operetta, especially Lehár, and composed a number of pieces himself.

Tausig, Carl (1841–71), Polish pianist and composer who settled in Germany. One of the greatest piano virtuosos of his day, he studied under his father (Aloys Tausig) and Thalberg, and from 1855–59 under Liszt at Weimar. He made his debut in Berlin at a concert conducted by von Bulow (1858), toured Germany (1859–60) and later lived in Dresden. He gave orchestral concerts of modern music in Vienna (1862) and settled in Berlin (1865), where he founded a school of advanced piano playing. He composed symphonic poems, a piano concerto and studies and transcriptions for piano, including some of Bach's organ music.

Taverner, opera in two acts by Peter Maxwell Davies, with a libretto by the composer based on the career of John Taverner, the 15th–16th century English composer, organist and heretic, and some say an agent of Thomas Cromwell and an enthusiastic destroyer of the monasteries. The opera was first performed at Covent Garden in 1971.

Taverner, John (c. 1490–1545), English composer. He was probably educated at the Collegiate Church of the Holy Trinity at Tattershall (Lincolnshire) and worked in London from at least 1514. In 1525 he was back at Tattershall as a clerk. From 1526 to 1530 he was master of the choristers at Cardinal College (later Christ Church), Oxford. He later settled in Boston where he was elected a member (1537) and a steward (1541) of the Guild of Corpus Christi. There is no firm historical basis for the widely accepted notion that he renounced composition in 1530 and worked as an agent of Thomas Cromwell in the suppression of monasteries. He composed eight Masses, three Magnificats, motets, and other church music, which has been published in *Tudor Church Music*, i (1923) and iii (1924).

He was one of the last and one of the greatest composers to write Masses, Magnificats and antiphons to the Virgin in the elaborate style practised by English composers in the first decades of the 16th century. Compared with his immediate predecessors, he makes greater use of imitation, a technique which became general in the work of Tye and Tallis. His Masses show an interesting variety of method. Three – *Corona spinea*, *Gloria tibi Trinitas*, and *O Michael* – are large works on a *cantus firmus* in the older style; *The Western Wynde* is a set of variations on the secular tune, a unique example of this way of designing a Mass on an adopted melody; three – *Playne song*, *Sine nomine* and *Small Devotion* – are in a 'familiar' (i.e. chordal) style, making use of divided choir technique (*see* CORI SPEZZATI) to some extent; and one, *Mater Christi*, is a parody Mass, being based in part on Taverner's antiphon of that name. The 'In nomine' section of the *Benedictus* of his Mass *Gloria tibi Trinitas* was the starting-point of the history of the English IN NOMINE. Four of the pieces printed in *Tudor Church Music*, iii as by Taverner are actually by other composers (Fayrfax, Aston and Tallis; for details *see* F. Ll. Harrison, *Music in Medieval Britain*, 1958, page 334).

D. JOSEPHSON: 'In Search of the Historical Taverner', in *Tempo*, ci (1972)

D. W. STEVENS: 'John Taverner', in *Essays in Musicology*, edited by G. Reese and R. J. Snow (1969)

Taylor, Joseph Deems (1885–1966), U.S. composer, critic and writer on music. He studied at New York University, and later became music critic, *New York World*, 1921–25; editor of *Musical America*, 1927–29;

musical adviser to the Columbia Broadcasting System from 1940. He wrote *Of Men and Music* (1938), made translations of French, Russian, German and Italian songs, and composed operas (*The King's Henchman*, 1927; *Peter Ibbetson*, 1931), a ballet, symphonic poems, suites (including one on *Through the Looking Glass* after Lewis Carroll) and other orchestral works, cantatas and other choral works and incidental music for plays.

Tchaikovsky, *see* CHAIKOVSKY

Tcherepnin, *see* CHEREPNIN

te, an English substitution for the Italian *si* (B), used in TONIC SOL-FA for the seventh note (or leading note) of the major scale.

Teagarden, Jack (1905–64), U.S. jazz trombonist, the most famous of his day. Though not a Negro (he was born in Texas, of American Indian stock), he created a style of playing the trombone which was the counterpart of Louis Armstrong's on trumpet. His heyday was the 1930s, when he appeared frequently with Ben Pollack and Paul Whiteman, as well as with his own bands. He also worked as a singer, often performing in partnership with Louis Armstrong.

Tebaldi, Renata (born 1922), Italian soprano, one of the most important to emerge since World War II. Toscanini chose her for the reopening of La Scala, Milan, in 1946. Her Covent Garden début was in performances of Verdi's *Otello* and the Requiem, conducted by Victor de Sabata. In that year she also made her first American appearance (as Aïda at San Francisco); from 1955 she sang regularly at the New York Metropolitan. She is specially associated with dramatic roles, by Verdi and Puccini, also with the title-role in Cilea's *Adriana Lecouvreur*, a work revived for her by several opera houses.

tecla (Sp.), a term for key and keyboard, dating from the 16th and 17th centuries. *Música para tecla* is music for keyboard instruments.

tedesca (It.), short for *danza tedesca*, 'German dance'. *See* ALLA TEDESCA, ALLEMANDE, DEUTSCHER TANZ

Te Deum (Lat.), the opening words of 'Te Deum laudamus' (We praise thee, God), a Christian hymn attributed to Nicetas (born c. 340), Bishop of Remesiana in Dacia. It is sung at Matins on festivals, on occasions of thanksgiving, and (in the English translation) at Morning Prayer in the Anglican service. The plainsong begins thus:

Among the choral settings written in the 16th century are those of Hugh Aston, John Taverner, Felice Anerio and Jacob Handl. There are organ settings for *alternatim* performance by John Redford, William Blitheman and Nicolas Gigault. Aston and Palestrina composed Masses on its plainsong. John Marbeck's adaptation of the plainsong to the English translation was printed in his *Booke of Common Praier noted* (1550; facsimile edition by J. E. Hunt, 1939).

The Lutheran form of the melody, for alternating choirs or for choir alternating with the congregation, set to Martin Luther's translation ('Herr Gott, dich loben wir'), was reprinted in von Winterfeld's *Martin Luthers geistliche Lieder* (1840). Organ settings, presumably intended to accompany this version, were composed by Scheidt (in four parts; *Complete Works*, volume i) and Bach (five parts; *Neue Bach-Ausgabe*, Ser. iv, Bd. iii, page 36).

Settings in festive style for voices and instruments have been written by Purcell (St. Cecilia's Day, 1694), Blow (1695), Handel (Peace of Utrecht, 1712 and Battle of Dettingen, 1743), Berlioz (Paris Exhibition of 1855), Bruckner (1884), Dvořák (1892), Verdi (1898), Stanford (Leeds Festival, 1898), Parry (coronation of George V, 1911), Vaughan Williams (coronation of George VI, 1936) and Walton (coronation of Elizabeth II, 1953).

See also SERVICE

Teil (Ger.), section, part (of a work). Thus, Erste Teil would be 'Part One' (of a work laid out in several sections).

Telemann, Georg Michael (1748–1831). German composer and writer. He published in 1773 an introduction to figured bass (*Unterricht im Generalbass-Spielen*) and composed trio sonatas, solo sonatas (published by Walsh), organ preludes, and church music. He became cantor at Riga about 1775.

His grandfather **Georg Philipp Telemann** (1681–1767), was a composer. Educated in Magdeburg and Hildesheim, he studied law at Leipzig University (where he founded a student *Collegium musicum*) but taught himself music and wrote compositions for the Thomaskirche and operas for the Leipzig Theatre. He was organist of the Neukirche and *Kapellmeister* to Prince Promnitz at Sorau, 1704. In 1708 he became *Konzertmeister* and later *Kapellmeister* at Eisenach (where he made friends with J. S. Bach). In 1712 he moved to Frankfurt, working as the *Kapellmeister* of the Katharinenkirche and later city music director. Later he became *Kapellmeister* to the Prince of Bayreuth and at the Barfusserkirche. From 1721 until his death he was cantor of the Johanneum and music director at Hamburg. He visited Paris in 1737 and made several visits to Berlin.

The most prolific composer in an age of prodigious production, he wrote twelve cycles of cantatas for the church year, 44 Passions, oratorios, and much other church music, forty operas, 600 French overtures (i.e. suites for orchestra), concertos, a great deal of chamber music in various forms, fantasies for harpsichord and short fugues for organ. He also published *Singe-, Spiel- und General-bass-Ubungen* ('exercises in singing, playing, and figured bass'), engraved by himself (1733–35). Among the modern editions of his works are: oratorio, *The Day of Judgement*, and cantata, *Ino*, in D.D.T., xxvii; 24 odes for solo voices and continuo in D.D.T., lvii; *Musique de Table* (three chamber suites, Hamburg, 1733) in D.D.T., lxi/lxii; violin concerto in F in D.D.T., xxix; twelve *Methodische Sonaten* Hamburg (1728, 1732) for transverse flute and continuo, edited by Max Seiffert (1951, the first volume of a collected edition); opera, *Pimpinone*, in E.D.M., vi.

Telemusik, work by Stockhausen, composed in 1966

and marking the start of a new phase in his career. It incorporates recorded *objets trouvés* from all over the world, but particularly from Japan, whose music and people had recently made a great impression on the composer.

Telephone, The, opera in one act by Menotti, first performed in New York in 1947. The libretto, by the composer, concerns a young man who has to compete with an incessantly ringing telephone for his beloved's attention.

television opera, (1) as a medium for opera performance, television has always been limited by its size of screen and quality of sound reproduction. The first experimental performance took place in Britain in 1937 (John Blow's *Venus and Adonis*); the United States followed four years later with *I Pagliacci*. In general, performances today are either telecast versions of theatre productions, such as those filmed at Glyndebourne, the New York Metropolitan, the Aix-en-Provence Festival, or one of the famous German opera houses; or else they are specially prepared studio presentations, like the B.B.C. productions of Britten's *Billy Budd* and *Peter Grimes*. The principal value of television opera performances is that they can reach a mass audience. When Germany televised Berg's *Wozzeck*, more people saw it in a single night than had previously seen it in the work's whole theatrical history. Similarly the televising of Prokofiev's *War and Peace* from Australia enabled the world to share in the opening of the Sydney Opera House in the autumn of 1973.

(2) work written specifically for television presentation. The first opera composed for this medium was Menotti's *Amahl and the Night Visitors*, sponsored by a U.S. commercial company and first televised in 1951 – later it also enjoyed a stage success. In Britain the first television opera was Richard Arnell's *Love in Transit* (1955). Other examples have been Arthur Benjamin's *Manana*, Bliss's *Tobias and the Angel* and, perhaps the most important work of its kind so far, Britten's *Owen Wingrave*.

Telmányi, Emil (born 1892), Hungarian violinist, now resident in Denmark, where he married a daughter of the composer Carl Nielsen. In 1949 he invented a 'Bach bow' for the performance of baroque music, one of its special features being that it enables chords to be played without spreading.

tema (It.), theme. *Tema con variazioni*, theme and variations.

temperament, a system of tuning in which intervals are 'tempered' (i.e. slightly lessened or enlarged) away from the 'natural' scale. It was devised when the gradual introduction of chromatic tones made inadequate systems based on physical laws (e.g. the Pythagorean system), where the intervals agree with those found by successive fractional division of a string.

After c. 1500 the system of mean-tone temperament was generally adopted for keyboard instruments, which was adequate for the normal chords of modal harmony and for keys which did not involve the use of more than two sharps or flats. If chords containing G sharp, D sharp or A sharp as major thirds were wanted, such expedients as separate chords had to be resorted to. With the use in composition of the complete cycle of major and minor keys, as in Bach's *The*

Well-Tempered Clavier, the system of EQUAL TEMPERAMENT began to be adopted, but was not universally accepted before c. 1850.

See DIESIS, FIFTH

J. M. BARBOUR: *Tuning and Temperament* (1951)

Tempest, The, (1) *The Tempest, or the Enchanted Island*, opera with dialogue by Purcell (1695), the text adapted from Shakespeare by Thomas Shadwell.

(2) opera in three acts by Gatty, libretto by Reginald Gatty (after Shakespeare). First performed, London, April 17th, 1920.

(3) operas by foreign composers based on the same play include Reichardt's *Die Geisterinsel* and Zumsteeg's setting of the same libretto (both 1798), Halévy's *La tempesta* (1850), Fibich's *Boure* (1895) and Lattuada's *La tempesta* (1922). Also opera by Frank Martin, based almost entirely on Shakespeare's text, produced in Vienna (1956).

(4) among 17th century composers in England who wrote music for the play were Banister, Humfrey, Reggio, Draghi, and Locke.

(5) incidental music for the play by Sibelius, op 109 (1926).

(6) symphonic fantasy by Chaikovsky, op 18 (1873), based on the play.

temple block, also known as the Chinese or Korean temple block, the first of these names being liable to cause confusion with the WOOD BLOCK, which is sometimes referred to as the Chinese block. Made of hard wood with slits and shaped like skulls, temple blocks are usually made in sets of five. They are played with sticks and the tone varies according to the hardness of these. It is in any case deeper and mellower than that of the wood block. Although usually treated as instruments with no definite pitch, temple blocks give out recognisable notes, some sets being tuned to a pentatonic scale.

tempo (It.), (1) time. The pace of a composition as determined by the speed of the beat to which it is performed. Until c. 1600 the beat (*see* TACTUS) in any composition in a particular style (e.g. motet, madrigal) was more or less uniform, and differences of pace were conveyed by the conventions of the notation. Towards the end of the 17th century the modern tempo indications, such as *largo*, *adagio*, *allegro*, *presto*, were adopted in Italy and gradually came into general use. They indicate in a general way the tempo of the beat, which is given by the lower figure of the TIME SIGNATURE. Within certain limits the tempo which they suggested remained a matter of convention based on the style of the music, on local custom, and on individual choice until the invention of the METRONOME. Even with both tempo and metronome marks the practice of performers and conductors is by no means uniform, and choice of tempo is generally regarded as an element in interpretation, dependent to some extent on conditions of performance.

F. ROTHSCHILD: *The Lost Tradition in Music: Rhythm and Tempo in J. S. Bach's Time* (1953)

C. SACHS: *Rhythm and Tempo* (1953)

(2) movement (of a sonata, symphony, etc.): *il secondo tempo*, the second movement.

temps (Fr.), beat. *Temps fort*, strong beat; *temps faible*, weak beat.

Tender Land, The, opera in two acts by Copland,

with a libretto by Horace Everett. Produced by the New York City Opera in 1954, it concerns a farmer's daughter who falls in love with a harvester on her father's Midwest farm.

Tenebrae, the Roman Catholic services of Matins and Lauds for Thursday, Friday and Saturday of Holy Week, in which are sung the LAMENTATIONS and the *Miserere* (Psalm 50), respectively. The name derives from the practice, laid down in the *Liber Usualis*, of gradually extinguishing the lights through the services.

tenendo (It.), sustaining.

teneramente (It.), tenderly.

tenor (from Lat. *tenere*, 'to hold'), (1) in psalmody, the note of recitation, also known as the dominant.

See RECITING NOTE

(2) in sacred polyphonic music (e.g. organum, motet, Mass) until c. 1450, the lowest part, which was most often derived from plainsong, and on which the composition was based. In a polyphonic *chanson* of the same period the part which formed, with the highest part (*cantus*), the two-part frame-work of the composition. It was as melodious as the *cantus* part, and could be used as the tenor of a Mass, e.g. Dufay's Mass *Se la face ay pale.*

See also CANTUS FIRMUS

(3) in music after c. 1450, when a bass part began to be used, the part above the bass in a four-part vocal composition (S.A.T.B.). The term was hence applied to the adult male voice intermediate between the bass and the alto.

(4) prefixed to the name of an instrument it indicates a size intermediate between the alto (or treble) member of the family and the bass, e.g. tenor saxophone, tenor trombone.

See also TENOR HAUTBOY

(5) English term for the viola (short for tenor violin), now obsolete.

(6) the tenor clef is the C clef on the fourth line:

used in the 16th and 17th centuries for the tenor voice and instruments of equivalent range, now usual only for the tenor trombone and the upper notes of the bassoon, cello and double bass. The tenor voice is now written, except in short score, in the G (treble) clef read an octave lower:

tenor-bass trombone, *see* TROMBONE

tenor bugle, the misleading Belgian name for the soprano SAXHORN.

tenor cor, a name sometimes given to the MELLOPHONE.

tenor drum (Fr., *caisse roulante*; Ger., *Rolltrommel* or *Rührtrommel*; It., *tamburo rullante*), a snareless drum larger than a side-drum but considerably smaller than a bass drum. Long used in military bands and those consisting of drums and fifes, its penetrating power is much less than that of a side-drum. It is only during the 20th century that it has found its way into the symphony orchestra, and even now its appearances are fairly rare.

Tenorfagotte (Ger.), TENOROON.

Tenor Flügelhorn, *see* FLÜGELHORN

Tenorgeige (Ger.), literally 'tenor violin', in other words the VIOLA.

tenor hautboy, obsolete English name for the *cor anglais* or English horn.

Tenor Horn, Tenorhorn (Ger.), names sometimes given to the tenor SAXHORN and occasionally the corresponding member of the FLUGELHORN family, although in Germany this is known as an ALTHORN.

tenoroon (Fr., *basson quinte*; Ger., *Tenorfagott*; It., *fagottino*), a tenor bassoon pitched a fifth higher than the normal instrument, which it resembled without equalling in tone. It is long since obsolete.

See OBOE

Tenorposaune (Ger.), tenor TROMBONE.

tenth, the interval of an octave plus a third, e.g.

In the theory of harmony and in figured bass it is treated as the equivalent of the third.

tento, *see* TIENTO

tenuto (It.), 'held'. Indication that a single note or chord should be held for its full value (or even longer) in a context in which the performer might be inclined to play it *staccato*. Generally abbreviated *ten..*

ternary form, a form, represented by the formula *ABA*, in which a first section is restated, with or without modifications or embellishments, after a middle section of different content. Where the restatement is without change it is often indicated by *da capo al fine* at the end of the middle section, as in the *da capo* aria and the minuet or scherzo with trio; where it is abbreviated, by *dal segno al fine*, or as in plainsong responds of the office by an asterisk or by quoting the word with which the restatement begins. Most of the short piano pieces of the romantic period (nocturne, impromptu, intermezzo, rhapsody, etc.) are in ternary form. SONATA FORM, having evolved from an earlier binary form, is a special case of ternary form in which the middle section is a development, the recapitulation involves a partial change of key, and the coda may be as long as each of the other sections.

Terradellas (Terradeglias), Domingo Miguel Bernabe (Domenico) (c. 1713–51), Spanish composer who studied at a Catalan monastery and under Durante at the Conservatorio Sant' Onoforio in Naples. He lived in London from 1746–7, visited Paris and returned to Rome, where he became *maestro di cappella* at S. Giacomo. He composed operas, of which *Artaserse*, the most important, was produced at Venice in 1744, and *Bellerofonte* in London in 1747, on which Burney remarked that 'crescendo is used in this opera, seemingly for the first time; and new effects are frequently produced by pianos and fortes'. He also composed some church music.

Terry, Charles Sanford (1864–1936), English historian. He studied at St. Paul's Choir School and King's College School, lectured at Newcastle and at Cambridge, and founded the first Prize Festival in Scotland at Aberdeen (1900), where he was appointed professor of history at the University in 1903. He published an English translation of Forkel's *Life of J. S. Bach*

(1920), *J. S. Bach, Cantata Texts* (1925), *J. S. Bach* (1928, revised 1933), *Johann Christian Bach* (1929), *The Origin of the Family of Bach Musicians* (1929), *Bach: The Historical Approach* (1930), *Bach's Orchestra* (1932), *The Music of Bach* (1933), essays on the B minor Mass, the Cantatas and Oratorios, the Passions, and on the Magnificat, Lutheran Masses, and Motets, and an edition of the *Coffee Cantata*.

Terry, Richard Runciman (1865–1938), English organist, composer and editor. He was organist at Westminster Cathedral, 1901–24. He gave many performances of early English church music, and edited Tudor motets and the *Westminster Hymnal* (1912). He published *Catholic Church Music* (1907, revised as *The Music of the Roman Rite*, 1931), and other books on church music, and a collection of sea shanties (*Shanty Book*, 1921, 1926). He composed five Masses, a Requiem and motets.

tertian harmony, harmonic system based on the third or triad, i.e. the standard western system of harmony.

Tertis, Lionel (1876–1975), English viola player and teacher. He studied at Leipzig and the Royal Academy of Music and settled in London. He toured in Europe and the United States and retired from the concert platform in 1936. Several contemporary composers, including Bax, Bliss and Cyril Scott, wrote music for him. He published *Beauty of Tone in String Playing* (1938), and laid down new technical specifications for the making of violas.

Terz (Ger.), third. *Terzdezime* is a thirteenth, or upper sixth.

terzetto (It.; Ger., *Terzett*), a vocal trio. The term is also applied, though rarely, to a piece for three instruments.

terzina (It.), triplet.

Teschner, Melchior (1584–1635), German church musician. He was a cantor at Fraustadt (1609) and pastor at Oberpritschen (1614). He was the composer of the hymn 'Valet will ich dir geben' (first published 1614), which is sung in England to the words 'All glory, laud and honour' (*English Hymnal*, no 622).

Teseo (*Theseus*), opera in five acts by Handel, with a libretto by Nicola Francesco Haym. It was first performed in London, January 21st, 1713.

Tessarini, Carlo (1690–c. 1762), Italian violinist and composer, probably a pupil of Vivaldi. He was violinist in Venice at St. Mark's (from 1729) and at SS. Giovanni e Paolo, and in Brno for Cardinal Wolfgang Hannibal (before 1738). He was orchestra leader at Urbino (1742) and played at Amsterdam (1762). His works include violin sonatas, trio sonatas, violin duets, *concertini* and *concerti grossi* for strings. His *Grammatica di musica* (1741) was published in French and English translations.

Tessier, Charles (born c. 1550), French composer and lutenist. He was chamber musician to Henry IV and visited England. He composed a book of *Chansons et airs de cour* for four to five voices (London, 1597) dedicated to Lady Penelope Riche (Stella in Sir Philip Sidney's sonnets), and *Airs et villanelles* for three to five voices (Paris, 1604). He also set a song from Sidney's *Astrophel and Stella* which was printed in Robert Dowland's *A Musicall Banquet* (1610; modern edition by P. Stroud, 1968).

tessitura (It.), 'texture'. The compass of a particular voice or of a vocal or instrumental part in a particular piece. The term is used mainly to denote the compass to which a singer's voice naturally inclines, or else the compass of a particular piece of music ('he, she, it has a high or low tessitura').

testo (It.), literally 'text'. The narrator in early ORATORIO.

testudo (Lat.), literally 'tortoise, tortoise-shell'. Hence (1) in the Graeco-Roman world a LYRE;
(2) in the 16th and 17th century a lute.

tetrachord (Gr., literally 'that which has four strings'), a segment of the scale of ancient Greek music, consisting of four notes descending through a perfect fourth in the order tone-tone-semitone, e.g. *A-G-F-E*. This, the diatonic tetrachord, was the basis of the complete diatonic scale. The chromatic tetrachord had two steps of a semitone above the lowest note, the enharmonic tetrachord two steps of a quarter-tone above the lowest note. *See* CHROMATIC, ENHARMONIC.

Tetrazzini, Luisa (1871–1940), Italian operatic soprano. She studied at the Liceo Musicale in Florence, sang in various Italian theatres, settled in Buenos Aires and was a member of a company in the Argentine (from 1898), and in Mexico City (from 1905). She gave many performances in European and American cities and in London at Covent Garden (from 1907), in New York at the Manhattan Opera (1908–10) and the Metropolitan (1910), and in Chicago at the Chicago Opera (1913–14). She sang in Italy for charity during the war and later taught singing in Milan. She published *My Life of Song* (1921) and *How to Sing* (1925).

Teutsch, *see* DEUTSCHER TANZ

Teyte, Maggie (1888–1976), British soprano, pupil of Jean de Reszke. Like her predecessor, Mary Garden, she achieved success on the French opera stage. She made her début in Monte Carlo in 1907, as Zerlina in *Don Giovanni*; the following year she sang her first Mélisande in Paris, having studied the role with Debussy. In Britain she appeared in the première of Holst's *The Perfect Fool* (1923). She was also famous as a recitalist, specializing in the French repertory of the late 19th and early 20th centuries.

Thaïs, opera in three acts by Massenet, to a libretto by Louis Gallet (based on Anatole France's novel). It was first performed in Paris in 1894. The work mingles sex with sanctimony, the heroine being a 4th century courtesan who becomes a nun. The score contains an orchestral interlude – the so-called 'Meditation from *Thaïs*', often performed out of context.

Thalben-Ball, *see* BALL

Thalberg, Sigismond (1812–71), Austrian pianist and composer, the natural son of Prince Moritz Dietrichstein and Baroness von Wetzlar. He studied in Vienna under Sechter and Hummel, made his début as pianist in 1826 and published his first works in 1828. He toured in Germany (1830), was chamber pianist to the Austrian Emperor (1834), and played in Paris (1835), where he was a rival of Liszt. He also gave concerts in London, Belgium, Holland, Russia, Spain, Brazil and the United States. His works include two operas, a piano concerto, a sonata, studies and many other piano pieces, transcriptions for piano and songs.

Thamos, König in Agypten, incidental music by Mozart (K 345) for a play by Tobias Philipp, Baron von Gebler. The music, dating from 1773, consists of choruses and entr'actes.

Thayer, Alexander Wheelock (1817–97), U.S. writer about music. He studied at Harvard University, where he worked in the library for several years. He made visits to Berlin, Bonn, Prague, Vienna and other cities, collecting material for a life of Beethoven, wrote for the *New York Tribunal* (1852) and was appointed U.S. Consul at Trieste (1865), where he lived until his death. He contributed to Dwight's *Journal of Music* and many other U.S. publications. His life of Beethoven, which is the standard biographical work on the composer, was published in German (Volume I, 1866, Volume II, 1872, Volume III, 1879; the projected fourth volume was not completed). The English edition in three volumes, translated and completed by H. E. Krehbiel, was published in 1921. Today it is printed in a single volume. Thayer also published a chronological index of Beethoven's compositions (1865).

theme, a musical entity (consisting of a group of notes, usually melodic) which is the chief idea, or one of the chief ideas, in a composition. It is used especially of an idea in an instrumental work which is used as the basis for discussion, development or variation, as are the themes in a sonata of the baroque period and in SONATA FORM, and a theme used for a series of VARIATIONS.

See also MOTIF

Theodora, oratorio by Handel, with a text by Thomas Morell, on the subject of the Christian martyr. The first performance was in London in 1750.

theorbo (Fr., *théorbe*; Ger., *Theorbe*; It., *tiorba*), a small bass lute or ARCHLUTE used in the 17th century as a continuo instrument in ensembles, and less frequently to accompany monodies. Besides the stopped strings it had a number of unstopped bass strings running from a separate peg-box. A tuning for a *liuto attiorbato* given by C. Saracini in 1614 was:

In his *Musick's Monument* (1676) Thomas Mace gives this tuning:

There is a late use of the theorbo in Handel's *Esther* (1732) for the accompaniment to 'Breathe soft, ye winds'.

theory of music, according to the period in which they were written, works on the theory of music may deal with one or more of the following aspects of the subject: acoustics, notation, melody, rhythm, harmony, counterpoint, composition, form, and musical aesthetics.

Thérémin, an electronic instrument invented by the Russian physicist Léon Thérémin (born 1896) and first demonstrated by him in 1920. The notes are produced by variations in the frequency of an oscillating electric circuit, controlled by movement of the player's hand in the air towards, or away from, an antenna. It is a purely melodic instrument.

Theresienmesse (Theresa Mass), Mass in B flat major by Haydn, composed in 1799 (Haydn Society, no 10; Novello's edition, no 16). No satisfactory explanation of the name has been advanced.

thesis, *see* ARSIS

Thibaud, Jacques (1880–1953), French violinist. After studying at the Paris Conservatoire, he joined the Colonne Orchestra, but rapidly made his name as a virtuoso. He toured widely as a soloist, and in association with Alfred Cortot (piano) and Pau Casals (cello). He was killed in an air crash in the Alps.

Thieving Magpie, The (It., *La Gazza ladra*), opera in two acts by Rossini, with a libretto by Gherardini after the play *La Pie Voleuse* by Baudouin d'Aubigny and Caigniez. The first production was at La Scala, Milan, in 1817. The story concerns a maidservant who is condemned to death for theft; but the thief is really a magpie, and the culprit is discovered in the nick of time. For many years the work was known only by its overture (which opens with a drum-roll and contains a choice example of the 'Rossini crescendo'); recently however, the whole opera has begun to regain its place in the repertory.

third, the interval comprised by two notes written on adjacent lines or spaces, e.g.:

A major third has two whole tones, a minor third a tone and a semitone, and a diminished third a whole tone:

The mode of a triad is determined by its third, as is the mode of a scale, since the sixth and seventh degrees are treated as variable in the harmonic minor and melodic minor scales.

thirteenth, the interval of an octave and a sixth, e.g.:

For the so-called 'chord of the thirteenth', *see* CHORD.

thirty-second note (U.S.), demisemiquaver.

Thoinan, Ernest (*nom de plume* of Antoine Ernest Roquet) (1827–94), French musical scholar who lived in Paris from 1844 as a businessman. He collected works of music and became a contributor to *La France musicale*, *L'Art musical* and other periodicals. He published many of his essays in pamphlet form.

Thomas, Arthur Goring (1850–92), English composer. He studied music in Paris under Emile Durand (from 1873), in London at the Royal Academy of Music under Sullivan and Prout (from 1877) and in Berlin under Bruch. He was commissioned by the Carl Rosa Opera Co. to write *Esmeralda*, which was first performed in 1883. He composed other operas (including *Nadeshda*, 1883), four concert-scenas, cantatas and other choral works, an orchestral *Suite de Ballet*, and many songs (chiefly to French words).

Thomas, Charles Louis Ambroise (1811–96), French composer. He studied at the Paris Conservatoire, where he won the *Prix de Rome* (1832), and under Kalkbrenner (piano) and Lesueur (composition). After three years in Italy he returned to Paris, where he wrote many operas for the Opéra-Comique and was appointed teacher of composition (1852) and director (1871) at the Conservatoire. His works include operas, ballets, a Fantasia for piano and orchestra, cantatas, two Masses, motets, chamber music, part-songs, songs and piano pieces. His most successful operas were *Mignon* (1866), which reached its 500th performance in 1878, and *Hamlet* (1868), which seems to have been the first opera in which a saxophone was used in the orchestra.

Thomas, Theodore (1835–1905), U.S. (German born) conductor and violinist who was almost entirely self-taught. His family moved in 1845 to New York, where he became a member of the New York Philharmonic (1854) and of the Mason-Thomas Quintet (1855), and orchestra leader and later conductor at the New York Academy of Music. He founded his own orchestra (1862). He was the conductor of the Brooklyn Philharmonic, 1866; New York Philharmonic, 1877; Chicago Symphony Orchestra, 1891 until his death. He gave many first performances in the United States of modern music and wrote *A Musical Autobiography* (edited by G. P. Upton, 1905).

Thomé, Francis (1850–1909), Mauritius born French composer, whose real first names were Joseph François Luc. He studied at the Paris Conservatoire, and composed numerous operas and operettas, incidental music to plays, and works for chorus. Today he is remembered principally for his piano piece, 'Simple Aveu'.

Thompson, Randall (born 1899), U.S. composer, pupil of Ernest Bloch. He has held many academic posts in the United States, including professorships at Princeton and Harvard. He has composed an opera, *Solomon and Balkis*, three symphonies, *Jazz Poem* for piano and orchestra and other orchestral works, choral works, chamber music, incidental music for the theatre, piano pieces and songs. After a study of music in U.S. universities he published *College Music* (1935).

Thomson, Virgil (born 1896), U.S. composer and music critic. He studied at Harvard University and was a pupil of Nadia Boulanger in Paris. He received several fellowships, was an instructor at Harvard (1920–5) and lived in Paris (1925–32), where he came under the influence of Eric Satie, Les Six, Cocteau, and Stravinsky. He became organist at King's Chapel in Boston and music critic for various U.S. publications and for the *New York Herald Tribune* (1940–54). He has written *The State of Music* (1939), *The Musical Scene* (1945) and *The Art of Judging Music* (1948), and has composed two operas – *Four Saints in Three Acts*, 1934, and *The Mother of us all*, 1947 (both to texts by Gertrude Stein) – two symphonies, a cello concerto, and other orchestral works, a ballet, choral works, chamber music, music for plays and for films, pieces for piano and for organ, and songs (many to French

words). He has also written a series of *Portraits*.

Thorne, John (died 1573), English composer. He was probably organist of York Minster from 1550 until his death and was mentioned as a 'practicioner' of music in Morley's *Plaine and Easie Introduction* (1597). His motet 'Stella coeli' was printed in Hawkins's *History of Music* (1875 edition, page 360).

thorough-bass, *see* FIGURED BASS

Three Choirs Festival, an annual festival, founded in 1724, given by the combined choirs of the cathedrals of Gloucester, Worcester and Hereford, and held in each cathedral in turn. It opens with a service on the first Sunday in September, and performances take place from the following Tuesday to Saturday. The scope of the programmes, which in the 18th century consisted largely of choral works by Handel, was enlarged during S. S. Wesley's tenure at Hereford (1832–42), and later in the century the festival played an important part in the English choral renaissance by giving performances of works by Parry and Elgar.

Three-Cornered Hat, The (Sp., *El Sombrero de Tres Picos*), ballet by Falla, based on Pedro de Alarcón's story with the same title (which also provided the story for Wolf's opera *Der Corregidor*). It was performed under the title *El Corregidar y la Molinera* (*The Magistrate and the Miller's Wife*) in Madrid. The revised version with the present title was first seen in London in 1919. The choreography was by Massine, and the settings and costumes were designed by Picasso.

Threepenny Opera, The (Ger., *Die Dreigroschenoper*), opera in a prologue and eight scenes by Kurt Weill. The text, by Bertolt Brecht, is a modern interpretation of *The Beggar's Opera*, based on a translation by Hauptmann, with lyrics (some of them drawn from Kipling and Villon) by Brecht himself. The first performance was in 1928 in Berlin, with Lotte Lenya in the leading role. The sweet-sour, jazz-tinged music includes a number of songs which have become familiar outside their context, the most popular being 'Mack the Knife'.

Threni, work for soloists, chorus and orchestra by Stravinsky, first performed in Venice in 1958. One of the milestones of his serial period, it is based on the ecclesiastical text of the *Lamentations* of Jeremiah, in its Latin version.

through-composed (Ger., *Durchkomponiert*), term applied to songs where the musical material is different from stanza to stanza. The word is therefore the opposite of 'strophic', where each stanza has the same music. Schubert's 'Der Erlkönig' is therefore through-composed, whereas 'Heidenröslein' is strophic. The term is also applied nowadays to operas where the music runs continuously, as in Wagner, instead of being divided into set numbers, as in Handel.

Thuille, Ludwig (1861–1907), German composer, pupil of Rheinberger at the Munich Conservatorium. He was a friend of Richard Strauss and of Alexander Ritter. His compositions include four operas (one unfinished), an overture and other orchestral works, works for female and for male choirs, chamber music, songs and piano pieces.

thump, early English word for plucking strings, especially on the lyra viol, now called *pizzicato*. It was sometimes used to describe a piece of music so performed.

thunder horn, an early and difficult to explain name for the 'folded' as opposed to the 'straight' TRUMPET.

thunder machine, device consisting of hard balls inside a large rotating drum. It is employed in theatres to imitate the noise of thunder, but also used by Strauss in his *'Alpine' Symphony*, and in a few works by other composers. Thunder effects are produced more often by shaking a large thin metal sheet. Such devices were part of theatre equipment until replaced by recorded thunder.

thunder stick, bull roarer, or **whizzer** (Fr., *planchette ronflante*; Ger., *Schwirrholz*), an instrument consisting simply of a flat piece of wood fastened to a piece of string. When swung rapidly around the head it produces a groaning or roaring sound varying in pitch with the speed it is swung at. It has long been in use among the North American Indians, the Australian aborigines, the peoples of central Africa, etc., but has made an appearance in a piece of chamber music, Henry Cowell's Ensemble for two violins, viola, two violoncellos, and two thunder sticks.

Thus spoke Zarathustra, *see* ALSO SPRACH ZARATHUSTRA

tibia (Lat., a pipe), (1) the Greek *aulos*.

(2) an organ stop, usually with some further qualifications, e.g. *tibia clausa*, a flue stop of large scale.

tie (Fr., *liaison*; Ger., *Bindung*; It., *legatura*), a curved line, also called a bind, joining two notes of the same pitch into a continuous sound.

Tiefland (*Lowland*), opera with a prologue and three acts by d'Albert. The libretto, by 'Rudolf Lothar' (i.e. Rudolf Spitzer), was founded on the play *Terra baixa* by the Catalan author, Angel Guimerá. First performed in Prague in 1903, the work is a melodrama of passion, betrayal and death – an example of German (as opposed to Italian) *verismo*.

tiento (Sp.; Port., *tento*), literally 'touch'. A term for *ricercar* used in the 16th century, e.g. by Cabezón in his *Obras de música* of 1578.

tierce de Picardie (Fr., literally 'Picardy third'), a major third used in the final chord of a composition in the minor mode, replacing the expected minor third. Before the 16th century a final chord almost invariably had no third; in the 16th century it became usual to have a major third in the last chord, whatever the mode. The earliest recorded use of the term is in J. J. Rousseau's Dictionary of 1764.

tierce flute, the 18th century name for a flute built a minor third higher than the normal form, also known as 'third flute'. Since it was treated as a transposing instrument it was therefore properly a flute in E flat; but since its natural scale was F major (the natural scale of the ordinary flute being D major) it was misleadingly described as 'flute in F'. The so-called 'flute in E flat' which was used in military bands until comparatively recent times was properly a flute in D flat, since its pitch was a semitone above that of the ordinary flute.

Tiersot, Jean Baptiste Elisée Julien (1857–1936), French historian and composer, pupil of Massenet and César Franck at the Paris Conservatoire. He wrote many books on musical history and folk-music, edited collections of folk songs, worked with Saint-Säens on the Pelletan edition of Gluck's works, and composed works for chorus and orchestra, a suite and other orchestral works, and incidental music for a play, Corneille's *Andromède*.

Tietjens, Therese (1831–77), German soprano. She made her début in Hamburg in 1849 singing the title role in Donizetti's *Lucrezia Borgia*. This was also, 28 years later, her final role, for she collapsed while singing it in London and never again appeared on stage. Between these two performances, however, she built up a substantial repertory, excelling in nineteenth century operas (especially Bellini's *Norma* and Weber's *Der Freischutz*) which she sang with great richness.

Tigrini, Orazio (c. 1535–91), Italian composer and theorist. He was *maestro di canto* at S. Maria della Pieve, Arezzo, around 1560, and was at the Cathedral there in 1562. From 1587 till his death he was *maestro di cappella* of the Cathedral. He composed a book of madrigals for four voices (1573) and two books for six voices (1582, 1591). He also wrote a four-volume work on counterpoint (*Compendio della musica*, 1588; facsimile edition, 1966), from which Morley quoted a number of examples, without acknowledgement, in his *Plaine and Easie Introduction* (1597; *see* the edition by R. A. Harman, 1952, page 241).

Tikhi Don, *see* QUIET FLOWS THE DON

Till Eulenspiegels lustige Streiche ('Tyll Owlglass's Merry Pranks'), symphonic poem by Richard Strauss, op 28 (1895), based on a 15th century German folk tale about the exploits of a lovable rogue. Usually known simply as *Till Eulenspiegel*, it was first performed in Cologne in 1895. An opera on the same subject has been written by Reznicek.

Tillyard, Henry Julius Wetenhall (1881–1968), scholar and authority in Byzantine music. He was one of the editors of the series *Monumenta Musicae Byzantinae*, and published a number of studies in Byzantine music and musical notation, including *Byzantine Music and Hymnography* (1923), *Handbook of the Middle Byzantine Musical Notation* (1936), *The Hymns of the Sticherarium for November* (1938), *The Hymns of the Octoechus* (two parts, 1940, 1949), and *Twenty Canons from the Trinity Hirmologium* (1952).

timbales, (1) (Fr.), TIMPANI.

(2) single-headed drums of Latin American origin. They are similar to BONGOS and CONGAS, but played with wooden sticks. Two such drums of different sizes are normally fastened to a single stand, but timbales are also made in threes. Since in France the word *timbales* means timpani, these instruments are named *timbales creoles*.

timbre (Fr.), quality of tone, also used in English as an alternative term for TONE-COLOUR. The German word is *Klangfarbe*.

timbrel, very rarely used English name for the TAMBOURINE.

time, the time of a piece of music is its division into beats per bar. Since about 1700 it has been indicated in musical notation by bar-lines and a TIME-SIGNATURE. Time in this sense may be duple (two beats in a bar), triple, quadruple, quintuple, and so on. Each of these is called 'simple' when the beat is a simple note-value, i.e. semibreve, minim, crotchet, etc. A 'compound' time is one in which the beat is a ternary note-value, which is always represented by a dotted note; thus six quavers in a bar is compound duple time, i.e. two dotted crotchets in a bar, and twelve quavers in a bar is compound quadruple time.

See also METRE, RHYTHM

time-signature, an indication at the start of a piece of music of the number and type of note-values in each bar. It consists of figures placed one above the other directly after the key signature – e.g. $\frac{3}{4}$ means three crotchets in the bar, $\frac{6}{8}$ means six quavers. The lower figure, therefore, gives the value of each beat in relation to the semibreve (or whole-note). The upper figure gives the number of beats in the bar.

Time-signatures are in effect signs of proportion based on the semibreve, which was the unit of time in the 17th century. Two signs which were a part of the time-signature system in use before 1600 and which were commonly combined with signs of proportion in the 17th century have survived in modern use: C as the equivalent of 4/4 time, and ₵ as the equivalent of 2/2 time, also called ALLA BREVE.

See also METRE

timpan, a string instrument used by the Irish in the early middle ages. It was played with the nails or a plectrum and was thus an early type of PSALTERY. In the later middle ages the strings were struck with a rod in the same way as those of the DULCIMER.

timpani (It.; Fr., *timbales*; Ger., *Pauken*), drums of Arabian origin, the most important of all orchestral percussion instruments. Although the term 'kettle-drums' is still in use, they are usually called by their Italian name in the English-speaking world; the word is plural, the singular *timpano* being very rare. The instructions *timpani coperti, timpani sordi* indicate muffled timpani.

The instrument consists of a basin-shaped shell of copper or brass across which is stretched a head, formerly of calfskin but nowadays a synthetic substitute. The shell is mounted on legs. The drums are played with two sticks, with heads most often of hard felt, although other materials are used when different effects are required, and the drums may be muffled or muted. The head's tension can be adjusted by screws, allowing accurate tuning and alterations of pitch within a limited compass.

The screw-tensioning device was added in the 17th century, and it was then that timpani found their way into the orchestra. Until Beethoven's time only two instruments were used, one tuned to the tonic and the other to the dominant of the piece being played. Their combined range was approximately an octave with the F below the bass stave as the lowest note. Beethoven contented himself with a pair of timpani, but he introduced other tunings and opened up new possibilities, sometimes bringing the instruments to the fore for solos, as in the fourth and ninth symphonies, the fifth piano concerto and the violin concerto.

BEETHOVEN, *Symphony no 4*

The next composer to increase the expressive range of timpani was Berlioz, who called for large numbers of them, with several performers. He often used them thus to produce chords, as in the *Fantastic Symphony*, where the sound of distant thunder is evoked. Although Sibelius used lesser numbers, he wrote for the timpani with great imagination, while Janáček treated them with such freedom that he sometimes caused tuning problems during performances. To overcome such problems, methods of tuning the drums mechanically by a foot pedal were introduced. On instruments with this device (pedal drums, pedal timpani, machine drums; Ger., *Pedalpauke*) the pitch can be changed instantly, so giving a virtually complete chromatic compass and allowing glissandi to be played. Bartók was one of the first to take full advantage of the new possibilities offered, in, for example, *Music for Strings, Percussion, and Celesta*. Today composers write with such instruments in mind, and demand a greater compass – orchestras now have a small drum extending the range up to middle C; still higher notes are occasionally written. The timpanist of today rarely has less than four instruments at his command.

H. W. TAYLOR: *The Art and Science of the Timpani* (1964)

Tinctoris, Joannes (c. 1435–1511), Flemish theorist and composer. He studied at the University of Louvain, where he became master in 1471. By 1476 he was a chaplain and singer in the chapel of Ferdinand I in Naples, and tutor to Ferdinand's daughter Beatrice of Aragon. He died as canon of Nivelles. In the dedication to Ferdinand of his *Liber de arte contra puncti* (1477; English translation by Albert Seay, *The Art of Counterpoint*, 1961) he remarked that no music written more than forty years before that time was thought worth hearing, and in the preface to the *Proportionale musices* (before 1476; English translation by Seay in *Journal of Music Theory*, i, 1957) observed that the 'fount and origin' of this new art was considered to be among the English, of whom Dunstable was the chief. In the same paragraph he pointed to the conservatism of the English composers of his own time, as compared to the French. He published (c. 1495) the first dictionary of musical terms, the *Terminorum musicae diffinitorium* (facsimile edition, 1966; modern edition with English translation by Carl Parrish, 1963) and *De inventione et usu musicae* about 1484. Eleven of his twelve treatises are printed in Coussemaker, *Scriptores*, iv, and English translations of the preface of the *Proportionale musices* and the dedication of the *Liber de arte contrapuncti* are in O. Strunk, *Source Readings in Music History* (1950). His compositions include four Masses, two motets, Lamentations and seven *chansons*. A complete edition was begun in 1960 by F. Feldmann.

Tin Pan Alley, U.S. slang expression (now obsolete) for the pop music industry. The term originated in the early years of this century, when popular song publishing was based largely in one street, West 28th Street, in New York City.

Tintagel, symphonic poem by Bax, written in 1917, and intended, according to the composer, to 'evoke a tone-picture of the castle-crowned cliff of Tintagel' on the Cornish coast.

tin whistle, sometimes known as a penny whistle, this instrument with six finger holes is made of metal and modelled on the RECORDER. Its shrill sound is a feature of Irish folk music.

tiorba (It.), theorbo.

Sir Michael Tippett

Tippett, Michael Kemp (born 1905), English composer. He studied at the Royal College of Music under Wood and Morris and subsequently became director of music at Morley College. Like Britten's, his music reveals a deep compassion for mankind, especially in works such as his oratorio, *A Child of Our Time* (1941), and the third symphony. Otherwise his music is very different from Britten's, being less fluent, more contrapuntal and 'chiselled'. His style has been influenced by the cross-rhythms of English 16th century composers, by the American Blues and also in his mature years by Beethoven – his third symphony and third piano sonata have distinct and conscious affinities with the works of Beethoven's last period. His output, though not enormous, is of almost consistently high quality. It includes four operas – *The Midsummer Marriage* (1955), *King Priam* (1962), *The Knot Garden* (1970), *The Ice Break* (1977) – all performed at Covent Garden; a cantata, *The Vision of St. Augustine* (1966); a *Concerto for Orchestra* (1963), piano concerto, and other orchestral works; also song cycles and instrumental music. The composer was knighted in 1966.

I. KEMP (ed.): *Michael Tippett* (1965)

tirade (Fr.), **tirata** (It.), a baroque ornamental scale passage linking two notes of a melody, or two chords. A late example of this ornament appears in bar four of the first movement of Beethoven's fourth piano concerto:—

tirasse (Fr.), a manual to pedal coupler on the organ. *See* COUPLER (3)

tiré (Fr.), the downward stroke of the BOW in string instruments.

Titelouze, Jean (1563–1633), French organist and composer. He lived in Rouen where he was organist at the Cathedral. He visited Paris to inaugurate the organ at the Abbey of Saint Denis (1604) and at Notre Dame (1610). He composed organ hymns, Magnificats and a Mass *In ecclesia*. His organ works have been reprinted in *Archives des maîtres de l'orgue* (edited by Guilmant and Pirro, i).

toccata (It., from *toccare*, to touch, play), (1) a piece for a keyboard instrument. Towards the end of the 16th century two types of toccata were written by Italian composers. The first, practised by A. Gabrieli, G. Gabrieli and L. Luzzaschi, and later by Frescobaldi, was in free style with a great deal of elaborate passage-work, as in the opening of the first toccata in Frescobaldi's second book of toccatas, canzonas, etc., of 1627:

The second, practised by Merulo, and later by Frescobaldi (e.g. the ninth toccata in his first book, 1637) and Michelangelo Rossi, used sections in this style alternating with sections in imitative style. This type, and the shorter toccatas to be played before a *ricercar* (*avanti il Ricercare*) in Frescobaldi's *Fiori musicali* (1635), may be considered two of the prototypes of the later toccata (or prelude) and fugue. The *Fiori musicali* also contain short toccatas in a quieter style to be played before Mass (*avanti la messa*) or at the Elevation.

Sweelinck and the German organists (e.g. Scheidt) adopted both of the Italian types, which were later cultivated by Froberger, Pachelbel and Buxtehude. One of Pachelbel's toccatas, a short piece in free style, is followed by a fugue; others were of a kind also written by Italian composers of his time (e.g. Pasquini) in which the free style became much less diffuse, and each piece tended to pursue one particular form of figuration. Bach's toccatas for harpsichord are of the alternating type, which he divides into three or more distinct sections. Of the organ toccatas, each of which precedes a fugue, that in F major is unique in combining the traditional characteristics of the genre with the utmost consistency of idea and clarity of design. Toccatas by later composers, for example Schumann, Widor, Ravel (in *le Tombeau de Couperin*), Prokofiev, are usually pieces in a fast tempo with a continuous rhythm based on one kind of figuration.

M. BRADSHAW: *The Origin of the Toccata* (1972)

(2) the word was also applied c. 1600 to a short piece with the character of a fanfare, for brass with or without other instruments (the English 'tucket'). In Italy this kind of toccata was usually played three times before a stage work, for example the toccata at the beginning of Monteverdi's *Orfeo*.

Toch, Ernst (1887–1964), Austrian born composer who later settled in the United States, becoming professor of composition at the University of Southern California in 1940. He composed *The Princess and the Pea* and three other operas, orchestral and other chamber works and, during his Hollywood years, a variety of film and radio music. His book, *The Shaping Forces in Music*, was published in 1948.

Tod und das Mädchen, Der, *see* DEATH AND THE MAIDEN

Tod und Verklärung, *see* DEATH AND TRANSFIGURATION

Toeschi, Carlo Giuseppe (1724–88), Italian born composer and violinist. A pupil of Johann Stamitz, he became violinist (1752) and leader (1759) of the MANNHEIM Court Orchestra and went with the court to Munich, where he was appointed music director (1780). He composed 63 symphonies, ballet music, chamber music, etc.

Togni, Camillo (born 1922), Italian composer and pianist, pupil of Casella. He has written choral music (including settings of T. S. Eliot), chamber music and piano works.

Tolomeo, Rè d'Egitto (*Ptolemy, King of Egypt*), opera in three acts by Handel, with a libretto by Nicola Francesco Haym, first performed in London in 1728.

Tolstoy, Count Theophil Matveivich (1809–81), Russian composer and critic. He studied in St. Petersburg, Naples and Moscow and began work as a music critic (under the *nom de plume* Rostislav) in 1850. His works include an opera and about 200 songs.

Tomašek, Václav Jan (Tomaschek, Wenzel Johann), (1774–1850), Bohemian composer and pianist, who visited Vienna and met Beethoven in 1814. His works include three operas, three Masses, two Requiems, cantatas, hymns, vocal scenes from works by Goethe and Schiller, a symphony, a piano concerto, chamber music, sonatas and other piano pieces, and many songs.

Tomasi, Henri (1901–71), French composer and conductor of Corsican parentage. His works include operas (*Sampiero Corso* and *The Silence of the Sea*), ballets, orchestral music and radio music.

Tomasini, Luigi (1741–1808), Italian born violinist and composer. He joined Prince Esterhazy's orchestra at Eisenstadt (1757), was appointed leader by Haydn (1761) and later became chamber music director. He moved with the court to Esterház in 1766. Haydn

wrote for him several violin concertos, string quartets, duets for two violins and 24 *Divertimenti* for baryton, violin and cello. His son, Luigi, was also a violinist in the Esterhazy orchestra.

tombeau (Fr.), 'tomb, tombstone.' A title used by French composers in the 17th century (e.g. Gaultier, L. Couperin, d'Anglebert) for a lament on the death of a notable person. Gaultier's *Tombeau* for lute for the lutenist de Lenclos, which is followed by a *Consolation aux amis du Sr. Lenclos*, is printed in Schering's *Geschichte der Musik in Beispielen*, no 215. The idea was revived by Ravel in his *Tombeau de Couperin*.

See also LAMENT

Tombelle, Fernand de la, *see* LA TOMBELLE

Tomkins, Thomas (1572–1656), English composer and organist. He studied under Byrd, and was organist of Worcester Cathedral from 1596 till 1646. He was also one of the organists at the Chapel Royal from 1621. He composed services (printed in *Tudor Church Music*, vii), 93 anthems, *Songs of 3, 4, 5 and 6 parts* (1622; modern edition in *English Madrigal School*, xviii), keyboard music (edited by S. D. Tuttle in *Musica Britannica*, v), and consort music including two three-part *In Nomines* and four six-part fantasias. He also wrote coronation music for Charles I (1625). His church music was published posthumously in *Musica Deo Sacra* (1668) and has been reprinted in a modern edition by Bernard Rose (three volumes, 1965–73). He was a master equally of the polyphonic style (his third service is a fine example of the more elaborate type of setting), of the verse anthem, and of the string fantasia, in which he wrote some effective passages of expressive chromaticism. His brother John (c. 1586–1638), organist of King's College, Cambridge (1606) and St. Paul's Cathedral (1619), composed some anthems and a set of keyboard variations on 'John come kiss me now'. His brother Robert, a musician in the household of Charles I (c. 1633–c. 1641), composed anthems.

I. ATKINS: *The early Occupants of the Office of Organist . . . of the Cathedral . . . Worcester* (1918)

D. STEVENS: *Thomas Tomkins* (1957)

Tommasini, Vincenzo (1878–1950), Italian composer. He studied at Santa Cecilia in Rome and under Bruch in Germany. He composed two operas, a ballet (on music by Domenico Scarlatti), orchestral suites and symphonic poems, choral settings of poems by Dante and others, chamber music, piano pieces and songs. One of his ambitions as a composer was to help to detach Italian music from its operatic connections.

tomtom, tom-tom, a snareless drum, usually with two heads but occasionally with only one. Tom-toms are rarely found singly, sets of seven being quite common. They range in diameter from about 30 to 54 centimetres and in depth from 20 to 50 centimetres. The largest sizes are supported on legs and the smaller ones are often clamped in pairs onto a special frame. They are used both as pitchless and tuned instruments, and in the latter case they are sometimes employed as an upward extension of the timpani. Stravinsky's *Agon* used them for this purpose. They have a clear tone which varies according to the type of stick used; for quiet passages they are often played by the tips of the fingers. The two heads can be adjusted separately and when no specific note is required they are deliberately tuned differently. On the other hand when a clear pitch is needed the lower of the two heads is generally removed.

ton (Fr.), (1) key, mode; (2) pitch; (3) *see* TONE (1); (4) *demi-ton*, semitone; (5) *ton de rechange*, crook (of a brass instrument).

Ton (Ger.), (1) sound, music: *Tondichter*, literally 'poet in sound', i.e. composer; (2) note; (3) *Ganzton*, *see* TONE (1); (4) *Halbton*, semitone; (5) quality of sound: *Tonfarbe*, tone colour; (6) *Kirchenton*, church mode.

tonada (Sp.), tune set to poem or dance, usually with contrasts between slow and fast tempi.

tonadilla (Sp.), the diminutive of TONADA. The word refers to a type of scenic cantata, often with vocal, choral and instrumental movements, used in Spanish stage entertainment. Originally, tonadillas were light intermezzi, presented between the acts of a play or serious opera. A famous exponent of the form was Luís Misón, a Spanish composer and flautist, who, from the 1750s onwards, wrote about 100 works in the form. Other tonadilla composers of the period were Pablo Esteve and Blas Laserna.

tonal answer, *see* FUGUE

tonality, *see* KEY, POLYTONALITY

Tonart (Ger.), key, mode.

tonary, a medieval catalogue of the chants performed in conjunction with psalm verses, classified by mode. Its purpose was to facilitate the selection of the correct TONE and termination for the relevant psalm recitation. An important early example is the tonary of Regino of Prüm (c. 900; printed in Coussemaker, *Scriptores*, ii, page 1).

> M. HUGLO: *Les Tonaires* (1971)

Tondichtung (Ger.), tone-poem.

> *See* SYMPHONIC POEM

tone, (1) the interval of a major second, e.g. between C and D, or E flat and F, sometimes known as a whole tone. It may be subdivided into two semi-tones. Some 20th century composers have divided it still further into quarter-tones and sixths of a tone, which can be played accurately on string instruments and the trombone but not on other instruments as normally constructed. On keyboard instruments the interval of a tone is always the same. If the major scale, however, is based on the notes of the HARMONIC SERIES there are slight differences according to the position of the notes in the scale. Thus in the scale of C major the ratio between C and D is 8:9, between D and E 9:10. The first of these intervals (C to D) is called in acoustics a major tone, the second (D to E) a minor tone. It is unfortunate that the terminology is ambiguous, 'major' and 'minor' being also used in quite another sense to distinguish intervals differing by a semitone, e.g. major third (three semitones), as well as the major and minor scales;

> *See* KEY, MAJOR, MINOR, SCALE, SECOND

(2) in the United States a musical note. In Britain used in this sense only in acoustics, e.g. a pure tone (a note without upper partials or overtones), resultant tone (a note produced by the combination of the frequencies of two other notes);

> *See* ACOUSTICS

(3) quality of sound, e.g. good tone, harsh tone, brittle tone;

(4) in plainsong a melodic formula used for the

recitation of the psalms, canticles and other parts of the liturgy (Lat., *tonus*). There are eight ordinary psalm-tones, corresponding to the eight MODES, and most of them have a number of alternative endings, e.g. in the SARUM RITE:

See PSALMODY, TONUS PEREGRINUS

(5) in the 17th century also used in the sense of 'key',

> 'If wee say a lesser Third consists of a Tone, and a Semi-tone; here by a Tone is ment a perfect Second, or as they name it a whole note: But if wee aske in what Tone is this or that song made, then by Tone we intend the key which guides and ends the whole song.'

> (Campion, *A New Way of making fowre parts in Counter-point*, c. 1618, printed in *Campion's Works*, edited by P. Vivian, page 192).

tone cluster, U.S. expression for note cluster.

tone-colour (Fr., *timbre*; Ger., *Klangfarbe*), the characteristic quality of tone of an instrument or voice. The effective combination of tone-colours is a chief part of the art of ORCHESTRATION. The investigation of the physical basis of tone-colour is a part of ACOUSTICS. The tone-colour of a note depends on the number, selection, and relative strengths of the overtones of which it is composed. In the flute and in the flue pipes of the organ the lower harmonics are relatively strong; the quality of reed instruments is determined by the relative strength of certain of the higher harmonics. Further, the tone quality of any individual instrument, e.g. a particular violin, depends on the extent to which the vibrations of the body of the instrument are in resonance with the overtones produced by the strings. The range in which these vibrations occur, which is a constant factor in each instrument, is called the 'formant' of the tone quality of the instrument.

tone poem, *see* SYMPHONIC POEM

tone-row, U.S. expression for note-row.

tongue, to tongue a note on wind instruments is to give impetus to its attack. Normally the first note in any phrase will be tongued, but whether those that follow will be similarly treated depends on the type of phrasing required. The degree of tonguing can vary from a sharp attack on each note in *staccato* passages to a barely perceptible accent.

> *See also* DOUBLE TONGUING, TRIPLE TONGUING, and FLUTTER TONGUING.

tonic, the first note of a scale (e.g. C in the case of C major and C minor) which is its key-note and the centre of its tonality, and the key-note of compositions written in that tonality.

tonic sol-fa, a system of ear-training and sight-singing in which the notes are sung to syllables and the ear is trained to recognise and reproduce, through the syllables, the intervals between the notes of the scale, and between each note and the tonic. In the British system, established and taught by John Curwen in the 1840s, the tonic of a major scale is always *doh*, whatever the key ('movable *doh*'), whereas in the French *solfege* (SOLFEGGIO) the syllables are fixed ('fixed *doh*'), C being always *ut*. The tonic of a 'natural' minor scale is *lah*, so that the same relation of intervals to syllables holds as in a major scale, and *ba* is used for the sixth degree of the ascending harmonic minor scale. The vowel *e* is used for sharps, and the vowel *a* for flats: e.g. in C major – A minor:

In tonic sol-fa notation the syllables are represented by their initial letters. The idea of tonic sol-fa and its syllables are derived from SOLMIZATION. Time values are represented by bar-lines and dots. The system was invented as an aid to schoolchildren and adult amateurs in singing choral music.

Tonkunst (Ger.), literally, 'art of sound', i.e. music.

Tonleiter (Ger.), scale.

tono or **tuono** (It.), key, mode, tone. The word can also mean thunder.

Tonreihe (Ger.), note-row, tone-row.

Tonstück (Ger.), a piece of music.

tonus peregrinus (Lat.), 'the strange (or alien) tone'. An additional psalm-tone to the eight regular tones (*see* PSALMODY), which is irregular in that the second half has a different dominant (reciting note) from the first half. In its Sarum form it is:

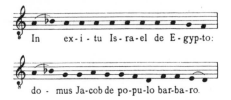

It is sung to Psalm 114 (113 in the Vulgate Bible), 'In exitu Israel', and has been adapted as an Anglican chant.

torch song, a sentimental ditty of unrequited love, usually sung by a woman, and with jazz or pop-music associations. The idea is that the singer is 'carrying a torch' for the loved one.

tordion (Fr.), a lively French dance, current in the 15th and early 16th centuries, used to form a contrast with the stately BASSE DANSE.

Torelli, Gasparo (died after 1613), Italian composer who taught at Borgo San Sepolcro, Lucca. He composed *I fidi amanti*, a pastoral fable in madrigal style for four voices (1600; reprinted in Torchi's *L'arte musicale in Italia*, iv), a book of madrigals for five voices (1598), and four books of *canzonette* mainly for three voices (1593–1608).

Tortelier, Paul (born 1914), French cellist, famous as soloist and in chamber music. His repertory ranges from Bach's solo suites to twentieth-century works such as Strauss's *Don Quixote* (with which he made his British début in 1947). He is also a composer, whose output includes a concerto for two cellos. Like Yehudi Menuhin, he is one of a family of gifted practising musicians.

Tosca, opera in three acts by Puccini, with a libretto by Giuseppe Giacosa and Luigi Illica (based on a play by Sardou). The first performance was in Rome in 1900. Angelotti (an escaped prisoner) hides in a church where Mario Cavaradossi (an artist) is painting. Mario helps him to escape. When Scarpia (the chief of police) arrives on the scene he is suspicious and has Cavaradossi arrested and sent to the torture chamber. Scarpia, who has become attracted by Tosca (Cavaradossi's mistress and a famous singer), promises her her lover's liberty in return for her favours. She finally grants pretended consent to his wishes, but as soon as he has written the orders for a mock execution of Cavaradossi she stabs him with a knife. At dawn she explains to Cavaradossi what has happened and tells him of the arrangements she has made for his escape after the mock execution. When the firing is over she hurries to his body and finds to her horror that she has been tricked and that he is dead. She realises her murder of Scarpia has been discovered. As a police agent attempts to arrest her she climbs the prison walls and leaps to her death.

Toscanini, Arturo (1867–1957), Italian conductor, one of the greatest in musical history. He began by studying the cello at the Parma Conservatorio and was appointed conductor of opera in Rio de Janeiro (1886). Later he became conductor of La Scala in Milan (1898–1903 and 1906–8) and of the Metropolitan Opera in New York (1908–15). He conducted the New York Philharmonic Orchestra (which was joined with the New York Symphony Orchestra in 1928) from 1926–36, at festivals in Bayreuth (1930 and 31) and at Salzburg (1933 and 1935–37), and was appointed conductor of the National Broadcasting Company Symphony Orchestra in New York in 1937. He lived during the latter part of his life in the United States, having refused to perform under German or Italian Fascism. Among his first performances was that of Puccini's *Turandot* in 1926. He was as renowned in German music as in Italian, his interpretations being characterized by their exceptional clarity and vigour. He appeared on two historic occasions in London, in 1938 and 1951. *See* illustration on p. 554.

Tosti, Francesco Paolo (1846–1916), Italian composer and singing master. He studied in Naples under Mercadante, and in 1880 settled in London as singing master to the royal family. His compositions consisted mostly of songs, of which his 'Farewell' is the most famous. He was knighted in 1908.

Tost Quartets, collective name for twelve string quartets by Haydn, composed between 1789 and 1790 and dedicated to a violinist called Johann Tost. The works are op 54, nos 1–3, op 55, nos 1–3, and op 64, nos 1–6.

tosto (It.), (1) quick, rapid. *Piu tosto*, faster;
    (2) quickly, soon. *Piu tosto* or *piuttosto*, sooner, rather.

Totenmesse (Ger.), Requiem Mass.

Arturo Toscanini, still active till shortly before his death at the age of 90.

Totentanz (Ger.), 'dance of death'. The title of a work by Liszt for piano and orchestra.

See also DANSE MACABRE.

Tote Stadt, Die, (*The Dead Town*), opera in three acts by Korngold, with a libretto by Paul Schott (from Georges Rodenbach's play *Bruges-la-Morte*). It was first performed, simultaneously, in Hamburg and Cologne in 1920.

touche (Fr.), (1) key of a keyboard instrument;

(2) fret on a lute, viol, guitar and other similar instruments;

(3) finger board of a stringed instrument. (It., *tasto*; Ger., *Griffbrett*). The direction *sur la touche*, meaning 'on the finger board', is an instruction to play above it, thereby producing a rather veiled tone.

Tournemire, Charles Arnould (1870–1939), French composer and organist, pupil of d'Indy. He was organist of Sainte-Clotilde (1898) and teacher of chamber music at the Conservatoire. His output included two operas, eight symphonies, choral works, chamber music, organ works, piano pieces and songs. In his organ music he was the leader of the movement towards a more liturgical use of the organ, and composed in his *L'Orgue mystique* a set of pieces for the Office for 51 Sundays of the church year (*Offices de l'annee liturgique*), based on their plainsong themes.

Tourte, François (1747–1835), French bowmaker. He studied his craft under his father, went into business with his elder brother, Xavier, and later by himself. He made many improvements in the violin bow, and was responsible for its modern form.

Tourte bow, invented by Francois Tourte (1747–1835), the normal type of bow used by string players. Unlike the earlier type the stick curves inwards towards the hair instead of outwards.

See BOW

Tovey, Donald Francis (1875–1940), English musical historian, pianist, composer and conductor. As a schoolboy, he was able to play Bach's Goldberg Variations from memory. He studied under Parratt and Parry and at Balliol College, Oxford (1894–8). After playing in London, Berlin and Vienna, and organising chamber music concerts in London, he became Reid professor of music at Edinburgh University in 1914. He founded the Reid Orchestral concerts in 1917 and was knighted in 1935. He composed an opera (*The Bride of Dionysus*), a symphony, a piano concerto, a cello concerto, nine string quartets and other chamber music, anthems, piano pieces and songs, but today he is renowned mainly for his essays, analyses and programme-notes, of exceptional penetration and wit. He wrote articles on music for the *Encyclopedia Britannica* (published in one volume, 1944), *A Companion to Bach's Art of Fugue* (1931), *A Companion to Beethoven's Pianoforte Sonatas* (1931), *Musical Form and Matter* (1934), *Essays in Musical Analysis* (seven volumes, 1935–44), *The Main Stream of Music* (1938), *Beethoven* (1944), *Essays and Lectures on Music* (edited by H. Foss, 1949), *Normality and Freedom in Music* (1936), *The Integrity of Music* (1941) and *Musical Textures* (1941). In addition, he composed a conjectural completion of the final unfinished fugue in Bach's *The Art of Fugue*.

M. GRIERSON: *Donald Francis Tovey* (1952)

toye, a term found occasionally in English instrumental music of the 16th and 17th centuries for a piece of a simple, playful character in dance rhythm.

Toye, Geoffrey (1889–1942), English conductor and composer. He conducted the Beecham Opera Company, the Royal Philharmonic Society Concerts (1918–19) and the D'Oyly Carte Opera. He was manager of the opera at Sadler's Wells, 1931–4 and managing director to the Royal Opera, Covent Garden, 1934–6. His works include an opera, a radio opera, two ballets, a masque (with his brother), a symphony and songs.

John Francis Toye (1883–1964), was an English music critic and author, brother of Geoffrey. He wrote *The Well-Tempered Musician* (1925), *Verdi* (1931), *Rossini* (1934), and a novel *Diana and the Two Symphonies* (1913).

Toy Symphony, an instrumental work with parts for toy instruments (cuckoo, rattle, etc.) added to the ordinary score. The earliest example, in three movements, is often attributed to Haydn, though the music exists also as part of a *divertimento* attributed to Leopold Mozart (the father of Wolfgang Amadeus Mozart). Among later examples the best-known is that by Andreas Romberg.

Trabaci, Giovanni Maria (c. 1575–1647), Neapolitan composer, a pupil of Jean de Macque. He was organist at the Royal Chapel in Naples (1603) and later choirmaster there. He composed motets for five to eight voices (1602), two books of madrigals for five voices (1606, 1611), Masses, psalms and two books of *Ricercate* and other organ pieces (1603, 1615). Twelve five-part motets, four six-part motets, four eight-part motets, and two Masses for double choir have been published in *Istituzioni e monumenti dell'arte musicale italiana*, v, edited by Guido Pannain (1934), and a *ricercar*, two *gagliarde*, two *partite*, a toccata, and a piece called *Consonanze stravaganti*, all from the *Ricercate, Canzone franzese, Caprice . . .* of 1603 in Torchi's *L'arte musicale in Italia*, iii.

tracker, a flat strip of wood used as part of the mechanism which connected the key of an organ with the lid ('pallet') which admitted wind to a pipe. Tracker action has now been universally replaced by some form of electric action.

tract, a part of the Proper of the Mass, which is sung in penitential seasons at the point where the Alleluia is sung at other times, that is after the Gradual. The tracts are among the oldest part of plainsong, and are all either in the second or eighth mode. Their words are taken from the psalms, and in one case ('Qui habitabit' for the first Sunday in Lent) consist of a complete psalm. Their music may preserve the form in which psalmody was sung until the 4th and 5th centuries.

> E. WELLESZ: *Eastern Elements in Western Chant* (1947), pages 127–140

Traetta, Tommaso Michele Francesco Saverio (1727–79), Italian composer and teacher. He was *Maestro di cappella* at the ducal court of the Infante Felipe of Spain in Parma, 1758; director of the Conservatorio dell'Ospedaletto in Venice, 1765; and musical director at the court of Catherine II of Russia, 1768–74. His prolific output of music included 42 operas, a *divertimento* for four orchestras, an oratorio for female choir, motets, a *Stabat Mater* for four voices and instruments, arias and duets.

tragédie lyrique (Fr.), a 17th century term for opera, especially those of Lully (also called *tragédie en musique*), all of which were settings of tragedies by Quinault and Corneille.

Tragic Overture, Brahms's *Tragische Ouvertüre*, op 81 (1880), a companion work to his *Academic Festival Overture*, op 80. It was not intended as the overture to any particular tragedy.

'Tragic' Symphony, Schubert's symphony no 4 in C minor, composed in 1816 and entitled *Tragische Symphonie* by the composer.

Tragoedia, work for wind quintet, string quartet and harp by Harrison Birtwistle, in which the composer seeks to capture the spirit of Greek tragedy without implying any specific events or plot. Written in 1965, it was intended to bridge the gap between absolute music and theatre music. Some of the material reappeared later in Birtwistle's opera *Punch and Judy*.

tranquillo (It.), calm.

Trans, orchestral work by Stockhausen, composed in 1971. It is one of several important works by him which reflect his Oriental experiences.

transcription, *see* ARRANGEMENT

Transfigured Night, *see* VERKLÄRTE NACHT

Transfiguration de Notre Seigneur Jésus Christ, La, large-scale work for chorus, orchestra, vocal and instrumental soloists by Messiaen, first performed in Lisbon in 1969. The work is a meditation on different aspects of the mystery of Christ's transfiguration, evoked by Biblical and other texts, sung in Latin. It consists of two large movements, each of which subdivides into a group of seven pieces and a closing chorale.

transition, (1) an incidental change of key in the course of a composition;

(2) a linking passage which involves (usually) a change of key.

transposing keyboards, devices whereby keyboard MANUALS could be moved in order to produce a higher or lower pitch. The player therefore had no need to transpose when music was required in the key other than the written one. Such keyboards were fitted to organs during the 16th century. The device was later applied to the piano.

transposing instruments, instruments which sound different notes than those written for them. One reason for this is to avoid large numbers of LEGER LINES. Consequently the music is written in a higher or lower key or octave than the notes produced. Music for the CELESTA is written in a lower octave, and that for the DOUBLE BASS and the GUITAR in a higher octave, while the GLOCKENSPIEL is usually notated two octaves below the required pitch. In the case of most transposing woodwind or brass instruments the written notes represent the fingering as opposed to the pitch, and this greatly eases the player's problems when switching from one instrument to another of a higher or lower pitch. Were this not the case a clarinetist, for instance, would have to learn totally different sets of fingerings for the instruments E flat, D, B flat and A, as well as for the basset-horn in F. As it is when he fingers C these notes result. Similarly the fingering on the *oboe d'amore* (in A) and *cor anglais* (in F) remains the same as on the oboe. Other instruments similarly affected include the piccolo and double bassoon (transposing an octave up and down respectively), alto flutes, saxophones, modern trumpets and cornets. With the horn, like the old type of trumpet in F, the situation is somewhat different, because before the invention of valves, the player was limited to the notes of the HARMONIC SERIES, and, in the case of the horn only those he could produce by hand stopping (*see* HORN). He could, however, alter the overall pitch of his instrument by using various crooks or pieces of tubing of different lengths. The harmonic series notated was always the one based on C and the crook used decided its actual pitch. With the invention of valves, giving the instrument a full chromatic compass, the standard horn and trumpet became those in F, although for a long time composers continued to treat them as if the crook method was still in use; this meant that players had to read one note, play another, and produce a third. Brass instruments with a fundamental note other than C are not necessarily transposing instruments. Trombones in E flat, B flat, G and F, have always been non-transposing, because they always have been fully chromatic. The bass tuba is similarly treated although the tenor is not. In brass bands, however, as opposed to symphony orchestras, all the instruments apart from the bass trombone, which is the only one to make use of the bass clef, are written for as transposing instruments. This naturally makes the scores very difficult to read, and since the same problem arises in symphonic works, particularly complex modern ones, many composers since Prokofiev write the sounds they require, these being transposed where necessary when the parts are written out.

transposition, the performance or writing down of music at another pitch, and therefore in a different key, from that in which it was originally written. Songs with piano are frequently published in three keys, high, medium, and low; a good accompanist should, however, be able to transpose an accompaniment when necessary. This ability is needed also in reading the parts for TRANSPOSING INSTRUMENTS (such as clarinet, English horn, French horn and trumpet) from an orchestral score. A. Schlick (1511) described an organ with movable manuals to effect transposition, and pianos with moveable keyboards were made during the 19th century. Some of the harpsichords made by the Ruckers family between 1600 and 1650 had two manuals which differed in pitch by a fourth.

transverse flute, the name at one time given to the modern flute to distinguish it from a recorder when the recorder was still in common use in chamber ensembles and small orchestras.

Trapassi, Pietro, *see* METASTASIO

Trapp, Max (1887–1971), German composer and pianist, pupil of Dohnanyi. He became professor at the Berlin Conservatorium in 1951. His output includes six symphonies and many other orchestral works, chamber music and songs.

traps, (1) the kit used by drummers in dance and jazz bands;

(2) in dance or theatre orchestras, devices used for special effects, e.g. whistles, whip crack, cowbell, etc..

Trauermarsch (Ger.), funeral march.

Trauer-Ode (Ger., *Funeral Ode*), Cantata no 198 by Bach (1727), with a text by Johann Christoph Gottsched. It was performed in Leipzig at the memorial ceremony of Christiane Eberhardine, Queen-Electress of Poland-Saxony, 1727.

Trauer-Sinfonie (Ger., *Mourning Symphony*), nickname for Haydn's Symphony no 44 in E minor (c. 1771–2). It is said that Haydn wanted the slow movement to be performed at his own funeral service.

Trauerwalzer (Ger., *Mourning Waltz*), the title given by the publisher to a piano composition by Schubert, op 9, no 2 (1816; published 1821). It was also known as *Le Désir* and was often attributed to Beethoven, since a corrupt version of it was published under his name.

Träumerei (Ger.), 'dreaming'. The title of a piano piece by Schumann, the most famous of his *Scenes of Childhood* (1838).

träumerisch (Ger.), dreamy.

traurig (Ger.), sad.

Trautonium, an electronic instrument similar to the SOLOVOX, invented in Germany in 1930. It could be attached to a piano, enabling the player to use one hand for each instrument, but it is limited to producing one note at a time.

Travers, John (c. 1703–58), English organist and composer, chorister at St. George's Chapel, Windsor. He studied under Greene and Pepusch, and became organist of St. Paul's, Covent Garden, London, c. 1725; later of Fulham Church; Chapel Royal 1737. He composed *The Whole Book of Psalms* for one to five voices with continuo for harpsichord (1750), anthems, services, a Te Deum, canzonets for two and three voices and voluntaries for organ and harpsichord.

traversa (It.), 18th century name for *flauto traverso*, the transverse flute (now known simply as *flauto*, flute).

Traviata, La (It., The Woman who was Led Astray), opera in three acts by Verdi, with a libretto by Francesco Maria Piave (after *La Dame aux camelias* by Alexandre Dumas the younger). The first performance was in Venice in 1853. Alfredo Germont, having fallen in love with the courtesan Violetta, succeeds in persuading her to give up her life of pleasure and retire with him to the country. His father, however, tells Violetta that her life with his son is a barrier to the marriage of Alfredo's sister and persuades her to leave him. Alfredo, believing that she has deliberately returned to her old life, follows her to Paris and publicly insults her at a ball. By the time he learns the truth it is too late: Violetta has been stricken by consumption and dies in his arms. The work was a failure at its first performance, but soon established itself as one of the best-loved works in the repertory. Patti, Melba, Tetrazzini, Galli-Curci and, more recently, Maria Callas have been famous exponents of the title-role.

traynour (Fr.), a term referred to by the Italian 14th century theorist Philippus de Caserta (*Tractatus de diversis figuris*, printed in Coussemaker's *Scriptores*, iii) as applied to the combination of different rhythmic groups, for example, four notes against three, nine against two. He remarks that such combinations are commonly called *trayn* or *traynour* by the French.

treble, (1) the highest voice in a choir, especially when sung by boys; otherwise 'soprano' is more often used. The term was first used in the 15th century, as the equivalent of the Latin *triplex*, for the third voice above the tenor (counting the tenor itself as the first voice, as with the *triplum* of the 13th century motet), the second voice being the 'meane';

(2) the G clef on the second line:

is commonly called the treble clef. The C clef on the first line:

is known as the soprano clef.

treble flute, an instrument approximately midway in pitch between the ordinary flute and the piccolo. Long regarded as obsolete, it is now being manufactured again.

> *See* FLUTE

treble recorder, treble trombone, *see* RECORDER TROMBONE etc.

tre corde (It.), 'three strings', a term used in piano music to indicate the release of the left-hand pedal. On the grand piano this normally has the effect of allowing the hammers to hit all the strings assigned to each note, instead of only one or two (*una corda*).

> *See* CORDA

La Traviata: the first London performance at Her Majesty's in 1856 with Piccolomini in the title role.

Tregian, Francis (c. 1574–1619), son of a Roman Catholic exile of the same name who had been deprived of his properties in Cornwall and died in Lisbon in 1608. The younger Tregian was educated at Eu and entered Douai College in 1586. From 1592 to 1594 he was chamberlain to Cardinal Allen in Rome. He returned to England to claim his father's lands, and was convicted as a recusant in 1608 or 1609 and committed to prison. While there he copied the manuscript of virginal music known as the Fitzwilliam Virginal Book, and two manuscripts (now British Library, Egerton 3665, and New York Public Library, Drexel 4302) which together contain over 2000 vocal and instrumental works in score, mainly by English and Italian composers.

> E. COLE: 'In Search of Tregian', in *Music and Letters*, xxxiii (1952)
>
> B. SCHOFIELD & THURSTON DART: 'Tregian's Anthology', in *Music and Letters*, xxxii (1951)

tremblement (Fr.), trill.

tremolo, rapid reiteration of a single note or alternation of two or more. On stringed instruments played with a bow the first of these effects is achieved by using a very fast succession of short up and down bowings, and on a harp by alternately plucking two adjacent strings tuned to the same note. The mandolin with its strings tuned in pairs is particularly suited to the tremolo. There are two methods of playing the second type of tremolo on bowed stringed instruments. If the interval between the notes is not too large, what is known as the fingered tremolo is employed. The bow performs a normal stroke and plays no part in effecting the tremolo, which is achieved by a rapid alternation of the two required fingerings on the same string. If, however, the interval exceeds an augmented fourth or at most a fifth, the two notes are fingered on adjacent strings, and then tremolo effect is achieved by the bow, which oscillates between them. Tremolos appear less frequently on wind instruments. Those involving the reiteration of the same note are performed by FLUTTER TONGUING, and in general it can be said that two-note tremolos are more effective and easier to play when the distance between the notes is small. On keyboard instruments the span of this type of tremolo is, of course, usually governed by the stretch of the hand.

tremulant, a device used on the organ to produce an effect resembling a VIBRATO by alternately increasing and decreasing the wind pressure. Though it has recently acquired an unsavoury reputation by mixing with bad company, it has a reputable history. Scheidt considered it an asset to the organ, and imitated its effect in his *Tabulatura nova* (1624) thus:

Later it was used on organs in France and Germany. Bach's organ at Arnstadt had a tremulant, and in his specification of the work to be done on the organ at Mühlhausen (1708) he suggested that the tremulant be 'made to vibrate properly'.

Trent Codices, six manuscript volumes (now numbered 87–92) of 15th century music which were discovered by Haberl in the chapter library of the Cathedral of Trent and a further volume (no 93) which came to light in 1920. They form the largest extant collection of music of the period, comprising over 1500 sacred and secular pieces by some 75 French, English, Italian and German composers. Facsimiles of the entire set were published in 1969 and 1970. Selections from the manuscripts have been published in *Denkmäler der Tonkunst in Osterreich*, xiv–xv, Jg. vii; xxii, Jg. xi (1); xxxviii, Jg. xix (1); liii, Jg. xxvii (1); lxi, Jg. xxxi; lxxvi, Jg. xl; and cxx.

Trepak, a Cossack dance in quick 2/4 time which occasionally appears in works of Russian composers, e.g. in Chaikovsky's 'Invitation to the Trepak', no 18 of the *Eighteen Pieces* for piano, op 72, and in the Trepak from the *Nutcracker* ballet.

Trésor musical, *see* MALDEGHEM

triad, a chord of three notes, the highest making the interval of a fifth (perfect, diminished or augmented) with the lowest, while the middle note is a third (major or minor) above the lowest. An example would be G-B-D, which is called the 'common chord' of G major. There are four different triads:

(1) major triad (major third and perfect fifth), e.g.:

(2) minor triad (minor third and perfect fifth), e.g.:

(3) diminished triad (minor third and diminished fifth), e.g.:

(4) augmented triad (major third and augmented fifth), e.g.:

See also CHORD, HARMONY, INVERSION

Trial by Jury, comic opera in one act by Sullivan, with libretto by W. S. Gilbert. This is the only Gilbert and Sullivan opera without spoken dialogue. It was first performed in London in 1875.

triangle (Fr., *triangle*; Ger., *Triangel*; It., *triangolo*), a percussion instrument consisting simply of a thin steel bar bent in the shape of a triangle but with one corner left open. Normally it is struck by a thin metal beater, but for a less brilliant sound a wooden stick is sometimes used. Although a tremolo is easily performed, fast-moving rhythmic patterns are unsuited to the instrument, and in general it can be said the simpler the part and the fewer notes it contains the more effective it will be. Nevertheless Liszt raised the

triangle to the status of a soloist in his E flat major concerto.

tricinium (Lat., from *tres*, three, and *canere*, to sing). A title used in the 16th and early 17th centuries for a short three-part piece, corresponding to BICINIUM for a two-part piece, as in Rhau's collection *Tricinia tum veterum tum recentiorum in arte musica symphonistarum, latina, germanica, brabantica et gallica* (1542). A tricinium on 'Ein' feste Burg' from Calvisius' *Tricinia; ausserlesene teutsche Lieder mit dreyen Stimmen zu singen, und sonst auff Instrumenten zu üben* (1603) is printed in Schering's *Geschichte der Musik in Beispielen*, no 160.

Triebschener Idyll, *see* SIEGFRIED IDYLL

trill (Fr., *cadence, tremblement, trille*, Ger., *Triller*, It., *gruppo, trillo*), (1) an ornament consisting of the rapid alternation of a note with the note a second above (also known as 'shake'). It occurs in English choral music early in the 16th century:

RICHARD DAVY, *O Domine coeli terraeque* (c. 1500)

which may be interpreted as an ornamentation of

and later in instrumental music, most frequently as an ornamentation of the suspension in a cadence, e.g.:

JOHN BULL, *Queen Elizabeth's Pavan* (c. 1600)

In the 17th and 18th centuries the trill was begun on the upper note, and was indicated *tr* or 〰 or 〰 or ⌇ (Purcell), e.g.:

played:

It might also begin with the upper appoggiatura, e.g.:

played:

with the lower appoggiatura, e.g.:

played:

or with a turn, e.g.:

played:

and might end with a turn, e.g.:

played:

The number of notes in a trill depended on the length of the note (it could be played as a turn if the note were very short), and the turn was frequently used to end it, whether indicated or not. This is also true of the modern trill, introduced early in the 19th century, which is begun on the principal note, e.g.:

played:

unless the beginning on the upper note is indicated by a grace note;

(2) in the Italian terminology of the early 17th century the trill was called *gruppo* or *tremolo*, and the term *trillo* (English 'plain shake') denoted the rapid reiteration of a note, given thus by Caccini (1602):

In his *Madrigales and Ayres* of 1632 Walter Porter gave this explanation:

> In the Songs which are set forth with Division where you may find many notes in a place after this manner

> in rule or space they are set to express the *Trillo*.

See also PRALLTRILLER, SCHNELLER

Trillo del Diavolo, Il, *see* DEVIL'S TRILL

Trinklied (Ger.), drinking song.

trio, (1) a composition for three parts, e.g. the trio sonata (*see* SONATA) of the baroque period for two instruments and continuo, and Bach's trio sonatas for organ;

(2) the middle section of a minuet or scherzo after which the first section is repeated. Such a trio was written earlier in three parts, as are the first trio (for two oboes and bassoon) and the second trio (for two horns and oboes) of the minuet in Bach's first Brandenburg concerto. The title was kept after the custom of writing in three parts had been dropped;

(3) an instrumental or vocal piece for three performers. The most frequent instrumental type is the piano trio (piano, violin, cello), which in its earliest state (e.g. J. C. Bach's *Six Sonates, pour le Clavecin, accompagnées d'un Violon ou Flûte Traversière et d'un Violoncelle*, op 2, 1763) was a keyboard sonata with optional violin and cello. The main interest of Haydn's trios, although most of them were written late in his life, is in the piano part though these in many cases are exceptionally fine and interesting works, whose full stature is only now being recognised. In Beethoven's trios, a true chamber music develops and there are many good examples of piano trios by later composers.

Haydn wrote three trios for piano, flute and cello, Mozart one trio and Schumann a set of four pieces (*Märchenerzählungen*) for piano, clarinet and viola; Beethoven's op 11 is for piano, clarinet and cello, Brahm's op 114 for piano, clarinet and cello, and his op 40 for piano, violin and horn.

Other types of instrumental trio are the string trio (violin, viola and cello; 21 or more by Haydn, five by Beethoven, one, the *Divertimento*, K 563, by Mozart, two by Hindemith), the woodwind trio (e.g. Mozart's five *Divertimenti* for two clarinets and bassoon, K App. 229, Beethoven's op 87 for two oboes and English horn), and the trio for woodwind and strings (e.g. nine by Haydn for two flutes and cello, one by Reger for flute, violin and viola, Debussy's sonata for flute, viola and harp, and Bax's *Elegy* for flute, viola and harp).

Triole (Ger.), **triolet** (Fr.), triplet.

Trionfi, a trilogy of three short operas or scenic cantatas by Carl Orff. The works, which can be (and usually are) performed separately, are *Carmina Burana*, *Catulli Carmina* and *Trionfo d'Afrodite*. The texts, by the composer, have their source in Catullus, Sappho and Euripides. The first performance of *Trionfi* as an entity was at La Scala, Milan, in 1953, with Herbert von Karajan as conductor.

Trionfo di Dori, Il (It., The Triumph of Doris), an anthology of 29 Italian madrigals by various composers, first published in Venice in 1592. The refrain 'Viva la bella Dori' (long live the fair Doris) is common to all the poems. It was the model for the English anthology, edited by Thomas Morley, THE TRIUMPHES OF ORIANA.

tripla, *see* NACHTANZ

triple concerto, a concerto for three solo instruments with orchestra, e.g. Beethoven's op 56, for piano, violin, cello and orchestra.

triple counterpoint, when three parts are so written that they may be disposed in any order, i.e. so that each will make a good bass to the others, they are in triple counterpoint. For example, the subject and the two counter-subjects of Bach's Fugue in C minor in the first book of the *Forty-eight* appear in these three ways in the course of bars 48–80:

triple croche (Fr.), demisemiquaver.

triple stop, any chord of three notes played on a bowed string instrument, whether or not all three strings are stopped by the fingers.

triplet (Fr., *triolet*; Ger., *Triole*; It., *terzina*), a group of three notes which is to be performed in the time of two: for an example see HEMIOLA. For the relation of its rhythm to the rhythm of a dotted note in the 18th century, *see* DOT.

triple time, time in which the number of beats in the bar is three, e.g. 3/8, 3/4, 3/2. If the beats are divisible by two, the time is 'simple'; if they are divisible by three, it is 'compound', e.g.

Simple triple time:

Compound triple time:

triple tonguing, a method of TONGUING on brass instruments in which the consonants T-K-T are articulated. This can be done at great speed, and passages involving or consisting entirely of triplets can be played much faster than would be possible with normal single tonguing. The method is also used on certain woodwind instruments, notably the members of the flute family; it is more difficult to accomplish on instruments with reeds, and only recently has become acknowledged as part of the technique of playing them.

triplum (Lat.), the third part above the tenor, counting the tenor itself as the first part, in the organum of the late 12th century and in the motet of the 13th century. For an example *see* PEROTINUS.

Tristan and Isolde (Ger., *Tristan und Isolde*), opera in three acts by Wagner, with a libretto by the composer, first performed in Munich, in 1865. Tristan, nephew of King Marke of Cornwall, has been sent to Ireland to bring back Isolde to be his uncle's bride. He is no stranger to her, since on a previous occasion she had tended him when he was severely wounded, in spite of the fact that he had killed her lover. Now, stung by what she considers to be Tristan's ingratitude, and in despair at the thought of her unwelcome marriage, she proposes that both she and Tristan should drink a poisonous draught. Her attendant Brangäne, however, substitutes a love-philtre.

In the palace gardens in Cornwall they declare their love, while the king is away on a hunting expedition. He returns to find them in each other's arms. A fight ensues between Tristan and Melot, one of the king's knights. Tristan, severely wounded, is taken off to Brittany by the faithful Kurwenal.

While his master lies by the shore in a feverish delirium, Kurwenal waits impatiently for Isolde, whom he has summoned from Cornwall. When she arrives, Tristan is so overcome by excitement that he tears off his bandages and collapses. A second ship arrives with the king and his attendants. Kurwenal, expecting a new attack, kills Melot and himself falls dead by Tristan's side. Marke has come to offer forgiveness, but it is too late. Tristan is dead, and Isolde, having sung for the last time the melody of their love, sinks to rest in death on his body.

The first performance of *Tristan* was so badly received that only the assistance of King Ludwig II, Wagner's patron, enabled it to survive three performances. In Vienna, after 77 rehearsals, it was abandoned as unperformable, but today it is established as one of the most important milestones of musical history.

Tristano, Lennie (born 1919), U.S. jazz pianist, conservatory trained. He is founder of an experimental school of jazz performers, specializing in free improvisation and in the breakdown of certain traditional features of jazz. Two of his most famous pieces,

Intuition and *Digression* (both recorded during the 1940s), are for a group of six musicians who begin playing with no pre-arranged time signature, chord sequence or key.

tritone, the interval comprising three whole tones, i.e. the augmented fourth. In EQUAL TEMPERAMENT it is identical in sound (though not in function) with its inversion, the diminished fifth, each interval representing exactly half an octave. The difference in function can be represented by examples of resolution. Thus:

is in the key of C and resolves thus:

If by a change of notation it is written as a diminished fifth:

it is in the key of F sharp and resolves thus:

The tritone or its inversion occurs most often as part of a dominant seventh chord, or of the chord on the leading note, e.g.:

in the key of C.

The tritone and its inversion were normally avoided in plainsong and, generally speaking, in medieval polyphony, though it is not certain to what extent singers supplied accidentals (*see* MUSICA FICTA) in the many cases where it occurs melodically in one part or as an interval between two parts.

Trittico, Il (*The Triptych*), a group of three one-act operas by Puccini – *Il tabarro* (libretto by Giuseppe Adami), *Suo Angelica* (libretto by Giovacchimo Forzano), and *Gianni Schicchi* (libretto again by Forzano). Their first performance as an entity was in New York in 1918.

Triumphes of Oriana, The, a collection of 25 five-part and six-part madrigals, perhaps in honour of Queen Elizabeth I, edited by Thomas Morley and published in 1601. The anthology, in which each madrigal ends with the refrain:

> Then sang the shepherds and nymphs of Diana:
> Long live fair Oriana,

was modelled on the Italian collection *Il trionfo di Dori* (1592), in which each piece has the refrain 'Viva la

bella Dori'. A modern edition by E. H. Fellowes is in *The English Madrigal School*, xxxii.

> J. KERMAN: *The Elizabethan Madrigal* (1962), pages 193–209

Triumphlied (*Song of Triumph*), a composition by Brahms, op 55, (1870–1) for chorus, orchestra and organ *ad lib.* to words from the Revelation of St. John. It was composed to celebrate the German victory in the Franco-Prussian war.

Triumph of Time and Enlightenment (It., *Il Trionfo del Tempo e del Disinganno*), oratorio by Handel, with a text by Cardinal Benedetto Pamfili. It was first performed in Rome in 1708; a revised version, *The Triumph of Time and Truth*, was performed in London in 1737.

Triumph of Time and Truth, The, oratorio by Handel. The text was translated by Thomas Morell from Handel's earlier work *Il trionfo de Tempo e della Verita* (1737), a revision of the still earlier *Il trionfo del Tempo e del Disinganno* (1708). Several of the movements were adapted from *Il trionfo del Tempo* and other works.

Troilus and Cressida, opera in three acts by Walton. The libretto by Christopher Hassall is mainly after Chaucer's not Shakespeare's version of the story. Its first performance was at Covent Garden in 1954.

Trojans, The (Fr., *Les Troyens*), opera in two parts by Berlioz (1856–8), with a libretto by the composer (after Virgil). The two parts are: (1) 'The Capture of Troy' (Fr., *La Prise de Troie*), first performed in German (*Die Eroberung Trojas*), in Karlsruhe in 1890, first performance of the original French text in Nice in 1891; (2) 'The Trojans at Carthage' (Fr., *Les Troyens à Carthage*), first performed in Paris. The first performance of the complete work (in German) was at Karlsruhe, December 6th and 7th, 1890; first performance in French, Brussels, December 26th and 27th, 1906.

This vast opera was Berlioz's masterpiece. The composer himself only heard the second part (the tragedy of Dido) performed, in a mutilated version. The failure of the performance did much to break Berlioz's spirit as a composer. The first British performance was in Glasgow in the 1930s. Since then the work has established itself in Britain and America, and its importance recognized there – if not fully in France. Part Two of *The Trojans* contains the famous interlude, *The Royal Hunt and Storm*, often performed in excerpt form. In recent years, however, there has been a growing understanding that the only way to do justice to Berlioz's opera with its contrast between the often stark music depicting Troy, and the warmer, more romantic music of the North African scenes, is to perform it uncut. See illustration on p. 562.

tromba (It.), trumpet. *Tromba cromatica, tromba ventile,* valve trumpet. *Tromba da tirarsi,* slide trumpet.

tromba da tirarsi, slide-trumpet.

See TRUMPET

tromba marina, a once very popular (from the middle ages to the 18th century) stringed instrument up to seven feet long and consisting of a single string mounted on a thin and slightly tapered box. The player, who used a bow, had to stand, and the only notes he could produce were natural harmonics, the bow playing above the 'stopping' point. Inside the box were twenty or so sympathetic strings. The bridge was the

The Trojans: Aeneas (Ronald Dowd) relates his story to Dido (Janet Baker): a scene from Scottish Opera's centenary production, only the third ever complete staging of the opera in English, but, curiously, the second in Glasgow.

instrument's most remarkable feature, with one foot fixed, and the other slightly shorter, drumming against the sound board. The sound produced was loud and trumpetlike, hence 'tromba', but no explanation has been found for 'marina'. The instrument was frequently played by nuns, hence one of its German names, '*Nonengeige*' (nun's fiddle). Antonio Vivaldi wrote solo parts for two tromba marinas in a concerto.

tromba ventile (It.), valve TRUMPET.

trombetta (Lat., diminutive of *tromba*), (1) an old name for the trumpet used by some 17th century composers (e.g. Buxtehude).

(2) given by Praetorius in his *Syntagma Musicum* (1618–19) as one of the Italian names for the tenor trombone (*gemeine rechte Posaune*). He also gives *trombetta piccola* as a name for the alto trombone.

trombone (Eng., Fr., It.; Ger., *Posaune*), the modern trombone is a brass instrument with two parts: one consists of a cylindrical bore expanding to a bell over the lower third of its length, with a cup-shaped mouthpiece; the other is a U-shaped slide which moves parallel to the first part to vary the effective length of the tube (*see* illustration under BRASS INSTRUMENTS).

Apart from the extra mechanism added in recent years to some, but by no means all, instruments, the trombone has remained basically unchanged for the last five hundred years or more. It is the old SACKBUT with a larger bell and the bore increased in size to provide the weightier tone required by orchestras, brass and military bands. Because they have always been fully chromatic trombones are non-transposing instruments.

By altering the length of tubing in use, the slide alters the pitch in the same way as the VALVES on trumpets and horns. There are seven slide positions,

which on the B flat tenor trombone give the following series of fundamental notes:

In practice only the upper three of these are used at all frequently and, until Berlioz showed otherwise, the lowest notes on the instrument were considered to be the first harmonics, an octave above these fundamentals (or pedal notes as they are usually called). Except that the low E can be 'lipped' down to E flat, there was no means of bridging the gap between the second harmonic in the seventh position (E) and the fundamental note in the first (B flat) until a valve operated mechanism, throwing into play an additional length of tubing, was added. This lowers the pitch of the tenor trombone from B flat to F, E or E flat. An instrument so equipped is often referred to as a tenor-bass trombone. A similar mechanism was also applied to the bass trombone, normally built either in F or G. The compass of the members of the trombone family is about three and a half octaves from the first pedal note, or four from the seventh, the highest note demanded from the tenor, and this only very rarely, being the F at the top of the treble stave.

Of the six members of the family the highest pitched or soprano trombone, often called a slide trumpet, is long since obsolete, as for many years was the alto in E flat which recently has enjoyed a revival. The tenor is by far the most frequently encountered especially now that the bass, at least in its old form, has virtually departed from the scene. It has been replaced by a large bore tenor, complete with extension mechanism, that is taking over the name as well as the function of the bass trombone. This instrument, with its ability to make use of the pedal notes on the F, E or E flat extension, also substitutes effectively for the contra-bass trombone, normally built in C but occasionally in B flat. This unwieldy instrument with two mechanically linked slides, one of which extended behind the player, was used by Wagner in the RING, and by D'Indy among others. The sixth member of the family is the valve trombone, which is still used very occasionally although not in symphony orchestras. It is a tenor, and the one advantage it has over the slide instrument is that successions of notes requiring extreme and rapid changes of slide position are negotiated more easily. This advantage, however, is limited to the low register where the notes of the harmonic series are widely spaced, and can be very nearly negated on slide instruments equipped with an additional mechanism. The valve instrument is, in fact, more of a brass trumpet than a true trombone.

trombone à pistons (Fr.), valve TROMBONE.

trombone stop, a sixteen foot reed stop on the organ with a powerful tone.

trombonino (It.), Alto TROMBONE

Trommel (Ger.), drum. *Grosse Trommel*, bass drum; *kleine Trommel*, side drum.

Trommelflöte, *see* FIFE

Trompete (Ger.), trumpet. *Ventiltrompete*, valve trumpet; *Zugtrompete*, slide trumpet.

tromp, trompe, trompede Béarn, trompe de Bern, trompe de Laquais, forms of JEW'S HARP.

trompette (Fr.), (1) trumpet. *Trompette a pistons*, valve trumpet.

(2) *trompette marine, see* TROMBA MARINA

tronco (It.), literally 'truncated'. A direction indicating that a note or chord is to be abruptly cut off.

trope (Lat., *tropus*), additional music and words which preceded, were interpolated with, or followed a piece of liturgical plainsong. Many such additions were written between the 9th and 11th centuries, most often to the Introit, Offertory, Communion and Gloria of the Mass. The words, whether poetry or prose, commented on and amplified the official text, as for example in the following translation of the St. Martial trope *Hodie Stephanus martyr* and its Introit *Etenim sederunt* (the text of the Introit is italicized):

> Today Stephen the martyr went up into heaven; of him the prophet once said, lifting up his voice: '*Princes sat, and spoke against me*, the Jewish people rose up against me wickedly, *and the wicked persecuted me*; full of hate, they crushed me with stones: *help me, O Lord my God*, take up my soul in peace, *for thy servant was exercised in thy justifications*.'

P. EVANS, *The Early Trope Repertory of Saint Martial de Limoges* (1970), page 57

The liturgical drama, from which the later medieval mystery plays developed, sprang directly from the trope; the earliest liturgical play is considered to be the enactment in the 10th century of the story of the three Marys coming to the tomb during the singing of the Easter Introit-trope *Quem quaeritis* (see Schering, *Geschichte der Musik in Beispielen*, no 8). The drama expanded with the addition of other Easter Day events, and attracted imitations on Christmas themes. The trope to the Introit for Christmas, *Hodie cantandus est* (attributed to Tuotilo, and printed in Schering, no 3),

in any case had dramatic implications, being in the form of a dialogue. Other New Testament subjects were also dramatized such as 'The Journey to Emmaus' (*Peregrinus* plays), 'The Raising of Lazarus' and 'The Conversion of St. Paul'. The only surviving Old Testament play complete with music is the magnificent and elaborate 12th century 'Play of Daniel' (modern edition by N. Greenberg, 1959) written at the cathedral school of Beauvais.

The expression 'trope' is also widely applied to the addition of new words to the existing words and music of the liturgy, but without historical justification. The early manuscripts use the Latin term 'prosula' for such additions, never 'tropus'. The more melismatic parts of the liturgy were particularly suitable for use as *prosulae*. The *Kyrie* for example, which still retains the name *Conditor Kyrie omnium* although it has been deprived of its added words since the 16th century:

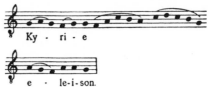

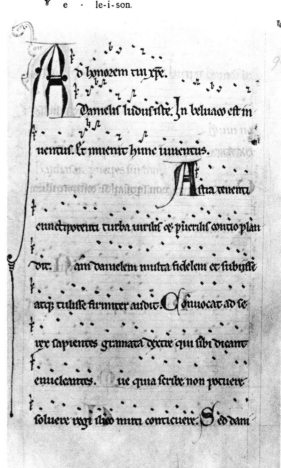

A Page from the 'Play of Daniel'

was sung at High Mass on Christmas Day in the Sarum rite in this form:

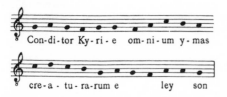

Con-di-tor Ky-ri-e om-ni-um y-mas

cre-a-tu-ra-rum e ley son

Other parts of the liturgy to which *prosulae* were sung included the *Ite missa est* at the end of Mass and the *Benedicamus Domino* at the end of Mass in Lent and Advent and at the end of the offices.

In the later middle ages polyphonic settings of the liturgy often incorporated additional unofficial sections of text. One of these, beginning *Virgo mater ecclesiae*, was included in virtually all the polyphonic settings of the antiphon SALVE REGINA by English composers from about 1400 until the Reformation. All additions of this kind were eliminated from the Roman liturgy by the decrees of the Council of Trent in the 16th century.

P. EVANS: *The Early Trope Repertory of Saint Martial de Limoges* (1970)

troppo (It.), too much. Thus *Allegro non troppo* means 'fast, but not too fast'.

troubadours (Fr., from the Provençal, *trobadors*), poet-musicians of the early middle ages who lived in the south of France and wrote in the *langue d'oc* (generally called Provençal). The origin of the word *trobador* is uncertain, but there is clearly a connection with the verb *trobar* (=*trouver*), 'to find'. Many of the troubadours (though not all) were of aristocratic birth. The first whose songs have survived is Guillaume, Count of Poitiers (1071–1127), who became Duke of Aquitaine in 1087. Others who were famous were Marcabru (early 12th century) and Bernard de Ventadour (12th century). The cultivation of lyrical song spread to the north of France in the late 12th century, the word *trobador* being translated into its French equivalent *trouvère*.

The music of the troubadours and *trouvères* was monophonic. Many songs show clearly the influence of Gregorian chant, while others, by their use of modes alien to the Roman church, seem to owe their musical style to a heritage of secular song which is now lost. The melodic styles had a considerable influence on the polyphonic motet of the 13th century, though the actual quotation of extensive passages is uncommon. The majority of troubadour and *trouvère* melodies have come down to us in a form which gives no indication of their rhythm, no doubt because they were never sung in strict time. Some modern editors interpret the notation in the light of the rhythm of the words and transcribe the songs in one or other of the RHYTHMIC MODES, although there is little evidence that they were so performed.

In German-speaking countries the art of the troubadours and trouvères was imitated by the MINNESINGER.

The following facsimile editions of troubadour and *trouvère* manuscripts (in some cases with transcriptions) have been published:

P. AUBRY: *Trouvères et troubadours* (1919; English edition, 1914); *Le Chansonnier de l'Arsenal* (1909, incomplete)

J. BECK: *Le Chansonnier Cangé* (two volumes, 1927)

J. and L. BECK: *Le Manuscript du Roi* (two volumes, 1938)

A. JEANROY: *Le Chansonnier d'Arras* (1925)

P. MEYER and G. RAYNAUD: *Le Chansonnier français de Saint-Germain-des-Prés* (1892)

U. SESINI: *Le melodie trobadoriche nel canzoniere provenzale della Biblioteca Ambrosiana R. 71 sup.* (1942)

H. VAN DER WERF: *The Chansons of the Troubadours and Trouvères* (1972)

J. A. WESTRUP: 'Medieval Song,' in *New Oxford History of Music*, ii (1954)

Trouble in Tahiti, opera in one act by Leonard Bernstein, with a libretto by the composer. First performed in 1952 at Waltham, Massachusetts, this comedy depicts a day of domestic strife between a married couple in a U.S. suburb.

Trouluffe (Truelove), John, 15th–16th century English composer who wrote, apparently with Richard Smert, carols and other sacred pieces in two and three parts. The carols are printed in *Mediaeval Carols* (*Musica Britannica*, iv, 1952).

Trout Quintet (Ger., *Forellenquintett*), the popular name of Schubert's quintet in A major for violin, viola, cello, double bass and piano, composed in 1819 and published posthumously in 1829 as op 114. The fourth movement consists of variations on Schubert's song *Die Forelle* (The Trout).

trouveres, *see* TROUBADOURS

Il Trovatore: illustration from the title-page of a contemporary piano version.

Trovatore, Il (It., *The Troubadour*), opera in four acts by Verdi, with a libretto by Salvatore Cammarano (based on a Spanish play by Antonio Garcia Gutierrez). It was first performed in Rome in 1853. The story takes place in the 15th century in Biscay and Aragon. Believing that a gypsy had bewitched one of his sons, the Count di Luna ordered her to be burnt at the stake. Azucena (the gypsy's daughter), wishing to avenge her mother, attempts to kill the boy, but by a mistake kills her own child and so kidnaps the Count's son and brings him up as her son. Years later the young Count di Luna (the brother of the kidnapped child) falls in love with Leonora but discovers that she is in love with Manrico (a troubadour who is the kidnapped child but does not know his identity). When Leonora is informed falsely that Manrico is dead, she resolves to become a nun, but he arrives to take her away from the altar while his men beat off the Count's, who are also attempting to kidnap her. The Count's men later capture Azucena and she is condemned to be burnt like her mother. When Manrico rushes to rescue her he is also captured. Leonora declares that she will give herself to the Count if he will free her beloved Manrico, but when he consents she secretly takes a slow poison. After she has taken a dying farewell of Manrico the Count breaks his vow and orders Manrico to be executed. Azucena finally has her revenge for her mother's death by telling the Count just before she dies that he has murdered his own brother.

In spite of its notoriously involved plot, *Il Trovatore* remains a favourite opera and is recognised as a milestone in Verdi's development. Its principal roles call for four outstanding voices.

Troyens, Les, *see* TROJANS

trumpet (Fr., *trompette*; Ger., *Trompete*; It., *tromba*, *clarino*), the name trumpet is applied to a wide variety of instruments, some of which have little in common apart from being made of metal (usually brass) and having a funnel-shaped mouthpiece. The trumpet's oldest ancestor was undoubtedly an animal's horn fitted with such a mouthpiece, but long before the Christian era this was replaced by the straight trumpet. It was during the 13th century that the folded trumpet made its first appearance, but instead of resembling the modern instrument it was at first shaped like a small saxophone. The familiar type of folded trumpet appeared only in the 15th century, and was usually referred to as the claro or clarion, the name trumpet being restricted to the straight variety. Being restricted to a selection of notes from the HARMONIC SERIES, trumpets were for long suited only to ceremonial and military occasions, but the invention of crooks gave them greater scope, and so paved the way for their admission into orchestras shortly after the turn of the 17th century. Monteverdi was probably the first composer of major significance to so use them. Crooks were lengths of tubing that could be inserted into the instrument, thereby altering the pitch. The limitations of the harmonic series remained, but the instrument could now be crooked in almost any key, and with two or more trumpets available the range of notes could be increased by using different crooks for each. Aided by shallow mouthpieces players developed a technique enabling them to exploit fluently the upper register, where the notes of the harmonic series lie close together. Thus during the baroque period the trumpet became a melodic instrument. The degree of virtuosity demanded is well illustrated by Bach's and Handel's more elaborate trumpet parts. For solo work the most usual key, and consequently crook, was the one in D, the F in Bach's Second Brandenburg Concerto being exceptional. This highly specialised technique apparently vanished during the mid-17th

century, presumably because composers ceased to demand it. As a consequence the trumpet now fulfilled a humbler role, using relatively few notes and often merely adding to the weight of sound of the full orchestra. These limitations led, during the last two decades of the 18th century, to experiments being made with keys similar to those on woodwind instruments. Basically this was reversion to the CORNETT method but with a system of keys replacing the finger-holes. It was for such an instrument that Haydn wrote his Trumpet Concerto in 1796. The keyed trumpet (Fr., *trompette à clefs*, Ger., *Klappentrompete*, It., *tromba a chiavi*) enjoyed only a brief existence, for early in the 19th century it was replaced by the valve trumpet (Fr., *trompette à piston*; Ger., *Ventiltrompete*; It., *tromba ventile*). Since this possessed a complete chromatic compass crooks were no longer needed, and the standard instrument became the F trumpet. Nevertheless composers continued to write as if crooks were still in use, thereby putting on players the burden of transposition. The large F trumpet (not to be confused with the small one used for such works as the Second Brandenburg Concerto) remained in general use until well into the 20th century; it appears, for instance, in scores by Vaughan Williams and Berg. Nowadays parts for it, as well as the ones for the earlier valveless instrument, are always played on modern instruments, usually those in C or B flat. These are very different instruments, being approximately half the size of the older F trumpet. Their range coincides because they use different sections of a harmonic series, the F trumpet sounding a fourth higher than the written note, and the B flat a tone lower. The open notes (those that do not necessitate the use of valves) on the two instruments are in actual sounds:

The valves allow the gaps between these notes to be filled in (see VALVE), and in the case of the B flat trumpet permit a downward extension to the sounding E (written F sharp), whereas the theoretically lowest notes on the F instruments, if they can be produced at all, are of very poor quality and no practical use. The smaller instrument is the more flexible and easier to manage, but something is undoubtedly lost when parts designed for the F trumpet are played on it, there being a marked difference in the tone quality. Many trumpets in C have an extension mechanism that puts them instantly into B flat; similarly B flat trumpets have one that lowers their pitch to A. The several higher pitched trumpets in use today all derive from, and use the same section of the harmonic series as, the B flat and C. The most frequently encountered are those in D and E flat (sounding a tone and a minor third above the written note), while the little F, despite being a modern invention, is often misleading referred to as the Bach trumpet, since it was designed with the

Second Brandenburg Concerto and other similar parts in mind. There is also a trumpet pitched in G, while the smallest of all those in common use is the 'piccolo B flat', which is an octave above the ordinary B flat; some models are equipped with a fourth valve that lowers the pitch to F.

The bass trumpet stemmed from Wagner, who at first envisaged a much larger counterpart of the F trumpet, then in everyday use. This proved impractical, and the modern bass trumpet corresponds instead to the B flat and C instruments, but sounds an octave lower. Beside these two keys it is also made in E flat, but it is in C that it usually appears in symphony orchestras on the comparatively rare occasions when the bass trumpet is required. This instrument, which comes close to being a valve trombone, is more often doubled by trombone than by trumpet players. Similarly the so-called slide trumpet, very rarely encountered today but used in the seventeenth century mainly to double choral soprano parts, is really a soprano TROMBONE or treble SACKBUT.

trumpet-cornet, an instrument which, although never prescribed, is manufactured in fairly large numbers and much used. As its name suggests it is a cross between the modern TRUMPET and the CORNET, and those who favour it consider it combines the tone of the former with the ease of playing of the latter.

trumpet stop, an eight foot reed stop on the organ.

Trumpet Voluntary, the popular name for a piece, falsely attributed to Purcell, which occurs among the harpsichord solos of Jeremiah Clarke (c. 1673–1707) under the title 'The Prince of Denmark's March' (modern edition in J. A. Fuller-Maitland, *At the Court of Queen Anne*).

Tsar's Bride, The, opera in three acts by Rimsky-Korsakov, first performed in Moscow in 1899. The libretto, by I. F. Tyumenev, is based on a play by Lev Alexandrovich Mey. The tsar is Ivan and his bride is Martha, who is loved by two other men. In the end she is not only poisoned but also (while dying) goes mad on hearing that the only man she loves has been beheaded by the tsar.

Tsarskaya Nevesta, *see* TSAR'S BRIDE

Tschudi, Burkhardt, *see* SHUDI

tuba, (1) a brass instrument of the saxhorn type which has a conical bore and three to five valves, and uses a cup-shaped mouthpiece. There are three sizes: (*a*) a bass-cum-tenor size, also called EUPHONIUM (Ger., *Barytonhorn*), in B flat with a range from

(*b*) a bass size a fourth or fifth lower, in F (the normal orchestral instrument) or E flat (used in military and brass bands) with a range from

or

(*c*) a double-bass size an octave lower than the first, in B flat with a range from

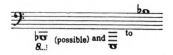

The two latter sizes are also called bombardon, or, if made in circular shape for marching, HELICON. Music for the tubas is normally written in the bass clef, with the actual sounds and key-signature (except in BRASS BAND music).

(2) The 'Wagner tubas' designed for use in the *Ring* are a group of five instruments consisting of two pairs and a bass. The upper pair are modified horns, with a funnel-shaped mouthpiece, in B flat with a range from

the lower pair similar instruments a fourth lower, in F, with a range from

Wagner wrote for these four as TRANSPOSING INSTRUMENTS; they are also used in Bruckner's last three symphonies. The bass of the group is a double-bass tuba.

A. CARSE: *Musical Wind Instruments* (1939)

(3) An organ stop of the reed type with a loud tone, chiefly used as a solo stop. The tuba of eight-foot pitch is sometimes called *tuba mirabilis*, that of four-foot pitch a *tuba clarion*.

(4) (Lat.), (*a*) trumpet. *Tuba mirum*, the opening words of the verse of the *Dies irae* which begins 'Tuba mirum spargens sonum' (the trumpet, spreading a marvellous sound); (*b*) the RECITING NOTE in the plainsong psalm tones.

tuba major, tuba mirabilis (often shortened to tuba), an eight-foot reed stop on the organ. The name is misleading since, although of great power, the range covered is considerably higher than that of the orchestral tuba.

tubaphone, or **tubophone,** a percussion instrument producing bell-like sounds when its metal tubes, which are laid out like a piano keyboard, are struck with hammers.

tubular bells, *see* BELLS

tuck, an early English word for the sound of a drum, particularly drum-taps.

tucket, an Elizabethan term for a fanfare of trumpets (Ger., Tusch), a corruption of the Italian TOCCATA.

Tudor, David (born 1926), U.S. composer and pianist, one of several disciples of John Cage experimenting with chance ideas.

Tudor Church Music, an edition of church music by English composers of the 16th and early 17th centuries published in ten volumes between 1923 and 1929. The contents are: Volume I, Masses by Taverner; Volume II, English church music by Byrd; Volume III, Magnificats and motets by Taverner; Volume IV, Services and anthems by Orlando Gibbons; Volume V, Latin and English church music by Robert White; Volume VI, Latin church music by Tallis; Volume VII, Byrd's *Gradualia* I and II; Volume VIII, Responses, psalms and services by Tomkins; Volume IX, Latin church music by Byrd; Volume X, compositions by Aston, Marbeck and Parsley. An appendix, containing supplements from sources discovered later, was published in 1948.

Tudway, Thomas (c. 1650–1726), English organist and composer. He was a chorister at the Chapel Royal under Blow from about 1660, and lay vicar at St. George's Chapel, Windsor, in 1664. He was an organist at Cambridge (from c. 1670) becoming professor of music there in 1705. For the Earl of Oxford he collected and edited six manuscript volumes of cathedral music by various composers (now in the British Library). He composed a Te Deum (1720), anthems and other church music.

tumbas, *see* CONGA DRUMS

Tunder, Franz (1614–67), German composer and organist. He was organist at the court of Gottorp from 1632 to 1641, and preceded his son-in-law, Buxtehude, as organist at the Marienkirche in Lübeck (from 1641), where he organized a group of instrumentalists for the church music. In the history of the Lutheran cantata his name is particularly associated with the form in which each verse of a chorale is based on the melody treated in a different way, a form sometimes called variation-cantata. An example is his setting of 'Ein feste Burg' (*Denkmäler deutscher Tonkunst*, iii, page 142).

tune, *see* MELODY

tuning, *see* TEMPERAMENT

tuning-fork (Fr., *diapason*, Ger., *Stimmgabel*, It., *corsita*), a two-pronged device for giving accurately the pitch of a single note, invented in 1711 by the trumpeter John Shore (died 1752). The sound given by a tuning-fork is practically a pure note, without overtones.

Tunsted, Simon (d. 1369), English musical theorist. He entered the Franciscan order at Oxford, studied theology, music and astronomy, and became head of the English branch of the Minorite Franciscans in 1360. He is the alleged author of *De quatuor principalibus musicae* (1351), a treatise on mensural music, printed in Coussemaker's *Scriptores*, iv, pages 200–98.

tuono, *see* TONO

Turandot, opera in three acts by Puccini, completed by Alfano after Puccini's death. The libretto is by Giuseppe Adami and Renato Simoni (after Gozzi) and the work was first performed in Milan in 1926 under Toscanini. Turandot (the beautiful Princess of China) delivers a proclamation that she will marry any man of noble blood who can answer three riddles which she will ask: if he fails he will be beheaded. After the Prince of Persia has been condemned to be executed, Calaf (the disguised son of the dethroned Tartar King) announces that he will try the test. To the Princess's dismay he succeeds. Her father insists that she must marry him, but Calaf promises to release her if she can discover his identity by dawn. The Princess orders that everyone must spend the night trying to find out his name. When she discovers that Liù (a slave who is secretly in love with Calaf) knows the stranger, she

demands that she be tortured until she reveals who he is. Liù stabs herself and finally Calaf himself tells the Princess that he is the enemy Tartar Prince. Turandot, overcoming her pride, suddenly realises that she has at last fallen in love and declares to her father that his name is 'Love'. Alfano's completion of the score consisted of one duet and the concluding scene.

Turandot, opera in two acts by Busoni, composed in 1917, with a libretto by the composer based on the Gozzi play which inspired Puccini nine years later. Other operas on the subject have been written by Blumenroeder (1810), Reissiger (1835), Vesque von Püttlingen (1838), Jensen (1864–5), Bazzini (1867) and Rehbaum (1888).

Turangalîla Symphony, large-scale work in ten movements by Messiaen, written for the Boston Symphony Orchestra and first performed in 1949. Turangalîla (pronounced with accent and prolonged sound on the last two syllables) is a Sanskrit word which the composer defines as meaning 'a love song, a hymn to joy, time, movement, rhythm, life and death.' The symphony is influenced by Indian music, and incorporates important parts for solo piano (written for the composer's wife, Yvonne Loriod) and for the Ondes Martenot (an electronic instrument with a keyboard).

turba (Lat.), crowd.

See PASSION

turca, alla (It.), 'in the Turkish style' (*see* JANISSARY MUSIC). Mozart's *Rondo alla turca* is the last movement of his piano sonata in A major, K 331.

Turchi, Guido (born 1916), Italian composer. His works include a *Concerto Brève* in memory of Bartók and *Five Comments on the Bacchae of Euripides* for orchestra.

Turco in Italia, Il (It., *The Turk in Italy*), opera in two acts by Rossini, to a libretto by Romani. It was first performed in Milan in 1814, and was revived in 1950 as a vehicle for Maria Callas; since then it has re-established itself in opera houses all over the world. The story is a conventional comedy of intrigue, enhanced by some captivating music.

Turges (Sturges), Edmund (c. 1450–after 1502), composer. He composed a three-part song celebrating the marriage (1501) of Prince Arthur and Catherine of Aragon and other secular songs, Masses, Magnificats and antiphons. Of his church music there have survived two settings of 'Gaude flore virginali' (in the Eton choirbook), a particularly elaborate setting of the Magnificat (in the Caius College choirbook), and a *Kyrie* and *Gloria*.

Turina, Joaquin (1882–1949), Spanish composer, pianist and conductor. He studied in Spain and later in Paris under Vincent d'Indy at the Schola Cantorum (1905–14) and under Moszkowski. He settled in Madrid as teacher and critic. His works include operas, symphonic poems, piano pieces and songs.

Türk, Daniel Gottlob (1756–1813), German composer and writer on music. He studied in Dresden, and in Leipzig under J. A. Hiller, and became a violinist at the opera and in Hiller's orchestra. He was cantor at St. Ulrich's Hall, 1776; director of music at the University, 1778; organist at the Liebenfrauenkirche, 1787. He published some useful text-books, including a *Klavierschule* (1789) and a treatise on figured bass

(1791). His compositions include piano sonatas, symphonies, songs and church music.

F. T. ARNOLD: *The Art of Accompaniment from a Thorough-Bass* (1931)

Turkish crescent, *see* PAVILLON CHINOIS

turn (Fr., *double, double cadence, brise,* Ger., *Doppelschlag,* It., *grupetto*). An ornament which makes a turn around a note, beginning with the note above. In the commonest forms it is indicated over a note thus:

and played thus:

or between two notes thus:

and played thus:

or thus:

played thus:

It may occasionally begin on the principal note, indicated by a grace note thus:

played

or be inverted, shown by the sign:

played

In music of the second half of the 18th century it may be more appropriate to play the first two notes of the turn more quickly than the others, in the manner

preferred by C. P. E. Bach. In that case

would be played

The sign $\widetilde{\mathbf{w}}$, used by Couperin, means the usual form of TRILL ending with a turn.

Turn of the Screw, The, opera in two acts by Britten, first performed at Venice in 1954. The libretto, by Myfanwy Piper, is based on the Henry James story about the ghostly possession of two children, and their relationship with their governess. The work is musically cast in the form of a theme and variations (the theme consisting of a twelve-note row, though the writing is not otherwise atonal).

Turner, William (1651–1740), English composer and singer. He was a chorister at Christ Church, Oxford, and at the Chapel Royal. In 1669 he was a Gentleman of the Chapel Royal. He was also vicar choral at St. Paul's and lay vicar at Westminster Abbey. He composed services, anthems, hymns, a masque, songs for plays, other songs, odes and catches.

Turnhout, Gerard de (c. 1520–1580), Flemish composer and singer. He was a singer (1545) and *Kapellmeister* (1563) at Antwerp Cathedral, and from 1572 was attached to the court of Philip II at Madrid. He composed a Mass, and a book of sacred and secular songs for three voices (1569; modern edition by L. J. Wagner, two volumes, 1970). His younger relative, Jean de Turnhout, was *maestro di capella* in the service of the Duke of Parma at Brussels from 1586 to 1618. He composed madrigals and motets.

tutte le corde (It.), 'all the strings'. A term used in piano music to indicate the release of the left-hand pedal. On grand pianos this normally has the effect of allowing the hammers to hit all the strings assigned to each note, instead of only one or two (*una corda*).

See CORDA

tutti (It.), 'all' (pl.). Term used, most often in concertos, to indicate an entrance of the full orchestra, as distinct from passages for the soloist.

Tveitt, Geirr (born 1908), Norwegian composer and pianist, also collector and arranger of Norwegian folk music. His prodigious output includes five operas, five piano concertos, some thirty piano sonatas, and orchestral arrangements of more than 100 folk tunes.

twelfth, (1) the interval of an octave plus a fifth, e.g.

(2) an organ stop of diapason quality and $2\frac{2}{3}$ foot pitch. The sounds produced are an octave and a fifth above the notes played.

twelve-note system (Ger., *Zwölftonsystem*), a method of composition, alternatively known as dodecaphony, formulated by Arnold Schoenberg about 1921 after a period of experimentation in writing music without tonality and without using the traditional ways of building chords. In it the basis of both melodies and chords of a composition is an arrangement of the twelve notes of the chromatic scale in a particular order, called a tone-row. This series is always used complete, but may be transposed to any one of the eleven other possible positions, inverted, reversed (RETROGRADE MOTION), or reversed and inverted. It thus has 48 forms, and in addition any note of the series may be used in any of its octaves. Both the melody and the chords, for example, of the last of the *Five Piano Pieces*, op 23, which begins:

are derived from this tone-row:

Schoenberg used the method much less rigidly in his later works than in the pieces written in the 1920s. It was adopted as a working basis by his pupils Anton Webern and Alban Berg, and later by Ernst Křenek and other composers. The tone-row on which Berg based his violin concerto (1935):

is quite tonal in its implications, being a series of thirds followed by three whole tones. In the last section of the work a modified form of this series is combined with the melody of J. R. Ahle's chorale 'Es ist genug' (It is enough), which begins with three whole tones, thus:

and the chorale is then continued by the woodwind in Bach's harmonisation from the cantata *O Ewigkeit, du Donnerwort*:

E. KŘENEK: *Studies in Counterpoint* (1940).
J. RUFER: *Composition with Twelve Notes* (1954).

twelve-tone system, a U.S. name for the Ger. *Zwölftonsystem*. In Britain the term is misleading, since it suggests the use of a scale consisting of twelve whole tones (*see* TONE), instead of a chromatic scale in which each note is potentially equal. The logical English version is TWELVE-NOTE SYSTEM.

Twilight of the Gods, *see* GOTTERDÄMMERUNG, RING DES NIBELUNGEN

Tye, Christopher (c. 1500–1573), English composer. He was educated at Cambridge, where he was a chorister and lay clerk at King's College. He was master of the choristers at Ely Cathedral from 1542 to 1561. He composed a four-part setting of the *Acts of the Apostles* (the first fourteen chapters) to a metrical translation by himself (London, 1553; reprinted in M. Frost, *English and Scottish Psalm and Hymn Tunes*, 1953, page 346), Masses, motets, anthems, services and In Nomines for strings.

tymbal, the early English name, deriving from the French *timbale,* for the kettle-drum or *timpano* (*see* TIMPANI).

tympani, an incorrect but still encountered spelling of TIMPANI.

tympanon (Fr.), dulcimer.

typophone (Fr.), DULCITONE.

Tyrolienne (Fr.), a country dance, akin to the *Ländler,* in slow waltz-time. Though believed to be of Tyrolean origin, it probably had its source in various 19th century operas and ballets, which sought to give a poetic impression of the music (complete with yodelling effects) popularly associated with the Tyrol. A typical *Tyrolienne* is to be found in Act 3 of Rossini's *William Tell*.

Tyrwhitt-Wilson, *see* BERNERS

tzigane, tsigane (Fr.), term for Hungarian gypsies and their music. Ravel used it as the title of a violin rhapsody (1924), which he wrote in two versions: one for violin and piano, and the other (much superior) for violin and orchestra.

Uber (Ger.), 'over', 'above'.

Ubung (Ger.), 'exercise'. Thus *Clavierübung*, keyboard exercise.

Ugolini, Vincenzo (c. 1570–1638), Italian composer. He was *maestro di cappella* at Santa Maria Maggiore in Rome from 1592 to 1603, at Benevento Cathedral in 1609, at San Luigi dei Francesi in Rome from 1616 to 1620 and from 1631, and at the Cappella Giulia of St. Peter's from 1620 to 1626. He composed Masses, motets, psalms, vespers and other church music, and madrigals.

uillean pipe, *see* UNION PIPE

ukelele or **ukulele,** a type of guitar but smaller and with only four strings, of Portuguese origin. It first came into vogue in the South Pacific Islands and, being easy to play, became popular in the United States and Europe shortly after the World War I. It is largely confined to playing chords and the notation for it, which merely indicates the position of the fingers, is a type of TABLATURE.

Uhr, Die, German title for Haydn's 'CLOCK' SYMPHONY.

Ulysses (It., *Ulisse*), opera by Dallapiccola, based on Homer; first performance, West Berlin, 1968. Mátyás Seiber's cantata of the same title was inspired not by Homer but by James Joyce's novel.

Umkehrung, German word meaning 'turning round', 'reversal', 'inversion'. A *'Kanon in der Umkehrung'* would be a canon by inversion.

Umlauf, Ignaz (1746–96), Austrian composer. He was violinist in the court theatre orchestra, Vienna, from 1772; director of the German national *Singspiel*, which he opened with his *Bergknappen* (1778), and from 1789 he was assistant *Kapellmeister* (under Salieri) for the court theatre orchestra and for the opera. He composed *Singspiele*, a comic opera, and incidental music.

His son, **Michael Umlauf** (1781–1842), was also a composer and conductor. He was violinist at the Vienna Opera and *Kapellmeister* at the two court theatres, 1810–25 and from 1840. From 1814 he gave the beat to the orchestra in performances of Beethoven's works, while the composer (who was then growing deaf) conducted. He composed twelve ballets, a *Singspiel*, an opera, church music and piano sonatas.

umore (It.), 'humour'. Thus *'Mit Umore'*, signifies 'with humour'.

una corda (It.), one string. A term used in piano music to indicate the use of the left hand pedal. On grand pianos this normally shifts the whole keyboard slightly to the right, so that the hammers can strike only one or two of the two or three strings assigned to each note. For other methods of achieving a similar effect on upright pianos, *see* CORDA

Una Cosa Rara (A rare thing), opera in two acts by Martin y Soler with libretto by Lorenzo da Ponte, based on a story by Luis Velez de Guevara. The opera was first performed at the Burgtheater, Vienna in 1786, six months after Mozart's *The Marriage of Figaro* (whose success it stole). Later, Mozart quoted an excerpt from Act 1 of Soler's opera in the Supper Scene of *Don Giovanni*, enabling Leporello to voice the reply: 'Bravi! *Cosa Rara*!' Though no longer a rival to Mozart's operas, *Una Cosa Rara* has achieved a few productions in recent years. The score contains one of the earliest examples of a Viennese waltz.

Una furtiva lagrima (a furtive tear), Nemorino's aria in Act 2 of Donizetti's *L'Elisir d'Amore*, in which he detects tears in his beloved Adina's eyes – proof, he hopes, that his love is returned.

Una voce poco fa, Rosina's aria in Act 1 of Rossini's *The Barber of Seville* in which she reads a love letter from Lindoro, the student who is really Count Almaviva in disguise. Though often sung by sopranos, the aria was conceived by Rossini for mezzo voice.

Un Ballo in Maschera, *see* MASKED BALL

Un bel di vedremo, aria in Act 2 of Puccini's *Madama Butterfly* in which Cio-Cio-San looks forward to the return of Pinkerton. It is famous in English translation as 'One fine day'.

unda maris (Lat.), 'wave of the sea'. An organ stop of soft tone which is tuned slightly flatter than the true pitch, or which has two ranks slightly mistuned, so that a beat results which has an effect similar to that of a vibrato. A stop of this type may also be called *voix céleste* or *vox angelica*.

Un di felice, love duet between Alfredo and Violetta in Act 1 of Verdi's *La Traviata*.

Undine, opera in four acts by Lortzing with a libretto by the composer, based on Friedrich de la Motte Fouqué's story of the same title. The first performance was in Magdeburg, in 1845. The story, of a water-nymph who lured her unfaithful lover to his death, also inspired operas by E. T. A. Hoffmann (1816), Mori (1865) and Sporck (1877) as well as a ballet by Hans Werner Henze.

'Unfinished' Symphony, the title given to Schubert's symphony no 8 in B minor (1822), of which he completed only two movements, though sketches for a third have survived. It was sent to the Musical Society at Graz in return for his election as an honorary member. It was recovered in 1865 and received its première in Vienna in that year, conducted by Johann Herbeck. There are various theories as to why the work is incomplete: Schubert may have meant to complete it later; or he did actually complete it, but the two final documents were mislaid; or he simply ran out of inspiration. Among scholars who incline to the last of these theories is Hans Gal. Nevertheless, a number of attempts have been made to complete the work, (most recently by the English scholar, Gerald Abraham, in 1971), though the symphony achieves perfection as it stands.

unichord, alternative name for the MONOCHORD.

Union pipe, a form of BAGPIPE, popular in Ireland from the early 18th century. It is blown by a bellows and has a relatively quiet tone which makes it suitable for indoor use. The modern instrument is very elaborate. 'Uillean pipe' is sometimes used as an alternative name, 'uillean' being the Gaelic for 'elbow'.

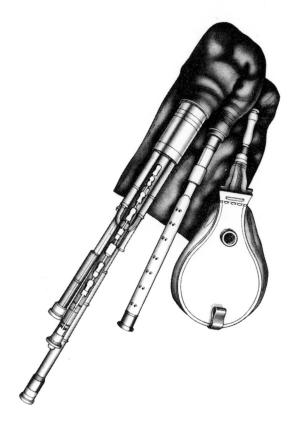

Union pipe

unison, the combined sound of two or more notes of the same pitch. The term 'singing in unison' is used when a song is performed by several voices, all of them at the same pitch (or, in the case of male and female voices, an octave apart).

unit organ, a small organ constructed to save space and expense, with certain pipes shared by different stops.

unruhig (Ger.), restless.

unter (Ger.), 'under', 'lower'.

Unterwerk (Ger.), choir organ.

up-beat, the upward movement of a conductor's baton or hand, indicating the beat before the main accent in a bar of music.

up bow, a bow stroke on a stringed instrument from the point to the heel.

upper partials, overtones produced by vibrating strings or (in the case of wind instruments) air columns.

Uppman, Theodor (born 1920), U.S. baritone. He sang the title-role in Britten's *Billy Budd* at the Covent Garden première in 1951.

upright piano, the ordinary domestic piano in which, to save space, the strings are laid out vertically instead of horizontally as in a grand piano.

See PIANO

Urio, Francesco Antonio (born c. 1660), composer and Franciscan monk. He was *maestro di cappella* of the Church of the Twelve Apostles in Rome (1690) and later of the Church of the Frari in Venice. He composed a *Te Deum* (modern edition, supplement no 2 to Chrysander's edition of Handel), oratorios, motets for voices and instruments, and psalms. A considerable amount of material from the *Te Deum* was used by Handel in his *Dettingen Te Deum*, *Saul*, *Israel in Egypt* and *L'Allegro*. The view, however, has been taken that Handel was himself the composer of the *Te Deum* attributed to Urio (*see* P. Robinson, *Handel and his Orbit*).

Usper, Francesco Spongia (died 1641), Italian organist, composer and priest. He lived in Venice, where he was organist at San Salvatore (c. 1614), deputy organist at San Marco (1621–23), and director of the school of St. John the Evangelist (1627). He composed church music, madrigals, *ricercari* and other instrumental pieces. He used the tremolo for violin in his instrumental works before its appearance in Monteverdi's *Combattimento di Tancredi e Clorinda* (1624).

Ussachevsky, Vladimir (born 1911), U.S. composer whose tape-recorder experiments in the 1950s made him one of the pioneers of U.S. electronic music.

Ut, French for the note C, *Ut majeur* being C major. It is also the first note of the Guidonian hexachord (*see* SOLMIZATION).

utility music (Ger., *Gebrauchsmusik*), term employed by Hindemith, Weill and other German composers of the 1920s, to describe works which were intended to have a social or political function rather than be music for music's sake. In writing pieces of this nature, composers tended to choose everyday subjects and to cultivate an everyday style.

Utopia Limited or **The Flowers of Progress**, comic opera in two acts by Sullivan with libretto by W. S. Gilbert. The first performance was in London in 1893. The story concerns a Utopia run on the lines of a British limited liability company.

Utrecht Te Deum, choral work by Handel, composed (along with a Jubilate) for the Peace of Utrecht. The first performance was in St. Paul's Cathedral, London, 1713.

Utrenja, a large-scale choral work by Penderecki, in two parts – *The Entombment of Christ* and *The Resurrection of Christ*. The title refers to the morning service of the Eastern Church, the work consisting mainly of settings of extracts from two such services, those for the Saturday and Sunday of Easter. Part 1 was originally conceived as an independent piece, in which form it had its première at Altenberg Cathedral in 1970. Part 2 was completed the following year.

V, as an abbreviation, V.=violin, voice. V.=verse (in Gregorian chant). Vc.=cello. Vla.=viola. Vln.= violin. V.S.=*volti subito* (turn over quickly – an instruction frequently found in manuscripts of orchestral parts.

Vaccai, Nicola (1790–1848), Italian opera composer, who studied under Paisiello at Naples. The most successful of his works was *Giulietta e Romeo* (Milan, 1825), the last scene of which came to be substituted for the corresponding section of Bellini's *I Capuleti ed i Montecchi* (Venice, 1830), a setting of the same libretto (after Shakespeare's *Romeo and Juliet*). His treatise on singing, *Metodo practico di canto italiano per camera*, had a considerable vogue.

Vaet, Jakob (1529–67), Flemish composer. He was in the service of Maximilian, King of Bohemia, on whose accession as emperor (Maximilian II) he was appointed *Kapellmeister* in Vienna. He composed a quantity of church music, some of which was published under the title *Modulationes quinque vocum* (*volgo motecta*) *noncupatae* (two volumes, 1562). A modern edition of his complete works was begun in 1961 by Milton Steinhardt in various volumes of the series *Denkmäler der Tonkunst in Osterreich* (beginning with volume xcviii).

Vakula the Smith, opera in four acts by Chaikovsky, with a libretto by Yakov Polonsky, after Gogol's story *Christmas Eve*. It was first performed at St. Petersburg in 1876, and was revised nine years later under the title of *Cherevichki* (*The Little Shoes*). In the latter form it had its première at Moscow in 1887.

Valen, Olav Fartein (1887–1952), Norwegian composer who spent his early years in Madagascar. He studied at the Oslo Conservatory and the Hochschule für Musik, Berlin, where he was a pupil of Reger. His compositions, in which he adapted Schoenbergian methods to his own purposes, include five symphonies, two string quartets, a violin concerto, choral works, piano music and songs.

Valkyrie, The, *see* WALKÜRE

Vallas, Léon (1879–1956), French music critic and teacher. He founded the *Revue musicale de Lyon*, 1903 (later *Revue française de musique* and *Nouvelle Revue musicale*), and wrote books on Debussy and d'Indy.

Vallin, Ninon (1886–1961), French soprano, who began her career as a concert singer (in Debussy's *La Damoiselle élue* and *Le Martyr de Saint Sébastien*). In 1912 she joined the Opéra-Comique in Paris, where she became a leading exponent of the title-roles in Charpentier's *Louise* and Massenet's *Manon*.

valse (Fr.), waltz.

Valse, La (Fr., *The Waltz*), poème choréographique for orchestra by Ravel, first performed in Paris, 1920.

Valses Nobles et Sentimentales (Fr., *Noble and Sentimental Waltzes*), a set of seven waltzes for piano

solo by Ravel. The title is an allusion to Schubert's *Valses nobles*, op 77, and *Valses sentimentales*, op 50, for piano solo. The set was first performed in Paris in 1911 at a concert where all the works in the programme were anonymous. It was subsequently orchestrated and performed as a ballet under the title *Adélaïde, ou Le Langage des fleurs*, Paris, 1912.

Valse Triste (Fr., sad waltz), orchestral piece by Sibelius, part of the incidental music to Arvid Järnefelt's play *Kuolema*, op 44 (1903).

valve (Fr., *piston*; Ger., *Ventil*; It., *pistone*), a device enabling brass instruments to command a complete chromatic compass. Valves are used on the horn, cornet, trumpet, Flügelhorn, saxhorn, euphonium, tuba and, less frequently, on a trombone, where the same result is normally achieved by means of a slide. They are of two kinds: (1) piston valves: (2) rotary valves. Each type consists of a cylinder, pierced with holes in the appropriate places, the first moving vertically inside a cylindrical case, and the second rotating. Both fulfil one of two functions. In the case of the first and more general of these the holes are so designed that when the valve is depressed the air column is compelled to pass through extra tubing and so lower the pitch. The second function is exactly the opposite. Lengths of tubing are cut off and the pitch consequently raised.

On a three-valved instrument – such as the F horn, trumpet, cornet and valve trombone – the first valve lowers the pitch a tone, the second a semitone, the first and second together (or the third alone) a minor third, the second and third together a major third, the first and third together a perfect fourth, and all three together a diminished fifth (or augmented fourth). The following example gives all the theoretical fingering possible, some of which are rarely, if ever, used, for a chromatic scale of one octave on the C trumpet (o represents an open note, i.e. without the use of valves):

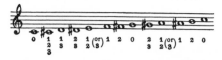

A fourth valve, lowering the pitch a perfect fourth, is usually added to euphoniums and tubas, and sometimes to the very high B flat trumpet pitched an octave above the normal instrument; this last is a recent innovation. Its main purpose is to fill the gap between the fundamental note and the augmented fourth above, these five notes being unobtainable on an instrument with only three valves. The same device is also applied to the slide trombone in B flat, which consequently becomes a double instrument. However the opposite applies in the case of the double horn, for here the fourth valve raises the pitch from F to the B flat a fourth above, thereby giving increased security in the upper register and also an extension of compass in the lower, since the B flat fundamental note can be produced whereas the F, to all intents and purposes, cannot. Certain deep instruments also possess a compensating valve. This introduces a very small length of extra tubing, and its purpose to assist correct intonation, rather more tubing being needed for this on 'valved notes' in the lower register than in the upper. It must be said that valve systems are in a constant state of flux, particularly on deep instruments. For instance, many B flat slide trombones have a second valve that, when used in conjunction with the first, puts the instrument down an augmented fourth to E. Other and more recent systems allow this instrument to change instantly from B flat to E flat or D as well as to F.

See also HORN, TROMBONE, TUBA

valve horn, valve trombone, etc., *see* HORN, TROMBONE, etc.

vamp, to improvise an accompaniment, usually to a song.

Vampyr, Der (Ger., *The Vampire*), opera in two acts by Marschner, produced at Leipzig in 1828. The libretto, by William August Wöhlbruck, derives from a story by John William Polidori. It tells how Lord Ruthven avoids death for three years by annually sacrificing a pure maiden to the spirits. In the end he is exposed as a vampire, and is struck down by a flash of lightning.

Van den Borren, Charles, *see* BORREN

Van Dieren, Bernard, *see* DIEREN

Vanessa, Samuel Barber's first opera, produced in 1958 at the New York Metropolitan and in the same year at the Salzburg Festival. The libretto, in four acts, is by Gian Carlo Menotti. It concerns three women (two of them baronesses), representing three generations of one family, and living in a castle in a northern country in 1905.

Va, pensiero, sull' ali dorate, patriotic chorus in Act 3 of Verdi's *Nabucco*, in which the Hebrew prisoners by the banks of the Euphrates sing of their lost homeland.

Vanhall, Johann Baptist, *see* WANHAL

Varèse, Edgard (also known, inaccurately, as Edgar) (1885–1965), French born composer who studied in Paris under D'Indy, Roussel, and Widor. As a young man he was encouraged by Debussy and in 1913 attended the première of *The Rite of Spring* at the Théâtre de Champs-Elysées, later declaring that Stravinsky's work 'seemed very natural to him'. During World War I, he served in the French army but his health failed to stand the strain. In 1916 he emigrated to the United States, where he later took U.S. citizenship. In 1921 he became one of the founders of the International Composers Guild, and for the rest of his career did much to further the cause of modern music in the United States. A dedicated experimentalist, he used the sound-quality – or what he liked to call the 'density' – of each instrument as the starting-point of his musical ideas, rather than harmony, melody or form. Wilfrid Mellers has aptly described Varèse's music as 'a polyphony of timbres' (*Man and his Music*, page 1059).

Varèse's most famous piece, and the one that embodies his musical philosophy at its purest, is his *Density 21.5* for solo flute (1936) – the title refers to the density of platinum, because the piece was written for a platinum flute. His other works, many of them making pioneering use of bold instrumental combinations, include *Ionisation* for thirteen percussionists (1933), *Ecuatorial* for chorus, brass, piano, organ, two ondes Martenot and percussion (1934, revised 1961), *Etude* and *Espaces* for chorus, two pianos and percussion (1947) and *Déserts* for orchestra and two tracks of 'organised sounds' on magnetic tape (1950–54). He also wrote a number of works for symphony orchestra, among them *Amériques* (1920–21) and *Arcana* (1926–27), both of which were first conducted by Leopold Stokowski.

F. OUELLETTE: *Edgard Varèse* (1966; English translation 1968)

variation, the process of modifying a theme, figure or passage in such a way that the resulting product is recognisably derived from the original.

The simplest type of variation consists in repeating a passage with modifications, e.g.:

CHOPIN, *Nocturne* no 15, op 55, no 1

Extended melodic variation occurs in 15th century motets in which the upper part is an embellished version of a familiar plainsong melody. In such cases the variation is heard without the theme on which it is based. Dunstable's motet 'Veni, sancte Spiritus' (*Musica Britannica*, viii, no 32), however, is an example of a piece in which the plainsong melody (of the hymn 'Veni, creator spiritus') is present (*a*) in its original form, in long notes, (*b*) in a melodic variation in the treble.

Variation of accompaniment is found in Spanish and French lute-songs of the 16th century. Two versions of the accompaniment are given, one simple, the other florid; the voice-part remains the same in both. Variation of accompaniment became a familiar practice of composers of strophic songs in the late 18th and 19th century: for an example see Osmin's first song in Mozart's *Die Entführung* (1782).

Variation of contrapuntal setting occurs in 15th and 16th century compositions based on a CANTUS FIRMUS: (*a*) in motets in which the *cantus firmus* is stated more than once, (*b*) in Masses, where the same *cantus firmus* serves as a basis for several movements. In such cases the rhythm of the *cantus firmus* may be altered, but melodically it remains the same, while the material of the other parts which compose the contrapuntal texture is constantly varied, though their melodic material may often be derived from the *cantus firmus*.

Melodic variation above a repeated bass occurs in the strophic monodies of the Florentine composers of the early 17th century: for an example see the prologue to Monteverdi's *Orfeo* (1607). In such cases the bass has no symmetrical structure but is used simply as a foundation for the melodies of the successive verses.

Melodic variation above a symmetrical bass is represented by the GROUND or *ostinato*, which was extremely popular in the 17th century and has remained an element in composition down to the present day. The origin of such variation is probably to be sought in popular dance music. Examples are to be found both in instrumental and vocal music. Allied forms are the CHACONNE and PASSACAGLIA, though here the persistent theme is not necessarily restricted to the bass (*see also* DIVISIONS).

The practice of writing a sequence of instrumental variations on a theme occurs first in the Spanish lute music of the early 16th century. Similar variations were also written by English composers for the virginals in the late 16th and early 17th centuries. The themes chosen were in many cases popular songs. From that time the 'theme and variations' has been a standard form of composition. As well as choosing popular songs composers have also borrowed themes from other composers (Beethoven's variations on a theme of Diabelli, Brahms's variations on a theme of Handel, Britten's variations on a theme of Frank Bridge) or provided their own (Mendelssohn's *Variations sérieuses*, Elgar's *Enigma* variations). Since one element in variation is elaboration, it is inevitable that variations for a solo instrument (as well as for chamber music ensembles and orchestra) should make some demands on virtuosity. The temptation to make virtuosity a mere excuse for variations has proved irresistible to some composers. Beethoven's exploration of more subtle methods of presenting a theme in new guises did not put an end to this tendency. Mendelssohn's *Variations sérieuses* were in fact written as a protest against the emptiness of so much of the work of early 19th century composers in this form. Later composers, e.g. Brahms and Elgar, have moved far away from the mere pursuit of brilliance: Elgar's *Enigma* variations have a unique psychological interest, in that they are not only variations on an original theme but also portraits in music of a number of his friends.

The basic elements to be found in a series of variations are: variation of melody; variation of figuration or texture; variation of rhythm; variation of tonality (e.g. minor for major, or vice versa); and lastly variation of harmony. Any or all of these may be combined in the same variation. The art of variation is, however, more complex than the mere exploitation of these basic types: it consists much more in using the theme as a source of inspiration and deriving from it suggestions which may superficially appear to have only a slight connection with it. The link is not necessarily to be sought on the surface but in the composer's imagination.

Variation has also been combined with other forms. In the 17th century variation suites were written, in which the several dance movements were thematically related and hence were in fact variations on a basic melody. From the late 18th century variations have frequently figured as a complete movement in a sonata, symphony, or similar composition. Schumann combined variations on a theme with sonata form in the first movement of his piano concerto. Strauss, in *Don Quixote*, wrote a symphonic poem in the form of an introduction, theme and variations, each of which illustrates an episode in the life of his hero. In a more general sense variation is an indispensable element in all symphonic writing. DEVELOPMENT of a theme or themes consists in realizing the possibilities inherent in the material and so is itself a form of variation.

See also DOUBLE

Variations on a Theme of Haydn, *see* HAYDN VARIATIONS

variazione (It.), variation; *tema con variazioni*, theme and variations.

Varnay, Astrid (born 1918), U.S. soprano, born in Stockholm, of Austro-Hungarian parentage. She made her début at the New York Metropolitan in 1941 as Sieglinde in *Die Walküre*, and subsequently established herself internationally as an outstanding exponent of Wagner and Strauss roles.

varsovienne (Fr., short for *danse varsovienne*), Warsaw dance. A dance in fairly slow 3/4 time, in mazurka rhythm, popular in the salons of Paris in the time of Napoleon III.

Vàsàry, Tamàs (born 1933), Hungarian pianist, who received his musical training at the Liszt Academy in Budapest. He is one of the finest Mozart and Chopin exponents of his generation.

Vassilenko, Sergei Nikiphorovich (1872–1956), Russian composer. He studied at the Moscow Conservatory, where he taught from 1906 to 1938. Beginning as a nationalist composer, he developed for a time a more cosmopolitan style, subsequently reverting, under the influence of Oriental melodies which he collected, to a characteristically Russian idiom. His compositions include the opera *Son of the Sun* (Moscow, 1929), the cantata *The Legend of the City of Kitezh* (later rewritten as an opera), four other operas, six ballets, four symphonies, the symphonic poems *The Garden of Death* (after Oscar Wilde) and *Witches' Flight* (*Hircus Nocturnus*) and other orchestral works, a violin concerto, incidental music, chamber music and songs.

vaudeville (Fr., origin uncertain), a popular song, in particular, a topical song to a well-known tune, sung in Paris in the early 18th century at the Théâtre de la Foire (Fair Theatre) and its successor the Opéra-Comique. The final *vaudeville* in such an entertainment often consisted of verses sung by each of the characters in turn. This practice was also imitated in opera, e.g. Mozart's *Die Entführung* (1782).

With the establishment of *opéra-comique* as an independent form with original music the term *vaudeville* came to be given to comedies interspersed with songs (originally *comédies mêlées de vaudevilles* or *comédies vaudevilles*). This type of entertainment flourished in the 19th century. More recently, Britten has used the term to describe his one-act stage work for boys, *The Golden Vanity*.

Vaudeville is now often used to describe a variety entertainment.

Vaughan Williams, Ralph (1872–1958), British composer, born at Down Ampney, Gloucestershire, and educated at Charterhouse and Cambridge. He studied at the Royal College of Music with Parry and Stanford, in Berlin with Max Bruch, and also for a short time with Ravel in Paris. Vaughan Williams held comparatively few official appointments. He joined the R.C.M. as teacher of composition in 1918, conducted the Bach Choir, 1920–6, and became president of the English Folk Dance and Song Society in 1932. He also for many years directed the Leith Hill Festival at Dorking. His interest in English folk song dated from the beginning of the century: he was active as a collector and discovered an affinity between the traditional melodies and his own aspirations. Folk song began to colour his work more and more, but this was combined with the influence of Tudor polyphony and restrained by an independence of outlook which gave to his mature work a wholly individual flavour. He made occasional use of POLYTONALITY, e.g. in *Flos campi*; but more frequently this arrived naturally as a result of turning single melodic lines into sequences of chords in block harmony – a process which results in strong passing dissonance when two independant sequences of this kind are combined. The range of expression of his work is considerable: brutal violence, robust jollity and an almost mystical tranquility – all these find a place, often in the same work. The contrasts between them are not contradictions but related facets of the same personality. In his published opinions on music – his own and others – he always expresses a profound distaste for shams and insincerity (but he could be wildly wrong, as when he described Mahler as 'a tolerable imitation of a composer'). His own work is the best evidence of the value of uncompromising honesty. Familiarity with its mannerisms does nothing to lessen respect for its integrity.

His principal compositions are:

(1) Orchestra: *A London Symphony* (1914; revised 1920); *A Pastoral Symphony* (1922); symphony in F minor (no 4; 1935); symphony in D major (no 5, 1943); symphony in E minor (no 6, 1948); *Sinfonia Antartica* (1953); symphony in D minor (no 8; 1956); symphony in E minor (no 9, 1958); three Norfolk rhapsodies (1906–7); Fantasia on a theme by Tallis (1910); *The Lark ascending*, for violin and orchestra (1914); *Flos campi*, for viola, orchestra and voices (1925); *Concerto accademico* for violin (1925); piano concerto (1933); suite for viola and orchestra (1934); *Five Variants of 'Dives and Lazarus'*, for strings and harp (1939); oboe concerto (1948).

(2) Choral works: *Toward the Unknown Region* (1907); *A Sea Symphony* (1910); *Five Mystical Songs* (1911); Fantasia on Christmas carols (1912); Mass in G minor (1923); *Sancta Civitas* (1926); *Benedicite* (1930); three choral hymns (1930); *Magnificat* (1932); *Dona nobis pacem* (1936); *Five Tudor Portraits* (1936); *Te Deum* (1937); *Serenade to Music* (1938); *The Sons of Light* (1950).

(3) Operas: *Hugh the Drover* (1914); *Riders to the Sea* (1927); *The Poisoned Kiss* (1928); *Sir John in Love* (1929); *The Pilgrim's Progress* (1951, incorporating most of the one-act *The Shepherds of the Delectable Mountains*, 1922).

(4) Other stage works: incidental music to *The Wasps*

Sir Ralph Vaughan Williams: a portrait study in which the composer might be reflecting on his comment on his fourth symphony: 'I don't know whether I like it or not, but it's what I meant.'

of Aristophanes (1909); ballets – *Old King Cole* (1923); *Job* (1930).

(5) Chamber music: piano quintet; two string quartets (G minor, A minor); fantasy quintet for strings.

(6) Songs: *The House of Life* (six sonnets by Rossetti); *Songs of Travel* (Stevenson); *On Wenlock Edge* (songcycle: Housman); and many individual songs. Also works for organ and piano, and film music.

He also published *National Music* (1934) and *Some Thoughts on Beethoven's Choral Symphony* (1953).

JAMES DAY: *Vaughan Williams* (1961)

A. E. E. DICKINSON: *An Introduction to the Music of R. Vaughan Williams* (1928)

H. FOSS: *Ralph Vaughan Williams* (1950)

F. HOWES: *The Music of Ralph Vaughan Williams* (1954)

MICHAEL KENNEDY: *The Works of Ralph Vaughan Williams* (1964)

S. PAKENHAM: *Ralph Vaughan Williams: a Discovery of his Music* (1957)

URSULA VAUGHAN WILLIAMS: *R.V.W., a biography* (1964)

P. M. YOUNG: *Vaughan Williams* (1953)

Vautor, Thomas, English composer of the early 17th century who published a volume of five-part and six-part madrigals (1619), dedicated to the Marquess (later Duke) of Buckingham. A modern edition is in *The English Madrigal School*, xxxiv.

Vauxhall Gardens, a house and grounds at Lambeth, opened to the public at the Restoration under the name 'Spring Garden' and used for concerts in the 18th century and also for dramatic entertainments with music in the early 19th century. The name 'Vauxhall Gardens' was first used in 1786. Roubiliac's statue of Handel (now at Messrs. Novello & Co., 160 Wardour Street) was erected there in 1738.

Vecchi, Orazio (1550–1605), Italian composer. He was *maestro di cappella* at Modena Cathedral from 1584 to 1585 and from 1596 to 1604, and at Reggio Cathedral in 1586. From 1586 he was canon at Correggio, becoming archdeacon there for the period 1591 to 1595. From 1598 to his death he was *maestro di cappella* to the Duke of Modena.

He published six books of *canzonette*, two books of madrigals, Masses, motets, and four collections for voices entitled *Selva di varia ricreatione* (The grove of varied recreation), *Convito musicale* (Musical banquet), *Amfiparnaso* and *Veglie di Siena* (Evening parties in Siena). Of these the best known is *Amfiparnaso* (modern edition in *Publikationen älterer praktischer und theoretischer Musikwerke*, xxvi, Jg. xxx, and L. Torchi, *L'arte musicale in Italia*, iv), in which characters from the *commedia dell' arte* are presented in a series of contrasted and frequently comic madrigalian compositions:

the characterization is left to the singers, since a stage presentation would not only be impossible but is expressly excluded by the composer.

Vecchi, Orfeo, late 16th-century Italian composer who was *maestro di cappella* at the church of S. Maria della Scala, Milan. His compositions – motets, Masses, psalms, etc. – are almost exclusively for the church.

veloce (It.), fast.

Venegas de Henestrosa, Luys (c. 1505–after 1557), Spanish musician who was in the service of Cardinal Juan de Tavera, archbishop of Santiago and later of Toledo. He compiled and published in 1557 *Libro de cifra nueva para tecla, harpa, y vihuela* (A book of new tablature for keyboard, harp and *vihuela*), a modern edition of which was published by H. Anglès in *La Música en la Corte de Carlos V* (*Monumentos de la Música Española*, ii). It contains several pieces by Cabezón.

Venetian Swell, a series of shutters, similar to the laths of a Venetian blind, used to control the volume produced by a keyboard instrument. It was first applied to the harpsichord by Burkat Shudi in 1769, and subsequently adapted for the organ.

See SWELL ORGAN

Venite (Lat.), the first word of Psalm 95, 'Venite, exultemus Domino' (O come let us sing unto the Lord), sung as a canticle before the psalms at Matins in the Anglican service. It was included in choral settings of

Vauxhall Gardens, in London's Lambeth, opened in May 1660 and closed in July 1859. Pepys found its entertainments 'mighty devertising'; but over 200 years the character of the eating, drinking, music, and dancing degenerated into notoriety. It is recorded that on one August night in 1833 over 20,000 thronged its booths and alleys.

the service by pre-Commonwealth composers (e.g. Tallis, Byrd, Gibbons), but since the Restoration has been sung as a chant, like the psalms.

Ventil (Ger.), valve.

Venus and Adonis, masque with a prologue and three acts by Blow. The librettist is unknown. It was first performed at the court of Charles II in about 1682. Modern editions exist by G. E. P. Arkwright (*Old English Edition*, no xxv) and by Anthony Lewis (1949).

Vêpres Siciliennes, Les, *see* SICILIAN VESPERS

Verbunkos, Hungarian military dance, once used to attract recruits for enlistment in the army. Its heyday was in the late 18th and early 19th centuries, when the Austrian government imposed conscription. Today it survives as a ceremonial dance. Its traditional musical layout of a slow introduction (*lassu*) followed by a rapid section (*friss*) has been used as the basis of a number of Hungarian rhapsodies (e.g. those of Liszt and Bartók).

Verdelot (also known as **Deslouges), Philippe,** 16th century Flemish composer, possibly born in the village of Les Loges, near Montmirail (part of the former province of Champagne). He spent most of his life in Italy and possibly died in Florence in the 1530s or 1540s. He was one of the earliest composers of Italian madrigals. Two books of madrigals by him were published, and many more appeared together with the works of other composers. He also composed two Masses and several motets. Two of his madrigals are in Schering's *Geschichte der Musik in Beispielen*, nos 97–8, and four are in Einstein's *The Italian Madrigal*, iii, nos 16–19. Several of his madrigals and motets are in *A Gift of Madrigals and Motets*, edited by H. C. Slim (1972). A complete edition of his works was begun in 1966 by Anne-Marie Bragard.

> A.-M. BRAGARD: *Etude bio-bibliographique sur Philippe Verdelot* (1964)

Verdi, Giuseppe (1813–1901), Italian composer. Born near Busseto, the son of a grocer, Verdi began his career playing the organ at the village church and acting as assistant conductor of the Busseto Philharmonic Society. Having failed to gain admission to the Milan Conservatorio in 1832, he studied privately with Lavigna, a repetiteur at La Scala. The staff of La Scala recognised Verdi's genius even if Milan's academics did not; and it was at La Scala that his first opera, *Oberto, Conte di S. Bonifacio,* was successfully produced in 1839. Merelli, the Scala's discerning administrator, immediately invited Verdi to write three more. Unfortunately the first of these, a comedy entitled *Un giorno di regno* (1840), was a flop. Moreover it coincided with the death from disease of Verdi's wife and two children, and as a result the composer vowed he would write no more music. In the end, however, the sympathetic Merelli managed to get him working again by showing him the libretto of *Nabucco*, a text (by Solera) whose patriotic fervour proved irresistible. The huge success of the finished work, with its chorus, 'Va, pensiero', which sent nationalist pulses racing, was the first big milestone in Verdi's career. From that time he devoted himself almost entirely to the composition of operas. Soon leading opera houses throughout Italy and elsewhere requested his services. *Rigoletto* (one of several works which ran him into censorship trouble because of politically controversial texts) was written for Venice

Giuseppe Verdi in his ripe old age – the period of his two greatest masterpieces, *Otello* and *Falstaff*

in 1851 and *Il trovatore* for Rome in 1853. The latter, said the composer in a manifesto as stirring as some of Wagner's declarations farther north, was to be 'a new sort of opera' in which arias, cabalettas, duets, ensembles, finales and so forth would not take precedence over drama. Though, at this stage in his career, he did not pursue his aims with quite Wagner's single-mindedness, *Il trovatore* can still seem a potent, forward-looking work when properly presented – not at all the glorification of 'the bad old style' it is often thought to be. *La traviata* (Venice, 1853), though initially a failure, soon established itself as the intimate obverse of *Trovatore*. In *A Masked Ball,* (*Un ballo in maschera*, Rome, 1859), *The Force of Destiny* (*La Forza del Destino*, St. Petersburg, 1862), *Don Carlos* (Paris, 1867) and *Simon Boccanegra* (Venice, 1857; revised, Milan, 1881) Verdi's Shakespearian qualities came to the fore. *Aida* (Cairo, 1871) was perhaps more of a 'grand opera', but it contains private scenes of an expressiveness that place it far above other works of its type. Then, after a sixteen-year gap during which (for the second time in his career) Verdi appeared to have abandoned the stage, came the two genuinely Shakespearian operas, *Otello* (Milan, 1887) and *Falstaff* (Milan, 1893) which crowned his achievement. In addition to these works, he also composed in his later years some church music (although he was not a churchgoer), including in 1873 the Manzoni Requiem in tribute to Italy's great poet, novelist and patriot. 'I would have knelt before him', declared Verdi, 'if men worshipped men'. Instead he commemorated him with one of the great choral requiems of the 19th century.

Brought up in the traditions of Italian opera, which exalted the singer at the expense of the orchestra, Verdi began his career by accepting them wholeheartedly and only gradually developed the form for his own use, until he reached supreme mastery in the operas of his old age – *Otello* and *Falstaff*. Though he himself dismissed his formative period as his 'years in the galleys', his early works are not to be disparaged. Even in his most immature works, Verdi had a gift for melody and a red-bloodedness that sweep the music along. One after another, these works have been revived in recent years and found to be still full of life.

Nevertheless, as he matured, Verdi's work showed a steady growth of musicianship, an increased sensitivity and, in particular, a resourceful and imaginative treatment of the orchestra. His orchestration was highly individual, picturesque, and completely clear, although some have criticised it (e.g. Bernard Shaw, who likened it to the sound of a big guitar). Verdi's principal compositions are:–

(1) Operas: *Oberto, Conte di San Bonifacio* (Milan, 1839); *Un giorno di regno* (Milan, 1840); *Nabucco*

A cartoon at the time of *Don Carlos*. Whatever may be thought of Verdi's early melodramas, the hurdy-gurdy hardly seems appropriate to a work which shows the composer at the peak of his dramatic maturity

(*Nabucodonosor*) (Milan, 1842); *I Lombardi alla prima crociata* (Milan, 1843; revised as *Jérusalem*, Paris, 1847); *Ernani* (Venice, 1844); *I due Foscari* (Rome, 1844); *Giovanna d'Arco* (Milan, 1845) *Alzira* (Naples, 1845); *Attila* (Venice, 1846); *Macbeth* (Florence, 1847; revised, Paris, 1865); *I masnadieri* (London, 1847); *Il corsaro* (Trieste, 1848); *La battaglia di Legnano* (Rome, 1849); *Luisa Miller* (Naples, 1849); *Stiffelio* (Trieste, 1850; revised as *Aroldo*, Rimini, 1857); *Rigoletto* (Venice, 1851); *Il Trovatore* (Rome, 1853); *La Traviata* (Venice, 1853); *Les Vêpres siciliennes* (Paris, 1855); *Simon Boccanegra* (Venice, 1857; revised, Milan, 1881); *Un ballo in maschera* (Rome, 1859); *La forza del destino* (St. Petersburg, 1862); *Don Carlos* (Paris,

1867); *Aida* (Cairo, 1871); *Otello* (Milan, 1887); *Falstaff* (Milan, 1893).

(2) Choral works: *Inno delle nazioni* (1862); *Messa da Requiem* (1874); *Pater Noster*; *Ave Maria* (1889); *Stabat Mater* (1898); *Te Deum* (1898); *Lauda alla Vergine Maria* (1898).

(3) Chamber music: string quartet (1873).

(4) Songs: sixteen songs and a part-song.

F. BONAVIA: *Verdi* (1930)
J. BUDDEN: *The Operas of Verdi* (volume one, 1973)
G. CESARI and A. LUZIO: *I copialettere di Giuseppe Verdi* (1913)
D. HUSSEY: *Verdi* (1940)
A. LUZIO: *Carteggi Verdiani* (four volumes, 1935–47)
G. MARTIN: *Verdi: His Music, Life and Times* (1963)
C. OSBORNE: *The Complete Operas of Verdi* (1969)
C. OSBORNE: *Letters of Giuseppe Verdi, selected, translated and edited from the copialettere* (1971)
F. WALKER: *The Man Verdi* (1962)
J. WECHSBERG: *Verdi* (1974)

Veress, Sándor (born 1907), Hungarian pianist, composer and critic, now living in Switzerland. He first appeared in public as a pianist in 1916, and as a composer in 1920. He studied at the Musical Academy of Buda and the State Academy of Music, Budapest, where his teachers included Bartók and Kodály. He was teacher of composition, Academy of Music, Budapest, 1943; Berne Conservatorium, 1950. His music has been influenced by his activity as a collector of folk songs, by the example of Bartók, and by Stravinsky's neo-classical style. His compositions include an opera for children, ballets, several choral works, two symphonies and chamber music, a violin concerto, piano concerto, and a Sinfonia Minneapolitana (for the Minneapolis Symphony Orchestra).

Veretti, Antonio (born 1900), Italian composer, pupil of Alfano. He has written music in diversified styles, including a Sinfonia Sacra for chorus and orchestra and a one-act opera-ballet, *Burlesca*.

verismo (It., from *vero*, 'true'), anglicized as 'verism'. An artistic movement originating in the late 19th century which aimed at a vivid and realistic representation of contemporary life. In opera this resulted in a melodramatic treatment which tended to exploit individual moments at the expense of development or structural unity. The best known examples are Mascagni's *Cavalleria rusticana* (1890), Leoncavallo's *I Pagliacci* (1892), and Charpentier's *Louise*; in all these the participants are people of humble birth. Such realism is different from that of Bizet's *Carmen* (1875), which, though it treats a down-to-earth subject, is in the tradition of the 19th century *opéra-comique*. The influence of *verismo* is to be seen in many of Puccini's operas such as *Il Tabarro* (The Cloak), set on a Paris barge, and *The Girl of the Golden West*, set in California at the time of the Gold Rush.

Verklärte Nacht (Ger., *Transfigured Night*), string sextet by Schoenberg, op 4, inspired by Richard Dehmel's poem about a moonlit walk by a man and a woman. Musically it derives from the erotic chromaticism of Wagner's *Tristan and Isolde* and at the same time points the way towards Schoenberg's later atonal style. It is thus a milestone in the development of modern music. The original version of the work (for two violins, two violas and two cellos) dates from 1899. Later it was arranged for full string orchestra. It has also served as the basis of a ballet, *Pillar of Fire*.

Vermeulen, Matthijs (1888–1967), Dutch composer and critic, at one time resident in France. His works include six symphonies, chamber music and songs.

Véronique, operetta in three acts by Messager, produced at the Bouffes-Parisiens in Paris in 1898. It remains the most popular of his seventeen or so operettas.

Verschiebung (Ger.), soft pedal of the piano.

Verschworenen, Die (Ger., *The Conspirators*), opera in one act by Schubert, inspired by the Aristophanes comedy *Lysistrata*. Its first production was at Frankfurt in 1861. Unlike most of Schubert's other operas, it is still performed from time to time today.

verse anthem, an anthem in which important sections are assigned to one or more solo voices with independent accompaniment.

Verset, an organ piece based on a plainsong melody and used to replace a verse of a psalm, Magnificat, or a section of an item of the Mass. The performance would thus alternate between choir and organ. Numerous examples of such verses by composers of the 16th, 17th and early 18th centuries have survived.

versicle, in the Roman Catholic and Anglican church, a short text (usually from the Bible) which is sung by the officiant, with responses from the choir or congregation.

vers mesuré, *see* MUSIQUE MESURÉE À L'ANTIQUE

verto, *see* OUVERT

Vespers, the service preceding Compline in the series of *horae diurnae* (daily hours) of the Office in the Roman rite. It includes a series of psalms with their antiphons, a hymn and the Magnificat. Examples of elaborate settings for voices and orchestra are those by Monteverdi (modern editions by H. F. Redlich and Denis Stevens) and Mozart (K 321 and 339). Rakhmaninov's Vespers (1915), one of his finest works, is scored for unaccompanied voices.

Vestale, La (Fr., *The Vestal Virgin*), opera in three acts by Spontini. The libretto, by Victor Joseph Etienne de Jouy, tells of a Roman general who discovers that his beloved has become a vestal virgin during his absence at war. She breaks her religious vows, is condemned to be buried alive, but is saved at the last moment by a flash of lightning interpreted as a sign that she has been forgiven by the gods. The work had its première in Paris in 1807. It is Spontini's most important opera, and in our own day has been revived as a vehicle for Maria Callas and other star sopranos.

Vesti la giubba, Canio's aria from Act 1 of Leoncavallo's *I Pagliacci*. Familiarly known as 'On with the motley', it bemoans the fate of a clown who has to act in comedy while his heart is breaking.

Via Crucis, a work for soloists, chorus and organ by Liszt, depicting the fourteen Stations of the Cross. The text, arranged by Princess Sayn-Wittgenstein, makes use of Biblical quotations, Latin hymns and German chorales, with solo parts for Jesus, Pilate and the mourning women. Completed in 1879, the music is harmonically adventurous, with use (some years before Debussy) of the whole-tone scale. Its experimentalism deprived it of a performance in Liszt's lifetime – it was neither performed nor published until

more than forty years after his death. Today it is regarded as the fulfilment of Liszt's aim, in his old age, to create a new form of church music.

Viadana, Lodovico (**Lodovico Grossi**) (c. 1560–1627), Italian composer. He was *maestro di cappella* at Mantua Cathedral from about 1589 until 1594, and became a Franciscan in 1596. His compositions include canzonets, instrumental ensemble music and church music. His *Cento concerti ecclesiastici, a una, a due, a tre, & a quattro voci* (1602, containing only the first instalment of the 100 pieces) is provided with an unfigured *basso continuo* and includes detailed instructions for its performance by the organist (see F. T. Arnold, *The Art of Accompaniment from a Thorough-Bass*, pages 2–5, 9–33).

    F. MOMPELLIO: *Lodovico Viadana*, Florence (1967)

Viaggio a Reims, Il (It., *The Journey to Rheims*), opera in two acts by Rossini, produced in Paris in 1825 for the coronation of Charles X. The performance was a failure but the composer salvaged much of the music, which reappeared three years later in *Le Comte Ory*.

vial, viall, alternative names for the viol.

Viardot-Garcia, Pauline (originally Michelle Ferdinande Pauline) (1821–1910), French mezzo soprano of Spanish parentage. She was the daughter of the singer Manuel del Popolo Garcia and sister of the prima donna Maria Malibran. She studied singing with her parents, piano with Liszt and composition with Reicha. She first appeared in public in Brussels in 1837. Subsequently, she sang with great success in opera in London, Paris, Berlin and elsewhere. She taught singing at the Paris Conservatoire from 1871 to 1875, and married the music critic and impresario Louis Viardot in 1841. Among her outstanding roles was that of Fidès in Meyerbeer's *Le Prophète*, which she sang at the first performance in Paris in 1849. Viardot-Garcia was a close friend of Turgenev (whose letters to her were published in 1907). She composed operettas to librettos by him.

vibraharp, alternative name, used mainly in the United States, for the VIBRAPHONE.

vibraphone, an instrument which probably developed from the GLOCKENSPIEL. It made its first appearance shortly after World War I. In appearance it resembles a XYLOPHONE, but the bars are made of metal instead of hardwood. Like the xylophone it has resonators underneath, and tuned to, each of the bars, but an addition is an electric or clockwork motor that sets discs in the resonators spinning. Their action helps to sustain the notes, and it adds a controllable vibrato to them. The motor is normally only brought into use when specified by the composer. The duration of the notes is also controlled by means of a damper pedal operated by the player. The vibraphone is capable of a substantial variety of tone colours, determined, apart from the motor, by the type of beaters used. The most commonly found models have a three-octave compass extending from the F in the bass stave to the F above the treble one, but both smaller and larger instruments are made. One of the first composers to avail himself of the vibraphone's characteristic sound was Berg, who wrote an extensive part for it in his opera *Lulu*. Chords, played by holding two beaters in one or both hands, are very effective.

vibrato (It.), literally 'shaking', but in the musical

sense the word is used to describe the method of giving expressive quality to a note by means of rapid and minute fluctuations of pitch. This is achieved in the following ways:

(1) on string instruments by oscillations of the left hand, which is used to stop the strings. Described by Leopold Mozart, *Versuch einer gründlichen Violinschule* (1756; translated by Editha Knocker as *A Treatise on the Fundamental Principles of Violin Playing*, page 203), as a 'natural quivering on the violin'. He calls it the TREMOLO, and adds: 'Because the tremolo is not purely on one note but sounds undulating, so would it be an error if every note were played with the tremolo. Performers there are who tremble consistently on each note as if they had the palsy.' One may assume that he would have condemned modern violin-playing, since it is now the practice to use *vibrato* more or less consistently wherever the notes are sufficiently long to make it possible.

(2) on the CLAVICHORD by repeating the pressure of the finger on a key without releasing it, the result being to vary slightly the tension, and hence the pitch, of the string. This practice is generally known by its German name, BEBUNG.

(3) on wind instruments by suitably manipulating the supply of air. This is done by the lips or EMBOUCHURE. An alternative and less satisfactory method, used particularly on valved brass instruments, is to shake the instrument slightly. On trombones a well controlled vibrato can be produced by means of a slide.

(4) in singing by a method similar to that used on wind instruments. This is often referred to as *tremolo*, a term which is properly applied to the rapid reiteration of the same note – a practice now obsolete but much cultivated in the 17th century and known then as the *trillo* (*see* TRILL). *Vibrato* is even more likely to be abused by singers than by string-players, particularly as it arises naturally from incomplete control and may as easily be a sign of defective technique as a deliberate means of expression.

Vicentino, Nicola (1511–1576), Italian composer and theorist, a pupil of Willaert. He was *maestro di cappella* to Duke Ercole d'Este from 1546 to 1549. Two books of five-part madrigals by him survive and an unscientific treatise entitled *L'antica musica ridotta alla moderna prattica* (1555; facsimile edition, 1959), in which he argued that the DIATONIC, CHROMATIC and ENHARMONIC *genera* of Greek music should be used as the basis for composition (*see* J. Hawkins, *A General History of the Science and Practice of Music*, 1875 edition, pages 41–5, 392–5). In pursuit of his theory he invented a keyboard instrument called the *arcicembalo* (with six manuals) and another called the *arciorgano*. His own description of the latter has been translated by H. Kaufmann in *Journal of Music Theory*, v (1961), pages 32–49. His complete works have been edited by Kaufmann (1963).

Vickers, Jon (born 1926), Canadian tenor. After studying in Toronto, he made his début at the Stratford (Ontario) Festival in 1956 as Don José in *Carmen*. His first Covent Garden appearance was in 1957, in Verdi's *A Masked Ball*. Since then he has established himself as one of the finest Verdi and Wagner singers of the day.

Victoria (**Vitoria, Vittoria**), **Tomás Luis de** (c.

1548–1611), Spanish composer. He was a student at the Collegium Germanicum at Rome in 1565 and organist at S. Maria di Monserrato in Rome in 1569. He was *maestro di cappella* at the Collegium Romanum in 1571 (in succession to Palestrina) and at the Collegium Germanicum from 1573 to 1578. In 1575 he was ordained as a priest, and from 1578 to 1585 he was chaplain at S. Girolamo della Carità. He became chaplain to the Empress Maria (sister of Philip II of Spain) in about 1580 and returned with her to Spain, where in 1596 he became director of music at the Convent of the Descalzas Reales, Madrid (to which he retired), holding the appointment until his death.

His compositions, exclusively for the church, appeared between 1572 and 1605, many of them in sumptuous folio editions. They include motets, Masses, Magnificats, hymns and psalms; among them are several elaborate works for eight to twelve voices with organ. A master of subtle and expressive polyphony, he is one of the outstanding figures among 16th century composers of church music and one of the most remarkable in the history of Spanish music. A complete edition of his works in eight volumes was edited by F. Pedrell (1902–13).

> R. CASIMIRI: *Il Vittoria: nuovi documenti* (1934)
> H. COLLET: *Le Mysticisme musical espagnol au XVIe siècle* (1913); *Victoria* (1914)
> R. MITJANA: *Estudios sobre algunas músicos espanoles del siglo xvi* (1918)
> F. PEDRELL: *Tomás Luis de Victoria abulense* (1918)

Vida Breve, La (Sp., *Life is short*), opera in two acts by Falla about a gipsy girl who discovers that the man she loves is about to marry someone else. She curses him, then, overcome with remorse, falls dead at his feet. The work, Falla's major achievement, has a Spanish libretto by Carlos Fernandez Shaw. It was, however, first performed in French, at Nice in 1913, in a translation by Paul Milliet. The opera's two Spanish dances are often performed separately.

vide (Fr.), empty. Thus *corde à vide* means open string.

vide (Lat.), literally 'see'. This term is employed to indicate an optional omission in a score. The syllables *Vi-* and *-de* are usually separately marked, to indicate for the performer(s) the extent of the optional cut.

vielle, vielle-a-manivelle, Fr. name for HURDY-GURDY.

vielle organisée (Fr.; It., *lira organizzata*), an 'organ' (not 'organized') HURDY-GURDY incorporating a set or sets of organ pipes. It was for this instrument that Haydn wrote eight double concertos in 1786.

Vienna Philharmonic Orchestra, a self-governing body of players founded in 1842 by members of the Vienna State Opera Orchestra. Their first conductor was Otto Nicolai, whose successors have included Hans Richter (1875–98), Gustav Mahler (1898–1901), Felix Weingartner (1908–27), Wilhelm Furtwängler (1927-30), Clemens Krauss (1930–33), Furtwängler and Bruno Walter (1933–38) and Furtwängler again (1938–54). At the first Edinburgh Festival, in 1947, the orchestra had a historic reunion with Bruno Walter. Its more recent conductors have included Herbert von Karajan, Karl Böhm and Claudio Abbado.

Viennese School, a general term for the composers active in Vienna in the late 18th and early 19th centuries, notably Haydn, Mozart, Beethoven and Schubert. The so-called Second Viennese School grew up in the present century with Schoenberg, Berg and Webern as its principal members.

Vie Parisienne, La (Fr., *Life in Paris*) one of a series of outstandingly successful operettas composed by Offenbach for Paris. Dating from 1866, it still holds its place in the repertory, in Paris and elsewhere.

Vier Grobiane, Die, *see* QUATTRO RUSTEGHI

Vierhebigkeit (Ger.), a term for musical phrases containing four bars or accents, or their multiples.

Vierne, Louis Victor Jules (1870–1937), French organist and composer, blind from birth. He studied at the Paris Conservatoire under Franck and Widor, and became organist at Notre Dame where he died while performing. His pupils included Joseph Bonnet, Marcel Dupré and Nadia Boulanger. In addition to compositions for the organ (six large-scale works entitled 'symphonies' and a large number of shorter pieces) he also wrote choral works, chamber music and a symphony for orchestra.

Viertel (Ger.), crotchet (U.S., quarter-note).

Vieuxtemps, Henri (1820–81), Belgian violinist and composer. He showed unusual precocity as a small boy, and by the age of thirteen was touring as a soloist. He studied for a time in Paris with de Bériot, but much of his excellence as a performer was due to his own industry. For many years he travelled widely in Europe and the United States. He settled in Brussels in 1871 as teacher at the Conservatoire, but was compelled to resign in 1873 in consequence of a paralytic stroke. He wrote a number of works for the violin, including several concertos, some of which are still in repertory.

vif (Fr.), lively.

vihuela, vihuela da mano (Sp.), the Spanish LUTE, which usually had six strings and was shaped like a guitar. It became obsolete towards the end of the sixteenth century. As its longer name suggests, it was plucked with the fingers most commonly, although sometimes a plectrum was used (*vihuela da pendola*). Still earlier the name 'vihuela' was used as the generic term to denote any form of stringed instrument.

vihuela de arco (Sp.), viol.

vihuela de flandes (Sp.), the ordinary as opposed to the Spanish lute (*vihuela*).

Village Romeo and Juliet, A, opera in six scenes by Delius. The libretto, by the composer, is based on a story by Gottfried Keller. The first performance was in Berlin in 1907 (in a German version). The London première, conducted by Sir Thomas Beecham, followed in 1910.

The lands of Manz and Marti (two farmers) are separated by a narrow strip of ground which has been allowed to run wild by the Dark Fiddler (the bastard son of its former owner). The farmers' children (Sali, the son of Manz, and Vrenchen, the daughter of Marti) use this strip of wild land as their playground until the farmers, each having encroached on the plot, finally have a violent quarrel over it and separate, taking their children with them. While their fathers are involved in a long and expensive law action, Sali and Vrenchen meet secretly on their beloved playground. But one day they are discovered together by Marti, who tries to drag his daughter from her lover's arms and is later sent to a lunatic asylum. Sali comes to visit the destitute Vrenchen on the last night she may spend in her old

home and they both dream that they are being married in a church. The next day they go to a fair, but being disturbed by the malicious tongues of local gossipers they walk to an inn, where they meet the Dark Fiddler and his vagabond friends, who invite them to join their company and live with them in the mountains. They refuse, feeling that this would not be the ideal life they both long for. Hearing a boatman's song they decide that they will also drift down the river and drift away for ever. They find a barge filled with hay moored to the river-bank, which Sali proclaims is their marriage bed. After drifting a little way down the river he pulls the plug from the bottom of the boat and throws it into the river. In the far distance is heard the voice of the boatman: 'Heigho, travellers we a-passing by'. The most famous section of the opera is the orchestra interlude entitled *The Walk to the Paradise Garden*, often performed out of context.

Villa-Lobos, Heitor (1887–1959), Brazilian composer, the first South American composer to become internationally famous. As a young man he earned his living as an orchestral player. Villa-Lobos visited Paris with a fellowship from the Brazilian Government, 1922–6. He became superintendent of Musical Education in Schools, Rio de Janeiro, in 1931, and was founder and director of Orfeão de Professores (a teacher's training college). His compositions, which are very numerous, show the influence of South American Indian music, which he studied in 1912, and Brazilian folk song: they include operas, symphonies, symphonic poems, a cello concerto, thirteen *choros* (serenades) for various media, chamber music, choral works, piano solos and songs. His most popular works, the series of *Bachianas Brasileiras*, are an attempt to evoke the spirit of Bach in Brazilian terms. One of them – no 5 for solo soprano and eight cellos – is especially picturesque.

villancico (Sp., from *villano*, rustic).

(1) a type of song in a popular but sophisticated style, current in Spain in the late 15th and 16th centuries. It is characterized by the fact that it begins with a refrain, which is subsequently repeated after each verse, as in the French *virelai* and the 13th century *cantigas* of Alfonso el Sabio. Examples for vocal ensemble are in F. Asenjo Barbieri, *Cancionero musical del los siglos xv y xvi* (1890), R. Mitjana, *Cancionero de Upsala* (1944), and *Monumentos de la Música Española*, iv, v, viii & ix. *Villancicos* were also set in the 16th century for solo voice with VIHUELA accompaniment.

(2) in the 17th and 18th centuries a cantata for soli and chorus with instrumental accompaniment, frequently on the subject of Christmas.

(3) in modern Spanish a Christmas carol.

villanella (It.), literally 'rustic song' (cf. VILLANCICO). A popular but sophisticated form of part song in 17th century Italy. It originated in Naples and was hence also known as *napolitana* (Neapolitan in English). The most popular type was for three voices, with frequent use of consecutive triads, e.g.:

vec-chie son ma - le - ci - o - se

Di Maio (in A. EINSTEIN, *The Italian Madrigal*, iii, no 38)

The words often parodied the elevated and sentimental style of the madrigal.

villanelle (Fr.), song or other vocal piece based on the words of a poem in *villanelle* form. It consists of three-line stanzas, in which the first and third lines of the opening stanza are repeated alternately as the third line of the succeeding stanzas. Not all *villanelles* conform with this rule, however, a notable exception being the *villanelle* (to words by Théophile Gautier) which opens Berlioz's song cycle, *Nuits d'Eté*.

Villi, Le (It., *The Witches*), Puccini's first opera, written in one act to a libretto by Ferdinando Fontana. Its first performance was at Milan in 1884. The story, set in the Black Forest, bears a resemblance to Adam's *Giselle*.

villota (It.), a form of popular part-song of North Italian origin current in the 16th century and cultivated in opposition to the more serious style of the madrigal. It was normally for four voices.

Vinay, Ramón (born 1914), Chilean tenor, previously a baritone. He studied in Mexico, where he made his début in 1938 as Count di Luna in *Il Trovatore*. Six years later he made his first appearance as a tenor, singing the title role in *Otello* with the National Opera Company of Havana. From 1962 he resumed baritone roles, appearing as Telramund in *Lohengrin* at Bayreuth and as Iago in *Otello* at Dallas, though he continued to retain some tenor roles in his repertoire.

Vinci, Leonardo (1690–1730), Italian composer. He studied in Naples, where he made his reputation as a composer of *opera buffa* and *opera seria*. He also wrote church music, and was one of the *maestri da capella* at the Neapolitan court from 1725. Leonardo da Vinci, the artist, was no relation.

Viñes, Ricardo (1875–1943), Spanish pianist, who studied in Barcelona and Paris. He gave the first performance of a number of works by Debussy and other 20th century French composers.

Vingt-Quatre Violons du Roi, Les (The King's 24 Violins), a string orchestra maintained by the French kings in the 17th and 18th centuries. The organization was copied by Charles II, who instituted a band of '24 violins'.

Vingt Regards sur l'Enfant-Jésus (Fr., *Twenty contemplations of the child Jesus*), a work for piano by Messiaen, composed in 1944. Its twenty movements, when performed complete, last about two and a half hours and are based on three cyclic themes: the 'Thème de Dieu', the 'Thème de l'Étoile et de la Croix' and the 'Thème d'accords'. The music makes use of Christian symbolism (a favourite subject of Messiaen's) and, to quote the composer, seeks 'a language of musical love'.

Vin Herbé, Le, chamber oratorio for twelve voices, seven strings and piano by Frank Martin, based on the legend of Tristan and Isolde (but treating it in a very

un-Wagnerian way). It was first performed at Zürich in 1940, and was presented in an extended version at the Salzburg Festival in 1948.

viol (Fr., *viole*: Ger., *Viole*; It., *viola*; Sp., *viheula de arco*), a family of bowed string instruments which was widely used in the sixteenth and seventeenth century and has been revived in modern times for the performance of music of the period. Sizes, tuning and shape varied considerably in the sixteenth century, but by the seventeenth there was some degree of standardization. Three sizes were normally used in chamber music and they were generally tuned as follows:

treble viol or discant-viol:

tenor viol or *viola de braccio*:

or

bass viol or *viola da gamba*:

The back was normally flat and the shoulders sloping. The bow was held above the palm of the hand. A series of gut frets on the fingerboard gave a clear tone to each stopped note.

In England a set of viols for ensemble playing was known as a 'chest of viols', from the cupboard in which they were kept: Thomas Mace, in *Musick's Monument* (1676), recommends two trebles, two tenors and two basses. The literature of ensemble music for viols is extensive, particularly in England in the mid 17th century, though it was rarely published there, except in mixed collections of vocal and instrumental music. The bass viol in particular was also cultivated as a solo instrument, especially for playing 'divisions' (or variations) on a GROUND. For this purpose a rather smaller instrument was used: the standard book on the subject is Christopher Simpson's *The Division-Violist* (1659), in which, it is interesting to note, he expresses a preference for a type of instrument with rounded shoulders, like the cello. A still smaller bass viol was used for playing 'lyra way', i.e. with a variety of different tunings to facilitate hand-playing; the problem of constantly using new fingerings was solved by writing the music in TABLATURE, as for the lute. The bass viol continued to be used as a solo instrument in the early 18th century. Bach wrote three sonatas for it, with harpsichord, and obbligato parts for it in the *St. Matthew Passion* and the *St. John Passion*. French composers of the early 18th century were particularly conservative in their attitude to the viol, writing not only for the bass but also for the treble and for the *pardessus de viole*, a high treble tuned a fourth above the normal instrument.

The bass viol had also an important function as an accompanying instrument in the 17th century. It was used to play the bass line of the continuo part (in association with the harpsichord or organ), not only in vocal music but also in violin sonatas and in trio sonatas for two violins and bass, where it was for long preferred to the cello. For the same reason the *violone* (or double-bass viol, an octave below the bass viol) was widely used in preference to the coarser double-bass violin. Monteverdi, in his opera *Orfeo* (1607), expressly writes for a *contrabasso de viola da gamba* to be used in association with an ensemble of *viole da braccio* (violins, violas and cellos). The double bass now used in the orchestra retains the shape of the *violone*, though it no longer uses frets.

G. R. HAYES: *Musical Instruments and the Music, 1500–1750. II. The Viols, and other Bowed Instruments* (1930)

viola (It.; Fr., *alto*; Ger., *Bratsche*), originally a generic term for àny bowed stringed instrument, the name *viola* is now used exclusively for the alto (or tenor) member of the violin family – it was once known in English as the tenor violin. The instrument is larger than a violin but smaller than would be expected from its pitch, which is a fifth lower and an octave above the cello; if it were made to the 'correct' size, the viola would be impossible to play in the violin position. The tuning is:

The alto clef is used except when, in the upper register, it is replaced by the treble to avoid leger lines. The tone of the viola differs markedly from that of both the violin and cello. Particularly characteristic is the dark colour of the bottom string, while the instrument as a whole displays an affinity, and consequently blends, with woodwind instruments; it can even deceive the ear into thinking they are playing. Being more restricted in its top register than either the violin or the cello, the viola has approximately the same range as the clarinet. It has been a member of the orchestra since the early 17th century, but its development in chamber music dates from Haydn's cultivation of the string quartet in the 18th. As a solo instrument it received only occasional attention before the 20th century; examples are a concerto by Karel Stamic (Carl Stamitz), Mozart's *Sinfonia Concertante* and Berlioz's *Harold in Italy*. In more recent times composers – often inspired by such distinguished players as Lionel Tertis, William Primrose, Frederick Riddle and Walter Trampler – have written extensively for the viola, none more so than Hindemith, who was himself an outstanding performer on the instrument. Among viola concertos the best known is Walton's, but Bartók left an unfinished one that was completed by Tibor Serly. Bloch, Bax and Bliss are among those who have written major works for viola and piano.

'*Viola*' is also the Italian for viol, hence *viola d'amore*, *da braccio*, etc.

viola alta (It.), an unusually large viola made in Germany during the 1870s especially for the Wagner Festivals at Bayreuth. Some twenty years later a fifth string was added to increase facility in the upper register; it was tuned to E, the same note as the violin's top string.

See also VIOLINO GRANDE, VIOLA POMPOSA

viola bastarda (It.), the instrument known in England as the lyra viol or the viol played 'lyra way' (*see* VIOL). It was a small-sized bass viol with six strings, the tuning of which was varied to suit the player's convenience. Being so small, it might have been regarded as a large tenor viol, despite its pitch; this is probably the origin of the name, which implies it was neither one thing or the other.

viola da braccio (It.), literally 'arm' viol, the tenor of the VIOL family and the largest of its members to be played held on the arm. Its modern equivalent is the viola.

viola da gamba (It.), literally 'leg' viol. Although the bass of the VIOL family, the *viola de gamba* was very much at home playing melodic passages in the treble register. Because of this it was much used as a solo instrument as well as a continuo. There are parts for gambas in Bach's fourth Brandenburg Concerto.

viola d'amore (It.; Fr., *viole d'amour*; Ger., *Liebesgeige*), literally 'love' viol. Although other reasons have been given, it is probably that the instrument's tender tone quality gave it its name. It is a tenor VIOL with seven instead of six strings that are normally tuned to the chord of D major.

In addition seven or fourteen other strings are tuned to the same note, but, instead of being played on, these merely vibrate in sympathy. Because of its distinctive and attractive tone, the instrument's use is not confined to old music, although its appearances elsewhere are fairly rare. Among 19th and 20th century composers who have written for it are Meyerbeer, Charpentier, Puccini, Janáček, Strauss and Hindemith.

viola da spalla, viola de spalla (It.), literally 'shoulder' viol. A portable cello, held by means of a shoulder strap, used by itinerant musicians in the 17th and 18th centuries.

viola di bordone (It.), literally 'drone' viol. Alternative names for both the VIOLA BASTARDA and the BARYTON.

viola di fagotto (It.), literally 'bassoon viola', an alternative name for the VIOLA BASTARDA.

viola pomposa (It.), a name which appears to have been given to three very different instruments that enjoyed a brief existence:

(1) a small cello with a fifth top string added. This is probably the violoncello piccolo for which Bach wrote the sixth and last of his Cello Suites;

(2) a viola with an additional top string and as such a predecessor of the VIOLA ALTO. This instrument would seem to be identical with the violino pomposo (*see also* VIOLINO GRANDE);

(3) a four-stringed instrument irregularly tuned, the lowest note being D below middle C.

viol d' amour, an open Diapason organ stop, similar to the Violin Diapason.

viol de gamba, an organ stop imitating string tone.

viol de gamboys, early English name for the VIOLA DA GAMBA.

viol d'orchestre, an organ stop similar to VIOL DE GAMBA.

viole (Fr. and Ger.), VIOL.

violet, an English name that was occasionally used for the VIOLA D'AMORE.

viole ténor (Sp.), a viola manufactured in Spain during the 1930s of a size that was proportionate to its pitch as compared with the violin. It could be played only in the cello position.

violetta (It., the diminutive of viola):

(1) G. M. Landfranco in 1533 gave the name *violetta da arco senza tasti* (little bowed viol without frets), or *violetta da braccio* (little arm viol) to an instrument with three strings which appears to be an early form of a violin;

(2) the name often given to the viola by 18th century German composers;

(3) Praetorius, in his *Syntagma Musicum* (1619), gives *violetta piccola* as the alternative name for the violin as well as the treble viol.

violetta marina (It.), literally 'little marine viol'. A rare and obsolete instrument, used by Handel in *Orlando*, was a modified and presumably smaller version of the VIOLA D'AMORE.

violetta piccolo (It.), literally 'little small violin', rare kind of small VIOL made in various shapes and having anything from three to six strings.

violin, (1) in the 17th century the name of a family of bowed string instruments (Fr., *violon*; Ger., *Geige*; It., *viola da braccio*; Sp., *vihuela de braço*). Thus in France the King's string orchestra was called *les vingt-quatre violons du roi* and in Restoration England the '24 violins'. In both cases the name refers to treble, alto (or tenor) and bass instruments. The members of the family differ from the VIOL family in several respects, notably: (*a*) they have slightly rounded backs and round shoulders, (*b*) there are normally only four strings, which are tuned in fifths, (*c*) there are no frets, (*d*) the smaller members (violin and viola) are held on the arm (hence the Italian name *viola da braccio*). The alto (or tenor violin) is now known as the VIOLA, the bass violin as the cello (an abbreviation of VIOLONCELLO). An instrument intermediate between the viola and cello existed in the late 17th century but is now obsolete: it is often referred to as the 'tenor violin' – a confusing nomenclature, since 'tenor violin' is the old English name for the viola. A double-bass violin also existed, but the double-bass viol was preferred (*see* DOUBLE BASS), and from this the modern double bass, though it has no frets, is derived.

The ancestry of the family is complex. A large number of bowed string instruments of various shapes existed in the middle ages, and from these the

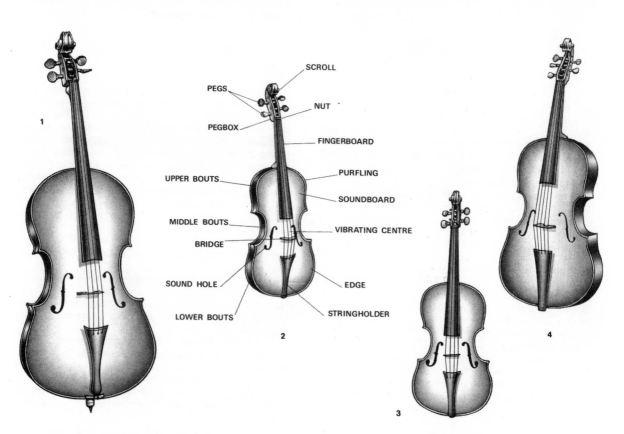

SCROLL

PEGS

NUT

PEGBOX

FINGERBOARD

UPPER BOUTS

PURFLING

SOUNDBOARD

MIDDLE BOUTS

VIBRATING CENTRE

BRIDGE

SOUND HOLE

EDGE

LOWER BOUTS

STRINGHOLDER

1

2

3

4

Violin family: (1) cello (2) violin (3) viola (4) *viola pomposa*

members of the violin family (at first with three, and
soon with four, strings) were evolved in the 16th
century. From the first they were used for ensemble
music, like the viols, and when orchestras became necessary for opera in the early 17th century the violin
family were preferred on account of their more incisive, brilliant tone. From that time they have
remained in all essentials the same, though such details
as methods of bowing, the shape of the bridge, and the
material of the strings have changed. In consequence
though wind-players prefer new instruments, old
violins, violas and cellos, fashioned by master-
craftsmen, are much sought after and highly valued.

(2) in particular, the treble of the violin family, to
which the name 'violin' (Fr., *violon*; Ger., *Violine*; It.,
violino) is now exclusively assigned. The standard
tuning is:

Other tunings were adopted in the 17th century to
facilitate chord-playing (*see* SCORDATURA). The violin
was used early in the 17th century as a solo instrument
and its capacity for virtuosity exploited. The solo
sonata and the trio sonata for two violins and continuo
developed side by side. The solo concerto appeared c.

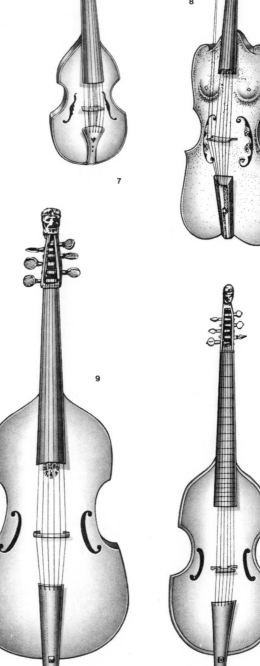

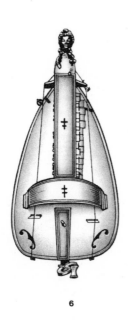

Violin family: (5) Hardanger fiddle (6) hurdy-gurdy (7) *viola d'amore* (8) *lira da braccio* (9) bass viol (10) lyra viol

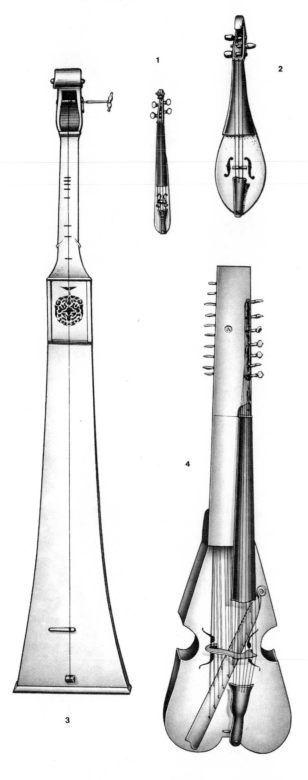

Violin family: (1) kit (2) rebec (3) tromba marina (4) baryton

1700. In view of the popularity of the form it is curious that so many 19th and 20th century composers – e.g. Beethoven, Mendelssohn, Schumann, Brahms, Chaikovsky, Dvořák, Elgar, Sibelius, Bartók and Walton – should have written only one violin concerto,

(3) a smaller violin was used in the 17th and 18th centuries (*see* VIOLINO PICCOLO).

> G. R. HAYES: *Musical Instruments and their Music, 1500–1750. II. The Viols, and other Bowed Instruments* (1930)
>
> E. VAN DER STRAETEN: *The History of the Violin* (two volumes, 1933)

Violin Diapason, an open Diapason organ stop imitating string tone.

Violine (Ger.), violin.

violino (It.), (diminutive of *viola*), (1) a name used indiscriminately in the 16th century for members of the viol and violin families;

(2) from the 17th century onwards it means 'violin', i.e. the treble of the violin family.

violino grande (It.), a large violin, now virtually obselete, with five strings, the lowest tuned to the C in the bass clef and the other four as on a normal violin. The instrument, which would seem to be identical with one form of the VIOLA POMPOSA, has been revived by Penderecki, who has written a concerto for it which he later adapted for the cello.

violino piccolo (It.; Ger., *kleine Discantgeige, Quartgeige*), a small violin used in the 17th and early 18th century. Praetorius, in his *Syntagma Musicum* (1619), gives the following tuning:

Monteverdi's *Orfeo* (1607) has parts for two *violini piccoli alla francese* (i.e. on the French model). Bach wrote solo parts for it in Cantata 140 and the first Brandenburg concerto, using a tuning a tone lower than that given by Praetorius:

and writing as for a transposing instrument (i.e. a minor third lower than the actual sounds), so that a player accustomed to a normal violin could use the same fingering. The instrument became obsolete in the latter half of the 18th century.

violon (Fr.), (1) in the 16th century used, like *violino*, for members both of the viol and of the violin family;

(2) in the 17th century the name of the violin family – treble, tenor and bass;

(3) now used exclusively for the treble of the violin family – the violin.

violoncello (It.; Fr., *violoncelle*; Ger., *Violoncell, Violoncello*), the bass of the violin family. The name is a diminutive of VIOLONE. The illogical but convenient abbreviation 'cello' is peculiar to non-Romance languages, e.g. English, Dutch, German and Swedish. It was originally known, in the 17th century, as *bassa* *viola da braccio*. It now has four strings, tuned:

but was also made with five in the 17th and early 18th century. The last of Bach's six suites for unaccompanied cello is for a five-string instrument, tuned:

Alternative tunings were used for the four-string instrument, as for the violin (*see* SCORDATURA): the fifth of Bach's suites requires the following tuning:

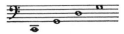

Music is written for the cello in the bass clef, except for the higher register, where the tenor and treble clefs are used, in order to avoid leger lines. The practice of writing in the treble clef an octave higher than the actual sounds is now obsolete, though often retained in modern editions of classical works.

For the greater part of the 17th century the cello was restricted to playing the bass line in the orchestra and in chamber music (though in the latter case the bass viol was often preferred). Solo music begins to appear at the end of the 17th century and is frequent in the 18th century in the form of concertos, sonatas and obbligatos in opera and oratorio. Concertos by 19th and 20th century composers include those by Schumann, Dvořák and Elgar. In Strauss's symphonic poem *Don Quixote* the solo cello represents the hero. The repertory of modern concertos is limited, since the combination of solo cello with the sonority of the modern orchestra presents problems which few composers have cared to solve.

E. VAN DER STRAETEN: *History of the Violoncello* (1915)

violoncello piccolo (It.), a small-sized cello for which Bach wrote obbligato parts in nine of his cantatas.

violon d'amour (Fr.), literally 'love violin', an obsolete instrument, used briefly during the 18th century. It resulted from an attempt to provide the violin family with the equivalent of a viola d'amore, albeit at a higher pitch. It had five playing strings and six sympathetic ones.

violone (It.), (augmentative of *viola*), (1) properly the double-bass viol (or *contrabasso da gamba*), a six-stringed instrument an octave below the bass viol.

(2) applied also in the 18th century to the double-bass violin: hence the diminutive *violoncello* for the bass violin.

See DOUBLE BASS

violotta, a modern and so far very little used stringed instrument pitched between the viola and the cello. Its lowest note is G on the bottom line of the bass clef, and its four strings are tuned an octave below those of the VIOLIN.

viol lyra way, *see* LYRA VIOL

Viotti, Giovanni Battista (1755–1824), Italian violinist and composer, a pupil of Pugnani. In 1780 he embarked on a tour of Europe, visiting Switzerland, Germany, Poland and Russia. He arrived in Paris in 1782 and remained for ten years, first as a soloist at the Concert Spirituel and later as joint director of the Italian opera at the Théâtre de Monsieur. The rest of his life, from 1792, he spent partly in London (where he played at Salomon's concerts and also conducted) partly near Hamburg and partly in Paris, where he was director of the Opéra, (1819–22). He had a great reputation as a performer, and his influence as a teacher was far-reaching. His compositions include 29 violin concertos and ten for piano.

Viozzi, Giulio (born 1912), Italian composer whose works include an opera, *Allamistakeo*, and a threnody for two pianos.

Virdung, Sebastian, late 15th and early 16th century German musician who published at Basle in 1511 an important work on musical instruments entitled *Musica getutscht* (facsimile editions, 1935 and 1970).

virelai (Fr.), a form of medieval French song, beginning with a refrain which was subsequently repeated after each verse. The same structure is found in the 13th century *cantigas* of Alfonso el Sabio and in the Spanish *villancico*.

virginal, virginals (both singular and plural occur), a member of the harpsichord family, first mentioned and described by Sebastian Virdung in his *Musica getutscht* (1511). The name (which was used also in the Netherlands) presumably implies that it was an instrument favoured by young ladies, who are in fact constantly represented performing on it in Dutch paintings, whereas men are shown playing the lute. It belongs properly to the oblong (or rectangular) SPINET, but English usage was inconsistent, and in the Tudor and Jacobean period any instrument of the harpsichord type was called 'virginal'. A clear distinction between harpsichord and virginal was not made until the Restoration.

English composers of the 16th and early 17th century were particularly active in writing for this instrument. Their compositions include variations, dance movements, fantasias and transcriptions of vocal pieces. The only printed collection was *Parthenia* (1611; facsimile edition, 1942), containing works by Byrd, Bull and Gibbons. There are, however, several substantial manuscript collections, notably: (1) The Fitzwilliam Virginal Book (modern edition by J. A. Fuller Maitland and W. Barclay Squire, 2 volumes, 1899), (2) My Ladye Nevells Booke, containing only pieces by Byrd (modern edition by Hilda Andrews, 1926), (3) Will Foster's Virginal Book (in the Royal Music Library), (4) Benjamin Cosyn's Virginal Book (also in the Royal Music Library), (5) Elizabeth Rogers's Virginall Booke (British Museum), and (6) a manuscript in the New York Public Library (Drexel 5612). A complete edition of English virginal music is in course of preparation for *Musica Britannica*. Byrd's keyboard works have been published in a modernized text by E. H. Fellowes, and Orlando Gibbons's by Margaret Glyn.

C. VAN DER BORREN: *The Sources of Keyboard Music in England* (1913)

M. H. GLYN: *About Elizabethan Virginal Music and its Composers* (1924)

E. W. NAYLOR: *An Elizabethan Virginal Book* (1905)

W. BARCLAY SQUIRE: 'Collections of Virginal Music', in Grove's *Dictionary of Music and Musicians*, article VIRGINAL MUSIC

virtuoso, a performer of uncommon skill and technical mastery. The word derives from the Latin *virtus* = virtuous or excellent, but is today sometimes used in a derogatory sense, the implication being that a performer who is 'merely' a virtuoso, or a composer who writes only virtuoso music, may be lacking in feeling and/or intelligence. In this respect, an Italian theorist once described in three words the path of musical damnation a performer or composer could easily follow if his taste and intelligence did not keep pace with his technique: *vittorioso, virtuoso, vitioso* (victorious, virtuous, vicious).

Vishnevskaya, Galina (born 1926), Russian soprano, born in Leningrad. After making her début in 1950 in Strelnikov's *Kholopka*, she joined the Bolshoi Opera in Moscow, where her roles have included Tatyana in Chaikovsky's *Eugene Onegin* and Marguérite in Gounod's *Faust*. In 1961 she made her New York Metropolitan début as Aïda, a role she sang the following year at Covent Garden. Britten's song cycle, *The Poet's Echo*, and the solo soprano part of the *War Requiem* were written for her. She is married to the cellist, Mstislav Rostropovich.

Vision of St. Augustine, The, mystical choral work by Michael Tippett, inspired by the two visions of the saint, 1500 years ago. Scored for solo baritone, chorus and orchestra, it was first performed in 1966 in London, with Dietrich Fischer-Dieskau as soloist.

Visions fugitives, set of twenty piano pieces by Prokofiev (op 22), composed between 1915 and 1917 and inspired by the poetry of Balmont. The movement headings range characteristically from *Ridicolosamente* to *Feroce* and *Presto agitatissimo e molto accentuato*. The music also exists in a version for string orchestra, prepared by Rudolf Barshai.

Visitation, The, opera in three acts by Gunther Schuller, commissioned by the Hamburg Opera, where it was first performed in 1966. The libretto, by the composer, is based on Kafka's *The Trial*, but the action is transferred to the Deep South of the United States, where Kafka's hero, Joseph K., becomes Carter Jones, a Negro student. The work's racial theme is underlined by the jazz-orientated style of Schuller's music.

Vitali, Filippo (c. 1590–1653), Italian composer. He was a singer in the Papal Choir in Rome in 1631 where he also enjoyed the patronage of Cardinal Barberini. In 1642 he was *maestro di cappella* at Florence Cathedral. His *L'Aretusa* (1620) was one of the earliest operas performed in Rome. He also published madrigals, arias for one or more voices with instrumental accompaniment, and church music.

Vitali, Giovanni Battista (1632–92), Italian violinist and composer. He was vice-*maestro di cappella* to the Duke of Modena in 1674 and *maestro di cappella* in 1684. One of the most important composers of chamber music in the 17th century, he published several collections of trio sonatas and dance movements for strings, as well as psalms for voices and instruments, and also composed operas and oratorios. Examples of his work are in L. Torchi, *L'arte musicale in Italia*, vii.

His son **Tommaso Antonio Vitali** (1663–1745) was also a violinist and composer. He was in the service of the Duke of Modena. His surviving publications – three sets of trio sonatas and *Concerto di sonate a violino, violoncello e cembalo* – are dated 1693, 1695 and 1701. A set of variations above an ostinato bass in G minor, for violin and continuo, described in the manuscript as 'Parte del Tomaso Vitalino', was attributed to him by Ferdinand David and published in a truncated and much edited version under the title 'Ciaccona' (Chaconne) in *Die hohe Schule des Violinspiels* (1867). A modern edition by D. Hellmann of this work was published in 1966.

vite (Fr.), fast, quick.

Vitoria, *see* VICTORIA

Vitry, Philippe de (1291–1361), French composer, poet and theorist. He was a diplomat in the service of the French court and became Bishop of Meaux in 1351. Only a few compositions by him survive, but enough to show that he was a master of the isorhythmic motet (*see* ISORHYTHM). A complete edition is in L. Schrade, *Polyphonic Music of the Fourteenth Century*, i. The title of his treatise *Ars nova* has been adopted by historians as a general term for the music of the 14th century. The treatise itself is printed in an edition by G. Reaney, A. Gilles and J. Maillard (1964) and has been translated by L. Plantinga in *Journal of Music Theory*, v (1961). Among the refinements of notation advocated by, or attributed to, him are the introduction of time signatures, the use of red notes (principally to indicate modifications of rhythm), the recognition of duple time, and the precise division of the semibreve into two or three minims by analogy with the division of the breve into semibreves.

Vittoria, *see* VICTORIA

vivace (It.), lively. *Allegro vivace*, quick and lively.

Vivaldi, Antonio (1675–1741), Italian composer and violinist, a pupil of his father Giovanni Battista Vivaldi, and Legrenzi. He was ordained priest in 1703, and was familiarly known as *il prete rosso* (the red-haired priest). For many years he was in the service of the Conservatorio dell'Ospedale della Pietà (a music school for girls in Venice). He travelled extensively and was one of the most prolific composers of his time. His surviving works include concertos for a wide variety of solo instruments with orchestra (he was one of the first composers to use clarinets), chamber music, secular cantatas, church music, an oratorio and operas. A catalogue is in the second volume of Pincherle's work (cited below). Despite his tremendous output he was by no means a conventional composer, and much of his instrumental work shows a lively and fertile imagination. Bach admired him, and transcribed some of his concertos, including a concerto for four violins which he arranged for four harpsichords. Since the 1950s, there has been an enormous revival of interest in Vivaldi's music, especially the concertos, among which four works for violin, collectively known as *The Four Seasons*, have become particularly popular. These form part of a cycle of twelve concertos, op 8, entitled *Il Cimento dell'armonia e dell'invenzione* (the contest between harmony and invention).

Antonio Vivaldi

M. PINCHERLE: *Antonio Vivaldi et la musique instrumentale*, two volumes (1948)

O. RUDGE: *Lettre e dediche di Antonio Vivaldi* (1942)

A. SALVATORI: *Note e documenti sulla vita e sulle opere di Antonio Vivaldi* (1939)

vivo (It.), lively.

Vlad, Roman (born 1919), Rumanian born Italian composer, pupil of Casella. His works include a ballet after Dumas, *La Dama delle Camelie*, three cantatas, a symphony, chamber music and film music. He has written books on Stravinsky and on the history of dodecaphony.

Vltava, the second of a cycle of six symphonic poems by Smetana, collectively entitled *Má Vlast* (My Country). Written in 1874, the music depicts the River Vltava as it travels from its source to Prague and then on towards the sea.

vocalise (Fr.), a wordless composition, or passage in a composition. The term is used often in connection with vocal exercises, though it can apply equally to concert works or to sections of an opera. Rakhmaninov wrote a song entitled *Vocalise*, op 34 no 14.

voce (It.), voice; *colla voce*, with the voice (an indication that the accompaniment must neglect strict time and follow the singer); *mezza voce*, medium voice, i.e. fairly quietly: *sotto voce*, under the voice, i.e. very quietly.

See also MESSA DI VOCE.

Voces Intimae (Lat., *Intimate voices*), title given by Sibelius to his D minor string quartet, op 56.

voces musicales (Lat.), 'musical notes'. The notes of the hexachord, sung to SOLMIZATION syllables, often used in the 16th century as a *cantus firmus* in vocal and instrumental pieces.

Vogel, Emil (1859–1908), German musicologist. He was director of the Musikbibliothek Peters, Leipzig, 1893–1901 and founder and editor of the *Jahrbuch der Musikbibliothek Peters*, 1894–1900. He published detailed studies of Monteverdi and Gagliano, both the product of the most thorough research, a catalogue of the music of the Ducal Library at Wolfenbüttel, and *Bibliothek der gedruckten Vokalmusik Italiens aus den Jahren 1500–1700* (two volumes, 1892). The last is indispensable for students of the period.

Vogel, Vladimir (born 1896), Russian born German composer, pupil of Busoni, but more influenced by Schoenberg and Berg. His most important work is his oratorio *Tyl Klaas*, completed in 1945 and more than four hours long, intended as a protest against dictatorship and the denial of human liberty. The first performance was conducted by Ernest Ansermet in Switzerland, where Vogel has lived since 1933. His other works include a large-scale *Epitaffio per Alban Berg* for solo piano (1936), *Arpiade* for soprano, speech chorus and five instruments (inspired by the Alsatian painter and author, Jean Arp), a Passacaglia for Orchestra, and *Sept Aspects d'une Série* for orchestra.

Vogelweide, Walther von der, late 12th and early 13th century MINNESINGER. Very few of his poems survive with music. His song of the crusader in Palestine, 'Nu alerst leb' ich mir werde', is one of the finest of all Minnesinger melodies: it has often been printed, for example in *Historical Anthology of Music*, edited by A. T. Davison and W. Apel, no 20b, and *New Oxford History of Music*, ii, page 253.

Vogl, Johann Michael (1768–1840), Austrian baritone. Having shown promise at school as a singer and actor, he was engaged to sing at the court opera in 1764 and was a regular member of the company from 1795–1822. Among the parts which he sang were Oreste in Gluck's *Iphigenie en Tauride* and the Count in Mozart's *Figaro*. He was for several years a close personal friend of Schubert and was first to sing 'Erlkönig' in public.

Vogler, Georg Joseph (1749–1814), German composer, organist and teacher, the son of a violin-maker. He studied law at Bamberg University, visited Italy, 1773–5, and was ordained priest in Rome, 1773. Later he became *Kapellmeister* in Munich, and *Kapellmeister* to the king of Sweden, 1786–99. He also directed music schools in Mannheim, Stockholm and Frankfurt. His compositions include many operas as well as church music and instrumental works, and books on harmony, organ playing, tuning of keyboard instruments, and so on. He advanced a number of ideas for improvement of organ-building, some of which were subsequently adopted by others, and was the inventor of the so-called Acoustic Bass stop, which produces the effect of a 32 foot stop by utilizing the combination of tones resulting from the simultaneous use of a $10\frac{2}{3}$ foot stop and a 16 foot stop (see ORGAN). Among his pupils were Weber and Meyerbeer. Mozart, who met him at Mannheim in 1778–9, described him as 'exceedingly conceited and rather incompetent' (see E. Anderson, *The Letters of Mozart and his Family*, p. 522). Against this, however, must be set the loyalty and friendship of a great number of his friends.

voice, (1) the sound produced by humans and many other animals by the vibrating of the vocal chords.

(2) a technical term used traditionally for an individual part or 'strand' in a contrapuntal composition (particularly a fugue), whether for voices or for

instruments. Thus a keyboard fugue for three voices is a fugue in a three-part counterpoint. The word is used in instrumental music because contrapuntal writing for instruments was originally imitated from similar writing for voices.

voice leading, literal U.S. translation of the German *Stimmführung* (part-writing).

voicing, the process of ensuring a good and uniform tone-quality from any particular set of organ pipes. This is done by making minor adjustments to the pipes after they have left the maker's hands, and demands not only a sensitive ear but also expert craftsmanship and long experience.

Voi, che sapete, the aria sung by Cherubino to the Countess in Act 2 of Mozart's *The Marriage of Figaro*

voix céleste (Fr.), literally 'heavenly voice', an organ stop.
> *See* UNDA MARIS

Voix Humaine, La, opera in one act by Poulenc, to a libretto by Jean Cocteau. First produced in Paris in 1959, it takes the form of a long scena for solo soprano and orchestra – the voice of the title being that of an abandoned woman talking to her lover over the telephone. The first exponent of the part was Denise Duval.

volante (It., *flying*), fast and light.

Volkslied (Ger.), (1) a folk song, in the generally accepted English sense of a traditional song of unknown authorship;

(2) a popular song, whether anonymous or by a known composer. The great majority of *Volkslieder* belong to this category. Their square-cut rhythm and symmetrical structure have had a considerable influence on German composers.

Volles Werk (Ger.), full organ.

Volo di Notte (It., *Night Flight*), opera in one act by Dallapiccola, after Antoine de Saint-Exupéry's novel, *Vol de Nuit*, about the early days of flying and the responsibility of an airline director for the safety of his pilots. This was Dallapiccola's first opera, written in a style somewhere between Puccini and Berg. Its first performance was at Florence in 1940.

volta (It.), 'turn' or 'time', (1) *Prima volta* (first time) and *seconda volta* (second time) are used when a composition or a section of a composition, is to be repeated with some change in the concluding bar or bars. Horizontal brackets above the stave indicate the bars affected: the first time the performer plays the bar or bars marked *prima volta* (or simply '1') and then goes back to the beginning, the second time he omits these bars and goes straight on to the bars marked *seconda volta* (or '2').

(2) A lively dance in 6/8 rhythm (*Fr.* volte) which was very popular in the late 16th and early 17th centuries, though condemned by moralists, since the men swung the women high in the air. Often referred to in English sources as *lavolta*. The following is an example:

volti (It.), turn over (the page). *Volti subito* = turn quickly.

voluntary, (1) in general a keyboard piece in a free style.

(2) in particular an organ solo played before or after the service in the Anglican church. The earliest use of the term appears to be in the mid 16th century 'Mulliner Book' (*Musica Britannica*, i).

von Bülow, *see* BÜLOW

Von Heute auf Morgen (Ger., *From Day to Day*), opera in one act by Schoenberg, written in an uncharacteristic comic vein. Produced at Frankfurt in 1930, it was Schoenberg's first opera employing twelve-note techniques. It also proved (against popular theory at the time) that it was possible to compose a twelve-note comedy. The libretto, by the composer's wife under the pseudonym of Max Blonda, concerns the ruses employed by a woman to prevent her husband from abandoning her.

Vorschlag (Ger.), appoggiatura.

Vorspiel (Ger.), prelude.

Votre Faust (Fr., *Your Faust*), opera in two acts by Henri Pousseur, composed between 1960 and 1967. The libretto, by Michel Butor and the composer, is a modernization of Goethe's drama. Unlike the latter, however, the work has alternative endings, which the audience is invited to choose between during each performance.

vox angelica, vox coelestis (Lat.), organ stops.
> *See* UNDA MARIS

vox humana (Lat.), a reed organ stop imitating the human voice.

Voyevoda, The, Chaikovsky's first opera, with a libretto by himself and Alexander Ostrovsky (author of *The Storm*). The first performance, at the Bolshoi, Moscow, in 1869, was a success with the audience, but the opera quickly fell from the repertoire. The composer later transferred some of the material to other works.

Vulpius, Melchior (c. 1570–1615), German composer who was cantor at Weimar. He published several volumes of church music for four to eight voices, settings of Lutheran chorale melodies, and a *St. Matthew Passion*. His own chorale melodies include 'Christus der ist mein Leben' and 'Jesu Leiden, Pein und Tod' (originally 'Jesus Kreuz, Leiden und Pein').

Vyšehrad, the first of a cycle of six symphonic poems by Smetana, collectively entitled *Má Vlast* (*My Country*). Composed between 1872 and 1874, the music portrays 'The High Castle', a rock in the River Vltava, formerly the seat of the royal house.

Vyvyan, Jennifer (1925–74), British soprano, pupil of Roy Henderson. She appeared at Covent Garden, Sadler's Wells and Glyndebourne, and was especially associated with Britten's operas, in which she created the role of the Governess in *The Turn of the Screw* and of Tytania in *A Midsummer Night's Dream*.

Wachet auf (Ger., 'Sleepers Awake'), title of Bach's cantata no 140, written for Trinity XXVII, first performed at the Thomaskirche, Leipzig, on 25 November 1731, and based on a hymn by Philipp Nicolai (1599).

Waelraut, Hubert (1517–95), Flemish composer and singer. His compositions, which had a great reputation in his day, include *chansons*, madrigals and motets.

Wagenseil, Georg Christoph (1715–77), composer to the Imperial Court, Vienna. His numerous compositions include symphonies, concertos, keyboard works, church music, oratorios and operas.

Wagner, Peter Josef (1865–1931), German musical historian and first president of the International Musicological Society (1927). His principal studies were in the field of Gregorian chant.

Wagner, (Wilhelm) Richard (1813–83), German composer. Born in Leipzig, he was the son of a civic clerk, who died a few months after the composer's birth. His mother then married the Jewish actor, Ludwig Geyer, who in turn died in 1821. At school in Leipzig, Wagner acquired a profound interest in drama and in Beethoven's symphonies. Though he learnt the piano, he preferred to study the vocal scores of operas. He was taught harmony and counterpoint by Weinlig at St. Thomas's School, Leipzig, and by the age of twenty had written several orchestral works. He also started an opera, *Die Hochzeit* (The Wedding), but soon abandoned this in favour of *Die Feen* (The Fairies), inspired by Gozz's comedy *La Donna Serpente*. By now he was beginning to gain practical experience, first as chorusmaster at the Würzburg theatre (1833), then as conductor at Magdeburg (1835), where Wagner met the actress Minna Planer, whom he married and with whom he moved on to the Konigsberg theatre, and to Riga (1837) and then to Paris (1839), where they lived for three years in wretched poverty. Nevertheless, during this period, Wagner managed to complete *Rienzi* and begin *The Flying Dutchman*. Both of these were accepted for performance at Dresden, where Wagner was appointed assistant conductor in 1842. *Tannhäuser* followed in 1845, and another opera (*The Saracens*) was begun. The latter, however, remained unfinished. After the abortive revolt in Dresden in 1848, Wagner, who had shown sympathy with liberal ideas, was threatened with arrest and fled to Zürich. There he started to work out his ideas for his great political tetralogy, *The Ring*. Meanwhile his friendship with Liszt resulted in the production of *Lohengrin* at Weimar in 1850 (though Wagner himself did not hear it until eleven years later). In 1859 he completed *Tristan and Isolde* at Lucerne, and the following year was allowed to return to Germany after more than a decade of exile. Marital and financial problems, however, kept his life as turbulent as ever. By 1864 he was

again being threatened with imprisonment, this time for debt; but Ludwig II of Bavaria, one of his deepest admirers, came to his rescue and invited him to Munich, giving him the facilities he needed to continue his work. *Tristan* was produced at Munich in 1865, none too successfully: its importance as one of the great turning points in operatic history was not to be recognised until later. During this period Wagner fell in love with Cosima von Bülow, Liszt's daughter and the wife of the conductor Hans von Bülow. A scandal ensued, and antagonism at court compelled Wagner to leave Munich for Switzerland, though *The Mastersingers* was performed at Munich in 1868. In spite of more financial problems he planned the construction of a special festival theatre for his operas at Bayreuth. It opened in 1876 with the first performance of *The Ring*. By this time Wagner had married Cosima von Bülow (Minna Wagner having died in 1866) and had built a villa at Bayreuth. Ill-health interrupted work on his last opera, *Parsifal*, which he completed in 1882. He died of a heart attack during a visit to Venice the following year.

Wagner's whole career was characterised by a determination to succeed as an opera composer: his other compositions are few and, apart from the *Faust* overture, the *Siegfried Idyll* and the *Wesendonk Lieder*, are of minor importance. He wanted to create a new type of dramatic work, in which all the parts – music, drama and spectacle – could be united in a significant whole – to be called 'music dramas' rather than operas. The fulfilment of this design necessitated the building of a special theatre at Bayreuth, which is still used for festival performances of his works every summer. The financial difficulties which this and other projects involved were alleviated by the persistent generosity of his friends, particularly Liszt, who continued to believe in him in spite of Wagner's irresponsibility in money matters.

The works which illustrate, in its different aspects, his theory of operatic construction and philosophy are *The Ring*, *Tristan*, *The Mastersingers* and *Parsifal*. The principal points in that theory are briefly: (1) traditional opera was at fault in its subject matter, its verse-forms and the domination of music over drama; (2) Beethoven had shown the significance of instrumental melody, but music needs to be complemented by poetry; (3) the subject-matter must be suitable, hence legends were more suitable than the everyday common-places of modern opera; (4) the importance of feeling, as opposed to mere understanding, necessitated emotionally evocative verse – written by the composer himself – to which music could add a further stimulus; (5) operatic conventions which were opposed to the creation of such direct impressions must be abandoned, e.g. the operatic ensemble; (6) the

Richard Wagner in 1877, the year after the first complete *Ring* at Bayreuth

orchestra should not merely accompany – it should express everything that the voice cannot, and should also make use of the powerful force of association; (7) above all, symphonic continuity was essential. These principles were carried out most consistently in the four operas which constitute *The Ring*, in which the force of association was maintained by a large number of short and reasonably simple thematic fragments, which recur constantly in varying forms, sometimes independently, sometimes in combination, and are woven together to form a continuous symphonic texture. In general Wagner's instinctive musicianship triumphed over the limitations of his theories. All his mature works exhibit a highly developed gift for melody, unusual inventiveness in harmony, and a mastery of orchestration which owes little to tradition.

He wrote the following operas (words and music):
Die Feen (1834; first performed posthumously, Munich, 1888); *Das Liebesverbot* (after Shakespeare's *Measure for Measure*; Magdeburg, 1836); *Rienzi* (1840; first performed, Dresden, 1842); *The Flying Dutchman* (1841; first performed, Dresden, 1843); *Tannhäuser* (Dresden, 1845); *Lohengrin* (1848; first performed, Weimar, 1850); *The Ring of the Nibelung*: (1) *The Rhinegold* (1854; first performed, Munich, 1869), (2) *The Valkyries* (1856; first performed, Munich, 1870), (3) *Siegfried* (1871; first performed, Bayreuth, 1876), (4) *The Twilight of the Gods* (1874; first performed, Bayreuth, 1876); *Tristan and Isolde* (1859; first performed, Munich, 1865; *The Mastersingers* (1867; first performed, Munich, 1868): *Parsifal* (Bayreuth, 1882).

His other compositions include *Eine Faust Ouvertüre* (1840) and *Siegfried Idyll* (1870) for orchestra, and

Das Liebesmahl der Apostel (The Love Feast of the Apostles, 1843) for chorus and orchestra. His numerous prose works were published in ten volumes, translated by W. A. Ellis in eight volumes, (1892–9). The following list is a small selection from the voluminous literature on Wagner: Newman's *Life* includes detailed bibliographies.

P. BEKKER: *Richard Wagner* (1931)
J. N. BURK: *Letters of Richard Wagner: the Burrell Collection* (1951)
R. DONINGTON: *Wagner's 'Ring' and its Symbols* (1963)
A. GOLDMAN and E. SPRINCHORN: *Wagner on Music and Drama: a selection from Wagner's prose works* (1964)
R. GUTMAN: *Richard Wagner: the Man, his Mind and his Music* (1968)
W. H. HADOW: *Richard Wagner* (1934)
R. L. JACOBS: *Wagner* (1935)
B. MAGEE: *Aspects of Wagner* (1968)
E. NEWMAN: *Wagner as Man and Artist* (1924); *The Life of Richard Wagner*, four volumes (1933–46)
R. M. RAYNER: *Wagner and 'Die Meistersinger'* (1940)

Wagner, Siegfried (originally Helferich Siegfried Richard)(1869–1930), German composer and operatic administrator, the son of Richard Wagner and Cosima von Bülow. He studied with Humperdinck and from 1899 onwards was active as an opera-composer. His most important work, however, was the part which he played in the direction of the festival theatre at Bayreuth (later controlled by his sons, Wieland and Wolfgang).

Wagner, Wieland (1917–67), German producer and designer, son of Siegfried Wagner and grandson of Richard. With his brother Wolfgang (born 1919), he controlled the artistic and financial welfare of BAYREUTH after World War II, ridding it of its Nazi associations and revolutionizing the style of Wagner production. His 1951 *Parsifal*, and subsequent productions of *Tristan and Isolde*, *The Ring*, and other works, were milestones in operatic history; in these productions, traditional naturalistic trappings gave way to a new, uncluttered, more abstract and symbolic style of presentation, with special emphasis on lighting. In Wieland's view, the lighting technician was as important as the conductor – an order of priorities his grandfather might not have agreed with, but would certainly have understood. Wieland also produced works by various composers in other German cities (his *Salome* and *Lulu* being specially notable). It can be said that he changed the face of opera production in the 20th century just as decisively as his grandfather changed the face of opera composition in the 19th. Of his numerous emulators, however, few have achieved their aims with comparable success.

Wagner tuba, *see* TUBA

wait, (1) another name for the medieval SHAWM, presumably derived from (2);
  (2) (Ger., *Stadtpfeifer*) a musician, most commonly a wind-player, employed by a municipality (and in earlier times by the king or noblemen), so called because his original function was to act as a watchman and to announce the hours at night. Companies of waits were maintained in England between the 14th and 18th

centuries. During the 16th century their primary purpose ceased to be protective, the emphasis changing to that of providing musical entertainment. At the same time their scope was extended to include players of string instruments and singers. The term 'waits' is now loosely applied to itinerant musicians who play in the streets at Christmas time;

(3) a piece of music played by the waits.

G. A. STEPHEN: *The Waits of the City of Norwich* (1933)

W. L. WOODFILL: *Musicians in English Society* (1953), pages 33–53, 74–108

Walcha, Helmut (born 1907), German organist especially associated with the music of Bach. He had weak eyes in childhood and subsequently became blind.

Waldhorn (Ger.), literally 'woodland horn', the old German for the orchestral horn. In some 19th century scores the term implies a natural horn as opposed to one with valves.

Waldmärchen (Ger., 'Forest Legend'), the first part of Mahler's cantata DAS KLAGENDE LIED.

Waldstein Sonata, Beethoven's piano sonata in C major, op 53 (1804), dedicated to his friend Count Ferdinand Ernst Gabriel von Waldstein (1762–1823). The slow movement (*Introduzione*) was an afterthought. The original slow movement, which it replaced, was published separately as *Andante favori.*

Waldteufel, Emil (1837–1915), French (Alsatian) composer. He studied at the Paris Conservatoire, and for a time was employed in a piano factory. His highly successful waltzes included *The Skater's Waltz*. He was pianist to the Empress Eugénie of France.

Walford Davies, *see* DAVIES.

Walker, Ernest (1870–1949), British composer, pianist and historian, born in India. He wrote *A History of Music in England* (1907), and composed choral works, chamber music and songs.

Walker & Sons, J. W., a firm of organ-builders, founded in London by George England in 1740 and acquired in 1820 by Joseph W. Walker (died 1870), a former apprentice in the business.

Walküre, Die (Ger., *The Valkyrie*), opera in three acts by Wagner, the second part of the cycle DER RING DES NIBELUNGEN. First performed, Munich, June 26, 1870.

Wallace, William (1860–1940), Scottish composer and writer on music. The son of a distinguished surgeon, Wallace studied medicine in Glasgow, Vienna and Paris, specializing in ophthalmology, but from the age of 29 he concentrated on music. His main sympathies were with Liszt, and his output as a composer reflected this. His six symphonic poems (a form he pioneered in Britain) were his main tribute to his idol. The first (*The Passing of Beatrice*, 1892) was inspired by Dante; Goethe, Rossetti and Villon were the source of subsequent works in this form. The Scottish side of his personality found an outlet in *Sir William Wallace* (not a self-portrait, but a study of the early Scottish hero) and *In Praise of Scottish Poesie*.

Wallace, William Vincent (1812–65), Irish composer. His opera *Maritana* (London, 1845) brought him immediate success. He spent several years travelling in Australia, New Zealand, India, Mexico and the United States. Of his other operas, the most successful was *Lurline* (London, 1860). He also wrote a violin concerto and piano music. Wallace died in the Hautes Pyrénées.

Waller, Thomas 'Fats' (1904–43), U.S. jazz pianist and composer, specializing in stride piano. A pupil of James P. Johnson, he was a famous and influential figure who performed with enormous exuberance and humour, often singing as well as playing. Many of his performances are preserved on tape, some of the finest being *The Minor Drag, Harlem Fuss, Truckin', B flat Blues, Ain't Misbehavin', Rosetta, Black Raspberry Jam* and *Jitterbug Waltz* (one of the first important examples of jazz in 3/4 time).

Wally, La, opera in four acts by Catalani, with libretto by Illica after Wilhelmine von Hillern's novel *Die Geyer-Wally.* The première was at La Scala, Milan, 1892. The opera ends with a famous scene in which the heroine, La Wally, and her lover, Hagenbach, die in an avalanche. Toscanini, who greatly admired the piece, named his daughter after the heroine.

Walsh, a firm of music publishers in London, founded by John Walsh (died 1736) and continued by his son, John Walsh the younger (died 1766). A large number of Handel's works were published by the firm.

Walter, Bruno (1876–1962), German born conductor, also pianist, composer and writer. Walter studied at the Stern Conservatorium, Berlin, then was successively conductor at opera houses at Cologne, Hamburg, Breslau, Pressburg (Bratislava), Riga, Berlin. His career includes periods with Vienna Opera, 1901–12; at Munich (general music director), 1913–22; Berlin Stadtische Oper, 1925–33; Gewandhaus concerts, Leipzig, 1930–33; Vienna Philharmonic, 1933–38. When the Nazis rose to power, he took French nationality; later he moved to the United States, becoming naturalized in 1946. As a conductor, he excelled in the music of Mozart, Mahler and Bruckner, and in opera (he played an important part in establishing the Salzburg Festival in the inter-war years). Walter was reunited with the Vienna Philharmonic at the first Edinburgh Festival (1947), where he gave a memorable performance of Mahler's *Song of the Earth* with Kathleen Ferrier. He composed symphonies, chamber music and songs; his reminiscences were published under the title *Theme and Variations* (1946), and he also published a book on Mahler.

Walther von der Vogelweide, *see* VOGELWEIDE

Walther (Walter), Johann (1496–1570), German composer, singer and choirmaster. In 1526 he was municipal cantor at Torgau. He was director of the chapel of Moritz of Saxony, Dresden, from 1548 to 1554. A friend of Luther, he played a prominent part in establishing the music of the Reformed Church. His publications include the first Protestant hymnbook, *Geystliche Gesangk-Buchleyn* (1524), and a number of other collections of religious music. A number of instrumental compositions survive in manuscript. A complete edition of his works was begun in 1953 by Otto Schröder.

G. B. SHARP: 'The Fathers of Lutheran Music: 1, Johann Walter', in *Musical Times*, cxii (1971), pages 1060–2

Walther, Johann Gottfried (1684–1748), German organist, composer and lexicographer. He was organist at St. Thomas's, Erfurt, in 1702, municipal organist at Weimar in 1707, and court musician at Weimar in

1720. He was a relative of J. S. Bach, who was a godfather to his eldest son. He excelled in the composition of choral preludes. His complete organ works are published in *Denkmäler deutscher Tonkunst*, xxvi–xxvii.

Walther, Johann Jakob (c. 1650–1717), German violinist and composer. He served successively the Elector of Saxony at Dresden and the Elector of Mainz. His compositions for violin include imitations of nature and of orchestral instruments.

Walton, William Turner (born 1902), English composer. Walton was a chorister at Christ Church, Oxford; as a composer he is mainly self-taught. He made his reputation by a string quartet performed at the festival of the International Society for Contemporary Music, Salzburg, 1923, and by *Façade*, a series of instrumental pieces designed to be played in conjunction with the recitation of poems by Edith Sitwell. He reached maturity with his viola concerto (1929) and the oratorio *Belshazzar's Feast* (1931). His work, even when most successful, gives the impression of having been created with effort, though this often gives it an extra edge of excitement: his later compositions have been relatively few, and sometimes seem to strive consciously to recreate, not without success, the atmosphere of their predecessors. He displays considerable assurance in handling large masses of sounds, as in *Belshazzar's Feast* and the first symphony, but his most characteristic work exploits a nostalgic vein which is seen at its best in the viola concerto. He has occasionally flirted with modern tonality, but in essentials his work is in the English tradition represented by Elgar, whose influence is apparent in spite of what is undoubtedly a personal idiom. Milestones in his output have been his two symphonies; his full-length opera *Troilus and Cressida* (1954); his concertos and his orchestral *Variations on a Theme of Hindemith* (1963). He also wrote a one-act opera, *The Bear* (1967), for the

Sir William Walton: a pencil drawing done by his artist friend Rex Whistler in 1929.

Aldeburgh Festival. Walton was knighted in 1951.

F. HOWES: *The Music of William Walton* (1965, rev. 1973)

waltz (Fr. *valse*, Ger. *Walzer*, It. *valzer*), a dance in triple time, slow or fast, with one beat in the bar. It first appeared in the late 18th century as a development of the old *Deutscher Tanz* (German dance). An early example is the waltz by Diabelli, on which Beethoven composed a set of variations (op 120) in 1823:

The development of the waltz as a dance-form in the 19th century was due principally to the Viennese composers Joseph Lanner and Johann Strauss, followed by Johann Strauss, the younger, composer of *The Blue Danube* (1867), and his brother Joseph. Sets of waltzes for piano (solo or duet) were also written by Schubert, Weber, Chopin and Brahms. Weber's *Invitation to the Dance* for piano solo is a programmatic piece consisting of a series of waltzes, with introduction and epilogue. The vogue of the waltz was not confined to instrumental pieces. Brahms wrote two sets of waltzes for piano duet, *Liebeslieder-Walzer* and *Neue Liebeslieder-Walzer*, with parts for four voices. The influence of the waltz is to be found in many songs and operas of the late 19th and early 20th centuries (e.g. the waltzes in Richard Strauss's *Der Rosenkavalier* and *Arabella*). Waltzes have also appeared as movements in symphonies, e.g. Berlioz's *Symphonie fantastique* and Chaikovsky's fifth symphony. Ravel's choreographic poem *La Valse* for orchestra is an impressionistic interpretation of the Viennese waltz.

Walzer (Ger.), waltz.

Wanderer Fantasia, the name popularly given to a *Fantaisie* for piano by Schubert, op 15 (1822). It is in four linked sections. In the second section (Adagio) the composer uses part of his song 'Der Wanderer', op 4, no 1 (1816). Liszt arranged the work for piano and orchestra (first performed 1851).

Wand of Youth, The, two orchestra suites by Elgar, op 1a and 1b. Written as incidental music for a play during the composer's childhood, the piece was revised and rescored in 1907.

Wanhal, Johann Baptist, German form of Jan Křtitel Vanhal (1739–1813), Czech composer. He studied under Dittersdorf in Vienna, and subsequently in Italy. Exceptionally prolific, Wanhal wrote about 100 symphonies, 100 string quartets, 23 Masses and numerous other instrumental and vocal works. He was a friend of Haydn and Mozart. His reputation, considerable in its day, extended to Britain, where his name was spelt Vanhall by British publishers.

War and Peace (Russ., *Voina i mir*), opera in five acts by Prokofiev, with a libretto by Myra Mendelson (the composer's wife) after Tolstoy's novel. The première was in Moscow, 1944, in concert form, and the first stage production in Leningrad, 1946. Prokofiev subsequently revised the work, and the final version was heard in Leningrad in 1955, two years after the composer's death. *War and Peace* was the opera chosen for the opening of the Sydney Opera House in the autumn of 1973.

Ward, John (1571–1638), English composer who was in the service of Sir Henry Fanshawe. He published a set of madrigals in 1613 (reprinted in *The English Madrigal School*, xix). He also wrote a number of anthems, fantasias for strings, and keyboard pieces. Ten pieces for strings are printed in *Musica Britannica*, ix.

Ward, Robert (born 1917), U.S. composer and conductor. He studied at the Eastman School of Music and Juilliard Graduate School, and learnt composition under Aaron Copland and Howard Hanson, among others. His most famous work is his opera, *The Crucible* (1961), based on the play by Arthur Miller. He has also written an opera on Leonid Andreyev's *He Who Gets Slapped*, four symphonies, choral music, and pieces for orchestra and band.

Warlock, Peter, pseudonym used by Philip Heseltine (1894–1930) English composer, editor and writer on music. Educated at Eton, Warlock founded and edited *The Sackbut* in 1920, and with Philip Wilson edited five volumes of *English Ayres, Elizabethan and Jacobean*. He was author (under his own name) of books on Delius (1923) and Gesualdo (in collaboration with Cecil Gray, 1926). His compositions, all published under the name of Warlock, include a song cycle, *The Curlew*, for tenor, flute, cor anglais and string quartet; an orchestral suite, *Capriol*; choral works and many songs. He committed suicide in London, where he was born.

Warren, Leonard (1911–60), U.S. baritone; he studied in New York and Milan, and made his début at New York Metropolitan in 1939 as Paolo in *Simon Boccanegra*. Subsequently, he sang all over the world, and was particularly admired for his Verdi portrayals. Warren died on the stage of the Met. during a performance of *The Force of Destiny*.

War Requiem, A, large-scale choral work by Britten, with important solo parts written for Galina Vishnevskaya, Peter Pears and Dietrich Fischer-Dieskau. Based on anti-war poems by Wilfred Owen and on the Latin Requiem (the two ingeniously intermingled), it was composed in 1962 for the new Coventry Cathedral, and had its première there that year.

washboard, laundry utensil, made either of wood or metal and played with a drumstick or occasionally with thimbles on the fingers. It was much used in early jazz bands and before that by Negro slaves. Such associations may have prevented it being considered

seriously by composers. All the same it has been known to appear as a substitute for the less powerful GUERO in Stravinsky's *The Rite of Spring*.

Wasielewsky, Joseph Wilhelm von (1822–96), German-Polish violinist, conductor and musical historian, born near Danzig. He was a pupil of Mendelssohn at the Leipzig Conservatorium, and played in the Gewandhaus Orchestra. Under Schumann he led the Düsseldorf Orchestra (1850), and he wrote a book on that composer (1858), as well as several books on the violin.

Water Carrier, The (Fr., *Les Deux Journées*), opera in three acts by Cherubini, in which the hero, Armand, is enabled by a water carrier to escape from Paris in a barrel. The libretto is by Jean Nicolas Bouilly; first performed in Paris, January 16th, 1800.

Water Music, orchestral suite by Handel, composed about 1715 for a royal procession on the Thames, and first published in 1740. Six of the twenty pieces were adapted for symphony orchestra by Sir Hamilton Harty in 1922, but today the music is more often performed in its original form.

water organ, *see* HYDRAULIS

Watson, Thomas (c. 1557–92), editor of an anthology of Italian madrigals, published with English texts in 1590. Most of the pieces are by Marenzio. The collection also includes two madrigals by Byrd, written at the editor's request.

> A. OBERTELLO: *Madrigali italiani in Inghilterra* (1949)
>
> J. KERMAN: *The Elizabethan Madrigal* (1962), pages 39–72

Wat Tyler, opera by the English communist composer Alan Bush about the leader of the Peasants' Revolt in England in 1381. The libretto is by the composer's wife, Nancy Bush. The work was completed in 1950 and first performed three years later in Leipzig, East Germany, where Bush's music is more widely admired than in his homeland.

wayte, wait, old name for the hautboy or OBOE.

Webbe, Samuel (1740–1816), English composer of glees and catches. He was librarian at the Glee Club, 1787, and secretary of the Catch Club, 1794. He also wrote motets and Masses. His son, **Samuel Webbe** (1770–1843), was a pianist, organist and composer of glees and church music.

Weber, Ben (born 1916), U.S. composer, influenced by Schoenberg and Berg. His works include a symphony on poems by William Blake for baritone and chamber orchestra; also a ballet, *Pool of Darkness*, chamber music and piano music.

Weber, Bernhard Christian (1712–58), German organist and composer. His *Well-tempered Clavier*, a set of preludes and fugues for organ in all the major and minor keys (which survives in manuscript in Brussels), was at one time thought to have preceded Bach's first set by 33 years. In fact it was written more than twenty years later.

Weber, Carl Maria Ernst von (1786–1826), German composer, conductor and pianist, second cousin of Aloysia, Constanze and Josepha Weber. He studied under his father, J. P. Heuschkel and Michael Haydn, under whom he became a chorister at Salzburg. After further study at Munich in 1798, he appeared as a solo pianist in several towns and wrote his first opera, *Das*

Waldmädchen (Freiburg, 1800). Weber settled in Vienna in 1803, where he studied further with Vogler. He was conductor at the theatre, Breslau, from 1804–6, and from 1807–10 was secretary to Duke Ludwig of Württemberg, Stuttgart; in 1810, he was banished by the King of Württemberg and moved to Mannheim, and thence to Darmstadt. After several concert tours he was appointed conductor at Prague in 1813, and at Dresden Opera in 1816. His most successful work, the opera *Der Freischütz*, was produced at Berlin in 1821. In 1826, he visited London to produce *Oberon*, written for Covent Garden Opera, and he died there nearly eight weeks after the first performance. Weber was virtually the creator of German romantic opera. *Der Freischütz*, a *Singspiel* with dialogue, shows the influence of German folklore and the German countryside in its two aspects, one homely, the other mysterious. *Euryanthe* (Vienna, 1823), an opera with continuous music, which suffers from an obscure libretto, recreates the atmosphere of medieval chivalry and may be regarded as the precursor of Wagner's *Lohengrin*. Weber's piano compositions show a fertile imagination and a brilliant technical command of the instrument. Other operas by him are *Peter Schmoll* (1803); *Silvana* (1810), and *Abu Hassan* (1811). He also composed choral works, two symphonies, two piano concertos, a *Konzertstück* for piano and orchestra, two clarinet concertos and a clarinet concertino, four piano sonatas, and many piano pieces and songs. He wrote on music, and even began a novel, *A Composer's Life*.

J. Benedict: *Weber* (1881)
A. Coeuroy: *Weber* (second edition, 1927)
E. Kroll: *Carl Maria von Weber* (1934)
W. Saunders: *Weber* (1940)
J. Warrack: *Carl Maria von Weber* (1968)

Weber, Gottfried (1779–1839), German lawyer, composer, and theorist. In his house Carl Maria von Weber (not a relation) found refuge after he had been banished from Württemberg in 1810. His compositions include church music, songs and instrumental pieces of various kinds. He also founded a conservatoire at Mannheim. He published *Versuch einer geordneten Theorie der Tonsetzkunst* and several other important works on the theory of music and acoustics.

Weber, Josepha (1758–1819), Austrian coloratura soprano, eldest of the three Weber sisters. She was married first to Hofer, a violinist, then to Meyer, a bass. Mozart wrote for her the part of the Queen of the Night in *The Magic Flute* (Vienna, 1791). **Aloysia Weber** (1760–1839) was also a soprano. Mozart, who had once been in love with her, wrote for her the part of Constanze in *Die Entführung aus dem Serail* (Vienna, 1782), and general concert arias. She married the actor, Joseph Lange, in 1790. **Constanze Weber** (1763–1842), married Mozart in 1782; he died in 1791, and she later married (1809) Georg Nikolaus Nissen, a Danish diplomat. She supervised the publication of Nissen's life of Mozart (1828). Translations of the letters written by her are in E. Anderson's *The Letters of Mozart and his Family*, volume iii. The sisters were second cousins to Carl Maria Ernst von Weber.

Webern, Anton von (1883–1945), Austrian composer. He was born in Vienna, and studied musicology under Adler and composition under Schoenberg. With Berg, he was Schoenberg's principal disciple. He began his career as a theatre conductor in Germany and Czechoslovakia, but settled near Vienna after World War I and conducted the concerts of Schoenberg's Society for Private Performances and the Workers' Symphony Concerts. He devoted most of his time, however, to teaching and composition. His first composition, a passacaglia (1908), revealed the influence of Mahler, and showed no sign of the absolute adoption of the TWELVE-NOTE SYSTEM which was to characterize his works from then on. His relatively few works, most for small chamber combinations (often of unusually grouped instruments) or voice, reduce music to the bare essentials, abandoning traditional harmonic concepts. He concentrated many isolated musical events, ordered by intricate contrapuntal and rhythmic patterns, into extremely brief time-spans. For example, his *6 Bagatelles* (1913) for string quartet lasts three minutes 37 seconds, and *Five Pieces for Orchestra* (1911–13) contains only 76 measures. Later works, e.g., *Variations* (1940) for orchestra, strove for total variation in opposition to traditional developmental techniques. Webern's style was individual, intensely poetic, and expressive. Since his death his music has had an important, original and growing influence on young composers, although while he lived he had pursued his goals in almost total isolation. His life was cut short by a tragic accident – he was shot by a sentry during the U.S. occupation of Austria.

Webern's works include: *Das Augenlicht* and Cantatas nos 1 and 2 for chorus and orchestra; two songs (settings of Goethe) for chorus and chamber orchestra; two symphonies, passacaglia, variations, 'Six Pieces' and 'Five Pieces' for orchestra; concerto for nine instruments; three works, including *6 Bagatelles*, for string quartet; canons for voice, clarinet and bass clarinet; and songs.

There is a biography of him by Friederich Wildgans (translated 1963), and a study by René Leibowitz (reprinted 1970).

Kolneder, W.: *Anton Webern. Einfuhrung in Werk und Stil* (1961)
Webern, A.: *Letters* (edited by Josef Polnauer, 1967); *Paths to New Music* (edited by Willi Reich, 1963); 'Schönbergs Musik', in *Arnold Schönberg* (1912)

Wechsel (Ger.), change. Thus *Wechseldominante* means 'exchange dominant' or dominant of the dominant, i.e. the note D in the key of C. *Wechselgesang* is alternating or antiphonal singing.

Weckerlin, Jean Baptiste Théodore (1821–1910), French composer and editor, born Alsace. He studied at the Paris Conservatoire, unsuccessfully, but was chorusmaster, Société de St. Cécile, 1850–5; archivist, Société des Compositeurs de Musique, 1863, and chief librarian, Paris Conservatoire, 1876–1909. His one-act opera, *L'Organiste dans l'embarras* (Paris, 1853), was very successful when it first appeared. He published many collections of old French songs.

Weckmann, Matthias (1621–74), German organist and composer. He was a chorister under Schütz at Dresden and studied further at Hamburg. He was court organist at Dresden in 1641, organist to the Crown Prince of Denmark in 1642, returned to his post in Dresden in 1647, and was organist at St. James's, Hamburg, in 1655. At Hamburg he helped to found the *Collegium Musicum*, which gave public performances. His reputation as an organist was considerable. Examples of his church cantatas are in *Denkmäler deutscher Tonkunst*, vi. A number of keyboard works have been edited by R. Buchmayer in *Aus Richard Buchmayers Historischen Klavierkonzerten* (1927); several others in M. Seiffert's collection *Organum*. See also *Das Erbe deutscher Musik, Landschaftsdenkmale, Schleswig-Holstein und Hansestädte*, iv.

Wedding, The (Russ., *Svadebka*), dance cantata in four scenes by Stravinsky, dedicated to Diaghilev and scored for chorus, four pianos and percussion. Based on Russian popular texts, it depicts a characteristic Russian peasant wedding of the early 19th century. Though first performed in Paris (by the Russian Ballet, in 1923), the work is not normally referred to by its French title, *Les Noces*, except in France.

'Wedge' Fugue, the nickname given to Bach's organ fugue in E minor whose opening subject proceeds in gradually widening intervals:

Weelkes, Thomas (c. 1576–1623), English composer. He was successively organist of Winchester College and Chichester Cathedral. His first published work – *Madrigals to 3, 4, 5, & 6 Voyces* – appeared in 1597. Four further volumes date from 1598 to 1608. A considerable amount of church music survives in manuscript, some of it incomplete. He was one of the most original and inventive of the English madrigalists, excelling particularly in the composition of works for six voices. A modern edition of his madrigalian works is in *The English Madrigal School*, ix–xiii. His collected anthems are published in *Musica Britannica*, xxiii.

D. BROWN: *Thomas Weelkes* (1969)

Wegelius, Martin (1846–1906), Finnish composer and conductor. After studying philosophy at Helsinki University, he turned to music and studied in Vienna and Leipzig. He became conductor at the Finnish Opera in Helsinki, 1878, and was founder and first director of the Conservatory (now the Sibelius Academy), 1882. Among his pupils were Sibelius, Järnefelt and Palmgren.

Weichsel, Elizabeth, *see* BILLINGTON

Weigl, Joseph (1766–1846), Austrian composer, son of a cellist in Prince Esterhazy's orchestra and godson of Haydn. Weigl worked as an opera conductor in Vienna, and composed more than thirty operas, ballets, church music and songs. An aria from his opera *L'Amor marinaro* was used by Beethoven as a theme for variations in the finale of his trio for clarinet, cello and piano, op 11.

Weigl, Karl (1881–1949), Austrian composer, pupil of Adler and Zemlinsky. He taught at the Neues Wiener Konservatorium, 1918, and settled in the United States, 1938. His works include two symphonies, piano concerto for left hand, violin concerto, choral and chamber music, and more than a hundred songs.

Weihe des Hauses, Die, *see* CONSECRATION OF THE HOUSE

Weihnachtsoratorium, *see* CHRISTMAS ORATORIO

Weihnachtssymphonie, *see* LAMENTATION SYMPHONY

Weill, Kurt (1900–50), German born composer. He was a pupil of Humperdinck in Berlin. Weill's early orchestral music was influenced by Schoenberg, but his first major success was *The Threepenny Opera* (*Die Dreigroschenoper*), a modern version of *The Beggar's Opera* written in collaboration with Bertolt Brecht (1928). With its fierce social conscience, its sweet-sour melodies and jazz-orientated accompaniments, this work was the musical equivalent of the caricatures drawn by the German artist George Grosz. A second and more ambitious opera, *Rise and Fall of the City of Mahagonny* (*Aufstieg und Fall der Stadt Mahagonny*), continued the vein, again with Brecht's collaboration (1930). But this exposure of social corruption, as well as the fact that Weill was a Jew, provoked increasing opposition from the Nazis. In 1933 Weill moved to Paris, where he wrote *The Seven Deadly Sins*, and in 1935 he settled in the United States, where his music lost some of its former 'bite'. In his later works, such as *Lady in the Dark* and *Down in the Valley*, he was content to employ the contemporary idioms of musical comedy. These pieces compare unfavourably with *Happy End* and *The Lindbergh Flight* (1927–9), two 'American' works dating from his German years.

Weinberger, Jaromir (1896–1967), Czech composer. His first important work (and the one for which he is still best known) was his opera *Schwanda the Bagpiper* (*Svanda dudák*). Written in Prague in 1927, it exploited a racy national idiom. Two excerpts from it, a polka and fugue, became popular concert pieces. Later operas included *The Outcasts of Poker Flat* (after Bret Harte) (1932) and orchestral Variations and Fugue on *Under the Spreading Chestnut Tree*. Weinberger settled in the United States in 1938.

Weiner, Leó (1885–1960), Hungarian composer, who taught at the Budapest National Academy from 1908. Weiner wrote for the orchestra and for the stage, but his most important compositions are chamber works, of which the second string quartet, op 13, won the Coolidge Prize in 1921.

Weingartner, Felix (1863–1942), Austrian conductor and composer. He studied in Graz and Leipzig, and with Liszt at Weimar. After working in numerous German opera houses, Weingartner succeeded Mahler as conductor of the Vienna State Opera in 1907. Later he travelled widely, and gained international fame for his finely-chiselled interpretations of the German classics. His own compositions, including several operas, symphonies, choral and chamber works, are now neglected. More important, perhaps, are his prose writings, especially his textbook on conducting and the editing of the complete works of Berlioz (1899).

Weinszweig, John Jacob (born 1913), Canadian composer, conductor and teacher. His most famous work is an orchestral suite, *The Land*, inspired by his native Canada.

Weisgall, Hugo (born 1912), Czechoslovakian born composer and conductor, resident in the United States since 1920. He studied at the Peabody Conservatory and the Curtis Institute, Philadelphia, and was a composition pupil of Roger Sessions. His most important works are for the stage. His operas include *The Tenor* (1950), *The Stronger* (1952) after Strindberg, and *Six Characters in Search of an Author* (1959) after Pirandello. He has also written ballets, orchestral pieces and songs.

Weiss, Amalie, *see* JOACHIM

Weiss, Sylvius Leopold (1686–1750), German lutenist and composer. He worked at the courts of Hesse-Cassel, Dusseldorf and Dresden, where his colleagues included Lotti, Hasse and Porpora. His compositions were principally for the lute. He was reckoned by his contemporaries to be the finest lutenist of his time. He was also famed as an improviser, and on one occasion, it is said, competed with Bach at Dresden.

welcome song, a composition for soli, chorus and orchestra used in Restoration times to mark the return to London of the King or other members of the royal family. Examples by Purcell are in the Purcell Society's edition, xv and xviii.

Welitsch, Ljuba (born 1913), Bulgarian soprano. A famous exponent of Salome (a role she first sang under Strauss in Vienna in 1944), Welitsch is also renowned for her performance as Donna Anna, Amelia, Aida and Tosca, which she portrayed to fiery effect. She was associated in the post-war years with Glyndebourne and the New York Metropolitan.

Wellesz, Egon (1885–1974), Austrian composer and musicologist, pupil of Adler and Schoenberg. He was appointed professor of musical history at Vienna University in 1913, and moved to Britain in 1938, when he became a research fellow at Oxford. As a composer he showed in his earlier work the strong influence of Schoenberg, but his later music is marked by a considerable simplification of harmony and a ready acceptance of Romantic idioms. His operas include a Schoenberg-influenced *Alkestis* (1924) and *Incognita* (1951), in which the style leans more towards Mozart and Strauss. He has also written ballets, symphonies, choral and chamber works, several books on Byzantine music, and an important study of Schoenberg.

Wellington's Victory, otherwise known as *The Battle of Victoria* or, simply, the *Battle Symphony*, this short *pièce d'occasion* by Beethoven was written in 1813 and depicts the British victory over Napoleon at Victoria, Spain. It quotes various popular tunes, including the British National Anthem.

Well-Tempered Clavier, The (Ger., *Das Wohltemperierte Clavier*), the title of two sets of preludes and fugues for keyboard by Bach, each set consisting of 24 preludes and 24 fugues in all the major and minor keys (together the two sets are familiarly known as 'the Forty-eight'). The first set, dating from 1722, is described as 'for the use and profit of young people who are desirous of learning, as well as for the amusement of those already skilled in this study'. It was also clearly designed as a practical demonstration of the advantage of tuning keyboard instruments in 'equal temperament'. This system, now universally employed, makes all the semitones equal (as opposed to the older system of mathematically precise tuning of the standard keys). The result is that, while every key is very slightly out of tune, it is possible to play as easily in one key as in another; whereas with the older system

of tuning, some keys were virtually impossible because they were so badly out of tune. Bach was undoubtedly influenced by a collection of twenty preludes and fugues by J. K. F. Fischer, entitled *Ariadne musica neo-organoedum*, and published about 1700.

The second set of *The Well-Tempered Clavier* dates from 1744 and is more in the nature of a compilation. It is known that some of the pieces were originally in other keys than those in which they now appear. Others have the air of transcriptions. There is no indication of the instrument for which *The Well-Tempered Clavier* was written. *Clavier* is a generic term for a keyboard instrument with strings and may equally well mean the harpsichord or the clavichord. The probability is that Bach intended the pieces to be available for either instrument.

Welsh National Opera, one of Britain's two leading companies outside London (the other being Scottish Opera); founded in Cardiff in 1946. Famous in its early days for its Verdi productions (especially *Nabucco*), but now has a repertory ranging from Mozart to Berg's *Lulu* and new Welsh works.

Welte Photophone, an electronic instrument involving the use of a photo-electric cell.

Werckmeister, Andreas (1645–1706), German organist successively at Hasselfelde, Quedlinburg and Halberstadt. As a writer on the theory of music he was much respected by his contemporaries and successors. In his *Orgelprobe* (1681) and *Musicalische Temperatur* (1691) he gave detailed instructions for the tuning of keyboard instruments.

Werle, Lars Johan (born 1926), Swedish composer. His opera, *Dreaming about Thérèse* (1965), was based on Zola and intended for performance 'in the round', with the orchestra surrounding the audience, and the audience surrounding the singers: in that form it had its première in Stockholm in 1965. A later opera, *Die Reih* (The Journey), made use of collage effects, including quotations from *The Magic Flute*. Other works include a ballet, *Zodiac*, and a Sinfonia da Camera.

Wert, Giaches de (1535–96), Flemish composer. He served the Duke of Mantua for many years. He was one of the most prolific madrigal-composers of the 16th century. His publications include eleven books of madrigals in five or more parts, one book of madrigals in four parts, *canzonette* and motets. A collected edition of his works by C. MacClintock, assisted by M. Bernstein, was begun in 1961.

C. MACCLINTOCK: *Giaches de Wert* (1966)

Werther, opera in four acts by Massenet. The original French libretto is by Edouard Blau, Paul Milliet and Georges Hartmann, based on Goethe's novel, *The Sorrows of Young Werther* (*Die Leiden des jungen Werther*). The plot concerns Werther's love for Charlotte and his suicide when he finds she has married his friend Albert. It was first performed (in German) in Vienna, 1892, and in Paris the following year.

Wesendonk Songs, five songs 'for female voice' by Wagner based on poems by Mathilde Wesendonk, the wife of a rich silk merchant, befriended by the composer in Zurich in 1852. The third and fifth songs each carry the description 'Study for Tristan and Isolde'. In 'Im Treibhaus' there are passages in common with the prelude to Act 3 of the opera. 'Träume' shares material with the love scene.

Wesley, Samuel (1766–1837), English organist and composer, a son of the hymn-writer Charles Wesley. He showed outstanding gifts as a child, and had written a considerable amount of music, both vocal and instrumental, before the age of twenty. His subsequent career was limited by the recurrent effects of an accident to the skull. His enthusiasm for the music of J. S. Bach did much to bring it to the notice of other musicians at a time when it was virtually unknown in Britain. In particular, he helped to produce an English edition of *The Well-Tempered Clavier*. His best-known composition is the eight-part motet 'In exitu Israel'.

His son **Samuel Sebastian Wesley** (1810–76), was an organist and composer. He was a chorister of the Chapel Royal, and held various appointments as organist at London churches between 1826 and 1832. Subsequently, he was organist at Hereford Cathedral (1832), at Exeter Cathedral (1835), at Leeds Parish Church (1842), at Winchester Cathedral (1849), and at Gloucester Cathedral (1865). His compositions, which are not without individuality, are mostly for the church.

Westrup, Jack Allan (1904–75), English musicologist, critic and composer. As an undergraduate at Oxford he edited Monteverdi's *Orfeo* and *The Coronation of Poppaea* for the Oxford University Opera Club. After six years as one of the *Daily Telegraph*'s music critics, he was successively lecturer in music at King's College, Newcastle (1941), professor of music at Birmingham University (1944–6), and professor at Oxford (1947–71). He chaired the editorial board of the *New Oxford History of Music*, and edited *Music and Letters* from 1959. His books include a study of Purcell and an introduction to musical history. He was knighted in 1961.

Weyse, Christoph Ernst (1774–1842), Danish composer and teacher. He wrote a number of operas, piano sonatas, and some studies which were much admired in the 19th century. Among his pupils were Gade and Hartmann.

Whale, The, a dramatic cantata by John Tavener, inspired by the Biblical allegory of Jonah and the whale. First performed in 1968, it is scored for mezzo-soprano, baritone, speaker, organ and Hammond organ, chorus and orchestra. It has been described as a 'fantasy' of exuberance and serenity in which hieratic austerity (it uses a Latin text) gives way to the deliberate banality of the 'belly music'.

When I am laid in earth, Dido's lament at the end of Purcell's *Dido and Aeneas*.

whiffle, an early English name for the FIFE.

whip, *see* SLAPSTICK

whistle, a general name for any instrument that when blown produces a sound approximating to human whistling. Some, like the TIN WHISTLE (used by Copland in *Billy the Kid*) can play several pitches, while others, such as a police whistle, have only one; even this type has occasionally found its way into an orchestral score, one example being the last movement of Ibert's *Divertissement*.

White, Robert, *see* WHYTE

whithorn, may-horn, a very primitive type of OBOE made from the bark and wood of a willow tree.

Whittaker, William Gillies (1876–1944), English conductor, teacher and composer. He was founder and conductor of the Newcastle upon Tyne Bach Choir in 1915. He was Professor at Glasgow, and Principal of the Scottish National Academy of Music, 1930. A lifelong campaigner for the works of Bach, many of which he edited for public performance, he also made numerous arrangements of other works (including many folk songs) for school and domestic use.

whittle and dub, early English name for the PIPE AND TABOR.

whizzer, *see* THUNDERSTICK

whole-note, U.S. for 'semi-breve'.

whole-tone scale, a scale consisting of a series of intervals of a tone. It may begin on any note. There is no tonic or any other implicit relationship between the notes of the series. The limitations of notation make it necessary to represent one of the intervals as a diminished third (*see* DIMINISHED INTERVALS), but on a keyboard instrument this is identical with a tone, e.g. A sharp to C is the same as A sharp to B sharp, or as B flat to C. Two such scales are possible, the notation of which may vary according to convenience:

A scale starting on D is obviously part of the same series as the one starting on C, and so on.

Debussy and other composers have featured the whole-tone scale extensively in their music, both harmonically and melodically.

The following passage shows the use of the whole-tone scale in an actual composition:

DEBUSSY, *Voiles* (*Préludes*, Book I)

whole-tube instruments, *see* BRASS INSTRUMENTS

Whyte, Ian (1901–60), Scottish conductor and composer; he was a pupil of Stanford and Vaughan Williams. Whyte developed musical broadcasting in Scotland, first as B.B.C.'s Head of Music in Scotland (1931–45), then as conductor of B.B.C. Scottish Orchestra (1945–60). His works include an opera, *Comala*, after Ossian. His ballet, *Donald of the Burthens*, was produced at Covent Garden in 1951 and made musical history through incorporating a part for bagpipes in an otherwise conventional orchestral score. Whyte also wrote symphonies, concertos, symphonic poems, chamber music and numerous songs. His many arrangements of Scottish traditional music were inspired, like the rest of his output, by his lifelong love for his homeland.

Whyte, Robert (c. 1535–74), English composer. He was master of the choristers at Ely Cathedral in 1562, at Chester Cathedral in 1566, and at Westminster Abbey in 1570. His compositions, of high quality, consist of Latin church music, a few English anthems, and instrumental music. A modern edition of the church music is in *Tudor Church Music*, v.

Whythorne, Thomas (1528–96), English composer and music teacher. In 1571 he published *Songes, for three, fower, and five voyces*, eleven of which have been reprinted by P. Warlock (1927). His *Duos, or Songs for two voices* (1590) include fifteen textless canons which have been edited by W. Bergmann (1955). He also wrote an autobiography containing rare information about the working life of a professional musician in the early years of Elizabeth's reign (modern edition by J. M. Osborn, 1961).

Widdop, Walter (1892–1949), English tenor. He first appeared as Radamès in *Aïda* with the British National Opera Company in 1923, and was later famed for his Wagner portrayals, especially Siegmund and Tristan.

Widor, Charles Marie Jean Albert (1845–1937), French composer and organist. He studied in Brussels, where he was a pupil of Lemmens and Fétis. From 1870–1934 he was organist at St. Sulpice, Paris. He wrote ten large-scale works for organ, described as 'symphonies'. His other compositions include three operas, of which *Les Pêcheurs de Saint-Jean* (Paris 1905) was the most successful, five symphonies (two with organ, one with final chorus), two piano concertos, cello concerto, *Une Nuit de Walpurgis* (chorus and orchestra), chamber works, piano solos, and songs. He also edited Bach's organ works, in collaboration with Schweitzer, and wrote a supplement to Berlioz's *Traité de l'instrumentation*.

Wieck, Clara, *see* SCHUMANN

Wieck, Friedrich (1785–1873), German piano teacher, Schumann's father-in-law. For some time proprietor of a piano-manufacturing business and lending library in Leipzig, Wieck settled in Dresden in 1840. He developed his own method of teaching the piano and practised it with great success. His pupils included Hans von Bülow and his daughter Clara, whose marriage to Schumann he initially opposed with considerable asperity.

wieder, (Ger.), 'again'.

Wiegenlied, cradle song. The cradle song often attributed to Mozart (*Schlafe, mein Prinzchen* – 'Sleep, my little prince') was in fact written by J. B. Flies.

Wieniawski, Henri (1835–80), Polish violinist. He studied at the Paris Conservatoire; from 1860 to 1872 he was violinist to the Czar, and he taught at the Brussels Conservatoire in 1875. He toured widely as a soloist, at first with his brother, Joseph, and later with Anton Rubinstein. One of the outstanding violinists of his time, his compositions include two concertos and pieces of a popular kind.

Wigmore Hall, a concert hall in Wigmore Street, London, famous for chamber concerts and recitals. It was built by the firm of Bechstein, piano makers, and opened as the Bechstein Hall in 1901. The name changed to Wigmore Hall in 1917.

Willaert, Adrian (c. 1485–1562), Flemish composer who, like many of his compatriots, made his career in Italy. He was *maestro di cappella* at St. Mark's, Venice, from 1527 till his death. According to Zarlino he was inspired by the existence of two organs at St. Mark's to write *cori spezzati*, or compositions for two antiphonal choirs: the practice of this form of church music remained one of the characteristics of Venetian composers. He was also one of the first composers of the typical polyphonic madrigal of the mid-16th century, and one of the first to issue collections of polyphonic *ricercari* (*see* RICERCAR) for instrumental ensembles. His compositions also include Masses, motets and *chansons*. A complete edition of his works, by H. Zenck and W. Gerstenberg, was begun in 1950.

Williams, Alberto (1862–1952), Argentinian composer, pianist, conductor and poet. He studied at Buenos Aires Conservatory and at the Paris Conservatoire under César Franck. He was active in Buenos Aires as a recitalist and conductor. His compositions, several of which are influenced by South American folk song, include nine symphonies and other orchestral works, chamber music, unaccompanied choral works, many piano pieces and songs.

Williams, Grace (1906–77), Welsh composer. A pupil of Vaughan Williams and Egon Wellesz, her output includes an opera, *The Parlour*, orchestral works, concertos and Welsh folk song arrangements.

Williamson, Malcolm (born 1931), Australian composer, resident in Britain from 1953. He studied in Sydney with Sir Eugene Goossens, then in London with Elisabeth Lutyens and Erwin Stein. His substantial output, in a varied but consistently direct idiom, includes several operas. Of these, *English Eccentrics*, *Our Man in Havana* and *The Violins of St. Jacques* have all achieved success, as have the children's operas, *The Happy Prince* and *Julius Caesar Jones*. He has also written orchestral works, chamber music, piano and organ pieces, and church music in a pop-song style. He was appointed Master of the Queen's Musick in 1975, succeeding Sir Arthur Bliss.

William Tell (Fr., *Guillaume Tell*), Rossini's last opera, a setting in four acts of Schiller's drama, with libretto by Victor Joseph Etienne de Jouy and Hippolyte Louis Florent Bis. Written for the Paris Opéra, where it was first performed in 1829. The story deals with the rebellion of the Swiss, led by William Tell, against their Governor, Gessler, whose son Arnold sides with the rebels. The fortunes of this imposing opera have fluctuated over the years, some authorities deeming it to be too long and clumsy, others hailing it as Rossini's masterpiece. Its overture, however, remains a perennial concert favourite.

Willis, Henry (1821–1901), English organ-builder and organist. He founded the firm, Henry Willis and Sons, which has built or restored a large number of cathedral organs in Britain, including that of Gloucester Cathedral (1847). Among the other organs built by him were those at the Great Exhibition of 1851, St. George's Hall, Liverpool, Alexandra Palace and the Royal Albert Hall.

Wilson, John (1595–1674), English instrumentalist, singer and composer. In his earlier years he seems to have appeared as a singer in plays; it is at any rate certain that he set songs for stage productions. He became one of Charles I's musicians in 1635. From 1646 onwards he lived in retirement for several years. In spite of his Royalist affiliations he was made professor of music at Oxford in 1656. At the Restoration he became one of Charles II's musicians and in 1662 a Gentleman of the Chapel Royal. Many of the song collections of the Commonwealth and early Restoration periods contain pieces by him. He also published *Psalterium Carolinum*, a memorial tribute to Charles I (1657), and *Cheerful Ayres or Ballads* (printed at Oxford in 1660). Thirteen songs by him are printed in *Musica Britannica*, xxxiii.

wind band, an ensemble consisting of mixed wind instruments as opposed to the brass band, which does not contain members of the woodwind family. A MILITARY BAND is sometimes referred to as a wind band.

wind chimes, *see* WOOD CHIMES

Windgassen, Wolfgang (born 1914), German tenor. The leading Wagnerian HELDENTENOR of his day, he sang Parsifal in the first post-war Bayreuth production and thereafter was associated particularly with that opera house and with Stuttgart.

wind instruments, *see* INSTRUMENTS

wind machine (Ger., *Windmaschine*; Fr., *éoliphone*), also known as an aeoliphone, the wind machine consists of a large circular frame covered with silk and rotated by means of a handle. When this happens the silk brushes against cardboard or thin wood, thereby imitating the sound of wind. The faster the handle is turned the higher the pitch. The instrument has been used by several composers, including Strauss in *Don Quixote* and the 'Alpine' *Symphony*, and Ravel in *L'Enfant et les Sortilèges*. Strictly speaking it is not a percussion instrument although it is always placed under this heading.

Winter, Peter von (1754–1825), German composer. He wrote more than thirty operas, of which the most famous and successful was *Das unterbrochene Opferfest* (Vienna, 1796), while *Das Labirint* (Vienna, 1798) is interesting as a setting of Schikaneder's sequel to *Die Zauberflöte* (set by Mozart, 1791). He also wrote church music and instrumental works, including concertos for clarinet and bassoon.

Winterreise, Die ('The Winter Journey'), a cycle of 24 songs by Schubert on the subject of unrequited love (1827). Words by Wilhelm Müller, who also wrote *Die schöne Müllerin*. The title of the songs are:

(1) *Gute Nacht* (Good Night)
(2) *Die Wetterfahne* (The weather-vane)
(3) *Gefrorne Thränen* (Frozen tears)
(4) *Erstarrung* (Numbness)
(5) *Der Lindenbaum* (The lime-tree)
(6) *Wasserfluth* (Flood)
(7) *Auf dem Flusse* (On the stream)
(8) *Rückblick* (Retrospect)
(9) *Irrlicht* (Will-o'-the-wisp)
(10) *Rast* (Rest)
(11) *Frühlingstraum* (Dream of spring)
(12) *Einsamkeit* (Loneliness)
(13) *Die Post* (The Post)
(14) *Der greise Kopfe* (The hoary head)
(15) *Die Krähe* (The crow)
(16) *Letzte Hoffnung* (Last hope)
(17) *Im Dorfe* (In the village)
(18) *Der stürmische Morgen* (The stormy morning)
(19) *Täuschung* (Illusion)
(20) *Der Wegweiser* (The sign-post)
(21) *Das Wirtshaus* (The inn)
(22) *Muth* (Courage)
(23) *Die Nebensonnen* (The mock-suns)
(24) *Der Leiermann* (The hurdy-gurdy man)

Winter Wind Study, the nickname given to Chopin's piano study in A minor, op 25 no 11.

Winter Words, song cycle by Britten for high voice and piano, based on eight lyrics and ballads by Thomas Hardy. First performed, by Peter Pears and the composer, at the Leeds Triennial Festival in 1953.

Wirbeltrommel (Ger.), TENOR DRUM.

wire brush(es), thin but stiff wires attached to small handles, much used by dance band drummers to obtain brushing effects from a side drum. The same device is occasionally found in symphonic works.

Wirén, Dag Ivar (born 1905), Swedish composer. He studied at the Stockholm Conservatory, and in Paris with Sabaneiev, and became music critic in Stockholm from 1938–46. His compositions include five symphonies, concert overtures, a cello concerto, string quartets and other chamber works, choral works, piano pieces, songs and film music.

Wise, Michael (c. 1648–87), English organist and composer. He was a chorister in the Chapel Royal after the Restoration, and a lay-clerk at St. George's Chapel, Windsor. He was organist at Salisbury Cathedral in 1668, a gentleman of the Chapel Royal in 1676, and master of the choristers at St. Paul's Cathedral in 1687. His compositions include anthems, services, songs and catches.

Wishart, Peter (born 1921), English composer. Pupil of Nadia Boulanger, his output includes operas, *The Captive* and *Two in a Bush*; also a violin concerto, organ and piano music.

Witt, Jeremias Friedrich (1771–1837), Austrian composer, whose so-called 'Jena' Symphony was at one time believed to be by Beethoven. The mistake occurred because the score, discovered at Jena in Germany in 1909, bore the inscription 'par Louis van Beethoven'. In 1957, however, J. F. Witt was established (by the musicologist Robbins Landon) as its composer.

Wittgenstein, Paul (1887–1961), Austrian pianist, studied in Vienna. He first appeared in public in 1913. Wittgenstein lost his right arm in the 1914–18 war, and subsequently devoted himself to playing compositions for the left hand alone. Among the many works specially written for him are Ravel's concerto for left hand, Strauss's *Parergon zur Symphonia Domestica*, and Britten's *Diversions on a Theme*. He lived in the United States from 1939.

Wolf, Hugo (1860–1903), Austrian composer. He studied at the Vienna Conservatorium, 1875–7, but was compelled to leave after a disagreement with the director. For some years he was forced to make a precarious living by teaching and by writing musical criticism for the *Wiener Salonblatt*. In 1897 he lost his reason and had to enter an asylum, where he died. He began writing songs in 1876 and this continued to be his principal activity for the rest of his creative life. He worked irregularly: a furious spate of composition would be succeeded by a completely fallow period. A fanatical admirer of Wagner, he lost no opportunity of expressing his prejudices in his criticism. Wagner's influence appears also in his song accompaniments, which often have the character of independent instrumental compositions to which a voice-part has been added. The reason for this is not that he regarded the singer as superfluous, but that a passion for exact declamation and a genius for interpreting in music the mood of the words constantly induced him to write a vocal line which, like Wagner's, is virtually recitative, sung in strict time above an accompaniment which ensures the continuity and logical development of the musical ideas. His principal compositions are:

    (1) Songs: *Nachgelassene Lieder* (youthful works, first published in 1936); twelve *Lieder aus der Jugendzeit* (1877–8); *Lieder nach verschieden Dichtern* (settings of poems by various authors, including Gottfried Keller, Ibsen, Robert Reinick and Michaelangelo, 1877–97); *Mörike-Lieder* (1888); *Eichendorff-Lieder* (1888); *Goethe-Lieder* (1889); *Spanish Songbook* (*Spanisches Liederbuch*) (1890); *Italian songbook* (*Italienisches Liederbuch*) (1891 & 1896);

    (2) Opera: *Der Corregidor* (Mannheim, 1896);

    (3) Choral works: *Christnacht* (1889); *Elfenlied* (1891); *Der Feuerreiter* (1892); *Dem Vaterland* (1898);

    (4) Orchestra: *Penthesilea* (symphonic poem, 1885); *Italian Serenade* (1892);

    (5) Chamber music: string quartet (1884); *Italian Serenade* (1887).

His collected musical criticisms were published by R. Batka and H. Werner (1911).

    E. NEWMAN, *Hugo Wolf* (1907)
    E. SAMS, *The Songs of Hugo Wolf* (1961)
    F. WALKER, *Hugo Wolf* (1951)

Wolf, Johannes (1869–1947), German musicologist. He studied in Berlin, where he was a pupil of Spitta. A lecturer at Berlin University in 1902, and professor in 1908, he became honorary professor in 1922. In 1915 he became librarian of the music section of Preussische Staatsbibliotek (the Prussian State Library), where he was director from 1928–34. He edited the complete works of Obrecht for the Society for the History of Music in the North Netherlands. His books include *Geschichte der Mensuralnotation von 1250–1460* (three volumes, 1905), *Handbuch der Notationskunde* (two volumes, 1913 & 1919), *Musikalische Schrifttafeln* (a portfolio of facsimiles illustrating the development of notation, 1923), and *Kleine Musikgeschichte* (three volumes, 1923–9) together with *Sing- und Spielmusik* (an anthology of examples, since reissued in the United States as *Music of Earlier Times*).

Wolff, Albert Louis (1884–1970), French conductor and composer. He studied at the Paris Conservatoire. He became conductor at the Opéra-Comique in 1911, and chief conductor in 1922. From 1928–34 he was conductor at the Lamoureux concerts, and at the Pasdeloup concerts from 1934. His compositions include the opera *The Blue Bird* (Fr., *L'Oiseau Bleu*), a setting of Maeterlinck's play (New York, 1919).

Wolf-Ferrari, Ermanno (1876–1948), Italian composer. Son of the German painter August Wolf and an Italian mother, he studied under Rheinberger in Munich from 1893–5. From 1902–12 he was director at Liceo Benedetto Marcello, Venice. He made his name as an opera composer, exploiting an attractive vein of lyricism, and showing a particular flair for comedy, in which he adroitly adapted the idioms of the

18th century to the 20th century stage. His most famous works are *I quattro rusteghi* (1906), *Susanna's Secret* (*Susannens Geheimnis*, 1909) and *The Jewels of the Madonna* (*Der Schmuck der Madonna*, 1911). He also wrote choral works, chamber music, songs and piano pieces. Although some of his operas were first performed in German versions, they were originally composed to Italian words.

Wolfrum, Philipp (1854–1919), German composer and organist. He studied at Altdorf and Munich. In 1884 he became university director of music and organist at Heidelberg, where he founded and conducted a Bach Choir. He became professor in 1898. His works include choral music, chamber music, organ pieces and songs. He also wrote a study of Bach in two volumes (1906).

Wolkenstein, Oswald von (1377–1445), German poet and composer, one of the last of the Minnesinger. His songs, some of which are for two and three voices, have certain affinities with folk song. A modern edition of them is in *Denkmäler der Tonkunst in Osterreich*, xviii, Jg. ix (1).

    W. SALMEN: 'Werdegang und Lebensfülle des Oswald von Wolkenstein', in *Musica Disciplina*, vii (1953).

WoO (Werk ohne Opus), identification tag applied to works by Beethoven which do not have opus numbers. Thus the Rondo in B flat for piano and orchestra is WoO 6, and the *Variations on a March by Dressler* WoO 63.

Wood, Charles (1866–1926), Irish organist and composer. He studied at the Royal College of Music, where he subsequently became a teacher. From 1889–94 he was organist at Gonville and Caius College, Cambridge, and in 1897 he became a lecturer at Cambridge, being appointed professor in 1924. His compositions include choral music, incidental music, string quartets and songs, the most famous being 'Ethiopia saluting the colours'.

Wood, Henry Joseph (1869–1944), English conductor; studied composition at the Royal Academy of Music. He began his career as an opera conductor in 1889. Wood inaugurated London's promenade concerts in 1895, and conducted them until his death. Initially they were held at the Queen's Hall (until its destruction in World War II), and subsequently at the Royal Albert Hall. He also conducted innumerable other symphony concerts and festivals in Britain, Europe, and the United States. He introduced to British audiences, particularly at the Promenade Concerts, a very large number of new works by British and foreign composers, and also gave young performers the opportunity of appearing in public. His meticulous technique and business-like methods at rehearsals enabled him to give finished performances under the most adverse conditions. His numerous arrangements and re-orchestrations of older music show a passion for vivid colouring which is rarely justifiable on either historical or aesthetic grounds. Wood was knighted in 1911; he published his autobiography under the title *My Life of Music* (1938), and also published a collection of singing exercises, *The Gentle Art of Singing*, in four volumes (1927–8).

Wood, Hugh (born 1932), English composer. Wood studied under Iain Hamilton and Matyas Seiber. His piano pieces, op 5, show the influence of Schoenberg. Although his output is by no means prolific, it is impressively consistent in quality. His works include *Scenes from Comus* (after Milton) for soprano, tenor and orchestra, a cello concerto and two string quartets.

Wood, Thomas (1892–1950), English composer. A pupil of Stanford, he wrote a number of choral works, with and without accompaniment; several of these are concerned with the sea, to which, as the son of a master mariner, he was naturally attracted. His literary skill found expression in his autobiography, *True Thomas* (1936), and *Cobbers* (1932), a book about Australia.

wood block, also known as the Chinese wood block, this is a rectangular piece of hard wood partially hollowed out. When played with side-drum sticks it gives a bright and penetrating sound and one that differs markedly from that of TEMPLE BLOCKS. Wood blocks have been much used by 20th century composers of all nationalities. A single wood block is usually used but occasionally composers ask for sets of two or more in varying sizes.

wood chimes, also known as bamboos or wind chimes. They consist of a very large number of different-sized hollow bamboo canes suspended together. They are played either with the hand or a wooden stick (or sometimes by the wind) and give out a dry sound that continues as long as the canes remain in motion and so hit each other. Occasionally hard wood is used instead of bamboo, in which case the sound is more brittle.

wood drums, although wood drums of various shapes and sizes exist in different parts of the world, few of these are ever seen in our concert halls. The most important are the log drum, slit drum, and wood-plate drum (Ger., *Holzplattentrommel*). The first of these, which is also known as the wooden gong, is large, cylindrical in shape and hollowed out. A slit runs almost the whole length of the centre. The slit drum is similar but differently shaped. Stockhausen used six in his *Gruppen* and required notes of definite pitch from them. Wood-plate drums are virtually tom-toms with a single head made of wood. They are higher pitched than either log or slit drums.

wooden gong, wooden-headed tom-toms, wood-plate drums, *see* WOOD DRUMS

Wooden Prince, The, ballet by Bartók, based on a scenario by Béla Balázs, who wrote the libretto of *Bluebeard's Castle*. It was first performed by the Budapest Opera and Ballet, 1917. Today it often forms part of a triple bill with Bartók's two other works for the stage, *Bluebeard's Castle* and *The Miraculous Mandarin*.

woodwind instruments, *see* INSTRUMENTS

Wooldridge, Harry Ellis (1845–1917), painter and musicologist. He published a new edition of W. Chappell's *Popular Music of the Olden Time*, under the title *Old English Popular Music* (two volumes, 1893), *Early English Harmony* (a volume of facsimiles, 1897) and *The Polyphonic Period* (volumes I and II of the *Oxford History of Music*, 1901 and 1905; new edition by P. C. Buck, 1929 and 1932). He was joint editor, with Robert Bridges, of *The Yattendon Hymnal* (1899), and, with G. E. P. Arkwright, of volumes XIV and

XVII (anthems) of the Purcell Society (1904 and 1907).

Wordsworth, William (born 1908), English composer, resident in Scotland since 1961. A descendant of Christopher Wordsworth, brother of the poet. His output, which reflects his belief in traditional tonality, includes five symphonies (the second of which won a competition sponsored by the Edinburgh Festival in 1950), six string quartets, and many vocal and instrumental works. The *Four Sacred Sonnets of John Donne* (1944) for baritone and piano, show his style at its strongest.

Worgan, John (1724–1790), English organist and composer. He was organist at St. Botolph's, Aldgate, and organist and composer at Vauxhall Gardens. His compositions include oratorios, church music, organ music and harpsichord works.

Wozzeck, opera in three acts by Berg, to a libretto from Georg Büchner's drama. It was first performed in Berlin, 1925. Wozzeck (a German soldier) is the servant of the captain of the garrison and also of the doctor, who experiments on his body and mind and tells him that he suffers from mental aberration. The captain claims that Marie (Wozzeck's mistress, by whom he has a son) is having an affair with the drum-major. Wozzeck, enraged by the drum-major's boastful words, fights with him but is defeated. He later stabs Marie near a pond, throws his knife into the water and drowns himself. When the news of Marie's death is announced, her child does not understand and goes on playing.

Wranitsky, Paul (1756–1808), Austrian violinist, composer and conductor. He studied in Vienna, where he became conductor at the Court Opera. In addition to a number of instrumental works, he composed several operas, which were very successful in Germany, particularly *Oberon, König der Elfen* (Vienna, 1789).

His brother, **Anton Wranitsky** (1761–1820), was a violinist and composer. Pupil of Albrechtsberger, Mozart and Haydn, he later became *Kapellmeister* to Prince Lobkowitz in Vienna, 1808. He composed numerous instrumental works, including symphonies, violin concertos and string quartets, and also church music. Anton's daughter, **Karoline Wranitsky** (1790–1872) was a soprano. She sang Agathe at the first performance of Weber's *Der Freischütz* (Berlin, 1821).

Wreckers, The, opera in three acts by Ethel Smyth. The original French libretto (from a Cornish drama, *Les Naufrageurs*) is by Henry Brewster. The work was first performed (in a German version, *Strandrecht*) at Leipzig, 1906, and in London, 1909, where it was conducted by Sir Thomas Beecham. The plot concerns a Cornish community which lives by wrecking; the heroine, Thirzen, is accused of warning ships off the coast, and in punishment is condemned to die with her lover.

wuchtig (Ger.), weighty, heavy.

Wuorinen, Charles (born 1938), U.S. composer who has worked extensively in the field of electronic music.

Wurlitzer organ, type of UNIT ORGAN that at one time was much used in large cinemas.

Wurstfagott (Ger.), literally 'sausage-bassoon'.
See RACKET

Xenakis, Iannis (born 1922), Greek composer, born in Romania. Xenakis has had a multiple career as architect, mathematician, logician, poet and musician. He studied at the Athens Polytechnic, and in Paris as a pupil of Honegger, Milhaud and Messiaen. As architect, he has worked with Le Corbusier, and in 1958 designed the Philips Pavilion at the Brussels Expo. Mathematics has had a powerful influence on his music; at sixteen he rewrote some of Bach's works in terms of geometrical formulae, and today he uses a computer to speed the creation of his own works. He has experimented with the idea of 'clouds', 'masses', and 'galaxies' of events in sound under the title of 'stochastic music', and with mathematical theory under the title of 'symbolic music'. His *ST/10* (1956–62) was his first work to rely on a computer – although it was scored, like most of his music, for conventional instruments of the orchestra. Other works with procedures involving computerized formulae are *Eonta*, for piano and five brass, and *Atrées*, for ten instruments. In the United States, Xenakis founded the Center for Mathematical and Automatic Music at Indiana University; in Paris, he founded a group called EMAM, composed of mathematicians, electronic engineers, psychologists and others, to further the use of mathematics in music.

Xerxes (It., *Serse*), comic opera by Handel, produced in London, 1738. The story (based on a libretto by Minato) concerns a Persian king. The music includes the famous aria, 'Ombra mai fù' (in praise of a tree's shade), meant by Handel to be satirical but subsequently solemnized under the world-famous title of 'Handel's Largo'. The composer marked the aria to be sung *larghetto*, implying a somewhat faster speed.

xylophone, a percussion instrument consisting of hardwood bars, laid out in the manner of a keyboard and set in a frame that is itself the stand. Nowadays, although not in the past, the instrument is fitted with tuned metal resonators that help to enrich and sustain the tone. They do so only to a limited degree in order not to counteract the characteristic hard and bright sound. When performing on the xylophone the player stands and uses mallets of various weights and hardness according to the quality of tone required. Chords can be played by holding two mallets in either or both hands. The range of the instrument and consequently its size varies from model to model. Large ones have a compass of four octaves upwards from middle C, but many in general use are limited to three octaves and a fifth or to three octaves and a tone; in both cases it is the lower range which is curtailed. Normally the xylophone is treated as a non-transposing instrument, but composers occasionally write for it an octave below the true pitch. Occasionally two players perform on it simultaneously.

Xylophones are used greatly in non-Western cultures, particularly Java and Africa (*see* GAMELAN, MARIMBA). Saint-Saëns imitated the rattling of skeletons with it in his *Danse Macabre*, and Shostakovich used it in his Fifth Symphony.

xylorimba, xylomarimba, despite its names this instrument is not a cross between a xylophone and a marimba, but a large xylophone with an extended compass down to the C in the bass stave. The reason for the name is that the range of five octaves covers those of both the xylophone and the marimba.

Yancey, Jimmy (1898–1951), U.S. boogie-woogie pianist, of uncommon sensitivity. He often based his style on tango and habanera rhythms, as in *Five o'clock Blues*.

Yankee Doodle, song used by British troops to deride the revolutionary colonial troops of North America, and later taken up by the revolutionists themselves. The tune dates back at least as far as 1778, when it was included in Aird's *Selection of Scottish, English, Irish and Foreign Airs*, published in Glasgow.

Yeomen of the Guard, The, comic opera in two acts by Sullivan with a libretto by William Schwenk Gilbert. First performed, London, October 3rd, 1888. The story is set in 16th century London, and the title refers to the warders of the Tower of London.

yodel (Ger., *Jodel*), form of singing found in Switzerland and the Austrian Tyrol, involving an alternation between natural voice and falsetto. The music tends to be cheerful, making use of simple dance rhythms.

Yonge, Nicholas (died 1619), editor of two volumes

of Italian madrigals. These were published in London with English texts under the title *Musica Transalpina* (1588 and 1597; facsimile editions, 1972).

A. OBERTELLO: *Madrigali italiani in Inghilterra* (1949)

J. KERMAN: *The Elizabethan Madrigal* (1962), pages 39–72

Youll, Henry, English madrigalist who published a volume of *Canzonets to three voyces* in 1608. A modern edition is in *The English Madrigal School*, xxviii.

Young France (Fr., *La jeune France*), a group of four French composers (Baudrier, Jolivet, Lesur, Messiaen) who in 1936 set out to promote a 'personal message' in their compositions.

Young, LaMonte (born 1935), U.S. composer. Pupil of Stockhausen, he is an exponent of the 'indeterminacy' school. His various vanguard works include *Poem for Chairs, Tables and Benches* (1960), *The Tortoise Droning Selected Pitches from the Holy Numbers for the Two Black Tigers, the Green Tiger and the Hermit* (1964) and *The Tortoise Recalling the Drone of the Holy Numbers as They Were Revealed in the Dreams of the Whirlwind and the Obsidian Gong, Illuminated by the Sawmill, the Green Sawtooth Ocelot, and the High-tension Line Stepdown Transformer* (1964).

Young, Lester (1909–59), U.S. tenor saxophonist and clarinettist. He worked with Count Basie's band in the 1930s and 1940s, his detached, oblique style foreshadowing the 'cool' jazz of the 1950s. Particularly associated with jazz singer Billie Holiday, with whom he established a deep musical rapport.

Young, William (died 1671), English violist and violinist who was one of the king's musicians at the Restoration. He published at Innsbruck in 1653 a collection of eleven sonatas for three, four, and five voices, dedicated to the Archduke Ferdinand (modern edition by W. G. Whittaker, 1930). The collection, which also includes dance tunes, is interesting as the earliest known set of sonatas for strings and continuo by an English composer.

Young Lord, The (Ger., *Der junge Lord*), comic opera in three acts by Henze, produced in Berlin, 1965. The

libretto is by Ingeborg Bachmann, based on a story by Wilhelm Hauff. A satire on German provincial snobbery, the opera concerns a young English aristocrat who is idolized by the townsfolk of Grunwiesel until he turns out to be a trained ape dressed up as a man.

Young Person's Guide to the Orchestra, The, variations and fugue by Britten on a theme from Purcell's *Abdelazer*. The score was commissioned in 1945 by the Ministry of Education as music for a film, *The Instruments of the Orchestra*, but soon established itself as a concert piece in its own right. Each of the thirteen variations spotlights a different instrument or group of instruments.

Yradier, Sebastián (1809–65), Spanish composer of popular songs and dances. The most famous of his songs is 'La Paloma' ('The Dove'). Another was adapted by Bizet for use as the 'Habañera' in *Carmen*.

Ysaÿe, Eugène (1858–1931), Belgian violinist, composer and conductor. He studied at Liège Conservatoire, and subsequently with Wieniawski and Vieuxtemps. Ysaÿe was a teacher at Brussels Conservatoire from 1886–97, and was founder and conductor of the Société des Concerts Ysaÿe, Brussels. He toured widely as a soloist and as leader of a string quartet, and gave the première of many works, including César Franck's violin sonata. His own output included six concertos and other pieces for violin. From 1918–22 he conducted the Cincinnati Symphony Orchestra.

Yun, Isang (born 1917), Korean composer. He studied in Osaka and Tokyo, taught from 1954–6 at the University of Seoul, then moved to Europe to continue his studies with Boris Blacher and Josef Rufer. In 1964 he settled in Berlin, but in 1967 was kidnapped by South Korean secret agents and sentenced to life imprisonment in his homeland. After two years, however, he was released and returned to Germany. His works, which mix eastern and western techniques, include *Om mani padme hum*, a setting of texts by Buddha, for baritone, chorus and orchestra (1964), and an opera, *The Butterfly's Widow* (1968). He has also written an orchestral piece, *Réak* (1966), and a keyboard work *Shao Yang Yin* (1966).

Zacconi, Lodovico (1555–1627), Italian singer, composer and theorist. He was for a time a member of the court chapel at Munich, but spent most of his life in Italy. His *Prattica di musica* (two volumes, 1592 and 1619) is one of the most comprehensive treatises of its time; the subjects dealt with include notation, counterpoint, musical form, the modes, instruments, and methods of performance. His manuscript works include a set of canons (with solutions) and *ricercari* for organ.

Zachow or **Zachau, Friedrich Wilhelm** (1663–

1712), German organist and composer. He was organist of the Liebfrauenkirche, Halle, from 1684 till his death. Handel as a boy was his pupil. His compositions include church cantatas and organ works (modern edition in *Denkmäler deutscher Tonkunst*, xxi–xxii).

Zadok the Priest, the first of four anthems composed by Handel for the coronation of George II in 1727. It is still sung at British coronation ceremonies.

Zaïde, opera in two acts by Mozart, written in 1779 but left unfinished. The libretto is by Johann Andreas Schachtner. It was first performed at Frankfurt, 1866, with additional material by Karl Gollmick and Anton André. The story resembles that of *Die Entführung aus dem Serail,* which Mozart composed three years later.

Zaira, opera in two acts by Bellini. Libretto by Felici Romani, based upon Voltaire's tragedy, *Zaïre.* The first performance was in Parma in 1829.

Zampa, opera in three acts by Hérold with libretto by Anne Honoré Joseph Mélesville; first performed in Paris, 1831. The story is an offshoot of *Don Giovanni.* Zampa (baritone) is a 16th century pirate who mockingly places a ring on the finger of a marble statue of a girl he has betrayed. Thereupon the statue drags him to his death at the bottom of the sea. The overture has long been a concert hall favourite.

zampogna (It.), Calabrian BAGPIPE.

Zandonai, Riccardo (1883–1944), Italian composer. He studied at the Liceo Musicale, Pesaro. Zandonai's first opera, *Il grillo del focolare,* after Dickens's *The Cricket on the Hearth,* was performed at Turin in 1908. Of his other operas, all written in traditional style, the most successful were *Conchita* (Milan, 1911), *Francesca da Rimini* (Turin, 1914) and *Giulietta e Romeo* (Rome, 1922), based on Shakespeare's *Romeo and Juliet.* He also composed a Requiem and other choral works, concertos for violin and cello, and songs.

zapateado, spirited Spanish dance, with three beats to the bar, in which stamping clogs replace the more usual castanets.

Zarlino, Gioseffo (1517–90), Italian theorist and composer, a pupil of Willaert. He was *maestro di cappella* at St. Mark's, Venice, in 1565. His reputation rests on his theoretical works, *Istitutioni harmoniche* (1558) and *Dimostrationi harmoniche* (1571), both of which have been reprinted in facsimile (1965). The subjects treated include the mathematical basis of music, counterpoint, and the modes. A translation by G. A. Marco and C. V. Palisca of part 3 of *Istitutioni* ('The Art of Counterpoint') was published in 1968. In 1588 he published *Sopplimenti musicali,* partly as a reply to Vincenzo Galilei, who had attacked Zarlino's theories in his *Dialogo della musica antica et della moderna* (1581) and was to do so again in his *Discorso intorno all'opere di messer Gioseffo Zarlino* (1589). Zarlino's few surviving musical compositions include three motets and a spiritual madrigal, edited by R. Flury in 1959 (*Das Chorwerk,* lxxvii), but they lack the originality of his theoretical writings.

zart (Ger.), tender. So *Zartheit,* tenderness, *Zärtlich,* tenderly.

Zar und Zimmermann, see CZAR AND CARPENTER

zarzuela, a characteristically Spanish type of opera with dialogue, so called from the La Zarzuela, a royal palace in the country outside Madrid, where representations were given in the 17th century. The earliest known example appears to be *Celos aun del ayre matan* (Jealousy, even of air, is deadly) by Juan Hidalgo, produced in 1660. The popularity of the *zarzuela* declined in the 18th century, but it was revived in the 19th century. The Teatro de la Zarzuela, in Madrid, specially built for such performances, was opened in 1856. The modern *zarzuela* is generally either a serious work in three acts or a comic opera, satirical in character, in one act.

G. CHASE: *The Music of Spain* (1941)

Zauberflöte, Die, see MAGIC FLUTE, THE

Zaubergeige, Die (Ger., *The Magic Violin*), opera in three acts by Egk with libretto by the composer and Ludwig Andersen, after a puppet play by Count Pocci. The première was in Frankfurt, 1935, with a revised version in Stuttgart, 1954. Egk's first opera and written in a folk song style, it concerns a violin whose owner, in return for its magic powers, must renounce love.

Zauberoper (Ger., magic opera), a type of opera popular in Vienna in the late 18th and early 19th centuries. The text tended to be based on a fairy-tale subject, which was usually treated comically and with sumptuous scenic effects. Mozart's *The Magic Flute* is the greatest and most famous work in the form. Few others have stayed the course, though Weber's *Oberon* holds a peripheral place in the repertory – fortunately, because (in spite of its feeble libretto) it contains some of his finest music.

Zazà, opera in four acts by Leoncavallo, with libretto by the composer, after the play by Simon and Berton. The première was at Teatro Lirico, Milan, 1900. The story concerns a café singer and her love affairs. The music includes 'Il bacio' ('The Kiss Duet').

Zeffirelli, Franco (born 1923), Italian producer and designer who worked for the spoken theatre and the cinema before turning to opera in 1948. His first successes were at La Scala, Milan, where he produced and designed works by Rossini and Donizetti in the early 1950s. His work at Covent Garden has included *Lucia di Lammermoor, Rigoletto, Tosca, Cavalleria Rusticana, Pagliacci* and *Falstaff,* all presented in the meticulously detailed, realistic vein which has become characteristic of his work.

Zeitmass (Ger.), tempo.

Zeitmasse (Ger., *Tempi*), work for woodwind quintet by Stockhausen, first performed by the Domaine Musical, Paris, 1956, under Boulez's direction.

Zeitoper (Ger., opera of the times), title applied to a type of opera composed in Germany, particularly in the 1920s. The most famous example of the form is Krenek's *Jonny spielt auf* (1927), which uses jazz-inspired techniques to convey its violent story and to create an atmosphere of 20th century social realism. Hindemith's *Hin und Zurück* (*There and back,* 1927) and *Neues vom Tage* (*News of the Day,* 1929) belong to the same genre.

Zelenka, Jan Dismas (1679–1745), Bohemian composer and double bass player. He studied in Prague, joined the court band at Dresden in 1710, then moved to Vienna to become a pupil of Fux in 1716. After travels in Italy, he returned to the Dresden court, to collaborate with Heinichen, whom he succeeded in 1729 as director of church music. Until recently he was reckoned to be one of the minor figures of the baroque era, but the resurrection of six fine trio sonatas (the source manuscripts of which are in Dresden) has revealed him to be a composer of considerable personality. The woodwind parts in these works have a vitality of invention that suggest him to have been scarcely inferior as a composer of chamber music to his slightly younger contemporary, J. S. Bach. Though these sonatas are the only ones by him that have come to light, he also wrote a variety of church music, including some twenty Masses, oratorios (*I penitenti al sepolcro, Il serpente di bronzo* and

Gesù al Calvario), a *Melodrama de Sancto Wenceslao*, cantatas, motets and psalms; some of these works, too, may establish themselves as baroque masterpieces, now that the sonatas have won deserved recognition.

Zelmira, opera seria in two acts by Rossini. The libretto is by Andrea Leone Tottola, after the *Zelmire* (1762) of Dormont de Belloy. The première was in Teatro San Carlo, Naples, 1822, with Isabella Colbran in the title role.

Zelter, Carl Friedrich (1758–1832), German composer, conductor and theorist. Originally a mason, he studied music while still a boy and rapidly became an accomplished musician. He was the accompanist in the Berlin Singakademie in 1792 and its conductor in 1800. He was also founder and conductor of the Königliche Institut für Kirchenmusik in 1820, and a friend of Goethe, many of whose poems he set to music, and Mendelssohn, who as a boy was his pupil. He revived Bach's motets with the Singakademie. Though at first opposed to Mendelssohn's revival of the *St. Matthew Passion* in 1829, he yielded to persuasion and allowed Mendelssohn to conduct it.

Zémire et Azor, opera (*comédie-ballet*) in four acts by Grétry, with libretto by Jean François Marmontel (based on Pierre Claude Nivelle de la Chaussée's comedy *Amour par amour*). It was first performed in Fontainebleau in 1771. The story is an adaptation of *Beauty and the Beast*: Azor is a prince whose selfishness and pride caused him to be transformed into a monster. Zémire is the woman whose love restores him to human form.

Zemire und Azor, (1) opera in four acts by Baumgarten. The libretto was translated by Karl Emil Schubert and the composer, from Marmontel's libretto of *Zémire et Azor*. It was first performed in Breslau in 1776;

(2) opera in three acts by Spohr with libretto by Johann Jakob Ihlee (based on the libretto of Marmontel's *Zémire et Azor*). It was first performed in Frankfurt in 1819.

Zemlinsky, Alexander von (1872–1942) Austrian composer and conductor. He studied at the Vienna Conservatorium. He conducted the Vienna Volksoper in 1906, the Vienna Opera in 1908, Mannheim in 1909, Prague in 1911, and the Berlin State Opera from 1927–30. He was rector of the Deutsche Musikakademie in Prague from 1920–7. He settled in the United States in 1934. Schoenberg was his pupil and wrote the libretto of Zemlinsky's first opera, *Sarema* (Munich, 1897). Other operas include *Eine florentinische Tragödie* (after Oscar Wilde; Stuttgart, 1917) and *Der Zwerg* (after Wilde's *The Birthday of the Infanta*; Frankfurt, 1921). He also composed two symphonies and other orchestral works, choral works, chamber music, piano pieces and songs. As a conductor, he was much admired by Stravinsky.

Zhizn za Tsara, see IVAN SUSSANIN

Ziani, Marc' Antonio (1653–1715), Italian composer. He was vice-*Kapellmeister* at Vienna in 1700 and *Kapellmeister* there in 1712. He was a prolific composer of operas, including the puppet opera *Damira placata* (Venice, 1680), and oratorios. Motets by him are printed in *Denkmäler der Tonkunst in Osterreich*, ci–cii. His uncle **Pietro Andrea Ziani** (c. 1620–84), was also a composer. He was organist at Venice and at

Bergamo. In 1669 he was appointed second organist at St. Mark's, Venice. From 1676 to 1684 he was in the Royal Chapel at Naples. He composed operas, oratorios, church music, and sonatas for instrumental ensemble.

ziemlich (Ger.), rather. Thus *Ziemlich langsam,* rather slow.

zilafone (It.), XYLOPHONE.

Zimbel (Ger.), medieval chime-bell.
See CYMBALS

Zimmermann, Bernd Alois (1918–70), German composer, pupil of Fortner and Leibowitz. His works include the multiple opera, *Die Soldaten* (*The Soldiers*), one of the most important and influential works written in Germany since the Second World War. He also composed four symphonies, a violin concerto and choral works (including a cantata, *In Praise of Stupidity*, on texts by Goethe), before committing suicide.

Zingarelli, Nicola Antonio (1752–1837), Italian composer. He studied at the Conservatorio Santa Maria di Loreto, Naples. Zingarelli's opera *Maestro di cappella* was performed in Milan Cathedral, 1792, in St. Peter's, Rome, 1804–11, and in Naples Cathedral, 1816. He was director of the Real Collegio di Musica, Naples, 1813. A prolific composer, he wrote 35 operas, numerous oratorios and cantatas (including *Isaiah* for the Birmingham Festival, 1829), and an enormous number of Masses, Magnificats and motets. His refusal to perform a Te Deum in 1811 to celebrate the birth of Napoleon's son (the King of Rome) led to his dismissal from St. Peter's.

zingarese, *see* ALLA ZINGARESE

Zinke (Ger.), CORNETT.

Zipoli, Domenico (1688–1726), Italian composer. Organist of the Jesuit church in Rome, he published *Sonate d'intavolatura per organo o cimbalo* (two volumes, 1716). *A third collection of toccatas, voluntaries and fugues* is an English reprint of part of the same collection.

zither, a flat instrument with up to about forty strings, very popular in Austria and Bavaria. Larger models are usually played on a table and smaller ones on the player's lap. There are two sets of strings both stretched over a sound box. The larger group consists of open strings and these serve accompanying purposes. The melodic strings, of which there are usually four or five, have a fretted fingerboard beneath them. They are stopped by the thumb of the left hand and plucked by a plectrum held in the right. The fingers of the left hand are used to pluck the open accompanying strings. As will be seen the technique is a fairly elaborate one and the best performers on the instrument are virtuosi in their own right. A notable use for the zither in a symphony orchestra occurs in Johann Strauss's *Tales from Vienna Woods*. See illustration on p. 608.

zither banjo, a small sized BANJO with wire strings.

Zitti, zitti, trio for Almaviva, Rosina and Figaro as they make ready to escape through the window of Dr Bartolo's house in Act 2 of Rossini's *Barber of Seville.*

Zolotoy Petushok, *see* GOLDEN COCKEREL, THE

zoppa, *see* ALLA ZOPPA

Zoroastre, opera in five acts by Rameau, to a libretto by Louis de Cahusac; first performed, Paris, 1749.

Zugposaune (Ger.), the slide as opposed to valve TROMBONE.

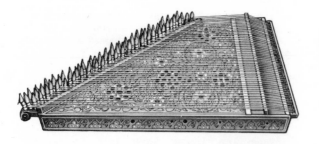

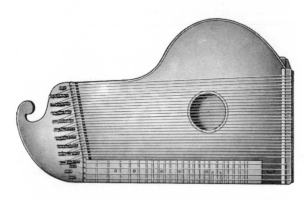

Zithers: (top) Arab *kanun*, modern form of the Middle Eastern zither from which the European psalteries developed; (bottom) 19th century German concert zither

Zugtrompete (Ger.), slide TRUMPET.

Zukunftsmusik (Ger., 'Music of the Future'), a term originally applied satirically by the critic Ludwig Bischoff to the music of Wagner, who had written an essay entitled *Das Kunstwerk der Zukunft* (The Artwork of the Future), and subsequently adopted by Wagner himself in his *Zukunftsmusik: Brief an einen französi-schen Freund* (Music of the Future: Letter to a French Friend).

Zumsteeg, Johann Rudolf (1760–1802), German composer. He was the son of a soldier, who became groom to the chamber at the Stuttgart court. Zumsteeg became court *Kapellmeister* at Stuttgart, 1792. He was famous for the composition of *Balladen* (extended solo songs with contrasted sections) which formed the model for some of Schubert's earlier works. He also wrote several operas, including *Der Geisterinsel* (Stuttgart, 1798; after Shakespeare's *The Tempest*), incidental music, church cantatas, and two cello concertos. The modern edition of selected songs is by L. Landshoff.

Zurich, Swiss city, famous for its opera company which in 1903 gave the first legal performance of Wagner's *Parsifal* outside Bayreuth. From 1937 to 1956, the opera house was directed by Hans Zimmermann, under whom the Zurich June Festival mounted the premières of Berg's *Lulu*, Hindemith's *Mathis der Maler*, Honegger's *Joan of Arc at the Stake*, and the European première of Gershwin's *Porgy and Bess*. In 1969, Henze's *King Stag* (*König Hirsch*) was conducted there by the composer. The company also has a well-established Richard Strauss tradition.

zuruckhaltend (Ger.), holding back, i.e. slowing down the tempo.

Zweiunddreissigstel (Ger.), demisemiquaver.

Zwischenspiel (Ger.), interlude, episode (e.g. in a fugue or rondo).

Zwölf (Ger.), twelve. Thus *Zwölftonmusik*, twelve-note music, *Zwölftonsystem*, twelve note system.

Zyklus (Ger., *Cycle*), piece for solo percussionist by Stockhausen, composed in 1959 for an instrumental competition at the Darmstadt Holiday Course in New Music. The music consists of 17 'periods', each of which, according to the player's whim, can serve as the beginning or end of the piece. The composer later suggested that the score could be performed jointly by two players.

Zymbelstern (Ger.), a percussion stop found in baroque organs.